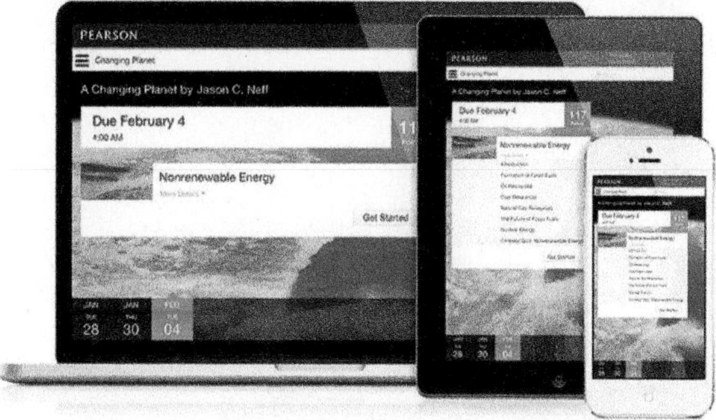

Enable learning anytime, anywhere The Revel mobile app lets students read, practice, and study—anywhere, anytime, on any device. Content is available both online and offline, and the app syncs work across all registered devices automatically, giving students great flexibility to toggle between phone, tablet, and laptop as they move through their day. The app also lets students set assignment notifications to stay on top of all due dates. Available for download from the App Store or Google Play. Learn more about the app at www.pearsonhighered/com/revel

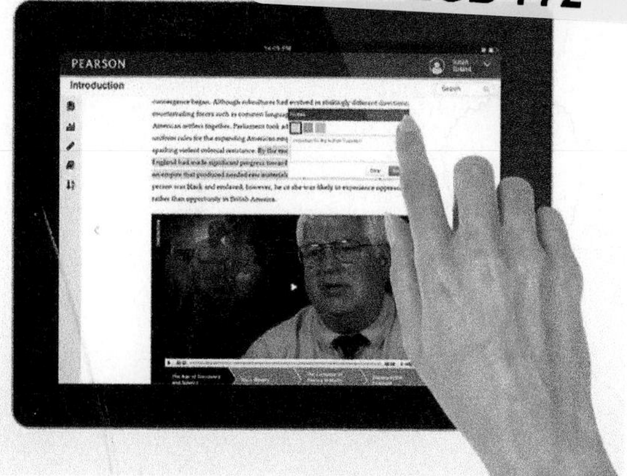

Provide an all-in-one solution Fully digital and highly engaging, Revel gives students everything they need for the course—all in one continuous, integrated learning experience. Highlighting, note taking, and a glossary let students read and study however they like. Educators can add notes for students, too, including reminders or study tips.

Foster critical thinking through writing The writing functionality in Revel, available in select courses, enables educators to integrate writing—among the best ways to foster and assess critical thinking—into the course without significantly impacting their grading burden. Writing features include:

- Self-paced Journaling Prompts throughout the narrative that encourage students to express their thoughts without breaking stride in their reading;
- Assignable Shared Writing Activities that direct students to share written responses with classmates, fostering peer discussion; and
- Essays integrated directly within Revel that allow instructors to assign the precise writing tasks they need for the course.

Superior assignability and tracking

Revel's assignability and tracking tools help educators make sure students are completing their reading and understanding core concepts.

Set the pace for progress Revel allows educators to indicate precisely which readings must be completed on which dates. This clear, detailed schedule helps students stay on task by eliminating any ambiguity as to which material will be covered during each class. When they understand exactly what is expected of them, students are better motivated to keep up.

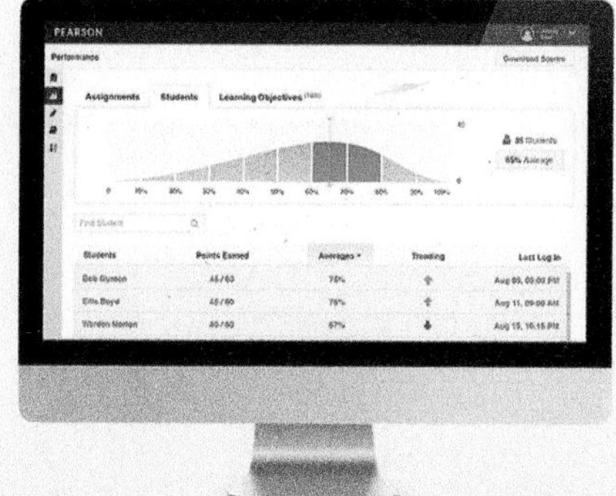

Focus your time and resources on students' needs Revel empowers educators to monitor class assignment completion as well as individual student achievement. Actionable information, such as points earned on quizzes and tests and time on task, helps educators intersect with their students in meaningful ways. For example, the trending column reveals whether students' grades are improving or declining, helping educators to identify students who might need help to stay on track.

Government by the People

Structure, Action, and Impact

2018 Elections and Updates Edition

Twenty-sixth Edition

David B. Magleby
Brigham Young University

Paul C. Light
New York University

Christine L. Nemacheck
The College of William & Mary

Pearson

Portfolio Manager: Jeff Marshall
Content Producer: Mary Donovan
Senior Content Developer: Jennifer Jacobson
Portfolio Manager Assistant: Christina Winterburn
Product Marketer: Candice Madden
Field Marketer: Alexa Macri
Content Producer Manager: Amber Mackey
Content Development Manager: Beth Jacobson
Managing Editor: Rebecca Green
Art/Designer: Kathryn Foot
Digital Studio Course Producer: Chris Fegan
Full-Service Project Manager: Vanitha Puela, SPi Global
Compositor: SPi Global
Printer/Binder: LSC Communications, Inc.
Cover Printer: LSC Communications, Inc.
Cover Design: SPi Global
Cover Credit: Library of Congress/ Getty Images

Acknowledgements of third party content appear on page 613, which constitutes an extension of this copyright page.

Library of Congress Cataloging-in-Publication Data.

Names: Magleby, David B., author. | Light, Paul Charles, author. | Nemacheck, Christine L., author.
Title: Government by the people : structure, action, and impact, 2018 midterm elections and updates edition 26th edition / David B. Magleby, Brigham Young University, Paul C. Light, New York University, Christine L. Nemacheck, The College of William & Mary.
Description: Twenty-sixth edition. | Hoboken : Pearson, [2018] | Includes bibliographical references and index.
Identifiers: LCCN 2018044891 | ISBN 9780135247396 | ISBN 013524739X
Subjects: LCSH: United States—Politics and government—Textbooks.
Classification: LCC JK276 .G68 2018b | DDC 320.473—dc23 LC record available at https://lccn.loc.gov/2018044891

1 18

Access Code Card:
ISBN 10: 0-13-517666-2
ISBN 13: 978-0-13-517666-5

Revel Combo Card:
ISBN-10: 0-13-558159-1
ISBN-13: 978-0-13-558159-9

Rental Edition:
ISBN-10: 0-13-524739-X
ISBN-13: 978-0-13-524739-6

Loose Leaf Edition:
ISBN-10: 0-13-524774-8
ISBN-13: 978-0-13-524774-7

Instructor's Review Copy:
ISBN-10: 0-13-524744-6
ISBN-13: 978-0-13-524744-0

Brief Contents

Part IV Rights and Liberties

Part V The Politics of National Policy

Contents

Part V The Politics of National Policy

To the Student

As the title of our book suggests, we view the idea of government by the people as a defining element of American politics and government. From the Mayflower Compact to the Declaration of Independence to the expansion of rights and liberties to more and more citizens in the last century, we have expanded on the idea of self-government. Too often, Americans take their basic rights to life, liberty, and the pursuit of happiness for granted. But these rights were guaranteed neither by those who wrote our Constitution nor by the citizens who have worked, one generation after another, to expand these rights and set our government's course. Rather, government by the people today depends on citizens who are informed and involved in the decisions and processes of our constitutional democracy. We have written this book with the aim of informing you about why you have a stake in our government. In this edition, we have gone a step further to argue that you can have an impact on government at all levels if you understand how government works—what we call structure—and if you are willing to act on your knowledge. Our idea can be summarized as follows: knowledge of structure + action = impact. We will develop this focus in each chapter.

The image we selected for our cover was chosen with our theme of structure, action, and impact in mind. Central to government by the people is the U.S. Capitol building. This physical structure, like our government, was built over time and was expanded as our country and government grew. By 1850, the Capitol could no longer accommodate the increasing numbers of senators and representatives from newly admitted states. The expansion seen here occurred between 1851 and 1865, though work was suspended temporarily from 1861 to 1862 due to the Civil War. The expansion of the Capitol is evidence of the government taking action. Over the course of U.S. history, there are many examples of government having an impact on people's lives. As you reflect on this image during your course of study, we hope it reminds you of the importance of structure, action, and impact.

The Framers of our Constitution warned us that we must always safeguard our rights, liberties, and political institutions. But we cannot do so without first understanding the basic rules of the game set by the Constitution. We must see the presidency, Congress, the federal bureaucracy, and the Supreme Court not as a remote "federal government" but as institutions that affect each of us every single day. Government by the people depends on people informing themselves and participating. It is not something that can be outsourced or that a generation can decide to take a pass on.

This new edition of *Government by the People* will help you embrace the legacy of constitutional government you have inherited, even as it gives you important insights into how you can shape the future direction of our country, guarantee a system that protects minorities, and all of our rights and liberties, and defend our government by the people from tyranny. In some ways, you can read this book as an "owner's guide" to American government and as a basic "repair manual" about how you can play a role in making our Constitution work. Whether you act on your own or with others on campus and in your communities, your participation alone will make American government work better. Our constitutional system depends on active engagement—win, lose, or draw. As the old saying goes, politics is a game for people who show up. We want you to get into the game.

Meet Your Authors

DAVID B. MAGLEBY is a distinguished professor of political science at Brigham Young University (BYU). He has been an American Political Science Association Congressional Fellow, as well as a Fulbright Scholar. He is recognized for his expertise on direct democracy, voting behavior, and campaign finance. Dave is also the recipient of many teaching awards, including the 1990 Utah Professor of the Year Award, the 2001 Rowman & Littlefield Award for Innovative Teaching in Political Science, and several department and university awards. He served as president of Pi Sigma Alpha, the political science honor society.

PAUL C. LIGHT is the Paulette Goddard Professor of Public Service at New York University's Wagner School of Public Service and the founding principal investigator for the Global Center for Public Service. In 2015, he received the American Political Science Association John Gaus Award for exemplary scholarship in Political Science and Public Administration. He has worked on Capitol Hill as a senior committee staffer in the U.S. Senate and as an American Political Science Association Congressional Fellow in the U.S. House of Representatives. Paul is the founding director of the Brookings Institution's Center for Public Service and continues his research on how to invite Americans to serve their communities through public service.

CHRISTINE L. NEMACHECK is an associate professor of government at The College of William & Mary, where she directs the Center for the Liberal Arts and co-directs the H. Stewart Dunn, Jr. Civil Liberties Project. Her research focuses on judicial selection, judicial federalism, and the role of the courts in a separation of powers system. Chris has received a number of awards for her teaching and research activity, including the Alumni Fellowship Award for excellence in teaching at The College of William & Mary. She is the former co-editor of the *Pi Sigma Alpha Undergraduate Journal of Politics*.

To the Instructor

The three of us remember well the first time we taught an introductory American government class. As teaching assistants in graduate school, we had given an occasional lecture. But to pull off our own first class seemed daunting. We also remember our desire for a well-written, carefully researched, well-illustrated, up-to-the-minute book that would help us jumpstart student interest in active citizenship.

We share a desire to make a difference through our teaching, and we care deeply about playing our own role in making American government work. Although we have provided many enhancements to this text that will help your students make a difference in their own way, the text itself lays the foundation for leading students forward into political science majors and public service.

These experiences inform our approach, as does the feedback you and your students pass along about what works and what does not. Long after teaching our first American government classes, we continue to share a common passion for teaching and for the study of American government. Because all of us still teach this course regularly, we recognize the challenges of engaging students and overcoming their cynicism about the subject and doubts about the relevance of the course to their lives. We see American government as a lively subject and make every effort to provide opportunities for debate and active learning in our own classes, using current examples and controversies to help show students the relevance of the topic. We know students won't learn what they don't read, and we believe we have written a book that gives them every reason to stick with each topic.

This book and the courses we teach are informed by our professional lives and academic research. We are actively engaged in research and publication on courts, campaigns, bureaucracy, the presidency, Congress, public opinion, campaign finance, judicial nominations, and policy making. Our engagement in studying how government and politics really work has interrupted our teaching careers as we pursued appointments as Congressional Fellows of the American Political Science Association, produced new information for many of the book's figures and charts, and wrote books on the core topics in each of our areas. All of us regularly conduct interviews with leading policy makers in the executive, legislative, and judicial branches, and we study implementation and ongoing controversies through frequent trips to the major centers of government activity across the country. This constant contact with history, theory, and reality buttresses our appreciation for American government and tempers our interpretations of the many contemporary events we use in this book. We care deeply about the challenges facing American government today but also rely on history and theory to put those challenges in context.

We are delighted that you are reading this edition of *Government by the People*. First published in the 1950s, the book has reached more than 2 million students during its 60-plus years in circulation. Given the distinguished coauthors who came before us, we always carefully anchor our writing in the long tradition of careful scholarship embedded in the very fiber of this book. We believe our coauthors were right on point when they decided to title this book *Government by the People*. They wanted to emphasize how important people are in our constitutional democracy, and we still make every effort to reinforce the point. Understanding American politics and government must include an understanding of the American people, their similarities and differences, their beliefs and attitudes, and their behaviors.

The constitutional democracy we have in the United States is exceedingly hard to achieve, equally hard to sustain, and often hard to understand, especially when contemporary experience seems to frustrate action on the problems we all care about. We know our democracy has evolved toward a greater and greater role for citizens and voters over the decades since the first edition of *Government by the People* was published. Citizens have more rights and political opportunities in 2019 than they had when early editions of this book were published, while social media has made politics available to everyone instantly by providing a deluge of information.

Given the conflicting opinions students often confront in their Web browsing, we frequently remind ourselves of the famous adage that everyone is entitled to their opinions, but not to their facts. That is why we work hard to set the record straight by providing a constitutional anchor for critical thinking, even as we make every effort to keep this book relevant through up-to-date examples, charts, chapter openers, photos, and exercises that challenge the instant analysis that sometimes distorts the real workings of American government.

Like your students, we are sometimes frustrated by the contemporary state of American government and the challenges in solving tough problems, and we are not reluctant to talk about the current level of public cynicism and polarization. In the book we emphasize the importance of learning the structure of American government and politics, and that when students act on that knowledge through participation they can have an impact on the future of their community, their state, the nation, and the world. We are committed to helping educate and activate the next generation of citizens who will take their place in honing the Framers' design to meet the challenges of the future, and we are hopeful that this edition of *Government by the People* will help them shape the future, each in his or her own most effective way.

New to This Edition

The 2018 Elections and Updates Edition of *Government by the People* builds on this book's long reputation for deep, accurate, accessible, and current coverage of the foundations of American government. We embrace the idea of government by the people and want students to understand how they can have an impact at any level of government. Our simple formulation is that students must first understand the structure of government and politics. Participation is a necessary step as well, but participation without knowledge of the structure of politics and government is not likely to be effective. But participation with an understanding of how government and politics works can have an impact. We integrate this theme throughout the book, provide examples of people who have made a difference, and suggest ways students in the class can make a difference.

As in previous versions, in this edition we integrate the latest in scholarship on American politics and government. We include comparisons of the United States with countries around the world, as well as analyses of recent political events, namely the first few two years of the Trump administration, including his many executive actions and his dealings with Congress and the judicial system. We also cover legislative controversies over economic, social, and defense and foreign policy and content on the Supreme Court, including the vacancy resulting from Justice Kennedy's retirement and Trump's appointment of Brett Kavanaugh, as well as recent Supreme Court decisions. The issues surrounding immigration, from expenditures to building a wall between the United States and Mexico, what to do about government actions toward children brought here years ago by their undocumented parents, and whether to separate children from parents in families seeking asylum are all included. The efforts by Russia to influence the outcome of the 2016 election through social media, leaked emails from the Clinton campaign and Democratic party, and efforts to hack into state level voter files are all important and integrated where relevant in the new text. Finally, we explore the growing partisan polarization and legislative gridlock, the use of big data in campaigns, the surge in spending by Super PACs and other outside money groups, and the increasing role of the Internet and social media in politics.

Throughout the 2018 Elections and Updates Edition, we have updated the content to make sure students can see American government as it is today. The following are some major changes we incorporated in this edition while keeping in mind both the current political context and the needs of the course:

- The content now provides a launchpad for discussing all the major issues in the headlines today, including the frequent tweets by Donald Trump, the implications of his presidency with high staff turnover, repeatedly expressed hostility toward the press, and preoccupation with the Justice Department inquiry into Russian interference in the 2016 election. Special attention is directed to the 2018 midterm elections, the War on Terrorism, the ongoing government debt debate, and the many current and unresolved questions on the basic performance of government.
- Just as social media and use of the Web in politics and government are explored throughout the material, we also use these resources—along with examples, photos, figures, tables, and critical-thinking exercises—to reinforce learning and encourage further analysis of what students can do to make a difference.
- Text, tables, figures, and all other material have been updated to reflect available current data. In cases where there have been new developments, as with Super PACs and 501(c) groups, textual and tabular summaries provide specific information—for example, in the case of Super PACs, where this money came from and for which sides it was spent.
- In the chapters on the courts, civil liberties, and civil rights, we discuss the Supreme Court's recent decisions regarding the extent to which private businesses can refuse to serve same-sex weddings, affirmative action, and abortion access, as well as other major legal developments, including the Court's consideration of how to protect religious liberties in light of contraception coverage under Obamacare.
- We have reviewed every table and figure to ensure that they contain the most recent information available and have also included many new items. We want students to see how public opinion, diversity, campaign finance, congressional action, presidential press conferences and approval, judicial decisions, and the federal budget have changed in the past two to four years and how they might change in the future. Examples of updated tables and figures include the continuing gender gap in voting, from what sources do candidates raise campaign funds, spending by Super PACs in 2012, 2014, and 2016, news sources for millennials, changes in the U.S. Supreme Court's caseload, diversity, and the public's evolving views on abortion access. New maps and figures include which states are likely to benefit in congressional seats from the 2020 census, a map of a Pennsylvania congressional district gerrymander, and turnout by age, race, gender, and education.
- We see photos as a powerful way to engage students with the material. We have reviewed every photo and replaced dozens of them to provide the most dynamic and engaging art program possible for your students. The 2018 Elections and Updates Edition features several new images including President Trump, the Women's March on Washington, new Supreme Court Justices Neil Gorsuch and Brett Kavanaugh, Tom Perez (new Chair of the Democratic National Committee), Ronna Romney McDaniel (new Chair of the Republican National Committee), and the summit between North Korean dictator Kim Jung-Un and President Trump. Other new images include the Bears Ears National Monument in Utah,

protests over the travel ban affecting those from majority Muslim countries, and the shootings in Las Vegas, Nevada and Parkland, Florida, images from the Russian Facebook ads run during the 2016 election, new Federal Reserve chair Jerome Powell, Mark Zuckerberg testifying in Congress over the role Facebook played in the 2016 election, children separated from parents as a result of the zero tolerance immigration policy in 2018, and the new U.S. Supreme Court as we approach 2019. We have retained the major iconic photos of the past but incorporated many new ones to capture the major events of the last few years and to create a visual narrative that enhances rather than repeats the text content.

Features

While upholding the long tradition of scholarship that has always made this book credible to the political science community, we have brought new perspectives, stories, and data into the text to make sure every student knows that American government is as relevant to his or her life today as it was when our book was first published. We are proud of what our coauthors produced over the first 26 editions, but at the same time, we have not rested on the past by merely updating what has come before. We want this book to live on as an exemplar of how to integrate the basic arguments about what the Framers created with what is happening now, while retaining a focus on what needs to be changed in the future.

Toward this goal, we continue to present the book in an accessible tier of increasingly detailed knowledge. We start with a clear introduction telling students what they will read and how we think and then pivot to the constitutional foundations and the basic elements of our federalist system. After that we provide a deep introduction to the American political landscape to make sure students understand the geographic, demographic (race and ethnicity, religion, gender, sexual orientation, family structure, education, age), and economic (wealth and income, occupation, social class) factors that shape American government. This foundation informs our chapters on political parties, interest groups' political participation, elections, and the media.

The book then turns to core chapters on American political institutions (Congress, the presidency, the bureaucracy and policy process, and the judiciary), follows with chapters on civil rights and liberties, and ends with chapters on economic, social, and defense and foreign policy. The book flows naturally from one section to the other, but we invite you to present these chapters in any order that fits with your own teaching plan.

We have placed definitions of key terms in the margins of every chapter to help students define new and important concepts at first encounter. For easy reference, key terms from the marginal glossary are repeated at the end of each chapter and in the end-of-book glossary.

These many tools and updates bring the book into the present. Students will never wonder what an example has to do with their reality. They will never question why the Constitution and history matter to solving big problems. And they will never ask how American government is being challenged today.

Ultimately, the book draws upon its own past to show students that others have made a difference before and that they can make their own difference today. We want all of your students to become active participants in our democracy, and we have written a book that gives them a broad invitation to engage. This is the enduring commitment of the book and one that we take very seriously when we sit down every two years to bring American government back into focus through a vibrant emphasis on what students need to know as they accept the call to public service.

Revel for Government by the People

Providing educational technology for the way today's students read, think, and learn, Revel is an interactive learning environment that offers a fully digital experience. It uses frequent updates of articles and data to illustrate the current state of government and politics in the United States. Students can interact with multiple types of media and assessments integrated directly within the authors' narrative:

- Chapter-opening **Current Events Bulletins** feature author-written articles that put breaking news and current events into the context of American government. Examples include Fake News; Russian Involvement in the 2016 U.S. Presidential Election; Affirmative Action and Asian Americans at Harvard; Conflicts of Interest in the Trump Administration; Trump and Putin; and Selective Attention and Selective Perception. The 2018 Elections and Updates Edition retains the popular blog, **Happening Now,** through which the authors offer weekly analyses of events. This blog appears before the first module quiz of each chapter.
- **Videos** bring to life chapter contents and key moments in American government. ABC news footage provides examples from both current and historical events, including President George W. Bush's "bullhorn speech," footage of 2016 primary and general election candidates like Hillary Clinton, Bernie Sanders, and Donald Trump on the campaign trail, and Gabby Giffords's "You Must Act" speech to Congress about gun control.

In addition, popular "Sketchnote" videos, two per chapter, walk students through difficult-to-understand concepts such as the Electoral College, reapportionment and redistricting, lack of success of minor party candidates and PACs and Super PACs. Through the visual storytelling approach, Sketchnote videos cater to visual and audio learners, but also activate a high level of engagement in all students, as they see the concepts come to life.

Also, ***Pearson Original for Political Science are compelling stories about contemporary issues.*** These short-form documentaries contextualize the complex social and political issues impacting the world today. In addition to helping students better understand core concepts, Pearson Originals inspire students to think critically as empowered citizens who can inspire social and political change. Explaining complex political issues in a simplified and entertaining way, Pearson Originals for Political Science help students become informed members of society. Videos include *Marijuana and Federalism: Who's in Charge?; Who Should Be Allowed to Call Themselves "American"?; and What Is the Emoluments Class and Why Should I Care About It?* In addition, videos from **Pearson's *Politics Hidden in Plain Sight* series** do exactly that—provide students with concrete examples of politics influencing the activities of their daily lives—from using their cellphones to going to a convenience store—even if they can't actually see the politics at work. Videos from both series are incorporated into the chapters and can also be easily accessed from the instructor's Resources folder within Revel.

- **Interactive maps, figures, and tables** feature Social Explorer technology which allow for real-time data updates and rollover information to support the data and show movement over time. The 2018 Elections and Updates Edition features visualizations with data current through July 2018, including data from American National Election Studies and David Leip. Examples of Social Explorer visualizations include: Figure 1.2 Trust in Government; Figure 4.1 State Population Changes and the Coming 2020 Reapportionment; Figure 5.4 PAC Contributions to Congressional Candidates, 1996–2016; Explore the Map: 2004, 2008, 2012, and 2016 Battleground States; Explore the Map: 2012 vs. 2016 Midwest Election Results; Figure 9.2 Americans Turning More to Mobile Devices for News; Figure 10.1 Public Approval of Congress; Figure 12.5 Uncontrollable Spending, 1962-2018; Figure 12.7 Does the Federal Government Have Too Much Power?: Figure 14.2

Public Opinion on Abortion Access; Figure 16.2: Where the Federal Income Came From and Where It Went in 2019; and Figure 17.3 Reducing the Threat of Terrorism.

- Dozens of other interactivities such as "click-to-reveals," enhanced maps, and images with hotspots bring important concepts to life.
- **Document prompts** incorporate primary source material into the narrative. Examples include the U.S. Constitution, excerpts from various Federalist Papers, Gideon's Petition, the Obergefell Petition, FDR's Executive Order 9066, and *Marbury* v. *Madison*.
- Interactive **Review the Chapter** summaries that utilize video, learning objectives, and flashcards featuring key terms and definitions allow students to review the chapters and reinforce the content.
- **Assessments** tied to primary chapter sections, as well as full chapter exams, allow instructors and students to track progress and get immediate feedback.
- **Integrated Writing Opportunities:** To help students reason and write more clearly, each chapter offers two varieties of writing prompts:
  - **Journal prompts** at the end of each major section ask students to consider critical issues that relate to topics at the module level. These questions are designed to reinforce the authors' main goal—to equip students to change the world.
  - **Shared writing prompts**, linked to each chapter's conclusion, encourage students to consider how to address challenges described in the chapter. Through these prompts, instructors and students can address multiple sides of an issue by sharing their own views and responding to each other's viewpoints.
  - **Essay prompts from Pearson's Writing Space**, allow instructors to assign both automatically graded and instructor-graded prompts. Writing Space is the best way to develop and assess concept mastery and critical thinking through writing. Writing Space provides a single place within Revel to create, track, and grade writing assignments; access writing resources; and exchange meaningful, personalized feedback quickly and easily to improve results. For students, Writing Space provides everything they need to keep up with writing assignments, access assignment guides and checklists, write or upload completed assignments, and receive grades and feedback—all in one convenient place. For educators, Writing Space makes assigning, receiving, and evaluating writing assignments easier. It's simple to create new assignments and upload relevant materials, see student progress, and receive alerts when students submit work. Writing Space makes students' work more focused and effective, with customized grading rubrics they can see and personalized feedback. Writing Space can also check students' work for improper citation or plagiarism by comparing it against the world's most ac-curate text comparison database available from Turnitin.
- **Learning Management Systems:** Pearson provides Blackboard Learn™, Canvas™, Brightspace by D2L, and Moodle integration, giving institutions, instructors, and students easy access to Revel. Our Revel integration delivers streamlined access to everything your students need for the course in these learning management system (LMS) environments. With *Single Sign-on*, students are ready on their first day. From your LMS course, students have easy access to an interactive blend of authors' narrative, media, and assessment. *Grade Sync:* Flexible, on-demand grade synchronization capabilities allow you to control exactly which Revel grades should be transferred to the LMS gradebook.
- The **Revel Combo Card** provides an all-in-one access code and loose-leaf print reference (delivered by mail).

Supplements

Make more time for your students with instructor resources that offer effective learning assessments and classroom engagement. Pearson's partnership with educators does not end with the delivery of course materials; Pearson is there with you on the first day of class and beyond. A dedicated team of local Pearson representatives will work with you to not only choose course materials but also integrate them into your class and assess their effectiveness. Our goal is your goal—to improve instruction with each semester.

Pearson is pleased to offer the following resources to qualified adopters of *Government by the People*. Several of these supplements, in addition to other teaching resources, are available to instantly download on the Instructor Resource Center (IRC); please visit the IRC at www.pearsonhighered.com/irc to register for access.

TEST BANK Evaluate learning at every level. Reviewed for clarity and accuracy, the Test Bank measures this book's learning objectives with multiple-choice, true/false, fill-in-the-blank, short-answer, and essay questions. You can easily customize the assessment to work in any major learning management system and to match what is covered in your course. Word, Blackboard and WebCT versions are available on the IRC, and Respondus versions are available upon request from www.respondus.com.

PEARSON MYTEST This powerful assessment generation program includes all of the questions in the Test Bank. Quizzes and exams can be easily authored and saved online and then printed for classroom use, giving you ultimate flexibility to manage assessments anytime and anywhere. To learn more, visit www.pearsonhighered.com/mytest.

INSTRUCTOR'S RESOURCE MANUAL Create a comprehensive roadmap for teaching classroom, online, or hybrid courses. Designed for new and experienced instructors, the Instructor's Manual includes learning objectives, lecture and discussion suggestions, activities for in or out of class, and essays on teaching American government. Available on the IRC.

LECTURE POWERPOINTS Make lectures more enriching for students. The accessible PowerPoint presentations include full lecture outlines and photos and figures from the book. Available within Revel and on the IRC.

LECTURE LIVESLIDE POWERPOINTS These PowerPoint presentations include full lecture outlines, photos, and figures from the book—with an exciting enhancement. Figures that are Social Explorer visualizations appear as dynamic LiveSlides. This gives you a direct path to the live Social Explorers in the Revel course. Social Explorer visualizations are data-rich interactive maps and figures that enable students to visually explore demographic data to understand how local trends impact them, while improving data and statistical literacy. Available within Revel and on the IRC.

Acknowledgments

Government by the People began in 1948 when two young assistant professors, James MacGregor Burns of Williams College and Jack W. Peltason of Smith College, decided to partner and write an American government text. Their first edition had a publication date of 1952. Their aim was to produce a well-written, accessible, and balanced look at government and politics in the United States. As new authors have become a part of this book, they have embraced that objective. Tom Cronin of Colorado College and David O'Brien of the University of Virginia have been coauthors and made important contributions to the book. As the current authors of *Government by the People*, we are grateful for the legacy we have inherited.

Creating this instructional design has required teamwork among many people. First, the coauthors have conversed often with each other about the broad themes, features, and focus of this material, and we have read and reviewed, as well as rewritten and revised, each other's work. We are grateful to one another for the commitment and dedication shown in this work.

Second, our research assistants have not only researched and investigated numerous details, but also have given us the perspective of current students. Research assistants for the current edition of *Government by the People* are Stephanie Perry Curtis, Benjamin Forsgren, John Geilman, Jake A. Jensen, Alena Smith, and Fred (Wen Jie) Tan of Brigham Young University.

Third, the editors and others at Pearson have provided essential professional assistance. We express appreciation to the superb Pearson team members who have been so supportive and worked so hard to produce this edition: Jeff Marshall, Portfolio Manager, and key members of his team, Mary Donovan, Tina Gagliostro, Peggy Bliss; Vanitha Puela at SPi Global. Special thanks are extended to Rebecca Green, Managing Editor and Jennifer Jacobson, Senior Managing Editor, who again provided exceptional skill in coordinating complex digital and print editorial and production processes. Their colleagues at Ohlinger Studios rounded out the team: Corinna Dibble, Program Manager, Caitlin Bonaventure, Digital Media Manager, and Allison Collins, Project Manager, as well as Mary Jackson, Maggie Barbieri, Dea Barbieri, Darcy Betts, April Cleland, Deb Coniglio, Natalee Sperry, and Kate Tully who collaborated on the digital assets for the Revel edition. Also, we appreciate Kim Norbuta's efforts with our Current Events Bulletins.

We also wish to thank the many professors and researchers who gave detailed feedback on how to improve content and who provided invaluable input during professional conferences and Pearson-sponsored events:

Spring 2018 Revel Editorial Workshops: Christopher Hallenbrook, Bloomsburg University; Ben Christ, Harrisburg Area Community College; Laci Hubbard–Mattix, Spokane Falls Community College–Pullman; Shobana Jayaraman, Savannah State University; Jeneen Hobby, Cleveland State University; John Arnold, Midland College; Reed Welch, West Texas A&M; Amanda Friesen, IUPUI; Thomas Ambrosio, North Dakota State; Ted Vaggalis, Drury University; Coyle Neal, Southwest Baptist University; Hanna Samir Kassab, Northern Michigan University; Julie Keil, Saginaw Valley State University; Henry Esparza, University of Texas at San Antonio; Sierra Powell, Mount San Antonio College; Edgar Bravo, Broward College; Alicia Andreatta, Angelina College; Robert Sterken, The University of Texas at Tyler; Jessica Anderson, University of Louisiana Monroe; Pat Frost, San Diego Miramar College; Scott Robinson, Houston Baptist University; Cessna Winslow, Tarleton State; Carrie Currier, Texas Christian University; Paul Jorgensen, University of Texas Rio Grande Valley; Steve Lem, Kutztown University; Meng Lu, Sinclair Community College; James Pearn, Southern State Community College; Blake Farrar, Texas State University; Carlin Barmada, NVCC; Michael Chan, California State University, Long Beach; Mehwish, SUNY Buffalo State; Daniel Tirone, Louisiana State University; Richard Haesly, California State University, Long Beach; Hyung Park, El Paso Community College; Jesse Kapenga, UTEP; Stephanie A. Slocum–Schaffer, Shepherd University; Augustine Hammond, Augusta University; Shawn Easley, Cuyahoga Community College; Darius Smith, Community College of Aurora; Robert Glover, University of Maine; Carolyn Cocca, State University of NY, College at Old Westbury; Benjamin Arah, Bowie State University; Ahmet Turker, Pima Community College; Eric Loepp, UW–Whitewater; Holly Lindamod, University of North Georgia; Denise Robles, San Antonio College; Asslan Khaligh, Alamo Colleges District–San Antonio College; Brandy Martinez, San Antonio College; Andrew Sanders, Texas A&M University, San Antonio; Mohsen Omar, Northeast Lakeview College; Heather Frederick, Slippery Rock University; Heather Rice, Slippery Rock University;

Leslie Baker, Mississippi State University; Jamie Warner, Marshall University; Will Jennings, University of Tennessee; Arjun Banerjee, University of Tennessee, Knoxville; Jonathan Honig, University of Tennessee; Rachel Fuentes, University of Tennessee Knoxville; Andrew Straight, University of Tennessee, Knoxville; Margaret Choka, Pellissippi State Community College; Christopher Lawrence, Middle Georgia State University; LaTasha Chaffin, College of Charleston; Jeff Worsham, West Virginia University; Cigdem Sirin–Villalobos, University of Texas at El Paso; Lyle Wind, Suffolk Community College; Marcus Holmes, College of William & Mary; Marcus Holmes, College of William & Mary; Kurt Guenther, Palm Beach State College; Kevin Wagner, Florida Atlantic University; Eric Sands, Berry College; Shari MacLachlan, Palm Beach State College; Sharon Manna, North Lake College; Tamir Sukkary, American River College; Willie Hamilton, Mt. San Jacinto College; Linda Trautman, Ohio University–Lancaster; Dr. William H. Kraus, Motlow State Community College; Kim Winford, Blinn College; Lana Obradovic, University of Nebraska at Omaha; Doug Schorling, College of the Sequoias; Sarah Lischer, Wake Forest University; Ted Clayton, Central Michigan University; Steven Greene, North Carolina State University; Sharon Navarro, University of Texas at San Antonio; Curtis Ogland, San Antonio College; Henry Esparza, UT San Antonio; Mario Salas, UTSA; Robert Porter, Ventura College; Will Jennings, University of Tennessee; Haroon Khan, Henderson State University; Brenda Riddick, Houston Community College; Julie Lantrip, Tarrant County College; Kyle C. Kopko, Elizabethtown College; Kristine Mohajer, Austin Community College (ACC); Dovie D. Dawson, Central Texas College; Joycelyn Caesar, Cedar Valley College; Daniel Ponder, Drury University

APSA TLC 2018: Mujahid Nyahuma, Community College of Philadelphia; Tahiya Nyahuma, NCAT; Christopher Lawrence, Middle Georgia State University; Jason Robles, University of Colorado; Tim Reynolds, Alvin Community College; Marilyn C. Buresh, Lake Region State College; Frances Marquez, Gallaudet University; Natasha Washington, Liberal Arts and Communications; Jonathan Honig, University of Tennessee, Knoxville; Ayesha Ahsanuddin, University of Tennessee, Knoxville; Arjun Banerjee, The University of Tennessee–Knoxville; Jesse R. Cragwall, Tusculum College Pellissippi State Community College; Ms. Amnah H. Ibraheem, University of Tennessee, Knoxville; Karl Smith, Delaware Technical Community College; Richard Waterman, University of Kentucky; Peggy R. Wright, ASU–Jonesboro; Christopher Hallenbrook, Bloomsburg University; Eric Loepp, UW–Whitewater; Robert Glover, University of Maine; Heather Rice, Slippery Rock University; Shawn Easley, Cuyahoga Community College; Benjamin Arah, Bowie State University; Andrew Straight, University of Tennessee; Rachel Fuentes, University of Tennessee at Knoxville; Stephanie A. Slocum–Schaffer, Shepherd University; Will Jennings, University of Tennessee

APSA 2017: Jooeun Kim, Georgetown; Leonard L. Lira, San José State University; Abigail Post, University of Virginia; Jamilya Ukudeeva, Chabot College; Shannon Jenkins, University of Massachusetts–Dartmouth; Matthew Platt, Morehouse College; Sara Angevine, Whittier College; Andy Aoki, Augsburg University; Stephen Meinhold, University of North Carolina–Wilmington; Manoutchehr Eskandari–Qajar, Santa Barbara City College; Clayton Thyne, University of Kentucky; Alice Jackson, Morgan State University; Mark Rom, Georgetown University; Krista Wiegand, University of Tennessee; Geoffrey Wallace, University of Washington; Precious Hall, Truckee Meadows Community College; Patrick Larue, University of Texas at Dallas; Margot Morgan, Indiana University Southeast; Patrick Wohlfarth, University of Maryland; Christian Grose, University of Southern California; Clinton Jenkins, George Washington University; Jeffrey W. Koch, US Air Force Academy and SUNY Geneseo; Albert Ponce, Diablo Valley College; Justin Vaughn, Boise State University; Joe

Weinberg, University of Southern Mississippi; Cindy Stavrianos, Gonzaga University; Kevan M. Yenerall, Clarion University; Katherine Barbieri, University of South Carolina; Elsa Dias, Metropolitan State University of Denver; Maria Gabryszewska, Florida International University; Erich Saphir, Pima Community College; Mzilikazi Kone, College of the Desert; Mary McHugh, Merrimack College; Joel Lieske, Cleveland State University; Joseph W. Roberts, Roger Williams University; Eugen L. Nagy, Central Washington University; Henry B. Sirgo, McNeese State University; Brian Newman, Pepperdine University; Bruce Stinebrickner, DePauw University; Amanda Friesen, IUPUI; LaTasha Chaffin, College of Charleston; Richard Waterman, University of Kentucky

MPSA 2018: Adam Bilinski, Pittsburg State University; Daniel Chand, Kent State University; Agber Dimah, Chicago State University; Yu Ouyang, Purdue University Northwest; Steven Sylvester, Utah Valley University; Ben Bierly, Joliet Junior College; Mahalley Allen, California State University, Chico; Christian Goergen, College of DuPage; Patrick Stewart, University of Arkansas, Fayettville; Richard Barrett, Mount Mercy University; Daniel Hawes, Kent State University; Niki Kalaf-Hughes, Bowling Green State University; Gregg R. Murray, Augusta University; Ryan Reed, Bradley University; Kimberly Turner, College of DuPage; Peter Wielhouwer, Western Michigan University; Leena Thacker Kumar, University of Houston/DTN; Debra Leiter, University of Missouri Kansas City; Michael Makara, University of Central Missouri; Ola Adeoye, University of Illinois–Chicago; Russell Brooker, Alverno College; Dr. Royal G. Cravens, Bowling Green State University; Vincent T. Gawronski, Birmingham–Southern College; Benjamin I. Gross, Jacksonville State University; Matthew Hitt, University of Northern Colorado; Megan Osterbur, New England College; Pamela Schaal, Ball State University; Edward Clayton, Central Michigan University; Ali Masood, California State University, Fresno; Joel Lieske, Cleveland State University; Patrick Wohlfarth, University of Maryland; Steven Greene, NC State; Will Jennings, University of Tennessee; Haroon Khan, Henderson State University; Kyle Kopko, Elizabethtown College; Hyung Lae Park, El Paso Community College; Linda Trautman, Ohio University–Lancaster.

2017–2018 Reviewers: Benjamin Gonzalez O'Brien, Highline Community College; Jennifer Sacco, Quinnipiac University; Royal Cravens, Bowling Green State University; Jerome Hunt, Long Beach City College; Maureen Kperogi, Kennesaw State University; Jason R. Jakubowski, Manchester Community College; Joshua Lader, Sinclair Community College

We also want to thank you, the professors, and students who use our book and who send us letters and email messages with suggestions for improving *Government by the People*. Please write us in care of Pearson Education or contact us directly:

David B. Magleby Distinguished Professor of Political Science,
Brigham Young University, Provo, UT 84602, david_magleby@byu.edu

Paul C. Light Paulette Goddard Professor of Public Service at
New York University, Wagner School of Public Service,
New York, NY 10012, pcl226@nyu.edu

Christine L. Nemacheck Wilson & Martha Claiborne Stephens
Associate Professor of Government at The College of William & Mary,
Williamsburg, VA 23187, clnema@wm.edu

CHAPTER 1

Constitutional Democracy

Self-government requires many actions on the part of citizens from obeying laws to casting ballots as is happening here. It includes serving on juries, volunteering in the community, and helping others with their participation as the election officials are doing here. People often take for granted the opportunity to govern themselves. But many people in the world today are not free to participate openly in their government.

LEARNING OBJECTIVES

1.1 Describe the nature of the "grand experiment in self-government" in America (Structure), p. 2.

1.2 Describe the importance of citizen participation in constitutional democracy (Structure), p. 4.

1.3 Describe democracy and the conditions conducive to its success (Structure), p. 7.

1.4 Identify pre-Revolutionary concepts central to the new government and the problems under the Articles of Confederation (Structure), p. 16.

1.5 Identify the issues resolved by compromise during the writing of the Constitution (Action), p. 18.

1.6 Evaluate the arguments for and against the ratification of the Constitution (Impact), p. 24.

Americans are often cynical about government, and students sometimes ask why they should take a course in American government. Our answer is that government can foster the freedom that makes higher education possible. More generally, American government, with all of its limitations, has enhanced the lives and prosperity of people not only in the United States, but in much of the world. We helped defeat fascism and communism, we helped establish democratic self-government in Germany and Japan after World War II, we extended civil rights and voting rights to more people, we dramatically expanded the reach of college education, we built the interstate highway system, and we successfully put astronauts on the moon. We often overlook the role of American government in reducing air and water pollution, extending health care to children and older Americans, reducing disease, and fostering technological advances like the Internet. In order to continue to be a positive force in the lives of its citizens and the world, the government needs the participation and help of civically knowledgeable and engaged young people—people just like you.

At the same time we are reminded daily that our country and the world faces many unresolved problems. Racial prejudice continues in our society. High youth unemployment and incarceration rates persist for black Americans. While the United States and our allies have been successful in reducing the territory held by the Islamic State in Iraq and Syria (ISIS), the ability of this and other groups to stage terrorist attacks continues. There is also the problem of home-grown violence; trust in government has dropped; and the September 11, 2001, attacks continue to cast a long shadow on the national consciousness. Many of America's achievements of the past are in trouble—our interstate highway system is straining under increased traffic and congestion; the environment is facing new threats; health care costs and student debt are rising; and mass shootings like those at a country music festival in Las Vegas, Nevada or a high school in Parkland, Florida, remind us of how an individual armed with an assault weapon can murder many innocent people. Looking to the future, many Americans wonder how we will solve the problems ahead.

The answers to some of these problems are already emerging. You and others like you are engaging in tough conversations about what unites and divides us, and finding your own solutions and ways to make a difference. You know that the world is much more complex than it was when your parents were born. Students like you have changed the way we communicate, learn, participate, and innovate. And you have already shown a deep commitment to changing the future. You have launched new programs to help vulnerable Americans, volunteered for great causes, and adapted the conversation about how we can get along. We are confident you can make a difference, and our goal in this book is to provide you with some of the knowledge you will need to create lasting impact.

Our Constitution provides the basic framework or structure of government of the United States, and it is within that structure that the next generation of achievement will be shaped, and it is within that structure that "we the people" must act to create policy and to make an impact. In each chapter of the book, we embrace that simple framework for understanding American government: STRUCTURE + ACTION = IMPACT in solving important national challenges such as economic growth, environmental pollution, access to health care and college, and protection from international threats and terrorism. *Structure* refers to the basic rules or framework of government set by the Constitution, the courts, and history, while *action* refers to the political behavior that occurs within the structure. Put these two elements together, and the result is *impact,* or the lack of it, in terms of policy aimed at solving tough problems.

A Grand Experiment in Self-Government (Structure)

1.1 Describe the nature of the "grand experiment in self-government" in America.

Government by the People is about the continuing grand experiment in self-government launched more than two centuries ago by the United States. In this book, we examine the historical context and current practices of the institutions and political processes of American government. As this book's title strongly suggests, we will focus on the role played by people like you in government. The idea of government by the people was important to the Pilgrims who wrote and signed the Mayflower Compact in 1620, the document in which they committed to a system of democratic government to promote the "general good of the colony."[1]

A century and a half later, a different group signed the Declaration of Independence claiming that government derived its powers from the people, and government violation of that public trust was a legitimate cause for revolution. After winning the Revolutionary War and recognizing the need for a stronger and more unified government, the authors of our most important political document, the Constitution, began their proposed framework with the words, "We the people," vividly emphasizing their commitment to self-governance.

After arriving in the New World but before departing the Mayflower to establish Plymouth, the settlers who were free men agreed to and signed a compact about how leaders would be selected and laws enacted. This Mayflower Compact is an early example of self-government.

Undergirding this experiment in self-government is what we might call the idea of America. More broadly, the idea of America includes individualism, a desire for self-government, the pursuit of opportunity, economic liberty, and a commitment to equality of opportunity and to freedom of religion. A list like this was identified by Alexis de Tocqueville, the French aristocrat who visited the United States in the 1820s and whose book *Democracy in America* (written for French readers and published in 1835) remains insightful. More recently, other writers have identified a similar set of ideas as enduring elements of the American political tradition.[2]

Securing an agreement on self-government and perpetuating that agreement is unusual in human history. In many nations, those in power got there because they were born into the right family or because they killed and jailed their opponents. During most of the world's history, no one, especially not oppositional political figures, could openly criticize the government, and any political opponent was treated as an enemy by the state. This is not the case in the United States. Periodically throughout history there had been instances of self-government, including in ancient Greece and the Italian city-states, with republics in Rome, and in England, where the Magna Carta granted by King John in 1215 provided some limits on the monarch and granted certain liberties for free men.

The American colonists had themselves practiced self-government in a limited way through their state legislatures. European philosophers had articulated ideas consistent with the idea of self-government long before the founders of the American republic declared their independence and enshrined these ideas into an agreed-upon constitutional structure. What distinguishes the American Revolution and Constitution is the dramatic scale of the experiment and the claim that ultimate sovereignty came from the people, rather than God or some other source.

The Framers of our republic acknowledged they had devised an imperfect constitution. We know this to be true because the Framers built into the Constitution the ability to change it through amendment or through the calling of another constitutional convention. But the United States has never exercised the option of a second constitutional convention, and only 27 constitutional amendments have been adopted. The experience of the United States in developing a constitutional framework for government and sustaining that framework over time is unusual and important enough to warrant your careful study. In contrast, it is not uncommon for other countries to have had multiple constitutions. For example, Nigeria has had nine constitutions in 24 years.[3]

Some of our early leaders assumed more fundamental change would occur from time to time. Thomas Jefferson, for example, said that "a little rebellion now and then is a good thing, and as necessary in the political world as storms in the physical."[4] Some of our adversaries assumed it would not take long for a monarch, presumably

George Washington, to assume power. England's King George III reportedly said that George Washington would be "the greatest man alive" if he were to voluntarily step down as president after two terms.[5] In this day and age, we take for granted that an officeholder who is defeated in an election will relinquish power to the candidate who won. Imagine what our early leaders would think of the fact that since the birth of the nation, we have held 115 presidential and midterm elections (as of the 2016 election), and we have witnessed the peaceful transfer of power from one party to another on dozens of occasions.

Constitutional self-government is more than a set of abstract principles detached from your life—this is your government too. "Government by the people" now includes you. You will have to protect and use our government of the people to solve the great problems of the day—from repairing the nation's broken roads and rusty bridges to restoring air and water quality, fixing our immigration policy and national defense, protecting the voting rights of all citizens, attacking new diseases, fixing Social Security and our expensive health care system, reducing the debt, making college affordable, caring for our veterans, and reducing the threat of global climate change and nuclear war.

As noted at the start of the chapter, our country has taken on great problems before, not the least of which was surviving the first decades of its existence. And it has produced great achievements in doing so. The air and water did become cleaner; diseases such as polio were conquered; the electorate was expanded to include women, all races, and 18–21-year-olds; Social Security has been repaired at least twice; and the right to marriage now exists for all couples. But even as the nation solved these problems, new problems have arisen. And it is now up to you to provide many of the answers and much of the pressure to solve them.

Constitutional self-government requires each successive generation to decide what parts of the Constitution to retain and what to change. So as *you* read this book and take this course, and beyond this term, ask *yourself* what should be retained and what should be changed. How would you go about defending what you like? How can you change what you don't like? How did we arrive at a constitution that has remained the largely undisputed government structure for more than two centuries? How have we overcome religious and other differences that are an extensive and enduring source of disagreement in Syria and many other countries? How have we come to see elections as the means to work out our differences and take for granted the peaceful transfer of political power from one party to another?

We believe the answers to these questions come from the people, including you and your peers. Without your engagement, the Constitution is only a collection of words. People must pay taxes, defend the nation, and vote and run for office for the structure to have meaning. In this book we emphasize the importance of citizen action. It is our good fortune to live in a country with an established democratic structure. We do not have to establish freedom; for us action often involves less dangerous forms of political participation. Our view is that active citizenship can have an impact, especially when the action is informed by an understanding of the structure of government.

U.S. Government and Politics in Context (Structure)

1.2 Describe the importance of citizen participation in constitutional democracy.

The United States of America, the oldest constitutional democracy in the world, has survived for more than two centuries, yet it is still a work in progress. We think of it as an enduring, strong government, but our political system actually stands on a delicate foundation. The U.S. Constitution and Bill of Rights survive, not because we still have the parchment they were written on, but because each generation of U.S. citizens has respected and worked to understand the principles and values found in these documents. Each generation has faced different challenges in preserving, protecting, and defending our way of **government**, meaning the procedures and institutions (that is, structures such as elections, courts, and legislatures) by which a people govern and rule themselves.

government
The processes and institutions through which binding decisions are made for a society.

We start to practice democracy from an early age, and often go to the polls with our parents or watch them cast their votes by mail to learn how elections work, and though we may be critical of the leaders we choose, we nevertheless recognize the need for political leadership. We also acknowledge the deep divisions and unsolved problems in the United States. For instance, many Americans are concerned about the persistence of racism, about religious bigotry, and about the gap in economic opportunities between rich and poor. We also want our government to defend us against terrorism and foreign enemies, and to address domestic problems like basic health care, education, and unemployment.

But what is this government of which we expect so much? The reality is that "government by the people" is built on the foundation of hundreds of thousands of our fellow citizens: the people we elect and the people they appoint to promote the general welfare, provide for domestic tranquility, and secure the blessings of liberty for us. Government involves **politics**, which, at least in our system of government, is the process by which people decide who shall govern and what policies shall be adopted. Research shows that many of you do not like politics, but politics still matters to your future. Research also shows that you are pioneering new methods for civic engagement using social networks.[6] Whatever tool you use, politics is a still a game for those who show up. If you do not participate, your interests will not be represented in such issues as taxes, U.S. policy in the Middle East, interest on student loans, or the environment.

politics
The process by which decisions are made and carried out within and among nations, groups, and individuals.

More than any other form of government, the kind of democracy that has emerged under the U.S. Constitution requires active participation and a balance between faith and skepticism. Government by the people does not, however, mean that everyone must be involved in politics and policy making, or that those who become involved need to do so through traditional avenues such as campaigning for a political candidate or interning in a representative's office. Some individuals run for office seeking to represent the voters, many of whom will always be too busy doing other, nonpolitical things, and some of whom will always be apathetic about government and politics. However, a fraction of the public must be sufficiently attentive, interested, involved, informed, and willing, when necessary, to criticize and change the direction of government.

Thomas Jefferson, author of the Declaration of Independence, third president of the United States, and founder of the University of Virginia. This statue of Jefferson is in Paris, France, where Jefferson was serving during the Constitutional Convention.

Thomas Jefferson, author of the Declaration of Independence and a champion of constitutional democracy, believed in the common sense of the people and in the possibilities of the human spirit. Jefferson warned that every government degenerates when it is left solely in the hands of the rulers. The people themselves, Jefferson wrote, are the only safe repositories of government. He believed in popular control, representative processes, and accountable leadership. But he was no believer in the participatory democracy of ancient Greece, where all eligible citizens were directly involved in decision making in the political process. Even the power of the people, Jefferson believed, must be restrained from time to time.

Jefferson also believed that education was essential to a successful democracy, and urged citizens to learn how government works. Even today, the vast majority of our leaders have bachelor's degrees—indeed, a college degree is almost a requirement for political life. If you do not know the structure, action, and impact of government, you will enter the process unprepared for its many twists and turns, and you will be locked out.

Government by the people requires faith in our common human enterprise, a belief that the people can be trusted with their own self-government, and an optimism that when things begin to go wrong, the people can be relied upon to set them right. But the people also need a healthy dose of skepticism. Democracy requires us to question our leaders and never entrust a group or institution with too much power. And even though constitutional advocates prize majority rule, they must think critically about whether the majority is always right. Constitutional democracy requires constant attention to protect the rights and opinions of others, and to ensure that our democratic processes serve the principles of liberty, equality, and justice. A peculiar blend of faith and caution is warranted when dealing with the will of the people.

politician
An individual who participates in politics and government, often in the service of a group or political community.

Constitutional democracy means government by **politicians** who represent the people; the elected officials who fulfill the tasks of overseeing and directing the government. A central feature of democracy is that those who hold power do so only by winning a free and fair election. In our political system, the fragmentation of powers requires elected officials to mediate among factions, build coalitions, and work out compromises among and within the branches of our government to produce policy and action.

We all expect our politicians to operate within the rules of democracy and to be honest, humble, patriotic, compassionate, well informed, self-confident, and inspirational. We want politicians, in other words, to be perfect, to have all the answers, and to have all the "correct" values (as we perceive them). We want them to solve our problems, yet we also make them scapegoats for the things we dislike about government: taxes, regulations, hard times, and limits on our freedom. Many of these ideals are unrealistic, and no one could live up to all of them. Like all people, politicians live in a world in which perfection may be the goal, but compromise, ambition, fund-raising, and self-promotion are necessary.

Citizens of the United States will never be satisfied with their political candidates and politicians. The ideal politician is a myth. Politicians become "ideal" only when they are dead. Politicians and candidates, as well as the people they represent, all have different ideas about what is best for the nation. Indeed, liberty invites disagreements about ideology and values. That is why we have politics,

Clay De Long (pictured center), a student at the University of California, Davis, studies a voter's guide as he waits to vote early at a campus polling site in Davis, California.

candidates, opposition parties, heated political debates, and elections. Sadly, the lack of agreement on many of these tough problems can drive down trust in government. Vast numbers of Americans have come to believe the worst about their leaders—that they are lazy, dishonest, and just not very smart.[7] But it is up to the same citizens to replace leaders they disapprove of and work to restore trust.

democracy
Government by the people, where citizens through free and frequent elections elect those who govern and pass laws or where citizens vote directly on laws; also called a *republic*.

direct democracy
Government in which citizens vote on laws and select officials directly.

direct primary
An election in which voters choose party nominees.

initiative
A procedure whereby a certain number of voters may, by petition, propose a law or constitutional amendment and have it submitted to the voters.

referendum
A procedure for submitting to popular vote measures passed by the legislature or proposed amendments to a state constitution.

recall
A procedure for submitting to popular vote the removal of officials from office before the end of their term.

Defining Democracy (Structure)

1.3 Describe democracy and the conditions conducive to its success.

The distinguishing feature of democracy is that government derives its authority from its citizens. In fact, the word comes from two Greek words: *demos*, "the people," and *kratos*, "authority" or "power." Thus **democracy** means *government by the people*, not government by one person (a monarch, dictator, or priest) or government by the few (an oligarchy or aristocracy).

The word *democracy* is not found in either the Declaration of Independence or the U.S. Constitution. Ancient Athens, a few other Greek city-states, and the Roman Republic had a **direct democracy**, in which citizens assembled to discuss and pass laws and select their officials. Most of these Greek city-states and the Roman Republic degenerated into mob rule and then resorted to dictatorial rule or rule by aristocrats. In 1787, James Madison, in *The Federalist*, No. 10, reflected the view of many of the Framers of the U.S. Constitution when he wrote, "Such democracies [as the Greek and Roman]...have ever been found incompatible with personal security, or the rights of property; and have in general been as short in their lives, as they have been violent in their deaths." Madison feared that empowering citizens to decide policy directly would be dangerous to freedom, minorities, and property and would result in violence by one group against another. In line with Madison's view, the Framers used the term *democracy* to describe unruly groups or mobs, and a system that encouraged leaders to gain power by appealing to the emotions and prejudices of the people.

Over time, our democracy has increasingly combined representative and direct democracy. The three most important forms of direct democracy were created roughly a century ago and include the **direct primary**, in which voters, rather than party leaders or other elected officials, select who may run for office; the **initiative** and **referendum**, which allow citizens to vote on state laws or constitutional amendments; and the **recall**, which lets voters remove state and local elected officials from office between elections. Initiatives and referendums are not permitted in all states, but where they are allowed and used, they have been important.

For example, in 2008, California's Proposition 8 divided the state on the issue of gay marriage. Proposition 8 was an initiative that defined marriage as a legal relationship solely between a man and a woman. More than $73 million was spent by the two sides in an intensely fought campaign. The measure was passed with 52 percent of the vote and was deemed constitutional by the California Supreme Court in 2009.[8] Since then it has been reversed by the federal courts.[9] This is not the first vote of the people to be overturned by the courts. In the 1960s, the U.S. Supreme Court reversed a ballot initiative enacted by California voters sanctioning racial discrimination in the sale of housing, sometimes called the "open housing initiative."[10]

Today, even if it were desirable, it is no longer possible to assemble the citizens of any but the smallest towns to make their laws or select their officials directly. Rather, we have invented a system of representation.

James Madison can be thought of as the architect of the Constitution. He was its principal author and one of its strongest supporters as a contributing author of *The Federalist Papers*.

Steve Marx stands up to speak at the Strafford Meeting Hall in Strafford, Vermont, during a town meeting. Since colonial times, many local governments in New England have held meetings at which all community members are invited to discuss issues with public officials.

representative democracy
Government in which the people elect those who govern and pass laws; also called a republic.

republic
Government in which the power is held by the people and their elected representatives.

Democracy today means **representative democracy**, or a **republic**, in which those who have governmental authority get and retain that power directly or indirectly by winning free elections in which all adult citizens are allowed to participate. These elected officials are the people who determine budgets, pass laws, and are responsible for the performance of government. The Framers used the term *republic* to avoid any confusion between direct democracy, which they disliked, and representative democracy, which they liked and thought secured all the advantages of a direct democracy while curing its weaknesses.

Many ideas that are found in the Constitution can be traced to philosophers' writings—in some cases, centuries before the American Revolution and the Constitutional Convention. Among those philosophers, the Framers would have read and been influenced by Aristotle, Thomas Hobbes, John Locke, and Montesquieu. Aristotle, a Greek philosopher writing in the fourth century BCE, provided important ideas on a political unit called a state, on constitutions, and on various forms of governing in his famous work *Politics.*[11] John Locke, an English philosopher, also profoundly influenced the authors of the Declaration of Independence and Constitution. Locke rejected the idea that kings had a divine right to rule, advocated for constitutional democracy, and provided philosophic justification for revolution.[12] Locke, like his fellow Englishman Thomas Hobbes, asserted that there was a social contract whereby people formed governments for security and to avoid what he called the state of nature, where chaos existed and where "everyone was against everyone."[13]

constitutional democracy
A government that enforces recognized limits on those who govern and allows the voice of the people to be heard through free, fair, and relatively frequent elections.

To fully define democracy, we need to clarify other terms. **Constitutional democracy** refers to a government (or structure) through which individuals exercise governmental power (act) as the result of winning free and relatively frequent elections. It is a government in which there are recognized, enforced limits on the powers of all governmental officials. Usually, it also includes a written set of governmental rules and procedures—a constitution. The practice in the United States of constitutional provisions limiting the power of one part of the government by having another part of the government balance or check it is another example of the Framers applying ideas from earlier thinkers—in this case, the French philosopher Charles de Montesquieu.[14] *Constitutionalism* is a term we apply to arrangements or structures designed to limit power and to require leaders to listen, compromise, and reach agreements before they make laws. The people can then hold them politically and legally accountable for the way they exercise their powers.

Like most political concepts, democracy encompasses many ideas and has many meanings. It is a way of life, a form of government, a way of governing, a type of nation, a state of mind, and a variety of processes. We can divide these many meanings of democracy into three broad categories: a system of interacting values, a system of interrelated political processes, and a system of interdependent political structures.

Democracy as a System of Interacting Values

A constitutional democracy is built on a foundation of the people sharing a set of core values, an agreed-upon structure of governance, and confidence in their ability to work out differences through the political process. Political scientists use the term **political culture** to refer to the widely shared beliefs, values, and norms citizens hold about their relationship to government and to one another. These beliefs, values, and norms provide the structure or context needed to understand American politics. We can discover the specifics of a nation's political culture not only by studying what its people believe and say, but also by observing how they behave. That behavior includes such fundamental decisions as who may participate in political decisions, what rights and liberties citizens have, how political decisions are made, and what people think about politicians and government generally.

political culture
The widely shared beliefs, values, and norms citizens hold about their relationship to government and to one another.

The founders of our nation claimed that individuals have certain **natural rights**—the rights of all people to dignity and worth—and that government must be limited and controlled because it is a threat to those rights. This belief in natural rights creates a system of interacting values that provides a foundation for public confidence. Among those values are personal and economic liberty, individualism, equality of opportunity, and popular sovereignty.

natural rights
The rights of all people to dignity and worth; also called *human rights*.

PERSONAL AND ECONOMIC LIBERTY No value in the American political culture is more revered than liberty. "We have always been a nation obsessed with liberty. Liberty over authority, freedom over responsibility, rights over duties—these are our historic preferences," wrote the late Clinton Rossiter, a noted political scientist. "Not the good man but the free man has been the measure of all things in this sweet 'land of liberty'; not national glory but individual liberty has been the object of political authority and the test of its worth."[15] The essence of liberty is self-determination, meaning that all individuals must have the opportunity to realize their own goals. Liberty is not simply the absence of external restraint on a person (freedom from something); it is also a person's capacity to reach his or her goals (freedom to *do* something). Not all students of U.S. political thought accept this emphasis on freedom and individualism over virtue and the public good, and in reality both sets of values are important.[16]

INDIVIDUALISM Popular rule in a democracy flows from a belief that every person has the potential for common sense, rationality, and fairness. Individuals have important rights; collectively, those rights are the source of all legitimate governmental authority and power. These concepts pervade democratic thought, and constitutional democracies make the individual—rich or poor, black or white, male or female—the central measure of value. Policies that limit individual choice generate intense political conflict. The debates over legalized abortion and universal health care are often framed in terms of our ability to exercise choices. Although American citizens support individual rights and freedoms, they also understand that their rights can conflict with another person's or with the government's need to maintain order or promote the general welfare.

Not all political systems put the individual first. Some promote a form of government based on centralized authority and control, especially over the economy. China, Vietnam, and Cuba, for example, take this approach. But, in a modern democracy, the nation, or even the community, is less important than the individuals who compose it.

EQUALITY Thomas Jefferson's famous words in the Declaration of Independence express the strength of our views of equality: "We hold these truths to be self-evident, that all men are created equal, that they are endowed by their Creator with certain unalienable rights that among these are life, liberty, and the pursuit of happiness." In contrast to Europeans, our nation shunned aristocracy, and our Constitution explicitly prohibits governments from granting titles of nobility. Although our rhetoric about equality was not always matched by our policy—for example, slavery and racial segregation in schools—the value of social equality is now deeply rooted.

American citizens also believe in *political equality*—the idea that every individual has a right to equal protection under the law and equal voting power. Although political equality has always been a goal, it has not always been a reality. In the past, African Americans, Native Americans, Asian Americans, and women were denied rights extended to white males.

equal opportunity
All individuals, regardless of race, gender, or circumstance, have the opportunity to participate in politics, self-government, and the economy.

Equality encompasses the idea of **equal opportunity**, especially with regard to improving our economic status. American adults believe social background should not limit our opportunity to achieve to the best of our ability, nor should race, gender, or religion. The nation's commitment to public education programs such as Head Start for disadvantaged preschool children, state support for public colleges and universities, and federal financial aid for higher education reflects this belief in equal opportunity.

American dream
A complex set of ideas that holds that the United States is a land of opportunity where individual initiative and hard work can bring economic success.

capitalism
An economic system based on private property, competitive markets, economic incentives, and limited government involvement in the production, pricing, and distribution of goods and services.

OPPORTUNITY AND THE AMERICAN DREAM Many of our political values come together in the **American dream**, a complex set of ideas that holds that the United States is a land of opportunity where individual initiative and hard work can bring economic success. Whether fulfilled or not, this dream speaks to our most deeply held hopes and goals. Its essence is expressed in our enthusiasm for **capitalism**, an economic system based on private property, competitive markets, economic incentives, and limited government involvement in the production, pricing, and distribution of goods and services.[17]

The concept of private property enjoys extraordinary popularity in the United States. Most cherish the dream of acquiring property and believe that the owners of property have the right to decide how to use it. And yet, the unequal distribution of property that James Madison highlighted in *The Federalist*, No. 10, is still a cause of faction or political division to this day.[18] The conflict in values between a *competitive economy*, in which individuals reap large rewards for their initiative and hard work, and an *egalitarian society*, in which everyone earns a decent living, carries over into politics. How the public resolves this tension changes over time and from issue to issue. Different generations, living under different conditions and constraints, have acted within the political structure to achieve their desired policy outcomes (impact).

Young Americans are still sorting out their positions on many issues, but are currently "unmoored" from the traditional political and social institutions that might give them some direction on their priorities. According to a 2014 survey of American generations, the millennial generation is less trusting of other people, less likely to see themselves as patriotic, and less likely to believe in God. However, they are no less likely to be partisan or to say they lean toward one of the two major parties.[19] At the same time, they are more likely than older Americans to support gay rights, bigger government, health coverage for all, a legal path to citizenship for undocumented immigrants, and to call themselves environmentalists. They are also more likely to be upbeat about their financial future. At the individual level, young people can have an impact on an even wider array of issues. The big question is which of these attitudes and positions are likely to endure and perhaps define the millennial generation the way the Great Depression did the 1930s, and the Vietnam War did the 1970s.

Though the American dream is important as an aspiration, it remains unfulfilled. The gap between rich and poor has grown in recent years, and a sharp income difference between whites and blacks remains tenacious.[20] For many, chances for success still depend on the family into which they were born, the neighborhood in which they grew up, or the college they attended. An underclass persists in the form of impoverished families, malnourished and poorly educated children, and the homeless.[21] Many cities are actually two cities, where some residents live in luxury and others in squalor.

Most people today support a semi-regulated or mixed free enterprise system that checks the worst tendencies of capitalism, but they reject excessive government intervention. Much of American politics centers on how to achieve this balance. Currently, most people agree that some governmental intervention is necessary to assist those who fall short in the competition for education and economic prosperity and to encourage ventures that, though they have substantial public benefit, might not be undertaken without government assistance.

POPULAR SOVEREIGNTY The animating principle of the American Revolution, the Declaration of Independence, and the resulting new nation was **popular sovereignty**—the idea that ultimate political authority rests with the people. This means that a just government must derive its powers from **popular consent**. A commitment to democracy thus means that a community must be willing to participate and make decisions in government. These principles sound unobjectionable, but often other people in positions of power disrupt or overturn self-government. In Egypt, the 2011 Arab Spring protests forced from power Hosni Mubarak, who had led the country for 29 years. Mubarak claimed to have been elected in Egypt, but the balloting was usually limited to returning him to power with no other option given to voters.[22] Before the protests of 2011, Mubarak showed no signs of relinquishing power, and his likely successor was presumed to be his son, Gamal Mubarak. The protests led to military responses in which hundreds were wounded, and at least seven died on the bloodiest day of clashes.[23] Mubarak then relinquished power to the military, which in turn announced a six-month plan to have elections and write a new constitution.

popular sovereignty
The idea that ultimate political authority rests with the people.

popular consent
The idea that a just government must derive its powers from the consent of the people it governs.

After more violent protests calling for a quicker transition to democracy, an election for a new parliament was held, and religious groups like the Muslim Brotherhood won a majority. Six months later, a presidential election was held in which a Muslim Brotherhood candidate, Mohammed Morsi, defeated Mubarak's former prime minister, Ahmed Shafik, becoming the first civilian to lead Egypt. Critics of Morsi and the new constitution then protested, and some of those protests turned violent. The military, headed by General Abdul-Fattah el-Sisi, expressed concerns about the way the new constitution was written and Morsi's failure to uphold democratic values.[24] Sisi removed Morsi from power and suspended the constitution. He was elected president in 2014 with 97 percent of the vote in an election described by some as "undemocratic."[25] Morsi was later charged with inciting the protests and riots and imprisoned. Egypt is not alone in having an elected government removed from power. This also happened in Thailand in 2014.[26] What happened in these countries demonstrates the difficulty of establishing a democratic process that consistently results in a stable government, protects individual rights, and accomplishes a peaceful transfer of power.

Democracy as a System of Interrelated Political Processes

In addition to meeting a few key conditions and having a consensus of core democratic values, a successful, democratic government requires a well-defined political process as well as a stable governmental structure. To genuinely practice democracy, a nation must incorporate democratic values into its political process, in the form of free and fair elections, majority rule, freedom of expression, and the right of its citizens to peaceably assemble and protest. Having a judiciary that applies the laws equally and fairly is also an important part of a successful democracy.

FREE AND FAIR ELECTIONS Democratic government is based on free and fair elections held at intervals frequent enough to make them relevant to policy choices. Elections are one of the most important devices used to keep officials and representatives accountable to the voters. The United States has never postponed an election; even in the middle of the Civil War, voters cast ballots as scheduled. We might take this record for granted, but it is far from universal. In recent years, for example, elections have been postponed in Cuba (2017),[27] Democratic Republic of the Congo (2016),[28] Liberia (2017),[29] and Venezuela (2018).[30]

In the United States, the date of national elections is set in the Constitution as the first Tuesday after the first Monday in November of even-numbered years. Even during the Civil War elections were not postponed. But in some democracies the government will postpone an election, as happened in Nigeria in 2015. Here, Nigerians are protesting that action.

Crucial to modern-day definitions of democracy is the idea that opposition political parties can exist, can run candidates in elections, and have a chance to replace those who currently hold public office. Thus political competition and choice are crucial to the existence of democracy. In 2018, the Chinese removed term limits for their president, Xi Jinping, opening the possibility that he may be president for life. This change strengthened Xi Jinping's hold on power.[31] Although free and fair elections do not imply that everyone will have equal political influence, they do imply that everyone will have equal voting power; each citizen—president or plumber, corporate CEO or college student—casts only one vote.

majority rule
Governance according to the expressed preferences of the majority.

plurality rule
The candidate or party with the most votes wins an election, not necessarily more than half.

MAJORITY AND PLURALITY RULE Governance according to the expressed preferences of the majority, or **majority rule**, is a basic rule of democracy. The majority candidate or party is the one that receives *more than half* the votes and so wins the election and takes charge of the government until the next election. In practice, however, democracies often function by **plurality rule**. Here, the candidate or party with the *most* votes wins the election, even though the candidate or party may not have received more than half the votes because votes were divided among three or more candidates or parties.

Should the side with the most votes always prevail? American citizens answer this question in various ways. Some insist that majority views should be enacted into laws and regulations. An effective representative democracy, however, requires far more than simply counting individual preferences and implementing the will of most of the people. In a constitutional democracy, the will of a majority may run counter to the rights of individuals.

The Framers of the U.S. Constitution wanted to guard against oppression of any one faction of the people by any other faction. The Constitution reflects their fear of tyranny by majorities, especially momentary majorities that spring from temporary passions. They insulated certain rights (such as freedom of speech) and institutions (such as the Supreme Court and, until the Constitution was changed in 1913, the Senate) from popular choice. Effective representation of the people, the Framers insisted, should not be based solely on parochial interests or the shifting breezes of opinion.

FREEDOM OF EXPRESSION Free and fair elections depend on voters having access to facts, competing ideas, and the views of candidates. This means that competing, nongovernment-owned newspapers, radio stations, and television stations must be allowed to flourish. If the government controls what is said and how it is said, elections cannot be free and fair, and there is no democracy. We examine free expression in greater detail in Chapter 14.

THE RIGHT TO ASSEMBLE AND PROTEST Citizens must be free to organize for political purposes. Obviously, individuals can have a greater impact if they join with others in a party, a pressure group, a protest movement, or a demonstration. The right to oppose the government, to form opposition parties, and to have a chance to defeat incumbents is a defining characteristic of a democracy.

JUSTICE AND THE RULE OF LAW Inscribed over the entrance to the U.S. Supreme Court are the words "Equal Justice Under Law." The rule of law means government is based on a body of laws applied equally and by just procedures, as opposed to arbitrary rule by an elite group whose whims decide policy or resolve disputes. In 1803, Chief Justice John Marshall summarized this principle: "The government of the United States has been emphatically termed a government of laws, not of men."[32] Americans believe strongly in fairness: everyone is entitled to the same legal rights and protections.

To adhere to the rule of law, government should follow these five rules in making and enforcing laws:

1. *Generality.* Laws should be stated generally and not single out any group or individual.
2. *Forward-looking.* Laws should apply to the present and the future, not punish something someone did in the past.
3. *Publicity.* Laws cannot be kept secret and then enforced.
4. *Authority.* Valid laws are made by those with legitimate power, and the people legitimate that power through some form of popular consent.
5. *Due process.* Laws must be enforced impartially with fair processes.

Democracy as a System of Interdependent Political Structures

Democracy is, of course, more than the values and processes we have discussed so far. Its third characteristic is political structures that safeguard these values and processes. The Constitution and its first 10 amendments, the **Bill of Rights**, set up an ingenious structure that both grants and checks government power. A system of political parties, interest groups, media, and other institutions that intercede between the electorate and those who govern reinforces this constitutional structure and helps maintain democratic stability. For example, the president, justices of the Supreme Court, and members of Congress all swear to uphold the Constitution. Moreover, individuals, groups, and the media also play a role in the functioning of the Constitution. Individuals, including elected officials, do not always secure their desired outcome in a particular matter, but by working within the constitutional framework, they reinforce it as the agreed-upon way to resolve differences.

Bill of Rights
The first 10 amendments to the Constitution that provide a guarantee of individual liberties and due process before the law.

The U.S. constitutional system has five distinctive elements:

1. *Federalism.* Federalism is the division of powers between the national and state governments.
2. *Separation of powers.* Powers are divided among the executive, judicial, and legislative branches.
3. *Bicameralism.* This refers to the division of legislative power between the House of Representatives and the Senate.
4. *Checks and balances.* Each branch is given the constitutional means, the political independence, and the motives to check the powers of the other branches so that a relative balance of power among the branches endures.
5. *Bill of Rights.* The Bill of Rights is a judicially enforceable, written document that provides a guarantee of individual liberties and due process before the law.

Conditions Favorable for Constitutional Democracy

Although it is hard to specify the precise conditions that consistently establish and preserve a democracy, we can identify some patterns that foster its growth. Conditions favorable for constitutional democracy include education, economic opportunity, social cohesion, ideological consensus, and stability.

EDUCATION The exercise of voting privileges requires an educated citizenry. A high level of education (measured by the number of high school diplomas and university degrees granted) does not guarantee democratic government, but voting makes little sense unless many of the voters can read and write and express their interests and opinions. The poorly educated and illiterate are often left out in a democracy. Direct democracy puts a further premium on education.[33]

ECONOMIC OPPORTUNITY A relatively prosperous nation, with an equitable distribution of wealth, provides the best context for democracy. Starving people are more interested in food than in voting. Where economic power is concentrated, political power is also likely to be concentrated; thus, well-to-do nations have a better chance of sustaining democratic governments than do those with widespread poverty. As a result, the prospects for an enduring democracy are greater in Canada or France than in Egypt (discussed earlier in this chapter) or many other new democracies.

Private ownership of property and a market economy are also related to the creation and maintenance of democratic institutions. Freedom to make economic choices is linked to other freedoms, like freedom of religion and the right to vote. Democracies can range from heavily regulated economies with public ownership of many enterprises, such as Sweden, to those in which there is little government regulation of the marketplace, such as the United States. But there are no democracies with a highly centralized, government-run economy and little private ownership of property. Examining experiments with democracy in other countries, we can find examples of democracies that struggled in settings with unfavorable economic conditions. For example, economic challenges during the Weimar Republic in Germany (1919–1933) undermined that short-lived experiment in self-rule.[34]

SOCIAL COHESION Economic development generally makes democracy possible, but proper social conditions are necessary to make it real.[35] In a society fragmented into warring groups that fiercely disagree on fundamental issues, government by discussion and compromise is difficult. When ideologically separated groups consider the issues at stake to be vital, they may prefer to fight rather than accept the verdict of the ballot box, as happened in the United States in 1861 with the outbreak of the Civil War.

In a society that consists of many overlapping associations and groupings, however, individuals are less likely to identify completely with a single group and give their allegiance to it. For example, think of yourself for a moment as an African American man, a member of the African Methodist Episcopal Church, a Texan, a Democrat, an electrician, and a member of the local Coalition of Black Trade Unionists, who makes $25,000 a year at a minimum-wage job. Then think of yourself for a moment as unaffiliated with any religion, a white woman, a Californian, a physician, an independent, and a member of the National Organization for Women making $150,000 a year. Or think of some other combination altogether. On some issues, you might think as an African American or supporter of unions, and on others as a physician and high-income professional. While you and your friends may differ on some issues and agree on others, you likely share an overriding common interest in maintaining democracy.[36]

IDEOLOGICAL CONSENSUS American adults have basic beliefs about power, government, and political practices—beliefs that arise from the educational, economic, and social conditions of their individual experience. From these conditions there must also develop general acceptance of the ideals of democracy and willingness of a substantial number of people to agree to proceed democratically. This acceptance, sometimes called democratic consensus, is a set of widely shared attitudes and beliefs about government and its values, procedures, documents, and institutions. Without such a consensus, attempts at democracy will not succeed. For example, China has made major strides in improving its educational and economic circumstances in recent years, but it lacks both democratic consensus and the institutions and liberties vital to a democracy.

STABILITY Political scientists have long tried to determine what factors contribute to stability in a democracy. Comparative studies have often linked factors such as national prosperity, education, and literacy to democratic success. Table 1.1 lists several different dimensions for the United States, seven other countries, and the world.

The basic values of democracy do not always coexist happily. Individualism may conflict with the collective welfare or the public good. Self-determination may conflict with equal opportunity. A media outlet's freedom to publish classified documents about foreign or defense policy may conflict with the government's constitutional requirement to "provide for the common defense."

Much of our political debate revolves around how to strike a balance among democratic values. How, for example, do we protect our unalienable rights of life, liberty, and the pursuit of happiness promised in the Declaration of Independence while also trying to "promote the general Welfare" as the Constitution proclaims?

We have discussed the values, political processes, and political structures that help foster constitutional democracy, as well as the conditions conducive to it. These provide a foundation on which we can assess governments throughout the world, as well as the extraordinary story of the founding and enlargement of constitutional democracy in the United States, to which we turn next.

TABLE 1.1 CONDITIONS FOR DEMOCRACY

These countries vary dramatically in many aspects. For example, note the extremely young population of Nigeria compared to the generally older population of Japan. *What are the implications of this difference for both governments?* Notice that the U.S. population is less than one-fourth that of China. *How might population size affect some of these factors?* Compare the differences in literacy between men and women in India, Nigeria, and China. *What do you think accounts for these differences?*

	World	UK	China	India	Japan	Mexico	Nigeria	US	Iran
Population (millions; July 2013 est.)	7,405.1	65.6	1,379.3	1,281.9	126.5	124.6	190.6	326.6	82.0
Median Age (years)	30.4	40.5	37.4	27.9	47.3	28.3	18.4	38.1	30.3
Life Expectancy (years)	69	80.8	75.7	68.8	85.3	76.1	53.8	80	74
Literacy:									
Male	89.8%	99	98.2	81.3	99	95.5	69.2	99	91.2
Female	82.6%	99	94.5	60.6	99	93.5	49.7	99	82.5
Government Type		Constitutional monarchy	Communist state	Federal republic	Constitutional monarchy	Federal republic	Federal republic	Federal republic	Theocratic republic*
GDP (purchasing power parity)**	127	2.88	23.12	9.45	5.41	2.406	1.12	19.36	1.63
Internet Users (% of population)	67	88	65	22	69	54	39	89	
Freedom House***		Free	Not Free	Free	Free	Partly Free	Partly Free	Free	Not Free

NOTES: *Theocratic government is a form of government in which a deity is recognized as the supreme civil ruler, but the deity's laws are interpreted by ecclesiastical authorities; **Calculated based on the country's official exchange rate in trillions of USD; ***For more on Freedom House's Freedom Index, see http://www.freedomhouse.org/report-types/freedom-world#.UyH46PldV8E.

SOURCE: Central Intelligence Agency, *The World Factbook*, at http://www.cia.gov/library/publications/the-world-factbook/geos/xx.html and Freedom House, *Freedom in the World 2018 The Annual Survey of Political Rights and Civil Liberties*, at http://www.freedomhouse.org/report-types/freedom-world#.UyH46PldV8E; #Jacob Poshter, "Smartphone Ownership and Internet Usage Continues to Climb in Emerging Economies." Pew Research Center, Global Attitudes & Trends, February 22, 2016, based on survey conducted in 2015. http://www.pewglobal .org/2016/02/22/smartphone-ownership-and-internet-usage-continues-to-climb-in-emerging-economies/.

The Roots of the American Constitutional Experiment (Structure)

1.4 Identify pre-Revolutionary concepts central to the new government and the problems under the Articles of Confederation.

Most of us probably consider having a democracy and a constitution as part of the natural order of history. Although we have essentially inherited a functioning system—the work of others, generations ago—we take pride in our ability to make it work. Our job is not only to keep the system going, but also to improve and adapt it to the challenges of our times. To do so, however, we must first understand it by recalling our democratic and constitutional roots.

Colonial Beginnings

Our democratic experiment might well have failed. The 13 original states (formerly colonies) were independent and could have gone their separate ways. Differences between them, based both on social and economic conditions, including slavery in the Southern states, were an obvious challenge to unity. Given these potential problems, how did democracy survive? The Framers of the Constitution had experience to guide them. For nearly two centuries, Europeans had been sailing to the New World in search of liberty, especially religious liberty, as well as the chance to own land and to an extent exercise self-governance in colonial legislatures. The experience of settling a new land, overcoming obstacles, and enjoying the fruits of their labors was also important to the spirit of independence in the colonies.[37]

theocracy
A form of government in which a deity is recognized as the supreme civil ruler, but the deity's laws are interpreted by ecclesiastical authorities.

But freedom in the colonies was limited. Ironically, given their concern for religious liberty, the Puritans in Massachusetts established a **theocracy**, a system of government in which religious leaders claimed divine guidance and in which other sects were denied religious liberty. Later, as that system was challenged, the Puritans continued to worry "about what would maintain order in a society lacking an established church, an attachment to place, and the uncontested leadership of men of merit."[38] Nine of the 13 colonies eventually set up a state church. Throughout the 1700s, Puritans in Massachusetts barred certain men from voting on the basis of church membership. Women, slaves, and Native Americans could not vote at all.

By the 1700s, editors in the colonies found that for the most part they could speak freely in their newspapers, dissenters could distribute leaflets, and agitators could protest in taverns or in the streets. And yet dissenters were occasionally exiled, imprisoned, and even executed, and some printers were beaten and had their shops closed. In short, the colonists struggled to balance stability and dissent, order, and liberty.

The Rise of Revolutionary Fervor

As resentment against British rule mounted during the 1770s, the colonists became determined to fight the British to win their rights and liberties. In 1776, a year after the fighting broke out in Massachusetts, the Declaration of Independence proclaimed, in ringing tones, that all men are created equal, endowed by their Creator with certain unalienable rights including "life, liberty, and the pursuit of happiness"; that to secure those rights, governments are instituted among men; and that whenever a government becomes destructive of those ends, it is the right of the people to alter or abolish it.

We have heard these great ideals so often that we take them for granted. Revolutionary leaders did not. They were willing to fight and pledge their lives, fortunes, and sacred honor for these rights. Indeed, by signing the Declaration of Independence, they were effectively signing their own death warrants if the Revolution failed.[39] In most cases, state constitutions guaranteed the underlying rights referred to in the Declaration: free speech, freedom of religion, and the natural rights to life, liberty, and property. All state constitutions spelled out the rights of persons accused of a crime, such as the right to know the nature of the accusation, confront their accusers, and receive a timely and public trial by jury.[40] Moreover, these guarantees were set out in writing, in sharp contrast to the unwritten British constitution.

Toward Unity and Order

As the war against the British widened to include all 13 colonies, the need arose for a stronger central government to unite them. In 1777, Congress established a new national government, the Confederation, under a written document called the **Articles of Confederation**.[41] The Articles were not approved by all the state legislatures until 1781, after Washington's troops had been fighting the British for six years.

Articles of Confederation
The first governing document of the confederated states, drafted in 1777, ratified in 1781, and replaced by the present Constitution in 1789.

The Confederation was more a fragile league of friendship than a national government. There was no national executive, no judiciary, and no national currency. Congress, with no direct authority over citizens, had to work through the states. It could not levy taxes or regulate trade between the states or other nations; neither could it prevent the states from taxing each other's goods or issuing their own currencies. The lack of a judicial system meant that the national government had to rely on state courts to enforce national laws and settle disputes between the states. In practice, state courts could overturn national laws.

With the end of the Revolutionary War in 1783, the sense of urgency that had produced unity among the states began to fade, and the national government was not equipped for what followed. Conflicts between states and between creditors and debtors within the various states grew intense. Foreign threats continued, especially from within the territories ruled by England and Spain that surrounded the weak new nation. As pressures on the Confederation mounted, many leaders became convinced that a more powerful central government was needed to create a union strong enough to deal with internal diversity and factionalism and to resist external threats.

In September 1786, under the leadership of Alexander Hamilton, supporters of a truly national government took advantage of the Annapolis Convention—a meeting in Annapolis, Maryland, on problems of trade and navigation attended by delegates from five states—to issue a call for a convention to consider basic amendments to the

Since 1928, an image of Alexander Hamilton, one of the authors of the Constitution and the first secretary of the treasury, has appeared on the $10 bill. In 2015, the Department of the Treasury invited input on who the first female should be to replace Hamilton on this currency. A groundswell arose to keep Hamilton, driven in part by the success of the Broadway play, *Hamilton*. In 2016, it was announced that Hamilton would remain on the front of the $10 bill, with the back having images of leaders of the women's suffrage movement. The Treasury Department under President Trump has not commented on changes to the $10 bill.

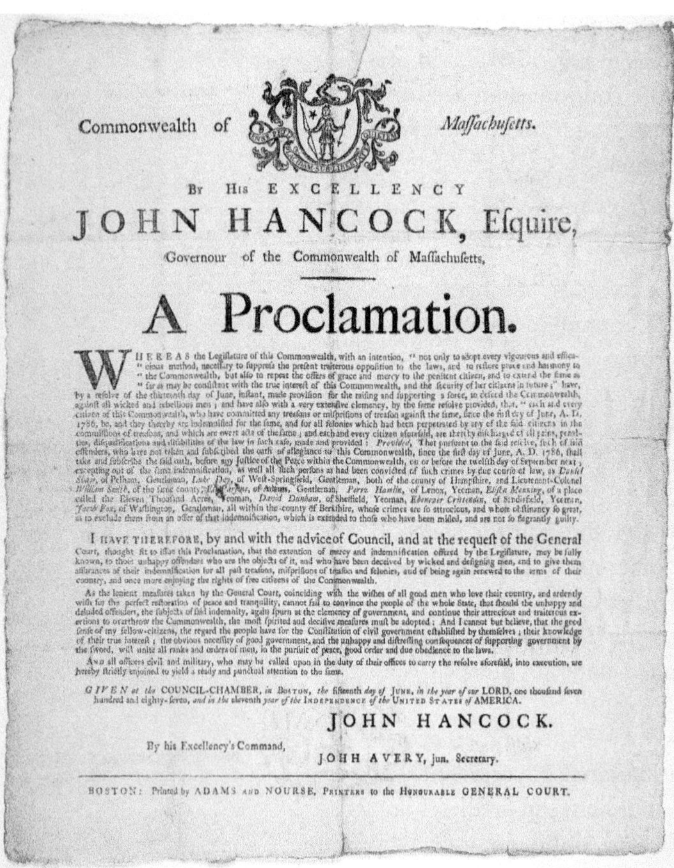

Commonwealth of *Massachusetts.*

By His EXCELLENCY

JOHN HANCOCK, Esquire,

Governour of the Commonwealth of Massachusetts,

A Proclamation.

WHEREAS the Legislature of this Commonwealth, with an intention, "not only to adopt every vigourous and efficacious method, necessary to suppress the present traiterous opposition to the laws, and to restore peace and harmony to the Commonwealth, but also to repeat the offers of grace and mercy to the penitent citizen, and to extend the same as far as may be consistent with the true interest of this Commonwealth, and the security of her citizens in future;" have, by a resolve of the thirteenth day of June, instant, made provision for the raising and supporting a force, to defend the Commonwealth, against all wicked and rebellious men; and have also with a very extensive clemency, by the same resolve provided, that, "each and every citizen of this Commonwealth, who have committed any treasons or misprisions of treason against the same, since the first day of June, A. D. 1786, be, and they thereby are indemnified for the same, and for all felonies which had been perpetrated by any of the said citizens in the commissions of treason, and which are overt acts of the same; and each and every citizen aforesaid, are thereby discharged of all pains, penalties, disqualifications and disabilities of the law in such case, made and provided: *Provided*, That pursuant to the said resolve, such of said offenders, who have not taken and subscribed the oath of allegiance to this Commonwealth, since the first day of June, A. D. 1786, shall take and subscribe the said oath, before any Justice of the Peace within the Commonwealth, on or before the twelfth day of September next; excepting out of the same indemnification, as well all such persons as had been convicted of such crimes by due course of law, as *Daniel Shays*, of Pelham, Gentleman, *Luke Day*, of West-Springfield, Gentleman, both of the county of Hampshire, and Lieutenant-Colonel *William Smith*, of the same county; *Eli Parsons*, of Adams, Gentleman, *Perez Hamlin*, of Lenox, Yeoman, *Elisha Manning*, of a place called the Eleven Thousand Acres, Yeoman, *David Dunham*, of Sheffield, Yeoman, *Ebenezer Crittenden*, of Sandisfield, Yeoman, *Jacob Fox*, of Washington, Gentleman, all within the county of Berkshire, whose crimes are so attrocious, and whose obstinancy so great, as to exclude them from an offer of that indemnification, which is extended to those who have been misled, and are not so flagrantly guilty.

I HAVE THEREFORE, by and with the advice of Council, and at the request of the General Court, thought fit to issue this Proclamation, that the extention of mercy and indemnification offered by the Legislature, may be fully known, to those unhappy offenders who are the objects of it, and who have been deceived by wicked and designing men, and to give them assurances of their indemnification for all past treasons, misprisions of treason and felonies, and of being again renewed to the arms of their country, and once more enjoying the rights of free citizens of the Commonwealth.

As the lenient measures taken by the General Court, coinciding with the wishes of all good men who love their country, and ardently wish for the perfect restoration of peace and tranquility, cannot fail to convince the people of the whole State, that should the unhappy and deluded offenders, the subjects of said indemnity, again spurn at the clemency of government, and continue their attrocious and traiterous exertions to overthrow the Commonwealth, the most spirited and decisive measures must be adopted: And I cannot but believe, that the good sense of my fellow-citizens, the regard the people have for the Constitution of civil government established by themselves; their knowledge of their true interest; the obvious necessity of good government, and the unhappy and distressing consequences of supporting government by the sword, will unite all ranks and orders of men, in the pursuit of peace, good order and due obedience to the laws.

AND all officers civil and military, who may be called upon in the duty of their offices to carry the resolve aforesaid, into execution, are hereby strictly enjoined to yield a ready and punctual attention to the same.

GIVEN at the COUNCIL-CHAMBER, *in* BOSTON, *the fifteenth day of* JUNE, *in the year of our* LORD, one thousand seven hundred and eighty-seven, *and in the eleventh year of the* INDEPENDENCE *of the* UNITED STATES *of* AMERICA.

JOHN HANCOCK.

By his Excellency's Command,

JOHH AVERY, jun. Secretary.

BOSTON: Printed by ADAMS AND NOURSE, PRINTERS to the HONOURABLE GENERAL COURT.

The rebellion of farmers led by Daniel Shays in 1787 added urgency to the Framers' efforts to draft a constitution that would protect property and the rule of law. Later, Governor John Hancock issued a pardon to participants in the rebellion providing they swore an oath to the Commonwealth of Massachusetts.

Articles of Confederation. The delegates were to meet in Philadelphia on the second Monday of May 1787 "to devise such further provisions as shall appear to them necessary to render the Constitution of the Federal Government adequate to the exigencies of the Union."[42] This meeting became the **Constitutional Convention**.

For a short time, all was quiet. Then, late in 1786, messengers rode into George Washington's plantation at Mount Vernon in Virginia with the kind of news he and other leaders had dreaded. Farmers in western Massachusetts, crushed by debts and taxes, were rebelling against foreclosures, forcing judges out of their courtrooms, and freeing debtors from jails. This came to be known as **Shays' Rebellion**, named for Daniel Shays, the leader of the insurrection. As a patriot and a wealthy landowner, Washington was appalled. "What, gracious God, is man?" he exclaimed.

Not all reacted as Washington did. When Abigail Adams, the politically knowledgeable wife of John Adams, the Revolutionary statesman from Massachusetts, sent news of the rebellion to Thomas Jefferson, the Virginian replied, "I like a little rebellion now and then." He noted that the "tree of liberty must be refreshed from time to time with the blood of patriots and tyrants. It is its natural manure."[43] But the rebellion highlighted the lack of a mechanism to enforce contractual obligations in the absence of a strong central government.

Some, like historian Charles A. Beard, have argued that the primary motive of the authors of the U.S. Constitution was the protection of their economic interests more than concern for other values.[44] Beard's views have been challenged.[45] Most agree that even though the early leaders of the United States were protecting their own economic interests, this was not their only motive.

Shays' Rebellion was defeated after the farmers attacked an arsenal and were cut down by cannon fire. The uprising, however, had threatened prosperity, established order, and the rule of law, and it reinforced the view that a stronger national government was needed. Congress issued a cautiously worded call to all the state legislatures to appoint delegates for the "sole and express purpose of revising the Articles of Confederation."[46] The call for a convention specified that no recommendation would be effective unless approved by Congress and confirmed by all the state legislatures, as provided by the Articles.

Constitutional Convention

The convention in Philadelphia, from May 25 to September 17, 1787, that debated and agreed on the Constitution of the United States.

Shays' Rebellion

A rebellion led by Daniel Shays of farmers in western Massachusetts in 1786–1787 protesting mortgage foreclosures. It highlighted the need for a strong national government just as the call for the Constitutional Convention went out.

The Constitutional Convention of 1787 (Action)

1.5 Identify the issues resolved by compromise during the writing of the Constitution.

Representing different constituencies and different ideologies, the Constitutional Convention devised a totally new form of government that provided for a central government strong enough to rule but still responsible to its citizens and to the member states.

Despite the limited purposes given for calling the convention of 1787, within five days of its opening, the convention voted—with only the Connecticut delegates dissenting—that "a national government ought to be established consisting of a

The convention to draft the constitution was held in this room in Independence Hall in Philadelphia, Pennsylvania. Here, a U.S. Park Ranger is conducting a tour of the building. The room is not large and the participants spent that hot summer here without air-conditioning and with the windows closed so their conversations could not be overheard. George Washington presided over the convention. You can see his chair at the far end of the room.

supreme legislative, executive, and judiciary." This decision profoundly changed the nature of the union, from a loose confederation of states to a true nation.

The delegates who assembled in Philadelphia in May 1787 had to establish a national government powerful enough to prevent the young nation from dissolving but not so powerful that it would crush individual liberty. What these men did continues to have a major impact on how we are governed. It also provides an outstanding lesson in political science, which is the study of the principles, procedures, and structures of government and the analysis of political ideas, institutions, behaviors, and practices.

The Delegates

The various states appointed 74 delegates, but only 55 arrived in Philadelphia. Of these, approximately 40 actually took part in the work of the convention. It was a distinguished gathering. Many of the most important men of the nation were there: successful merchants, planters, bankers, lawyers, and former and present governors and congressional representatives (39 of the delegates had served in Congress). Most had read the classics of political thought. Most had experience constructing local governments. Many had also worked hard to create and direct the national confederation of the states. Eight of the delegates' names were among the 56 signatures on the Declaration of Independence.

The convention was as representative as most political gatherings were at the time: the participants were all white male landowners. These well-read, well-fed, well-bred, and often well-wed delegates were mainly state or national leaders, for ordinary people were not likely to participate in politics in the 1780s. (Even today, farm laborers, factory workers, and truck drivers are seldom found in Congress—although a haberdasher, a peanut farmer, and a movie actor have made their way to the White House.)

Educated men of the period considered science, as well as politics and economics, within their sphere of knowledge. Influenced by Isaac Newton's discoveries, they were fascinated by machinery that operated by balancing forces one against another. The Framers thought the Constitution should embody the principles of such machines, with each part of government exerting force upon the others. Newton's success in describing physical laws reinforced the Framers' belief that they could identify, understand, and harness forces in human nature.

Although active in the movement to revise the Articles of Confederation, George Washington had been reluctant to attend the convention and accepted only when persuaded that his prestige was needed for its success. He was selected unanimously to preside over the meetings. According to the records, he spoke only twice during the deliberations, but his influence was felt in the informal gatherings as well as during the sessions. Everyone understood that Washington favored a more powerful central government led by a president. In fact, the general expectation that he would be the first president played a crucial role in the creation of the presidency. "No one feared that he would misuse power.... His genuine hesitancy, his reluctance to assume the position, only served to reinforce the almost universal desire that he do so."[47]

To encourage everyone to speak freely and allow delegates to change their minds after debate and discussion, the proceedings of the convention were kept secret and delegates were forbidden to discuss them with outsiders. The delegates also knew that if word of the inevitable disagreements got out, it would provide ammunition for the enemies of the convention.

Consensus

Critical to the success of the Constitutional Convention were its three famous compromises: the compromise between large and small states over representation in Congress, the compromise between North and South over the regulation and taxation of foreign commerce, and the compromise between North and South over how to count slaves for the purposes of taxation and representation. There were other important compromises, but on many significant issues most of the delegates were in agreement.

All the delegates publicly supported a republican form of government based on elected representatives of the people. This was the only framework the convention seriously considered and the only form acceptable to the nation. Equally important, all the delegates opposed arbitrary and unrestrained government. Most of the delegates were in favor of balanced government in which no single interest would dominate and in which the national government would be strong enough to protect property and business from outbreaks like Shays' Rebellion.

Benjamin Franklin, the 81-year-old delegate from Pennsylvania, favored extending the right to vote to all white males, but most of the delegates believed landowners were the best guardians of liberty. James Madison feared that if given the right to vote, those without property might combine to deprive property owners of their rights. Delegates agreed in principle on limited voting rights but differed on the kind and amount of property owned as a prerequisite to vote. The Framers recognized that they would jeopardize approval of the Constitution if they made the qualifications to vote in federal elections more restrictive than those of the states. As a result, each state was left to determine its own qualifications for electing members to the House of Representatives, the only branch of the national government that was to be elected directly by the voters.

Few dissented from proposals to give the new Congress all the powers of the old Congress, plus all other powers necessary to ensure that state legislation would not challenge the integrity of the United States. After the delegates agreed on the extensive powers of the legislative branch and the close connection between its lower house and the people, they also agreed that a strong executive, which the Articles of Confederation had lacked, was necessary to provide energy, direction, and a check on the legislature. They also accepted an independent judiciary without much debate. Other issues, however, sparked conflict.

Conflict and Compromise

Serious differences among the various delegates, especially between those from the large and small states, predated the Constitutional Convention. With the success of the War of Independence, the United States gained the formerly British land west of

FIGURE 1.1 WESTERN EXPANSION, 1791

Tension between small states and large states was intensified by the dispute over claims to western land acquired after the Revolutionary War.

the colonial borders. States with large western borders, such as Virginia, claimed that their borders should simply be extended, as depicted in Figure 1.1. Colonies without open western borders, such as New Jersey and Connecticut, took exception to these claims, reinforcing the tension between the colonies. The matter was resolved in the Land Ordinance of 1785 and the Northwest Ordinance of 1787, when all states agreed to cede the western lands to the national government and permit them to eventually become part of new states rather than expand the borders of existing states. But the rivalries between the former colonies remained sharp at the convention in Philadelphia in 1787. For example, the large states also favored a strong national government (which they expected to dominate), while delegates from small states were anxious to avoid being dominated.

This tension surfaced in the first discussions of representation in Congress. Franklin favored a single-house national legislature, but most states had had two-chamber legislatures since colonial times, and the delegates were accustomed to this system. **Bicameralism**—the principle of a two-house legislature—reflected the delegates' belief in the need for balanced government. The Senate, the smaller chamber that would represent the states, and to some extent the wealthier classes, would offset the larger, more democratic House of Representatives that represented the people.

bicameralism

A legislature in which power is divided between two chambers. In the United States, this is the Senate and the House of Representatives.

THE VIRGINIA PLAN The Virginia delegation, especially James Madison, took the initiative. They presented 15 resolutions known collectively as the **Virginia Plan**. This plan called for a strong central government with a legislature composed of two

Virginia Plan

The initial proposal at the Constitutional Convention made by the Virginia delegation for a strong central government with a bicameral legislature dominated by the big states.

chambers. The voters were to elect the members of the more representative chamber, which would choose the members of the smaller chamber from nominees submitted by the state legislatures. Representation in both houses would be based on either wealth or population. Wealth was based on a 1783 law where "general expenses were apportioned on the basis of land values with their improvements." The more wealthy states were also the more populous ones—Massachusetts, Pennsylvania, and Virginia—which gave them a majority in the national legislature.

The Virginia Plan would have created a Congress with all the legislative power of its predecessor under the Articles of Confederation, as well as the power "to legislate in all cases in which the separate States are incompetent," which is understood to mean areas that concerned the states collectively;[48] to veto state legislation that conflicted with the proposed constitution; and to choose a national executive with extensive jurisdiction. A national Supreme Court, along with the executive, would have a qualified veto over acts of Congress. In sum, the Virginia Plan would have created a strong national government with disproportionate power to the more populous states.

New Jersey Plan

The proposal at the Constitutional Convention made by William Paterson of New Jersey for a central government with a single-house legislature in which each state would be represented equally.

THE NEW JERSEY PLAN The Virginia Plan dominated the discussion for the first few weeks. That changed when delegates from the small states put forward their plan. William Paterson of New Jersey presented a series of resolutions known as the **New Jersey Plan**. Paterson did not question the need for a strengthened central government, but he was concerned about how this strength might be used. The New Jersey Plan would give Congress the right to tax and regulate commerce and to coerce states, and it would retain the single-house or unicameral legislature (as under the Articles of Confederation) in which each state, regardless of size, would have the same vote.

The New Jersey Plan contained the beginnings of what eventually came to be a key provision of our Constitution: the supremacy clause. The national Supreme Court was to hear appeals from state judges, and the supremacy clause would require all judges—state and national—to treat laws of the national government and the treaties of the United States as superior to the constitutions and laws of each of the states.

For a time, the convention was deadlocked. The small states believed that all states should be represented equally in Congress, especially in the smaller "upper house" if there were to be two chambers. The large states insisted that representation in both houses be based on population or wealth, and that voters and not state legislatures should elect national legislators. Finally, the so-called Committee of Eleven—a committee of 11 men, one from each of the member states—was elected to devise a compromise.[49] On July 5, this committee presented its proposals, including what came to be known as the Great or Connecticut Compromise.

Connecticut Compromise

The compromise agreement by states at the Constitutional Convention for a bicameral legislature with a lower house in which representation would be based on population and an upper house in which each state would have two senators.

THE CONNECTICUT COMPROMISE The **Connecticut Compromise** (so labeled because of the prominent role the Connecticut delegation played in its construction) called for one house in which each state would have an equal vote, and a second house in which representation would be based on population and in which all bills for raising or appropriating money—a key function of government—would originate. This proposal was a setback for the large states, which agreed to it only when the smaller states made it clear this was their price for union. After the delegates accepted equality of state representation in the Senate, most objections to a strong national government dissolved. (Table 1.2 outlines the key features of the Virginia Plan, the New Jersey Plan, and the Connecticut Compromise.)

NORTH–SOUTH COMPROMISES Other issues split the delegates from the North and South. Southerners were afraid that a northern majority in Congress might discriminate against southern trade. They had some basis for this concern. John Jay, a

TABLE 1.2 THE CONSTITUTIONAL CONVENTION: CONFLICT AND COMPROMISE

	Virginia Plan	New Jersey Plan	Connecticut Compromise
How Is Legitimacy Derived?	Derived from citizens, based on popular representation	Derived from states, based on equal votes for each state	Derived from citizens and the states
What Type of Legislature?	Bicameral legislature, representation in both houses determined by population	Unicameral legislature, representation equal by state	Bicameral legislature with seats in the Senate apportioned by states and seats in the House apportioned by population
How Many Executives and to Whom Accountable?	Executive size undetermined, elected and removable by Congress	More than one person, removable by state majority	Single executive elected by Electoral College, not removable by state majority
What Is the Role of the Judiciary?	Judicial life tenure, able to veto state legislation	No federal judicial power over states	Judicial life tenure, able to veto state legislation that is in violation of Constitution
Would the Constitution Be Superior to the States?	Legislature can override state laws	Government can compel obedience to national laws	Constitution is the supreme law of the land
How Would the Constitution Be Ratified?	Ratification by citizens	Ratification by states	Ratification by states, with process open to citizen ratification

New Yorker who was secretary of foreign affairs for the Confederation, had proposed a treaty with Great Britain that would have given advantages to northern merchants at the expense of southern exporters of agricultural products such as tobacco and cotton. To protect themselves, the southern delegates insisted that a two-thirds majority in the Senate be required to ratify a treaty.

One subject that appears not to have been open for resolution was slavery. The view widely shared among historians is that the states with greater reliance on slaves would have left the convention if the document had reduced or eliminated the practice. The issue did arise on whether to count slaves for the purpose of apportioning seats in the House of Representatives. To gain more representatives, the South wanted to count slaves; the North resisted. After heated debate, the delegates agreed on the **three-fifths compromise**. Three of every five slaves would be counted for purposes of apportionment in the House and of direct taxation. This three-fifths fraction was chosen because it maintained a balance of power between the North and the South. The compromise also included a provision to eliminate the importation of slaves in 20 years, which Congress did in 1808. The issue of balance between North and South would recur in the early history of our nation as territorial governments were established and territories that applied for statehood decided whether to permit or ban slavery.

three-fifths compromise
The compromise between northern and southern states at the Constitutional Convention that three-fifths of the slave population would be counted for determining direct taxation and representation in the House of Representatives.

OTHER AGREEMENTS Delegates also argued about other issues. Should the national government have lower courts, or would one federal Supreme Court be enough? This issue was left to Congress to resolve. The Constitution states that there shall be one Supreme Court and that Congress may establish lower courts.

How should the president be selected? For a long time, the convention favored allowing Congress to pick the president, but some delegates feared that Congress would then dominate the president, or vice versa. The convention also rejected election by the state legislatures because the delegates distrusted the state legislatures. The delegates finally settled on election of the president by the Electoral College, a group of individuals equal in number to the U.S. senators and representatives. Originally, it was thought electors would exercise their own judgment in selecting the president. But the college quickly came to reflect partisanship, and today, for most states, electors cast ballots for the candidate who wins the popular vote of that state. (We discuss the Electoral College in greater detail in the chapter on campaigns and elections.) This was perhaps the delegates' most novel contribution as well as the most contrived, and it has long been one of the most criticized provisions in the Constitution.[50] (See Article II, Section 1, of the Constitution.)

After three months, the delegates stopped debating. On September 17, 1787, all but three of those still present signed the document they were recommending to the nation. Others who opposed the general drift of the convention had already left. Their work well done, the delegates adjourned to the nearby City Tavern to celebrate.

According to an old story, a woman confronted Benjamin Franklin as he left the last session of the convention.

"What kind of government have you given us, Dr. Franklin?" she asked. "A republic or a monarchy?"

"A republic, Madam," he answered, "if you can keep it."

To Adopt or Not to Adopt? (Impact)

1.6 Evaluate the arguments for and against the ratification of the Constitution.

The delegates had gone much farther in creating a new government than even they expected. Indeed, they had disregarded Congress's instruction to do no more than revise the Articles of Confederation. In particular, they had ignored Article XIII, which declared the Union to be perpetual and prohibited any alteration of the Articles unless Congress and every one of the state legislatures agreed—a provision that had made it impossible to amend the Articles. The convention delegates, however, boldly declared that their newly proposed Constitution should go into effect when ratified by popularly elected conventions in nine states.

They turned to this method of ratification for practical considerations as well as to secure legitimacy for their proposed government. Not only were the delegates aware that there was little chance of winning approval of the new Constitution in all state legislatures, but many also believed that a constitution approved by the people would have higher legal and moral status than one approved only by a legislature. The Articles of Confederation had been a compact of state governments, but the Constitution was based on the will of the people (recall its opening words: "We the People…"). Still, even this method of ratification would not be easy.

Federalists Versus Anti-Federalists

Federalists
A group that argued for ratification of the Constitution, including a stronger national government at the expense of states' power. They controlled the new federal government until Thomas Jefferson's election in 1800.

Anti-Federalists
Opponents of ratification of the Constitution and of a strong central government generally.

Supporters of the new government, by cleverly appropriating the name **Federalists**, forced their opponents to be known as the **Anti-Federalists** and pointed out the negative character of the arguments opposing ratification. In advocating a strong national government but also retaining state prerogatives, the Federalists took some of the sting out of charges that they were trying to destroy the states and establish an all-powerful central government.

The split was in part geographic; seaboard and city regions tended to be Federalist strongholds, while backcountry regions from Maine (then part of Massachusetts) through Georgia, inhabited by farmers and other relatively poor people, were generally Anti-Federalist. The underlying regional and economic differences led to fears by those opposing the new form of government that it would not protect individual rights, and reinforced the "Anti-Federalist charge that the Constitution was an aristocratic document."[51] But as in most political contests, no single factor completely accounted for the division between Federalists and Anti-Federalists. Thus, in Virginia, the leaders of both sides came from the same general social and economic class. More urban New York City and Philadelphia strongly supported the Constitution, yet so did predominantly rural New Jersey and Connecticut.

The Federalist
Essays promoting ratification of the Constitution, published anonymously by Alexander Hamilton, John Jay, and James Madison in 1787 and 1788.

The great debate between Federalists and Anti-Federalists was conducted through pamphlets, newspapers, letters to editors, and speeches. It provides an outstanding example of a free people publicly discussing the nature of their fundamental laws. As discussed, out of the debate came a series of essays known as ***The Federalist***, written under the pseudonym Publius by Alexander Hamilton, James Madison, and John Jay to persuade the voters of New York to ratify the Constitution. *The Federalist* is still "widely regarded as the most profound single treatise on the Constitution ever written and as among the few masterly works in political science produced in all the centuries of history."[52]

Anti-Federalists opposed the creation of a strong central government. They worried that, under the Constitution, Congress would "impose barriers against commerce," and they were concerned that the Constitution did not do enough to ensure "frequent rotation of office," worrying that elected officials would not be recalled through elections and over time would become less concerned with their constituents.[53]

The Anti-Federalists' most telling criticism of the proposed Constitution was its failure to include a bill of rights.[54] The Federalists believed a bill of rights was unnecessary because the proposed national government had *only* the specific powers that the states and the people delegated to it. Thus, there was no need to specify that Congress could not, for example, abridge freedom of the press because the states and the people had not given the national government power to regulate the press in the first place. Moreover, the Federalists argued, to explicitly provide protections for some liberties might lead to the denial of others not explicitly included. The Constitution itself already protected some important rights—the requirement of trial by jury in federal criminal cases, provided for in Article III, for example. Hamilton and others also insisted that paper guarantees were feeble protection against governmental tyranny.

The Anti-Federalists were unconvinced. If some rights were protected, what could be the objection to providing constitutional protection for others? Without a bill of rights, what was to prevent Congress from using one of its delegated powers to abridge free speech? If bills of rights were needed in state constitutions to limit state governments, why did the national constitution not include a bill of rights to limit the national government? This was a government farther from the people, they contended, with a greater tendency to subvert natural rights than was true of state governments.

The Politics of Ratification

The absence of a bill of rights in the proposed Constitution dominated the struggle over its adoption. In taverns, churches, and newspaper offices, people were muttering, "No bill of rights—no Constitution!" This feeling was so strong that some Anti-Federalists who were far more concerned with states' rights than individual rights joined forces with those wanting a bill of rights in order to defeat the proposed Constitution.

The Federalists began the debate over the Constitution as soon as the delegates left Philadelphia in mid-September 1787. Their tactic was to secure ratification in as many states as possible before the opposition had time to organize. The Anti-Federalists were handicapped because most newspapers supported ratification. Moreover, Anti-Federalist strength was concentrated in rural areas, which were underrepresented in some state legislatures and in which it was more difficult to arouse the people to political action. The Anti-Federalists needed time to organize, while the Federalists moved in a hurry.

Most of the small states, now satisfied by getting equal Senate representation, ratified the Constitution without difficulty. Delaware was the first, and by early 1788, Pennsylvania, New Jersey, Georgia, and Connecticut had also ratified. In Massachusetts, however, opposition was growing. Key leaders, such as John Hancock and Samuel Adams, were doubtful or opposed. The debate in Boston raged for most of January 1788 and into February. But in the end, the Massachusetts Convention narrowly ratified the Constitution in that state, 187 to 168.

By June 21, 1788, Maryland, South Carolina, and New Hampshire had also ratified, giving the Constitution the nine states required for it to go into effect. However, two big hurdles remained: Virginia and New York. Even with the necessary nine ratifying states, it would be impossible to begin the new government without the consent of these two major states. Virginia, as the most populous state and the home of Washington, Jefferson,

Patrick Henry's famous cry of "Give me liberty or give me death!" helped rally support for the revolution against Britain. Later, he was an outspoken opponent of ratification of the Constitution and was instrumental in forcing adoption of the Bill of Rights. This statue is on the state capitol grounds in Richmond, Virginia.

and Madison, was a link between North and South. The Virginia ratifying convention rivaled the Constitutional Convention in the caliber of its delegates. Madison, who had only recently switched to favoring a bill of rights after saying earlier that it was unnecessary, captained the Federalist forces. The fiery Patrick Henry led the opposition. In an epic debate, Henry cried that liberty was the issue: "Liberty, the greatest of earthly possessions...that precious jewel!" But Madison promised that a bill of rights embracing the freedoms of religion, speech, and assembly would be added to the Constitution as soon as the new government was established. Washington tipped the balance with a letter urging ratification. News of the 89–79 Virginia vote for ratification was rushed to New York.[55]

The great landowners along New York's Hudson River, unlike the southern planters, opposed the Constitution. They feared federal taxation of their holdings, and they did not want to abolish the profitable tax New York had been levying on trade and commerce with other states. When the convention assembled, the Federalists were greatly outnumbered, but they were aided by Alexander Hamilton's strategy and skill, and by word of Virginia's ratification. New York approved by a margin of three votes. Although North Carolina and Rhode Island still remained outside the Union (the former ratified in November 1789, the latter six months later), the new nation was created. In New York, a few members of the old Congress assembled to issue the call for elections under the new Constitution. Then they adjourned without setting a date for reconvening.

At the Constitutional Convention in 1787 and later in the first Congress, the Framers had begun the hard work of confronting the challenges of creating a government, writing a Constitution, and drafting a bill of rights that would protect rights to life, liberty, and self-government for themselves and subsequent generations. The way they approached their work demonstrated an understanding of the importance of the structure of the new government they were creating. They needed to preserve some important prerogatives for the states while creating a much stronger national government. They did that in part through the structure of the Senate and the limited powers of the Constitution. They did not want too much power to go to the executive, and they wanted to further check the power of the legislature. Hence, they created a government structure with checks, balances, and bicameralism.

In *The Federalist*, No. 10, Madison claims it is possible and important to understand human nature, because out of that understanding come ways to limit people's negative tendencies. Madison identified the following aspects of human nature that need to be considered in designing a government: "zeal for different opinions,...attachment to different leaders,...[and the] propensity of mankind to fall into mutual animosities most commonly concerning the unequal distribution of property."[56] Madison, borrowing from Locke, connected understanding of human nature to constitutional structure, as follows: "If men were angels, no government would be necessary. If angels were to govern men, neither external nor internal controls on government would be necessary."[57] In other words, human nature as Madison understood it required some type of government to regulate citizens' behavior and some type of control over that government to regulate citizen-politicians' behavior, as well.

Madison's idea of harnessing the human capacity for evil found its fullest expression in the constitutional provisions for dividing powers among the branches. The president cannot sit in the legislature; a senator cannot also be in the House. The president shares in legislation with the power to sign and veto bills. Congress shares in the executive power by providing all the money, but the spending is done by the executive branch. The president has the power to conduct foreign relations and wage war, but Congress must ratify treaties and provide declarations of war. Most appointments are made by the president, but Congress must ratify these candidates. The judiciary can check both of the other branches by determining if executive or legislative actions are consistent with the Constitution. The executive has the power to appoint federal court judges, and the Senate must consent to these appointments. Each branch thus is given ways to check the others. For Madison, the science of politics included understanding human nature and designing constitutional mechanisms to channel power to good, and not bad, ends.

In addition to understanding the importance of structure, the Framers also knew that an active citizenry was essential to the new government's success. They knew, as we also know, that passive allegiance to ideals and rights is never enough. Every generation must become responsible for nurturing these ideals by actively renewing the community and nation of which it is a part. This was more than an abstract interest of the Framers; their presence in Philadelphia demonstrated a willingness to engage in public affairs. So, did structure coupled with action equal impact for those who wrote the Constitution? The answer is clearly yes.

Although the ratified Constitution had limitations and shortcomings, it is an extraordinary governing document to this day. It allowed the states to unite, it provided a workable structure, and it protected fundamental rights and liberties. Over the centuries since it was ratified, it has been amended and interpreted by succeeding generations to meet changing needs and circumstances. It provides a clear structure for governing the nation that sets out the rules and boundaries for action toward solving important national problems. The Framers made sure to provide a governing structure allowing for citizen action and participation that can substantially impact public policy.

CONCLUSION

When the colonists declared their independence in 1776, they did so in part because of their conception that the British government had disregarded their rights as citizens. However, their assertion that there were certain inalienable rights like life, liberty, and property had never before been given as a reason for a free and independent government. The colonists defeated a superior army and achieved independence. But the legacy of separate colonies and a limited and ineffectual confederation of the colonies meant the newly free colonies lacked a viable national government that could pay its loans to foreign allies, manage interstate commerce, and defend the country.

James Madison arrived at the Constitutional Convention in 1787 with a plan for a new and much stronger national government. His proposed structure, however, gave too much power to the large states at the expense of the small states. An important lesson from the Framers' resolution of this issue is that meaningful action in politics often requires compromise.

It is one thing to form a new government, and another for that government to endure through time. Throughout history, many such governments have failed, only to be replaced by anarchy or tyranny. As Americans, we take for granted an established structure within which to work out our political differences, and we assume that the people, and not the military, will have the final say in our government. Yes this is not the case throughout the world. Sometimes democracy emerges, but lacking established institutions and processes (structures), these new democracies often fail and either new dictators emerge or old dictators return to power, promising a return to order.

Our constitutional democracy has endured in part because of a widely held set of democratic values (like liberty and political equality), agreed-upon processes to resolve our differences (like elections and popular sovereignty), and political structures that the people see as legitimate (courts, legislatures, executives). Central to the continuity of this remarkable experiment in self-government is citizen action, which has the possibility to impact the present and future. The signers of the Declaration of Independence took action and achieved a remarkable impact—independence. Those who hammered out our constitutional structure took action and achieved an impact—a constitutional republic that over time has acted to extend rights and liberties to more and more people. Achieving government by the people is an ongoing process that can be informed by the past but must be applied in the present and the future if it is to endure and be improved.

To do this, people of all generations (including millennials) must overcome the very low levels of trust in government found in data from the Pew Research Center (See Figure 1.2). And yet the data also show that when the country faces large challenges, like after the September 11, 2001, terrorist attacks, the level of trust in government rises, especially for millennials. Is this reaction to an external threat to self-government an indication that more fundamentally Americans prefer their form of government, however imperfect, or does it mean something else?

FIGURE 1.2 TRUST IN GOVERNMENT

While the trend over time is clearly for trust in government to decline, note the rise in trust in the 2001–2002 period. This reflects a changed perspective on government. By 2006, however, the trend lines are lower than they were before the 2001–2002 rise. Note that the Millennial and Generation X cohorts both start around the same level and follow the pattern of declining trust similar to other generational groups such as the Silent and Greatest generations. By 2017, millennials express levels of trust lower than Gen X or the Silent generations, and differences between generations are largely absent.

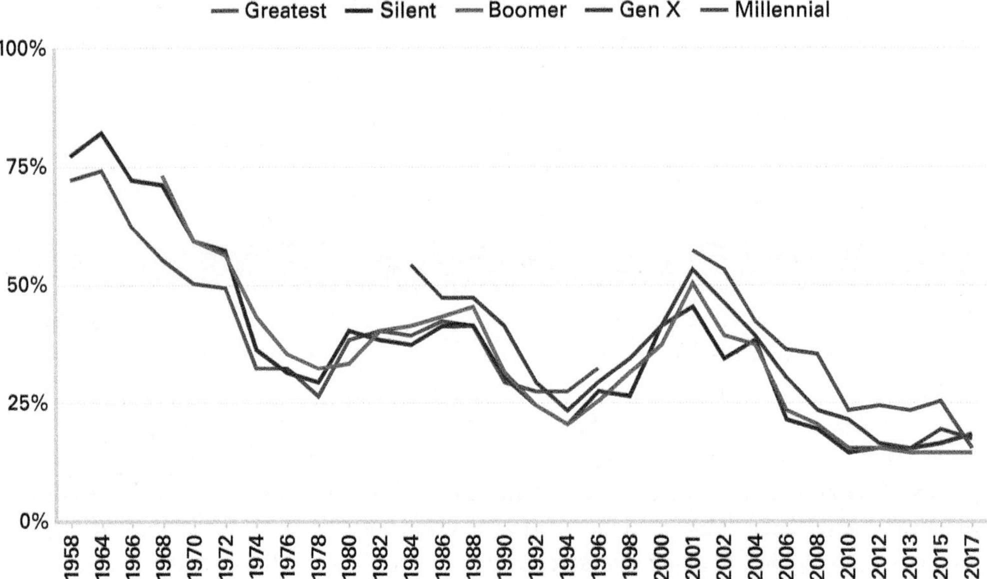

SOURCE: Pew Research Center, U.S. Politics & Policy. "Public Trust in Government: 1958-2017. http://www.people-press.org/2017/05/03/public-trust-in-government-1958-2017/ Data summarized in chart from Pew, CBS/New York Times, CNN, Gallup, American National Election Study, ABC/Washington Post,

QUESTION: Percent who trust government in Washington always or most of the time.

You will decide whether to retain the governmental structure we have today, or modify it by amendment. While we have not adopted a new constitution in nearly 220 years, prior generations have made important changes to the Constitution through amendments approved by two-thirds of both houses of Congress and three-quarters of the states. People like you are proposing particular amendments and some are calling for a constitutional convention. Among the changes being debated: who should be counted in apportioning the U.S. House of Representatives? Should all religions be allowed to worship? Should people born in the United States automatically be U.S. citizens? If you choose not to participate in these decisions, you are, by your inaction, allowing others to decide for you. While changing our structure of government is difficult, history teaches us that sustained action can have an impact. Examples of enduring impact from those taking action include abolishing slavery, extending the right to vote, and protecting rights and liberties from governments at all levels.

REVIEW THE CHAPTER

A Grand Experiment in Self-Government (Structure)

1.1 Describe the nature of the "grand experiment in self-government" in America, p. 2.

While it was Abraham Lincoln who made the phrase "government of, by and for the people" famous in his Gettysburg address, the idea of people governing themselves is central to the settlement of places like Plymouth, Massachusetts, to Thomas Jefferson's argument in the Declaration of Independence, and to the U.S. Constitution, which begins with the words, "We the people." The idea that the people have the right to form their own government and make their own laws brings with it the need for each generation to take ownership of their government and help shape it. Prior generations have done this and accomplished remarkable things, but also made some mistakes and left unfinished work for today's citizens. Active participation informed by an understanding of the structure of government, we believe, can have an impact.

U.S. Government and Politics in Context (Structure)

1.2 Describe the importance of citizen participation in constitutional democracy, p. 4.

The United States operates under a constitutional democracy. In our system, the Constitution lays out the basic rules of the game under which politicians act to accomplish their different agendas. *Politics* is a broad term that can be used to describe what happens between these politicians in pursuit of their goals. *Government* is another broad term that encompasses the many different institutions enumerated by the Constitution in which the politicians function. Political science studies the interaction among politics, politicians, the government, and, within the American context, our constitutional democracy. A recurrent theme in the book is that knowledge of the *structure* of government and politics combined with citizen *action* can result in *impact.*

Defining Democracy (Structure)

1.3 Describe democracy and the conditions conducive to its success, p. 7.

In the United States, we often use the term *democracy* to describe our form of government. This description is true to an extent, but a more accurate term would be *representative democracy* or *republic.* The politicians in our system are elected representatives meant to stand up for the interests of their constituents. Representative democracy differs from direct democracy in the level of citizen participation.

Scholars have identified several conditions that may help democratic governments form and consolidate. Among these, the most important are educational, economic, social, and ideological conditions. These conditions further democratic values such as a belief in personal liberty, respect for the individual, equality of opportunity, and popular consent. Established processes like elections and an impartial judiciary also are important to a stable democracy. Our representative democracy functions through political structures including courts, legislatures, the executive, administrative agencies, federalism, and the principle of limited government. Also important to our tradition is the rule of law and freedom of expression.

The Roots of the American Constitutional Experiment (Structure)

1.4 Identify pre-Revolutionary concepts central to the new government and the problems under the Articles of Confederation, p. 16.

In the formative years of American democracy, several competing factions worked, sometimes at cross purposes, to develop the Constitution. Some of the most divisive issues that the Framers had to address were the challenges presented by a federal system. Small states, for instance, had real concerns about their role in a democratic system. Other issues had more to do with geography and economics. The divide between the North and the South on slavery, for example, was important at the convention.

The Constitutional Convention of 1787 (Action)

1.5 Identify the issues resolved by compromise during the writing of the Constitution, p. 18.

The Framers came up with some brilliant compromises to address the issues of slavery and large states versus small states, such as the Connecticut Compromise, which led to our current bicameral legislative branch. Other issues were put on hold. For example, the Framers postponed dealing with slavery and compromised on counting slaves as three-fifths of a person for purposes of apportionment.

To Adopt or Not to Adopt? (Impact)

1.6 Evaluate the arguments for and against the ratification of the Constitution, p. 24.

Some of the same themes that dominated the debate over ratification can still be heard today. Federalists argued for a central government that would be strong enough to make the newly United States capable of standing up to the great powers of the time. Anti-Federalists worried about what might come of a strong central government and were particularly concerned about the lack of any bill of rights in the document.

LEARN THE TERMS

government, p. 5
politics, p. 5
politician, p. 6
democracy, p. 7
direct democracy, p. 7
direct primary, p. 7
initiative, p. 7
referendum, p. 7
recall, p. 7
representative democracy, p. 8
republic, p. 8
constitutional democracy, p. 8
political culture, p. 9
natural rights, p. 9
equal opportunity, p. 10
American dream, p. 10
capitalism, p. 10
popular sovereignty, p. 11
popular consent, p. 11
majority rule, p. 12
plurality rule, p. 12
Bill of Rights, p. 13
theocracy, p. 16
Articles of Confederation, p. 17
Constitutional Convention, p. 18
Shays' Rebellion, p. 18
bicameralism, p. 21
Virginia Plan, p. 21
New Jersey Plan, p. 22
Connecticut Compromise, p. 22
three-fifths compromise, p. 23
Federalists, p. 24
Anti-Federalists, p. 24
The Federalist, p. 24

CHAPTER 2

Constitutional Foundations

Debates over the definition of citizenship have important consequences, especially to families of undocumented immigrants with children born on U.S. soil. These are not debates that can be answered solely by the language of the U.S. Constitution.

LEARNING OBJECTIVES

- **2.1** Describe the framework for government expressed in the Constitution (Structure), p. 33.
- **2.2** Describe the constitutional foundations of the federal judiciary and judicial review (Action), p. 39.
- **2.3** Describe the process by which the Constitution can be changed (Impact), p. 41.

The Statue of Liberty has greeted immigrants arriving in New York Harbor since its dedication in 1886. Its famous inscription welcomes the world's tired, poor, "huddled masses yearning to breathe free." Historically, the United States has had one of the most open immigration policies in the world, even encouraging immigration as a way to settle land as the country expanded westward. Indeed, immigrants have been essential in developing the United States into the world leader that it is today.

Immigration was a major issue in the 2016 presidential campaign and has continued to be a focal point for the Trump administration during his first two years in office. Debate centered on the president's long-promised wall along the U.S.–Mexico border, the fate of undocumented immigrants in the United States and those covered by the Obama-era Deferred Action for Childhood Arrivals (DACA), the policies of so-called sanctuary cities, and broader reform of general U.S. immigration policy. After campaigning on the border wall and contending that Mexico would pay for its construction, President Trump was finally able to secure initial funding through a March 2018 spending bill. A far cry from the $25 billion the president requested, the March legislation provided just $1.6 billion for "border security" measures, and just $641 million for the wall itself.[1]

These immigration debates are not new. Indeed, the story of U.S. immigration policy is not one in which those "huddled masses yearning to breathe free" have always found open doors. In the wake of the "Great Wave" of immigration that brought over 24 million people to the United States from 1900 to 1920, Congress enacted a national origins immigration system that limited immigration from each country based on their representation in past U.S. census reports. Those quotas significantly limited immigration, even in the years leading up to World War II, when the United States refused to accept Jewish immigrants from Nazi Germany. In one notorious case, when a ship carrying over 900 mostly Jewish passengers arrived off the Florida coast in 1939, the United States refused entry and the ship was forced to return to Europe. Over a quarter of those passengers died in the Holocaust. And, of course, much more recently, debate has focused on improving enforcement of existing policies and whether to offer amnesty to some portion of undocumented immigrants.

During President Obama's 2008 election campaign, he promised to introduce immigration reform that would provide for greater border security and a path to citizenship for undocumented immigrants. But, throughout his presidency, attempts to secure congressionally enacted comprehensive immigration reform largely failed. As a result, in 2012, President Obama announced that the Department of Homeland Security would implement a temporary program that would defer deportation to a subgroup of undocumented immigrants, in particular individuals whose parents brought them to the United States as children. President Trump had long argued that the program represented executive overreach and in November 2017, he announced an end to DACA as of March 5, 2018. A lower federal court judge ruled that the plan the Justice Department developed to end DACA is problematic and that the U.S. Supreme Court has refused to intervene at this point.

What do you think the Constitution means when it refers to United States citizenship? One significant aspect of the immigration debate concerned the treatment of children born on U.S. soil to undocumented immigrant parents. Are these persons citizens? There are legal theories and historical precedent to help answer this question, but depending on how you and your classmates understand and interpret the Constitution, you might reach different conclusions. This is just one example of many for which the Constitution's lack of clarity can lead to reasonable disagreements on its meaning.

What is the most appropriate understanding? How does that understanding influence your views on immigration policy? Should policies differ depending on the reason for immigrating to the United States? Should immigrants fleeing crime and violence in Mexico and other Central American countries be treated differently than Syrian immigrants fleeing civil war and terrorism in the Middle East? Your generation will have to answer these questions, and there's a lot riding on your answers: economic stability and national security, the position of the United States in the global community, and the protection of human rights.

In this chapter, we discuss the structure of our constitutionally arranged system of separation of powers and checks and balances. You will see how the judiciary has acted strategically to expand its limited structural authority and the impact of that action on all three branches of government, which have widely accepted the judiciary as the final interpreter of constitutional meaning. Although they have accepted the judiciary's authority, the executive and the legislature also have used the Constitution's structure to pursue their own ends. Finally, the chapter will help you understand the difficult process through which we, the people, can act to change the structure of the Constitution itself. As the Framers intended, achieving such an impact is no small feat, but it has been an important factor in the stability of our Constitution.

Constitutional Framework (Structure)

2.1 Describe the framework for government expressed in the Constitution.

The United States Constitution is the oldest written constitution in the world; it is also one of the shortest. The original Constitution contains only 4,543 words. In comparison, India's constitution has more than 117,000 words, and the longest state constitution—that of Alabama—totals more than 380,000 words.[2] The Framers had long deliberations over the appropriate wording of the document, and in the end, it was not ratified until they promised to add 10 amendments, the Bill of Rights, during the first congressional session. The Constitution established an enduring system of government that has been altered only 17 more times in over 225 years. But that stability masks a great deal of debate over its meaning—debate that continues today.

The requirement for presidents to be natural born citizens without clarification of the phrase's meaning is one example of the Constitution's lack of specificity, which is both its genius and a flaw. In composing the Constitution, the Framers were conscious that they were writing a document that needed to withstand the test of time. By not specifying how, exactly, one qualifies as a natural born citizen, they designed a document that others could apply to changing circumstances. This generality, however, also has resulted in continuing debates, including debates about the appropriate authority of the governing branches and the extent of national government authority over the states and individuals. The power of the courts to determine what exactly the Constitution means has also led to scrutiny of the ways in which they reach those decisions.

Citizens can view the original U.S. Constitution on display at the National Archives in Washington, D.C.

The Constitutional Structure of American Government

The Constitution's basic structure is straightforward. Article I establishes a bicameral Congress, with a House of Representatives and a Senate, and empowers it to enact legislation; for example, governing foreign and interstate commerce. Article II vests the executive power in the president, and Article III vests the judicial power in the Supreme Court and other federal courts that Congress may establish. Article IV guarantees the privileges and immunities of citizens and specifies the conditions for admitting new states. Article V provides for the methods of amending the Constitution, and Article VI specifies that the Constitution and all laws made under it are the supreme law of the land. Finally, Article VII provides that the Constitution had to be ratified by 9 of the original 13 states to go into effect. In 1791, the first 10 amendments, known as the Bill of Rights, were added, and another 17 amendments have been added since.

Despite its brevity, the Constitution firmly established the Framers' experiment in self-government, something that each generation reinterprets and renews. That is why after more than 225 years we have not had another written constitution—let alone two, three, or more—like other countries around the world. Part of the reason is the public's widespread acceptance of the Constitution. But the Constitution also has endured because it is a brilliant structure for limiting government and one that the Framers designed to be adaptable and flexible.

As the Constitution won the support of citizens in the early years of the Republic, it took on the aura of natural law—law that defines right from wrong, which is regarded to be higher than human law. Like the Crown in Great Britain, the Constitution became a symbol of national unity and loyalty, evoking both emotional and intellectual support from Americans, regardless of their differences. The Framers' work became part of U.S. culture.[3] The Constitution stands for liberty, equality before the law, limited or expanded government—indeed, it stands for just about anything anyone wants to read into it. Even today, U.S. citizens generally revere the Constitution, although many do not know what is in it. A national survey conducted by the Annenberg Public Policy Center found that just 36 percent of Americans could name all three branches of government, 35 percent could not name a single branch, and over 20 percent of respondents thought that Supreme Court cases decided by a 5-to-4 margin were sent to Congress for reconsideration.[4]

The Constitution is more than a symbol, however. It is the supreme and binding law that both grants and limits powers. "If men were angels," James Madison argued in *The Federalist,* No. 51, "no government would be necessary. If angels were to govern men, neither external nor internal controls on government would be necessary."[5] But the Framers knew well that people are not angels, and thus, to create a successful government, they would need to create a government of *limited* authority. How? Within the government, competing interests would check each other, and externally, the governed would check the government through elections, petitions, protests, and amendments.

This chapter examines a number of questions that are still being asked long after the Framers completed their work. How does the constitutional structure limit the power of the government? How can it be used to create governmental power? How has it managed to serve as a great symbol of national unity and, at the same time, as an adaptable instrument of government? The secret is in part an ingenious separation of powers and a system of checks and balances that limits power with power. But, the Constitution is adaptable enough to accommodate dramatic economic, social, and technological changes. You and your peers inherit the structure of a government with limited powers but also the obligation to find ways to adapt that government to current and future challenges.

The Framers wanted a stronger and more effective national government than they had under the Articles of Confederation. But they were keenly aware that the people would not accept too much central control. Efficiency and order were important, but liberty was more important. The Framers wanted to ensure domestic tranquility and prevent future rebellions; they also wanted to prevent the emergence of a homegrown King George III. Accordingly, they allotted certain powers to the national government and reserved the rest for the states, thus establishing the system that is American federalism. But even this was not enough. The Framers believed additional restraints were needed to limit the national government.

The most important means they devised to make public officials observe the constitutional limits on their powers was free and fair elections, through which voters can remove anyone who abuses power. Yet the Framers did not fully trust the people's judgment. "Free government is founded on jealousy, and not in confidence," said Thomas Jefferson. "In questions of power, then, let no more be heard of confidence in man, but bind him down from mischief by the chains of the Constitution."[6]

No less important, the Framers feared a majority might deprive minorities of their rights. This risk was certainly real at the time of the framing, as it is today. For example, although public support for harsher restrictions on gun ownership often increases in the wake of a mass shooting, the Second Amendment protects citizens' right to own guns. That was true of the December 2012 tragedy in Newtown, Connecticut, where 27 people, mostly first graders, were killed. In a Gallup Poll released immediately following the Newtown shooting, 58 percent of respondents supported more severe laws restricting firearms sales.[7] Although popular support of gun control did fall in the years following the Newtown shooting (down to 47 percent in October 2014), support for stricter limits on the sale of firearms reached 67% in March 2018, the highest level in 25 years.[8] That increase came on the heals of the Parkland Florida High School shooting in which 17 students and adults were murdered by a former student wielding an assault-style rifle. Popular support for stricter gun limits has resulted in some state and local laws limiting gun sales, but recent U.S. Supreme Court decisions have affirmed Second Amendment protections and struck down some of these laws.[9] Madison predicted as much in *The Federalist*, No. 51, when he wrote that "[a] dependence on the people is, no doubt, the primary control on the government, but experience has taught mankind the necessity of auxiliary precautions."[10] It is to those "auxiliary precautions" that we now turn.

Separation of Powers

The first step against potential tyranny of the majority was the **separation of powers** that distributed constitutional authority among the three branches of the national government. In *The Federalist,* No. 47, Madison wrote: "No political truth is certainly of greater intrinsic value, or is stamped with the authority of more enlightened patrons of liberty, than that... the accumulation of all powers, legislative, executive, and judiciary, in the same hands... may justly be pronounced the very definition of tyranny."[11] Chief among the "enlightened patrons of liberty" to whose authority Madison was appealing were the eighteenth-century philosophers John Locke and Montesquieu, whose works most educated citizens knew well.

separation of powers
Constitutional division of powers among the legislative, executive, and judicial branches, with the legislative branch making law, the executive applying and enforcing the law, and the judiciary interpreting the law.

The intrinsic value of the dispersion of power, however, is not the only reason the Framers included it in the Constitution. It had already been the general practice in the colonies for more than 100 years. Only during the Revolutionary period did some of the states concentrate authority in the hands of the legislature, and that unhappy experience as well as that under the Articles of Confederation confirmed the Framers' belief in the merits of the separation of powers. Many attributed the evils of state government and lack of energy in the central government to the lack of a strong executive who would check legislative abuses and give energy and direction to administration. Still, the Framers wondered whether the nation needed more protection from tyranny. Separating power by itself was not enough to protect the people. It might not prevent the branches of the government and officials from pooling their authority and acting together, or from responding alike to the same pressures—from the demand of a majority to restrict handgun ownership, for example, or to impose high taxes on the rich. What else could be done?

Checks and Balances: Ambition to Counteract Ambition

The Framers' answer was a system of **checks and balances**. Madison's idea to avoid concentration of power was to give each branch the constitutional power to check the others. "Ambition must be made to counteract ambition."[12] Each branch therefore has a role in approving or rejecting the actions of the other branches (see Table 2.1 on the next page).

checks and balances
A constitutional grant of powers that enables each of the three branches of government to check some acts of the others and therefore ensures that no branch can dominate.

TABLE 2.1 THE SEPARATION OF POWERS AND CHECKS AND BALANCES

Although the branches have checks on each other, they do not always use them, even when they disagree. But, the mere possibility that they *could* be used can act as a powerful constraint on each branch.

Branch	Power	Exercise of Checks and Balances, 1789–2018
Executive	Veto	Presidents have vetoed nearly 2,600 acts of Congress. Congress has overridden presidential vetoes more than 100 times.
Legislature (House)	Votes on articles of impeachment	The House of Representatives has impeached two presidents, one senator, one secretary of war, and 15 federal judges; the Senate convicted eight of the judges but neither president.
Legislature (Senate)	Confirms cabinet appointments Conducts impeachment trials	The Senate has refused to confirm nine cabinet nominations. Many other cabinet and subcabinet appointments were withdrawn because the Senate seemed likely to reject them.
Judiciary	Judicial review	The Supreme Court has ruled more than 180 congressional acts or parts thereof unconstitutional.

SOURCE: Vetoes: http://www.senate.gov/reference/Legislation/Vetoes/vetoCounts.htm; Impeachments: http://www.senate.gov/artandhistory/history/common/briefing/Senate_Impeachment_Role.htm; Nominations: http://www.senate.gov/artandhistory/history/common/briefing/Nominations.htm; Acts of Congress Unconstitutional: https://www.congress.gov/content/conan/pdf/GPO-CONAN-2017-11.pdf.

Congress enacts legislation, which the president must sign into law or veto. The Supreme Court can declare laws passed by Congress and signed by the president unconstitutional, but the president appoints the justices and all the other federal judges, with the Senate's approval. The president administers the laws, but Congress provides the money to run the government. Moreover, the Senate and the House of Representatives have absolute veto power over each other because both houses must approve bills before they can become law.

Not only does each branch have some authority over the others, but each is also politically independent of the others. Voters in each local district choose members of the House; voters in each state choose senators; and through the Electoral College, voters in all the states elect the president. With the consent of the Senate, the president appoints federal judges who remain in office until they retire or are impeached.

The Framers also ensured that a majority of the voters could win control over only part of the government at one time. In an off-year (nonpresidential) election where a new majority might take control of the House of Representatives, the president still has at least two more years, and senators hold office for six years. Finally, independent federal courts exercise their own powerful checks.

Distrustful of both the elites and the masses, the Framers deliberately built into our political system mechanisms to make changing the system difficult. They designed the decision-making process so that the national government can act decisively only when there is a consensus among most groups and after all sides have had their say. In the words of Justice Louis D. Brandeis, "[t]he doctrine of the separation of powers was adopted by the convention of 1787, not to promote efficiency but to preclude the exercise of arbitrary power. The purpose was not to avoid friction, but, by means of the inevitable friction incident to the distribution of the governmental powers among three departments, to save the people from autocracy"—a system in which one person has control over the populace.[13] Still, even though the fragmentation of political power written into the Constitution remains, topics not addressed by the Constitution and developments since its ratification have modified the way the system of checks and balances works.

National Political Parties and Interest Groups

Political parties—the Republican and Democratic parties being the largest—can serve as unifying institutions, at times drawing the president, senators, representatives, and sometimes even judges together behind common programs. When parties do this, they help bridge the separation of powers. But parties can be splintered and weakened by having to work through a system of fragmented governmental power, and special-interest groups enjoy increasing influence. As a result, it is unlikely that parties will become so strong and cohesive that they threaten liberty.

When one party controls Congress or one of its chambers and the other party controls the White House, **partisanship** is intensified, and Congress is inclined to more closely monitor the executive branch. A recent example involved seven separate congressional investigations of the 2011 terrorist attacks in Benghazi, Libya, that took the life of Ambassador J. Chris Stevens. Critics of the investigation, including some committee staff, complained that the intent was to call attention to the failures of former Secretary of State Clinton in handling the incident. Indeed, House Majority Leader Kevin McCarthy may have cost himself the speakership by acknowledging the political purpose of at least some of these investigations. As Secretary Clinton's testimony at the hearing unfolded, however, no new criticisms emerged and she was able to defend her perspective. Conflicts like these are to be expected during divided government, but even when one party controls both branches, the pressures of competing interest groups may make cooperation among legislators difficult.

partisanship
Strong allegiance to one's own political party, often leading to unwillingness to compromise with members of the opposing party.

Because of this competition between the legislative and executive branches, each is prone to encroaching on the power of the other when given the opportunity.[14] Thus we have battles over the budget and angry confirmation hearings for the appointment of Supreme Court justices, lower federal court judges, and members of the executive branch; as a result, some might suspect that less would be accomplished during periods of divided government. The division of powers also makes it difficult for the voters to hold anyone or any party accountable. "Presidents blame Congress...while members of Congress attack the president....Citizens genuinely cannot tell who is to blame."[15]

Yet when all the shouting dies down, political scientist David Mayhew concludes, there is just as much important legislation passed when one party controls Congress and another controls the presidency (**divided government**) as when the same party controls both branches (**unified government**).[16] As one noted expert on Congress and the presidency argues, conflict across the branches is precisely what the voters appear to have wanted through much of our history.[17] Divided government frequently occurs when the president's party loses congressional seats in the midterm elections.

divided government
Governance divided between the parties, especially when one holds the presidency and the other controls one or both houses of Congress.

unified government
Governance in which one party controls both the White House and both houses of Congress.

Expansion of the Electorate and the Move Toward More Direct Democracy

The **Electoral College** was another provision of the Constitution meant to provide a buffer against the "whims of the masses" (see *The Federalist*, No. 10). The Framers wanted the Electoral College—wise, independent citizens free of popular passions and hero worship—to choose the president rather than leave the job to ordinary citizens. Almost from the beginning, though, the Electoral College did not work this way.[18] Rather, voters actually do select the president because the presidential electors that the voters choose pledge in advance to cast their electoral votes for their party's candidates for president and vice president, with rare instances of faithless electors who defect. Nevertheless, presidential candidates may occasionally win the national popular vote but lose the vote in the Electoral College, as happened in 2016, when Hillary Clinton won the popular vote but lost the Electoral College; Clinton earned 227 electoral votes compared to Donald Trump's 304. Only 16 years earlier, Clinton's co-partisan, Al Gore, also won the popular vote but lost the Electoral College race to George W. Bush by five votes (271 to 266).

Electoral College
The electoral system used in electing the president and vice president, in which voters vote for electors pledged to cast their ballots for a particular party's candidates.

Changes in Technology

Because of new technologies, today's system of checks and balances operates differently from the way it did in 1789. There were no televised congressional committee hearings in 1789; no electronic communications; no *The Daily Show* with Trevor

In December 2017, the FCC voted to repeal the Open Internet Rule, which required net neutrality. Here FCC Chairman Ajit Pai announced that decision. However, the United States Court of Appeals for the District of Columbia Circuit will hear oral arguments challenging the FCC's actions in February 2019. That court could vacate the FCC's repeal and reinstate net neutrality.

Noah; no *New York Times, USA Today,* CNN, Fox News, or C-SPAN; no Internet; no nightly news programs with national audiences; no presidential press conferences; no Facebook or Twitter; and no live coverage of wars and of U.S. soldiers fighting in foreign lands. Nuclear weapons, social media, smart phones, and virtual reality—these and other innovations create conditions today that are unimaginably different from those of two centuries ago. We live in a time of instant communication and polls that tell us what people are thinking about public issues almost from one day to the next.

In 2015, for example, you and your friends changed the debate about Internet access after watching *Last Week Tonight with John Oliver*. On his HBO program, Oliver railed against proposals to end net neutrality by giving Internet service providers the ability to prioritize certain Internet traffic and charge consumers for faster connections. Oliver urged his audience to take advantage of the Federal Communication Commission's notice and comment period and send comments to their Web site. In the week before Oliver's show aired, the FCC received just over 3,000 comments; in the week following the show, that number was nearly 80,000.[19] The result in 2015 was that the FCC voted to approve net neutrality. However, with a change in membership, the FCC voted to repeal those net neutrality rules in December 2017. Although Congress had the opportunity to reverse the FCC's latest decision, it failed to do so and net neutrality officially ended on June 11, 2018.

In some ways, these new technologies have added to presidents' powers by permitting them to appeal directly to millions of people and giving them immediate access to public opinion. In turn, they have enabled interest groups to target thousands of letters, emails, and calls at members of Congress; to orchestrate campaigns to write letters to editors; and to organize and mobilize on the Internet. New technologies also have given greater independence and influence to nongovernmental institutions such as interest groups and the press. They have made it possible for wealthier people to bypass political parties and carry their message directly to the electorate—an action the Republican Party feared Donald Trump might take if he had not been chosen as the party's 2016 nominee for president.

The Growth of Presidential Power

Today, problems elsewhere in the world—North Korea, Syria, and Iran, for example—often create crises for the United States. The need to deal quickly with perpetual emergencies has concentrated power in the hands of the chief executive and the presidential staff. As a result, the president of the United States has emerged as the most significant player on the world stage, and media coverage of summit conferences with foreign leaders enhances the president's status. Headline-generating events give the president a visibility no congressional leader can achieve.

In response, presidents have occasionally seized (or have been given by Congress) greater latitude than the system of checks and balances typically permits in order to provide a measure of national unity. As the need to respond immediately to global threats has emerged, presidents have drawn on political justifications to take action. This is most apparent in international affairs, where modern presidents have claimed that being Commander in Chief and the obligation to provide for the nation's defense take priority over the need to secure a declaration of war from Congress. The Obama administration argued strongly for recognizing the authority of the executive, particularly given national security concerns. In fact, many of his supporters were disappointed that President Obama's policies did not diverge more significantly from those of his predecessor, George W. Bush, who asserted that he had authority to wiretap U.S. citizens' communications without court-approved search warrants.[20]

Judicial Review and Constitutional Interpretation (Action)

2.2 Describe the constitutional foundations of the federal judiciary and judicial review.

The judiciary has become so important in our system of checks and balances that it deserves special attention. Judges did not claim the power of **judicial review**—the power to review a law or government regulation and determine whether it conflicts with the Constitution—until some years after the Constitution had been adopted. Many understood, however, that judges would provide an important check on the other branches. Alexander Hamilton, for example, emphasized the importance of judicial independence for protection "against the occasional ill humors in the society."[21]

judicial review
The power of a court to review laws or governmental regulations to determine whether they are consistent with the U.S. Constitution, or in a state court, the state constitution.

Judicial review is a major contribution of the United States to the art of government, one that many other nations have adopted. In Canada, Germany, France, Italy, and Spain, constitutional courts have the power to review laws referred to them. The degree to which the courts utilize this power, however, and the point in the legislative process at which it occurs, vary across countries.[22]

Origins of Judicial Review

The Constitution says nothing about who should have the final word in disputes that may arise over its meaning. Today, most scholars agree that the Framers intended the Supreme Court to have the power to declare acts of the legislative and executive branches unconstitutional. But in the years following ratification, the scope of the Court's power remained uncertain.

The **Federalists**—who urged ratification of the Constitution and controlled the national government until 1801—generally supported a strong role for federal courts and thus favored judicial review. Their opponents, the Jeffersonian Republicans (called *Democrats* after 1832), were less enthusiastic. In the Kentucky and Virginia Resolutions of 1798 and 1799, respectively, Jefferson and Madison (who by this time had left the Federalist camp) came close to arguing that state legislatures—and not the Supreme Court—had the ultimate power to interpret the Constitution. These resolutions seemed to question whether the Supreme Court even had final authority to review *state* legislation, a point about which there had been little doubt.

Federalists
A group that argued for ratification of the Constitution, including a stronger national government at the expense of states' power. They controlled the new federal government until Thomas Jefferson's election in 1800.

Chief Justice John Marshall (1755–1835) was our most influential Supreme Court justice. Appointed in 1801, Marshall served until 1835. Earlier he had been a staunch defender of the U.S. Constitution at the Virginia ratifying convention, a member of Congress, and a Secretary of State. He was one of the rare people who served in all three branches of government. This statue resides in John Marshall Memorial Park in Washington, D.C.

When the Jeffersonians defeated the Federalists in the election of 1800, the question of whether the Supreme Court would actually exercise the power of judicial review was still undecided. Then in 1803 came *Marbury* v. *Madison,* the most pathbreaking Supreme Court decision of all time.[23]

Marbury v. *Madison*

President John Adams and fellow Federalists did not take their 1800 defeat by Thomas Jefferson easily. Not only did they lose control of the executive office, but they also lost both houses of Congress. That left the judiciary as the last remaining Federalist stronghold.

To further shore up the federal judiciary, the outgoing Federalist Congress created 42 new judgeships. Working quickly to "pack" the posts with loyal Federalists, Adams nominated, and the Senate confirmed, all of the new judges just before Jefferson was due to become president on March 3, 1801. Outgoing Secretary of State and newly confirmed chief justice of the Supreme Court, John Marshall, was responsible for making sure that all of the signed and sealed commissions were delivered. With time running out, Marshall left the last few on a table in the Department of State to be delivered sometime in the next few days. However, in one of his first acts as president, Jefferson refused to deliver the last of the commissions, including a justice of the peace commission for a loyal Federalist named William Marbury.[24]

When Marbury realized he would never receive his commission, he decided to seek action from the courts. Section 13 of the Judiciary Act of 1789 authorized the Supreme Court "to issue writs of *mandamus*," orders directing an official like the Secretary of State to perform a duty, such as delivering a commission. Marbury went directly to the Supreme Court and, citing section 13, made his request.

Marbury's request presented Chief Justice John Marshall and the Supreme Court with a difficult dilemma. On the one hand, if the Court issued the writ, Jefferson and Madison would probably ignore it. The Court would be powerless, and its already low prestige might suffer a fatal blow. On the other hand, by refusing to issue the writ, the judges would appear to support the Jeffersonian Republicans' claim that the Court had no authority to interfere with the executive. Would Marshall issue the writ? Most people thought he would; angry Republicans even threatened impeachment if he did so.

On February 24, 1803, the Supreme Court delivered what is still considered a brilliantly written and politically savvy decision. Marshall, writing for a unanimous Court, first took Jefferson and Madison to task. Marbury was entitled to his commission, and Madison should have delivered it to him. Moreover, the proper court could issue a writ of mandamus, even against so high an officer as the Secretary of State.

Marshall concluded, however, that section 13 of the Judiciary Act, giving the Supreme Court original jurisdiction to issue writs of *mandamus,* was in error. It impermissibly expanded the Court's original jurisdiction, which is detailed in Article III of the Constitution. Marshall concluded that the grant of original jurisdiction in Article III was meant to be limited to those cases explicitly mentioned: when an ambassador, foreign minister, or a state is a party. Because none of these was at issue in Marbury's request for the writ of mandamus, the Court deemed section 13 of the Judiciary Act contrary to the Constitution. Given that Article VI provided that the Constitution is the "supreme Law of the Land," and judges took an oath to uphold the Constitution, any law in conflict with it could not withstand the Court's review.

Although the Federalists suffered a political loss when they failed to seat all their "midnight judges" on the bench, Marshall and the Court gained a much more important power: to declare laws passed by Congress unconstitutional. Subsequent generations might have interpreted *Marbury* v. *Madison* in a limited way, such as that the Supreme Court had the right to determine the scope of its own powers under Article III, but Congress and the president had the authority to interpret their powers under Articles I and II. But throughout the decades, building on Marshall's precedent, the Court has taken the commanding position as the authoritative interpreter of the Constitution.

There are several important consequences of Marshall's argument that judges are the official interpreters of the Constitution. The most important is that people can challenge laws enacted by Congress and approved by the president, as did a variety of states and parties in a number of challenges to the Patient Protection and Affordable Care Act (also known as Obamacare). Simply by bringing a lawsuit, those who lack the clout to get a bill through Congress can often secure a judicial hearing. And organized interest groups often find they can achieve goals through litigation that they could not attain through legislation. For example, religiously devout owners of secular businesses turned to the courts to successfully obtain exemptions to the requirement that their employer-provided health insurance must cover contraceptive care after they failed to secure that exemption through the legislative or rule-making process.[25] Litigation thus supplements, and at times even takes precedence over, legislation as a way to make public policy.[26]

Changing the Letter of the Constitution (Impact)

2.3 Describe the process by which the Constitution can be changed.

As careful as the Constitution's Framers were to limit the powers they gave the national government, the main reason they assembled in Philadelphia was to create a stronger national government. Having learned that a weak central government was a danger to liberty, they wished to establish a national government with enough authority to meet the country's needs. They made general grants of power, leaving it to succeeding generations to fill in the details and organize the structure of government in accordance with experience.

Hence our formal, written Constitution is only a skeleton. It provides the structure for government, but it is filled out in numerous ways that we must consider part of our constitutional system in a larger sense. In fact, our system is kept up-to-date primarily through changes in the informal, unwritten Constitution. These changes exist in certain basic statutes and historical practices of Congress, presidential actions, and court decisions. They are the results (or impact) of the action taken by these political actors.

Congressional Elaboration

Because the Framers gave Congress authority to provide for the structural details of the national government, it is not necessary to amend the Constitution every time a change is needed. Rather, Congress can create legislation to meet the need with what we refer to as *congressional elaboration*, and by this process adapt the Constitution to current needs. The Judiciary Act of 1789, for example, laid the foundations for our national judicial system, just as other laws established the organization and functions of all federal executive officials subordinate to the president and enacted the rules of procedure, internal organization, and practices of Congress.

Another example of this congressional elaboration of our constitutional system is the use of the impeachment power. The structure provides for the exertion of this power, but in order for the impeachment process to begin, some congressional representatives must be willing to take action. An **impeachment** is a formal accusation against a public official and the first step in a process for removing him or her from office. Constitutional language defining the grounds for impeachment is sparse. In fact, the last time the House of Representatives formally accused a president of an impeachable offense, President Bill Clinton in 1998, House members had nearly 20 scholars testify before them as to the clause's meaning, and they still did not reach consensus on it. Although the Constitution provides for the basic procedural structure of impeachments, it leaves to Congress the determination of when a president's actions amount to an impeachable offense.

impeachment
A process for removing the president, judges, and other civil officials from office for committing treason, bribery, and other high crimes and misdemeanors. The House is responsible for approving the articles of impeachment by a majority vote, while the Senate is responsible for convicting or acquitting the president by a two-thirds vote.

A more recent example of congressional elaboration involves the debate over health care reform and whether Congress has the power to mandate that American citizens purchase health insurance. Part of that debate has centered on congressional authority under the commerce clause (Article I, Section 8). Although the Constitution is clear that Congress has the authority to regulate "commerce...among the several States," just what "commerce" is and how far congressional authority to regulate it extends are topics on which many experts disagree. In arguments before the U.S. Supreme Court, the U.S. government contended that Congress has commerce clause authority to regulate health insurance, which accounts for 17 percent of the U.S. economy. Opponents of the reform argued that the commerce clause does not give Congress the power to require American citizens, who would not otherwise do so, to engage in commerce (that is, purchase health insurance).[27] In its decision, the Court ruled that Congress had unconstitutionally exceeded its authority under the commerce clause when it required all individuals to purchase health insurance or face a financial penalty. But, the Court still upheld that key provision of the Patient Protection and Affordable Care Act based on Congress's taxing authority.[28] Although President Trump made repealing the Affordable Care Act a focus of his 2016 election campaign, once in office, he was unable to directly repeal the legislation. He was, however, able to include a repeal of the individual mandate, widely understood to be essential to the program's survival, as a provision in his Tax Cut and Jobs Act of 2017.

Presidential Practices

Although the formal constitutional powers of the president have not changed, the office is dramatically more important and more central today than it was in 1789. Vigorous presidents—George Washington, Thomas Jefferson, Andrew Jackson, Abraham Lincoln, Theodore Roosevelt, Woodrow Wilson, Franklin Roosevelt, Harry Truman, Lyndon Johnson, Bill Clinton, George W. Bush, and Barack Obama—have boldly exercised their political and constitutional powers, especially during times of national crisis such as the war against international terrorism and the 2008 economic crisis. Their actions and practices have established important precedent, building the power and influence of the office.

A major presidential practice is the use of **executive orders**, which carry the full force of law but do not require congressional approval, though they are subject to legal challenge. Executive orders direct the executive branch to take some action, such as President Franklin Roosevelt's 1942 order to intern Japanese Americans during World War II and President Truman's order to integrate the armed forces in 1948. Not all executive orders are as path breaking as these two examples, but even so they belong to the executive, not Congress. For example, President Trump issued 55 executive orders during his first year in office, including orders placing a ban on travel into the United States from seven predominantly Muslim countries, creating a 90-day freeze on federal government hiring, reversing the Obama administration's "clean coal" environmental protections, and creating national commissions on the opioid crisis and voting fraud. Presidents have long used these orders to achieve goals that may lack congressional support. Nevertheless, they can be challenged in the federal courts, as were President Trump's 2017 travel bans, and can be overturned through legislation, though the president can veto such legislation. In June 2018, the U.S. Supreme Court upheld the president's travel ban that had been repeatedly struck down in the lower courts.

executive order
A formal instruction that tells the executive branch how to execute a specific law or broader presidential policy; executive orders carry the force of law, but can be revoked by the next president.

executive privilege
A constitutionally supported right that allows presidents the right to keep executive communications confidential.

impoundment
A decision by the president not to spend money appropriated by Congress, now prohibited under federal law.

Other practices fall under **executive privilege**, which includes the right to confidentiality of executive communications, especially those that relate to national security; **impoundment** by a president of funds previously appropriated by Congress; the power to send armed forces into hostilities; and the authority to propose legislation and work actively to secure its passage by Congress.

Foreign and economic crises as well as nuclear-age realities and the war against international terrorism have expanded the president's role. A respected scholar of presidential power has noted, "When it comes to action risking nuclear war, technology has modified the Constitution: the President, perforce, becomes the only such man in the system capable of exercising judgment under the extraordinary limits now imposed by secrecy, complexity, and time."[29] The presidency also has become the pivotal office for regulating the economy and promoting the general welfare through an expanded federal bureaucracy. In addition, the president has become a leader in sponsoring legislation as well as the nation's chief executive.

Judicial Interpretation

In its decision in *Marbury* v. *Madison* (1803),[30] the Supreme Court established that it was the judiciary's responsibility to interpret the Constitution. The courts have made far-reaching decisions that have settled, at least for a time, what some of the vague clauses of the document mean. For example, the Supreme Court ruled that segregation by race, even when equal facilities were provided, violated the requirements of the equal protection clause (*Brown* v. *Board of Education* [1954]),[31] and that Americans have a constitutionally protected right to privacy, even though the word *privacy* appears nowhere in the Constitution (*Griswold* v. *Connecticut* [1965]).[32] In both of these cases and a myriad of others, the Court's definition of what the Constitution means led to changes in our political system without any amendment to the document itself. In such cases, the courts have acted on their structural authority to impact

The Supreme Court's 2008 decision affirming an individual citizen's right to own guns makes it more difficult to restrict gun ownership than would have a decision recognizing a right to own guns only as a member of a military organization. Despite mass shootings in Newtown, Connecticut, San Bernardino, California, and Orlando, Florida, Las Vegas, Nevada, and Parkland, Florida, Congress has thus far refused to act to limit access to guns in ways that would be consistent with the Court's ruling. In February 2018, a former student opened fire in Marjory Stoneman Douglas High School in Parkland, Florida, killing 17. Here family and friends anxiously await word from their loved ones who were in the school at the time of the shooting.

significant policy changes. Although there is relatively little current debate over the judiciary's authority to interpret the Constitution, there is substantial disagreement over *how* it should be read.

originalist approach

An approach to constitutional interpretation that envisions the document as having a fixed meaning that might be determined by a strict reading of the text or the Framers' intent.

Two broad categories of constitutional interpretation are the originalist approach, taken by those who believe the text and structure of the Constitution are primary and unchanging, and the evolutionary approach, taken by those who see the Constitution as evolving in one way or another. In the **originalist approach**, constitutional meaning is deciphered through a strict reading of the text. If the exact wording of the document does not provide a conclusive answer, an originalist might consider other factors, such as the Framers' intent, the context of the times in which the words were written, and the literal meaning of the text when it was written. Especially important are writings or speeches by the Framers themselves or by proponents of subsequent amendments.

evolutionary approach

A method used to interpret the Constitution that understands the document to be flexible and responsive to the changing needs of the times.

The second approach to interpreting the Constitution sees it as an evolving document that provides a basic structure for government but that allows, and even encourages, new generations to interpret ideas such as "equal justice" and "due process" in light of the needs of their time. This **evolutionary approach** may mean that subsequent generations will interpret the same document differently from prior generations.

Varying interpretations of the Second Amendment right to bear arms highlight the differences between these two approaches. The late Justice Antonin Scalia, who embraced originalism, concluded that since the Second Amendment mandates that "the right of the people to keep and bear Arms, shall not be infringed," strict gun regulations like the one challenged in *District of Columbia* v. *Heller* (2008) impermissibly restricted citizens' constitutional right to own handguns. Justice Stephen Breyer, on the other hand, typically favors a more evolutionary view of constitutional interpretation. In his dissent to the Court's *Heller* decision, Justice Breyer argued that the Court must consider the District of Columbia's restriction on handguns in light of present-day conditions, such as the public safety concerns raised by gun violence. Justice Breyer weighed an individual's right to own a handgun against the District's responsibility to protect its citizenry, and believed that the Court should have upheld the District of Columbia's handgun restrictions.[33]

The idea of a constantly changing system disturbs many people. How, they contend, can you have a constitutional government when the Constitution is constantly being twisted by interpretation and changed by informal methods? This view fails to distinguish between two aspects of the Constitution. As an expression of *basic and timeless personal liberties*, the Constitution does not and should not change. For example, a government cannot destroy free speech and still remain a constitutional government. In this sense, the Constitution is unchanging. But when we consider the Constitution as an *instrument of government* and a positive grant of power, we realize that if it did not grow with the nation it serves, it would soon be irrelevant and ignored.

The Framers could not anticipate the problems facing our nation's government today. Although the general purposes of government remain the same—to establish liberty, promote justice, ensure domestic tranquility, and provide for the common defense—the powers of government that were adequate to accomplish these purposes in 1787 are simply insufficient more than 230 years later. The Framers knew that future experiences would call for changes in the text of the Constitution and that it would need to be formally amended. In Article V, they gave responsibility for amending the Constitution to Congress and to the states. The president has no formal authority over constitutional amendments; presidential veto power does not extend to them, although presidential influence is often crucial in getting amendments proposed and ratified.

Proposing Amendments

The Constitution provides two methods for proposing amendments. Dozens of resolutions proposing amendments are introduced in every session, but Congress has proposed only 31 amendments, of which 27 have been ratified (see Figure 2.1).

FIGURE 2.1 FOUR METHODS OF AMENDING THE CONSTITUTION

The first method of proposing a constitutional amendment, and the only one used so far, is by a two-thirds vote of both houses of Congress.

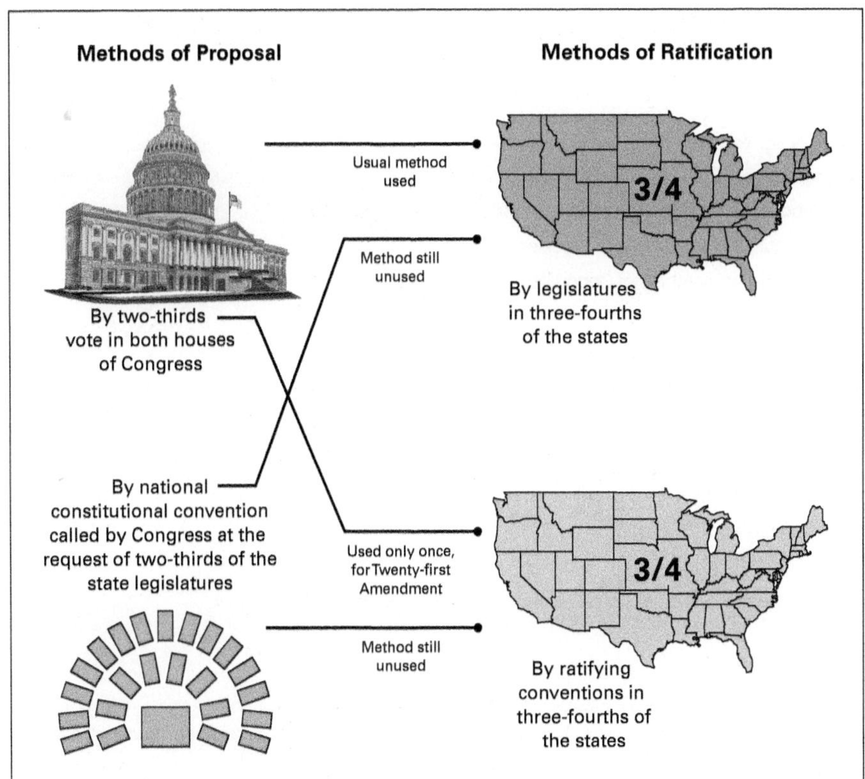

Why is introducing amendments to the Constitution so popular? Amendments may be introduced for different reasons: because the nation needs to make government more responsive to changing times; because groups frustrated by their inability to get things done in Congress hope to bypass it; or because Congress, the president, interest groups, or the public want to overturn unpopular Supreme Court decisions. All of these parties were involved in an effort to overturn the Supreme Court's decision to strike down a Texas law barring flag burning (*Texas* v. *Johnson* [1989]).[34] Though Congress attempted to bypass the decision with the Federal Flag Protection Act of 1989, which prohibited intentionally burning or defiling the flag, the Court struck down that law as well (*United States* v. *Eichman* [1990]).[35] In doing so, the Court ruled that the First Amendment protects burning the flag as a form of political speech.

Though many Americans would like to see the flag protected from being burned in protest, the Supreme Court's decisions continue to allow flag burning as a form of political expression. Here, protestors burn a flag outside of New York City's Trump Tower the day after Donald Trump won the 2016 presidential election. In the wake of Trump's victory, protests erupted in cities across the United States.

Following its failure to overturn the decision through new laws, Congress has made repeated efforts to send a constitutional amendment banning flag burning to the states.[36] The House of Representatives has voted seven times since the early 1990s on an amendment prohibiting the "physical desecration of the flag of the United States," but the Senate has been unable to garner the necessary two-thirds vote. It came close to succeeding in June 2006, but the vote fell one short of the number required to send the amendment to the states for ratification.[37] See Table 2.2 on the next page to see how the amending power has been used.

The second method for proposing amendments is a constitutional convention. Although this method has never been used, it was established

TABLE 2.2 THE AMENDING POWER AND HOW IT HAS BEEN USED

While there have been few formal changes to the Constitution, those that have been made have significantly transformed our governing structure. Leaving aside the first 10 amendments (the Bill of Rights), constitutional amendments have served several purposes.

Purposes of Constitutional Amendments
To Increase or Decrease the Power of the National Government
The Eleventh took some jurisdiction away from the national courts.
The Thirteenth abolished slavery and authorized Congress to legislate against it.
The Sixteenth enabled Congress to levy an income tax.
The Eighteenth authorized Congress to prohibit the manufacture, sale, or transportation of liquor.
The Twenty-first repealed the Eighteenth and gave states the authority to regulate liquor sales.
The Twenty-seventh limited the power of Congress to set salaries for members of Congress.
To Expand the Electorate and Its Power
The Fifteenth extended suffrage to all male African Americans over the age of 21.
The Seventeenth took the right to elect U.S. senators away from state legislatures and gave it to the voters in each state.
The Nineteenth extended suffrage to women over the age of 21.
The Twenty-third gave voters of the District of Columbia the right to vote for president and vice president.
The Twenty-fourth outlawed the poll tax, thereby prohibiting states from taxing the right to vote.
The Twenty-sixth extended suffrage to otherwise qualified persons age 18 or older.
To Reduce the Electorate's Power
The Twenty-second took away from the electorate the right to elect a person to the office of president for more than two full terms.
To Limit State Government Power
The Thirteenth abolished slavery.
The Fourteenth granted national citizenship and prohibited states from abridging privileges of national citizenship; from denying persons life, liberty, and property without due process; and from denying persons equal protection of the laws. This amendment has come to be interpreted as imposing restraints on state powers in every area of public life.
To Make Structural Changes in Government
The Twelfth corrected deficiencies in the operation of the Electoral College that the development of a two-party national system had revealed.
The Twentieth altered the calendar for congressional sessions and shortened the time between the election of presidents and their assumption of office.
The Twenty-fifth provided procedures for filling vacancies in the vice presidency and for determining whether presidents are unable to perform their duties.

under Article V of the Constitution, and does not require presidential approval. This method presents difficult questions, including whether state legislatures must apply for a convention to propose specific amendments on one topic, or a convention with full powers to revise the entire Constitution.[38] There have been congressional efforts to clarify how this process would work: each state would have as many delegates to the convention as it has representatives and senators in Congress, and a constitutional convention would be limited to considering only the subject specified in the state legislative petitions and described in the congressional call for the convention. Scholars are divided, however, on whether Congress has the authority to limit what a constitutional convention might propose,[39] and to date Congress has not passed any legislation on the topic.

Ratifying Amendments

After Congress has proposed an amendment, the states must ratify it before it takes effect. The Constitution provides two methods of ratification, and Congress may choose which to use: approval by the legislatures in three-fourths of the states or approval by special ratifying conventions in three-fourths of the states. Congress has submitted all amendments except one—the Twenty-first (to repeal the Eighteenth Amendment on prohibition)—to the state legislatures for ratification.

Seven state constitutions specify that their state legislatures must ratify a proposed amendment to the U.S. Constitution by majorities of three-fifths or two-thirds of each chamber. Although a state legislature may change its mind and ratify an amendment after it has voted against ratification, the weight of opinion is that once a state has ratified an amendment, it cannot "unratify" it.[40]

The Supreme Court has said that ratification must take place within a "reasonable time" so that it is "sufficiently contemporaneous to reflect the will of the people."[41] When Congress approved ratification of the Twenty-seventh Amendment, however, the amendment had been before the nation for nearly 203 years, so there seemed there might be no limit on what it considers a "reasonable time" (see Figure 2.2). Congress has since stipulated that ratification must occur within seven years of the date it submits an amendment to the states, and will probably continue to do so.

FIGURE 2.2 THE TIME FOR RATIFICATION OF THE 27 AMENDMENTS TO THE CONSTITUTION

The ratification process ordinarily takes place rather quickly—one-third of all amendments were ratified within about one year, and 80 percent were ratified within about two years.

SOURCE: http://www.lexisnexis.com/constitution/amendments_timeline.asp.

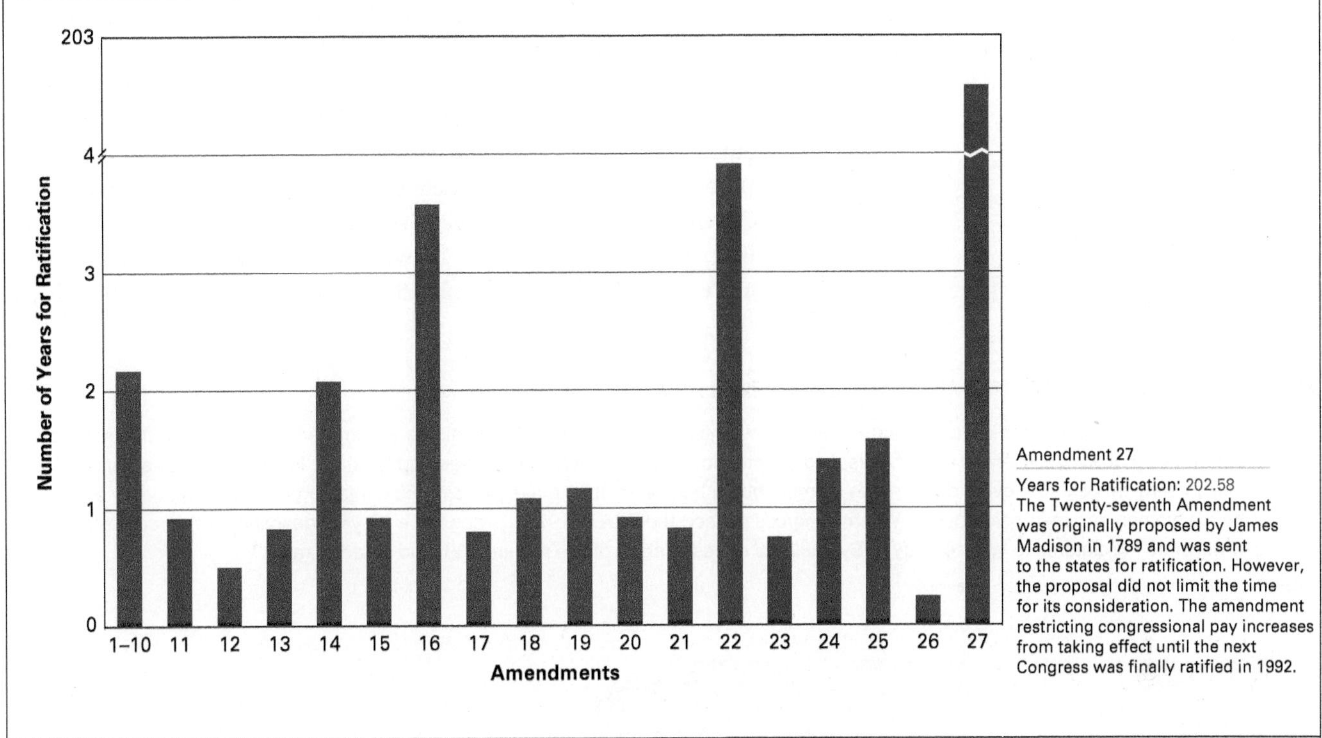

The failure to ratify the Equal Rights Amendment (ERA) provides a vivid example of the pitfalls of ratification. First introduced in 1923, the ERA did not get much support until the 1960s. By the 1970s, the ERA had overwhelming support in both houses of Congress and in both national party platforms. Every president from Harry Truman to Ronald Reagan, and many of their wives, endorsed the amendment. More than 450 organizations with a total membership of more than 50 million were on record in support of the ERA.[42] The ERA provided for the following:

Section 1. Equality of rights under the law shall not be denied or abridged by the United States or by any State on account of sex.

Section 2. The Congress shall have power to enforce, by appropriate legislation, the provisions of this article.

Section 3. This amendment shall take effect two years after the date of ratification.[43]

Soon after Congress passed the amendment and submitted it to the states in 1972, many legislatures ratified it—sometimes without hearings—and by overwhelming majorities. By the end of that year, 22 states had ratified the amendment, and it appeared that the ERA would soon become part of the Constitution. But because of opposition organized under the leadership of Phyllis Schlafly, a prominent spokesperson for conservative causes, the ERA became controversial.

Opponents not only argued that the amendment would force women to join the military and even serve in combat, but also claimed that women would be pushed into the labor force. These opponents came chiefly from the same cluster of southern states that had opposed ratification of the Nineteenth Amendment, which gave women the right to vote. In the end, despite extensions on the deadline to ratify the ERA, the amendment fell 3 states short of the 38 needed for ratification.

America changed in spite of the ERA's defeat. For example, women did enter the military. In 1973, for example, women were already in the military but were not allowed to serve in combat. By 2016, women were officially allowed to serve in combat; 15 percent of all active-duty military personnel were women, as were 17 percent of all active-duty officers, and women now serve in close quarters on all Navy vessels, including nuclear submarines.[44] Although women military personnel are far more likely than men to report sexual harassment and assault, they have shown no reluctance to fight on their country's behalf. Almost 1,000 women were wounded in the Iraq and Afghanistan wars, and 140 were killed.

Women also entered the workforce in large numbers. In 1973, approximately 76 percent of all men were employed in the civilian labor force compared with only 42 percent of women. And unemployment figures for women seeking work during that year were 50 percent higher than for their male counterparts. By 2016, however, approximately 57 percent of all women were employed in the civilian labor force, compared with 69 percent of men. Although women continue to trail men in pay (see Figure 2.3) and work in lower-paying jobs, they have been able to keep their jobs

FIGURE 2.3 WHAT A WOMAN MAKES FOR EVERY DOLLAR A MAN MAKES

Persistent inequality continues in the wages paid to men and women across the United States. The average American woman makes just 82.5 cents for every dollar the average man makes, and substantial variation exists in the wage gap by state. In New York, for example, women make nearly 87 cents for every dollar made by men, but in Louisiana, they make just over 65 cents for each dollar made by a man. In no state are women and men paid equally. When Congress passed the ERA in 1972, it imposed a 10-year deadline for the required three-fourths of the state legislatures to vote to ratify it. By 1982, 35 states, 3 short of the required 38, had voted to ratify.

SOURCE: http://nwlc.org/resources/wage-gap-state-state

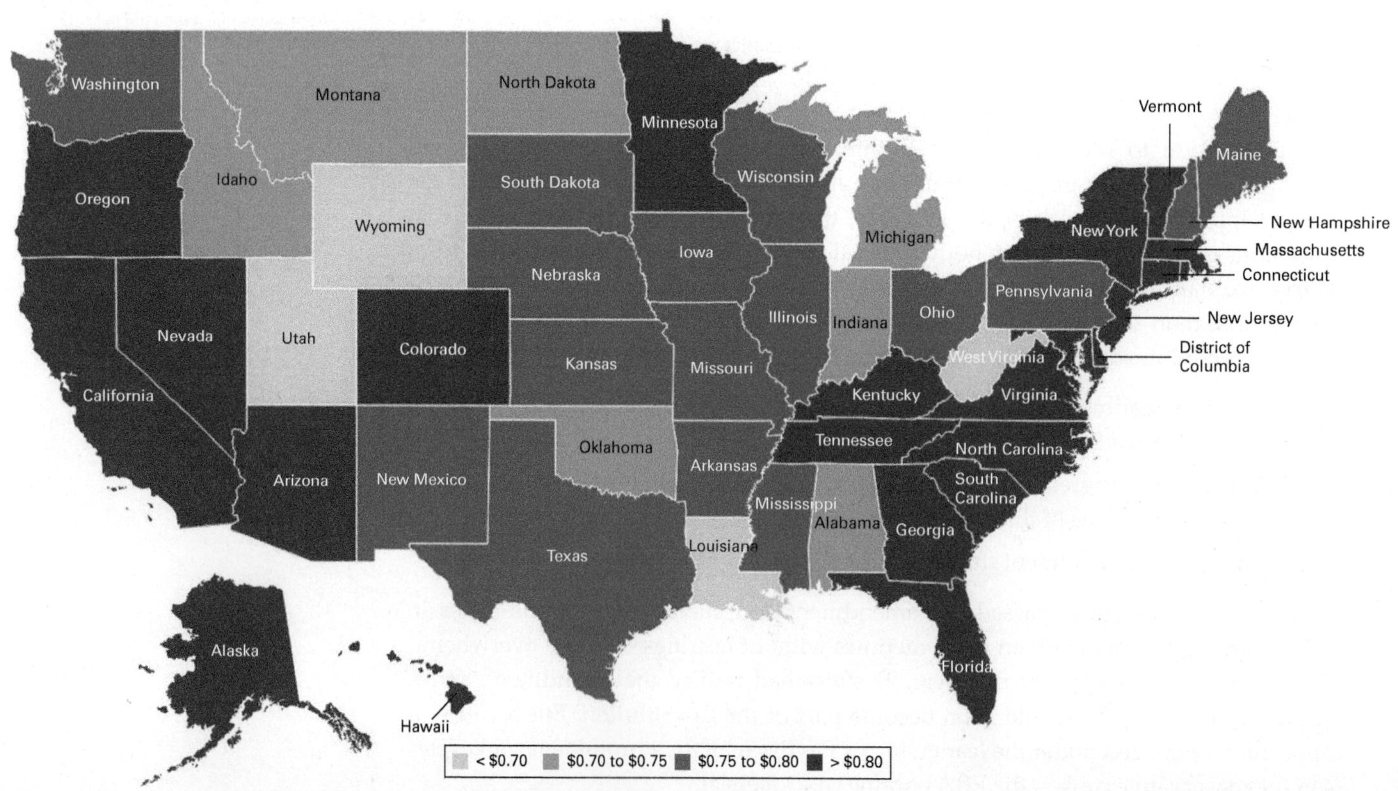

during good times and bad. Unemployment figures for both men and women declined as the economy began to recover from the 2008 economic crisis; at the end of 2015, just over 6 percent of both women (6.1 percent) and men (6.3 percent) who were actively seeking work were unable to get it.[45]

Despite women's presence in the workforce, income inequality between male and female employees persists. When Congress passed the ERA, one of the proponents' primary goals was removing that income inequality. For every dollar the average male worker makes, however, the average female worker makes only 82.5 cents, even after controlling for the type of employment. For example, in 2014, the median weekly salary for men in computer and mathematical occupations was $1,435 compared to $1,165 for their female counterparts.[46]

CONCLUSION

The current and divisive debate on immigration policy and the meaning of the word "citizen" continued long after the 2016 presidential election was over. But candidates, politicians, and the public all realize the importance of our constitutional structure in affecting political debate and creating impact in American politics. Depending on your (and a majority of the Supreme Court's) understanding of constitutional structure, you can best determine how to act to impact policy.

The Framers believed the constitutional structure would withstand the test of time. Toward that end, there are many clauses in the document that lack specificity and, as is clear from the disagreement over the definition of a "natural born" citizen, debate persists. Whether first, second, third, fourth, or even tenth generation, it's most likely that you and most of your classmates are immigrants yourselves. Perhaps you or your neighbors are undocumented immigrants or are the American-born children of undocumented immigrants; if the latter, are you or your neighbors "natural born" U.S. citizens? Americans are fond of saying that anyone could grow up to become president of the United States. But given our current understanding of the natural born citizenship requirement, that is not actually true. Do we need a constitutional amendment to clarify the term or to redefine our understanding of citizenship in an increasingly diverse political landscape? Your answers to these and other questions will affect immigration policy and the lives of current and future U.S. immigrants throughout the twenty-first century.

Debate over the definition of "natural born" citizen persists. Some Americans even continued to question President Obama's citizenship throughout his time in office. In an attempt to end continued allegations that he was not born in the United States, the Obama administration released his "long form" birth certificate, pictured here, in 2011.

STATE OF HAWAII — CERTIFICATE OF LIVE BIRTH — DEPARTMENT OF HEALTH

FILE NUMBER 151 61 10641

1a. Child's First Name (Type or print): BARACK | 1b. Middle Name: HUSSEIN | 1c. Last Name: OBAMA, II

2. Sex: Male | 3. This Birth: Single ☒ Twin ☐ Triplet ☐ | 4. If Twin or Triplet, Was Child Born 1st ☐ 2nd ☐ 3rd ☐ | 5a. Birth Date: Month August, Day 4, Year 1961 | 5b. Hour 7:24 P.M.

6a. Place of Birth: City, Town or Rural Location: Honolulu | 6b. Island: Oahu

6c. Name of Hospital or Institution (If not in hospital or institution, give street address): Kapiolani Maternity & Gynecological Hospital | 6d. Is Place of Birth Inside City or Town Limits? If no, give judicial district. Yes ☒ No ☐

7a. Usual Residence of Mother: City, Town or Rural Location: Honolulu | 7b. Island: Oahu | 7c. County and State or Foreign Country: Honolulu, Hawaii

7d. Street Address: 6085 Kalanianaole Highway | 7e. Is Residence Inside City or Town Limits? If no, give judicial district. Yes ☒ No ☐

7f. Mother's Mailing Address | 7g. Is Residence on a Farm or Plantation? Yes ☐ No ☒

8. Full Name of Father: BARACK HUSSEIN OBAMA | 9. Race of Father: African

10. Age of Father: 25 | 11. Birthplace (Island, State or Foreign Country): Kenya, East Africa | 12a. Usual Occupation: Student | 12b. Kind of Business or Industry: University

13. Full Maiden Name of Mother: STANLEY ANN DUNHAM | 14. Race of Mother: Caucasian

15. Age of Mother: 18 | 16. Birthplace (Island, State or Foreign Country): Wichita, Kansas | 17a. Type of Occupation Outside Home During Pregnancy: None | 17b. Date Last Worked

I certify that the above stated information is true and correct to the best of my knowledge. | 18a. Signature of Parent or Other Informant: Ann Dunham Obama | Parent ☒ Other ☐ | 18b. Date of Signature: 8-7-61

I hereby certify that this child was born alive on the date and hour stated above. | 19a. Signature of Attendant: David A Sinclair | M.D. ☒ D.O. ☐ Midwife ☐ Other ☐ | 19b. Date of Signature: 8-8-61

20. Date Accepted by Local Reg.: AUG - 8 1961 | 21. Signature of Local Registrar | 22. Date Accepted by Reg. General: AUG - 8 1961

23. Evidence for Delayed Filing or Alteration

APR 25 2011

I CERTIFY THIS IS A TRUE COPY OR ABSTRACT OF THE RECORD ON FILE IN THE HAWAII STATE DEPARTMENT OF HEALTH

Alvin T. Onaka, Ph.D.
STATE REGISTRAR

REVIEW THE CHAPTER

Constitutional Framework (Structure)

2.1 Describe the framework for government expressed in the Constitution, p. 33.

The U.S. Constitution's first three articles establish the legislative, executive, and judicial branches of government. The Bill of Rights, the first 10 amendments to the Constitution, provides protections from federal government infringement on individual liberties. Power is separated among the three branches: the legislature has the power to create law; the executive enforces the law; and the judiciary interprets the law. None of the branches depends on the others for its authority, and each branch has the power to limit the others through the system of checks and balances.

Competing interests within this structure check and balance one another. Political parties may sometimes overcome the separation of powers, especially if the same party controls both houses of Congress and the presidency. Typically this is not the case, however, and a divided government intensifies checks and balances. Presidential power, which has increased over time, has sometimes overcome restraints the Constitution imposes on it.

Judicial Review and Constitutional Interpretation (Action)

2.2 Describe the constitutional foundations of the federal judiciary and judicial review, p. 39.

Judicial review is the power of the courts to review acts of Congress, the executive branch, and the states and, if necessary, strike them down as unconstitutional. This authority provides the judiciary a powerful check on the other branches of government. In deciding that it lacked the jurisdiction to order a judicial commission to be delivered, the Supreme Court, in *Marbury* v. *Madison*, established its authority to rule an act of the federal legislature unconstitutional. The Court's decision was politically savvy and greatly enhanced the role of the judiciary in a separation of powers system.

Changing the Letter of the Constitution (Impact)

2.3 Describe the process by which the Constitution can be changed, p. 41.

The Constitution provides the structure of government. The constitutional system has been modified over time, adapting to new conditions through congressional elaboration, presidential practices, and judicial interpretation. Some jurists believe the Constitution is unchanging and should be interpreted using an originalist approach. Others consider the document's meaning to be flexible with time and changing circumstances. They pursue an evolutionary approach.

Although adaptable, the Constitution itself needs to be altered from time to time, and the Framers provided a formal procedure for its amendment. An amendment must be both proposed and ratified: proposed by either a two-thirds vote in each chamber of Congress or by a national convention called by Congress on petition of the legislatures in two-thirds of the states; ratified either by the legislatures in three-fourths of the states or by special ratifying conventions in three-fourths of the states.

LEARN THE TERMS

separation of powers, p. 35
checks and balances, p. 35
partisanship, p. 37
divided government, p. 37
unified government, p. 37
Electoral College, p. 37
judicial review, p. 39
Federalists, p. 39
impeachment, p. 42
executive order, p. 43
executive privilege, p. 43
impoundment, p. 43
originalist approach, p. 44
evolutionary approach, p. 44

American Federalism

CHAPTER 3

Thirteen Minnesotans were killed and another 90 injured in August 2007 when a U.S. interstate highway bridge collapsed high above the Mississippi River. The state government was responsible for repairing the bridge, but the federal government was responsible for assuring its safety. As of February 2018, almost 10 percent of the nation's 600,000 bridges had at least one structural flaw. Most of these bridges are still usable, but they must be repaired or replaced to be safe into the distant future.

LEARNING OBJECTIVES

America has always relied on its highway system to keep its economy growing. The nation's highways anchor the nation's extensive economic infrastructure that belongs to all Americans, even those who rarely or never use them. The highway system is built and maintained by national, state, and local government. Although the U.S. Constitution gave the national government the power to build postal roads to deliver the mail, all three levels of government have worked together to build the most complex transportation infrastructure in the world.

Today's national highway system covers more than four miles of roads, including 47,000 miles of interstate highways.[1] Although the U.S. Bureau of Public Roads originally proposed the network in 1939, President Dwight David Eisenhower is given credit for pushing the idea forward in 1956. The massive construction project put millions of Americans to work and is still considered one of the national government's greatest achievements since World War II.[2] Although the system is considered finished, there may yet be new interstate highways, including an Interstate 11 between Phoenix and Las Vegas.

This infrastructure is currently threatened by decades of neglect.[3] The American Society of Civil Engineers recently gave the nation a grade of D+ on the current condition of the roads, rails, waterways, and other infrastructure that keeps the economy moving. The society blamed all levels of government for the growing number of accidents, traffic jams, and frustration, and calculated that American families lose $3,400 each year because the economy is not moving at full speed.[4]

This neglect causes more than the headaches that come with traffic jams. According to the White House Council of Economic Advisers, Americans spend more than $120 billion in lost time stuck in traffic a year, businesses spend $27 billion in shipping freight, and road conditions contribute significantly to the nation's staggering number of traffic fatalities.[5] Even more significantly, the U.S. Department of Transportation estimates poor road conditions cause 14,000 highway deaths a year.[6]

The national government pays for about a third of the nation's infrastructure system, while states and localities pay the rest. In 2018, for example, the national government paid for 25 percent of highway construction and maintenance costs, while local governments paid 35 percent, and state governments paid the final 40 percent. Some of the funding comes from the gasoline tax, but much also comes from property taxes, tolls, and the cost of buying a car.[7] The national government relies in part on general funding to cover its share of the total, but also draws upon gasoline taxes for construction and repair.[8] The 18-cents-per-gallon tax has not been raised since 1993, which means that the nation's transportation infrastructure must fight for budget dollars against more immediate government needs like the war on the Islamic State in Iraq and Syria (ISIS), Social Security, environmental protection, medical research, and education reform.

President Trump and Congress know that the infrastructure needs help, but have been unable to balance their appetite for tax cuts with the $1.5 trillion that many experts believe is the lowest possible price tag for a transportation overhaul. Transportation is only part of the repair bill, however. The nation also needs expensive overhauls in its water and sanitation systems, hospitals, electric power grid, and waterways. This work cannot be done without national, state, and local governments cooperation within our federalist system.

This chapter will help you prepare to make these decisions by introducing you to the structure of the federalist system and making you aware of available options to take action so that you can impact these kinds of issues. Our national government will drive decisions on how to repair the system, but states and localities will shoulder a great responsibility in absorbing the costs and aiding residents in dealing with frustration. You must be ready to play an active role in making choices and paying costs related to taxes and being late for work or class.

Readers should note that many Americans confuse the terms "federalism" and "federalist" with the term "federal." However, "federalism" and "federalist" refer to a system of government, while "federal" refers to the nation's government in Washington. This chapter will use the term "national" to describe what most Americans think of as the federal government in Washington, which is how we will use the term throughout the rest of this book.

The Constitutional Foundations of Federalism (Structure)

3.1 Explain the constitutional foundations of federalism.

The Constitution provides the structure that governs the relationship between the national government in Washington and the 50 states. Both levels of government must work together if the nation is to prosper, but they must maintain boundaries that define who does what.

The Framers drew these boundaries by using a form of government called federalism that divides authorities and powers between a national government and states or provinces. In turn, states create cities, townships, school districts, and the special districts that run facilities like airports, toll roads, water systems, and even mosquito control services. The U.S. Constitution created the foundations for our separate but unified system of government that gives substantial powers to the national and state levels, including the power to collect taxes and to pass and enforce laws regulating the conduct of individuals, like "death with dignity" or "assisted suicide," but gives the national level the greatest authority to govern the nation as a whole.[9]

The Framers understood that the people would be more strongly attached to their state and local governments than to the national government and that they would not support reserving all power to that national government. Alexander Hamilton even called the states "the great cement of society." Thus, the Framers provided hopeful reassurance in the Tenth Amendment, which promises "powers not delegated to the United States by the Constitution, nor prohibited by it to the States, are reserved to the States respectively, or to the people."[10]

This wording has left a question about how to resolve ongoing disputes over national and state power. The Federalists argued that the national government received the most significant and certainly the most detailed powers, while the Anti-Federalists argued that the states retained the most important powers. Whatever the initial balance, however, most experts would argue that the national government has grown more powerful with its expanding agenda, budget, and international role.

Powers Delegated to the National Government

Before turning to the division of powers between the national government and the 50 state governments, it is important to understand that federalism divides powers between the two levels. The Framers provided a long list of powers to the national government but reserved all powers not mentioned in the Constitution for the states. Therefore, it is impossible to count specific powers or easily calculate which level of government received the greatest authority under the Constitution's brand of federalism.

The Constitution gives the national government a list of **delegated powers** that provide the authority to act on behalf of the nation and its states. Three kinds of delegated powers are found either in the Constitution's specific lists or are implied in other constitutional clauses: (1) **enumerated powers**, such as the power to coin money and to tell each branch of government (executive, legislative, judicial) what it can and cannot do—these are so carefully outlined that they are sometimes called "express powers"; (2) broad and unwritten **implied powers**, such as the power to pass a budget that Congress uses to make the leap from its enumerated powers to actually making laws; and (3) even broader unwritten **inherent powers**, such as the power to monitor the Internet for terrorist messages, that all three branches believe are essential for protecting the nation from great threats that might destroy it.

The national government, however, has authority that goes beyond the Constitution's delegated powers. The Framers gave the national government additional strength through a series of decisions that resulted in: (1) the supremacy clause,

delegated powers
Powers given to the national government.

enumerated powers
Powers that are specifically given to a branch of the national government; sometimes called "express powers."

implied powers
Broad and unwritten powers that Congress uses to carry out its enumerated powers.

inherent powers
Broad and unwritten powers of the national government essential for protecting the nation from domestic and foreign threats. An unwritten extension of the take care clause that presidents occasionally use to claim authority to take action without congressional or judicial authority.

Protestors in Texas show their support for eliminating all national government funding for Planned Parenthood family planning centers in Texas in the wake of false allegations that Planned Parenthood sold tissue from aborted fetuses to research institutions. Although states do not receive national funding for abortions, many accept support for Planned Parenthood family planning and health centers. In May 2018, the Trump administration issued a proposed rule that would prohibit funding for any family planning programs affiliated with any organizations that also provided abortion services.

(2) the war power, (3) the commerce clause, and especially (4) the power to tax and spend for the general welfare. Each of these pillars is discussed in more detail in the following text. Together these pillars have permitted a steady expansion of the national government's authority to the point where some states complain they have lost the power to regulate their own actions.

The federal courts play an important role in limiting the range of federal and state authority, but generally side with the federal government on laws that Congress and the president deem necessary and proper for protecting the nation. Although the Supreme Court can and does limit federal laws that conflict with constitutional rights such as free speech, it generally upholds federal laws that remedy state-level violations of guarantees to freedoms such as due process and equal protection of the laws.

supremacy clause

Contained in Article IV of the Constitution, the clause gives national laws the absolute power even when states have enacted a competing law.

THE SUPREMACY CLAUSE The **supremacy clause** may be the most important pillar of U.S. federalism. Found in Article VI of the Constitution, the clause is simple and direct: "This Constitution, and the Laws of the United States which shall be made in Pursuance thereof; and all Treaties made…under the Authority of the United States, shall be the supreme Law of the Land; and the Judges in every State shall be bound thereby; any Thing in the Constitution or Laws of any State to the Contrary notwithstanding."

preemption

The right of a national law or regulation to preclude enforcement of a state or local law or regulation.

In simple terms, the supremacy clause prevents states from enacting laws in conflict with national law. It also provides the constitutional foundation for **preemption** of state laws, which means that the state laws are neither valid exercises of state powers nor enforceable. Moreover, the supremacy clause warns states not to legislate in areas that are to be regulated, or occupied, by the national government, such as interstate commerce.

Because national and state responsibilities so often overlap, preemption is one of the most widely used concepts in the national courts today. Can states set higher safety standards for nuclear power plants than the national government does? Can they put tougher warnings on cigarette packages than the national government does? Can they permit civil unions between same-sex couples, or raise the minimum wage far above the national level? Can they allow the use of medical marijuana to alleviate pain and suffering by victims of cancer? These are some of the questions that have been asked in recent years in attempts to resolve ongoing disputes over national and state power.[11]

The answers to such questions are provided by the national courts, which must balance a state's right to use its own powers and the national government's right to exercise its enumerated, inherent, and implied powers. In terms of individual rights or limits on interstate commerce, for example, states may provide greater protection than the national government does, but never less.

There are times, however, when states make the first move in creating laws that the national government might eventually adopt for the rest of the nation. In December 2015, for example, Connecticut imposed a sweeping ban on the sale of any assault rifles to any citizen who was listed by the national government's as a possible terrorist. Few states followed Connecticut's lead, the absence of national laws on the issue meant any state was entirely free to set any limits it deemed appropriate. And, in the wake of mass shootings in Las Vegas, Nevada, Parkland, Florida, and Santa Fe, Texas, there was renewed interested in state action.[12]

Students at Leon High School in Tallahassee, Florida, gather to prepare for a march at the state capitol in February 2018. Although gun advocates argued that gun laws violate the Second Amendment's right to bear arms, the Florida legislature eventually enacted a new law raising the minimum age required to purchase a firearm to 21 years, while requiring a three-day waiting period between a purchase and delivery and providing more state funding for school police officers and mental health services.

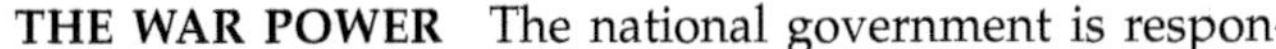

THE WAR POWER The national government is responsible for protecting the nation from external threats, whether from other nations or from terrorists who do not consider themselves citizens of any nation at all. The government's power to maintain national security includes the power to wage war. In today's world, military strength depends not only on the presence of troops in the field, but also on the ability to mobilize the nation's industrial might and harvest any scientific and technological knowledge for defense. As the Supreme Court's chief justice, Charles Evans observed in 1930: "The power to wage war is the power to wage war successfully."[13] At times the national government must take control of activities ordinarily reserved for the states. Federalism is of no value if the nation is defeated in war.

THE POWER TO REGULATE COMMERCE Congressional authority extends to all commerce that affects more than one state. Commerce includes the production, buying, selling, renting, and transporting of goods, services, and properties. The **commerce clause** (Article I, Section 8, Clause 1) packs a tremendous constitutional punch; it gives Congress the power "to regulate Commerce with foreign Nations, and among the several States, and with the Indian Tribes." In these few words, the national government has found constitutional justification for regulating a wide range of human activity because few aspects of our economy today affect commerce in only one state. In one recent issue, however, the Supreme Court ruled in 2012 that the national government's authority under the commerce clause does not extend so far as to require Americans to purchase health insurance; but the Court did allow the national government to penalize people who decide not to purchase insurance as an exercise of the national government's taxing authority.[14]

commerce clause

The clause in the Constitution (Article I, Section 8, Clause 3) that gives Congress the power to regulate all business activities that cross state lines or affect more than one state or other nations.

THE POWER TO TAX AND SPEND Congress lacks constitutional authority to pass laws solely on the grounds that the laws will promote the general welfare, but it may raise taxes and spend money for this purpose. For example, even when the national government lacks the power to regulate education or agriculture directly, it still has the power to appropriate money to support education or to pay farm subsidies. By attaching conditions to its grants of money, the national government creates incentives that affect state action. If states want the money, they must accept the strings.

Some of this power involves threats to withhold funds if states do not follow national policies. For example, the national government will not provide funds for any program that denies benefits because of race, color, sex, or physical disability. The national government also has used this power to withhold highway construction funds to force states to increase the drinking age to 21.

In addition, the national government can require states to provide services, such as nutrition assistance to low-income Americans, under **national mandates** that set

national mandates

Requirements the national government imposes as a condition for receiving national funds.

EMPLOYEE RIGHTS
UNDER THE FAIR LABOR STANDARDS ACT

FEDERAL MINIMUM WAGE
$7.25 PER HOUR
BEGINNING JULY 24, 2009

The law requires employers to display this poster where employees can readily see it.

OVERTIME PAY At least 1½ times the regular rate of pay for all hours worked over 40 in a workweek.

CHILD LABOR An employee must be at least 16 years old to work in most non-farm jobs and at least 18 to work in non-farm jobs declared hazardous by the Secretary of Labor. Youths 14 and 15 years old may work outside school hours in various non-manufacturing, non-mining, non-hazardous jobs with certain work hours restrictions. Different rules apply in agricultural employment.

TIP CREDIT Employers of "tipped employees" who meet certain conditions may claim a partial wage credit based on tips received by their employees. Employers must pay tipped employees a cash wage of at least $2.13 per hour if they claim a tip credit against their minimum wage obligation. If an employee's tips combined with the employer's cash wage of at least $2.13 per hour do not equal the minimum hourly wage, the employer must make up the difference.

NURSING MOTHERS The FLSA requires employers to provide reasonable break time for a nursing mother employee who is subject to the FLSA's overtime requirements in order for the employee to express breast milk for her nursing child for one year after the child's birth each time such employee has a need to express breast milk. Employers are also required to provide a place, other than a bathroom, that is shielded from view and free from intrusion from coworkers and the public, which may be used by the employee to express breast milk.

ENFORCEMENT The Department has authority to recover back wages and an equal amount in liquidated damages in instances of minimum wage, overtime, and other violations. The Department may litigate and/or recommend criminal prosecution. Employers may be assessed civil money penalties for each willful or repeated violation of the minimum wage or overtime pay provisions of the law. Civil money penalties may also be assessed for violations of the FLSA's child labor provisions. Heightened civil money penalties may be assessed for each child labor violation that results in the death or serious injury of any minor employee, and such assessments may be doubled when the violations are determined to be willful or repeated. The law also prohibits retaliating against or discharging workers who file a complaint or participate in any proceeding under the FLSA.

ADDITIONAL INFORMATION

- Certain occupations and establishments are exempt from the minimum wage, and/or overtime pay provisions.
- Special provisions apply to workers in American Samoa, the Commonwealth of the Northern Mariana Islands, and the Commonwealth of Puerto Rico.
- Some state laws provide greater employee protections; employers must comply with both.
- Some employers incorrectly classify workers as "independent contractors" when they are actually employees under the FLSA. It is important to know the difference between the two because employees (unless exempt) are entitled to the FLSA's minimum wage and overtime pay protections and correctly classified independent contractors are not.
- Certain full-time students, student learners, apprentices, and workers with disabilities may be paid less than the minimum wage under special certificates issued by the Department of Labor.

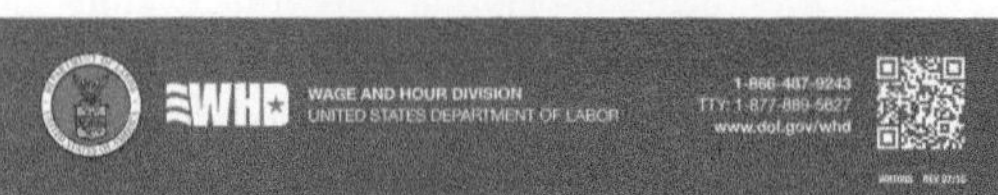

The Constitution's commerce clause gives Congress the power to regulate all business activities that cross state lines or affect more than one state or other nations. Congress uses this power to regulate many parts of the U.S. economy, including the power to regulate the minimum wage that workers receive. Congress last raised the minimum wage in 2009 when it moved up 70 cents to $7.25. States are free to set their minimum wage higher. Eighteen states and 20 cities raised their minimum wages on January 1, 2018, for example. New York set the nation's highest mark in the nation at $11.50 per hour with California and Maine close behind at $11 and $10 respectively. Local governments are also free to set higher minimums for businesses within their jurisdictions. El Cerrito, California, raised its minimum wage to the nation's highest mark at $13.60 an hour in 2018.

three types of requirements: (1) program requirements that establish exactly what state governments must do to provide a given service, (2) process requirements that establish exactly how state governments are to provide a service, and (3) restraints that limit the extent of action by states in certain areas, such as highway speed limits or texting while driving. The national government often provides the funding needed for action, but sometimes asks states to implement mandates without any national dollars at all. States often follow these unfunded mandates despite the cost to their budgets because they worry that if they do not, there may be future national cuts in other funding programs.

Powers Reserved to the States

As noted, the Tenth Amendment to the Constitution reserves all powers not delegated to the national government (for example, the power to declare and wage war), nor denied (for example, the power to coin money), to the states. States use these **reserve powers** to create schools and local governments, for example, which are not listed among the national government's express powers. States can exercise these reserve powers as long as their decisions do not conflict with the supremacy and commerce clauses, or any of the express powers given to the national government.

reserve powers
All powers not specifically delegated to the national government by the Constitution. The reserve power can be found in the Tenth Amendment to the Constitution.

The national and state governments also share powers. These **concurrent powers** allow the states to levy taxes and regulate commerce within state boundaries. States also are free to use these concurrent powers to tax the same products that the national government targets, including income, alcohol, and gasoline. However, states cannot use their concurrent powers to "unduly burden" commerce among the states, interfere with a function of the national government, complicate the operation of a national law, or abridge the terms of a treaty of the United States. (See Table 3.1 on next page for the constitutional division of powers.)

concurrent powers
Powers that the Constitution gives to both the national and state governments, such as the power to levy taxes.

Congress and the president decide whether the nation needs a national law to solve a significant problem, while the national courts decide whether a state law places an "undue burden" on interstate commerce. When Congress is either silent or unclear about the proper balance between national and state powers, the Supreme Court must resolve the issue. In general, the lack of national law is viewed as permission for state action.

Powers Denied to the National Government and the States

The Constitution imposes restraints on both the national and the state governments in an effort to check and balance one against the other.

RESTRAINTS ON THE NATIONAL GOVERNMENT Although the Framers clearly supported a strong central government, the Constitution nonetheless restrains the national government from reaching too far into state activities.[15] As the national government has grown, the Supreme Court has become the most important check on national power, holding that the national government may not enact laws that command states to enforce national laws. In *Printz* v. *United States,* the Court held that states were not required to conduct instant national background checks prior to selling a handgun.[16] Referring broadly to the concept of dual federalism (discussed later in this chapter), the Supreme Court said that the national government could not "draft" local police to do its bidding. But, as previously discussed, even if the national government cannot force states to enforce certain national laws, it can threaten to withhold its funding if states do not comply with national policies, such as by lowering the minimum drinking age or speed limit.

The national government also has the responsibility to protect states against domestic insurrection. Congress has delegated to the president the authority to

TABLE 3.1 THE CONSTITUTIONAL DIVISION OF NATIONAL AND STATE POWERS

The Framers divided government powers to give states strong authority over issues that are close to home, and the national government powers to protect the nation as a whole. They also gave some powers to both the national government and the states, which occasionally creates conflict between national and state action.

Powers Delegated to the National Government	Powers Reserved for State Governments
Regulate trade and interstate commerce	Create local governments
Declare war	Police citizens
Create post offices	Oversee primary and elementary education
Coin money	
Concurrent Powers Shared by the National and State Governments	
Impose and collect taxes and fees	
Borrow and spend money	
Establish courts at their level of government	
Enact and enforce laws	
Protect civil rights	
Conduct elections	
Protect health and welfare	

dispatch troops to put down such insurrections when the proper state authorities request them.

RESTRAINTS ON THE STATES The Constitution is quite specific about what states cannot do, in part to protect the national government's authority, and in part to prevent divisions and even wars between the states. Toward these ends, states are prohibited from (1) making treaties with foreign governments, (2) coining their own money or any other "legal tender" that might be used for paying debts, (3) taxing imports or exports, (4) raising their own armies and building navy ships, and (5) waging wars.

Despite the ban on creating state armies and navies, the Framers gave states authority to form and arm their own militias to supply troops to the U.S. military when needed. These militias became even more closely tied to the U.S. military in 1903, when Congress created the outlines of today's Army and Air National Guard. Members of the National Guard hold regular jobs during the week but train regularly on weekends; they can be called into service by their state governor in times of crisis, such as natural disasters and civil unrest, and can be ordered into war by the president.

State militias are a particularly important exception on the list. State governors ordinarily command the National Guard and have the power to call it into action at any time. The president, however, controls the recruitment and training of each Guard member, and can order the National Guard to act in national emergencies. The president also can call the Guard to service in war. Many National Guard units fought in the Iraq and Afghanistan wars after they were "federalized" into action, and almost 500 Army National Guard troops died.[17]

In 2016, the Supreme Court ruled that Texas did not have the constitutional authority to limit access to abortion clinics. Texas had limited access under a law that put tough restrictions on who could perform abortions and set specific conditions that required immediate access to hospital care in the event of a medical crisis. The Supreme Court ruled that the restrictions were an unconstitutional exercise of state rights in the absence of a compelling reason for the limits.

Despite the Supreme Court defeat, Texas passed an even more restrictive anti-abortion law in May 2017. The new law required that abortion providers bury or cremate all tissue from unborn fetuses, prohibited the donation of fetal tissue for use in medical research, banned "partial-birth abortions" after the first 13 weeks of pregnancy, and prohibited the use of state insurance for any abortion procedure.

Opponents of the bill argued that these provisions were unconstitutional under the 2016 Supreme Court decision but failed to convince anti-abortion advocates. Texas legislators were ready to pass another version of the bill whenever the Supreme Court might act.

Powers That Help States Work Together

Alongside the divisions of national and state power, the Constitution regulates state-to-state relationships. Using provisions taken directly from the Articles of Confederation, Article IV requires states to give full faith and credit to each other's public acts, records, and judicial proceedings; extend all privileges of state citizenship to residents of other states; and return anyone who flees justice in another state to that state.

full faith and credit clause
The clause in the Constitution (Article IV, Section 1) requiring each state to recognize the civil judgments rendered by the courts of the other states and to accept their public records and acts as valid.

FULL FAITH AND CREDIT The **full faith and credit clause** (Article IV, Section 1), one of the more technical provisions of the Constitution, requires state courts to enforce the civil judgments of the courts of other states and to accept their public records and acts as valid.[18] It does not require states to enforce the criminal laws or legislation and administrative acts of other states; in most cases, for one state to enforce the criminal laws of another would raise constitutional issues. The clause applies primarily to enforcing judicial settlements and court awards.

INTERSTATE PRIVILEGES AND IMMUNITIES Under Article IV, Section 2, individual states must give citizens of all other states the privileges and immunities they grant to their own citizens, including the protection of the laws, the right to engage in peaceful occupations, access to the courts, and freedom from discriminatory taxes. Because of this clause, states may not impose unreasonable residency requirements; that is, withhold rights to American citizens who have recently moved to the state and thereby have become citizens of that state.

EXTRADITION In Article IV, Section 2, the Constitution asserts that, when individuals charged with crimes have fled from one state to another, the state to which they have fled is to deliver them to the proper officials on demand of the executive authority of the state from which they fled. This process is called extradition. "The obvious objective of the Extradition Clause," the courts have claimed, "is that no State should become a safe haven for the fugitives from a sister State's criminal justice system."[19] Congress has supplemented this constitutional provision by making the governor of the state to which fugitives have fled responsible for returning them.

INTERSTATE COMPACTS The Constitution requires states to settle disputes with one another without the use of force. States may carry their legal disputes to the Supreme Court, or they may negotiate interstate compacts. Such compacts can be seen as treaties between the states, and often establish interstate agencies to handle problems affecting an entire region. Congress must approve most interstate compacts before they can take effect. Then the compact becomes binding on all states that sign it, and the national judiciary can enforce its terms. A typical state may belong to 20 compacts dealing with such subjects as environmental protection, crime control, water rights, and higher-education exchanges.[20]

Federalism and Its Alternatives (Structure)

3.2 Distinguish federalism from other forms of government.

The constitutional foundation was only the starting point for an effective national system. The formal rules were generally clear, but the national and state governments had to learn the boundaries to create effective federalism. The Constitution set the core principles for federalism, but there is still disagreement about which entity should be allowed to do what today.

The Framers actually drew some of their ideas on how federalism would work from the failed Articles of Confederation; they even copied some of the old language. They wanted to give the states enough authority to create support for the new Constitution, but not so much authority that the new national government would be too weak to act. Hence, the Framers often argued that the states would have even greater freedom to set their own course under a "firm union" than as separate members of a weak confederacy that could not protect them from foreign or domestic threats. Although the states would lose a long list of powers, they would gain a much longer list of protections from what Hamilton described as the "perpetual vibration between the extremes of tyranny and anarchy."[21] The heated controversy about the ability of the national government and the states to work together continues to this day.

In 2012, for example, the national and state governments went to the Supreme Court to decide how much states can do to regulate unlawful immigration. The case hinged on whether Arizona could impose a "show-me-your-papers" provision that required citizens to prove their U.S. citizenship when stopped by the police. Although the Supreme Court let the provision stand, it forbade Arizona from creating its own immigration system. The state could help the national government by turning over non citizens to the U.S. Immigration and Customs Bureau, but could do nothing more. After apprehending an undocumented immigrant, the national government takes over.[22]

Systems for Dividing Power Across Levels of Government

Federalism is not the only way to divide and distribute powers across states and regions. The Framers could have created a **unitary system** of government, in which a constitution vests all governmental power in the central government. The central government, if it so chooses, may delegate authority to constituent units, but what it delegates, it may take away. China, France, the Scandinavian countries, and Israel have unitary governments.

The Framers also could have created a much stronger central government within a less powerful **confederation**. Under a confederation, the central government makes regulations for state governments, but does so only at their direction. The 13 states under the Articles of Confederation operated in this manner, as did the southern Confederacy during the Civil War.

The Framers chose federalism instead, entirely because the confederation created under the Articles of Confederation had been such a dismal failure. A federalist system was politically necessary. The states had experienced independence not only from England but also from each other, and so room had to be allowed for some state differences if the states were to agree to become a United States of America.

Even among nations that call themselves federations, there is no single model for dividing authority between national and state governments. Some countries have no federalism at all, whereas others have different variations of power sharing between the national and state governments. Indeed, even the United States has varied greatly over time in its balance of federal–state power.

The British government, for example, is divided into three levels: national, county, and district governments. County and district governments deliver roughly one-fifth of all government services, including education, housing, and police and fire protection. As a rule, most power is reserved for the central government on the theory that there should be "territorial justice," which means that all citizens should be governed by the same laws and standards. In recent years, however, Great Britain has devolved substantial authority to Scotland, Wales, and Northern Ireland.

Types of Federalism

The mere existence of a strong national government and clearly defined state powers does not create **federalism**. Rather, federalism involves a division of powers between the national government and state or regional governments in which each is given

unitary system
A constitutional arrangement that concentrates power in a central government.

confederation
A constitutional arrangement in which sovereign nations or states, by compact, create a central government but carefully limit its power and do not give it direct authority over individuals.

federalism
A constitutional arrangement in which power is distributed between a central government and states, which are sometimes called provinces in other nations. Both the national government and the states exercise direct authority over individuals.

A young girl places flowers on the grave of an unknown soldier at Gettysburg National Cemetery. The Battle of Gettysburg was a defining battle in the Civil War over slavery. The war took the lives of more than 600,000 Americans.

clearly defined functions. Neither the central nor the regional government receives its powers from the other; both derive them from a common source—the Constitution. No ordinary act of legislation at either the national or the state level can change this constitutional distribution of powers. Both levels of government operate through their own agents and exercise power directly over individuals.

Constitutionally, the national structure of the United States consists of only the national government and the states. However, the national and state governments oversee thousands of county, city, and town governments; school districts; and special authorities that include airports, subway systems, and hospitals. As Figure 3.1 shows, the number of school districts has fallen dramatically since the end of World War II, while the number of municipalities, townships, and counties have held steady.[23]

As the figure also shows, special districts have grown dramatically in recent districts. These authorities, as they are sometimes called, generally operate with significant freedom to raise and spend money on behalf of the citizens they serve, and are usually governed by independent boards appointed by the state governor. Some operate airports, others build and manage sports stadiums, and still others manage electric grids, cemeteries, sewer systems, fire districts, libraries, and even mosquito control programs.

Power is shared among these 90,000 governments by using one or more of six types of federalism:

1. *Dual, or "layer-cake," federalism:* This form involves a strict separation of powers between the national and state governments, in which each "layer" has its own responsibilities and reigns supreme within its constitutional realm. Dual federalism was the favored form until the national government took the dominant role in addressing the nation's great economic crisis during the 1930s.
2. *Cooperative, or "marble-cake," federalism:* As its name suggests, cooperative federalism involves a much more flexible relationship between the national and state governments in which both work together to address shared goals such as providing education and health care.[24] Cooperative federalism was the preferred approach beginning after World War II and continuing through the 1970s.
3. *Competitive federalism:* This form is seen as a way to improve government performance by encouraging state and local governments to compete against each

FIGURE 3.1 UNITS OF GOVERNMENT IN THE UNITED STATES, 1942–2012

The number of state and local governments may look steady over the last 60 years, but there has been a great deal of movement underneath the surface. The number of school districts has declined as local governments try to save money through larger schools, while the number of special districts has increased dramatically as local governments use these districts to generate revenues for their communities through economic and community development. In 1942, there were 155,000 units of government; 82,000 units of government in 1982; and 90,000 units of government in 2012. The number of governments changes so slowly that the Census Bureau only takes a count every five years. The 2017 totals will be released by early 2019.

SOURCE: U.S. Census Bureau, Government Units by State, factfinder.census.gov.

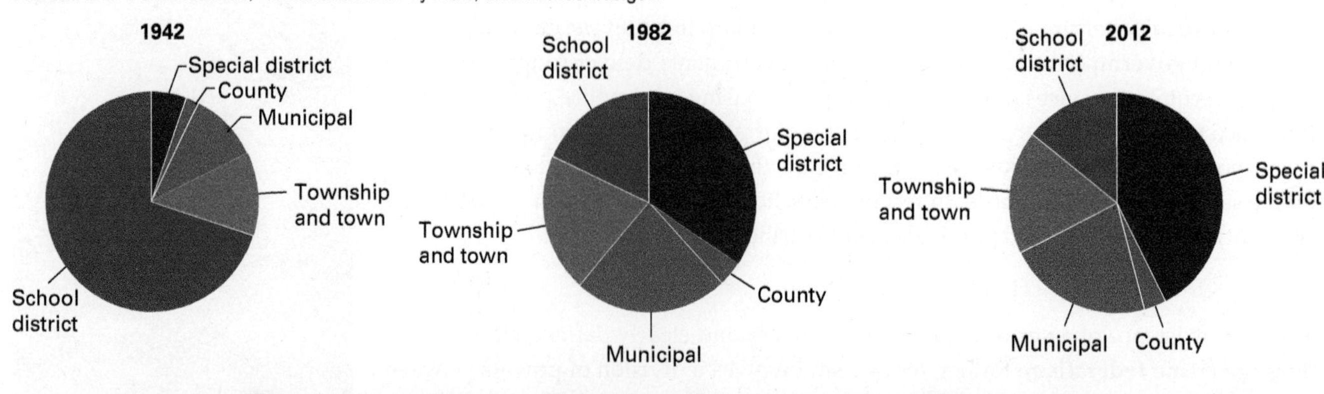

other for residents, businesses, investment, and national funding.[25] Competitive federalism has become more popular in recent decades as a way to promote state action in return for incentives such as large federal prizes and grants, such as ther-ecent "Race to the Top" grants given to states for innovation in public education.[26]

4. *Restrictive federalism:* The national government uses restrictive federalism to force states to follow its lead. Although states are always free to ask the national government for permission to use their own rules, restrictive federalism is based on the argument that the national government has the sole power to grant the request.[27] Restrictive federalism was the preferred approach to sorting national and state responsibilities from the 1930s to the 1990s, but was often mixed with other forms on this list.
5. *Coercive federalism:* This is the strongest form of top-down federalism, and is often called "centralized federalism" to suggest a blend of tough control from the very top of the national government. As the term "coercive" implies, this form of federalism imposes strict control of the states through orders or even the use of force. Coercive federalism was used during the 1960s to enforce racial integration in states that refused to obey the Civil Rights Act.
6. *New federalism:* President Richard Nixon created this blend of the other types of federalism in 1969 as a way to return, or **devolve**, responsibilities to the states. Promising "more money and less interference," Nixon launched new programs that gave states a greater share of national funding to spend as they wished, and more freedom to make the rules on nationally funded programs such as community economic development.[28] Although Nixon's brand of the new federalism unraveled after he resigned from office in disgrace, it still influences national government decisions today.[29]

devolve
To return national powers to the states.

The Constitution does not favor any one type of federalism, nor do Congress and the president have to use the same type for every policy. As a result, the choice of one form of federalism over another varies more with events and politics than the Constitution. Moreover, the national government often changes its mind on which type is best for dividing power on the same issue.

In 2001, for example, President George W. Bush combined restrictive and coercive federalism to reform public education under his No Child Left Behind Act. Although Republicans generally support dual federalism and states' rights, Bush decided that a blend of federalism allowing more top-down control was the only way to get all states to follow the new rules on standardized testing and school discipline.

States soon rebelled against the law because it limited their freedom to set their own educational standards, use their own tests, and manage their schools.[30] Although the No Child Left Behind Act provided national funds to help states implement the reforms, the act also threatened to withdraw the funds if states did not punish failing schools. Many Republicans also argued that the act violated states' rights under dual federalism to run their own schools.

Bush was gone from office when Republicans led a revolt against the act in late 2015.[31] The national government had already given many states waivers from the act's most restrictive provisions, parents were fighting against the rising amount of student testing, and a new generation of conservative Republicans was demanding a return to the party's historical support for dual federalism. Even Democrats who believed the law was a reasonable use of coercive and restrictive federalism to improve the nation's failing public schools came to believe that the act had gone too far in stripping the states of their authority to run their schools.

In early December 2015, strong majorities from both parties voted to replace the No Child Left Behind Act with the Every Student Succeeds Act. Although states are still required to test their students regularly, the new law reduced the role of test scores on teacher evaluations, and gave parents more access to teachers.

The end of No Child Left Behind also restored the two-party balance on federalism. Democrats returned to their historic support for cooperative federalism,

Republicans returned to their historic support for dual federalism, and states regained significant control of what they always believed was their primary responsibility: education. Under their authority to control education, many states have now adopted the "common core" curriculum that also relies on heavy testing to achieve its goals.

The Trump administration offered its own education reforms early in his administration by ordering the Department of Education to review, modify, and repeal any rules and guidance that limited state authority to oversee public and private schools. Building even further on the president's campaign promises to return education decisions to the states, the administration gave states more choices in how to spend federal grants for specific programs such as access to health care and food for the poor. The administration also revoked environmental regulations on clean air, power plant emissions, methane emissions, and water quality, while promising to fight California's regulations designed to increase automobile mileage requirements. In reversing these federal rules, the Trump administration gave states more power to reduce the regulations they had enacted to support the Obama administration's environment programs, while punishing states that had received permission to raise their own standards beyond federal requirements.

The U.S. Courts and Federalism (Action)

3.3 Trace the evolution of federalism from ratification to the present.

Like so much in American government, federalism is still evolving. There are still strong opinions about how powers should be distributed between the national government and the states, and inevitable conflicts about how economic, social, and international problems should be solved and at what level. As noted earlier, the Constitution provides the framework, but the political process ultimately decides how power will be divided, or at what level of government the action will take place, national or state. This process often requires an umpire to make the final calls about which level of government should do what, for whom, and to whom. The nation's highest court claimed this role in the celebrated case of *McCulloch* v. *Maryland.*

McCulloch v. *Maryland*

The Supreme Court had its first chance to define federalism in 1819 when it ruled in *McCulloch* v. *Maryland.*[32] Congress had established the Bank of the United States, but Maryland opposed any national bank and levied a $15,000 tax on any bank not incorporated in the state. James William McCulloch, the cashier of the bank, refused to pay on the grounds that a state could not tax an instrument of the national government.

Maryland was represented before the Court by some of the country's most distinguished lawyers, including Luther Martin, who had been a delegate to the Constitutional Convention. Martin said the Constitution did not expressly delegate to the national government the power to create a bank. Martin maintained that the Necessary and Proper Clause gives Congress only the power to choose those means and to pass those laws absolutely essential to the execution of its expressly granted powers. Because a bank is not absolutely necessary to the exercise of its delegated powers, Martin argued, Congress had no authority to establish it.

The national government was also represented by some of the country's distinguished lawyers, including Daniel Webster, one of the country's greatest orators. Webster conceded that the power to create a bank was not one of the express powers of the national government. However, the power to pass laws necessary and proper to carry out Congress's express powers is specifically delegated to Congress. Webster argued that the Constitution leaves no room for doubt as to which level of government has the final authority. According to the supremacy clause, when national and state laws conflict, Webster argued, the national law must be obeyed.

Speaking for a unanimous Court, Chief Justice John Marshall rejected every one of Maryland's contentions. He summarized his views on the powers of the national government in these now-famous words: "Let the end be legitimate, let it be within the scope of the Constitution, and all means which are appropriate, which are plainly adapted to that end, which are not prohibited, but consistent with the letter and spirit of the Constitution, are constitutional." Because the constitutional structure delegated to Congress the powers to coin money and regulate commerce, congressional action establishing a national bank was properly within its authority.

Having decided that the national government has implied powers, Marshall proceeded to outline the concept of national supremacy. No state, he said, can use its taxing powers to tax a national instrument. Relying on the supremacy clause, he wrote that "The power to tax involves the power to destroy.... If the right of the States to tax the means employed by the general government be conceded, the declaration that the Constitution, and the laws made in pursuance thereof, shall be the supreme law of the land, is empty and unmeaning declamation."

McCulloch v. *Maryland* immediately became the linchpin of a unified national economy. Maryland's arguments would have limited the national government's ability to deal with the interstate problems that confronted a rapidly expanding nation, and if upheld would have made the nation much weaker today.

The U.S. Courts and the States

National courts' authority to review the activities of state and local governments has expanded dramatically in recent decades because of modern judicial interpretations of the Fourteenth Amendment, which forbids states to deprive any person of life, liberty, or property without due process of the law. States may not deny any person the equal protection of the laws, and that includes congressional legislation enacted to implement the Fourteenth Amendment. Almost every behavior by state and local officials is now subject to challenge before a national judge as a violation of the Constitution or of national law.

Throughout U.S. history, the national courts' decisions have sometimes favored the states, but more generally they have upheld the national government's authority against state challenges. The rationale has been that constitutional rights and liberties need to be understood and enforced uniformly across the states. As Supreme Court Justice Oliver Wendell Holmes argued in 1913, national laws are less likely to threaten the constitutional foundations of federalism than state laws, in large part because states have less reason to consider the needs of the nation as a whole. "I do not think the United States would come to an end if we lost our power to declare an Act of Congress void. I do think the Union would be imperiled if we could not make that declaration as to the laws of the several States."[33]

The U.S. Supreme Court and the Commerce Clause

From 1937 until the 1990s, the Supreme Court essentially removed national courts from what had been their role of protecting states from acts of Congress. The Supreme Court broadly interpreted the commerce clause to allow Congress to do whatever it thought necessary and proper to promote the common good, even if national laws and regulations infringed on the activities of state and local governments. As with its understanding of congressional power under the commerce clause, the Marshall Court set the rules that still give the national government the power to control the states.

Even though national laws are supreme, at times state governments adopt different rules. Although marijuana is an illegal drug under the national government's Controlled Substances Act, several states now allow its use to reduce the effect of cancer treatments, while other states and the District of Columbia have legalized the sale of marijuana for recreational use. The legalization movement accelerated after the Obama administration relaxed tough federal laws on possession in 2013, but began to retreat when the Trump administration decided to tighten enforcement as part of its campaign against the opioid crisis. Here customers shop for marijuana at a dispensary in Colorado.

GIBBONS* V. *OGDEN The 1824 case *Gibbons* v. *Ogden* recognized this authority.[34] The case involved a New York state license that gave Aaron Ogden the exclusive right to operate steamboats between New York and New Jersey. Using the license, Ogden asked the New York state courts to stop Thomas Gibbons from running a competing ferry. Although Gibbons countered that his boats were licensed under a 1793 act of Congress governing vessels "in the coasting trade and fisheries," the New York courts sided with Ogden. Just as the national government and states both have the power to tax, the New York courts said they both had the power to regulate commerce.

Gibbons appealed to the Supreme Court to answer a simple question: which government has the ultimate power to regulate interstate commerce? The Supreme Court gave an equally simple answer: the national government.

By ruling that states may not discriminate against each other, *Gibbons* v. *Ogden* was immediately heralded for promoting a national economy. For 200 years, the Supreme Court's definition of *commerce* as "intercourse among the states" provided the basis for national regulation of "things in commerce"[35] that now include an expanding range of economic activities, such as the sale of lottery tickets,[36] prostitution,[37] radio and television broadcasts,[38] and regulation of the Internet.

The U.S. Supreme Court and the Continued Contest over Federalism

The tight balance between liberals and conservatives on the Supreme Court has created victories and defeats for the states. Although the Court generally sided with the states during the 1990s and early 2000s, its recent decisions suggest a shift toward a more liberal position.

In 2015, for example, a 5-to-4 majority overturned state laws banning same-sex marriage. Ruling in *Obergefell et al.* v. *Hodges,* the Supreme Court relied on the Constitution's Fourteenth Amendment provision that no state shall "deprive any person of life, liberty, or property, without due process of law" to strike down state bans on same-sex marriage as unconstitutional.[39] Reading the Fourteenth Amendment broadly, the Court majority concluded that the right to dignity was embedded in the amendment's overall intent, and therefore ruled that same-sex couples had the same right to marry as all other couples based on "equal dignity in the eye of the law."[40]

In 2016, a 5-to-3 majority also ruled that Texas could not deny access to abortion by imposing strict rules on who can perform abortions and where the procedure had to take place. Under the Texas law, doctors would have been unable to perform abortions unless they were affiliated with nearby hospitals and only in clinics that met the highest levels of care for surgical centers. Ruling in *Whole Woman's Health et al.* v. *Hellerstedt,* the Court concluded that these two restrictions would impose an "undue burden" on a woman's ability to seek and obtain an abortion and would therefore violate its past decisions limiting state interference with access. According to the Court, neither of the restrictions offered enough medical benefit to outweigh the burden on abortion. The ruling sent a clear signal to states with similar laws that their statutes were likely to be held unconstitutional, too.[41]

Despite these more recent decisions, the most important recent Supreme Court decision on federalism came in 2010 on the constitutionality of the Patient Protection and Affordable Care Act, better known as "Obamacare." Passed by Congress with little Republican support in March 2010, the act contained a number of popular provisions for health care reform. In *National Federation of Independent Business et al.* v. *Sebelius,* the Supreme Court was asked whether the national government had the power to enforce two of the most important pieces of the Affordable Care Act.[42]

First, did the Necessary and Proper Clause provide authority to order states to expand their Medicaid programs for the poor? The national government gave states extra funding to increase the reach of their Medicaid programs for low-income Americans. At the same time, they were told that they would lose all Medicaid funding if they failed to implement the expansion.

Second, did the commerce clause provide authority to order individual Americans to buy health insurance? Congress and the president understood that younger, healthier Americans were less likely to buy health insurance than older, more vulnerable Americans. And if young Americans did not buy insurance, the program could collapse as costs rose with an aging population. As Congress and the president argued, absent the requirement, the new health program would cost so much that interstate commerce would be disrupted by cash-strapped state insurance programs.

The Supreme Court answered "no" to both questions. The Court declared that because the Medicaid expansion was such a large program, states had to be given the option to accept the national money or continue running the program as usual. Congress was free to "alter" or "amend" any program, but could not create an entirely new program without a state's willingness to participate. This shift clearly gave states more power to decide which national funding to accept in the future. As of January 2018, Republicans had unified control of the governments in 16 of the 18 states that had decided not to expand their programs.[43]

The Supreme Court likewise rejected use of the commerce clause as a justification for the insurance requirement. As Chief Justice John Roberts argued, in explaining the 5–4 decision, Congress has used the commerce clause to create a number of large national programs over the years, including Medicaid itself; however, it has never used the commerce clause to "compel individuals not engaged in commerce to purchase an unwanted product.... If the power to 'regulate' something included the power to create it, many of the provisions in the Constitution would be superfluous."[44] In the end, Chief Justice Roberts joined the four liberals on the Court to uphold the compulsory coverage requirement as a tax penalty, and the decision may yet lead states to challenge other congressional uses of the commerce clause.

Both the *Gibbons* v. *Ogden* and *National Federation of Independent Business et al.* v. *Sebelius* decisions limited the national government's authority over the states, and laid the basis for future cases. If not a full rejection of restrictive federalism, these decisions contain elements of support for the dual federalism that once shaped national behavior.

Federalism in Practice (Action)

3.4 Analyze the impact of federalism on the relationships among national, state, and local levels of government.

Despite all the historical work, federalism is still a contested system. The national government and states continue to argue about the appropriate exercise of power at both levels. This does not mean that federalism prevents action, however. Governments make decisions every day without the slightest controversy, and often work together to reach agreements on major issues. Nevertheless, ongoing debates about the balance of power will continue far into the future.

Early in 2018, for example, Attorney General Jeff Sessions charged that California state officials were undermining the Trump Administration's effort to police immigration. Speaking at a convention of California police officers, Sessions called the president's immigration policy "the supreme law of the land" and announced that the Justice Department was filing suit to force the state to identify and report undocumented immigrants to federal authorities.

California responded by reminding Sessions that the federalist system does not require states to act as agents of the federal government. States cannot ignore federal laws such as the minimum wage or environmental standards, but neither can they be forced to help the federal government impose a dragnet on citizens. They are free to allow local governments to designate themselves as sanctuary cities, as long as the term is not defined as freedom to ignore federal laws. If past Supreme Court decisions hold in the case, the federal government's laws will still be supreme in California, but California will not be forced to become an agent of the federal enforcement system.

The Continuing Debate Between Centralists and Decentralists

From the beginning of the Republic, there has been an ongoing debate about the "proper" distribution of powers, functions, and responsibilities between the national government and the states. Did the national government have the authority to outlaw slavery in the territories? Did the states have the authority to operate racially segregated schools? Can Congress regulate labor relations? Does Congress have the power to regulate the sale and use of firearms? Does Congress have the right to tell states how to clean up air and water pollution?

centralists
People who favor national action over action at the state and local levels.

decentralists
People who favor state or local action rather than national action.

Today, the debate continues between **centralists**, who favor national action on issues such as environmental protection and gun control, and **decentralists**, who defend the freedom of states to make their own decisions about major policy issues such as civil rights and environmental protection.

THE CENTRALIST POSITION Centralists support a strong national government built on constitutional authority, not state permission. Presidents Abraham Lincoln, Theodore Roosevelt, Franklin Roosevelt, and Lyndon Johnson were particularly strong advocates of centralism, and received strong support from the Supreme Court until the 1990s.

Centralists reject the idea of the Constitution as an interstate compact. They see the Constitution as a document of, by, and for all the people. Although they agree that the Tenth Amendment reserves some powers for the states, they believe that the Framers favored a strong national government and wrote the supremacy clause precisely to stop the states from interfering with the good of the nation.

states' rights
Powers expressly or implicitly reserved to the states.

THE DECENTRALIST POSITION Decentralists generally believe in **states' rights** as originally designed by the Anti-Federalists who opposed the Constitution. In recent years, the decentralist position has been supported by conservatives such as Ronald Reagan, former Supreme Court Chief Justice William H. Rehnquist, and Justices Antonin Scalia and Clarence Thomas.

Many decentralists contend that the Constitution is a compact among sovereign states that created the central government and gave it limited authority. Thus the national government is little more than an agent of the states, and every one of its powers should be narrowly defined. Any question about whether the states have

Decentralists believe the national government exercises too much control over state and local responsibilities such as running airports. However, even strong decentralists wanted the national government to build and operate a new screening system after the September 11 terrorist attacks. Although even centralists no doubt complain about the long lines in airports such as Chicago O'Hare, they nonetheless believe that the national government should protect Americans against terrorist attacks on the nation's airlines and their passengers.

given a particular function to the central government or reserved it for themselves should be resolved in favor of the states.

Decentralists believe that the national government should not interfere with constitutional powers reserved for the states. Their argument is based on the Tenth Amendment: "The powers not delegated to the United States by the Constitution, nor prohibited by it to the States, are reserved to the States respectively, or to the people." Decentralists insist that state governments are closer to the people, and thereby reflect the people's wishes more accurately than the national government does.

For example, decentralists were at the center of the fight against school integration in the 1950s and 1960s following the Supreme Court's rulings to end racial segregation. The fight was led in part by Alabama's fiery governor, George C. Wallace, who "stood in the schoolhouse door" to block African American students who tried to register for classes at the University of Alabama in 1963. President Kennedy forced Wallace to step aside by ordering U.S. troops to protect the students, under national law upheld by past Supreme Court rulings.

Decentralists have been particularly supportive of the devolution revolution that emerged from the new Republican Congress in 1995.[45] The revolution was designed to give states more control over programs such as welfare; President Clinton proclaimed, "The era of big government is over." However, he tempered his comments by adding, "But we cannot go back to the time when our citizens were left to fend for themselves," and despite its dramatic name, the revolution has fallen short of the hoped-for results.

To the contrary, the national government has continued to enact laws regulating behavior within the states. At the same time it created the national passenger screening system shown in the airport photo, Congress also passed a long list of laws giving states specific responsibilities for defending homeland security, including the implementation of national criteria for issuing driver's licenses. It also has ordered states not to sell any citizen's personal information to private companies, ended state regulation of mutual funds, replaced state laws that restricted telecommunication competition, and expanded the national criminal code to include crimes that previously had been solely state and local crimes, including carjacking and acts of terrorism.

States often argue that they have the power to *nullify*, or ignore, national laws—and even vote to do so, as when several states voted to nullify Obamacare after it passed—but such votes are symbolic only. Nullification is clearly unconstitutional under the supremacy clause.

The Pros and Cons of Federalism

At first glance, federalism seems ideally suited to a diverse and rapidly growing nation that favors unity but not uniformity, especially during a period when the two parties are deeply split. It offers five significant advantages for creating impact on solving difficult problems at all levels of government.

1. *Federalism protects the nation against tyranny:* Although federalism was clearly rejected by the 11 states that seceded from the Union during the Civil War, it was restored with the Union winning the war at Appomattox, and remains strong today.[46] When one political party loses control of the national government, it is still likely to hold office in a number of states and can continue to challenge the party in power at the national level. The Framers saw the diffusion of power as a check against factions. They believed that federalism would make it more difficult for any one ideological group to impose its will on the nation as a whole.
2. *Federalism allows unity without uniformity:* The national government cannot solve every issue that divides the states, be it abortion, same-sex marriage, gun control, capital punishment, welfare financing, or assisted suicide. Instead, these issues are debated in state legislatures, county courthouses, and city halls.

Information about state action spreads quickly from government to government, especially during periods when the national government is relatively slow to respond to pressing issues.

3. *Federalism encourages innovation:* As Justice Louis Brandeis once argued, states can be laboratories of democracy.[47] If they adopt programs that fail, the negative effects are limited; if programs succeed, they can be adopted by other states and by the national government. Georgia, for example, was the first state to permit 18-year-olds to vote; Wisconsin was a leader in requiring welfare recipients to work; California moved early on global warming; and Massachusetts created one of the first state programs to provide health insurance to all its citizens.[48]
4. *Federalism produces new leaders:* Federalism allows state and local leaders to gain experience before moving to the national stage. Presidents Jimmy Carter, Ronald Reagan, Bill Clinton, and George W. Bush previously served as governors of the respective states of Georgia, California, Arkansas, and Texas. All told, 20 of the nation's 45 presidents served as governor at some point before winning the presidency. In addition, nine current or former governors (John Kasich, Jeb Bush, Jim Gilmore, Chris Christie, Mike Huckabee, George Pataki, Bobby Jindal, Scott Walker, and Rick Perry) ran for the Republican Party's nomination for president in 2016.
5. *Federalism promotes government by the people:* By providing numerous arenas for decision making, federalism provides many opportunities for Americans to participate in the process of government and helps keep government closer to the people. Every day, thousands of U.S. adults serve on city councils, school boards, neighborhood associations, and planning commissions. Federalism also builds on the public's greater trust in government at the state and local levels. The closer the specific level of government is to the people, the more citizens trust the government.

Even though federalism offers a number of advantages in creating impacts, it also creates at least three potential barriers as citizens seek answers to their problems.

1. *Federalism confuses citizens:* Just as federalism encourages cooperation between federal, state, and local governments, it can confuse citizens about which government to ask for help. Where do they go to ask about better schools? Whom do they ask for help in getting health insurance? What kind of job training is available from their federal, state, and/or local government? The answers are often confusing, thereby undermining the sense that federalism works for the citizens.
2. *Federalism weakens accountability:* Federal, state, and local cooperation can improve implementation of federal laws, but can also weaken the public's ability to hold public officials accountable for their actions. Hurricane Katrina is just one of several recent examples of such potential confusion. All levels of government were responsible for responding to the massive hurricane that roared ashore just outside New Orleans in 2005, and all levels seemed to fail. The national government did not do its job in coordinating the response, thereby leaving thousands of people trapped in the Superdome football stadium without food and water for days. The state government did not do its job in evacuating citizens in time to avoid the storm. And the city did not do its job in providing emergency response in time to prevent the loss of life that followed the breach of the levees that protected much of the city. All levels of government were responsible for the failures, but none could be held fully responsible. The federal government was more effective in 2017 when Hurricanes Harvey (Houston), Irma (Florida), and Maria (Puerto Rico) hit the United States, but the damage continued to plague Puerto Rico well in 2018 because of longstanding problems with the territory's aged power grid.
3. *Federalism creates inequality:* The freedoms that stimulate innovation across governments can create inequality in states that set lower standards for education, health care, gun ownership, financial assistance, and even licensing for

morticians. Companies seeking to do business across state lines must learn and abide by many different sets of laws, while individuals in licensed professions must consider whether they face recertification if they choose to relocate to another state. Where national laws do not exist, it is tempting for each state to try to undercut another state's regulations to gain a competitive advantage in such areas as attracting new industry, regulating environmental concerns, or setting basic eligibility standards for welfare or health benefits.

The U.S. Budget and Federalism (Impact)

3.5 Analyze the impact of federalism on the budget.

Congress authorizes programs, establishes general rules for how the programs will operate, and decides whether room should be left for state or local discretion and how much. Most important, Congress appropriates the funds for these programs and generally has a bigger budget and debt than all of the states combined. This process reflects the interaction embedded in the structural framework of federalism, with individuals in both the national and state governments acting to impact policy to their best advantage.

National grants are one of Congress's most potent tools for influencing policy at the state and local levels. Funding provides a clear path from structure to action and impact—the Constitution sets the boundaries, competing definitions of federalism create the potential for action, and dollars create the impact.

Types of Grants

The national government has an enormous impact on national problems by sending money to the states through four types of grants: (1) categorical, (2) formula, (3) project, and (4) block. The U.S. government spent $450 billion on all grants to the states in 2017, and estimates show the amount rising to $600 billion by 2020. Two-thirds of this spending flows through categorical grants to the states that can only be used for specific benefits such as housing for low-income citizens, Medicaid health care for low-income families, and job training for the disabled.[49]

However, these grants are only part of the funding that the national government provides to the states, not the least of which is the direct spending that goes to low-income citizens. In 2018 alone, Medicaid cost about $375 billion, and estimates show the number rising to $450 billion by 2020. As Figure 3.2 on the next page shows, spending on grants and other support for some states can be much greater than the amount of federal taxes that they pay. The result is a sense that some states are paying more than their fair share of the national burden for all low-income citizens, while other states are not paying enough.

CATEGORICAL GRANTS Categorical grants are given to the states for specific purposes such as health care for low-income Americans, nutrition assistance, and childcare. These grants are tightly monitored to ensure that the money is spent exactly as directed. Categorical grants have the most strings attached—state and local governments need to conform to all aspects of the funding legislation in order to receive the national funds. Although states have leeway in deciding how some categorical grants can be spent for programs such as highway construction, the national government often attaches strings to the overall category. In addition, many categorical grants require states to match the national dollars to some degree.

FORMULA GRANTS Formula grants are distributed to the states based on procedures set out in the granting legislation. The simplest formula is by population—each

FIGURE 3.2 HOW STATES RANK ON TAXES PAID AND BENEFITS RECEIVED

Many states get more from the national government in benefits than they pay in taxes, but this is often because they are poor. They pay less because they make less, and get more because their citizens need more help from government in paying their bills, covering unemployment, and providing access to health care. Many of these states are also likely to be conservative, which may be the result of the poverty, and the anger toward the national government that sometimes goes with it.

SOURCE: Pew Research Center analysis of data from the U.S. Census Bureau, 2016 Annual Survey of State Government Finances, and U.S. Census Bureau analysis of 2016 Annual American Community survey.

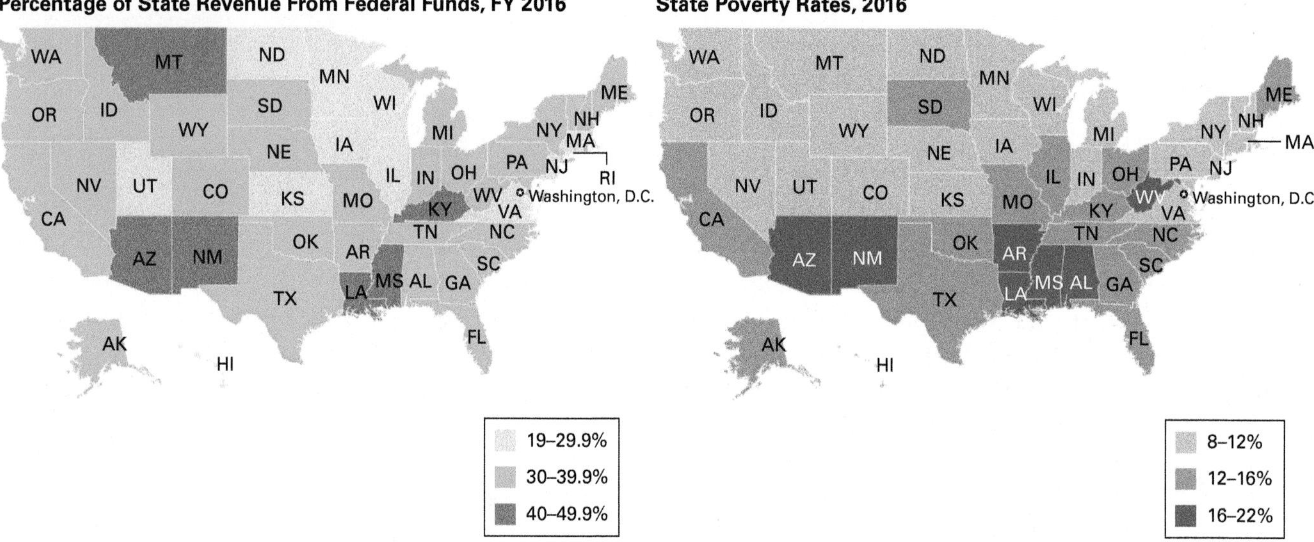

recipient government receives a certain number of dollars for each person who lives in the jurisdiction. More complex formulas might define the target population—for example, the number of people below the poverty line or above the age of 65. Other formulas do not involve people at all, but specific measures of a problem, such as the number of boarded-up houses in a state. Early rounds of homeland security funding were based largely on a population formula, while the most recent rounds have taken both population and the risk of a terrorist attack into consideration in granting funds to state and local governments.

PROJECT GRANTS The national government also provides funding to the states through project grants for specific activities, such as scientific research, homeland security, and some education programs. Most project grants are awarded through a competitive application process. Project grants are generally restricted to a fixed amount of time and can be spent only within tight guidelines. Many university medical schools rely on project grants to support their efforts to cure life-threatening diseases such as cancer and heart disease. In order for a state or local government to receive funding through a project grant, the state or local government must apply for the funding. This gives the grantor the discretion to approve some applications and reject others based typically on the technical requirements of the individual grant program.

BLOCK GRANTS Block grants, which are sometimes called flexible grants, support broad policy goals such as public assistance, health services, childcare, or community development. By definition, these blocks of funding are provided with very few requirements attached. States have great flexibility in deciding how to spend block grant dollars, but are limited to specific amounts set by the national government.

How Grants Create Impact

The four types of grants are occasionally combined within a single program area. Some categorical grants contain formulas, for example, while block grants are generally restricted to a broad issue such as education or assistance to the poor. As the following examples demonstrate, the national government often mixes and matches the grant types to accomplish its goals:

- The National School Lunch Program is both a categorical and formula grant—school districts receive funding for each meal served to a qualified student. To receive the funding, the school district must guarantee that the lunches meet U.S. Department of Agriculture nutrition standards.
- The Community Development Block Grant (CDBG) program is both a formula and block grant—states receive funding from the national government based on a formula that includes a number of need-based variables, but the money flows in a block grant that sets few requirements.
- Homeland Security funding for state and local preparedness for attacks is both a categorical and project grant—states receive their funding within a specific category, and then allocate the dollars to localities based on project proposals such as the purchase of new equipment and training.

The National College Athletic Association (NCAA) received a project grant from the national government to help build a $30 million database to understand how to prevent sports concussions that plague hard-hitting sports such as football. Here, Alabama Crimson Tide quarterback Tua Tagovailoa is sacked in the 2018 NCAA National Championship game with the University of Georgia Bulldogs. The NCAA does not know for sure how many concussions go unreported in any given season, but there is growing evidence that hard hits can result in lasting brain damage.

National grants have a noticeable impact on state and local schools, including both public and private universities. In the 1940s and 1950s, for example, World War II veterans received individual grants to cover college tuition under the GI Bill. These tuition grants, not loans, helped thousands of veterans get better jobs, purchase homes, and rebuild the economy, which was suffering from a postwar slump.

Out of 15 million eligible veterans, 8 million went to college or training programs. In 1947 alone, veterans accounted for nearly half of all college students. According to past research by Congress, every dollar invested over the life of the program generated between $5 and $12.50 in tax revenues from veterans whose college education gave them better jobs and higher salaries than they otherwise would have had.[50]

The national government also gives states the funding to build public schools, create new charter schools, and support college students as they work toward their degrees. In 2001, for example, Congress passed the No Child Left Behind Act, which set national math and reading standards tied to national funding for public schools. The act was replaced by the Every Student Succeeds Act in December 2015. The new act gives the states much greater flexibility to set their own standards and tests for measuring student math and reading skills.

The GI Bill, No Child Left Behind Act, and Race to the Top show how federalism can help all levels of government accomplish broad national goals from homeland security to disaster relief and educational reform. Sometimes the national grants can play a large role, as in Race to the Top, but even the relatively small amount of funding that actually reaches an individual public school can have significant impact.

The Politics of National Grants

Republicans have long favored grants that carry fewer strings and greater flexibility.[51] Democrats have generally been less supportive of broad discretionary block grants, instead favoring more detailed, federally supervised spending. The Republican-controlled Congress in the 1990s gave high priority to creating block grants, but it ran into trouble when it tried to lump together welfare, school lunch and breakfast programs, prenatal nutrition programs, and child protection programs into one block grant.

The battle over national versus state control of spending tends to be cyclical. As one scholar of federalism explains, "Complaints about excessive national control tend to be followed by proposals to shift more power to state and local governments. Then, when problems arise in state and local administration—and problems inevitably arise when any organization tries to administer anything—demands for closer national supervision and tighter national controls follow."[52]

HOW GRANTS ARE MADE Each of the national government's 1,700 grants is the direct result of a U.S. law that creates a new program through an authorization and allocates money through a congressional spending appropriation. At first glance, the grant-making process seems very simple: (1) Congress and the president create the grant; (2) the national bureaucracy writes the rules for implementing the grant; (3) the bureaucracy transfers the grant to state governments; and (4) the states either keep the funding for statewide programs or transfer the funding to counties, cities, school districts, and other local government units.

However, with more than billions of dollars of funding at stake, it is hardly surprising that state and local governments might exploit their political connections at each stage of this process to win their share of the money, especially in setting the formulas that dictate funding within many grants. State governments often intervene at several points in the funding process by reminding their own members of Congress that the money matters, hiring lobbyists to pressure the executive branch or president, or creating pressure through their national trade associations such as the National Conference of State Legislatures.

First, states work hard to influence the specific instructions Congress develops in allocating formula grants. Small changes in the terms—or the weight that the terms carry—in a given formula can advantage some states and disadvantage others. It is now a simple matter for states to analyze various proposed formulas in new legislation and to calculate how well they will do using each of the rival formulas.

Second, state and local governments sometimes lobby their members of Congress to push national agencies toward their project proposals. The project grant process, however, is generally insulated from outside influence. Often it is very difficult to apply for a national project grant, if only because the proposals must be very detailed and are subject to intense review by outside panels of experts. Therefore, the more professional the proposal, the more likely that it will be approved, regardless of whether it is backed by a member of Congress.

Third, state officials generally prefer (and lobby Congress for) block grants, which have fewer restrictions on how the states can spend the funding than the categorical grants that have more restrictions. State lobbying was central to the creation of general revenue sharing in 1972. Created as part of Nixon's new federalism in 1972, revenue sharing dedicated a relatively small percentage of national income for each state to spend as they wished. The program lasted until it was phased out in favor of large block grants in 1987.

UNFUNDED MANDATES Smaller national grants do not necessarily mean smaller national demands. As noted earlier in this chapter, the national government has imposed sweeping mandates on state and local governments in return for national funds, and occasionally imposed such mandates without any funds at all. State and local officials fought these unfunded mandates for decades before Republicans pushed through the Unfunded Mandates Reform Act of 1995.

The 1995 law requires Congress to identify and report unfunded mandates to the two chambers, and imposes mild constraints on Congress itself. A congressional committee that approves any legislation containing a national mandate must draw attention to the mandate in its report and describe its cost to state and local governments. If the committee intends any mandate to be partially unfunded, it must explain why it is appropriate for state and local governments to pay for it.

At least during its first 15 years, the act reduced the number of unfunded mandates.[53] According to the National Conference of State Legislatures, the national government has enacted only 11 laws since 1995 that imposed unfunded mandates. Three of these unfunded mandates required states to raise the minimum wage for all government employees under their jurisdiction, including county, city, town, school district, and special district workers.[54]

Mandates require states to adopt national programs and rules under the broad national powers listed in the Constitution, or in return for receiving federal funds. In 1984, for example, the national government set a mandatory drinking age of 21, and threatened to reduce highway funding by 10 percent for any state that refused to comply. The law was supported by Mothers Against Drunk Driving, and has been followed in all but a handful of states, and even then under almost all circumstances. Here, Los Angeles students cry at the end of their school's "Every 15 Minutes" program, which simulates the effects of drunk driving on their friends.

The Politics of Federalism (Impact)

3.6 Link the growth of the national government to federalism.

The formal structures of federalism have remained mostly unchanged since 1787, but the political realities of a changing world have altered how the national and state governments solve important problems. There are times when each level of government works toward impact on its own, but many times federal, state, and local levels have to work together to achieve progress.

The national government has grown dramatically since the founding, and now has a large policy agenda that impacts much of what states do and do not do. Yet, even as it has grown, the national government has asked states to do more on its behalf through grants and mandates. States have pressed back against the national government, however, and continue to fight for their authority to use powers that are reserved for them under the Constitution.

The national government grew in part because Americans wanted a strong national government to address economic, social, and foreign threats. Moreover, government obligations that were local in 1789, in 1860, or in 1930 are now national, even global. State governments can supervise the relationships between small merchants and their few employees, for instance, but only the national government can supervise relationships between multinational corporations and their thousands of worldwide employees, many of whom are organized into powerful interest groups and political parties.

The growth of the national economy and the creation of national transportation and communications networks have altered people's attitudes toward the national government. Before the Civil War, citizens saw the national government as a distant, even foreign, entity. Today, in part because of television and the Internet, most people know more about Washington than they know about their state capitals, and they often know more about the president and members of Congress than their governor, their state legislators, or even the local officials who run their cities and schools. Voter turnout in local elections is generally lower than in state elections, and it is lower in state elections than in presidential elections.

The Great Depression of the 1930s stimulated extensive national action on welfare, unemployment, and farm surpluses. World War II brought national regulation of wages, prices, and employment, as well as national efforts to allocate resources,

States are responsible for registering voters, but the national government is responsible for assuring that state registration rules are constitutional. States are also responsible for setting the time and place of elections, but the national government determines the size of congressional districts and sets the minimum voting age in national elections. States are responsible for counting ballots for national officials, but the national government has its own process for settling disputed congressional and presidential results.

train personnel, and support engineering and inventions. After the war, the national government helped veterans obtain college degrees and inaugurated a vast system of support for university research. The United States became the most powerful leader of the free world, maintaining substantial military forces even in times of peace.

Although economic and social conditions created many of the pressures for expanding the national government, so did political claims. Once established, national programs generate groups with vested interests in promoting, defending, and expanding them. Associations are formed and alliances are made. "In a word," a famous political scientist named Aaron Wildavsky has argued, "the growth of government has created a constituency of, by, and for government."[55] The national budget can become a negative issue for Congress and the president if it grows too large, however. In 2011–2013, for example, Congress and the president adopted deep cuts in national aid to the states in an effort to reduce the national deficit. The cuts were needed to reassure financial markets that the United States was making progress to reduce its rapidly increasing debt. Similar cuts were proposed in 2017–2018 to pay for the Trump administration's $1.5 trillion tax cut, but were stalled as the midterm elections approached.

The politics of federalism are changing, and Congress is being pressured to reduce the size and scope of national programs, even while dealing with the demands for homeland security. Meanwhile, the cost of entitlement programs such as Social Security and Medicare is rising, and states and localities are under enormous pressure to balance their budgets during a time of continued economic stress.

The Future of Federalism

Despite the long history of national growth, the rising national debt has created larger funding deficits and a steady weakening of national government performance. This pause, if not decline, has created an opening for state governments to retake lost responsibilities. Most states have improved their governmental structures, taken on greater roles in funding education and welfare, launched programs to help distressed cities, expanded their tax bases by allowing citizens to deduct their state and local taxes from the national income tax, and assumed greater roles in maintaining homeland security and in fighting corporate corruption.

After the civil rights revolution of the 1960s, segregationists feared that national officials would work for racial integration. Thus, they praised local government, emphasized the dangers of centralization, and argued that the protection of civil rights was not a proper function of the national government. As one political scientist observed, "Federalism has a dark history to overcome. For nearly 200 years, states' rights have been asserted to protect slavery, segregation, and discrimination."[56]

Today, the politics of federalism, even with respect to civil rights, is more complicated than in the past. The national government is not necessarily more sympathetic to the claims of minorities than state or city governments are. Rulings on same-sex marriages and "civil unions" by state courts interpreting their state constitutions have extended more protection for these rights than has the Supreme Court's interpretation of the U.S. Constitution. At the same time, other states are passing legislation that would eliminate such protections, and opponents are pressing for a constitutional amendment to bar same-sex marriages.

The national government is not likely to retreat to a more limited role. Indeed, international terrorism, the wars in Afghanistan and Iraq, and rising deficits substantially alter the underlying economic and social conditions that generated the demand for national action. In addition to such traditional challenges as helping people find jobs and preventing inflation and depressions—which still require national action—combating terrorism and surviving in a global economy based on the information explosion, e-commerce, and advancing technologies have added countless new issues to the national agenda.

Few Americans know what the term *federalism* means, but they seem to want what federalism delivers: a strong government in Washington that protects the nation against threats to the future such as economic collapse and terrorism, and strong governments in their states and cities to provide basic services such as education, health care, and police and fire protection. Yet, even though they want the best of federalism, most Americans have very different views on the three levels of government.

On the one hand, Americans express high levels of approval toward state and local governments because they like the governments they know best, and also because state and local governments do most of their jobs very well. On the other hand, Americans express very low approval toward the national government in Washington largely because their political leaders cannot reach consensus on pressing problems such as the national debt, immigration, and climate change, and also because they have come to believe that the national government is wasteful and inefficient. Thus, even as approval of state and local government has remained relatively stable over the past 15 turbulent years, approval of the government in Washington has tumbled. (See Figure 3.3 on the next page for the trend in public approval toward national, state, and local government dating back to 1997.)

The trends in approval strongly suggest that Americans trust the governments they know best, and disapprove of the national government's lack of action on issues such as immigration, tax reform, and terrorism. If the national government wants to reverse the recent declines in approval, it might take a lesson from the state and local trend lines. Impact on problems that matter to ordinary citizens keeps trust high, while government shutdowns, insults, and polarization drive trust down.

CONCLUSION

After years of delay and worry, the national government finally took a tiny first step toward repairing America's economic infrastructure at the very end of 2015 when Congress passed the $305 billion Fixing America's Surface Transportation Act, or FAST Act. On the positive side, it was the first time in a decade that the national government had been able to commit to more than a short-term package of fixes, and it did contain a tiny bit of funding for building bike lanes and encouraging self-driving cars.

FIGURE 3.3 APPROVAL OF FEDERAL, STATE, AND LOCAL GOVERNMENT, 1997–2018

Public approval of the national government plunged after the war in Iraq began. Although approval had surged as all Americans rallied around the president and national government immediately after the September 11 attacks, the long war and growing partisanship in Washington cut into public confidence. Meanwhile, the states and localities retained considerable support.

SOURCE: Pew Research Center survey results online, available at http://assets.pewresearch.org/wp-content/uploads/sites/5/2018/04/15160829/4-26-2018-Democracy-release1.pdf.

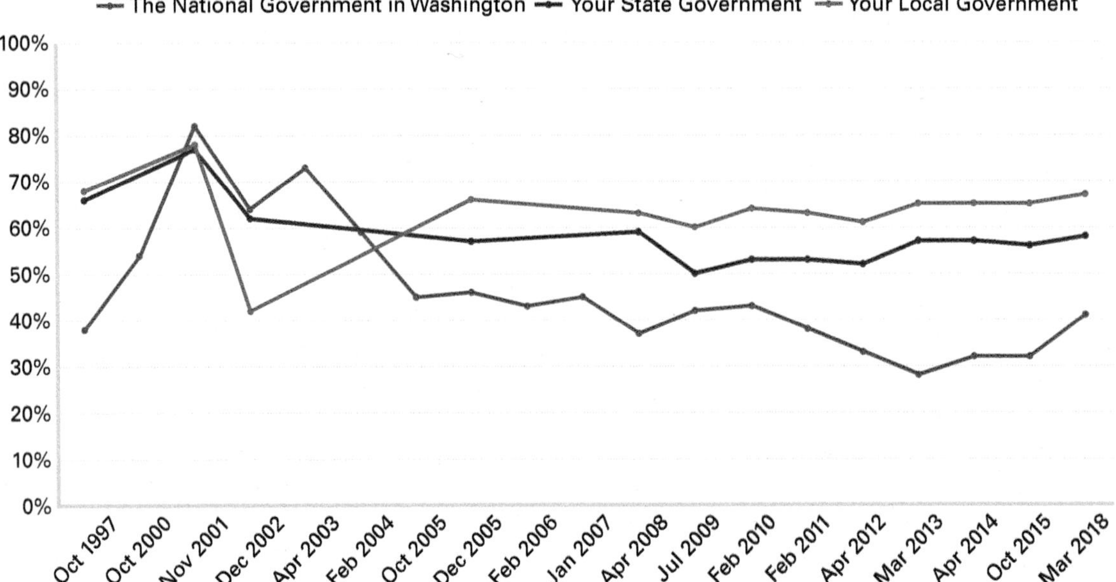

On the negative side, even the title of the act stated its narrow purpose. The $305 billion is less than one-tenth of the $3.6 trillion needed to fix the nation's vast infrastructure, which led some advocates to grade the effort a "D." Moreover, the FAST Act only covers roads and bridges,[57] leaving states and localities to wonder where to find the money to fix their tunnels, subways, water pipes, dams, and even storm drains.

Given all that you have learned about how federalism works, the challenge is to find some way for the national and state governments to pool their energies and find the funding to keep the infrastructure running. Some argue that the answer is a new "infrastructure bank" that would give states low-interest, very long-term loans to repair their systems. Others argue that the recent decline in gasoline prices has created more than enough room to double or even triple the federal gasoline tax to build up a reserve for massive projects.[58] Europe has done both in its own efforts to modernize its infrastructure and has worked closely across national boundaries to make sure that the repairs fit together. The United States could do the same thing by building some kind of system to raise more money and pull states together into regional authorities to make sure the infrastructure repairs make sense.

As the answers to these complicated problems emerge over time, you will be the ones who have to approve tax increases and loans, and foster the cooperation needed to fix the system. Self-driving cars will help, perhaps, and biking will no doubt reduce some of the stress, but $3 trillion problems demand $3 trillion answers. You will have to decide how federalism can work for the nation to avoid wasting years in traffic jams and subway delays because you and your leaders refused to act.

REVIEW THE CHAPTER

The Constitutional Foundations of Federalism (Structure)

3.1 Explain the constitutional foundations of federalism, p. 53.

The Framers gave the longest list of powers to the national government, but reserved all powers not mentioned in the Constitution for the states. Therefore, it is impossible to put the two sets of powers on a scale and decide which level of government received the greatest authority under federalism.

The Constitution gives the national government delegated powers in three forms: (1) enumerated, or listed, powers that tell each branch what they can and cannot do, (2) implied powers that Congress uses to make the leap from the enumerated powers to actually making the laws, and (3) inherent powers that all three branches believe are essential for protecting the life of the nation. The Constitution also instructs states to cooperate. The national government's power over the states also stems from a set of specific constitutional limits on the states, including the supremacy clause, which makes national law supreme in spite of contrary state laws; limits on state war powers and on the power to regulate interstate commerce; and the congressional power to make any laws that are necessary and proper to promote the general welfare and to provide for the common defense.

Federalism and Its Alternatives (Structure)

3.2 Distinguish federalism from other forms of government, p. 58.

The Framers could have created a unitary system of government that put the national government in charge of states and localities. They also could have created a stronger central government within a confederacy. But they went to Philadelphia for the Constitutional Convention precisely because the confederation created under the Articles of Confederation had failed so dramatically, and so the format they chose was federalism. Over time, federalism has changed shape and now includes six different types: (1) dual federalism, (2) cooperative federalism, (3) marble-cake federalism, (4) competitive federalism, (5) coercive federalism, and (6) a new federalism (which may be considered a variation of dual federalism), produced by events in recent years, that has shifted national programs back to the states.

The U.S. Courts and Federalism (Action)

3.3 Trace the evolution of federalism from ratification to the present, p. 62.

The U.S. courts umpire the relationship between the national government and the states. The Marshall Court, in decisions such as *McCulloch* v. *Maryland* and *Gibbons* v. *Ogden*, asserted the power of the national government over the states and promoted a national economic common market. These decisions reinforced the supremacy of the national government over the states. Since the 1990s, the Supreme Court has drifted back toward a more decentralist position on national power. Although it approved Obamacare in *National Federation of Independent Business et al.* v. *Sebelius*, it restricted the use of both the Necessary and Proper Clause and the interstate commerce clause as instruments of strong national control.

Federalism in Practice (Action)

3.4 Analyze the impact of federalism on the relationships among national, state, and local levels of government, p. 65.

There is still an active debate about how federalism works. Centralists favor strong national powers and limited state powers, while decentralists favor more limited national powers and stronger state powers based on states' rights and the Tenth Amendment. Decentralists have won several recent battles as part of the devolution revolution that has returned at least some national programs to the states. Despite these debates, federalism offers significant advantages to the nation. It protects the nation from tyranny, permits local variation in policy, builds a pipeline of future leaders, encourages innovation, and promotes government by the people; however, it also creates problems with confusion among citizens about where to get help, in determining exactly which level of government is responsible for what goes right and wrong in government performance, and by at times creating the inequality that it is supposed to remedy.

The U.S. Budget and Federalism (Impact)

3.5 Analyze the impact of federalism on the budget, p. 69.

The major instruments of national intervention in state programs have been various kinds of financial grants-in-aid, of which the most prominent are (1) categorical grants, (2) formula grants, (3) project grants, and (4) block grants. Categorical, formula, and project grants often carry tight national rules on implementation, while block grants give states much more freedom to use national funds as they wish. Although the national grant system is relatively simple, states battle hard to win their share of national funding. States often lobby for the best terms on formula grants, and have fought against unfunded mandates in which the national government forces states to implement new programs without any national support.

The Politics of Federalism (Impact)

3.6 Link the growth of the national government to federalism, p. 73.

Federalism remains a key element of the constitutional system, but it has been challenged by the growth of the national government. The national budget is much larger than all of the states' budgets combined, and the power of the national government to affect state and local conduct often seems unmatched. Although the future will continue to produce debates about its shape, federalism has proven to be an effective method for allocating power.

LEARN THE TERMS

delegated powers, p. 53
enumerated powers, p. 53
implied powers, p. 53
inherent powers, p. 53
supremacy clause, p. 54
preemption, p. 54
commerce clause, p. 55
national mandates, p. 55
reserve powers, p. 56
concurrent powers, p. 56
full faith and credit clause, p. 58
unitary system, p. 59
confederation, p. 59
federalism, p. 59
devolve, p. 61
centralists, p. 66
decentralists, p. 66
states' rights, p. 66

The American Political Landscape

CHAPTER 4

Immigration has long been a contentious issue in American politics, and was a major focus in the 2016 elections. After years of legislative inaction, President Obama issued an executive order calling for deferred action for childhood arrivals (DACA) permitting children brought into the country illegally to stay if they met certain conditions. President Trump later rescinded the order forcing the issue onto the legislative agenda and into federal courts.

LEARNING OBJECTIVES

4.1 Assess the role of geography, natural resources, and type of community in building a national and local identity (Structure, Action, and Impact), p. 81.

4.2 Analyze how such social and demographic factors such as race and ethnicity, religion, gender, family structures, education, and age affect American politics (Structure, Action, and Impact), p. 86.

4.3 Describe the importance of income, wealth, occupation, and social class in American politics (Structure, Action, and Impact), p. 100.

On September 5, 2017, Attorney General Jeff Sessions announced President Trump's decision to end the federal government's program for Deferred Action for Childhood Arrivals (DACA). Created by President Obama in June 2012, DACA gave about 800,000 undocumented individuals who came to the United States as children special protections from being sent back to their country of origin. In June 2018 the immigration issue generated new controversy as the Trump administration began separating children from parents of families seeking asylum as they came across the border to the United States.

DACA was intended to protect a group of immigrants often called "dreamers," individuals who entered the United States before age 16, have lived in the United States for at least five years, graduated from high school or the equivalent or served honorably in the military, and do not have a criminal record. DACA status removes the threat of deportation, grants two-year renewable work permits, and allows access to driver's licenses. Depending on the state, dreamers may qualify for in-state college tuition, which defenders of DACA point to as good for dreamers and the economy. Given the scope of the program, most college students have likely had DACA classmates.

Trump's decision gave Congress six months to pass legislation restoring the plan, but Congress failed to act by his March 2018 deadline.[1] The Senate debated proposed legislation, in part in response to the Democrats forcing a three-day government shutdown over the issue in January 2018. After a week of debate in the Senate none of the bills passed; President Trump's own proposal mustered only 39 votes.

President Trump's self-imposed deadline on Congress to come up with a legislative solution to his concerns with DACA became somewhat less urgent when multiple federal courts ruled that the Trump administration erred in ending DACA. The Trump administration announced its reversal of DACA just before a deadline imposed by the Texas Attorney General and nine other states to sue the federal government if it did not end DACA by September 5.[2] Only days after the administration's announcement, the University of California and a dozen state attorneys general filed separate lawsuits challenging the legality of terminating the DACA program. In reviewing the administration's actions, federal courts ruled that "the administration had abused its discretion and had acted arbitrarily and capriciously in rescinding the program."[3] The administration appealed the district court ruling directly to the U.S. Supreme Court, but it refused to hear the case on expedited review. That ruling meant that DACA would remain in effect pending review by the federal courts of appeals and a likely return trip to the U.S. Supreme Court. In May 2018, the 9th Circuit Court of Appeals became the first appellate court to hear arguments in a DACA case.

Obama's DACA order came after years of failed efforts to enact comprehensive immigration reform. Republicans criticized the order as being politically motivated and timed to help him in the 2012 presidential election. Obama countered that it was unfair to leave in limbo young persons who had been brought to the United States as children and knew no other country as their home. Conservatives argued that DACA was an unconstitutional overreach of executive authority, a theme Attorney General Sessions repeated when announcing the deadline for legislative action.

President Trump has given mixed statements on DACA and the dreamers' immigration status. During the 2016 campaign Trump said he would terminate DACA, but after the election he said that dreamers should "rest easy."[4] Some Republicans including House Speaker Paul Ryan as well as business interests including the U.S. Chamber of Commerce, Apple, and Facebook urged the president not to revoke DACA. Others, like commentator Laura Ingraham, expressed concern about Trump's willingness to work with Democrats on a solution and referred to the president as "amnesty Don," a claim that permitting dreamers to stay in the United States amounted to legal amnesty.[5]

Although President Trump's first two years in office saw intense debate over immigration policy, often motivated by vitriolic and at a minimum racially insensitive comments, arguably racist comments by the president himself, discriminatory treatment in immigration policy is not new. Over the course of U.S. history discrimination has been directed at blacks, Asians, and persons from southern and eastern Europe.[6]

Race and ethnicity are only part of the American political landscape discussed in this chapter. However, you will see yourself in many of the trends discussed and we encourage you to consider how you fit into the landscape and what you think about the continuing debates about economic fairness and inequality, education and diversity, and religion and families. How does our system limit or create opportunities for all Americans?

This chapter will continue to use our "structure," "action," and "impact" theme as we consider the particular characteristics and attributes of people that matter in American politics. Rather than focusing individual sections on structure, action, or impact, this chapter explores all three in the context of the characteristic or attribute of people under consideration. For example, individuals have come to expect a right to public education through high school (structure). Researchers have documented that education is highly correlated with political participation (action) and that educated people are more confident and persistent in pursuing their political agendas (impact).

Geography, Natural Resources, and the Importance of Where We Are From (Structure, Action, and Impact)

4.1 Assess the role of geography, natural resources, and type of community in building a national and local identity.

American politics have been influenced by the geography and natural resources of the nation. The Atlantic and Pacific Oceans largely separated the new nation from world powers during our formative period in our experiment with self-government. Plentiful natural resources reinforced our sense of independence from other nations. Our climate was conducive to agriculture, which was important to our economic development and self-sufficiency.

The American landscape is also varied, with navigable rivers and lakes, which fostered different kinds of economic development and settlement patterns. Regions and states have developed their own political cultures and traditions. Over time, population movements led to cities and suburban areas with some continuing rural communities. These different places are also important to our politics.

Geography

The United States is a geographically large and, for much of its history, isolated country. In the 1830s, French writer Alexis de Tocqueville observed that the country had no major political or economic powers on its borders "and consequently no great wars, financial crises, invasions, or conquests to fear."[7] Geographic isolation from the major powers of the world during our government's formative period helps explain American politics.[8] The Atlantic Ocean served as a barrier to European meddling, giving the United States in this formative period time to establish our political tradition and develop our economy. Although geographic location may have previously provided a substantial buffer from foreign attack, technological advances since the 1950s made that less the case, with long-range missiles and aircraft able to travel long distances. As we learned in the 2016 election, foreign adversaries can mount cyberattacks on the United States as Russia did on some state voter systems[9] and on the Hillary Clinton presidential campaign.[10]

Remarkably few foreign enemies have successfully struck within U.S. continental borders: most notably, England in the War of 1812 and the Japanese in the attack on Pearl Harbor in the territory of Hawaii in 1941. More recently terrorists have attacked the United States, when they bombed the World Trade Center in 1993, and when they crashed jet airliners into the Pentagon and World Trade Center on September 11, 2001, killing nearly 3,000 people.[11] These attacks changed the nation's sense of vulnerability to terrorist attacks and changed the way we fly, where we travel, and what we think about threats in our own communities. Terrorist attacks like these and others around the world are reminders that terrorists have the ability to harm the United States and other countries, especially if they are willing to die along with their victims. As a result, providing for the national defense and homeland security poses new and difficult challenges.

Geographical size also confers an advantage in protecting the nation. As a result of winning the Revolutionary War, the new United States secured former British-held territory largely between the Appalachian Mountains and the Mississippi River. This provided the new country with land into which it could expand. Some of this land was given to veterans of the Revolutionary War in exchange for their military service. The frontier west of the Mississippi gave the expanding population of the United States additional room to spread out and defused some political conflicts arising from religion, social class, and national origin because groups could isolate themselves from one another. Moreover, plentiful and accessible land helped foster the perspective that the United States had a **manifest destiny** to be a continental nation reaching from the Atlantic to the Pacific Ocean. Early settlers used this notion to justify taking land from Native Americans, Canadians, and Mexicans, especially the huge territory acquired after victory in the Mexican-American War (1846–1848).

manifest destiny
A notion held by nineteenth-century Americans that the United States was destined to rule the continent, from the Atlantic to the Pacific.

Natural Resources

The United States has abundant natural resources, especially coal, iron, uranium, oil, and precious metals. We have rich farmland, which not only feeds our population but also makes us the largest exporter of food in the world.[12] All of these resources enhance economic growth, provide jobs, and stabilize government. Wealth and opportunity in the United States are in part due to these abundant natural resources.[13] Parts of the United States are wonderfully suited to agriculture, others to mining or ranching, and still others to shipping and manufacturing. These differences produce diverse regional economic concerns, which in turn influence politics. For instance, a person from the agricultural heartland may see foreign trade differently from the way a software engineer in Seattle sees it. However, unlike many other countries, geography and the distribution of natural resources has *not* generally reinforced ethnic or religious divisions in the United States. All the Serbians in the United States do not live in one place, nor do all French-speaking Catholics or Hispanic immigrants. Sectional or regional differences in the United States are primarily geographic, not ethnic or religious.

Where We Are From

Within the United States, when you are asked where you are from your likely answer is the state you grew up in. Americans have strong identity with their state, but they also often see themselves as from the West, the South, or the Northeast. In large states, the sense of where we are from may be a part of the state, like Northern California or Southern California. All of this underscores the importance of understanding what impact where we are from has on our politics.

REGIONAL DIFFERENCES The most distinct section of the United States remains the South, although its differences from other parts of the country are diminishing. From the beginning of the Republic, the agricultural South differed from the North, where commerce, and later manufacturing, were more significant. But the most important difference between the regions was the institution of slavery. Northern opposition to slavery, which grew increasingly intense by the 1850s, reinforced sectional economic interests. The 11 Confederate states, by deciding to secede from the Union, reinforced a common political identity. After the Civil War, Reconstruction and the problems of race relations reinforced regional differences. The Civil War made the Democratic Party the party of the South, and the Republican Party (the party of Lincoln) the party of the North. The Democratic "solid South" remained a fixture of American politics for more than a century.

In other ways the South is becoming less distinct. In addition to undergoing tremendous economic change, the large number of people moving to the South from other regions has diminished the sense of regional identity. The civil rights revolution of the 1960s eliminated legal and social barriers that prevented African Americans from voting, ended legal segregation, opened up new educational opportunities, and helped integrate the South into the national economy.

Since the mid-1960s, the South has become more reliably Republican. The GOP Southern strategy sought to exploit the national Democratic party's support of civil rights legislation, hoping enough whites would vote Republican to more than compensate for the larger share of the African American vote going to the Democrats; as a result, the region became competitive and eventually Republican.[14] In 1992 and 1996, even with two Southerners on the ticket—Bill Clinton and Al Gore—Democrats won only four of the 11 former Confederate states. In 2000 and 2004, Republican George W. Bush carried all 11 Southern states, including Al Gore's home state of Tennessee in 2000 and vice presidential candidate John Edwards's home state of North Carolina in 2004. In 2008, Barack Obama made some inroads by winning in Florida, Virginia, and North Carolina, but in both North Carolina and Florida the margins were close. In 2012 Obama failed to carry North Carolina.

In 2016, the trend of Republican voting strength in the South continued with Donald Trump reclaiming Florida for the Republicans and winning every former

In March 1956, the Reverend Martin Luther King, Jr. led a group of civil rights demonstrators protesting the denial of voting rights on a march from Selma, Alabama to Montgomery, Alabama. While crossing the Edmund Pettus Bridge in Selma, Alabama, the demonstrators were attacked by police officers using clubs and tear gas. News reports of the police attack helped galvanize support for the 1965 Voting Rights Act.

Confederate state except Virginia. North Carolina had highly contested presidential, senatorial, and gubernatorial races. Even though the Clinton campaign ran ads and set up field offices in Georgia, it remained solid for Trump. However, in a 2017 Alabama special election to fill the vacancy created by Senator Jeff Sessions having become Attorney General, Democrats staged an upset when their candidate Doug Jones defeated Republican Roy Moore. The race garnered national interest with substantial spending. Multiple women made allegations that Moore had sexually assaulted them, some when they were teenagers.[15] Jones' victory was the first for a Democrat in an Alabama senate race in some 25 years and narrowed the Republican majority in the U.S. Senate to a one-seat margin.

The partisan shift in the South is evident in the rising percentage of U.S. representatives who are Republicans, which grew from about 10 percent in the 1960s to 77 percent in 2015.[16] The increase in GOP seats in the House of Representatives is in part due to success at the state legislative level, which helped create more safe Republican congressional districts. The Republican share of Southern state legislators in the House and Senate rose from 5 percent and 4 percent, respectively, in 1960 to 61 percent and 63 percent in 2016.[17] In 1961, Democrats controlled all 11 governorships of the former Confederate states. In 2016, Republicans controlled nine of them.[18] In the state legislatures, remnants of the old Democratic "solid South" remain, but Republicans have made major inroads, and politics in the region are becoming more predictably Republican.

Sun Belt

The region of the United States in the South and Southwest that has seen population growth relative to the rest of the country and which, because of its climate, has attracted retirees.

Bible Belt

The region of states in the South and states bordering the South with a large number of strongly committed Protestants who see a public role for religion.

Rust Belt

States in the Midwest once known for their industrial output, which have seen factories close and have experienced relatively high unemployment.

Another sectional division is the **Sun Belt**—it includes most of the 11 former Confederate states plus New Mexico, Arizona, Nevada, and the southern half of California. Sun Belt states are growing much more rapidly than the rest of the country (see Figure 4.1). Reapportionment has shifted seats in the House of Representatives to the Sun Belt, which has tended to help the Republican Party. Some of the states in the Sun Belt are also part of the **Bible Belt**, a region long known for having more committed Protestants as measured by church attendance and more acceptance for public displays of religion, such as school prayers.[19] The Bible Belt includes the former Confederate states plus nearby states like Kentucky, Oklahoma, and West Virginia.

Other sectional groupings of states include the **Rust Belt** of states in the Midwest, where industrial production and jobs have left the region, leaving rusting factories vacant. States in the Rust Belt include Ohio, Pennsylvania, Michigan, and parts of Indiana and New York. The interior western states are another section with economic and political similarities. Much of the land in the West is owned by the federal government, which causes tension between state and local governments and the federal government.

STATE AND LOCAL IDENTITY Within the regions discussed above, individual states also have distinctive political cultures that affect public opinion and policies. Individuals often have a sense of identification with their state.[20] Part of the reason for enduring state identities is that we elect members of Congress and the president at the state level. States such as Iowa and New Hampshire play important roles in narrowing the field of presidential candidates seeking their party's nomination. Differences in state laws relating to driving, drinking, gambling, and taxes reinforce the relevance of state identity. Colleges and universities may have the same effect of reinforcing competition between different states. California specifically stands out in American politics today, if only because nearly one of eight U.S. citizens lives in the state.[21] In economic and political importance, California is in a league by itself.

urban

A densely settled territory that is often the central part of a city or metropolitan area.

suburban

An area that typically surrounds the central city, is often residential, and is not as densely populated.

rural

Sparsely populated territory and small towns, often associated with farming.

URBAN AND RURAL POPULATIONS Where we live can be categorized as one of three types of areas: **urban**, which is defined by the Census Bureau as "densely settled territory," often also the central part of a city; **suburban**, which is typically less densely settled and surrounds the central city; and **rural**, which is more sparsely populated

FIGURE 4.1 STATE POPULATION CHANGES AND THE COMING 2020 REAPPORTIONMENT

The United States as a whole had an average population increase over the decade between 2000 and 2012 of nearly 10 percent. This increase was due to increasing life expectancy, children being born, and immigration from outside the United States. Population growth has continued and the exact rate of growth will be determined by the 2020 census. Demographers have projected how much reapportionment of congressional seats is likely to occur after the 2020 census in the map below. Texas and Florida are likely to gain two or more seats in 2022, with Oregon, Arizona, Colorado, and North Carolina likely to gain one seat. Illinois may lose two seats while Alabama, Ohio, Michigan, Pennsylvania, New York, Rhode Island, and West Virginia are likely to lose one seat. If this projection using data from 2017 holds, the Rust Belt states will again see a reduction in seats while some Sun Belt states will gain in representation.

SOURCE: U.S. Census Bureau, Statistical Abstract of the United States, 2012, p. 19.

Issues of state and local identities are also called into play when Washington is seen to be interfering in local affairs. In December 2016, President Obama announced he was using powers granted him by the Antiquities Act to create a national monument in southeastern Utah, which includes two buttes known as Bears Ears. The area of the monument included 1.35 million acres including Native American ruins and rock art, red sandstone buttes and spires, and expansive vistas. After calling for a review of the monument, President Trump ordered the monument be reduced by 85 percent, as well as 45 percent reduction to another Utah national monument, the Grand Staircase Escalante. President Trump's action was immediately challenged in court. Much of the western United States is land owned and managed by the national government and when that land is designated a national park or monument, the use of the land is more restricted. To rural westerners, the moves by President Clinton with the Grand Staircase Escalante and by President Obama with Bears Ears were seen as "land grabs" intended to limit future grazing and other uses of public lands.

and where farmers often reside. Four of five people in the United States now live in urban areas.[22] During the early twentieth century, the movement of population was from rural areas to central cities, which we call *urbanization,* but the movement since the 1950s has been from the central cities to their suburbs. Today the most urban states are California and New Jersey (both have about 95 percent of their population living in cities or suburbs). Vermont is the least urban, with only 39 percent living in cities or suburbs.[23] Regionally, the West and Northeast are the most urban, and the South and Midwest the most rural.

People move from cities to the suburbs for many reasons—better housing, new transportation systems that make it easier to get to work, a lower cost of living, the desire for cleaner air and safer streets. Another reason is "white flight," the movement of white people away from the central cities so children can avoid being bused for racial balance and attend generally better schools. White, middle-class migration to the suburbs has made American cities increasingly poor, African American, and Democratic.

Who We Are (Structure, Action, and Impact)

4.2 Analyze how such social and demographic factors such as race and ethnicity, religion, gender, family structures, education, and age affect American politics.

demography
The study of the characteristics of human populations.

ethnocentrism
Belief in the superiority of one's nation or ethnic group.

This chapter is also about the nation's **demography**, the study of population characteristics. Some differences are part of a person's identity and can be important to politics. Albert Einstein, who himself immigrated to the United States from Germany in the 1930s, once said that most people are incapable of expressing opinions that differ much from the prejudices of their social upbringing.[24] This **ethnocentrism**—selective perception based on our background, attitudes, and biases—is not uncommon. People often assume that others share their economic opportunities, social attitudes, sense of civic responsibility, and self-confidence, so in this chapter we consider how our social and economic environment explains, or at least shapes, our opinions and prejudices, and emphasize that to understand how people behave politically requires us to move beyond ethnocentrism.

reinforcing cleavages
Divisions within society that reinforce one another, making groups more homogeneous or similar.

cross-cutting cleavages
Divisions within society that cut across demographic categories to produce groups that are more heterogeneous or different.

In some cases, social and economic differences that split society into groups reinforce each other, for example, whether the rich are of one religion and the poor of another. Social scientists call these **reinforcing cleavages**; they can make political conflict more intense and society more polarized. In this context cleavage means a division or grouping along some perceived difference. Nations can also have **cross-cutting cleavages**, where, for example, there are rich and poor in all religious groups. Here, instead of reinforcing each other, multiple differences further pull societal groups in different directions. American diversity has generally been more of the cross-cutting than the reinforcing type. This chapter lays the foundation for understanding how different aspects of who we are as people influence how we behave politically.

From a demographic standpoint, most nations consist of groups of people who have lived together for centuries and who speak the same language, embrace the same religious beliefs, and share a common history. Most Japanese citizens are Japanese in the fullest sense of the word, and this sense of shared national identity is generally as strong in Sweden, Saudi Arabia, and China. The United States is different. We have attracted the poor and oppressed, the adventurous, and the talented from all over the world, and we have been more open to accepting strangers than many other nations. How the United States should respond to the refugee crisis in the Middle East and Europe in 2015 and 2016 became a subject of debate in the 2016 presidential election. The United States has been admitting more than 50,000 refugees from all over the world, and in 2016 under the Obama administration 15,479 Syrian refugees were admitted, with the new Trump administration the number of Syrian refugees admitted dropped to 3,024 in 2017.[25] Opponents of admitting Syrian refugees express concerns about whether these refugees might include terrorists, a concern that was amplified by the terrorist attacks in Paris and Brussels in 2016. In 2018, images of asylum-seeing families, with parents being separated from children, raised the issue again of how to treat people seeking to flee violence. President Trump frequently claimed that terrorists and criminals were among those who were part of the caravan of asylum-seekers fleeing Honduras. Frequent news coverage and Trump's focus on the caravan made the issue a rallying point for Republican campaigns.

Early in his administration, President Trump issued an executive order that suspended all refugee admissions for 120 days and denied admission to the United States for 90 days to persons from six Muslim-majority countries (Iran, Iraq, Libya, Somalia, Sudan, and Yemen). At airports in several cities outside the United States, individuals from these countries, or refugees from any country, were not allowed to board flights going to the United States. Simultaneously, at U.S. airports, individuals covered by the order were blocked from entry, and some were sent back overseas until a judge ordered that individuals who had landed in the United States should not be required to leave immediately.[26] The order prompted large protests in several U.S. cities, often centered at airports and many organized through social media. Legal challenges to the Trump travel ban arose, with the most important challenge coming from the state of Washington where a U.S. District Court judge ruled the ban unconstitutional. Six weeks later, in March 2017, President Trump issued a new travel ban, dropping Iraq from the list of targeted countries and changing the indefinite ban on Syrian refugees to 120 days.[27] Federal courts again ruled the ban unconstitutional. The Trump administration issued a third travel ban in September 2017; it was immediately challenged in the federal courts. The lower federal courts again found that the ban "continues to exhibit a primarily religious anti-Muslim objective."[28] The U.S. Supreme Court, which allowed the third iteration of the ban to go into effect while the courts considered its constitutionality, decided in 2018 the ban was within the president's national security powers and therefore was constitutional.[29]

Where we are from does less to distinguish one American from another than it did a century or even a half-century ago. Today we are more likely to define ourselves by a number of other characteristics, each of which may influence how we vote or think about candidates, issues, or policies. In recent elections, both parties have developed the ability to target individual voters based on computer models they have developed from historic patterns of the relationships between particular individual characteristics and political behaviors, as well as large-sample-size polls that assess attitudes towards issues and candidates in a particular election environment. Individuals fitting a certain profile by their age, gender, religion, and race may be targeted for particular communications, a process known as "micro-targeting." Other variables like education, sexual orientation, partisanship, ideology, and even the kind of car people own or what types of magazines they read, when combined with other variables, may be predictive of political attitudes and behaviors.

Race and Ethnicity

Racial and ethnic differences have always had political significance. By **race**, social scientists may mean classifications of human beings with distinctive physical characteristics determined by genetic inheritance,[30] while others see it as more culturally determined.[31] The Census Bureau defines race by the respondents self-classification and does not "to define race biologically, anthropologically or genetically."[32] **Ethnicity** is a social division based on national origin, religion, and language, often within the same race, and includes a sense of attachment to that group. Many retain an identity with the land of their ancestors, even after three or four generations. Families, churches, and other close-knit ethnic groups foster these ties. Examples of ethnic groups with enduring relevance to American politics include Italian Americans, Irish Americans, Polish Americans, and Korean Americans, though most race and

race

A grouping of human beings with distinctive characteristics determined by genetic inheritance.

ethnicity

A social division based on national origin, religion, language, and often race.

TABLE 4.1 CHANGING RACIAL COMPOSITION OF THE U.S. POPULATION, 1950–2060

	1950	1990	2010	2030	2060
White	89.5%	83.9%	72.4%	75.6%	70.8%
Non-Hispanic White	—	75.7	63.7	57.5	47.3
African American	10.0	12.2	12.6	13.5	14.4
Native American, Inuit, Aleut	0.2	0.8	0.9	1.3	1.3
Asian and Pacific Islander	0.2	3.0	5.0	6.7	9.7
Hispanic	—	9.0	16.3	20.3	28.6

NOTE: Percentages do not equal 100 because Hispanics can be of any race. Figures for 2030 and 2060 are projections. Categories from the 1950 census are different from those used in the last several decades. For example, the 1950 census did not provide a classification for Hispanic, Native Americans were classified as "Indian," and Asians were separated into Japanese and Chinese.

SOURCE: All figures from U.S. Bureau of the Census, Population Division. See Jonathan Vespa, David M. Armstrong, and Lauren Medina. "Demographic Turning Points for the United States: Population Projections for 2020 to 2060. Table 3. p. 7. https://www.census.gov/content/dam/Census/library/publications/2018/demo/P25_1144.pdf

ethnicity issues in the United States today focus primarily on African Americans, Asian Americans, Native Americans, and Hispanics.

There are more than 43 million African Americans in the United States, making up 13.3 percent of the population. Native Americans, including native Alaskans and native Hawaiians, comprise about 1.4 percent.[33] Asian Americans are the fastest growing U.S. ethnic group, constituting 5.7 percent of the population and growing at a rate of 3 percent annually.[34] Most American Hispanics classify themselves as white, although Hispanics can be of any race. For example, a person from South America may be black (race) and given his national origin consider himself Hispanic (ethnicity). At more than 57 million, Hispanics constitute more than 17 percent of the population and are the second largest ethnicity in the United States.[35] Because of differences in immigration and birthrates, non-Hispanic whites will decrease to about 50 percent of the population by 2044.[36] Table 4.1 illustrates how the racial composition of the U.S. population has changed since 1950 and how it is predicted to change through 2060.

NATIVE AMERICANS The original inhabitants of what became the United States have played an important role in its history and continue to be important to the politics of states like South Dakota, New Mexico, Alaska, and Oklahoma. More than half the names of states and hundreds of the names of cities, rivers, and mountains in the United States are Native American in origin. In U.S. Senate elections in South Dakota and Alaska, the Native American vote has been important.[37] More than one-in-four (26 percent) Native Americans and Alaskan Natives have an income below the federal poverty level. This percent is higher than those for African Americans and Hispanics.[38] Many Native Americans still live on reservations, areas of land managed by a Native American tribe. Some tribes have developed casinos on their reservations and secured added revenues, but many reservations have higher infant mortality, lower life expectancy, and greater poverty than the state as a whole in which the reservation is located.[39]

AFRICAN AMERICANS Most Americans are descendants of immigrants who chose to come to this country in search of freedom and opportunity. In contrast, most African Americans are descendants of slaves who came to America against their will. Although the Emancipation Proclamation and Thirteenth Amendment ended slavery in the 1860s, and the civil rights movement in the 1960s resulted in great strides forward, racial divisions still affect American politics.

Some of the divisions reflect geography. In 1900, more than 90 percent of all African Americans lived in the South; 110 years later, that figure was 55 percent.[40]

FIGURE 4.2 THE 2 TO 1 RATIO

This figure shows unemployment by race in America over the last 40 years. Note the persistence of a roughly 2 to 1 gap during good times and bad. We explore some of the reasons for this difference in this chapter: education being among the most important factors. Even though unemployment reached modern lows in 2018, the disparities between whites and blacks remained.

SOURCE: U.S. Bureau of Labor Statistics.

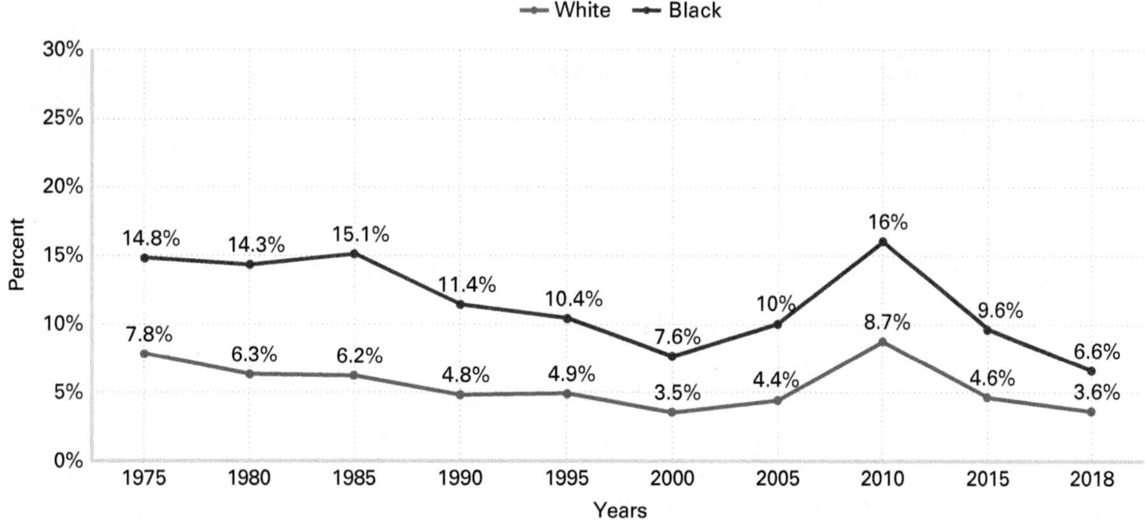

Many African Americans left the South hoping to improve their lives by settling in the large cities of the Northeast, Midwest, and West. But what many of them found was urban poverty. More recently, African Americans have been returning to the South, especially to states like Mississippi, Florida, Georgia, Texas, Virginia, and North Carolina,[41] and African American millennials are moving in larger numbers to Georgia, Florida and North Carolina.[42]

Race is also related to economic well-being. The median weekly earnings for African Americans was $673 in early 2016, compared with $857 for whites.[43] In turn, unemployment for African Americans was 9 percent, compared with 4.6 percent for whites. This 2 to 1 ratio in unemployment has been steady for at least the past half-century—unemployment rates change for whites and African Americans at about the same speed through economic booms and busts, but always remain about twice as high for African Americans. (See Figure 4.2.)

Race is also related to economic opportunity. Nearly a quarter of African American families live below the poverty level, compared to about 10 percent of white families.[44] However, African Americans have made slight gains in recent years: 41 percent of African American households earned more than $50,000 in 2016, compared to 32 percent in 1990.[45]

Finally, race is related to education. Although the proportions of African Americans who go on to college after high school graduation is now only 7 percent lower than for white Americans,[46] 33 percent of whites graduate from college, compared with about 23 percent of African Americans.[47] The African American population is much younger than the white population; the median age for whites in 2016 was 39.1 years, compared to 31.7 for African Americans.[48]

African Americans had little political power until after World War II. Owing their freedom from slavery to the "party of Lincoln," most African Americans initially identified with the Republicans, but this loyalty started to change in the 1930s and 1940s under President Franklin D. Roosevelt, who insisted on equal treatment for African Americans in his New Deal programs.[49] After World War II,

African Americans came to see the Democrats as the party of civil rights. The 1964 Republican platform position on civil rights espoused *states' rights*—at the time, the creed of Southern segregationists—in what appeared to be an effort to win the support of Southern white voters. Virtually all African Americans voted for Lyndon Johnson in 1964, and in presidential elections between 1984 and 2016, their Democratic vote averaged nearly 89 percent.[50]

In 2008, with an African American running for president, 95 percent of blacks voted for Obama, and in 2012 the proportion was 93 percent.[51] In both years, African Americans were 13 percent of all voters, up from 10 percent in 2000 and 11 percent in 2004.[52] In 2016, African Americans were 12 percent of all voters and 88 percent of them voted for Hillary Clinton.[53] Evidence of growing African American political power comes in the dramatic increase in the number of African American state legislators, which rose from 168 in 1970 to 659 in 2015.[54] In 2015, Georgia and Alabama legislatures were more than one-fifth African American.[55] In 2017–2018 African Americans held 11 percent of seats in the U.S. House of Representatives.[56]

HISPANICS Hispanic Americans are not a monolithic group, and although they share a common linguistic heritage in Spanish, they often differ by the country from which they or their forebears emigrated. Cuban Americans, for instance, tend to be Republicans, like 2016 presidential candidates Marco Rubio and Ted Cruz, while Mexican Americans and Puerto Ricans living on the mainland are disproportionately Democrats.[57] Hispanics are politically important in a growing number of states. Nearly two-thirds of Cuban Americans live in Florida, especially in greater Miami. Mainland Puerto Ricans are concentrated in and around New York City; many Mexican Americans live in the Southwest and California. More than 15 million Hispanics live in California.[58]

In 2012 Obama received 71 percent of the Hispanic vote, up from the 65 percent he received in 2008. In 2004 John Kerry, the Democratic candidate, received 58 percent of the Hispanic vote. In 2016, national exit polls had Clinton winning 66 percent of Latino voters and Trump with 28 percent, one point higher than Mitt Romney had in 2012.[59] But more detailed analysis of voting patterns in California suggest the national exit poll which is not designed to be representative of sub-populations like Latinos, underestimated the Latino vote. These scholars estimate that Clinton won more than 80 percent of the California Latino vote rather than the 71 percent estimate from the exit polls.[60]

Should the Democratic partisan advantage become the norm it will be a boost to Democrats, in part because of the growth in the Hispanic population and because Hispanics are concentrated in some battleground states like Colorado and Nevada. However, the many noncitizen Hispanics and the relative youth of the Hispanic population also diminish the group's political power. For example, 13.9 million foreign-born Hispanics are not citizens,[61] and of the estimated 11 million unauthorized immigrants, three-fifths are from Mexico.[62] This group lacks the political power of the vote and, while important to the U.S. economy, lives in fear of deportation. The median age of the U.S. Hispanic population in 2014 was 29, more than 10 years younger than whites (40 years) and four years younger than African Americans.[63] Moreover, some states have yet to print voting guides in both English and Spanish, which also reduces Hispanic voter registration and turnout.

Both major parties are aggressively cultivating Hispanic candidates. Several Hispanics have been cabinet members. R. Alexander Acosta, the son of Cuban refugees, was appointed by President Trump as the Secretary of Labor in 2017. Likewise, Thomas Perez became Secretary of Labor in 2013 and is of Dominican descent. He was elected Chairman of the Democratic National Committee in 2017. Ernest Moniz, the Secretary of Energy under President Obama became a key participant in negotiating the nuclear agreement with Iran. Moniz is a physicist from the Massachusetts Institute of Technology. Alberto Gonzales served as Attorney General in the George W. Bush administration. In 2009, President Obama appointed and the Senate confirmed

Sonia Sotomayor became the third female and first Latina U.S. Supreme Court justice in 2009. She attended Yale Law School where she was an editor of the *Yale Law Journal*. Before entering private law practice, she was an assistant district attorney in New York. Appointed to the U.S. District Court for the Southern District of New York by President George H. W. Bush, she was appointed to the U.S. Supreme Court by President Barack Obama.

Sonia Sotomayor to the U.S. Supreme Court. Sotomayor became the first Hispanic U.S. Supreme Court justice.

The 2016 presidential nomination contest among Republicans was marked by strong rhetoric on the subject of illegal immigration from candidates such as Donald Trump and Ted Cruz. Trump and Cruz favored what Cruz's Web site labeled "deportations and returns" of undocumented persons.[64] During the campaign Trump frequently referred to his plans to build a wall between Mexico and the United States to keep out undocumented persons that would be paid for by the Mexican government. Trump also spoke of Mexican leaders exporting "the crime and poverty in their own country" to the United States.[65] In 2018, Trump laid out a four part plan on immigration reform: a path to citizenship for "Dreamers" and others who might have qualified for DACA but had not yet applied (about 1.8 million people); a $25 billion trust fund to pay for the U.S.–Mexico border security including a wall; replacing the visa lottery with a merit-based immigration system; and replacing family reunification as a priority for immigrants with priority going only to spouses and children.[66]

In 2017, Puerto Rico experienced two hurricanes. Irma, a category 5 storm, impacted the northern side of the island and three weeks later Maria, a category 4 storm with winds up to 175 miles per hour, devastated the entire island killing as many as 5,000 people, and knocking out all power on the island. The restoration of power was slower than in other U.S. localities impacted by hurricanes like Harvey which did substantial damage to Houston in 2017.[67] The storm disrupted some fundamental supplies, but there were also fewer Federal Emergency Management (FEMA) personnel in place, and unlike Houston relief supplies and personnel were not positioned ready to provide relief soon after the storm ended. Congress and the president were slow to agree on funding for disaster relief, delaying recovery.[68]

ASIAN AMERICANS The U.S. Census Bureau classifies persons of Chinese, Japanese, Indian, Korean, Vietnamese, Filipino, and Thai origin, as well as persons from the Pacific Islands, together as Asian Americans for statistical purposes. Many Asian Americans have done well economically and educationally. Their income is well above the national median, and 50 percent have graduated from college, compared to 32 percent of whites and 22 percent of African Americans.[69]

Like Hispanics, Asian Americans exhibit significant differences in culture, language, and political experience in the United States.[70] For example, Japanese Americans are more likely to register as Democrats than Korean Americans or other Asian Americans, and they are also more likely to vote than other Asian ethnic groups.[71]

However, Asian Americans as a whole do not have particularly strong alliances to either political party—in fact, just over a third reported that they did not identify with any party in 2016. Nevertheless, nearly three-quarters of Asian Americans voted for Barack Obama in 2012, which was a noticeable increase over Obama's share in 2008 and an even larger increase over the two previous Democratic presidential candidates, John Kerry in 2004[72] and Al Gore in 2000.[73] Hillary Clinton received 65 percent of the Asian American vote in 2016.[74]

Obama's strong showing among African Americans, Hispanics, and Asian Americans led some Republicans following the 2012 election to call for their party to focus even more than in the past with white voters by resisting immigration reform. Patrick Buchanan argued that with respect to immigration reform, this means "No amnesty, secure the border, enforce laws against businesses that hire illegals, and impose a moratorium on new immigration."[75] Other Republican strategists, like Karl Rove, who is most identified with the George W. Bush campaigns of 2000 and 2004 and a Super PAC he started in 2010, had a very different view, saying, "If the GOP leaves non-white voters to the Democrats, then its margins in safe districts and red states will dwindle."[76] Rove's views were shared by a group of prominent Republicans who following the 2012 presidential election defeat prepared a report on how the party should change. The Growth and Opportunity Report calls on the party to strengthen outreach to minority groups, especially Hispanics.[77] This has not been a major priority of the party or Trump administration.

Religion

In many parts of the world, religious differences, especially when combined with disputes over territory or sovereignty, are a source of violence. The conflict between Israelis and Palestinians has motivated suicide bombers who kill Israeli civilians along with themselves, and Israelis who attack Palestinian settlements and leaders. The war between India and Pakistan over Kashmir is largely a religious battle between Muslims and Hindus, and the Shiite–Sunni conflict among different branches of Islam threatens the stability of the Middle East. Predominantly Sunni Saudi Arabia competes with heavily Shia Iran for power in the region, and the conflict has surfaced in warfare in Syria, Iraq, Lebanon, and Yemen.[78]

Jews have often been the target of religious discrimination and persecution (anti-Semitism), which reached its greatest intensity in the Holocaust of the 1940s, during which the Nazis murdered an estimated 6 million Jews.[79] The United States has not been immune from such religious discrimination, despite its principle of religious freedom. In 1838, Governor Lilburn W. Boggs of Missouri issued an extermination order that made legal the killing of any Mormons in the state.[80]

Our government is founded on the premise that religious liberty flourishes when there is no predominant or official faith, which is why the Framers of the Constitution did not sanction a national church. The absence of an official church does not mean that religion is unimportant in American politics; indeed, there were established churches in individual states in this country until the 1830s. At one time, people thought voters' religious preferences could prevent a Catholic from being elected president. John F. Kennedy's election in 1960 resolved that question. Nevertheless, a candidate's religion may still become an issue today if the candidate's religious convictions on sensitive issues such as abortion threaten to conflict with public obligations.

Religion has also been a historically important catalyst for political change. The Catholic Church helped overthrow communism in parts of Eastern Europe.[81] Black churches provided many of the leaders in the American civil rights movement. More recently, political activity among fundamentalist Christians has increased. Led by ministers such as Pat Robertson and Focus on the Family founder James Dobson, evangelicals, sometimes called **fundamentalists**, are an important force in the Republican Party and in some local governments.[82] For example, more than three-fifths of the Iowa Republican caucus goers in 2016 were self-described evangelicals.[83] Their agenda includes returning prayer to public schools, outlawing abortion, restricting homosexual rights, opposing gun control, and opposing the teaching of evolution and sex education in public schools.

fundamentalists
Conservative Christians who, as a group, have become more active in politics in the last two decades and were especially influential in the 2000 and 2004 presidential elections.

Many American adults take their religious beliefs seriously—more than do citizens of other democracies.[84] Thirty-six percent attend houses of worship at least once a week, 33 percent attend monthly or yearly, and 30 percent seldom or never attend.[85] Religion, like ethnicity, is a shared identity. People identify themselves as Baptist, Catholic, Jewish, Buddhist, or no religion at all. Sometimes religious attendance or nonattendance, rather than belonging to a particular religion or denomination, determines attitudes toward issues.

The United States includes tremendous variety in religious denominations. Approximately two-fifths of the people in the United States describe themselves as Protestant (see Figure 4.3). Because Protestants are divided among so many different churches, Catholics have the largest single membership in the United States,

FIGURE 4.3 RELIGIOUS GROUPS IN THE UNITED STATES

The U.S. population is religiously diverse. While predominantly Christian, there are different types of Protestants, Catholics, and other Christian faiths. Jews are the largest non-Christian religion in the United States, but there are growing numbers of Muslims, Buddhists, and Hindus. Another growing category is the unaffiliated (a category different from atheists). This group is now more than one-fifth of the U.S. population.

SOURCE: Pew Research, Religion & Public Life Project, http://www.pewforum.org/religious-landscape-study/.

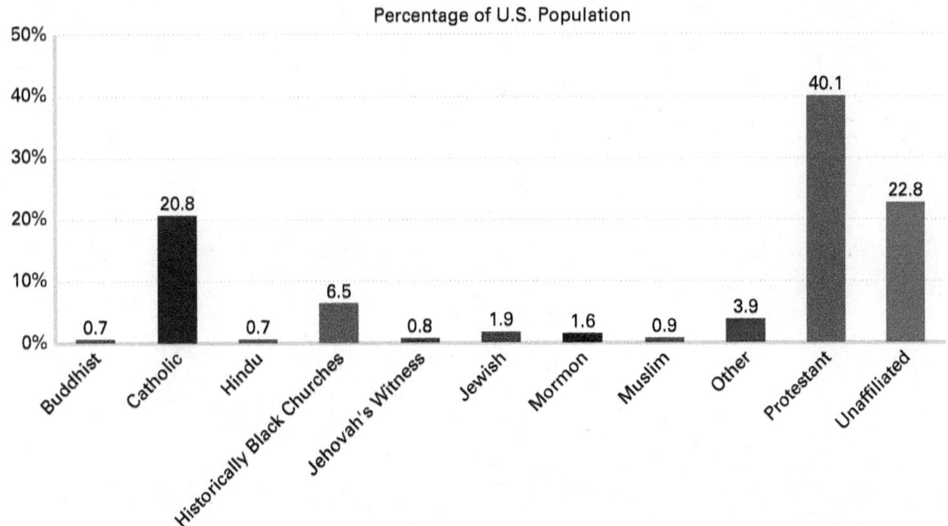

constituting just over a fifth of the population.[86] Jews represent less than 2 percent of the population,[87] and Muslims number just under 1 percent.[88]

Religion is important in American politics in part because people of particular religions are often concentrated in a few states. Catholics constitute 42 percent of the population of Rhode Island. Baptists represent 9 percent of the American population, yet they account for more than a quarter of the populations of Mississippi (26 percent) and Alabama (31 percent). Mormons represent less than 2 percent of the American population, but constitute 55 percent of the population of Utah. The state of New York has the highest percentage of Jews with 7 percent.[89] Religious groups vary in their rates of political participation. In recent elections Jews have the highest rate of reported voter turnout among any religious group, while those who claim no religious affiliation have the lowest, an average of roughly 70 percent in recent elections.[90] In recent presidential elections, most Evangelical Protestants voted Republican, while Jews and African American Protestants voted Democratic; other Protestants and Catholics were more evenly divided.[91] In 2012, Romney got 52 percent of the Protestant vote. Obama did better among Protestants in 2008 than Kerry in 2004 and received a majority of the Catholic vote in both 2008 and 2012. In 2012, Romney argued that the Obama administration had not been as supportive of Israel. Obama's share of the Jewish vote declined from 84 percent in 2008 to 63 percent in 2012; his share of the Catholic vote also dropped from 74 to 53 percent.[92] In 2016, Clinton got about 33 percent of the Protestant vote, 80 percent of the Jewish vote, and almost 50 percent of the Catholic vote, with much of this coming from Hispanic Catholics.[93]

Gender

For most of U.S. history, politics and government were men's business. Women first gained the right to vote primarily in the western territories, beginning with Wyoming in 1869 and Utah in 1870, and then in Colorado and Idaho before 1900.[94] The right was not extended nationally to women until 1920 with passage of the Nineteenth Amendment.

For a half-century after gaining the right to vote, American women voted at a lower rate than women in other Western democracies.[95] In 2016, as in the prior four presidential elections, a higher percentage of women than men voted in the

Seen here are the women members of the U.S. House of Representatives for 2017–2018. After the 2018 midterm elections, the number of female members of the House increased from 84 to more than 100 (as of press time).

presidential elections, and the same has been the case in recent midterm elections.[96] Women have chosen to work within the existing political parties and do not overwhelmingly support female candidates, especially if they must cross party lines to do so.[97] Each party has found that running a female nominee for vice president does not necessarily motivate women to vote for that ticket. The share of women voting Republican in 2008 when Republicans selected Sarah Palin as their vice presidential nominee dropped when compared to 2000 or 2012 when no women were running. In 2018, with Democrats having the first female nominee for president from a major party, the percent of women voting for Clinton was one percent lower in 2016 than the percent of women voting for Obama in 2012 and two percent lower than it was in 2008.[98]

The number of women in Congress has increased in recent years, but the number of men still far exceeds the number of women serving. At the beginning of 2019, there were 9 female governors, at least 23 women serving in the Senate, and at least 101 women in the House.[99] The proportion of women serving in the House of Representatives and in the Senate is 23 percent. In contrast, some state legislative chambers, like those in Colorado and Vermont, are between 30 to 40 percent women.[100]

Is there a **gender gap**, or a persistent difference between men and women in voting and in attitudes on important issues? Since 2000, women have consistently voted for Democratic presidential candidates more than men, and in 2012 the gap was 10 percent (see Figure 4.4).[101] In 2016, it rose to 12 percentage points for Clinton over Trump. Clinton received 90 percent of the vote of Democratic women and 4 percent more than Trump among Independent women.[102] In 2008, men also gave Obama more votes than McCain, with 49 percent of men voting for Obama and 48 percent for McCain.

gender gap
The difference between the political opinions or political behavior of men and of women.

The women's movement in American politics seeks equal opportunity, education, jobs, skills, and respect in what has long been a male-dominated economy.[103] Women are more likely than men to oppose violence in any form, and are more likely to favor government-provided health insurance and family services. In recent elections female voters were more prone than men to consider issues such as abortion, economic inequality, the environment, and health care important.[104] There are serious income inequalities between men and women. Nearly twice as many women as men have an annual income of less than $15,000, while men are two times more likely than women to make more than $75,000 a year.[105] Because an increasing number of women today

FIGURE 4.4 GENDER AND THE VOTE FOR PRESIDENT, 2016

As in the past, there was a gender gap in the presidential vote in 2016. In 2012, Obama got 55 percent of the female vote while Romney got 52 percent of the male vote. In 2016, Clinton got 54 percent of the female vote while Trump got 53 percent of the male vote.

SOURCE: "Exit Polls 2012: How the Vote Has Shifted," *Washington Post*, http://www.washingtonpost.com/wp-srv/special/politics/2012-exit-polls/table.html and http://www.cnn.com/election/results/exit-polls.

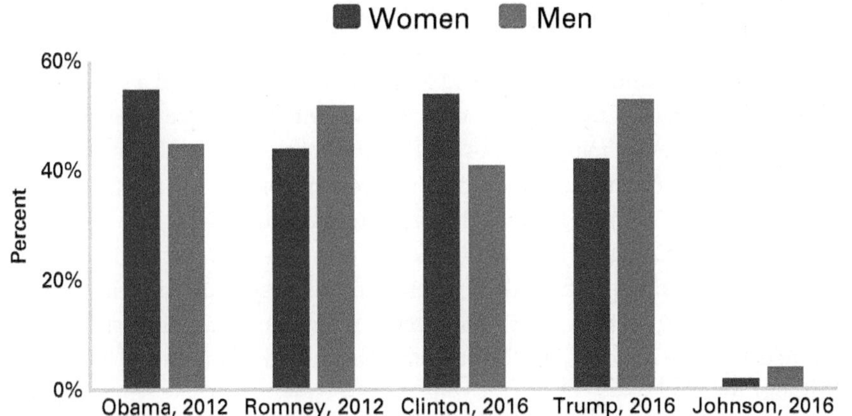

are the sole breadwinners for their families, the implications of this income inequality are especially significant. On average, women earn less than men for the same work. After controlling for characteristics such as job experience and education, a U.S. Census Bureau study shows that the wage difference between the genders is 80 cents on every dollar.[106] But, unemployment in the economic recession of 2008–2010 affected more men than women. Four out of the five jobs lost in the recession were jobs held by men in such industries as manufacturing and construction.[107] However, during the recovery unemployed men were more likely to find jobs than unemployed women.[108]

Sexual Orientation and Gender Identity

The modern movement for expanded rights for the lesbian, gay, bisexual, and transgender and queer plus community (LGBTQ) traces its roots to 1969, when New York City police raided the Stonewall Inn, a bar in Greenwich Village, and a riot ensued.[109] Since then LGBTQ Americans have become more active and visible in pushing for legal rights and protections.

The precise size of the LGBTQ community in the United States is unclear. Estimates range from 2 to 10 percent of the U.S. population, with about 4 percent probably the most accurate estimate.[110] Whatever its overall size, the LGBTQ community has become politically important in several cities, most notably in San Francisco. Its lobbying power has increased noticeably in many states and at the national level as well, and being gay, lesbian, bisexual or transgender is no longer a barrier to election in many places.

The political agenda for LGBTQ advocacy groups includes fighting discrimination. Victories have included removing laws criminalizing consensual adult homosexual conduct and ending the "don't ask don't tell" policy in the military. In 2011, President Obama signed legislation allowing gays and lesbians to serve in the military without having to hide their sexual orientation,[111] and in 2016 the ban on transgender troops serving in the military ended. Despite a Presidential Memorandum signed by President Trump on August 25, 2017, reintroducing the ban on transgender troops serving in the military, Secretary Mattis stated that transgender troops will be allowed to remain in service pending further studies and recommendations.[112] In recent years, the LGBTQ agenda has included enacting antidiscrimination laws at the local, state, and national levels, including a legislative victory in 2013 when the Senate passed the Employment Non-Discrimination Act (ENDA), a bill making discrimination based on sexual orientation in housing and employment impermissible. Since then, the Military Equal Opportunity policy has been expended to protect gay and lesbians from discrimination because of sexual orientation.

In 2015, the Supreme Court ruled in *Obergefell* v. *Hodges* that marriage was a fundamental right, in effect legalizing same-sex marriage.[113] The decision came after several years of intense disagreement on the question in state legislatures, among voters deciding ballot propositions, and in the lower courts. A turning point for gay rights came in 2012 when three states voted in support of legalizing same-sex marriage (Washington, Maine, and Maryland) and Minnesota voters rejected a proposed constitutional ban on same-sex marriage. These votes were the first time a majority of voters had supported same-sex marriage. As is often the case, rights and liberties may be in conflict. That was true in a Colorado case where a baker refused to bake a cake for a gay marriage. The Colorado Civil Rights Commission sued the baker for discrimination. The Supreme Court, in June 2018, decided the case very narrowly and in doing so, did not answer the question as to whether a business could discriminate against gay customers based on their First Amendment religious freedoms. Instead, the Court determined that the state's Civil Right Commission had not afforded the baker, Jack Phillips, fair review.[114]

Salt Lake City elected Jackie Biskupski (left) mayor in 2015. She is the city's first openly gay mayor and second female mayor. She is seen here with her fiancé, Betty Iverson whom she married in 2016. Together, Jackie and Betty have two adopted children.

Family and Fertility

Throughout the past half-century, the traditional American family (mother and father married, with children in the home) has become anything but typical. The traditional family had several key characteristics: it married early, had children, and stayed together through thick and thin. However, the number of American adults who lived with someone of the opposite sex without being married was 7 percent of adults in 2016.[115] Marriage also used to occur earlier in life, but people now marry later: the average age for first marriage for men is 29.5; for women it is 27.4.[116]

Children were also essential to the traditional families, but fertility rates have been falling since the 1960s, when more birth control options became available. In the early 1960s when the baby boom was at its peak, women averaged 118 births per 1,000. By 2016 the number had fallen to 62 births per 1,000, slightly below the rate needed to replace the population as a whole.[117] These rates vary slightly by race, with 70.6 births per 1,000 among Hispanic women, 63.3 per 1,000 among African Americans, and 62.7 per 1,000 among American Indian or Alaska Native Americans.[118] Fertility rates have risen slightly since the end of the recent economic collapse; this "baby bounce" shows the relationship between economic growth and the willingness to take on the cost of having a child.

Finally, the traditional family stayed together, but the divorce rate has grown from 2.2 per 1,000 people in 1960 to 3.2 per 1,000 people in 2016.[119] Today it is estimated that between one-third and one-half of marriages end in divorce.[120] This is one reason why the number of households headed by women has risen.

Education

Differences in education affect not only economic well-being but political participation and involvement as well. Thomas Jefferson wrote of education, "Enlighten the people generally Most American students are educated in public schools. Almost nine of every ten students in kindergarten through high school attend public schools, and more than three of, and tyranny and oppressions of body and mind will vanish like evil spirits at the dawn of day."[121] Most American students are educated in public schools. Almost nine of every ten students in kindergarten through high school attend public schools, and more than three of four college students are in public institutions.[122]

For the first time, in 1992 the number of American college graduates surpassed the number of persons who did not graduate from high school.[123] Though many college students assume that almost everyone goes to college, over half of all U.S. adults have not, and attendance rates vary substantially by race. Approximately 37 percent

FIGURE 4.5 EDUCATION ATTAINMENT IN THE UNITED STATES

Differences in the level of education between men and women are now small compared to differences between Hispanics and blacks and non-Hispanic Whites and Asians. Holding aside 18–24-year-olds, those over the age of 65 and especially those over the age of 75 are more likely to have not completed high school. Given the importance of education in politics, differences like those we find among Hispanics and blacks and the oldest and youngest eligible voters are important.

SOURCE: Author supplied data set from U.S. Census Bureau, Educational Attainment in the United States: http://www.census.gov

	Not a High School Graduate	High School Graduate	Bachelor's Degree	Advanced Degree
Male	14.2	52.1	21.0	12.7
Female	23.5	52.8	21.6	13.1
Asian	10	35.2	30.5	24.3
Black	15.8	60.3	15.1	8.8
Non-Hispanic White	8.6	53.2	23.8	14.4
White	13.8	51.7	21.8	12.7
Hispanics	32.6	50.1	12.2	5.1
25–34	10.9	51.8	25.7	11.6
35–54	13.1	50.1	22.5	14.3
55+	14.8	54.9	18.1	12.2

of whites are college graduates, compared to 23 percent of African Americans and 16.4 percent of Hispanics; roughly 11 percent of African Americans and 31.5 percent of all Hispanics left school before completing high school (see Figure 4.5).[124]

Education is one of the most important variables in predicting political participation, confidence in dealing with government, and awareness of issues. Education is also related to the acquisition of democratic values. People who have not learned the prevailing norms of American society are far more likely to express opposition to democratic and capitalist ideals than those who are well educated and politically knowledgeable.[125]

Age

The "graying of America" has become a new force in American politics as the number of older citizens is increasing rapidly (Figure 4.6).[126] This demographic change has increased the proportion of the population over age 65 and increased the demand for medical care, retirement benefits, and a host of other age-related services.[127] Persons over age 64 constitute approximately 15 percent of the population yet account for more than 40 percent of the top 5 percent of medical spenders.[128] With birth rates decreasing, the graying of America has given rise to concern about maintaining an adequate workforce in the future.

Older adults are more politically aware and vote more often than younger ones, making them a potent political force. Their vote is especially important in South western states and in Florida, the state with the largest proportion of people over age 65.[129] In contrast to the high participation among older Americans, younger Americans are much less likely to participate. The League of Women Voters, Rock the Vote, and TurboVote are all working to make voting easier for younger Americans. Turnout among those aged 18–29 rose from 33 percent in 1996 to 45 percent in 2004, to 48 percent in 2008, before dropping to 41 percent in 2012 and 43 percent in 2016.[130] Recent studies find that while youth voting is always lower in midterm elections, but rises in all elections in states that offer same-day voter registration. Young voters appear to focus on the coming election later than older voters, in part because they are focused on pressing issues such as staying current on their class readings in college.[131]

FIGURE 4.6 PERCENTAGE OF POPULATION OVER THE AGE OF 65, 1900–2060

The percent of the population over the age of 65 grew in each decade through 1990–2000. It then leveled off between 10 and 15 percent of the population. It is expected to grow again by 2020 before again leveling off. Consider the share of the population that is 65 years old and eligible for Social Security in 1930 and in 2020, and you will see that the share of the population that is of retirement age will have nearly tripled.

SOURCE: U.S. Census Bureau, "2017 National Population Projections Tables, Table 2. Projected Age and Sex composition of the Population." https://www.census.gov/data/tables/2017/demo/popproj/2017-summary-tables.html.

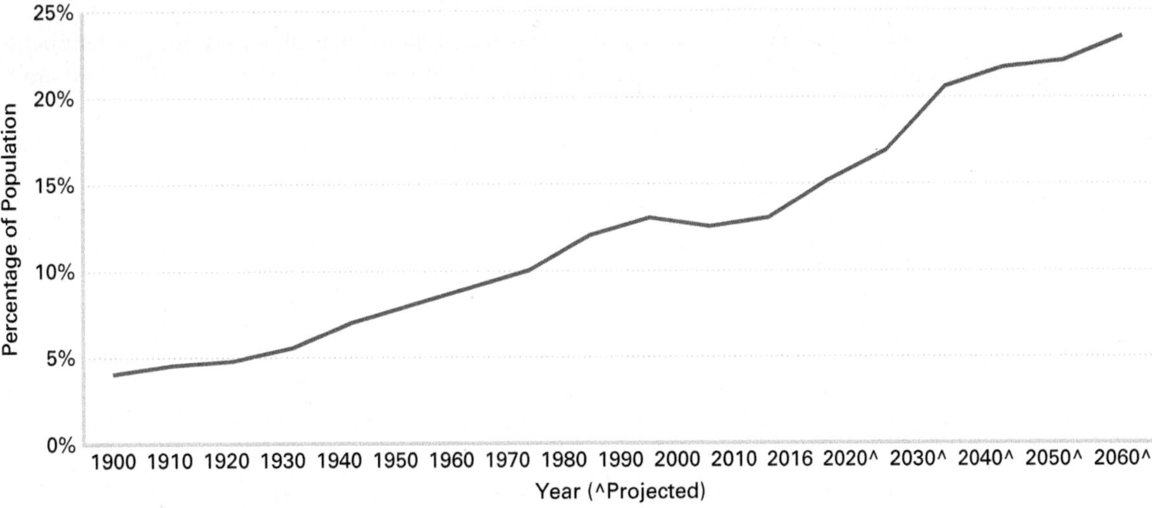

Age is important in terms of politics in two additional ways: lifecycle and generational effects. *Lifecycle effects* have shown that as people become middle-aged, they become more politically conservative, less mobile, and more likely to participate in politics. As they age further and rely more on the government for services, they tend to grow more liberal.[132] Young people, in contrast, are more mobile and less concerned about the delivery of government services.

Generational effects in politics arise when a particular generation has had experiences that make it politically distinct. For example, for those who lived through it, the Great Depression of the 1930s shaped their lifelong views of political parties, issues, and political leaders. Some members of this generation saw Franklin D. Roosevelt as the leader who saved the country by pulling it out of the Depression; others felt he sold the country down the river by launching too many government programs. Another event that shaped a generation was World War II. Following the war, the nation's 15 million veterans needed education, homes, jobs, health care, and cash when they got home, and their families needed new schools, hospitals, roads, and transportation. Congress and President Franklin Roosevelt provided it all in a giant package of social and economic programs through the Servicemen's Readjustment Act of 1944, known to World War II veterans as the GI Bill of Rights.

This group is sometimes referred to as the Greatest Generation. They created new families and brought 76 million children into the world between 1946 and 1964. The "Baby Boom" also had great impact on American society. The boomers filled the schoolrooms, studied in the same buildings as their parents, and reshaped the social and cultural rules of the nation. Boomers were named *Time's* Man of the Year in 1967, helped put civil rights and women's rights on the national agenda, held the first Earth Day demanding environmental protection, and fought to end the Vietnam War.[133]

However, the baby boomers were also criticized for being self-absorbed slackers who cared more about having a meaningful philosophy of life than making money. They also earned a reputation for caring more about new products and rock and roll than getting ahead. They were the original "me" generation, but eventually settled down and went to work.

The baby boomers became parents of an even larger generation called the millennials that has already made its own impact on society by embracing new technologies, peer-to-peer businesses such as Uber and Etsy, and a host of new communication channels.[134] Although the millennials are criticized in similar ways as their parents were, they are actually more likely than their parents to volunteer in their community, boycott products that they believe hurt the environment or undermine human rights, get their news online, and say that government should do more to solve problems in society.[135] More of them attend college but they also face unprecedented student loan debt. They are also remaking the social and cultural rules of society, just as their baby boomer and Generation X parents did.[136,137] If you were born before 1995, you are a millennial. If you were born after 1995, demographers and marketers have not yet labeled your generation. Some demographers are referring to this youngest cohort as Generation Z," others use "iGen." How this generation is different from millennials is also the subject of current study.[138]

The millennial generation also reflects many of the trends reshaping the American political landscape. They are part of the most racially diverse generation in American history, more likely than previous generations to still live with their parents after leaving college, and enter a much more competitive job market. They are also more likely to be Democrats,[139] stay with the same employer longer, and defer marriage and having children until the economy improves. Yet, there is a reason why *Time* magazine said that the millennials will save us all: they have the skills to solve the tough problems ahead, and the willingness to change their own behavior to make the world a better place to live.[140]

How Much We Own (Structure, Action, and Impact)

4.3 Describe the importance of income, wealth, occupation, and social class in American politics.

The extent to which a society is divided along economic lines and people feel they and their children can improve their economic standing are important to democratic stability. The United States has long been known as a land of economic opportunity. This chance to own property and improve one's standard of living, along with freedom more generally, drew many immigrants to America.

A group of children begins the day in the federal government's Head Start program. Head Start was created in 1965 to help low-income children prepare for school and has shown consistent benefits in the first few years of K–12 education. In his proposed 2019 budget, Donald Trump proposed a 5 percent cut in education by removing discretionary grant programs.

Many of our political values come together in the **American dream**, a complex set of ideas that holds that the United States is a land of opportunity where individual initiative and hard work can bring economic success. Whether fulfilled or not, this dream speaks to our most deeply held hopes and goals. It is also the case that while recognizing its imperfections, Americans value free markets and **capitalism**, an economic system based on private property, competitive markets, economic incentives, and limited government involvement in the production, pricing, and distribution of goods and services.[141] Capitalism also means there are winners and losers in the economy. Much of the political debate in 2012 and 2016 was about the economy and the extent to which people at different income levels were hurt or advantaged by government policies. To put this important debate in context we need to understand how social scientists measure the economic standing of individuals.

American dream
A complex set of ideas that holds that the United States is a land of opportunity where individual initiative and hard work can bring economic success.

capitalism
An economic system based on private property, competitive markets, economic incentives, and limited government involvement in the production, pricing, and distribution of goods and services.

Wealth and Income

The United States is a wealthy nation. Indeed, to some knowledgeable observers, "the most striking thing about the United States has been its phenomenal wealth."[142] Most American citizens lead comfortable lives. They eat and live well and have first-class medical care. However, the unequal distribution of wealth and income results in political divisions and conflicts.

Wealth, the total value of someone's possessions, is more concentrated than income (annual earnings). The wealthiest families hold most of the property and other forms of wealth such as stocks and savings. Historically, concentrated wealth fosters an aristocracy. The framers of the Constitution recognized the dangers of an unequal concentration of wealth. "The most common and durable source of factions has been the various and unequal distribution of property," wrote James Madison in *The Federalist*, No. 10. Economic differences often lead to conflict, and we remain divided politically along economic lines. Income may be the single most important factor in explaining partisanship, views on issues, and ideology. Most rich people are Republicans, and most poor people are Democrats—something that has been true since at least the Great Depression of the 1930s.

Between the 1950s and the 1970s, U.S. inflation-adjusted income doubled, but since then it has fluctuated, with no substantial change over time.[143] In 2016, 12.7 percent of Americans fell below the income threshold that the federal government uses to measure poverty. Although some researchers believe the line understates the true amount of poverty, the 2018 line was set at $12,140 a year for a single person living alone, and $25,100 for a family of four living together.[144]

Poverty can be measured in both percent and number terms. Measured by percentage, families headed by a single parent are more than twice as likely to be poor than families headed by married parents, but measured by numbers, the two are almost equal. Measured by percentage, African American, Hispanic, and American Indian children are twice as likely to be poor than white and Asian American children, but measured by number, white children are almost twice as likely to be poor as African American children, and slightly more likely to be poor than Hispanic children.[145] Regardless of family status or race, many children appear to be trapped in a cycle of poverty, in which they are born into poverty and remain in poverty through most of their lives. The poor lack political power at least partially because they vote less than wealthier people, are less confident and organized in dealing with government, and rarely contribute to candidates.

For several years, scholars have been describing the growing economic inequality in the United States. During the 1950s and 1960s, economic growth did not lead to greater economic inequality. That period retained a relatively flat income distribution.[146] Since 1967, however, the real pre-tax income of the top 5 percent of households has grown more than 90 percent, while that of the lowest 60 percent of households has only grown by about 20 percent.[147] This trend continues today: in 2016, the income of the lowest 20 percent of families grew by about 0.5 percent from 2015, the income of families in the middle experienced a decrease of about 1 percent, while that of the top 5 percent of families grew by almost 3 percent (the disparity was even larger in previous years).[148]

This large difference in who reaps benefits from policy choices is central to the current debate about tax policy, public spending, the minimum wage, and the role of government. Political Scientist Larry Bartels attributes the persistent and growing inequality to "the policies and priorities of Republican presidents."[149] Bartels also argues that inequality may have "deleterious social implications in the realms of family and community life, health and education."[150] Others who have studied inequality have come to different conclusions. They see economic inequality as a natural consequence of a free market that rewards initiative, creativity, and hard work, and that may lead to big gaps between rich and poor. This view holds that for government, as a matter of policy, to try to close those gaps will likely result in less economic growth, potentially hurting everybody.[151] The 2017 tax cut provides a much lower benefit in terms of the percent of income after taxes given to those with lower incomes. Households with income between $500,000 and $1 million are projected to see a 4.3 percent rise in after tax income, four times greater than those making $40,000 a year.[152]

A gap in income and wealth is not new. Writing in the early 1980s, political scientist Robert Dahl observed: "it is a striking fact that the presence of vast disparities in wealth and income, and so in political resources, has never become a highly salient issue in American politics or, certainly, a persistent one."[153] For 30 years after Dahl wrote these words, his description of the limited attention given to the income and wealth gaps remained true; but in the last few years that changed.

Many commentators argue that income inequality has now reached levels we have not seen since the 1920s, though it appears to depend, in part, on how inequality is measured.[154] Economists and political candidates alike have debated the causes of the growing income and wealth gap. Some economists point out that market forces like increased trade and technological advances have allowed well-educated and highly skilled individuals to demand more pay. The argument is that today's marketplace rewards creative people with technical skills. Many of those skills are gained in undergraduate and graduate education, so colleges and universities are not only pathways to higher pay, but a screening mechanism that helps identify talented people.[155] Others argue that deregulation, tax policy, and the decline of unions have allowed the

Proponents of a ballot initiative to raise the minimum wage and mandate employers offer paid sick leave in the state of Washington talk to the media before turning in their petitions for measure 1433. The initiative was approved by voters in November 2016. It raises the minimum wage over four years to be $13.50 in 2020.

well-off to become better-off.[156] Both parties in recent elections have emphasized their different approaches to economic growth and who should benefit from that growth.

President Obama and the Democrats sought to roll back the tax cuts enacted during the George W. Bush administration and to pay for broad-based tax relief with higher taxes on individuals earning $250,000 or more per year. Republicans have countered, sometimes criticizing the Democrats for "class warfare," arguing that higher taxes hurt the economy and create unemployment. In the debate over the 2017 tax cuts, Republicans argued that the tax cuts provided needed relief to corporations and would lead to higher wages. Democrats countered that the economy was not needing additional stimulus, that the cuts were so deep as to risk inflation, and that the benefits of the tax cuts went largely to the rich.[157]

Democrats in recent years have pushed for an increase in the minimum wage as a modest step in reducing income inequality. In 2018, the federal minimum wage was $7.25 per hour, but some states and cities had a higher minimum wage. For example, the minimum wage in Washington, D.C., is $12.50 an hour, and in California it was $10.50.[158] In 2014, voters in five states approved raising the minimum wage in their state, and in 2016 voters in Arizona, Colorado, Maine, and Washington voted to increase the minimum wage in their state, while voters in South Dakota voted to retain the increase in minimum wage for teenagers passed previously by the legislature.[159] This pattern continued in 2018, as the Massachusetts and Delaware legislatures enacted measures to increase the state minimum wage, while voters in Arkansas and Missouri also voted for similar measures.

Opposition to raising the minimum wage is largely based on the argument that such a minimum is bad for economic growth generally and leads to fewer jobs particularly. As former U.S. House Speaker Boehner said of the Obama/Democratic proposal to raise the minimum wage, "Why would we want to make it harder for small employers to hire people?"[160] A more fundamental argument against the minimum wage is that the marketplace is disrupted by the government mandating a minimum wage rather than allowing the employer and employee to negotiate the wage without such a minimum. Another argument is that raising the minimum wage will raise prices, which again hurt the people a minimum wage is supposed to help.[161]

Supporters of raising the minimum wage counter that there is little evidence that raising the minimum wage dampens job growth and that low-paying jobs have not left higher-minimum-wage states for lower-minimum-wage states. Supporters also point to rising corporate profits with a declining share of corporate income going to labor.[162] More broadly, proponents argue that a wage of $7.25 an hour is not a "livable wage." As of 2016, almost 80 million U.S. workers were paid on an hourly rate, but the vast majority made more than $7.25 on average, because many states and employers set a higher minimum.[163]

The five lowest-paying jobs in what economists call the nation's "low-wage workforce" are food workers, dishwashers, cashiers, restaurant hosts and hostesses (on an average hourly basis), and amusement park attendants.[164] All of these jobs pay $8–$10 per hour, and very few provide benefits such as health insurance. About 5 percent of these and other low-wage workers are teenagers, almost three quarter are white, more than, 50 percent are women, around 55 percent have some post–high school education, and approximately 20 percent have a college degree.[165]

The distribution of income in a society can have important consequences for democratic stability. If enough people believe that only the few at the top of the economic ladder can hope to earn enough for an adequate standard of living, domestic unrest and, in extreme cases, even revolution may follow.

Occupation

In Jefferson's day and for several generations after, most people in the United States worked primarily on farms, but by 1900, the United States had become the world's leading industrial nation. As workers moved from farms to cities to find better-paying

FIGURE 4.7 THE DECLINE OF THE MANUFACTURING INDUSTRY

A frequent topic on the campaign trail in 2016 was the reason for the decline in U.S. manufacturing jobs. This chart shows the magnitude of the change and the fact that the decline has been steady over time. As recently as 1967 about one-quarter of all U.S. jobs were in manufacturing. Since about 2003 the percent had dropped by more than half to under 10 percent. Many of the lost jobs have gone to countries with lower labor costs and fewer environmental protection rules. The impact of the lost jobs has been most concentrated in the Rust Belt.

SOURCE: U.S. Department of Commerce, Bureau of Economic Analysis, Table 6.4D: Full-Time and Part-Time Employees by Industry, http://www.bea.gov/iTable/iTable.cfm?reqID=9&step=1#reqid=9&step=3&isuri=1&903=181.

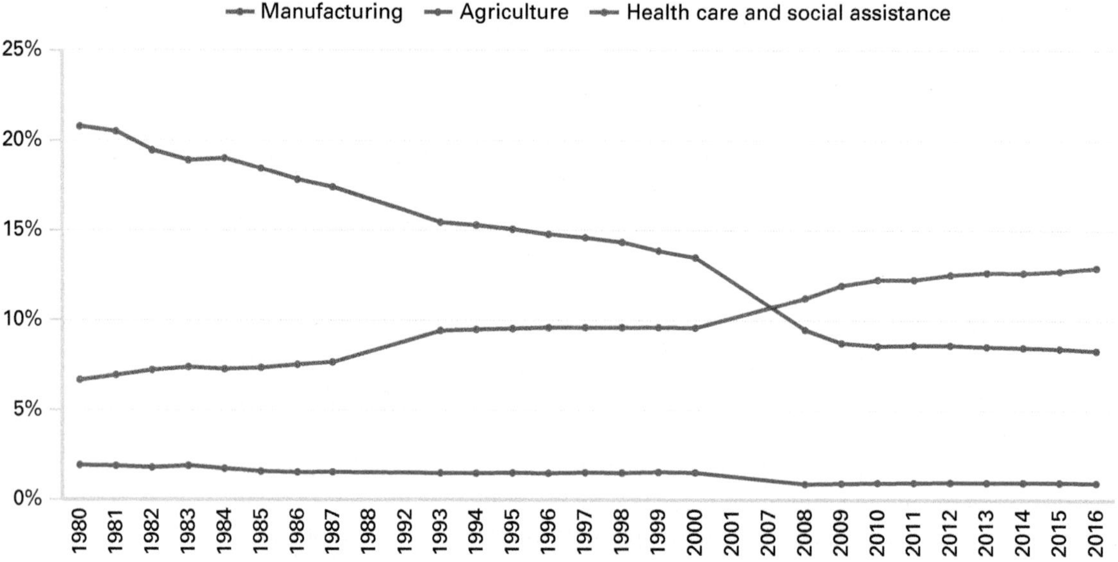

gross domestic product (GDP)
The total output of all economic activity in the nation, including goods and services.

jobs, the cities grew rapidly. Labor conditions, including child labor, the length of the work-week, and safety conditions in mines and factories, became important political issues. New technology, combined with abundant natural and human resources, meant that the American **gross domestic product (GDP)** rose by more than 564 percent from 1960 to 2017, after adjusting for inflation.[166] Gross domestic product is one measure of the size of a country's economy. It is the total market value of goods and services produced in that country in a specified period of time. Even as the overall output of the economy has grown the types of goods and services produced has changed. There has been, for example, a shift from manufacturing to technology and services (see Figure 4.7).

The United States has entered what Daniel Bell, a noted sociologist, labeled the "postindustrial" phase of its development: "A postindustrial society, being primarily a technical society, awards less on the basis of inheritance or property … than on education and skill."[167] *Knowledge* is the organizing device of the postindustrial era. Postindustrial societies have greater affluence and a class structure less defined along traditional labor-management lines.

The white-collar sector of our economy has grown tremendously in the past 50 years. This sector includes managers, accountants, and lawyers, as well as professionals and technicians in rapid-growth areas such as computers, communications, finance, insurance, and research. A dramatic decline in the number of people engaged in agriculture and a more modest decline in the number of people in manufacturing (which together make up the blue-collar sector) has accompanied this shift. In 2016, agriculture employed approximately 1 percent of working adults, down from 4 percent in 1980,[168] and manufacturing employs approximately 7 percent.[169] Federal, state, and local governments employ just under 13 percent of jobholders,[170] while government expenditures account for slightly less than 18 percent of our gross domestic product.[171]

The U.S. Bureau of Labor Statistics estimates that department store cashiers are among the lowest-paid workers in America, as are movie ticket takers and fast-food workers. All of these jobs pay minimum wage and offer limited employee benefits. They are sometimes referred to as part of the "down wage" economy.

Social Class

Why do U.S. citizens not divide themselves into social classes as Europeans do? American workers have not formed their own political party, nor does class seem to dominate our political life. Karl Marx's categories of *proletariat* (those who sell their labor) and *bourgeoisie* (those who own or control the means of production) are far less important here than they have been in Europe. Still, we do have social classes and what social scientists call **socioeconomic status (SES)**—a division of the population based on occupation, income, and education.

socioeconomic status (SES)
A division of population based on occupation, income, and education.

Conventionally the terms used to describe social class are "upper class," "middle class," and "lower class." Most American adults say they are middle class. Few see themselves as lower class or upper class. In many other industrial democracies, large proportions of the population think of themselves as "working class" rather than middle class.[172]

What constitutes the middle class in the United States is highly subjective. For instance, some individuals perform working-class tasks (such as plumbing), but their income places them in the middle class or even the upper-middle class. A schoolteacher's income is below that of many working-class jobs, but in terms of status, teaching ranks among middle-class jobs.

CONCLUSION

Our geographic isolation, relative wealth, prosperity, and sense of destiny have fostered a view that the United States is different from the rest of the world. This **American exceptionalism**, a term first used by de Tocqueville in 1831, has historically been defined as "the perception that the United States differs from other developed nations, because of its unique origins, national credo, historical evolution, and distinctive political and religious institutions."[173] As we have discussed in this chapter, America is also a diverse country. People bring to the American experiment in self-government different demographics, backgrounds, and religions or no religion at all, and more people are allowed to participate in American elections today than was the case for much of our history. Young people today bring their own distinct beliefs into the American experiment as both millennials and citizens in the national landscape as a whole.

American exceptionalism
The view that due to circumstances of history, the Constitution, and liberty, the United States is different from other nations.

As remarkable as American diversity is, the existence of a strong and widely shared sense of national unity and identity may be even more remarkable. It was this unity that led millions of Americans to defend the nation in World War II, support the GI Bill of Rights, build families and have children, and eventually become grandparents to many of you. In its own way, government action to help our veterans rebuild their lives paved the way for your own journey to this class.

Economic and social mobility have unified much of the U.S. population. Education has been an important part of this, as was the nationalizing influence of World War II. We are united by our shared commitment to democratic values, economic opportunity, work ethic, and the American dream. Social scientists used to speak of the "melting pot," meaning that as various ethnic groups associate with other groups, they are assimilated into U.S. society and come to share democratic values such as majority rule, individualism, and the ideal of the United States as a land of opportunity. Critics have argued that the melting pot idea assumes there is something wrong with differences between groups, and that these distinctions should be discouraged. In its place, they propose the concept of the "salad bowl," in which every ingredient enriches the whole.

As this chapter has demonstrated, regional, social, and economic differences have important political consequences. They influence public opinion, participation, voting, interest groups, and political parties. At the same time, it is impressive that our country has achieved a sense of unity despite our remarkable diversity.

In this chapter we have examined several social and economic differences in the American public and explored their political significance today. James Madison engaged in this kind of analysis when trying to, persuade others to support ratification of the Constitution. In *The Federalist*, No. 10 he states that "the most common and durable source of factions has been the various and unequal distribution of property."[174] Madison was correct—economic differences remain among the most important predictors of political behavior.

In the 2012 and 2016 presidential elections there was sustained attention to income inequality in part because of a statement Mitt Romney made that "These are people who pay no income tax; 47 percent of Americans pay no income tax. So our message of low taxes doesn't connect."[175] In the 2016 presidential race, Democrat Bernie Sanders made a center piece of his campaign the issue of growing income inequality. When announcing his candidacy he said, "The issue of wealth and income inequality is the great moral issue of our time, it is the great economic issue of our time, and it is the great political issue of our time."[176] Donald Trump's campaign emphasized making American great again, a broad theme which included bringing back good paying jobs to parts of the country with stagnant economies and securing trade agreements that put American workers first. In his inaugural address, President Trump reinforced these themes when he said: "every decision on trade, on taxes, on immigration, on foreign affairs will be made to benefit American workers and American families. We must protect our borders from the ravages of other countries making our products, stealing our companies and destroying our jobs."[177] But political behavior is based on more than income or wealth. Education, age, gender, and other characteristics also matter.

From its inception, the structure of our government fostered the kind of diversity so characteristic of the United States. The fact that the Constitution does not provide for a state church is one reason we have such a remarkable array of religious faiths. The Framers also abandoned primogeniture, which in Europe had meant all of the property and wealth in a family went to the eldest son. This structural difference plus the abundant land to settle helped foster a more democratic culture. But the structure of government was also important. Over the course of history we have become more egalitarian (often with changes to our structure through constitutional amendments), which has allowed women, younger persons, African Americans, and others greater access to rights and liberties. With increased education and wealth have come greater opportunities for action. It is also the case that action has been essential to the inclusion of once excluded groups in our democratic experiment. The ways our country has changed to include more people in the process and expand opportunity is an important example of our theme that structure plus action equals impact.

REVIEW THE CHAPTER

Geography, Natural Resources, and the Importance of Where We Are From (Structure, Action, and Impact)

4.1 Assess the role of geography, natural resources, and type of community in building a national and local identity, p. 81.

The United States is a continental nation, which has provided ample land for population growth and access to both the Atlantic and Pacific Oceans. Our people have benefited from abundant natural resources. These characteristics help explain American politics and traditions, including the notions of manifest destiny, ethnocentrism, and isolationism. Social and economic differences can foster conflict and violence.

For much of U.S. history, the South has been a distinct region in the United States, in large part because of its agricultural base and its history of slavery and troubled race relations. Today, the region is Republican and conservative. Other regional clusters that have political relevance include the upper-Midwest states, which once had a strong manufacturing economy but more recently have been in decline (Rust Belt), and the West, with large open spaces and with much of the land under the control of the federal government. Other regions include the Bible Belt and Sun Belt. People also live in communities that are classified as urban, suburban, and rural. These differences have political significance, as these living environments foster different kinds of issues and concerns and different styles of politics. Recently, the most significant migration in the United States has been from cities to suburbs. Today, many large U.S. cities are increasingly poor, African American, and Democratic, surrounded by suburbs that are primarily middle class, white, and Republican.

Who We Are (Structure, Action, and Impact)

4.2 Analyze how such social and demographic factors as race and ethnicity, religion, gender, family structures, education, and age affect American politics, p. 86.

Race has been and remains among the most important of the differences in our political landscape. Although we fought a civil war over freedom for African Americans, racial equality was largely postponed until the latter half of the twentieth century. Ethnicity, including the rising number of Hispanics, continues to be a factor in politics. The United States has many religious denominations, and these differences, including between those who are religious and those who are not, help explain public opinion and political behavior. Gender, sexual orientation, and family structures have become more important in politics. Women who once lagged behind men in voting now surpass them. Laws relating to sexual orientation reflect the changing public opinion landscape and the growing influence of gay rights organizations. Age and education remain very important to understanding political participation.

How Much We Own (Structure, Action, and Impact)

4.3 Describe the importance of income, wealth, occupation, and social class in American politics, p. 100.

Throughout U.S. history one of the most important sources of political division has been the unequal distribution of income and wealth. Although some people in America continue to achieve great wealth and there remains a large middle class, the gap between the most affluent and the remainder of society has grown in recent decades. It became the source of protest and conflict in the Occupy Wall Street movement. At the same time and in part due to the recession of the 2008–2010 period, poverty has grown, especially among African Americans, Native Americans, Hispanics, and single-parent households. Women as a group continue to earn less than men, even in the same occupations.

LEARN THE TERMS

manifest destiny, p. 82
Sun Belt, p. 84
Bible Belt, p. 84
Rust Belt, p. 84
urban, p. 84
suburban, p. 84
rural, p. 84
demography, p. 86
ethnocentrism, p. 86
reinforcing cleavages, p. 86
cross-cutting cleavages, p. 86
race, p. 87
ethnicity, p. 87
fundamentalists, p. 93
gender gap, p. 95
American dream, p. 101
capitalism, p. 101
gross domestic product (GDP), p. 104
socioeconomic status (SES), p. 105
American exceptionalism, p. 105

Interest Groups

CHAPTER 5

As part of its annual convention the National Rifle Association (NRA) has an exhibit space where firearms are displayed and sales promoted. The NRA is a powerful interest group in protecting and extending gun rights Here attendees walk past a display by SOTA Arms, a manufacturer of parts and accessories for assault rifles (AR-15's and AR-10's), weapons like those used in the mass shootings at the Newtown, Connecticut elementary school in 2012; a nightclub in Orlando, Florida in 2016; a music festival in Las Vegas, Nevada in 2017; and the Marjory Stoneman Douglas High School in Parkland, Florida in 2018, among others.

LEARNING OBJECTIVES

5.1 Describe why interest groups form and how they attract members (Structure), p. 110.

5.2 Describe different types of interest groups (Action), p. 114.

5.3 Analyze the methods and activities that interest groups use to influence political outcomes (Action), p. 120.

5.4 Evaluate the factors that affect the relative success of interest groups (Impact), p. 126.

5.5 Assess the effectiveness of regulations designed to control interest groups (Impact), p. 134.

The National Rifle Association (NRA) is among the most powerful interest groups in American politics. The lobbying arm of the NRA is the NRA Institute for Legislative Action (NRA-ILA). The NRA takes a keen interest in congressional and presidential elections. In 2016, for example, the NRA spent more than $30 million in support of Donald Trump, triple what it spent in the 2012 presidential election for Mitt Romney. When we include spending by its Super PAC, the NRA spent a combined $54 million on the 2016 elections, including spending in races for other federal offices.[1] While its membership is not as large as some other organizations, the NRA members feel passionately about access to firearms and are willing to take action and make voting decisions on the issue. Based on candidates' gun-related voting record and the group's questionnaire, the NRA assigns a letter grade from "A" to "F" to candidates for offices ranging from the state legislature to the president. The NRA then sends candidate grades to all NRA members in a personalized form that includes each candidate on that member's ballot and their grades. In the 2016 presidential debates, Republican party candidates occasionally mentioned their own NRA grades, or criticized others for low grades. Most GOP contenders had A or A+ grades, but New Jersey governor Chris Christie, who dropped out of the race early in February 2016, had only a C+. Democratic candidates Bernie Sanders had a D- and Hillary Clinton an F.[2] Not surprisingly, candidates with low NRA grades, may face opposition from NRA members and friends, as well as substantial independent spending against them from NRA affiliated groups.

One reason the NRA has long dominated the politics of gun legislation is that there are not equally powerful interest groups on the other side of the issue. That has started to change as former New York Mayor Michael Bloomberg formed a group, Everytown for Gun Safety, and Americans for Responsible Solutions, groups that spent over $180,000 and $54 million, respectively, in direct contributions and independent expenditures in 2016.[3] After another horrific school shooting in which 17 people were killed in February 2018, some families of students at Parkland, Florida's Marjory Stoneman Douglas High School, formed a new Super PAC and nonprofit group to counter the NRA. The group is named, "Families vs. Assault Rifles."[4] In addition to these groups, Stoneman Douglas students also organized "March for Our Lives" rallies in Florida, Washington, D.C., and around the United States, drawing significant attention and support for sensible restrictions on guns, particularly assault rifles.

While groups are important to organizing in a democracy, they can also be a threat to self-government. If one group becomes so dominant that it can intimidate or exclude other groups from forming, then liberty itself is at risk. Having a set of agreed-upon processes helps protect everyone from such abuses. In the sensitive area of workers and employers, groups over time have worked out laws and practices that protect both sides. An active news media reporting on what groups seek to accomplish and who is promoting them is also important. Protecting basic political rights like freedom of speech, of the press, and of assembly are also part of what is needed to protect against too much concentration of power in any one group.

Striking a balance in providing freedom to form and participate in groups and encouraging competition between groups while not permitting them to become so dominant that they can erode liberty is an ongoing challenge. You will have to decide when a group needs protection from a larger and more powerful adversary. For example, in campaign finance, should corporations be given the same rights as individuals to spend their money independently in campaigns? Should those injured by a defective product or hurt in an accident be limited in how much their attorney can win in a court settlement? The competition between interests impacts everyone all the time.

The founders understood that individuals would organize themselves around common interests. At the same time, since the founding, observers have been concerned about the power of groups that focus on their self-interest at the expense of the general public. Therefore, our governmental structure provides some checks on interest groups, one of which is disclosure of who is part of a group and how much they are spending on elections (structure). Restraining the negative tendencies of interest groups while protecting their liberty is not easy. It is mostly through groups that citizens seek to influence government (action). In this chapter, we examine the full range of interest group activities as well as what difference they make in politics and policy (impact). Finally, we also assess efforts to limit their potentially negative influences, including reforming campaign finance regulations (action).

You have the good fortune of having substantial freedom to organize and participate in groups. An understanding of how groups function and pursue political aims will prepare you for participation that is more effective. This may be useful in college, neighborhood, city, state, or national matters. You may form a group yourself or join an existing group. In either case, you and others involved can shape the group and play a role in its activities. More broadly, all citizens have a stake in making sure no one group or set of groups is "rigging the rules" to their benefit. This means you not only need to be concerned with your particular interest but also the broader interest of good democratic practices.

The Reasons Interest Groups Endure and the "Mischiefs of Faction" They Produce (Structure)

5.1 Describe why interest groups form and how they attract members.

It may come as a surprise that you are already represented by several interest groups because of personal characteristics like your gender, race, ethnicity, or religion. As a student, you are assumed to be part of a group concerned about issues such as student loans and the cost of tuition. Your hobby of flying drones probably means you have connected with other drone enthusiasts to oppose limits on what you see as safe and fun. If you happened to apply for a credit or debit card, a car loan, or a mortgage or rental agreement, you were likely asked to provide your Social Security number, driver's license number, employer, income, and bank account information.as well as your full name, address, and telephone number. In 2017, Equifax, one of the companies that collects and stores this information for lenders and calculates credit ratings on individuals, was hacked and that the security of this information on as many as 143 million Americans was compromised. You, and many others, were suddenly part of a group concerned about possible identity theft. Pressure from citizens and elected officials led to the resignation of the CEO of Equifax.[5] Over time, almost all Americans will find themselves working with others who share common interests and seek similar outcomes. The structure of American government and modern communications tools make forming interest groups easy, and these groups often take action and have an impact.

As humans, we naturally form groups. This may come from an evolutionary basis, where people had a better chance of survival as groups than as individuals.[6] Individuals also understand that groups often help them accomplish their goals. We also turn to groups for social acceptance.[7] The utility of groups in politics was recognized long before the founding of the United States, but the structure of our government encourages people to associate in groups, while at the same time the Constitution seeks to limit the potential negative consequences of groups becoming too powerful. For example, federalism provides multiple points of access for groups to seek to influence policy, the structure of Congress means each person has two senators and one House member as well as the president, whom they can seek to persuade to their point of view. Freedom of the press, association, and petition allows groups to take their message to the public.

From the beginning of our experiment with self-government, Americans have organized into groups to achieve their political goals. The importance of the freedom to form and participate in groups is found in the structure of the Bill of Rights, which guarantees freedom of assembly. As the economy, society, and politics have changed, so have the array of groups active in politics. During our more agrarian period, farm groups were especially important. When women won the right to vote in 1920, the

League of Women Voters was formed with the objective of helping women "carry out their new responsibilities as voters."[8] Today the League is important in fostering good government efforts and election activities like candidate debates. People often form groups around particular issues—medicinal marijuana, funding for the arts, or restrictions on what landlords can do to renters, for instance.

The founders of the Republic were very worried about groups with common interests, which they called **factions**. (They also thought of political parties as factions.) For the Framers of the Constitution, the daunting problem was how to establish a stable and orderly constitutional system that would both respect the liberty of free citizens and prevent the tyranny of the majority or of a single dominant interest.

faction
A term the founders used to refer to political parties and special interests or interest groups.

As a talented practical politician and a brilliant theorist, James Madison offered both a diagnosis and a solution in *The Federalist*, No. 10. He began with a basic proposition: "The latent causes of faction are ... sown in the nature of man." All individuals pursue their self-interest, seeking advantage or power over others. Acknowledging that we live in a maze of group interests, Madison argued that the "most common and durable source of factions has been the various and unequal distribution of property." Madison defined a faction as "a number of citizens, whether amounting to a majority or minority of the whole, who are united and actuated by some common impulse of passion, or of interest, adverse to the rights of other citizens, or to the permanent and aggregate interests of the community." For Madison, "the *causes* of faction cannot be removed, and ... relief is only to be sought in the means of controlling its *effects*."[9]

A Nation of Interests

Some U.S. citizens identify with groups distinguished by race, gender, ethnic background, age, occupation, religion, or sexual orientation. Others form voluntary groups based on their opinions about issues such as gun control or tax reduction. When such associations seek to influence government, they are called **interest groups**.

interest group
A collection of people who share a common interest or attitude and seek to influence government for specific ends. Interest groups usually work within the framework of government and try to achieve their goals through tactics such as lobbying.

Interest groups are also sometimes called "special interests," implying that they are not concerned with the good of all. Politicians and the media often use this term in a pejorative way while not specifying what makes an interest group "special." The term is highly subjective. One person's *special* interest is another's *public* interest. However, so-called public interest groups such as Common Cause or the League of Women Voters support policies that not everyone agrees with. Politics is best seen as a clash among interests, with differing concepts of what is in the public interest, rather than as a battle between the special interests on one side and "the people" or the public interest on the other.

In fact, the term "special interest" conveys a selfish or narrow view, one that may lack credibility. For this reason, we use the neutral term "interest groups." An interest group simply speaks for some, but not all, of us. A democracy includes many interests and many organized interest groups. The democratic process exists to decide among them.

Attracting Members

Madison was correct in his view that humans, when involved in politics, naturally form groups. Individuals join groups because of a common interest, because of a shared identification, or because of an issue or concern. James Q. Wilson and Peter B. Clark have taken Madison's idea and expanded it to identify three primary sets of incentives for individuals to join groups: material, solidary, and purposive incentives.[10] *Material* incentives have to do with a tangible reward, often monetary, that can result from joining the group. Taxpayer groups, labor unions, and business associations are all examples of organizations whose members join because they see the government as helping or hurting them in material ways and they see the group as beneficial to securing this benefit. *Solidary* incentives give individuals a sense of belonging or status from their group association. Here the incentive is more social than economic. The Veterans of Foreign Wars is a group that veterans join out of a sense of group identity that also seeks to influence how our government treats veterans. The third motivation to form a group, *purposive* incentives, is driven more by the goals of the organization and how they relate to an individual's issue concerns. People who feel strongly about the environment may join the League of Conservation Voters, while those wanting to limit abortion may become involved with right-to-life groups. This set of motives is not exhaustive. A broad generalization is that Americans have a proclivity to form groups, and often these groups become involved with seeking to influence government.

Social Movements

social movement
A large body of people interested in a common issue, idea, or concern that is of continuing significance and who are willing to take action. Movements seek to change attitudes or institutions, not just policies.

Interest groups sometimes begin as social movements. A **social movements** consists of many people interested in an issue, idea, or concern who are willing to take action to support or oppose it. Examples include civil rights, environmental causes, anti-tax groups, animal rights, women's rights, the Christian Right, LGBTQ rights, anti-immigration movements, and antiwar movements. In some respects, the Tea Party groups that formed in 2009 and 2010 and remained active through the 2012 election are examples of social movements. The Tea Party began in early 2009, not long after Barack Obama took office; groups started forming to protest the $787 billion economic stimulus package, officially known as the American Recovery and Reinvestment Act of 2009. These groups adopted the name Tea Party, a reference to the Boston Tea Party of 1773, when colonists rebelled against what they thought to be unfair British taxes on tea. The group's general concerns are about increasing government spending and growing government power. While exhibiting many characteristics of a social movement, the Tea Party has also become part of the Republican Party. In 2017, a social movement against sexual harassment and assault known as #metoo, gained widespread attention. Press reports about sexual misconduct allegations against Hollywood producer Harvey Weinstein focused attention on the issue. The press played an important role in uncovering patterns of abuse in prominent figures in politics, media, the arts, and the corporate world. The 2018 shooting of fourteen high school students, a teacher, administrator. and coach in Parkland, Florida, became a national movement for changes in gun laws. The students used social media to organize national demonstrations, including hundreds of school walkouts in the United States. Their advocacy for gun law changes was successful in Florida.[11]

The Bill of Rights protects movements, popular or unpopular, by upholding free assembly, free speech, and due process. Consequently, those who disagree with government policies do not have to engage in violence or other extreme activities in the

Stella Artois partnered with Water.org and its cofounders, Matt Damon and Gary White, on a campaign to increase awareness of the 660 million people around the world who live without access to clean water. Water.org is an international nonprofit organization working to encourage the rising generation to be the one that ends the global water crisis.

United States, as they do in some countries, and they need not fear prosecution for demonstrating peacefully. In a democratic system that restricts the power of government, movements have considerable room to operate *within* the constitutional system.

Mischiefs of Faction

James Madison played a critical role in drafting and enacting the Constitution, and many of its provisions are aimed at limiting the "mischiefs of faction," where groups would seek to gain power over other groups, be concerned about self-interest more than national interest, and restrict liberty. These provisions include separation of powers, checks and balances, bicameralism, and federalism, which make it hard for a faction to change the direction of government. Staggered terms of office make it necessary for a faction to endure. Rather than trying to encourage one or another faction, the Constitution encourages competition between them. Indeed, checks and balances arguably function best when factions within the branches work to counter one another. The Constitution envisions a plurality of groups competing with each other, an idea that has been called **pluralism**.

pluralism
A theory of government that holds that open, multiple, and competing groups can check the asserted power of any one group.

But a well-organized and well-funded faction may be able to exploit checks and balances to block government action, even if a majority favors it. One example is the efforts to expand background checks for gun buyers after the Newtown, Connecticut, shooting in December 2012.[12] Despite a strong push by President Obama and overwhelming public support for action on guns, Congress failed to act in part due to the power of the NRA. After the shooting in Parkland, Florida, however, students successfully pressured the Florida legislature to change the state's gun laws by raising the minimum age to buy guns to 21 from 18, establishing a 3 day waiting period to buy guns, banning bump stocks, providing additional funds for school security, including arming school employees, and to expanding mental health services.[13] Gun control groups did not have as much success in Congress where they failed to get legislative action.

Rights for persons with disabilities are now taken for granted, but for much of U.S. history they received little attention. Legislation like the Americans with Disabilities Act made it law that buildings and facilities be accessible to persons with limited mobility. Here at a 2010 March for Jobs, Peace & Justice Organized by United Auto Workers and Rainbow Push in Detroit, Michigan, called attention to the need for jobs for persons with disabilities.

How well pluralism has worked in practice is debated.[14] We will see that over time, government has sought to regulate factions as a response to the power some groups such as corporations, unions, and wealthy individuals have had in American government. The debate about how to check their power without damaging their liberty is an enduring one. As we will discuss later in this chapter and others, other possible mischiefs of faction are their role in supporting candidates or those opposing them through large campaign expenditures.

Types of Interest Groups (Action)

5.2 Describe different types of interest groups.

Some interest groups are formal associations or organizations, like the National Association of Home Builders (NAHB); others have no formal organization, like airline passengers. Some are organized primarily to persuade public officials on issues of concern to the group, such as reducing greenhouse gases; others conduct research or influence public opinion with published reports and mass mailings.

We can categorize interest groups into several broad types: (1) economic, including business, trade, labor, and professional associations; (2) ideological or single-issue; (3) public interest; (4) foreign policy; and (5) public sector interest groups or government itself. Obviously, these categories are not mutually exclusive.

Most American adults are represented by a number of interest groups, even if they do not know it. For instance, people age 50 and older may not know that the AARP (which began as the American Association of Retired Persons) claims to represent *all* older citizens, not only those who are actually members. Similarly, the American Automobile Association (AAA) claims to represent all motorists, not only those who join. The varied and overlapping nature of interest groups in the United States has been described as *interest group pluralism,* meaning that competition among open, responsive, and diverse groups helps preserve democratic values and limits the concentration of power in any single group. We look at each category of interest group next.

Economic Interest Groups

There are thousands of economic interest groups: agriculture, consumers, plumbers, the airplane industry, landlords, truckers, bondholders, property owners, and more. Economic interest groups pursue what benefits them both financially and politically.

BUSINESS The most familiar business institution is the large corporation. Corporations range from one-person enterprises to vast multinational entities. General Motors, AT&T, Microsoft, Coca-Cola, McDonald's, Wal-Mart, Wall Street banks, investment firms, and other large companies exercise considerable political influence, as do hundreds of smaller corporations. For example, as Microsoft and Wal-Mart came under heightened government and public scrutiny, their political contributions expanded in an effort to enhance their access to policy makers.[15] Corporate power and a changing American and global economy make business practices important political issues.

Cooperation between groups can increase their effectiveness, giving even small business an important voice in public policy. The Commerce Department, for example, includes a Small Business Administration. Small businesses are also organized into groups such as the National Federation of Independent Business (NFIB) that help elect pro-business candidates and persuade the national government on behalf of members.

TRADE AND OTHER ASSOCIATIONS Businesses with similar interests join together as *trade associations,* which are as diverse as the products and services they provide. Businesses of all types are also organized into large nationwide associations such as the National Association of Realtors, and smaller ones like the American Wind Energy Association.

The broadest business trade association is the Chamber of Commerce of the United States. Organized in 1912, the Chamber is a federation of thousands of local Chambers of Commerce representing millions of businesses. Loosely allied with the Chamber on most issues is the National Association of Manufacturers, which, since 1893, has tended to speak for the more conservative elements of American business.

LABOR Workers' associations have a range of interests, including professional standards, wages, and working conditions. The level of unionization has policy consequences. For example, a nation's minimum wage rates increase with unionization. Labor unions are one of the most important groups representing workers, yet the American workforce is among the least unionized of any industrial democracy.[16] (See Figure 5.1.)

Throughout the nineteenth century, American workers organized political parties and local unions. Their most ambitious effort at national organization, the Knights of Labor, registered 700,000 members in the 1890s. But by approximately 1900, the American Federation of Labor (AFL), a confederation of strong and independent-minded national unions mainly representing craft workers, was the dominant organization. During the 1930s, unions more responsive to industrial workers broke away from the AFL and formed a rival national organization of industry groups, the Congress of Industrial Organizations (CIO). In 1955, the AFL and CIO reunited. In 2005, more than a third of AFL-CIO members (4.5 of 13 million members) affiliated

FIGURE 5.1 UNION MEMBERSHIP IN THE UNITED STATES COMPARED TO OTHER COUNTRIES

Compared to other industrialized countries the United States has a much lower level of unionization. Scandinavian countries have the highest level of union membership with more than two-thirds of the workforce in unions. Much of the rest of Europe is between 25 and 50 percent unionized. Germany and Japan, two large economies, are 18 percent unionized. The United States has long had lower percentages of the workforce in unions but recent declines in union membership has increased the difference with other nations.

SOURCES: https://stats.oecd.org/Index.aspx?DataSetCode=TUD; https://www.forbes.com/sites/niallmccarthy/2017/06/20/which-countries-have-the-highest-levels-of-labor-union-membership-infographic/#5882597133c0.

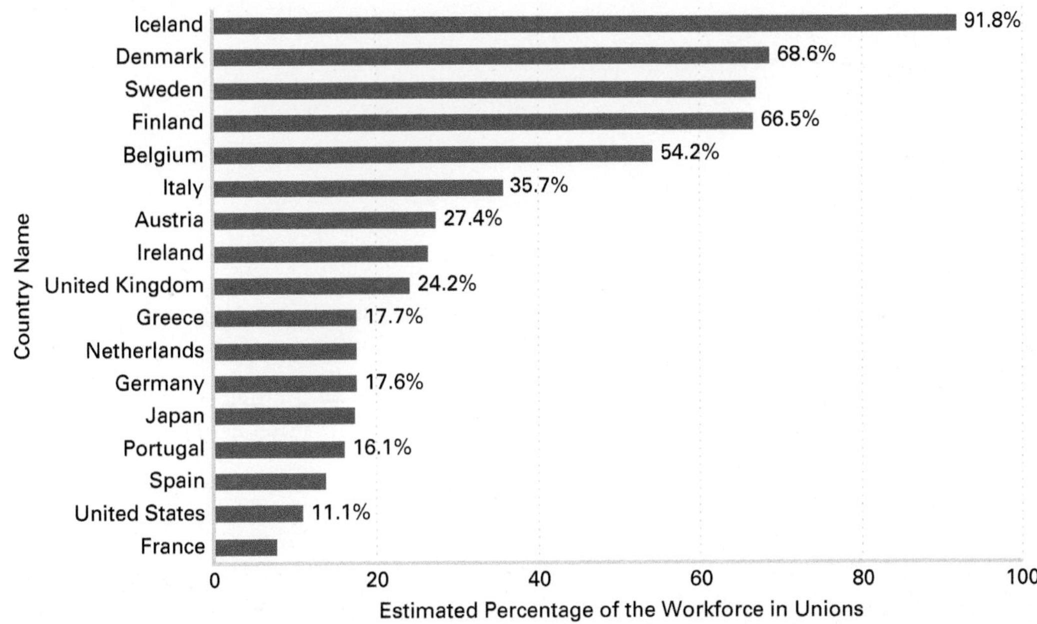

with the Service Employees International Union (SEIU), the International Brotherhood of Teamsters, and two other unions split off from the AFL-CIO, forming a new group named the Change to Win Federation.[17] Unions today are thus less unified, but by 2007, dues paid to the AFL-CIO exceeded levels before the division.[18] Unions have been at the forefront in using personalized appeals to their members and are seen as among the most effective groups in voter mobilization.[19] The AFL-CIO speaks for approximately three-fourths of unionized labor,[20] and unions represent about 11 percent of the nation's workforce (see Figure 5.2).[21]

open shop
A company with a labor agreement under which union membership cannot be required as a condition of employment.

closed shop
A company with a labor agreement under which union membership can be a condition of employment.

collective bargaining
The process in which a union represents a group of employees in negotiations with the employer about wages, benefits, and workplace safety.

free rider
An individual who does not join a group representing his or her interests yet receives the benefit of the group's influence.

Union membership is optional in more than half of the states, where laws permit **open shop** companies, in which workers cannot be required to join a union as a condition of employment. Kentucky was the latest state to adopt open-shop rules in 2017. In **closed shop** states, workers may be required to join a union to be hired at a particular company if most employees at that company vote to unionize. In both cases, the unions negotiate with management, and all workers share the benefits the unions gain, a process known as **collective bargaining**. In open-shop states, many workers may choose not to affiliate with a union because they can secure the same benefits that unionized workers enjoy without incurring the costs of joining the union. When a person benefits from the work or service of an organization like a union (or even a public TV or radio station) without joining or contributing to it, this condition is referred to as the **free rider** problem. For example, unions that achieve wage concessions from management do so for all workers in and out of the union. This results in little incentive to join the union or support it financially.

As large membership organizations, unions have long been important participants in election campaigns. Since 1998, unions have emphasized direct contact with members and their families through mail, email, on the phone, and in person. They have organized get-out-the-vote drives and paid for television advertising. Unlike in 2000, when unions were important to securing Al Gore's nomination,[22] in the 2004 and 2008 Democratic presidential primaries they were divided. In 2008, some unions such as SEIU and the Change to Win Federation supported Senator Barack Obama, whereas the United Steel

FIGURE 5.2 UNION MEMBERSHIP AMONG ALL WAGE AND SALARY WORKERS

The proportion of the U.S. workforce belonging to unions has fallen, in part because of the shift from an industrial to a service and information economy. Dwindling membership limits organized labor's influence.

Sources: © 2018 by Barry T. Hirsch and David A. Macpherson. 1930–1972: Richard B. Freeman, "Spurts in Union Growth: Defining Moments and Social Processes"; 1973–2017: Hirsch and Macpherson, www.unionstats.com.

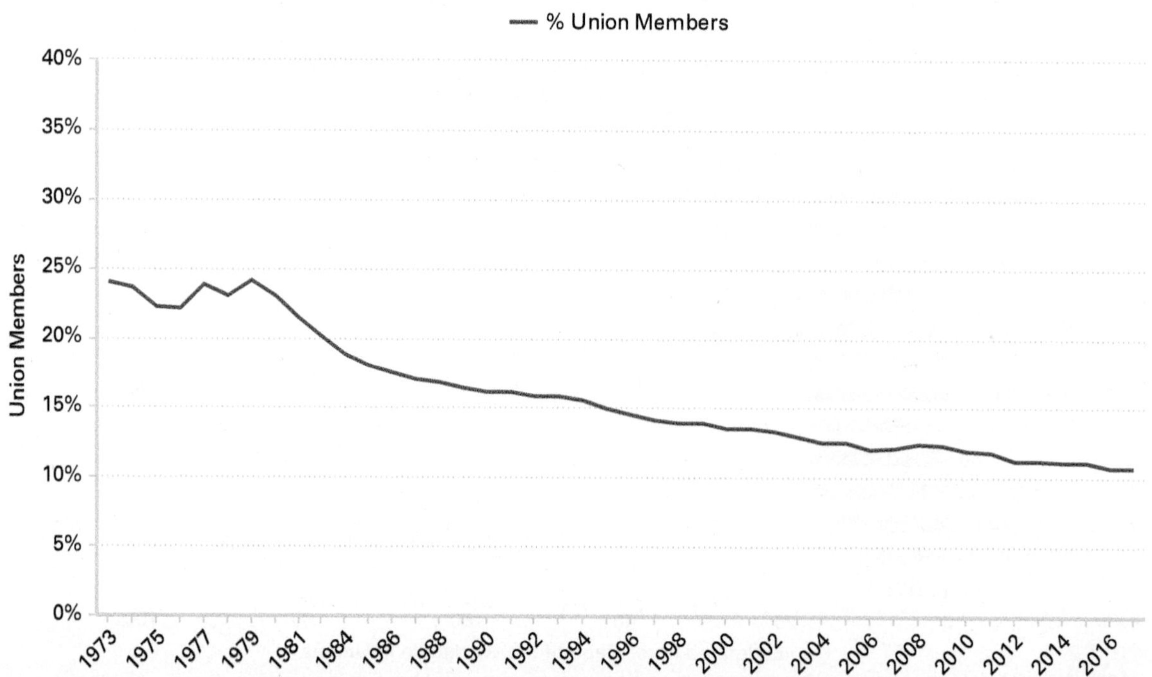

Workers supported John Edwards, and the American Federation of State, County, and Municipal Employees (AFSCME) supported Senator Hillary Clinton. In 2016, AFSCME along with SEIU and NEA endorsed Hillary Clinton early in the Democratic nomination contest against Bernie Sanders. The Communications Workers of America and the National Nurses United, the largest U.S. nurses' union, supported Bernie Sanders. A Super PAC associated with the nurses' union spent more than $2.5 million in support of Sanders.[23] In the 2016 general election, unions overwhelmingly backed Clinton through contributions and independent expenditures. In the 2012 general election, unions were unified in backing Obama, and in 2016 Clinton received most union endorsements, including the major unions. An exception was the Firefighters Union.

Traditionally identified with the Democratic Party, unions have not enjoyed a close relationship with Republican legislatures or executives. Given labor's limited resources, one option for unions is to form temporary coalitions with consumer, public interest, liberal, and sometimes even industry groups, especially on issues related to foreign imports. Unions opposed the Trans Pacific Partnership (TPP) trade agreement in 2016. President Obama supported the agreement but both Hillary Clinton and Donald Trump opposed it during the 2016 election campaign. Once elected, President Trump withdrew from TPP and entered into negotaitions on changes to NAFTA. Labor has been unsuccessful in blocking free trade agreements like the North American Free Trade Agreement (NAFTA) and it opposed the TPP in 2016.[24] Weeks before the 2018 midterm elections, the U.S., Mexico, and Canada agreed to a new trade agreement named the "United States-Mexico-Canada Agreement" (USMCA), which President Trump pointed to as evidence that his approach to trade was working.

PROFESSIONAL ASSOCIATIONS Professional people join **professional associations** such as the American Medical Association (AMA) and the American Bar Association (ABA), which serve some of the same functions as unions. Other professions are divided into many subgroups. Teachers and professors, for example, belong to the National Education Association, the American Federation of Teachers, and the American Association of University Professors, and also to subgroups based on specialties, such as the Modern Language Association and the American Political Science Association.

professional associations
Groups of individuals who share a common profession and are often organized for common political purposes related to that profession.

Government, especially at the state level, regulates many professions. Lawyers are licensed by states, which, often because of pressure from lawyers themselves, set standards of admission to the state bar. Professional associations also use the courts to pursue their agendas. In the area of medical malpractice, for example, doctors lobby hard for limited-liability laws, while trial lawyers resist them. Teachers, hairstylists, and marriage therapists are licensed by states and work for or against legislation that concerns them. It is not surprising, then, that groups representing professional associations such as the AMA and the National Association of Home Builders are among the largest donors to political campaigns.

Ideological or Single-Issue Interest Groups

Ideological groups focus on issues—often a single issue. Members generally share a common view and a desire for government to pursue policies consistent with it. Such *single-issue* groups are often unwilling to compromise. Right-to-life and pro-choice groups on abortion fit this description, as do the NRA and anti-immigration groups.

Countless groups have organized around other specific issues, such as civil liberties, environmental protection, nuclear energy, and nuclear disarmament.[25] Such associations are not new. The Anti-Saloon League of the 1890s was devoted solely to barring the sale and manufacture of alcoholic beverages, and it did not care whether legislators were drunk or sober as long as they voted dry. One of the best-known single-issue groups today is the NRA, with almost 4 million members committed to protecting the right to bear arms.[26] Other single-issue groups include the Club for Growth, a generally libertarian and anti-tax group, and Planned Parenthood, a pro-choice on abortion group.

Planned Parenthood is a nonprofit organization providing reproductive health care. It grew out of the first birth control clinic in the United States, founded in 1916. It is the largest provider of reproductive health services, including abortion, in the country. The group is also active in politics, contributing nearly $1 million to candidates and parties in 2016, and spending another $15 million independently. In this photo, Carolyn Williamson and others express support for Planned Parenthood and opposition to a health care act being considered in Congress.

Environmental groups are among the most active interest groups. Among the best known of these groups is the Sierra Club. Founded in 1892, the Sierra Club is the oldest and largest environmental organization. The Sierra Club is active in environmental protection efforts in states and local communities, and it has a lobbying presence in Washington, D.C. Another group known for its efforts to elect pro-environment candidates is the League of Conservation Voters (LCV). The Environmental Defense Fund, Environment America, National Resources Defense Council, Sierra Club, World Wildlife Fund, and a host of other environmental groups have members and paid staff committed to protecting wildlife and securing, preserving, and protecting wilderness.

Single-issue groups often align with other groups on either the left or the right. Groups that are more liberal include the environmental, pro-choice, and labor groups. Groups that are more conservative include business, anti-tax, pro-life, and pro-gun groups. Some groups focus on multiple issues. For example, on the conservative side are groups like Heritage Action and American Conservative Union, and on the left are groups like MoveOn.org and People for the American Way.

Public Interest Groups

Out of the political ferment of the 1960s came groups claiming to promote "the public interest." For example, Common Cause campaigns for electoral reform, for making the political process more open and participatory, and to stem media consolidation. Its Washington staff raises money through direct-mail campaigns, oversees state chapters of the group, and publishes research reports and press releases on current issues, and lobbies Congress and government departments.

After uncovering design flaws in the Ford Pinto in 1977 that resulted in 180 deaths, consumer activists like Ralph Nader charged Ford "with sacrificing human lives for profit."[27] Ralph Nader was instrumental in forming organizations to investigate and report on governmental and corporate action—or inaction—relating to consumer interests. Public interest research groups (PIRGs), as these groups are called, today seek to influence policy on Capitol Hill and in several state legislatures on environmental issues, safe energy, and consumer protection.

Foreign Policy Interest Groups

Interest groups also organize to promote or oppose foreign policies to Congress and the president. Among the most prestigious is the Council on Foreign Relations in New York City. Some of these interest groups have been trying to influence American policy regarding China's refusal to grant independence for Tibet. Human rights groups have been calling on the U.S. government to close the prison at Guantanamo, Cuba.[28] Other groups support or oppose free trade. Foreign policy groups should not be confused with foreign governments and interest groups in other nations, which are banned from making campaign contributions but often seek to influence policy through lobbying firms.

One of the most influential foreign policy groups is the American Israel Political Action Committee (AIPAC), with more than 100,000 members.[29] Because AIPAC's primary focus is influencing government directly, not distributing campaign funds, it is not required to disclose where its money comes from or goes. AIPAC's successes include enactment of aid packages to Israel, passage of the 1985 United States–Israel Free Trade Agreement, emergency assistance to Israel in the wake of the 1992 Gulf War, and promoting moving the U.S. Embassy to Jerusalem.[30] Its counterpart, the Arab American Institute, lobbies to support Arab causes. Efforts to secure a negotiated settlement between the Palestinians and Israel have kept U.S. interest groups on both sides visible and important.

Nongovernmental organizations (NGOs), nonprofit groups that operate outside the institutions of government but often pursue public policy objectives and lobby governments, are another type of foreign policy interest group. The most common are social, cultural, or environmental groups such as the Boys and Girls Clubs of America, CARE, Red Cross, Save the Children, and the Humane Society of the United States.

nongovernmental organization (NGO)
A nonprofit association or group operating outside government that advocates and pursues policy objectives.

Public Sector Interest Groups

Governments are themselves important interest groups. Many cities and most states retain Washington lobbyists, individuals who advocate on behalf of the city or state before Congress and with the executive branch of the federal government. Governors are organized through the National Governors Association, cities through the National

A lawsuit brought by the family of a deceased victim in Georgia led to the discovery that General Motors had installed faulty ignition switches that led to engine shutoffs and airbags not deploying. The number of people who died in accidents due to the defect exceeded 100. GM knew about the defect for at least a decade before the 2014 recall, which involved more than 29 million cars in North America. Here a family member at a hearing of a subcommittee of the Senate Commerce and Transportation Committee holds a photo of Kelly Ruddy and a photo of the Chevrolet Cobalt in which she died.

League of Cities, and counties through the National Association of Counties. Other officials—lieutenant governors, secretaries of state, mayors—have their own national associations as well.

Government employees form a large and well-organized group. The National Education Association (NEA), for example, has 3.2 million members.[31] The NEA endorses politicians from both parties but more typically supports Democrats. In 2008 and 2012, the NEA endorsed Barack Obama for the presidency. In 2016, the NEA and AFSCME endorsed Hillary Clinton for the Democratic nomination, and were part of her general coalition as well.[32] The NEA fits the definition of a professional association, labor union, and public sector interest group. Donald Trump was endorsed by the Fraternal Order of the Police,[33] and by the National Border Patrol Council (the union representing border patrol agents), a group which had not previously made a presidential endorsement.[34] Once in office, however, he issued several executive orders to curtail the influence of unions that represent federal employees, including a June 2018 order reducing the amount of time union officials can spend representing their members.

Other Interest Groups

American adults are often emotionally and financially engaged by a wide variety of groups: veterans' groups, nationality groups, and religious organizations, among others. Women's organizations have long been important in advocating for equal rights, most notably for the right to vote. Among the best-known group in the area of political rights for women is the League of Women Voters, formed in 1920 and with chapters in all 50 states. Some groups adopt a narrower focus on gender and politics and would be classified as a single-issue group. Interest groups with a focus on reproductive rights include NARAL Pro-Choice America or Planned Parenthood. More broadly focused is the National Organization of Women (NOW).

Characteristics and Power of Interest Groups (Action)

5.3 Analyze the methods and activities that interest groups use to influence political outcomes.

An important aspect of the relative power of groups is the size and cohesion of their membership. Securing the participation of individuals in groups—what economist Mancur Olson labeled **collective action**[35] and others describe as **public choice**[36]—is challenging because often the benefits from the group efforts are shared with everyone, including those who do not participate in the work of securing the benefit. This creates the *free rider* problem. Groups seek to counter the free rider problem by providing incentives or benefits to only those individuals who join the group (selective benefits), communicate about the purposes of the group hoping to motivate participation on this basis, and by making group activity socially desirable.[37] Another marker of interest group power is how well the group does in influencing policy making and implementation. Individuals who try to influence policy decisions and positions, often representing groups, are called **lobbyists**. The term "lobbying" was not generally used until around the mid-nineteenth century in the United States. This refers to the lobby or hallway outside the House and Senate chambers in the U.S. Capitol and to those who hung around the lobby of the old Willard Hotel in Washington, D.C., when presidents dined there. The noun "lobby" is now used as a verb.

collective action
How groups form and organize to pursue their goals or objectives, including how to get individuals and groups to participate and cooperate. The term has many applications in the various social sciences such as political science, sociology, and economics.

public choice
Synonymous with "collective action," specifically studies how government officials, politicians, and voters respond to positive and negative incentives.

lobbyist
A person who is employed by and acts for an organized interest group or corporation to try to influence policy decisions and positions in the executive and legislative branches.

Despite their negative public image, lobbyists perform useful functions for government. They provide information for decision makers in all three branches of government, help educate and mobilize public opinion, help prepare legislation and testify before legislative hearings, and contribute a large share of the costs of campaigns. However, many people fear that lobbyists have too much influence on government and add to legislative gridlock by stopping action on pressing problems.

Who Are the Lobbyists?

The typical image of policy making is of powerful, hard-nosed lobbyists who use a combination of knowledge, persuasiveness, personal influence, charm, and money to influence legislators and bureaucrats. Often former public servants themselves, lobbyists are experienced in government and often go to work for one of the interests they dealt with while in government, or for a lobbying firm.

Moving from a government job to a job with an interest group—or vice versa—is so common that this career path is called the **revolving door**. Although it is illegal for former national government employees to lobby directly the agency from which they came, their contacts made during government service are helpful to interest groups. Many former members of Congress use their prior congressional experience as full-time lobbyists. Of those who left Congress or lost seats in the 2014 or 2016 election and have found new employment, 46 percent are employed by lobbying firms and 18 percent are employed by lobbying clients.[38]

revolving door
An employment cycle in which individuals who work for government agencies that regulate interests eventually end up working for interest groups or businesses with the same policy concern.

In 2007, Congress passed the Honest Leadership and Open Government Act, which requires more disclosure of employment history of lobbyists, sets stricter limits on lobbyist activities, requires senators to wait two years before lobbying, and requires staff to wait one year before lobbying any Senate office. The Obama administration used this lobbying list to prohibit any registered lobbyists from serving in any White House or executive branch jobs.

Many lobbyists participate in **issue networks** or relationships among interest groups, congressional committees and subcommittees, and government agencies that share a common policy concern. Personal relationships among members of these groups can sometimes allow these networks to become so strong and mutually beneficial that they almost form a separate branch of government.

issue network
Relationships among interest groups, congressional committees and subcommittees, and the government agencies that share a common policy concern.

Legal and political skills, along with specialized knowledge, are so crucial in executive and legislative policy making that they have become a form of power in and of themselves. Elected representatives increasingly depend on their staffs for guidance, and these issue specialists know more about "Section 504" or "Title IX" or "the 2012 amendments"—and who wrote them and why—than most political and administrative leaders, who are usually generalists.[39] New laws often need specific rules and applications spelled out in detail by the agencies charged to administer them. In this rule-making activity, interest groups and issue networks assume even more significance.

Techniques for Exerting Influence

Our separation-of-powers system provides many access points for any group attempting to influence government. They can present their case to Congress, the White House staff, state and local governments, and federal agencies and departments. They can also challenge actions in court. Groups also become involved in litigation, protests, and election activities, and even establish their own political parties. Groups vary in the extent to which they have widespread support that comes directly from the people (grassroots) versus calls for action that are generated by lobbying groups made to look like real grassroots activity (Astroturf).[40]

PUBLICITY, MASS MEDIA, AND THE INTERNET One way to attempt to influence policy makers is through the public. Interest groups use the media—television, radio, the Internet including Web sites and social media, newspapers, leaflets, signs, direct mail, and word of mouth—to influence voters during elections and motivate them to contact their representatives between elections. Businesses enjoy a special advantage because, as large-scale advertisers, they know how to deliver their message effectively or can find an advertising agency to do it for them. But organized labor is also effective in communicating with its membership through shop stewards, mail, phone calls, and personal contact.

Mobilization increasingly occurs through the Internet, especially through social media such as Facebook and Twitter. Business organizations like the Business and Industrial Political Action Committee (BIPAC) use the Internet to communicate with members and employees of affiliated businesses. BIPAC's Web site provides downloadable forms to request absentee ballots and the roll call votes of legislators on issues of interest to their businesses.[41] Some groups, such as MoveOn.org, operate almost exclusively online, while massive forums such as DailyKos.com and Townhall.com act as a clearinghouse for left- and right-wing causes. As one scholar noted, much of what modern interest groups do "could not work without the Internet."[42]

The Internet helps interest groups in two ways. First, it allows citizens to easily organize themselves for rallies, marches, letter-writing drives, and other kinds of civic participation. Second, the Internet opens new, exclusively online forms of political action, such as sending mass emails, posting videos, joining Facebook groups, donating money online, commenting on articles, and blogging. We discuss these developments in greater detail in the media chapter.

MASS MAILING/EMAILING One means of communication that has extended the reach and effectiveness of interest groups is computerized and targeted mass mailing.[43] Before computers, interest groups could either call lists of people to contact from telephone directories and other sources or send mailings indiscriminately. Today's computerized communication technology can target personalized letters and emails to specific groups and individuals. Environmental groups make extensive use of targeted mail and email. The Obama campaign had a list of over 13 million email addresses after the 2008 campaign,[44] which it used to communicate messages during Obama's first term and which provided the foundation for the email list for the 2012 reelection campaign and for his second term as well.

DIRECT CONTACT WITH GOVERNMENT Organized groups have ready access to the executive and regulatory agencies that write the rules implementing laws passed by

When President Trump issued an executive order banning entry in the United States to citizens of seven Muslim countries traveling to the United States, protests broke out at several U.S. airports, including Los Angeles, as seen in this photo. Social media played an important role in mobilizing people, in some cases thousands, to go to the airports to protest.

Congress. Government agencies publish proposed regulations in the ***Federal Register*** and invite responses from all interested persons before the rules are finalized—in the "notice and comments period."[45] Well-staffed associations and corporations use the *Register* to obtain the specific language and deadlines for pending regulations. Lobbyists prepare written responses to the proposed rules, draft alternative rules, and make their case at the hearings.

Federal Register
An official document, published every weekday that lists the new and proposed regulations of executive departments and regulatory agencies.

LITIGATION When groups find the political channels closed to them, they may turn to the courts.[46] They do this by challenging laws, administrative rules, or other actions in lawsuits. The legal challenge to Obamacare, for example, was brought by the National Federation of Independent Business (NIFB).[47] The Legal Defense and Educational Fund of the National Association for the Advancement of Colored People (NAACP), for example, initiated and won numerous court cases in its efforts to end racial segregation and protect the right to vote for African Americans. Urban interest groups, feeling underrepresented in state and national legislatures, turned to the courts to press for one-person, one-vote rulings to overcome the disproportionate power rural interest groups had in legislatures and to otherwise influence the political process.[48] The Campaign Legal Center, among others, played a key role in the litigation over partisan gerrymandering in 2018. Individuals and groups opposed to campaign finance reform have challenged federal, state, and local laws in this area and in recent years have been able to overturn laws and regulations.[49]

In addition to initiating lawsuits, associations can gain a forum for their views in the courts by filing ***amicus curiae* briefs** (literally, "friend of the court" briefs), presenting arguments in cases in which they are not direct parties. It is not unusual for courts to cite such briefs in their opinions. *Amicus* briefs have been found to influence decisions on whether to review cases.[50] While it is common for cases heard by the Court to be accompanied by at least one *amicus* brief, particularly prominent cases typically have more. For example, the marriage equality cases, decided in 2015, set the current record of 147 *amicus* briefs filed.[51]

***amicus curiae* brief**
Literally, a "friend of the court" brief, filed by an individual or organization urging the Supreme Court to hear a case (or discouraging it from doing so) or, at the merits stage, to present arguments in addition to those presented by the immediate parties to a case.

PROTEST To generate interest and broaden support for their cause, movements and groups often use protest demonstrations. For example, on the day after the inauguration of President Trump, a group in the hundreds of thousands held the Women's March on Washington. The idea for the protest came from Teresa Shook, a resident of Hawaii, who created a Facebook event and invited friends to march with

Getty Images/David McNew

Protest has long been a tactic of interest groups, including those seeking women's rights and civil rights. Sometimes protests are focused, as was the case here, where a group of University of California students stage a sit-in protest against college tuition increases and state budget cuts in 2010.

her in Washington in protest. Other Facebook pages arose, and the groups combined efforts. Others organized over four hundred local marches on the same date to advocate women's rights, health care reform, and other issues. In 2018, another Women's March was held in many American cities with an estimated million or more individuals involved.[52] In 2018, the Women's March became international with marches in Germany, Uganda, Japan, London, Rome, and other cities. As with protests generally, the likelihood of the protest actually leading to a set of specific policy changes is uncertain, but the magnitude of the marches clearly demonstrated widespread interest and the fact that so much of it was spontaneous is noteworthy.

More recently, there were large protests following the acquittal of George Zimmerman in the shooting death of African American teenager Trayvon Martin in 2013 in Sanford, Florida, and the deaths in 2014 of two African American teens, Michael Brown in Ferguson, Missouri, and Eric Garner in New York City. These and other incidents have helped galvanize groups across the country concerned about the use of deadly force by police and more broadly racial profiling by police and how minorities are treated in the criminal justice system. One of these groups, Black Lives Matter, staged protests during the 2016 election campaign.[53] Protests occurred at both of the major parties' nominating conventions, but none disrupted the proceedings. In the months that followed, protesters were removed from some Trump events, and one event in Chicago was canceled. Black Lives Matter in 2017 helped organize a counterprotest to a White supremacist protest of the removal of a statue of confederate General Robert E. Lee in Charlottesville, Virginia.[54] Other movements or groups that have used protest include the civil rights movement and antiwar, environmental, and antiglobalization groups.[55]

CONTRIBUTIONS TO CAMPAIGNS Individuals clearly associated with an interest group also contribute to campaigns as individuals in ways that make clear to the candidate the interest of the donor. Often one party gathers contributions from several individuals and then gives the checks made out to the candidate's campaign in a bundle, a process called **bundling**. Interest groups also form **political action committees (PACs)**, which are the legal mechanism for them to contribute money to candidates, political party committees, and other political committees. PACs link two vital techniques of influence—giving money and other political aid to politicians and persuading officeholders to act or vote "the right way" on issues. Thus, PACs are one important means by which interest groups seek to influence which legislators are elected and what they do once they take office.[56]

bundling
A tactic in which PACs collect contributions from like-minded individuals (each limited to $2,000) and present them to a candidate or political party as a "bundle," thus increasing the PAC's influence.

political action committee (PAC)
The political arm of an interest group that is legally entitled to raise funds on a voluntary basis from members, stockholders, or employees to contribute funds to candidates or political parties.

Super PAC
Independent expenditure-only PACs are known as Super PACs because they may accept donations of any size and can endorse candidates. Their contributions and expenditures must be periodically reported to the FEC.

section 501(c) groups
Section 501(c) groups are organized under this section of the Internal Revenue Code. Some of these groups have spent heavily in recent campaigns. Because donors to these groups are not disclosed they are attractive to some donors.

We categorize PACs according to the type of interest they represent: corporations, trade and health organizations, labor unions, ideological organizations, and so on. One of the oldest PACs is the Committee on Political Education (COPE) of the AFL-CIO, but business groups and others have long existed to direct money to favored candidates. PACs also encourage other PACs to contribute to favored candidates, occasionally hosting joint fundraisers for candidates. In 2010, a new type of PAC, a **Super PAC**, was allowed to form. A Super PAC can spend money supporting or opposing candidates with no limitations as to the amount of money individuals, corporations, or unions could contribute. Several of these groups were active in the Republican presidential nomination contest in 2012 and 2016, in the presidential general election in those same years, and in several congressional election campaigns since 2010.

Interest groups also support candidates, parties, and issue campaigns through various associations, often organized under section 501(c) of the tax code and labeled **section 501(c) groups**. These groups are tax-exempt and fall under various classifications. Trade associations fall under the classification of 510(c)(6) groups. An example of a trade association is the U.S. Chamber of Commerce, which represents businesses nationally and campaigns for and against candidates for Congress. Funding for these efforts comes from corporations, but that spending is done in the name of the Chamber and not the corporation, making it impossible to know which corporation funded the advertisement. Since 2010 there has been growth in what are called "social welfare organizations" or Section 501(c)(4) groups. The primary purpose of these groups is intended to be "the common good and general welfare of the people of the community." They may "engage in political activities so long as that is not its primary activity."[57] The IRS and courts have not defined what is meant by "political activity" nor "primary activity," often making regulation of these groups difficult. Groups appear to believe they can spend up to half of their expenditures on campaign ads, but some spend more. For those who contribute to these groups there is the advantage that they do not make public who gave them money. In 2012 and 2016, Section 501(c) groups spent hundreds of millions of dollars on the presidential campaigns. These ways of spending money expand the potential of interest groups to impact elections.

CANDIDATE SUPPORT/OPPOSITION Most large organizations are politically engaged in some way, though they may be, or try to be, *nonpartisan.* Most organized interest groups try to work through *both* parties and want to be friendly with the winners, which often means they contribute to incumbents. However, as competition for control of both houses of Congress has intensified and with presidential contests also hotly contested, many interest groups invest mostly in one party or the other.

Many interest groups also publicly endorse candidates for office. Ideological groups like Americans for Democratic Action and the American Conservative Union publish ratings of the voting records of members of Congress on liberal and conservative issues. Other interest groups, such as the U.S. Chamber of Commerce and the League of Conservation Voters, create scorecards of key legislative votes and report to their members how their representative voted on those issues.

NEW POLITICAL PARTIES Another interest group strategy is to form a political party, often more to publicize a cause than win an election. Success in such cases may occur when a major party co-opts the interest group's issue. The Free Soil Party was formed in the mid-1840s to work against the spread of slavery into the territories, and the Prohibition Party was organized two decades later to ban the sale of liquor. Farmers have formed a variety of such parties. More often, however, interest groups prefer to work through existing parties. This is also true for factions like the Tea Party, which is closely identified with the Republican Party.

Today, environmental groups and voters for whom the environment is a central issue must choose between supporting the Green Party, which has yet to elect a candidate to federal office, an Independent candidate such as Ralph Nader in 2008, or one of the two major parties. Sometimes minor-party candidates can spoil the chances of a major-party candidate. In a New Mexico congressional special election in 1997, the Green Party candidate won 17 percent of the vote, taking some votes from the Democrat and thereby helping to elect a Republican to what had formerly been a Democratic seat. The Tea Party Movement became a rallying cry for some candidates in 2010. However, although more closely identified with Republicans than Democrats, the Tea Party Movement is not currently a party.

In 2015 and early 2016, former New York City mayor Michael Bloomberg actively considered running for president in 2016 as a third-party candidate. He met with consultants, commissioned polls, and indicated he would be willing to spend up to $1 billion of his own money on the race. By March 2016, he announced he would not run, in part because it might help the chances of Donald Trump or Senator Ted Cruz.[58] Bloomberg has since turned his attention to supporting congressional candidates, promising to spend $80 million from his personal fortune to help Democrats retake the House majority in 2018.[59]

COOPERATIVE LOBBYING Like-minded groups often form cooperative groups. In 1987, the Leadership Conference on Civil Rights and People for the American Way brought together many groups to defeat the nomination of outspoken federal judge Robert Bork to the U.S. Supreme Court.[60] Different types of environmentalists work together, as do consumer and ideological groups on the right and on the left.

lobbying
Engaging in activities aimed at influencing public officials, especially legislators, and the policies they enact.

The larger the coalition, the greater the chance that members may divide over specific issues and no longer be able to pursue cooperative **lobbying**.

Since 2004, a group of pro-Democratic interest groups, under pressure from some major donors, have come together to share information and campaign support plans with each other on an ongoing basis during the campaign. The coordinating group is named America Votes and those who coordinate with each other include Planned Parenthood, EMILY's List, Sierra Club, League of Conservation Voters, several unions, MoveOn.org, and other groups.[61] Republicans for a time had their own coordinating group, called the Weaver Terrace Group, named after the street where a former George W. Bush administration advisor resided who was instrumental in forming the group.[62] Since 2014, coordination among Republican groups has been more informal and one set of active conservative groups, those funded by Charles and David Koch, prefer not to coordinate with other groups. Another example of a cooperative group is the Business Roundtable, an association of chief executive officers of the 200 largest American corporations, which promotes policies that help large businesses, such as free trade and less government regulation.

What Explains Interest Group Success? (Impact)

5.4 Evaluate the factors that affect the relative success of interest groups.

Groups vary in their goals, methods, and power. Among their most important characteristics are size, incentives to participate, resources, cohesiveness, leadership, and techniques. As we will demonstrate, these different resources and objectives help us understand how and when interest groups have an impact.

Size and Resources

Obviously, size is important to political power; an organization representing 5 million voters has more influence than one speaking for 5,000. Perhaps even more important is the number of members who are active and willing to fight for policy objectives. Interest groups often provide tangible incentives to join, sometimes called selective benefits, such as exclusive magazines, travel benefits, professional meetings and job opportunities, and discounts on insurance, merchandise, and admission to cultural institutions. Some are compelling enough to attract the potential free rider. Other times a shared benefit like local fireworks on the Fourth of July has to be canceled because of a lack of funding.

Many government programs provide services that benefit everyone, such as clean air, national defense, and streetlights. One solution to the free rider problem is to pay for these widely shared benefits through taxes. Nongovernment service providers can require a number of people to pay for the service before providing it. It is then in everyone's interest to pay for the service or face the prospect that no one will have it. Groups rarely overcome the risk of free riders and sometimes attempt to sanction or punish free riders, which is why unions prefer that only union workers be employed in a given firm or industry. When this is not possible, group leaders try to reduce the free rider problem through persuasion or group pressure.

Although the size of an interest group is important to its success, so is its *spread*—the extent to which membership is concentrated or dispersed. Because automobile manufacturing is concentrated in Michigan and a few other states, the auto industry's influence does not have the same spread as the American Medical Association, which has an active chapter in virtually every congressional district. Concentration of membership in a key battleground state, however, such as Cuban Americans in Florida or ethanol producers in Iowa, enhances that group's influence.

Finally, groups differ in the extent of their *resources*—money, volunteers, expertise, and reputation. Some groups can influence many centers of power—both houses of Congress, the White House, federal agencies, the courts, and state and local governments—whereas others cannot. The U.S. Chamber of Commerce has a broad reach, with active "chambers" at the local, state, and national levels. An even larger group, the AARP, touts its large national membership in policy debates. Particular industries, such as citrus growers, have a spread that includes only a few states.

Cohesiveness

Most mass-membership organizations include three types of members: (1) a relatively small number of formal leaders who may hold full-time, paid positions or devote much time, effort, and money to the group's activities; (2) a few hundred people intensely involved in the group who identify with its aims, attend meetings, pay dues, and do much of the legwork; and (3) thousands of people who are members in name only and cannot be depended on to vote in elections or act as the leadership wants. A fourth group could be people who are not members of the group but who benefit from the activities of the group. When members share common views on the aims of the organization, the group is more cohesive; single-issue groups typically enjoy strong cohesion among their members. An example of a cohesive group with strong organizational structures is Planned Parenthood, which operates offices all over the country and has a clear purpose that its supporters understand well. In 2012, when one financial supporter announced it was no longer contributing to Planned Parenthood, the reaction was swift and strong and the sponsor reversed itself and resumed funding the organization. Following the 2016 election, Planned Parenthood provided staff and organizational support for the Women's March which took place the day after the Trump inauguration. At least 600 cities nationwide had marches and Planned Parenthood saw growth in online contributions and volunteers to the organization.[63] Planned Parenthood picked up additional support in spring 2018 when the Trump administration proposed reductions in federal funding for family planning for any organization with affiliates that offer abortion services. Although the new policy faced many hurdles before formal adoption, Planned Parenthood took immediate action to active its members against the proposal.

Actor Jeff Bridges attends a 2014 AARP (American Association of Retired Persons) luncheon in his honor and is seen here standing next to the cover of *AARP The Magazine* that featured him. Bridges, like any person over 50 years of age, can join the AARP which is active on issues of concern to older Americans.

Leadership

In a group that embraces many attitudes and interests, leaders may either weld the various elements together or sharpen their disunity. The leader of a national business association, for example, must tread cautiously between big business and small business, between exporters and importers, between chain stores and corner grocery stores, and between the producers and the sellers of competing products.

The group leader is in the same position as a president or a member of Congress; he or she must know when to lead and when to follow. An example of an effective group leader is Thomas J. Donohue, the president of the U.S. Chamber of Commerce. Under Donohue's leadership, the Chamber has grown in size and influence. He has also met with President Obama, even though the Chamber and the president are often on opposing sides.

Helping Those They Represent

Thousands of lobbyists are active in Washington, but few are as glamorous or as unscrupulous as the media suggest. Nor are they necessarily influential. One limit on their power is the competition among interest groups. As we have seen, rarely does any one group have a policy area all to itself.

To members of Congress, the single most important thing lobbyists provide is money for their next reelection campaign. "Reelection underlies everything else," writes political scientist David Mayhew.[64] Money from interest groups is the most important source funding this driving need among incumbents. Interest groups also provide volunteers for campaign activity. In addition, their failure to support the opposition can enhance an incumbent's chances of being reelected.

Beyond their central role in campaigns and elections, interest groups provide information of two important types, political and substantive. *Political information* includes such matters as who supports or opposes legislation, including the executive branch, and how strongly they feel about it.[65] *Substantive information,* such as the impact of proposed laws, may not be available from any other source. Lobbyists often provide technical assistance for drafting bills and amendments, identifying persons to testify at legislative hearings, and formulating questions to ask administration officials at oversight hearings.[66] An example of a group that not only lobbied for legislation but also has drafted laws that were introduced as written in four states is named the American Legislative Exchange Council (ALEC). The group is funded by oil companies and other corporations.

Interest groups sometimes attempt to influence legislators and regulators by going directly to the people and urging them to contact public officials. They sometimes do this through television advertising, but also through mail, email, and banner ads on the Internet. During the long debate over health care reform in 2009–2010, multiple groups took their message directly to the people, not only to influence public opinion on possible legislation, but also as a way to try to pressure Congress. In 2010, an estimated $200 million was spent in TV advertising on health care.[67]

Funding Campaigns

Interest groups also seek to influence politics and public policy by spending money on elections and by mobilizing members or employees.

Helping to elect candidates creates a relationship between the interest group and the elected official that a group may later exploit. At a minimum, substantial involvement in the election process helps provide access to policy makers.[68] We discuss the dynamics of campaign finance and efforts to reform or regulate it in a later chapter. Here, we discuss the most important ways interest groups organize and participate in funding campaigns and elections.

POLITICAL ACTION COMMITTEES (PACS) PACs grew in number and importance in the 1970s, in part because of campaign finance reform legislation enacted in that decade. The number of PACs registered rose from 608 in 1974 to nearly 9,000 today, some of which make no contributions, but also including Super PACs which have seen the greatest growth.[69] Corporations and trade associations contributed most to this growth; today, their PACs constitute the majority of all PACs. Labor PACs, by contrast, represent less than 4 percent of all PACs.[70] But the increase in the number of PACs is less important than the intensity of PAC participation in funding elections and lobbying (see Figure 5.3). Note in the figure the pattern of PAC contributions over time. The increase is noteworthy because PAC contribution limits have been the same since 1975 and PACs, as we will discuss, can spend money to influence elections in ways beyond contributions to candidates.

Surprisingly, considering that the growth in numbers of PACs has occurred mainly in the business world, organized labor invented this device. In the 1930s, John L. Lewis, president of the United Mine Workers, set up the Non-Partisan Political League as the political arm of the newly formed Congress of Industrial Organizations (CIO). When the CIO merged with American Federation of Labor (AFL), the new labor group established the Committee on Political Education (COPE), a model for PACs. The most active business PAC today is the one affiliated with the National Association of Realtors.[71] Table 5.1 lists the most active PACs in elections since 2000.

INDEPENDENT EXPENDITURES The Supreme Court in 1976 declared that limits on independent expenditures were unconstitutional when the contributions or expenditures were truly independent of a party or candidate. Hence, groups, like individuals, can campaign for or against a candidate, independent of a party or candidate committee and in addition to contributing to candidates and party committees

FIGURE 5.3 TOTAL PAC CONTRIBUTIONS TO CANDIDATES FOR U.S. CONGRESS IN MILLIONS OF DOLLARS, 2015–2016.

The amount of money contributed by PACs to congressional candidates in 2016 dipped slightly from $446 million in 2012 to $441 million in 2016. One reason for this may be that with recent court and administrative decisions, interest groups have more ways to help fund candidates in the most competitive races where the money may be the most important to election outcomes.

SOURCES: Harold W. Stanley and Richard G. Niemi, Vital Statistics on American Politics 2009–2010 (CQ Press), p. 92; Federal Election Commission, "Political Action Committee (PAC) Data Summary Tables: PAC Contributions," https://www.fec.gov/press/campaign_finance_statistics.shtml.

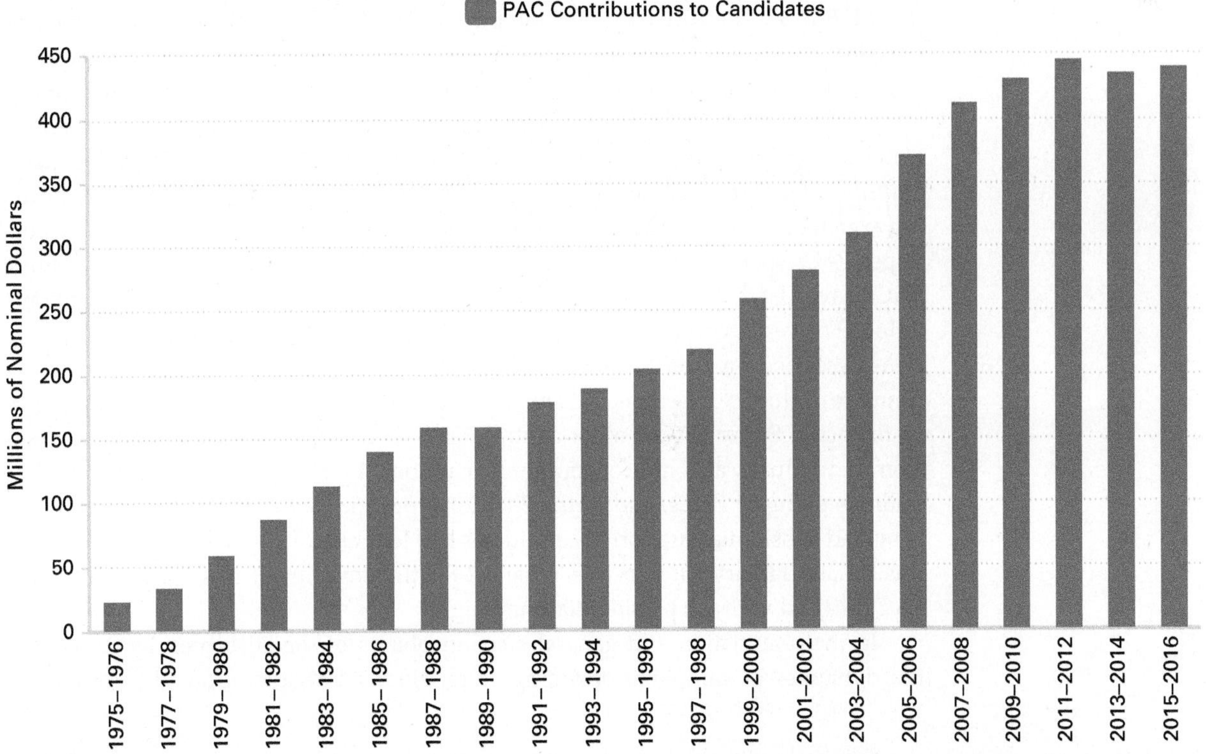

TABLE 5.1 PACS THAT GAVE THE MOST TO FEDERAL CANDIDATES, CUMULATIVELY, 2000–2016 (MILLIONS OF DOLLARS)

Half of the ten largest PACs in money given to federal candidates since 2000 have been unions. Business interests like realtors, beer wholesalers, and auto dealers have also been active. Note that all of the top ten PACs gave more money in 2014 than in any prior cycle and they repeated that behavior in 2016. The largest increases in spending in 2016 were among unions. Take for example the Service Employees International Unions (SEIU) which spent $1.82 million in 2012, $3.36 million in 2014, and $6.87 million in 2016. SEIU and the Laborers Union were the two PACs that contributed the most in 2016.

PAC	2000	2002	2004	2006	2008	2010	2012	2014	2016	Total
1. National Association of Realtors	$3.42	$3.65	$3.77	$3.75	$4.01	$3.79	$3.96	$4.97	$5.24	$36.56
2. International Brotherhood of Electrical Workers	$2.46	$2.21	$2.30	$2.78	$3.33	$2.98	$2.89	$4.20	$4.71	$27.86
3. National Beer Wholesalers Association	$1.87	$2.07	$2.29	$2.95	$2.87	$3.30	$3.39	$4.09	$4.26	$27.09
4. National Auto Dealers Association	$2.50	$2.58	$2.58	$2.82	$2.86	$2.48	$3.07	$3.31	$3.61	$25.81
5. American Federation of Teachers	$1.58	$1.58	$1.70	$2.08	$2.27	$2.33	$2.21	$5.66	$5.57	$24.98
6. Laborers Union	$1.79	$2.25	$2.25	$2.32	$2.05	$1.73	$1.82	$3.50	$6.90	$24.61
7. AT&T	$1.29	$1.47	$1.79	$1.77	$3.12	$3.26	$3.62	$3.60	$4.49	$24.41
8. International Brotherhood of Teamsters	$2.49	$2.33	$1.89	$2.07	$2.20	$2.31	$2.08	$3.69	$5.05	$24.11
9. Honeywell International	$0.22	$0.17	$0.40	$0.79	$2.52	$3.66	$4.81	$5.13	$5.67	$23.37
10. Service Employees International Union	$1.89	$1.88	$1.93	$1.44	$2.29	$1.83	$1.82	$3.36	$6.87	$23.31

SOURCE: Federal Election Commission, "Top 50 PACs by Contributions to Candidates," includes activity through 12/31/16, https://www.fec.gov/press/campaign_finance_statistics.shtml.

independent expenditures
The Supreme Court has ruled that individuals, groups, and parties can spend unlimited amounts in campaigns for or against candidates as long as they operate independently from the candidates. When an individual, group, or party does so, they are making an independent expenditure.

from their PAC. These conventional **independent expenditures** come from funds raised with the same contribution limits as the funds used for PAC contributions but they are unlimited in amount spent. The spending must be disclosed to the Federal Election Commission (FEC). In 2016, for example, the NRA, Affiliated Federal, State, County, and Municipal Employees (AFSCME), and End Citizens United were the most active groups in making independent expenditures, spending between $13.7 and $19.3 million independently.[72] This spending dwarfs what groups can do through PAC contributions. Groups making independent expenditures receive credit with their members for their activity because the source of independent expenditures is clearly communicated.

SUPER PACS The 2016 elections saw further development of Super PACs, which can only make independent expenditures but can spend unlimited amounts of money in support of or opposition to federal candidates. Super PACs came into existence in 2010 after the U.S. Supreme Court declared limits on corporations' or unions' spending from their general funds on campaign communications unconstitutional in *Citizens United* v. *FEC*.[73] In the 2010 election cycle, Super PACs spent over $60 million, a training exercise for some of them in anticipation of even more spending thereafter. In 2012, Super PACs spent $607 million, and in 2016 Super PACs spent over 1 billion.[74] Super PACs have also been very active in U.S. Senate races; they spent nearly 700 million in 2016.[75] For years, corporations and unions had PACs that made the limited contributions described previously, but they had not been able to use their profits or general funds to influence elections.[76] How large a role did corporations and unions play in financing Super PACs? Most contributions to Super PACs since 2010 have been from individuals, and not corporations or unions. But individuals gave hundreds of millions to Super PACs, and in the 2015-2016 presidential election these Super PACs provided substantial support to candidates like Jeb Bush, Ted Cruz, Marco Rubio, John Kasich, and Hillary Clinton. See Table 5.2 for the amounts of money spent by Super PACs aligned with the presidential campaigns.

In the nomination and general election phases of the 2016 presidential contest, the dynamics of campaign spending were different because Donald Trump relied

TABLE 5.2 CANDIDATE AND ALLIED SUPER PAC SPENDING IN 2016 PRESIDENTIAL ELECTION

Super PACs supporting Hillary Clinton and Donald Trump spent in excess of $100 million for their preferred candidate but this was down from the nearly $250 million spent by Super PACs supporting Mitt Romney in 2012. Hillary Clinton had more than double the amount spent for her by her Super PAC than Barack Obama did in 2012. As you can see in Table 5.2, Jeb Bush, Marco Rubio, and Chris Christie all had more money spent to support them by their aligned Super PAC than they were able to raise and spend through their campaign committees.

Candidate/Supporting Super PAC	Candidate Spending	Super PAC Spending
Clinton/Priorities USA Action	$585,346,281	$133,408,056
Trump/Get Our Jobs Back	343,056,732	50,010,166
Bush/Right to Rise USA	35,435,885	86,817,478
Rubio/Conservative Solutions PAC	51,557,701	55,443,629
Cruz/Stand for Truth	94,304,803	9,523,815
Carson/The 2016 Committee	64,530,285	6,167,228
Kasich/New Day for America	19,534,124	11,189,336
Christie/America Leads	8,718,080	18,579,148
Trump/Future45	*	24,264,041
Trump/Rebuilding America Now	*	19,763,237
Trump/Make America Number 1	*	13,454,942

NOTE: This does not include all candidates or all Super PACs.

SOURCE: Compiled from Federal Election Commission data (https://www.fec.gov/finance/disclosure/candcmte_info.shtml [May 7, 2017]).

heavily on generating news coverage and less on campaign spending. In the nomination phase, he and Democrat Bernie Sanders made a point of not affiliating with a Super PAC. In the general election, Trump did not endorse a Super PAC but his campaign did have a close relationship with the Rebuilding America Now PAC. Compared to Mitt Romney in 2012, Trump had much less Super PAC spending on his behalf. During the general election, Trump showed increased willingness to receive Super PAC support. Overall, Super PACs raised more than $60 million dollars to help elect Donald Trump, compared to approximately $190 million dollars raised by Super PACs favoring Hillary Clinton.[77]

Elected officials also form their own PACs to collect contributions from individuals and other PACs and then contribute to candidates and political parties. These committees, called leadership PACs, were initially a tool of aspiring congressional leaders to curry favor with candidates in their political party. For example, in 2016 leadership PACs associated with the Republican and Democratic U.S. House leaders (Speaker Paul Ryan and Minority Leader Nancy Pelosi) and Senate leaders (Mitch McConnell and Chuck Schumer) raised nearly $250 million through their Super PACs for races their Super PACs thought critical.[78]

HOW PACS INVEST THEIR MONEY PACs are important because, not only do they contribute such a large share of the money congressional candidates raise for their campaigns, but they also contribute disproportionately to incumbents, committee chairs, and party leadership and give so little to challengers (see Figure 5.4). PACs often give not only to the majority party, but also to key incumbents in the minority. In the 2016 election cycle, incumbent congressional candidates raised more than 12 dollars from PACs for each one dollar raised from PACs by challengers.[79] Senate incumbents not only raise proportionately more from individuals than do House incumbents, but also enjoy a fundraising advantage among PACs compared to Senate challengers. One reason members of Congress become entrenched in their seats is that PACs fund their campaigns.

FIGURE 5.4 PAC CONTRIBUTIONS TO CONGRESSIONAL CANDIDATES, 1996–2016 (MILLIONS OF DOLLARS)

The amount of money given by PACs to incumbents has increased in a near linear fashion since 1996, while the amounts given to challengers and open seat candidates have changed very little over time. The PAC incumbency fundraising advantage relative to challengers and open seat candidates was greater in 2016 than in any prior cycle.

SOURCE: Federal Election Commission, "PAC Contributions to Candidates," https://www.fec.gov/press/campaign_finance_statistics.shtml.

NOTE: Includes all House and Senate candidates.

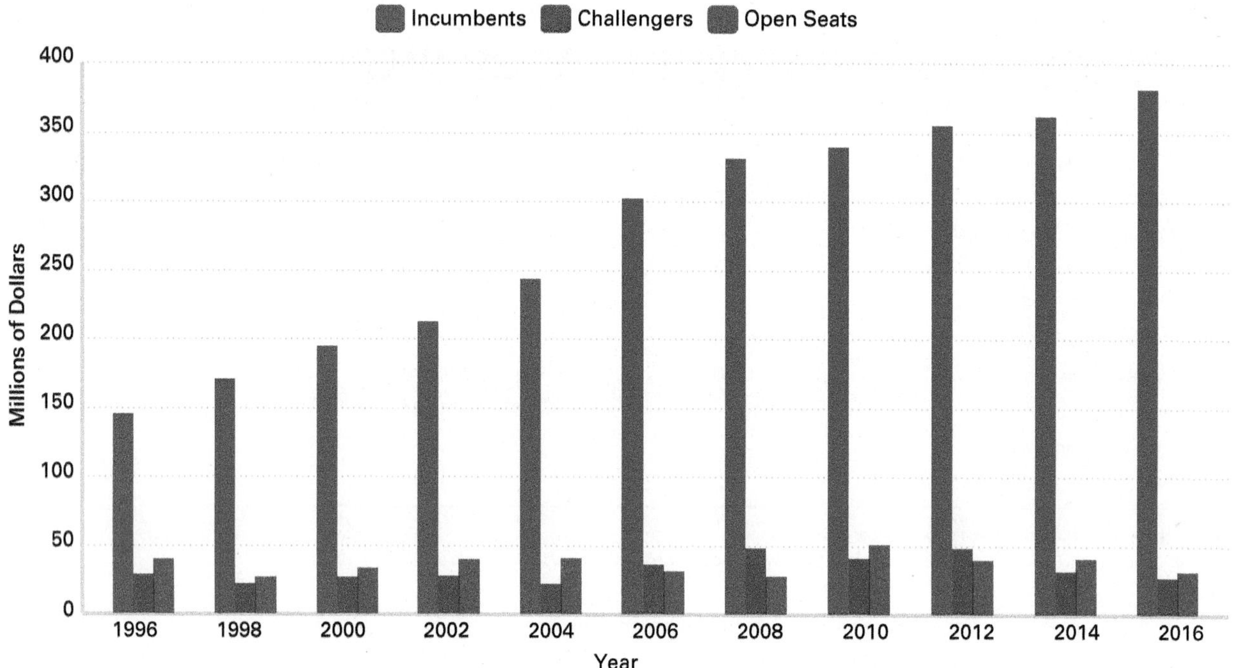

One important reason PACs give to committee chairs and party leaders is to secure access to meet with them about policies they care about. To reinforce this relationship, the Republicans in the 1990s developed a strategy, the "K Street Project," to do even better in getting PAC contributions. House GOP leaders pushed lobbying firms to hire more lobbyists that are Republican and to contribute more money to Republicans. K Street in Washington, D.C., houses many of the lobbying and law firms that represent trade associations and corporations that contribute.[80]

After the Democratic Party took control of Congress in 2007, some PACs changed loyalties. In the House, approximately 60 percent of PAC money went to Democrats and 40 percent to Republicans.[81] Before Congress changed hands, just the opposite was true—approximately 60 percent of PAC money went to Republicans. The same pattern followed the Republican recapture of Congress in 2010: the following election cycle, they received 56 percent of all PAC contributions.[82] In the Senate, Republicans once received more PAC money than Democrats did, but in recent elections there has been relatively more parity in PAC giving to the two parties,[83] likely because the close balance of power between the parties means either party could be in the majority after the next election.

NONPROFIT AND TRADE ASSOCIATIONS Some groups that are important to the financing of electons that are not organized as PACs and spend their funds independently of the candidates are nonprofit groups whose primary purpose is not elections and trade associations like the U.S. Chamber of Commerce, or the National Football League. These organizations are organized under section 501(c)(6) of the Internal Revenue Code. In the 2012, 2014, and 2016 elections the U.S. Chamber spent a total of over $100 million on federal elections. The Chamber is the most visible group representing business interests in the United States. Other trade associations that are important include the National Association of Realtors and the National Rifle Association. Some like the NRA, also have a PAC which makes contributions to candidates and party committees.

Vice President Mike Pence addresses the U.S. Chamber of Commerce in the spring of 2017. Although the Chamber opposed the Trump administration's tariffs on foreign goods such as steel and aluminium, it is a steadfast supporter of conservative economic causes, and a "must-stop" convention for national leaders.

In recent elections, a second form of outside group has been increasingly active in spending independently of candidates and parties, these are often called "social welfare organizations" and are organized under section 501(c)(4) of the Internal Revenue Code. The code requires that these organizations not have politics as their primary purpose, rather the primiary purpose is to be social welfare. Spending by these gropes has been substantial in recent years. Between 2012 and 2016, American Crossroads/Crossroads GPS/ and One Nation, which are different forms of the same underlying group spent over $100 million in federal elections. Over the same time period another conservative group linked to the Koch brothers spent $53 million.[84] These groups can form very late in a contest and may have only a few donors. For example, 45 Committee formed in 2016 and spent $21 million supporting Donald Trump in the 2016 race. 45 Committee "was reportedly funded by some of the same people who funded the Future 45 Committee, a Super PAC that started out as an anti-Hillary Clinton Super PAC, but later became a pro-Trump Super PAC."[85] Because the reporting schedule for section 501(c)(4)s is different from that of political committees, their overall activity is often not known until months after an election.

MOBILIZING EMPLOYEES AND MEMBERS Another way interest groups can influence the outcome of elections is by persuading their employees, members, or stockholders to vote in a way consistent with the interests of the group or corporation. They accomplish this mobilization through targeted communications at the workplace, through the mail, on the telephone, or on the Internet. As we discuss elsewhere in this chapter, labor unions have been especially effective in member communications. Corporations and business associations have been following labor's lead. Membership organizations such as the NRA have also been able to mobilize their members, as well as allied individuals and groups.[86]

OTHER MODES OF ELECTIONEERING For a time, citizens, journalists, and scholars had a complete picture of who was giving what to whom, and who was spending money and in what ways, to influence elections. That changed in 1994 and 1996, when interest groups found a way to circumvent disclosure and contribution limits through **issue advocacy**. They simply made election ads without words like "vote for" or "vote against," and then they spent millions attacking or promoting particular candidates. Labor unions were the first to exploit this tactic in a major way, spending an estimated $35 million in 1996, mostly against Republican candidates.[87] Corporations and ideological groups quickly followed labor's lead, spending millions on issue ads in 1996–2002, before they were limited by the 2002 **Bipartisan Campaign Reform Act (BCRA)**.[88]

issue advocacy
Promoting a particular position or an issue paid for through unlimited and undisclosed spending by interest groups or individuals but not candidates. Much issue advocacy is often electioneering for or against a candidate, avoiding words like "vote for" or "vote against," and until 2004 had not been subject to any regulation.

Bipartisan Campaign Reform Act (BCRA)
Largely banned party soft money, restored a long-standing prohibition on corporations' and labor unions' use of general treasury funds for electoral purposes, and narrowed the definition of issue advocacy.

Another way unlimited contributions and expenditures grew in importance was through soft money. Until the 2004 election cycle, interest groups and individuals could avoid the contribution limitation to political parties by contributing so-called **soft money** to political parties. Originally justified as an exception to contribution limits to help the political parties by funding get-out-the-vote drives or party appeals that are not specific, soft money came to be used for candidate-specific electioneering.[89] BCRA also banned party soft money.

soft money

Money raised in unlimited amounts by political parties for party-building purposes. Now largely illegal except for limited contributions to state or local parties for voter registration and get-out-the-vote efforts.

The Supreme Court in 2007 declared parts of BCRA relating to these kinds of ads unconstitutional, allowing corporations and unions again to spend their general funds on ads that advocate a point of view on political issues, which may affect elections.[90] Later in their 5-to-4 decision in *Citizens United* v. *FEC* in 2010, discussed above, allowed corporations and unions to use unlimited general funds for election-specific ads and has resulted in much greater spending by corporations and unions in this mode of electioneering in competitive federal election contests.[91] Interest groups can avoid disclosure if they communicate with voters through the mail, in newspaper ads, on billboards, on the phone, and by email.

Limiting the Mischiefs of Faction (Impact)

5.5 Assess the effectiveness of regulations designed to control interest groups.

The law limits the amount of money that PACs, like individuals, can contribute to any single candidate in an election cycle. But raising money from PACs was for many years more efficient for a candidate than raising it from individuals. Since the 1970s, PAC contributions to any federal candidate have been limited to $10,000 per election cycle (primary and general elections), whereas until 2004 individuals were limited to $2,000 per candidate per election cycle. The BCRA doubled individual contribution limits and mandated that they increase with inflation while leaving PAC contribution limits unchanged. The contribution limit for 2015–2016 was $5,400 (primary and general elections combined). This means two individuals giving the maximum allowable can now exceed the maximum allowable PAC contribution. This probably reflected the view of the legislators that actual corruption or the appearance of it is more likely to come from organized interests such as unions, trade associations, and businesses than from individuals.

We have said that because PACs give more money to incumbents, challengers have difficulty funding their campaigns and have to rely more on individual contributors. This holds true even with the larger individual contribution limits allowed in 2004 and since; most challengers still had much less money than their incumbent opponents.

How much does interest group money influence election outcomes, legislation, and representation? Candidates for president in 2016 in both parties criticized the way elections are financed and the particular role of interest groups in that process. Texas Senator Ted Cruz accused the "Washington Cartel" of supporting "cronyism and corporate welfare in order to get votes." In addition, that the government "listens to one voice: … the voice of the Washington Cartel, of the lobbyists on K street, of the big money and big corporations."[92]

Donald Trump was equally explicit when he said in 2016, "There is total control of the candidates.… I know it better than anybody. And I will tell you this: I know the system far better than anybody else and I know the system is broken.… I was on both sides of it. I was on the other side all my life and I've always made large contributions."[93] Democratic candidate Hillary Clinton said, "We have to end the flood of secret, unaccountable money that is distorting our elections, corrupting our political system, and drowning out the voices of too many everyday Americans."[94] And Bernie Sanders, who spoke often of the evils of large donors, said, "We are talking about a rapid movement in this country toward a political system in which a handful of very wealthy people and special interests will determine who gets elected or who does not get elected."[95] "I will tell you that our system is broken," Trump said of the campaign finance system in a 2016 televised GOP debate in 2016. "I gave to many people before this—before two months ago I was a businessman. I give to everybody. When they call, I give. And you know what, when I need something from them two years later, three years later, I call them. They are there for me. That's a broken system."[96]

Although a candidate may receive a great amount of interest group money, only a fraction of that total comes from any single group. It is also debatable how much campaign contributions affect elections, and there is no guarantee that money produces a payoff in legislation. What the substantial spending by Super PACs showed in 2012 and 2016, however, is that allowing an individual to spend unlimited amounts through a Super PAC in support of a candidate can allow that candidate to continue to stay in the race. Without Super PAC support, it is doubtful that Gingrich or Santorum would have been able to stay in the race as long as they did in 2012, or Jeb Bush, Marco Rubio, or Chris Christie in 2016. Because Super PACs are often funded by a small number of individuals giving large sums of money, the concern about donors having influence over the candidate's policy is amplified.

Numerous groups seek to mobilize their membership in elections. They create Web sites for members to obtain information about their view of candidates and provide voter registration materials and absentee ballot request forms. How effective is electioneering by interest groups? In general, mass-membership organizations fail to mobilize their full membership in elections, although they can effectively mobilize when their interests are directly attacked.[97] More typically, too many cross-pressures operate in the pluralistic politics of the United States for any one group to assume a commanding role. Some groups reach their maximum influence only by allying themselves closely with one of the two major parties. They may place their members on local, state, and national party committees and help send them to party conventions as delegates, but forming such alliances means losing some independence.

Enduring Concerns with Interest Group Power

If James Madison were to return today, neither the existence of interest groups nor their variety would surprise him. However, the varied weapons of group influence, the deep investment of interest groups in the electoral process, and the vast number of lobbyists in Washington and the state capitals might come as a surprise. Moreover, doubtless, Madison would still be concerned about the power of interest groups and possible "mischiefs of faction," especially their tendency to foster instability and injustice.

Concern about the evils of interest groups has been a recurrent theme throughout U.S. history. President Dwight Eisenhower used his Farewell Address to warn against the "military-industrial complex," the alliance of defense industries and the U.S. military formed to pursue more spending on weapons. President Ronald Reagan in his farewell address warned of the power of "special interests."[98]

Single-issue interest groups organized for or against particular policies—abortion, handgun control, tobacco subsidies, animal rights, and so on—have aroused increasing concern in recent years. "It is said that citizen groups organizing in ever greater numbers to push single issues ruin the careers of otherwise fine politicians who disagree with them on one emotional issue, paralyze the traditional process of governmental compromise, and ignore the common good in their selfish insistence on getting their own way."[99] But which single issues reflect narrow interests? Women's rights—even a specific issue such as sexual harassment or abortion—are hardly "narrow," women's rights leaders contend, because women represent more than half the population. These issues may seem different from those related to subsidies for dairy farmers, for example.

One of the main arguments against interest groups is that they do not represent people equally. For example, fewer interest groups represent young or low-income people than represent senior citizens or corporations. Further, some groups are better organized and better financed, allowing them a decided advantage over more general groups. In addition, the existence of a multiplicity of interests often leads to incoherent policies, inefficiency, and delay as lawmakers try to appease conflicting interests. In addition, the propensity of interest groups to support incumbents in elections increases the advantages of incumbency, which is often seen as undesirable.

Checking the Power of Interest Groups

What—if anything—should we do about factions? For decades, American citizens have tried to find ways to keep interest groups in check. They have agreed with James Madison that the "remedy" of outlawing factions would be worse than the disease. It would be absurd to abolish liberty simply because it nourished faction. And the Constitution solidly protects the existence and activity of interest groups and lobbies. Moreover, interest groups provide important services. They supply needed and accurate information to government officials. But by safeguarding the value of liberty, have we allowed interest groups to threaten equality, the second great value in our national heritage? The question remains: how can we regulate interest groups in a way that does not threaten our constitutional liberties? Should we?

The United States has generally responded to this question by seeking to regulate lobbying in general and political money in particular. At the federal level, the most enduring effort to regulate lobbying has been mandatory disclosure of what lobbyists spend on specific activities. Regulations also require lobbyists to register with the government, and Congress and the executive branch have rules barring former officials from becoming lobbyists for a specified period of time.

After the Republicans won control of Congress only two years after Bill Clinton became president in 1992, Congress passed the first major overhaul of lobbying laws since 1946. Under the Lobbying Disclosure Act of 1995, the definition of a lobbyist was expanded to include part-time lobbyists, those who deal with congressional staff or executive branch agencies, and those who represent foreign-owned companies and foreign entities. The number of registered lobbyists peaked in 2007 at nearly 15,000 but declined with the recession, and in 2015 was 11,504.[100] The act also included specific disclosure and information requirements.

During his administraton, President Obama banned staff in his administration from accepting gifts from lobbyists and for those who leave the administration imposed a ban on lobbying former colleagues and agencies they worked with for at least two years.[101] President Trump began his administration issuing an executive order requiring appointees to sign a pledge that they would not be involved in matters such as regulations or contracts involving their former employer or former clients, he also reduced the length of time appointees were banned from lobbying former colleagues and agencies to one year. Some of President Trump's appointees had served as lobbyists before entering his administration, a reversal of the policy in the Obama administration which barred appointees who had been registered lobbyists in the previous year.[102]

The Trump presidency has also faced an ethics challenge because of the president possibly receiving the equivalent of gifts from foreign governments through their use of his properties, especially his Trump International Hotel in Washington, D.C. The Constitution includes an emoluments clause which bans the president and other federal officials "without the consent of Congress, [to] accept any present, emolument, office or title of any kind whatever, from any king, prince, or foreign state."[103] The state of Maryland and the District of Columbia have sued President Trump both personally and as president.[104]

Ethics concerns in the Trump presidency also include cabinet officials. Scott Pruitt who headed the Environmental Protection Agency was subject to at least a dozen investigatons over possible ethics violations. Among the possible violations reported in the press are that Pruitt asked a federal employee to find a job for his spouse from groups doing business with his agency, that he asked his staff to obtain a used mattress from the Trump International Hotel, and that he rented an apartment at below market value from the spouse of a person who lobbies the EPA.[105] Pruitt resigned in July 2018.[106] Concern over the use of money—especially corporate funds—to influence politicians goes back more than a century, to the administration of Ulysses S. Grant in the 1870s, when members of Congress promoted the Crédit Mobilier construction company in exchange for the right to make huge profits by buying its stock below market value. In the Progressive Era during the first two decades of the twentieth century, Congress legislated against corporate contributions in federal elections and required disclosure of the use of the money (Tillman Act, 1907, and Federal Corrupt Practices Act, 1925).[107] But federal legislation was not very effective and was only loosely enforced. Many candidates filed incomplete reports or none at all. The reform mood of the 1960s and the Watergate scandal of 1972 brought basic changes. The outcome was the Federal Election Campaign Act of 1971 (FECA), amended in 1974. We discuss FECA and the more recent Bipartisan Campaign Reform Act in greater detail in the chapter on campaigns and elections.

But as the 2012 and 2016 elections highlighted, disclosure was incomplete or came after key election contests. For example, a group led by Republican political professionals, Crossroads GPS, spent in excess of $20 million on anti-Obama ads in 2012 without having to disclose its donors because the group ostensibly was a section 501(c)(4) social welfare organization.[108] A similar section 501(c)(4) organization, Conservative Solutions Project, spent at least $10 million on advertising largely against Florida senator Marco Rubio's opponents in the 2016 presidential nomination contest.[109] Super PAC donors, unlike section 501(c)(4) donors, are disclosed, but often that happens after voters have cast their ballots. For example, the disclosure of Super PAC donors' giving in the critical month of February did not come in most cases until February 29, 2016, which was after the New Hampshire and South Carolina primaries and the Nevada caucuses. Participants in those contests did not know who was funding the last-minute multimillion-dollar advertising campaigns being run in their states.

At the same time, interest groups provide important opportunities for individuals to work together to pursue common objectives. Sometimes, this means that individuals join existing groups; at other times, they form new ones. Interest groups not only foster healthy competition in our politics, but they also teach important lessons about self-government. While the potential for abuse by interest groups is real, they serve critical functions in American government.

CONCLUSION

Recognizing the reality that people have interests and will want to organize in groups to pursue common interests, our structure of government protects freedom of association and the right to petition government. James Madison and the others who wrote our Constitution saw interest groups as inevitable. Their hope was that the competition between groups would not allow any one group to become dominant. An extension of this structured competition is the need for transparency in who is supporting which groups and which policy makers.

Competition between interest groups has become an important feature of American politics. We expect there to be disagreement between environmental groups and energy companies, between unions and employers, and between banks and credit unions. However, competition is not always present and the broader public interest may not have an organized group participating in the debate. The success of this system of interest group competition depends on individuals like you forming or joining groups and pursuing your interests.

Another challenge to self-government is the ability of some individuals and groups to use their wealth to try to influence elections through campaign spending and the process through lobbying. The 2016 presidential election in both parties included a call to "clean up" the system of campaign finance and the "cartel" of special interests in Washington, D.C. Some reform ideas may require a constitutional amendment. How you and other citizens see the balance between freedom of speech and association and the need for free and fair election outcomes will be important as these decisions are made.

The challenges of balancing freedom of association, petition, and speech with the desire of interest groups to become more and more powerful will be an ongoing challenge at the local, state, national, and international levels. The choices that you and others will be called on to make will have important consequences for the way society is organized and the government is run. History teaches that self-interest will propel some interest groups, but whether other individuals and interests also organize is critically important.

REVIEW THE CHAPTER

The Reasons Interest Groups Endure and the "Mischiefs of Faction" They Produce (Structure)

5.1 Describe why interest groups form and how they attract members, p. 110.

The founders worried about the dangers of factions (interest groups and political parties) and hoped the structure of government would limit their "mischiefs." Interest groups form when a collection of people share similar political goals and organize to achieve them. Sometimes, these groups are based on a shared group identity, such as race, ethnicity, gender, or sexual orientation. Others are based on specific policy issues, such as reducing taxes or combating global warming. Still others claim to operate in the public interest on broad issues, such as educating voters or reducing the federal deficit. Interest groups sometimes begin as social movements, which consist of many people at the grassroots level who are interested in a significant issue, idea, or concern and take action to support or oppose it.

Types of Interest Groups (Action)

5.2 Describe different types of interest groups, p. 114.

Interest groups can be categorized as economic, ideological or single-issue, public interest, foreign policy, or government itself. Economic groups include corporations, labor unions, and professional and trade associations; they lobby officials and campaign for candidates whose trade, tax, and regulation policies favor their perspective. Interest groups often offer benefits to members to overcome the free rider problem. Ideological groups typically pursue a single policy goal through many means; for example, the ACLU pursues civil liberties cases. Public interest groups are presumably more broadly based, including watchdog groups and charities. Foreign policy groups work to influence some area of the United States' international affairs. Finally, government groups include public sector unions and other government entities.

Characteristics and Power of Interest Groups (Action)

5.3 Analyze the methods and activities that interest groups use to influence political outcomes, p. 120.

Size, resources, cohesiveness, leadership, and techniques, especially the ability to contribute to candidates and political parties and to fund lobbyists, affect interest group power. The actual power of an interest group stems from how these elements relate to the political and governmental environment in which the interest group operates. Interest groups typically include people with many other cross-cutting interests, which both reduce and stabilize their influence.

Lobbyists represent organized interests before government. Lobbying involves communicating with legislators and executive-branch officials, making campaign contributions, and assisting in election activity, especially through political action committees (PACs). Interest groups also communicate their message directly to the public through mass mailings, advertising, and online media.

What Explains Interest Group Success? (Impact)

5.4 Evaluate the factors that affect the relative success of interest groups, p. 126.

The size, cohesion, political interest, and resources of the interest group are important to predicting success in influencing policy. Interest groups spend money to lobby government officials and to support or defeat candidates, especially through the expanded use of PACs. Groups that lack money typically struggle to get their message out to the public and fail to influence public officials.

Interest groups can be important in influencing the outcome of elections. In recent elections, groups like the League of Conservation Voters, the U.S. Chamber of Commerce, and others were important in competitive contests. The influence of groups in the legislative process is greatest when there is an absence of strong groups on the other side of the issue and when members of Congress do not have a strong constituency interest.

Limiting the Mischiefs of Faction (Impact)

5.5 Assess the effectiveness of regulations designed to control interest groups, p. 134.

Congress has enacted laws to regulate and reform excesses of interest groups in electoral democracy. Often the reforms came after a scandal. The Federal Election Campaign Act (FECA) was passed in the 1970s in response to the Watergate scandal, and the Bipartisan Campaign Reform Act (BCRA) was passed in 2002 in response to soft money and other abuses by political parties and interest groups. Court decisions have removed some of the restrictions on interest group activities during elections.

Congress has also enacted laws requiring more disclosure by lobbyists, restricted gifts they can give office holders, and generally tried to make lobbying more transparent. Presidents have also issued executive orders banning staff from accepting gifts from lobbyists and requiring that those who leave the administration must wait at least two years before they can lobby former colleagues and agencies they worked with while in office.

LEARN THE TERMS

faction, p. 111
interest group, p. 111
social movement, p. 112
pluralism, p. 113
open shop, p. 116
closed shop, p. 116
collective bargaining, p. 116
free rider, p. 116
professional associations, p. 117
nongovernmental organization (NGO), p. 119
collective action, p. 120
public choice, p. 120
lobbyist, p. 120
revolving door, p. 121
issue network, p. 121
Federal Register, p. 123
amicus curiae brief, p. 123
bundling, p. 124
political action committee (PAC), p. 124
Super PAC, p. 124
section 501(c) groups, p. 124
lobbying, p. 126
independent expenditures, p. 130
issue advocacy, p. 133
Bipartisan Campaign Reform Act (BCRA), p. 133
soft money, p. 134

CHAPTER 6

Political Parties

Political parties have become more ideologically divided and more hostile to cooperation and compromise. One exception to this political division has been the tradition of an annual congressional baseball game with participants from both parties and both chambers participating. The 2017 game was delayed a day after a gunman shot five members of the Republican team as they practiced for the annual event. Here, members of both the Democratic and Republican teams pause for prayer before the game, with the Chaplain of the U.S. House of Representatives offering a prayer. Almost 25,000 people attended the game in a show of support for bipartisanship. The young man with crutches in the photo is Zack Barth, an aid to Congressman Roger Williams of Texas. He was wounded in the shooting.

LEARNING OBJECTIVES

6.1 Trace the development of political parties in the United States (Structure), p. 142.

6.2 Identify the functions of political parties and their structure at the national, state, and local levels (Action), p. 147.

6.3 Evaluate the role of minor parties in the U.S. electoral system (Action), p. 159.

6.4 Describe the significance of party identification in America today (Impact), p. 162.

6.5 Assess the reasons for the persistence of the two-party system (Impact), p. 166.

Some years ago, a community college district in Los Angeles held a nonpartisan election for its trustees in which any registered voter could run if he or she paid the $50 filing fee and gathered 500 valid signatures on a petition. Each voter could cast up to seven votes. Political parties were not allowed to nominate candidates, and party labels did not appear on the ballot. In addition, because the community college district was newly created, none of the candidates were incumbents. As a result, incumbency—another frequently used voting cue—was also absent. A total of 133 candidates ran, and they were listed alphabetically.

So how do people vote in an election without the party labels that typically help voters get a sense for the candidates? The answer is that some voters decide on random information such as the spelling and sound of the candidate's first name. Based on the election results, candidates with a Mexican American surname had an advantage, while those whose names began with the letters A to F did better than those later in the alphabet. Having a well-known name also helped. One of the winners, E. G. "Jerry" Brown Jr., was the son of a former governor.[1] Winning this election launched his political career; later he was elected California governor in 1975 and then again in 2010. Endorsements by the *Los Angeles Times* also influenced the outcome, as did campaigning by a conservative group.

Clearly, parties play an important role in facilitating voting by organizing elections and simplifying choices. Rarely are American voters asked to choose from among 133 candidates. E. E. Schattschneider, a noted political scientist, once said, "The political parties created democracy, and modern democracy is unthinkable save in terms of the parties."[2] This view that parties are essential to democracy runs counter to a long-standing and deeply seated distrust of parties. But without parties, voters would face the daunting challenge of choosing between scores of candidates for each office, as happened in Los Angeles. They would need to research the policy positions of each individual candidate in order to make an educated choice.

This chapter begins by examining the structural evolution of American political parties and how that structure influences elections today. We then examine why parties are so vital to the functioning of an active democracy. Our election rules make it difficult for minor parties to win the election itself, but even so, minor parties do influence electoral agendas and politics more generally. Although U.S. political parties have changed over time, they remain important institutions on their own and within government. We will look at the way parties have an impact in elections and whether they will remain relevant in the future.

A Brief History of American Political Parties (Structure)

6.1 Trace the development of political parties in the United States.

The Constitution makes no mention of parties, and some of the Framers and early leaders of the country worried about parties, which they sometimes called "factions." George Washington in his farewell address warned that parties "may become potent engines, by which cunning, ambitious and unprincipled men will be enabled to subvert the power of the people and to usurp for themselves the reins of government."[3] John Adams, our second president, also "dreaded" political parties, which he considered "evil."[4] Given these strong anti-party sentiments it is not surprising that there is no mention of political parties in the Constitution. While not part of the constitutional structure, parties play an important structural role in facilitating citizen action and voting by organizing elections and simplifying choices.

The parties also provide a structure to facilitate action; you can volunteer in campaigns and get-out-the-vote efforts, and even provide transportation to get your fellow citizens to the polls on Election Day. The impact of political parties, and your action within those parties, is difficult to overstate. Without the structure parties provide, it would be more difficult to impact the political system through your actions.

Parties are both a consequence of democracy and an instrument of it. In addition to narrowing voters' choices, they make national and state elections work.[5] American voters take for granted the peaceful transfer of power from one elected official to another and from one party to another; yet in new democracies where holding power may be more important than democratic principles, the peaceful transfer of power after an election is often a problem. Well-established parties help stabilize democracy.

To the founders of the young Republic, parties meant bigger, better-organized, and fiercer factions, which they did not want. Benjamin Franklin worried about the "infinite mutual abuse of parties, tearing to pieces the best of characters." And Thomas Jefferson said, "If I could not go to heaven but with a party, I would not go there at all."[6]

How, then, did parties start?

The Nation's First Parties

Political parties emerged largely out of practical necessity. The same early leaders who so frequently stated their opposition to them also recognized the need to organize officeholders who shared their views so that government could act. In 1787, parties began to form as citizens debated ratifying the U.S. Constitution. To get Congress to pass its measures, President George Washington had to fashion a coalition among factions. This job fell to his Treasury secretary, Alexander Hamilton, who built an informal Federalist party, while Washington stayed "above politics."

Secretary of State Jefferson and other officials, many of whom despised Hamilton and his aristocratic ways as much as they opposed the policies he favored, were uncertain about how to deal with these political differences. Their overriding concern was the success of the new government; personal loyalty to Washington was a close second. Despite his opposition to Washington's policies, Jefferson stayed in the cabinet through most of the first term. When he left the cabinet at the end of 1793, many who joined him in opposition to the administration's economic policies remained in Congress, forming a group of legislators opposed to Federalist fiscal policies and eventually to Federalist foreign policy, which appeared "soft on Britain." This party was later known as Republicans, then as Democratic-Republicans, and finally as Democrats.[7]

Realigning Elections

American political parties have evolved and changed over time, but some underlying characteristics have been constant. Historically, we have had a two-party system with occasional minor parties. Our parties are moderate and accommodative, meaning they are open to people with diverse outlooks. Political scientist V. O. Key and others have argued that our party system has been shaped in large part by **realigning elections**. Also called *critical elections,* these turning points define the agenda of politics and the alignment of voters within parties during periods of historic change in the economy and society.

realigning election
An election during periods of expanded suffrage and change in the economy and society that proves to be a turning point, redefining the agenda of politics and the alignment of voters within parties.

Realigning elections are characterized by intense voter involvement, disruptions of traditional voting patterns, changes in the relationships of power within the broader political community, and the formation of new and durable electoral groupings. They have occurred cyclically, about every 32 years, and tend to coincide with expansions of suffrage or changes in the rate of voting.[8] Political scientists generally agree that there have been four realigning elections in American party history: 1824, 1860, 1896, and 1932. Although some argued that the United States was due for another in the 1970s and 1980s,[9] there is little evidence that such an election has yet occurred.

1824: ANDREW JACKSON AND THE DEMOCRATS Party politics were invigorated following the election of 1824, in which the leader in the popular vote—the hero of the Battle of New Orleans in the War of 1812, Democrat Andrew Jackson—failed to achieve the necessary majority of the Electoral College votes and was defeated by John Quincy Adams in the runoff election in the House of Representatives. Jackson, brilliantly aided by Martin Van Buren, a veteran party builder in New York State, later knitted together a winning combination of regions, interest groups, and political doctrines to win the presidency in 1828. By the time Van Buren, another Democrat, followed Jackson into the White House in 1837, the Democrats had become a large, nationwide movement with national and state leadership, a clear party doctrine, and a grassroots organization. The Whigs, who succeeded the Federalists as the opposition party, were nearly as strong: in 1840 they put their own man, General William Henry Harrison ("Old Tippecanoe"), into the White House. A two-party system had been born.

1860: THE CIVIL WAR AND THE RISE OF THE REPUBLICANS Out of the crisis over slavery evolved the second Republican Party—the first being the National Republican Party that existed for barely a decade in the 1820s. The second Republican Party ultimately adopted the nickname "Grand Old Party" (GOP).[10] Abraham Lincoln was elected in 1860 with the support not only of financiers, industrialists, and merchants, but also of many workers and farmers. For 50 years after 1860, the Republican coalition won every presidential race except for Grover Cleveland's victories in 1884 and 1892. The Democratic Party survived with its durable white-male base in the South.

1896: A PARTY IN TRANSITION Economic changes, including industrialization and hard times for farmers, led to changes in the Republican Party in the late 1800s.[11] Some Republicans insisted on maintaining their Reconstruction policies into the 1890s, until it became obvious it would jeopardize their electoral base.[12] A combination of western and southern farmers and mining interests sought an alliance with workers in the East and Midwest to "recaptur[e] America from the foreign moneyed interests responsible for industrialization. The crisis of industrialization squarely placed an agrarian-fundamentalist view of life against an industrial-progressive view...."[13] William Jennings Bryan, the Democratic candidate for president in 1896, was a talented orator but lost the race to William McKinley.[14] The 1896 realignment differs from the others, however, in that the party in power did not change hands. In that sense, it was a *converting realignment* because it reinforced the Republican majority status that had been in place since 1860.[15]

The Progressive Era, the first two decades of the twentieth century, produced a wave of political reform led by the Progressive wing of the Republican Party. Much of the agenda of the Progressives focused on the corrupt political parties. Civil service reforms shifted some of the patronage out of the hands of party officials. The direct primary election took control of nominations from party leaders and gave it to the rank and file. In addition, a number of cities instituted nonpartisan governments, totally eliminating the role of a party.

Equally important, the Progressive Era produced major changes in political power. In 1913, voters won the right to choose their senators through popular vote under the Seventeenth Amendment to the Constitution; in 1920, women won the right to vote under the Nineteenth Amendment. Thus, in a short time, the electorate changed, the rules changed, and even the stakes of the game changed. Democrats were unable to build a durable winning coalition during this time and remained the minority party until the early 1930s, when the Great Depression overwhelmed the Republican Hoover administration.[16]

1932: FRANKLIN ROOSEVELT AND THE NEW DEAL ALIGNMENT The 1932 election was a turning point in U.S. politics. In the 1930s, the United States faced a devastating economic collapse. Between 1929 and 1932, the gross national product fell more than 10 percent per year, and unemployment rose from 1.5 million to more than 12 million, with millions more working only part-time.[17]

With the economic crisis deepening, Franklin D. Roosevelt and the Democrats were swept into office in 1932 on a tide of anti-Hoover and anti-Republican sentiment. Roosevelt promised that his response to the Depression would be a "New Deal for America." After a century of sporadic government action, the New Dealers fundamentally altered the relationship between government and society by providing government jobs for the unemployed and using government expenditures to stimulate economic growth.

The dividing line between Republicans and Democrats was the role of government in the economy. Roosevelt Democrats argued that the government had to act to pull the country out of the Depression. Republicans objected to enlarging the scope of government and intruding into the economy. This basic disagreement about whether the national government should play an active role in regulating and promoting our economy remains one of the most important divisions between the Democratic and Republican parties today, although with time, the country and both parties accepted many of the New Deal programs.

The Last Half-Century

Major shifts in party demographics have occurred in recent decades. The once "Solid South" that Democrats could count on to bolster their legislative majorities and help win the White House has now become the "Republican South" in presidential and congressional elections. Republican congressional leaders have often been from southern states that once rarely elected Republicans. This shift is explained by the movement of large numbers of white people out of the Democratic Party, in part because of the party's position on civil rights but also because of national Democrats' stance on abortion and other social issues. The rise of the Republican South reinforced the shift to conservatism in the GOP. This shift, combined with the diminished ranks of conservative southern Democrats, made the Democratic Party, especially the congressional Democrats, more unified and more liberal than in the days when more of its congressional members had "safe" southern seats.[18]

Since 1953, **divided government**, with one party controlling Congress and the other the White House, has been in effect twice as long as united government, in which one party controls both legislative and executive branches. At other times, Congress has had divided control with one party having a majority in the House and the other in the Senate. For 34 of the last 50 years the United States has had a divided government.

divided government
Governance divided between the parties, as when one holds the presidency and the other controls one or both houses of Congress.

The 1932 election is seen as a "critical election" resulting in an enduring realignment. Franklin Roosevelt and the Democrats enlarged the role of government in response to the Great Depression. Roosevelt is seen here greeting farmers in Georgia in October 1932 as he campaigned for the presidency.

The current system of party identification is built on a foundation of the New Deal and the critical election of 1932, events that took place more than three-quarters of a century ago. Elections during the past few decades have seen power change hands many times without any long-term shifts in the population in party allegiance. There has been some sorting, with Southern whites now more consistently Republican, African Americans more consistently Democratic, and Hispanics, women, and younger voters increasingly Democratic. But the fundamental party divide has remained remarkably stable. Some wondered whether 2016 would be the long-awaited realigning election or at least the beginning of a realigning era.[19] The number of registered voters expanded steadily during the 2008 election, suggesting high levels of voter interest and a possible start to a realignment. But in 2012, turnout dropped by nearly five percentage points nationwide, an indication that the public was less engaged.[20] Turnout in 2016 was higher than in 2012 but remained 2 percent lower than in 2008, making 2008 look less like a realignment. In 2016, like 2008 and 2012, Democrats retained their large advantage among racial minorities, women, and younger voters, giving them an advantage in presidential elections, as long as their constituents turn out to vote. In 2018, Democrats regained the House majority, picking up over 30 seats, many of them in suburban areas.[21]

While Democrats have broadened their party base, Republicans have found energy in a new faction within their party. The 2008 election produced an immediate backlash among conservative voters that later became known as the Tea Party Movement. Although most Tea Party activists were also Republicans, they were particularly concerned about growing deficits, health care reform, illegal immigration, protecting gun rights, and big government. They saw Barack Obama even more unfavorably than other Republicans. The Tea Party was seen as helping the GOP secure a majority in the House of Representatives in 2010.

The Tea Party faction since 2010 has had success in challenging some Republicans for renomination.[22] Tea Party Republicans in the House are known as the Freedom Caucus, and they have pushed fellow congressional Republicans in a more conservative direction. For example, in 2013 they insisted that the Senate adopt a House-passed government-spending bill that would have delayed the Affordable Care Act. When the Senate did not pass that version of the bill the government was forced to shut down for lack of funding as the new budget year began. The Freedom Caucus has remained occasionally at odds with House Republican leadership, especially Speaker John Boehner, but were less contentious with Speaker Paul Ryan. With Ryan's decision not to seek reelection in 2018, the different factions within the Republican House caucus will test the ability of a new leader to hold the party together. Following the Republican loss of the majority in 2018, the party faced a contested election for majority leader.

Following the 2012 presidential election defeat of Mitt Romney, Republican Party leaders expressed a desire to broaden the appeal of the party to younger voters, women, and minorities. Barack Obama had done well with these groups in 2008 and 2012. But the Trump campaign did not activate these demographic groups; rather, it appeared to be driven by lower- and middle-income white males. Moreover, the rhetoric of the 2016 Republican nomination contest, including mentions of deporting undocumented persons, building a wall to better secure the border with Mexico, punishing women who pursue abortions, and halting the immigration of Muslims, may have a lasting negative impact on these groups' support for the GOP.

In 2016, Donald Trump won the presidency but failed to win the popular vote. However, his coalition included citizens who had not voted in recent elections and some who had voted for Barack Obama. Trump ran as a different kind of politician who has the potential to reshape the Republican Party around his message of America first in foreign policy and his populist approach to domestic issues. Whether there is an enduring Trump effect in the Republican Party is uncertain as his approach to foreign policy and international trade is counter to what has been the traditional Republican position. There is also the possibility that opponents of Trump may activate new and less active voters to oppose Republicans in 2018 or 2020.

Within the Democratic Party, the 2016 nomination contest was about where the party stood on reducing income inequality by increasing taxes on affluent people and spending more on government programs like health care, college tuition, and infrastructure. Bernie Sanders, like Donald Trump, ran as an outsider, in this case seeking to make the Democratic Party more liberal. Over the course of the nomination campaign Hillary Clinton's positions moved towards those of Bernie Sanders on trade, college education, and taxing the wealthy to protect social security.

The 2016 general election focused largely on negative attributes of Donald Trump and Hillary Clinton. This was in part the strategy of both candidates. Clinton and her supporting groups tried to depict Trump as unqualified and inexperienced. Trump and his allies also made negative attributes of Clinton their main focus. For example, they often criticized her having used a private computer server for her emails while she was Secretary of State, possibly breaking the law. Candidate attacks like these are election specific and not likely to lead to a realignment. Following Clinton's defeat, Democrats found themselves controlling neither chamber of the Congress nor the Presidency, and their party had also suffered major losses over several elections in state and local races. What unified Democrats was opposition to Donald Trump. The new president gave them political openings to showcase opposition on some of his appointments, on controversies like the firing of FBI Director James Comey, and on Trump's disclosure of top secret intelligence in a meeting with Russian Foreign Minister Sergi Lavrov and other Russian officials. The investigation of the Trump campaign's possible involvement with Russia during the 2016 campaign remained a topic for frequent news coverage throughout 2018. Another major focus of Trump's first two years in office was the high turnover of his staff and appointees, some leaving amid alleged ethics violations.

What Parties Do for Democracy (Action)

6.2 Identify the functions of political parties and their structure at the national, state, and local levels.

American political parties serve a variety of political and social functions, some well and others not so well. The way they perform them differs across time and place. But the parties remain important because they are among the most widely used organizations that help citizens take action.

Party Functions

Political parties play an important role in organizing elections, simplifying choices for voters, and helping elect people who will help their party's positions and philosophy become public policy.

political party
An organization that seeks political power by electing people to office so that its positions and philosophy become public policy.

ORGANIZE THE COMPETITION Parties exist primarily as organizing mechanisms to win elections and thus win control of government. They recruit and nominate candidates for office; register and activate voters; and help candidates by training them, raising money for them, providing them with research and voter lists, and enlisting volunteers to work for them.[23]

At one time parties helped organize electoral competition by providing the ballots on which people voted. For most of the first century of U.S. history, ballots were not provided by the government, but printed by the parties on different-colored paper or distributed in partisan newspapers. In this system, voters turned in their ballots and observers knew how they voted, making it possible for parties to reward or punish individuals based on how they voted. Other voting systems in our early history included voting orally or casting a pebble or bean into a hat.[24]

Australia was the first country to adopt secret ballots in 1857; the trend later spread to other English-speaking countries and was first proposed in the United States in 1882. An article by Henry George, a writer and politician, published in the *North American Review*, argued that the secret ballot would prevent the bribery or intimidation of voters fostered by the party ballot system. Opponents of the reform contended that state-printed ballots distributed at voting places would take too long, resulting in long lines, and would cost the taxpayers too much money.[25]

Massachusetts was the first state to adopt the system in 1888, and by 1896 all but six states were using secret ballots. Different states adopted different formats for their ballots. Some organized the ballots by party, others by office. The organization of the ballot can be important in fostering more or less partisan voting. Later, some states permitted voters to vote via machines, and today, many states use electronic voting machines. How people vote in other types of elections, like whether or not to unionize, has generated controversy in recent years. But a voting system that protects the privacy of the act of voting, provided at state expense, is now taken for granted.

Parties no longer print the ballots but they play other important functions in organizing elections and structuring candidate choices. Party labels typically help voters get a sense for the candidates; even without knowing anything about the individual candidate, voters can still make reliable assumptions about a candidate's positions based on the party label. But, not all elections are partisan. In some settings, as with the Los Angeles Community College District election discussed at the beginning of the chapter, people vote without knowing a candidate's party label. Without a party label, other factors, at least some of which are entirely unrelated to the positions the candidate is likely to hold, may play a bigger role in voting decisions. Party labels do important work for voters. They may not know much about a particular candidate, but knowing the candidate is a Republican or a Democrat provides some information.

nonpartisan election
An election in which candidates are not selected or endorsed by political parties, and party affiliation is not listed on ballots.

Most local and judicial elections are **nonpartisan elections**, which gives parties little opportunity to influence the outcome. Advocates of nonpartisan elections contend that partisanship is not relevant to being a good judge, mayor, or school board member. But, just as in the Los Angeles community college district election, without knowing candidates' party affiliations, voters rely on name familiarity, ballot order, or incumbency. These local elections are also often held at times other than when state or federal elections are held. As a result, fewer voters tend to turn out for nonpartisan elections than for standard partisan elections.[26]

UNIFY THE ELECTORATE Parties are often accused of creating conflict, but they actually often help unify the electorate and moderate conflict, at least within the party. Parties have a strong incentive to resolve their internal differences and come together to take on the opposition. Moreover, to win elections, parties need to reach out to voters outside their party and gain their support. This action also helps unify the electorate, at least into the two large national political parties in the American system.

Parties have great difficulty building coalitions on controversial issues such as immigration, abortion, or gun control. Not surprisingly, candidates and parties generally try to avoid defining themselves or the election in single-issue terms. Rather, they hope that if voters disagree with the party's stand on one issue, they will still support it because they agree on other issues.

ORGANIZE THE GOVERNMENT Political parties in the United States are important when it comes to organizing state and national governments. Congress is organized along party lines: the party with the most votes in each chamber elects the officers of that chamber, selects committee chairs, and has a majority on all the committees. State legislatures, except Nebraska, are also organized along party lines. For four decades, the Democrats had majorities in the U.S. House, but since 1994 Republicans have been in the majority in all but four years (2007–2011). Over the same time period in the U.S. Senate, party control has changed five times with control of the chamber possible in most election cycles. In the 2016 election, Republicans had a net loss of two seats—one in New Hampshire and one in Illinois—but retained the Senate majority. As a result, in 2017 the GOP controlled both houses of Congress and the Presidency for the first time since 2005. Divided government returned after the 2018 election with the Democrats taking control of the House of Representatives and the Senate retaining a Republican majority.[27]

Political parties and candidates attempt to personally contact in person or on the phone as many likely supporters as they can. Here a volunteer for Bernie Sanders is calling people urging them to attend the Nevada caucus for Senator Sanders.

The party that controls the White House, the governor's mansion, or city hall gets **patronage**, which means its leaders can select party members as public officials or judges. Such appointments are limited only by civil service regulations that restrict patronage typically to the top posts, but these posts, which number approximately 3,000 in the federal government (not including ambassadors, U.S. marshals, and U.S. attorneys), are also numerous at the state and local levels. Patronage provides an incentive for people to become engaged in politics and gives party leaders and elected politicians the loyal partisans in key positions they need to help them achieve their policy objectives. Patronage, sometimes called the *spoils system,* has declined dramatically in importance due to civil service reform, which we discuss later in this chapter and in the chapter on the bureaucracy and policy.

MAKE POLICY One of the great strengths of our democracy is that even the party that wins an election usually has to moderate what it does to win reelection. Public policy seldom changes dramatically after elections. Nonetheless, the party that wins the election has a chance to enact its policies and campaign promises.

American parties have had only limited success in setting the course of national policy, especially compared to countries with strong parties. The European model of party government, which has been called a *responsible party system,* assumes that parties discipline their members through their control over nominations and campaigns. Officeholders in such party-centered systems are expected to act according to party wishes and vote along party lines—or they will not be allowed to run again under the party label, generally preventing their reelection. Candidates also run on fairly specific party platforms and are expected to implement them if they win control in the election.

patronage
The dispensing of government jobs to persons who belong to the winning political party.

In the United States, because candidates can win nominations from voters directly in primaries it is more difficult for parties to discipline members who express views contrary to those of the party.[28] The American system is largely *candidate centered*; politicians are nominated largely on the basis of their qualifications and personal appeal, not party loyalty. In fact, it is more correct to say that in most contests, we have *candidate* politics rather than *party* politics. As a consequence, party leaders cannot guarantee passage of their program, even if they are in the majority.

honeymoon
The first six months or so of a new presidential administration when the president enjoys generally positive relations with the press and Congress, his or her supporters are still celebrating victory, and the public focuses on the inaugural festivities and presidential agenda.

PROVIDE LOYAL OPPOSITION The party out of power closely monitors and comments on the actions of the party in power, providing accountability. When national security is at issue or the country is under attack, parties restrain their criticism, as the Democrats in Congress did for some time after September 11, 2001. There is also usually a polite interval following an election—known as the **honeymoon**—after which the opposition party begins to criticize the party that controls the White House, especially when the opposition controls one or both houses of Congress.[29] The length of the honeymoon depends, in part, on how close the vote was in the election, the contentiousness of the new administration's agenda, and the leadership skills of the new president. Honeymoons have grown shorter throughout the past few decades as candidates from the president's own party and the opposition party get ready for the next presidential election. This puts pressure on the new president to move quickly to set the legislative agenda. Early success in enacting policy can prolong the honeymoon; mistakes or controversies can shorten it.

In the early months of his presidency, Donald Trump issued many executive orders which he linked to campaign promises, including controversial ones like the ban on refugees from predominantly Muslim countries. But he did not go as far as some religious conservatives wanted regarding LGBTQ rights in his executive order on religious liberty, nor did he immediately withdraw from the North American Free Trade Agreement as some assumed he would do given his campaign rhetoric. However, Trump fulfilled two of his most important campaign promises with the nomination and confirmation of Neil Gorsuch to the U.S. Supreme Court, and passage of a large tax cut, especially aimed at reducing taxes for corporations and high-income individuals.

The Nomination of Candidates

From the beginning, parties have been the mechanism by which candidates for public office are chosen, although parties have used various means to choose candidates. And, as mentioned above, today elections are largely candidate-centered. Candidates run as Democrats or Republicans, but they appeal directly to constituents who typically vote for the party's candidate in primary elections.

caucus

A meeting of local party members to choose party officials or candidates for public office and to decide the platform.

THE CAUCUS The **caucus** played an important part in pre-Revolutionary politics and continued to be important in our early history, as elected officials organized themselves into groups or parties and together selected candidates to run for higher office, including the presidency. This method of nomination operated for several decades after the United States was established.

As early as the 1820s, however, critics were making charges of "secret deals." Moreover, the caucus was not representative of people from areas where a party was in a minority or nonexistent, as only officeholders took part in it. The *mixed caucus* was an effort to make the caucus more representative of rank-and-file party members. It brought in delegates from districts in which the party had no elected legislators.

Not long after Democratic voters arrive at their neighborhood caucus in Iowa, they are asked to divide into groups based on their preferred candidate. Local representatives of the presidential candidates seek to persuade undecided voters, like those seen here, to join their candidate group and possibly secure more delegates from that ward (the name Iowa uses for voting district). Republicans do not form groups by candidates, rather they vote early in the meeting by secret ballot.

Some states have retained a caucus system that indirectly selects nominees. Voters participate by attending a meeting at a set time and explaining their candidate and policy preferences. The meeting usually includes a vote for preferred presidential candidates in presidential election years. In 2016, 13 states used caucuses to determine delegates for the presidential nominations for at least one party.[30]

The best-known example of a caucus system is Iowa, which is the first state where voters may vote for their preferred candidate. Because it is first, a great deal of attention by the candidates and media is given to Iowa. In 2016, Ted Cruz won the Iowa Republican Caucus, with Hillary Clinton very narrowly winning among Democrats.

THE PARTY CONVENTION During the 1830s and 1840s, a system of **party conventions** was instituted. Delegates, usually chosen directly by party members in towns and cities, selected the party candidates, debated and adopted a platform, and built party spirit by celebrating noisily. Party conventions, once dominated by party bosses and machines, are now gatherings of delegates elected at the state level either through a complex process of caucuses or primaries that may lead to county and state conventions where the actual delegates are chosen. To draw more voters and reduce the power of the bosses, most states now have the **direct primary**, in which people can vote for the party's nominees for office. As a result, delegates have little freedom to change their votes during the initial balloting at the convention.

party convention
A meeting of party delegates to vote on matters of policy and, in some cases, to select party candidates for public office.

direct primary
An election in which voters choose party nominees.

The 2016 presidential nomination contest called attention to the differing rules for selecting delegates to attend the national nominating convention. Winning a primary or caucus does not necessarily result in convention delegates from a state. Rather, candidates often must continue to do well in state party conventions where the actual persons who will serve as delegates are selected. This is something Ted Cruz did much better at than Donald Trump. Cruz had more extensive networks of supporters who would attend conventions and vote for his delegates. For example, Ted Cruz won more than half of the delegates in Louisiana's 2016 presidential primary despite losing the popular vote to Donald Trump. Cruz did this by winning enough votes to receive an equal number of delegates (Louisiana awards them proportionally) and by courting the five "unbound" delegates (according to state rules, they can vote for the candidate of their choice), as well as the five delegates who had previously been committed to Marco Rubio. Trump criticized state processes like this as "a rigged system."[31]

Both parties provide for some automatic delegate slots that go to officeholders and elected party officials. The Democrats have more of these "super delegates" than do the Republicans. Hillary Clinton had locked up most of the Democratic super delegates early in the nomination process, even from states that Bernie Sanders won in a landslide. Speaking of these delegates, he said, "[they] ought to seriously reflect on whether they should cast their super delegate vote in line with the wishes of the people of their state."[32] In March 2018, the Democratic National Committee took the first step to "revise the role and reduce the perceived influence" of superdelegates.[33]

THE DIRECT PRIMARY Primaries spread rapidly after Wisconsin adopted them in 1905—in the North as a Progressive Era reform, and in the South as a way to bring democracy to a region that had seen no meaningful general elections since the end of Reconstruction in the 1870s because of one-party Democratic rule. By 1920, direct primaries were the norm for some offices in nearly all states.

Today, the direct primary is the typical method of picking party candidates. Primaries vary significantly from state to state in terms of (1) who may run in a primary and how he or she qualifies for the ballot; (2) whether the party organization can or does endorse candidates before the primary; (3) who may vote in a party's primary—that is, whether a voter must register with a party to vote in that party's primary; and (4) how many votes are needed for nomination—the most votes (a plurality), more than 50 percent (a majority), or some other number determined by party rule or state law. The differences among primaries are not trivial; they have an important impact on the role played by party organizations and on the strategy used by candidates. In the 2018 midterm election House Democratic leaders and the Democratic Congressional Campaign Committee was more active in party primaries. This was due in part to a surge in individuals seeking the Democratic nomination.[34] In states with **open primaries**, any voter, regardless of party, can participate in the primary of whichever party he or she chooses. This kind of primary permits **crossover voting**—Republicans and Independents helping to determine the Democratic nominee, and vice versa. Other states use **closed primaries**, in which only persons already registered in that party may participate. In 2016, Sanders and Trump did better in open primaries while Cruz and Clinton did better in closed primaries.

open primary
A primary election in which any voter, regardless of party, may vote.

crossover voting
Voting by a member of one party for a candidate of another party.

closed primary
A primary election in which only persons registered in the party holding the primary may vote.

Participation in primaries is generally higher than participation in caucuses, and typically the earlier caucuses or primaries have higher rates of participation than later ones because in many election years the nominee is determined well before the later states vote. In 2016, overall turnout was projected to rival the record set in 2008. However, turnout for the 2016 Democratic nomination was lower in the contests through May 1 than in 2008. Democrats were at 9.5 percent of the voter-eligible population voting in 2016, down from 16.9 percent in 2008. Republicans, in contrast, were up slightly in 2016 (11 percent) over both 2008 (9.8 percent) and 2012 (7.8 percent). Clearly the 2008 Democratic nomination contest involved more voters than the GOP that year or in either party since then.[35]

Some states, such as Washington and California, experimented with *blanket primaries*, in which all voters could vote for any candidate, regardless of party. They could vote for a candidate of one party for one office and for a candidate from another party for another office, something not permitted under either closed or open primaries. But, in 2000, upon challenge from the California Democratic Party, the Supreme Court held that the blanket primary violated its members' free association rights.[36] In 2010 and 2012, California voters invented another new form of primary voting when they overwhelmingly passed an initiative to allow voters to cast their primary ballot for a candidate from any party, with the top two vote getters then running in the general election. This has come to be known as the top two primary, gaining national attention in the 2018 California primaries. Proponents of the **top two primary** see it as fostering more moderate politics.[37] In neither California nor Washington was the "top two" primary used in the 2016 primaries for president; rather, voters selected from among candidates from one party.[38] But in contests for the U.S. House or U.S. Senate there are several examples in recent years of the top two candidates coming from the same party.

top two primary
A type of primary election in which all candidates are listed on the same ballot with the two receiving the most votes, regardless of their party, going onto the general election ballot. This may mean the general election will be between two candidates from the same party.

Along with modern communications and fund-raising techniques, direct primaries have diminished the influence of leaders of political parties. Many critics believe this change has had some undesirable consequences. Party leaders now have less influence over who gets to be the party's candidate, and candidates are less accountable to the party both during and after the election.

Party Structure

Like other institutions of government—Congress, the presidency, and the courts—political parties have rules, procedures, and organizational structure. What are the institutional characteristics of political parties?

NATIONAL PARTY LEADERSHIP The supreme authority in both major parties is the **national party convention**, which meets every four years for four days to nominate candidates for president and vice president, to ratify the party platform, and to adopt rules.

national party convention
A national meeting of delegates elected in primaries, caucuses, or state conventions who assemble once every four years to nominate candidates for president and vice president, ratify the party platform, elect officers, and adopt rules.

In charge of the national party, when it is not assembled in convention, is the *national committee*. In recent years, both parties have strengthened the role of the national committee and enhanced the influence of individual committee members. The committees are now more representative of the party rank and file. But in neither party is the national committee the center of party leadership.

Each major party has a *national chair* as its top official. The national committee formally elects the chair, but in reality this official is the choice of the presidential nominee. For the party that controls the White House, the chair actually serves at the pleasure of the president and does the president's bidding. Party chairs often change after elections. Since 2017, the Republican National Committee (RNC) has been chaired by Ronna Romney McDaniel who had previously been chair of the Michigan Republican party. After the 2012 presidential election defeat, the RNC released a detailed report on how the party could become more competitive in presidential elections.[39] The report included recommendations that the party expand its appeal to racial minorities, women, and members of the LGBTQ community, establish a shorter presidential primary season, and catch up with the Democrats in the use of campaign tools that help to identify and mobilize voters likely to support the party.[40] In 2016, the Trump campaign focused its campaign themes and issue positions on appealing to and mobilizing a larger share of non-college educated whites. At the same time, Clinton and her allies did not achieve the same turnout levels as Obama did among non-whites, young, and lower-income potential voters.

Between 2012 and 2016, Florida congresswoman Debbie Wasserman Schultz chaired the Democratic National Committee (DNC). She was the third woman to head the Democratic National Committee and the first sitting congresswoman to do so. In 2016, she was accused of favoring the candidacy of Hillary Clinton over Bernie Sanders by scheduling only six debates on holiday weekends televised on networks with limited reach. In addition, in a controversial move, the DNC briefly suspended the Sanders campaign's access to the shared Democratic voter file, an essential tool of campaigns, after a Sanders staffer accessed Clinton campaign data that should have not been accessible to the Sanders campaign from a vendor hired by the Democratic National Committee.[41] Wasserman Schultz eventually restored access to the data, but not before Sanders's campaign sued the DNC for breach of contract.[42] As Democrats gathered for their convention in Philadelphia in July 2016, the Web site WikiLeaks released emails from within the DNC that showed a bias against Bernie Sanders. The emails had been obtained by hackers, with a Russian hacker claiming credit.[43] The controversy of some DNC staff bias against Sanders led to Wasserman Schultz's resignation and the appointment of longstanding Democratic operative Donna Brazile as chair.

Ronna Romney McDaniel became Chair of the Republican National Committee in 2017. She was President Trump's recommendation for the position after he selected the prior chair, Reince Preibus to be his White House Chief of Staff. She is seen here at a Trump campaign rally in Washington Township in 2018.

Following the 2016 election defeat, the Democrats elected former Secretary of Labor Tom Perez to head the DNC. Tom Perez, who was the Secretary of Labor under President Obama, was elected DNC chair in February, 2017. Perez defeated U.S. Representative Keith Ellison who was supported by party leaders who had favored Bernie Sanders in 2016. Both Perez and Ellison had pledged to change the culture of the DNC.

What do national party organizations do? They are often agents of an incumbent president in securing his renomination. When there is no incumbent president seeking reelection, the national party committee is generally neutral until the nominee has been selected. National committees play an important role for the Republicans in organizing and coordinating the party get-out-the-vote (GOTV) efforts and were significant in 2004 and to a lesser extent in 2008.[44] The 2012 Obama campaign built a voter operation in many ways similar to its 2008 operation, with roughly twice as many field offices, more staff, and more volunteers compared to the Romney/RNC effort. Both sides targeted individuals based on past behavior and used sophisticated computer models to predict which individuals would be most likely to vote. Democrats continue to rely heavily on allied groups like unions, environmentalists, and pro-choice groups to get the vote out. In 2016, Clinton built on Obama's data-driven approach to voter mobilization. Trump's get-out-the-vote operation relied heavily on the Republican National Committee. Though his program was not as well funded or expansive, Trump and his party mobilized enough voters to win the Presidency.

In addition to the national party committees, there are national congressional and senatorial campaign committees. These committees work to recruit candidates, train them, make limited contributions to them, and spend independently in some of the most competitive contests.[45] The National Republican Senatorial Committee (NRSC) and Democratic Senatorial Campaign Committee (DSCC) are led by senators elected to two-year terms by their fellow party members in the Senate. The National Republican Campaign Committee (NRCC) and Democratic Congressional Campaign Committee (DCCC) have leaders chosen in the same manner by fellow partisans in the House. Chairs of campaign committees are nominated by their party leadership and typically ratified by their party caucus.

platform

Every four years the political parties draft a document stating the policy positions of the party. This party platform details general party-wide issue stances. The process sometimes engenders disputes among fellow partisans but is rarely an election issue and often is written to avoid controversy.

PARTY PLATFORMS Although national party committees exist primarily to win elections and gain control of government, policy goals are also important. Every four years, each party adopts a platform at the national nominating convention. The typical party **platform**—the official statement of party policy that hardly anyone

Tom Perez, former Secretary of Labor under President Obama, was elected Chair of the Democratic National Committee in February 2017. Perez defeated U.S. Representative Keith Ellison who was supported by Vermont Senator and 2016 presidential candidate Bernie Sanders. During and after the 2016 campaign Sanders and his supporters pointed to unfair treatment by the DNC, leaving the party divided following Secretary Clinton's defeat. Perez, after winning the ballot to be chair, moved that Ellison be DNC Deputy Chair. Perez pledged to change the culture of the DNC. As suggested by the message on the podium where he is speaking, he seeks to unify the party.

FIGURE 6.1 DIFFERENCES IN PERCEPTION OF WHAT THE PARTIES STAND FOR, 2016

A National Election survey tracks responses to the question, "Do you think there are any important differences in what the Republicans and Democrats stand for?" Voters in 2016 reported seeing important differences between the parties more than in any election in this time series. This continues a trend started in 1998. The candidacies of Donald Trump and Hillary Clinton appear to have called attention to party differences for voters.

SOURCES: http://www.electionstudies.org/nesguide/toptable/tab2b_4.htm. 2004 National Election Study, "Important Difference in What Democratic and Republican Parties Stand For, 1952–2004" (Center for Political Studies, University of Michigan, 2004); 2008 National Election Study (Center for Political Studies, University of Michigan, 2008); and 2012 National Election Study (Center for Political Studies, University of Michigan, 2012)."

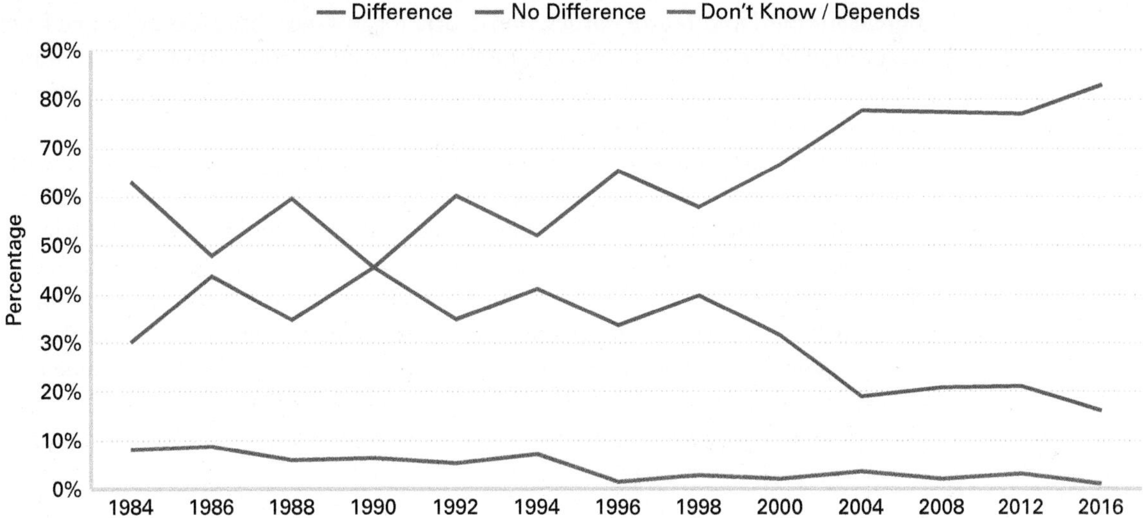

reads—is often a vague and ponderous document, the result of many meetings and compromises between groups and individuals. Platforms are ambiguous by design, giving voters few obvious reasons to vote against the party (see Figure 6.1).[46] In 2016, the Republican platform heavily emphasized reforming the broken system for which President Obama and career politicians like Hillary Clinton were blamed. The Trump Republican's call for an institutional reform to "drain the swamp," as Trump described Washington, resonated with voters who felt marginalized by the current system.

Many politicians contend that platforms rarely help elect anyone, but platform positions can hurt a presidential candidate. Because the nominee does not always control the platform-writing process, presidential candidates can disagree with their own party platform. But the platform-drafting process gives partisans, and generally the nominee through people he or she appoints, an opportunity to express their views. It spells out the most important values and principles on which the parties are based. Once elected, politicians are rarely reminded of their platform position on a given issue. Even so, the winning party actually seeks to enact much of its party platform.[47] One major exception was former President George H. W. Bush's memorable promise not to raise taxes if elected in 1988, "Read my lips—no new taxes." He was forced to eat those words when taxes were raised in 1990.[48]

In 2016 neither party had a contested platform on the convention floor. Hillary Clinton's campaign supported including free community college education and language that health care is a right and not a privilege as a gesture to the Sanders delegates. The Republican platform departed from such longstanding GOP positions as removing the call for a two-state solution to the Israeli-Palestinian conflict, and while denouncing the Supreme Court's decision making same-sex marriage legal, did not call for a constitutional amendment restoring marriage as between a man and a woman.

PARTIES AT THE STATE AND LOCAL LEVELS The two major parties are decentralized. They have organizations for each level of government—national, state, and local. The state and local levels are structured much like the national level. Each state has a *state committee* headed by a *state chair*. State law determines the composition of the state committees and regulates them. Members of state committees are usually elected from local areas.

Despite much state-to-state variation, the trend is toward stronger state organizations, with Republicans typically being much better funded.[49] Some states have significant third and fourth parties. New York, for instance, has a Conservative Party in addition to the Democratic and Republican parties. The role that minor parties play in statewide elections can be important, even though, just as in national elections, they rarely win offices themselves.

Below the state committees are *county committees*, which vary widely in function and power. These committees recruit candidates for such offices as county commissioner, sheriff, and treasurer. Often this means finding a candidate for the office, not deciding among competing contenders. For a party that rarely wins an election, the county committee has to struggle to find someone willing to run. When the chance of winning is greater, primaries, not the party leaders, usually decide the winner.[50] Some county organizations are active, distributing campaign literature, organizing telephone campaigns, putting up posters and lawn signs, and canvassing door-to-door. Other county committees do not function at all, and many party leaders are just figureheads.

Parties in Government

Political parties are central to the operation of our government. They help bridge the separation of powers and facilitate coordination between levels of government in a federal system.

IN THE LEGISLATIVE BRANCH Members of Congress take their partisanship seriously, at least while in Washington. Their power and influence are determined by whether their party is in control of the House or Senate; they also have a stake in which party controls the White House. The chairs of all standing committees in Congress come from the majority party in that chamber, as do the presiding officials of both chambers. Partisans in both houses sit together on the floor and in committee. Political parties help bridge the separation of powers between the legislative and executive branches by creating partisan incentives to cooperate. Partisanship can also help unify the two houses of Congress.

Congressional staffs are also partisan. Members of Congress expect their staffs—from the volunteer intern to the senior staffer—to be loyal, first to them and then to their party. Should you decide to go to work for a representative or senator, you would be expected to identify yourself with that person's party, and you would have difficulty finding a job with the other party later. Employees of the House and Senate—elevator operators, Capitol Hill police, and even the chaplain—hold patronage jobs. With few exceptions, such jobs go to persons from the party that has a majority in the House or the Senate.

Following the 2016 election, Republicans had control of both houses of Congress and the presidency. Unified government had not been in place since the first two years of the Obama administration. President Trump and Republican congressional leadership shared an agenda that included repealing and replacing the Affordable Care Act, tax cuts, and spending on infrastructure, plus the routine budget processes. They moved first on health care and suffered an embarrassing defeat in the House when one faction of the party, the Freedom Caucus, objected to the bill, forcing the leadership to pull it. Weeks later a modified bill passed the House, but fell one vote short of passage in the Senate. This episode called attention to the challenge of maintaining a majority in both chambers.

IN THE EXECUTIVE BRANCH Presidents select nearly all senior White House staff and cabinet members from their own party. In addition, presidents typically surround themselves with advisers who have campaigned with them and proved their party loyalty. Partisanship is also important in presidential appointments to the highest levels of the federal workforce. Party commitment, including making campaign contributions, is expected of those who seek these positions. However, presidents usually fill at least one or two senior posts with members of the opposition party. It is a time-honored way to emphasize bipartisanship. President Trump departed from this pattern, appointing only Republicans and limiting this selections to persons who had not opposed his candidacy publicly.

IN THE JUDICIAL BRANCH The judicial branch of the national government, with its lifetime tenure and political independence, is designed to operate in an expressly nonpartisan manner. Judges, unlike members of Congress, do not sit together by party. But the appointment process for judges has always been partisan. The landmark case establishing the principle of judicial review, *Marbury* v. *Madison* (1803), concerned Federalists' efforts to stack the judiciary with fellow partisans before leaving office.[51] Today, party identification remains an important consideration when nominating federal judges. The importance of partisanship in the process of confirming Supreme Court appointees is evident in the way the Senate responded in early 2016 to the death of Justice Antonin Scalia. President Obama's nomination of Judge Merrick Garland to replace Scalia led to an intense partisan battle over how the Republican-controlled Senate would treat the nomination; Republicans refused to hold hearings or allow a vote on Garland. Donald Trump's presidential victory and the ability of Republicans to preserve a Senate majority in 2016 allowed President Trump to nominate Neil Gorsuch for the Scalia vacancy and the Senate Republicans confirmed his selection. This suggests that the GOP decision to hold up the Garland nomination paid off and that Democrats may behave similarly if vacancies arise for a Republican president when they are next in the majority.

AT THE STATE AND LOCAL LEVELS The importance of party in the operation of local government varies among states and localities. In some states, such as New York and Illinois, local parties play an even stronger role than they do at the national level. In others, such as Nebraska, parties play almost no role. In Nebraska, the state legislature is expressly nonpartisan, although factions perform like parties and still play a role. Parties are likewise unimportant in the government of most city councils. But in most states and many cities, parties are important to the operation of the legislature, governorship, or mayor's office in large cities. Judicial selection in most states is also a partisan matter. The 2000 Bush campaign made much of the fact that six of the seven Florida Supreme Court justices deciding the 2000 ballot-counting case in favor of former Vice President Gore were Democrats. Similarly, Democrats noted that the five U.S. Supreme Court justices whose decision ended the Florida recount and led to Bush's election were nominated by Republican presidents. The death of Justice Antonin Scalia in early 2016 and President Obama's nomination of Judge Merrick Garland to replace him prompted an intense partisan battle over whether the Republican-controlled Senate would hold hearings and vote on the nominee. Donald Trump's presidential victory and the ability of Republicans to preserve a Senate majority suggest that the GOP decision to hold up the Garland nomination paid off. The 2016 election did little to change the Republican dominance at the state level. Republicans retained majorities in 32 state legislative chambers and picked up governors hips in Missouri, New Hampshire, and Vermont, offices which had been held by Democrats. In 2018, Democrats picked up key governorships in the Midwest: Illinois, Michigan, and Wisconsin but also Kansas, Maine, New Jersey, New Mexico and Nevada. Democrats gained new majorities in six state legislative chambers.

Raise and Spend Money

Although parties cannot exert tight control over candidates, their ability to raise and spend money has had a significant influence. Political parties, like candidates, rely on contributions from individuals and interest groups to fund their activities. Because of the close connection political parties have with officeholders, the courts have long permitted regulation of the source and amount of money people and groups can contribute to parties, as well as the amount parties can spend with or contribute to candidates.

Under the reforms enacted after President Richard Nixon resigned from office following the Watergate scandal, contributions to the parties from individuals were limited to $20,000, whereas the limit for political action committees (PACs) was $15,000.[52] PACs are more inclined to give to candidates than party committees.

After the 1976 election, both parties pressed for further amendments to FECA, claiming that campaign finance reforms resulted in insufficient money for generic party activities such as billboard advertising and get-out-the-vote drives. The 1979 amendments to FECA and the interpretations of this legislation by the Federal Election Commission (FEC) permitted unlimited **soft money** contributions to the parties by individuals and PACs for these party-building purposes. Unions and corporations were also allowed to give parties unlimited amounts of soft money. Two decades later, in 1996, parties found ways to spend this soft money to directly influence electoral outcomes by advertising for and against particular candidates. By the elections of 2000, all party committees combined raised $500 million in soft money, a feat they repeated in 2002. This money was spent in large amounts in the most competitive races.

soft money

Money raised in unlimited amounts by political parties for party-building purposes. Now largely illegal except for limited contributions to state or local parties for voter registration and get-out-the-vote efforts.

After failed efforts in one or both houses of Congress for 15 years, Congress successfully banned party soft money under the Bipartisan Campaign Reform Act (BCRA) in 2002. In the same act, Congress doubled contribution limits for individuals giving to candidates and parties and indexed those new limits to inflation. Although some parts of BCRA were later declared unconstitutional because money spent in campaigns represents speech, and is therefore protected by the constitution, the soft money ban remains in effect.

In 2014, the Supreme Court expanded the ability of parties to raise and spend money by declaring unconstitutional the BCRA aggregate party contribution limits. In *McCutcheon* v. *FEC*[53] the Court retained the limit on what an individual could give to a party committee, which in 2014 was $32,400, but struck down the prior aggregate party committee contribution limit, which was $74,600. The Court's decision meant an individual could give $97,200 to national party committees ($32,400 to each of the three national party committees) and another $500,000 to state party committees.[54] *McCutcheon* also struck down the aggregate contribution limit to candidates, and because candidates and party committees can form joint fund-raising committees, an individual could give more than $3.6 million to a single party joint fund-raising committee for the 2014 or 2016 elections. A likely consequence of the decision is an effort on the part of both parties to court large donors who can make large contributions.

Parties, like individuals and groups, can now also spend unlimited amounts for and against candidates, as long as the expenditures were independent of the candidate or a party committee.[55] Unlike soft money, **party-independent expenditures** must use money raised with normal **hard money** contribution limits. Those making independent expenditures may not coordinate with candidates about the content, timing or placement of the advertisement. As long as the party committees could use soft money, independent expenditures were of lesser importance, but with the BCRA ban on soft money, there has been a surge in party-independent expenditure activity. This will likely only grow in the wake of *McCutcheon* v. *FEC*.

party-independent expenditures

Spending by political party committees that is independent of the candidate. The spending occurs in relatively few competitive contests and is often substantial.

hard money

Political contributions given to a party, candidate, or interest group that are limited in amount and fully disclosed. Raising such limited funds was harder than raising unlimited soft money, hence the term *hard money*.

In 2016, the Hillary Clinton campaign and a joint fundraising committee with the Democratic National Committee and 38 state party committees raised nearly $530 million. Donald Trump, along with the Republican National committee and 21 state party committees, had two joint fundraising committees which together raised $372 million. Individuals contributed as much as $1.95 million to one of these joint fundraising committees.[56] The Clinton campaign launched its joint committee much earlier than did Donald Trump, and Trump's campaign was slower than was Clinton's to ramp up fundraising, even from large donors. Future campaigns will be more likely to follow the Clinton approach by fundraising from large donors early. We will explore this topic in greater detail in Chapter 8.

During the debate over BCRA, and in the court case on its constitutionality, some speculated that BCRA's soft money ban would weaken political parties.[57] The surge in individual contributions has demonstrated the opposite; the DNC and RNC could and did find an alternative to unlimited soft money. It remains to be seen whether the four congressional party committees can make up for the loss of soft money, but the surge in individual contributions to them has largely filled this gap. With the Supreme Court dramatically increasing aggregate individual contribution limits, party committees will likely again emphasize individuals who can contribute millions of dollars. The independent expenditure option allows parties to continue to direct money well in excess of the normal limits to races they think are more competitive.

The Role of Minor Parties (Action)

6.3 Evaluate the role of minor parties in the U.S. electoral system.

Although we have a two-party system in the United States, we also have minor parties, sometimes called *third parties*. Candidate-based parties, which arise around a candidate, usually disappear when the charismatic personality does. In most states, candidates can get their names on the ballot as an Independent or minor party candidate by securing the required number of signatures on a nomination petition. This is hard to do. Former New York City Mayor Michael Bloomberg considered launching a third-party candidacy in 2016. After doing polling, investigating laws about getting on the ballot, and assessing his likely impact on the outcome, he decided not to run. Concluding that his candidacy would help Donald Trump, Bloomberg stated, "I love our country too much to play a role in electing a candidate who would weaken our unity and darken our future—and so I will not enter the race for president of the United States."[58]

Minor parties organized ideologically usually persist over a longer time than those built around a particular leader. Communist, Prohibition, Libertarian, Right to Life, and Green parties are of the ideological type. Minor parties of both types come and go, and several minor parties usually run in any given election. Some parties arise around a single issue, like the Right to Life Party active in some states like New York. The Green Party is another example of an ideological third party. Although they are occasionally visible, minor parties have never won the presidency (see Table 6.1) or more than a handful of congressional seats.[59] They have done only somewhat better in gubernatorial elections.[60] They have never shaped national policy from *inside* the government, and their influence on national policy and on the platforms of the two major parties has been limited.[61]

Although the United States has had several **minor parties**, only the two major parties have much of a chance to win elections. Multiparty systems are almost always found in countries that have a parliamentary government, in contrast to our presidential system. Parliamentary systems usually have a *head of state*, often called the president, but they also have a *head of the government*, often called the prime minister or chancellor, who is the leader of one of the large parties in the legislature.

minor party
A small political party that persists over time that is often composed of ideologies on the right or left, or centered on a charismatic candidate. Such a party is also called a *third party*.

Parliamentary democracies often operate with multiparty systems. These systems often have fierce competition among many parties for even small numbers of seats, because winners are determined through **proportional representation**, in which the parties receive a proportion of the legislators corresponding to their share of the vote. Even small percentages of votes can produce enough seats to give a party bargaining power in forming a coalition to run the government. Minor parties can gain concessions—positions in a cabinet or support of policies they want implemented—in return for joining a coalition. Major parties need the minor parties and are therefore willing to bargain. Thus, the multiparty system favors the existence of minor parties by giving them incentives to persevere and disproportionate power if they will help form a government.

proportional representation
An election system in which each party running receives the proportion of legislative seats corresponding to its proportion of the vote.

TABLE 6.1 MINOR PARTIES IN THE UNITED STATES

Third-party candidates have not won electoral votes since Alabama Governor George Wallace did in 1968. Ross Perot secured a higher percentage of the popular vote in 1992 (19 percent) than Wallace did in 1968 (14 percent), but did not carry a single state. Libertarian Gary Johnson received the highest percent of the vote (3.3 percent) of any third-party candidate since 1996 when Ross Perot received 8.4 percent of the vote. Since 2000, no third-party candidate has gotten above 3.3 percent of the popular vote.

Year	Party	Presidential Candidate	Percentage of Popular Vote Received	Electoral Votes	Percentage of Electoral Votes
1832	Anti-Masonic	William Wirt	8%	7	2%
1856	American (Know-Nothing)	Millard Fillmore	22%	8	3%
1860	Democratic (Secessionist)	John C. Breckinridge	18%	72	24%
1860	Constitutional Union	John Bell	13%	39	13%
1892	People's (Populist)	James B. Weaver	9%	22	5%
1912	Bull Moose	Theodore Roosevelt	27%	88	2%
1912	Socialist	Eugene V. Debs	6%	0	0%
1924	Progressive	Robert M. La Follette	17%	13	2%
1948	States' Rights (Dixiecrat)	Strom Thurmond	2%	39	7%
1948	Progressive	Henry A. Wallace	2%	0	0%
1968	American Independent	George C. Wallace	14%	46	9%
1980	National Unity	John Anderson	7%	0	0%
1992	Independent	Ross Perot	19%	0	0%
1996	Reform	Ross Perot	8%	0	0%
2000	Reform	Pat Buchanan	0%	0	0%
2000	Green	Ralph Nader	3%	0	0%
2004	Reform	Ralph Nader	0%	0	0%
2008	Independent	Ralph Nader	0%	0	0%
2012	Libertarian	Gary Johnson	1%	0	0%
2016	Libertarian	Gary Johnson	3%	0	0%
2016	Green	Jill Stein	1%	0	0%

NOTE: Only includes parties that received electoral votes at least once, or more than 3 percent of the popular vote at least once.

SOURCES: Dave Leip's Atlas of U.S. Presidential Elections. http://uselectionatlas.org/RESULTS/national.php?year=2016&off=0&elect=0&f=0 Compiled by the author from the Web site 270towin, http://www.270towin.com/1968_Election/index.html.

winner-take-all system
An election system in which the candidate with the most votes wins.

The United States has a single-member district, **winner-take-all system**, where only the candidate with the most votes in a district or state takes office.[62] Because a party does not gain anything by finishing second, minor parties in a two-party system can rarely overcome the assumption that a vote for them is a wasted vote.[63] For this reason, in an election system in which the winner is the candidate in a single-member district with the plurality deciding the winner, there is a tendency to have two parties. This regularity is called *Duverger's law*.[64]

In multiparty systems, parties at the extremes are likely to have more influence than in our two-party system; and in nations with a multiparty system, legislatures more accurately reflect the full range of the views of the electorate. In contrast, our two-party system tends to create *centrist* parties that appeal to moderate elements and suppress the views of extremists in the electorate. Moreover, once elected, our parties do not form as cohesive a voting bloc as ideological parties do in multiparty systems.

Multiparty parliamentary systems often make governments unstable as coalitions form and collapse. In addition, swings in policy when party control changes can be dramatic. In contrast, two-party systems produce governments that tend to be stable and centrist, and as a result, policy changes occur incrementally.

Third parties in a winner-take-all system like that in the United States face the obstacle that a vote for a third-party candidate with little chance of winning may be a wasted vote. In several close elections, including the 2000 presidential election, the vote cast for one or another minor party, if cast for the likely second choice of those voters, would have changed the outcome of the election. Ralph Nader, for example, received 92,241 votes in Florida; if 537 of them had been cast for Al Gore and none for George W. Bush, Gore would have won the election. A more recent example of a candidate who won office but failed to gain a majority was Nevada Republican Senator Dean Heller, who received 46 percent of the vote in 2012, while Democrat Shelly Berkeley got 45 percent. Other minor-party candidates together got 9 percent of the vote.[65] In such a situation, should voters care more about influencing who wins an election or more about casting a vote for a candidate whose views are closest to their own, even if that candidate has little chance of winning?

Following the 2016 election, some thought that Jill Stein had cost Hillary Clinton the victory. Her Green Party received 1 percent of the vote in Wisconsin and 1.1 percent of the vote in Michigan. In Michigan, if 10,705 of Stein's 51,463 voters had voted for Clinton instead of Stein, Clinton would have won the state. In Wisconsin, it would have taken 22,748 out of Stein's 30,980 voters switching for Clinton to have carried the state. But even if this had happened, it would have taken nearly all of Stein's Pennsylvania voters to switch to Clinton for Clinton to have won in the Electoral College. Had some of Stein's voters known the election would be as close as it turned out to be, they might have voted for Clinton, but it is also the case that some Stein voters may have not voted at all if Stein had not been on the ballot. Exit polls found that 65 percent of voters who voted for third-party candidates would not have voted if the choice had been between only Clinton and Trump.[66]

Those who see the vote as a largely symbolic exercise will likely vote for a minor party candidate who has little chance of winning. The problem is that the more electable candidate who is clearly preferred over the other more competitive alternative may not win office at all if a voter does not consider electability. The winner-take-all system makes this trade-off more consequential. In a system in which proportional representation is possible, a voter is more likely to be able to translate policy preferences into a vote for representatives. But in our system, voters must often vote for their second choice in order to avoid letting their third choice win office. Interest groups, like environmental groups, often find themselves not endorsing a minor party candidate who may be closer to their views because they want to avoid helping to elect a competitive alternative candidate whose views they abhor.

The leaders of two of the world's most important democracies are women, Prime Minister Theresa May of Great Britain, on the left, and Chancellor Angela Merkel of Germany, on the right. They are seen here after a meeting between the two in Berlin. Merkel has served as chancellor since 2005, having assembled governing coalitions four times, most recently following the 2017 election. May became Prime Minister in 2016, having served previously as Home Secretary. Although women lead only 38 percent of the world's nations, their numbers have been growing in recent decades. As of 2016 there were 56 women heads of state.[67]

One way to lessen the influence of minor party candidates is to require a runoff election of the top two vote getters if no candidate receives a majority. Although this would force another election in some instances, it would also force people who vote to decide among the more viable options. A counterargument is that many people who support minor party candidates would opt out of an election without this chance to express their preferences, and so such a runoff is already accomplished with the plurality-winner system we now have.

Parties in the Electorate (Impact)

6.4 Describe the significance of party identification in America today.

Political parties would be of little significance if they did not have meaning to the electorate, and if that meaning did not have an impact on outcomes. Adherents of the two parties are drawn to them by a combination of factors, including their stand on the issues; personal or party history; religious, racial, or social peer grouping; and the appeal of their candidates. The emphases among these factors change over time, but they are remarkably consistent with those that political scientists identified more than 40 years ago.[68]

Party Registration and Activity

Political parties are in part private associations, but because they also are involved in elections they are subject to state laws. One important area of election law that relates to parties is whether or not the state provides for voters to designate a party when they register to vote. Voters may decline to declare their party in such states, but that may limit their ability to participate in selecting party nominees. Citizens vary widely in their level of party involvement. For most people most of the time, politics is not their primary concern. But for some especially politically active people the parties are high priority.

party registration
The act of declaring party affiliation; required by some states when one registers to vote.

PARTY REGISTRATION For citizens in most states, "party" has a particular legal meaning—**party registration**. When voters register to vote in these states, they are asked to state their party preference. They then become registered members of one of the two major parties or a third party, although they can change their party registration. The purpose of party registration is to limit the participants in primary elections to members of that party and to make it easier for parties to contact people who might vote for their party.

PARTY ACTIVISTS People who invest time and effort in political parties are often called party activists. They tend to fall into three broad categories: party regulars, candidate activists, and issue activists. *Party regulars* place the party first. They value winning elections and understand that compromise and moderation may be necessary to reach that objective. They also realize that it is important to keep the party together because a fractured party only helps the opposition. In 2016, some of these party regulars were also called the party establishment by Donald Trump and Bernie Sanders.

Candidate activists are followers of a particular candidate who see the party as the means to elect their candidate. Candidate activists are often not concerned with the other operations of the party—with nominees for other offices or with raising money for the party. Candidate activists may have a strong ideological orientation, which means they take a strong interest in the party platform debates and the issue positions of the eventual nominees. For example, many people who supported Ron Paul in his unsuccessful run for the presidency as a Republican in 2008 and 2012 were candidate activists. Paul, a Libertarian Republican congressman from Texas, had previously run for the presidency as a Libertarian. His son, Kentucky senator Rand Paul, ran for the presidential nomination in 2016 and also had committed candidate activists.

Issue activists wish to push the parties in a particular direction on a single issue or a narrow range of issues: the wars in Iraq and Afghanistan, abortion, taxes, school prayer,

The 2018 midterm election saw a surge in female candidates seeking their party's nomination for the U.S. House of Representatives. This was coupled by ideological divides in both parties. In the South Carolina Republican primary, Katie Arrington, with support from the Trump faction of the party and a tweet from President Trump, defeated incumbent Congressman Mark Sanford. However, following a very tight race, Arrington lost to Democrat Joe Cunningham in the general election—the first time that the seat has been held by a Democrat in more than 40 years.[69]

the environment, or civil rights, among others. To issue activists, the party platform is an important battleground because they want the party to endorse their position. Issue activists are also often candidate activists if they can find a candidate willing to embrace their position. Some candidates, like Bernie Sanders, attract both candidate and issue activists.

Party Identification

Party registration and party activists are important, but many voters are not registered with a political party. Most American adults lack the partisan commitment and interest needed for active involvement. This is not to say that they find parties irrelevant or unimportant. For them, partisanship is what political scientists call **party identification**—a psychological attachment to a political party that most people acquire in childhood from their parents.[70] This type of voter may sometimes vote for a candidate from the other party, but without a compelling reason to do otherwise, most will vote according to their party identification. Peers and early political experiences reinforce party identification as part of the political socialization process.

party identification
An affiliation with a political party that most people acquire in childhood. The best predictor of voting behavior in partisan candidate elections.

Political scientists and pollsters use the answers to the following questions to measure party identification: "Generally speaking, in politics, do you usually think of yourself as a Republican, a Democrat, an Independent, or what?" Persons who answer Republican or Democrat are then asked, "Would you call yourself a strong or a not very strong Republican/Democrat?" Persons who answer Independent are asked, "Do you think of yourself as closer to the Republican or the Democratic Party?" Persons who do not indicate Democrat, Republican, or Independent to the first question rarely exceed 2 percent of the electorate and include those who are apolitical or who identify with one of the minor political parties.

When these questions are combined in a single measure, there are seven categories of partisan identification: (1) strong Democrats, (2) weak Democrats, (3) Independent-leaning Democrats, (4) pure Independents, (5) Independent-leaning Republicans, (6) weak Republicans, and (7) strong Republicans. During the more than 50-year period in which political scientists have been conducting such surveys, partisan preferences of the public as a whole have remained remarkably stable, even though new voters have been added to the electorate—minorities and 18- to 21-year-olds (see Table 6.2). For some sub-populations like Protestants and Catholics, partisan allegiances have changed over time (see Table 6.3).

TABLE 6.2 PORTRAIT OF THE ELECTORATE

Since 1964, the distribution of party identification has shifted from more than two-thirds Democrats over Republicans to Democrats having less than a 10 percent greater share of the public in 2016. The change is most evident in the South and among Catholics where Republicans do much better now than they did in 1964.

	1964			2016		
	Republican	Democrat	Independent	Republican	Democrat	Independent
Sex						
Male	30%	61%	8%	43%	42%	15%
Female	30	61	7	36	51	13
Race						
White	33	59	8	48	39	13
Black	8	82	6	8	81	11
Hispanic	—	—	—	24	58	18
Age						
18–34	26	64	9	34	49	17
35–45	32	59	8	35	50	15
46–55	26	65	8	43	44	13
56–64	28	66	6	44	42	13
65+	43	49	6	46	44	10
Religion						
Protestant	34	58	7	57	34	8
Catholic	22	70	9	41	47	12
Jewish	11	76	13	24	66	10
Other	28	55	16	48	36	16
Region						
Northeast	36	54	10	31	57	13
North-Central	36	55	8	43	45	12
South	20	71	7	43	41	16
West	30	63	7	37	50	13
Total	30	61	8	39	47	14

NOTE: Numbers may not add to 100 because of rounding. Independents that lean toward a party are classified with the party toward which they lean. Race is defined by the first race with which a respondent identifies. Income is classified as the respondent's household income.

SOURCES: *1964 National Election Study* (Center for Political Studies, University of Michigan, 1964); 2012 National Election Study (Center for Political Studies, University of Michigan, 2012 and 2016 National Election Study (Center for Political Studies, University of Michigan, 2016).

TABLE 6.3 COMBINED PARTY IDENTIFICATION BY DECADES, 1950s–2010s

Party Identification has been quite stable over time. Look, for example, at the percent of Strong Democrats and Strong Republicans. The share of the public classifying themselves as strong partisans has barely changed between the 1950s (36 percent) and 2010s (35 percent). Greater changes can be seen among Independent leaning partisans and pure Independents where there are 13 percent more of these three types of Independents in the 2010s than there were in the 1950s.

Decade	Strong Democrat	Weak Democrat	Independent-Leaning Democrat	Independent	Independent-Leaning Republican	Weak Republican	Strong Republican	Other
1950*	23%	23%	8%	7%	7%	15%	13%	4%
1960	22	25	8	10	7	15	12	2
1970	17	24	12	14	10	14	9	2
1980	18	26	11	12	11	14	11	2
1990	18	19	13	10	12	15	13	1
2000†	18	16	16	10	12	13	14	2
2010^	19	19	12	14	11	13	12	1

*1950s percentages based on years 1952, 1956, and 1958.
†2000s percentages based on years 2000, 2002, 2004, and 2008.
^2010s percentages based on 2012 and 2016.

NOTE: Data may not sum to 100 percent because of averaging. *How has the strength of party identification changed over time?*

SOURCES: *National Election Study* (Center for Political Studies, University of Michigan, 1952–2012). National Election Study Cumulative File (Center for Political Studies, University of Michigan, 2005); 2008 National Election Study (Center for Political Studies, University of Michigan, 2008); 2012 National Election Study (Center for Political Studies, University of Michigan, 2012); and 2016 National Election Study (Center for Political Studies, University of Michigan, 2016).

Recall from our earlier discussion of voting that party identification is the single best predictor of how people will vote.[71] Unlike candidates and issues, which come and go, party identification is a long-term element in voting choice. The strength of party identification is also important in predicting participation and political interest. Strong Republicans and strong Democrats participate more actively in politics than any other group, are generally better informed about political issues, and are most predictably partisan in their voting behavior. Pure Independents are just the opposite; they vote at the lowest rates and have the lowest levels of interest and awareness of any of the categories of party identification. This evidence runs counter to the notions that persons who are strong partisans are unthinking party adherents and that Independents are informed and ideal citizens.[72] However, Independents who acknowledge party leanings tend to vote for the party toward which they lean. Weak partisans are less reliably partisan and vote at lower rates than strong partisans or some Independents with partisan leanings.

Partisan Dealignment?

As we noted, partisan identification has been stable for more than six decades, despite such changes to the electorate as adding minorities and 18- to 21-year-olds. In addition, as Figure 6.2 suggests, Americans have shown no consistent preference for one party over the other in their votes in presidential elections. In a time of electoral volatility, the basics of politics determine the winners and losers: who attracts positive voter attention, who strikes themes that motivate voters to participate, and who communicates better with voters.

However, some experts argue that Independents are increasing in number, suggesting that the party system may be in a period of **dealignment**, in which partisan preferences are weakening and there is a rise in the number of Independents. Indeed, the number of self-classified Independents has increased from 22 percent in the 1950s to approach 40 percent in the last decade. However, two-thirds of all

dealignment
Weakening of partisan preferences that point to a rejection of both major parties and a rise in the number of Independents.

FIGURE 6.2 PRESIDENTIAL VOTE BY PARTY

Notice the closeness between the red and blue lines in 1948, 1960, 1976, and since 2000. These quite competitive contests are distinct from elections where Republicans dominated (1952, 1956, 1972, 1980, 1984, 1988) and from 1964, when Democrats won big. While Ross Perot did well enough to pull the winning candidate below 50 percent, he did not alter the outcome. Neither Hillary Clinton nor Donald Trump exceeded 50 percent in 2016 and, as with the 2000 election, the winning candidate in terms of popular vote did not win in the Electoral College.

SOURCE: Stanley and Niemi, pp. 20–21. 2016 data from http://uselectionatlas.org/RESULTS/national.php?year=2016&off=0&elect=0&f=0.

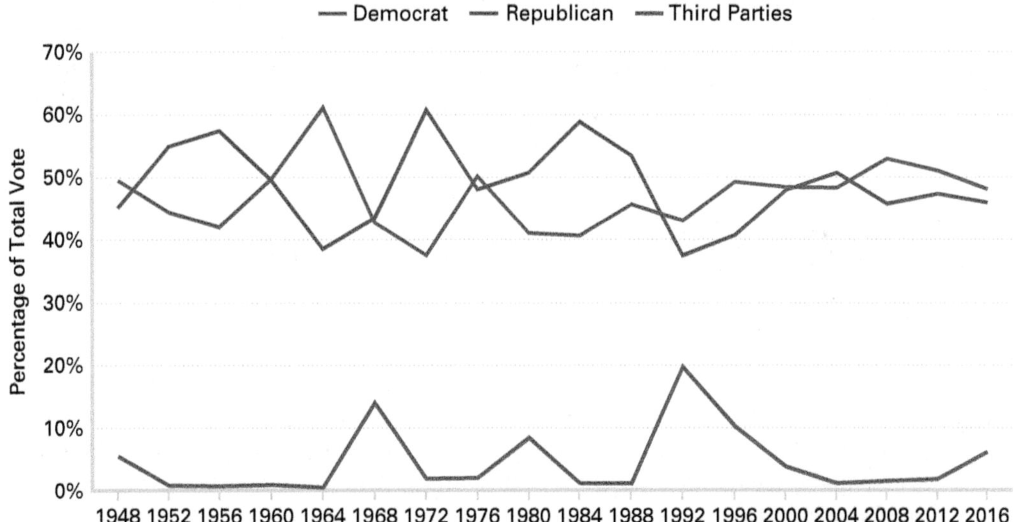

TABLE 6.4 VOTING BEHAVIOR OF PARTISANS AND INDEPENDENTS, 1992–2016

Across even presidential elections party identification strongly predicts presidential voting. Strong partisans are loyal to their party more than 90 percent of the time and weak and independent-leaning partisans 80 percent or more of the time. Only pure independents are more unpredictable. The tendency of weak and independent partisans to vote for their party became even more pronounced in 2012.

	Percent Voting for Democratic Presidential Candidate						
	1992	1996	2000	2004	2008	2012	2016
Strong Democrats	94%	96%	97%	98%	95%	98%	97%
Weak Democrats	69	84	85	85	86	83	76
Independent-Leaning Democrats	70	74	78	88	91	88	82
Pure Independents	41	39	45	58	55	46	32
Independent-Leaning Republicans	11	23	14	15	18	9	9
Weak Republicans	14	21	16	11	12	12	16
Strong Republicans	3	4	2	3	4	3	2

	Percent Voting for Democratic House Candidate								
	1994	1996	1998	2000	2002	2004	2008	2012	2016
Strong Democrats	90%	88%	83%	89%	92%	91%	92%	93%	86%
Weak Democrats	72	72	63	73	69	86	84	78	72
Independent-Leaning Democrats	66	72	65	73	68	80	83	81	82
Pure Independents	51	42	46	52	38	57	43	46	46
Independent-Leaning Republicans	25	20	25	26	28	34	21	9	20
Weak Republicans	22	20	27	17	27	17	22	9	16
Strong Republicans	8	3	8	12	8	10	7	4	11

SOURCES: National Election Study (Center for Political Studies, University of Michigan, 1952-2012); National Election Study Cumulative File (Center for Political Studies, University of Michigan, 2005); 2008 National Election Study (Center for Political Studies, University of Michigan, 2008); and 2012 National Election Study (Center for Political Studies, University of Michigan, 2012); and 2016 National Election Study (Center for Political Studies, University of Michigan, 2016).

self-identified Independents are really partisans in their voting behavior and attitudes. Table 6.4 summarizes voting behavior in recent contests for president and the House of Representatives. One-third of those who claim to be Independents lean toward the Democratic Party and vote Democratic in election after election. Another third lean toward Republicans and just as predictably vote Republican. The remaining third, who appear to be genuine Independents, do not vote consistently and appear to have little interest in politics. Thus, despite the reported growth in numbers, pure Independents make up approximately the same proportion of voters today as in 1956.

The Persistence of Political Parties (Impact)

6.5 Assess the reasons for the persistence of the two-party system.

Critics of the U.S. party system typically make four allegations against it: (1) parties do not take meaningful and contrasting positions on most issues, (2) party membership is essentially meaningless, and (3) parties are so concerned with accommodating the middle of the ideological spectrum that they are incapable of serving as an avenue for social progress, or the opposite, that (4) extremes have captured both parties and this polarization results in deadlock in Congress and between Congress and the president. Are these statements accurate? And if they are accurate, are they important? Note that critics sometimes express opposite criticisms of the parties.

The view that parties are indistinguishable is overstated. True, parties compete in a winner-take-all system where voters in the middle can be important to winning often forcing candidates to moderate their positions. But on issues like health care, abortion, global warming, and LGBTQ rights, the parties have clear differences.

Party affiliation is not less important today than in prior decades. Voters rely on party labels to simplify voting choices (see the example at the beginning of the chapter). Party also matters in legislatures, Congress, governorships, the presidency, and in judicial selection.

Parties are built to win elections and need to appeal to enough voters to do so. This often means moderating some issue stances. However, candidates with more extreme ideologies, like Ted Cruz and Bernie Sanders in 2016, often criticize the "party establishment" and propose more ideological positions. Hillary Clinton declared, "I'm a progressive, but I'm a progressive who likes to get things done." Though their most extreme ideas may appeal to the smaller segments of the population that participate in primaries, voters in a general election are not as ideological and may be less willing to vote for less moderate candidates. It is true that there is an ongoing conflict in both parties over issues. This surfaced in Congress when a faction of the Republican Party called the Freedom Caucus threatened to force the party to shut down the government over federal funding for Planned Parenthood. This enduring rancor ultimately forced John Boehner, the Speaker of the House, to resign, and may have been a factor in the decision by Paul Ryan, Boehner's successor as speaker, to not seek reelection in 2018. The intra-party struggle between ideologues and moderates will continue to shape the day-to-day workings of Congress and presidential races despite who ultimately wins the presidential election.

Some analysts fear that parties are in severe decline or even mortally ill. They point first to the long-run adverse impact on political parties of the Progressive movement reforms early in this century, reforms that robbed party organizations of their control of the nomination process by allowing masses of Independent and "uninformed" voters to enter the primaries and nominate candidates who might not be acceptable to party leaders. They also point to the spread of nonpartisan elections in cities and towns and to the staggering of national, state, and local elections that made it harder for parties to influence the election process. States like New Jersey and Virginia elect their legislature and state officers in odd-numbered years.

Legislation limiting the viability and functions of parties was bad enough, say the party pessimists, but parties suffer from additional ills. The rise of television and electronic technology and the parallel increase in the number of campaign, media, and direct-mail consultants have made parties less relevant in educating, mobilizing, and organizing the electorate. Television, radio, the Internet, telephones, and social media have strengthened the role of candidates and lessened the importance of parties. Advocates of strong parties counter that there are signs of party revival, or at least the persistence of party. The national party organizations own permanent, modern buildings in Washington, D.C., located a few blocks from the U.S. Capitol, and remain capable of providing assistance to candidates in competitive races and to state and local party organizations.

Reform Among the Democrats

In Chicago in 1968, the Democratic National Convention saw disputes inside the hall and riots outside, largely because of protests against the country's policy in Vietnam. Responding to the disarray and to disputes about the fairness of delegate selection procedures, members of the party agreed to a number of reforms. They established a process that led to greater use of direct primaries for the selection of delegates to the national convention to select the presidential nominee and greater representation of younger voters, women, and minorities as elected delegates. Another reform was the abolition of the winner-take-all rule (the *unit rule*) that gave all delegates to the primary or convention winner. This rule was replaced by a system of *proportionality* in which candidates won delegates in rough proportion to the votes they received in the primary election or convention in each state. These rule changes became important in 2008, as proportionality rules meant that neither Hillary Clinton nor Barack Obama could benefit from the "winner-take-all" rules that helped propel John McCain to the Republican Party's nomination. In 2016, the proportionality rules helped prolong the nomination contest between Hillary Clinton and Bernie Sanders.

The reforms following 1968 achieved greater diversity of representation among delegates and, as noted, meant that more states adopted primaries. But the new process also meant that elected officials who wanted a voice in determining presidential candidates had to run to become a delegate to the national convention. Some elected officials feared losing in their own party process, and others wanted to delay endorsing a candidate. Responding to this criticism, the party created "super delegate" positions for elected officials and party leaders who were not required to run for election as delegates. Initially in 2008, most super delegates favored Clinton, but by late May 2008, a majority of them supported Obama. They were decisive in determining the nominee, as neither Hillary Clinton nor Barack Obama had enough delegates selected in primaries or caucuses to win the nomination. As discussed earlier, in

Chicago police officers push a protestor's head against the hood of a car as they restrain him after he climbed onto a wooden barricade near the headquarters of the 1968 Democratic National Convention and waved a Vietcong flag during anti–Vietnam War demonstrations, August 1968.

2016, Hillary Clinton had secured the support of super delegates early in the process, which became a source of contention as Sanders had a streak of victories, mostly in caucus states. Sanders characterized the process as in need of reform, claiming he was "entitled" to votes from super delegates from states he had won like Minnesota and Washington.[73]

Reform Among the Republicans

Republicans have not been immune to criticism that their conventions and procedures were keeping out the rank and file. They did not make changes as drastic as those made by the Democrats, but they did have more and more states adopt primaries. Republicans have more states with winner-take-all rules, and a smaller share of all delegates are super delegates.[74]

After a disappointing loss by Romney to Obama in 2012, Republicans made some rule changes with the intent to secure a winner earlier in the process and attempting to limit the damage Republican candidates would do to each other by having fewer televised candidate debates in 2016. In 2011 and 2012 there were 22 televised presidential candidate debates during the nomination phase. In 2016, there were 12. The party encouraged winner-take-all contests after March 15. In 2016, there were eight of these contests, compared to six in 2012. Winner-take-all primaries help narrow the field and determine a nominee sooner. The success of outsider Donald Trump in winning the nomination in 2016 may prompt the established Republican Party to evaluate the rules yet again before the 2020 presidential election.

The Republican Party has long been better organized than the Democrats. In the 1970s, the GOP emphasized grassroots organization and membership recruitment. Seminars taught Republican candidates how to make speeches and hold press conferences, and weekend conferences were organized for training young party professionals. The Democrats have become better organized and more professional than they were previously.[75] Until 2004, Republicans had cultivated a larger donor base and were less reliant on the large-donor soft money contributions that became so controversial between 1996 and 2002. Since then, however, the Democratic committees closed the donor gap, with 45 percent of their money raised from small donors, compared to 46 percent from small donors among the Republican committees. The trend toward small donors continued in 2008 and 2012, especially in the Obama campaign, which set new records not only for total contributions but also for the number of individuals contributing to the campaign. Many of these donors were new donors making contributions that did not exceed $200.

In the 2010 election cycle, the Democratic Party committees all raised and spent more than the Republican Party committees, a gap that was filled in part by interest groups, which were more active on the Republican side. But in 2012, in part due to Romney's successful fund-raising, the RNC raised $100 million more than the DNC. The Democratic congressional committees, however, raised more than the Republican committees again in 2012 and 2014. It was long the case, Republicans have done better in securing small donors to the party committees than the Democrats. This was again the case in 2012 for the RNC and NRSC but not the NRCC.[76] In 2014, the RNC raised more from small donors than the DNC, but the DSCC and DCCC raised more than double the amount from small donors as did the NRSC and NRCC, and the same pattern held in 2016.[77]

Continued Importance of Parties

As we have demonstrated in this chapter, political parties are vital to the functioning of democracy. They organize electoral competition, unify large portions of the electorate, simplify democracy for voters, help transform individual preferences into policy, and provide a mechanism for opposition.

Hillary Clinton's acceptance speech at the Democratic National Convention came on the fourth night of the convention. Speakers on the prior nights included Bernie Sanders, Barack Obama, Michelle Obama, Bill Clinton, and Joe Biden. Clinton was introduced by her daughter, Chelsie Clinton. In her speech she sought to unify the party and contrast her candidacy with that of her opponent Donald Trump.

Donald Trump's acceptance speech at the Republican National Convention framed the election in terms of the country needing strong new leadership that he could provide. His focus ranged from crime to national security to trade to immigration. His speech was more scripted than his campaign speeches generally were before and after the convention. To underscore the theme of his speech there were scores of American flags behind him.

Parties are just as important in organizing the government. They help straddle the separation of powers as party members cooperate between the executive and legislative branches or between the House and Senate. Senior government appointees get their jobs in part because of party loyalty.

Parties also provide an important way for citizens to influence government. Because they are the means by which politicians secure office, participation in the parties can impact the course of American government. Parties also provide opportunities to learn about how other people see issues and to learn to compromise. Rather than being an impediment to democracy, they make government by the people possible.

CONCLUSION

The U.S. electoral system includes functions provided by state governments, like the provision of ballots or voting machines, setting the date of elections, and determining who may vote and what they need to do in order to vote. State and local governments, by performing these functions, provide important support for self-government. On those occasions when there are not enough ballots or voting machines, or as in Florida in 2000 when there were widespread problems with voting, we are reminded of the generally good service these officials provide.

Political parties, as we have shown, also provide very important functions. Citizenship is not a spectator sport, and parties have long been a means for people to impact government. Your ability to make a difference is enhanced if you become involved with a political party. It is likely that one of the parties is already a preferred option for you. But the party closer to you probably does not represent your views in all areas. The reality is that parties are permeable organizations, meaning they adapt to the views of those who become involved with them. You and other like-minded people can influence the direction of a party. Those supporting Ronald Reagan did this to the Republican Party in 1976 and 1980, and those who supported Bill Clinton did this to the Democratic Party in 1992 and 1996. This same principle applies to parties at the state and local levels.

Although they are not mentioned in the Constitution, political parties are an important part of the structure of government. They have been especially important in organizing the legislative and executive branches of government. Parties provide multiple avenues through which Americans may take action to impact policy outcomes. They organize the competition of elections by recruiting, training, and helping fund candidates. They simplify elections for many citizens by providing meaningful "brand labels." Parties are malleable organizations that are quite responsive to citizen input. But, American adults typically take political parties for granted.[78] If anything, you may be like most people, who are critical or distrustful of them. Some see parties as corrupt institutions, interested only in the spoils of politics. Critics charge that parties evade the issues, fail to deliver on their promises, have no new ideas, follow public opinion rather than lead it, or are just one more special interest.

Still, as we have shown in this chapter, parties are necessary. You likely want party labels kept on the ballot, at least for congressional, presidential, and statewide elections. There is a high probability that you think of yourself as a Democrat or a Republican and typically vote for candidates from that party. In 2015–2016, you may even have given $10 or $20 to a candidate or party, you may have attended an event or rally for a candidate, or you may have responded through social media to a Facebook posting or tweet. Having read the material in this chapter, you have likely come to appreciate that parties are necessary to run a democracy in a large, modern country. Both the Democratic and Republican national parties and most state parties are moderate in their policies and leadership.[79] Successful party leaders must be diplomatic; to win presidential elections and congressional majorities, they must find a middle ground among competing and sometimes hostile groups. Members of the House of Representatives, to be elected and reelected, have to appeal to a majority of the voters from their own district. As more districts have become "safe" for incumbents, the House has had fewer moderates and is prone to more partisan ideological clashes than the Senate.

REVIEW THE CHAPTER

A Brief History of American Political Parties (Structure)

6.1 Trace the development of political parties in the United States, p. 142.

Despite their reservations about political parties, the founders became early leaders of a two-party system. Since then, American parties have experienced critical elections and realignments. Most political scientists agree that the last realignment occurred in 1932. During the last half-century, the two parties have been fairly evenly matched, with both parties able to win elections and with divided government more common than unified government. During the 2008 and 2012 elections, Democrats did well among racial minorities, women, and the young, possibly signalling a long-term voting majority at the presidential level. Among Republicans the Tea Party added enthusiasm in 2010 and in some House races in 2012, but some Tea Party-backed candidates fared poorly in Senate elections.

What Parties Do for Democracy (Action)

6.2 Identify the functions of political parties and their structure at the national, state, and local levels, p. 147.

Political parties are essential to democracy. They simplify voting choices, organize electoral competition, unify the electorate, help organize government by bridging the separation of powers and fostering cooperation among branches of government, translate public preferences into policy, and provide loyal opposition.

As institutions, they are governed by their national and state committees, which are led by the party chairs, and they recruit and elect candidates, promote their party's principles, and keep the party organized. In government, Congress is organized around parties, and judicial and many executive branch appointments are based in large part on partisanship.

With the rise of soft money in the 1990s and early 2000s, parties had more resources to spend on politics. In 2002, Congress passed the Bipartisan Campaign Reform Act (BCRA), which banned soft money except for some narrowly defined and limited activities. The parties adapted to BCRA by building a larger individual donor base. The Supreme Court in 2014 again opened the door to parties seeking funds in large amounts by striking longstanding individual aggregate contribution limits.

The Role of Minor Parties (Action)

6.3 Evaluate the role of minor parties in the U.S. electoral system, p. 159.

Our electoral rules foster a two-party system because of our single member districts and winner-take-all system. Nevertheless, minor parties have persisted and occasionally been important to election outcomes, most often as spoilers. One result is that when they get a few percent of the vote the winner may be a plurality winner rather than a majority winner. Countries like Germany that have a proportional representation system have more parties, and the government is often comprised of a coalition of parties.

Parties in the Electorate (Impact)

6.4 Describe the significance of party identification in America today, p. 162.

In the electorate, parties actively seek to organize elections, simplify voting choices, and strengthen individuals' party identification. Party identification has remained the best predictor of voting choice, and most Americans have a party preference, especially if Independent leaners are included with partisans. In recent years, there has been an increase in the number of persons who call themselves Independents. This trend is sometimes called dealignment, but most Independents are closet partisans who vote fairly consistently for the party toward which they lean. In the United States voting in all but one state requires voters to register with the state, and in many states individuals also register by party.

The Persistence of Political Parties (Impact)

6.5 Assess the reasons for the persistence of the two-party system, p. 166.

Frequent efforts have been made to reform our parties. The Progressive movement saw parties, as then organized, as an impediment to democracy and pushed direct primaries as a means to reform them. Following the 1968 election, the Democratic Party took the lead in pushing primaries and stressing greater diversity among the individuals elected as delegates. Republicans have also encouraged broader participation, and they have improved their party structure and finances. There has been some party renewal in recent years as party competition has grown in the South and the parties themselves have initiated reforms.

LEARN THE TERMS

realigning election, p. 143
divided government, p. 145
political party, p. 147
nonpartisan election, p. 148
patronage, p. 149
honeymoon, p. 149
caucus, p. 150
party convention, p. 151
direct primary, p. 151
open primary, p. 152
crossover voting, p. 152
closed primary, p. 152
top two primary, p. 152
national party convention, p. 152
platform, p. 154
soft money, p. 158
party-independent expenditures, p. 158
hard money, p. 158
minor party, p. 159
proportional representation, p. 159
winner-take-all system, p. 160
party registration, p. 162
party identification, p. 163
dealignment, p. 165

CHAPTER 7

Public Opinion, Ideology, Participation, and Voting

Even with the 1964 Civil Rights Act in place, widespread discrimination in voting registration continued. In early 1965, the Reverend Martin Luther King, Jr. and others encountered strong resistance to their efforts to register African Americans in Selma, Alabama. To call attention to these obstacles, civil rights leaders organized a march from Selma, Alabama, to the state capitol in Montgomery. Seen here is a group of three young women who joined the march. Those in the march met sometimes violent resistance from state and local authorities. News coverage of the march helped call attention to the continuing challenges with voting rights and the need for additional legislation. This and other protests helped move Congress to pass the landmark 1965 Voting Rights Act.

LEARNING OBJECTIVES

- **7.1** Explain how the agents of socialization influence the development of political attitudes (Structure), p. 176.
- **7.2** Describe public opinion research and modern methods of polling (Structure), p. 181.
- **7.3** Assess the influence of political ideology on political attitudes and behaviors (Structure), p. 188.
- **7.4** Identify the factors that influence political participation (Action), p. 195.
- **7.5** Analyze why people vote the way they do (Action and Impact), p. 207.

During the twentieth century the United States successfully expanded the right to vote to millions of citizens and ensured it was protected for millions more. From constitutional amendments aimed at extending the vote to women and to Americans between the ages of 18 to 21, to ending the poll tax and enacting the 1965 Voting Rights Act, the United States achieved greater equity at the voting booth than ever before.

If you had been a college student in 1970 you probably would not have been old enough to vote. People under the age of 21 gained the right to vote through the Twenty-sixth Amendment, which took effect with the 1972 election. This change added about 11 million new voters.[1]

Over the prior decade the right to vote also became a reality for African Americans residing in the 11 former Confederate states and several border states. While given the right to vote by the Fifteenth Amendment in 1870, states effectively denied the right to vote through literacy tests, taxes on those who tried to vote but whose grandfathers had not had the right, and threats of physical violence including lynching. This grandfather clause effectively meant the tax was applied primarily to children of former slaves. These barriers were so effective that in 1962 less than 7 percent of African Americans were registered to vote in Mississippi. In a dramatic reversal of nearly a century of discrimination, the Twenty-fourth Amendment was adopted in 1964, banning the poll tax, and the following year Congress passed and the president signed the 1965 Voting Rights Act. Together, these actions made possible voting participation by African Americans in the South. Only three years after the Act was in force, voter registration had risen to 68 percent in Mississippi, a 10-fold increase.[2]

Voting rights were extended nationally to women by the Nineteenth Amendment, ratified in 1920; but for decades after this change, the rates of female voter participation lagged behind men. Today more women than men vote, and women vote at a higher rate than men.[3] In 2008 and 2012, a higher percentage of African Americans than whites voted for president, in part a response to the first African American running as the nominee of a major party. This growing participation by women and African Americans and other minorities speaks to a growing political equality in the United States.

Although the franchise has been greatly expanded and barriers to voting have been lowered, not all barriers have been removed, and there are concerns about laws that could result in decreasing voting turnout. For example, laws requiring photo identification, ostensibly enacted to limit fraud at the voting booth, make it more difficult for some individuals to exercise their right to vote. In the 2016 presidential election, 17 states had new voting restrictions in place, including cutbacks in early voting and new restrictions on voter registration.[4]

Of all the expansions in voting rights, one group of recently enfranchised voters has been consistently less active: 18- to 29-year-olds. You may be part of this group, and so you likely understand some of the reasons people your age do not vote as much as other people. Young people are more mobile, sometimes moving two or more times in a year. As you move you may not change your voter registration, or if you do, you may not think about registering at your new address as early as needed to vote in the next election. You may question the importance of voting, especially compared to more pressing priorities. You probably have heard the argument that any one person's vote does not really matter anyway. Yet as we demonstrate throughout this book, individuals can have an impact on public policy if they understand how government works (structure) and participate meaningfully (action).

Put simply, elections matter for you. The 2016 election, for example, focused on such pressing matters as the tax system, immigration policy, college tuition and student loans, and the future direction of the Supreme Court. Consider this last example and the numerous court decisions discussed in this book. In 2017 and 2018, federal courts overturned the Trump administration's Muslim immigration bans which barred immigrants from seven Muslim-majority countries, and issued an injunction against the administration's termination of the Deferred Action for Childhood Arrivals (DACA) program, which permitted undocumented persons who came to the United States illegally as children to remain if they met certain conditions. In 2018, the Supreme Court in a 5-4 decision upheld the Trump ban on travel from mostly-Muslim countries. The decision affirmed presidential powers extended to decisions about limiting travel from based on legitimate national security concerns. The majority acknowledged President Trump's characterization of the ban as a "Muslim ban," but focused on the actual wording of the executive order. The dissenting justices saw the majority decision as the decision in World War II that permitted the detention of Japanese-Americans.[5]

The justices appointed to the state and federal courts play an important role in the lives of all Americans and President Trump has been acting very quickly to fill the federal courts with his nominees. As a result of Donald Trump's Electoral College victory and the Republicans holding the U.S. Senate in 2016, Justice Antonin Scalia's seat was filled by Neil Gorsuch rather than Merrick Garland who had been nominated by Barack Obama, but never got a hearing, much less a vote in the Senate. Through late 2018, Republicans had filled a second Supreme Court vacancy, and 82 other openings in federal courts with 29 of those being appellate judges. Recent decisions on gay marriage, college admissions, and lawsuits regarding technology and privacy all affect some aspect of our daily lives. Who can make these decisions, however, comes as a result of who is elected governor, president, and members of the legislative bodies that confirm a judge or justice's appointment. Politicians also tend to pay more attention to groups who vote; this is one reason why people over the age of 60 have much greater influence on policy than those under 30.

Turnout in the 2018 midterm elections was up substantially over turnout in the midterms of 2010 and 2014. Overall, turnout increased 10 percent from 2014. In some highly competitive states, turnout approached presidential election levels. The surge in turnout was greater for Democrats but was also evident for Republicans. Among Democrats, the increase was driven by opposition to President Trump. Among Republicans, the increase came later and appears to have been driven by concerns over immigration and judicial confirmations.

As we will discuss in this chapter, to meaningfully participate in politics you must understand the structure of elections. You will need to register to vote not only for general elections, but also for the primary elections: it is important to help choose who runs for office as well as who will serve in office. You will also need to balance the importance of ensuring that all who have the right to vote can exercise that right while also maintaining a fair election process. And even though many of your peers may claim that your vote does not matter, you will soon realize the magnified impact you can have as you participate and as you encourage other like-minded individuals to participate in this complicated, yet fundamental, political process. We begin by looking at how we develop our political opinions and values.

Forming Political Opinions and Values (Structure)

7.1 Explain how the agents of socialization influence the development of political attitudes.

political socialization
The process—most notably in families and schools—by which we develop our political attitudes, values, and beliefs.

No one is born with political views. Rather, they are learned and acquired through experience and association with other people. **Political socialization**—the way in which we come to see society and ourselves and learn to interact with other individuals and in groups—provides the foundation for political beliefs, values, ideology, and partisanship. It is a process that continues throughout our lives. People's views on political issues can change, but our core values and beliefs seldom do. More transitory opinions, say, on banking regulation, tend to be volatile, whereas core values on such things as liberty or freedom tend to remain more stable. This difference is important for understanding the varied levels on which people think about politics.

Political Socialization

You developed your political attitudes from many mentors and teachers through a process that starts in childhood, making families and schools our two most important political teachers. We learn about our culture in childhood and adolescence, but we reshape our opinions as we mature.[6] A common element of political socialization in most cultures is *nationalism,* a consciousness of the nation-state and of belonging to it.

People gain confidence as citizens as they interact with others about politics. The idea of people coming together, listening to each other, exchanging ideas, learning to appreciate each other's differences, and defending their opinions is sometimes called **deliberation** and builds what has been called **social capital**. Robert Putnam has defined social capital as "features of social organization such as networks, norms, and social trust that facilitate coordination and cooperation for mutual benefit."[7] Such interaction is thought to foster and strengthen community and relationships in ways that do not happen when citizens only cast ballots. More specifically, social scientists have distinguished between two types of social capital.

deliberation
The idea of people coming together, listening to each other, exchanging ideas, learning to appreciate each other's differences, and defending their opinions.

social capital
The value of social contacts, associations, and networks individuals form that can foster trust, coordination, and cooperation.

The first, bonding social capital, occurs when similar people build relationships with one another. Participating in a university club of your choice could be an example of this, as you gather with the other individuals that hold similar beliefs and values. Your family, religious group, or even social media friends can all be examples of this as well. In recent years, political campaigns have used social media networks to identify people with similar interests, preferences and politics. Facebook, Instagram, and Twitter all have data on users that vthey sell to advertisers for these kinds of marketing purposes.[8] These same kind of data on social media networks was used by the Russians in the 2016 election to try and defeat Hillary Clinton and elect Donald Trump.[9] The second, bridging social capital, is harder to develop and consequently less common in individuals' lives. This type of social capital occurs when groups of people associate together even though there are major differences like race, religion, or social class. As a push for diversity on university campuses has historically prevailed in the admittance process, the composition of your student body is an attempt to bring various backgrounds into one organization where you can learn from and grow with each other, hopefully resulting in increased bridging social capital. This type of social capital helps build trust—something less common among millennials when compared to older Americans. For example about 40 percent of baby boomers believe that "most people can be trusted," while less than half as many (19 percent) of millennials have this view.[10]

The pluralistic political culture of the United States makes the sources of our views immensely varied. Political attitudes may stem from religious, racial, gender, or ethnic backgrounds, or economic beliefs and values. But we can safely make at least one generalization: we form our attitudes through participation in *groups.* Close-knit groups such as the family are especially influential. At an early age, children in the United States adopt common values that provide continuity with the past and that legitimate the U.S. political system. Young children know what country they live in, and they quickly develop national loyalty. Although the details of our political system may elude them, most young citizens acquire a respect for the Constitution and for the concept of participatory democracy, as well as an initially positive view of the most visible figure in our democracy, the president.[11]

FAMILY Most social psychologists agree that family is the most powerful socializing agent.[12] What we first learn in the family is not so much specific political opinions as basic **attitudes**, broad or general, that shape our opinions about our neighbors, political parties, other classes or types of people, particular leaders (especially presidents), and society in general. Attitudes are understood to be "a propensity in an individual to

attitudes
An individual's propensity to perceive, interpret, or act toward a particular object in a particular way.

perceive, interpret, and act toward a particular object in particular ways."[13] Attitudes are often seen as positive or negative toward the object, person, or idea.

American children typically show political interest by age 10, and by the early teens their awareness may be fairly high. Studies of high school students indicate a strong correlation between their partisan identification and their parents' political party that continues throughout life. In other words, people tend to belong to the same political party as their parents. Does the direct influence of parents create the correspondence? Or does living in the same social environment—neighborhood, church, and socioeconomic group—influence parents and children? The answer is *both*. One influence often strengthens the other.

SCHOOLS Schools also mold young citizens' political attitudes. U.S. schools see part of their purpose as preparing students to be citizens and active participants in governing their communities and the nation. Especially important in fostering later political involvement are extracurricular activities such as student government and debate.[14]

From kindergarten through college, students generally develop political values consistent with the democratic process and supportive of the U.S. political system. In your study of U.S. history, you were likely introduced to our nation's heroes and heroines, important events, and the ideals of U.S. society. Other aspects of your experience, such as the routine recitation of the Pledge of Allegiance and school programs or assemblies, reinforce respect for country. Children also gain practical experience in the way democracy works through elections for student government. In many states, high school and even college students are required by law to take courses in U.S. history or government to graduate.

Do school courses and activities give young people the skills needed to participate in elections and democratic institutions? A study of 18- to 24-year-olds commissioned by the National Association of Secretaries of State, the state officials generally in charge of administering elections, found that young people "lack any real understanding of citizenship … information and understanding about the democratic process … and information about candidates and political parties."[15] Furthermore, the Secretaries of State report noted that "most young people do not seek out political information and that they are not very likely to do so in the future."[16] You and your classmates are not a representative sample, in part because you have more interest and knowledge than most people. Recent surveys comparing millennials with older generations find younger people today less interested in politics compared to older groups. It is true that in 2008, those ages 18–29 were significantly more interested and more likely to vote than in 2012, 2014, or 2016.[17] Others have argued that young people today are engaged in different—and new—forms of political activism. The advent of the Internet and social media is changing the nature of politics.[18]

PEERS AND FRIENDS People of all ages learn from peers and friends, but for younger people they are especially important. For example, friends help with adaptation to school, including college. The influence of friends and peers stems from the human desire to be like people around us.[19] Peer groups not only define fashion and social norms, they reinforce or may challenge what has been experienced in families. One study suggests that college students are more likely than non-college students of the same age to be knowledgeable about politics, more in favor of free speech, and more likely to talk and read about politics.[20]

Technology has expanded the ways we interact with peers through Facebook, Twitter, Snapchat, Instagram, or other types of social media. Some scholars have found that users of social networking sites "are no more knowledgeable about politics (in general and about the field of presidential candidates) than are their counterparts and, in fact, seem to be less so. Their political participation, as such, seems to be limited to Internet activity, and they do not seem to be more likely to vote."[21]

These images are from the 470 Facebook accounts used by the Russian Internet Agency seeking to influence the 2016 presidential election. As a result of the investigation being led by Special Counsel Robert Mueller, indictments were issued against the Russian Internet Agency and 13 of its employees for breaking U.S. laws. The names adopted by the Russians speak to their target audiences: "Back the Badge" emphasizing law and order themes; "South United" with a confederate flag calling for the South to rise again; "Blacktivist" which sought to dampen African American turnout; and "Being Patriotic" which had multiple ads, one saying, "Benghazi victim's mother wishes Hillary to 'burn in hell.'" Facebook was paid in Russian rubles for some of these four ads.

MASS MEDIA Like everyone else, young people are exposed to a wide range of media—school, local, and national newspapers, the Internet, movies, radio, and television—all of which influence what they think. And like everyone else, young people often pick and choose the media with which they agree, a process called **selective exposure**. The mass media also serve as agents of political socialization by exposing individuals to the values and behavior of others. Media influence is greater on attitudes about issues and individual politicians than on underlying values.[22]

selective exposure
Individuals choosing to access media with which they agree or avoiding media with which they disagree.

OTHER INFLUENCES Religious, ethnic, and racial backgrounds, as well as the workplace, can also shape opinions, both within and outside the family. Some scholars have found, for example, that the religious composition of a community has a direct impact on knowledge, discussion, and self-confidence among students in dealing with politics.[23] However, even though generalizations about how people vote are useful, we have to be careful about stereotyping. For example, not all African Americans vote Democratic, and many Catholics disagree with their church's opposition to abortion. It is a mistake to assume that because we know a person's religious affiliation or racial background, we know his or her political opinions.

Stability and Change

Adults are not simply the sum of their early experiences, but adults' opinions do tend to remain stable. Even if the world around us changes rapidly, we are slow to shift our loyalties or to change our minds about things that matter to us. In general, people who remain in the same place, in the same occupation, and in the same income group throughout their lives tend to have stable opinions. People often carry their attitudes with them, and families who move from cities to suburbs often retain their big-city attitudes after they have moved, at least for a time.

Political analysts are becoming more interested in how adults modify their views. A harsh experience—a war, an economic depression, or an event like the terrorist attacks of September 11, 2001—may be a catalyst that changes attitudes and opinions.[24]

Because they are part of our core values, views on abortion, the death penalty, and doctor-assisted suicide, for example, tend to remain stable over time. On issues

FIGURE 7.1 PRESIDENTIAL APPROVAL NUMBERS AND ABORTION ATTITUDES

Public opinion on some matters is quite stable as is the case with how the public sees abortion. In this figure the percent who report they are pro-choice hovers around 48 percent. But the share of the public who approve of the way a president is performing shows much greater variability. Note the surge in public approval of President George W. Bush after the terrorist attacks of September 11, 2001. The more typical pattern is for approval to be in a rather steady decline over the course of a presidency. Late in his presidency, Barack Obama enjoyed resurgence in popularity. You can see that in the blue line in the figure. Mid-way through his last year in office his approval was at 50.9 percent, up from 44 percent two years earlier.

NOTE: Question wording for Presidents Bush, Obama, and Trump: "Do you approve or disapprove of the way Donald Trump [George W. Bush, Barack Obama] is handling his job as president?"

QUESTION wording for abortion: "With respect to the abortion issue, would you consider yourself to be pro-choice or pro-life?"

SOURCES: On abortion: http://news.gallup.com/poll/1576/abortion.aspx http://www.gallup.com/poll/191834/americans-attitudes-toward-abortion-unchanged.aspx; on George W. Bush, http://news.gallup.com/poll/116500/presidential-approval-ratings-george-bush.aspx; on Barack Obama, http://news.gallup.com/poll/116479/barack-obama-presidential-job-approval.aspx; and on Donald Trump, http://news.gallup.com/poll/203198/presidential-approval-ratings-donald-trump.aspx.

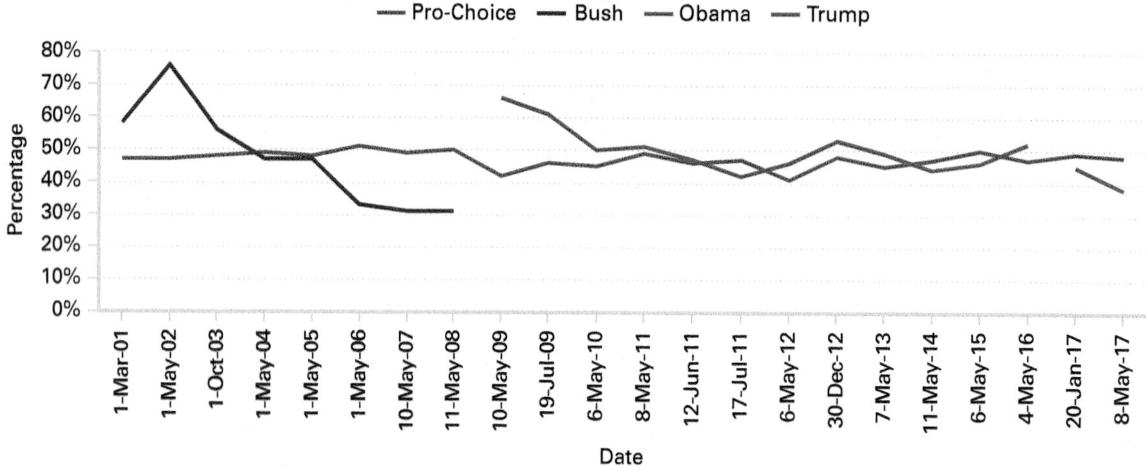

less central to our values, such as how a president is performing, opinions can change substantially. Figure 7.1 contrasts the public's opinion toward Presidents George W. Bush and Barack Obama with its views on abortion over time. Although the electorate's opinion of Presidents Bush and Obama changed noticeably over time, opinions on abortion remained remarkably stable. On many issues, opinion can change once the public learns more about the issue or perceives another side to the question. These are the issues politicians can help shape by calling attention to them and leading the debate.

Awareness and Interest

Many people find politics complicated and difficult to understand. And they should, because democracy is complicated and difficult to understand. The mechanics and structures of our government, such as how the government operates, how the Electoral College works, how Congress is set up, and the length of terms for the president and for members of the Senate and House of Representatives, are examples of such complexity that are important to our constitutional democracy.

Younger adults who remember learning the details in school typically know most about how the government works. In general, however, adults fare poorly when quizzed about their elected officials.[25] Slightly more than a third of the public know the names of the congressional candidates from their district.[26] With so few voters knowing the candidates, it is not surprising that "on even hotly debated issues before Congress, few people know where their Congress member stands."[27] In 2017, only 12 percent could identify John Roberts as the chief justice of the U.S. Supreme Court.[28] The public knows even less about important public policy issues.

Fortunately, not everyone is uninformed or uninterested. Approximately 25 percent of the public is interested in politics most of the time.[29] This is the **attentive public**, people who know and understand how the government works. They vote in most elections, read a daily newspaper, and talk politics with their families and friends. They tend to be better educated and more committed to democratic values than other adults.

attentive public
Citizens who follow public affairs carefully.

At the opposite end of the spectrum are *political know-nothings,* people who are rarely interested in politics or public affairs and seldom vote. About one-third of American adults have indicated that they are interested in politics "only now and then" or "hardly at all."[30]

Between the attentive public and the political know-nothings are the *part-time citizens,* roughly 40 percent of the U.S. public. These individuals participate selectively in elections, voting in presidential elections but usually not in others. Politics and government do not greatly interest them, they pay only minimal attention to the news, and they rarely discuss candidates or elections with others.

Democracy can survive even when some citizens are passive and uninformed, as long as others serve as opinion leaders and are interested and informed about public affairs. It may seem to you that there is not enough time to become part of the attentive public. But becoming attuned to the politics around you is simpler than you think. It can be as easy as building on the basics you are learning in this class in whatever areas interest you—local politics, education policy, the environment, etc. Staying informed both generally and on the area you are specializing in is greatly facilitated by news apps you can use on your phone or tablet. Indeed, the Internet makes being informed less time consuming. As you become interested and involved, you will have much greater impact than your less-active fellow citizens.

Public Opinion: Taking the Pulse of the People (Structure)

7.2 Describe public opinion research and modern methods of polling.

All governments in all nations should be concerned with public opinion. Even in nondemocratic nations, unrest and protest can topple those in power. We saw this in 2014 as mass protests brought down the government of Ukrainian President Viktor Yanukovych after he failed to complete an agreement with the European Union, which had been a goal of previous governments, and instead signed a treaty with Russia. That led to large protests where some protesters were shot. Yanukovych fled to Russia and a new government was formed.[31] Public dissatisfaction with the performance of Ukrainian government remains high but not at the level found in 2014.[32] In a constitutional democracy, citizens can express opinions in a variety of ways, including through demonstrations, in conversations, by writing to their elected representatives and to newspapers, through the use of social media like Twitter and Facebook, and by voting in free and regularly scheduled elections. In short, democracy and public opinion go hand in hand.

Following prolonged protests and the shooting of some protesters, the president of Ukraine fled to Russia. That led to a new government. Here, thousands gather in Kiev's Independence Square to hear the names of the new pro-Western cabinet.

What Is Public Opinion?

public opinion
The distribution of individual preferences for or evaluations of a given issue, candidate, or institution within a specific population.

Politicians frequently talk about what "the people" think or want. But social scientists use the term "public opinion" more precisely: **public opinion** is the distribution of individual preferences for or evaluations of a given issue, candidate, or institution within a specific population as measured by public opinion surveys. *Distribution* means the proportion of the population that holds a particular opinion, compared to people who have opposing opinions or no opinion at all. The most accurate way to study public opinion is through systematic measurement in polls or surveys. For instance, final 2016 pre-election polls by CBS News found that among likely voters, 45 percent said they were voting for Hillary Clinton, 41 percent said they were voting for Donald Trump, and 7 percent said they were voting for someone else. The actual vote was Clinton, 48 percent; Trump, 47 percent; and 11 percent for all others.[33] Final pre-election polls in 2016 generally had Hillary Clinton up by 1 to 7 points over Donald Trump. Those who projected the Electoral College vote also overestimated Clinton's projected electoral votes.

A committee of the American Association for Public Opinion Research released a report on polling accuracy following the 2016 election. They found that national polls collectively predicted a Clinton victory of about 3 percent, only 1 percent above her 2 percent victory in the popular vote. State polls, which are more relevant in determining who wins the presidency given the role played by the Electoral College, showed a competitive race, with the polls on average having Clinton ahead but Trump within one state of winning.[34] Other studies of the 2016 polls found that polls which used both landline and cellphone samples with high quality samples only overestimated the Clinton vote by 1 percent. The problem is not all polls have reliable samples and national polls do not predict the state level results which are determinative in presidential elections. In some key states in 2016, polls were often not scientific and also done only a few times in the general election period.[35]

Measuring Public Opinion

In a scientific public opinion poll, a relatively small number of people can accurately represent the opinions of a larger population if the researchers use *random sampling*. In a **random sample**, every individual in the group has a known and equal chance of being selected. For instance, a survey of 18- to 24-year-olds should not consist solely of college students because nearly half of this age group does not attend college.[36] If only college students are selected, everyone in this age group does not have an equal chance of being included. A reliable way to draw a sample today is with random-digit dialing, in which a computer generates phone numbers at random, allowing the researcher to reach unlisted numbers and cell phones as well as home phones. When properly conducted, exit polls are administered to voters at random as they leave the polls at a randomly selected set of precincts.

random sample
In this type of sample, every individual has a known and equal chance of being selected.

Even with proper sampling, surveys have a **margin of error**, meaning the sample accurately reflects the population only within a certain range—usually plus or minus 3 percent for a sample of at least 1,000 individuals. If, for example, a pre-election poll had one candidate getting 50 percent of the vote and another 48 percent, and the margin of error was plus or minus 3 percent, the first candidate's share of the vote could be as high as 53 percent or as low as 47 percent, and the second candidates could be as high as 51 percent or as low as 45 percent. In such a race, the result would be within the margin of error and too close to accurately conclude which candidate was ahead. If the sample is sufficiently large and randomly selected, these margins of error would apply in about 95 of 100 cases.

margin of error
The range of percentage points in which the sample accurately reflects the population.

The *art of asking questions* is also important to scientific polling. Questions can measure respondents' factual knowledge, their opinions, the intensity of their opinions, or their views on hypothetical situations. The type of questions asked should be determined by the kind of information desired by the researcher. *Open-ended questions* permit respondents to answer in their own words rather than by choosing responses from set categories. These questions are harder to record and compare, but they allow respondents to express their views more clearly and may provide deeper insight into their thinking. Most polls rely on closed-ended questions where respondents select from a set of alternative responses. The way questions are

In addition to polls conducted in advance of the election by Gallup, Pew, and media organizations, a group of newspapers and TV networks together conduct exit polls interviewing voters as they leave voting places. Because more and more people vote early or by mail, reliable exit polls now also do surveys by telephone of a sample of voters who have voted early. Exit polls are helpful to researchers. You will see them cited in this book, for example.

TABLE 7.1 THE WAY YOU ASK THE QUESTION MATTERS

The way you ask a polling question can make a lot of difference in the way people answer it. In the 2016 presidential election, the issue of immigration was frequently discussed in debates. Within a short period of time all major national polls asked questions on the topic of illegal immigration. However, different sources asked slightly different questions, which led to different interpretations of public opinion. Consider the following questions about illegal immigration, each of which was asked between June 15 and August 2, 2015. Read each question and consider how you would have responded if asked by an interviewer.

1. When it comes to legal immigration, do you believe the United States allows too many, too few, or about the right number of each of the following? The number of legal immigrants as a whole.

Date	**Too many**	**Too few**	**About the right amount**	**Don't Know/No Opinion**
	%	%	%	%
August 3–6, 2017	33	12	39	16

SOURCE: Politico National Tracking Poll, August 03–06, 2017, N=1992, Margin of Error: ±2%, https://www.politico.com/f/?id=0000015d-c4ac-dd39-a75d-cfbfbc3e0002.

2. Do you think that legal immigration to the United States should be increased, decreased, or kept about the same as it is now?

Date	**Increased**	**Decreased**	**Kept about the same**	**Unsure/No answer**
	%	%	%	%
2/2–5/18	24	17	54	6

SOURCE: PollingReport.com, May 3–6, 2018, N=1,101, Margin of error ± 3%, http://www.pollingreport.com/immigration.htm

3. Next, we'd like to know how you feel about the state of the nation in each of the following areas. For each one, please say whether you are very satisfied, somewhat satisfied, somewhat dissatisfied, or very dissatisfied. If you don't have enough information about a particular subject to rate it, just say so. How about—the level of immigration into the country today?

	Very satisfied	**Somewhat satisfied**	**Somewhat dissatisfied**	**Very dissatisfied**	**No opinion**
	%	%	%	%	%
2018	8	32	27	27	7

(Asked of those dissatisfied with level of immigration into United States) Would you like to see the level of immigration in this country increased, decreased, or remain about the same?
Combined responses: satisfaction with immigration levels + follow-up of those dissatisfied

	Total satisfied	**Dissatisfied, want increase**	**Dissatisfied, want decrease**	**Dissatisfied, remain same**	**No opinon**
	%	%	%	%	%
2018	40	11	28	15	7

SOURCE: Gallup, March 1–8, 2018, N=1.024, Margin of error ± 4%, http://news.gallup.com/poll/1660/immigration.aspx

4. In your opinion, about how many legal immigrants should be admitted to the United States each year?

None	1 to less than 250,000	250,000 to 499,999	500,000 to less than 1 million	1 million to less than 1.5 million	1.5 million to less than 2 million	2 million to less than 2.5 million	2.5 million or more
9%	35%	19%	18%	7%	3%	1%	8%

SOURCE: Harvard-Harris Poll, January 17–19, 2018 2018, N=980, margin of error NA., http://harvardharrispoll.com/wp-content/uploads/2018/01/Final_HHP_Jan2018-Refield_RegisteredVoters_XTab.pdf

worded and the order in which they are asked can influence respondents' answers (see Table 7.1). Researchers should pretest their questions to be sure they are as clear and as specific as possible. Professional interviewers should read the questions exactly as written and without any bias in their voices.

Scientific polls also require thorough *analysis and reporting of the results.* Such polls must specify the sample size, the margin of error, and when and where the poll was conducted. Moreover, because public opinion can change, polls are really only snapshots of opinion at a particular point in time. One way to track opinion *change* is to interview the same sample more than once. Such surveys are called *panel surveys.* Although they can be informative, it can also be difficult and expensive to contact respondents for a second or third set of interviews, and the fact that those in the sample know they will be interviewed again may influence their responses.

The mass shooting in February 2018 at Marjory Stoneman Douglas High School in Parkland, Florida, created a national protest of gun laws. Here student survivors of the shooting deliver petitions to the office of Florida Governor Rick Scott. The legislature later passed a law raising the minimum age for purchasing most guns in the state and allocated additional funds for school security, including funds to arm school staff and teachers. Governor Scott signed the legislation. For the governor and legislature this marked a major change in their position on gun laws.

Defining public opinion as the distribution of *individual preferences* emphasizes that the unit of measurement is *individuals*—not groups. The **universe** or *population* is the group of people whose preferences the researcher wants to measure. The sample of whom we ask the questions in the survey should be representative of this universe. When a substantial percentage of a sample agrees on an issue—say, that we should honor the U.S. flag—there is a **consensus**. But on most issues, opinions are divided. When two opposing sides feel intensely about an issue and the difference between the major alternatives is wide, the public is said to be **polarized**. On such issues, it can be difficult to compromise or find a middle ground. The Vietnam War in the 1960s and 1970s was a polarizing issue. A more recent example is gay marriage. Neither those who favor legalizing gay marriage nor those who unequivocally oppose it see much room for compromise. Somewhere in the middle were those who opposed gay marriage but favored giving gay couples legal rights through "civil unions." (See Table 7.2. on the next page)

universe
The group of people whose preferences we try to measure by taking a sample; also called population.

consensus
A substantial percentage of a sample that agrees on an issue.

polarized
A wide, intense difference between two opposing sides regarding an issue; often used to describe public opinion regarding an issue.

INTENSITY The degree to which people feel strongly about their opinions, or **intensity**, produces the brightest and deepest hues in the fabric of public opinion. For example, some individuals mildly favor gun control legislation, others mildly oppose it; some people are emphatically for or against it; and some have no interest in gun control at all. Others may not have even heard of it. People who lost their jobs or retirement savings because of corporate scandals are likely to feel more intensely about enhanced regulation of corporations and financial institutions than those not directly affected. We typically measure intensity by asking people how strongly they feel about an issue or about a politician. This type of question is often called a *scale*.

intensity
A measure of how strongly an individual holds a particular opinion.

LATENCY When people hold political opinions but do not fully express them, the opinions are described as **latent**. These opinions may not have crystallized, yet they are still important, because they can be aroused by leaders or events and thereby motivate people to action. Latent opinions set rough boundaries for leaders who know that, if they take certain actions, they will trigger either opposition or support from millions of people. If leaders understand people's unexpressed wants, needs, and hopes, they will know how to mobilize people and draw them to the polls on Election Day. A prominent example of a latent opinion is the concern for security from foreign enemies, which had not been an issue in the United States before the terrorist attacks of September 11, 2001. The need for homeland security has now become a **manifest opinion**, a widely shared and consciously held view.

latency
Political opinions that are held but not yet expressed.

manifest opinion
A widely shared and consciously held view, such as support for abortion rights or for homeland security.

TABLE 7.2 DIFFERING OPINIONS ON GAY MARRIAGE

This table looks at opinions on gay marriage for different categories of persons and compares opinion change on this question between 2012 and 2016. First, for purposes of comparison, look at the percentage points difference between categories of different variables on the "Gay marriages should be allowed" response column. Men and women are not very different, nor are there many differences for people with different levels of education. But large differences exist between the never married and the currently married as well as between Democrats and Republicans. As church attendance increases, support for gay marriage decreases, and there is a clear relationship between age and support for gay marriage, with younger people most supportive and older people most opposed.

Between 2012 and 2016 there were major changes in attitudes towards gay marriage. In 2012, 43 percent of the public favored gay marriage being allowed. In 2016, the percent holding this view had risen to 58 percent. The shift in opinion was often double digits in percentage terms. In 2016, those opposed to gay marriage were most concentrated among people who attend church weekly, African Americans, Republicans, and conservatives.

	Gay Marriage Should Not Be Allowed (Percent)		Gay Marriage Should Not Be Allowed, but Civil Unions Should Be Allowed - (volunteered response) (Percent)		Gay Marriage Should Be Allowed (Percent)	
	2012	2016	2012	2016	2012	2016
Total -	24	18	33	23	43	58
Gender: Men	25	18	34	26	41	57
Gender: Women	23	19	33	20	45	61
Region: Northeast	21	7	33	20	47	73
Region: North Central	24	20	31	25	46	56
Region: South	30	26	33	24	37	50
Region: West	17	12	37	22	47	66
Age: 18–29	17	15	25	14	57	71
Age: 30–44	18	15	33	18	49	67
Age: 45–64	27	20	36	27	37	53
Age: 65+	33	21	39	30	29	49
Church Attendance: Every Week	45	42	39	30	16	28
Church Attendance: Almost every week	27	26	47	33	26	41
Church Attendance: Once or twice a month	25	15	33	32	42	53
Church Attendance: A few times a year	16	12	35	23	49	65
Church Attendance: Never	14	8	25	16	61	76
Race: White	23	16	34	24	42	60
Race: African American	30	29	34	18	36	53
Race Hispanic	24	19	30	23	46	58
Race: Other	20	17	24	22	56	60
Party: Republican	40	25	39	34	20	41
Party: Democrat	17	12	25	15	58	73
Party: Independent	18	19	37	18	45	63
Political Philosophy: Conservative	38	28	46	36	20	36
Political Philosophy: Moderate	19	17	33	20	48	63
Political Philosophy: Liberal	8	5	22	10	70	85
Political Philosophy: Do not know/Have not thought about it	29	31	26	16	45	53
Marital Status: Married	28	19	37	27	35	54
Marital Status: Widowed	29	28	38	22	33	49
Marital Status: Divorced	22	17	33	24	45	59
Marital Status: Separated	19	30	34	22	47	48
Marital Status: Never married	16	14	24	15	60	71
Education: High school or less	30	24	29	21	41	55
Education: Some College	26	19	35	25	41	56
Education: College degree or more	15	10	38	23	47	67

NOTE: Question wording: 1. Gay and lesbian couples should be allowed to legally marry; 2. Gay and lesbian couples should be allowed to form civil unions but not legally marry; 3. There should be no legal recognition of a gay or lesbian couple's relationship.

SOURCES: 2016 American National Election Study (ANES; www.electionstudies.org). The ANES 2016 Time Series Study [dataset]. http://electionstudies.org/studypages/download/datacenter_all_datasets.php.

SALIENCE Issues that people believe are important to them are **salient**. Most people are more concerned about personal issues such as paying their bills and keeping their jobs than about national issues, but if national issues somehow threaten their security or safety, their salience rises sharply. Salience and intensity, though different, are often correlated on the same issue.

salience
An individual's belief that an issue is important or relevant to him or her.

The salience of issues may change over time. During the Great Depression of the 1930s, people were concerned mainly about jobs, wages, and economic security. By the 1940s, with the onset of World War II, foreign affairs came to the forefront. In the 1960s, problems of race and poverty were important to many. In the 1970s, Vietnam and then the Watergate scandals became the focus of attention.

Public opinion on same-sex marriage changed a great deal between 2012 and 2016, perhaps due to the Supreme Court decision on the constitutionality of same-sex marriage. As noted in Table 7.2, the percent saying same-sex marriage should be allowed rose from 43 percent in 2012 to 58 percent in 2016, and the growth was the same for men and women. The share of the public holding the view that same-sex marriage should not be allowed dropped from 24 percent in 2012 to 18 percent in 2016. The region with the largest change was the Northeast, where 73 percent saying same-sex marriage should be allowed. Not surprisingly two-thirds of more of liberals, Democrats, persons under age 45, college educated and never married all think same-sex marriage should be allowed. The increase in percent saying same-sex marriage should be allowed came from declines in the percent saying same sex marriage should not be allowed and from those who held the middle position that same-sex marriage should not be allowed but that civil unions should be. Those that hold the view that same-sex marriage should not be allowed remain, with at least 20 percent holding this view include persons over age 45, church attenders (regular or almost every week), people from the South, or North Central states, African Americans, Republicans, conservatives, those who do not have an ideology, widows, who are separated from spouse, and who have high school or less education.

Public Opinion and Public Policy

For much of human history, public opinion has been difficult to measure. "What I want," Abraham Lincoln once said, "is to get done what the people desire to be done, and the question for me is how to find that out exactly."[37] Politicians today do not face such uncertainty about public opinion—far from it.[38] Polling informs them about public opinion on all major policy issues. Politicians can commission polls themselves, or they can turn to public or media polls. All national and some local newspapers and television stations conduct or commission their own polls.[39]

Many examples from history show how public opinion can shape policy and, in turn, how policies shape opinion. On May 3, 2003, the day after President Bush announced "Mission Accomplished" in the Iraq War, 72 percent of American adults approved of the way he had handled the situation in Iraq. About one year later, after revelations of torture by U.S. soldiers in the Abu Ghraib prison and repeated attacks on U.S. forces in Iraq, Bush's approval rating had fallen to 34 percent,[40] and in 2008, it fell to less than 30 percent.[41] Obama began his presidency with a 69 percent approval rating, only to see that drop to 49 percent in 2010, not long after Congress enacted health care reform, and fall further to 38 percent in 2011.[42] In October 2012, Obama had an approval rating of about 50 percent, which was similar to positive ratings between 48 percent and 52 percent that George Bush had in October 2004 as he sought reelection.[43] Obama's approval rating was 53 percent as the country went to the polls in 2016 to select his successor. President Trump's approval rating rose slightly before the 2018 midterm election to the mid-40 percent range. Compared to other presidents, his approval rating had little variation.

Typically, elected officials focus on issues of importance to the public.[44] In a sense, they follow public opinion by using polls to learn how to talk about issues in ways that resonate with the public. Members of Congress who want to win reelection pay greater attention to public opinion as Election Day looms.[45] Candidates use polls to determine where, how, and even whether to campaign. The decision in 2016 about which states and districts the two parties and allied interest groups most contested in the presidential and congressional races was driven by the polls. Even less populous states such as New Hampshire and Nevada received substantial attention because outcomes have been more evenly divided in these "swing states." Larger states such as New York, California, Illinois, and Texas were taken for granted because one side or the other was so far ahead in each and gaining a plurality in the national popular vote was a secondary objective to securing 270 electoral votes.

Polls are no substitute for elections. With a choice between candidates before them, voters must now translate their opinions into concrete decisions and decide what is important and what is not. Democracy is more than the expression of views, a simple mirror of opinion. It is the thoughtful participation of people in the political process. Elections are the critical link between the many opinions "We the People" hold and how we select our leaders.

Political Ideology and Attitudes Toward Government (Structure)

7.3 Assess the influence of political ideology on political attitudes and behaviors.

political ideology

A constant pattern of ideas or beliefs about political values and the role of government, including how it should work and how it actually does work.

One central component of public opinion is ideology. **Political ideology** refers to a consistent pattern of ideas or beliefs about political values and the role of government, including how it should work and how it actually does work.

Two major schools of political ideology dominate American politics: *liberalism* and *conservatism*. Two less popular schools of thought—*socialism* and *libertarianism*—also help define the spectrum of ideology. We measure ideology by asking people a question like, "When it comes to politics do you usually think of yourself as extremely liberal, liberal, slightly liberal, moderate or middle of the road, slightly conservative, conservative, extremely conservative, or haven't you thought much about this?"[46] People rather consistently self-classify themselves as liberal or conservative and are also willing to report the strength of their views (e.g., extremely conservative, slightly liberal, etc.). At the same time a large group of people respond to the question by saying they are "moderate" or "have not thought much about this." (See Table 7.3.)

Liberalism

In the eighteenth and nineteenth centuries, classical liberals favored *limited government* and sought to protect people from governmental harassment in their political and economic lives. Over time, the liberal emphasis on individualism has remained constant, but the perception of the need for government changed.

liberalism

A belief that government can bring about justice and equality of opportunity.

CONTEMPORARY LIBERALS In its current U.S. usage, **liberalism** refers to a belief that government can bring about justice and equality of opportunity. Modern-day liberals typically wish to preserve the rights of the individual and the right to own private property, yet they believe that some government intervention in the economy is necessary to remedy the shortcomings of capitalism. Liberals advocate equal access to health care, housing, and education for all citizens. They generally believe in affirmative action programs, protections for workers' health and safety, reducing income inequality, tax rates that rise with a person's income, and unions' rights to organize and strike. Liberals are generally more inclined to favor greater environmental protection and individual choice in such matters as same-sex marriage and abortion.

TABLE 7.3 DIFFERENCES IN POLITICAL IDEOLOGY

This table compares ideology for a variety of variables like sex, race, age, religion, education, and political party. For example, people over age 45 are more conservative than persons younger than 45, and those over 65 are even more likely to be conservative. Another interesting comparison is the proportion in each category who don't know or have not thought about their ideology. Note that African Americans, those with high school diplomas or those who did not finish high school, and pure Independents are much more likely to not know or not have thought about their own ideology.

	Conservative	Moderate	Liberal	Don't Know/Haven't Thought About It
Sex				
Male	36	21	22	21
Female	27	20	26	27
Race				
White	36	20	25	20
Black	12	21	22	45
Hispanic	28	19	23	30
Other	27	21	26	26
Age				
18–29	23	19	32	26
30–44	25	19	26	30
45–64	35	22	22	22
65+	39	20	20	21
Religion				
Protestant	48	18	20	14
Catholic	33	24	20	23
Jewish	16	18	58	8
Other	27	21	16	35
Education				
Less than high school	22	21	18	39
High School Diploma	27	18	16	39
Some College	33	23	21	23
Bachelor's Degree	39	21	30	10
Advanced Degree	31	18	45	6
Party				
Democrat	8	21	46	26
Independent	14	32	12	43
Republican	65	16	4	15

SOURCE: Center for Political Studies, University of Michigan, *2016 American National Election Study Guide to Public Opinion and Electoral Behavior.*

Liberals generally believe that the future will be better than the past or the present—that obstacles can be overcome and the government can be trusted to, and should, play a role in that progress.[47] Liberals led in expanding civil rights in the 1960s and 1970s and favor affirmative action today. They seek ways to reduce the growing income inequality and tend to favor a certain minimum level of income for all. Rather than placing a cap on wealth, they want to build a floor beneath the poor. If necessary, they favor raising taxes to achieve these goals. In the recent health care reform debate, liberals favored a public insurance plan providing something like Medicare for all citizens.

CRITICISMS OF LIBERALISM Critics say liberals rely too much on government, higher taxes, and bureaucracy to solve the nation's problems. Moreover, once a government program is started it is very rarely removed, and as a result government

In recent years liberals have pressed for an increase to the minimum wage. Here in 2017 supporters of raising the minimum wage to $15 in Minneapolis rally to show their support for the change. The City Council adopted the change which will rise to $15 by 2022.

grows ever larger. Government is not as well suited to solving many problems, they contend, as the private sector. They argue that liberals have forgotten that government has to be limited if it is to serve our best interests.

Critics also contend that liberals lack fiscal responsibility and are largely responsible for an increasing national debt. Too much dependence on government can corrupt the spirit, undermine self-reliance, and make people forget those personal freedoms and property rights the Republic was founded to secure and protect. In short, critics of modern liberalism contend that the welfare and regulatory state liberals advocate will ultimately destroy individual initiative, the entrepreneurial spirit, and the very engine of economic growth that might lead to true equality of economic opportunity.

Finally, some critics of liberals are concerned with trends in society they see being promoted by liberals. These included permissiveness in the media, a tolerance for immoral lifestyles, a willingness to legalize marijuana, and a disregard for the sanctity of life. Opponents frequently cite liberals' support for abortion rights and same-sex marriage as examples of liberals' ideological extremity. Since the late 1960s, Republicans have made liberalism a villain while claiming that their own presidential candidates represent the mainstream.

Conservatism

conservatism
A belief in private property rights and free enterprise.

Belief in private property rights and free enterprise are cardinal attributes of contemporary **conservatism**. In contrast to liberals, conservatives want to enhance individual liberty by keeping government small, especially the national government, although they support a strong national defense. Conservatives take a more pessimistic view of human nature than liberals do.[48] Given that a primary task of government is to ensure order, they maintain that people need strong leadership, firm laws, and strict moral codes. Conservatives also believe that people are the architects of their own success or failure.

TRADITIONAL CONSERVATIVES Conservatives are pro-business. They favor tax cuts and resist all but the minimum antitrust, trade, and environmental regulations on corporations. They believe that the primary functions of government should be to protect the nation from foreign enemies, preserve law and order, enforce private contracts, encourage economic growth by fostering competitive markets and free and fair trade, and promote family values. Traditional conservatives favor dispersing power throughout the political and social systems to avoid an overly powerful national government; they believe that the market, not the government, should provide services. These views were tested by the Bush administration's advocacy of the massive government bailout of America's financial institutions in 2008, and more broadly by concerns about government spending and increased budget deficits during the Bush and Trump administrations.

Conservatives opposed the New Deal programs of the 1930s, the War on Poverty in the 1960s, many civil rights and affirmative action programs, and the Obama administration's push for a larger government role through the Affordable Care Act. Families and private charities, they say, have the primary responsibility to take care of human needs and social and economic problems. They further argue that government social activism has been expensive and counterproductive. State and local government should address those social problems that need a government response. Conservatives, especially those in office, do, however, selectively advocate government activism, often expressing a desire for a more effective and efficient government.

SOCIAL CONSERVATIVES Some conservatives focus less on economics and more on morality and lifestyle. **Social conservatives** favor strong governmental action to protect children from pornography and drugs. They generally want to overturn or repeal judicial rulings and laws that permit abortion, same-sex marriage, and affirmative action programs. This brand of conservatism—sometimes called the New Right—emerged in the 1980s. Social conservatives share with traditional conservatives a love of freedom and support an aggressive effort to defend American interests abroad.

social conservatives
Focus less on economics and more on morality and lifestyle.

A defining characteristic of social conservatism is a strong desire to impose *social controls*. Christian conservatives, who are disproportionately evangelical, seek to preserve traditional values and protect the institution of the family. In 2016, the connection between Christian conservatives and the GOP was further reinforced by the candidacy of Texas senator Ted Cruz, who strongly emphasized his religion and Christian religious values in his campaign.[49]

CRITICISMS OF CONSERVATISM Not everyone agreed with Ronald Reagan's statement that "government is the problem." Indeed, critics point out that conservatives themselves urge more government when it serves their purposes—to regulate pornography and abortion, for example—but are opposed to government when it serves somebody else's. Conservatives also tend to have fewer objections to big

A defining issue for conservatives has been the repeal of the Affordable Care Act, Obamacare, which has been brought to a vote more than 60 times in the House of Representatives. Seen here on May 4, 2017, are Republican Representatives Jim Jordan of Ohio, center, Mo Brooks of Alabama, left, and Justin Amash of Michigan, right, as they leave the House Republican Conference meeting prior to the House voting to repeal the act. The vote was 217 to repeal and 213 not to repeal, with all Democrats voting in opposition. On July 28, 2017, with a 52 to 48 seat majority in the Senate, the Senate voted 51-49 to reject legislation undoing major portions of the law.

government when individuals have a choice in determining how government will affect them. Vouchers for schools, choices in prescription-drug benefit plans, and options to manage Social Security savings are examples of such choices.[50]

Conservatives' great faith in the market economy often puts them at odds with labor unions and consumer activists and in close alliance with businesspeople, particularly large corporations. Hostility to regulation and a belief in competition lead conservatives to push for deregulation. This approach has not always yielded positive results, as illustrated by the collapse of many savings and loan companies in the 1980s[51] and the 2008 financial crisis, brought about by troubled subprime mortgages and other risky lending practices.[52] Conservatives counter that overall it is still best to rely on the free market.

The policy of lowering taxes is consistent with the conservative hostility to big government. Many conservatives embrace the idea that if the rich pay fewer taxes, they will spend and invest more, and the benefits of this increased economic activity will "trickle down" to others including the poor. But Democrats and liberals argue that most of the growth in income and wealth that followed 1980s tax cuts was largely concentrated among the well-to-do and that reduced taxes and increased government spending, especially for defense, tripled the deficit during the 1980s, when conservatives were in control.[53] The temporary tax cuts pushed by President George W. Bush during his first term have been extended three times.[54] Republicans and conservatives favor making the cuts permanent, and all of the 2016 Republican presidential candidates favored even more extensive tax cuts.

Liberals counter that the Bush tax cuts should be repealed because they further benefit the rich while hurting everyone. They have proposed increasing taxes for those making more than $1 million, a reform sometimes called "the Buffett Rule," named after billionaire Warren Buffett, who endorsed higher taxes for the wealthy.[55] Who should pay what in taxes was a central issue in the 2016 elections and shows the enduring ideological divide over taxing and government spending.

socialism

A governmental system where some of the means of production are controlled by the state and where the state provides key human welfare services like health care and old-age assistance. Allows for free markets in other activities.

Socialism and Communism

Socialism is an economic and governmental system based on public ownership of some of the means of production and exchange and a wider role for government in providing social programs meeting such needs as health care and old-age assistance.

Conservatives often present their views in moralistic or religious terms, as is being done here by talk show personality Glenn Beck at a campaign event for Ted Cruz in Iowa City shortly before the 2016 Iowa Caucus. Beck is discussing the importance of prayer at critical times in U.S. history: George Washington at Valley Forge, Abraham Lincoln during the Civil War, and in 2016 on the eve of the presidential election.

Socialism allows for capitalism in many economic sectors, but favors more government regulation. The nineteenth-century German philosopher Karl Marx once described socialism as a transitional stage of society between capitalism and communism. In a capitalist system, the means of production and most property are privately owned; under **communism** the state owns property in common for all the people, and a single political party that represents the working classes controls the government.

communism
A belief that the state owns property in common for all people and a single political party that represents the working classes controls the government.

In communist countries such as Cuba and China, the Communist Party allows no opposition. Some countries, such as Sweden, have combined limited government ownership and operation of business with democracy. Most western European countries and Canada have various forms of socialized or government-run medical systems and sometimes telecommunications networks, while keeping most economic sectors private.

American socialists favor a greatly expanded role for the government, but argue that such a system is compatible with democracy. They would nationalize certain industries, institute a public jobs program so that all who want to work could work, tax the wealthy much more heavily, and drastically cut defense spending.[56] Canada and most of the democracies of Western Europe are more influenced by socialist ideas than we are in the United States, but they remain, like the United States, largely market economies. Debate will continue about the proper role of government and what the market can do better than government can.[57] Younger Americans (age 18–29) are more likely to have a positive view of socialism (55 percent) than the U.S. public generally.[58]

The most visible person who has used the term socialist as part of a self-classification in American politics today is Vermont U.S. senator Bernie Sanders, a candidate for the Democratic nomination for president in 2016. Sanders was elected in Vermont as an Independent and continues to describe himself as a democratic socialist. To him, "democratic socialism means that we must create an economy that works for all, not just the very wealthy" that does not include government control of the means of production, but instead gives "the middle class and the working families who produce the wealth of America . . . a fair deal."[59]

libertarianism
Would limit government to such vital activities as national defense while fostering individual liberty. Unlike conservatives, libertarians oppose all government regulation, even of personal morality.

Libertarianism

Libertarianism is a political ideology that cherishes individual liberty and insists on sharply limited government. Libertarians oppose nearly all government programs. They favor massive cuts in government spending and an end to the Federal Bureau of Investigation (FBI), the Central Intelligence Agency (CIA), the Internal Revenue Service (IRS), and most regulatory commissions. They typically oppose American participation in the United Nations and favor armed forces that would defend the United States only if directly attacked. They oppose *all* government regulation, including, for example, mandatory seat-belt and helmet laws, in part because they believe individuals will all benefit more from an undistorted free market, and more generally because they embrace the attitude "live and let live." Unlike social conservatives, libertarians would repeal laws that regulate personal morality, including abortion, pornography, prostitution, and illicit drugs. The Libertarian Party has gained a following among people who share this perspective. Ron Paul, who ran as a Libertarian for president in 1988, continued to espouse many of the positions identified with Libertarians in his 2008 and 2012 bids to become the Republican nominee for president.[60]

Senator Bernie Sanders speaks at a rally in 2011 in support of Social Security in Washington, D.C. At the rally he spoke against proposals to raise the retirement age and to privatize Social Security. Sanders is among the most liberal senators and the only one elected as a Democratic Socialist.

Despite the twists and turns of American politics, the distribution of ideology in the nation has been remarkably

FIGURE 7.2 SEVEN POINT IDEOLOGY SCALE

While attention is often focused on conservatives and liberals, the reality is that the modal American is not ideological, meaning they classify themselves as moderate or indicate they don't know or have not thought about their ideology. To the extent these individuals vote, they will pull candidates more to the center in hopes of picking up their support. Relatively few Americans are extreme conservatives or extreme liberals.

SOURCES: 2016 American National Election Study (ANES; https://www.electionstudies.org). The ANES 2016 Time Series Study [dataset]. http://electionstudies.org/studypages/download/datacenter_all_datasets.php.

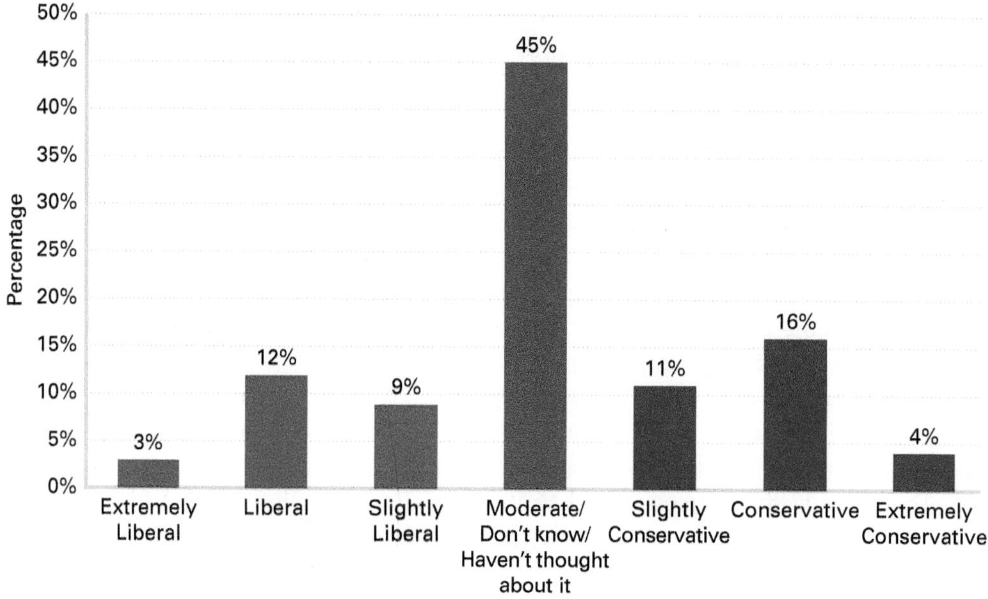

consistent (see Figure 7.2). Conservatives outnumber liberals, but the proportion of conservatives did not increase substantially with the decisive Republican presidential victories of the 1980s or the congressional victories of the 1990s. Moreover, in the United States most people consider themselves to be moderates. In recent years only 2–3 percent of Americans viewed themselves as extreme liberals, while extreme conservatives ranged from 2 to 4 percent.

United States Senator Rand Paul from Kentucky ran for the presidency in 2016, as his father did in 2008 and 2012. His father also ran as a Libertarian for president in 1988. Both Ron and Rand Paul appeal to the more libertarian wing of the Republican party. They favor lower taxes and a less aggressive military, and are opposed to security measures like those used by the National Security Agency, such as listening to cell phone conversations.

Participation: Translating Opinions into Action (Action)

7.4 Identify the factors that influence political participation.

United States citizens influence their government's actions in several ways, many of which the Constitution protects. In addition to voting in elections, they participate in Internet political blogs, join interest groups, go to political party meetings, ring doorbells, urge friends to vote for issues or candidates, sign petitions, write letters to newspapers, and call radio talk shows. This kind of "citizen-to-citizen" participation can be important and may become more so as more people use the Internet and its social capital-building applications, such as social networking sites.[61]

Protest is also a form of political participation. Our political system is remarkably tolerant of protest that is not destructive or violent. Boycotts, picketing, sit-ins, and marches are all legally protected. Rosa Parks and Martin Luther King, Jr. used nonviolent protest to call attention to unfair laws. Relative to voting, few people participate in protests, but the actions of those who do can substantially shape public opinion, as the Tea Party activities demonstrated in 2010 and 2012, and the Occupy Wall Street protesters demonstrated in 2011 and 2012. In extreme cases, people may feel so strongly about an issue that they would rather fight than accept the verdict of an election. The classic example is the American Civil War.

For most people, politics is a private activity. To say that politics is private does not mean that people do not have opinions or will not discuss them when asked by others, including pollsters. But many people avoid discussing politics with neighbors, coworkers, or even friends and family because it is too divisive or upsetting. Typically, fewer than two persons in five attempt to influence how another person votes in an election,[62] although that number has been higher since 2000,[63] and even fewer people contribute financially to a candidate.[64] Fewer still write letters to elected officials or to newspapers for publication or participate in protest groups or activities. Yet, despite the small number of people who engage in these activities, they can make a difference in politics and government. An individual or small group can generate media interest in an issue and thereby expand the issue's impact.

Levels of political participation rose during the 2008 presidential election, in part because of increased use of the Internet to persuade and mobilize voters (see Figure 7.3). Candidates' Web sites allowed individuals to register with the campaign and be connected with other politically active individuals in their area. They also provided calling lists for volunteers to call from their own phones. Local campaign leaders in turn used the Internet to contact individuals in the area who had expressed an interest in working with the campaign. The Internet helped campaigns organize more effectively and made it easier for interested people to participate. From its peak in 2008, turnout more generally declined in 2012 and further declined in 2016. In 2016, there were warning signs that elements of the Obama/Clinton voting coalition were not voting at 2008 levels, and late visits by Trump to Michigan signaled greater potential from Trump supporters than had been expected. The Clinton campaign banked on their data-driven voter mobilization to foster turnout. The Trump campaign relied on large rallies to gather media attention and encourage supporters.

Candidates' Web sites make it easy for individuals to donate and to invite their friends to donate through email, Facebook, Snapchat, Instagram, and other social-networking Web sites. The Obama campaign was especially innovative in its use of the Internet in 2008 and 2012. ActBlue, a liberal political action committee, has used the Internet to make it much easier for people to donate to the Democratic candidates of their choice, while Slatecard has tried to achieve the same for Republicans. Bernie

FIGURE 7.3 POLITICAL PARTICIPATION IN THE UNITED STATES

There is a large difference between the more active forms of participation like making a financial contribution, visiting a candidate's Web site, or displaying a button or sticker, and voting or following campaigns online or on TV. The exception is that about two in five people try to persuade another person to vote a particular way.

SOURCES: a. 2016 American National Election Study (ANES; https://www.electionstudies.org). The ANES 2016 Time Series Study [dataset]. http://electionstudies.org/studypages/download/datacenter_all_datasets.php; b. *Michael McDonald*, http://www.electproject.org/2016g; c. 2016 Cooperative Congressional Election Study (CCES).

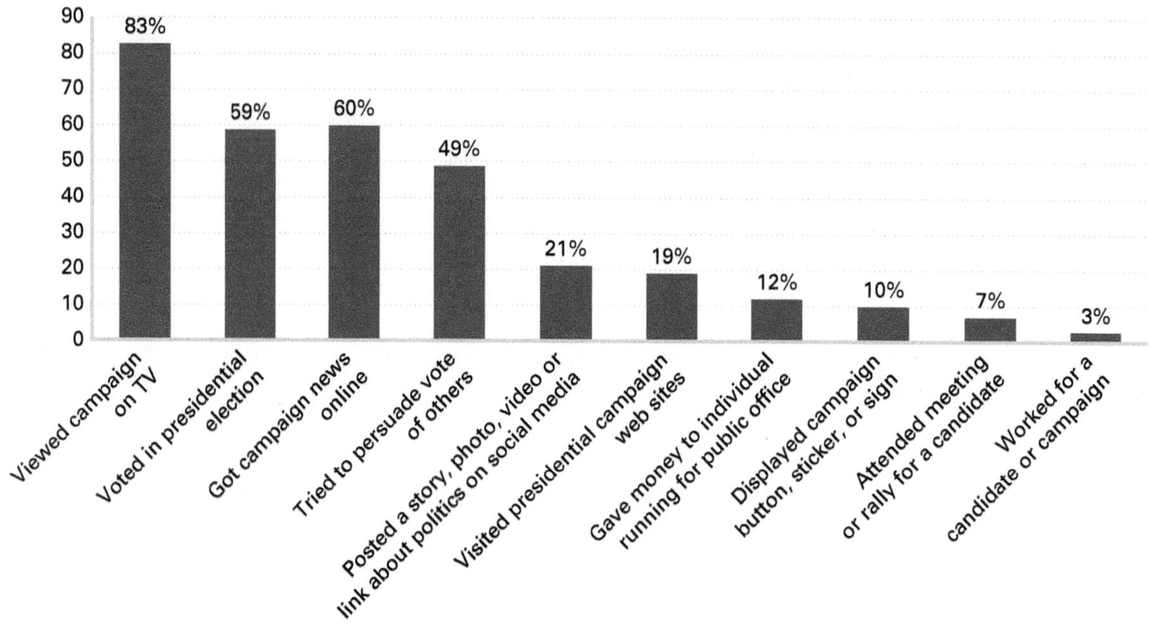

Sanders's 2016 campaign for the presidency is reported to have exceeded Obama's campaigns in the number of online donations, and during some periods of the 2016 campaign, Sanders raised more money than Hillary Clinton did.[65] On the Republican side in 2016, Ben Carson made extensive use of Facebook and a large proportion of his contributions were under $200.[66] In 2018, Democratic candidates experienced success raising funds from small donors via the Internet. Candidates like Beto O'Rourke in Texas and Heidi Heitkamp in North Dakota achieved notable success. Some called the surge in internet driven fundraising the "green wave."

Voting

For most people, politics and elections are of secondary importance, and if they become involved at all, they do so by voting. The United States is a constitutional democracy with more than 200 years of free and frequent elections. Elections have consequences resulting in the peaceful transfer of power between competing groups and parties. But who may vote and what we vote for has changed over time. Our ideas about suffrage and the right to vote have changed from a belief that only property-owning white men should be allowed to vote to a conviction that all adult citizens, excluding felons in some states, should have the right; as an example see the women's suffrage time line (see Table 7.4). The role of voters has also expanded. Citizens now may vote in party primaries to select nominees for office instead of having nominees chosen by party leaders.

Originally, the Constitution left it to the individual states to determine who could vote, and qualifications for voting differed considerably from state to state. Most states did not permit women, African Americans, or Native Americans to vote, and until the 1830s, property ownership was often a requirement. By the time of the Civil War (1861–1865), however, every state had extended the franchise to white male citizens. Since that time, eligibility standards for voting have been expanded seven times by congressional legislation and constitutional amendments (see Table 7.5).

TABLE 7.4 WOMEN'S SUFFRAGE TIME LINE*

Time line	Change
1821	Emma Willard founds the Troy Female Seminary, the first school to offer girls classical and scientific studies on a collegiate level.
1833	Oberlin College is founded as the first coeducational institution of higher learning.
1837	Mount Holyoke, the first college for women, is founded by Mary Lyon in South Hadley, MA.
1839	Mississippi becomes the first state to grant women the right to hold property in their own name.**
1848	The first woman's rights convention is held in Seneca Falls, New York. The state legislature passes a law that gives women the right to retain possession of property they owned prior to their marriage.
1869	National Woman Suffrage Association is founded with Elizabeth Cady Stanton as president. Wyoming Territory grants suffrage to women.
1890	Wyoming joins the union as the first state with voting rights for women.
1912	Suffrage referendums are passed in Arizona, Kansas, and Oregon.
1916	Jeannette Rankin, a Republican from Montana, is elected to the House of Representatives and becomes the first woman to serve in Congress.
1920	The Nineteenth Amendment to the U.S. Constitution, granting women the right to vote, is adopted.
1936	Federal court rules birth control legal for its own sake, rather than solely for prevention of disease.
1960	FDA approves birth control pills.
1964	Civil Rights Act prohibits job discrimination on the basis of race or sex and establishes Equal Employment Opportunity Commission to address discrimination claims.
1972	After nearly 50 years, Equal Rights Amendment passes both houses and is signed by President Richard Nixon. Title IX prohibits sex discrimination in educational programs and activities.†
1973	In *Roe* v. *Wade*, U.S. Supreme Court affirms women's right to first-trimester abortions without state intervention.
1981	Sandra Day O'Connor is appointed first woman U.S. Supreme Court justice.
1993	The Family and Medical Leave Act requires employers to provide up to 12 weeks of unpaid leave within one year of the birth of a child.‡
2007	Democratic Representative from California, Nancy Pelosi, elected as first women speaker of the U.S. House of Representatives.
2016	Hillary Clinton nominated as first woman presidential candidate of a major party.

*Unless otherwise indicated, drawn from Susan B. Anthony Time Line, Anthony Center for Women's Leadership at the University of Rochester, http://www.rochester.edu/sba/suffragetimeline.html. All rights reserved.
**http://www.wearewoman.us/p/us-womens-rights-history.html.
†Title IX is a portion of the Education Amendments of 1972, Public Law No. 92-318, 86 Stat. 235 (June 23, 1972), codified at 20 U.S.C. sections 1681 through 1688nces.ed.gov/fastfacts/display.asp?id=93.
‡https://www.dol.gov/whd/fmla/.

The civil rights movement in the 1960s made voting rights a central issue. In 1964, President Lyndon Johnson pushed for passage of the Twenty-fourth Amendment, which banned poll taxes, and in 1965, for passage of the National Voting Rights Act, which outlawed the use of literacy tests as a requirement for voting. Anticipating that some state or local governments would change election rules to foster discrimination, the act also required that any changes to voting practices, requirements, or procedures must

TABLE 7.5 CHANGES IN VOTING ELIGIBILITY STANDARDS SINCE 1870

For nearly a century amendments to the Constitution were not used to extend voting rights. That changed in 1870 with the Fifteenth Amendment. But since 1920 and especially since 1961, amendments to the Constitution have repeatedly been used to expand suffrage.

Time line	Change
1870	Fifteenth Amendment forbade states from denying the right to vote because of "race, color, or previous condition of servitude."
1920	Nineteenth Amendment gave women the right to vote.
1924	Congress granted Native Americans citizenship and voting rights.
1961	Twenty-third Amendment permitted District of Columbia residents to vote in federal elections.
1964	Twenty-fourth Amendment prohibited the use of poll taxes in federal elections.
1965	Voting Rights Act removed restrictions that kept African Americans from voting.
1971	Twenty-sixth Amendment extended the vote to citizens age 18 and older.

be cleared in advance with the Department of Justice or the U.S. District Court for the District of Columbia. The ban on the poll tax and the provisions of the Voting Rights Act resulted in a dramatic expansion of registration and voting by African Americans. Once African Americans were permitted to register to vote, "the focus of voting discrimination shifted … to preventing them from winning elections."[67] In southern legislative districts where African Americans are in the majority, however, there has been a "dramatic increase in the proportion of African American legislators elected."[68] The number of African Americans in the U.S. House of Representatives from all states hit a new high of 44 following the 2014 election, plus two delegates who are also African American.[69]

voter registration

A system designed to reduce voter fraud by limiting voting to those who have established eligibility to vote by submitting the proper documents, including proof of residency.

REGISTRATION One legal requirement—**voter registration**—arose as a response to concerns about voting abuses, but it also discourages voting.[70] It requires voters to take an extra step—usually filling out a form at the county courthouse, when renewing a driver's license, or with a roving registrar—days or weeks before the election and every time they move to a new address. Average turnout in the United States is more than 30 percentage points lower than in countries such as Denmark, Germany, and Israel where voter registration is not required.[71] This was not always the case. In fact, in the 1800s, turnout in the United States was much like that of these countries today. It began to drop significantly around 1900, in part as a result of election reforms like voter registration (see Figure 7.4).

Laws vary by state, but every state except North Dakota requires registration, usually in advance of Election Day. Idaho, Maine, Minnesota, New Hampshire, Wisconsin, and Wyoming permit Election-Day registration. The most important provision regarding voter registration may be the closing date. Until the early 1970s, closing dates in many states were six months before the election. Now, federal law prevents a state from closing registration more than 30 days before a federal election.[72] Other important provisions include places and hours of registration, and some states require that voters show photo identification before voting.[73]

FIGURE 7.4 VOTER TURNOUT IN PRESIDENTIAL ELECTIONS, 1789–2016

Voting participation peaked and stayed relatively high from the 1840s through 1900 and then started a decline before leveling off again in the 1930s. Part of the explanation for this is changes in the rules of voting, most notably that voters needed to be registered in order to vote and the end of the parties printing the ballots, often on different colors, which meant voting was not secret.

SOURCE: Howard W. Stanley and Richard G. Niemi, *Vital Statistics on American Politics, 2015–2016* (CQ Press, 2015), pp. 4–5; for 2016 see Michael McDonald, http://www.electproject.org/2016g.

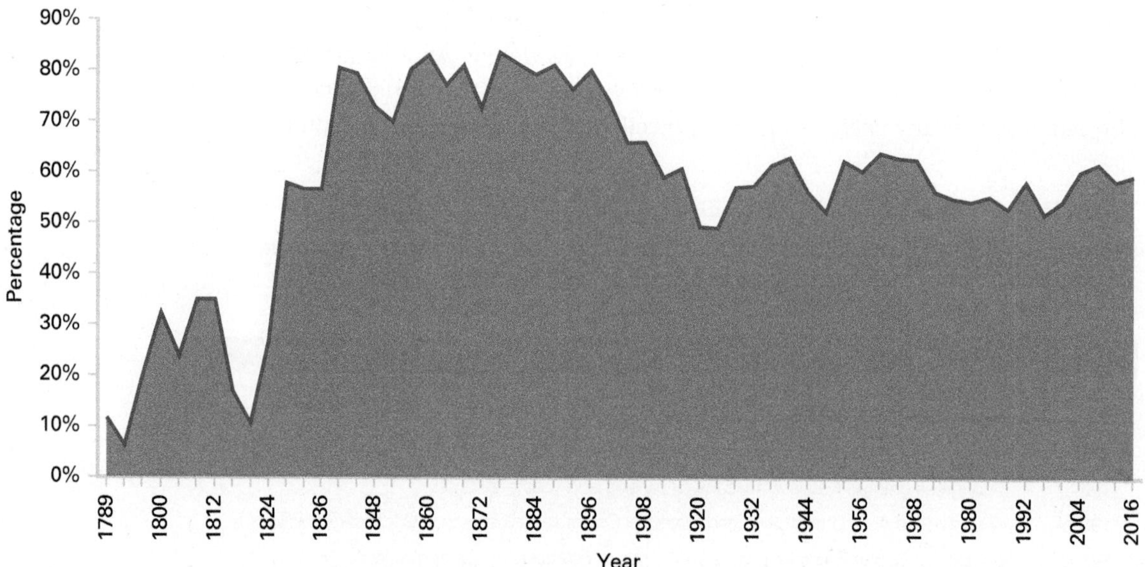

MOTOR VOTER In 1993, the burdens of voter registration were eased a bit with the National Voter Registration Act—called the "Motor Voter" bill—which allows people to register to vote while applying for or renewing a driver's license. Offices that provide welfare and disability assistance can also facilitate voter registration. States may use public schools, libraries, and city and county clerks' offices as registration sites. The law requires states to allow registration by mail using a standardized form. To purge the voting rolls of those who may have died or changed residence, states must mail a questionnaire to voters every four years. But Motor Voter forbids states from purging the rolls for any other reason, including solely for not voting in multiple previous elections.

The Supreme Court ruled on the process of purging voting rolls in June 2018 when it upheld Ohio's system for doing so. A U.S. Navy veteran, Larry Harmon, went to vote at his regular voting location in 2015 and was told he was no longer on the voting roll. Harmon, who had lived at the same address for 16 years, challenged Ohio's process. Harmon argued it violated the National Voter Registration Act, which details how voters can be removed from voting rolls. Under the Ohio system, one of the most aggressive in the nation, voters were removed from the registration lists if they (1) have not voted in *any* election over two consecutive years, (2) and failed to respond to a state notice asking them to affirm they still lived at the address where they were registered to vote, and (3) failed to vote for an additional period of four consecutive years, including two general elections. The 5-to-4 Court majority ruled that the purging system was consistent with controlling federal law—it did not purge a voter *solely* for nonvoting; the voter also had to fail to respond to the state notice. Supporters of Ohio's system argued that it prevented voter fraud by people who had left the state, while opponents said that Ohio's system would disproportionately purge mi-nority and low-income voters. Opponents also warned that other states would respond to the decision by tightening their registration removal systems.[74]

As a result of this law, more new voters have registered.[75] Data on the impact of Motor Voter suggest that neither Democrats nor Republicans are the primary beneficiaries because most new voters who have registered claim to be Independent.[76] Yet Motor Voter alone does not appear to have increased turnout. Instead, when states actively invite citizens to register at the time they renew their driver's license, there is a boost in turnout of 4 percent.[77]

ABSENTEE AND EARLY VOTING Growing numbers of people choose not to vote in person at their local voting places on Election Day. Instead they use *absentee voting* to vote early by mail. Absentee voting has been used since the Civil War[78] and has recently become more popular. More than four in ten voters in 2012 and 2016 cast their vote away from a traditional, Election-Day polling location, the most in the history of the United States.[79] In 1998, Oregon was the first state to switch to statewide elections done through the mail, an experiment that was widely seen as a success in that state. Since then Washington and Colorado have moved to vote statewide by mail.[80]

Advocates of vote-by-mail argue that it lowers cost and is easier to administer than an in-person voting process held on only one day. Vote-by-mail has been found to increase turnout, at least in the initial period after adoption,[81] and in Oregon it continues to foster greater turnout in presidential general elections.[82] However, opponents of vote-by-mail worry about potential abuses of the process, where people might fraudulently cast the ballot of another person or bribe a person to vote a certain way and then mail in that person's ballot. Some see value in casting a ballot in public with other voters on a designated day. More fundamentally, some question the value of making it easier for people to vote, which voting by mail does. This viewpoint is based on the perceived importance of citizens being willing to invest time and effort, which in-person voting requires.

Another innovation designed to make voting easier is allowing people to vote early but at a convenient polling location like a shopping mall. This change was in part the result of concerns about having insufficient voting machines for Election Day. In 2016, 37 states and the District of Columbia allowed early voting, either through the mail or in person at polling locations, without needing to claim travel, work, or other reasons to vote early.[83] But in 2016, 15 states had new voting restrictions ranging from photo ID requirements to reduced time for early voting to changes in voter registration rules.[84]

As is often the case, changes in the laws about who may vote and when they may cast their ballots were challenged in court in 2016. For the first time since 1968, this happened in a context in which Section 5 of the Voting Rights Act of 1965 that required state and local governments that had exhibited a pattern of racial discrimination in voting to submit changes in voting laws to the Department of Justice for preclearance.[85] Reasoning that the Act was no longer needed and a breach of federalism, a 5-to-4 majority of justices overturned this part of the Act. States like North Carolina that would have been subject to Section 5 shortened early voting, passed photo-ID requirements, and other limitations. Federal courts overturned the new law as unconstitutional, a decision not reversed by a tie vote (4-4) in the Supreme Court. In other states, courts allowed new restrictions. For example, in Arizona a law banning a practice called ballot harvesting was upheld. This practice involves individuals or groups gathering completed mail ballots and delivering them to election offices. The cases illustrate the important role the courts play in deciding what limits can and cannot be placed on voting.

Some states require state-issued photo identification in order to vote. Here a Kentucky voter is showing a form of photo identification. The requirement to provide photo ID and a reduction in the number of days voters could cast early ballots were important to the context of the 2016 election. In 2018, states largely continued to tighten voter ID requirements, and some states saw a reduction in the number of polling places.

REQUIRING VOTER IDENTIFICATION Unlike in many countries, citizens in the United States do not have a state-issued national identification card. And while the constitutional amendments related to voting say that states may not exclude from voting those citizens who are 18 years or older, women, or who did not pay their poll taxes, in all states except North Dakota various voter registration laws require citizens to submit state-issued forms in advance of voting, sometimes days or weeks in advance of the election. Some states even require valid identification in order to vote in person. When asked to present such identification, most people display their driver's license or, in some situations, a passport. But not everyone has a passport or driver's license. By some estimates, as much as 11 percent of the population and 25 percent of African Americans, as well as more than 15 percent of Hispanics, the elderly, and those earning less than $35,000 per year, do not have a state-issued form of voter identification.[86] In response to worries about possible voter fraud, often defined as people voting more than once in an election or people claiming to be someone else when voting, 34 states have enacted voter identification requirements, typically mandating a state-issued photo ID.[87] Persons without such identification not only need to be sure they are registered to vote but have the added hurdle of securing the ID in order to be able to vote. Some may not be able to afford the costs of securing birth certificates and marriage licenses, which some states require for verification of identity. There is also the challenge of finding the time and having the means of transportation to go to the government office to complete this requirement. The effect of voter identification on turnout is difficult to measure and some research finds there to be little effect.[88]

Credible studies of possible fraud have found that "the best available evidence shows that voter fraud is a minor issue in American elections.[89] There is little hard evidence that it occurs, even less evidence that it is widespread, and almost no indication that it has altered election outcomes."[90] The absence of evidence of widespread fraud has not deterred states from imposing the identification requirements. The possibility of widespread voter fraud in 2016, as was frequently asserted by President Trump, led to his forming a commission charged with investigating the matter. The commission generated controversy and lawsuits by asking states to provide voter lists, some of which included confidential information. The president later disbanded the commission, but retained his claim that there was "substantial evidence of voter fraud."[91]

The broader question posed by the debate over how much early voting to permit, how difficult to make voter registration, and whether a particular kind of personal identification is needed is the question of whether voting should be made more or less difficult and whether we effectively exclude some citizens from participating by making it more difficult. Extending the right to vote to women, African Americans, and young people, as discussed at the beginning of the chapter, was a major accomplishment. At each election you have a choice whether or not to vote, and more broadly you have a voice that should be heard on how we protect the integrity of the electoral process without excluding citizens who would like to vote.

Turnout

The United States holds more elections for more offices than any other democracy. That may be why U.S. voters tend to be selective about the elections in which they vote. We elect officeholders in **general elections**, determine party nominees in **primary elections**, and replace members of the House of Representatives who have died or left office in *special elections*.

general election
Election in which voters elect officeholders.

primary election
Election in which voters determine party nominees.

Elections held in years when the president is on the ballot are called **presidential elections**; elections held midway between presidential elections are called **midterm elections**, and elections held in odd-numbered calendar years are called *off-year elections*. Midterm elections (such as the ones in 2010 and 2014) elect one-third of the U.S. Senate, all members of the House of Representatives, many governors, other statewide officeholders, and state legislators. Many local elections for city council members and mayors are held in the spring of odd-numbered years.

presidential election
Election held in a year when the president is on the ballot.

midterm election
Election held midway between presidential elections.

Turnout—the proportion of the voting-age public that votes—is higher in general elections than in primary elections, and higher in primary elections than in special elections. It is also higher in presidential general elections than in midterm general elections, and higher in presidential primary elections than in midterm primary elections (see Figure 7.5).[92] Presidential elections attract greater interest and awareness. Turnout is also higher in elections in which candidates for federal office are on the ballot (U.S. senator, member of the House of Representatives, and president) than in state elections in years with no federal contests. Some states—for example, New Jersey, Virginia, and Kentucky—elect their governor and other state officials in odd-numbered years in part to separate state politics from national politics. The result is generally lower turnout. Finally, local or municipal elections have lower turnout than state elections, and municipal primaries generally have the lowest rates of participation.

turnout
The proportion of the voting-age public that votes, sometimes defined as the number of registered voters that vote.

Turnout reached more than 65 percent of those eligible to vote in the presidential election of 1960, but it declined to slightly more than 60 percent in 2004, and rose to 61.7 percent in 2008.[93] It was 59.3 percent in 2016.[94] In midterm elections, turnout

FIGURE 7.5 VOTER TURNOUT IN PRESIDENTIAL AND MIDTERM ELECTIONS, 1992–2016

There is a long-noted regularity of turnout surging in presidential years and declining in midterm elections. This is due to the greater interest and attention given presidential elections. In this period, turnout peaked in the 2008 presidential election and was lowest in the 1996 presidential election. For midterms, turnout was lowest in this period in 2014. The composition of the electorate in presidential years is different from midterm years as well.

SOURCES: Howard W. Stanley and Richard G. Niemi, *Vital Statistics on American Politics*, 2015–2016 (CQ Press, 2015), pp. 4–5; for 2016 see Michael McDonald, http://www.electproject.org/2016g.

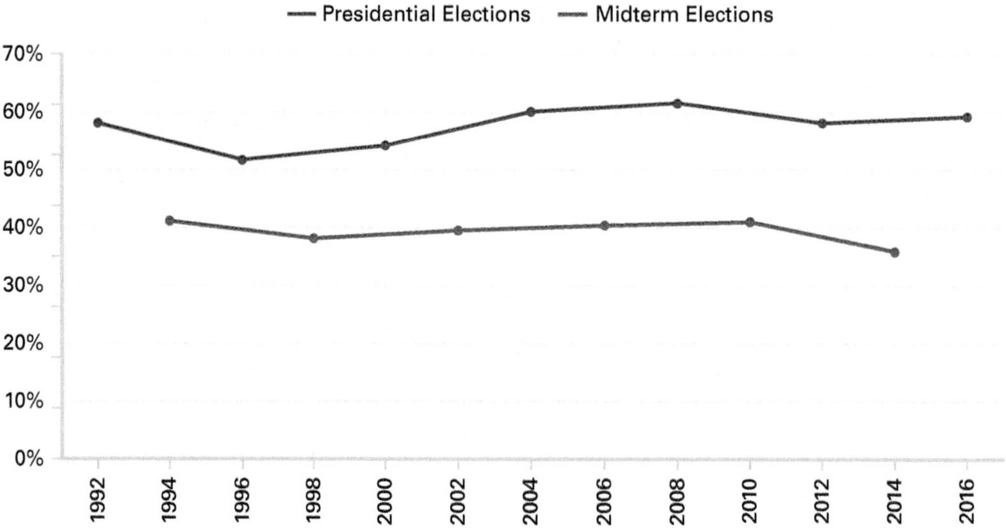

was 35.9 percent nationally in 2014, the lowest it has been in 72 years. More competitive elections generate more interest among the public and more spending by the candidates, which in turn stimulate participation. However, more than 100 million eligible citizens failed to vote in the 2016 presidential election, and even more did not vote in midterm, state, and local elections.[95] Turnout rose in 2018 by more than 12 percent over turnout in 2014. Turnout was especially high in battleground states like Florida where it rose by more than two million voters. The increase was greater for Democrats, but both parties saw higher turnout than had been the norm. In some democracies, like Brazil, Greece, and the Philippines, voting is mandatory,[96] while in the United States it is voluntary and requires more effort on the part of voters in keeping their voter registration current.

Who Votes?

The extent of voting varies widely among different groups. Level of education is an important predictor in whether people will vote; as education increases, so does the propensity to vote. According to one study, education gives people the ability to understand complicated topics like politics, and an understanding of the meaning of civic responsibility. Education also gives students experience with bureaucracy and large organizations—like you, other college students have learned to meet deadlines, fill out forms, fulfill requirements, and go to interviews.[97]

Race and ethnic background are linked with different levels of voting, largely because they correlate with education. In other words, racial and ethnic minorities with college degrees vote at approximately the same rate as white people with college degrees. As a group, African Americans vote at lower rates than Caucasians, though not surprisingly in 2008 and 2012 African American turnout reached historic highs (12 percent of votes in 2008 and 13 percent in 2012).[98] In the 2016 election, African American turnout dropped by 7 percent compared to 2008, reinforcing the sense that having Obama on the ballot was important to African American voters.[99]

In recent elections, both parties mounted major efforts to register and mobilize Hispanic voters, as Hispanics have become the largest minority group in the United States. Despite these efforts, the proportion of Hispanics voting in 2008 was up only slightly over 2004: 49.9 percent as compared to 47.2 percent.[100] As the illegal immigrant issue took center stage in 2006, Democrats, Republicans, and allied groups again sought to expand the number of Hispanic voters. Exit polls found that 9 percent of voters in 2008 were Latinos, with two-thirds of them voting for Obama.[101] In 2012, Latinos were 10 percent of the vote, and 71 percent of them voted for Obama.[102] The Hispanic share of the vote in 2010 was 8 percent,[103] but in 2014 it rose to 11 percent.[104] and then fell to 9.2 percent in 2016 with 66 percent voting for Hillary Clinton.[105]

Women, another historically underrepresented group, have voted in greater numbers than men since 1984.[106] Women's higher turnout is generally attributed to increasing levels of education and employment. Interest groups, including prominent pro-choice groups, have sought to mobilize female supporters of their agenda in recent elections.

Age is also highly correlated with the propensity to vote. As age increases, so does the proportion of persons voting. Older people, health permitting, are more likely to vote than younger people. The greater likelihood that older persons vote amplifies the importance of this group as baby boomers age and retire. The number of young people voting was up substantially.[107] In 2016, there were 700,000 more voters under the age of 30 than voters in this age group in 2008. But as noted, this group voted less in 2016 than in 2008.[108]

In 2012, nearly one in five voters (19 percent) was under the age of 29, and they voted heavily for Obama (60 percent). Latino voters also voted more in 2012. Racial minorities, younger voters, and women were important to Obama's winning coalitions in 2008 and 2012. Despite losing, Hillary Clinton took similar percentages with 55 percent of voters under 30, 54 percent of female voters, and the majority of votes from all minority groups.[109] In battleground states, these voters stood in long lines both on Election Day and at early voting sites.[110]

The number of people who cast ballots in 2016 was higher than in 2012, but as a share of eligible voters, turnout was down about 2 percent from 2012 and 5 percent from 2008. In 2016 more voters cast early ballots than in prior cycles, even despite some states reducing early voting options. What explains the decline in 2016 turnout is a substantial drop in Election Day voting. A drop in African American, Hispanic, and young voters especially hurt Clinton. As is generally the case, turnout is higher in competitive states where candidates spend more time and far more money on persuasion and mobilization.

Mobilization

In a nation as evenly divided politically as the United States has been in recent years, candidates must also mobilize their most loyal supporters, or their "base." To do this, they reaffirm their support for issues or groups that matter to the base. In 2016, Donald Trump did this by calling for building the wall on the border with Mexico, for bringing jobs back to the United States, and for more limits on abortion. On the Democratic side, Hillary Clinton argued for tax increases on those making more than $250,000, expansion of health care coverage, and supported abortion rights, same-sex marriage, and immigration reform.

In the 2016 "battleground" states where polls showed the race to be close, postcards urging residents to vote and phone calls reminding them it was Election Day bombarded voters. In addition, the candidates and parties mobilized their supporters to vote early in states where it was possible. This effort, sometimes called "banking the vote," reduced the list of people the campaigns needed to mobilize on Election

Oregon Democratic Governor Kate Brown applauds as Darren Harold-Golden casts his ballot in the 2018 Oregon primary. The governor and others are wearing green shirts with the words "vote" and a map of the state on the front. Oregon votes by mail, but voters can submit ballots at voting boxes as is the case here at Portland State University. Mobilizing voters to register, and later cast their ballots is a key to electoral success.

Day, when poll watchers would track those who had not yet voted and would urge those who had pledged support to vote.

Campaigners learn which issues matter to potential voters and which candidates these voters prefer by conducting interviews on the telephone or in person, a process called a canvass. Individuals who are undecided and probable voters in competitive Senate and House races are likely to receive communications designed to persuade them to vote for a particular candidate. Interest groups, including Super PACs and political parties in 2016, also conducted a canvass, followed by mail and phone calls that often reinforced the same themes the candidates themselves express.

Undecided or "swing voters" are a major focus of mobilization efforts, and they received a lot of attention in competitive states in recent elections. Both sides intensely courted these voters through numerous person-to-person contacts, mailings, telephone calls, and efforts to register new voters. Candidates, groups, and parties are all part of this "ground war." The volume of communication in competitive contests and battleground states in recent elections has been extraordinary.[111]

How Serious Is Nonvoting?

Although voters can hardly avoid reading or hearing about political campaigns, especially during an election as intensely fought as recent presidential elections, about 40 percent of all eligible citizens fail to vote. This amounts to approximately 80 million people.[112] Who are they? Why don't they vote? Is the fact that so many people choose not to vote a cause for alarm? If so, what can we do about it?

There is considerable disagreement about how to interpret low voter turnout. The simplest explanation is that people are lazy and voting takes effort, but there is more to it than that. Of course, some people are apathetic, but most are not. Paradoxically, we compare favorably with other nations in political interest and awareness, but for a variety of institutional and political reasons, we fail to convert this interest in politics into voting (see Table 7.6 on the next page).

In the United States, voting is more difficult and takes more time and effort than in other democracies. As we have seen, in our system people must often have photo identification, register to vote, and then decide how to vote, not only for many

TABLE 7.6 WHY PEOPLE DO NOT VOTE

Consistent with a point made earlier about the U.S. requirement of voter registration lowering turnout, the most frequent reason people do not vote is that they are not registered to vote. Beyond this, voters provide a range of reasons they did not vote in 2016 ranging from dislike of the candidates to inconvenient voting places.

Not registered	30%
Didn't like the candidates or campaign issues	25%
Not interested, felt vote would not make a difference	15%
Too busy or conflicting schedule	14%
Illness or disability	12%
Other	11%
Out of town or away from home	8%
Registration problems	4%
Forgot to vote	3%
Transportation problems	3%
Inconvenient hours or polling places	2%

SOURCES: Gustavo Lopez and Antonio Flores, "Dislike of Candidates or Campaign Issues Was Most Common Reason for Not Voting in 2016." Pew Research Center, June 1, 2017. http://www.pewresearch.org/fact-tank/2017/06/01/dislike-of-candidates-or-campaign-issues-was-most-common-reason-for-not-voting-in-2016/; for data on the percent of the public registered to vote, see, U.S> Census Bureau, Voting and Registration in the Election of November 2016. Table 1. https://www.census.gov/data/tables/time-series/demo/voting-and-registration/p20-580.html

different offices but also often for referendums on public policy or constitutional amendments. The United States also holds elections on weekdays, when people are at work, rather than on holidays or weekends as other countries often do. Another factor in the percentage decline of voter turnout since the 1960s is, paradoxically, the Twenty-sixth Amendment, which increased the number of eligible voters by lowering the voting age to 18. Young people are the least likely to vote, and after the amendment was ratified in 1971, turnout in the presidential election fell from 62 percent in 1968 to 57 percent in 1972.[113]

Some political scientists argue that nonvoting does not change the outcome, as nonvoters closely resemble voters in policy views.[114] "Nonvoting is not a social disease," wrote Austin Ranney, a noted political scientist. The late Senator Sam Ervin of North Carolina provided a rationale for registration when he said, "I don't believe in making it easy for apathetic, lazy people to vote."[115]

Those who argue that nonvoting is a serious problem cite the "class bias" of those who do vote. The social makeup and attitudes of nonvoters differ significantly from those of voters and hence distort the representative system. "The very poor... have about two-thirds the representation among voters than their numbers would suggest." Thus, the people who need the most help from the government lack their share of electoral power to obtain it.[116] Some may contend that younger voters, the poor, and minority citizens do not vote because politicians pay less attention to them. But politicians understandably cater to people who vote more than to people who do not.

How might increased voter turnout affect national elections? It might make a difference because there are partisan differences between different demographic groups, and poorer persons are more likely to be Democrats. Candidates would have to adjust to the demands of this expanded electorate. A noted political scientist pointed out that if the large nonvoter population decided to vote, it could overturn the balance of power in the political system.[117] Others contend that the difference may not be that pronounced, because on many issues, nonvoters have much the same attitudes as voters. Finally, for better or worse, low voter turnout may indicate approval of the status quo, whereas high voter turnout may signify disapproval and widespread desire for change.

Style No.

State of Maine Sample Ballot
Democratic Primary Election, June 12, 2018
for

Instructions to Voters

To vote, fill in the oval like this ●

To rank your candidate choices, fill in the oval:

- In the 1st column for your 1st choice candidate.
- In the 2nd column for your 2nd choice candidate, and so on.

Continue until you have ranked as many or as few candidates as you like.

Fill in no more than one oval for each candidate or column.

To rank a write-in candidate, write the person's name in the write-in space and fill in the oval for the ranking of your choice.

Governor	1st Choice	2nd Choice	3rd Choice	4th Choice	5th Choice	6th Choice	7th Choice	8th Choice
Cote, Adam Roland Sanford	O	O	O	O	O	O	O	O
Dion, Donna J. Biddeford	O	O	O	O	O	O	O	O
Dion, Mark N. Portland	O	O	O	O	O	O	O	O
Eves, Mark W. North Berwick	O	O	O	O	O	O	O	O
Mills, Janet T. Farmington	O	O	O	O	O	O	O	O
Russell, Diane Marie Portland	O	O	O	O	O	O	O	O
Sweet, Elizabeth A. Hallowell	O	O	O	O	O	O	O	O
Write-in	O	O	O	O	O	O	O	O

Rep. to Congress District 2	1st Choice	2nd Choice	3rd Choice	4th Choice	5th Choice
Fulford, Jonathan S. Monroe	O	O	O	O	O
Golden, Jared F. Lewiston	O	O	O	O	O
Olson, Craig R. Islesboro	O	O	O	O	O
St. Clair, Lucas R. Hampden	O	O	O	O	O
Write-in	O	O	O	O	O

Turn Over for Additional Contests

11 21 40 41 42 43 51

Maine - Government and Politics

Voters sometimes complain they wish they had more choices of candidates and that they did not have to only select only one candidate to vote for. In 2018 in the primary, Maine experimented with a ranked choice ballot. Under this system if no candidate receives a majority of the first choice votes, the last place candidate's votes are redistributed to his or her voters' next choices until a candidate exceeds 50 percent. Voters in the primary also approved keeping ranked choice voting for future Maine elections.

Voting Choices (Action and Impact)

7.5 Analyze why people vote the way they do.

Why do people vote the way they do? Political scientists have identified three main elements of the voting choice: party identification, candidate appeal, and issues. These elements often overlap.

Voting on the Basis of Party

Party identification is our sense of identification or affiliation with a political party; it often predicts a person's stand on issues. It is part of our national mythology that we vote for the person and not the party. But, in fact, we vote most often for a person *from the party we prefer.*

party identification
An informal and subjective affiliation with a political party that most people acquire in childhood.

The number of self-declared Independents since the mid-1970s has increased dramatically, and today, Independents outnumber Republicans and Democrats. But two-thirds of all Independents are, in fact, partisans in their voting behavior. There are three distinct types of Independents: Independent-leaning Democrats, Independent-leaning Republicans, and Pure Independents. Independent-leaning Democrats are predictably Democratic in their voting behavior, and Independent-leaning Republicans vote heavily Republican. In fact, Independent "leaners" vote for the party toward which they lean at approximately the same rate, or even more so, than weak partisans do. Independent leaners are thus different from each other and from Pure Independents. Pure Independents have the lowest rate of turnout, but most of them generally side with the winner in presidential elections. Independent leaners vote at about the same rate as partisans and more than Pure Independents.

This data on Independents only reinforces the importance of partisanship in explaining voting choice. When we consider Independent-leaning Democrats and Independent-leaning Republicans as Democrats and Republicans, respectively, only 10 percent of the population was Pure Independents in 2004.[118] In 2008, that number had risen slightly to 11 percent.[119] This proportion is consistent with earlier election years; however, it fell slightly in the 2016 election when the proportion was recorded as 8 percent.[120] In short, there are few genuinely Independent voters.

Although party identification has fluctuated in the past 40 years, it remains more stable than attitudes about issues or political ideology. Fluctuations in party identification appear to come in response to economic conditions and political performance, especially of the president. The more information voters have about their choices, the more likely they are to defect from their party and vote for a candidate from the other party.[121]

Voting on the Basis of Candidates

Although long-term party identification is important, it is clearly not the only factor in voting choices. Otherwise, the Democrats would have won every presidential election since the last major realignment in partisanship, which occurred during the Great Depression in the election of Franklin Roosevelt in 1932. In fact, since 1952, there have been five Democratic presidents elected and the same number of Republicans.[122] The reason is largely found in a second major explanation of voting choice—**candidate appeal**.

candidate appeal
How voters feel about a candidate's background, personality, leadership ability, and other personal qualities.

Candidate-centered politics means that rather than relying on parties or groups to build a coalition of supporters for a candidate, the candidates make their case directly to the voters. In many races, the parties and groups also make the candidate the major focus of attention, minimizing partisanship or group identification.[123] The fact that we vote for officials separately—president/vice president, senator, governor, state attorney general, and so on—means voters are asked repeatedly to choose from

Ronald Reagan projected positive candidate appeal. People could relate to him and he seemed to understand them. The image here is of him working on his ranch during his presidency, doing ordinary work, something he routinely did when on the ranch. In his speeches, especially his 1980 speech accepting the Republican nomination, he skillfully reached out to union members, Democrats, and Independents.

among competing candidates. Although the party of the candidates is an important clue to voters, in most contested races voters also look to candidate-specific information.

Candidate appeal often includes an assessment of a candidate's character. Is the candidate honest? Consistent? Dedicated to "family values"? Does the candidate have religious or spiritual commitments? In recent elections, the press has sometimes played the role of "character cop," asking questions about candidates' private lives and lifestyles. The press asks these questions because voters are interested in a political leader's background—perhaps even more interested in personal character than in a candidate's political position on difficult-to-understand health care or regulatory policy issues.

Candidate appeal, or the lack of it—in terms of leadership, experience, good judgment, integrity, competence, strength, and energy—is sometimes more important than party or issues. Many voters saw Bill Clinton in 1992 and 1996 as a regular working-class person who had risen against the odds. Dwight Eisenhower, who was elected president in 1952 and reelected in 1956, had positive candidate appeal. He was a five-star general, a legendary hero of the Allied effort in World War II. His unmilitary manner, his moderation, his personal charm, and his appearance of seeming to rise above partisanship appealed across the ideological spectrum. Most voters in 2016 viewed both Hillary Clinton and Donald Trump negatively. Exit polls had 54 percent viewing Hillary Clinton unfavorably and 56 percent viewing Donald Trump unfavorably. According to CBS, voters saw the 2016 campaign as the most negative campaign in the history of that network's polling. In October 2016, 82 percent of voters said the campaign was more negative than previous presidential elections, a 45 percent increase over 2012.[124]

Increasingly, campaigns today focus on the negative elements of candidate's history and personality. Opponents and the media are quick to point out a candidate's limitations or problems. The election in 2016 was perhaps the most negative in history as two unpopular candidates fought tooth and nail for the presidency. In 2016, Republicans attempted to define Hillary Clinton as a dishonest career politician that said whatever she thought was popular, exhibited poor foreign policy judgment, and disregarded the law to achieve her own ends. Democrats, in turn, focused on Donald Trump's controversial statements against Muslims, Mexicans, women, disabled persons, and veterans, as well as his failed business ventures and his lack of clear policy positions. Despite both candidates' high unfavorability ratings, Democrats were ultimately more successful in defining Trump negatively. Exit polls in 2016 found that more voters had unfavorable views of Trump than they did of Clinton. More voters also saw her as better qualified to be president and as having the temperament to be president. Nearly half of voters (45 percent) were concerned about Clinton's use of a private email server, and these voters overwhelmingly voted for Trump (87 percent). The other 55 percent of voters who were not concerned about Clinton's emails voted for Clinton by large margins. Seventy percent of all voters were concerned with Trump's treatment of women, and among these voters, 65 percent voted for Clinton. One overall question captures the underlying mood of the electorate: when asked if the country was headed in the right direction or was on the wrong track, 62 percent said wrong track. Trump, more than Clinton, was able to speak to that sense of a need for change.

Voting on the Basis of Issues

Most political scientists agree that issues, though important, have less influence on how people vote than party identification and candidate appeal do.[125] This occurs partly because candidates often intentionally obscure their positions on issues—an understandable strategy.[126] When he was running for president in 1968, Richard Nixon said he had a plan to end the Vietnam War, which was clearly the most important issue that year, but he would not reveal the specifics. By not detailing his plan, he stood to gain votes both from those who wanted a more aggressive war effort and those who wanted a cease-fire. In 2008, Obama and the Democrats emphasized change from the Bush administration, a general theme that exploited public sentiment.

For issue voting to become important, a substantial number of voters must find the issue itself important, opposing candidates must take opposite stands on the issues, and voters must know these positions and vote accordingly. Rarely do candidates focus on only one issue. Voters often agree with one candidate on one issue and with the opposing candidate on another. In such cases, issues will probably not determine how people vote. But voters' lack of interest in issues does not mean candidates can take any position they please.[127]

Political parties and candidates often look for issues that motivate particular segments of the electorate to vote and on which the opposing candidate or party has a less popular position. These issues are sometimes called *wedge issues.* In recent elections, wedge issues have been gay marriage, the minimum wage, and abortion. One way to exploit a wedge issue is to place an initiative to decide a proposed law or amendment on the issue on the ballot. Both parties and allied groups are expanding their use of ballot initiatives in this way.

More likely than **prospective issue voting**—voting based on what a candidate pledges to do about an issue if elected—is **retrospective issue voting**, or holding incumbents, usually the president's party, responsible for past performance on issues, such as the economy or foreign policy.[128] In times of peace and prosperity, voters will reward the incumbent. If the nation falls short on either, voters are more likely to elect the opposition.

prospective issue voting
Voting based on what a candidate pledges to do in the future about an issue if elected.

retrospective issue voting
Holding incumbents, usually the president's party, responsible for their records on issues, such as the economy or foreign policy.

However, good economic times do not always guarantee that an incumbent party will be reelected, as Vice President Al Gore learned in 2000 when he was the Democratic candidate for president.[129] His inability to effectively claim credit for the good economic times hurt him, especially when Republicans contended that the American people, not the government under President Bill Clinton, had produced the strong economy. Neither do bad economic times guarantee defeat for an incumbent. In 2012 President Obama overcame slow economic growth and chronically high unemployment to win a second term.

The state of the economy is often the central issue in both midterm and presidential elections. Studies have found that the better the economy seems to be doing, the more congressional seats the "in" party retains or gains. The reverse is also true. The worse the economy seems to be doing, the more seats the "out" party gains.[130] Political scientists have been able to locate the sources of this effect in the way individual voters decide to vote. Voters tend to vote against the party in power if they perceive that their personal financial situations have declined or stagnated.[131]

When a party holds the White House for two terms, that party rarely wins the next election. Republicans won the presidency after two terms of Clinton, while Democrats won the presidency after two terms of George W. Bush and Republicans again won the presidency after Obama's two terms The exception was George H. W. Bush who won after Ronald Reagan's two terms. Often the country has seemed inclined to change the party in power, which played out as part of the dynamic of the 2016 election.

The Donald Trump candidacy was unusual in several respects. He had no prior experience in government or the military. He ran an unconventional campaign with less campaign staff and less paid advertising. His approach to generating turnout appeared to be driven more by large events and extensive free media coverage. The Clinton candidacy was more conventional in approach, with an extensive operation on the ground in competitive states and heavy reliance on paid advertising funded by her campaign and supportive Super PACs. Clinton won the popular vote but lost in the Electoral College. Trump's success in activating voters in key battleground states made the difference. Students of campaigns and elections will study the decisions of both campaigns for years to come.

CONCLUSION

The distribution of public opinion, as well as how strongly people hold their opinions, is important in assessing how elected officials respond to public opinion. In our representative form of government, elected officials closely monitor public opinion and generally reflect the positions of their constituents on issues where there is a clearly preferred position. On some issues opinion changes little over time; for example, attitudes on the death penalty or abortion are quite stable. However, an issue like same-sex marriage has seen large shifts in public opinion. Over time, and especially since the 2012 election, the public has become more supportive of changing laws to permit same-sex marriage. This is also an issue where voter participation may have helped reinforce the shifts in public opinion, as for the first time, in 2012, a majority of voters in three states voted to permit same-sex marriage, and in a fourth voters rejected a move to ban same-sex marriage in the state constitution. In addition, the U.S. Supreme Court's 2015 decision striking down state bans on same-sex marriage has likely reinforced changes in public opinion. On other issues where most of the public is unaware and uninformed on the issue, elected officials are less constrained by public opinion.

For public opinion to have an impact, individuals need to act on their opinions either by voting in elections or some other form of participation. In the 2010 and 2014 midterm elections, many of those who had supported Democrats, including Barack Obama, in 2008 and 2012 stayed home and did not vote. The result was that the Republicans won the majority in the House of Representatives with several Tea Party conservatives who then repeatedly voted to repeal Obamacare and were instrumental in the 2013 government shutdown. In 2014, Republicans regained control of the U.S. Senate, putting both houses under GOP control. In 2018, turnout rose substantially over 2014 which helped Democrats win a majority in the House. Democrats made health care a major issue, and this time, Republicans were on the defensive having voted to repeal Obamacare which guaranteed coverage for people with pre-existing conditions.

Government by the people is most frequently exercised by voting. This is why, when younger persons do not vote, they allow others to make decisions about important parts of their lives. Government, directly or indirectly, has a bearing on educational opportunity, taxes, and the environment, to name only a few examples. Elected officials are most attuned to the will of those who vote, and so when people fail to vote, they lessen their impact and enlarge the voice of those who do register and vote. Candidates and campaigns are important to the voting choice. Given the frequency of elections in the United States and the number of offices people vote for, it is not surprising that voters look for simplifying devices such as partisanship to help them decide how to vote. Effective campaigns give them reasons to vote for their candidate and reasons to vote against the opposition.

Campaigns are a team sport, with the political parties and interest groups also important to the process of persuading and motivating voters.[132] Groups and parties are heavily engaged in all aspects of campaigns, and their efforts are often indistinguishable from the candidates' campaigns.

Although having enough money is necessary to run a competitive campaign, spending more money does not guarantee that a candidate will win. Effective campaigners find ways to communicate with voters that are memorable and persuasive.

Campaigns are not for the faint of heart. Electoral politics are intensely competitive, and campaigns are often negative and personal. Campaigns give voters a sense of how politicians react to adversity because most competitive races involve adversity. Skills learned in the campaign environment, in some respects at least, carry over into the skill set needed to govern. Perhaps you will consider running for office. You could make a significant difference serving on a school board, in local government, in the state legislature, or even running for federal office. There are more ways than simply voting to get involved in the political process.

Who votes and how they do so has changed dramatically throughout the course of U.S. history. Our process has become more democratic, and citizens today have a wider array of candidate contests and ballot questions to decide than ever before. This opportunity to influence policy is open to you, and you can magnify your voice by encouraging others to participate with you. Although there has been progress in making voting easier, challenges remain. It is important that every vote be counted and counted accurately. Your active involvement could help achieve this goal.

REVIEW THE CHAPTER

Forming Political Opinions and Values (Structure)

7.1 Explain how the agents of socialization influence the development of political attitudes, p. 176.

People's political attitudes form early in life, mainly through the influence of family. Schools, the media, social groups, and changing personal and national circumstances can cause attitudes to change, although most of our political opinions remain constant throughout life. Most people do not follow politics and government closely and have little knowledge of political issues.

Public Opinion: Taking the Pulse of the People (Structure)

7.2 Describe public opinion research and modern methods of polling, p. 181.

Public opinion is the distribution across the population of a complex combination of views and attitudes that individuals hold, and we measure it through careful, unbiased, random-selection surveys. Public opinion takes on qualities of intensity, latency, consensus, and polarization—each of which is affected by people's feelings about the salience of issues.

Sometimes, politicians follow prevailing public opinion on policy questions; in other cases, they attempt to lead public opinion toward a different policy option. Major events, such as economic crises and wars, affect both public opinion and government policy. Citizens who wish to affect opinion, policy, or both, can take action by voting or engaging in other forms of political participation.

Political Ideology and Attitudes Toward Government (Structure)

7.3 Assess the influence of political ideology on political attitudes and behaviors, p. 188.

The two most important ideologies in American politics are liberalism, a belief that government can and should help achieve justice and equality of opportunity, and conservatism, a belief in limited government to ensure order, competitive markets, and personal opportunity while relying on free markets and individual initiative to solve social and economic problems. Critics of liberalism contend that liberals, by favoring government solutions to problems, limit the capacity of markets to function well and create large and unmanageable bureaucracies. Critics of conservatism contend that some problems require government to become part of the solution and that too much faith in the market to solve the problem is misplaced. Socialism, which favors public ownership of the means of production, and libertarianism, which puts a premium on individual liberty and limited government, attract only modest followings in the United States.

Participation: Translating Opinions into Action (Action)

7.4 Identify the factors that influence political participation, p. 195.

One of the hallmarks of democracy is that citizens can participate in politics in a variety of ways. Citizens who are dissatisfied with government can protest. Individual citizens participate by writing letters to elected officials, calling radio talk shows, serving as jurors, voting, or donating time and money to political campaigns. The Internet has allowed individuals to volunteer for campaigns in a wider variety of ways, to donate money more easily, and to produce content that can be uploaded onto the Internet and viewed by any interested person.

Better-educated, more affluent, and older people, as well as those who are involved with parties and interest groups tend to vote more. While young people voted at higher rates in 2008 and 2012 than previously, the young still vote the least. Voter turnout is usually higher in national elections than in state and local elections, higher in presidential elections than in midterm elections, and higher in general elections than in primary elections. Close elections generate interest and efforts to mobilize voters and thus have higher turnout than uncompetitive elections.

Voting Choices (Action and Impact)

7.5 Analyze why people vote the way they do, p. 207.

Party identification remains the most important element in determining how most people vote. It represents a long-term attachment and is a "lens" through which voters view candidates and issues as they make their voting choices. Candidate appeal, including character and record, is another key factor in voter choice. Less frequently, voters decide on the basis of issues.

LEARN THE TERMS

political socialization, p. 176
deliberation, p. 177
social capital, p. 177
attitudes, p. 177
selective exposure, p. 179
attentive public, p. 181
public opinion, p. 182
random sample, p. 183
margin of error, p. 183
universe, p. 185
consensus, p. 185
polarized, p. 185
intensity, p. 185
latency, p. 185
manifest opinion, p. 185
salience, p. 187
political ideology, p. 188
liberalism, p. 188
conservatism, p. 190
social conservative, p. 191
socialism, p. 192
communism, p. 193
libertarianism, p. 193
voter registration, p. 198
general election, p. 201
primary election, p. 201
presidential election, p. 201
midterm election, p. 201
turnout, p. 201
party identification, p. 207
candidate appeal, p. 207
prospective issue voting, p. 209
retrospective issue voting, p. 209

Campaigns and Elections

CHAPTER 8

Voters on their way to cast ballots in 2018 at the Sierra 2 Center for the Arts and Community in Sacramento, California. Official signs, like the ballots themselves, need to be printed in multiple languages depending on the location.

LEARNING OBJECTIVES

- **8.1** Outline the procedures for presidential and congressional elections (Structure), p. 216.
- **8.2** Assess how well American elections are administered (Structure), p. 221.
- **8.3** Evaluate the influence of money in elections and the main approaches to campaign finance reform (Action), p. 223.
- **8.4** Assess the influence of redistricting, incumbency, partisanship, and candidate appeal on the outcome of congressional elections, (Action) p. 230.
- **8.5** Outline how presidential campaigns are organized and evaluate methods for reaching voters (Action), p. 237.
- **8.6** Describe common criticisms of presidential elections and evaluate proposed reforms to address them (Impact), p. 247.

Candidates put themselves on the firing line because elections matter. You and millions of other Americans collectively have the power to decide who will lead the country, your state, and your local governments. Americans underestimate how unusual it is for people to have this power. The 2016 election provided you with a choice between two candidates with very different positions on issues and governing styles, and yet no one doubted that the winner would take office. The two-century-old peaceful transfer of power from one president to another, often from one party to another, is a testament of our commitment to self-government. Similarly, power has changed hands in both houses of Congress frequently in our history, and especially in recent years, as the close party balance means both parties are competitive. During the final presidential debate of the 2016 campaign Donald Trump did not commit to accepting the outcome of the election if he was defeated, saying he wanted to leave debate viewers and the media "in suspense." This prompted a strong reaction from the Clinton campaign but also from several Republican leaders like RNC chair Reince Priebus. After Trump won in the Electoral College, both Hillary Clinton and President Obama called on the country to accept the election outcome and the transfer of power commenced. As this reaction again demonstrated, you are part of a system of self-government that means ordinary Americans get to decide their future.

The party that wins the presidency sets the national political agenda, and if that party also controls Congress it may be able to enact much of that agenda. In the period after the 2008 election, Democrats controlled both houses of Congress and the White House and were able to enact the Affordable Care Act, something that would not have been possible after Republicans won a majority in the House of Representatives in the 2010 midterm election. Some Tea Party conservatives were angry with Republicans for not reversing the Affordable Care Act after the GOP regained control of the Senate in the 2014 election. But in our system of checks and balances it takes more than a majority to override a presidential veto, which President Obama was certain to use even if Congress had successfully repealed the act.

Elections also matter because they determine the kind of persons nominated and confirmed for the Supreme Court and other federal courts. The 2016 election was unusual in that it took place with a Supreme Court vacancy because Senate Republicans refused to act on President Obama's nomination to fill the seat left vacant by Justice Antonin Scalia's death in February 2016. Republicans, arguing that the voters should decide who would choose the next Supreme Court justice, refused to vote, or even hold a hearing, on Washington, D.C. Circuit Court of Appeals Chief Judge Merrick Garland. Both parties saw the Supreme Court vacancy as critical because the new justice could tilt the Court's ideological balance on a closely divided court. Early in his presidency, Donald Trump nominated and the Senate confirmed Tenth Circuit Court of Appeals Judge Neil Gorsuch to fill that vacancy. Trump and his supporters consistently referred to the appointment as the president's most significant accomplishment in his first 100 days.[1] Senate Republicans' refusal to consider Judge Garland—President Obama's nominee—left conservatives with a likely 5-to-4 majority on the Court's most closely divided cases. With the retirement of Justice Anthony Kennedy in late June 2018, President Trump was able to nominate a second Supreme Court justice. He selected Brett Kavanaugh, who had served in the George W. Bush White House and on the Circuit Court of Appeals for the Washington, D.C. Circuit. Late in the Kavanaugh confirmation process, charges of sexual assault when Judge Kavanaugh was in high school arose. Later, other accusations of inappropriate sexual activity surfaced. After a dramatic hearing that included testimony from Kavanaugh's principal accuser followed by a passionate defense from Kavanaugh, the committee and full Senate voted to confirm him to the U.S. Supreme Court.

Our system of federalism means we hold elections at the national, state, and local levels of government. Citizens of the United States have the opportunity to vote more often and for more offices than citizens of any other democracy. We hold thousands of elections for everything from community college directors to county sheriffs. Approximately half a million persons hold elected state and local offices.[2] In November 2018, Americans elected 35 U.S. senators,[3] all 435 members of the U.S. House of Representatives, 36 state governors, and many state treasurers and judges, and Secretaries of State. In addition to electing people, voters in 27 states are allowed to vote on laws or constitutional amendments put on the ballot by petition (initiatives or popular referendums). In every state except Delaware, voters must approve all changes to the state constitution.[4]

Although our democratic system has much to applaud, it is not without faults. There were many elections that took place on November 6, 2018, but not all races were competitive. Without viable challengers, voters are not actually given a true choice at the polls. The complexities of the nominating process present challenges for voters as well as the parties. In 2016, what would have happened if the Republican Convention had been "contested" as many political pundits thought it would be? The structure of the Electoral College, as we will discuss later in this chapter, also changes the nature of presidential campaigns and poses a challenge for democratic theory more generally. And, of course, the amount of money spent on political campaigns continues to grow along with concerns over its influence. Should campaign spending be reined in? Can reasonable limits be placed on campaign spending when the Supreme Court has recognized it as a constitutionally protected form of speech? You and your generation will have to deal with these questions, and your actions will affect the political climate in which you live.

In this chapter, we explore our election rules and how they structure our democratic republic. In part because of your college education, you are acquiring the knowledge and self-confidence to become an active participant in our democratic system. Voting is one of the ways you can take action in our government. In addition to voting, you might decide to become a campaign volunteer for a candidate you feel strongly about. Campaigns depend on volunteers and donors working to help elect a candidate who shares their concerns and reflects their values. Getting involved in a campaign is a way you can directly impact government policy. Our system provides ample opportunities to select a race and a candidate you can support.

Elections: The Rules of the Game (Structure)

8.1 Outline the procedures for presidential and congressional elections.

The rules of the game—the electoral game—impact participants' strategy and affect the outcome. Although the Constitution sets certain electoral conditions and requirements, consistent with federalism, state law determines most electoral rules and procedures. For example, the Constitution dictates the timing of elections, the length of terms for members of the House of Representatives, Senate, and presidency, and the limited (for the president) and staggered terms for federal offices. The Constitution also sets limits on who may run for these offices. More broadly the Constitution and Bill of Rights provide a context of free and fair elections by guaranteeing freedom of speech, press, and assembly. Finally, constitutional amendments have expanded who may participate in elections.

Who May Vote?

The Constitution left to the states the job of determining who may vote. However, amendments to the Constitution prohibit states from restricting the right to vote based on race, sex, and for citizens between 18 and 21 years of age. In all but North Dakota, citizens are required to register with local election officials, often in advance of Election Day, to be able to vote.[5] Voter registration systems came about in the late 1800s and early 1900s due to concerns about duplicate voting and voter fraud often attributed to political machines in large cities. Voter registration may have limited duplicate voting, but it also permitted those running elections to exclude groups with requirements like poll taxes or by closing voter registration several months before the election.[6]

Several states have adopted new voter identification rules that go beyond simple voter registration and instead require voters to show a form of government-issued photo identification. Defenders of the photo identification requirement argue it is necessary to lessen voter fraud. Opponents argue that these rules discriminate against poorer and minority citizens who are less likely to possess such identification. As you assess the United States electoral process, it is important to remember that voting rules are the subject of intense political conflict.

Regularly Scheduled Elections

In our system, elections are held at fixed intervals that the party in power cannot change. It does not make any difference if the nation is at war, as we were during the Civil War, or in the midst of a crisis, as in the Great Depression; when the calendar calls for an election, the election is held. Elections for members of Congress occur on the first Tuesday after the first Monday in November of even-numbered years. Although there are exceptions (for special elections or peculiar state provisions), participants know *in advance* exactly when the next election will be. In most parliamentary democracies, such as Great Britain and Canada, the party in power can call elections at a time of its choosing. The predetermined timing of elections is one of the defining characteristics of democracy in the United States.

Primary, General, and Sometimes Special Elections

Americans vote more often and for more offices than do the citizens of any other democracy. Foreign observers are often puzzled that we have elections to decide who can run under a party label in the general election. These primary elections generally determine who can run as the candidate for the Democratic or Republican Party for Congress, president, and state and local offices. Primaries generally have lower turnout and they have become ideological battlegrounds in recent years, especially between factions within the Republican Party. General elections determine who takes office. When a Senator dies or otherwise leaves office, typically the governor from that state can appoint a replacement to serve until the next regularly scheduled election. But when a House member dies or leaves office, a special election is held to determine the new replacement.

A result of our structure of federalism is that state officials are often on the same ballot with federal office seekers. At the state level it is more common to vote not only for governor but also for lieutenant governor and other statewide offices like attorney general. This may mean a governor is elected from one party but other statewide officials are from the other party.

Fixed, Staggered, and Sometimes Limited Terms

Our electoral system is based on *fixed terms,* meaning the length of a term in office is specified, not indefinite. The Constitution sets the term of office for the U.S. House of Representatives at two years, the Senate at six years, and the presidency at four years.

Our system also has *staggered terms* for some offices; as a result, not all offices are up for election at the same time. All House members are up for election every two years, but only one-third of senators are up for election at the same time. Because presidential elections can occur two or four years into a senator's six-year term, senators can often run for the presidency without fear of losing their seat, as John Kerry did in 2004 and John McCain, Barack Obama, and Joe Biden (for the vice presidency) did in 2008, and Tim Kaine (for vice presidency) did in 2016.

But when a senator or representative's term expires the same year as the presidential election, many states have laws that require them to give up their Senate or House seat to run for president, vice president, or any other position. However, some states permit a candidate to run for election to two offices, as does Wisconsin, where Paul Ryan was reelected to the House of Representatives in 2012 even though he lost in the vice presidential race. Had he been victorious in both campaigns, he would have resigned his House seat.[7]

The Twenty-second Amendment to the Constitution, adopted in 1951, limits presidents to two terms. Although George Washington had set the two-term precedent as the nation's first president, Franklin D. Roosevelt rejected the precedent in winning third and fourth terms. Republicans pushed the amendment forward in part to guarantee that no future president could ever repeat Roosevelt's dominant role in reshaping government. Knowing that a president cannot run again changes the way members of Congress, the voters, and the press regard the chief executive. A politician who cannot, or has announced he or she will not, run again is called a *lame duck.* Lame ducks are often seen as less influential because other politicians know that these officials' ability to bestow or withhold favors is coming to an end. Efforts to limit the terms of other offices have become a major issue in several states. The most frequent targets have been state legislators and the most frequent limit is eight years.[8] One consequence of term limits is more lame ducks.

Term limits at the state level were largely adopted during the 1990s. Currently, 15 states have term limits for state legislatures. Six states have rescinded term limits either through legislation or state court rulings. Despite their popularity at the state level, Congress has repeatedly failed to pass proposals for term limits on federal legislators. The Supreme Court, declared that a state does not have the constitutional power to impose limits on the number of terms for which its members of the U.S. Congress are eligible, either by amendment to its own constitution or by state law.[9] Congress has refused to propose a constitutional amendment to impose a limit on congressional terms.

Winner Take All

winner-take-all system
An election system in which the candidate with the most votes wins.

An important feature of our electoral process is the **winner-take-all system,** sometimes referred to as "first past the post."[10] In most U.S. electoral settings, the candidate with the most votes wins. The winner does not need to have a *majority* (more than half the votes cast); in a multicandidate race, the winner only needs a *plurality* (the largest number of votes). Plurality-rule elections with single-member districts most often lead to two-party systems. In 2016, six U.S. Senate candidates won their races with less than 50 percent of the vote, the largest number of plurality winners in more than four decades. The plurality winners included Lisa Murkowski in Alaska (44.4 percent), Catherine Cortez Masto in Nevada (47.1 percent), Maggie Hassan in New Hampshire (48 percent), Pat Toomey in Pennsylvania (49 percent), Roy Blunt in Missouri (49.2 percent), and Michael Bennet (49.97 percent).[11] In 2018, plurality winners include Laura Kelly, who was elected governor in Kansas (48 percent), and Ned LaMont, elected governor in Connecticut (49 percent).

Winner-take-all electoral systems tend to reinforce moderate and centrist candidates because they are more likely to secure a plurality or a majority of the votes. Candidates in a winner-take-all system often stress that a vote for a minor party candidate is a wasted vote that may actually help elect the voter's least desired candidate.

single-member district
An electoral district in which voters choose one representative or official.

Most U.S. electoral districts are **single-member districts,** meaning that in any district for any given election—senator, governor, U.S. House, and state legislative seats—the voters choose *one* representative or official.[12] When the single-member district and winner-take-all systems are combined, minor parties find it especially hard to win and a two-party political system is virtually guaranteed. For example, even if a third party gets 25 percent of the vote in several districts but not a plurality in any, it still gets no seats. The single-member districts and winner-take-all system are different from a system of **proportional representation,** in which political parties secure legislative seats and power in proportion to the number of votes they receive in the election. Countries that practice some form of proportional representation include Germany, Israel, Italy, and Japan.

proportional representation
An election system in which each party running receives the proportion of legislative seats corresponding to its proportion of the vote.

Proportional representation more accurately reveals the division of voter preferences and gives those who do not vote with the plurality some influence as a result of their vote. For this reason, proportional representation may encourage greater turnout

Alaska Republican U.S. Senator Lisa Murkowski won reelection by a plurality in 2016. She received 44 percent of the vote, the Libertarian candidate received 29 percent, followed by an Independent candidate with 13 percent, and a Democrat at 12 percent. Murkowski is not the only plurality winner serving in the Senate. In 2016, there were 14 plurality winners, but her percent of the vote was lowest of those plurality winners. Here, Murkowski campaigns on Election Day in Anchorage

for people who identify with parties that rarely win elections under winner-take-all rules, such as Democrats in Utah or Republicans in Massachusetts. Proportional representation may also encourage issue-oriented campaigns and enhance the representation of women and minorities.

However, proportional representation can cause problems. It may make it harder to determine a clear winner, especially if minor parties win seats. As a result, it may encourage the proliferation of minor parties. Opponents of proportional representation worry that it can contribute to political instability and ideological extremism.

The Electoral College

We elect our president and vice president not by a national vote but by an indirect device known as the **Electoral College**. The Framers of the U.S. Constitution devised this system because they did not trust the choice of president to a direct vote of the people. Under this system, each state has as many electors as it has representatives and senators. California therefore has 55 electoral votes (53 House seats and 2 Senate seats), whereas seven states and the District of Columbia only have 3 electoral votes each.

Electoral College
The electoral system used in electing the president and vice president, in which voters vote for electors pledged to cast their ballots for a particular party's candidates.

Each state legislature is free to determine how it selects its electors. Each party nominates a slate of electors, usually longtime party activists. They are expected to cast their electoral votes for the party's candidates for president and vice president if their party's candidates get a plurality of the vote in their state. In our entire history, no "faithless elector"—an elector who does not vote for his or her state's popular vote winner—has ever cast the deciding vote, and the incidence of a **faithless elector** is rare.[13] However, there were seven faithless electors in 2016, the most since 1872 when 63 electors voted for someone other than Horace Greeley (who had died before the Electoral College vote). Two faithless electors defected from Trump and five from Clinton. The Trump defectors voted for John Kasich and Ron Paul, while three Clinton defectors voted for Colin Powell, one for Bernie Sanders, and one for Faith Spotted Eagle (an activist opposed to the Dakota Access and Keystone XL Pipelines).[14]

faithless elector
In the Electoral College an elector who does not vote for the candidate who should receive the electoral vote based on the popular vote in the presidential election in his or her state or district is a faithless elector.

Candidates who win a plurality of the popular vote in a state secure all of that state's electoral votes, except in Nebraska and Maine, which allocate electoral votes to the winner in each congressional district plus two electoral votes for the winner of the state as a whole. Winning electors go to their state capital on the first Monday after the second Wednesday in December to cast their ballots. These ballots are then sent to Congress, and early in January, Congress formally counts the ballots and declares who won the election for president and vice president.

It takes a majority of the electoral votes to win. If no candidate gets a majority of the electoral votes for president, the House chooses among the top three candidates, with each state delegation having one vote. If no candidate gets a majority of the electoral votes for vice president, the Senate chooses between the top two candidates, with each senator casting one vote.

When there are only two major candidates for the presidency, the chances of an election being thrown into the House are remote. But twice in our history, the House has had to act: in 1800, the House had to choose in a tie vote between Thomas Jefferson and Aaron Burr; and in 1824, the House picked John Quincy Adams over Andrew Jackson. The 1800 election prompted the Twelfth Amendment, ratified in 1804, requiring that electors in the Electoral College vote for one person as president and for another as vice president.

As we were reminded in 2000 and again in 2016, our Electoral College system makes it possible for a pres-idential candidate to receive the most popular votes, as did Al Gore in 2000 and Hillary Clinton in 2016, respectively, and yet not get enough electoral votes to be president. Gore lost the Electoral College vote 271 to 266, and George W. Bush became president.[15] In 2016, Clinton lost the Electoral College vote 227–304 to Donald Trump. This also happened in 1824, when Andrew Jackson won 12 percent more of the vote than John Quincy Adams; in 1876, when Samuel Tilden received more popular votes than Rutherford B. Hayes; and in 1888, when Grover Cleveland received more popular votes than Benjamin Harrison. It almost happened in 1916, 1960, and 1976, when the shift of a few votes in a few key states could have resulted in the election of a president without a popular majority.

Questions about the Electoral College arise every time a serious third-party candidate runs for president. If no candidate receives a majority in the Electoral College and the decision is left to Congress, which Congress casts the vote, the one serving during the election, or the newly elected one? The answer is the newly elected one, the one elected in November and taking office the first week in January. Because each state has one vote in the House, what happens if a state delegation's vote is tied? The answer: its vote does not count. Would it be possible to have a president of one party and a vice president of another? Yes, if the election were thrown into the House and Senate, and a different party controlled each chamber.

In two of the four elections in which the winner of the popular vote did not become president, the Electoral College did not decide the winner. The 1824 election was decided by the U.S. House of Representatives. In the controversial 1876 presidential election between Rutherford B. Hayes and Samuel Tilden, the electoral vote in four states was disputed, resulting in the appointment of an electoral commission to decide how those votes should be counted. The Electoral Commission of 1877, depicted in the drawing, met in secret session, and after many contested votes, Hayes was elected.

TABLE 8.1 2004, 2008, 2012, AND 2016 BATTLEGROUND STATES

As the table shows, some battleground states shifted to Obama from Bush but then back to Trump. Others were only won by Obama in 2008 but were otherwise Republican. Some states like Wisconsin went for Kerry, Obama twice, and then Trump. Hence, they are called battleground states because candidates spend so much time and money trying to win these states.

State	Electoral Votes in 2012–2020	Percent Difference in 2004 Popular Vote	Percent Difference in 2008 Popular Vote	Percent Difference in 2012 Popular Vote	Percent Difference In 2016 Popular Vote
Michigan	16	3.4 Kerry	16.5 Obama	9.5 Obama	0.2 Trump
Pennsylvania	20	2.5 Kerry	10.3 Obama	5.4 Obama	0.7 Trump
New Hampshire	4	1.4 Kerry	9.6 Obama	5.6 Obama	0.4 Clinton
Wisconsin	10	0.4 Kerry	13.9 Obama	6.9 Obama	0.8 Trump
Iowa	6	0.7 Bush	9.5 Obama	5.8 Obama	9.4 Trump
New Mexico	5	0.8 Bush	15.1 Obama	10.2 Obama	8.2 Clinton
Ohio	18	2.1 Bush	4.6 Obama	3.0 Obama	8.1 Trump
Nevada	6	2.6 Bush	12.5 Obama	6.7 Obama	2.4 Clinton
Florida	29	5.0 Bush	2.8 Obama	0.9 Obama	1.2 Trump
Missouri	10	7.2 Bush	0.1 McCain	9.4 Romney	18.6 Trump
Virginia	13	8.2 Bush	6.3 Obama	3.9 Obama	5.3 Clinton
North Carolina	15	12.4 Bush	0.3 Obama	2.0 Romney	3.7 Trump
Indiana	11	20.7 Bush	1.0 Obama	10.2 Romney	19.1 Trump
Minnesota	10	3.5 Kerry	10.2 Obama	7.7 Obama	1.5 Clinton

SOURCE: Federal Election Commission, "Election Results," http://www.fec.gov/pubrec/electionresults.shtml; "President Map" *The New York Times*, November 8, 2012, http://elections.nytimes.com/2012/results/president and http://www.nytimes.com/elections/results/president.

The Electoral College strongly influences presidential campaigns. To win a presidential election, a candidate must appeal successfully to voters in populous states such as California, Texas, Ohio, Illinois, Florida, and New York because their electoral votes far exceed other states. For example, California's electoral vote of 55 in 2016 exceeded the combined electoral votes of the 15 least populous states plus the District of Columbia. Sparsely populated states such as Wyoming and Vermont also have disproportionate representation in the Electoral College because each has one representative, regardless of population. When the contest is close, as it has been in recent elections, every state's electoral votes are crucial to the outcome, and so greater emphasis is given to states in which the contest is close (see Table 8.1).[16]

Counting Votes (Structure)

8.2 Assess how well American elections are administered.

Until the 2000 election, most citizens assumed they could cast a vote and have it count. They registered to vote, showed up at their local polling place ready to decide, waited in line to be given a ballot, cast their secret ballot, and assumed it would be counted. They did not expect to be challenged for special identification, or questioned about how they had registered to vote. And they certainly did not expect their ballot to be lost or miscounted.

Votes are counted in the United States according to state law as administered by local officials. The technology used in voting varies greatly between and within states. In Florida in 2000, some counties used paper ballots, others voting machines, others punch-card ballots, and at least one county used ballots that a computer could scan. More recently, states have moved from touchscreen computerized voting systems to paper ballots that can be optically scanned. Reasons for this include lower costs for optical scan machines and a paper ballot makes recounts easier.

Voter identification requirements and heightened scrutiny over the voter registration process have become more common since the 2010 election. In 2012, Democrats and allied groups successfully challenged in courts the new voter identification laws in several states, as well as cutbacks on the number of early voting days in some of these same states. In some cases, the challenges resulted in delaying implementation of the law until after the election. In 2016, as many as 20 states had seen some new voter identification requirements or limits on early voting compared to 2010.[17] The trust voters had in how ballots are counted changed after the 2000 election, when the nation waited for weeks to find out whether George W. Bush or Al Gore would be president. The outcome hinged on a few damaged ballots that were cast and counted or not counted in Florida. Not only did the dispute raise important questions about how votes are counted, it also opened a broad debate about how votes are cast. Even before the votes were counted in elections since 2000, both parties had deployed thousands of lawyers to observe the voting and ballot counting and to launch legal challenges if necessary. Ultimately the votes are counted, and we see the peaceful transfer of power from one individual or party to another. This, especially after contested elections, is an important and culminating event in electoral democracy.

Another lesson the recent ballot-counting controversies have reinforced is that in every election, in every jurisdiction, and with every technology, voting is imperfect. Touch-screen software can be manipulated; people can miscount paper ballots; punch cards may not always be completely perforated; and so on. The goal in election administration is to minimize errors and eliminate as much bias and outright fraud as possible.

But how we count votes is more complicated than how we cast votes. Election officials have to make judgment calls about incomplete or flawed ballots. Decisions about which ballots to count and which ones not to count matter in an election decided by only 537 votes, as Florida's presidential election was in 2000. With the growth in absentee voting, and with military personnel and civilians living abroad voting by mail, a close election may not be decided until days after the polls officially close.

When voters appear in person to vote at one of the nation's thousands of voting places, or *polls*, they are greeted and given a ballot by citizens from their own neighborhood. These volunteer poll workers arrive at the polls hours before voting starts to set up equipment and ensure that the voter lists, ballots, and voting equipment are ready to go. Recent research has found that poll workers can greatly influence the security, efficiency, and overall environment of polling locations. Those who receive high-quality training and are confident in both their expertise and the accuracy of the polling location create an overall environment that makes voters feel more confident.[18]

Who is and who is not allowed to vote on Election Day is also a source of controversy. In most states, persons must be registered voters in order to vote. Voters are expected to vote in designated voting places. In 2012, as a result of the 2010 redistricting, some voting places and precincts in parts of the country changed, which confused some voters who went to the wrong place to vote. The law permits voters who think they should be allowed to vote but who are not on the rolls to cast what are called provisional ballots. These ballots are counted only if the voter is, in fact, registered to vote. States often have laws removing individuals from the voter rolls if they have not voted in recent elections, a process called the purge. Ohio has the most aggressive voter purge law in the nation. If a voter does not vote in any election in two consecutive years they are sent a postcard asking them to confirm they are still living at the address where they are registered to vote. If they do not

Judge Robert Rosenberg of the Broward County Canvassing Board uses a magnifying glass to examine a dimpled chad on a punch-card ballot, November 24, 2000, during a vote recount. The presidential election in 2000 in Florida was plagued with vote counting and ballot problems. For example, several counties used punch cards, and some voters failed to make their vote clear by successfully punching out the "chad" for the choice selected. This led to discussion of "dangling chads" and "dimpled chads." In other counties, the format of the ballot itself was confusing. The Florida problems led to passage of the Help America Vote Act.

return the post card and do not vote in the next four consecutive years including two general elections, their names are removed from the rolls and they must register again to vote in subsequent elections. As discussed in Chapter 7, the Supreme Court upheld the Ohio law in 2018.[19]

Following the 2000 and 2004 elections, federal and state governments invested billions of dollars in new voting technology, established new rules on provisional ballots, and modernized voting methods. Interest groups, political parties, and candidates have made the integrity of the voting process a high priority. In 2012 and 2014, with some states adding photo identification requirements in order to vote and some more actively purging their voter lists of presumed illegal immigrants, more attention was given to who may and may not vote. Groups established toll-free hotlines for voters to call if they felt they were not being treated fairly, and in key jurisdictions, lawyers were on call to file immediate challenges when a person's right to vote was contested.

The issue of possible voter fraud in 2016 was frequently mentioned by candidate and later President Donald Trump. For example, he tweeted on October 17, 2016, "Of course there is large scale voter fraud happening on and before Election Day. Why do Republican leaders deny what is going on? So naïve!"[20] In May 2017, President Trump signed an executive order creating a "Presidential Advisory Commission on Election Integrity," with Vice President Mike Pence as chair and Kansas Secretary of State, Kris Kobach, as the vice chair. The commission generated controversy when it requested state governments share voter registration lists, including personal information like Social Security numbers. Some states complied in part, withholding some information deemed confidential, others declined to send the lists. The commission was also subject to a number of lawsuits.[21] In January 2018 the commission was disbanded. The dispute over how much voter fraud there actually is continues, but the politics of this matter will remain largely at the state level.

Money in U.S. Elections (Action)

8.3 Evaluate the influence of money in elections and the main approaches to campaign finance reform.

Election campaigns cost money, and the methods of obtaining that money have long been controversial. Campaign money can come from a candidate's own wealth, political parties, supportive individuals, or interest groups. Money is contributed to candidates for a variety of reasons, including ideology, group identification and support, self-interest, and because the donor really does not like the other candidate. Concern about campaign finance stems from the possibility that candidates or parties, in their pursuit of campaign funds, will decide it is more important to represent the will of their financial contributors than that of their own conscience or the voters as a whole. Courts have ruled that this potential for corruption or the appearance of corruption is a valid reason for Congress to legislate in this area.[22]

Scandals involving the influence of money on policy are not new. For example, a cabinet member was convicted of accepting bribes in 1922 for arranging for the lease of federal land in Wyoming and California for private oil developments.[23] Responding to what then became known as the Teapot Dome scandal, Congress passed the Corrupt Practices Act, which required disclosure of campaign funds but was "written in such a way as to exempt virtually all [members of Congress] from its provisions."[24]

Similarly, the 1972 Watergate scandal—in which persons associated with the Nixon campaign broke into the Democratic Party headquarters to steal campaign documents and plant listening devices—led to media scrutiny and congressional investigations, discovering that large amounts of money from corporations and individuals had been deposited into secret bank accounts outside the country for political and campaign purposes. The public outcry from these discoveries prompted Congress to enact the body of reforms that still largely regulate the financing of federal elections.[25]

Efforts at Reform

Reformers have tried three basic strategies to prevent abuse in political contributions: (1) imposing limits on giving, receiving, and spending political money; (2) requiring public disclosure of the sources and uses of political money; and (3) giving governmental subsidies to presidential candidates, campaigns, and parties to reduce their reliance on campaign contributors. By 2012, all three of these strategies had been limited by court and administrative decisions and by changing campaign dynamics. Of the three, disclosure remains the primary strategy still in place.

THE FEDERAL ELECTION CAMPAIGN ACT In 1971, Congress passed the Federal Election Campaign Act (FECA), which limited amounts that candidates for federal

The Watergate scandal not only led to the resignation of President Nixon, it also called attention to the role of large undisclosed campaign contributions. This in turn helped motivate Congress to pass comprehensive campaign finance reform.

office could spend on advertising and required disclosure of the sources of campaign funds and how they are spent. It also required political action committees to register with the government and report all major contributions and expenditures.

In 1974, the Watergate scandal helped push Congress to amend FECA in the most sweeping campaign reform measure in U.S. history. These amendments established more realistic limits on contributions and spending by candidates and party committees, strengthened disclosure laws, created the **Federal Election Commission (FEC)** to administer the new laws, and provided for partial public funding for presidential primaries and a grant to major-party presidential general election candidates. The money to fund the presidential candidates comes from taxpayers who choose to allocate $3 of their income taxes by checking a box on their tax returns. The FEC, which has six commissioners, three from each party, is often deadlocked along partisan lines.

Federal Election Commission (FEC)

A commission created by the 1974 amendments to the Federal Election Campaign Act to administer election reform laws. It consists of six commissioners appointed by the president and confirmed by the Senate. Its duties include overseeing disclosure of campaign finance information, public funding of presidential elections, and enforcing contribution limits.

The 1974 law was extensively amended after the Supreme Court's 1976 *Buckley* v. *Valeo* decision, which overturned several of its provisions on grounds that they violated the First Amendment free speech protection.[26] The *Buckley* decision still allowed limitations on contributions and full and open disclosure of fund-raising and campaign spending by candidates for federal office, as well as the system of public financing for presidential elections.[27] However, the Supreme Court made a distinction between campaign spending and campaign contributions, holding that the First Amendment protects spending; therefore, although Congress may limit how much people contribute to somebody else's campaign, legislatures may not limit how much of their own money people spend on their own campaigns or that they spend independent of a candidate or political party.

One of the success stories of FECA was that for 20 years presidential candidates of both parties chose to accept the limitations on fund-raising and campaign spending that were part of the public financing provisions. During the nomination phase, candidates receive federal matching funds for campaign contributions up to $250. Accepting the federal matching funds means candidates accept state-by-state spending limits for the caucuses and the primaries. Until 2000, presidential candidates (except a few wealthy, self-financed candidates) accepted the voluntary limitations that come with partial public financing of presidential nomination campaigns. In 2012, the number of candidates in both parties who turned down the matching funds in the primaries increased and included Barack Obama, Mitt Romney, Rick Santorum, Ron Paul, Newt Gingrich, Tim Pawlenty, Michele Bachmann, Rick Perry, and Herman Cain. Why the change between 1996 and 2012? Candidates began viewing the spending limits associated with matching funds as too constrictive, and once the first candidate rejects matching funds, politically, it becomes easier for other candidates to do so as well. Rather than focusing on the small (under $250) matchable contribution, candidates have started focusing more on the max-out donors who gave four times that amount in 2000 and eight or more times that amount in subsequent elections.[28]

Public funding in the presidential general election is a grant that, if accepted, requires candidates to stop fund-raising for their own campaign. However, if candidates accept public funding, they can continue to raise money for the national party. In 2008, Obama was the first major party candidate since the system was created in 1974 to reject taxpayers' money for the general election; he ultimately had access to much greater funds than did his opponent, John McCain. In 2012, both Obama and Romney turned down the public grant and both led the pack in money raised in the early stages of the 2012 campaign. In 2016, Clinton and Trump declined the public funding grant. Some candidates have taken advantage of the absence of any limits on the use of their personal funds in running for president. For example, Mitt Romney gave his campaign $35.4 million in 2008.[29] In 2016, Donald Trump stated that he planned on spending $100 million of his own money on his campaign. The actual amount he spent was $66 million.[30]

The entertainment media has long been a major source of funds for Democratic candidates. However, some of the fund-raising events hosted by movie stars and producers lead to negative press for their organizers. George Clooney came under fire after hosting a $33,400-per-plate fund-raising dinner for Hillary Clinton in April 2016. Clooney appeared the following weekend on the Sunday morning news programs, where he criticized the "obscene" amount of money that funds campaigns but did not apologize for hosting the event.[33] Here Clooney relaxes in Cannes, far from the ongoing controversy about the cost of campaigns.

THE BIPARTISAN CAMPAIGN REFORM ACT (BCRA) After years of legislative debate, Senate filibusters, and even a presidential veto, Congress passed and President Bush signed into law the **Bipartisan Campaign Reform Act (BCRA)** in 2002. This legislation, often known as the McCain–Feingold bill, after its two chief sponsors in the Senate, was written with the understanding that it would immediately be challenged in court—and it was. The Supreme Court upheld most of the provisions of BCRA in *McConnell* v. *FEC*.[31] But subsequent decisions have reversed much of BCRA.

BCRA is best understood as incremental change. It continued the public financing of presidential campaigns with funds from the income tax check-off. It left unchanged the limits on spending by candidates for presidential nominations (on a state-by-state basis and in total) and in the presidential general elections for those candidates who accept public funding. Although recognizing that individuals are free to spend unlimited amounts on their own campaigns, BCRA provided increased contribution limits for candidates running against an opponent who was spending substantial amounts of his or her own money, a provision later declared unconstitutional by the Supreme Court.[32] Finally, it left unchanged the limits on the amounts the national parties can spend on presidential campaigns and on individual congressional and senatorial campaigns. Now these limits have largely been eliminated by court rulings.

BCRA made individuals more important as sources of money to candidates because it increased the amount they could give and indexed those limits to inflation. In the election cycles since BCRA took effect, there has been substantial growth in individual contributions, especially to the Democrats, who once were more reliant on soft money, the money political parties could raise in unlimited amounts, which was intended to be for limited purposes but was later used in candidate promotion or attack ads. As we discuss below, soft money is, for the most part, now prohibited.

The limits under BCRA for 2017–2018 for individuals giving to candidates were $2,700 for each primary, general, or runoff election. Runoffs are rare in the United States, so for most individuals the total contribution limit to a candidate in 2017–2018 was $5,400. Until the 2014 *McCutcheon* v. *FEC* ruling, individuals also had an aggregate two-year election cycle limit for money given to candidates, party committees, and PACs. Before the decision, the 2014 inflation-adjusted aggregate individual contribution limits to candidates, party committees, and PACs was $123,000. But after the decision the amount could reach as much as $13.7 million.[34] BCRA had already given party committees an opportunity to appeal to "max-out" donors, something both parties pursued. Individuals could also contribute unlimited amounts to independent expenditure-only PACs (Super PACs), and some gave several million dollars, calling into question the contribution limits to candidates, party committees, and conventional PACs. Both parties now seek to raise even larger sums from individuals as a result of the McCutcheon decision. While the parties are still adapting to their ability to raise much more money from large donors, it has been the Republican party committees who have benefited the most to date.[35] BCRA also had a major impact on stopping novel ways to evade the campaign finance laws. One particularly effective tool involved party efforts to register voters and run generic party ads for what were called "party building purposes."[36] This money came to be defined as **soft money**,[37] in contrast to the limited and more-difficult-to-raise **hard money** contributions to candidates and party committees that are committed to candidate-specific electoral activity. Over time, soft money became more important. The 1996 election saw aggressive soft money fund-raising by the Clinton–Gore campaign, including opportunities for donors to have meetings with the president, to fly with him on Air Force One, and to spend the night in the Lincoln Bedroom at the White House. Much of this money was spent on candidate specific

Bipartisan Campaign Reform Act (BCRA)
Largely banned party soft money, restored a long-standing prohibition on corporations and labor unions from using general treasury funds for electoral purposes, and narrowed the definition of issue advocacy.

soft money
Money raised in unlimited amounts by political parties for party-building purposes. Now largely illegal except for limited contributions to state or local parties for voter registration and get-out-the-vote efforts.

hard money
Political contributions given to a party, candidate, or interest group that are limited in amount and fully disclosed. Raising such limited funds is harder than raising unlimited funds, hence the term "hard money."

election ads.[38] A congressional investigation into these and related concerns about campaign finance in the 1996 election cycle reinforced the case for reform.[39] From the perspective of the voter, the advertising purchased by soft money was indistinguishable from other campaign expenditures.[40]

After 1996, both parties continued to make raising and spending soft money a major priority, and soft money spending rose dramatically. All national party committees combined raised more than $509 million of soft money in the 1999–2000 election cycle, and nearly that much again in 2001–2002,[41] up from $110 million adjusted for inflation in 1991–1992.[42] Banning soft money became the primary objective of reformers and was one of the more important provisions in BCRA. Soft money enabled large donors to be major players in campaign finance. It also strengthened the power of the national party committees, which allocated the money to state parties and indirectly to candidates. To the Supreme Court, which upheld the BCRA soft money ban, one of the major problems with soft money was that it purchased access to elected officials, and with that access can come influence and the possibility or appearance of corruption.[43]

Resisting Reform

Despite the Supreme Court's decisions to uphold much of FECA and BCRA, the fight to reverse campaign finance reform has continued for almost three decades. Opponents have fought the limits in the courts, Congress, and the Federal Election Commission, hoping to overturn or weaken the laws.

ISSUE ADVOCACY Much of the fight against campaign finance reform has tried to exploit the Supreme Court's 1976 ruling in *Buckley* v. *Valeo*, which challenged restrictions on campaign advertisements that were about issues and not candidate campaigns. The Supreme Court agreed with this challenge and decided that groups were free to run advertisements during the campaign season as long as the ads did not use such words as "vote for" or "vote against" a specific candidate. The Supreme Court's 1976 *Buckley* v. *Valeo* decision defined election communication as "communications containing express words of advocacy of election or defeat, such as 'vote for,' 'elect,' 'support,' 'cast your ballot for,' 'Smith for Congress,' 'vote against,' 'defeat,' and 'reject.'"[44] Communications that did not use these "magic words" were defined as issue ads, presumably because they deal with issues not candidates, and thus are not subject to disclosure required by FECA restrictions. Not surprisingly, interest groups and media consultants found a way to form groups that avoid disclosure and to communicate an electioneering message without using the magic words.

The 1996 election saw a surge in candidate-specific **issue advocacy**. Issue ad spending in some U.S. House races exceeded $1 million. A prominent example of issue advocacy against a candidate was the ad campaign by Republicans for Clean Air, formed by two Texans attacking John McCain in some 2000 presidential primaries.[45] Legislation to limit groups doing electioneering through the guise of issue ads was struck down by the courts, so that today there are groups able to spend money against or for a candidate masking their identity behind some obscure name like Citizens for Freedom.

issue advocacy
Promoting a particular position or an issue paid for through unlimited and undisclosed spending by interest groups or individuals but not candidates. Much issue advocacy is often electioneering for or against a candidate, avoiding words like "vote for" or "vote against," and until 2004 had not been subject to any regulation.

Like soft-money ads, issue advertisements sponsored by interest groups are largely indistinguishable from candidate-run advertisements.[46] In some competitive contests, interest groups and parties spent more money than the candidates themselves. Typically, these party and group ads are even more negative than the ads run by candidates. Though many candidates disavowed ads intended to help them and hurt their opponent, determining who is accountable for the content of the non-candidate ads is difficult in an election context. Issue ads have been run by businesses, labor unions, health care organizations, environmental groups, energy groups, pro- and anti-gun groups, pro- and antiabortion groups, and the pharmaceutical industry.

INDEPENDENT EXPENDITURES The Supreme Court made clear in its ruling on FECA in 1976 that individuals and groups have the right to spend as much money as they wish for or against candidates as long as they are truly independent of the candidate and the money is not corporate or union treasury money. BCRA does not constrain **independent expenditures** by groups, political parties, or individuals, as long as the expenditures by those individuals, parties, or groups are independent of the candidate and fully disclosed to the FEC. Some groups, such as the American Medical Association, the National Education Association, and the National Rifle Association, have long tried to influence elections independently rather than through a party committee or a candidate's campaign. The Supreme Court, in 1996, extended to political parties the same right to make independent expenditures afforded to groups and individuals.[47]

independent expenditures
Money spent by individuals or groups not associated with candidates to elect or defeat candidates for office.

In recent election cycles, independent expenditures by the party committee were important in several competitive contests. For example, in the 2014 North Carolina U.S. Senate race, Democratic challenger Kay Hagan had $8.9 million spent on her behalf by the Democratic Senatorial Campaign Committee, only to lose to Republican challenger Thom Tillis whose party spent $6.3 million in support of his candidacy.[48] In 2010, Republicans and Democrats received roughly equal amounts of independent expenditures in U.S. House races, while the Democrats received substantially more in U.S. Senate races than did the Republicans.[49] In 2012, Republicans surpassed Democrats, while in 2014 both parties benefited from similar amounts of outside spending. In 2016, Clinton benefited from an $84 million spending advantage by Democratic party committees over what the Republicans spent in support of Trump. This does not include another $43 million Clinton advantage over Trump in candidate joint fundraising with the national party committee. In congressional races, Democrats were able to spend over $50 million more on their congressional candidates with party funds than were the Republicans Super PAC spending helped Republicans in battleground contests, helping fill this gap.[50] Individuals have also made large independent expenditures. Michael Goland, a California entrepreneur, spent $1.1 million against Senator Charles Percy (R-IL) in the 1984 election because he considered Percy unfriendly to Israel. In the 2000 presidential election, Stephen Adams, owner of an outdoor advertising firm, spent $2 million to support George W. Bush.[51] In 2004, billionaire George Soros, who gave millions to organizations opposing the reelection of Bush, also spent $2.3 million in independent expenditures against the president. In 2016, Stephen Adams, who made a fortune in billboards, spent over $1.6 million in support of Donald Trump and other GOP candidates.[52]

SUPER PACS Opponents of campaign finance reform achieved a major legal shift in campaign finance when in 2010, the Supreme Court, in a 5-4 decision in *Citizens United* v. *FEC*, rejected the long-standing ban on unions and corporations using their general funds on ads about the election or defeat of a candidate.[53] The application of this decision and a subsequent decision in *SpeechNow, Inc.* v. *FEC* led to **Super PACs**, a type of organization that can receive unlimited money from individuals, unions, and even corporations. Since 2010, individuals have been the major contributors to Super PACs. In 2010, since Super PACs were legalized late in the cycle, only two individuals gave more than $5 million to a Super PAC. By 2012, that number increased to nine, where it remained in 2014. By the end of the 2016 election, the number of individuals who gave $5 million or more to a Super PAC was 30. Some individuals gave $5 million or more in several of these cycles: Robert J. Perry (2010, 2012); Fred Eshelman (2010, 2012); Sheldon and Miriam Adelson (2012, 2014); Fred Eychaner (2012, 2014); Michael Bloomberg (2012, 2014, 2016); John Ricketts (2012, 2014, 2016); James Simons (2012, 2014, 2016); Robert Mercer (2012, 2014, 2016); Thomas Stayer (2014, 2016); and Paul Singer (2014, 2016). Candidates have become increasingly reliant on spending by Super PACs and other outside groups in their quest for office (see Figure 8.1 on the next page).

Super PAC
An independent expenditure-only committee first allowed in 2010 after court decisions allowing unlimited contributions to such PACs. Super PACs were important in the 2010 and 2012 elections.

Since 2010, Super PACs played an important role in prolonging presidential nomination contests, attacking candidates of both parties in battleground congressional races, and helped Mitt Romney match Barack Obama in overall spending in 2012.

FIGURE 8.1 PRESIDENTIAL CANDIDATES AND OUTSIDE MONEY SPENDING THROUGH JUNE 30, 2016

With the exception of Bernie Sanders, presidential candidates included in Figure 8.1 relied on Super PAC support, and some had more Super PAC money spent on their behalf than their own candidate campaign committees spent. Examples of heavy Super PAC reliant candidates are Rick Perry, Carly Fiorina, Chris Christie, Scott Walker, John Kasich, Jeb Bush, Marco Rubio, and Donald Trump. Super PACs supporting Trump entered the race later than did most other candidate specific Super PACs.

SOURCE: Compiled from Federal Election Commission data (https://www.fec.gov/finance/disclosure/candcmte_info.shtml [May 9, 2017])..

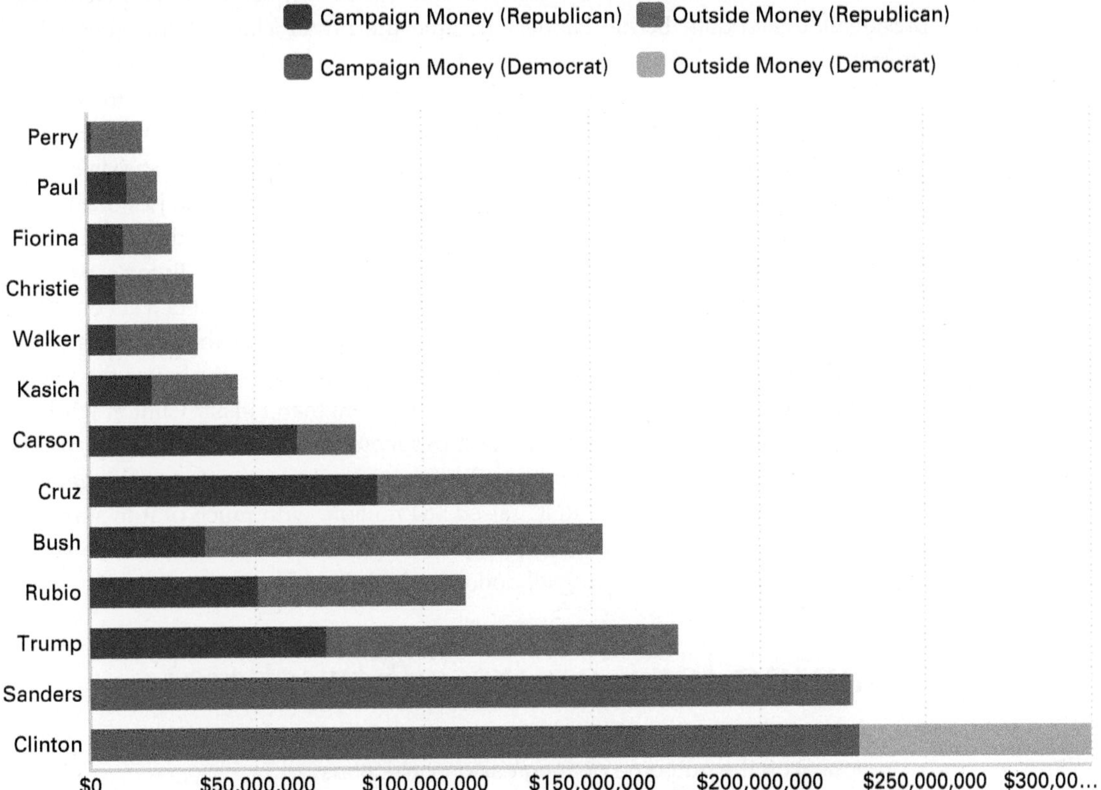

But their effectiveness was questioned for failing to put Mitt Romney in the White House and restore Republicans to the majority in the U.S. Senate in 2012.[54] Karl Rove, a former Bush strategist and FOX News commentator, joined a team to organize American Crossroads and Crossroads Grassroots Policy Strategies, while other prominent Republicans organized American Action Network and other groups. These groups coordinated their spending with other GOP allied groups like the Chamber of Commerce, Club for Growth, and the National Rifle Association. Some groups organized under sections of the law that allowed them to avoid disclosing their donors, or Section 501(c) groups. These groups target unlimited expenditures to many of the same battleground states, and their spending is often substantial.[55]

Small Donors and the Internet

By banning party soft money, BCRA pushed candidates to turn more to individuals for contributions, and because BCRA increased the individual contribution limit, candidates turned first to donors able to contribute the new maximum, which in the first election after BCRA took effect was $2,000 for the primary and $2,000 for the general election. Mitt Romney's campaign made max-out donors their major focus in 2012.[56]

Some candidates also expanded their small-donor fund-raising efforts in an attempt to boost total contributions. Raising money from small donors has been enhanced by skillful use of the Internet. Starting in 2000 with the McCain presidential campaign and then expanding with Howard Dean's campaign for president in 2004, individuals started giving to candidates via the Internet. But it was the Obama campaign in 2008 that demonstrated the extraordinary power of the Internet as a means to reach donors and a way for people to contribute to a candidate.[57] Obama built on his 2008 success in Internet fund-raising in 2012, and while Romney closed the gap between Republicans and Democrats in Internet fund-raising, it remains a large Democratic advantage.[58] As former senator Tom Daschle said, the Internet "is an evolution away from Washington's control, away from the power that big money and big donors used to have a monopoly on."[59] It is clear that the Internet has the potential to change the way campaigns are funded.

Combining the power of the Internet and a focus on small donors, Democratic presidential candidate Bernie Sanders became the poster child of this fund-raising strategy during the 2016 election cycle. "Take our country back from the billionaire class"[60] became his slogan directed at the young and the middle class, to call these people to donate $27 each, what Sanders touted as his average individual contribution. The Sanders campaign saw impressive results. During his victory speech after the New Hampshire primaries, 2,689 people donated an average of $34 in just one minute. Within 23 hours after his speech, he had amassed $6.3 million,[61] with almost another $4 million in donations the next day.[62] Comparing his campaign to Clinton's, Sanders's $95 million trailed Clinton's $127 million in February 2016, and Sanders went on to raise more money than Clinton in March.[63] A lingering question after the primaries of 2016 was to what extent Hillary Clinton or Donald Trump could effectively use the Internet as Obama and Sanders did. It was Donald Trump more than Hillary Clinton who used the Internet to tap into small donors in the 2016 general election. He did this by working with the Republican National Committee in a joint fundraising effort and together in July 2016 his campaign and the RNC raised $64 million, with much of it in small contributions.[64] Trump and the RNC continued to emphasize the Internet and he and his party raised $238.6 million from small donors in 2015–2016.[65]

Running for Congress (Structure)

8.4 Assess the influence of redistricting, incumbency, partisanship, and candidate appeal on the outcome of congressional elections.

How candidates run for Congress differs depending on the nature of their district or state, on whether candidates are incumbents or challengers, on the strength of their personal organization, on how well known they are, and on how much money they have to spend on their campaign. There are both similarities and differences between House and Senate elections. For example, most House elections are not close (see Figure 8.2).

Representatives run in districts whose boundaries are typically drawn by the state legislature following the once-a-decade census. Districts are now drawn to be approximately equal in population. But they are also often drawn in ways that enhance party control and incumbent reelection, a process called *partisan gerrymandering*. Party identification is an important predictor of voting in congressional elections. In districts where most people identify with one party or where incumbents are popular and enjoy fund-raising and other campaign advantages, there is often little competition.[66] Those who believe that competition is essential to constitutional democracy are concerned that so many officeholders have **safe seats**. Some contend that when officeholders do not have to fight to retain their seats, elections are not performing their proper role.[67] The Supreme Court considered the constitutionality of partisan gerrymandering in several much anticipated cases in 2018. But, rather than decided the central question, the Court sent the cases back to the lower courts on procedural grounds—primarily whether those who brought suit had the right, or standing, to do so.

safe seat
An elected office that is predictably won by one party or the other, so the success of that party's candidate is almost taken for granted.

Competition is more likely when both candidates have adequate funding, which is not often the case in U.S. House elections because incumbents can raise money more easily and are better known than their challengers. Elections for governor and for the

FIGURE 8.2 SAFE AND COMPETITIVE HOUSE SEATS, 2000–2018

With the exception of 2010 when the number of safe seats dropped by 39 seats from the average for the 2000–2014 period, the number of safe seats has not varied much. In prior decades the election after redistricting, which in this figure would be 2002 and 2012, saw more competitive contests. When only a few contests are competitive as in 2014, it is not surprising that there is very little change in the partisan composition of the House.

NOTE: Competitive seats include both toss-up, lean Republican, and lean Democrat.

SOURCES: Charlie Cook, "National Overview," *Cook Political Report*, October 16, 2008, p. 6; Charlie Cook, "Competitive House Race Chart," *Cook Political Report*, http://cookpolitical.com/house/archive/chart/house/race-ratings/2010-10-11_15-22-53; Charlie Cook, "2012 House Race Ratings for October 11, 2012," *Cook Political Report*, October 11, 2012, http://cookpolitical.com/house/charts/race-ratings (accessed October 15, 2012); Charlie Cook, *Cook Political Report*, October 17, 2014, http://cookpolitical.com/house/charts/race-ratings/6346 (accessed October 30, 2014); Charlie Cook, *Cook Political Report*, October 14, 2016, http://cookpolitical.com/house/charts/race-ratings/10085; *Charlie Cook, Cook Political Report*, October 17, 2018, https://www.cookpolitical.com/ratings/house-race-ratings/186618.

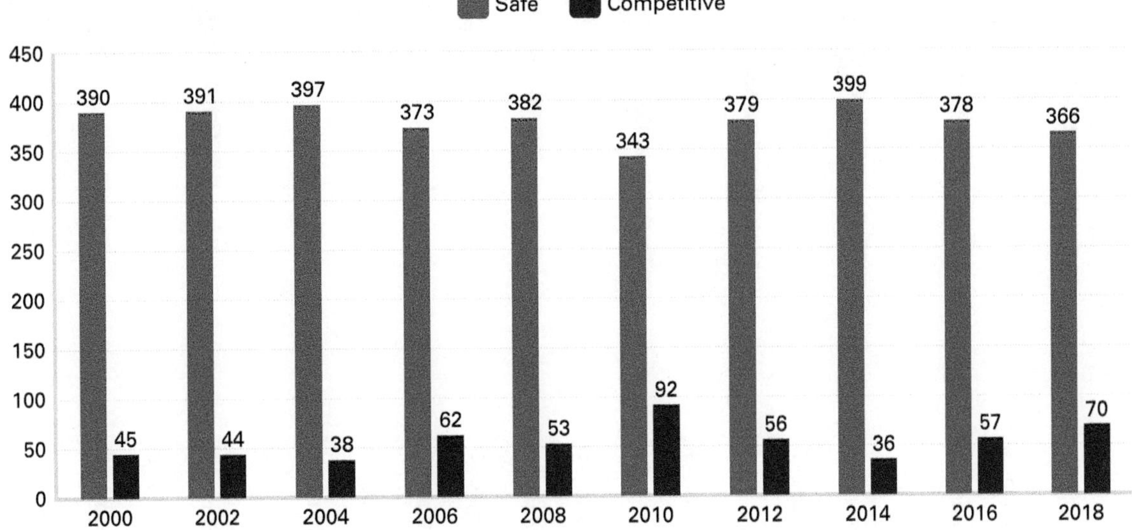

U.S. Senate are more seriously contested and more often adequately financed than those for the U.S. House.

Presidential popularity affects both House and Senate races during both presidential and midterm elections. The boost candidates get from running at the same time as a popular presidential candidate from their party is known as the **coattail effect**. But winning presidential candidates do not always provide such a boost. The Republicans suffered a net loss of six House seats in 1988 even though George H. W. Bush won the presidency, and the Democrats suffered a net loss of 10 House seats in 1992 when Bill Clinton won the presidential election. On the coattails of Barack Obama's convincing presidential win in 2008, the Democrats saw a net gain of 21 House seats and 8 Senate seats. In 2012 Democrats gained two seats in the Senate and eight in the House. In 2016 neither Clinton nor Trump appeared to have coattails, with some Republicans distancing themselves from Trump. Among the Senate Republican candidates who distanced themselves from Trump were Joe Heck in Nevada and Kelly Ayotte in New Hampshire. Both were defeated. Some who did not endorse Trump like Pennsylvania's Pat Toomey, ended up winning. Overall, "measurable coattail effects continue to appear," according to congressional elections scholar Gary Jacobson, but their impact is "erratic and usually modest."[68]

coattail effect
The boost that candidates may get in an election because of the popularity of candidates above them on the ballot, especially the president.

In midterm elections, presidential popularity and economic conditions have long been associated with the number of House seats a president's party loses.[69] These same factors are associated with how well the president's party does in Senate races, but the association is less strong.[70] Figure 8.3 shows the number of seats in the House of Representatives and U.S. Senate gained or lost by the party controlling the White House in midterm elections since 1954. In all of the midterm elections between 1934 and 1998, and since 2006, the party controlling the White House lost seats in the House. But in 1998 and 2002, the long-standing pattern of the president's party losing

FIGURE 8.3 SEATS GAINED OR LOST BY THE PRESIDENT'S PARTY IN MIDTERM ELECTIONS, 1942–2018

The pattern of the president's party losing seats in midterm elections is clear. For Bill Clinton (1994) and Barack Obama (2010) the number of net seats lost was especially high. It is not the case that the second midterm of a presidency has more net seats lost; see Harry Truman (1950), Ronald Reagan (1986), Bill Clinton (1998), and Barack Obama (2014). Presidents are more likely to have a net gain in Senate seats than House seats, but the more predictable pattern is for them to lose Senate seats in midterms as well.

SOURCE: Harold W. Stanley and Richard G. Niemi, *Vital Statistics on American Politics 2015–2016* (CQ Press, 2015), p. 31. Post-election estimates by author, November 12, 2018.

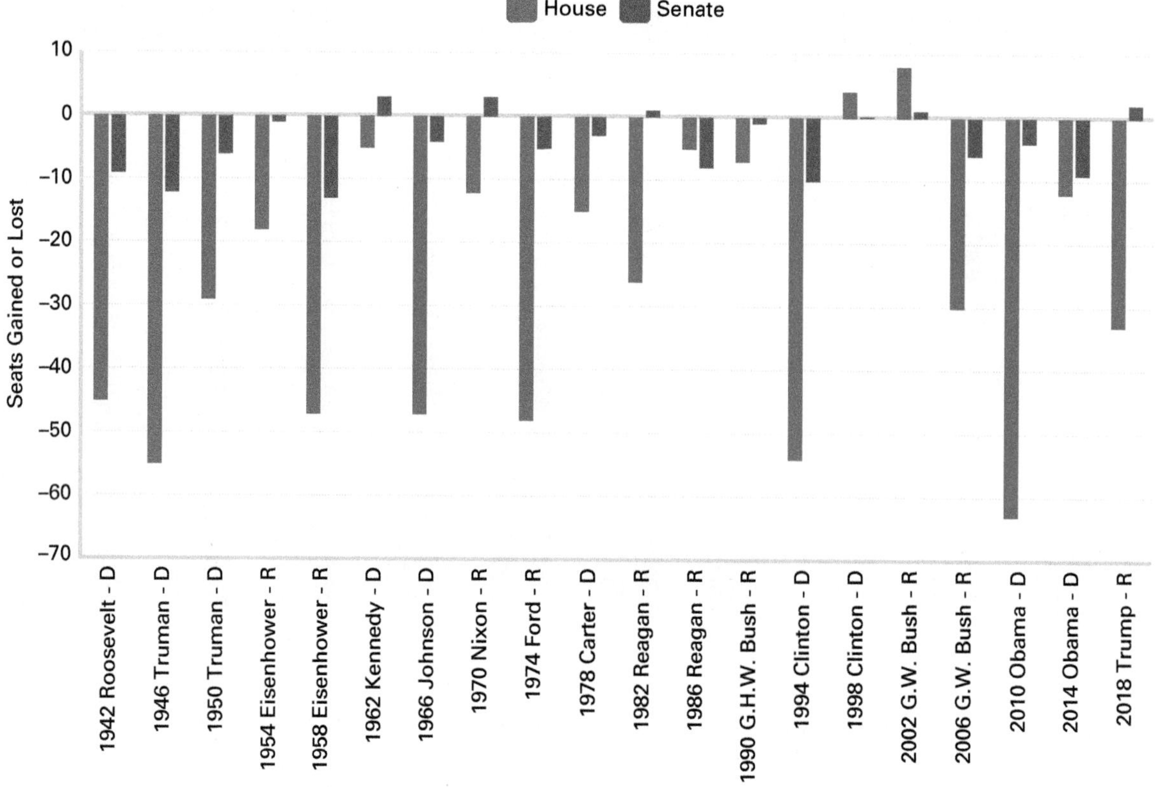

seats in a midterm election did not hold. In 2010, Democrats lost a net of 63 seats in the House and 6 U.S. Senate seats. In 2014, Democrats lost a net of 9 seats in the Senate and 12 in the House. The Senate defeats returned the Republicans to the majority, and the House defeats enlarged the GOP majority over what it was after the 2012 presidential election.[71] The 2018 midterm was intensely fought with record setting spending and higher than normal turnout for a midterm election. Democrats picked up between 33 and 35 House seats, and Republicans gained between 1 and 3 Senate seats depending on recounts in very close races. Democrats made health care their major issue, while President Trump emphasized immigration. The GOP tax cut was not a major issue.

The House of Representatives

Every two years, as many as 1,000 candidates—including approximately 400 incumbents—campaign for Congress. Challengers from other parties running against incumbents rarely encounter opposition in their own party,[72] and the same has been true for incumbents. In the 1990s, for example, on average only two House incumbents were denied renomination, what some have labeled being "primaried," in each election. That changed with the Tea Party success in the 2010 election, when four House incumbents were denied renomination.[73] In 2012, 13 House incumbents were denied renomination (5 by Tea Party challengers and 8 by other incumbents due to redistricting).[74] Only four incumbents were denied renomination in 2014, three of which were Republicans. The Tea Party staged a major upset in 2014 when House Majority Leader Eric Cantor, once seen as a likely speaker of the House, was defeated in a 2014 Virginia primary election by Tea Party–supported David Brat.

The Tea Party has been even more visible in Senate contests, with early success in denying renomination to incumbent senators Robert Bennett in Utah (2010), Lisa Murkowski in Alaska (2010), and Richard Lugar in Indiana (2012). Republicans now worry more about the threat of being seriously challenged for renomination, or "primaried." In 2017, President Trump's former chief political strategist announced an effort to unseat Senate Republicans in 2017 and 2018. His first target was to replace Luther Strange who had been appointed to fill the remainder of Senator Jeff Sessions term when he was named Attorney General. Bannon's candidate, Judge Roy Moore, defeated Strange in the GOP primary but lost in the general election to Doug Jones. Others on Bannon's target list for 2018 included Arizona Senator Jeff Flake, Nevada Senator Dean Heller, Mississippi Senator Roger Wicker, and Tennessee Senator Bob Corker. Despite strong support from Trump, Heller lost the Nevada seat in 2018. Senators Flake and Corker did not run in 2018, making both states competitive, and Wicker won handily in Mississippi.

In 2018, it was not so much the Tea Party that played a role in some GOP primaries as President Trump who made a point to send a tweet criticizing Republican Representative Mark Sanford of South Carolina. Trump's tweet read in part, "Mark Sanford has been very unhelpful to me in my campaign to MAGA (Make America Great Again). He is MIA and nothing but trouble."[75] Katie Arrington who defeated Sanford, thanked Trump in her victory speech and said, "We are the party of Donald J. Trump"[76] but Arrington was defeated in the general election. In 2018, it was more the Democrats than the Republicans who faced intraparty contests with more liberal candidates running against candidates they claimed were not liberal enough. This happened in New York's 14th Congressional District where Alexandria Ocasio-Cortez, a self-described Democratic Socialist, defeated Joseph Crowley, a 20 year incumbent and fourth in line in the House Democratic leadership.[77] This tension was most present in districts that had previously been carried by Republicans. In some districts the national party had recruited and signaled that they were backing a particular candidate for the race, only to have other candidates object.[78]

MOUNTING A PRIMARY CAMPAIGN The first step for would-be challengers wanting to mount a serious campaign is to raise hundreds of thousands of dollars or more. This requires asking friends and acquaintances as well as interest groups for money. Candidates need money to hire campaign managers and technicians, buy television and other advertising time, conduct polls, and pay for a variety of campaign activities. Parties can sometimes help, but they shy away from giving money in primary contests. The party organization usually stays neutral until the nomination is decided. Given the earlier success of Tea Party challenges to incumbents, this policy changed in 2014, when the Republican Party campaign committee actively supported Senators Cochran and McConnell for renomination.

Alexandria Ocasio-Cortez, seen here on MSNBC the morning after defeating 10-term incumbent Joseph Crowley in New York's 14th Congressional District Democratic primary. Ms. Ocasio-Cortez, age 28, won the nomination in her first race for public office. She was a campaign organizer for Bernie Sanders in 2016. In her successful 2018 campaign, she emphasized providing Medicare for all and to abolish the current Immigration and Customs Enforcement agency. In the 2018 midterm elections, Ocasio-Cortez became the youngest woman ever elected to Congress.

Another early step is to build a *personal organization*. A congressional candidate can build an organization while holding another office, such as a seat in the state legislature, by serving in civic causes, helping other candidates, and being conspicuous without being controversial.

A candidate's main hurdle is gaining visibility. Candidates work hard to be mentioned by the media. In large cities with many simultaneous campaigns, congressional candidates are frequently overlooked, and in all areas television is devoting less time to political news.[79] Candidates rely on personal contacts, on hand shaking and door-to-door campaigning, and on identifying likely supporters and courting their favor—the same techniques used in campaigns for lesser offices. Despite these efforts, the turnout in primaries tends to be low, except in campaigns in which large sums of money are spent on advertising and mobilizing voters.

CAMPAIGNING FOR THE GENERAL ELECTION The electorate in a general election is different from that in a primary election. Many more voters turn out in general elections, especially the less-committed partisans and Independents. Party identification is more important in a general election, as many voters use party as a simplifying device to select from among candidates in the many races they decide. Not surprisingly, candidates in districts where their party is strong make their partisanship clear, and candidates from a minority party deemphasize it. General elections also focus on **candidate appeal**, the strengths and weaknesses of the candidates and their background, experience, and visibility.

candidate appeal

The tendency in elections to focus on the personal attributes of a candidate, such as his or her strengths, weaknesses, background, experience, and visibility.

Issues can also be important in general elections, but they are often more local than national in focus. Occasionally, a major national issue can help or hurt one party. Candidates who have differentiated themselves from their party or its leader can reduce the impact of such a **national tide** if it is negative. Some elections for Congress or the state legislature are in part referendums on the president or governor, but public opinion concerning the president or governor is rarely the only factor in play. It will be debated whether there was a "tide" for Democrats in 2018. Republicans picked up some seats in the Senate but lost at least 33 seats in the House giving the Democrats a majority. Democrats also won key governorships in states like Illinois, Michigan, Nevada, and Wisconsin which will be important to the 2020 presidential election.

national tide

The inclination to focus on national issues, rather than local issues, in an election campaign. The impact of a national tide can be reduced by the nature of the candidates on the ballot who may have differentiated themselves from their party or its leader if the tide is negative, as well as competition in the election.

As mentioned, most incumbent members of Congress win reelection.[80] Since 1970, 93.4 percent of incumbent House members seeking reelection have won; the percentage dipped to 86 percent in 2010, but was back to 93 percent in 2012 and 95 percent in 2014, and 97 percent in 2016.[81] This lends credibility to the charge that we have a "permanent Congress." Why is reelection to a House seat so much easier than defeating an incumbent or winning an open seat? One reason is incumbents have a host of advantages. They are generally better known than challengers, something called **name recognition**, and benefit from years of media coverage of their generally positive efforts on behalf of the district.

name recognition

Incumbents have an advantage over challengers in election campaigns because voters are more familiar with them, and incumbents are more recognizable.

Incumbents also win so often because they are able to outspend challengers in campaigns by approximately three to one in the House and more than two to one in the Senate in 2014 and 2016 although in 2010 and 2012 the differences were not as large.[82] In 2014, the ratios returned to about three to one in the House and two to one in the Senate.[83] Most challengers run campaigns that are much less visible than incumbents, contact fewer voters, and lose badly. Many potential challengers are scared away by the prospect of having to raise more than $1 million in campaign funds, and some do not want to face the media scrutiny that comes with a serious race for Congress. Nonetheless, in each election, a few challengers mount serious campaigns because of the incumbent's perceived vulnerability, the challengers' own wealth, party or political action committee efforts, or other factors. In those competitive House races, the party committees, Super PACs, and outside groups often spend as much as the candidates on mostly attack advertising.[84] In addition, incumbents generally win because of the way their district boundaries are drawn: the party in control of the state legislature typically draws them so as to unify partisan support for the incumbent. Retirements and redistricting create *open seats,* which can result in more competitive elections. If, however, the district is heavily partisan, the predominant party is likely to retain the seat, and once elected, the incumbent then reaps the other incumbency advantages as well. In these cases, the contest for the nomination in the predominant party effectively determines who will be the new representative.

RISING COSTS OF CAMPAIGNS The U.S. ideal that anyone—even a person of modest or little wealth—can run for public office and hope to win has become more myth than reality.[85] Serious presidential candidates in the future are likely to bypass public funding and instead try to replicate the kind of fund-raising success Barack Obama had in 2008 and 2012. Rising costs also mean that incumbents spend more time raising funds and less time legislating and representing their districts. Since FECA became law in 1972, total expenditures by candidates for the House of Representatives have more than doubled after controlling for inflation, and they have risen even more in Senate elections (see Figure 8.4). A major reason for escalating costs is television advertising. Organizing and running a campaign is expensive and effectively limits

FIGURE 8.4 AVERAGE CAMPAIGN EXPENDITURES OF HOUSE CANDIDATES, 1988–2014. RUN FOR DEMOCRATS AND REPUBLICAN GE CANDIDATES ONLY. (NOMINAL DOLLARS)

Among candidates for the U.S. House, incumbents on average raise much more than do challengers in both parties. In some years, open seat candidates raise more money on average than incumbents, as happened with Democrats in 2016. Because so many incumbents seek reelection, the number of open seats is low. When open seats arise, more money is often spent on them because both parties may see the contest as competitive.

SOURCES: Federal Election Commission, "FEC Reports on Congressional Financial Activity for 2000," press release, May 15, 2001; Federal Election Commission, "Financial Activity of General Election Congressional Candidates - 1992-2010", includes activity through 12/31/10, www.fec.gov/press/2010_Full_summary_Data.shtml; 2012-2016 data compiled from www.fec.gov/files/bulk-downloads/index.html, June 23, 2018.

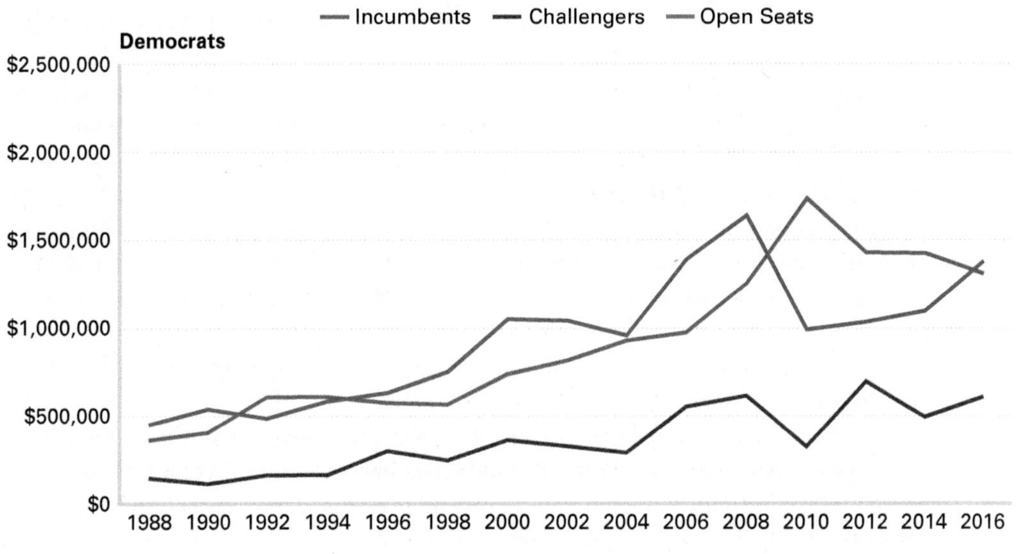

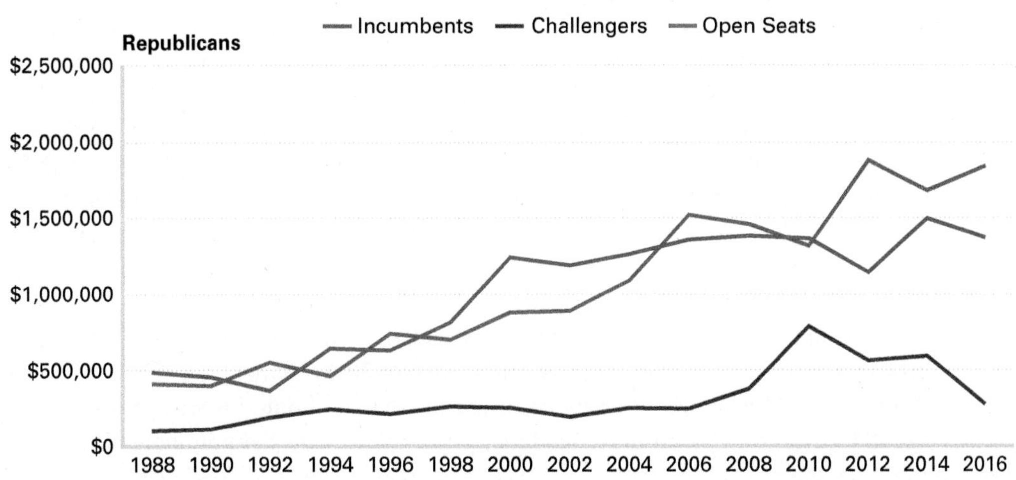

the field of challengers to those who have their own resources or are willing to spend more than a year raising money from interest groups and individuals.

DECLINING COMPETITION Unless something is done to help finance challengers, incumbents will continue to have the advantage in seeking reelection. Nothing in BCRA addressed this problem. Challengers in both parties are typically underfunded. House Republican and Democratic challengers averaged just over $349,000 in spending in 2016, while the average for incumbents was nearly $2.5 million.[86] In today's expensive campaigns, candidates are generally invisible if they spend much less than $500,000.

The high cost of campaigns dampens competition by discouraging individuals from running for office. Potential challengers look at the fund-raising advantages incumbents enjoy—at incumbents' campaign war chests carried over from previous campaigns.[87] Following the 2016 election, South Dakota Senator John Thune whose next election is 2018 had over $10 million in his account and Ohio Representative Patrick Tiberi having had $5.2 million in unspent funds, and at the time it will take them to raise enough money to launch a minimal campaign—and they decide not to run. Moreover, unlike incumbents, whose salaries are being paid while they are campaigning and raising money, most challengers have to support themselves and their families throughout the campaign, which for a seat in Congress often lasts more than one year.

The Senate

Running for the Senate is generally more high-profile than running for the House. The six-year term, the fact that there are only two senators per state, and the national exposure many senators enjoy make a Senate seat a glittering prize. Individual Senate campaigns cost more than individual House races and are more likely to be seriously contested; though in the aggregate, because there are so many more House races, overall spending on House races surpasses overall spending on Senate races (see Figure 8.5 on the next page).[88] The essential tactics are to raise large amounts of money, hire a professional and experienced campaign staff, make as many personal contacts as possible (especially in states with smaller populations), avoid giving the opposition any ammunition to use against you such as extreme or insensitive comments, and have a clear and consistent campaign theme. Incumbency is an advantage for senators, although not as much as it is for representatives.[89] Incumbent senators are widely known, but often so are their opponents, who generally raise and spend significant amounts of money.[90]

When one party controls the Senate by only a few seats, as has been the case in recent years, both parties and the White House become more involved in recruiting competitive candidates. Sometimes, a contender or the party leadership attempts to "clear the field" by discouraging other candidates from running. The reasons to clear the field include not having to spend as much money in the primary, saving funds for the competitive general election, and not having negative ads run in the primary that may damage the primary winner in the general election. In 2014, Colorado Republican U.S. Senate candidate Cory Gardner was able to persuade other declared candidates to drop out of the race, giving him a clear shot at the nomination.[91] Also in 2014, Montana Democrats paved the way for a candidate for U.S. Senate when Democratic governor Bullock appointed his lieutenant governor, John Walsh, to fill the remainder of the term of Democratic Senator Max Baucus, who had been named ambassador to China.[92] In 2018, party leaders including President Trump urged Danny Tarkanian to not challenge incumbent Nevada Republican Senator Dean Heller.[93] Tarkanian instead ran for the U.S. House in Nevada. Also in 2018, Democratic House Minority Whip, Steny Hoyer, was secretly recorded by the candidate he was trying to persuade to drop out.[94] The party leadership candidate won the nomination. The cost

FIGURE 8.5 RISING CAMPAIGN COSTS FOR WINNING CONGRESSIONAL CANDIDATES, HOUSE, SENATE, TOTAL FOR 2016. (MILLIONS OF NOMINAL DOLLARS)

Since 1976, the pattern has been for there to be an increase in total spending by the winning congressional candidates (House and Senate). The exceptions are 1988 and 1990 when there was little overall change but spending by Senate candidates dropped, and 2002 when spending by Senate winners dropped. Note that by 2012 and since, winning congressional candidates collectively have spent in excess of $1 billion. The overall spending appears to rise following passage of the higher contribution limits which took effect with the 2004 election cycle.

SOURCES: 1976–1998: Harold W. Stanley and Richard G. Niemi, Vital Statistics on American Politics 2007-2008 (CQ Press, 2008), p. 101; 2000–2016: Center for Responsive Politics, "Winning vs. Spending," https://www.opensecrets.org/overview/bigspenders.php (accessed May 11, 2017).

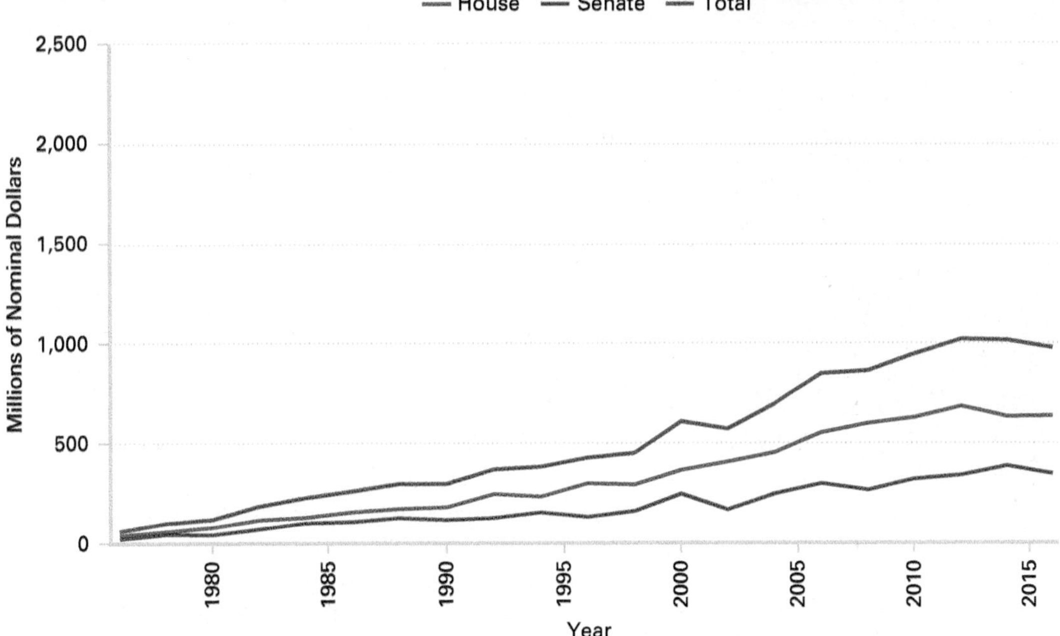

of Senate campaigns can vary greatly. California has nearly 70 times the number of potential voters as Wyoming; not surprisingly, running for a seat from Wyoming is much cheaper than running for a seat from California. As a result, interest groups and parties direct more money to com-petitive races in small states where their campaign dollars have a greater potential impact.[95]

Running for President (Action)

8.5 Outline how presidential campaigns are organized and evaluate methods for reaching voters.

Presidential elections are major media events, with candidates seeking as much positive television coverage as possible and trying to avoid negative coverage. The formal campaign has three stages: winning the nomination, campaigning at the convention, and mobilizing support in the general election.

Stage 1: The Nomination

Presidential hopefuls must make a series of critical tactical decisions. The first is when to start campaigning Some candidates begin fundraising and visits to early caucus or primary states like Iowa and New Hampshire, soon after the last presidential election.[96] On the day of his inauguration in 2017, President Trump filled the paperwork for his renomination campaign, and only days later hosted his first fundraiser for 2020 at the Trump International Hotel in Washington, D.C. This is the earliest any president has announced his campaign for reelection.[97] Mitt Romney's 2012

The Nevada caucuses took place in February 2016, and featured tight battles in the Democratic and Republican races. Like other caucuses, Nevada voters gathered in their communities to discuss their party's candidates, and cast their ballots. Hillary Clinton won the Democratic caucus by a slim margin, while Donald Trump won the Republican caucus by a large margin. Here, Clinton engages voters in a MSNBC/Telemundo debate with Bernie Sanders.

nomination opponents often quipped that he had been running for president for more than six years. Looking to the 2020 election, several possible candidates have made visits to Iowa and New Hampshire to meet with party activists and possibly prepare the way for a candidacy. Candidates generally formally announce their candidacy in March or April of the year before the presidential election. For 2016 most had announced by mid-June 2015. Campaigning begins well before any actual declaration of candidacy, as candidates try to line up supporters to win caucuses or primaries in key states and to raise money for their nomination effort. This period in the campaign has been called the "invisible primary."[98] Before the era of Super PACs, early announcements of candidacy were seen as necessary to raise money and assemble an organization. In 2016, former Florida governor Jeb Bush, while active on the campaign trail, delayed his official announcement of candidacy, in part to allow him to continue raising money for his Super PAC.[99] He raised $103 million for Right to Rise, his Super PAC, before he officially announced his candidacy.[100]

One of the hardest jobs for candidates and their strategists is calculating how to deal with the complex maze of presidential primaries and caucuses that constitute the delegate selection system. Nominees are selected by their national party convention, made up of delegates selected at the state level. The system for electing delegates to the national party convention varies from state to state and often from one party to the other in the same state. In some parties in some states, for example, candidates must provide lists of delegates who support them months before the primary.

In 2012, for example, both Rick Santorum and Newt Gingrich failed to secure sufficient petition signatures to qualify for the Virginia primary.[101] Santorum's campaign also lost delegates he would otherwise have won in Ohio to Romney because he failed to file a full slate of delegates.[102] Another decision candidates must make is whether to participate in partial public financing of their primary campaigns. The presidential campaign finance system provides funds to match small individual contributions during the nomination phase for candidates who agree to remain within spending limitations. However, serious candidates now decline public funding so they are free to spend money they raise without the accompanying spending limitations. For example, George W. Bush declined federal funds in the 2000 and 2004 nomination phase, as did Democrats John Kerry and Howard Dean in 2004. Since then, most candidates turned down matching funds and in 2016, only Martin O'Malley, former governor of Maryland, accepted them.

delegate

A person selected by local citizens to represent them in selecting party leaders and nominees, and in deciding party positions.

superdelegate

Delegates to national party nominating conventions who are not selected through the normal caucus or primary process. They are often state or local party leaders or elected officials.

PRESIDENTIAL PRIMARIES You may not realize this, but in a presidential primary, you are typically not directly voting for your favored presidential candidate.[103] Instead, your vote helps determine how many delegates to the national convention will be won by candidates who meet a minimum threshold. A **delegate** is a person chosen by local partisans in a caucus or primary to represent them in selecting nominees, party leaders, and party positions. These delegates will then go to your party's national convention and vote for their designated candidate. As states, rather than the federal government, have the right to determine how primaries and caucuses are run, every state has different rules for how delegates are assigned to candidates. In 2016, 72 percent of the Democratic delegates and 82 percent of the Republican delegates were chosen in primaries.[104] The rest of the delegates were chosen by state party caucuses or conventions or were party leaders who served as "**superdelegates**," a term describing delegates not typically elected through the primaries or caucuses but who are delegates due to their holding an elective office or party position. States have different means of determining different types of delegates, using the following systems:

- *Proportional representation:* Some delegates to the national convention are allocated based on the percentage of votes the candidates received in a primary. In many states, a candidate must receive a minimum threshold, say 15 percent, of votes in order to receive any delegates. This system was used in most of the states, including several of the largest ones. The Democrats mandate proportional representation for all of their primaries, with 85 percent of the states' delegates elected in primaries determined by the proportional vote in congressional districts. Republicans somewhat followed suit in 2016 when more than half (54.5 percent) of their delegates were determined proportionally, including those in 29 states plus Washington, D.C. and Puerto Rico.
- *Winner take all:* Whoever gets the most votes, even if it is less than 50 percent, wins all of that state's delegates. Republicans still used the winner-take-all system at the state level in eight states and two territories in 2016, including Ohio, Florida, Arizona, Delaware, Nebraska, Montana, New Jersey, and South Dakota. Florida was by far the largest state to use a winner-take-all primary in 2016. Winning all the delegates of a big state such as Florida is an enormous bonus to a candidate.
- *Hybrid Primaries:* Used only by the Republican Party, hybrid primaries are some of the more complicated delegate selection processes. This system usually includes combinations of proportional and winner-take-all systems that can sometimes be quite complex. For example, in Connecticut statewide delegates (also called at-large delegates) are proportionally awarded with a 20 percent threshold. However, if a candidate wins more than 50 percent of the statewide vote, these delegates are all awarded as if in a winner-take-all system. On the other hand, Connecticut district delegates are awarded on a winner-take-all system from the start. Ten states, including South Carolina, Illinois, Missouri, Wisconsin, Maryland, Pennsylvania, and California, had hybrid systems in 2016.
- *Superdelegates and delegate selection without a commitment to a candidate:* Following the 1972 election, when some elected officials and party leaders were not elected delegates, there was an effort to give more influence in selecting the presidential candidate to party leaders and elected officials. These superdelegates were not required to commit to support a particular candidate based on the vote in the state. In 2016, Republicans had two states with 10 or more unbound delegates or superdelegates and Democrats had 21.[105] In 2008 and 2016, a lot of attention was paid to Democratic superdelegates. They cast the deciding vote for Obama in 2008 because no candidate secured a majority of all delegates through the primary and caucus process. In 2016, most Democratic superdelegates committed early to vote for Hillary Clinton, giving Clinton a 45-1 lead on Sanders in superdelegate votes.[106] The GOP has its form of unbound delegates consisting of Republican National Committee members; but there are not nearly as many, nor are they as influential in the nomination process when compared to Democratic superdelegates. In 2018, the DNC voted not to allow superdelegates to vote on the first ballot at the national convention if no candidate has won a majority of the elected delegates. Since the party created superdelegates, all nominees have had a majority of elected delegates. The Obama and Clinton race in 2008 was close with Obama having 51 percent of elected delegates

Voters in states such as Iowa and New Hampshire, which are the first states to pick delegates, bask in media attention for weeks and even months before they cast the first ballots in the presidential sweepstakes. Because these early contests have had the effect of limiting the choices of voters in states that come later in the process, states have tended to move their primaries up in a process called "front loading." California, which traditionally held its primary in June, moved it to March in 2000 and 2004. The change cost California taxpayers, as the state had two primaries, the presidential primary in March and the primary for other offices in June. In a cost-saving move, California returned to June as the date again in 2012 and 2016. but has moved the date for 2020 to March 3, 2018.[107]

As states have competed more aggressively for early positioning in shaping primary contests, the parties have sought to prevent too much front loading. In 2008, when Florida and Michigan moved their primaries up to January 29 and January 15 (respectively) ahead of what party rules allowed, the Democratic National Committee (DNC) voted that delegates so selected would not be seated.[108] The controversy was resolved by giving each Florida and Michigan delegate a half vote, but at the convention, the party relented and each delegate was given a full vote. In 2012, Florida moved up its GOP primary and the national party took away half of the state's delegates as a punishment, but unlike in 2008, this punishment was not rescinded.[109] In 2016, the RNC condensed the primary season and had their national convention earlier.[110] Both parties held their conventions in July 2016, ahead of the Summer Olympics.

caucus
A meeting of local party members to choose party officials or candidates for public office and to decide the platform.

CAUCUSES AND CONVENTIONS A meeting of party members and supporters of various candidates who may elect state or national convention delegates, who in turn vote for the presidential nominee, is called a **caucus**. In 2016, one or both parties used a caucus or convention system (or both) to choose delegates in 15 states and 3 territories.[111] Each state's parties and legislature regulate the methods used.[112] The caucus or convention is the oldest method of choosing delegates, and unlike the primary system, it centers on staffing local party positions such as voting district chair, and often includes party discussions of issues and candidates in addition to a vote on delegates to the county or state convention, who in turn elect delegates to the national convention where the nominee is selected.

The best-known example of a precinct meeting or caucus is in Iowa, because Iowa has held the earliest caucuses or primary since 1972. In January or early February in a presidential election year, Iowans have the opportunity to attend Republican and Democratic precinct meetings or caucuses.[113] In 2016, Bernie Sanders outperformed Hillary Clinton in Democratic caucuses, winning 12 to Clinton's 2. Clinton did better in primaries, winning 26 compared to 10 for Sanders. In the Republican race, Ted Cruz won in Iowa and five other caucuses, while Donald Trump carried 33 primaries, including the one in Indiana, which knocked Cruz and Ohio governor John Kasich out of the race.[114]

STRATEGIES Presidential hopefuls face a dilemma: to get the Republican or Democratic nomination, a candidate has to appeal to the more intense ideological partisans, but during a general election a candidate has to appeal to more moderate voters. For example, those who voted in Republican caucuses and primaries and actively supported campaigns were different from the general population in 2016, in that they were more likely to be male (51 percent), white (90 percent), hold a college degree (51 percent), and make more than $100,000 annually (37 percent).[115]

On the opposite side, Democratic hopefuls had to appeal to the liberal wing of their party as well as to minorities, union members, and environmental activists. Democratic primary voters and caucus goers were different from the general population in 2016, in that they were more likely to be female (57 percent), African American (27 percent), live in urban areas (33 percent), and make less than $30,000 (19 percent).[116]

Once they win their party's nomination, candidates have to win support from moderate and pragmatic voters in the general election, many of whom do not vote in the primaries. If candidates position themselves too far from the moderates in their nomination campaign, they risk being labeled extreme in the general election and losing these votes to their opponents. In 2016, for example, Donald Trump's position on illegal immigration, abortion, and environmental regulation was more conservative than some of his primary opponents like Senator Marco Rubio, former governor Jeb Bush, and Governor John Kasich. Later, during the general election campaign, Clinton and her allies used Trump's earlier statements to portray him as extreme in his views.

Trump did the same thing to Clinton with positions she took during her protracted nomination contest with Bernie Sanders.

The pre-nomination debates are an important element of the campaign when no incumbent is running. The Republican contest for the nomination in 2016 had a series of 12 televised debates (down from 27 in 2012), which generally lasted more than two hours each, with opportunities for some candidates to shine and others to stumble. Because so many sought the GOP nomination in 2016, candidates whose polling numbers fell below a threshold were relegated to the debate earlier in the evening, while candidates with better polling numbers participated in the debate held later in the evening—the more desirable timeslot. Polling also determined the position on the stage, and because Donald Trump was ahead in the polls, he was consistently center stage. He made himself the center of the debate in a second way—he frequently criticized his opponents with disparaging labels, reinforcing negative images of them. When a candidate tried to fight back as Marco Rubio did, that candidate often appeared ineffective in the exchange. The Democrats had nine debates in 2016. Bernie Sanders saw this as the party leadership favoring Hillary Clinton because more debates gave her less well-known opponents more exposure.[117] The party initially planned on six debates and increased the number later in the election cycle.

Strategies for securing the nomination have changed over time. Most candidates choose to run hard in Iowa and New Hampshire, hoping that early showings in these states, which receive a great deal of media attention, will move them into the spotlight for later contests. In recent elections some candidates have chosen to skip some of the earlier contests and enter first in states where their strength lies. John McCain pursued such a strategy in 2000 and again in 2008, ignoring Iowa and concentrating on New Hampshire. John Kasich followed suit in 2016. As a more moderate Republican candidate, Kasich correctly assumed that he would do much better among the many Independent voters in New Hampshire than the very conservative caucus goers of Iowa. Kasich's strong finish in New Hampshire gave him the coveted media attention he had wanted.

During this early phase of the election cycle, the ability of candidates to generate momentum by managing the media's expectations of their performance is especially important. As a result, candidates may intentionally seek to lower expectations so that "doing better than expected" will generate momentum for their campaign. The media and pollsters generally set these expectations in their coverage of candidates. For example, in 2016, Senator Marco Rubio tried to set low expectations for his campaign in Iowa. To the media, he noted that frontrunners Cruz and Trump were spending more time and money in the state. His aim was to make his coming in a strong third place a "better-than-expected" outcome and a sign that he should be taken seriously. Senator Rubio's plan worked. He came in third but still gathered momentum from the Iowa caucus when, immediately after the results were all but in, he delivered a televised victory speech to an excited crowd of supporters. It was as if people forgot that he had only finished in third place.

Donald Trump pursued a novel strategy to secure the 2016 Republican presidential nomination. Initially he was roundly dismissed as a celebrity candidate, one not to be taken seriously. It turned out that celebrity appeal helped generate crowds and a great deal of media attention. One estimate of the free media attention, sometimes called earned media, Trump received valued it at $2 billion through mid-March 2016.[118] Trump received this media attention because of a series of attention-getting actions like garnering the endorsement of Sarah Palin, boycotting an Iowa debate and holding his own event to benefit veterans at the same time, and tweeting about his opponents, even the Pope. Trump also attacked his opponents' spouses and family members. He made disparaging statements about immigrants, Muslims, and women, particularly Fox News anchor Megyn Kelly. He defied convention by not having a large staff and having very few field offices. He preferred large events to the small group gatherings famous in early state caucuses and primaries. In debates, he made himself the center of attention, not by the substance of his answers as much as by the way he belittled his opponents.

The 2016 Republican presidential nomination debates had frequent exchanges when the candidates interrupted each other and tried to speak over one another. Sometimes these exchanges included personal insults, like the one between Marco Rubio and Donald Trump where Trump called Rubio "Little Marco" and Rubio responded that Trump has "little hands," which was interpreted to be an attack on Trump's masculinity. Trump generally got the better of these exchanges.

Stage 2: The National Party Convention

national party convention
A national meeting of delegates elected in primaries, caucuses, or state conventions who assemble once every four years to nominate candidates for president and vice president, ratify the party platform, elect officers, and adopt rules.

The delegates elected in primaries, caucuses, or state conventions assemble at their **national party convention** in the summer before the election to pick the party's presidential and vice presidential candidates. Conventions follow standard rules, routines, and rituals. Usually, the first day is devoted to a keynote address and other speeches touting the party and denouncing the opposition; the second day to committee reports, including party and convention rules and the party platform; the third day to presidential and vice presidential balloting; and the fourth day to the presidential candidate's acceptance speech.

In 2016, Trump had secured enough delegates to win the nomination before the convention although some unsuccessful last ditch attempts were made to derail his candidacy. Absent from the convention were former GOP nominees Mitt Romney and John McCain, and both Presidents Bush, but the 1986 nominee Robert Dole did attend. Democrats who met the week after the Republicans appeared more unified, and Clinton benefited from the support of party leaders like the president and Mrs. Obama and Joe Biden.

National party conventions were once events of high excitement because there was no clear nominee before the convention. In the past, delegates also arrived at national nominating conventions with differing degrees of commitment to presidential candidates; some delegates were pledged to no candidate at all, others to a specific candidate for one or two ballots, and others firmly to one candidate only. Because of reforms encouraging delegates to stick with the person to whom they are pledged, there is now less room to maneuver at conventions, and for half a century, conventions have ratified a candidate who has already been selected in the primaries and caucuses. The focus on delegates and whether they are required to vote for a particular candidate became a subject of debate in the Republican party in 2016, as individuals and groups tried unsuccessfully to engineer a "dump Trump" movement.

Despite the lack of suspense about who the nominee will be, conventions continue to be major media events. For many potential voters the conventions provide an opportunity to learn more about the presidential and vice presidential nominee, emphasizing positive candidate appeal. The conventions can also assist in motivating more partisan voters to join the campaign effort of the nominee. The parties feature their most important speakers and highlight their most important messages in the time the networks give them. As recently as 1988, the major networks gave the Democratic and

Republican National Conventions gavel-to-gavel coverage, meaning that television covered the conventions from the beginning of the first night to the end of the fourth night. The long-term decline in viewership and the reduced hours of coverage have altered the parties' strategies. Now, the major networks leave comprehensive coverage to C-SPAN. In 2008, coverage and viewership of the conventions increased; this was especially the case for the Obama, Palin, and McCain acceptance speeches. An estimated 40 million people viewed the McCain speech, slightly higher than the number who saw Obama's acceptance speech.[119] In 2012, viewership declined in both parties.[120] In 2016, Donald Trump had 32.2 million view his acceptance speech, up from Mitt Romney by 2 million. Hillary Clinton had 29.8 million watch her acceptance speech, down from Barack Obama's 35.7 million viewers in 2012.[121]

Acceptance speeches provide the nominees with an opportunity to define themselves and their candidacy. An example of an acceptance speech that worked more to the benefit of the opposition was Barry Goldwater's speech to the Republican convention in 1964, when he said, "Extremism in the defense of liberty is no vice."[122] This helped to define Goldwater as "dangerous" and "extreme," themes his opponent, Lyndon Johnson, exploited. Democrats hoped Ronald Reagan would also self-destruct in 1980, but instead Reagan came off as warm and confident. At two places in his acceptance speech, he quoted Franklin D. Roosevelt, once by name. Candidates of one party rarely quote a president of the other party in favorable terms as Reagan did.[123] This was clearly an effort to reach out to Democrats. In 2016 it was Hillary Clinton and the Democrats who made overtures to Republicans by featuring a speech by a General, showcasing the parents of a heroic veteran killed in Iraq, and inviting a Republican, Michael Bloomberg, former mayor of New York, to speak. While there were some signs of disunity at the Democratic convention, it was at the Republican convention where a divided party was more evident with Trump delegates booing Texas Senator Ted Cruz when he failed to endorse Donald Trump in his prime-time speech.

THE PARTY PLATFORM Delegates to the national party conventions decide on the *platform,* a statement of party perspectives on public policy. Why does anyone care what is in the party platform? Critics have long pointed out that the party platform is binding on no one and is more likely to hurt than to help a candidate by advocating positions unpopular to moderate or Independent voters, whose support the candidate may need to win in the general election. But presidential candidates, as well as delegates, take the platform seriously because it defines the direction a party wants to take. Also, despite the charge that the platform is ignored, most presidents try to implement much of it.[124]

THE VICE PRESIDENTIAL NOMINEE The choice of the vice presidential nominee garners widespread attention. Rarely does a person actually "run" for the vice presidential nomination, because only the presidential nominee's vote counts. However, there is a good deal of maneuvering to capture that one vote. Sometimes the choice of a running mate is made at the convention—not a time conducive to careful and deliberate thought. But usually it is made before, and the announcement is timed to enhance media coverage and momentum going into the convention. The last time a presidential candidate left the choice of vice president to the delegates was the Democratic convention in 1956.

Presidential candidates often weigh the ability of possible running mates to help them win in the Electoral College. John F. Kennedy's selection of Lyndon Johnson as his running mate was in part an effort to shore up Texas for Democrats.[125] For six of nine presidential elections between 1952 and 1984, Republicans had a Californian on the ticket. Given California's large number of electoral votes this strategy made sense. President Trump is reported to have selected Mike Pence as his running mate in 2016 in part because of his strong support on the Christian right.[126] Presidential candidates have made compatibility a more important criterion as vice presidents like Al Gore, Dick Cheney, and Joe Biden have been more fully integrated into the governing process.

THE VALUE OF CONVENTIONS Why do the parties continue to have conventions if the nominee is known in advance and the vice presidential nominee is the choice of one person? What role do conventions play in our system? For the parties, they are a time of "coming together" to endorse a party program and to build unity and enthusiasm for the fall campaign. For candidates, as well as other party leaders, conventions are a chance to capture the national spotlight and further their political ambitions. For nominees, they are an opportunity to define themselves in positive ways. The potential exists to heal wounds festering from the primary campaign and move into the general election united, but it is not always realized. Conventions can be potentially divisive, as the Republicans learned in 1964 when conservative Goldwater delegates loudly booed New York governor Nelson Rockefeller, and as the Democrats learned in 1968 in Chicago when the convention spotlighted divisions within the party over Vietnam, as well as ugly battles between police and protesters near the convention hotels.

(Top) Donald Trump selected Mike Pence, governor of Indiana, as his running mate. Pence, who served in the U.S. House of Representatives before being elected governor, helped reassure restive Republicans about Trump's candidacy. Pence helped balance the GOP ticket because of his strong conservative stand on social issues. (Bottom) Hillary Clinton selected Virginia Senator Tim Kaine as her running mate. Kaine served as Virginia governor before being elected to the U.S. Senate. More liberal wings of the party were hoping Clinton would select Massachusetts Senator Elizabeth Warren or her primary opponent Bernie Sanders. Supporters of Kaine's selection pointed to his ability to help with blue-collar white voters and Catholics. He was also seen as helping Clinton in the battleground state of Virginia.

NOMINATION BY PETITION There is a way to run for president of the United States that avoids the grueling process of primary elections and conventions—if you are rich enough or well-known enough to use it. Third-party and Independent candidates can qualify for the ballot by meeting each state's ballot access requirements. This takes time, organization, and money. In 2016, the petition process was as simple as submitting the signatures of 1,000 registered voters in Washington State or by paying $500 or securing petition signatures in Colorado or Louisiana, and as difficult as getting the signatures of currently registered voters equal to 2 percent of total votes cast in the last election in North Carolina.[127] Of course, to stand a fighting chance in the election, these independent candidates need to meet the bar set by each one of the 50 states.

Stage 3: The General Election

The national party convention adjourns immediately after the presidential and vice presidential candidates deliver their acceptance speeches to the delegates and the national television audience. Traditionally, the time between the end of the nominating contest and Labor Day was a time for resting, for binding up wounds from the fight for the nomination, for gearing up for action, and for planning campaign strategy. In recent elections, however, the candidates have not paused after effectively securing the nomination but launched directly into all-out campaigning. In 2016, especially in battleground states, the two candidates their vice presidential running mates and supportive groups and individuals made numerous campaign appearances. For example, Hillary Clinton and Tim Kaine went on a bus tour of Rust Belt states while Donald Trump and Mike Pence traveled to campaign events in Colorado.

PRESIDENTIAL DEBATES Televised presidential debates are a major feature of presidential elections. Since 1988, the nonpartisan Commission on Presidential Debates has sponsored and produced the presidential and vice presidential general election debates. The commission includes representatives from such neutral groups as the League of Women Voters. Before the commission became involved, there was often a protracted discussion about the format, the timing, and even whether to have debates. No detail seemed too small to the candidates' managers—whether the candidates would sit or stand, whether they would be able to ask each other questions, whether they would be allowed to bring notes, and whether a single journalist, a panel of reporters, or a group of citizens would ask the questions. By negotiating in advance many of the contentious details and arranging for debate locations, the commission now facilitates the presidential and vice presidential debates.

The format of the 2016 presidential debates had two presidential debates with a standard format and one with a town hall format, and one vice-presidential debate with a standard format. In 2016, the first of the three debates between Donald Trump and Hillary Clinton was the most watched of any presidential debate in history, with 84 million viewers.[128] An estimated 259 million viewers watched the three presidential debates and one vice-presidential debate in 2016, also a record total audience. In the second debate, which followed the release of the Access Hollywood tape in which Trump bragged about groping women, Trump appeared to want to shift the focus to former President Bill Clinton by inviting and seating in a prominent place four of the women who had accused Bill Clinton of sexual assault. When asked about the Access Hollywood Tape, Trump referenced Bill Clinton saying, "Mine are words, his was action."[129] As he had done in the Republican primary debates, he personally attacked Hillary Clinton, saying that if elected he would put her in jail for her handling of the State Department emails.[130] According to the Gallup Poll, Clinton won all three debates in the eyes of the public.[131]

Minor party candidates often charge that those organizing debates are biased in favor of the two major parties. To be included in presidential debates, such candidates must have an average of 15 percent or higher in the five major polls the commission uses for this purpose.[132] Candidates must also be legally eligible and on the ballot in enough states to be able to win at least 270 electoral votes.[133] In recent elections, no minor-party candidate has participated in the debates. Including or excluding minor party candidates remains a contentious issue. Including them takes time away from the major-party candidates, especially if two or more minor-party candidates are invited. It may also reduce the likelihood of both major parties' candidates participating. But excluding them raises issues of fairness and free speech.

Although some critics are quick to express their dissatisfaction with presidential candidates for being so concerned with makeup and rehearsed answers, the debates have provided important opportunities for candidates to distinguish themselves and for the public to weigh their qualifications. Candidates who do well in these debates are at a great advantage. When candidates do not do well, as was the case with Obama in the first debate with Romney in 2012, it can change the campaign dynamic. Obama did damage control personally after the first 2012 debate when he called supporters and said, "This one's on me."[134] Obama bounced back in the second debate and his online contributions spiked in the day or two after that debate. Candidates have to be quick on their feet, seem knowledgeable but not overly rehearsed, and project a positive image. Most presidential candidates are adept at these skills.

TELEVISION AND RADIO ADVERTISING Presidential candidates communicate with voters in a general election and in many primary elections through broadcast television, radio, cable television, and satellite radio. Approximately 630,000 commercials were run across the country during the 2004 presidential election,[135] in 2008 the number rose to 782,782,[136] and in 2012 it hit 1,015,615 ads and in 2016, it was little changed at 1,030,069.[137] Spending on television across federal races has risen from $623 million in 2000 to nearly $2 billion in 2012, before dropping to $1.835 billion in 2016.[138]

As with campaign activity generally, the competitive or battleground states see much more activity, including candidate visits and mail or phone calls about the candidates. Candidates and their consultants believe that advertising on television and radio helps motivate people to vote and persuade voters to vote for them—or against their opponent. With the growth in cable television, candidates can target ads to particular audiences—people who watch the Golf Channel or Fox News, for instance. Political party committees and interest groups also run television and radio ads for and against candidates.

THE GROUND GAME With many millions of citizens voting in general elections, candidates and others seeking to persuade voters emphasize tools like television ads, sometimes called the "air war." But campaigns also pursue a "ground game" that emphasizes direct voter contact at the workplace, home, on the phone, and through social media. The objective of the voter contact is to persuade the person to register to vote if they are not already registered and to vote for a particular candidate. Rather than communicate with whole neighborhoods or all registered voters, campaigns now target individual voters with personalized appeals.

The Obama campaign of 2008 and 2012 set a new and high standard for identifying voter support of Obama and helping get these voters to the polls. They did this through an investment in building a large database of prospective supporters and engaging volunteers to communicate with many people individually on the phone, in person, and through social media.[139] Clinton built on the Obama approach in 2016 and Trump utilized field offices and staff that had previously been deployed by the RNC.[140]

THE OUTCOME Though each election is unique, politicians, pollsters, and political scientists have collected enough information to agree broadly on a number of basic factors they believe affect outcomes. The state of the economy probably has the most to do with who wins a presidential election, and in 2016 the economic issues gave Democrats a slight advantage. Exit polls found party identification remained very important in 2016, with 90 percent of Republicans voting for Trump and 89 percent of Democrats voting for Clinton.[141] With both candidates viewed unfavorably, neither nominee dominated on candidate appeal. The state of the economy is the issue that often has the most to do with who wins a presidential election. In 2016 even though the economy had improved in most states since the great recession of 2008, Trump used frustration with trade deals, stagnant wages, and the idea that the system was rigged against working people to build support in states like Wisconsin, Michigan and Ohio, Pennsylvania. But as we have noted, most voters vote primarily on the basis of party and candidate appeal.[142]

Who wins also depends on voter turnout, and here the strength of party organization and allied groups is important. The Democrats' long-standing advantage in the number of people who identify themselves as Democrats has declined in recent years and is mitigated by generally higher voter turnout among Republicans.

In 2016, the Clinton campaign assumed turnout among key demographic groups that were key to electing Barack Obama would turnout at the same levels in 2016 as they did in 2012 and that they would vote for Clinton in similar proportions to how they had voted for Obama. Neither case turned out to be true. Blacks, Hispanics, women, and younger voters turned out less in 2016 than in 2012, and they gave Clinton a smaller percentage of their votes. Among white voters, the share who voted for Trump was slightly higher than had been the case in 2012 with Romney. Among white voters without college degrees, Trump received two-thirds of the vote, far more than any other Republican since 1980. Finally, Clinton's 18-point advantage among voters age 18 to 29 was less than Obama's 24-point advantage with this group in 2012 and his 34-point advantage in 2008.[143]

While attention to vote share among different segments of the population is informative, Trump won the presidency by winning states, which in turn led to his Electoral College victory. His ability to assemble pluralities in enough states to surpass 270 electoral votes was the key to his victory. The outcome of the 2016 election is a reminder of the ways federalism is woven into the fabric of American democracy.

Improving Elections (Impact)

8.6 Describe common criticisms of presidential elections and evaluate proposed reforms to address them.

A combination of party rules and state laws determines how we choose nominees for president. Reformers agree that the current process is flawed but disagree about which aspects should be changed. Concern over how we choose presidents now centers on the number, timing, and representativeness of presidential primaries and caucuses, and the role of the Electoral College, including the possibility that a presidential election may be thrown into the House of Representatives.

Reforming Campaign Finance

The continuing problems with federal election fund-raising are easy to identify: dramatically escalating costs, spending by Super PACs and other outside groups, some of which are not required to disclose their donors, congressional candidates' dependence on PAC money, challengers' low visibility and lack of competitiveness (especially in House races), and the advantage wealthy individuals have in funding their own campaigns or their preferred candidates. The potential danger posed by large contributions directly influencing lawmakers was reduced by the BCRA, but the Supreme Court struck down much of that legislation, resulting in a campaign finance structure that is increasingly deregulated.[144] The upshot is that individuals and interest groups have been given much greater latitude to attempt to influence election outcomes. While there have been some examples of foreign individuals seeking to influence U.S. elections, the involvement of Russia in funding campaign efforts against Hillary Clinton and for Donald Trump in 2016 is unprecedented.

SUPER PACS AND 501(C) GROUPS Donald Trump and Bernie Sanders both made much of the fact that unlike their competitors for their party's nomination, they did not have Super PACs. Further, they thought they should be prohibited. After securing the nomination, Trump stepped back from his strong opposition to Super PACs, Hillary Clinton, who did have a Super PAC, frequently said that she thought the *Citizens United* opinion should be overturned, a reference to banning Super PACs.

Because Trump and Sanders spurned Super PACs and still were competitive, some question Super PACs' importance. At the same time, however, Super PACs were crucial in helping sustain the candidacies of Rubio, Christie, Carson, and Kasich.

While Super PACs can spend large amounts of money and empower wealthy donors, the spending and donors are fully disclosed (see Figure 8.6). That is not the case with Section 501(c) groups. Candidates made greater use of these groups in 2016 and, as long as the IRS does not appear to be investigating their compliance with the law, it is likely more and more candidates will make use of these groups as well. The major advantage of 501(c) groups is they do not have to disclose their donors, nor do they have to report some types of expenditures. Should reform be seriously considered in the future it is likely that changes in the IRS code about section 501(c)(4) groups will be on the agenda.

FOREIGN FUNDING OF ELECTIONEERING How campaigns are funded is, as we have shown, a contentious topic. But one aspect of campaign finance is widely agreed upon as essential: the campaign contributions to candidates, parties, and interest groups seeking to influence the outcome of U.S. elections come from U.S. citizens and not from foreign individuals, corporations, or governments. Although some scholars argue that one of every ten dollars donated to political campaigns come from foreigners working through lobbyists, more direct means of foreign donations

Opposition to Super PACs often focuses on the wealthy donors who fund Super PACs and 501(c)(4) groups. Here actress Rosario Dawson takes part in a demonstration on Capitol Hill in Washington, D.C. She and other protestors also called for restoration of the Voting Rights Act and statehood for the District of Columbia.

FIGURE 8.6 SPENDING BY OUTSIDE GROUPS IN 2012, 2014, AND 2016.

Spending by outside groups has been substantial since the Supreme Court permitted independent expenditure only committees (Super PACs) in 2010. Note the substantial increase in Super PAC spending in 2016 was over 2012. Some of the spending by 501(c)(4) groups is not disclosed and some is only reported months after the election, so this reported spending in 2016 is incomplete.

SOURCE: "Outside Spending," *Center for Responsible Politics*, http://www.opensecrets.org/outsidespending/fes_summ.php?cycle=2016 (accessed November 16, 2016).

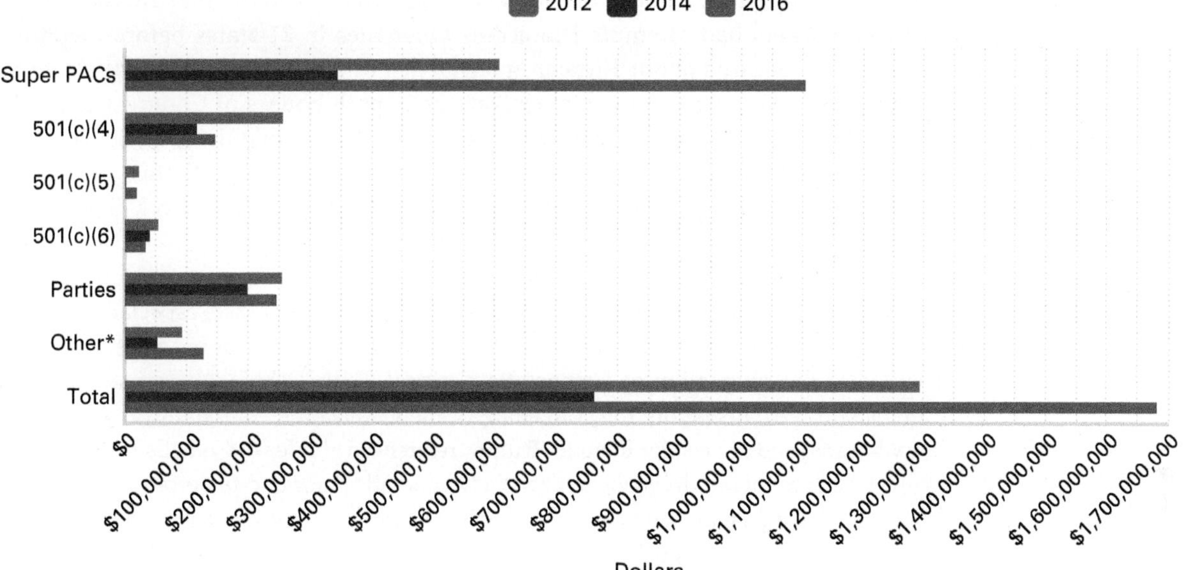

NOTE: *Other indicates individuals, corporations, and other groups.

or interventions in American elections are highly controversial and viewed by many as threatening to the American democratic system.[145] While the 2016 election is a prominent example of controversial foreign donations and involvement, this issue has arisen in previous campaigns. In 1996, news reports highlighted the Department of Justice investigations into whether foreign nationals had given funds to the Democratic National Committee, the Bill Clinton Defense fund, or the Clinton–Gore 1996 campaign.[146] Several individuals involved were convicted of campaign finance violations.[147] While some of the campaign funds were returned when their source was discovered to be foreign nationals, the issue remained prominent for years and was part of opposition ads in the 2000 campaign as Al Gore, the Democratic nominee in 2000, had been involved in the 1996 scandal.

In a series of revelations that might be mistaken for the plot line of an espionage novel, the U.S. Central Intelligence Agency (CIA) concluded and announced one week before the Electoral College voted in December 2016 that the Russian government sought to help elect Donald Trump in the 2016 U.S. presidential election. The Federal Bureau of Investigation (FBI) agreed that there was compelling evidence of Russian actions against the Democratic Party, and with the intent to help elect Donald Trump.[148] The intelligence agencies agreed that the Russians had attempted to hack into both national political parties as well as the personal email of John Podesta, Hillary Clinton's campaign manager, though they only leaked materials damaging to Clinton and the Democrats. The FBI investigation into such illegal activity expanded to encompass members of the Trump campaign, including Michael Flynn, who had become National Security Advisor in the Trump administration. After only 24 days on the job, Flynn resigned his position at the request of President Trump amid concerns that Flynn had misled White House officials about the details of a phone conversation with the Russian ambassador.

The investigation into Russian interference in the 2016 election took an unexpected turn when President Trump fired FBI Director James Comey, who was heading the investigation into Russian meddling in the 2016 election, in early May 2017. Comey's firing led to bipartisan calls for a Special Counsel to take charge of the investigation. Former FBI director Robert Mueller was selected to head the investigation. Mueller's investigation is complex and ongoing.

The extent of Russian meddling in the election was extensive. Months after the election, the Department of Homeland Security disclosed that Russian government hackers had attempted to access voter files in 21 states before the 2016 election.[149] Concerns about Russian interference in the 2016 presidential election led to congressional committee investigations in both houses of Congress in 2017. Late in his administration, President Obama ordered the expulsion of 35 Russian diplomats, the closure of two Russian compounds in the United States, and some additional sanctions against Russia as a response to the Russian 2016 U.S. election interference.[150]

The Russians used the leaks from the hacked emails to embarrass Clinton and the Democrats, and their content became issues in the presidential race, especially as they were timed to accomplish maximum damage to the Democrats. For example, the leaks that led to the resignation of Democratic National Chair Debbie Wasserman Schultz came just three days before the convening of the Democratic National Convention.[151] Republicans, and especially Donald Trump, referenced the leaked emails on the campaign trail to point out divisions within the Democratic Party and to perpetuate concern about the private email server used by Hillary Clinton during her service as Secretary of State. Trump expressed his hope that Russia would find and publish the Clinton emails that, due to their personal nature, had not been shared with investigators. At a news conference about the Clinton emails, Trump directly urged Russia to hack into and release Clinton's emails. Trump critics responded, saying it was, "a serious threat against the security of the West" for a presidential candidate to invite a foreign adversary to intervene in an election by conducting illegal espionage against a political opponent.[152]

Russian involvement in the 2016 presidential election extended to direct contact with voters via Facebook, Twitter, and other social media. The nature and extent of this activity was only learned months after the election and the full story of this involvement remains unknown. In October 2017, Facebook disclosed that 126 million people saw content from the Internet Research Agency, a Russian firm with connections to the Russian government.[153] What is known is that the Russian campaign was sophisticated, using trolls within Facebook, for example, to target particular segments of the population with messages intended to influence whether they would vote at all and, if they decided to vote, for whom they voted. The Russians' efforts were not limited to Facebook. There were an estimated 288 million automated, election related tweets after Labor Day paid for by Russian accounts. Some of these tweets falsely told people they could "vote by text."[154] Although our understanding of Russian involvement in the 2016 election continues to develop, the gradually unfolding revelations have stunned and perturbed the American public.

This is the building in St. Petersburg, Russia where it is believed the Internet Research Agency mounted its efforts to interfere in the 2016 U.S. presidential election. The agency ran ads on Facebook, Twitter, Instagram, and other platforms. It also ran a "troll factory."

In May 2018, *The New York Times* reported that Robert Muller's investigation includes the possible involvement of the United Arab Emirates and Saudi Arabia in the 2016 election, and efforts after the election to build relationships with the new Trump administration. The pre-election involvement centers on a meeting at Trump Tower in New York City with Donald Trump, Jr. the president's son, and an emissary for two wealthy Arab princes, along with a Republican donor and private security contractor. Much less is known about what, if anything, came from this meeting.[155]

Americans take pride in their ability to elect leaders. Efforts by a foreign adversary to interfere with voter files, provide disinformation to voters, actively seek to hurt one presidential candidate, and thereby help a preferred candidate is new in American politics. Russian involvement in the U.S. presidential election will likely have profound institutional and international ramifications and many questions remain unanswered. How will it influence the role of intelligence agencies in the Trump administration? How will Congress conclude the multiple ongoing investigations of this matter, and how will President Trump respond? Will Russian involvement result in retaliation from the U.S government? How will the media treat what is in some ways a story stranger than fiction?

DEPENDENCE ON PACS FOR CONGRESSIONAL INCUMBENTS Most House incumbents' campaign money comes from PACs. In recent years, about half of incumbents seeking reelection raised more money from PACs than from individuals (see Figure 8.7).[156] Senators get a smaller percentage of their campaign funds from PACs, but because they spend so much more, they need to raise even more money from PACs than do House incumbents. PACs are pragmatic and give largely to incumbents. The BCRA left intact the cap for PAC contributions at $10,000 for the primary and general election combined. Incumbents will continue to rely on PACs because relatively few individuals have the means to give $5,400 to a campaign, as they could have in 2015–2016. It also often takes less time to raise money from PACs than from individuals.

To be sure, PACs and individuals spend money on campaigns for many reasons. Most of them want certain laws to be passed or repealed, certain funds to be appropriated, or certain administrative decisions to be rendered. At a minimum, they want access to officeholders and a chance to talk with members before key votes.

FIGURE 8.7 HOW PACS AND OTHERS ALLOCATED CAMPAIGN CONTRIBUTIONS TO HOUSE CANDIDATES, 2015–2016

The two major funders of U.S. House candidates are individuals and PACs. PACs give primarily to incumbents. Individuals give more to incumbents but much more to challengers and open seat candidates. When the blue bars in Figure 8.7 are combined, the advantage enjoyed by incumbents in fundraising is striking.

SOURCE: Compiled from Federal Election Commission data.

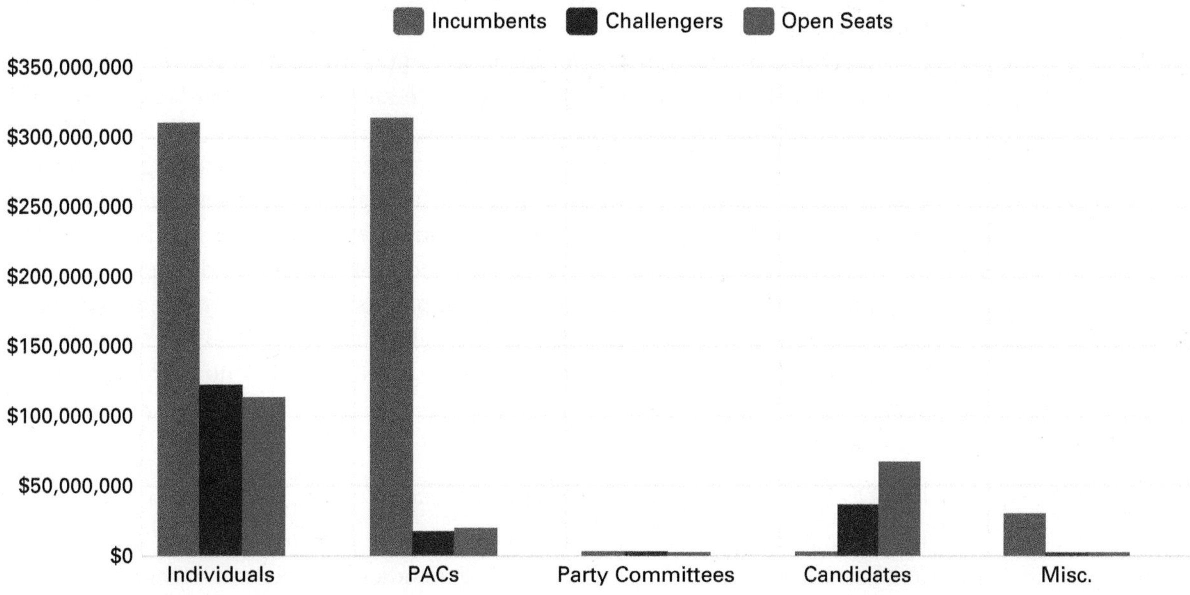

Defenders of PACs point out that there is no evidence for a causal relationship between contributions and legislators' votes.[157] But influence in the legislative process depends on access to staff and members of Congress, and most analysts agree that campaign contributions give donors extraordinary access. PACs influence the legislative process in other ways as well. Their access with friendly legislators may help them block some items from the legislative agenda and may lead to input on the drafting of legislation or amendments to existing bills.

CANDIDATES' PERSONAL WEALTH Campaign finance legislation cannot constitutionally restrict rich candidates—the Rockefellers, the Kennedys, the Perots, the Clintons, the Romneys, the Bloombergs, or the Trumps—from spending heavily on their own campaigns. Big money can make a big difference, and wealthy candidates can afford to spend big money. In presidential politics, this advantage can be most meaningful before the primaries begin. The personal wealth advantage also applies to congressional and gubernatorial races. Investment banker Jon Corzine spent $133.5 million in one decade on his own gubernatorial and U.S. Senate campaigns, winning two of the three races.[158] Meg Whitman, the unsuccessful Republican candidate for governor of California in 2010, spent over $140 million of her own money on her campaign, breaking the previous record held by New York Mayor Michael Bloomberg ($109 million). Donald Trump emphasized in his nomination campaign that he was different from his opponents because no donors owned him. He gave his own campaign about $50 million in the period before July 2016.[159] He later said he planned on spending $100 million of his own money on his candidacy. The amount he actually loaned his campaign in 2016 was $66 million.[160]

DEREGULATION VERSUS MORE AGGRESSIVE REFORM The BCRA's incremental reforms and the subsequent Supreme Court decisions have not resolved the issues of campaign finance. Among the unresolved issues are how presidential campaigns will be financed, the role of Super PACs, the adequacy of disclosure, and the long-term strength and viability of the political parties. More broadly, the FEC's inability to reach decisions because of its frequent partisan deadlock, as demonstrated by its inaction on Super PACs, has generated growing pressure to reform the commission itself.

Proponents of deregulation portray post-BCRA elections as further evidence that limiting money in elections is impossible. The surge in individual donors in 2008 and 2012 is also cited as further evidence that public financing is unnecessary. Those favoring deregulation will continue to push for disclosure as the sole regulatory aim of government in this area.

In contrast to deregulation proponents, others argue for even more aggressive reforms than those found in BCRA. They argue for banning Super PACs, restructuring public financing of presidential elections, providing incentives for individual contributions to candidates and parties, and prohibiting foreign corporations and others doing business with the government from spending money on federal elections. While there is near consensus on the importance of disclosing donors' contributions, there are still ways for individuals and groups to avoid doing so. Enhanced disclosure, including requirements that campaigns electronically file contributions more frequently, is a first step for reformers. Both sides are likely to agree that the Federal Election Commission needs to be changed, but will not agree on how to change it.

Reforming the Nominating Process

In 2008 and 2012, the importance of voters in early primary or caucus states such as Iowa and New Hampshire continues to generate controversy, as these early states are not broadly representative of the country or of their respective parties. Voters in primaries and caucuses also tend to be more ideological than voters generally, a further bias in the current nominating process. As in 2008, the 2016 nomination contest pushed to the forefront controversy over whether the Democrats' proportionality rules made it more difficult to have a winner emerge from the process. On the Republican side, the election of delegates at conventions was criticized, especially the Colorado Republicans' use of the state and district conventions rather than a primary or caucus to select delegates for the national convention. Ted Cruz out-organized Trump and other candidates to win all 34 Colorado delegates despite Trump leading in state polls. Finally, the role of superdelegates in the Democratic nomination contests raised concerns about their role compared to delegates selected through a democratic process.

What would the critics substitute for state presidential primaries (see Figure 8.8)? Some argue in favor of a *national presidential primary* that would take the form of a single nationwide election, probably held in May or September, or separate state primaries held in all the states on the same day.[161] Supporters contend that a one-shot national presidential primary (though a runoff might be necessary) would be simple, direct, and representative. It would cut down the wear-and-tear on candidates and the media coverage would attract a large turnout. Opponents argue that such a reform would worsen the present system by enhancing the role of showmanship and gamesmanship and hurting the chances of candidates who lack strong financial backing due to its enormous expense.

A more modest proposal is to hold *regional primaries,* possibly at two- or three-week intervals across the country. Regional primaries might bring more coherence to the process and encourage more emphasis on issues of regional concern. But such primaries would retain most of the disadvantages of the present system—especially the emphasis on money and media. Clearly, they would give an advantage to candidates from whatever region held the first primary, encouraging regional candidates and increasing polarization among sections of the country.

FIGURE 8.8 VOTER TURNOUT IN THE 2016 PRESIDENTIAL PRIMARIES

In 2016, as in 2008, the presidential nomination contest did not have an incumbent president or vice president seeking the nomination. Even though both parties had spirited contests for the nomination, most states did not have voter turnout over 25 percent, and in six states turnout was under 10 percent. Only in the first primary state, New Hampshire, was turnout above 50 percent. In Iowa, the first caucus state, turnout was 16 percent.

SOURCE: Michael McDonald, "2016 Presidential Nomination Contest Turnout Rates," U.S. Election Project http://www.electproject.org/2016P.

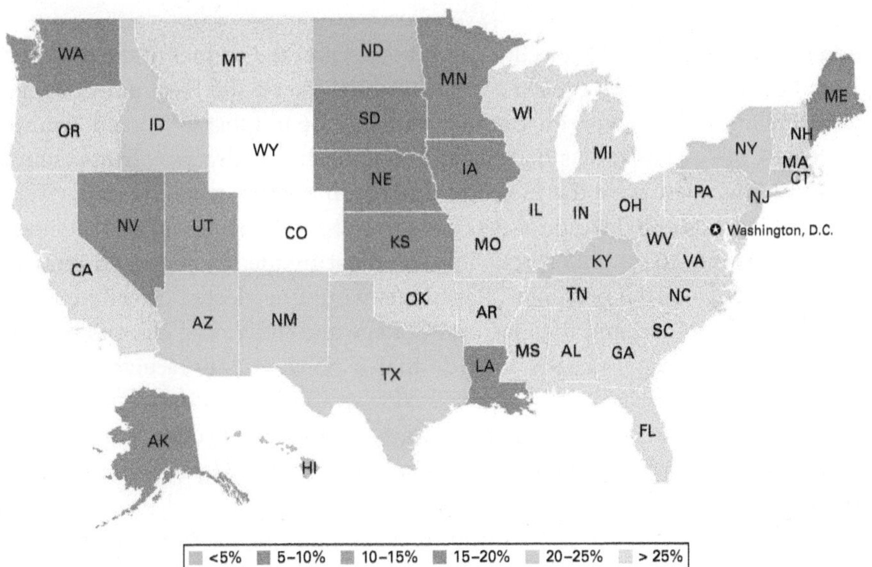

A different proposal is to ban caucuses and replace them with primaries. Critics of caucuses point to the restriction that only those who can attend a meeting at a designated time are allowed to vote. What about people who have to work at that time? What about people who need to be traveling on that day? Some individuals do not like the nature of the caucus, which is more like a meeting than standard in-person voting. For these reasons, critics contend, caucuses are less representative of the party or public than primaries where voters can cast absentee ballots and can vote in person throughout Election Day.

Bernie Sanders and Donald Trump both benefited when primaries or caucuses were open to Independents, as was the case in New Hampshire. Should nomination contests be limited to registered partisans? The argument for only party registrants (closed primaries or caucuses) is that choosing the party's nominee should be up to the party and if people want a voice in the party they should register with the party. Those who favor open processes where Independents can vote argue that this broadens the party and demonstrates which candidates have broader electoral appeal. Speaking of the New York closed primary, Bernie Sanders said, "Three million people in the state of New York who are Independents have lost their right to vote in the Democratic or Republican primary. That's wrong. You're paying for this election. It's administered by the state. You have a right to vote. And that's a very unfortunate thing which I hope will change."[162] On the Republican side, the New York closed primary rule meant two of Donald Trump's children could not vote because they had not changed their registration from Independent to Republican in time.[163]

Given the problems with the current nomination process, why has it not been reformed? Part of the answer is strong resistance from the states that benefit from the current system. In our federal system, imposing a national or regional primary means certain states would lose power.

Does the present nominating process help or hurt candidates and parties? News coverage of candidates in nomination contests allows voters to evaluate the candidates' political qualities and their abilities to organize campaigns; communicate through the media; stand up under pressure; avoid making mistakes (or recover when mistakes are made); adjust their appeals to shifting events and to different regions of the country; control and utilize their staffs; and be decisive, articulate, resilient, humorous, informed, and ultimately successful in winning votes. In short, supporters of the current system claim that primaries test candidates on the very qualities they must exhibit in the presidency.[164]

Reforming the Electoral College

The Florida recount after the 2000 election, and the fact that the winner of the popular vote did not become president, renewed a national debate on the Electoral College. The fact that Hillary Clinton won the popular vote in 2016 but lost to Donald Trump in the Electoral College has intensified the call to abolish this process. Trump himself called for doing away with the Electoral College in a tweet when he said, "The Electoral College is different. I would rather have the popular vote because it's, to me, it's much easier to win the popular vote."[165] The most frequently proposed reform is *direct popular election* of the president. Presidents would be elected directly by the voters, just as governors are, and the Electoral College and individual electors would be abolished. Such proposals usually provide that if no candidate receives at least 40 percent of the total popular vote, a *runoff election* would be held between the two contenders with the most votes. Supporters argue that direct election would give every voter the same weight in the presidential balloting in accordance with the one-person, one-vote doctrine.

Opponents contend that the plan would further undermine federalism, encourage unrestrained majority rule and political extremism, and hurt the most populous and competitive states, which would lose some of their present influence. Others fear that the plan would make presidential campaigns more remote from the voters; candidates might stress television and give up their forays into diners and shopping centers.[166]

From time to time, Congress considers proposals for a constitutional amendment to elect presidents directly.[167] Such proposals seldom get far, however, due to strong opposition from those who believe they may be disadvantaged by such a change, especially small states and minority groups whose role is enlarged by the Electoral College. Groups such as African Americans and farmers, for example, fear they might lose their swing vote power—their ability to make a difference in key states that may tip the Electoral College balance.

Another alternative to the Electoral College is sometimes called the National Bonus Plan. This plan would add another 102 Electoral College members to the current 538. These 102 members would be awarded on a winner-take-all basis to the candidate with the most votes, so long as that candidate received more than 40 percent of the popular vote. This system would avoid elections being thrown into the House of Representatives and would help ensure that the candidate who won the popular vote became president. The most serious liabilities of this plan are that it is complicated and that it requires a runoff election if there is no winner.

Two states, Maine and Nebraska, have already adopted a district system in which the candidate who carries each congressional district gets that electoral vote and the candidate who carries the state gets the state's two additional electoral votes. This quasi-proportional representation system has the advantage of not shutting out a candidate who is strong in some areas of a state and not others, but otherwise it does not address the larger concerns with the Electoral College.

The failure of attempts to change the system points to an important conclusion about procedural reform: U.S. voters normally do not focus on procedures. Even after the intense controversy on the outcome of the 2000 election, including the role of the Electoral College, reform was not seriously considered.

CONCLUSION

Elections in the United States occur frequently. This is due in part to our voting on who may run under the party label (primary elections) as well as who may serve in office (general elections). Federalism remains important in elections, as is evident by the different and complex state rules for candidates seeking the presidency.

As discussed at the beginning of the chapter, the United States has been innovative in finding ways to inform voters through news media, social media, and notably, candidate debates. Voters have come to expect debates for president and statewide offices like governor or U.S. Senator. Presidential debates have a large viewing and listening audience and can help shape public perceptions. One important advantage of debates is they provide you with a direct comparison of the two major-party nominees in a live format. But some candidates will want to avoid debates, especially incumbents. You can make a difference by encouraging media outlets to televise debates and to join with others in pressing candidates to debate.

It is clear that elections matter in a constitutional democracy. They determine who holds office and what policies the government adopts. Elections are complex, and the rules of the game affect how it is played. Our winner-take-all system is an example of a rule that has influenced the nature of our party system, the strategy of candidates, and the stability of our institutions. Over time, the rules of the electoral game have been changed. Today, party nominees are largely selected by voters in primaries, whereas early in our nation's history candidates were selected by party caucuses. Over time, our system has expanded the role of citizens and voters, as illustrated by the predominance of primaries. The expansion of suffrage and of the role of voters in deciding nominees and ballot questions means you have more control over your government.

Central to the functioning of a constitutional democracy, like that in the United States, is a well administered system of fair elections so that the outcome has legitimacy. Voter trust and confidence in elections centers on the kinds of issues we have examined in this chapter. Over time, we have learned ways to make elections better, including the secret ballot, the disclosure and limitation of campaign contributions, and the expansion of the role of citizens through primaries. As important as these structural and institutional changes are, without the participation of people in politics, the system will not function well. The involvement of the Russian government and foreign nationals in the 2016 campaign working to defeat a candidate and the efforts to hack into voting systems were unprecedented. What actions the government will take to reduce the threat of election hacking and prosecute those who broke the law are going to be ongoing concerns.

Although there have been great improvements in the way we run elections, there are still problems to be solved and new issues will emerge. As we discussed earlier in this chapter, there has been a substantial change in how campaigns are financed; candidate spending is now increasingly overshadowed by Super PACs, Section 501(c) organizations, and others. In 2016 these groups spent heavily in battleground Senate and House races. Should Super PACs face additional regulations? Should it be mandatory that donor information and contribution amounts be made public? Some candidates are seeking to counter the role of large donors with more small individual contributions. Given the importance of the Supreme Court in this policy area and others we have discussed, you now know to push your senators for their views on who should serve on the Court. Should Court nominees have to explain their views on campaign finance? These are questions you will have to confront, and your action (or inaction) will impact the quality of the electoral process.

You can make a difference in elections in many ways. You can vote, volunteer with the political party or candidate of your choosing, contribute financially to a candidate, or join a group around a common interest, such as reducing the money spent on political campaigns. You can also influence how your friends and neighbors vote since they are more likely to respond positively to a personal request to vote for a candidate or ballot proposition than they are to generic party requests or from an unknown campaign worker. New technologies like mobile payment apps on smartphones make participation easier for you than any prior generation. And in the future you may well be able to vote via the Internet; another change that could alter the way you make a difference.

REVIEW THE CHAPTER

Elections: The Rules of the Game (Structure)

8.1 Outline the procedures for presidential and congressional elections, p. 216.

The U.S. electoral system is based on winner-take-all rules, typically with single-member districts. These rules encourage a moderate, two-party system. Fixed and staggered terms of office add predictability to our electoral system. Although term limits have been popular with the public, Congress has not introduced any term limits to its members.

The Electoral College is the means by which presidents are elected. To win a state's electoral votes, a candidate must have a plurality of votes in that state. Except in two states, the winner takes all. Thus, candidates cannot afford to lose the popular vote in the most populous states. The Electoral College also gives disproportionate power to the largest states, especially if they are competitive. It has the potential to defeat the national popular vote winner.

Counting Votes (Structure)

8.2 Assess how well American elections are administered, p. 221.

Ballot-counting irregularities, equipment shortages and problems, and voter registration challenges have been problems in recent elections. Standardizing election administration; replacing old voting machines with computers, the Internet, and vote-by-mail elections; and reforming registration procedures are all potential solutions to election problems.

Money in U.S. Elections (Action)

8.3 Evaluate the influence of money in elections and the main approaches to campaign finance reform, p. 223.

The rising costs of campaigns have led to declining competition for congressional seats and increasing dependence on PACs and wealthy donors. Because large campaign contributors are suspected of improperly influencing public officials, Congress has long sought to regulate political contributions. The main approaches to reform have been (1) imposing limitations on giving, receiving, and spending political money; (2) requiring public disclosure of the sources and uses of political money; and (3) giving governmental subsidies to presidential candidates, campaigns, and parties, including incentive arrangements. Present regulation includes all three approaches.

Running for Congress (Structure)

8.4 Assess the influence of redistricting, incumbency, partisanship, and candidate appeal on the outcome of congressional elections, p. 230.

Candidates for Congress must raise money, develop a personal organization, and increase visibility in order to be nominated for the election. Incumbents have significant advantages over their challengers, with House incumbents having stronger advantages than their Senate counterparts, whose challengers often have strong name recognition and more easily raise money. The cost of elections and incumbency advantages make congressional elections widely noncompetitive.

Running for President (Action)

8.5 Outline how presidential campaigns are organized ssand evaluate methods for reaching voters, p. 237.

The three stages in a presidential election are winning enough delegate support in presidential primaries and caucuses to secure the nomination, campaigning at the national party convention, and mobilizing voters in enough states to get the most votes in the Electoral College. The nomination phase is dominated by more partisan and often more ideological voters. Early contests are often important, which means candidates start early. The connection phase is important in defining candidates for less engaged voters. The general election concentrates candidate time and money in a relatively few contested states.

Improving Elections (Impact)

8.6 Describe common criticisms of presidential elections and evaluate proposed reforms to address them, p. 247.

The present presidential selection system is under criticism because of its length and expense, because of uncertainties and biases in the Electoral College, and because it seems to test candidates for media skills less needed in the White House than the ability to govern, including the capacity to form coalitions and make hard decisions. Reform efforts center on presidential primaries, the Electoral College, and campaign finance.

LEARN THE TERMS

winner-take-all system, p. 218
single-member district, p. 218
proportional representation, p. 218
Electoral College, p. 219
faithless elector, p. 219
Federal Election Commission (FEC), p. 225
Bipartisan Campaign Reform Act (BCRA), p. 226
soft money, p. 226
hard money, p. 226
issue advocacy, p. 227
independent expenditures, p. 228
Super PAC, p. 228
safe seat, p. 230
coattail effect, p. 231
candidate appeal, p. 234
national tide, p. 234
name recognition, p. 234
delegate, p. 238
superdelegate, p. 238
caucus, p. 240
national party convention, p. 242

CHAPTER 9

The Media and U.S. Politics

During the 2016 presidential campaign Russian government sponsored groups ran Facebook ads and posts targeted at particular voters. This was one of the Russian ads, falsely claiming the image was from a group called "Army of Jesus," when it really came from the Russian funded Internet Research Agency. The post was sent to people who followed topics on Facebook like Jesus and conservatism in the United States, the Bible, Christianity, Laura Ingraham, Bill O'Reilly, and Mike Huckabee. As noted in the comment forwarded with the ad, the posting was intended to persuade others that Hillary Clinton was Satanic and though Donald Trump was "not a saint," he was moral and deserving of the vote in 2016. The Russian use of Facebook through ads and posts like this may have been seen by as many as 126 million Americans.

LEARNING OBJECTIVES

9.1 Explain the origins, structure, and functions of the news media, and the nature of constitutional protections of Freedom of the Press (Structure), p. 260.

9.2 Describe the effect of recent trends in how Americans get their news (Action), p. 265.

9.3 Assess the influence of the news media on American public opinion and elections (Impact), p. 275.

9.4 Describe the news media's relationship to governance in the United States (Impact), p. 282.

Just as with radio in the 1930s and television in the 1960s, social media is transforming American politics today. This was evident in the 2016 election as Donald Trump used Twitter to drive news coverage and amass a large advantage in news coverage over his opponents in the nomination contest and over Hillary Clinton in the general election. Political scientists refer to this as "earned media," and Trump exploited the news media's interest in reporting on his latest label for his opponents like "big Looser" (Marco Rubio), "crazy" (Bernie Sanders), "low energy" (Jeb Bush), "crooked" (Hillary Clinton) or "Lyin'" (Ted Cruz).[1]

After the election, the public also learned of an extensive effort by Russia to communicate directly with voters in the United States through Facebook, Twitter, Google, and Instagram. Inflammatory and attention getting ads like the one captured in a screen shot from a Russian financed group was targeted to American voters. The message in this ad was aimed at Christian conservatives,[2] but the Russians also targeted Facebook users who liked human rights or Malcolm X from a site named Blacktavist.[3]

In January 2017, U.S. intelligence agencies collectively concluded that the Russian Ordered "Influence Campaign" aided Donald Trump in the election.[4] Over the next several months the scope of the Russian interference was more fully acknowledged. Facebook founder and CEO Mark Zuckerberg, initially expressed scepticism that Russia used Facebook, but he later disclosed that its 2016 posts may have reached up to 1.8 million users. Instagram, Google. Twitter, and YouTube were also part of this Russian effort, reaching collectively millions more Americans.[5] At the same time, the Russians were attempting to hack into the voting lists and systems of as many as 21 states,[6] and compromised the voting systems in seven states.[7]

Testifying before the Senate Intelligence Committee, former FBI Director James Comey conveyed the seriousness of the Russian effort as follows: "We're talking about a foreign government, that using technical intrusion, lots of other methods, tried to shape the way we think, we vote, we act. That is a big deal. And people need to recognize it. It's not about Republicans and Democrats. They're coming after America."[8]

In this chapter, we examine how the media acts within the constitutional structure to impact important public policy problems. Although many functions served by the news media have not changed substantially over time, technology and consumer preferences for consuming news media have changed significantly. Internet news technology, for example, provides for much greater immediacy in news reporting and much greater opportunities for individuals to act on the news by responding to tweets, blogs, or articles posted online. It also raises significant questions about how the constitutional structure shapes media behavior and even whom we think of as "the media" or as "journalists." Finally we will explore the ways the media can facilitate individual citizen's actions in affecting government policy.

The Structure and Functions of the News Media and the Constitutional Protections of Freedom of the Press (Structure)

9.1 Explain the origins, structure, and functions of the news media, and the nature of constitutional protections of Freedom of the Press.

A free press was important to the Framers of our government. They were aware of the impact of pamphlets like *Common Sense,* Thomas Paine's call for independence from Great Britain in making the case for the separation.[9] They also used the press as a means to persuade the people of the states and their representatives to ratify the Constitution through a series of essays now known as *The Federalist Papers.*

While the Constitution does not speak of the news media, it includes several important protections for a free press. The First Amendment to the Constitution contains the most important reference to a free press, as follows: "Congress shall make no law ... abridging the freedom of speech, or of the press.... That freedom of the press is included along with religion, speech, and assembly as a fundamental right shows its importance to the Framers. This amendment was added as part of the Bill of Rights as a way to garner further support for the Constitution as some of the states pushed for more protection from a strong central government. The amendment was based on the 1769 writings of the highly-regarded William Blackstone, who wrote that "every freeman has an undoubted right to lay what sentiments he pleases before the public: to forbid this, is to destroy the freedom of the press."[10] Benjamin Franklin, himself a printer by trade, was a strong advocate for a free press. In editorials published in *The Pennsylvania Gazette,* Franklin recognized that a consequence of a free press is that some will be offended by what is printed. He observed, "if all Printers were determin'd not to print anything till they were sure it would offend nobody, there would be very little printed."[11] Speaking to the role the press plays in a free society, Franklin later wrote, "it is a principle among Printers that when Truth has fair Play, it will always prevail over Falsehood."[12]

Article I of the Constitution also provides important structural protections for a free press, by giving Congress the power to "promote the Progress of Science and useful Arts, by securing for limited Times to Authors and Inventors the exclusive Right to their respective Writings and Discoveries." This authority allowed Congress to give writers, artists, and inventors protections against plagiarism, forgeries, and outright theft of their ideas. Congress used this authority to create today's patents and trademarks system, which assigns full protection to the written word in books, magazine articles, and newspaper stories. Protecting the authors and publishers of news allowed compensation for reporters and publishers and reinforced the structure of an independent news media based on an ability to make a profit for what it produced.

The Framers also wrote extensively about freedom of the press and used it themselves to encourage ratification of the Constitution. Recall that their *Federalist* essays were published in newspapers and only later were assembled into a set that is now known as *The Federalist Papers.* The scope of the protection for the press includes the press as a business—newspapers, television stations, and networks, etc.—but more broadly to "protect everyone's use of the printing press (and its modern equivalents) as a technology."[13] Early state constitutions express this more expansive view of the freedom of every person to "speak, write and print on any subject."[14]

In practice, the meaning of a free press has been the subject of a long list of cases in which the courts interpreted the protections afforded by the First Amendment, particularly surrounding controversial newspaper stories about wars, spying, and scandals. In the 1970s, for example, the *New York Times* published what had been secret documents about the War in Vietnam. Although President Richard M. Nixon's administration claimed executive privilege and national security concerns, the U.S. Supreme Court decided those concerns were not significant enough to bar the newspaper's actions.[15] Indeed, the courts have been altogether reluctant to allow the government to restrict press publications.

The Changing Role of U.S. News Media

The news media, in particular the print media, have been called the "fourth estate" and the "fourth branch of government."[16] U.S. Supreme Court Justice Potter Stewart wrote, "the primary purpose of the constitutional guarantee of a free press was ... to create a fourth institution outside the Government as an additional check on the three official branches."[17] Although the media are sometimes called the "fourth branch" of government because it is so important for getting news to the people, it is not part of government. It has its own structure, similar to the way each of the three official branches have their own structure. But, the media still must work within the governmental framework and First Amendment protections; it must be independent to do its job, which includes playing government watchdog. An independent news media is a defining characteristic of a free society.

The news media has changed dramatically throughout the course of U.S. history. When the Constitution was being ratified, newspapers consisted of a single sheet, often published irregularly by merchants to hawk their services or goods. Delinquent subscribers and high costs meant that newspapers rarely stayed in business more than a year.[18] Despite this high turnover rate, the Framers understood the importance of the press as a watchdog of politicians and government, and so the Bill of Rights guaranteed freedom of the press. The new nation's political leaders, including Alexander Hamilton and Thomas Jefferson, recognized the need to keep voters informed. Political parties as we know them did not exist, but the support the press had given to the Revolution had fostered a growing awareness of the political potential of newspapers. Hamilton recruited staunch Federalist John Fenno to edit and publish a newspaper in the new national capital of Philadelphia. Jefferson responded by attracting Philip Freneau, a talented writer and editor and a loyal Democratic-Republican, to do the same for the Democratic-Republicans. (Jefferson's Republicans later became the Democratic Party.) The early U.S. press served as a mouthpiece for political leaders. Its close connection with politicians and political parties offered the opportunity for financial stability—but at the cost of journalistic independence.

news media
Means of communication about the news that reach the public, including newspapers and magazines, radio, television (broadcast, cable, and satellite), and electronic communication.

There is plentiful evidence that the media influences our culture and politics. The **news media** are made up of newspapers, magazines, radio, television (broadcast, cable, and satellite), and the Internet.[19] The mass media, including the news media as well as films, recordings, books, and electronic communication, reach nearly everyone. News programs often have entertainment value, and entertainment programs often convey news. Programs in this latter category include TV newsmagazines such as *60 Minutes*; talk shows with hosts such as Sean Hannity; and Trevor Noah's parody (formerly Jon Stewart's parody) of the news on *The Daily Show* and *Last Week Tonight with John Oliver,* respectively. In this chapter our primary focus is on the news media.

Comedian, political commentator, television host, John Oliver, is famous for his rants on issues from Donald Trump to Televangelists to FIFA which frequently go viral on YouTube and other social media. On his HBO show *Last Week Tonight*, he challenged viewers to petition the Federal Communications Committee to maintain net neutrality, an effort that resulted in tens of thousands of public comments to the FCC. However, the effort was ultimately unsuccessful. When Trump appointed commissioners took their seats in 2017, the FCC overturned the Obama era rule, ending net neutrality.

THE BUSINESS OF NEWS The news media are a business that must make a profit to survive. To make money, the news media disseminates messages to a large and often heterogeneous audience. Additionally, because they must have broad appeal, their messages are often simplified, stereotyped, and predictable. While the media has changed a great deal over the course of U.S. history, the need to make a profit and the implications of a mass audience have remained constant and are important to understanding the changing definition of the news and how it is delivered. How much political clout do the news media have? Two factors are important in answering this question: the media's pervasiveness, and their role as a link between politicians and government officials and the public.

During the Jacksonian era of the late 1820s and 1830s, the right to vote was extended to all free white adult males through the elimination of property qualifications. The press began to shift its appeal away from elite readers and toward the mass of less-educated and less politically interested readers. Thus, increased political participation by the common people—along with the rise of literacy—began to alter the relationship between politicians and the press.

Rather than relying on annual subscription fees, which most readers could not afford, most newspapers started charging a penny a paper, paid on delivery. The "penny press," as it was called, expanded circulation and increased advertising, enabling newspapers to become financially independent of the political parties. The changing finances of newspapers also affected the definition of news. Before the penny press, all news was political—speeches, documents, and editorials—and directed at politically interested readers.[20] The penny press reshaped the definition of news as it sought to appeal to less politically aware readers with human interest stories and reports on sports, crime, trials, fashion, and social activities.

Newspapers today still seek to appeal to broad audiences, which is one reason why sports and style often are in separate sections and have substantial coverage. Profitability for newspapers was generated not only through subscription or newsstand sales but also through advertising, including classified ads. Ownership was often local, but over time larger newspapers purchased smaller ones and became more important. Because of their early entry into the marketplace, newspaper owners were also well positioned to establish local radio stations and later television stations as well.

NEWS MEDIA CONSOLIDATION AND FRAGMENTATION When television was in its infancy, radio networks and newspapers were among the first to purchase television stations. These mergers established cross-ownership patterns that persisted until recently, when large media conglomerates separated their print business from their television and digital media business. Rupert Murdoch, an Australian-born U.S. citizen and founder of the FOX Network and owner of the *Wall Street Journal*, split his publishing businesses from his entertainment companies in 2013. In 2015, the Gannett Company separated *USA Today* and its 81 local newspapers from more than 40 television stations and online businesses like Cars.com and CareerBuilder. That same year the Tribune Company, owner of the *Chicago Tribune* and Times-Mirror, publisher of the *Los Angeles Times*, divided its nine newspapers from its 24 television stations including superstation WGN, one radio station, and its online businesses. This move to divide print from TV and digital divisions can be attributed to financial losses associated with declining newspaper profits.[21] Tensions between managers and both editors and reporters as well as difficulties achieving profitability were seen as reasons the Tribune Company in early 2018 sold the *Los Angeles Times* and *San Diego Union-Tribune* to Patrick Soon-Shiong who had previously owned part of the newspapers.[22] Ownership of television stations has become more consolidated, but some consolidation deals fall through as happened in 2018 when Tribune Media Company, which owned 42 television stations, declined Sinclair Broadcast Group's desire to buy its stations.[23]

While major media companies have recently split off their newspapers from their other communications businesses, it remains the case that most print media today are owned by a few large corporations. This is a big change from the time when most newspapers were locally owned. Questions are often raised when owners with a perceived ideological agenda acquire news media, such as newspapers and television stations. This happened when Rupert Murdoch, a visible and active conservative, acquired the *Wall Street Journal* in 2007.[24] At the time of the purchase, the publisher of the *Wall Street Journal* pledged "the same standards of accuracy, fairness and authority will apply to this publication, regardless of ownership."

One of Murdoch's British newspapers, *News of the World*, was forced to cease publication in 2011 and paid millions of dollars in damages after it was discovered that reporters at the paper had used telephone wiretaps or "hacking."[25] Similar concerns about persons with a strong point of view purchasing newspapers arose in 2015 when Las Vegas billionaire Sheldon Adelson purchased the major newspaper in Las Vegas, the *Review Journal.* Some reporters at the paper and in the community expressed concern about whether the newspaper would fairly report on Mr. Adelson and his businesses.[26] Adelson also owns a free daily paper in Israel.[27]

MEDIA REGULATION The government has regulated the actions of broadcast media since their inception. Due to the limited number of television and radio frequencies, the national government oversees their licensing and financing through the Federal Communications Commission. Concerns about decreased news coverage and possible bias in news reporting are most evident in cities that once had two or more competing daily papers and now have only one newspaper.[28] Although the number of local broadcast stations has not declined to the same extent, conglomerates without ties to the community now own more of these stations.

At the same time, on the national level, the cable networks—CNN, Fox News, and others such as C-SPAN—have expanded the number of news sources available to the 87 percent of households receiving TV cable or satellite service.[29] The courts and the Federal Communications Commission (FCC)—an independent regulatory commission charged with licensing stations—are reinforcing the trend toward media conglomeration by relaxing and striking down regulations that limit cable and television network ownership by the same company.[30] In June 2018, a federal judge ruled that the proposed merger between AT&T, the large telecommunications company, and Time/Warner, a large entertainment company that owns HBO and CNN, could merge. This set off other merger deals with large communications and media companies.[31] Because they use the public airwaves, the FCC is also involved in regulating some content shown by broadcast stations. For example, the FCC fined CBS for broadcasting as part of its 2004 Super Bowl halftime show an incident in which Justin Timberlake removed part of Janet Jackson's costume, exposing her right breast.[32] However, the FCC's regulatory power has been challenged on free speech grounds by the broadcast media, who contend that the absence of government regulation of media outlets like HBO and Showtime have created a double standard for broadcast and cable providers.[33] In 2012, the Supreme Court refused to address the free speech issue head-on and instead decided a case challenging stricter FCC regulations on procedural grounds.[34]

NEW YORK POST 25 CENTS
LATE CITY FINAL
KERRY'S CHOICE
Dem picks Gephardt as VP candidate
EXCLUSIVE
FULL STORY: PAGE 4

NEW YORK POST 25 CENTS
LATE CITY FINAL
KERRY'S CHOICE
Dem picks Edwards as VP candidate (REALLY)
NOT EXCLUSIVE
FULL STORY: PAGES 4-9

The news media are intensely competitive, and getting the story first is one of the ways media outlets distinguish themselves. In the 2000 presidential election, NBC initially called Florida for Gore but then later said the race was too close to call, which history showed to be true. Here the *New York Post,* in a race to break the story of John Kerry's selection of a running mate, ran with a front-page story saying that Kerry had selected Congressman Dick Gephardt of Missouri. They later changed that front page to reflect John Kerry's eventual selection, North Carolina senator John Edwards.

How Americans Get the News (Action)

9.2 Describe the effect of recent trends in how Americans get their news.

The invention of new communications technologies, such as the Internet, satellites, and cable television, has changed how people learn about politics and government. These technologies eliminate the obstacles of time and distance and increase the volume of information viewers can store, retrieve, and watch. They have also reduced the impact of single sources of broadcast or cable news.

More than nine-in-ten U.S. adults follow national news closely, with just over eight-in-ten following local news closely, and about two-thirds follow international news closely. These percentages are generally higher than in other countries.[35,36] There are substantial differences in where people of different ages go for news. For example, when asked where they went for news about politics and government over the previous week, the most common response for millennials was Facebook (61 percent), followed by CNN (44 percent). Generation X also listed Facebook more than any other source (51 percent). Baby boomers turned to local television (60 percent), with 39 percent citing Facebook. Respondents could list more than one news source, which is why the percentages do not add to 100 percent (see Figure 9.1). The fact that young people like you turn so heavily to Facebook has not been lost on other Internet sources. Twitter has been growing in importance as a news source and has its "Moments" platform. Apple and Google have also become news aggregators with Apple News and Google's Accelerated Mobile Pages.[37]

FIGURE 9.1 TOP SOURCES OF POLITICAL NEWS FOR MILLENNIALS, AND OTHERS

People in different age groups turn to different sources for news. For baby boomers, the local TV news is the source used most frequently. Millennials and generation X rely on Facebook the most, but millennials by an even wider margin. Three of the top 10 news sources for millennials are found on the Internet: Yahoo, Google, and Facebook.

SOURCES: Pew Research Center, Millennials & Political News: Social Media—the Local TV for the Next Generation?" p. 8. American Trends Panel (wave1). Survey Conducted March 19–April 29, 2014. Q22, q24A. Based on online adults. http://www.journalism.org/files/2015/06/Millennials-and-News-FINAL-7-27-15.pdf.

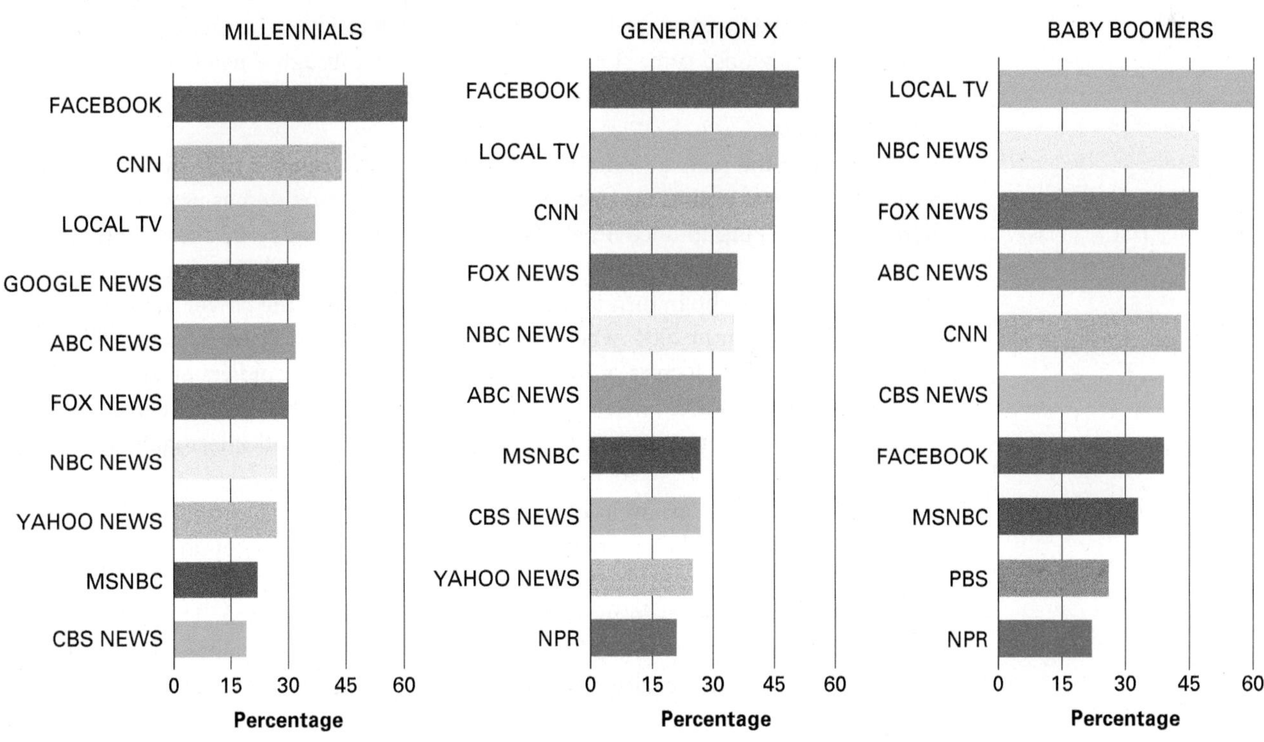

Whether Facebook, Twitter, and the other products delivered by technology companies are news media providers is open to debate. Some tech companies see themselves as distribution networks for news reports coming from other media outlets, delivering what their users want to see or hear. But the frequency with which people turn to Facebook and the other providers makes them important filters for what the public sees. About two-thirds of U.S. adults use Facebook, with even greater use among women (74 percent) and 81 percent of Americans between 18 and 29 years of age use the platform. And the use is frequent, with "most Facebook users visiting the site at least once a day."[38] Will these platforms exclude some stories or advertisers and on what basis? Facebook, for example, has decided it would ban private sales of guns on its site[39] and Facebook announced a new policy in April 2018 that it would start "forcing people who want to buy political or 'issue' ads to reveal their identities and verify where they are."[40] Finally, what objectionable content, like recruiting terrorists or encouraging violence, will be excluded? Because you and others like you often use these resources will be important not only for your online behavior, but also for policies you support or oppose about the use of the Internet.

The Transition from a Partisan Press to Objective Journalism

For much of our first century as a nation, newspapers were expressly partisan, even including the party name in the newspaper's name, like *The National Democrat* or the *Daily Republican.* But by the early twentieth century, many journalists began to argue that the press should be independent of the political parties. *New York Tribune* editor Whitelaw Reid eloquently expressed this sentiment in 1872: "Independent journalism! That is the watchword of the future in the profession. An end of concealments because it would hurt the party; an end of one-sided expositions...; an end of assaults that are not believed fully just but must be made because the exigency of party warfare demands them."[41] Objective journalism was also a reaction to exaggeration and sensationalism in the news media, something called *yellow journalism* at the time.

As journalists began to view their work as a profession, they established professional associations with journals and codes of ethics. This professionalization reinforced the notion that journalists should be independent of partisan politics. Further strengthening the trend toward objectivity was the rise of the wire services, which were news reporters whose print stories were distributed through a news service, such as the Associated Press (AP) and Reuters, which remained politically neutral to attract more customers.

As part of the shift to more objective news, there came a shift from journalists reporting on what politicians or government agencies provided as news to reporters aggressively seeking to uncover stories. News reporters today do more than convey the news; they investigate it, and their investigations can check government action by informing citizens who in turn take action. One example of the power of investigative journalism comes from 2004, when an investigative team at *60 Minutes* of CBS News broke the story of the torture of Iraqi prisoners held by U.S. soldiers at Abu Ghraib.[42] Another comes from 2005, when Dana Priest of the *Washington Post* revealed the existence of secret CIA prisons that were being used to hold and interrogate suspected terrorists.[43]

Another excellent example of investigative journalism comes from 2013, when a British newspaper, the *Guardian*, broke the story that one of the U.S. government's most secretive spy agencies had been collecting detailed information on almost all phone calls made by U.S. citizens since the September 11, 2001, terrorist attacks on New York City and Washington, D.C.[44] This huge database of phone calls allowed the National Security Agency (NSA) to search for information on potential communications between alleged terrorists. The *Guardian* later revealed its source to be Edward Snowden, a U.S. citizen who had been a private consultant to the NSA and Central Intelligence Agency.[45] The American public and allied leaders like German Chancellor Angela Merkel had no idea that their phone records were being accessed and reviewed by the U.S. government.[46]

Newspapers continue to experience business challenges, but some have built on their past reputations for investigative reporting in recent years. One area where newspapers and magazines have had a large impact in recent years is in reporting on individuals who had exhibited a pattern of sexual harassment or assault. Jodi Kantor and Megan Twohey, New York Times reporters who wrote the story, found different accusers with very similar stories of Harvey Weinstein's sexual misconduct, and neither accuser knew the other. Another reporter, Ronan Farrow, using similar reporting methods, was pursuing the same story about Weinsten, and his reporting confirmed the findings of Kantor and Twohey. Legal action against Weinstein is pending.

Other print reporters have published well documented stories of sexual harassment, intimidation, or assault since the Weinstein story broke. Alabama U.S. Senate Republican candidate Roy Moore was accused of initiating sexual activity with women as young as 14.[47] In the coming months elected officials including a U.S. Senator and Congressmen from both parties as well as actors, news reporters and editors, business leaders, artists, conductors, and others were accused of impropriety The consistent pattern in these accusations was multiple accusers coming forward with similar stories of inappropriate behavior followed by the quick resignation or firing of the alleged offender

One reason this and other stories on prominent individuals moved quickly is the #MeToo movement. In 2006, Tarana Burke founded #MeToo as a Twitter account to support survivors of sexual violence.[48] When the New York Times broke the story of film producer Harvey Weinstein's decades of sexual harassment and abuse in October, 2017, other women came forward with accusations of their own against Weinstein. Actress Alyssa Milano tweeted a screenshot of #MeToo with the message "If you've been sexually harassed or assaulted write 'me too' as a reply to this tweet." Overnight 30,000 people had responded and within 48 hours the hashtag had been tweeted nearly one million times, with the response through other social media also large.[49]

Though these examples illustrate the important power of investigative journalism, the most striking example is still the Watergate scandal that drove President Richard Nixon to resign from office.[50] Without persistent reporting by columnist Jack Anderson and two young *Washington Post* reporters, Robert Woodward and Carl Bernstein, the story would probably have been limited to a report of a failed burglary of the

Winners of the Pulitzer Prize award for public service in 2018 included Ronan Farrow of *The New Yorker*, and Beth Reinhard, Stephanie McCrummen, and Alice Crites of *The New York Times*, for their reporting on Harvey Weinstein and other powerful and wealthy sexual predators. The 2018 award in public service was also given to Beth Reinhard, Stephanie McCrummen, and Alice Crites of the *Washington Post* for their reporting on charges of sexual impropriety by Alabama U.S. Senate candidate Roy Moore against teenage women.

headquarters of the Democratic National Committee at the Watergate building.[51] The news reports, coupled with congressional investigations, put a spotlight on the inner workings of the Nixon White House and the Nixon reelection committee, which had funded the attempted burglary and other political dirty tricks.[52]

The Transformation of Media Platforms

Changes in technology and the economy have meant that Americans now have a much wider array of media they can use to learn about what is happening in the world. For much of our history as a nation news was limited to word-of-mouth and printed form. The discovery of radio, and then television, changed that and brought an immediacy to those who could afford these broadcast sources of news.

More recently we have undergone another major transformation with the invention of computers and the Internet. As computers have become more accessible and more mobile, the ability of people to access a large number of news sources on a mobile device has expanded the choices individuals have for news content. While access to these new tools of communication was once quite limited, that has changed, and now many Americans have access to online news.

Today, 43 percent of Americans report getting news online, only 7 percent lower than the 50 percent who often get their news from television. For 18–29-year-olds, twice as many get news online (52 percent) compared to on television (23 percent).[53] However, many people do not know that the high-speed electronic communications network they use for everything from communicating to shopping to consuming the day's news started as a government research endeavor. The role of the U.S. government in inventing the Internet and fostering its widespread availability is a remarkable accomplishment. What eventually became the Internet was developed in response to fears of a possible enemy nuclear attack destroying the defense department communications systems. To make communica-tions more secure, researchers created a system that could function even if parts were destroyed. This was accomplished by the creation of a network of multiple "nodes," an approach sometimes called distributed communications. This system was intended for researchers and the military to be able to transmit information to each other and share the use of computers.

For decades the government did not make access to the new technology generally available. Later, Congress passed legislation allowing commercial development, and by the mid-1990s, several commercial networks were in existence. There are now almost 3.5 billion Internet users,[54] and more than 284 million active domains have been registered. These new technologies have been more readily adopted by younger

Edward Snowden, the former U.S. intelligence contractor who brought to public attention the surveillance activities of the National Security Agency (NSA), received asylum in Russia, allowing him to evade prosecution by the U.S. government. Snowden's revelations gained worldwide news coverage. Some of his revelations included that U.S. surveillance had included people outside the United States, like German Chancellor Angela Merkel. Snowden is seen here with Glenn Greenwald of *The Guardian* newspaper who was one of the reporters who broke the story of NSA surveillance.

people. Millennials rely on Facebook for news far more than older persons. Does this description fit you? How often do you turn to Facebook for news as compared to cable TV, Google News, or Yahoo News? It will not surprise you that political campaigns increasingly use the Internet and social media to persuade through advertising and to enlist individuals to volunteer. How do you think the Internet influenced your interest in the 2016 or 2018 elections, choice of candidates, desire to vote?

THE IMPORTANT ROLE OF NEWSPAPERS AND THE DECLINE OF NEWSMAGAZINES Daily newspaper circulation has been declining for more than 20 years but leveled off in 2012 and remains steady today. Circulation was more than 62 million nationwide in 1990 but dipped below 35 million in 2016—the lowest levels in over six decades.[55] The percentage of Americans who said they had read a newspaper yesterday dropped from 40 percent in 1999 to just 17 percent in 2014.[56]

After a decade of little to no profits, and with subscriptions declining, the Graham family, who had held the controlling interest in the *Washington Post* for four generations, in 2013 sold the highly respected newspaper to Jeffrey P. Bezos, founder of Amazon .com.[57] Bezos pledged to not change the newspaper's values,[58] but has expanded the coverage to include international affairs, made content more available online and through mobile devices, and invested heavily in research and development.[59] The *Washington Post, New York Times,* and *Wall Street Journal* are among the newspapers that have moved to a digital subscription fee for online information.[60] Although newspapers have been struggling to remain profitable, they have remained authoritative news media sources, often able to provide more depth of reporting than other sources. Their opinion columns also have broad importance, especially to elites.

Newspapers have become less profitable because of declining circulation, in part because the Internet provides instantly available information for free.[61] The Internet has also hurt newspapers' bottom lines most by providing an alternative medium for retail advertisers, and particularly for classified ads via sites such as Craigslist (see Figure 9.2). Newspapers earned about $20 billion in revenue from classifieds in 2000; today they receive under $5 billion.[62] (See Figure 9.2.) With the decline in revenue,

FIGURE 9.2 NEWSPAPER AD REVENUE FROM DIGITAL AND PRINT

After having hit nearly $50 million in combined print and digital ad revenue in 2005 and 2006, newspapers have been on a steady decline in combined ad revenue. While the share of ad revenue from digital has been growing, the rate of decline in ad revenue form printed newspapers is now less than half of what it was a decade before.

SOURCE: From Pew http://www.journalism.org/files/2015/06/Millennials-and-News-FINAL-7-27-15.pdf.

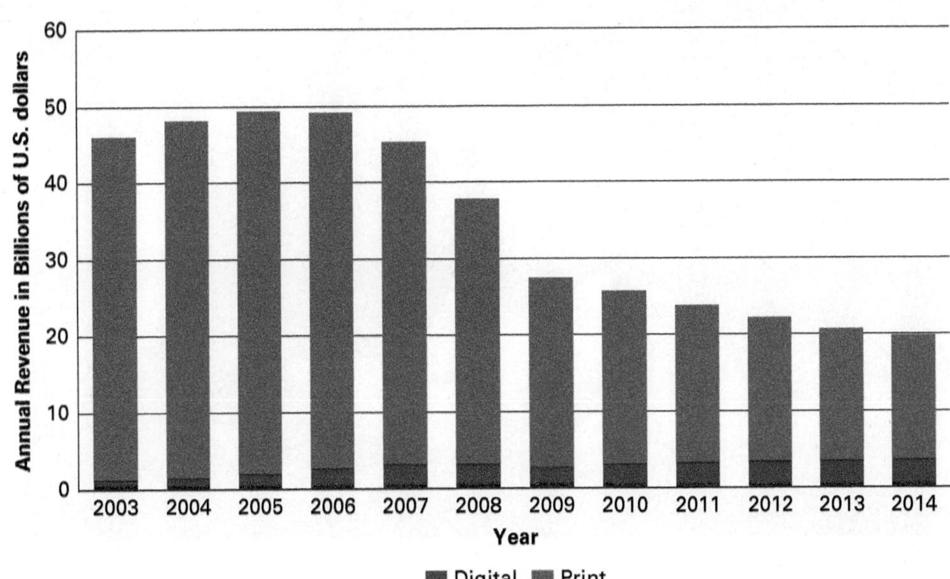

newspapers have had to "reduce newsroom staff while expanding only modestly on the digital side."[63] One exception to this has been the *New York Times,* where "circulation revenue exceeds advertising revenue."[64]

In addition to metropolitan and local newspapers, Americans now have at least three national newspapers to choose from: *USA Today,* the *Wall Street Journal,* and the *New York Times.* With a circulation of nearly 2.3 million, the *Wall Street Journal* has replaced *USA Today* as the top-circulating U.S. newspaper.[65] Newsmagazines, like newspapers, have also undergone major changes in recent years. Magazines such as *Time* have experienced substantial declines in circulation and become less profitable.[66] *Newsweek* has gone through multiple owners since 2010 when it was sold for $1, with the buyer agreeing to take on an estimated $70 million in debt owed by the publication.[67] It ceased publication in 2012 but returned to newsstands two years later.[68] Newsmagazines which once were widely subscribed to have greatly diminished in circulation. In 2018, *Newsweek* was not among the top 20 magazines in reach which includes print and digital editions, while *Time* lagged well behind *ESPN the Magazine* and *People Magazine.*[69]

BROADCAST MEDIA While radio made immediate access to changing news events possible and allowed the public to hear leaders in their own homes, it also foreshadowed the even more dramatic transformation in media platforms that followed. Those platforms added the possibility to see important news events and provided far more choices for access to news. Radio and television broadcasts nationalized and personalized the news. People could now follow events as they were happening rather than waiting for the publication of a newspaper.

From the 1920s, when radio networks were formed, radio carried political speeches, campaign advertising, and coverage of political events such as national party conventions.[70] Politicians could now speak directly to listeners, bypassing the screening of editors and reporters. Beginning in 1933, President Franklin Roosevelt used radio with remarkable effectiveness. Before then, most radio speeches were formal orations, but Roosevelt spoke to his audience on a personal level, seemingly in one-on-one conversations, "as though he were actually sitting on the front porch or in

President Franklin Roosevelt was the first to use broadcast media to communicate regularly with large audiences. He is pictured here giving a fireside chat on the radio. Later presidents would use TV to speak directly to the American people from the White House.

the parlor with them."[71] These "fireside chats," as he called them, established a standard that politicians still follow today.

Television and the Internet have not displaced radio. On the contrary, radio continues to reach more U.S. households than television does. The most recent data suggest that over 90 percent of Americans over the age of 12 listened to the radio in the past week.[72] The reach of radio has only grown as the number of people with access to mobile online devices has increased. A study by Edison Research found that more than half of Americans over the age of 12 listen to the radio online.[73] People listening to podcasts, particularly programming on National Public Radio, has also grown in recent years.[74] Many consider the radio an essential companion when driving. Listeners who tune in to talk or news shows on the radio get more than "the facts"; they also get analysis and opinion from commentators and talk show hosts.

Political campaigns continue to use radio to communicate with particular types of voters. This was especially the case in the 2016 Iowa caucus campaign.[75] Because radio audiences are distinctive, campaigns can target younger or older voters, women, Hispanics, and so on. Many candidates in 2012 used radio to "micro-target" particular audiences in this way.[76] As a respected annual review of the media noted, "presidential election-year advertising dollars kept the AM/FM industry above water in 2012."[77] One particularly important source of news on the radio is National Public Radio (NPR). An estimated audience of 14.65 million people listen to programs such as *Morning Edition.*[78] NPR rivals conservative radio commentator Sean Hannity for size of audience. Rush Limbaugh's show has one of the largest audiences, slightly lower than NPR's *Morning Edition.*[79]

Television added a dramatic visual dimension, which increased audience interest in national events and allowed viewers to witness lunar landings and the aftermath of political assassinations, as well as more mundane events. By 1963, the two largest networks at the time, CBS and NBC, had expanded their evening news programs from 15 to 30 minutes. Today, news broadcasting has expanded to the point that many local stations provide 90 minutes of local news every evening as well as a half-hour in the morning and at noon. However, recent studies have found that local news is less and less about politics or government (3 percent) and more and more about traffic, weather, and sports (40 percent).[80]

Television has changed U.S. politics more than any other invention. With its immediacy, visual imagery, and drama, television has an emotional impact that print media can rarely match.[81] It cuts across age groups, educational levels, social classes, and races. It provides instant access to news from around the country and the globe, permitting citizens and leaders alike to observe events firsthand. In contrast, newspapers provide more detail about the news and often contain opposing points of view, especially on the editorial pages. The average American watches nearly five hours of television a day, and most homes have more than two television sets.[82] Campaigns have adapted to the different ways Americans watch television. Based on extensive research, some campaigns target very particular demographic segments with their ads. A married Democratic male who prefers brown liquor, has kids in the house, goes to church weekly, consumes media mostly on a phone or tablet and graduated from college is thought by a political firm to watch *CSI: Crime Scene Investigaton* and also Comedy Central. A Republican male with the same other characteristics is thought by a political firm to watch Blue Bloods, and shows on the AMC movie network.[83]

CABLE Cable television created the round-the-clock **24/7 news cycle**, which is a term that refers to the opportunity to present news 24 hours a day, 7 days a week. Providing this much original news content is challenging and often leads to the same

24/7 news cycle
News is now constantly updated and presented via Internet sites like the *New York Times* or *Wall Street Journal* and cable news sources like CNN, Fox News, and MSNBC.

stories being repeated over and over again. It also means that some cable networks such as FOX and MSNBC have moved into programming with more commentary overemphasizing a particular ideological perspective. For example, opinion fills 85 percent of MSNBC's airtime.[84] Those who prefer news with a more ideological slant, often consistent with their own views of politics, have entered what some observers call an "echo chamber," because they get the news in ways that reinforce their prior views.[85]

The growth of cable television and more viewing options is one of the most important developments in recent years. Until the late 1980s, the network news programs on CBS, NBC, and ABC captured more than 90 percent of the audience for television news in the morning and early evening. Twenty-five years later, fewer than 33 percent of those using television during prime time were actually watching one of the "big three."[86] While network news programs have more competition for viewers they remain well ahead of cable network news programs in terms of numbers of viewers. In 2014, the networks' evening news audience was on average approximately 23.7 million evening news viewers,[87] whereas the cable news networks CNN, Fox News, and MSNBC had average combined audiences of about 2.8 million evening viewers.[88]

INTERNET AND SOCIAL MEDIA Many other news sources, like *The New York Times* and CNN, now provide 24/7 news coverage on the Internet. No longer must people wait for the morning paper to learn about current events: they can immediately turn to Internet news sources or cable TV. The news media now routinely send out "news alerts" via email to inform those who seek reports of breaking news. This has reinforced the trend of individuals using smart phones, tablets, or computers as sources for news over more traditional sources (See Figure 9.3).

FIGURE 9.3 AMERICANS TURNING MORE TO MOBILE DEVICES FOR NEWS

By 2017, three-quarters of Americans either often or sometimes use their mobile devices to get the news. This percent is up from 60 percent in 2016 and 40 percent in 2013.

SOURCE: Michael Barthell and Amy Mitchell, "Americans' Attitudes About the News Media Deeply Divided Along Partisan Lines." Pew Research Center. May 20, 2017. http://www.journalism.org/2017/05/10/americans-attitudes-about-the-news-media-deeply-divided-along-partisan-lines/pj_2017-05-10_media-attitudes_0-03/.

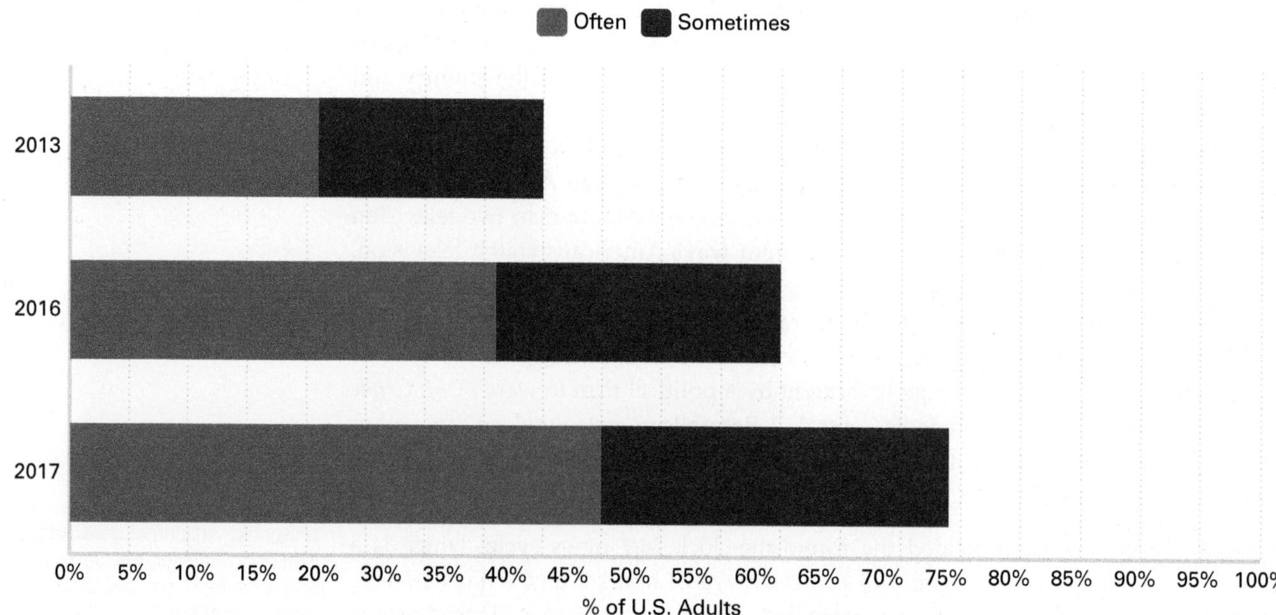

Just as television revolutionized American politics in the 1950s and 1960s, the Internet is bringing major changes to American politics today. From its humble beginnings as a Pentagon research project in the 1960s,[89] the Internet has blossomed into a global phenomenon. There are now more than 130 trillion unique URLs indexed on Google,[90] and almost 300 million domain names registered worldwide.[91] In 2018, more than two-thirds of Americans reported they used Facebook and nearly three-quarters used YouTube, and a majority of Facebook users report they visit the site several times a day. Among 18–24-year-olds, the preferred social media in 2018 was Snapchat (78 percent reporting use) and Instagram (71 percent reporting use), and a majority of these users report accessing the platform multiple times per day.[92] This high rate of usage is one reason political advertising on social media has grown in recent years. As the controversy over Russian use of Facebook ads in the 2016 election grew, and as attention was turned to the use of personal information made available by Facebook to advertisers, some advocated giving up use of social media. In a 2018 survey, 59 percent of all social media users said it would not be hard for them to give up social media, but 51 percent of those 18–24 said it would be hard.[93]

The Internet allows people to access multiple news sources instantly, including political videos on YouTube and other similar sites. The Internet also allows people to communicate with friends about politics via Facebook, Twitter, and other social networking sites. As use of the Internet on wireless and mobile devices has grown the impact of the Internet has expanded.[94]

More than three-quarters of Americans now own a smart phone and even more own a cellphone of some kind.[95] As individuals have been able to use the Internet on mobile devices, its impact has grown. More than four-fifths of all Americans (85 percent) have used a mobile device to access news,[96] and minutes spent on mobile devices accessing the Internet were much more frequent than minutes spent using a device with fixed internet access.[97] The Internet is a primary source of news for half of the public.[98] As noted, Internet users can also interact with politicians or other people about politics through email, social networking sites, and blogs. The Internet is also increasingly used for schoolwork by students of all ages, but is there a "homework gap" between those with and without Internet access? The answer is about 83 percent

M4OS Photos/Alamy Stock Photo

The Internet allows an individual to access news from conventional news sources such as online newspapers, seen here. Other sources such as blogs, Twitter, Reddit, YouTube, and customized news summaries also open up large amounts of information in an efficient manner. Here a reader is online accessing the Huffington Post.

of American homes with school-age children have broadband access. But in low-income households (household income under $50,000) nearly a third lack broadband access, with the gap wider in low income black and Hispanic households.[99] This raises questions about a technology gap between those with and without Internet access, and an even wider gap between those with high-speed Internet access and much slower or no access. Over 95 percent of households with income exceeding $100,000 have wired Internet access at home, compared to 53 percent of households with incomes below $30,000. Two-thirds of Americans with incomes over $100,000 have smart phones, desktop computers, and a tablet, while only 17 percent of those with incomes under $30,000 have all of these ways of accessing the Internet.[100] This almost certainly puts students without Internet at home at a disadvantage. Although much is still unknown about the impact of the Internet on the news media, it has given those with access additional sources of information, and it has the potential to limit the influence of other media.[101]

Nearly three-fifths of Twitter users turn to it to keep up with news about an event as it was happening, or at about twice the rate of Facebook users (31 percent).[102] Using Twitter in this way had long been the case among news organizations. In the 2016 election, reports on tweets from candidates, pollsters, and reporters occurred frequently. All of the major networks and most major newspapers have Twitter feeds, and in many cases news anchors and reporters have their own feeds as well. Twitter provides an additional means for news organizations to communicate and build followings, and also to receive feedback from their viewers.[103]

Campaigns not only sent messages out via Twitter, but also used the platform as "an early warning signal" of what reporters and the public were tweeting about. The Romney campaign, for example, monitored the Twitter stream from reporters covering the campaign not only to anticipate questions that might be asked of the candidate, but also to communicate the campaign's view of events.[104] The Obama campaign of 2008 and 2012 were among the most successful in applying these tools to a campaign. Following the 2012 election, the Republican Party acknowledged the need to make better use of these tools in future campaigns.[105] Candidates in 2016 not only used Twitter to speak to their supporters, but even debated with one another directly through tweeted correspondence. Democratic candidate Bernie Sanders's hashtag #feelthebern came to be one of the most defining elements of his campaign, especially as it dealt with tech-savvy young voters.[106]

As discussed earlier in this chapter, Donald Trump had a large earned media advantage throughout the 2016 election. One estimate of the value of Trump's earned media in the nomination contest was $2 billion by March 2016.[107] His earned media advantage over Clinton in the general election was over $3 billion, with Clinton's earned media valued at $2.8 billion and Trump's valued at $5.9 billion.[108] Since taking office, President Trump has used tweets to communicate his often negative views on other politicians and media personalities, policy issues, and even to fire his Secretary of State.[109] Sean Spicer who served as press secretary to President Trump saw the president's tweets as follows: "I do look [at Trump's overnight tweets] first, because that's what's going to drive the news . . . I think there's this misconception . . . that he's just randomly tweeting. He knows exactly where he wants to end up on a particular subject . . . He understands the strategic value in certain actions to achieve a goal."[110]

President Trump has used Twitter in novel ways. For example, he announced on Twitter that Secretary of State Rex Tillerson was being replaced by Mike Pompeo. Secretary Tillerson first learned of the change when an aid showed him this tweet. Generally, such an announcement would have been preceded by a meeting or a phone call.

The 1960 televised debate between Vice President Richard Nixon and Senator John F. Kennedy was the first to use this medium in this way in a presidential election. This debate was held in a TV studio rather than in front of a live audience. Contrast the setting of this debate with what you have seen in the 2016 presidential debates. The 1960 debate is widely seen as helping Kennedy. The 2016 presidential general election televised debates had the most viewers of any series of televised debates, not accounting for viewers who watched the debates online. The unusual candidacy of Donald Trump and his unpredictable style may have boosted viewership.

The Influence of the News Media on Public Opinion and Elections (Impact)

9.3 Assess the influence of the news media on American public opinion and elections.

Through the power of visual images, the news media have the ability to influence public opinion and elections. In the 1960s, as television news reports showing the brutal treatment of civil rights protesters in the South were shown, the issues of segregation and voting rights rose in importance and had an impact on public opinion on these issues.[111] More recently, when dramatic events such as the terrorist attacks on September 11, 2001, occur, we realize television's power to have an impact by bringing world events into our lives. Other events, like the terrorist attacks in Paris and Belgium, and the Las Vegas and Parkland shootings were dramatic and left a lasting impression.

The news media impacts American elections as well as influencing public opinion. The debate between then senator John F. Kennedy and Vice President Richard Nixon was a turning point in Kennedy's election campaign, and more recently candidates have struggled with restraining their smirks and fumbling their words in televised debates. In 2016 the Republican nomination process had debates that were often contentious and personal. A notable example was an exchange between Florida Senator Marco Rubio and New Jersey Governor Chris Christie. Christie had criticized Rubio for "truancy" in missing votes in the U.S. Senate, and Rubio's response included the phrase "dispel with this fiction that Barack Obama doesn't know what he is doing. He knows exactly what he is doing." Christie then said that phrase was part of a memorized 25-second speech. Rubio fired back, ending again with the phrase about Obama, only to have Christie say, "There it is. There it is—the memorized 25-second speech."[112] Christie was successful in putting Rubio on the defensive, but he fared poorly in the New Hampshire vote. Christie came in sixth and then dropped out of the race.

Because the public is exposed to news coverage and paid media advertising, candidates, political parties, and interest groups invest much time and money in their media communications. In advertising much of the messaging is negative, in part because people remember these messages and because they more often move voters.

The News Media and Public Opinion

The pervasiveness of newspapers, magazines, radio, and television confers enormous influence on the individuals who determine what we read, hear, and see because they can reach so many people so quickly and because they decide what is reported. The news media have also assumed the role of speaking for the people. Journalists report what "the people" want and think, and then they tell the people what politicians and policy makers are doing about it. Politicians know they depend on the news media to reach voters, and they are well aware that a hostile press can hurt or even destroy them. That explains why today's politicians spend so much time developing good relationships with the press.

For a long time, analysts argued that political leaders wielded more influence in U.S. politics than the news media did. Franklin D. Roosevelt's radio fireside chats symbolized the power of the politician over that of the news editor. President John F. Kennedy's use of televised press conferences established similar direct contact with the public. President Ronald Reagan was nicknamed "the Great Communicator" because of his ability to talk with the people persuasively and often passionately about public policy issues through television.

Now the news media are more aggressive in newsgathering. Controversy over the justification for going to war with Iraq became a major focus of the news media in George W. Bush's second term and helped explain the declining public assessment of his performance. In addition, the news media can exert significant influence on public opinion through *agenda setting* and *issue framing*. This is amplified by the repeated airing of the same story on cable news due to the need for content to fill the 24-hours-a-day, seven-days-a-week news cycle.

AGENDA SETTING By calling public attention to certain issues, the news media impact which topics will become subjects of public debate and legislation.[113] However, the news media do not have absolute power to set the public agenda. The audience and the nature of any particular issue limit it.[114] According to former Vice President Walter Mondale (1976–1980), "If I had to give up … the opportunity to get on the evening news or the veto power, I'd throw the veto power away. [Television news] is the president's most indispensable power."[115]

Communicating through the news media works, especially when the communication is—or at least appears to be—natural and unscripted. When President Bush first visited the scene of the destruction of the World Trade Center in New York City in September 2001, he took a bullhorn and said, "I can hear you. The rest of the world hears you, and the people who knocked these buildings down will hear all of us soon."[116] This action projected presidential leadership and reassured a nation that was still shocked by the attacks.

ISSUE FRAMING Politicians, interest groups, and political parties all try to frame issues to win support. The news media provide the means to frame issues, so politicians try to influence the "spin" the news media will give to their actions or issues. The news media, conscious of the desire of politicians to influence reporting, often turn to each other for interpretations of events. This has been described as *pack* journalism, meaning reporters work in packs and follow leaders. With more ideological cable news, we now have multiple news media issue frames operating on the same issue at the same time. Thus MSNBC may be emphasizing some aspects of the Special Counsel investigation into the Russian interference in the 2016 U.S. elections like the indictments of former Trump campaign officials, while FOX News may be emphasizing questions about the impartiality of the FBI during this same time period. One result of the competing issue frames from more ideological news media is that people tend to watch the news media source they agree with.

The News Media and Elections

News coverage of campaigns and elections is greatest in presidential contests, less in statewide races for governor and U.S. senator, and least for other state and local races. There has been a shift away from the news media being the source of reports on the character and records of presidential candidates and toward the campaigns and outside groups being the primary sources of these messages. Although in 2016 the press coverage of both major party nominees was negative in tone and consistently so throughout the general election campaign. One study estimated that the tone of news coverage of Trump in this period was 77 percent negative and for Clinton 64 percent negative. When both candidates are characterized in such negative terms, voters may find it hard to distinguish between the candidates.[117] Generally, the more news attention given the campaign, the less likely voters are to be swayed by any one source. Hence, news coverage is likely to be more influential in a city council contest than in an election for president or the Senate. For most city elections, there are only one or two sources of information about what candidates say and stand for; there are many sources for statewide and national contests.

The proliferation of diverse media outlets also lessens the ability of any one medium to influence the outcome of elections. Newspaper publishers, once seen as key figures in state and local politics, are now less important because politicians and their media advisers are no longer so dependent on newspapers to communicate their messages. Candidates can use ads on radio and television, direct mail, phone, the Web, and cable television to reach voters directly. In local contests, or even in larger settings such as the Iowa caucuses or the New Hampshire primary, personal contact can also be important. Here, as in other respects, Donald Trump took a different path in Iowa and New Hampshire, relying more on appearances to larger audiences rather than the kind of personal contact presidential candidates are known for in these contests.[118]

CHOICE OF CANDIDATES The extensive use of television has made looking and sounding good on television much more important. It has also led to the growth of the political consulting industry and made *visibility* the watchword in politics. Television strongly influences the public's idea of what traits are important in a candidate. Since television became so important in American politics, it has been assumed that being telegenic was important to candidate success. But as 2016 illustrated, some atypical candidates can also be successful. Vermont Senator Bernie Sanders did much better than expected against Hillary Clinton in the Democratic presidential contest, in part because he was seen as authentic. Donald Trump not only was a master at drawing the near constant attention of the media, but his rhetoric and style resonated with a set of voters who continue to see him favorably despite his unpredictability and sometimes abrasive style.

Although the news media insist that they pay attention to all candidates who have a chance to win, they also influence who gets such a chance. Consequently, candidates have to come up with creative ways to attract news media attention. As former Minnesota Democratic Senator Paul Wellstone said in his 1990 campaign advertisements, "Unlike my opponent I don't have 6 million dollars so I'm gonna have to talk fast."[119] His witty commercial became a news event itself—getting Wellstone additional coverage, and helping him win the election.

Exit polls from voters in the 2016 presidential election found very few voters who saw both Clinton and Trump favorably, while about one-in-five saw them both unfavorably. Clinton voters did not like Trump and Trump voters did not like Clinton.

The 2016 presidential race had unusual media elements. One involved an investigation, later reopened, by the FBI of Secretary of State Clinton's use of a private email server. FBI Director Comey, seen on the right, announced no criminal charges would be brought. But the "email" issue remained much discussed throughout the campaign.

This same pattern applied to candidate attributes like honesty, temperament, and being qualified for the office. A concern for about two-thirds of voters was Clinton's use of a private computer to access government emails, some of which contained sensitive, classified information.[120] In the words of FBI Director Comey, Secretary of State Clinton's use of the private server did not present "clear evidence" of an intent "to violate laws governing the handling of classified information, there is evidence that they were extremely careless in their handling of very sensitive, highly classified information."[121] Of those were bothered a lot about this, 86 percent voted for Trump. An even higher percentage, 70 percent, were bothered by Donald Trump's "treatment of women." Among those who were bothered a lot by Trump in this way, 83 percent voted for Clinton.[122] The issue of Trump's treatment of women grew in intensity with the release of a video of Donald Trump on the set of a television program, Access Hollywood, where he made vulgar comments about how he treated women.[123]

In this 2005 frame from video, Donald Trump prepares for an appearance on *Days of Our Lives* with actress Arianne Zucker (center). He is accompanied to the set by Access Hollywood host Billy Bush. (Obtained by the *Washington Post* via Getty Images)

CAMPAIGN EVENTS Candidates schedule events—press conferences, interviews, and "photo ops"—in settings that reinforce their verbal messages and public image. In 2008 and 2012, Barack Obama skillfully used a backdrop of young and diverse voters for his rallies. In contrast, other candidates were often surrounded by older and less diverse political leaders from the state or community. By 2016 it was standard practice for candidates in both parties to surround the candidates with a diverse group. Many campaign events fail to get reporters' attention because there are other more newsworthy stories, or because the media may sense that they have been staged to generate news coverage.

The parties' national conventions used to capture national attention. However, because party primaries now select candidates, the conventions no longer provide much suspense or make news, except perhaps over who will be the vice presidential nominee. This is one reason the networks have cut back their coverage of presidential nominating conventions. In 1952, the average television set was tuned to the political conventions for 26 hours, or an average of more than three hours a night for the eight nights of convention coverage.[124] In recent elections, by contrast, the major networks provided only one or two hours of prime-time coverage each evening. But cable channels now carry extensive coverage of the proceedings.[125]

In 2016, the conventions were in successive weeks with the Republicans going first. Mr. Trump's adult children and his wife Melania spoke. Mrs. Trump's speech was later found to contain passages from Michelle Obama's 2008 Democratic convention speech.[126] Texas Senator Ted Cruz, who had challenged Trump throughout the primaries, was given a prime-time speaking slot. When Cruz failed to endorse Trump in his remarks, he was roundly booed. Trump's acceptance speech focused on the need for change with regards to law and order, immigration, international trade and the U.S. economy, and America's role in the world.

The Democratic convention in 2016 showcased the Clinton family and included speeches from the president and Michelle Obama, and Vice President Biden. Many Sanders delegates arrived at the convention still angry about how their candidates had been treated and periodically during the convention they would express opposition. The Clinton campaign was poised to out-chant the Sanders delegates and much of this was not seen by the viewing audience.[127] In her speech, Hillary Clinton emphasized the need for unity within the Democratic Party and country and spoke of the needs of the middle class, while also criticizing Donald Trump. One short speech that became a controversy for days and weeks afterward was given by Khizr Kahn and his wife, Ghazala Kahn, who lost a son while he was serving in the Army in Iraq. Mr. Kahn, a Muslim, criticized Trump's position on Muslims and his understanding of the Constitution. Donald Trump called more attention to the speech by tweeting that Mrs. Kahn had been forbidden to speak at the convention and objecting to what he called Mr. Kahn's "vicious attacks." The back and forth between Mr. Trump and Mr. Kahn lasted for days after the convention and was a major distraction for the Trump campaign.

SOCIAL MEDIA AND CAMPAIGNS Although the expense associated with television advertising contributed to the skyrocketing costs of campaigning, it also made politics more accessible to more people. Blogs, Facebook posts, tweets, and other social media messages from the candidates further extend the campaign's reach.[128] More campaigns have used the Internet and email to reinforce voter preferences or answer voter questions than to persuade more passive citizens, but this may change given the success of the Obama campaign in 2012 and the expanded use of social media by candidates from both parties in 2016. In 2012, the Obama reelection campaign expanded its use of the Internet and social media. Drawing on the expertise of computer scientists and others, it used large databases with information on voter registration, consumer preferences, and data from other sources—what is sometimes called "big data"—to target persuadable voters and get them to vote early, by absentee, or on election day. Obama's data analytics operation was reported to be 10 times larger than Romney's. Obama also made much greater use of online ads than did Romney.[129] In 2016, the Internet was even more widely used, especially by Trump in the general election and social media was a major part of Trump's victory. In addition to the Russian use of social media, the Trump campaign used Facebook extensively for fundraising and voter persuasion.[130]

Just as communication moves faster on social media, so do mistakes. In 2008, Barack Obama speaking to a group of donors in San Francisco and unaware that he was being recorded said of unemployed people in states like Pennsylvania that "it is not surprising they get bitter, they cling to guns or religion or antipathy toward people who aren't like them or are anti-immigrant or anti-trade sentiment as a way to explain their frustrations."[131] This statement put Obama on the defensive with his rivals accusing him of not appreciating small-town values. In 2012, something similar happened to Republican presidential candidate Mitt Romney when a cellphone video of him speaking to Republican donors hit the Internet after he characterized 47 percent of the public as "dependent on government" and unwilling to "take personal responsibility."[132]

The Internet provides an inexpensive way for candidates and campaigns to communicate with volunteers, contributors, and voters, and promises to become an even larger component of future campaigns. Candidates' Web sites not only offer extensive information about the candidates themselves and their stances on issues, but also are tools for meeting fellow supporters, for receiving news and materials from the campaign, for volunteering, and for setting up personalized home pages. This is in addition to candidates' YouTube channels, emails, social networking profiles, tweets, and affiliated blogs.

Social media was important to the 2016 presidential election not only as a way to communicate with those using it but because it became a recurrent issue in the broader campaign environment. Donald Trump's tweets were so frequently covered and so controversial that *The New York Times* devoted a full two-page spread to tweets he sent during his candidacy. The Trump campaign characterized the story as "a liberal hatchet job." What is not in dispute is the way Mr. Trump used Twitter to generate media coverage of himself and his views of his opponents. Trump's use of social media surpassed Hillary Clinton on Twitter and Facebook, and this does not take into account how conventional news reporting covered his tweets. Trump was not alone in using Twitter—an estimated one-billion plus election-related posts were tweeted between the first presidential debate and election day.[133] Trump was not alone in his vast social media use in 2016. The Clinton campaign used it as well; and in the primaries, Ben Carson made extensive use of Facebook and Ted Cruz of Facebook and Twitter.[134]

IMAGE MAKING AND MEDIA CONSULTANTS Consistent with the media's focus on personality is its highlighting of mistakes and gaffes by candidates and officeholders. Long before *The Daily Show,* print and broadcast news media devoted considerable attention to such things as Gerald Ford mistakenly classifying Poland as a free country in the 1976 presidential debates.[135] In 2012, Texas governor and presidential hopeful Rick Perry had a memory lapse in a Republican presidential candidate debate when he said there were three agencies in Washington, D.C., he would close if elected but then could only name two of them.[136]

The ability of television and the Internet to reach a mass audience and the power of the visual image on television have contributed to the rise of new players in campaign politics, most notably *media consultants*—campaign professionals who provide candidates with advice and services on media relations, advertising strategy, and opinion polling.[137] A primary responsibility of a campaign media consultant is to present a positive image of the candidate and to reinforce negative images of the opponent. Both parties have scores of media consultants who have handled congressional, gubernatorial, and referendum campaigns.

Today, consultants coach candidates about how to act and behave on television and what to discuss on the air. Consultants report the results of *focus groups* (small sample groups of people who are asked questions about candidates and issues in a discussion setting) and *public opinion polls,* which in turn determine what the candidate says and does. Some critics allege that political consultants have become a new "political elite" that can virtually choose candidates by determining in advance which men and women have the right images, or at least images that the consultants can restyle for the widest popularity.[138] But political consultants who specialize in media advertising and image making know their own limitations in packaging candidates. As one media consultant put it, "It is a very hard job to turn a turkey into a movie star; you try instead to make people like the turkey."[139]

Impact on Voter Choice

As television and the Internet have become increasingly important to politics—and reforms such as primary elections have weakened the political parties and made news coverage of candidates more important—the question arises: what difference does the media make? Does it seem to affect your opinions and choices?

PERSONALITY OVER SUBSTANCE Some critics think reporters pay too much attention to candidates' personality and background and not enough attention to issues and policy. Others say character and personality are among the most important characteristics for readers and viewers to know about. The public appetite for stories on candidates' personal strengths and weaknesses is not new and is likely to persist.

The influence of the media on the public varies by level of sophistication of the voters. Better-informed and more-educated voters are less swayed by new information from the media.[140] But for the public generally, other scholars contend that "television news is news that matters."[141] The expanded use of social media as a news source has made political coverage more personality driven and more sensational,[142] especially tweets from Donald Trump in 2016.

THE HORSE RACE A common tendency in the news media is to comment less on a candidate's position on issues than on a candidate's position in the polls compared with other candidates—what is sometimes called the **horse race**. "Many stories focus on who is ahead, who is behind, who is going to win, and who is going to lose, rather than examining how and why the race is as it is."[143] Reporters focus on the tactics and strategy of campaigns because they think such coverage interests the public.[144] The news media's propensity to focus on the "game" of campaigns displaces coverage of issues.

horse race
A close contest; by extension, any contest in which the focus is on who is ahead and by how much rather than on substantive differences between the candidates.

NEGATIVE ADVERTISING Paid political advertising, much of it negative in tone, is another source of information for voters. Political advertising has always attacked opponents, but recent campaigns have taken on an increasingly negative tone. The rule of thumb used to be to ignore the opposition's charges and thus avoid giving them, or the opposition, importance or standing. More recently, media advisers recommend responding quickly and aggressively to attacks. One criticism of John Kerry, who was the Democratic nominee for president in 2004, and Mitt Romney, who was the GOP standard bearer in 2012, is that neither candidate effectively challenged attacks from groups opposing them. Kerry failed to respond to attacks on his record of military service, and Romney's record at Bain Capital, an investment banking group, was also attacked without adequate response.

Spending on advertising by groups not directed or controlled by the candidates has grown in recent years and includes spending by Super PACs and other groups.[145] As with ads in earlier cycles, this outside spending is most often negative in tone. In 2014, for example, the proportion of negative ads was double the proportion of positive ads.[146] In 2016, presidential campaign advertising declined compared to prior cycles, a change largely explained by the much lower level of television advertising by Donald Trump's campaign and supporting groups. The ads from Clinton supporting groups were almost all negative in tone, while the ads from groups supporting Trump were about 60 percent negative, with an additional 30 percent contrasting ads with some negative messaging on Clinton but some discussion of Trump's position.[147] The emphasis on negative messages has meant some specialized Super PACs now collect video clips from candidates to be used in attack ads later in the campaign.

Voters say the attack style of politics is offensive, but most campaign consultants believe that negative campaigning works. This seeming inconsistency may be explained by evidence suggesting that negative advertising may discourage some voters from voting who would be inclined to support an opposing candidate (a phenomenon known as *vote suppression*) while making your supporters more likely to vote.[148] Other research suggests that negative advertising is more informative than positive advertising and does not discourage voter turnout, but it does alienate people from government.[149] Finally, in some contexts at least, negative ads may stimulate individuals to contribute to both the candidate attacked by the ad as well as the candidate running, while positive ads that include partisan content only increase donations to the candidate running the ad.[150]

MAKING A DECISION Newspapers, television, and the Internet seem to have more influence in affecting the outcome of primary elections than of general elections,[151] probably because voters in a primary are less likely to know about the candidates and have fewer clues about how they stand. By the November general election, however, party affiliation, incumbency, and other factors diminish the impact of media messages. The mass media are more likely to influence undecided voters, who, in a close election, can determine who wins and who loses.

ELECTION NIGHT REPORTING Election returns from the East Coast come in three hours before the polls close on the West Coast. Because major networks often project the presidential winner well before polls close in western states, it can affect western voters. When one candidate appears to be winning by a large margin, it may make voters believe their vote is meaningless and dampen voter turnout. In a close presidential election, however, such early reporting may stimulate turnout because voters know their vote could determine the outcome.

Controversy over exit polls grew after the 2000 election, when television networks projected that Al Gore had won Florida, only to later retract that prediction. Hours later, Fox News projected Bush winning Florida. The truth was that the vote in Florida was by every measure too close to call. In 2004, leaks of early exit polls in the news media showed John Kerry winning Ohio,[152] a state carried by Bush. Despite these problems, exit polls are generally accurate and inform the public about who voted and why people voted the way they did. For example, exit polls are one source of data used in this book.

The News Media and Governance (Impact)

9.4 Describe the news media's relationship to governance in the United States.

The launch of the Affordable Care Act (Obamacare) in October 2013 produced a great deal of news media coverage on failures in the program's Web site, https://www.healthcare.gov. In some ways the roll-out of Obamacare was not unlike other new programs. What made Obamacare different was the size of the new program, the intense opposition to it by some, and the fact that the president's name was associated with the program. More commonly the press does not give much attention to how new laws are implemented.[153]

Lack of press attention to the way policies are implemented impacts what we know about how government officials go about their business. Only in the case of a scandal, such as the Obamacare Web site problems, does the press take notice of how policies are implemented.[154] The reverse is also the case; sustained news media attention on congressional inaction or deadlock between Congress and the president impacts how the public sees these institutions.

Some critics contend that the media pressure on policy makers to provide immediate answers forces them to make hasty decisions, a particular danger in foreign policy. If an ominous foreign event is featured on television news, the president and his advisers feel pressured to respond almost as soon as the crisis happens. The longer the president delays, the easier it is for opponents to attack him for indecisiveness, while portraying themselves as capable and unflappable in a crisis.[155]

Political Institutions and the News Media

Presidents and members of Congress develop relationships with the press they hope will pay off in positive media coverage. In contrast, the federal courts, whose judges are appointed and have long believed it important to distance themselves from politics, do not often engage with the media directly and instead let their written opinions be their primary mode of communication.

PRESIDENT Presidents have become the governmental stars for the news media, particularly television, and have made the news media their forum for setting the public agenda and achieving their legislative aims. Presidential news conferences command attention (see Figure 9.4). Every public activity a president engages in, both professional and personal, is potentially newsworthy; a presidential illness can become front-page news, as can the president's vacations and pets. President Trump, more than any prior president, has used Twitter to communicate his view of topics in the news, as well as criticisms of his political opponents, and even his political allies.

Well before the Trump presidency, governmental institutions at all levels, including the White House, used the Internet as a way to engage the public in online discourse. While President Trump likes to send out messages, his administration has not been as keen on receiving public input. For example, in mid-December 2017, the White House took down the popular "We the People" petitions Web site with the promise that it would be restored by "late January."[156] The site, after undergoing maintenance was operating in early February.[157] This White House public input site was started by President Obama and has generated serious proposals as well as many which involved pop culture like proposing that Justin Bieber be deported

FIGURE 9.4 PRESIDENTIAL PRESS CONFERENCES: JOINT AND SOLO SESSIONS, 1913–2018

Because presidents since Woodrow Wilson have varied in the total months in office, from a low of 30 for Gerald Ford to a high of 145.5 for Franklin Roosevelt, it makes sense to standardize the use of press conferences over time in the number per month in office. Using this metric, Calvin Coolidge had the highest number per month in office with 7.78, followed by two others who served after him, Hoover (5.56) and Roosevelt (6.55). Ronald Reagan, despite his reputation as the great communicator, had the fewest press conferences in this period, with 0.48 per month.

NOTE: In a joint press conference, the president answers questions along with someone else, most often a foreign leader. In a solo session, only the president answers questions. There are three missing transcripts for Roosevelt and one for Johnson, which makes it impossible to determine whether those sessions were solo or joint ones.

SOURCE: Martha Joynt Kumar, email correspondence November 2018; Gerhard Peters, "Presidential News Conferences," *The American Presidency Project*, eds. John T. Woolley and Gerhard Peters. Santa Barbara, CA: University of California. 1999–2016, available online at http://www.presidency.ucsb.edu/data/newsconferences.php.

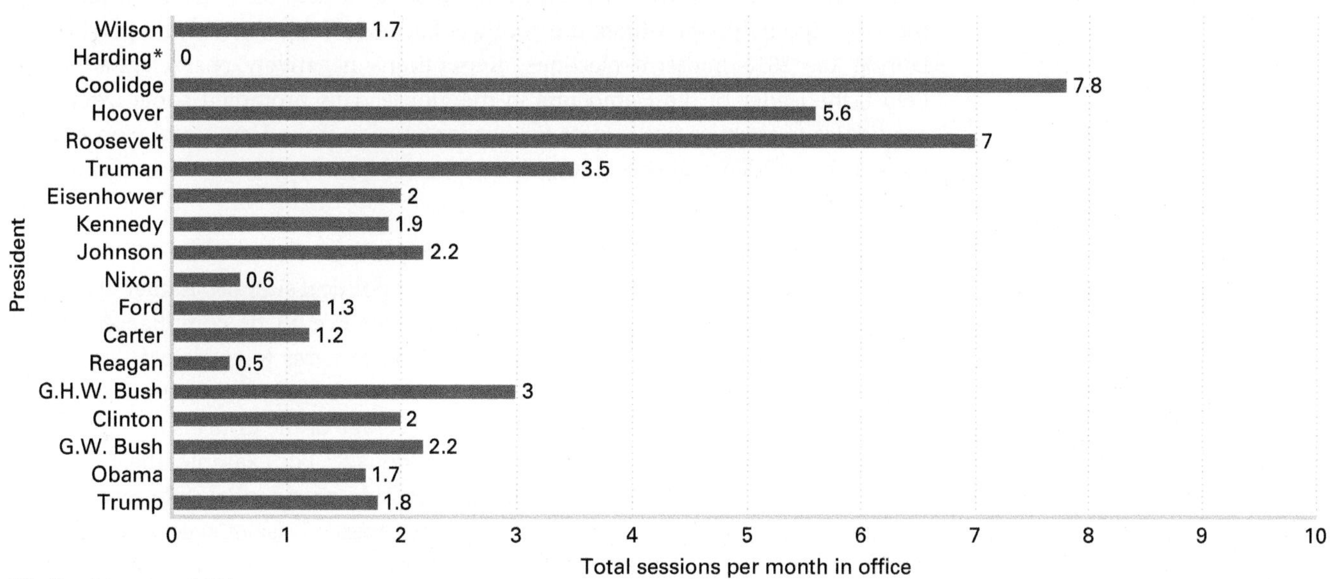

(*Harding data not available)

due to bad behavior. More serious petitions have led to actions like a proposal that cell phone users be able to transfer their phones to a different network, a White House call to end gay conversion therapy, and the granting of a Presidential Medal of Freedom to former baseball player Yogi Berra." The Web site pledges that the White House will respond to the petition when a threshold of 100,000 signatures is reached. The Obama White House was criticized for waiting two years to respond to a petition asking for a pardon of Edward Snowden, before saying "no."[158] President Trump's White House has not responded to any of the petitions that have exceeded the signature threshold since he took office. Among the petitions awaiting a response are ones calling on the president to release his tax returns, to repeal the National Firearms Act of 1934, and to put his business and financial assets in a blind trust.[159]

A president attempts to manipulate news coverage to his benefit, as in the Bush administration's decision to embed reporters with U.S. forces during the early stages of the Iraq War. Presidents and their staffs also leak information to reporters. Presidents use speeches to set the national agenda or spur congressional action. Presidential travel to foreign countries usually boosts popular support at home, due to largely favorable news coverage.

CONGRESS Members of Congress have long sought to cultivate positive relationships with news reporters in their states and districts. They typically have a press relations staffer who informs local news media of newsworthy events, produces press releases, and generally tries to promote the senator or representative.[160] Congress also provides recording studios for taping of news segments, and both parties have recording studios near the Capitol explicitly for electoral ads. Finally, politicians often appear on talk radio, which they can readily do from their offices in Washington. The focus of this news media cultivation is on the individual member and not on the institution of Congress as a whole.

Congress is more likely to receive negative coverage than either the White House or the Supreme Court. Unlike the executive branch, it lacks an ultimate spokesperson, a single person who can speak for the whole institution.[161] Congress does not make it easy for the press to cover it. Whereas the White House attentively cares for and feeds the press corps, Congress does not arrange its schedule to accommodate the news media; floor debates, for example, often compete with committee hearings and press conferences.[162] Singularly dramatic actions rarely occur in Congress; the press therefore turns to the president to describe the activity of the federal government on a day-to-day basis and treats Congress largely as a foil to the president. Most coverage of Congress is about how it acts on pressing matters, with some focus on legislative process, especially when there are conflicts between Congress and the president.[163] During the 2018 midterm elections, Republicans negatively characterized Nancy Pelosi, the leader of the Democrats in the House. This prompted some Democratic candidates to promise not to vote for her for Speaker if the Democrats won a majority—further evidence of strong negative partisanship, which is one reason Congress is held in such low regard.

JUDICIARY The federal judiciary is least dependent on the press. The Supreme Court does not rely on public communication for political support. Rather, it depends indirectly on public opinion for continued deference to or compliance with its decisions.[164] The Court does not allow television cameras to cover oral arguments, controls the release of audiotape, and bars reporters as well as anyone other than the justices when it meets to discuss cases. Press coverage of the Court is far more subtle and complex than that of the other two institutions.[165] For example, the complexity of the Supreme Court's decision in the 2000 Florida presidential vote recount case, with multiple dissents and concurrences and no press release or executive summary, made broadcast reporting on the decision difficult.

Factors That Limit News Media Influence

Despite the varied means the media has for influencing public opinion, people are not just empty vessels into which politicians and journalists pour information and ideas. The way we interpret political messages depends on a variety of factors: political socialization, selectivity, needs, and our ability to recall and comprehend the message.

POLITICAL ORIENTATION People respond to the news media having already developed an orientation to politics. We develop our political attitudes, values, and beliefs through an education process social scientists call **political socialization.**[166] Individual perceptions begin to be shaped by family values and attitudes at a very young age. By the time the media enters as a socializing force to shape public perceptions and knowledge, citizens already view information through the lens formed by their early political socialization.

political socialization
The process by which we develop our political attitudes, values, and beliefs.

PARTY IDENTIFICATION Party identification is one lens through which people view the media. Similarly, political ideology can influence where we go for political news and how we interpret the news. Strong party identification also acts as a powerful filter.[167] A conservative Republican from Arizona may watch the "liberal eastern networks" and complain about their biased news coverage while sticking to her own opinions. A liberal from New York will often complain about right-wing talk radio, even if he listens to it occasionally (see Figure 9.5). Additionally, face-to-face and social media contact with friends and business associates (*peer pressure*) can have far more impact than the information or views we get from an impersonal television program or newspaper article.

SELECTIVITY All human beings engage in **selective exposure**—screening out messages that do not conform to our own biases. We subscribe to newspapers or magazines or turn to television and cable news outlets that support our views.[168] For example, between 69 and 78 percent of the audience of Sean Hannity, Rush Limbaugh, and Bill O'Reilly are conservatives.[169] We also practice **selective perception**—perceiving what we want to in news media messages.[170] People do this by overlooking stories or parts of stories that are not consistent with their strongly held views.

selective exposure
The process by which individuals screen out messages that do not conform to their own biases.

selective perception
The process by which individuals perceive what they want in news media messages.

NEEDS People read newspapers, listen to the radio, or watch television for different reasons.[171] News media affect people differently depending on whether they are seeking information about politics or want to be entertained. Members of the broader audience are also more likely to pay attention to news that directly affects their lives, such as interest rate changes or the price of gasoline.[172]

AUDIENCE FRAGMENTATION As discussed above, the growth of cable television and new media such as the Internet has reduced the dominance of broadcast media and newspapers in transmitting information. Because there are more press outlets that cover politics in varied ways, the impact of the press has become more diffuse. Fragmentation of the news media audience has tended to counteract the impact of news media conglomeration. But as news media giants acquire both cable and broadcast stations and outlets and promote their own online sites, the importance of news media conglomerates such as NBC, CNBC, and MSNBC will increase.

PERCEIVED NEWS MEDIA BIAS One limitation on the impact of the media is the perceived bias of some news media. We tend to blame the news media for being either too conservative or too liberal. Conservatives often complain that the news media are too liberal. Radio talk show host Rush Limbaugh observed that "back in the day before we existed, they [the liberals] owned it [the news media], they had

FIGURE 9.5 IDEOLOGY AND TRUSTED NEWS SOURCES

Consistent conservatives trust Fox News and commentators like Hannity, Rush Limbaugh, and Glenn Beck while consistent liberals trust PBS, The *New York Times*, and network and cable TV news stations other than Fox News. Liberals have a wider set of news sources they trust, conservatives fewer. Less than one-third of consistent conservatives trust the *Wall Street Journal.*

QUESTION: Of the sources you have heard of, click on all that you generally TRUST for news about government and politics."

SOURCE: Political Polarization & Media Habits: From Fox News to Facebook, how Liberals and Conservatives Keep Up with Politics, Pew Research Center, October 21, 2014. http://www.journalism.org/files/2014/10/Political-Polarization-and-Media-Habits-FINAL-REPORT-7-27-15.pdf.

News Source	Total Sample	Consistently Liberal	Mostly Liberal	Mixed	Mostly Conservative	Consistently Conservative
CNN	54	56	66	61	39	14
ABC News	50	52	59	56	40	18
NBC News	50	56	59	54	37	16
Fox	44	6	28	47	72	88
CBS News	46	51	55	50	36	16
MSNBC	38	52	48	39	6	7
PBS	38	71	50	31	23	8
NY Times	34	62	45	29	17	3
Wall Street Journal	31	35	34	28	32	30
Hannity	12	0	1	6	28	62
Limbaugh	12	0	2	6	27	28
Beck	10	0	1	4	24	51

a monopoly."[173] Some liberal critics contend that the news media reflect a conservative bias not only in what they report, but also in what they choose to ignore. They point to Fox News as an example of conservative cable television.

In fact, most U.S. news media are committed to being unbiased. Newspapers and television management go to some lengths to insulate reporters from their advertising and business operations, in part to reduce criticism about favorable editorial treatment of large advertisers or the corporate owners. In 2007, when the management of the *Los Angeles Times* attempted to foster closer relationships between the business and news divisions, they were criticized out of a concern that advertisers would influence news coverage.[174]

The news media's alleged political bias is also a frequent target of criticism, in part because the journalists tend to be more liberal than the rest of the public. In a survey conducted in 2017 by the Newseum in Washington, D.C., 43 percent agreed with the statement that "the news media reports without bias." This was a substantial increase over 2015 and 2016. It may be that talk of fake news has actually led to more widespread public confidence in the news. Only one-quarter of the public thinks the news media reports without bias, a large drop over the 2013 survey (see Figure 9.6 on the next page). The question of whether there is an ideological bias in the news media has not been authoritatively answered. News reporters' worldview, some contend, may govern their choice of issues to cover and the way they cover them.[175] Critics counter that conservative forces in the news media, such as corporate ownership, lead to disproportionate time and influence given to conservative pundits. A further question is whether bias, if it exists and whatever its direction, seeps into the content of the news. Here too, the answer remains unclear. One source that seeks to inform news media consumers about detecting news media bias is a group named Fairness and Accuracy in Reporting (FAIR).[176]

FIGURE 9.6 DOES THE NEWS MEDIA REPORT WITHOUT BIAS?

Over the past decade or so the percent who disagree that the news media tries to report without bias has consistently been above 50 percent and sometimes as high as 75 percent. This level of distrust may help explain why people seek out media they agree with.

SOURCE: Newseum Institute, "The 2015 State of the First Amendment," available at http://www.newseuminstitute.org/wp-content/uploads/2015/07/FAC_SOFA15_report.pdf.

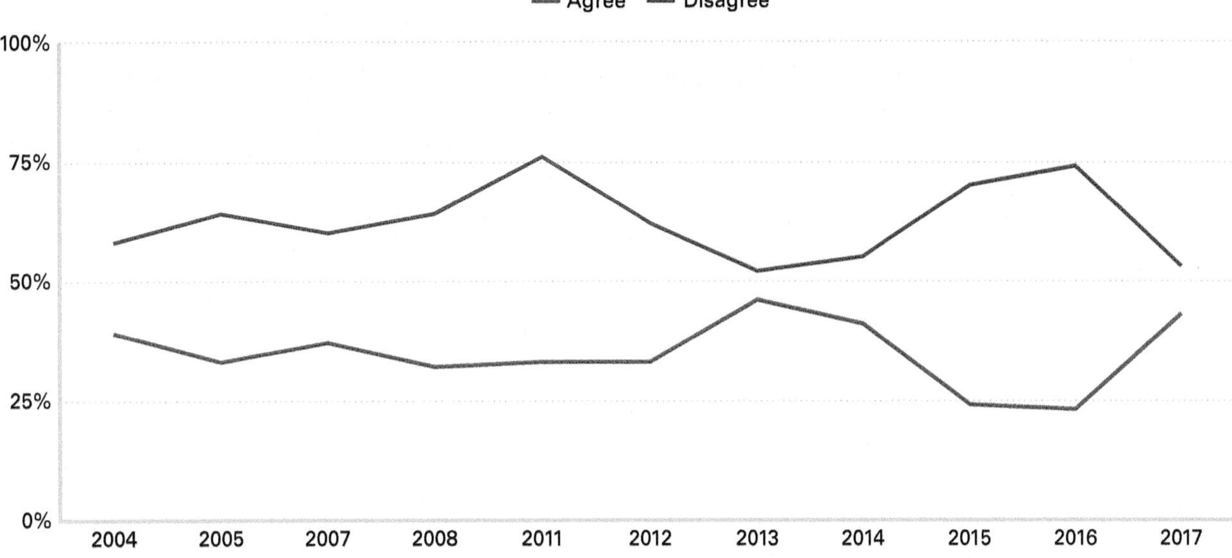

One bias that does not have a partisan or ideological slant is the bias toward sensationalism. Scandals happen to liberals and conservatives, Republicans and Democrats. Once the province of tabloids like the *National Enquirer,* stories about sex, drugs, or other scandals involving celebrities and politicians have become commonplace in the mainstream news media.

CONCLUSION

The government's development of the Internet has had an incredible impact on the way Americans communicate individually and as a society. You benefit from the government's investment in the Internet many times throughout the day. Beyond getting your news about what is going on in the world, you utilize Internet search tools to find out about what candidates stand for and to watch them in action via YouTube and other platforms. Candidates and groups also use the Internet to contact individuals and communicate messages about politics to them. The Internet is also a way to gauge public opinion through Twitter and various tracking methodologies. But as discussed at the beginning of this chapter, not all democracies are as open to using the Internet for political communication as is the United States. Voters in South Korea and Japan, for example, are much less free to communicate about candidates, and those not of voting age may not legally do so.

However, the benefits of the Internet do not accrue without drawbacks. As we become increasingly dependent on the Internet, we are more susceptible to hackers, and there are more opportunities for individual privacy to be violated. The expanded use of the Internet also raises a number of possibilities for changes in the political system.

If a technology could be developed that could not be hacked, should we permit people to vote online? There already has been extensive use of the Internet for political fundraising, with the Democrats having a substantial advantage in this new tool through the 2008 and 2012 elections. What, if any, limits should be placed on Internet political participation?

The government needs the news media to communicate with the public, but the news media has roles beyond simply relaying government officials' press releases. In some cases it is to discover and report news the government would rather not have you know. The Internet is one way people like you have helped report on news events. You may post videos of politicians making troubling comments. Given the frequency of shootings, should police officers be required to wear body cameras? These are questions you will have to decide. In a world of ever-advancing technology, there are likely to be even more complex questions we have not yet contemplated. How, or if, these advancements are regulated will have profound effects on the information we have about the government and, in turn, the information the government has about each of you.

REVIEW THE CHAPTER

The Structure and Functions of the News Media and the Constitutional Protections of Freedom of the Press (Structure)

9.1 Describe the origins, structure, and functions of the news media, and the nature of constitutional protections of Freedom of the Press, p. 260.

The news media include newspapers, newsmagazines, radio, television, and electronic communications in all their forms. These means of communication have been called the "fourth branch of government," for they are a pervasive feature of U.S. politics. The news media provide and carry information among political actors, the government, and the public. Our modern news media emerged from a more partisan and less professional past. Since the advent of broadcast media, the government has played a role in licensing radio and television stations that use the airwaves to send their signal to the public. Cable television and satellite radio stations that are not subject to these regulations now provide a broader set of news outlets.

Included in the Bill of Rights is Freedom of the Press. Our governmental structure thus envisions an active news media to inform citizens and serve as an additional check on government at all levels. The constitutional structure also protects authors and inventors, showing that since its inception, the founding document of U.S. government fosters freedom of thought and expression.

How Americans Get the News (Action)

9.2 Describe the effect of recent trends in how Americans get their news, p. 265.

Journalists today strive for objectivity and also engage in investigatory journalism. Corporate ownership and consolidation of news media outlets raise questions about news media competition and orientation. Radio and television broadcasting have changed the news media, and more recently so has social media. The media, which include news media plus films, recordings, and books, can also be important in shaping public opinion and social values.

Newspaper circulation has been decreasing, and although radio use has persisted, the Internet and social media have become increasingly more popular places to go for news. The Internet has emerged as a new source of both information and political participation. Television remains an important news source.

The Influence of the News Media on Public Opinion and Elections (Impact)

9.3 Assess the influence of the news media on American public opinion and elections, p. 275.

The mass media's influence over public opinion is significant but not overwhelming. People tend to filter the news through their political socialization, selectivity, needs, and ability to recall or comprehend the news. News media coverage dominates presidential campaigns, and candidates depend on news media exposure to build name recognition, a positive image, and thereby votes. Election coverage by the news media emphasizes the contest as a game or "horse race." Although conservatives charge that the news media are too liberal and liberals charge that the news media are captive to business interests, little evidence exists of actual, deliberate bias in news reporting. The news media's influence is most strongly felt in their ability to determine what problems and events will come to the public's attention and how those issues are framed.

The News Media and Governance (Impact)

9.4 Describe the news media's relationship to governance in the United States, p. 282.

The press serves as both observer and participant in politics as a recorder, watchdog, agenda setter, and check on the abuse of power. Examples include Watergate and the disclosure of large-scale government data collection on cell phone and Internet use. The presidency is the subject of more news attention than the Congress, the courts, or the bureaucracy. The news media rarely give much attention to the implementation or administration phases of the policy process. One exception is the start of Obamacare, which had Web site and other start-up problems. The influence of the media is limited by audience fragmentation, selective attention, and selective perception.

LEARN THE TERMS

news media, p. 262
24/7 news cycle, p. 271
horse race, p. 281
political socialization, p. 285
selective exposure, p. 285
selective perception, p. 285

Congress

CHAPTER 10

The nation's military remains a top priority for Congress and the president, and is well represented on Capitol Hill by the Joint Chiefs of Staff. The Joint Chiefs represent all four military services and the National Guard, and are frequently called to testify before Congress on the defense budget, military strategy, recruitment, and policy issues such as the Trump administration's decision to ban some transgender applicants from enlisting in the military. Here, members of the Joint Chiefs rise for the president's State of the Union Address before Congress on January 31, 2018.

LEARNING OBJECTIVES

The U.S. Congress has always played a central role in keeping the nation safe from foreign threats by building a strong national defense. Although the president is the military's Commander in Chief and has the constitutional authority to wage war, Congress is responsible for declaring war, organizing the military, and caring for veterans of war.

The United States already had the strongest national defense in the world at the end of World War II, but it needed to become even stronger to win its 30-year cold war against communism and the Soviet Union. With the Soviet Union moving quickly to build its first nuclear bomb, Congress merged the old departments of the army, navy, and air force into a new Department of Defense, and raised the military budget from $9 billion in 1948 to $300 billion in 1989, when the Soviet Union finally collapsed and the Berlin Wall was torn down.[1]

Even after the cold war ended, the United States continued to invest heavily in maintaining a strong national defense. It spends more money today on defense than the next seven world powers combined, and has 1.5 million Americans on active duty.[2] It also has the most sophisticated, high-tech, battle-ready armed services of any nation, and may well need all of it despite frequent calls for a less ambitious global agenda. As an old military saying goes, "You may not have an interest in war, but war may have an interest in you."

Experts disagree about the nation's readiness for the rapidly changing nature of possible military engagement. Recent assessments suggest that the United States is well prepared to fight a traditional war—it has more than enough troops, ships, aircraft, and heavy ground equipment such as tanks and armored personnel carriers.

But the United States must be prepared for the smaller conflicts that involve very fast moving adversaries such as the Islamic State in Iraq and Syria (ISIS). These wars often call for specially trained troops because superior U.S. air power alone is of limited use without incurring large numbers of civilian casualties. But given the protracted wars recently fought in the Middle East, the idea of committing U.S. troops on the ground is not popular. These realities mean you and your elected representatives will have to make trade-offs between a more limited war against ISIS or a commitment of U.S. forces to the conflict for an uncertain period of time. More broadly, you will have to vote for or against more spending for national defense.[3]

The United States still has the world's strongest national defense, but the big question today is how much to spend and what to buy to keep it. In 2018, for example, Congress and the president increased the defense budget 10 percent, or $70 billion dollars, but also began debating deep cuts in education, environmental protection, and health care for 2019. Much of the increase was set aside for higher military pay and new weapons systems such as fight aircraft and modernization of the nation's nuclear weapons arsenal. Faced with a growing budget deficit, Congress and the president will have to decide where to find the dollars to cover its priorities, while asking how to balance the need for increased defense spending with longstanding priorities such as student loan funding.[4] Because the defense budget changes slowly, the decisions you will need to make about what to keep and cut will have long-term consequences.

If you decide that cutting the defense budget is the way to go, you may also have to fight the defense industry itself. Members of Congress know that legislative votes for budget cuts are often used against them during tough campaigns, and that the defense industry creates good jobs in their states and districts. They also know that the defense industry provides millions in campaign contributions and puts great pressure on Congress through its lobbying.[5]

This chapter will help you understand and make these decisions by showing you how Congress members balance the public interest with the desire to keep their jobs through the advantage of incumbency that comes from defense spending and other policy choices. You will also learn how the legislative process works, why so many members of Congress are reelected, and what influences their legislative votes. Armed with knowledge about congressional structure, action, and impact, you will be able to make decisions on a host of legislative issues that may or may not strengthen the nation.

The Constitutional Foundations of Congress (Structure)

10.1 Describe the constitutional foundations of Congress.

The Framers expected that Congress, not the president or the judiciary, would be the most important branch of government, which is why they defined it in the first article of the Constitution, Article I, Section 1.[6] They knew that laws would matter greatly to the young nation's survival, and designed a lawmaking structure based on clear rules and powers.

Because they were convinced that the legislative authority has the greatest power in a government ruled by laws, as James Madison argued in *Federalist,* No. 51, the Framers gave Congress more than enough authority to lead the nation but also checked the powers to prevent tyranny.

A Divided Branch

The Framers made their most important decision about Congress late in the Constitutional Convention when they created a two-house legislature. Although they had originally settled on a one-house legislature, they embraced this **bicameralism** as a way to satisfy small and large states alike by giving each an edge in one chamber. Small states were guaranteed the same number of senators as large states, while large states were guaranteed more representatives than small states.

bicameralism
The division of the legislative branch into two chambers that have the power to check and balance each other.

These and other early decisions gave Congress great power to make the laws, but also checked this power by giving each chamber a different structure. Having argued that the legislature would "predominate" over the executive and judiciary, Madison and Hamilton wrote 10 separate papers on Congress that described the methods for electing senators and representatives, the rules governing how each chamber would make the laws, the relationship between the House and Senate, and checks and balances with the executive.

enumerated powers
The list of specific constitutional powers given to Congress in Article I, Section 8.

Each of the papers was carefully designed to refute claims that the legislature was too powerful. As Hamilton wrote in *Federalist,* No. 59, for example, the Constitution gives the states responsibility for determining the manner of congressional elections, but Congress itself can alter the state rules at any time. "Nothing can be more evident," Hamilton wrote in *Federalist,* No. 59, "than that an exclusive power of regulating elections for the national government, in the hands of the State legislatures, would leave the existence of the Union entirely at their mercy."[7]

Each chamber meets in its own wing of the Capitol Building; each has offices for its members on separate sides of Capitol Street; each has its own committee structure, its own rules for considering legislation, and its own record of proceedings (even though the records are published together as the *Congressional Record*); and each sets the rules governing its own members.[8]

Anyone can attend a congressional hearing provided they make it through heavy screening at the entrance to the U.S. Capitol Visitor Center. Here, advocates of funding for Planned Parenthood stand in line for a seat at a House hearing on the federal budget in 2017.

Congressional Powers

All congressional powers trace back to Article I, section 8 of the Constitution and its list of **enumerated powers**. Because the Revolutionary War had been sparked by unfair taxation, the power "to lay and collect Taxes" was the first of the specific powers Congress would use to protect the young nation. The long list of powers falls into five broad categories:

1. *The Power to Raise, Make, and Borrow Money.* Congress has the power to tax, borrow money, issue currency, and coin money.
2. *The Power to Regulate Commerce.* Congress has the power to regulate commerce between the United States and other nations, as well as between the states. It can also set standards for determining the value of products through weights and measures, establish uniform bankruptcy laws that govern private businesses, and promote the arts and sciences by granting copyright protection to authors and patents to inventors.
3. *The Power to Unify the Country.* Congress has the power to create post offices and postal roads, which link the states together; to determine the rules for becoming a citizen; and to acquire, manage, and dispose of federal land.
4. *The Power to Declare War.* Congress has the power to declare war, raise armies, and build ships; organize, arm, discipline, and call on state militias to act on the nation's behalf; execute laws suppressing civil unrest; and repel foreign invasions. However, even with these powers to declare and ready the nation for war, Congress does not have the power to command the military—this duty belongs to the president.
5. *The Power to Create the Federal Judiciary.* Congress is responsible for creating all "inferior" courts below the Supreme Court and for determining their jurisdiction, as well as the appellate jurisdiction of the Supreme Court.

power of the purse
The congressional power to appropriate and raise money for government programs and administration.

The Constitution also gave Congress the power to make laws to spend money. Writing in *Federalist,* No. 58, Madison called this **power of the purse** "the most complete and effectual weapon with which any constitution can arm the immediate representatives of the people, for obtaining a redress of every grievance, and for carrying into effect every just and salutary measure."[9] Congress uses the power of the purse to raise taxes, control spending, and provide the government funding to support programs such as the Affordable Care Act, sometimes called Obamacare. Congress passed the act in 2009, and the Supreme Court declared that its tax and spending provisions were constitutional in 2012. But, as part of the Tax Cut and Jobs Act of 2017, Congress repealed the Act's individual mandate, which required Americans to have health insurance or pay a tax. Just as Congress can use the power of the purse to raise taxes, it can also cut those taxes and the programs they supported.

impeachment power
The formal charges of treason, bribery, or other high crimes and misdemeanors against the president enacted by the House by majority vote.

articles of impeachment
The formal House document that lists the charges against the president for treason, bribery, or high crimes and misdemeanors.

Beyond the spending power, the Framers also gave Congress two powerful checks against the president: (1) the power to override a president's decision to veto a bill, and (2) the power to remove the president and federal judges from office. The **impeachment power** is one of the most important checks in the Constitution and is divided between the House and Senate to make sure it is never abused. Under the power, the House has the authority to charge, or impeach, a president for treason, bribery, or other "high crimes and misdemeanors," or a federal judge for failing to serve during "good behavior," but the Senate has the responsibility to conduct the trial to determine guilt or innocence. The **articles of impeachment** are forwarded to the Senate by a majority vote of the House, while a two-thirds vote of the Senate is required for a final conviction.

No U.S. president in history has ever been convicted of an impeachable offense, but two presidents, Andrew Johnson and Bill Clinton, were impeached by the House, tried by the Senate, and acquitted, and one other president, Richard Nixon was on the precipice of impeachment when he resigned from office. Impeachment reached the headlines again in 2017 when President Trump came under investigation for possible collusion with the Russian government during the 2016 presidential campaign. Democratic members of Congress also accused Trump of interfering with the investigation.[10]

The investigation continued through the 2018 midterm elections but hit a roadblock when Trump fired Attorney General Jeff Sessions only hours after the polls closed. Trump had wanted to remove Sessions since early 2017 but feared that the firing might affect Republican chances in the elections. He replaced Sessions with a temporary officer who had criticized the investigation in the past, which provoked Democratic concerns in the House and Senate.

Congress did return to Washington after the midterm elections, and while some members expressed outrage over the firing, the Senate showed little interest in legislative action or hearings. While the outgoing Republican House majority was still in charge of the agenda, both chambers were in "lame duck" mode, a term that refers to weakened birds that cannot keep up with the flock. A lame-duck Congress can produce major legislation on pressing issues such as the federal budget but generally steers clear of controversial action as it awaits the arrival of its new members on January 3 and prepares to say adieu to departing colleagues. Congress holds few hearings, curtails floor action, and stalls bigger issues for the new Congress. Trump took action against Sessions in part because he knew that a lame-duck Congress would not act.

The Framers also gave the House and Senate a handful of separate powers, thereby reinforcing the bicameral system (see Table 10.1). The House has the sole power to "originate" all revenue bills, largely because it would give the people "taxation with representation," while the Senate has the sole authority to ratify treaties by a two-thirds vote, and confirm the president's nominees by a simple majority vote. Even here, however, the Framers created checks and balances between the House and Senate. The Constitution clearly invites the Senate to offer amendments on House revenue bills, for example, while the House must do its part in making the laws, requiring the president to report on the State of the Union, and creating the bureaucracy that contains the principal officers of government. Checks balance checks, thereby creating balance.

The Necessary and Proper Clause

Having vested these legislative powers in Congress, the Framers needed only one more power to pull the whole list together. They needed a way to convert the powers into laws. It is one thing, after all, to tell Congress that it "shall have the power" to borrow money or regulate commerce, and quite another to give Congress the leverage to do so.

The Framers solved the problem by adding the **Necessary and Proper Clause** at the very end of Section 8. Under the clause, the Constitution gives Congress authority to "make all Laws which shall be necessary and proper for carrying into Execution the foregoing Powers, and all other Powers vested by this Constitution in the Government of the United States, or in any Department or Officer." This clause gives Congress a set of **implied powers** that are never spelled out in the Constitution, but that are widely interpreted as any powers that the legislative branch needs to fulfill its duties to the nation. Given its broad grant of every authority Congress would need to make the laws, the Necessary and Proper Clause was essential for converting the broad structure of Congress into action. "Without the SUBSTANCE of this power," Madison wrote of the Necessary and Proper Clause, "the whole Constitution would be a dead letter."[11]

Necessary and Proper Clause
The constitutional authority given to Congress to make all laws deemed necessary and proper for executing its duties.

implied powers
Unwritten constitutional powers that Congress assumes are needed to implement the Necessary and Proper Clause

TABLE 10.1 HOW HOUSE AND SENATE DIFFERENCES AFFECT THE LEGISLATIVE PROCESS

The House and Senate share the Capitol Building and come together in joint session for special events such as the president's annual State of the Union Address, but have different numbers of members, operate under different election calendars, make their versions of the laws under different rules, give their leaders different levels of authority, hold their debates and cast their votes using different systems, and even have different tools for killing legislation. Despite different structures, they must both pass the same version of a law to send it on to the president for final approval, and they cannot override a presidential veto unless they can each muster a two-thirds vote. Although the two chambers often disagree on legislation, they work together in national emergencies to make quick decisions to protect the nation.

	HOUSE	SENATE
NUMBER OF VOTING MEMBERS	435 seats with at least one per state; additional seats allocated by population	100 seats with only two per state; no additional seats unless new states are admitted to the Union
ELECTORAL PRESSURE	Two-year terms	Six-year terms
	All seats are open for election at the end of every term	One-third of seats are open for each election every two years
	Elected in districts divided by equal population	Elected by states as a whole
LEGISLATIVE ACTION	Responsible for moving first on revenue bills	Responsible for ratifying treaties and confirming presidential nominees
	Legislation cannot reach the floor for final consideration without a "rule," or ticket from the House Rules Committee; the decision to accept the rule is made through a majority vote	Legislation cannot reach the floor without the unanimous consent of all senators, which is based on a unanimous consent agreement that sets the terms of the debate
		Any senator can prevent a bill from reaching the floor by either threatening or launching a filibuster, in essence by "holding" the floor until forced to leave by a cloture motion
	Amendments to legislation only approved before floor debate as part of a rule	Amendments to legislation are generally spelled out in the unanimous consent agreement, but may be offered on the Senate floor under specific circumstances without prior review
LEADERSHIP POWER	House leaders receive their power through the majority party	Senate leaders receive their power through the majority party and unanimous consent of all senators
	Legislative action is controlled by the Speaker of the House, majority party leader, and a long list of lower-level leaders	Legislative action is loosely controlled by the majority party leader and a short list of lower-level leaders
	Committee leaders have more power to control decisions	Committee leaders have less power to control decisions
TERMS OF DEBATE	Strict limits on debate; the terms of debate are established by a rule	Flexible limits on debate; the terms of debate are established by the consent of all senators
	A single member cannot interrupt debate or floor procedures of any kind	A single member or group of members can interrupt debate once it begins and stop debate until the Senate takes action to stop interruption
FINAL VOTE	All final votes for amendments and final passage are either taken electronically with each member's vote publicly recorded or by voice without any member's vote recorded	All votes for amendments passage are either taken by reading the Senate roll in alphabetical order (roll call) with each member's vote publicly recorded or by voice without any member's vote recorded
	Passage of a bill requires a simple majority of all members present and voting	Passage of a bill requires a simple majority of all members present and voting
	Overriding a veto requires a two-thirds majority of all members present and voting	Overriding a veto requires a two-thirds majority of all members present and voting
	The House has no role in ratifying treaties	Ratification of a treaty requires a two-thirds vote of all members present and voting
	The House does not allow filibusters	A motion to invoke cloture to stop a filibuster requires 60 votes regardless of the number of members present and voting

SOURCES: Christopher M. Davis, "The Legislative Process on the House Floor: An Introduction," Congressional Research Service, December 1, 2016; Valerie Heitshusen, "The Legislative Process on the Senate Floor: An Introduction," Congressional Research Service, April 10, 2017.

Congressional Elections (Structure)

10.2 Describe the congressional election process and the advantages it gives incumbents.

The Framers did more than divide Congress into two chambers. As already noted, the Framers also gave the House and Senate their own checks and balances against each other, starting with very different rules governing the electoral process. This electoral structure is particularly important for understanding how members of Congress run for office and represent their districts and states.

How the House and Senate Are Elected

Article I begins with a description of House and Senate elections, not powers. Congress cannot make the laws until it is elected. Once again, the Framers honored the basic principle of separate powers by giving the House and Senate different qualifications for office, constituents, and terms of office.

COMPETING QUALIFICATIONS The Framers started dividing the chambers by setting different age and residency rules for future candidates. House members must be 25 years old at the time they take office and must have been citizens for at least seven years, whereas senators must be 30 years old and have been citizens for nine years. House and Senate candidates must be residents of the states from which they are elected.

The Framers set higher qualifications for the Senate because they wanted the chamber as a check against what they saw as the less predictable House. Concerned about the "fickleness and passion" of the House of Representatives, James Madison in particular saw the Senate as "a necessary fence against this danger."[12]

COMPETING CONSTITUENCIES The Framers further divided the chambers by giving House members and senators different constituents, the group of citizens they represent. House members serve in districts carved from within states, while senators serve their states as a whole. Every state is guaranteed two senators, but only one House member.

States earn additional districts by population, which is measured every 10 years by the constitutionally prescribed national census. States can win new House seats if their population increases relative to other states between each census, but can lose seats if their population declines or other states increase faster. As a result, small states end up with the same number of Senate seats as big states, but big states end up with many more House seats than small states.

Once they agreed to elect House members by districts, the Framers decided how many citizens to assign to each district, thereby determining the number of House seats per state. The Framers hoped that this first **apportionment** would create just enough districts to keep the House close to the people without clogging the lawmaking process. Toward this end, the Constitution set the initial number of citizens per district at 30,000, and required the **reapportionment** of districts every 10 years in "such manner" as the House directed by law. Apportionment is generally defined as the outcome of the process of determining how many representatives each state will have, while reapportionment refers to the process of dividing the population into districts. However, the two terms are sometimes used interchangeably.

apportionment
A general term used to describe the assigning of the 435 House seats to the states based on the total U.S. population. All states are guaranteed at least one seat regardless of population.

reapportionment
The reassignment of the 435 House seats to the states based on the most recent census of the U.S. population.

As states entered the Union and the nation's population grew, so did the size of the House. By 1883, the House had 330 districts with 152,000 citizens per district on average. Facing bitter conflict over the creation of new seats, the House refused to add seats to the body after the 1920 census, and thereby capped the number of members at 435. As a result, future reapportionments would be based on shifting populations among the states. Based on a new average of 710,000 citizens per district in 2010, Texas earned four new districts, Florida earned two, and six states earned one. In turn, New York and Ohio each lost two, and eight states lost one. Most states (32) held steady, including seven that had one district each.

COMPETING CAMPAIGNS The final and most important difference between House and Senate elections involves the term of office, and the resulting electoral calendar. Whereas all 435 House members serve for two years and stand for election at the same time, all 100 senators serve for six years, but only a third stand for election at the same time.

The 115th Congress takes the oath of office on January 3, 2017, with the most demographically diverse class in history. Despite the diversity, Congress is still a mostly white, male, highly educated institution. Some experts believe that a more diverse Congress would also be more effective in solving the problems that face the nation, while others believe that the wealthy and interest groups will always have the stronger position, and still others ask whether more diversity will change Congress at all.

The Framers gave House members two-year terms as a compromise between competing proposals for one-year and three-year terms, and made sure that House elections would be "by the People" to hold members more accountable to the public. In theory, the entire House can be voted out in any given election. In reality, most members of Congress who run for reelection are reelected.[13]

In turn, the Framers gave senators six-year terms to somewhat insulate them from the public. They also assured that only a third of the Senate could be turned out in any given election by creating a phased, one-third on, two-thirds off election calendar. Finally, they directed state legislatures, not the public, to elect their two senators, thereby reassuring the states that the Senate would represent their interests.

The Seventeenth Amendment removed a piece of insulation on this list in 1913 by requiring senators to stand for election by the people, not state legislatures. The amendment was designed to make the Senate more accountable to the people, but left the rest of the insulation in place—senators still have six-year terms, and no more than a third stand for election every two years.

These differences were clearly designed to check the passionate House with a more temperate Senate. Pressed by Thomas Jefferson to explain these differences between the House and Senate, George Washington asked his future Secretary of State why he had just poured his tea into his saucer. "To cool it," Jefferson replied. "Even so," Washington explained, "we pour legislation into the senatorial saucer to cool it."[14]

Drawing the Lines

The Constitution gives states, not Congress, the power to draw House district lines for the number of seats within their borders. As discussed above, the U.S. Congress is responsible for dividing the 435 districts into a specific number for each state—every state wins or loses seats based on its population, but all states are guaranteed at least one member regardless of their size. Once the number of districts per state is apportioned, it is up to each state to draw the lines for each district through **redistricting**.[15] Every district must contain an equal number of citizens, but the geographical size of each district varies greatly between urban and rural areas.

redistricting
The division of the total number of House seats within a state into specific districts based on an equal number of citizens per district. State legislatures are responsible for redistricting.

gerrymandering
The drawing of legislative district boundaries to benefit a party, group, or incumbent.

The state legislature's majority party often uses redistricting to increase its hold on House elections. This process for designing districts to favor one party or the other is sometimes called **gerrymandering**, a term dating to the early 1800s,

Congressional redistricting is subject to judicial oversight at both the state and federal level, and occasionally involves judicial review at both levels. In late summer 2018, a three-judge panel of federal district court judges ruled that North Carolina's 13 congressional districts had been unfairly drawn to favor Republican candidates. The panel ruled that the map violated the Constitution's 14th amendment by giving Republicans a greater say in the selection of the state's congressional representatives. As of September 1, the ruling was winding its way to the Supreme Court for review, while the panel considered action to redraw the maps before the November midterm elections. Here, two North Carolina Republican state senators examine the map before approving it.

when Massachusetts governor Elbridge Gerry won passage of a redistricting plan that created a salamander-shaped district drawn to help his party win another seat.

Redistricting shapes the demographic and economic profile within each House district. Republican districts in the 115th Congress in 2017–2018 were more likely than Democratic districts to have more white citizens, cover more land, and have lower unemployment rates. Not surprisingly, they were more likely to have more registered Republicans.[16]

The Incumbency Advantage

Despite these differences in qualifications, constituencies, and election campaigns, House members and senators share one very important goal: reelection. After all, it only takes one defeat to end a House or Senate career, which is a lesson learned by even the most protected members from time to time. This belief that members of Congress are "unsafe at any margin" explains the constant effort to create **safe seats** that are won by the party that already holds the post.[17]

safe seat
An elected office that is predictably won by one party or the other, so the success of that party's candidate is almost taken for granted.

This does not mean that congressional elections are irrelevant, however. A few dozen defeats in any given election can change the House majority, and even fewer can alter the balance of power in the smaller Senate. Moreover, substantial numbers of House and Senate members retire before each election, thereby creating open seats that offer at least some opportunity for a competitive election.

However, most House and Senate campaigns favor incumbents over challengers, in part because incumbents face little or no opposition. In the 2018 midterm elections, only 50 of the 435 House seats up for election were considered competitive, either because an incumbent was running for reelection or because no candidate from the other party was in the race.

Senate incumbents have historically faced tougher reelection battles than their House colleagues. Whereas House incumbents often outspend their opponents by wide margins, Senate candidates are more evenly matched, in part because Senate elections are so visible nationally. With only one-third of the Senate up for reelection at any one time, the public can pay closer attention to campaign issues and advertisements, and the two parties can invest more money in their candidates.[18] Despite these challenges, Senate incumbents still achieve impressive reelection rates, and have done as well as their House peers in recent elections. In the 2018 midterm elections, just 11 of the 26 Democratic Senate seats and 5 of the 9 Republican seats were considered competitive.

incumbency advantage
The electoral strength that incumbent members of Congress gain through increased visibility, popularity, and campaign funding.

This general tendency to reelect incumbents is called the **incumbency advantage**. The advantage comes from a mix of electoral resources such as higher public approval ratings, more campaign money, and greater name recognition. Consider the following list as a sampling of the sources of this general advantage:

casework
A source of incumbent advantages based on member efforts to help constituents receive better service and benefits from the federal bureaucracy.

franking privilege
Free postage Congressional members receive by simply putting their signature, or frank, on any mail back home.

- Incumbents often start the electoral cycle having done more **casework** helping constituents receive better service and benefits from federal agencies such as the Social Security Administration and Department of Veterans Affairs.
- Incumbents also maintain a visible presence back home through emails, tweets, letters, local meetings, and social media. Members of Congress use the **franking privilege** to send mail home without paying any postage, and stay in touch through their district or state offices, which often have more employees than a member's Washington office.
- Incumbents often use their committee and subcommittee positions to influence legislation to help their districts create jobs, build federal office buildings, repair roads and bridges, and make loans to local businesses. They also provide internships for local college students, give any constituent a free American flag that has been flown over the Capitol, and make nominations to the military academies.
- Incumbents receive more "free media" from newspapers and television than their opponents, which produces very high name recognition in their districts.
- Incumbents tend to be skilled candidates, having won many campaigns during their careers. The more elections they win, the better they are known, the more experienced they become, and the more connections they build.

earmarks
Special spending projects that are set aside on behalf of individual members of Congress for their constituents.

- Incumbents also have considerable influence over federal spending in their districts through **earmarks** that reserve funding for special projects back home.[19] An earmark tells the federal bureaucracy to spend money for a specific project that benefits a member's district or state. The House Republicans imposed a moratorium on earmarks in the 112th Congress (2011–2013), but many members still ask the bureaucracy to give their districts small amounts of funding, and the bureaucracy usually complies.[20]
- Incumbents often enter elections with a large edge in campaign funding. House incumbents outspent their opponents by more than $1 million in 2018, while Senators outspent their opponents by more than $10 million.[21]

Alongside traditional tools such as press conferences, mailings, speeches, and one-to-one conversations at the local diner, members of Congress are becoming much more effective in reaching out to their constituents through social media. Most senators and members of the House now have Facebook pages that are loaded with photos, statements, YouTube videos, and links to their committee work. And many tweet regularly to keep their constituents interested in their work. According to a recent study of congressional activity, 83 percent of House members are now registered with Twitter, and 90 percent have a Facebook page.[22]

Despite this constant contact, public approval of Congress continues to plummet. As Figure 10.1 shows, approval is now at its lowest mark since the failed impeachment of Bill Clinton in 1998. Even though the U.S. economy was booming, many Americans felt that Congress was wasting the nation's time with its investigation of the president's sex life. Public approval roared back in 2001 when the war on terrorism was

FIGURE 10.1 PUBLIC APPROVAL OF CONGRESS, 1996–2018

Public approval of Congress is measured through public opinion surveys using the following question: "Do you approve or disapprove of the way Congress is handling its job?" Although the number of Americans who disapprove of Congress has been rising, it is interesting to follow the trend line in the percentage of Americans who say they are unsure of their opinion. This percentage has moved up and down somewhat over the years, often tracking the economy, but has been dropping over the past decade or so.

SOURCE: Polling data from CBS News/*New York Times* polls taken in January of each year.

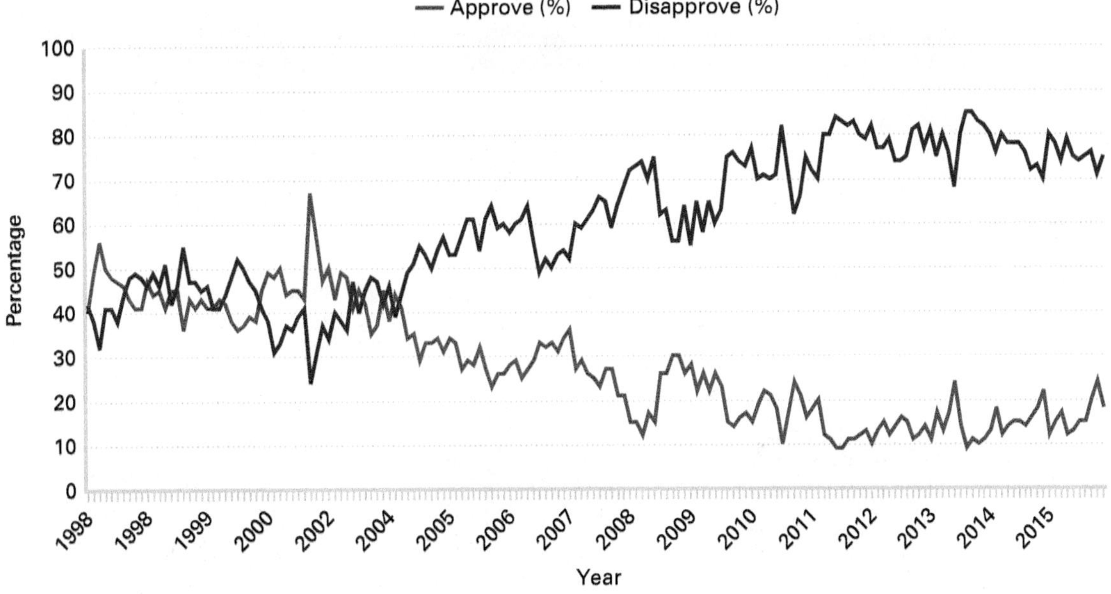

launched, but soon began to plummet as the economy began to collapse and the two congressional parties entered the current period of gridlock. Incumbents are still winning reelection at very high rates, but continued party conflict has pulled Congress down to record levels of disapproval with no rebound in sight. As the old saying goes, the American public hates Congress, but loves its member of Congress. The question is whether incumbency advantages can save individual members for much longer.

The Changing Face of Congress

In the early republic the House and Senate shared a characteristic in common: all members were to be white and male. After all, women, slaves, and freed slaves could not vote, let alone hold office.

The Framers would therefore be surprised by the demographics in today's Congress. The House had a record number of 89 women in 2018, while the Senate had a record of 23 women, including Minnesota's Tina Smith who replaced Al Franken after he resigned his post in the wake of a sexual harassment case and Mississippi's Cindy Hyde-Smith who was appointed to replace Sen. Thad Cochran when he resigned due to poor health April 1, 2018. Both chambers also made progress in raising their numbers of African Americans, Hispanic or Latino members, Asian/Pacific Islanders, and Native Americans. Both chambers also made progress in raising their racial diversity. Three of the four women who were elected to the Senate added to the chamber's diversity, including two African-Americans, the chamber's first Latina, and its first senator of Thai heritage. The Senate also seated the first Southern African-American Republican since the reconstruction era that followed the Civil War.[23]

The increased diversity appears to make a difference in both policy positions and legislative decisions. In 2013, for example, a small group of women senators came together to draft a three-point plan for ending a budget stalemate. "I don't think it's

FIGURE 10.2 CONGRESSIONAL DIVERSITY

Congress has become more diverse over time, but is still a mostly white, male, highly educated institution. Some experts believe that a more diverse Congress would also be more effective in solving the problems that face the nation, while others believe that the wealthy and interest groups will always have the stronger position, and still others ask whether more diversity will change Congress at all.

SOURCE: Congressional Research Service, "Membership of the 115th Congress: A Profile," January 17, 2018.

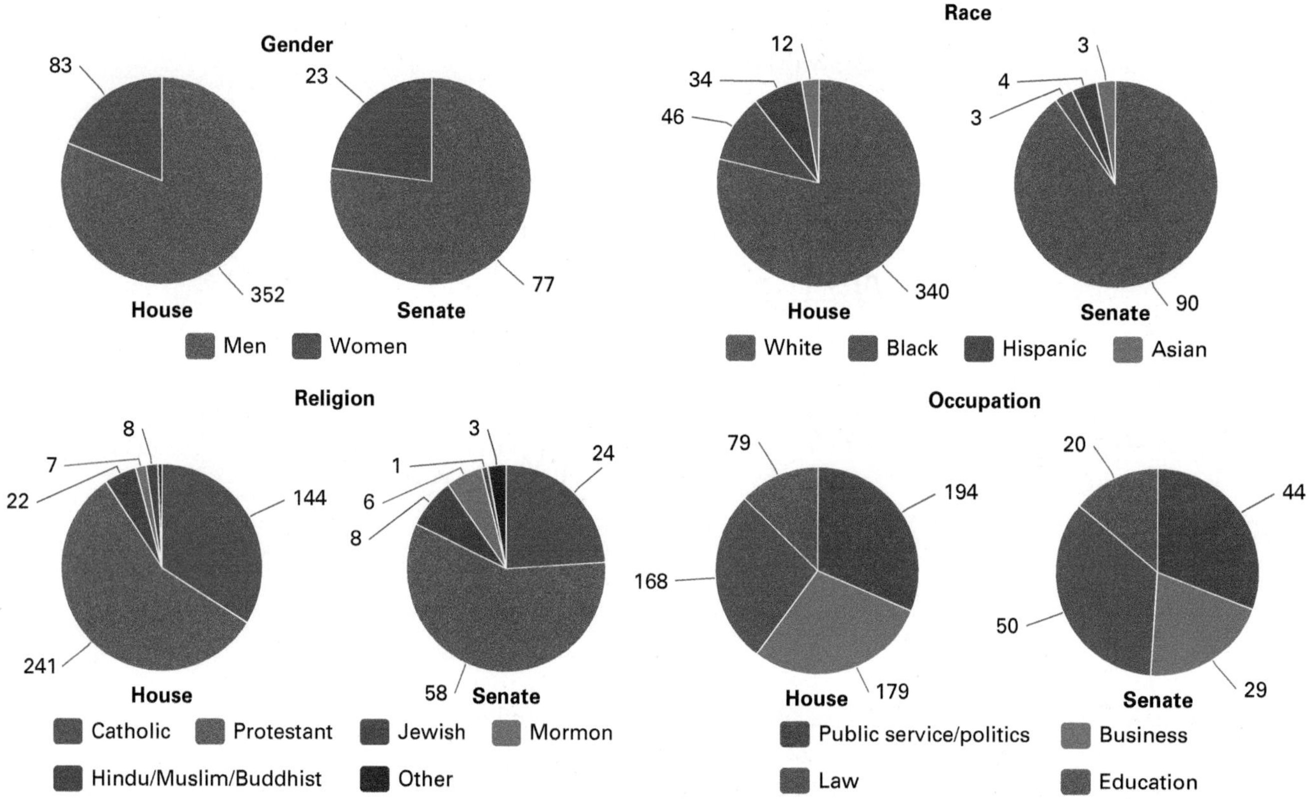

a coincidence that women were so heavily involved in trying to end this stalemate," said Senator Susan Collins (R-ME). "Although we span the ideological spectrum, we are used to working together in a collaborative way." As one of the final negotiators joked as government went back to work, "The women are taking over."[24]

Although Congress is becoming more diverse by race and gender, it still remains very different from the rest of the United States, and the differences are even greater in terms of income and occupation (see Figure 10.2). One-half of the House members and senators who served in the Congress that ended in January 2017 were millionaires, while 36 percent of House members and 54 percent of senators held law degrees, but both sets of percentages were down somewhat from 2014. As House members and senators retire or are defeated, their replacements are on average younger. New House members elected in 2014 were about five years younger than the House average, while new senators were more than 10 years younger.[25]

These changes suggest more room for younger, more diverse, and less wealthy candidates as the millennial generation and its younger siblings start running for office. Given the incumbency advantages discussed earlier in this chapter, you will have to start building momentum by learning how to run and win. Campaign experience fosters future victory, and the best way to gain experience is from practice. Another building block is public service. Join the Peace Corps—four House members did it somewhere along the way. Become a teacher—100 members of today's Congress started out teaching. Become a congressional staffer—102 started out that way. Become a state legislator—267 started out that way. Then run for office—41 House members and senators started out as mayors. In other words, you can start just about anywhere, but you cannot reach Congress unless you start.

The 2018 Congressional Elections

Despite intense media coverage of the 2018 midterm elections as a referendum on Donald Trump and the Republican agenda, the November 6 vote produced few surprises. Presidents usually lose seats in their first midterm elections, the parties begin testing campaign themes for the next presidential election, and the initial phase of the presidential election campaign begins.

These patterns held in 2018—with several recounts still underway days later, Democrats had already flipped enough Republican seats to capture the House, and Republicans added at least one and potentially more Senate seats to their razor-thin majority by exploiting fears of immigration and punishing Democrats who had opposed the Supreme Court nomination of Brett Kavanaugh in early October. In addition, voters supported record numbers of women candidates, and campaign spending soared to $5.2 billion, exemplified by the Florida Senate race between Democrat Bill Nelson and Republican Rick Scott, which ran to almost $200 million. Trump kept the midterms forefront in the public's consciousness by stoking fears of an immigrant invasion at the U.S. southern border and testing the boundaries of civility, and the final results matched predictions dating back to early summer.

Democrats, however, started the 2018 campaign with greater goals than just flipping the House back to their control. They also wanted to retake the Senate and turn the election into a referendum on Trump. Although Democrats had to defend 26 Senate seats, they believed they could lose one or two seats and still claim a Senate majority with wins in Arizona, Florida, and Nevada. They also hoped to ride a "blue wave" of Democratic victories in the House to create a super-majority that just might have the votes to impeach Trump for high crimes and misdemeanors. Their hopes did not come true—Democrats lost three Senate seats and only picked up one, thereby giving Republicans a slightly larger small majority. Democrats did get their blue wave, but it was limited to gaining the House and key governorships in Michigan and Wisconsin while holding onto Pennsylvania and Minnesota—which were all key to Trump's 2016 victory.

Republicans also started the campaign with great expectations. The U.S. economy was on fire—unemployment was at modern lows, pay checks were rising, and the stock market had added billions to the economy during Trump's first two years in office. They hoped to marry that prosperity to a hopeful message about the future and cement their House and Senate majorities. Although Trump's public approval rating stayed in the mid to low 40-percent range, they believed they could reduce

Nevada Republican Senator Dean Heller, directly to the president's left in the photo, was considered the most vulnerable Senate incumbent at the start of the 2018 midterm campaign. He faced a tough nomination battle just to run for reelection, a highly-motivated Democratic electorate ready to vote for his opponent, and lingering questions about whether he was too conservative in a state that Hillary Clinton won in 2016. He made every effort possible to leverage his close ties to President Trump, including a visible spot at the rally following passage of the president's tax cut in December 2017, but entered the election year with an approval rating under 40 percent in the state. Heller lost his reelection bid to Nevada Congresswoman Jacky Rosen, whom Trump derided as "wacky Jacky" during the campaign.

the number of Republican women and college-educated suburbanites who seemed ready to reject the president. But, their hopes did not come true either. Trump rejected the peace-and-prosperity message as too soft, deciding instead on a hard-right, anti-liberal message designed to ignite his base. The tough message may have increased conservative turnout in deep red states and some big states such as Ohio, but it also may have ignited a backlash among moderate Republicans in suburban districts, thereby accounting for many of the 30-plus seats lost to the Democrats.

Even though the election results were not surprising, they did produce a large number of firsts, including the youngest member of Congress ever elected (New York's Alexandria Ocasio-Cortez, age 29), the first Native American women elected to Congress (Kansas's Sharice Davids and New Mexico's Deb Haaland), the first Texan Latinas elected to Congress (Veronica Escobar and Sylvia Garcia), the first Muslim women elected to Congress (Michigan's Rashida Tlaib and Minnesota's Ilhan Omar), and, as of press-time, likely the first Korean-American woman elected to Congress (California's Young Kim). These firsts are part of what will be record numbers of women in Congress: women will occupy almost a quarter of all House and Senate seats in the 116th Congress, up from 20 percent in the 115th.

The elections broke other records, including the total number of candidates who ran for higher office, campaign spending totals, and the highest rate of early voting turnout and turnout among young Americans in a non-presidential election. According to early returns, voters aged 18–29 cast 13 percent of the midterm votes, up from 11 percent in 2014, and turnout appeared to reach even higher marks in key battleground states such as Texas and Nevada.

The midterms set the stage for a bitter standoff between the House and Senate over national policy, while provoking stern warnings from the president about taking a "wartime footing" against the Democrats if the House dares to launch a wave of investigations into Trump's finances, business dealings, and tax returns. At the same time, Trump also celebrated the potential for House cooperation on infrastructure reform, health care, trade, and immigration, and even talked about what he described as a "beautiful bipartisan type of situation." He even encouraged Democrats to reelect Nancy Pelosi as Speaker of the House, but his long post-election press conference featured the same viral name-calling that had characterized the campaign and suggested a tough two years ahead. Americans gave the Democrats a check on the president's power in the House, but did not offer a clear consensus on the future direction of the country.

Virginia's Abigail Spanberger became one of more than 100 women elected to Congress in 2018. Spanberger is a former CIA agent who promised to heal the nation's divisions and protect affordable health care. "We are breaking up the typical," she said of her campaign. "You can tell a child they can be anything they want, but until they see a broad spectrum of the country—someone who looks like them—they feel one step apart."

Organizing Congress (Action)

10.3 Compare and contrast the leadership systems used in the House and Senate, and explain how work is done through congressional committees.

Just because the House and Senate share the same view of Washington from Capitol Hill does not mean they share the same organization structure. Whereas the House gives its large number of representatives little room to maneuver, the Senate gives its smaller number of senators greater freedom to act.

Structure clearly shapes this kind of action, but politics bends the rules to the separate needs of each chamber. Whether because of size, qualifications, terms, calendars, debate, or passage, the bicameral system and separate powers have created a House and Senate that are both alike and different. Hence, it is best to address the structure and operation of House and Senate leadership organizations before turning to the role of committees.

Leading the House

The House of Representatives has a more powerful leadership system than the Senate, in large part because it has so many more members with much shorter terms of office. It is arguably easier to guide 100 senators who serve six-year terms and enter office one-third at a time than 435 House members who serve two-year terms and enter office at the same time. Thus out of necessity, House leaders are given more power to control the actions of their members than Senate leaders are.

THE SPEAKER OF THE HOUSE The most important member of Congress is the **Speaker of the House**. Selected by the majority party, the Speaker has enormous power to reward and punish individual members, set the legislative agenda, influence congressional campaigns, and control the flow of legislation through the House Rules Committee. The Speaker also becomes president in the event that both the president and vice president are unable to fulfil their constitutional duties.[26]

Speaker of the House
The presiding officer in the House of Representatives, formally elected by the House but selected by the majority party.

The Speaker has the greatest power when members of the majority party are willing to work together, but can be driven from office if the party is divided among competing factions. Rep. John Boehner (R-OH) learned this lesson in late 2016 when he was forced to resign when his party split between 40 ultra-conservatives who refused to negotiate with Republican moderates. Boehner was replaced by Paul Ryan, (R-WI), who decided to retire from Congress at the end of 2018 after similar fights with conservatives.

Nancy Pelosi (D-CA) gave the House leader's gavel to Paul Ryan (R-WI) in October 2015 after he became Speaker of the House. After Democrats won the House majority in the 2018 midterm elections, Pelosi planned to take the gavel back in January 2019. As of press-time, hurdles to Pelosi's rise to Speaker had emerged.

In theory, the party's large majority should have given Boehner significant power, and historically it would have. In reality, his more conservative members were generally inflexible on the budget, immigration, or health care reform. As a result, he was unable to confidently negotiate with House Democrats and the president, and was widely viewed as a Speaker without a following.

THE PARTY CAUCUS The House makes many of its most important decisions when Democrats and Republicans meet, or caucus, separately. Candidates who are elected as Independents must decide whether to caucus with the Democrats or Republicans, thereby declaring their allegiance, if not absolute loyalty, to one or the other.

Each party caucus, or formal gathering of members, plays its most important role when it selects the party's leaders at the start of a two-year Congress. However, each caucus also exerts significant influence when controversial legislation reaches the floor. The majority party caucus wields more power because it selects the Speaker, approves the basic organization of its chamber, approves the committee list, and sets the number of majority and minority members on each committee.

The minority party caucus can be nearly as influential if it can maintain party discipline on key votes, especially if the majority party caucus is divided between moderates and conservatives. In 2017–2018, for example, the House was frozen between strong conservatives on the Republican side of the aisle and equally committed liberals on the Democratic side. The only way to pass legislation was to bring a relatively small number of moderate Republicans together with the Democrats, an exceedingly uncomfortable position for then House Speaker Boehner.

OTHER HOUSE LEADERS The majority party also selects the House majority leader, who helps plan party strategy, confers with other party leaders, and tries to keep party members in line, while the minority party elects the minority leader. Each party also selects its own legislative whips to pressure party members to support the Speaker's position on specific votes by "whipping up" a majority. The majority and minority whips are generally given a list of members to keep in line on particularly controversial issues.

Leading the Senate

The Senate has the same basic committee structure, elected party leadership, and committee-based power as the House, but does not have a Speaker largely because it is smaller and less formal. Indeed, it is often said that the Senate has 100 separate power centers and is so splintered that party leaders have difficulty arranging the day-to-day call to order, let alone routine debates over noncontroversial legislation.[27] The Senate also has much stronger norms, or expectations that create more cooperation than the House.

The majority party selects the Senate's most important leader. When the president and the Senate majority leader are from the same party, the president becomes the party's most visible leader on Capitol Hill and in the nation as a whole. However, when the majority leader and the president are from different parties, the Senate majority leader is considered his or her party's national spokesperson. Senator Harry Reid (D-NV) was elected as Senate majority leader in 2006 after Democrats won a one-seat majority with 51 seats that year but lost his post to Senator Mitch McConnell (R-KY) after Republicans took the majority in 2014.

One of the last traditional filibusters occurred in 1965 when the Civil Rights Act came to a vote in the Senate. The Senate stayed in session day and night for 54 days as opposing senators held the floor, and members slept on cots just outside the chamber. The filibuster was finally broken on June 10, and the bill was passed hours later.

The majority leader has the power to persuade party members, but cannot control debate without unanimous consent of the entire Senate. Unless the vice president makes a rare appearance at the helm of the chamber to cast a tie-breaking vote, Senate floor debates are actually led by a president pro tempore, usually the most senior member of the majority party. Presiding over the Senate on most occasions is a thankless chore, which is why the president pro tempore regularly delegates this responsibility to junior members of the chamber's majority party.

The Senate's party machinery is similar to that of the House. Like the House, each of the Senate parties convenes at the start of a new Congress and selects its own leadership. Each party also appoints members of its policy committee that helps set the legislative agenda. Also like the House, each of the Senate parties has a policy committee that helps the leadership monitor legislation and provides policy expertise.

Unlike the House, however, senators have the power to bring the chamber to a complete standstill through a **filibuster**. Taken from the Dutch word meaning "pirate" and first used in 1841, a filibuster is often described as "talking a bill to death."[28] As the phrase suggests, a senator rises to speak and does not stop until the rest of the Senate either capitulates to the speaker's demands or invokes **cloture**, which is a French term meaning "closure." In most cases, cloture requires a three-fifths vote of all Senators and imposes strict limits on further debate after cloture is formally invoked. However, even the threat of a filibuster can be enough to force a delay in legislative business, especially when the threat comes from a small group of senators who can operate as a tag-team in occupying the Senate floor.

filibuster
A procedural practice in the Senate whereby a senator refuses to relinquish the floor and thereby delays proceedings and prevents a vote on a controversial issue.

cloture
A procedure for terminating filibusters in the Senate.

Despite the Senate's tradition of long debates, the number of successful cloture votes has actually increased in recent decades as the chamber has confronted a surge in filibuster threats on seemingly trivial issues. There were just four successful cloture votes during the 1960s, for example, but 174 between 2001 and September 2012.[29] Senate Democrats finally convinced a handful of Republicans to change the filibuster rules in late 2013.

Under the "nuclear option," the Senate currently allows a simple majority of its members to invoke cloture against filibusters of the president's cabinet officers. This option does not apply to other Senate business, and often raises a backlash when the Senate and presidency are held by different political parties. The Democratic majority used the option to prevent Republican filibusters against President Obama's judicial appointments in 2013–2014, while the Republican majority used it to prevent Democratic filibusters against President Trump's judicial appointments in 2017–2018.[30] The option assured Brett Kavanaugh's confirmation as an associate justice of the Supreme Court in October 2018. Democrats could have easily prevented his confirmation under the cloture rules that had existed before the Obama administration. Kavanaugh was confirmed on a 50–48 vote in the midst of sexual abuse allegations dating back to his high school years.

Congressional Committees

Committees do much of the work in Congress. They draft legislation, review presidential nominees, conduct investigations of executive branch departments and agencies, and are usually responsible for ironing out differences between House and Senate versions of the same legislation. Almost all congressional committees have subcommittees that help do their work.

TYPES OF COMMITTEES In theory, every **congressional committee** must be created from scratch in each new Congress. In reality, however, most continue from Congress to Congress without change, although new committees are sometimes created as new issues, such as homeland security, demand greater attention. There are three types of committees: (1) standing or full committees that continue from one Congress to the next, and produce most bills, (2) special or select committees that are created to

congressional committee
Separate units of each chamber of Congress composed of a specific number of members and chartered to examine legislative proposals and conduct oversight of past decisions in specific areas of concern such as appropriations, taxation, the budget, foreign policy, and domestic issues.

tackle a specific problem such as domestic spying by the National Security Agency, or provide ongoing oversight of relatively narrow legislative issues that do not fit the standing committee structure, and (3) joint committees that belong to both the House and the Senate and exist either to study an issue of interest to the entire Congress or pursue an investigation. Of the various types of committees, standing committees are the most important for making laws and representing constituents. (There is a special kind of joint committee called a conference committee that will be discussed later in the chapter.)

Standing committees and their subcommittees are organized to address different policy issues such as energy, the environment, foreign affairs, human services, and government management. Several also have administrative roles in running the House or Senate. These roles cover six different legislative tasks:

rule
A precise statement of how a law is implemented.

1. *Rules and Administration Committees* These determine the basic operations of their chamber—for example, how many staffers individual members get and what the ratio of majority to minority members and staff will be. However, the House Rules Committee is much more powerful than its Senate twin because it provides the **rule** that must be granted to a bill before it can reach the floor. The rule provides for both the length of the floor debate and whether or not the bill is subject to amendment. We discuss this in greater detail later in the chapter.
2. *Budget Committees* The House and Senate each have a budget committee. The two budget committees were created as permanent standing committees in 1974 to give each chamber greater information and discipline on the overall federal budget. They set broad targets for spending and taxes at the start of each session of Congress and push authorizing and appropriations committees to follow those guidelines as they work on legislation that involves any federal spending or revenue activities.
3. *Authorizing Committees* Authorizing committees pass the laws that tell government what to do. The House and Senate education committees consider legislation regarding student loan programs and efforts to improve public schools, while the House Ways and Means Committee and Senate Finance Committee consider legislation for raising taxes. Authorizing committees are also responsible for reviewing and reauthorizing programs that are about to expire. In the Senate, authorizing committees also hold confirmation hearings for the president's nominees for senior government posts and judgeships.
4. *Appropriations Committees* Appropriations committees make decisions about how much money government can spend on authorized programs. Although there is only one appropriations committee in each chamber, each appropriations committee has one subcommittee for each of the 13 appropriations bills that must be enacted each year to keep government running. Even if an authorizing committee calls for a large amount of money for a specific program, the appropriations committee actually decides the final amount, which is sometimes less.
5. *Revenue Committees* Revenue and budget committees deal with raising the money appropriating committees spend. Because it exists to raise revenues through taxes and also authorizes legislation that affects Social Security and oversees the Internal Revenue Service, the House Ways and Means Committee is one of the most powerful committees in Congress. Although the appropriations committee determines how much is spent on specific programs, the Ways and Means Committee is the only committee in either chamber that can originate tax and revenue legislation. It is also responsible for making basic decisions on the huge Social Security and Medicare programs.
6. *Oversight Committees* There are two major oversight committees in Congress: the House Oversight and Government Reform Committee and the Senate Homeland

Security and Governmental Affairs Committee. Both committees have wide latitude to investigate the performance of government. They are also free to authorize programs for fixing government-wide management problems.

CONFERENCE COMMITTEES The Framers imagined an orderly legislative process in which a bill would move from chamber to chamber until the House and Senate passed the same bill with the same bill number. But the first members of Congress soon discovered that this legislative ping-pong was both inefficient and frustrating, and they invented an entirely new method for resolving differences called a **conference committee.**

conference committee
A committee appointed by the presiding officers of each chamber to adjust differences on a particular bill passed by each chamber in different form.

Sometimes called the "Third House of Congress," conference committees are designed to create a compromise between the House and Senate without the endless back and forth.[31] Each party in each chamber appoints its own conference committee members, but the majority party is given more slots to fill. Typically the conference committee is composed of members of the committee that reported the bill.

Conference committees are created to handle just one bill, and are generally given 10 to 20 days to complete their work. If they reach an agreement, the members, or conferees, send their agreement to the House and Senate floors for passage. If they fail, the House or Senate can either instruct them to continue work, or simply agree to disagree.

Although there are relatively few conference committees per Congress, they have significant power to add and delete provisions of a bill in the search for an agreement. As President Reagan once joked, "If an orange and an apple went into conference consultations, they might come out a pear."[32]

MEMBER CAUCUSES In contrast to the party caucuses that select party leaders, **member caucuses** are informal groups of senators and/or House members that come together to promote shared legislative interests such as the arts, arthritis, children, defense, immigration, tax reform, women's rights, veterans, and a host of industries such as corn, lumber, rice, shellfish, and steel. Although they do not have any authority to review legislation or make legislative decisions, caucuses provide an opportunity for members to show their support for specific ideas. There are almost 300 member caucuses in Congress, many of which have Democratic and Republican members who work together on behalf of their states.[33]

member caucus
A meeting of the members of a party in a legislative chamber to select party leaders and to develop party policy.

Awarding Committee Seats

Each political party controls the selection of standing committee members. Because some committees are more prestigious than other committees, the debate over committee assignments can be intense. Members often ask for assignments that help build incumbency advantages in their home districts, and fight for seats to powerful committees such as House Ways and Means that allow them to claim credit for major legislation that might pass.

Each party in each chamber selects its own committee members. The selections are generally based on a blend between what the party needs on each committee and what its members want. The majority party selects the chair of each committee, while the minority party selects the ranking member.

Most committee chairs are selected on the basis of the **seniority rule,** meaning that the member of the majority party with the longest continuous service on the committee becomes chair upon the retirement of the current chair or a change in the party in control of Congress. The seniority rule lessens the influence of states or districts where the two parties are more evenly matched and where there is more turnover.[34] Although the Senate allows members to serve on more committees, no Senator is allowed to chair more than one committee. Senior members must choose which committee to chair, allowing others to chair the other committees.

seniority rule
A legislative practice that assigns the chair of a committee or subcommittee to the member of the majority party with the longest continuous service on the committee.

The Congressional Staff

Before turning to the question of how a bill becomes a law, it is important to note that the congressional leadership and committee system could not function without help from the congressional staff. Once again, the structure of the Constitution's bicameral system matters greatly to congressional action.

The Senate as a whole has 4,000 personal staffers, for example, but averages 40 per state, while the House has 7,000, but averages just 16 per district. Except for the seven small states with just one House member, each senator has more miles to cover and more constituents to serve. Moreover, the personnel budgets for all House staffers in a large state with a half-dozen members or more often dwarfs the budget for Senate staffers. Each of California's 53 House members has a staff budget of $1 million for example, while each of the state's senators has a staff budget of $3 million that adds up to just $6 million.[35]

Congressional staffers are responsible for everything from writing tweets for individual members to drafting legislation for committees and subcommittees. However, the staffs tend to be divided into those who work in Washington, and those who work in state or district offices back home. Personal staffers in Washington and the districts are almost entirely dedicated to constituent service, often in the form of casework on citizen problems, while committee and party staffers in Washington handle the larger legislative agenda.

The number of House and Senate personal staffers has remained mostly unchanged over the past two decades, but the percentage of those staffers assigned to home offices has increased rapidly as members work to build their incumbency advantage. The number of House staffers deployed at the district level rose from 23 percent in 1972 to nearly 50 percent in 2010, while the number of Senate staffers deployed at the state level increased from 13 percent to 41 percent over the same period.

How a Bill Becomes a Law (Action)

10.4 Describe the process of lawmaking in Congress.

The constitutional and electoral structure that checks the two chambers against each other is clearly linked to legislative decisions (action). Follow a bill, any bill, through the legislative process, and the odds are that it will die long before the next election. Barely one out of every 10 bills even receives a hearing, let alone time on the floor.

Legislative time is precious because each sitting of Congress only lasts for two sessions, each lasting one year. If a bill has not passed by the end of the second, and last, session of a Congress, it must work its way through the entire legislative process again. Every Congress operates for two years, and Congresses are numbered back to the 1st Congress in 1789. Thus, the 115th Congress was gaveled into session on January 3, 2017, 228 years after the 1st.

During the first session of the 115th Congress from January 3, 2017 to January 3, 2018, for example, House and Senate met for a combined total of almost 390 days, spent more than 390 hours in session, produced more than 18,000 pages of floor proceedings, and held almost 700 votes, yet passed just 100 laws, or less than one-tenth of one percent of the bills introduced.[36] (See Figure 10.3 for the trend line on how many bills became law in each Congress from 1974 to 2018.)

How Ideas Become Bills

The House and Senate have one major constitutional obligation: to make the laws. But a law cannot be made until a member, committee, or a chamber as a whole has an idea for action.

Legislative ideas can come from almost anywhere, including the lobbying groups that often approach members about special problems, family members who see important problems in their own work, constituents who raise concerns at town hall meetings, and think tanks that supply so much of the research that ends up in congressional testimony.

FIGURE 10.3 TRENDS IN LEGISLATIVE PASSAGE

According to historical trends, the number of bills introduced has remained relatively high over time, while this figure shows that the number of bills enacted into law has been falling. At the same time, the percentages have been relatively stable, meaning that the number of bills introduced has been the more important factor in driving down the number of laws enacted. The question, therefore, is why the number of bills introduced has been falling. One answer is that members of Congress are less interested in writing laws than in taking positions against the other party. Another is that the federal budget is so tight that there is no support for legislation that might require more federal spending. Why did so many proposals receive a vote over time, while so few actually passed? And why were so many of the votes on party lines?

SOURCE: GovTrack.US, "Historical Statistics about Legislation in the U.S. Congress: Bills and Resolutions," available at https://www.govtrack.us/congress/bills/statistics.

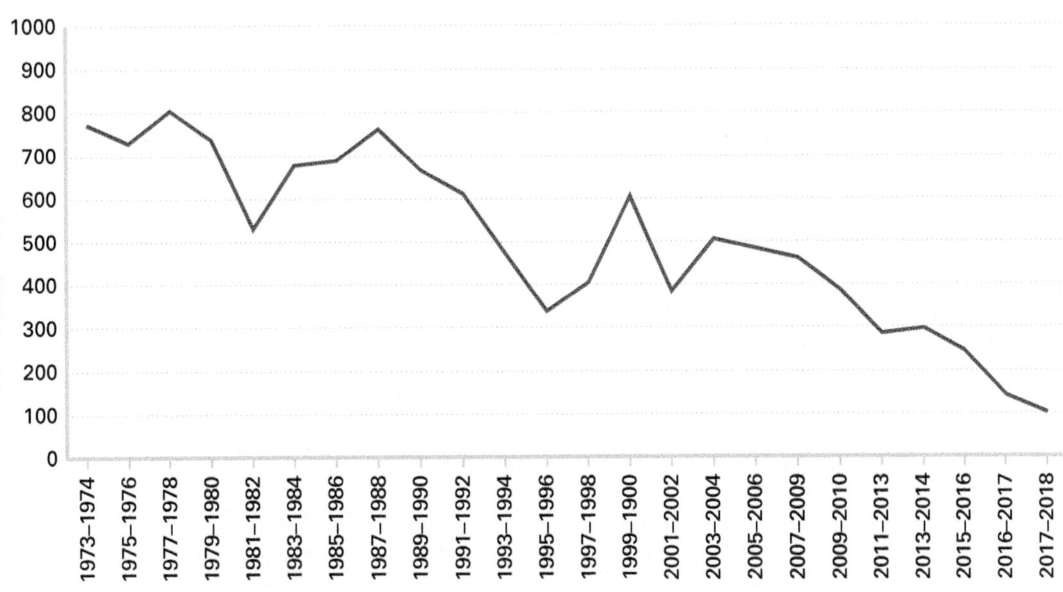

Members also bring their ideas to the legislative process. Senator John McCain (R-AZ) often spoke against the "enhanced interrogation techniques" that were used during the Iraq War against terrorists because he was tortured as a prisoner of war during the Vietnam War; Senator Edward Kennedy (D-MA) frequently rallied support for the National Cancer Institute in Washington, D.C., because of his son's long battle with bone cancer. Kennedy, himself, died from brain cancer in 2009.

The House and Senate usually follow the carefully designed process described below but occasionally skip some of the preliminary steps to save time or to address a crisis. Republicans skipped many of the early steps in 2017 to pass their party's longstanding promise to repeal and replace the Obama administration's health insurance program. The compromise moved so quickly through the House that many members of both parties later reported that they did not read the long proposal.

The original proposal was defeated only weeks before when conservative House Republicans refused to support the president and their own majority because the replacement for Obama's program was too expensive and contained too many rules on how states could spend federal funding for poor Americans under the Medicaid program. The conservatives rallied to the bill when the cost was cut by almost $1 trillion and the rules were eliminated. The new bill was introduced on a Thursday and passed the next day without a hearing or markup. However, the bill stalled when it reached the Senate. Under pressure to include Democrats in the process, Senate Republicans took the more traditional path for drafting, introducing, advancing, and passing a bill, thereby exposing the plan to the nine tests described in the next section.

How Bills Become Laws

A proposal must survive nine tests to become a law: it must be (1) introduced, (2) referred to a committee for further review, (3) reviewed by the committee and subcommittee, (4) "marked up" by the committee and subcommittee before it goes to the floor, (5) debated and amended on the floor, (6) passed by each chamber, (7) if necessary, redrafted by a conference committee to resolve any differences between the House and Senate versions, (8) passed a final time in each chamber as a conference report, and (9) either signed into law or rejected by the president through a **veto**. And if it is vetoed through a regular veto, the House and Senate can override the president's decision on a two-thirds vote in each chamber.[37] (See Figure 10.4 for a diagram of the process.)

veto
A formal decision by the president to reject a bill passed by Congress

INTRODUCING A BILL House members introduce bills by simply dropping them into the "hopper" on the clerk's desk at the front of the House chamber. In turn, senators

FIGURE 10.4 HOW A BILL BECOMES A LAW

The legislative process presents a long list of checks and balances that reduce the odds of passage. However, as this chart from USA.gov shows, there are only five steps from start to finish. The chart was designed by the federal government to help citizens understand the basic rules, but bypasses important detours such as efforts to repeal a law that can be raised through a simple motion on the House or Senate floor or the failure to reach an agreement between the two chambers during the final negotiations. This version of the process may lead citizens to think that the legislative process is much easier than it actually is, thereby increasing public distrust toward Congress after members kill popular legislation.

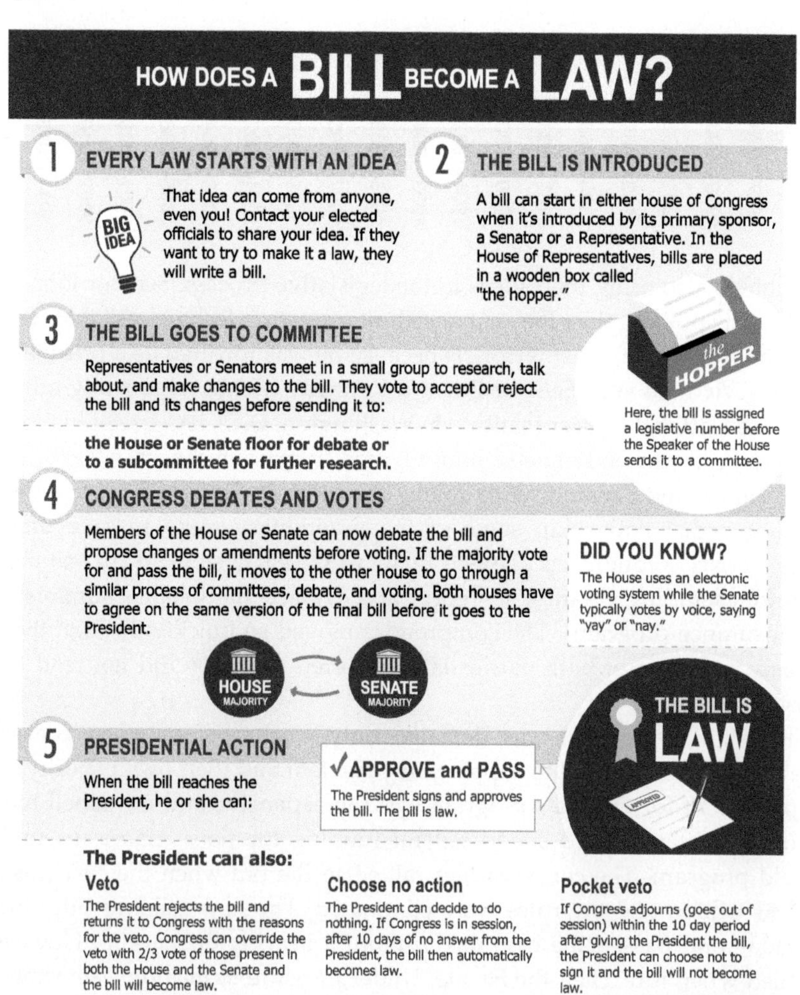

introduce a bill by handing it to one of the clerks who work at the front of the Senate chamber.

House bills are automatically numbered in sequence with an "H.R." at the start, while Senate bills are automatically numbered in sequence with an "S" followed by its number. There are times, however, when both chambers reserve the number H.R.1 and S.1 for particularly important legislation such as the Tax Cuts and Jobs Act of 2017 that eventually became part of the $1.5 trillion cut Trump signed three days before Christmas, 2017.

In the more informal Senate, members sometimes short-circuit these formalities by introducing a bill as an amendment to pending legislation. Presidents have no authority to introduce legislation, although they recommend many proposals that are in turn introduced as bills by legislators.

REFERRAL Once a bill has been introduced in either chamber, it is read into the daily congressional record as a formal proposal and referred by the House or Senate parliamentarian to a specific committee—tax bills to Ways and Means or Finance; farm bills to Agriculture; technology bills to Science, Space, and Technology; small business to Small Business; and so forth. The committee often refers the bill to a specific subcommittee. The House and Senate parliamentarians are career employees of Congress, and are not chosen by the parties. However, they must be careful not to anger one party or the other as they make difficult decisions, and they can be fired by the majority.

COMMITTEE REVIEW Most bills go to committees and subcommittees, and are never seen again. However, at least some are subject to committee and subcommittee hearings, and eventual passage. In general, committees pass these proposals down to highly specialized subcommittees, where most bills die. For a bill to move forward, hearings are held, the bill is marked up, and a majority of the subcommittee must support the bill.

If a subcommittee votes for a bill, its version is sent back up the chain of approval to the full committee for another round of hearings and review. This step is another likely point at which bills die—hearings are only held on the most important legislation. Committees and subcommittees only have so much time to review bills, and must choose which ones to consider.

Most bills die in subcommittee or committee without either a hearing or a markup, but the House does allow members to force a bill to the floor if a majority signs a petition demanding action. Because most members share a strong sense of reciprocity, or mutual respect toward other committees, House discharge petitions are rarely successful. The Senate does not allow discharge petitions, but often allows its members to offer entirely new bills as amendments to pending legislation.

MARKUP Once a committee or subcommittee decides to pass the bill, it "marks it up" to modify or amend its version of the bill. The term "markup" refers to the pencil marks that members literally make on the final version of the bill before it is typed into the text. Each change to the bill, which can be as little as adding a punctuation mark or deleting a word, must be approved by a majority of the subcommittee or committee doing the markup. Bills are rarely marked up unless they have a very high probability of floor action.

Once a markup is over and the committee passes the bill, it moves forward toward floor consideration. If the bill is moving through the House, it can only move to the floor if the powerful Rules Committee issues a formal rule, which sets the length of time for floor debate and whether a bill can be amended (open rule) or not (closed rule). If it is moving through the Senate, it is automatically forwarded to the full chamber for scheduling by unanimous consent.

Each bill is sent to the floor with a legislative report that summarizes the bill, makes the case for action, and provides an estimate of the bill's cost. These reports are rarely read before the final vote, but they do contain instructions to the executive branch on what each section of a bill requires. These instructions tell the bureaucracy what Congress intended, which often helps the bureaucracy write the regulations needed to implement the law.

FLOOR DEBATE Once a bill is reported to the full chamber directly from committee in the Senate or through the Rules Committee in the House, it is usually scheduled for floor action.

The House Rules Committee makes the decision to move a bill to the floor, while the Senate makes the decision through unanimous consent of all members. Recall that a single senator can deny action by withholding his or her consent, thereby requiring a cloture vote for further action. Most bills that reach the floor have already survived many tests along the way and are scheduled without controversy.

The House and Senate have different procedures for amending a bill before final passage. Both make their decisions before a bill reaches the floor, but each has a somewhat different process for allowing amendments.

If it grants a rule at all, the House Rules Committee decides whether a bill can be amended and, if so, what the amendment can say. Most House bills are considered under either a "structured rule" that limits debate to a small number of amendments with strict time limits, or a "closed rule" that only allows amendments approved by the committee that requested the rule. Only a handful of bills are considered under either an "open rule" or "modified open rule" that allow specific amendments and freer debate. The number of open rules has fallen steadily over the past two decades as the House has become more sharply divided, while the number of closed, or restricted rules has increased dramatically. In 2017, House Republicans set a new record in the number of closed rules for a single session of Congress.

In contrast, the Senate decides whether a bill can be amended by unanimous consent. Although Senate amendments must technically be "germane," or relevant to the legislation being considered, the rule is sometimes ignored.

Once recognized to speak, senators usually follow the rules embedded in the unanimous consent agreement and make the case for their amendment within the agreed time limits. However, once all unanimous-consent amendments are debated, any senator is free to offer other amendments, including amendments to amendments, which provides the opportunity to delay action or add unrelated issues to a popular bill that is sure to pass. Most Senate amendments are added to bills through majority vote.[38]

FINAL PASSAGE Both chambers use three types of votes for final decisions: (1) voice votes, (2) division, or standing, votes, and (3) roll call votes that call for each member's decision. The presiding officer in each chamber determines the results of voice or standing votes, but the names and votes of individual members and senators are not recorded.

In contrast, House and Senate roll call votes are recorded by member or senator by name and involve slightly different systems in each chamber. Voice and division votes are generally for routine business, while roll call votes are used for controversial rules and legislation.

Because of its sheer size, the House uses an electronic system to call the membership roll. Once a vote is announced by a series of bells that ring throughout the House, members arrive on the floor, insert their identification cards at an electronic voting terminal, and push the "yea," "nay," or "present" button. (A "present" vote does count toward passage or defeat.) The results are immediately tallied on a voting board located above the Speaker's chair at the front of the House chamber. Members are declared absent if they have not voted by the end of the 15-minute voting period.

Members can change their votes at any time when voting is open, but some wait until the last moment to see whether their "yea" or "nay" is needed to pass or defeat a particularly controversial bill that may affect their electoral future. In both houses when the vote is presumed close, members will have communicated their preferences to their respective party whip. This allows the whip to know how many votes must change to secure victory for the majority, as well as which members might be willing to change their position to help the majority win.

Bells also announce Senate votes, but the roll call is conducted in alphabetical order. Senators cast their "yea," "nay," or "abstain" votes in person standing at the front of the Senate chamber. The presiding officer tallies the vote on a checklist and announces the final margins only at the very end of the agreed-upon time period.

CONFERENCE (IF NEEDED) As noted earlier, conference committees are designed to resolve differences between two versions of a bill. Most conference committees produce a final bill that must go to each floor for passage. Members generally accept the results, if only because they might serve on a future conference committee and ask for the same accommodation.

THE PRESIDENT'S SIGNATURE Once a bill has passed both houses in identical form, it is printed on parchment paper and delivered to the president. The president must either approve or veto the bill. The president can always decide not to do anything at all, but even this nondecision can kill a bill.

The president can approve a bill by either (1) signing it into law, or (2) ignoring it for 10 days (not including Sundays). If Congress stays in session during the 10 days that the president fails to act, the bill automatically becomes law.

In turn, the president can reject a bill by either (1) returning it to Congress with a list of objections, or (2) ignoring it for 10 days (not including Sundays again). If Congress adjourns during the 10 days that the president fails to act, the bill is automatically rejected. Both of these decisions constitute a veto, which comes from a Latin phrase that means "I forbid." However, the first is sometimes called a regular veto, while the second is called a **pocket veto**, from a saying that means "the president puts the bill in his or her pocket."

pocket veto
A veto exercised by the president after Congress has adjourned; if the president takes no action for 10 days, the bill does not become law and is not returned to Congress for a possible override.

Even here, the Framers checked the veto power. Although Congress can override a regular veto by passing the original bill by two-thirds vote in both chambers, Congress cannot override a pocket veto because it is no longer in session to receive the president's list of objections. The only way to overturn a pocket veto is to reintroduce the bill in the next session of Congress and push it through the normal legislative process.

President Trump arrives in the White House Diplomatic Room before signing the 2,200 page, $1.3 federal spending bill on March 23, 2018. Trump told the press that he wanted to veto the "ridiculous" bill, but decided that the increase in military spending outweighed the increases in many domestic programs. "Nobody read it," he said. "I looked very seriously at the veto. As a matter of national security, I have signed this omnibus bill." The veto would have been the first of his term. As of November 2018, the president still had not vetoed a single bill of Congress.

The process is not over once a bill becomes a law, however. Laws are sometimes repealed, amended, or even ignored. House Republicans have tried for years to repeal Obamacare, for example, and the Department of Justice has long ignored the federal government's harsh marijuana laws in favor of state decisions. However, both laws came under tougher scrutiny with the unified Republican control of Congress and the presidency as the Trump administration toughened marijuana controls on the states, while the Republican Congress repealed the Obamacare requirement that all citizens purchase health insurance.

Making Legislative Choices (Impact)

10.5 Describe the factors that influence how members of Congress make decisions.

Members of Congress can have an impact on important issues in many ways, including representing citizens, solving bureaucratic problems, and casting votes on legislation. Their jobs often involve weekly travel to and from their districts and states, nearly constant fund-raising for the next election, and exhausting schedules.

Many historians argue that the job has become much more difficult, or at least time consuming, over the decades. The first members of Congress went to Washington for a few years and soon returned home to resume their lives. Congressional pay was low, living and office space was cramped, and Washington itself was a dreary, hot, and humid city.[39]

However, the job became more significant over time, as Congress began meeting more frequently in the late 1800s. Washington, D.C., was still hot and humid, but pay increased, and being a member became increasingly attractive.[40] As the number of members who retired after each election dropped steadily and reelection rates increased, being a member of Congress became a much more important job.[41]

As members became more attached to their jobs, they established a set of norms that shaped their actions. These norms were simple. Members were supposed to specialize in a small number of issues (the norm of specialization), defer to members with longer tenure in office (the norm of seniority), never criticize anyone personally (the norm of courtesy), and wait their turn to speak and introduce legislation (the norm of apprenticeship). As longtime House Speaker Sam Rayburn once said, new members were to be seen and not heard.

These norms began to collapse in the 1970s as campaigns became more expensive, and members started to exploit their incumbency advantages. Instead of retiring at the end of a few years, members decided to stay for long careers. New members wanted to be both seen and heard, and began criticizing their colleagues, fighting against the seniority rule, and rising to speak whenever they could.[42]

The Legislator's Job

These changes have created two Congresses, one that makes the laws with great care, and the other that fights for attention and electoral security. The two roles often exist side-by-side in the same debates as members of Congress move back and forth between two views of how to do their jobs. Some legislators believe they should serve as **delegates** for their constituents, and act on the basis of their opinions. Others see themselves as **trustees** who make decisions based on what they think is best for their district, state, and country, even if their constituents oppose that position.

delegates
An official who is expected to represent the views of his or her constituents even when personally holding different views; one interpretation of the role of the legislator.

trustees
An official who is expected to vote independently based on his or her judgment of the circumstances; one interpretation of the role of the legislator.

Most legislators shift back and forth between the delegate and trustee roles, depending on their perception of the public interest, their standing in the last and next elections, and the pressures of the moment. Most also view themselves more as free agents than as instructed delegates for their districts. And recent research suggests they often *are* free to vote as they please. Although approximately half of citizens do not know how their representatives voted on major legislation, most still believe their representative voted with the district or state.

Still, members of Congress also spend a great deal of time worrying about how a vote on a controversial issue will "play" back home, and sometimes admit that they might take a different position if they were free from constituent pressure.[43] They must be trustees on some votes, but delegates on others. The difference often resides in the salience of the issue back home—the more constituents care about an issue, the more likely that their member of Congress will be a delegate.

Influencing Votes

Only a fraction of all bills may reach the floor, but Congress still takes hundreds of votes each year. Although most of these votes involve routine issues, members often make tough decisions that involve great national debates about war and peace, taxes and spending, and national priorities such as health and welfare.

As members come to a final position on a controversial bill, they face pressure from both inside and outside of Congress. However, members make most of their decisions after asking what colleagues, constituents, party, president, and interest groups want. They also consider their own beliefs and ideology, and may even seek counsel from international leaders.

The final decision usually involves more than one of these factors. There are times when members make their decisions based on a last-second request from an old friend, other times when ideology shapes the call, and still other times when party or the president determine the choice. Moreover, members pay attention to different pressures depending on the type of vote at hand—party may be the most important factor on procedural votes that set the terms of a debate, while ideology, constituents, and personal beliefs may be more important for the final choice.[44]

In general, however, political scientists tend to agree that ideology and party exert the greatest influence on final votes. Even here, however, it is not clear whether party is the result of ideology, or ideology the product of strong party pressure, especially during primary campaigns. Moreover, ideology and party are clearly influenced and reinforced by colleagues, constituents, interest groups, and the president, all of which may play the leading role on a given vote.

The political and economic environments that surround American government also shape final votes. Political scientists have long argued that wealthy Americans have a much stronger voice in shaping the kind of policies that Congress makes. Affluent citizens and their preferences have much greater say over what gets done in government.

It is best to think of roll calls as a series of separate opportunities to serve colleagues, constituents, ideology, party, and/or the president. Sometimes, all of these factors add up to a uniform position; other times, members must choose between one or another depending on the situation at hand.

1. *How Colleagues Matter* Members of Congress often look for advice from other members of Congress, and pay particular attention to opinions from the committee members and primary sponsors of the legislation up for a vote.[45] Members also trade votes with their colleagues in a time-honored practice called logrolling to get a bill (log) moving. Some vote trading takes place to build coalitions so that members can "bring home the bacon" to their constituents. Other vote trading reflects reciprocity in congressional relations or deference to colleagues' superior information or expertise.

   Former colleagues also influence congressional decisions. Former members of Congress have access to the floor of their former chamber, and often work for lobbying groups and law firms to make the case for action to old friends and allies. On January 30, 2013, for example, former Rep. Gabrielle Giffords (D-AZ) testified before the Senate Judiciary Committee to support new guncontrol laws. Giffords had suffered a severe brain injury when she was shot in the head at a meet-and-greet event

Congress always meets in joint session when the president arrives to present the annual State of the Union Address. However, it also meets in joint session to receive international leaders. Here, Pope Francis addresses the House and Senate in joint session in September 2015 to issue a call to action on global environmental threats. His recommendations were well received by liberals and dismissed as meddling by conservatives.

back home. The injury did not stop her from returning to Capitol Hill as a former member to make the case for action. Members of the committee no doubt felt empathy for Giffords, but her plea for increased gun control protections was unsuccessful, and the proposed measures died in Congress without a vote.

2. *How Constituents Matter* Members of Congress invariably say they vote with their constituents on major legislation, but the evidence suggests that only certain constituents actually matter to the outcome. According to one recent study of thousands of congressional votes on major policy, wealthier constituents were more likely to be represented in Congress than average citizens. Bluntly put, after exhaustive statistical analysis, Martin Gilens and Benjamin Page conclude that "the preferences of the average American appears to have only a minuscule, near-zero, statistically non-significant impact upon public policy."[46]

The study raises more questions than it answers, however. To what extent do average constituents matter when an issue is very close to home? Do their opinions make more of a difference when the local economy is in trouble or the nation is at war? And do their opinions matter even more when their member is facing a tough reelection campaign? The answers are still unclear. There are times when members do pay more attention to their wealthier constituents, and times when most of their constituents do not care one way or the other about a specific vote.

3. *How Ideology Matters* Despite often-intense pressure from both inside and outside their chambers, members of Congress are influenced by their political ideology as they confront specific issues such as gay marriage, gun control, and taxes.[47] Generally measured on a scale from liberal to conservative, ideology is a powerful predictor of legislative votes and party cohesion.

Ideology is particularly important at the margins of major policy issues such as the federal budget. In 2013, for example, a large number of conservative Republicans pulled together to stop Congress from passing a budget for the coming year. Calling themselves members of a new "Tea Party" in reference to the 1773 Boston Tea Party, the group jumped to the national stage in 2010 when it helped Republicans regain the House majority with dozens of unexpected victories. Although most of these members were in their first or second terms when the budget stalemate occurred, they had strong public support back home, high media visibility, and absolute personal loyalty to the cause.

Ideology also matters in the traditional stand-offs between the two parties, especially when one party controls Congress and the other holds the presidency. Conservative Republicans held together against the Obama administration's agenda before recapturing the House majority in 2010 and Senate majority in 2014, and held together to support the Trump administration's tax plan in 2017. However, Republicans could not maintain party unity in 2017 on Trump's promise to repeal and replace Obamacare. Republican members from more moderate states denied their party a majority on the proposal in a late night vote in July.

4. *How Interest Groups Matter* Interest groups influence the legislative process through a mix of high-pressure tools that they have been using since the early 1800s, when they waited for members of Congress in the lobby outside the House and Senate chambers—thus earning the name "lobbyist." However, today's lobbyists do much more than talk to members of Congress. They also draft legislation, organize protests, make campaign contributions, oversee legislative decisions, build alliances with other

interest groups, and communicate with the public through advertising and social media, including ads targeted to the constituents of particular members.

Like any citizen or civic group, lobbyists have a constitutional right to use the First Amendment's right to petition government for a redress of grievances. But they have one clear advantage that most ordinary citizens lack: money. And they use that money to participate fully, and quite legally, in every way possible to get their point across, including making campaign contributions to members who support them and spending money against those who do not.

The 2018 Parkland High School shootings provoked student protest across the United States. Much of the student anger focused on the National Rifle Association and its supporters in Congress. The NRA is one of the nation's strongest lobbying groups. It has 5 million members, runs campaign ads against gun control candidates, and works hard to dilute even modest reforms. Although the NRA gives money to congressional candidates, its greatest strength comes from its voter turn-out campaign in conservative states and districts. Here, shooting survivors and their families address protestors at the March for Our Lives rally in Washington, D.C., on March 24, 2018. Rallies were held across the country to force gun control onto the legislative agenda by declaring enough is enough.

Interest groups often cancel each other out by taking opposing positions on issues. The result may be the death of the bill. Although some of this maneuvering occurs at the subcommittee level and is almost invisible to the public, it is always visible to the interest groups themselves and to Congress. "The result," Senator Joe Lieberman (I-CT) said before he retired in 2012, "is that everyone on Capitol Hill is keeping a close eye on everyone else, creating a self-adjusting system of checks and balances."[48]

Nevertheless, the amount of interest-group lobbying has been rising in recent years, and creates the appearance, if not absolute evidence, that outside groups have a significant voice on Capitol Hill. According to research by the nonpolitical Center for Responsive Politics, corporations, interest groups, and even universities, colleges, and local school systems spent $2.4 billion lobbying federal, state, and local officials in 2017, up from $1.4 billion in 1996. The U.S. Chamber of Commerce was the top spender at $64 million, followed by the American Medical Association and the National Association of Realtors both at $23 million, Blue Cross/Blue Shield at $17 million, and the Boeing Company at $16 million. Tracked by industry, the pharmaceutical sector, or "Big Pharma" as it is sometimes called, spent $178 million in 2015, followed by the insurance industry at $118 million, and oil and gas companies at $97 million.[49] Although heavy lobbying does not guarantee an industry's ultimate success, it does create the conditions that make support easier, if only because lobbying is so often accompanied by campaign contributions.[50]

At least some of the spending goes to former congressional staffers who leave Capitol Hill for high-paying lobbying posts. According to one recent report, these "revolving door" lobbyists who exchange their legislative and government knowledge for much higher-paying lobbying jobs accounted for almost all of the increased spending described above. These former officials bring special expertise to their jobs, not the least of which is knowledge about how to pass or kill a bill.[51]

You can check your own college or university's lobbying by entering its name in the search bar at the very top of https://www.opensecrets.org. Doing so is one way you can ask whether the spending is making any difference, and whether it might be better spent on other priorities.

5. *How Party Matters* Democrats and Republicans have historically voted against each other on major legislative issues. However, this historical division between the two parties has become sharper over the past two decades in the House and Senate, in part because both parties have become more ideologically pure. Since the 107th Congress in 2001, nearly 90 percent of Democrats and Republicans have voted with their party on key legislative votes, compared with 80 percent in the 1980s, and 70 percent during the 1970s.

FIGURE 10.5 PARTY UNITY SCORES, 1961–2014

Party unity scores show each party's strength in holding its members in line. Strictly defined, a party's unity score is calculated as the percentage of total votes in the House or Senate in which half or more members of one party vote against half or more of the other party. The score has been used for decades to show the amount of conflict within the House and Senate. As the score rises, the potential for agreement on policy issues declines.

SOURCE: "CQ Vote Studies: Party Unity," *CQ Magazine*, February 12, 2018.

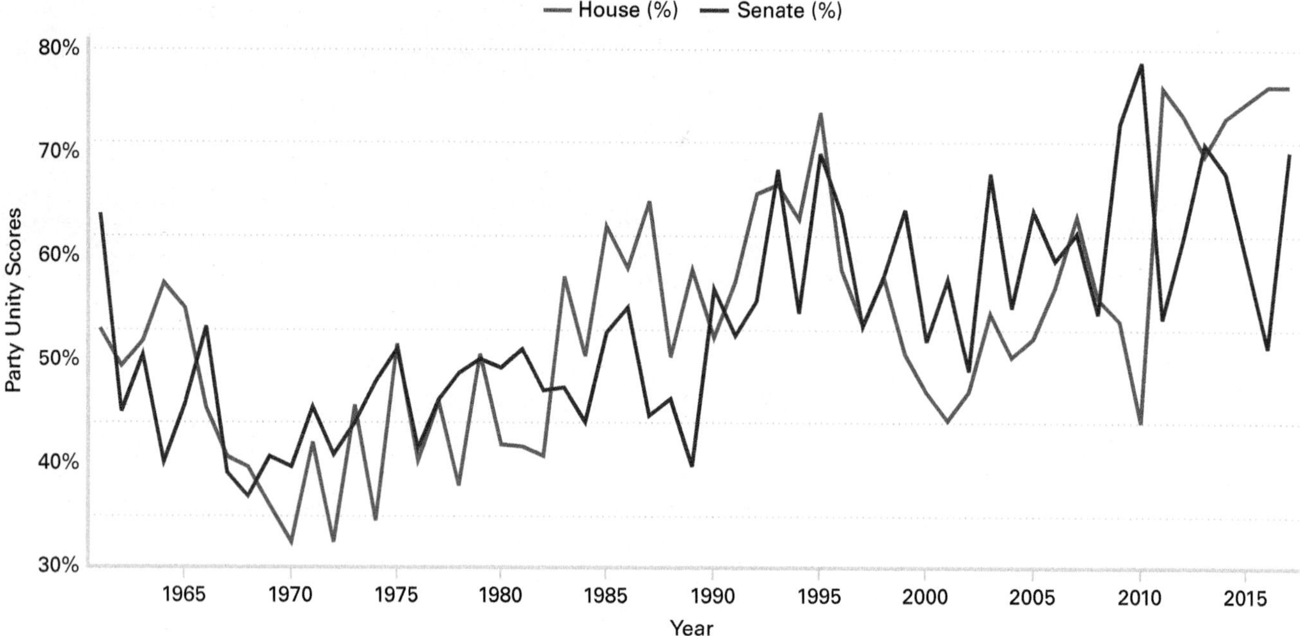

The standard measure of party influence is called the party unity score. As the name suggests, the measure tracks the number of times that each party held together in opposition to the other.[52] Experts often use party unity as a measure of party "polarization." The more that each party votes as a block, the more likely they are to disagree at other stages of the legislative process. As Figure 10.5 shows, the amount of party-unity voting has been increasing for decades, but is moving ever closer to the 100 percent party-against-party mark.[53]

6. *How Presidents Matter* Presidents have a long list of tools for influencing members of Congress, including the ability to distribute government resources to districts and states. Presidents also help set the legislative agenda through their annual State of the Union Address, the budget, and assorted legislative messages, and they lobby Congress on particularly important issues.

When asked why they vote one way or the other, members of Congress tend to deny the president's influence. Presidents work hard to influence public opinion, and they have a long list of incentives to encourage congressional support, not the least of which are invitations to special White House dinners and federal grants to support key projects back home. Trump used these perquisites and his command of Twitter in 2017 to set a modern record for presidential influence with Congress by winning 98.7 percent of the votes on issues he supported. Obama had set the previous record in 2009 with a 96.7 mark also by attaching his influence to issues he cared about.[54] These high scores reflect each president's party control of Congress, and the reluctance of their party leaders to bring particularly controversial items to the floor for votes. Obama lost influence when Republicans captured the 2010 midterm elections, while Trump began losing influence in 2018 as predictions of a "blue wave" of Democratic victories took hold.

Congressional Ethics

Under the Constitution, each chamber of Congress is responsible for disciplining its own members. Although some members are subject to federal prosecution for bribery and other criminal acts, the House and Senate set the more general rules for ethical conduct and investigate all complaints of misbehavior.

Members of Congress have faced tighter ethics rules after a series of scandals involving bribes and petty corruption linked to interest groups. Under new rules enacted in September 2007, members of Congress may not accept gifts, trips, hotel accommodations, or sports tickets from lobbyists, nor any payments for making a speech, providing a special briefing, attending an event, or writing an article.[55] These rules were expanded under the Stock Act of 2012, which prohibits members of Congress from buying or selling stocks based on "inside information" gleaned from their contacts in government.[56]

Despite these rules, some congressional members and staffers still find ways to outfox the House and Senate ethics committees. The committees are composed of members of Congress who are often reluctant to discipline their own members, and must enforce highly complicated rules that contain a host of loopholes and definitional ambiguity. Just what constitutes "inside information," for example, and what if members receive free travel and accommodations to learn more about a specific issue pending before a committee? The ethics rules are just murky enough to frustrate compliance.

Congress at a Crossroads (Impact)

10.6 Analyze the ability of members to represent their constituents.

As noted, members of Congress have many choices as they seek to represent their constituents, including the bicameral system, the election process, and the pressures on their decisions. They often face cross-pressures between their desires to represent their constituents as delegates and trustees, too.

More than two centuries after the creation of Congress, its members continue to face the barriers to impact that are embedded in their divided institution. Congress has become much more complex, more partisan, and much more active. Although most incumbents are easily reelected, most still campaign constantly to stay in office, creating what some observers have called the "permanent campaign."[57] Members appear driven by their desire to win reelection, so that much of what takes place in Congress seems mainly designed to promote reelection.

The permanent campaign may have paid off richly in high reelection rates, but not in congressional approval. Indeed, even with a $1.5 trillion tax cut showing up in their paychecks in of February 2018, only 15 percent of Americans approved of the way Congress was handling its job, yet another record low in a long decline that began in the 1970s.

This record-low level of approval is clearly related to the rising conflict between the two parties in Congress. As noted earlier, party members frequently vote as a block today, and are more likely to lean to the ideological extremes. Moreover, the percentage of moderates in the House and Senate peaked in the 1930s and 1940s, and reached a record low in 2014, too. (See Figure 10.6 for the trend lines.)

This is not the first time that moderates have been in the distinct minority, however. The number of moderates was very low in the 1920s, for example, high during the 1930s, and low in the 1980s. This fall-and-rise-and-fall pattern suggests that members of Congress behave more like moderates during periods of national crisis and less during years of party conflict. Congress is quite capable of enacting laws to address urgent threats such as wars and economic crisis, but tends to fall into conflict when the news is good.

Once past a nod of gratitude to the Framers for creating a system that prevents tyranny even at the cost of legislative action, the question remains whether Congress has become so divided that it is failing to do its job in addressing domestic and international threats. Many Americans undoubtedly believe the answer is yes, especially with the current level of partisan gridlock.

FIGURE 10.6 MODERATES IN CONGRESS, 1971–2015

Moderates are particularly important when the two parties are divided. The number of moderates in Congress reveals the potential for creating compromise across the party lines. Moderates are often viewed as boundary-spanners who can build compromises on controversial issues such as the budget, health care, stem cell research, and climate policy that both parties can accept. Moderates are particularly important when party unity scores are very high. If the number of moderates falls too far, there is little opportunity to create the negotiations that produce legislative agreement.

SOURCE: Data from Keith T. Poole and Howard Rosenthal, available at voteview.com.

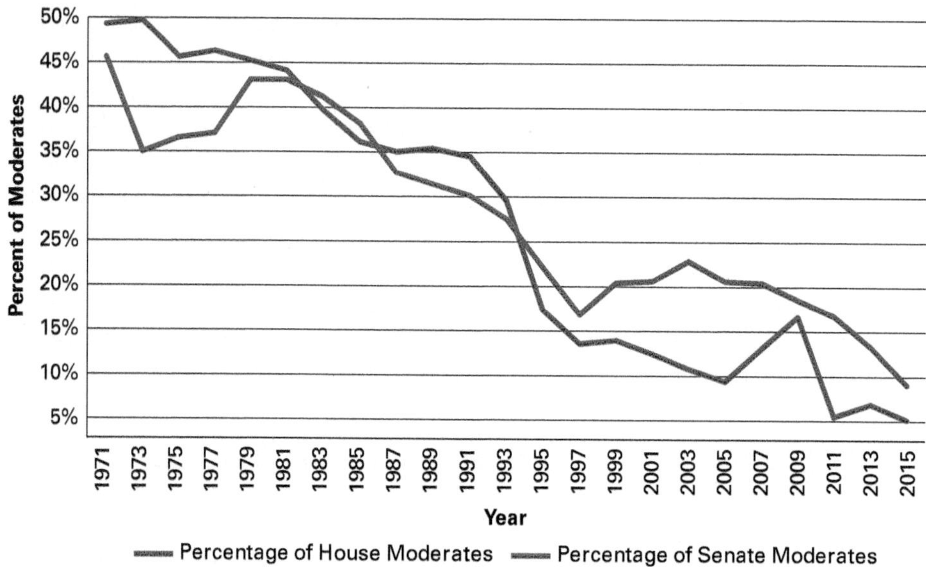

CONCLUSION

The U.S. national defense is currently protecting the nation from a staggering array of international threats. Russia is becoming increasingly provocative as its leader, Vladimir Putin, becomes more aggressive; the Islamic State in Iraq and Syria is expanding its reach to other nations in the Middle East, Africa, and Southeast Asia; North Korea claims to have tested a hydrogen bomb; Iran and Saudi Arabia are locked in a struggle over the future of the Persian Gulf; India and Pakistan continue to struggle over territory and policy; China continues to build its own cyber warfare capacity; and homegrown terrorism is rising.

The national defense must be ready to meet all of the threats at the same time, but cannot always tell Congress and the American public just what it needs in order to do so. Nor can it always know how much it must spend to get what it needs. Congress is enormously sensitive to defense-industry pressure, and has a well-deserved reputation for overspending on complex weapons that may be poorly suited for an uncertain world. Congress also has a well-deserved reputation for protecting defense programs that even the Defense Department does not want.

Given your own experience with new technologies and innovation, you have an important perspective on how to make America safe without breaking the budget. You also know a great deal about monitoring what is happening in the world.

With the knowledge you now have about how Congress works, you also have the ability to confront at least some of the barriers to making tough legislative decisions. To succeed you will need passion and persistence to push for congressional action. You may be one of the millions of Americans who have lost faith in Congress, but you are also part of a generation that is about to take over Congress. You have something to say about how to build a national defense that can protect the United States from uncertain threats, and you can make a difference by becoming one of the small donors or active constituents who can push Congress to act. There are many paths to action. You just have to pick one.

REVIEW THE CHAPTER

The Structure and Powers of Congress (Structure)

10.1 Describe the constitutional foundations of Congress, p. 293.

The Framers expected Congress to be the most important branch of government, and created a set of legislative powers that seem to dwarf those of the presidency and judiciary. Before they listed the powers, they divided Congress into a two-house, bicameral legislature that continues to divide Congress to this day. The Constitution contains a long list of legislative powers, including (1) the power to raise, make, and borrow money, (2) the power to regulate commerce, (3) the power to unify the country, (4) the power to declare war, and (5) the power to create the federal judiciary. It also lists the authority to make the laws by spending money through the power of the purse. The Constitution reinforced these powers through the Necessary and Proper Clause, which gives Congress the power to make the laws to enforce the powers. The Constitution also gives the House and Senate a handful of separate powers.

Congressional Elections (Structure)

10.2 Describe the congressional election process and the advantages it gives incumbents, p. 296.

The congressional election process begins with three basic differences between the two chambers: qualifications, constituencies, and campaigns. House members serve for two-year terms and all stand for reelection at the same time, while senators serve for six-year terms and stand for reelection one-third at a time. House members serve in districts, while senators serve the entire state. House districts are apportioned and reapportioned to each state by population, and districts are carved from the states through redistricting. House members and senators have many incumbency advantages in the drive for reelection, including constituent services, legislation, and earmarks.

Organizing Congress (Action)

10.3 Compare and contrast the leadership systems used in the House and Senate, and explain how work is done through congressional committees, p. 305.

The two chambers have slightly different organizational structures based on their own needs and behaviors as separate powers. The larger House is built around a tighter party structure led by the Speaker, a majority and a minority leader, and party whips, while the smaller Senate is built around a looser party system led by a majority and a minority leader. The Senate is more difficult to lead because of its greater individualism, sometimes expressed through the use of holds and filibusters to control the legislative process. Most of the work in Congress is done through standing committees and subcommittees that cover six different legislative tasks: (1) rules and administration, (2) budget, (3) appropriations, (4) authorizing, (5) revenue, and (6) oversight. The House Rules Committee is the most powerful committee in Congress as a whole because it controls the rules that structure debates in the much larger chamber.

How a Bill Becomes a Law (Action)

10.4 Describe the process of lawmaking in Congress, p. 310.

A bill moves through a difficult process to become a law, if ever it becomes a law at all. It must be (1) introduced, (2) referred to a committee for further review, (3) reviewed by the committee and subcommittee, (4) "marked up" by the committee and subcommittee before it goes to the floor, (5) debated and amended on the floor, (6) passed by each chamber, (7) if necessary, redrafted by a conference committee to resolve any differences between the House and Senate versions, (8) passed a final time in each chamber as a conference report, and (9) either signed into law or rejected by the president. Although all bills are referred to committees for consideration, very few receive a hearing, even fewer are marked up and sent to the floor, and fewer still are enacted by both chambers and signed into law by the president. In addition, the legislative obstacle course sometimes includes the fight over tickets to the floor, amendments to amendments, filibusters, riders, holds, and the president's decision to approve or veto a bill.

Making Legislative Choices (Impact)

10.5 Describe the factors that influence how members of Congress make decisions, p. 316.

Legislators must balance the needs of their constituents against the national good. In addressing constituent needs, they often act as representatives of public opinion in their home districts. In addressing national issues, they often act as trustees of the greater good. Members must balance these two roles, even as they balance the six sources of influence on their final decisions: (1) colleagues, (2) constituents, (3) ideology, (4) interest groups, (5) the party, and (6) presidents. These six factors sometimes come together on a single vote, but more often they influence a specific issue. In general, however, ideology and party are seen as the most powerful factors on final decisions.

Congress at a Crossroads (Impact)

10.6 Analyze the ability of members to represent their constituents, p. 321.

Congressional approval has recently hit new lows, raising questions about whether Congress can even do its job. Some experts argue that party conflict is the reason, and often track the number of moderates as an indicator of the divisions. Others argue that approval has fallen because of intense conflict and bitterness. And still others suggest that the problem resides in the number of safe seats, which stimulates more ideological primary elections that drive candidates toward the extremes of their party's supporters. Whatever the reason, Americans are right to wonder whether Congress can still do its job.

LEARN THE TERMS

bicameralism, p. 293
enumerated powers, p. 293
power of the purse, p. 294
impeachment power, p. 294
articles of impeachment, p. 294
Necessary and Proper Clause, p. 295
implied powers, p. 295
apportionment, p. 297
reapportionment, p. 297
redistricting, p. 298
gerrymandering, p. 298
safe seat, p. 299
incumbency advantage, p. 300
casework, p. 300
franking privilege, p. 300
earmarks, p. 300
Speaker of the House, p. 305
filibuster, p. 307
cloture, p. 307
congressional committee, p. 307
rule, p. 308
conference committee, p. 309
member caucuses, p. 309
seniority rule, p. 309
veto, p. 312
pocket veto, p. 315
delegates, p. 316
trustees, p. 316

CHAPTER 11

The Presidency

President Donald Trump won the presidency in part by promising to overturn the Obama administration's environmental policies. He called global warming a "hoax" and ridiculed scientists who warned that climate change would increase both the number and severity of hurricanes, cyclones, and droughts. Hurricane Harvey seemed to side with the scientists when it struck Houston, Texas in August 2018 with record-setting wind and flooding. Here, rescuers prepare to journey into a Houston neighbourhood to rescue stranded residents. One of the worst storms to ever come ashore, Harvey dropped more than 50 inches of rain on Houston and lingered over the city for days. Scientists argued that warmer ocean temperatures provided much of the fuel for the storm, while predicting increased risks of similar disasters in the future.

LEARNING OBJECTIVES

11.1 Identify the constitutional foundations of the presidency (Structure), p. 327.

11.2 Analyze the scope of presidential power (Structure), p. 332.

11.3 Describe the organization and functions of the Executive Office of the President (Action), p. 344.

11.4 Examine the relationship between the president and the public (Action), p. 349.

11.5 Describe the relationship between the president and the Congress (Impact), p. 353.

11.6 Identify the sources of presidential greatness (Impact), p. 356.

The president has been a key participant in strengthening the nation's response to environmental pollution. Presidents have been working with Congress since the end of World War II to promote environmental protection, and now oversee a large federal bureaucracy that regulates air and water quality. Democratic and Republican presidents strongly embraced early laws alike as both parties pushed passage of laws such as the 1970 Clean Air and 1972 Clean Water Acts.

President Donald Trump endorsed both efforts during the 2016 campaign but also promised to oppose the international movement to control global warming. He followed through on his opposition by appointing a mix of pro-environmental protection and anti-climate change advocates to develop his agenda.

Experts generally agree that the nation's air and water are much cleaner today than when polluters spewed toxins into the air and disposed of dangerous chemicals into hidden dumps or directly into the water. During the past 30 years, the levels of most of the air pollution covered by the Clean Air Act have fallen dramatically as presidents and the Environmental Protection Agency (EPA) have established ever-tighter rules promoting more efficient automobiles and cleaner-burning fuels. Aside from seasonal inversions in some cities, the dense smog that used to blanket U.S. cities is mostly gone, cars are getting much better mileage, and coal-fired electric power plants are producing less of the carbon monoxide that is blamed for the rising global temperature even as clean solar and wind energy are growing as green replacements.[1] People are living longer because of these positive changes.[2]

Similarly, it is hard to find a single body of water or a river that is not significantly cleaner because of the Clean Water Act. The 1972 law had set a goal of "zero discharge" of pollution, and the president and Congress sought to expand the coverage by prohibiting ocean dumping and by passing the Safe Drinking Water Act two years later. However, polluters have found many ways to get rid of their toxic waste, and still dump pollutants into unsafe collection pits that leak into the groundwater.

The nation will have to discuss many of the new threats to clean air and water, including the corroded pipes that deliver unsafe drinking water to citizens in aging cities such as Flint, Michigan. And you must deal with a global temperature crisis that many scientists believe will threaten the world's very existence in the next century. Global temperatures are clearly rising, the question being how far they can go before changing the world irreversibly. Environmental threats have become more complex. Old pollutants are being replaced today by much more toxic chemicals that are both hard to detect and eliminate. Responding to these challenges will cost money. Many conservative economists believe that higher mileage standards for cars, trucks, and even airplanes will damage the economy and reduce long-term job opportunities.[3]

Trump made this case when he revoked many of the Obama administration's new environmental rules during his first year. He nominated a bitter environmental opponent as administrator of the Environmental Protection Agency (EPA) on January 18, 2017, ordered the Commerce Department to approve two stalled oil pipeline projects on January 24, removed all references to climate change from the White House Web site on January 25, ordered the EPA to begin the process for unwinding Obama's new rules protecting streams and wetlands on February 28, approved deep cuts to EPA's budget on March 26, launched a full-scale review of Obama's clean power plan on March 28, and continued to challenge environmental air and water regulations throughout his first two years.[4]

Trump's most significant reversal came on June 1 when he announced America's withdrawal from the international agreement to reduce global temperatures. The accord was signed by 194 other nations in 2015 in an effort to lower "planet-warming" greenhouse gases to keep average temperatures from rising past a "tipping point" where the environmental damage rising sea levels, severe weather, and record-setting heat would be irreversible. Trump argued that the United States was paying too high a price for its participation, and often argues that climate change is a "hoax." He also encouraged Americans to fight the costs of environmental protection. Trump may yet reverse his decision, but the American public is increasingly resistant to the costs of compliance.

This chapter will give you the knowledge to understand how Trump and other presidents use their authority and influence to shape the laws, make difficult decisions, and address crises. As Trump has shown, presidents can make significant impact in stopping the federal government from acting on issues such as environmental protection, but they are also subject to checks and balances. As Obama has learned, even the most carefully drafted laws and executive orders can be reversed by Congress and the judiciary, and Trump is learning the same lesson as many of his early actions have been reversed in the courts. This chapter will help you understand the structure of the presidency, its sources of action, and its potential impact. You will be able to use this knowledge to help the president make tough choices related to the environment and a host of other pressing issues such as immigration, terrorism, and economic growth.

The Constitutional Foundations of the Presidency (Structure)

11.1 Identify the constitutional foundations of the presidency.

Although the Framers of the Constitution did not know what threats the republic would face, they designed the presidency to handle problems as diverse as the Islamic State in Iraq and Syria, global climate change, and economic uncertainty. At the same time, they also created many checks and balances to protect against the possibility of presidential tyranny.

The Constitution establishes the executive's structure. It confers presidential powers and provides the basic expectations for action. It also sets the ground rules for selecting a president and vice president. The Framers clearly wanted a strong president at the center of government. They knew firsthand how the Articles of Confederation had lengthened the Revolutionary War by creating only ceremonial, one-year presidents of Congress, and they knew the nation would always be vulnerable without someone like George Washington at the helm.

The Framers also wanted a president who would avoid factions and favoritism, enforce the laws passed by Congress, handle communications with foreign governments, and help states put down disorders. They believed the "jarrings of parties" in Congress were perfectly appropriate in making the laws, but not in fighting wars and running the executive branch. As Alexander Hamilton argued in *The Federalist*, No. 68, which explains the presidency in detail, "A feeble executive implies a feeble execution of the government. A feeble execution is but another phrase for a bad execution: and a government ill executed, whatever it may be in theory, must be in practice a bad government."[5]

Donald Trump's victory in the 2016 presidential campaign was announced on billboards in New York City's Times Square only hours after midnight on November 9. Although Trump had won enough Electoral College votes to secure his victory in battleground states such as Pennsylvania, Ohio, North Carolina, and Florida, his election was assured when Wisconsin finally finished its vote count at 1:00 a.m. Former Secretary of State Hillary Clinton won the popular vote, but could not string together enough state victories to reach a 270 electoral vote majority.

Presidential Powers

Much as they wanted a strong executive, the Framers rightly worried that the states might reject the Constitution if the president had the powers of a king. Perhaps that is why they gave the president fewer and less specific powers than Congress, described in four choppy paragraphs giving the president three broad powers that create the structure for action:

1. *The power to command the nation's armed forces during peace and war, and to make treaties with other nations.* The president, not Congress, is the Commander in Chief of the military, and the presidency, not Congress or state governments, is to be the fulcrum of negotiation with other countries.
2. *The power to appoint the principal officers of government, and to require their written opinions on any subject related to their duties.* The president is the chief executive of government, and supervises every employee by appointing the principal officers and holding them accountable in writing. Congress has long given the president authority to appoint the lower level, or "inferior," officers of government (discussed later in this chapter).
3. *The power to give Congress information on the state of the union, recommend new laws considered necessary and expedient, and convene Congress under extraordinary circumstances.* The president cannot introduce legislation, but may recommend measures to Congress, and can convene Congress to take action during emergencies. The president can also pardon individuals convicted of federal crimes such as fraud, counterfeiting, and bribery.

These three powers laid the foundation for what Alexander Hamilton called "energy in the executive." As he argued in *The Federalist*, No. 69, energy was central to nearly every priority facing the nation: "It is essential to the protection of the community against foreign attacks; it is not less essential to the steady administration of the laws; to the protection of property against those irregular and high-handed combinations which sometimes interrupt the ordinary course of justice; to the security of liberty against the enterprises and assaults of ambition, of faction, and of anarchy."[6] He made this case for an energetic executive even more forcefully in *The Federalist*, No. 70.

Choosing the President

The Framers made their most important decision about the presidency in mid-July, when they decided to create a single executive instead of a council of some kind. Despite worries that a single president might lay the groundwork for a future monarchy, the Framers had seen how a lack of energy in the executive had left the nation unable to respond to crises under the Articles of Confederation.

Once they created a single executive as the head of a separate branch of government, the Framers had to make a series of added choices establishing the basic rules about who could run for president, who would choose the president, how long the president and vice president would serve, and how to remove the president.

QUALIFICATIONS FOR OFFICE According to Article II, no person can serve as president unless he or she is (1) a natural born citizen, (2) at least 35 years old, and (3) has lived in the United States for 14 years. The Framers created the citizenship and residency requirements to prevent the election of wealthy foreigners who might move to the United States just to run for the presidency.[7]

There have never been any significant challenges about the age and residency limits, but there have been occasional arguments about what constitutes "natural-born" citizenship. Most of the arguments have surrounded the place of birth. President Chester A. Arthur was forced to prove his citizenship after he became president in 1881 because he may have been born in Canada, while Arizona senator and 2008

Republican presidential candidate John McCain was also challenged on his citizenship during the 2008 campaign because he was born on a military base in Panama before it became a U.S. territory

Most recently, Obama was challenged about his citizenship throughout his presidency because of persistent allegations that he was born in Kenya to a Kenyan father, not in Hawaii where his birth was registered. This "birther" scandal was occasionally raised during Obama's 2008 campaign, but received a burst of national attention in 2012 when Trump tweeted that he had information from "an extremely credible source" that Obama's birth certificate was "a fraud."[8] Obama eventually produced his birth certificate, but many Republicans continue to doubt his citizenship.[9]

The nation's 45 presidents entered office with a wide variety of skills and service. Twenty-six were trained as lawyers, 22 had served in the military, including 9 who were Army generals, 18 had served in Congress, 14 had been vice presidents, and 6 had business experience, including a mining investor (Herbert Hoover), a clothing sales clerk (Harry Truman), a peanut farmer (Jimmy Carter), a Hollywood actor (Ronald Reagan), an oil executive (George H. W. Bush), and a managing partner of a baseball team (George W. Bush). Truman and Reagan are considered great or near-great presidents, while Hoover is rated among the worst.

Trump was the first real estate tycoon and reality television star to win office, but had been politically active in politics for many years before launching his campaign. He argued that he would make the "best deals" as president and promised to use his negotiating skills to bring Democrats and Republicans together to make America great. However, he was widely criticized for recording-setting White House staff turnover, and earned a reputation for changing positions without notice in congressional negotiations on the budget and immigration—43 percent of Trump's senior staff exited during his first year, including six of the president's 12 "Tier One" positions such as chief of staff, press secretary, and White House counsel.[10] Trump saw the turmoil as a source of good decisions, not instability. "I like conflict," he said in early March 2018. "I like having two people with different points of view, and I certainly have that. And then I make a decision. But I like watching it, I like seeing it, and I think it's the best way to go. I like different points view."[11] Franklin D. Roosevelt used a similar style in forging his New Deal agenda in 1932, but did not wear out his staff at anywhere near the same pace as Trump.

THE TERM OF OFFICE The Framers were sharply divided between a fixed or flexible term of office. Some delegates favored a single seven-year term with no option for reelection, others favored a four-year term with reappointment by Congress, and Hamilton favored an unlimited single term that could last for decades. The Framers eventually gave the president and vice president four-year terms of office without any mention of a limit.

Written as such, the Framers allowed presidents to serve for as many terms as the public would permit. As Hamilton explained in *The Federalist*, No. 70, the Framers believed that elections created "safety in the executive" by giving the public a chance to remove the president from office.[12] If presidents were doing a good job, the public could keep them in office; if not, the public could remove them.

As we will note later in this chapter, presidents are now limited to two terms in office under the Twenty-second Amendment.

PRESIDENTIAL SELECTION The Framers had two options for choosing the president, one based on the British model, and the other uniquely American. First, they could have left the choice to the majority party in Congress by creating some variation of **parliamentary government**. Although parliamentary governments have three branches of government, the legislature is usually divided between a mostly ceremonial upper house and a lower house elected by the people, which holds the real power.

parliamentary government
A form of government in which the chief executive is the leader of the majority party in the legislature.

The chief executive is usually called the prime minister and is the majority leader of the parliament's lower house, called the House of Commons. Once the votes are counted after an election and the majority party is determined, the party leader automatically becomes the prime minister. **Prime ministers** have similar authority to U.S. presidents, but are limited by the size of their parliamentary majority—the smaller the majority, the less power they have.

prime minister
In the United Kingdom, the leader of a parliamentary government elected by the majority party in the House of Commons, which is the lower house of the parliament.

Parliamentary elections are called on a regular basis, but may occur after the parliament expresses "no confidence" in the majority's government by a two-thirds vote. If the majority party holds the parliament, the prime minister's agenda is more likely to pass—after all, the prime minister is the parliament's leader.

Second, the Framers could have created a selection process true to the separate powers system they had already created. Some of the delegates favored direct election by the people, others supported selection by state governors, and a handful even favored election by Congress. The delegates rejected all three proposals in favor of the Electoral College: voters would cast their ballots for competing slates of electors, who would in turn cast their electoral votes for president. The Framers also decided that the House would decide the outcome if no candidate received a majority of electors.

In turn, the Framers decided to award the vice presidency to the losing candidate under what can be called the "runner-up rule." Since the loser already had the qualifications to be president, the Framers seemed to believe that putting the two at the top of government might help calm the public.

Congress changed the rule after it was used in three of the first four presidential elections, which awarded first place to John Adams, and second place to Thomas Jefferson. Adams never consulted Jefferson on an issue of national significance, while Jefferson saw the vice presidency as an opportunity to spend "philosophical evenings in the winter and rural days in the summer."[13] In short, the runner-up rule had turned a weak office into a waste of time.

presidential ticket
A requirement created under the Twelfth Amendment in 1803 that requires the presidential and vice presidential candidates of the same party to run for election as a single choice.

The Framers fixed the runner-up rule in the Twelfth Amendment to the Constitution. Ratified in 1804, electors were allowed to cast separate votes for the president and vice president. This new practice encouraged candidates to run together as members of a **presidential ticket** that lists the presidential and vice presidential candidates first and second.

REMOVAL FROM OFFICE Much as they hoped that every president would serve with dignity, the Framers protected the nation against the possibility that a president might engage in corruption or even treason. The question, therefore, was how to remove a president who violates the law. The Framers decided on a process called impeachment that begins with a list of charges called **articles of impeachment** passed by a majority vote in the House, and then goes to a formal trial with the Senate as the jury and the Supreme Court's chief justice as the presiding judge, with conviction by a 67-vote majority or acquittal by less than that total.

articles of impeachment
The formal House document that lists the charges against the president for treason, bribery, or high crimes and misdemeanors.

British Prime Minister David Cameron decided to resign his post after the public voted to leave the European Union in a tight national referendum on the "Brexit." His party remained in power, but he had campaigned against the referendum and resigned to respect the public will.

The House is responsible for launching the impeachment process by charging the president with one of three offenses: (1) treason, (2) bribery, or (3) other high crimes and misdemeanors. Bribery and treason are easy to define, but "high crimes and misdemeanors" can cover everything from personal misconduct to violating a federal law. The House has impeached two presidents for high crimes and misdemeanors: Andrew Johnson was impeached in 1868 for violating a federal law limiting his authority to remove a principal officer of government, while Bill Clinton was impeached in 1998 for lying about his affair with a White House intern named Monica Lewinsky.

Once approved by a simple majority vote in the House, the resolution containing the specific articles of impeachment is forwarded to the Senate for a formal trial. The chief justice of the Supreme Court presides over the trial, every senator serves as a member of the jury, a team of senior House members who favor impeachment presents the case, and the White House counsel defends the president. If two-thirds of the Senate votes to convict the president of the charges, the president is removed from office. Johnson was acquitted by just one vote, while Clinton was acquitted by 11 votes.

Impeachment returned to the headlines in June 2017 when Trump fired FBI director, James Comey in the midst of the bureau's investigation of Russian meddling in the 2016 election. Some Democrats saw the firing as qualifying as a high crime and misdemeanor, while some Republicans viewed the firing as a scandal but not to the point of being an impeachable offense. Although Trump's advisors saw impeachment as unlikely, they convinced the president to build a legal team and launch a media campaign to convince the public that the investigation was a political "witch hunt."

Having secured multiple indictments and convictions during its first eighteen months, the investigation disappeared from the headlines during the 2018 campaign to avoid influencing the outcome of the election. It returned to the front pages soon after the election as the president's lawyers prepared for a final report before the end of the year. Although Democrats won enough seats in the House to charge the president with high crimes and misdemeanors, they did not have the votes to secure conviction in the Senate and would have to balance the political cost of a failed impeachment against their obligation to hold the president to account.

Impeachment was the only way to remove a president from office until the Twenty-second Amendment was ratified in 1951. Promoted by Republicans still angry about Franklin Delano Roosevelt's four-term victory streak, the amendment prohibits any person from winning the presidency more than twice. This means a president can only serve eight years total, which thereby removes that president from ever running again. The amendment also limits vice presidents who succeed a sitting president in the middle of a term to no more than 10 years in the office of the presidency.

Congress added another way to remove the president temporarily when the Twenty-fifth Amendment was ratified in 1967. Promoted by both parties to cover emergencies that might injure, but not kill, a president, the amendment allows for the temporary removal of the president from his or her responsibilities due to illness or disability. The president can only be removed temporarily if (1) the vice president and (2) a majority of either Congress or the president's own department secretaries declare the president to be unable to discharge the powers and duties of office. During the temporary removal of the president, the vice president becomes the acting president. If the president dies or resigns, the vice president becomes the president and must nominate a new vice president. The new president's choice for vice president must be confirmed by majority votes in both the House and Senate.

The amendment has been triggered six times, most notably in 1973 when Gerald Ford became vice president after his predecessor Spiro Agnew resigned in disgrace, and in 1974 when Nelson Rockefeller then became vice president after Ford became president. The other four incidents were due to routine medical procedures that involved anesthesia.

Here, Capitol Hill Police begin unloading the evidence that the House used to impeach President Clinton on December 19, 1998. Clinton was charged with lying under oath and obstruction of justice in a case that involved an extramarital affair with a White House intern. He was charged on a 222 to 212 vote by the House, and later acquitted by a margin of 55 to 45, far short of the two thirds vote needed to convict.

The President's Job Description (Structure)

11.2 Analyze the scope of presidential power.

The president's job description is a more specific form of structure, and affects everything from the decision to deploy U.S. troops to the government's budget. When presidents hear the term *Commander in Chief*, for example, they think of a specific set of responsibilities that add up to a very significant job.

The Framers designed the presidency with George Washington in mind, and he did not disappoint them, as he converted the Constitution's powers into a set of specific jobs for action. Elected as the first president of the United States, without opposition and by a unanimous electoral vote, Washington acted with energy, dispatch, and calm as the untested government navigated a period of great domestic and international uncertainty.

Washington did more than take action in a time of turbulence, however. He showed how the presidency should work. He negotiated the new government's first treaty, appointed its first judges and department heads, received its first foreign ambassadors, issued its first vetoes, and signed its first laws. Washington also showed how presidents could expand presidential power through hard work and bold ideas.

The Evolution of Presidential Power

Presidential power has expanded slowly but steadily since Washington returned to Mount Vernon after his two terms in office. Although many presidents were content with the presidency they inherited, roughly a third expanded its powers to act:

- Thomas Jefferson increased the president's reach by almost single-handedly doubling the nation's size through the Louisiana Purchase.
- Andrew Jackson taught future presidents how to engage the "common people" in the call for change, and set new precedents for helping the president's party reap the "spoils of victory."

- Abraham Lincoln invented entirely new powers to win the Civil War and end slavery, and showed the power of sheer eloquence, raw courage, and perseverance for creating change.
- Theodore Roosevelt used the presidency as a "bully pulpit" to attack greed and corruption, while building the United States into an international power by "speaking softly and carrying a big stick."
- Woodrow Wilson implemented the federal government's new income tax in his first term, led the United States into World War I, and unsuccessfully pushed to create a League of Nations to promote international cooperation.
- Harry S. Truman led the United States into the Korean War, integrated the armed services, nationalized the steel industry to prevent an economic crisis, and launched the Cold War against communism.
- Lyndon Johnson won historic victories on civil rights, Medicare for older Americans, and a long list of antipoverty programs, even as he edged the nation into the Vietnam War.
- Ronald Reagan sparked a revolution against big government with deep budget and tax cuts, and helped the United States win the Cold War, bring down the Berlin Wall, and unravel the Soviet Union.

George W. Bush and Barack Obama extended presidential power, too, by embracing the concept of the **unitary executive**. According to advocates of this unchecked executive authority, presidents are responsible not just for executing the laws faithfully, but also for protecting the presidency from Congress. This means that presidents can order departments and agencies to act in ways presidents deem essential for protecting the nation even if Congress says "no."[14] Trump also gave early notice that he intended to use presidential authorities to the maximum extent possible, even suggesting at times that neither Congress nor the federal courts could constrain his power as Commander in Chief.

unitary executive
An assertion that presidents have complete authority to exercise any and all powers they deem appropriate to protect the nation from imminent threats.

Bush, Obama, and Trump relied in part on their oath of office to argue they must protect the presidency. Their oath contained in Article II is quite specific: "I do solemnly swear (or affirm) that I will faithfully execute the Office of President of the United States, and will to the best of my Ability, preserve, protect and defend the Constitution of the United States." The oath is not just about the laws, but also about the Office of the President itself. By pushing their power to the edge of constitutional permission, Bush and Obama did their part to extend presidential power during the war on terrorism just as Lincoln did during the Civil War, while Trump put his own stamp on the unitary theory with his early executive orders.[15]

No president did more to lay the groundwork for these actions than Franklin Roosevelt. Roosevelt dominated Congress in the early years of his presidency as he secured a response to the Great Depression, led the nation to unequivocal victory in World War II, and created a host of major programs such as Social Security and unemployment insurance.

Roosevelt also harnessed the powers of the presidency to create an enduring personal relationship with the U.S. public using his radio broadcast "fireside chats" to calm the public during the darkest days of the economic depression and calling the nation to action during the early days of World War II. In doing so, he became the nation's communicator in chief, starting each broadcast with the simple phrase, "My friends."

How Presidential Powers Create Impact

Article II of the Constitution framed the president's job description by "vesting all executive power in a President of the United States." Although there are multiple checks and balances on presidential power, the Framers left no doubt that presidents were in charge of the executive branch. Indeed, presidents often use this **vesting clause** to argue that they control everything that happens after a bill becomes law.[16]

vesting clause
A constitutional provision in Article II that gives the president authority to execute the laws.

Under the vesting clause and the broad powers granted under the Constitution, the president has four key jobs: (1) Commander in Chief, (2) diplomat in chief, (3) administrator in chief, and (4) legislator in chief. Although each of the roles is checked and balanced by the legislative and judicial branches, the president has the most visible job description in government, especially when threats such as natural disasters, economic crises, and international threats rise to the top of the agenda.

COMMANDER IN CHIEF The Constitution explicitly states that the president is to be Commander in Chief of the army and navy, but the Framers were not entirely sure who would declare war.[17] Some wanted the president to do both, others wanted the Senate to make the decision, and still others wanted the House to make the call because it is closest to the people who would be called to fight.

Having moved back and forth about the war power as they created a government of checks and balances, the Framers eventually decided to give it to Congress. Much as they wanted the president to move quickly to protect the nation, they worried about giving any chief executive the power to both declare and wage war.[18] After all, they had won independence after fighting a war against just such an executive, the king of England. Faced with the choice between speed and tyranny, the Framers divided the war power between the two branches, and checked it three times: Congress would declare war, but the president would wage it with the armies, ships, and supplies that Congress would provide.

However, even this triple check did not stop presidents from ordering U.S. troops into battle without congressional permission. Nor did it prevent presidents from authorizing undeclared military action over the decades. The United States waged an undeclared naval war with France in 1798, for example, sent troops to Argentina in 1833 to protect U.S. interests, made a display of force in 1853 during the "opening of Japan" to international commerce, sent Marines to Nicaragua in 1867 to punish the murder of the crew of an American commercial ship, protected American citizens when Panama fought for independence from Columbia in 1930, and went to war in Vietnam without a congressional declaration.[19]

Congress finally took action to strengthen control over presidential military powers after learning about the secret bombings of Cambodia during the undeclared Vietnam War.[20] Angered about other unauthorized U.S. military interventions over the years, Congress passed the **War Powers Resolution** on November 7, 1973, thereby establishing a new process that would allow presidents to take quick action while giving Congress a clear role in the decisions.

War Powers Resolution
A 1973 law that limits the presidential use of U.S. military power without (1) a prior declaration of war by Congress, (2) a congressional resolution approving the use of force, or (3) an emergency.

Under the resolution, a president can commit the armed forces only (1) after a declaration of war by Congress, (2) by specific statutory authorization, or (3) in a national emergency. Under the resolution, the president must inform Congress whenever force might be used. Once notified, Congress must authorize this use of force within 60 days. If Congress does not authorize the action, the president must withdraw the troops in 30 days. Despite their claims that the resolution violates their inherent powers, presidents have followed it more than 130 times since passage, and Congress has never forced an early withdrawal.[21]

However, the congressional war power remains in doubt. In 2002, for example, President Bush merely asked Congress to give him the authority to deploy U.S. forces as he determined "necessary and appropriate" to defend national security against the threat posed by Iraq. The House passed the resolution on October 10 on a 297-to-133 vote, and the Senate followed just after midnight with a 77–23 vote. Despite the votes, White House lawyers had already argued that the president had the authority with or without the votes.[22] Moreover, it is important to note that Congress had only authorized the use of force, but never declared war in what became one of the longest wars in American history.[23]

treaty
A formal agreement between the United States and other nations that requires a two-thirds vote of approval from the Senate.

DIPLOMAT IN CHIEF The Constitution also makes the president the nation's top diplomat through the treaty power. A **treaty** is a binding agreement between the

United States and one or more nations that sets a common agenda of mutual action. Presidents are free to negotiate all the treaties they wish, but treaties are not binding on the United States until the Senate provides its consent with a two-thirds vote.

Even if a treaty is decades in the making, the Senate is not required to take a vote on any treaty, and can kill a treaty by simply ignoring it. This power to ignore also limits the president's power to appoint the principal officers of government, and recommend legislation to Congress.

Presidents are also free to make **executive agreements** with other nations. Unlike treaties, executive agreements are negotiated without Senate participation. In 2003, for example, the Bush administration negotiated a 22-item executive agreement with Mexico to create a "smart border" that would limit the movement of illegal aliens into the United States, while improving the flow of goods between the two nations. Although some executive agreements are secret, most are made public.

executive agreement
A binding pact between the U.S. president and an international leader or leaders that does not require Senate approval.

Presidents turn this power into action through tough conversations with world leaders, which increasingly occur during foreign visits. Eisenhower took just six foreign trips during his two terms, compared to 20 by Clinton, 22 by George W. Bush, and 26 by Obama in his first term alone. Most of these trips involved informal conversations with other world leaders, but not treaties or any other agreements.

take care clause
A constitutional requirement that presidents take care that the laws are executed faithfully.

Trump followed tradition with carefully choreographed trips to the Middle East and Southeast Asia, and early visits to Europe. He broke with tradition, however, by using Twitter to warn North Korea's unpredictable dictator, Kim Jong-un to shelve his nuclear weapons program. Having told North Korea that its nuclear program would be met with "fire and fury" if it became a threat to U.S. territories, Trump escalated the conflict by calling him "little rocket man," "short and fat," "a madman," a "sick puppy," and warning that the United States had a much bigger nuclear button than North Korea. Jong-un replied with his own wave of insults, calling Trump an "old dotard," "fat," and "mentally deranged."[24]

Foreign policy experts worried that the exchanges increased the odds of an accidental nuclear exchange, but Trump pressed forward in public and private to force Jong-un to the bargaining table. He seemed to win an early sign of success when Jong-un expressed his readiness to meet face-to-face on the nuclear stalemate. The insults may have violated tradition, but appeared to produce a possible breakthrough on ending North Korea's nuclear program. The success was short-lived, however, when the United States learned that North Korea was still enriching nuclear fuel. Trump blamed China in part for the reversal, but stopped celebrating the summer's success.

Every president has a favorite way to recover from the stress of the job. Obama liked to play pick-up basketball with White House staffers and invited guests, George W. Bush liked to clear brush at his ranch, and Reagan liked to chop wood. Trump spends his free weekends at one of his golf resorts and often eats dinner at his Washington, D.C. hotel. Some nonpartisan watchdog groups have argued that the president's hotels and golf resorts have come to rely on income from private groups and guests who spend money at Trump properties to curry favor.

Despite these setbacks, the president continued to promote his friendship with a brutal dictator he had once called "Rocket Man." He also continued to attack China for undermining U.S. influence in the region and told Americans that his strong relationship with Kim Jong-un would eventually open North Korea to U.S. influence and trade opportunities. Trump also escalated his trade war against China as part of a broad effort to protect U.S. industries.

ADMINISTRATOR IN CHIEF The Framers put presidents in charge of the executive branch, whether by allowing them to appoint the principal officers of government or by putting the **take care clause** into the Constitution, giving the president the power and responsibility to "take care that the laws be faithfully executed." Presidents may not like all the laws they must execute, but they must either make every effort to implement each one, or defer action because the federal government does not have the resources to act.

Obama and Trump both drew upon interpretations of the take care clause in decisions about children who enter the United States illegally through no choice of their own. Acting in 2012 as administrator in chief, Obama suspended the deportation of these children by issuing his Deferred Action for Childhood Arrivals (DACA) order. Although the deferral was temporary, Obama made no secret of his intent to protect the "Dreamers" until Congress acted. Trump saw DACA as an unconstitutional exercise of presidential authority and rescinded the order in September 2017, thereby putting the Dreamers on notice that they must eventually return to their home countries.[25] Despite his criticism of Obama's executive actions, Trump came under fire in late 2018 for using the same authority to take action against a large caravan of asylum seekers who approached the U.S.–Mexico border just before the 2018 election. His executive order was challenged in the federal courts, too, and remained unresolved as Congress returned to Washington in January 2019.

inherent powers
Broad and unwritten powers of the national government essential for protecting the nation from domestic and foreign threats. An unwritten extension of the take care clause that presidents occasionally use to claim authority to take action without congressional or judicial authority.

Presidents sometimes interpret the take care clause to claim that they have unwritten **inherent powers** to protect the nation from harm.[26] Jefferson drew on this broad notion in finalizing the Louisiana Purchase before presenting it to Congress, while Lincoln extended the concept to create the Emancipation Proclamation, suspend citizen rights, impose a blockade of Confederate shipping, and expand the size of the army beyond authorized ceilings, all without prior congressional approval as required under the Constitution's law-making power.

The president's job as administrator in chief involves more than broad interpretations of constitutional text, however. It also involves the power to appoint the principal officers of government, issue executive orders, shape the national budget, and keep secrets.

Appointing the Principal Officers of Government Presidents do not have the time to make or implement every decision. Instead, they use the presidential appointment power to nominate high-level government officials such as department

Obama meets with a small group of Dreamers in 2013. Trump's decision to rescind the deferral put the Dreamers, as they came to be called, on notice that they would have to leave the country starting in March 2017. However, the federal judiciary suspended such action until the case could be resolved on constitutional grounds.

secretaries, judges, ambassadors, and other officers of the executive branch. Presidents choose their appointees based on two broad categories: (1) characteristics of the appointee—the appointee's ability to do the job, support for the president and party, past campaign support, and their ideology; and (2) characteristics of the political environment such as interest group support, party leaders, Congress, and the public. Although presidents nominate the principal officers of government, each one must be confirmed by a majority vote of the Senate before they can be sworn into office.[27]

As noted earlier, Congress has historically given the president the wide latitude in appointing the inferior officers of government—those who work in between the principal officers at the top of departments and agencies and the employees such as forest rangers, student loan officers, and census workers who deliver goods and services to the public. None of these 2,500 "inferior," but very important, jobs require Senate confirmation, and rarely do they provoke any controversy. Although this number is only a fraction of the federal government's 2 million employees, the group is very influential in controlling what government does. The principal officers tend to make the broad decisions, while the inferior officers convert them into action.[28]

The Senate does not always give its advice and consent quickly. In fact, the Senate appointments process has grown so wearisome that some nominees must wait more than a year to learn of their fate. In 2016, for example, Senate Republicans refused to vote for Judge Merrick Garland, whom Obama nominated for the U.S. Supreme Court. They argued that the appointment should be made by the next president, while President Obama argued that the delay was unprecedented in U.S. history. The Republicans won the debate when President Trump was inaugurated and withdrew the Garland nomination. President Trump withdrew the Garland appointment after his inauguration and made his own nomination.

If the wait becomes unbearable, presidents can make an appointment when the Senate adjourns for a break. These **recess appointments** give presidents the chance to fill important offices quickly. Even here, however, there are constitutional checks. Recess appointees can only serve until the end of the next session of Congress, and the Senate can frustrate the president by staying in session through holiday breaks and summer vacation; a recess appointment can only occur during a recess, after all.

recess appointments
A type of presidential appointment that allows the president to appoint principal officers of government when the Senate is recessed.

The key question recently facing the federal judiciary is when a recess actually occurs. Presidents have argued that recesses occur whenever the Senate is on a break of any kind, including the Christmas period, but the Senate has recently been holding sessions chaired by just one senator during these breaks to prevent just these kinds of presidential appointments. The Supreme Court dealt with this question in 2014 when it ruled that a "recess" should be understood as a substantial interruption in Senate action. Short pro forma sessions were not to be considered recesses; instead, 10 days was to be a reasonable lower limit for a break in Senate action to be deemed a recess.[29]

Taking Executive Action Presidents direct the federal government through **executive actions** that tell government how to faithfully interpret and execute the laws. The term covers a range of formal and informal presidential decisions that can change the government's direction. Some executive actions involve signed orders that carry the force of law in telling the government exactly what it should or should not do regarding a specific issue such as automobile mileage standards, other executive actions involve memorandums that generally address routine administrative issues such as how to make government jobs more attractive to young Americans, and still other administrative actions involve informal instructions that can expand or limit existing government programs by reinterpreting past interpretations and targets.

executive action
A presidential directive to a federal government agency or agencies that tells government how to faithfully interpret and execute the laws. The term covers a range of formal and informal presidential decisions that can change the government's direction; some executive actions involve signed orders that carry the force of law in telling the government exactly what it should or should not do regarding a specific issue.

executive order

A presidential directive to a federal government agency or agencies that implements or interprets a federal statute, a constitutional provision, or a treaty; executive orders carry the force of law but can be revoked by the next president.

The most powerful executive actions involve **executive orders**. Executive orders are signed by the president, published in the federal record, and subject to judicial review. Under past Supreme Court decisions, executive orders generally carry the force of a law unless they violate the Constitution or reverse an existing federal law. Executive orders also take effect immediately, and remain in place until they are reversed by a future executive order, overturned by the federal judiciary, or reversed by a new law.

Once issued and signed by the president, each executive order is numbered on a list dating back to Herbert Hoover. Although experts have culled presidential records to count the total number of orders dating back to George Washington, presidents have used many different terms to describe this powerful form of executive action.[30] Between Washington's first order that established Thursday, November 26, as Thanksgiving, presidents issued more than 14,000 executive orders in total, including 291 issued by George W. Bush, 276 by Obama, and 82 by Trump in the first 20 months of this term.

The more frequently presidents used executive orders, the more powerful and influential orders became. Although presidents still use executive orders for relatively minor issues such as declaring days of celebration, they also use them to set broad policy by telling the federal bureaucracy what to do. (See Figure 11.1 for the number of executive orders issued by recent presidents.)

Presidents often issue their first executive orders within days of taking office, and occasionally use the opportunity to make a statement about how they intend to govern. Jimmy Carter used his first executive order in 1977 to pardon every American who evaded military service during the Vietnam War, while George W. Bush used

FIGURE 11.1 AVERAGE NUMBER OF EXECUTIVE ORDERS ISSUED PER YEAR, FROM DWIGHT EISENHOWER TO BARACK OBAMA

Presidents often use executive orders and other forms of executive action either to implement important laws or to create new policies that Congress opposes. The number of orders has fallen over the past 50 years as presidents have chosen to move more quickly toward both kinds of action. Trump exceeded Obama's pace in his first year, but did so in part by reversing a long list of Obama orders—it generally takes an executive order or an act of Congress to reverse a past order.[31]

SOURCE: U.S. National Archives, Executive Orders Disposition Tables, available at http://www.archives.gov/federal-register/executive-orders/disposition.html.

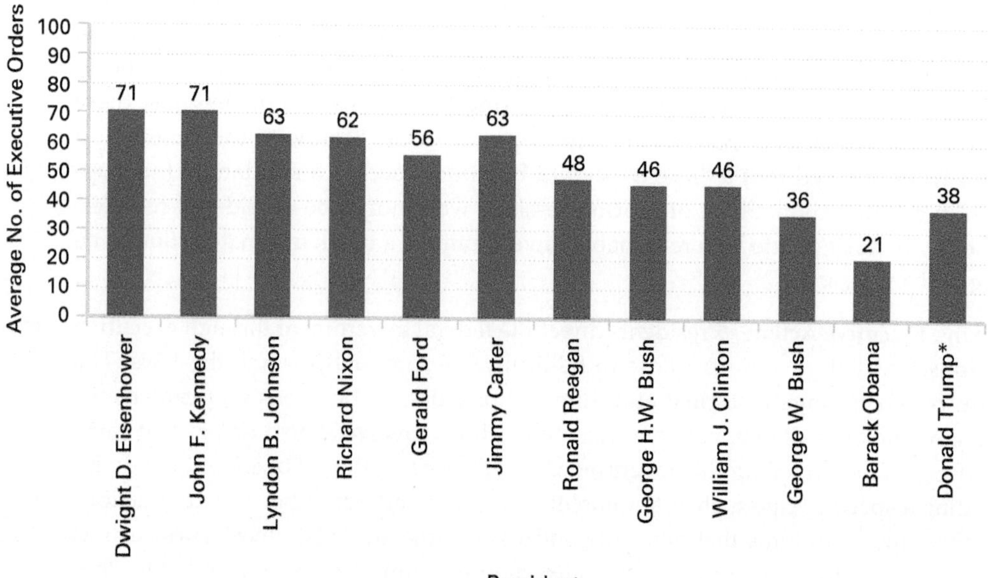

his first executive order in 2001 to help faith-based religious organizations compete for federal dollars, and Obama used his first to establish his control over presidential information, and his third to prohibit the use of "enhanced interrogation techniques" to extract information from individuals detained in armed conflicts.[32] Ironically, Bill Clinton used his first executive order in 1993 to bind all of his presidential appointees and White House staff to a strict ethics program, and he used one of his very last just before he left office in 2001 to revoke it.

Trump has been particularly active in using executive action to advance his agenda. Whereas Obama issued just 276 executive orders during his eight years in office combined, Trump issued 20 in his first two weeks alone, putting him on pace to issue more orders in his first year than any president since World War II. Trump's orders were designed to put his stamp on government by launching new policies such as suspending travel to the United States from areas of the world with a history of terrorism or revoking Obama administration policies such as prohibiting drilling the Artic. Trump quickly showed that while presidents can issue all the orders they wish with executive orders, these are not substitutes for formal laws. Presidents can issue orders with the stroke of a pen, but future presidents will be able to revoke his orders with the same pen.

Trump also discovered that executive orders are subject to judicial review by the federal judiciary. His January 27 travel ban was suspended by a federal district court only two days after Trump signed it, and was rejected two weeks later by a federal appeals court. The Trump administration issued a somewhat less restrictive ban in February, but it was suspended again at a different district court in March and at another federal appeals court in late May.

As noted above, executive orders are only one of several forms of presidential control as administrator in chief. Presidents also have the authority to issue **executive memorandums** that guide executive branch decisions. An executive memorandum is based on the Constitution's take care clause, and was once reserved for small-scale executive branch tinkering, such as moving employees from one agency to another. Like executive orders, executive memorandums have the force of law, but are not covered by government requirements for publication and reporting.

executive memorandum
A formal instruction that acts like an executive order, but that is much less visible to the public and potentially more significant in shaping broad policies.

Because they are just as powerful as executive orders, executive memorandums are increasingly popular for exerting presidential power. They are often called "executive actions" as a way to make them seem less important than they truly are. According to one painstaking count of every memorandum buried in presidential papers and other documents, the number of presidential memorandums has gone up over the past 50 years even as the number of executive orders has gone down.[33]

Obama was particularly aggressive in using executive memorandums to shape policy, sparking complaints that he governed as both a Congress and a president.[34] According to one inventory created by *USA Today*, Obama issued a slightly higher number of executive memorandums in his first six years than executive orders, and was more likely to use memorandums than legislation to set broad policy on guns, immigration, environment, the minimum wage, and clean energy.[35] Even former solicitor general and now Supreme Court Justice Elena Kagan has noted that this kind of "executive action" is a more important source of presidential power during periods of congressional stalemate than orders, in part because presidents face no limits on the range of these instruments.[36]

Presidents have one last tool for taking significant administrative action: they can simply instruct a department or agency to change priorities within a specific program. Obama did just that in November 2014 when he told the Department of Homeland Security to put its highest priority on finding and deporting the nation's most dangerous undocumented immigrants while deferring action on deporting undocumented

President Obama and former President George W. Bush join each other in prayer for the five police officers killed in Dallas in July 2016. "I'm here to insist that we are not as divided as we seem," he told the nation. "I know because I know America." Nevertheless, Obama recognized that the nation was in pain. "It's as if the deepest fault lines of our democracy have suddenly been exposed, perhaps even widened," Mr. Obama said. "And although we know that such divisions are not new, though they have surely been worse in even the recent past, that offers us little comfort . . . Dallas, I'm here to say we must reject such despair."

immigrants who posed no threat to the nation. He did not use an executive order or memorandum to give the instruction, however. He simply told the department to raise one priority and lower another. The department responded by creating a plan called "Deferred Action for Parents of Americans and Lawful Permanent Residents," or DAPA. Under the plan four million undocumented immigrants would be given work permits and allowed to remain in the U.S. indefinitely.

Texas and 25 other states responded almost immediately by asking the federal courts to declare DAPA an undue burden on their budgets and a violation of the government's process for creating new rules. The states never argued that Obama had exceeded his authority to administer the federal government, but did argue that he was violating the nation's immigration law by giving one group of undocumented immigrants favored status over another. The states also argued that DAPA would impose an unfair burden on their budgets, and asked the federal courts to halt the program.

The states eventually won their case in June 2016 on a tie vote in the Supreme Court. The tie meant that DAPA could not be implemented until the issue was resolved at some unknown point in the future.[37] The Trump administration removed any doubts about DAPA the day after the Supreme Court decision when Homeland Security Secretary John Kelly rescinded Obama's order as "just house cleaning."[38]

Obama also strengthened gun control laws through further executive actions. His efforts include stopping the purchase of armor-piercing bullets, and expanding and toughening background checks. Although Obama did not have the authority to stop gun owners from carrying concealed weapons onto your campus, he seemed to have authority to put more federal agents on the street to enforce bans on illegal gun sales and possible conspiracies to attack large numbers of citizens. The question on many campuses is whether these laws will make students safer, or whether guns on campus might prevent the kind of violence recently seen in Oregon.

Building the Federal Budget The Constitution gives Congress express power to appropriate money, but presidents are responsible for actually spending it on specific activities such as environmental protection, airport security, interstate highways, and homeland security.

Presidents are also responsible under federal law for developing a draft budget proposal for congressional review. This proposal tells Congress exactly how much the president wants to spend on every program in the federal government, and where the president wants to get the money.[39] Presidents rarely get every increase or cut they want, but the draft budget does set the debate in motion.

Congress is no longer dependent on the president for basic information about the budget, however. Under the 1974 Budget and Impoundment Control Act, Congress created its own process for reviewing the president's budget proposal, established the Congressional Budget Office (CBO) to reduce its reliance on the president for economic and spending forecasts, and required the president to submit detailed requests to Congress for any proposed cancellation of a congressional appropriation.

The new process did not stop members of Congress from adding money to the budget for their states and districts, however. Frustrated by rising budget deficits in 1996, Congress eventually voted to give the president greater budget power through the **line item veto**, which allowed presidents to strike out specific sections of an appropriations bill while signing the rest into law. In essence, the line item veto is a more efficient form of rescission. Although many governors have the line item veto, the Supreme Court decided the law disturbed the "finely wrought" procedure for making the laws and declared it unconstitutional in a 6-to-3 vote in 1998. If Congress wanted a new procedure for making the laws, Justice John Paul Stevens wrote for the majority, it would have to pursue a constitutional amendment.[40]

line item veto
A form of veto that allows the president to strike, or veto, specific provisions within a bill before signing it into law. The line item veto was declared unconstitutional in 1998.

Keeping Secrets The courts have long recognized that presidents have the broad authority called **executive privilege** to keep secrets, especially if doing so is essential to protect national security or confidential White House conversations about public policy.

executive privilege
A constitutionally supported right that allows presidents the right to keep executive communications confidential.

Some experts argue that there is no constitutional basis for executive privilege.[41] Yet presidents have withheld documents from Congress dating back to 1792, when President George Washington temporarily refused to share sensitive documents with a House committee that was investigating one of his military commanders.

Most scholars, the courts, and even members of Congress agree that a president has the implicit, if not constitutionally explicit, right to withhold information that could harm national security. However, presidents cannot assert executive privilege in either congressional or judicial proceedings when it means refusing to cooperate in investigations of their own personal wrongdoing.

Nixon brought this issue to the Supreme Court in 1974 by using executive privilege to protect himself during the Watergate scandal.[42] The scandal began with an attempted burglary of the Democratic National Committee's headquarters in the Watergate building, and eventually escalated to Nixon's possible impeachment for covering up his role in the crime. The case rested on Nixon's refusal to release secret White House tape recordings that proved his guilt.

In a unanimous decision, the Supreme Court acknowledged that presidents do have the power to claim executive privilege if the release of certain information would be damaging to national security. But the Court held that such claims are not exempt from review by the courts. More importantly for Nixon's future, the Court also held that national security was not threatened by the public release of the Watergate tapes. The Court ordered Nixon to yield his tapes, effectively dooming his presidency. Nixon resigned before he could be impeached and convicted.[43]

LEGISLATOR IN CHIEF The president is often described as the nation's "legislator in chief," but the Constitution provides relatively little power to force congressional action. Presidents are welcome to inform Congress "from time to time" about the state of the union, recommend measures they deem "necessary and expedient," and convene Congress on "extraordinary occasions."

Johnson became legislator in chief to deliver a powerful speech on voting rights before a joint session of Congress after a violent confrontation between African Americans and the police in Selma, Alabama. His powerful rhetoric, along with the civil rights advocacy work of Dr. King and others, moved Congress to pass the Voting Rights Act of 1965. "There is no constitutional issue here," Johnson told Congress on

March 15, 1965. "The command of the Constitution is plain. There is no moral issue. It is wrong—deadly wrong—to deny any of your fellow Americans the right to vote in this country. There is no issue of States rights or national rights. There is only the struggle for human rights. I have not the slightest doubt what will be your answer."[44]

Johnson was right. The Voting Rights Act of 1965 passed 333 to 85 in the House and 79 to 18 in the Senate.

Despite strong speeches, presidents cannot succeed as legislators in chief without the power to persuade (discussed later in this chapter). And they have few better ways to persuade Congress than by approving, rejecting, or even refusing to implement a law.

Approving Laws Presidents can turn a final bill into a public law in two ways. First, presidents can sign the bill with pen and ink, be it in a grand public ceremony or in private. Second, assuming Congress remains in session for 10 days (excluding Sundays), the president can simply ignore the bill and it will become law automatically.

Rejecting Laws Just as there are two ways to approve a bill, presidents can kill a bill in two ways. First, they can veto the bill by sending it back to Congress with a list of objections. Second, assuming that Congress adjourns before the 10 days expire (excluding Sundays again), presidents can simply ignore the bill and it will be automatically rejected through a pocket veto. Figuratively speaking, presidents simply put the bill in their pocket, and wait for Congress to leave town.

A veto does not necessarily kill a bill for good—once again, there is a check on the check. If Congress is still in session, it can reject the veto decision by a two-thirds vote in each chamber. If this override vote is successful, the bill becomes law without the president's signature. However, if Congress is not in session, it must pass the bill again, prepare for a near-certain presidential veto, and stay in session long enough to override it.

Vetoes are relatively rare, and overrides even rarer. Moreover, presidents are much more likely to approve a bill than reject one. Presidents approved almost 11,000 new laws between 1974 and 2016, while vetoing just 281, which is an approval-to-veto ratio of about 40 to 1.[45] And of the 270 they vetoed, Congress overrode just 30, which is a veto-to-override ratio of 9 to 1. (See Figure 11.2 for the historical trends.)

The veto is a powerful legislative tool, but only if the president is willing to use it. If recent history is a guide, the veto may be fading somewhat, perhaps because Congress is passing fewer bills, or because presidents are stopping more bills from getting to their desk by threatening a veto. Whereas Ronald Reagan vetoed 78 bills in his two terms from 1981 to 1988, George H. W. Bush vetoed 44, Bill Clinton vetoed 37, George W. Bush did not veto a single bill in his first term and only 11 in his second, and Barack Obama issued just 2 vetoes in his first term and 10 in his second. Trump did not veto a single bill during his first two years in office largely because his Republican congressional majority had enough votes to prevent passage of any legislation that might provoke presidential opposition. Trump did threaten to veto a $1.5 trillion, 2,232-page spending bill in March 2018, but the package had passed with enough votes to promise a tough fight to prevent an override. A Trump veto also would have forced the federal government to shut down for the third time in the year, which would have added to the sense that the White House had lost control of the legislative process despite unified party control.[46]

Presidents do not always issue vetoes because they think a bill is "ridiculous," as Trump described the 2018 spending package. They often issue their first veto merely to show Congress they are serious about being legislator in chief, and often veto bills to honor a promise they made during the campaign, support their party leadership, dare their opponents to waste time trying to build a two-thirds majority, or to simply take a stand against an idea just because they think it is wrong.

FIGURE 11.2 PRESIDENTIAL VETOES AND CONGRESSIONAL OVERRIDES, FROM KENNEDY TO OBAMA

The number of presidential vetoes dropped since World War II, in part because presidents are reluctant to veto legislation when both branches are controlled by their own party. The number of overrides is also low during "unified government" under one-party control. Finding enough votes to override a veto is difficult under any condition unless the two parties can find common cause in asserting their demand for action. Congress overrode Nixon's veto of the War Powers Resolution, for example, in a unified effort to assert the institution's power.

SOURCE: Gerhard Peters, "Presidential Vetoes," The American Presidency Project," John T. Woolley and Gerhard Peters, made available at http://www.presidency.ucsb.edu/data/vetoes.php. Figures are through June 8, 2016.

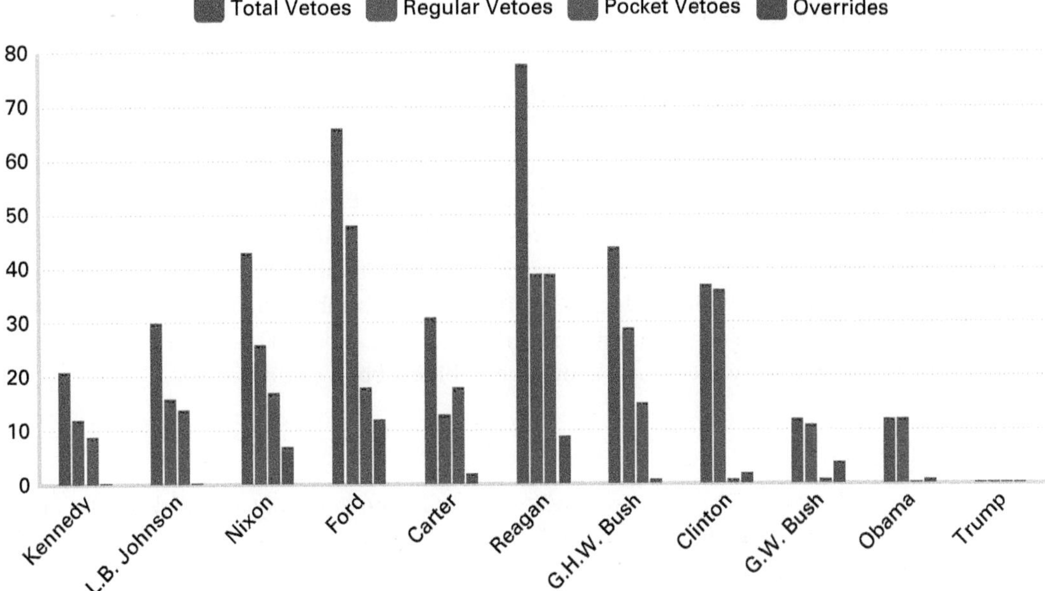

Whatever the number, presidents will still issue vetoes for political, electoral, ideological, and even personal reasons. They may want to, for example, show Congress they are serious about being legislator in chief, honor a promise they made during the campaign, support their party leadership, dare their opponents to spend mostly wasted time trying to build a two-thirds majority, or simply take a stand against an idea just because they think it is wrong. They may even look for a veto opportunity early in their term just to show Congress they know how to use their legislative muscle.

Refusing to Implement a Law The line item veto may be unconstitutional, but presidents have other ways to alter implementation. Presidents often do so by leaving senior posts vacant, slowing down the budget process, and requiring more information before the executive branch moves forward. Although presidents are required to take care to execute the laws faithfully, the Framers never defined the term *faithfully* to mean quickly, and, in fact, never defined the term at all.

Presidents can do more than slow down the process, however. They can promise not to implement specific provisions of a law even as they sign it, and increasingly do so by issuing **signing statements** when they approve a law.[47] Most of these signing statements apply to provisions buried in huge spending bills, but they clearly warn Congress that the president believes something about that provision is unconstitutional or would limit other jobs such as Commander in Chief.

signing statement
A statement issued by a president refusing to implement a provision of a law deemed unconstitutional or a violation of presidential powers.

On January 2, 2013, for example, Obama signed a massive defense appropriations bill that contained a provision reversing his order to allow gays in the military. "Our Constitution does not afford the president the opportunity to approve or reject statutory sections one by one," he explained. "I am empowered either to sign the bill, or reject it, as a whole. In this case, though I continue to oppose certain sections of the Act, the need to renew critical defense authorities and funding was too great to ignore." Calling section 533 of the 600-page bill "unnecessary and ill-advised," Obama told Congress that his order would stand.[48]

How the Presidency Works (Action)

11.3 Describe the organization and functions of the Executive Office of the President.

Presidents have the constitutional foundations and an energetic job description, but they need plenty of help to convert structure into the action required for impact. Their job is just too big to do alone.

Some of that help comes from the president's inner circle of close advisers, friends, and family, but most of it resides in a vast infrastructure of presidential appointees that extends beyond the West Wing of the White House to the far corners of the executive branch. In 2014, Obama had 10,000 appointees ready to give him help all across government, including 400 principal officers subject to Senate confirmation, 2,500 inferior officers chosen without further review, and 7,000 who served on scientific panels, advisory boards, task forces, and blue-ribbon commissions.

Organizing the Staff

The president's staff has grown steadily since George Washington relied on one personal assistant as the first president.[49] Today's presidents rely on 450 to 500 personal aides in the West Wing of the White House and ornate Old Executive Office Building just next door. The president also oversees 2,000–6,000 aides who work in the large number of buildings just beyond the White House gates. The president does not know all of these assistants by name obviously, but their work is essential as more senior White House aides shape the briefing papers that the president takes upstairs to the executive residence every night.

Every president uses a slightly different approach to organizing the flow of advice and counsel across this large team. Although presidents always put their most important aides just down the hall from the Oval Office, they generally follow one of three approaches for managing the staff as a whole.[50]

COMPETITIVE Among the 13 modern presidents elected after 1932, Roosevelt, Truman, and Johnson primarily used the competitive approach for managing the White House staff, which encourages the president's closest advisers to argue their positions vigorously, and Johnson sometimes gave different advisers the same assignment, hoping that the competition would produce a better final decision.

Trump's competitive management style became more chaotic in 2018 as he continued to hire and fire White House staff at a record-setting pace. "I think everybody would agree this is turmoil, it's confusion, it's not good for anything," one senior Republican said of the firings. "We always believe that there should be an orderly process, and of course government is not clean or orderly—ever. But this seems to be beyond normal." Others argued that Trump was simply moving from a competitive approach to a greater focus on getting results. "He wants to make things that he's been discussing for a while happen," press secretary Sarah Huckabee Sanders said. "He's tired of the wait game."[51]

COLLEGIAL Kennedy, Carter, Clinton, both Bushes, and Obama used the collegial approach, encouraging aides to work together toward a common position. It is a friendlier way to work but may have the serious drawback of producing what some experts call "groupthink," which is the tendency of small groups to stifle dissent in the search for common ground.[52]

Obama has generally adopted the collegial approach, but also used a bit of hierarchy by creating a long list of "policy czars" within the White House. These czars help coordinate executive branch decisions on health care, drug policy, unemployment, energy, and education, but also appear to supervise some department and agency heads. Republicans criticized the czars as an unconstitutional expansion of the president's power to appoint the principal officers of government, while Obama's own department secretaries complained that the czars shut them out of key decisions. The czars were still in business as Obama approached the end of his presidency.[53]

HIERARCHICAL Finally, Eisenhower, Nixon, Ford, and Reagan all used the hierarchical, or centralized, approach, in which the president establishes strict lines of authority and "choke points" for controlling the flow of information and meetings. Presidents who use this approach usually rely on a "gatekeeper," or trusted adviser such as the chief of staff, to keep the staff under control. The advantage is less chaos, but there is more risk that the president will miss a key issue or make a mistake that could have been prevented through more thorough debate. Some experts argue that George W. Bush used the hierarchical model to make the Iraq War decision by pulling together a very small team of equally committed advisers.[54]

Presidential Personality

Presidential personality plays a central role in the choice of a supervisory style, and also shapes each president's approach to presidential power. Some presidents put energy into the job (active) and love politics (positive), while others are exhausted by the job (passive) and almost wish they had never been elected (negative).

When these two categories are combined, they produce four types of presidents: (1) active-positives who love their work and are very engaged in taking action on their agendas; (2) active-negatives who work hard, but try to avoid conflict and an aggressive agenda, and bring great anger to their jobs; (3) passive-positives who avoid hard work and most forms of political engagement, but enjoy the ceremonial duties of being president and seek approval and affection; and (4) passive-negatives who also avoid hard work, but also dislike their jobs and avoid the give-and-take of compromise and action.

This theory of presidential character can be used to describe recent presidents as follows: Roosevelt, Truman, Kennedy, Carter, and Clinton were active-positives; Johnson, Nixon, George W. Bush, and Barack Obama were active-negatives; Ford, Reagan, and George H. W. Bush were passive-positives; and Eisenhower was the only recent president in the passive-negative category. Obama appears to fit best as an active-negative chief executive. He worked very hard but avoided the give-and-take of politics, and rarely befriended members of Congress and other allies to win support. He was a talented political leader but was also distant from the process.

Presidential personality does not necessarily determine a president's actions in every case, however. Some observers argue that George W. Bush entered office as a passive-positive president but became an active-positive president for several years after the 9/11 terrorist attacks as he fought the war on terrorism. Bush began to enjoy the job of being president and certainly understood the need to rally the public around the Iraq War. However, he retreated to his passive-positive president instincts in his second term as the Iraq War stalled, Congress returned to Democratic control, and his legislative agenda was sidetracked by the economic crisis.

The Executive Office of the President

Executive Office of the President (EOP)

Created in 1939, the EOP contains the president's most important staff support, including the Office of the White House, National Security Staff, and Office of Management and Budget.

The **Executive Office of the President (EOP)** was created in 1939 to help presidents oversee the sprawling federal government created during Franklin Roosevelt's furious first 100 days in office. "The president needs help," Roosevelt's own Committee on Administrative Management reported. "His immediate staff is entirely inadequate."[55]

The EOP consists of a long list of offices, but the most important are the Office of the Vice President, the White House Office, the Office of Management and Budget, the Council of Economic Advisers, the National Security Council, the Office of the United States Trade Representative, and the Office of the First Lady.

No one is quite sure how many people work in the EOP, although many staffers are on the White House budget; the EOP staff also includes between 2,000 and 6,000 staffers who are *detailed*, or loaned, to the White House by departments and agencies of government. Because they are still paid by their departments and agencies, these staff members do not show up on the traditional counts of EOP employees.[56]

THE OFFICE OF THE VICE PRESIDENT This office supports the vice president's work with the president, and depends entirely on the vice president's relationship with the president. Although vice presidents are next in line to be president, they are often ridiculed as essentially unimportant to the nation. "It is a doomed office," historian Arthur Schlesinger, Jr., wrote in 1974. "The Vice President has only one serious thing to do: that is, to wait around for the President to die."[57]

Schlesinger was right that vice presidents have no power to act without presidential permission, but presidents have been asking them to do more since Walter Mondale became Carter's vice president in 1976.[58] As a former governor and Washington outsider, Carter needed a Washington insider to help him lead the nation, and gave Mondale the power and prestige to become an active partner in the presidency. He also made sure Mondale had his own staff, gave him an executive office just down the hall from the Oval Office, and met with him frequently on pressing policy issues.

Carter also understood that vice presidents must know the job, if only because there is nearly a one-in-three chance they will become president themselves. After all, 14 of the 44 U.S. presidents were vice presidents before they became president—nine moved into the post after their president died or resigned in office, another four were

Here, Michele Obama helps plant the White House garden as part of her "Let's Move" campaign to encourage Americans to eat healthy food and get more exercise. The EOP contains the Office of the First Lady, which provided support for the First Lady's travel, press activities, and policy work. First Ladies have always been active in selected social causes, but have been increasingly engaged in addressing difficult national problems such as health care access and education reform. The office currently provides support to Melania Trump in her campaign against cyberbullying.

elected immediately after their president left office at the end of a term, and one was elected eight years after leaving office.

Vice President Dick Cheney is generally considered the most influential vice president in history, in part because he was a Washington insider matched with a former governor and Washington outsider. He is said to have been responsible for helping to convince Bush to go to war in Iraq after 9/11, he took on significant responsibilities in directing the president's reelection campaign, and he supported the use of "enhanced interrogation techniques," which many human rights groups call "torture," to extract information from terrorist suspects. Most of Cheney's work was kept secret, but his role has been confirmed by other staffers and secret documents leaked to the press.

Vice President Joe Biden was given a very different role in the Obama administration. He was a strong voice in the president's Afghanistan decision, and he was in charge of the effort to stimulate the economy. He also met regularly with the president and was often consulted by the White House before the president made his decisions. He was also deeply involved in negotiating with the Senate on the 2013 budget compromise.

Unlike Cheney and Biden, Vice President Mike Pence did not take on a portfolio of policy issues after he entered office. As he did during the campaign, he acts as an ambassador to the evangelical religious community.[59] Like his predecessors, however, Pence has a substantial staff.

THE WHITE HOUSE OFFICE The White House Office reports solely and independently to the president, oversees the rest of the EOP, and contains the president's most trusted aides and political advisers, none of whom are subject to Senate confirmation. The president's **White House chief of staff** heads the office, and is the president's most important adviser. The chief of staff has the most meetings with the president, the most information to compress, and the most White House staff to supervise, and often puts in the longest days. The chief works just down the hall from the president, and must be ready to assist in the Oval Office at any moment. It is no surprise that chiefs of staff burn out quickly.[60]

White House chief of staff
The president's most trusted staff aide in the White House.

Once past the very top tier of close aides, the president gets help from two kinds of White House offices: political and policy.

1. *Political offices.* Political organizations help the president run for reelection, control the national party, write the president's speeches and talking points, schedule the president's travel, conduct the political polling, and keep a tight watch on political trends. A deputy chief of staff usually oversees these responsibilities, and is generally viewed as the president's most important political adviser.
2. *Policy offices.* Policy offices help the president manage economic, domestic, foreign, and defense policy. They are also responsible for developing policy proposals, monitoring events that might affect the president's legislative agenda, building public support for specific proposals, and coordinating executive branch implementation of new programs such as education reform. The list of policy offices includes the National Economic Council, which coordinates the president's economic agenda; the National Security Council, which helps set foreign policy; and the Office of Faith Based and Community Initiatives, which encourages the use of religious institutions to help address community problems.[61]

Presidents occasionally appoint their own children and in-laws to the White House staff. Trump appointed his daughter Ivanka and her husband, Jared Kushner to senior advisory posts and gave each one substantial policy roles in office. Both came under fire early in the administration for potential conflicts of interest involving the sale of

Ms. Trump's luxury fashion line and Kushner's connection with the real estate industry. Kushner was unable to secure a top-secret security clearance in the White House during his first 18 months in the White House, but was eventually approved after further investigation of his past connections to foreign real estate interests.

Office of Management and Budget (OMB)
The presidential staff agency that serves as a clearinghouse for budgetary requests and management improvements for government agencies. The OMB drafts the president's annual budget message to Congress and oversees the basic operations of the executive branch.

THE OFFICE OF MANAGEMENT AND BUDGET This very large office is technically listed as part of the White House office, but generally operates as if it is a part of the Executive Office of the President. The **Office of Management and Budget (OMB)** has more employees than all of the other White House offices combined, handles a much larger agenda, and wields enormous power over the executive branch as the government agency that shapes the president's annual budget proposal. Its director advises the president in detail about the hundreds of government agencies—how much money they should be allotted in the budget and what kind of job they are doing.[62]

The OMB has more responsibilities than any other organization in the EOP. It pulls together the first draft of the president's budget proposal, resolves appeals from the various departments and agencies for more money, writes the president's budget message to Congress, monitors all expenditures, tracks government compliance with its rules, reviews all new rules and regulations to make sure they provide more benefit than cost, sets the policy for government purchasing, promotes careful measurement of government performance, and writes a year-end summary of how the government actually spent its money.

cabinet
An informal advisory group composed of cabinet heads and a handful of agency administrators who meet with the president on occasion.

THE CABINET The president's **cabinet** is neither a unit within the EOP nor a separate organization. Rather, it is a loosely designated body composed of the heads of the departments of government and selected major agencies such as the Environmental Protection Agency. However, the cabinet rarely meets, is rarely consulted before major decisions, and is more a source of photo opportunities than serious action. Although the cabinet is not specifically mentioned in the Constitution, every president since 1789 has had one. Washington's consisted of his Secretaries of State, treasury, and war, plus his attorney general. Because the cabinet is now so large, presidents often reserve cabinet meetings for general announcements, not specific debates.

The president's cabinet secretaries have become more diverse since Franklin Roosevelt appointed the first woman in 1933 (Francis Perkins at the Department of Labor), Lyndon Johnson appointed the first African American in 1966 (Robert Weaver at the Department of Housing and Urban Development), Ronald Reagan appointed the first Hispanic in 1988 (Lauro Cavazos at the Department of Education), and Bill Clinton appointed the first Asian American in 2000 (Norman Mineta at the Department of Commerce). Despite these breakthroughs, every Defense and Treasury secretary in history has been a male, and only one of the males has been a minority group member.

Diversity in the presidential cabinet has been increasing over the last 30 years as presidents have searched for talented appointees from every community. Here, members of Trump's cabinet rise to applaud the president during his first State of the Union Address on January 30, 2018. Trump's cabinet was one of the least diverse in recent history.

This increasing diversity brings great assets to the White House. It lends greater creativity and diverse life histories to the discussion of key issues such as economic growth, climate change, and health care reform. It also sends the message that a government of the people involves more than white males. Trump's first cabinet was less diverse than any cabinet since Ronald Reagan in 1981, but did include the first Indian-American appointed to a cabinet-rank position, Nikki Haley. She came to Washington as a two-term governor of South Carolina and quickly established herself as a forceful advocate as U.S. Ambassador to the United Nations. Trump's lower-level political appointees were also less diverse than any subcabinet in recent history.[63]

Presidents and the Public (Action)

11.4 Examine the relationship between the president and the public.

Presidents have always had a special relationship with the public, in part because there is only one president at a time. By creating a single executive instead of a council, the Framers guaranteed that presidents would become the center of attention. And by allowing reelection, they guaranteed that presidents would want to stay at the center.

If the Framers thought presidents would fade into the background of Congress, they were soon disappointed. Washington's first inauguration was a national event celebrated with bells, cannon salutes, and toasts; Jefferson's first inauguration was the model of simplicity, but his second produced an inaugural parade and open house; and Jackson's first inauguration took place on the Capitol's new East Portico that has been used for inaugurations ever since.

The president's relationship with the public has become more complex as the world has embraced the Internet and its vast array of information. However, the president's relationship still depends on two sources: (1) public approval, and (2) presidential action. Each of these sources gives presidents the power to persuade.

Public Approval

Presidential inaugurations are particularly exciting for the president's party but are even better when the president takes the oath after a landslide election, and with high public approval and a party lock on Congress. Presidents often combine these factors with their general sense of conquest to claim a **mandate** to govern. Andrew Jackson was the first president to use that term to argue that the public had expressed its demand for action, while Obama used just two words in 2009 to tell the Republicans that he had a mandate to act: "I won."[64]

mandate
A postelection claim that the public has given its support to the president's agenda for action, but a claim that is credible only if the president has enough election votes to prove it, and the public approval and party seats in Congress to enforce it.

Trump claimed a mandate of his own in November 2016 based on his surprise victory in the wake of opinion polls that predicted he would almost certainly lose his outsider campaign.

Four years later, this mandate was gone as Obama's congressional majority and public approval evaporated as the economic crisis dragged on. As a result, Obama began his second term with a modest mandate at best. In the 2008 election, he won the electoral vote by 18 percentage points, and entered office with two new Democrats in the Senate and eight in the House. But, in his reelection race, he won the popular vote by four percentage points, barely increased his public approval, and still faced an angry Republican House, albeit one with eight fewer seats. Given this weak election endorsement, Obama decided to invest his mandate in immigration reform, action on global warming, and securing the future of his national health program, which is often referred to as Obamacare.

Once past the inauguration, presidents rely on public approval as a resource for legislative action. Higher levels of approval also give members of Congress a reason to pay attention to the president's policy priorities as they start to think about the next election. As Figure 11.3 on the next page shows, presidents often start their first and second terms with a **honeymoon** created by high levels of approval. However, the honeymoon starts to end by early summer at the latest, and public approval begins to fall.

honeymoon
The first six months or so of a new presidential administration when the president enjoys generally positive relations with the press and Congress, his or her supporters are still celebrating victory, and the public focuses on the inaugural festivities and presidential agenda.

Some experts call the quick erosion of early presidential support the "honeymoon-hangover" effect. Presidents can soothe the hangover of disappointment with charismatic leadership, but the public will always ask "what have you done for me lately?" As the term wears on, the answer is often "not much."[65] Although members of the president's party remain loyal throughout the term, Independents and members of the opposing party peel away, the president's political strength dissipates, and economic performance may decline.

FIGURE 11.3 PRESIDENTIAL PUBLIC APPROVAL RATINGS, 1961 TO 2018

Presidential approval is a key resource for success, but tends to erode over time. This "cycle of decreasing influence" undermines the president's ability to win support for legislative initiatives, negotiate with other nations, and influence congressional and gubernatorial elections. Ironically, the longer presidents serve, the more they learn about the job. This "cycle of increasing effectiveness" gives them better judgment in their decisions. Together, these two cycles mean that presidents are the most popular when they have the least experience, and most experienced when they have less public support.

SOURCE: Data from the Gallup Presidential Approval Center as recorded at https://www.polling report.com.

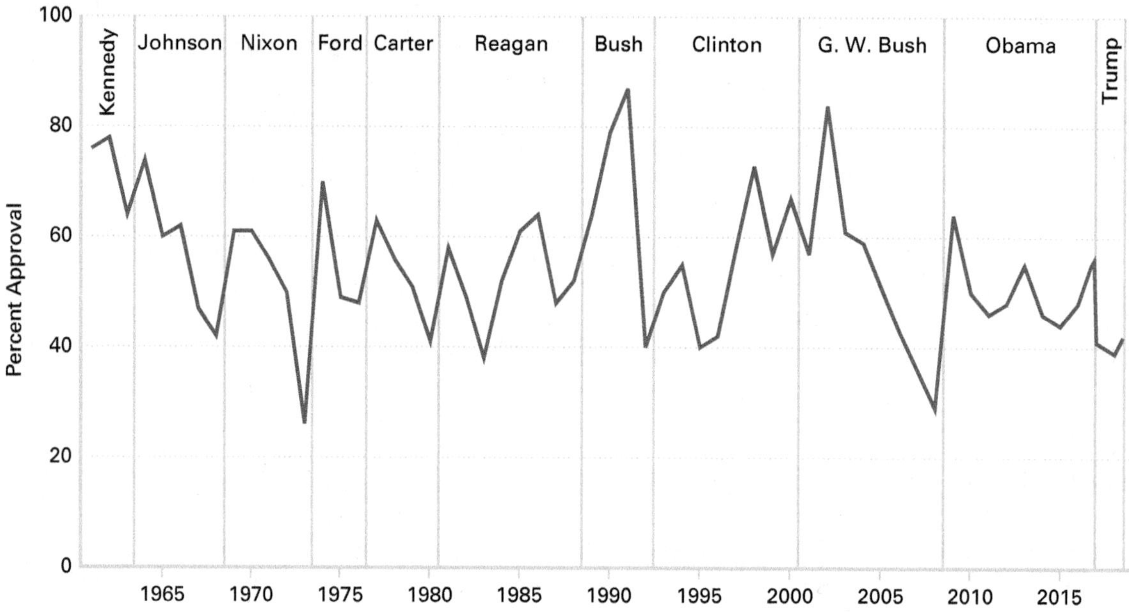

The reasons for the decline can seem random. One president might alienate a large constituency group with a single statement or tough decision; another might make a major mistake in handling a natural disaster or an international crisis; and yet another may face allegations of scandal and corruption.

Presidential Action

Moreover, the media almost always starts thinking about the next election well before the end of the term, opponents may start running negative advertisements against the president's legislative priorities, and the public often gets bored with the same, increasingly older president at the podium. Nevertheless, presidents do have at least some tools for slowing the decline by rallying the public, reaching out to the public, and maintaining contact with the nation.

rally point
A significant jump in presidential approval that occurs during a national crisis; the term refers to the tendency of Americans to "rally 'round the flag" and the chief executive when the nation is in trouble.

RALLYING SUPPORT Although presidential approval generally moves up or down in small increments, the gains are often related to the president's handling of unexpected events such as 9/11 and national tragedies that bring Americans together for a short time. These **rally points** do not last long, but do give presidents a chance to move quickly to create impact. Donald J. Trump's approval was 42 percent on July 1, 2018.

As Figure 11.4 on the next page shows, George W. Bush's ratings jumped almost 30 percentage points after 9/11, but fell back almost immediately. In contrast, Obama did not have any rally points during his first term, in part because his major crisis was the persistent effect of the 2008 financial collapse on the economy. Moreover, his approval ratings barely changed after the mastermind of the 9/11 attacks was tracked down and killed in 2011. Although Osama bin Laden had been hunted for years, the public was far more concerned with the economy and high unemployment, while the news story about bin Laden's death was short-lived. Figure 11.4 also shows the relationship between the Clinton and Obama rally points.

FIGURE 11.4 PRESIDENTIAL RALLY POINTS, FROM CLINTON TO OBAMA

Presidential approval can rise dramatically during sudden crises such as an international attack or a domestic catastrophe. These rally points reflect the public's desire to support the president's role as a morale builder and Commander in Chief.

SOURCE: Data from the Gallup Presidential Approval Center.

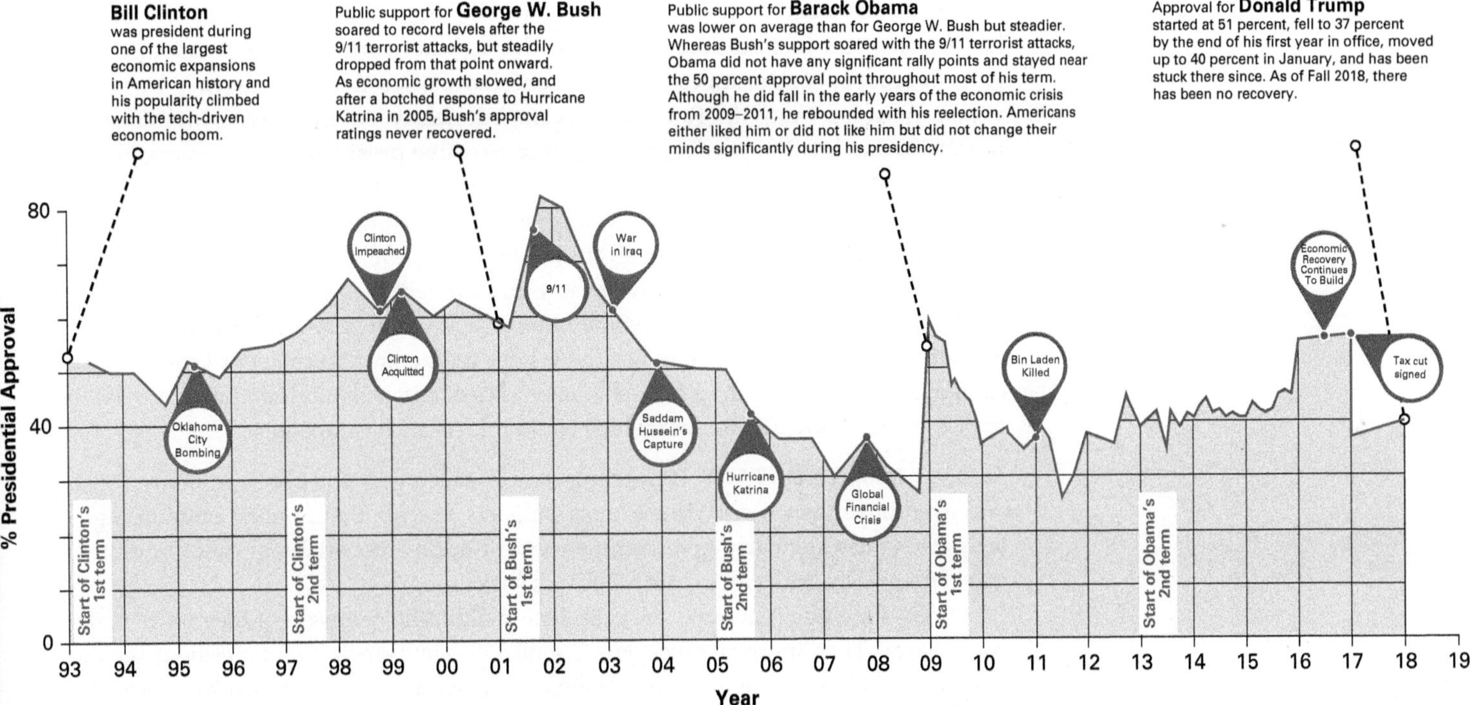

GOING PUBLIC Due to the structural limitations on their power, presidents may have difficulty getting Congress to enact their policy proposals, particularly when the opposition party controls one or both houses. In those cases, presidents might opt to take their case directly to the public, particularly during periods when they enjoy relatively higher public approval ratings (see Figures 11.3 and 11.4). This is referred to as **going public.**[66]

going public
A presidential strategy for increasing public approval by reaching out to congressional constituents by going over the heads of the Washington media and interest groups.

Going public is simple: instead of trying to pressure Congress through the Washington media or interest groups, presidents go public to put pressure on members by reaching out to their home districts without any interference from the Washington media and interest groups. This is sometimes called "going over the heads of Washington." The more popular the president is in the home district or state, or so the theory goes, the more likely members of Congress will support the president's demand for action even if the Washington media and interest groups do not. After all, members of Congress care most about the next election. Not only does going public make sense politically, it actually works. According to study after study, presidents who go public are more likely to succeed on key legislative votes than presidents who focus on Washington alone.[67]

Trump changed the rules for going public even before he took the Oath of Office. He was the first president to use Twitter to shape the news, defend his decisions, and announce the firing of senior aides and even his Secretary of State, Rex Tillerson. He also earned a reputation for fire and fury in his tweets, and left few subjects untouched among the 3,000 tweets he sent during his first 14 months in office. (Trump's tweets are recorded in a searchable Web site at http://www.trumptwitterarchive.com/.) As of April 1, he had sent 249 tweets that contained the word "fake," 234 with "lose," 222 with "dumb" or "dummy," 2014 with "terrible," 183 with "stupid," 115 with "dishonest," and 101 with "lightweight." Many commentators complained that the tweets degraded civic life and promoted "tribalism" between Democrats and Republicans, and red states and blue states. But the number of followers suggest that Trump was mining deep fissures in the public discourse, while changing expectations for future presidents. "He has this direct pipeline to the American people, where he can talk back and forth," his first press secretary said in 2017. Twitter allows him to "put his thoughts out and hear what they're thinking in a way that no one's ever been able to do before."[68]

Press conferences are one way to go public, but have lost effect as the public has lost interest in traditional coverage through network television and newspapers. Moreover, the number of press conferences has declined sharply over the years. Whereas Franklin Roosevelt averaged nearly seven press conferences a month during his dozen years in office, the past five presidents have averaged less than two per month.

Going public clearly fits with changes in the electoral process. Presidents now have the staff, the technology, and the public opinion research to tell them how to target their message, and they have nearly instant media access to easily speak to the public. And, as elections have become more image oriented and candidate centered, presidents have the incentive to use these tools to operate a permanent White House campaign. Figure 11.5 shows how characteristics of a presidential candidate are likely to be viewed by the public, data which could inform such campaigns.

MAINTAINING CONTACT Presidents stay in touch with the public in many ways, and even have their own White House pollsters feeding them public opinion regularly. They also regularly give commencement addresses, celebrate new programs, travel frequently, and stay in touch through social media.

Most of the public contacts the president in old-fashioned ways, if they try to make contact at all. They are always welcome to send letters and emails to the president, but the volume of such contact is so high that almost no one receives a personal response. The White House receives 65,000 letters, 100,000 emails, 1,000 faxes, and between 2,500 and 3,500 phone calls per day, but only a handful of these messages end up on the president's

FIGURE 11.5 WHAT AMERICANS WANT IN THEIR PRESIDENT, 2016

The public views favorably presidential candidates who have served in the military, were governors, or who had been business executives. A majority are less likely to support a candidate who is an Atheist or never held office. Nowadays, large majorities report that it would not matter to them if the president is a woman, in his or her 40s or 70s, Catholic, had attended a prestigious university, or used marijuana. According to these opinions, Trump would have benefited from his experience as a business executive, but damaged by his inexperience and extramarital affairs.[69]

SOURCE: Pew Research Center, "For Hopefuls, Washington Experience Could Do More Harm than Good," May 16, 2014, at http://www.people-press.org/2014/05/19/for-2016-hopefuls-washington-experience-could-do-more-harm-than-good/5-16-2014-12-22-25-pm.

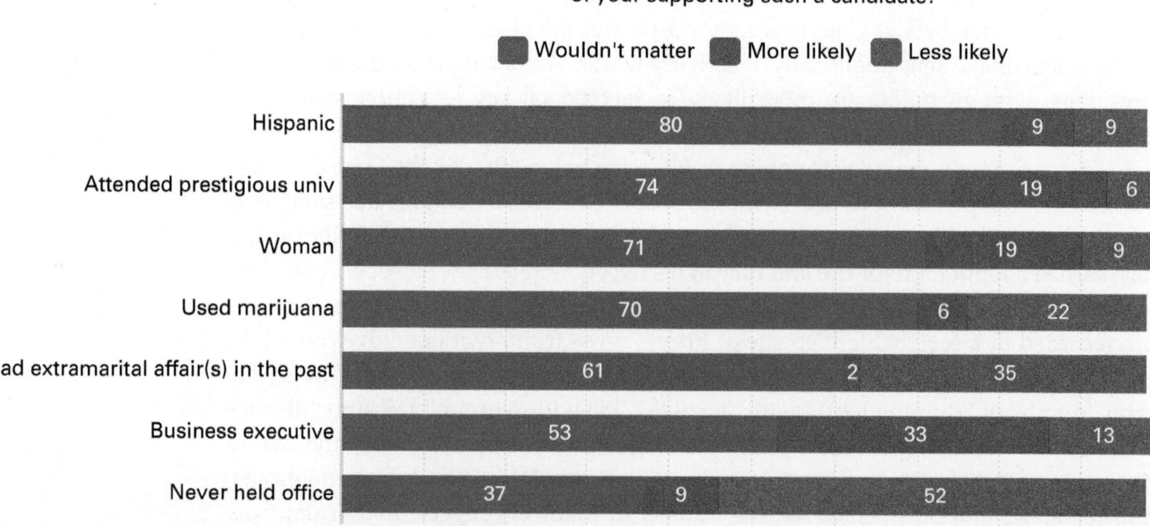

desk. Yet, Americans still pay great attention to what the president says and does, and let the president know what they think either directly or through social media. By March 2018, for example, Trump had 25 million Facebook friends and 50 million Twitter followers.

Presidents respond to public contact in different ways. At the start of his administration, for example, Obama asked the White House mailroom to give him 10 letters from ordinary Americans every day. Obama has been particularly interested in receiving real stories about the nation's current condition. "These letters, I think, do more to keep me in touch with what's happening around the country than anything else," Obama said in a White House video about the sorting process. "Some of them are funny, some of them are angry, a lot of them are sad or frustrated about their current situation.[70]

Trump does not have a formal process for writing letters, but does reach out through short notes, letters, and occasional messages delivered by his press secretary. Like all presidents before him, Trump also meets with constituents, members of Congress, and small groups of citizens one on one. In March 2018, for example, Trump met with a small group of Parkland High School students to talk about gun control. He listened carefully and empathically to the student stories and even carried notes to himself on the need to tell the group that he heard their concerns. He also told students he would support tough gun control legislation, and even scoffed at members of Congress who were scared of the National Rifle Association. "Some of you people are petrified of the NRA," he told members of Congress days later. "You can't be petrified. They have great power over you people, they have less power over me." A week later still, Trump abandoned the reforms, telling his Twitter followers there was "not much support (to put it mildly)."[71]

Presidents and Congress (Impact)

11.5 Describe the relationship between the president and the Congress.

Legislation is the central source of presidential impact. Although presidents have other significant sources of impact such as executive orders, memorandums, agreements, and their powers to shape the national agenda, laws put their ideas into action, and outlast their time in office.

Congress and presidents have been arguing since 1789. Although they often work closely to address crises like the 2008 financial collapse, they are also quite capable of a stalemate on tough issues such as the 2013 government shutdown. Given the separation of powers, it may seem remarkable that Congress and the president ever agree at all, which is exactly what the Framers intended. The Framers did not want the legislative process to work like an assembly line. Rather, they wanted ambition to counteract ambition as a way to prevent tyranny.

To the extent that they designed the legislative process to work inefficiently, the Framers clearly succeeded. Presidents work hard to enact their top priorities, but often complain that Congress is not listening. However, Congress listens more closely to its constituents, especially when the president's public approval is low. This is why so many of the Obama administration's priorities never reached the floor of the House or Senate.

Why Congress and Presidents Disagree

Congress and the president disagree for many reasons, in part because members of Congress focus on long careers, and presidents focus on their two-term limit. They also disagree because of competing constituencies, election calendars, and campaign strategies.

COMPETING CONSTITUENCIES The Framers laid the framework of disagreement by giving the two branches of government radically different collections of voters. The House and Senate represent districts and states respectively, while the president represents the nation as a whole. Although these constituencies often overlap in states that are solidly Democratic (blue) or Republican (red), members of Congress spend more time worrying about how voters feel about issues back home than the president's agenda. Indeed, some actively distance themselves from the president's priorities by refusing to identify themselves by party.

COMPETING CALENDARS The Framers also ensured that Congress and the president would be on a different election timetable, sometimes running together and other times running separately. Recall that presidents can serve a maximum of eight years before leaving office, whereas senators and members of the House can serve for decades. Presidents enter office wanting everything passed at once, whereas members of Congress have plenty of time to wait.

COMPETING CAMPAIGNS Finally, the Framers almost guaranteed that Congress and the president would run different kinds of election campaigns. Most members of Congress finance their election campaigns with only minimal assistance from their national political party. They usually run independently of the president or national party platform. Even members of the president's own party have been known to ask the president not to visit their districts or states in particularly tight elections or when the president's public approval is falling. Whenever possible, members try to make elections about local, not national, issues, which means the president is often ignored during the campaign.

How Presidents Create Congressional Impact

As noted earlier in this chapter, presidents have substantial authority to shape the congressional agenda. However, these powers are not enough to guarantee action, let alone even passing attention. Presidents are free to ask for anything they want, but Congress can and does say "no," especially when one party controls Congress and the other controls the presidency. Although the two branches can produce major laws during divided government, they just as frequently fail to act.[72] Thus, the key question for presidents is not whether they can ask Congress to act, but how they can convince Congress to answer "yes."

According to Richard Neustadt's famous book, *Presidential Power,* a president's constitutional powers as a whole add up to little more than a menial job, or a "clerkship," in his terms.[73] The real power resides in the president's ability to twist arms, bargain for passage, offer favors, and focus congressional and public attention on the need to act. Doing so involves many of the same tactics used in building public approval, including carefully timed speeches designed to frame the debate about a bill at the agenda-setting stage, push bills to the floor, and build support during the final votes.[74] Timing is everything in securing passage, as is the veto threat.

Presidents wrap these messages in four types of rhetoric: (1) mandate rhetoric that tells Congress the president has the public's support, (2) bipartisan appeals based on the need to act for the good of the nation, (3) signaling rhetoric that focuses congressional attention on the president's most important priorities, and (4) agency input through testimony and legislative drafts.[75]

political capital
The political influence a president can use to push forward on the legislative agenda; it is generally composed of public approval and party seats in Congress, and is expended over time.

However, presidents cannot use the power to persuade without enough **political capital** to reward friends and punish adversaries. Some experts argue that this capital relies in part on personal gestures such as "state dinners" with world leaders and celebrities, flights on Air Force One, private meetings in the president's study, a game or two at the White House bowling alley, and even the little boxes of M&Ms that congressional staffers take home after a lunch served by uniformed soldiers in the White House "mess." Although these are little more than trinkets that cannot change bitter opposition into support, presidents know that arms twist more easily after a cordial handshake.

Trump's reminders to himself for the February 21, 2018 "listening session" with Florida students and teachers from Parkland, Florida which experienced a school shooting where 17 were killed. His note reminded him to ask what the students thought would help them feel safe and to tell them he was listening.

Presidents can also create more success by helping their party win more seats in the next election. Every seat counts when the president's party is in the minority, and the president can help by endorsing candidates, raising campaign cash, directing government grants to swing districts, and spending time in the district or state.

This influence varies greatly in the general versus midterm elections, however. Presidents tend to gain seats in the general election as their party rises with them, and they can even produce **coattails** of electoral success by creating such large margins of victory in a district or state that they pull some members into office on the tails of the presidential vote. By definition, these coattails do not exist in the midterm election, which helps explain why the president's party tends to lose seats with the president off the ballot. Presidents can still retain a House or Senate majority after a midterm loss, but the sense that the president is losing congressional support can undermine his or her power to persuade.

coattails
The ability of a winning presidential candidate to pull party members into Congress by running ahead of them and creating coattails in the general election.

The president's power to persuade Congress is generally measured by **presidential support scores**. These scores are calculated by counting the number of congressional votes on which the president takes a position and wins. Johnson won 94 percent of these key votes in the House and 93 percent in the Senate in the year after his landslide victory in 1964, while Obama won 94 percent in the House and 97 percent in the Senate after he won the presidency in 2008. Obama's House score plunged to 31 percent in 2011 in the House after his party lost its House majority in 2010, but his Senate support remained relatively high in both 2015 and 2016 even though his party lost its Senate majority in 2014. Obama's continued Senate success reflected his care in taking positions on votes that were almost certain to win.[76]

presidential support score
The most frequently used measure of a president's success in convincing Congress to act; the score measures the president's percentage of victories on key votes.

Despite similar starting points, Johnson's scores stayed high throughout his term, largely because his party continued to control both chambers, while Obama's scores plummeted in the House, largely because Republicans retook the House majority in 2010, and enforced tough discipline against the president from 2011 until he left office.

Whereas Johnson had large party majorities in Congress throughout his term, Obama faced an angry Republican House majority committed to confrontations over the budget and the president's health insurance program, Obamacare.

Presidential Greatness (Impact)

11.6 Identify the sources of presidential greatness.

History is the ultimate judge of a president's impact, and presidents pay a great deal of attention to what history will think of them. In many ways, this concern about historical greatness is a check on every presidential decision.

Presidents rise and fall in the historical rankings based on a number of factors. Some rise because they led the nation through periods of intense domestic or international crisis; others rise because they had a distinctive vision of where the nation should go on issues such as civil rights, social policy, or the economy. Rankings also include at least some assessment of how presidents fared as political and moral leaders of the nation.

History tends to judge wars and international crises as the most significant test of a president's leadership. Wars that end in stalemate tend to diminish a president's greatness, whereas wars that end in victory raise a president's ranking, especially when the nation's survival is threatened. Abraham Lincoln (the Civil War), Woodrow Wilson (World War I), and Franklin Delano Roosevelt (World War II) rank among the great presidents because of their leadership during just such wars, whereas Lyndon Johnson ranks much lower because of his role in the Vietnam stalemate.

Corruption and inability to deal with economic problems are sure paths to presidential failure. Warren Harding and Richard Nixon both rank as failures because of scandals that tarnished their presidencies, while Herbert Hoover is ranked a failure because of his lack of leadership at the start of the Great Depression. Although Lyndon Johnson launched a number of great domestic programs such as Medicare for older citizens and helped secure civil rights for African Americans, his decision to escalate the Vietnam War continues to cast a shadow on his presidential greatness.

Ultimately, a president's place in history is determined decades after he or she leaves office. By reminding themselves that there is a future accounting, presidents can find some inspiration for making the hard and sometimes unpopular choices that have led to greatness among their predecessors. Thus, the judgment of history may be one of the most important sources of accountability the nation has on its presidents.

Ratings of recent presidents may change, over time, but they provide some context for holding presidents accountable for radical breaks with historical norms and practices. The ratings also set the mark for new presidents in fashioning their behavior. In March 2018, for example, scholars of the American presidency already ranked Obama among the top 10 presidents in American history.[77] He was a studious and charismatic leader, secured passage of major policies such as national health care reform, remained steady in the face of crises, helped the nation grieve after national tragedies, guided the economy through the Great Recession that he inherited from his predecessor, and worked to end the wars in Iraq and Afghanistan. In his last State of the Union Address he acknowledged one failure, saying, "It is one of the few regrets of my presidency—that the rancor and suspicion between the parties has gotten worse rather than better. There's no doubt a president with the gifts of Lincoln or Roosevelt might have better bridged the divide."[78]

In contrast, political scientists ranked George W. Bush far below at number 30 out of 44. Bush responded to the 9/11 terrorist attacks with a reassuring call to duty, but took the nation into an open-ended war, oversaw soaring budget deficits driven by tax cuts and military spending, and ended his second term in the midst of an economic crisis and stock market collapse.

As of March 2018, these same scholars rated Trump as the worst president in history. The rankings varied by party identification among the scholars: Democrats put Trump at the very bottom of their list, Independents put him just one president above the bottom, and Republicans put him four levels up. The differences were slight, however, and can be viewed as a failing grade for Trump's rough year. As the authors of the study note, Trump's grade is not yet set. Other presidents have started slowly and corrected course to national applause, not to mention landslide reelection. Moreover, even as he struggles to manage controversy and alleged wrongdoing, Trump is resetting the norms of presidential conduct. Whether his approach to the presidency will alter future candidates and expectations is uncertain, he has clearly operated at the edges of past practice, be it in going public through Twitter or creating chaos through policy and staff turnover.

CONCLUSION

Presidents have worked hard to improve the environment for decades, and have used aggressive executive action to strengthen government enforcement, increase the federal budget to hire more regulators, sign international agreements, and set tougher goals for cutting pollution and the greenhouse gases that are warming the planet. Congress has played an equally important role by passing important laws such as the Clean Air Act and Clean Water Act, but presidents have used the take care clause to execute the laws faithfully and aggressively.

There is no doubt that this work has paid off in the form of lower pollution and greater public health. But you now face an entirely new generation of environmental goals. Global climate change is almost surely going to reshape the world by raising sea levels and creating vast deserts devoid of water; population growth is threatening endangered wildlife; clean drinking water is at risk as new chemicals penetrate even the deepest aquifers; and the world's oceans are on the brink of collapse because of the lack of a national ocean policy that future presidents must address.

You will have to make decisions on how to solve these problems. Much as you can take some comfort from successes such as the Paris agreement on climate change that Secretary of State John Kerry helped negotiate, the future of the environment depends on the many choices you make every day. Are you doing everything you can to keep the environment clean? Are you paying attention to what you buy, where it was made, and whether it can be reused? And is your university doing its best to save energy and take good care of the environment in which you live?

These are not the only questions you will face in the coming years. Saving the environment is expensive, and you will decide how much you are willing to pay and do to take even bolder steps to assure a clean, healthy world for the future. The past 50 years show that this nation is capable of tough choices that cost money in the short run for new technologies such as solar panels, wind power, and higher gas mileage. This chapter has shown you how the structure of the presidency, its tools for action, and its great potential for impact can reshape the world for good. You will decide whether to support these and the other tools you learn in this book to deal with a host of tough issues, but you can look back to the days when air and water pollution seemed unsolvable, and see that change is possible if the tools are used well.

REVIEW THE CHAPTER

The Constitutional Foundations of the Presidency (Structure)

11.1 Identify the constitutional foundations of the presidency, p. 327.

The Framers gave the president three sets of powers that create the foundations for action: (1) command the nation's armed forces during peace and war, and make treaties with other nations; (2) appoint the principal officers of government and require their opinions in writing on any subject related to their duties; and (3) give Congress information on the state of the union, recommend new laws deemed necessary and expedient, and convene Congress on extraordinary occasions. The Framers also created a single executive with a four-year term; a set of qualifications such as citizenship, age, and residence; election through the Electoral College; and the power to remove the president through impeachment.

The President's Job Description (Structure)

11.2 Analyze the scope of presidential power, p. 332.

The Framers gave the president four major jobs in protecting the nation from domestic and international threats: (1) Commander in Chief, (2) diplomat in chief, (3) administrator in chief, and (4) legislator in chief. Each of these jobs has specific tools for success.

How the Presidency Works (Action)

11.3 Describe the organization and functions of the Executive Office of the President, p. 344.

Presidents manage the executive branch with the assistance of an intensely loyal White House staff, a much larger Executive Office of the President (EOP) that is anchored by the Office of the Vice President, the White House Office, Office of Management and Budget (OMB), and the cabinet of department secretaries and selected administrators that oversees the federal bureaucracy. Presidential personality plays a significant role in how these helpers work.

Presidents and the Public (Action)

11.4 Examine the relationship between the president and the public, p. 349.

The public expects the president to be both a friend and strong leader, while presidents need the public's approval as a key resource for creating impact. Presidents generate public approval by handling crises, going public, matching words and deeds, and staying in touch; but public approval tends to drop over the president's term regardless of what he or she does. However, public opinion often rises dramatically when the nation faces particularly serious threats such as an international crisis or war.

Presidents and Congress (Impact)

11.5 Describe the relationship between the president and the Congress, p. 353.

The president and Congress often have a tense relationship because of competing constituencies, calendars, and campaigns. Although presidents have the power to persuade, their greatest resource for influencing Congress resides in the number of seats controlled by their party.

Presidential Greatness (Impact)

11.6 Identify the sources of presidential greatness, p. 356.

Presidential greatness is hard to define. Historians, political scientists, and the American public consider Washington, Jefferson, Lincoln, and Franklin Roosevelt as their greatest presidents. Greatness depends in part on how presidents deal with crises and war.

LEARN THE TERMS

parliamentary government, p. 329
prime minister, p. 330
presidential ticket, p. 330
articles of impeachment, p. 330
unitary executive, p. 333
vesting clause, p. 333
War Powers Resolution, p. 334
treaty, p. 334
executive agreement, p. 335
take care clause, p. 335
inherent powers, p. 336
recess appointments, p. 337
executive action, p. 337
executive order, p. 338
executive memorandum, p. 339
line item veto, p. 341
executive privilege, p. 341
signing statement, p. 343
Executive Office of the President (EOP), p. 346
White House chief of staff, p. 347
Office of Management and Budget (OMB), p. 348
cabinet, p. 348
mandate, p. 349
honeymoon, p. 349
rally point, p. 350
going public, p. 351
political capital, p. 354
coattails, p. 355
presidential support score, p. 355

The Federal Bureaucracy and Public Policy

CHAPTER 12

Spencer Platt/Getty Images

Driven by easy access to a new generation of cheap synthetic painkillers, the nation's opioid epidemic took the lives of more than 40,000 Americans in 2017 and showed no signs of slowing down. Using his authority as the nation's top health officer, the U.S. Surgeon General issued a public health advisory on April 5, 2018, urging more Americans to carry the fast-acting opioid antidote, naloxone. "We should think of naloxone like an EpiPen or CPR," Dr. Jerome Adams said. "Knowing how to use naloxone and keeping it within reach can save a life." Here, a health clinic bulletin board promotes the use of naloxone in an emergency. Naloxone can be bought at most pharmacies without a prescription.

LEARNING OBJECTIVES

12.1 Outline the development of the federal bureaucracy (Structure), p. 362.

12.2 Describe how the federal bureaucracy is organized and staffed (Structure), p. 364.

12.3 Describe the roles and responsibilities of the federal bureaucracy (Action), p. 375.

12.4 Identify the means of controlling the federal bureaucracy (Action), p. 379.

12.5 Explain public policy and identify the key steps in making public policy (Impact), p. 381.

12.6 Identify the challenges the federal government faces in implementing public policy (Impact), p. 387.

The federal bureaucracy affects Americans every day, whether by protecting the water they drink, the roads they travel, or the food they eat. But perhaps the greatest impact of government bureaucracy has been its effort to improve public health. Americans live longer in part because Congress and presidents made large investments in fighting life-threatening diseases and gave the bureaucracy the authority to act.

The federal government's campaign to improve public health began long before World War II. The government created the Public Health Service to prevent cholera in 1798, appointed the nation's first surgeon general to set national medical priorities in 1871, and created the Food and Drug Administration (FDA) in 1906. These and other early efforts laid the foundation for the federal government's disease-fighting efforts today.

The fight against disease accelerated dramatically after 1945, when Congress and the president began creating medical research institutions and the National Institutes of Health (NIH) to study the cause of deadly diseases such as heart attacks and cancer. One year later, the Centers for Disease Control (CDC) were created to protect the nation from communicable diseases that have included polio, small pox and, more recently, Ebola and Zika. The CDC has also taken the lead in providing widespread access to vaccines against now-preventable diseases such as polio and smallpox. For more than half a century, the surgeon general has led the fight to stop smoking.

These efforts have produced longer, healthier lives for all Americans. Since 1930 life expectancy has jumped by 23 years for women and 14 years for men.[1] The federal bureaucracy cannot take all of the credit for the gains, but it remains central to what is called "avoidable mortality," or death at young and middle age, by implementing vaccines and reducing smoking, along with lower rates of mortality among older Americans through better health care and fitness.

Despite these shared gains, many Americans still face shortened lives due to where they live, learn, work, and play. People who live in low-income neighborhoods have less reliable access to health care, have longer commutes to more dangerous jobs, are more likely to go to school hungry, face higher crime rates, and often go to bed in unsafe buildings.[2] Dozens of federal departments and agencies have a role in fighting these social predictors of poor health—the Health and Human Services departments contains dozens of programs to attack disease and provide health care, while the Justice Department enforces the laws against illegal drugs such as the synthetic narcotics that fuel the opioid epidemic, the Agriculture Department provides access to healthier low-income communities, the Labor Department polices workplace safety, and the Environmental Protection Agency regulates air and water pollution.

Some experts argue that American health care is too expensive and poorly coordinated, but the gains will affect young Americans well into the future. Young people today are healthier than any generation in history. People are eating healthier food, paying more attention to exercise, and taking tough stands on smoking and food preservatives, and are even starting to ask hard questions about genetically modified foods.

There are public policy consequences that come with Americans generally living longer. Social Security and Medicare were designed to provide support for older Americans when life expectancy was much shorter. These gains for your parents and grandparents mean they will be receiving health care and retirement benefits longer than any generation in U.S. history; as a result, you may have to pay higher taxes and work longer than other generations to secure those benefits.

The federal bureaucracy is one constant in these predictions. It is likely to remain large, complicated, and an active influence on major policy decisions for the future. This chapter will introduce you to the basic structure of the federal bureaucracy and the ways in which it affects American life through the implementation of major policies. This chapter will also cover the basic steps involved in making policy decisions. You will learn that government bureaucracy can be slow, inefficient, and poorly managed, but also fast and effective in faithfully executing the laws that affect your lives for the good every day. To make bureaucracy effective means citizens like you need to combine an understanding of the structure of bureaucracy with a willingness to take action.

The Constitutional Foundations of the Bureaucracy (Structure)

12.1 Outline the development of the federal bureaucracy.

The Framers clearly understood that the new national government would need departments, agencies, employees, and military personnel to protect the young republic from foreign and domestic threats. They knew principal officers would be at the top of government, inferior officers at the middle, and government employees at the bottom. They asked the executive branch as a whole to faithfully execute the laws, but they provided very little constitutional structure and few rules to guide future presidents as they made choices about how to make an impact through administrative action.

bureaucracy

A form of organization that operates through impersonal, uniform rules and procedures.

bureaucrat

A negative term for describing a government employee.

As the executive branch evolved over time, the departments and agencies of government became known as the **bureaucracy**, and their employees as **bureaucrats**. Both words are based on the French word for the cloth covering government desks. Add a short suffix to "bureau" and the term *bureaucracy* becomes "government by people at desks."

Although bureaucracy and bureaucrats are often criticized as slow and expensive, a bureaucracy is simply a form of organization that delivers goods and services at the lowest cost through specialization of jobs, close supervision of employees, and clear rules for decision making. Indeed, at one time in history, the term *bureaucracy* actually meant fast and efficient. Writing in 1921, German sociologist Max Weber described bureaucracy as nearly perfect for getting work done: "It is superior to any other form in precision, in stability, in the stringency of discipline, and in its reliability. It thus makes possible a particularly high degree of control for the heads of the organization and for those acting in relation to it. It is finally superior both in intensive efficiency and in the scope of its operations, and is formally capable of applications to all kinds of administrative tasks."[3] The question is whether Weber would describe the federal bureaucracy as "superior" today.

Building the Federal Bureaucracy

The Framers did their work long before Weber, of course, but they recognized that government would need a strong president at the top. After all, they gave the president absolute responsibility to "take Care that the Laws be faithfully executed," to put the laws into action. Although the Framers did not tell the president exactly how to build the bureaucracy, they did give the president authority to nominate the principal officers of government and require their opinions in writing. Together, these two constitutional powers give the president general authority to lead the bureaucracy, as well as the inherent power to act as administrator in chief.

The Framers believed that the federal bureaucracy would remain relatively small. They also expected Congress to establish the same departments that had existed under the Articles of Confederation: war, state, treasury, and the postal service.[4] Nevertheless, the Framers made three key decisions about executing the laws that continue to shape federal administration to this day.

First, they prohibited members of the House and Senate from holding executive branch positions in Article I, Section 6, of the Constitution. Under that provision, Congress cannot create executive branch jobs for its members.[5]

Second, as noted earlier, the Framers gave the president authority to nominate the principal officers of government. At the same time, they gave the Senate authority, under its advice and consent power, to confirm or reject the president's nominees. They also gave Congress the power to create new departments and agencies through legislation signed by the president, and the power to determine the number of federal employees, the budgets they administer, and the taxes they collect.

Third, and most importantly, the Framers made the president the bureaucracy's administrator in chief. Once the laws are passed, employees are hired, and budgets and taxes are set, the president is responsible for making sure the laws are implemented and obeyed. Hamilton believed the electoral process would produce a president who would meet the key test of good government. Writing in *The Federalist*, No. 68, he explained the true test of good government: "its aptitude and tendency to produce a good administration."[6]

This does not mean, however, that the president has unlimited discretion in implementing the laws. Recall that Congress, not the president, has the power to create the departments and agencies of government in the first place, as well as the responsibility for appropriating the money to administer programs and hire government employees; and the Senate has the power to confirm certain presidential appointees. The Framers clearly expected both houses of Congress to monitor the workings of the executive branch.

Framing Principles

The Constitution did not contain many rules about the bureaucracy, but the Framers had very clear ideas about how the bureaucracy should work. Alexander Hamilton spelled the rules out one by one starting in *The Federalist,* No. 76, where he first discussed the president's power to nominate the senior officers of government, and explained the Senate's role in confirming each nomination as an "excellent check upon a spirit of favoritism in the President, and would tend to prevent the appointment of unfit characters. . . ."[7]

Hamilton believed that the aptitude and tendency to pass his test of a good government resided in an energetic bureaucracy built on six principles:

1. *Government should have a big mission.* As Hamilton argued in *The Federalist,* No. 72, government exists to pursue "extensive and arduous enterprise for the public benefit."[8] He did not see government as a passive instrument that would only react to threats, but as a force for strengthening the nation's economic, political, and social infrastructure.
2. *Government should have a clear chain of command from the top to the bottom.* Hamilton saw that clear links between the executive and the officers of government were essential for both effective administration and accountability to the public, and believed that the officers should be under the president's direct control. In turn, the federal service would, by implication, also be subject to the direct control of the senior officers of government, who would supervise day-to-day operations of post offices, revenue offices, and army garrisons.
3. *Government should be led by the best and the brightest.* Hamilton repeatedly referred to the officers of government as the extension of an energetic executive. He did not believe these officers would be perfect, but he did believe that the president's appointees would have the "moderation, firmness, and liberality with exactness" to ensure a government well executed.[9] Although George Washington paid attention to political loyalty in recruiting appointees, his primary focus was on finding persons with merit and expertise who were drawn from the highest ranks of society.[10]
4. *Government employees should act with "vigor and expedition."* Executive control would involve more than clear direction from the top; it also would involve a commitment to effective execution of the laws down the hierarchy. Hamilton did not believe, however, that civic duty would supply the needed incentive for faithful execution of the laws. Instead, he argued that adequate compensation and the opportunity for promotion would do so.[11]

5. *Young Americans must accept the call to service.* Hamilton believed that young Americans would form the core of the government workforce, whether in the army and navy, or as government employees. He understood that government would have to make its jobs attractive by offering competitive salaries, promotions, and a measure of political protection on the way up. He also believed that government had to provide the education and training for high performance in the public's benefit. Indeed, some of you may find yourselves working for the government or pursuing advanced education as part of government training.
6. *Government should be open to inspection.* Hamilton believed that government must be transparent. Having defined safety in "the republican sense" as a due dependence on and responsibility to the people, Hamilton defined accountability as the public's ability to detect, censure, and punish "national miscarriage or misfortune," which would be infinitely easier to prevent under a single, not plural, executive.[12]

Organizing the Bureaucracy (Structure)

12.2 Describe how the federal bureaucracy is organized and staffed.

Guided by Hamilton's words and actions as the first secretary of the treasury, the federal bureaucracy began as a very small operation. Indeed, the entire federal bureaucracy of 1790 consisted of nothing more than a handful of clerks, a board to oversee a government treasury that had no money, and an army of just 840 soldiers.[13] (See Figure 12.1 for recent trends in the number of federal employees who work in the defense and domestic bureaucracy.)

Congress had intended to keep government small and even fought to restrict the president's authority to fire appointees. President Washington won the arguments, however, and settled any remaining worries about his judgment by appointing Thomas

FIGURE 12.1 TOTAL NUMBER OF FEDERAL EMPLOYEES AND DEFENSE EMPLOYEES AS PERCENT OF TOTAL, 1981–2018

The number of federal government employees has remained relatively steady at about two million over the past three decades, but the share of defense and non-defense employees has changed significantly. The number of defense employees has been dropping in recent decades as war fighting has become more precise and the number of military personnel needed to wage war has declined. In the meantime, the number of non-defense federal employees has increased somewhat as new departments of government were created, such as the Department of Homeland Security.

SOURCE: Office of Management and Budget (OMB), *Budget of the U.S. Government, Fiscal Year 2019*, Historical Tables (U.S. Government Printing Office, February 2018), Table 16.1, available at https://www.whitehouse.gov/omb/historical-tables/.

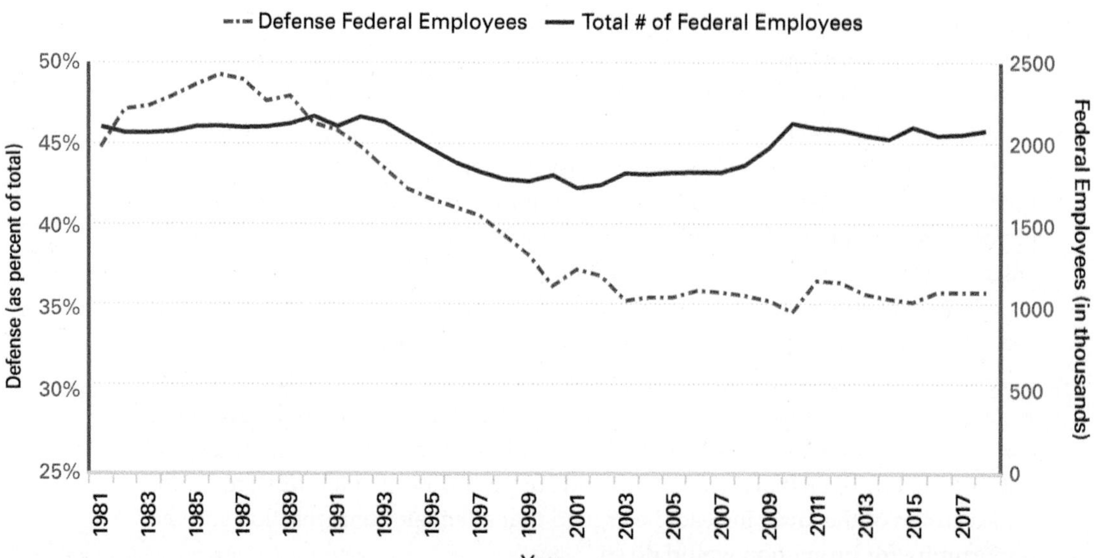

Jefferson as Secretary of State, Alexander Hamilton as secretary of the treasury, and Henry Knox as secretary of war. All three were easily confirmed and quickly went about the business of running their departments. At roughly the same time, Congress also created the Post Office Department and allowed for the appointment of a U.S. attorney general.

Even though the federal bureaucracy was tiny, it was not long before presidential candidates began promising smaller government. Indeed, Jefferson made waste in government a centerpiece of his first Inaugural Address in 1801, promising "a wise and frugal government, which shall restrain men from injuring one another, shall leave them otherwise free to regulate their own pursuits of industry and improvement, and shall not take from the mouth of labor what it has earned." Jefferson also wanted a government that taxed lightly, paid its debts on time and in full, and sought "economy in the public expense."

Ironically, Jefferson may have done more to build a bigger federal bureaucracy than any of the early presidents by negotiating the Louisiana Purchase. Not only did the purchase double the nation's size, but it also laid the groundwork for a vast expansion of the federal bureaucracy to oversee land grants, road and railroad construction, and the armed forces to protect settlers. Moreover, Jefferson embraced at least some features of Weber's bureaucracy, writing at one point that "it is by division and subdivision of duties alone that all matters, great and small, can be managed to perfection."[14]

Presidents oversee the bureaucracy as administrators in chief, but Congress creates every federal organization, approves all budgets, and makes the laws that allow the bureaucracy to hire and supervise federal employees. Although President Trump froze federal hiring during his first three months in office and was able to revoke many of the Obama administration's executive orders, only Congress could make the budget cuts needed to reduce the number of government employees and streamline the bureaucracy.

The odds of congressional approval for the needed budget cuts dropped sharply over Trump's first months in office as the Justice Department's special investigation of Russia's involvement in the 2016 election gained momentum. Like many presidents before him, Trump soon found that he had little power to control the bureaucracy without Congress on his side. He also learned that he did not have the same power to make snap decisions that he had in building his business empire. He was the chief executive officer of government but worked for a very strict board of directors on Capitol Hill and was subject to close review by external reviewers in the judicial branch.

Types of Federal Organizations

Federal employees work for departments and agencies, which are classified into four broad types: (1) departments, (2) independent stand-alone agencies, (3) independent regulatory commissions, and (4) government corporations. Each type is discussed in the following text.

DEPARTMENTS Departments are the most visible organizations in the federal bureaucracy. Today's 15 departments employ more than 70 percent of all federal civil servants and spend 93 percent of all federal dollars. Secretaries head 14 of the departments, while the attorney general heads the Department of Justice.

Measured by their total number of employees, the five largest departments are the Defense Department, which governs the armed services; the Department of Veterans Affairs, which helps veterans return to civilian life after military service; the Department of Homeland Security, which helps protect the nation from terrorism, runs the airport screening lines, and manages the response to natural disasters such as hurricanes; the Department of the Treasury, which oversees expenditures and raises revenues through the Internal Revenue Service; and the Department of Justice, which enforces laws by representing the nation in court cases and investigates crime through the Federal Bureau of Investigation.

inner cabinet
The four departments of government that are most important to the president: Defense, Justice, Treasury, and State.

outer cabinet
The departments of government that are less important to the president than those in the inner cabinet.

Measured by their importance to the president, the Departments of Defense, Justice, State, and Treasury are considered part of the **inner cabinet**, that is central to the president's political and administrative success, while the **outer cabinet** composed of the other 11 departments is considered to be less important to the president. Presidents meet with the secretaries of the inner cabinet frequently, but meet with the secretaries of the outer cabinet only when an emergency arises or a key policy issue is under review by Congress or the judiciary.

The structure of the 15 current federal departments was created using one of four different approaches.

1. *Merge already existing agencies into a new organization* In 2002, for example, Congress merged 22 separate agencies and 170,000 employees into a new Department of Homeland Security. The Trump administration made a similar proposal in June 2018 to move the Agriculture Department's food and nutrition assistance programs into the Department of Health and Human Services, but faced intense resistance from the congressional committees that would lose power over these large programs. (Figure 12.2 shows the department's organization chart as of January 1, 2012.)
2. *Break an existing department into two or more new departments.* In 1979, for example, Congress split the Department of Health, Education, and Welfare into the new departments of Education, and Health and Human Services.

FIGURE 12.2 THE DEPARTMENT OF HOMELAND SECURITY

The Department of Homeland Security was created in 2002 in response to the 9/11 attacks. The merger was the largest in federal government history, involved the movement of 22 different agencies, and the transfer of more than 200,000 federal employees. The U.S. Customs and Border Protection Bureau, Citizenship and Immigration Services, and Immigration and Customs Enforcement all handle different elements of immigration. The Coast Guard patrols that nation's territorial waters, the Secret Service protects the president and other federal officials, and the Federal Emergency Management Agency responds to domestic disasters such as hurricanes and earthquakes, while the Transportation Security Administration is responsible for airport, rail, subway, and other transportation systems.

SOURCE: Department of Homeland Security: https://www.dhs.gov/sites/default/files/publications/17_1219_DHS_Organizational_Chart.pdf.

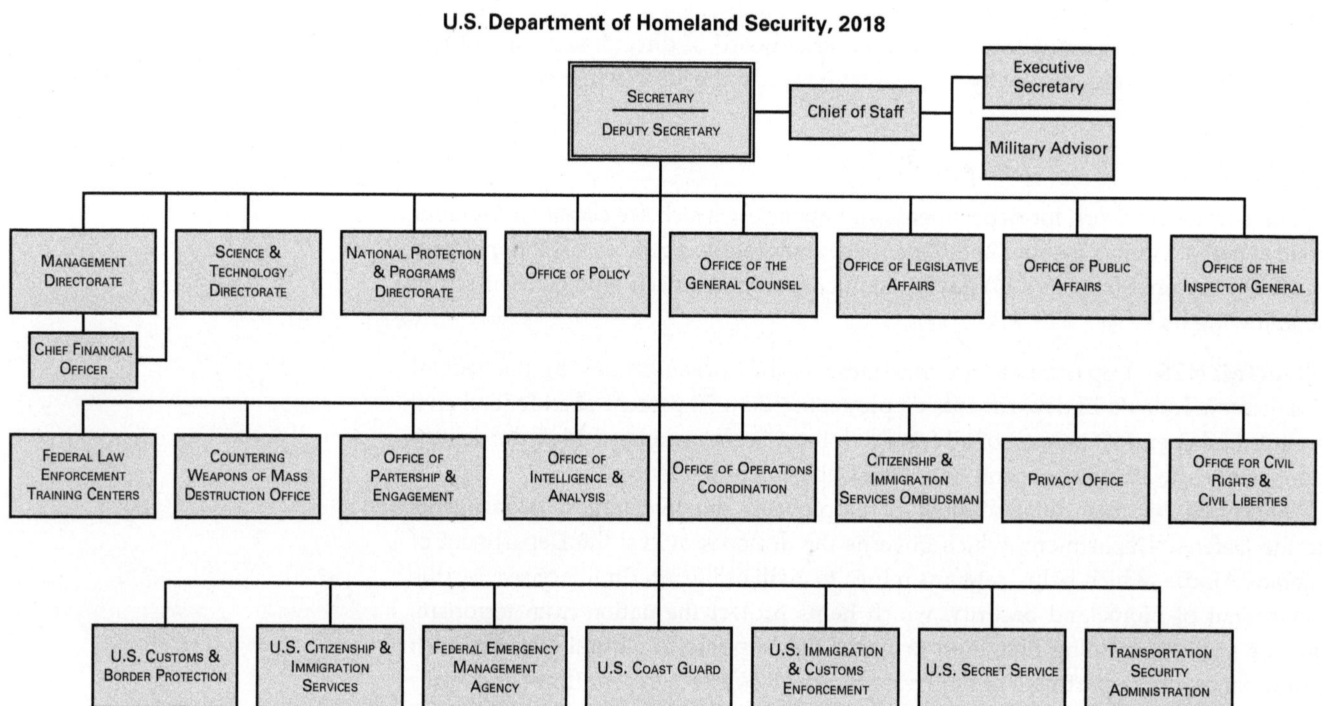

3. *Elevate an independent stand-alone agency to department-level status.* In 1988, for example, Congress elevated the Veterans Administration to cabinet status as the new Department of Veterans Affairs.
4. *Create an entirely new department to address a new issue.* The Department of Labor was created in 1913 as the nation grappled with a rapidly expanding industrial economy and the rise of labor unions. Although it did contain an independent stand-alone agency called the Bureau of Labor Statistics, the department was designed to administer an emerging agenda of immigration, worker safety, women's employment, railroad labor, and fair pay laws.

INDEPENDENT STAND-ALONE AGENCIES The word *independent* means at least two things in the federal bureaucracy. Applied to a regulatory commission, it means the agency is outside the president's control. Applied to a stand-alone agency of government, it merely means the agency is either smaller, younger, less visible, mostly hidden from the public, or less important than a traditional department. **Independent regulatory commissions** do not report to the president, but independent stand-alone agencies do.

independent regulatory commission
A government agency or commission with regulatory power whose independence is protected by Congress.

Independent stand-alone agencies usually are designed to address specific issues such as environmental protection (the Environmental Protection Agency), international aid (the U.S. Agency for International Development), national security (the National Security Agency), the administration of visible national programs such as Social Security (the Social Security Administration), the collection of intelligence (the Central Intelligence Agency), and service (the Peace Corps).

More than 50 of these agencies exist today, but most are small and almost invisible. There are times, however, when these agencies become so large and important to the president that they are elevated to cabinet status, which is why the Veterans Administration became a department in 1988.[15]

The use of independent stand-alone agencies can add to confusion about who is responsible for what in the federal government. More than a decade after federal intelligence agencies missed the advance warnings of the September 11 terrorist attacks, the federal government still has more than 15 different intelligence agencies, including the CIA, the Defense Intelligence Agency, the FBI, and the National Security Agency. Although Congress and the president created an Office of the Director of National Intelligence in 2004 to coordinate these agencies, they keep secrets from each other to this day.

INDEPENDENT REGULATORY COMMISSIONS The federal bureaucracy contains a relatively short list of independent regulatory commissions that are distinct from other government organizations in three ways: (1) they are headed by a small group of commissioners, not a single administrator; (2) the commissioners must make majority decisions to act; and (3) the commissions are not subject to strict congressional review. Almost all of these organizations have an odd number of commissioners to avoid tie votes on major issues.

The first independent regulatory commissions were created in the late 1880s to police interstate competition, and expanded rapidly in the early 1890s to cover a long list of particularly controversial issues such as labor and economic policy. Although the president appoints all independent regulatory commissioners and the Senate confirms each one separately, these appointees have fixed terms of office and generally are independent from the two branches once they are sworn into office. Commissioners cannot be removed from office without cause, which is defined by law to mean inefficiency, neglect of duty, or unethical behavior. As a result, independent regulatory commissions are generally insulated from political pressure.

Independent regulatory commissions, however, are not completely free to act without oversight. Congress and the president must approve their annual budgets, and the judiciary is often asked to review their decisions. Moreover, presidents often nominate commissioners on the basis of party loyalty, which means that commissions can be highly political. And at least one, the Federal Election Commission, has an even number of commissioners appointed to represent the two political parties equally, which often results in tie votes on campaign regulations.

Nevertheless, independent regulatory commissions still have considerable influence on daily life in the nation. The Consumer Product Safety Commission keeps dangerous toys off the market, the Securities and Exchange Commission (SEC) regulates banking behavior, the Federal Communications Commission oversees the news media and the sale of airways for new uses such as digital television, the Federal Trade Commission monitors business advertising, the Federal Reserve Board controls the supply of money and sets interest rates, and the Nuclear Regulatory Commission makes sure nuclear power plants are safe.

Independent regulatory commissions tend to be much less visible than other government organizations until a crisis occurs on their watch. The SEC was on the front pages for three years, for example, as one corporation after another disclosed accounting fraud in their annual reports to investors. The SEC was created in the 1930s to restore investor confidence in the stock market after the Great Depression, but it was accused of being negligent in monitoring accounting practices at big companies such as Enron and WorldCom in the early 2000s, and ignoring the financial scandals that led to the 2008 financial collapse.

GOVERNMENT CORPORATIONS Government corporations are the least understood organizations in the federal bureaucracy. Because they are intended to act more like businesses than like traditional government departments and agencies, they generally have more freedom from the internal rules that control traditional agencies. They often have greater authority to hire and fire employees quickly and are allowed to make money through the sale of services such as train tickets, stamps, or home loans.[16]

The Postal Service is a government corporation that is supposed to make money just like a business, but it is also required to deliver to every remote corner of the nation for the price of a single stamp, which makes it operate at a loss. Here, U.S. Postal Worker Oscar Zamora collects tax returns as cars drive past the San Francisco Post Office on tax day, which is the last day that taxes can be postmarked to meet the annual deadline.

Government corporations cover a wide range of policy issues, such as public radio and television (the Corporation for Public Broadcasting), mail delivery (the U.S. Postal Service), train travel (the National Railroad Passenger Corporation, which is better known as Amtrak), national service (the Corporation for National and Community Service), and a host of financial enterprises that make loans to banks and other institutions (the Federal National Mortgage Association, or Fannie Mae).

Government corporations are supposed to turn a profit just like a private corporation, but in reality, they rarely succeed. Amtrak loses more than $1 billion a year, for example, in large part because it operates a number of routes that generate little revenue. The bulk of its income comes from relatively short routes between large metropolitan areas such as Boston, New York, Philadelphia, and Washington, D.C., and on scenic routes in the Northwest and through the Rocky Mountains. Amtrak ridership has grown in recent years, but its speed remains slow compared to government and private rail systems in other nations such as Japan. Even though it is a business, it cannot make money unless it has the freedom to abandon unprofitable but politically protected routes.[17]

The U.S. Postal Service has also been losing money for decades. Although the USPS made almost $70 billion in 2017 and increased its package business, it still lost almost $3 billion as first-class mail volume continued its long decline. The losses prompted a series of presidential tweets criticizing Amazon for "costing the United States Post Office massive amounts of money for being their Delivery Boy." However, USPS financial reports show that Amazon has been a source of significant earnings, suggesting that it may have come under Trump's fire because its owner, Jeff Bezos, also owns the *Washington Post*, which often criticized the president's agenda.[18]

Types of Federal Employees

As the federal government's mission has grown from a relatively small list of laws in 1800 to thousands of laws today, so has its bureaucracy. By 2018, the federal bureaucracy was composed of 15 departments, 50 independent regulatory commissions, stand-alone agencies, the U.S. Postal Service, and the three branches of the armed services (Air Force, Army, and Navy).

Together, these departments and agencies employed almost 4 million people in 2018, including 500,000 postal workers, more than 2.2 million federal civilian employees, and 1.4 million uniformed members of the armed services. The federal bureaucracy also employed millions of private-sector employees under contracts to private firms such as Lockheed Martin and Boeing.[19] Although private contractors made many of the mistakes that led to the crash of https://www.healthcare.gov in 2013, they also provide highly technical skills that are in short supply inside the federal bureaucracy. Private contractors often pay higher salaries for these skills, and can also move faster than the federal bureaucracy in hiring and firing workers.

Americans have adopted a number of myths about the federal workforce, not the least of which is that most federal employees work in Washington, D.C. (Figure 12.3 on the next page dispels this myth.) Many Americans believe that most federal employees work for huge spending programs such as Social Security and Medicare, and that most are lower-level workers. The realities are much different:

- Only 15 percent the federal government's civilian employees work in the Washington, D.C., area. More federal employees work in California, Georgia, and Texas, for example, than in Washington.
- More than 25 percent of the bureaucracy's civilian employees work for the army, navy, or air force, while another 20 percent work for the U.S. Postal Service.

FIGURE 12.3 FEDERAL EMPLOYEES BY LOCATION

The majority of federal government employees do not work in Washington but in regional centers in large cities such as New York City, Los Angeles, and Kansas City. They also work in smaller cities and even small towns in local post offices and social security centers. Federal employees are strong supporters of the government and generally vote for candidates who support better working conditions and fair pay increases, and oppose job and spending cuts.

SOURCE: Office of Personnel Management, Federal Employment Statistics, September 2014, and U.S. Department of Labor, Bureau of Labor Statistics, Quarterly Census of Employment, March 2014. Researched and compiled by Janet Kopenhaver of Eye on Washington.

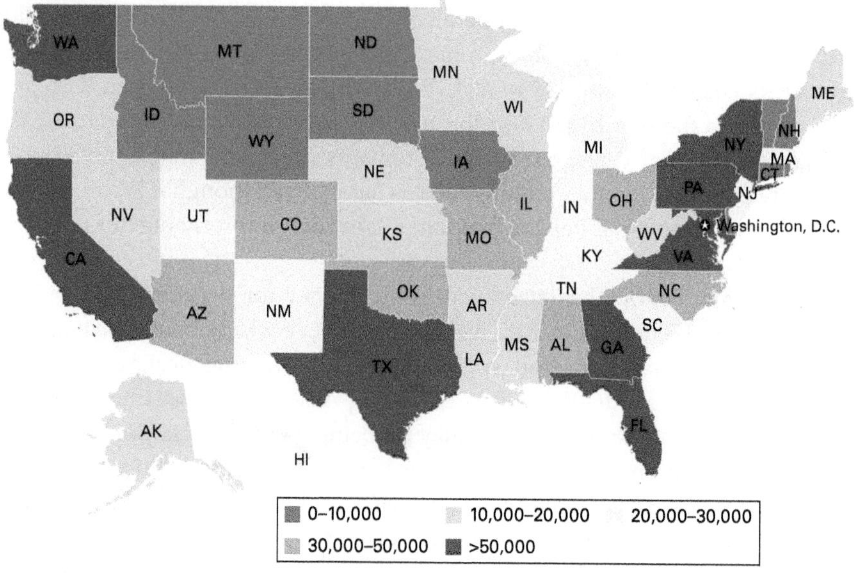

- Social programs such as Social Security and Medicare consume a very large portion of the U.S. budget, but employ just 10 percent of the federal workforce.
- The vast majority of workers occupy professional and technical positions as lawyers, physicians, economists, engineers, and auditors.

Finally, although the public believes most bureaucrats come to work for the security, paycheck, and benefits of their employment, most care deeply about making a difference for their country. According to annual surveys conducted by the president's personnel office, the vast majority of federal employees say they contribute to their agency's mission, and half say their organizations are very good at helping people. Most federal employees also say the people they work with are open to new ideas, willing to help other employees learn new skills, and concerned about their organization's mission.[20]

The federal bureaucracy has three different levels of employees: (1) a small number of presidential appointees who work directly for the president, (2) a somewhat larger number of Senior Executive Service (SES) members who help translate policy into action, and (3) a large number of long-serving employees who are selected on the basis of merit to implement policy under the direction of presidential appointees and senior executives.

The federal government also employs two types of non–civil service employees: (1) 1.5 million members of the armed services, all of whom receive federal government pay and benefits along with their responsibilities as members of the armed services; and (2) 500,000 postal workers and other employees who work for government corporations.

PRESIDENTIAL APPOINTEES Federal departments and agencies are led by about 4,000 presidential appointees, including one-third who are nominated by the president under Article II of the Constitution and confirmed by the Senate by majority vote, and two-thirds who serve "at the pleasure of the president," which means they are appointed by the president without Senate confirmation. The president has the constitutional power to ask any of these appointees for their written opinions

President Trump nominated Dr. Jerome Adams in June 2017 as the nation's 20th Surgeon General, the Senate Health Education and Labor and Pensions Committee held hearings on the nomination in late July, and the Senate confirmed his appointment on August 4. Here, the Surgeon General talks with U.S. Vermont National Guard medivac pilots about their work rescuing St. Croix hurricane victims in October. Although Adams moved through process quickly, the Trump administration was the latest in recent history to fill its top jobs. As of April 18, 2018, only half of the Trump appointees had been confirmed, and a quarter had yet to be nominated to the Senate.

on any issue, which provides the centralized control that Hamilton wrote about in *The Federalist,* No. 76. The number includes all department secretaries, stand-alone agency administrators, independent regulatory commissioners, government corporation heads, and ambassadors to foreign nations.

Because they are both selected and supervised by the president, these 4,000 presidential appointees are the most important leaders of the federal bureaucracy. As the principal officers of government, presidential appointees generally serve until the president leaves office or asks them to leave, although most leave long before the end of an administration to pursue other careers, including lobbying.[21] Under federal law, however, presidential appointees are not allowed to have any contact with their former departments and agencies until they finish a one-year "cooling-off" period.

THE SENIOR EXECUTIVE SERVICE Presidential appointees work closely with about 7,000 members of the **Senior Executive Service (SES)**, who are selected on the basis of their professional and technical skills, and spend most of their careers in government. Members of the SES help presidential appointees manage their agencies, translate information up and down the bureaucracy, and make sure the bureaucracy helps the president faithfully execute the laws. As such, they must understand what presidents want the bureaucracy to do, while protecting the bureaucracy from illegal political interference. They also are responsible for managing the relationship between the president's appointees and the career civil servants. The president is allowed to appoint 10 percent of the SES as presidential appointees without review.

Senior Executive Service (SES)
Established by Congress in 1978 as a flexible, mobile corps of senior career executives who work closely with other presidential appointees to manage government.

THE CIVIL SERVICE The Framers understood that the federal government would need employees, and that many of these employees would stay with government until they retired. The Framers believed that these members of what is now called the **civil service** would outlast each administration, thereby maintaining the "institutional memory" of government.

civil service
A term that describes federal employees who are hired under a competitive, nonpolitical selection process.

For the first 100 years, however, civil servants were chosen mostly on the basis of party loyalty. President Andrew Jackson substantially expanded this "to-the-victor-belong-the spoils" system after his election in 1829. Jackson believed that every job in government was a potential opportunity for employing his political allies.

Jackson's **spoils system** gave the president's party complete control over almost every government job, from cabinet secretaries down to post office clerks. Under this method of filling jobs through political connections, presidents strengthened their control of the

spoils system
A system of public employment based on rewarding party loyalists and friends.

bureaucracy, but sacrificed the expertise needed to execute the laws. After all, political allies were not necessarily skilled administrators. In 1883, Congress abolished the spoils system in favor of today's **merit system**. Under the merit system, employees are selected on the basis of their qualifications for the position, not their political connections.[22]

merit system
A system of public employment in which selection and promotion depend on demonstrated performance rather than political patronage.

Congress and the president expanded the system year after year until almost all federal employees are now selected on the basis of merit. The Office of Personnel Management (OPM) administers civil service laws and rules, whereas the independent Merit Systems Protection Board is charged with protecting the integrity of the federal merit system and the rights of federal employees. Individual departments and agencies, however, are responsible for making all hiring decisions, and must list job openings on https://www.USAjobs.gov.

Under OPM rules, most prospective government employees apply for jobs by identifying a job through the USA jobs Web site, submitting a formal application, and taking a civil service test. Some also must also be reviewed for a security clearance if their jobs involve access to secret information.

Federal organizations must keep careful records about each candidate and justify their decisions when challenged. Although everyone is free to compete for a federal job, veterans are always given extra points in the process in honor of their service. All applicants are free to challenge the final decision, but few enter this time-consuming and rarely successful path.

Once hired, federal employees receive a generous benefit package that includes health insurance, a retirement plan, vacation time, and unpaid leave to take care of a sick parent, spouse, or child. According to the Congressional Budget Office, which is an agency that works for Congress, federal employee benefits cost about $20 per hour worked, compared with $14 for private-sector employees, while federal salaries appear to be about 2 percent higher.[23]

However, these figures are in dispute, in part because federal salaries shift over time with education and job responsibilities. As federal employees get older and move into more complex jobs, they do receive higher salaries. They are also subject to broad pay freezes and cutbacks that often reduce their purchasing power. According to the Governmental Accountability Office, which also works for Congress, federal employees tend to be better educated and in jobs that require greater skills, both of which contribute to higher pay. According to this analysis, federal employees receive about the same total pay and benefits as private employees on an apples-to-apples basis.[24]

In addition, most civil servants are allowed to join employee unions. However, even though they have the same rights as citizens to petition government on issues such as salaries, hours, or working conditions, they are not allowed to strike, or walk out on government. To the contrary, presidents have the power to fire any federal employee who fails to show up for work without due cause. In 1981, for example, President Reagan fired 12,000 federal air traffic controllers after they left their posts on strike for higher wages and better working hours. Although Reagan's decision snarled air traffic as the National Aviation Administration struggled to hire and train new controllers, most of the strikers never worked in government again.[25]

Trump entered office promising to cut thousands of pages of needless rules, and later claimed that he had cut more regulations in his first year in office than any president in history. *Bloomberg Businessweek* later reported that most of the cuts came from stopping rules that had never reached the *Federal Register*. However, Trump deserved credit for slowing the number of new rules largely by pausing the regulatory process and demanding the elimination of at least two existing rules for every one rule created under new laws. Here, Trump illustrates his claim on December 14, 2017, by cutting a ribbon wrapped around stacks of reports meant to illustrate the federal government's regulatory burden.

Civil servants are not the only employees working for the government. The federal government also relies on a very large indirect workforce of private contractors, nonprofit grantees, and state and local government employees who deliver goods and services under the federal government's direction. The federal government has relied on this mixed workforce since the Revolutionary War when American soldiers fought side-by-side with contractors and foreign mercenaries to win the nation's independence. The estimated ratio between contract and military forces during the Revolutionary War was one to six, one to three during the

Korean War, one to one during most of the Iraq War, and one to four at the height of the Afghanistan War.[26] Contractors not only fight side-by-side with military personnel, they also pay the ultimate sacrifices for their service.

The total number of federal civil services has averaged two million total over the past 70 years, but the number of contractors, grantees, state and local government employees who work for the federal government rises and falls with the federal mission. In 2002, for example, the total federal government employed almost 8 million people, including 1.8 million civil servants, 1.4 million military personnel, 800,000 postal workers, 2.4 million contractors, and 1.4 million grantees, all of whom worked to faithfully execute the laws. Eight years later, in 2010, the total had grown to 11.3 million as the wars in Iraq and Afghanistan pushed the number of contractors much higher and the Obama administration increased grant spending to stimulate the economy. Almost eight years later again, in October 2017, the total had fallen to 9 million as wars in Iraq and Afghanistan wound down and federal grant spending fell. Throughout, all the number of federal civil servants remained steady at two million, meaning that the contractors, grantees, and state and local government employees answered the call for increased federal action during the 2000s and bore the cuts during the 2010s. What had risen with war and economic calamity fell during peace and economic growth.[27]

Diversity in Government

The federal bureaucracy is more representative of the American demographic landscape today than it was in the 1950s, when most of its employees were white and most female employees were clerk-typists. Women held 43 percent of all federal jobs at the end of 2016, whereas minorities held slightly more than one-third at 35 percent.[28] Even though the number of women and minorities in the federal workforce is at an all-time high, both groups still face barriers in rising to the top.

First, women and minorities are not equally represented in all departments and agencies. They tend to be concentrated in departments with strong social service missions such as Education, Health and Human Services, Housing and Urban Development, and Veterans Affairs. Military and technical departments such as Defense, Energy, and Transportation have far fewer female employees.

Second, women and minorities are not fully represented at all levels of the federal bureaucracy. Women held two-thirds of lower-paying technical and clerical positions in 2016, and minorities were also concentrated at the bottom of government. Together, women and minorities held barely 15 percent of the top jobs. Nevertheless, they are moving into the top jobs at a fast rate. Between 1994 and 2018, the number of women and minorities in professional and managerial jobs increased considerably, in part because of the retirements of older, white males.[29]

The federal government is struggling to recruit young employees. Many younger Americans see federal government jobs as boring work with low pay. However, research shows that federal employees say they do important work, care about their organization, and feel like they make a difference in their work. Just 7 percent of all federal employees were under 30 years old when the most recent numbers were gathered, but they represented 20 percent of all new hires; and just 27 percent of all federal employees were under 40 years old in 2016, but they accounted for 43 percent of new hires.[30] As employees retire, there will be opportunities for younger applicants.

The negative perceptions people have about federal government bureaucracy has meant that employee morale has declined. However, recent surveys show that federal morale has fallen in recent years as budget cuts, layoffs, pay freezes, and partisanship have taken their toll on employee satisfaction and commitment. Many federal employees believe they are being asked to do more with less every year, and less than half of federal employees recently reported that they were satisfied with the recognition they received for doing a good job.[31]

Diversity also involves recruitment at the top of government with the president's most senior appointees. Recent presidents made significant progress in bringing more women and appointees of color into their cabinets, but the Trump administration reversed course in appointing the least diverse group of senior officials since the Reagan administration in 1981. George W. Bush appointed 11 white men to his first 24-member cabinet, Obama appointed 8, and Trump appointed 18. However, none of the three presidents was particularly effective in recruiting women. Bush appointed just 4 women to his first cabinet, Obama appointed 7, and Trump appointed 3. Moreover, despite well qualified women in finance and the military, a woman has yet to serve as Secretary of the Treasury or Defense.

Regulating Employee Conduct

Because federal employees administer so many laws that can affect election outcomes, they are subject to tight regulations regarding most forms of political participation. In 1939, Congress passed the Act to Prevent Pernicious Political Activities, otherwise known as the **Hatch Act**. Under the original act, federal civil servants were prohibited from raising money for candidates or wearing campaign buttons during their off-work hours; they were prevented even from putting "vote-for" signs on their own private lawns. They also were prohibited from running for political office.[32]

Hatch Act
A federal statute barring federal employees from active participation in certain kinds of politics and protecting them from being fired on partisan grounds.

Under pressure from federal employee unions, Congress overhauled the Hatch Act in 1993 to permit greater political participation. The revised act still bars federal officials from running for political offices at the federal, state, or local level, but does permit most federal civil servants to hold party positions and involve themselves in party fund-raising and campaigning. Many advocates of this policy change argued that the old act discouraged political participation by two million people who otherwise might be vigorous political activists.[33]

But the new Hatch Act maintains restrictions on federal employees: they cannot raise money for candidates when they are at work, and those employed in highly sensitive federal agencies such as the Central Intelligence Agency, the Federal Bureau of Investigation, and certain divisions of the Internal Revenue Service are specifically barred from nearly all political activity on behalf of a candidate or party. In August 2012, for example, two senior managers at the Federal Aviation Administration were disciplined for telling their employees that Mitt Romney would cut their jobs, while Obama would not. These messages clearly violated the Hatch Act's rules against campaign activity.

The Hatch Act is only one of many laws that cover executive ethics. All federal employees from the very top to the bottom must obey basic rules regarding gifts and favors. Employees may not accept anything of value given because of their position. The definitions of gifts and favors are quite specific, and cover everything from a sandwich to a trip, hotel stay, car ride, or souvenir. In 2018, for example, Trump's Environmental Protection Agency administration, Scott Pruitt came under intense criticism for renting an inexpensive Capitol Hill apartment from the wife of an energy lobbyist. Although the rent was just $50 a night, it could be considered a thing of great value given prevailing rents of similar rooms in the neighborhood. Pruitt was also criticized for taking first-class flights and using private jets to travel on public business, including $1,641 for a brief flight from Washington, D.C., to New York City. Pruitt argued that he had to fly first class because he was being harassed for his positions on environmental issues by passengers in economy.[34] Pruitt resigned under increasing investigatory pressure on July 5, 2018.

Former Secretary of State Hillary Clinton responds to tough House questions regarding her role in the 2012 terrorist attack in Benghazi, Libya, that took the lives of U.S. Ambassador J. Christopher Stevens and three other Americans. The hearing lasted 11 hours, and focused on whether she did enough as Secretary of State to protect the Libyan diplomatic post given the terrorist threats that she had received during the months before the violent attack. Although the hearing took place in late 2015, more than three years after the attack, it is nonetheless an example of fire alarm oversight created by a crisis.

The Bureaucracy's Job (Action)

12.3 Describe the roles and responsibilities of the federal bureaucracy.

Whatever their size or mission, all federal organizations share one job: to faithfully execute the laws. Although the Framers did not provide much constitutional structure to accomplish this job, they gave the president responsibility to act, albeit with congressional checks on everything from appointments to the power of the purse. And that structure has been expanded to include judicial review of actions taken by the bureaucracy.

Implementation is the process of converting a policy into action. It covers a broad range of activities, such as writing checks at the Social Security Administration, inspecting job sites for the Occupational Safety and Health Administration, swearing in new citizens at the Citizenship and Immigration Services, and monitoring airline traffic for the Federal Aviation Administration.

implementation
The process of putting a law into practice through bureaucratic rules or spending.

Because Congress and the president could never pass laws with enough detail to address every aspect of implementation, these two branches give federal departments and agencies **administrative discretion** to implement the laws in the most efficient and effective manner possible. This freedom varies from agency to agency, depending on both past performance and congressional politics. Political scientist Theodore Lowi believes that Congress often gives the federal bureaucracy vague directions because it is unable or unwilling to make the tough choices needed to resolve conflicts that arise in the legislative process. Congress gets the credit for passing a law, but the federal workforce gets the challenge of implementing it.

administrative discretion
Authority given by Congress to the federal bureaucracy to use reasonable judgment in implementing the laws.

Whether a law is clear or ambiguous, most agencies implement its provisions with three primary tools: (1) **rules** for enforcing the law, which are produced through the **rule-making process**; (2) revenues collected from individuals and corporations through taxes; and (3) spending programs for providing benefits to society through Social Security and Medicare, and hiring employees such as military personnel. The bureaucracy also helps to resolve disputes between individuals and government, provides expertise to Congress and the president in making policies, and helps congressional constituents with specific problems, thereby reinforcing the incumbency advantage.

rule
A precise statement of how a law is implemented.

rule-making process
The detailed process for drafting a rule.

Making the Rules

Rules are designed to convert policies into action by providing detailed instructions to government and the nation. These rules tell citizens, corporations, and government itself what they can and cannot do, as well as what they must or must not do. Another word for rules in this context is regulations. Politicians often criticize rules and regulations, but the reality is they are necessary if laws are to be implemented.

Rules are drafted and reviewed under the Administrative Procedure Act of 1946, which is widely considered to be one of the most important laws regulating the bureaucracy in history. The act requires that all proposed rules be published in the ***Federal Register***.

Federal Register
The official record of what the federal bureaucracy does.

Publication marks the beginning of the public "notice-and-comment" period, which gives all individuals and parties affected or interested in the proposed rule the chance to make their opinions known to the agency. As we will discuss later in the public policy section of the chapter, the process can take years from start to finish and consume thousands of pages of records. Some agencies even hold hearings and take testimony from witnesses in the effort to build a strong case for a particularly controversial rule. Comment periods can last up to 180 days, but generally are closed after 60.

Many Americans have no idea where rules come from, and how they might affect the process. However, Americans can have enormous impact if they act together either in support or against a proposed rule. In 2014, for example, millions of Americans came together to stop a Federal Communications Commission (FCC) proposal to create fast and slow lanes on the Internet based on willingness to pay. The host of HBO's "Last Week Tonight," John Oliver, did his part to call young Americans into action to defend net neutrality in spring 2014. The movement was pushed forward by a handful of underfunded organizations such as Demand Progress, Free Press, and Fight for Freedom.

Few gave the net neutrality advocates a chance against $250 million in lobbying from Internet giants such as AT&T, Comcast, and Verizon. The coalition did not need millions to fight the "pay-to-play" initiative, however. They had millions of supporters ready to join a loose coalition that tweeted, retweeted, marched online and in person, and eventually crashed the FCC platform with 3.7 million comments in favor of retaining net neutrality. The advocates of net neutrality won their fight in early 2015 when the FCC voted 3-2 in favor of an open Internet.[35]

The fight over net neutrality returned to the agenda after the Trump administration appointed a pay-to-play advocate as chairman of the five-member commission in January 2017. The FCC soon followed with a 3-2 vote to reverse net neutrality in favor of pay-to-play, thereby igniting a new wave of protests that were still active as voters went to the polls in the 2018 midterm elections.

The Trump administration also pushed hard for rollbacks on a long list of environmental rules. Although it was able to reverse action on the pesticide use, automobile tailpipe emissions, water pollution, and clean coal, many of the decisions were immediately challenged in the courts. "In their rush to get things done," said one expert on environmental law, "they're failing to dot their i's and t's. They're producing a lot of short, poorly crafted rulemakings that are not likely to hold up in the courts."[36]

As the net neutrality and environmental cases show, the rule-making process does not end with formal bureaucratic approval. The process is public and every rule is subject to the same judicial review that governs formal laws, thereby creating a check against potential abuse of power when agencies exceed their authority to faithfully execute the laws. The *Federal Register* also identifies particularly significant rules in its pages. These major rules are defined as any proposal that would cost the economy $100 million or more, push consumer prices and manufacturing costs significantly higher, or reduce employment, innovation, and productivity.

At least at the start of the process, the public and lobbyists get the same information at the same time, and are free to comment on any rule they favor or oppose. All they need to do is visit regulations.gov and search for their target. (Figure 12.4 on the next page shows the increase in the number of pages published in the *Federal Register* dating back to the 1970s.)

Moreover, there is always an opportunity to reverse a rule through legislative action in the future. Although rules are essential for telling individuals, industries, and states what they must do to achieve economic and social goals, each one carries a cost. These costs have prompted a backlash against further regulation based on two complaints. First, government rules impose costly paperwork and reporting burdens on industry. Second, industries spend a great deal of money on obeying the rules through what experts call **compliance costs**. Building cleaner, more efficient power plants is expensive, for example, as is designing fuel-efficient cars. It also costs money to pay employees a minimum wage, provide family leave for the birth of a child or care for an aging parent, prevent workplace accidents, provide benefits such as health care coverage for employees with preexisting medical conditions, and seek federal approval for mergers with other corporations.

compliance costs
The costs involved in obeying a federal rule.

These industry concerns and associated lobbying by heavily regulated industries eventually sparked a 30-year effort to deregulate a long list of industries. Although this **deregulation movement** achieved its greatest success in the late 1970s with airline, trucking, and railroad deregulation, it came to an abrupt halt after banking deregulation in 1999 produced the rise of financial institutions that were "too big to

deregulation movement
The effort starting in the late 1970s to reduce rules in the airline, trucking, railroad, banking, and other heavily regulated industries.

FIGURE 12.4 PAGES IN THE *FEDERAL REGISTER*

The number of pages in the *Federal Register* expanded rapidly during the 1960s as the Johnson administration added a large number of new programs such as Medicare to the federal government's agenda. The number dropped during the Carter and Reagan administrations as Congress and both presidents rolled back regulations on industries such as trucking and airlines. It dropped again during the George W. Bush administration with another period of deregulation, rose significantly after the passage of national health insurance during the Obama administration, and began falling in 2017 as the Trump administration launched a broad deregulation campaign.

SOURCE: U.S. Office of the Federal Register, "Federal Register Pages Published Annually."

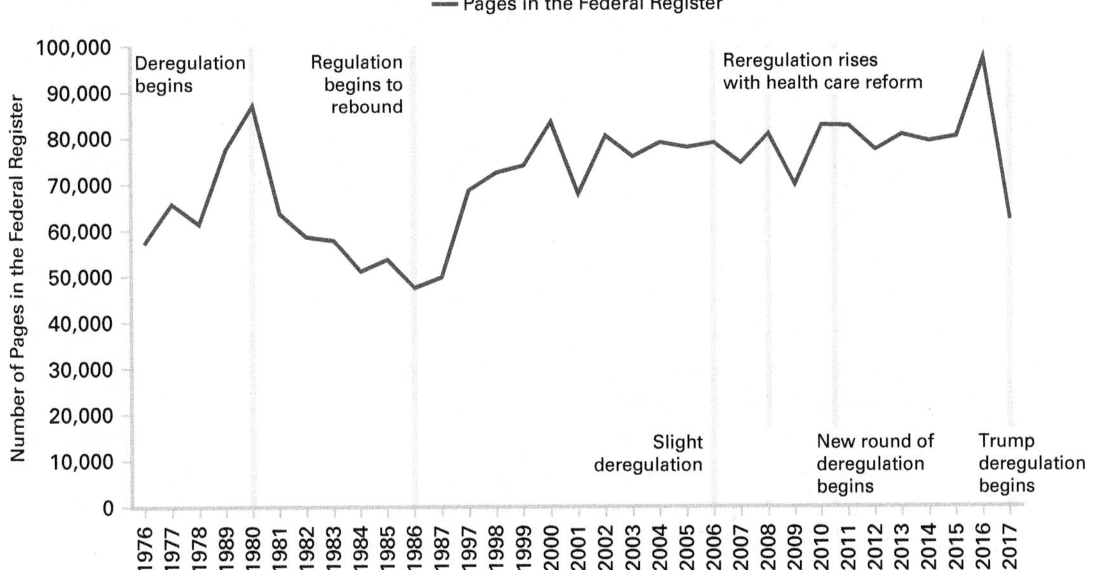

fail" but failed nonetheless as the United States slipped into a deep economic crisis.[37] The effort to reduce regulatory costs is still alive, but has shifted toward new forms of regulation that "nudge" businesses and individuals to do the right thing naturally through incentives rather than through the threat of punishment and fines.[38]

Raising and Spending Revenue

The federal bureaucracy also implements laws by raising and spending money, which have important effects in shaping economic and social impact. Some programs, such as Social Security, require a great deal of revenue in order to meet promised spending, while others are relatively inexpensive.

RAISING MONEY The federal bureaucracy is responsible for collecting all revenue, including individual and corporate income taxes; payroll taxes for Social Security, Medicare, disability programs, and unemployment insurance; leases on federal lands; fees on exports and imports; and even camping permits at national parks and forests. The vast majority of federal tax revenues are collected by the Internal Revenue Service, which is housed within the Treasury Department. The federal government uses four major taxes to collect its revenue:

1. *Individual income taxes.* The federal government was given authority to collect income taxes under the Sixteenth Amendment, which was ratified in 1913. Individual income taxes accounted for 50 percent of the federal government's tax revenue in 2018.[39]
2. *Payroll taxes.* Payroll taxes to pay for social insurance (Social Security and Medicare) accounted for more than a third of the federal government's revenue in 2018, and are the fastest-growing source of revenue. Most workers pay more in Social Security taxes than in individual income taxes.

3. *Corporate income taxes.* Corporate income taxes have fallen steadily from their historic high of almost 40 percent of all federal revenues during World War II to just 7 percent in 2018. Tax cuts account for most of the decline.
4. *Excise taxes.* Federal excise taxes cover specific products such as liquor, tobacco, gasoline, telephones, air travel, and other so-called luxury items. They accounted for just 3 percent of all federal revenues in 2014.

budget deficit
The result of a budget with lower revenues than spending.

national debt
The cumulative amount of money the federal government owes for past borrowing.

When the federal government cannot raise enough revenue to cover all its services, the only way to cover the resulting **budget deficit** is to borrow money by selling Treasury notes and savings bonds to individual citizens, investment firms, banks, and even foreign governments. Borrowing adds to the **national debt**, which is the total amount of money the federal government owes for past borrowing at any given point in time. Foreign nations currently own about half of the federal government's debt.[40] Treasury notes are best viewed as an "I-Owe-You" source of revenue—the federal government borrows money in the short term, but must repay the buyer when the notes come due, usually through taxes. federal government owed its borrowers more than $20 trillion at the start of 2019.

Congress and the president often mix and match these revenue sources to achieve specific economic goals. Higher tariffs on specific imports can protect young industries from foreign competition long enough to gain a share of the international market, for example, while increased borrowing and lower taxes can push more money into the economy during slowdowns.

progressive tax
A tax that falls more heavily on individuals with higher incomes.

regressive tax
A tax that falls equally on all taxpayers regardless of income.

Congress and the president can also mix and match revenue sources to make sure all citizens and corporations pay a reasonable share of government costs. The federal income tax, for example, is considered a **progressive tax** that lays a higher percentage on individuals with higher incomes, while the federal payroll tax is considered a **regressive tax** that lays an equal percentage on individuals regardless of their income. Liberals tend to prefer progressive tax policies, while conservatives tend to support regressive taxes.

SPENDING MONEY The federal bureaucracy also implements policy by spending money, whether by writing checks to millions of Social Security recipients, buying billions of dollars' worth of military equipment, or making grants to state governments and research universities.

uncontrollable spending
The portion of the federal budget that must be spent on programs that provide guaranteed benefits.

entitlement programs
Programs such as unemployment insurance, disaster relief, and disability payments that are provided to all eligible citizens.

A significant share of the federal budget is protected against cuts by strong federal laws and intense public support. This portion of the federal budget is composed of **uncontrollable spending**, meaning that the amounts cannot be cut without an act of Congress. Much of this spending is used for **entitlement programs** such as Social Security and Medicare for older citizens, hospital care for wounded veterans, and unemployment insurance for the poor. They are referred to as entitlement programs since all people are entitled to benefits if they fit program eligibility criteria such as age, military service, income, poverty level, or unemployment. Interest payments on the national debt also are uncontrollable. (See Figure 12.5.)

Social Security and Medicare spending increased dramatically between 1962 and 2012, as health costs increased and Social Security benefits went up with automatic annual inflation adjustments. The biggest cause of the increase, however, is the growing number of older Americans who are entitled to coverage. Not only are Americans living longer, but the large baby-boom generation is also now reaching retirement age. Because the baby-boom generation is so large compared to earlier generations, it is drawing down a much larger amount of federal dollars. The two programs are already the largest in the federal budget and will eventually account for more than half of all federal spending.

discretionary spending
The portion of the federal budget that is spent on programs that Congress and the president can change from year to year.

In contrast to uncontrollable spending, Congress and the president do control **discretionary spending**, which is the term used to cover the expenditures that can be changed through the annual budget process. This controllable part of the federal

FIGURE 12.5 UNCONTROLLABLE SPENDING, 1962–2018

The amount of uncontrollable spending has increased dramatically over the decades as Congress and the president have added new policies to the budget. However, Social Security and Medicare have been the most significant source of the increase. Both programs provide benefits to all Americans who qualify, and are expanding even faster today as the number of older Americans grows. By 2050, almost twice as many Americans will be 65 years of age or older than today, which will increase the amount of uncontrollable spending even more.

SOURCE: Office of Management and Budget (OMB), *Budget of the U.S. Government, Fiscal Year 2019*, Historical Tables (U.S. Government Printing Office, February 2018).

budget includes spending for programs such as health research, highway construction, student loans, and defense spending, all of which are subject to yearly increases or cuts by Congress and the president. Although this controllable spending is flexible, the amount has fallen dramatically over the past 70 years, again because Social Security and Medicare have grown so large over time. Between 1962 and 2018, the amount of controllable spending in the budget dropped from about 70 percent to just 28 percent of the annual total.[41]

RAISING AND SPENDING MONEY TOGETHER The federal bureaucracy has a final source of revenue called **tax expenditures**. This very large, and often hidden, source of revenue is actually a mix of both raising and spending money at the same time by using the tax code to provide incentives or benefits to individuals and businesses for economic goals such as homeownership, retirement savings, and college education. These expenditures are generally provided through deductions and credits buried in the tax code that reward individuals and corporations by reducing their taxes. The federal government spent more than $500 billion through tax expenditures in 2014, including $212 billion in corporate income tax deductions for employee health care and insurance, and just over $100 billion for individual income tax deductions for interest on home mortgage loans.[42]

tax expenditures
Spending that occurs through tax deductions and incentives that are largely hidden from public view.

Controlling the Federal Bureaucracy (Action)

12.4 Identify the means of controlling the federal bureaucracy.

Every president enters office promising to improve bureaucratic execution. Jimmy Carter promised to create a government as good as the people, Ronald Reagan promised to reduce waste in government, Bill Clinton promised to reinvent government, George W. Bush promised to make government friendlier to citizens, and Barack Obama promised to create a twenty-first-century government that would be both efficient and competent.

Who Controls the Bureaucracy?

Modern presidents often argue that they have absolute control of the executive branch as commanders in chief and administrators in chief. After all, the constitutional structure provides that presidents are responsible for taking care that the laws be executed faithfully, which presidents interpret as complete control over the basic decisions of government organizations.

Moreover, the Constitution gives presidents considerable influence over the bureaucracy under the take care clause, the authority to nominate and require the opinions of the principal officers of government, and the implied powers to shape the budget and oversee the day-to-day operations of each department and agency. Presidents also can influence the bureaucracy by issuing executive orders, signing statements, sending presidential memoranda telling departments and agencies to shift their attention, and even delaying the rule-making process by requiring further reviews by the Executive Office of the President.[43]

Congress, however, also has a share of control over the bureaucracy through the powers to create agencies, spend money, confirm or deny presidential appointees, and make the laws that determine what the bureaucracy can and should do. Much of this authority is used to help constituents as they battle federal red tape. Members of Congress earn political credit by influencing federal agencies on behalf of their constituents.

The Role of Oversight

oversight
Legislative or executive review of a particular government program or organization that can be in response to a crisis of some kind or part of routine review.

Congress and the president spend a great deal of time and energy monitoring the federal bureaucracy through **oversight**, the technical term for their ongoing efforts to ensure faithful execution of the laws.

central clearance system
The Office of Management and Budget (OMB) process for overseeing all executive branch communication with Congress.

PRESIDENTIAL OVERSIGHT Presidents use the Office of Management and Budget (OMB) to conduct most oversight. Under OMB's review process, departments and agencies must get the president's approval before giving congressional testimony on pending legislation, making legislative proposals, or answering congressional inquiries about their activities. Under this **central clearance system**, OMB makes sure that all executive branch communication with Congress is "in accordance" with the president's program (indicating the highest presidential support), "consistent with" the president's program (indicating at least moderate presidential support), or submitted "without objection" (indicating little or no presidential interest).

CONGRESSIONAL OVERSIGHT Congress has a number of tools for overseeing the federal bureaucracy, not least of which are the individual members of Congress themselves, who are free to ask agencies for detailed information on just about any issue. Congress, however, tends to use the Government Accountability Office or the Congressional Budget Office to conduct a study or investigation of a particular program. Often Congress conducts its most effective oversight during the authorization and appropriations process when new programs are created and spending is reviewed.

Types of Oversight

police patrol oversight
Oversight that is triggered by regular, noncontroversial contact with the federal bureaucracy through the authorization and appropriations process.

fire alarm oversight
Oversight that is triggered by urgent events or highly visible government failures.

Together, Congress and the president conduct two basic types of oversight: (1) **police patrol oversight**, and (2) **fire alarm oversight**.[44] Using "police patrol" oversight, the two branches watch the bureaucracy through routine reviews. Congressional spending committees and the president's budget office conduct most of the police patrol oversight in government during the annual budget process, when agencies make their case for funding. Congress and the president also keep track of ongoing agency performance through specific measures required under federal laws. The goal of police patrol oversight is to deter problems before they arise or catch them before they cause significant damage.

The other form of oversight is triggered by "fire alarms," in which the two branches react to the federal government's response to urgent events such as the 2010 Gulf of Mexico oil spill or Russian meddling in the 2016 presidential election. The media play a particularly important role in such oversight; using the Freedom of Information Act to gain access to documents the federal bureaucracy keeps secret, often they can uncover a scandal before a routine "police patrol" reveals an urgent problem.

Defining and Making Public Policy (Impact)

12.5 Explain public policy and identify the key steps in making public policy.

As noted earlier, the federal bureaucracy has one mission: to engage in extensive and arduous enterprise for the public benefit. This search for impact has been its mission since the first government officers and employees were selected in 1789. Name any economic, social, foreign policy, or defense problem that the United States has faced during its history, and the federal government almost certainly has been asked to solve it. Indeed, the U.S. Constitution itself was a solution to the problems associated with a weak government that was unable to protect itself.

The federal government works to solve problems through **public policy**, which is broadly defined as a formal instruction that tells the nation who is going to get what, when, and how from the federal government. Public policy comes in many forms, including formal laws, executive orders, and court decisions, but all tell the nation what it can and cannot do.

public policy
A specific course of action that government takes to address a problem.

Types of Public Policy

Public policies do not all have the same impact on society. Some public policies benefit all groups of citizens, others benefit one group of citizens by taking something away from another, and still others take resources from all groups in an effort to create a better society for everyone. These choices create two types of public policy.[45]

The first type of policy provides benefits to all citizens through **distributive policy**. In theory, everyone benefits from national parks, air traffic control, the interstate highway system, education funding, national defense, and Social Security. Although some citizens may get more benefit from a particular program such as Social Security, which is designed to provide a higher rate of return on taxes among low-income beneficiaries, every group receives at least something through distributive policy.

distributive policy
A public policy such as Social Security that provides benefits to all groups in society.

The second type of policy takes benefits from one group in society, and gives them to another group through **redistributive policy**. Welfare, poverty programs, and Head Start for poor preschool children help lower-income citizens by moving resources from the rich to the poor, while budget and tax cuts often help wealthier Americans by moving resources from the poor to the rich.

redistributive policy
A policy that provides to one group of society while taking away benefits from another through policy solutions such as tax increases to pay for job training.

Rule makers often use tools such as cost-benefit analysis to compare and contrast policy proposals. For example, electric cars reduce the nation's need for oil (benefit) but increase the demand for the electricity produced by coal-fired plants (cost). Similarly, new restrictions on carbon emissions from power plants approved in 2012 reduce global warming (benefit), but also increase the cost of electricity (cost) and may even weaken the economy (another cost).

Social Security was designed as a "pay-as-you-go" insurance system that transfers taxes from current workers to current beneficiaries. However, lower-income beneficiaries receive a higher percentage of their past contributions than higher-income beneficiaries, which makes the program redistributive. Here, young Americans march against any cuts in this benefit formula, and in favor of higher taxes on wealthier Americans to build up a reservoir of funding for the future. House Republicans had begun discussing the need for Social Security cuts as the federal budget deficit soared in 2018.

The Eight Steps in Making Public Policy

Whatever its form, a public policy develops in eight steps: (1) deciding to act, (2) making assumptions about the size and nature of the problem, (3) adding the problem to the agenda, (4) deciding how much to do, (5) choosing a solution to the problem, (6) deciding who will implement the policy, (7) adopting the policy, and (8) implementing the policy (see Figure 12.6).

STEP 1. DECIDING TO ACT The decision to act at all is the most important and difficult step in making public policy. Often it is far easier to do nothing by deciding not to act than to fight for action in Congress and the courts. Moreover, the federal government has only so much time, energy, and money to spend on public policy, which means that its leaders must ignore many problems if they are to focus on any problems at all.[46]

Thus, the fact that a problem exists does not mean that Congress, the president, or the judiciary will try to solve it. Some problems help policy makers achieve their personal or political goals, such as reelection or a place in history, in which case they decide to act; whereas others do not, in which case policy makers pick other problems to solve. Although these "nondecisions" are largely hidden from view and therefore difficult to influence, they are nonetheless important.[47]

FIGURE 12.6 THE EIGHT STEPS IN MAKING PUBLIC POLICY

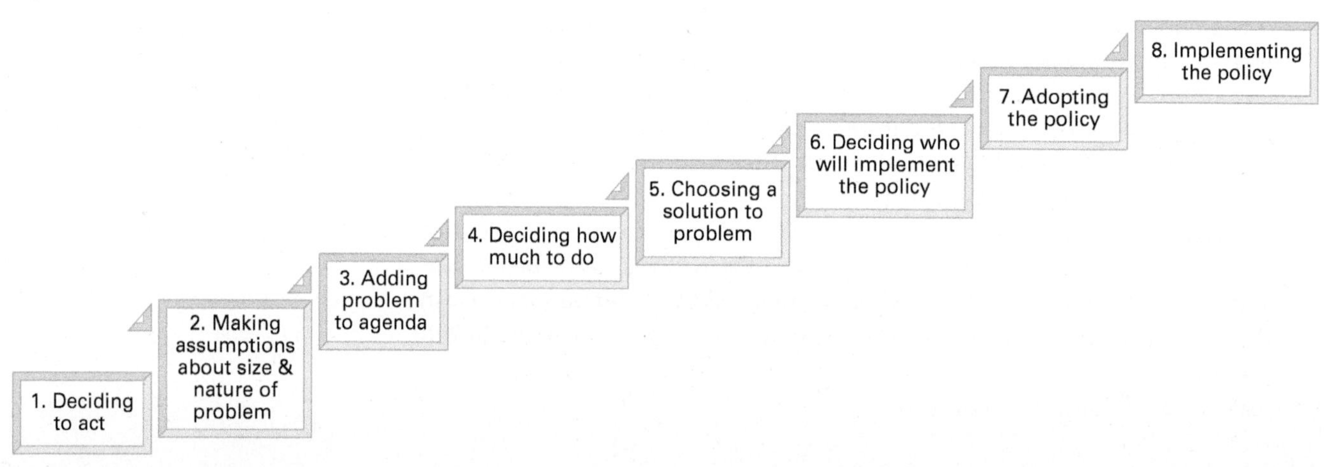

Policy makers also understand that public pressure for action ebbs and flows over time. In fact, writes political scientist Anthony Downs, "American public attention rarely remains sharply focused upon any one domestic issue for very long—even if it involves a continuing problem of crucial importance to society." According to Downs, public opinion follows an **issue-attention cycle** in which each problem "suddenly leaps into prominence, remains there for a short time, and then—although still largely unresolved—gradually fades from the center of public attention."[48]

issue-attention cycle
The movement of public opinion toward public policy from initial enthusiasm for action to realization of costs and a decline in interest.

- *Pre-problem stage.* The cycle starts with what Downs described as the "pre-problem stage": the rise of some "highly undesirable social condition," such as undisclosed and unlimited election spending by outside groups, that has yet to capture public attention.
- *Public awareness of the issue.* The issue-attention cycle continues with "alarmed discovery and euphoric enthusiasm": the sudden emergence of an issue as a topic for public debate. Books are written, documentaries made, speeches retooled, and campaigns rebuilt, all based on the sudden passion that generates public concern.
- *Realization of sacrifices and costs.* The cycle moves onward with the realization that action will require sacrifices and new costs. It is one thing to worry about money corrupting elections and officeholders and quite another to limit such spending without impeding freedom of speech and association. One solution would be to have full public financing of election campaigns, as is done in some other democracies, but that would cost money. The greater the cost of solving a problem, especially if it means tax increases or benefit cuts, the more strongly people pull back from their euphoric view of change.
- *Decline of public interest.* The cycle continues with the "gradual decline of intense public interest." Having pressed hard for action on an issue, such as universal health insurance, the public may begin to realize that change is nearly impossible given the array of political forces fighting for a nondecision.
- *Post-problem stage.* The cycle ends with what Downs calls the "post-problem stage." The problem moves into "prolonged limbo—a twilight realm of lesser attention or spasmodic recurrences of interest."

Public interest can always rise again as an old problem, such as unlimited and undisclosed spending by outside groups in elections, returns to the headlines, as this problem did following Supreme Court decisions and bureaucratic deadlock at the Federal Election Commission. But if citizens expect big problems to be solved immediately, they will usually be disappointed. Although issues such as campaign finance seem to demand that Congress and the president take immediate action before the public loses even more confidence in democracy, the two branches rarely stay engaged if support has drifted away.

STEP 2. MAKING ASSUMPTIONS ABOUT THE PROBLEM Every government decision involves assumptions about the size of the problem. Is the economy going to get stronger? If so, perhaps employment will go up and the costs of supporting the unemployed will go down. Is terrorism going to increase? If so, perhaps the federal government needs to inspect more cargo ships in search of bombs and other threats. Answers to questions about the future shape decisions about what the federal government might do.

Making even short-term assumptions about how the world will change is difficult, however. As one senior Reagan administration official once remarked, "I'm beginning to believe that history is a lot shakier than I thought it was. In other words, I think there are random elements, less determinism, and more discretion in the course of history than I ever believed before."[49] For example, the economy can change very quickly, which can increase joblessness overnight, which can put more pressure on the social safety net, which can demand higher taxes, and so on. Many experts were completely surprised in 2007–2008 when the mortgage market collapsed in the wake of billions of dollars of bad loans. They simply had not predicted it could happen.

policy agenda
The list of congressional and presidential priorities that are being considered for action.

STEP 3. SETTING THE AGENDA Choosing the problem to be solved is the essential decision in setting the policy agenda. The **policy agenda**, as political scientist John W. Kingdon defines it, "is the list of subjects or problems to which governmental officials, and people outside of government closely associated with those officials, are paying some serious attention at any given time."[50]

Defined this way, the agenda is a direct product of politics and reflects broad social goals embraced by the people and their government, such as liberty, equality, individualism, and respect for the common person. These values are core to the ideology that shapes the policy agenda, but they often conflict with each other as ideas move toward public policies. Everyone wants the American dream, for example, but we often disagree on how to get it. Politics affects the rise and fall of these ideologies through elections, party identification, interest group pressure, and a variety of other political expressions.

Problems are distinct from politics and reach the list of possible agenda items from a variety of sources. Some arise from events such as the September 11, 2001, terrorist attacks or Hurricane Katrina. Others become prominent through newspaper or television stories about controversial issues such as gay marriage, and still others because of interest group pressure for benefits such as prescription drug coverage for older citizens. Some emerge from congressional investigations of issues such as cigarette smoking, drilling accidents, hurricane damage, car safety, or government fraud.

The federal bureaucracy also monitors many issues for signs of potential trouble. For example, the government regularly reports data on the state of the economy as measured by unemployment, inflation, or new housing starts. These markers can show the beginnings of an economic slowdown or of an improving economy. Readers need only visit USA.gov to see the range of information the government provides to policy makers, investors, and the public. Through these different venues, policy makers latch on to particular problems or solutions depending on the readiness for action.

Nevertheless, the public's attention span can be very short as economic, social, and international problems compete for action. Problems such as global warming may be obvious and urgent to the world's leading scientists and a top priority for environmental interest groups, but can provoke endless disagreements about the evidence underpinning the case for action. The longer these esoteric debates continue, the less interested the public seems to become. Thus, even as former Vice President Al Gore was accepting the Nobel Peace Prize in 2007 for his work on global warming, a group of scientists challenged much of the evidence on which his work was based. Once the economy collapsed and Americans were faced with a trade-off between jobs and environmental protection, the global warming debate cooled off and has yet to be reenergized.

Policy makers set the agenda using many of the same criteria they apply to other political decisions—public opinion, interest group pressure, their own beliefs, ideology, party affiliation, and loyalty to their institution. In recent years, they also have come to rely on a small number of research organizations to help them sort through the stream of possible problems. These think tanks are, to some extent, universities without classes, and are sometimes partisan and other times independent. Many are located in Washington, D.C., so that they can be closer to the national political process. Unlike a college or university, which also produces policy research, a think tank exists almost entirely to influence the immediate agenda. Thus, many are described as either liberal or conservative.

Public interest in environmental protection generally rises when the economy is doing well, but falls when the economy begins to stall. Americans are willing to give up some growth for a clean environment, but not if they believe their own jobs are at risk. Here, a Bethlehem, Pennsylvania, steel plant awaits conversion into an art and concert space as part of an urban renovation in the city. The Trump administration has blamed environmental regulation for the decline of the American steel industry, but the more likely cause is access to lower cost energy sources such as natural gas.

STEP 4. DECIDING HOW MUCH TO DO Once the federal government decides it wants to do something about a problem, the next difficult decision is how much to do. The choice involves two options: (1) an **incremental policy** that makes slight adjustments in existing programs and budgets, or (2) a breakthrough policy that creates a dramatic change in the national agenda. This is essentially a choice between expanding a smaller program bit by bit over time versus launching a comprehensive program such as Social Security or Medicare.

incremental policy
A policy that makes small-scale adjustments to an existing public policy or the budget.

Incremental policies are generally the easiest to create, if only because they build on past decisions in very small ways, such as increasing the amount of federal support for colleges by a few hundred dollars. In contrast, breakthrough policies, such as providing national prescription drug coverage for older adults, often require citizens, interest groups, political parties, and policy makers to mobilize in a broad movement for change.[51] Because of the constitutional structure of checks and balances, incremental policy is often the easiest course of action to advance an idea.

STEP 5. CHOOSING A SOLUTION The federal government generally uses three tools for solving most public policy problems: (1) making rules to encourage or prohibit behavior through standards, incentives, or penalties; (2) using taxes both to raise money and to encourage certain behaviors; and (3) spending money to purchase goods and services or provide benefits to the public as a whole or to specific populations such as the elderly or children.[52]

These three solutions are designed to produce two types of benefits for the nation: (1) material or (2) symbolic. Material benefits can be seen and measured, and come in the form of tangible results (such as new roads, bridges, schools, and hospitals) or less tangible results (such as higher pay, greater safety, better education, and cleaner air and water) that can only be felt. In theory, for example, action to increase education loans should produce more educated workers who can fill the jobs created in the growing technology sector.

Symbolic benefits are intangible and often come in changing views on issues such as women's rights, a general sense of pride in the nation's accomplishments, or demands for future action. In theory, symbolic benefits highlight an emerging issue and create citizen action. In reality, they are sometimes a way to make a nondecision as policy makers merely express their concern and move on to other tangible policies.

It is not yet clear, for example, just how much global warming is caused by sources beyond government's control, but action to reduce global warming through international treaties can give the public a sense that the world is getting better.[53]

STEP 6. DECIDING WHO WILL IMPLEMENT THE POLICY Part of selecting a solution to implement a policy is deciding who will actually implement the program. The answer is not always a federal employee.[54] Although federal employment has been steady at roughly two million workers since the early 1990s, the federal agenda has continued to grow. As a result, in addition to the work of departments and agencies discussed earlier in the chapter, the government often depends on private firms, colleges and universities, state and local governments, and charities to achieve its policy goals. In fact, almost every institution in the nation is a potential implementer if called to action.

STEP 7. ADOPTING THE POLICY Public policy is often made and adopted by Congress through laws, presidents through their many roles such as Commander in Chief, and the judiciary through formal rulings. As noted previously, public policy also can involve decisions not to adopt a public policy.

Final adoption of a law, presidential action, and even a judicial decision is often propelled forward by alliances of citizens, interest groups, political parties, private businesses, government agencies, congressional committees, and others who come together to place an issue on the agenda and push for or against change. Political scientists generally refer to two types of alliances that affect adoption: **iron triangles** that exist for decades, and **issue networks** that come together for a relatively short period and quickly disband after adoption occurs.

iron triangle

A policy-making instrument composed of a tightly related alliance of a congressional committee, interest groups, and a federal department or agency.

issue network

A policy-making instrument composed of relationships among loosely related interest groups, congressional committees and subcommittees, presidential aides, government agencies, and other parties, all of whom share a common policy concern.

An iron triangle has three sides that hold together for long periods of time: (1) a federal department or agency, (2) a set of loyal interest groups, and (3) a congressional committee. Each side supports the other two sides. Loyal congressional committees work to protect or increase the agency's budget, allowing the agency to flourish, and pass legislation to support the interest groups, providing benefits for its members. Agencies give special services to the interest groups, keeping their members happy, and ensure the congressional constituencies are provided for, aiding in congressional approval ratings. Interest groups give contributions and endorsements to loyal members of Congress, aiding in their reelection, and support the activities and requests of the agency, enhancing their legitimacy. Policy making for veterans, for example, is achieved through an iron triangle composed of the Department of Veterans Affairs, the House and Senate Veterans Committees, and a long list of interest groups that represent veterans, such as the American Legion and Veterans of Foreign Wars.

Iron triangles have been largely replaced by much looser collections of participants in issue networks. As political scientist Hugh Heclo has argued, the notion that iron triangles make all policy was "not so much wrong as it was disastrously incomplete" in today's complicated policy environment.[55] The increasing number of small, highly specialized interest groups makes an iron triangle nearly impossible to create, if only because Congress and federal agencies can no longer identify a steady occupant for the third corner of the triangle. They have to find temporary allies, depending on the issue. There is nothing "iron" about such coalitions: they last only as long as an issue is hot.

Issue networks concentrate power in the relatively small number of individuals who organize and maintain them as the issue-attention cycle moves forward. These networks are composed of interest groups, members of Congress, and outside lobbyists, pollsters, and organizers. Some political scientists thus refer to the rise of well-financed issue networks—such as those that promote prescription drug coverage for older consumers or tax cuts for business—as a form of elitism, not pluralism, in which a very small number of actors accelerate or delay action. Medicare prescription drug coverage, for example, engaged an issue network of drug companies, the AARP, and hospitals.

STEP 8. IMPLEMENTING THE POLICY The policy process ends with formal implementation of a law. Although rules are an important way to implement the laws, implementation also can involve the hiring of new government employees, building new Web sites, increasing the size of benefit checks or reducing taxes, creating new departments and agencies, and even writing contracts for the purchase of goods and services.

In a sense, the implementation process never ends, in part because Congress, the president, and the judiciary are often making new policies that change the implementation of existing programs. Making public policy is often an unpredictable process. It can start with any step and skip back and forth as politics shapes everything from the decision to act to running the program.

Does the Bureaucracy Work? (Impact)

12.6 Identify the challenges the federal government faces in implementing public policy.

Despite complaints about big government, most Americans do not support massive cuts in popular programs such as Social Security and Medicare, nor do they support deep cuts in defense, transportation, or education. Although most Americans believe the federal bureaucracy and its employees create important policy, many also believe the impact of that policy comes with too much waste and too many errors.

This is not to argue that the federal bureaucracy always makes mistakes. Indeed, the federal government accomplishes the impossible every day, and many departments and agencies such as the National Aeronautics and Space Administration (NASA) and Centers for Disease Control receive high marks from the public.

Nevertheless, the federal bureaucracy faces significant challenges in helping the president faithfully execute the laws. And it is coming close to violating all six of Hamilton's principles for effective government, which we discussed at the beginning of this chapter, in the following ways:

1. *The government's mission is too big to execute.* The federal government cannot faithfully execute the laws without the resources to do so. But those resources have been difficult to find in an era of aggressive efforts to reduce federal spending and employment. At the same time, Congress and the president have shown no reluctance to give the federal bureaucracy new jobs to do, including the administration of national health care.
2. *The government is too cluttered to command.* The federal bureaucracy is burdened with too much duplication and overlap between departments and agencies that share many of the same tasks, but do not have full control over implementation. In 2014, for example, the federal organization chart contained more than 100 programs dealing with transportation policy, 82 that sought to improve education quality, 80 to support economic development, 47 that focused on job training for the unemployed, 20 that were devoted to homelessness, and 17 that supported more disaster preparedness.[56]
3. *The Senate takes too long to confirm the senior officers of government.* Presidents cannot guide the government unless their senior officers are nominated and confirmed quickly. The presidential appointments process, however, has become so slow and cumbersome that many senior posts remain vacant for months at the start of a new administration. Whereas the Kennedy administration was up and running within three months of Inauguration Day in 1960, the Obama administration was not fully staffed until the start of its second year in 2009.
4. *The government has too little vigor and not enough expedition.* The federal government is under increasing criticism for being too bureaucratic to act, but it also has absorbed large cuts in its operating budgets. The government shutdown was not

the only source of frustration for citizens who needed government's help. Federal employees were ordered to stay home on unpaid leave throughout 2013 and 2014, for example, while their agency operating budgets for needed supplies were frozen.

5. *Young Americans are less interested in government jobs.* Most college graduates still believe that the federal bureaucracy offers good salaries and benefits, but are increasingly worried about its reputation and job security, especially in the wake of the recent government shutdown. However, as noted earlier, the "bureaucrat bashing" by angry members of Congress and frustrated citizens may have contributed to the declining interest in federal service among young Americans. Despite all the bad press on how little young Americans care about helping others, most members of the "millennial generation" actually care a great deal about creating impact with their lives and are searching for meaningful work in government, the private sector, and among nonprofit charities. But increasingly they believe that the federal bureaucracy will not meet this goal.
6. *Government keeps too many secrets.* The federal bureaucracy has a legitimate duty to protect the nation's secrets from our adversaries. But recent experience with the National Security Agency's domestic surveillance of ordinary Americans suggests that the government may be keeping too many secrets, and collecting too much unnecessary information.

Many of these problems can be traced to the recent conflict over the role of the federal government in today's complex world. Liberals tend to argue that the public wants more of virtually everything the bureaucracy delivers, from Social Security to the mail, and that public demand for less government is just a reaction to conservative smear tactics. For their part, conservatives tend to argue that the bureaucracy spends too much money on too many programs with too much waste and intrusion into private life. Whatever the public's view, the more Congress and the president fight about the resources needed for faithful execution of the laws, the less likely it is that the bureaucracy can do its job. And as the ability to do its job declines, the more doubts the public has about the bureaucracy's performance.

The 9/11 terrorist attacks killed 3,000 Americans and sparked the war on terrorism. It also produced dozens of new laws designed to protect the nation, including new agencies such as the Department of Homeland Security and Directorate of National Intelligence, new laws authorizing the Iraq and Afghanistan wars, and new fears of domestic terrorism. Here, a firefighter weeps after the World Trade Center towers collapsed on 9/11.

This conflict framed the 2017 budget debate. The Trump administration's budget contained deep cuts in federal spending matched with equally dramatic cuts in taxes on high-income Americans. The $4 trillion budget included cuts to popular programs such as Meals on Wheels and cancer research, while concentrating its tax cuts at the highest income levels as a way to stimulate the economy. The budget appealed to Trump's conservative base but was declared dead-on-arrival by both congressional parties in favor of incremental spending adjustments that remain the traditional option for deciding how much to do. Americans may believe government wastes their taxes, but most want government to deliver more of the services they favor.

These doubts have increased in recent years. As shown in Figure 12.7, many Americans believe that the federal government has too much power. Much of the increase is related to the conflict between the president and Congress over the national budget, but there is also growing concern about government performance. Thus, the percentage of Americans who say the government wastes too much money and is inefficient has grown over the past two decades. Finally, the percentage of Americans who do not trust the federal government to do the right thing has risen steadily since 2001.

Improving public confidence in the bureaucracy depends in part on public engagement. Citizens can make a great difference in shaping rules, monitoring bureaucratic performance, and prompting Congress and the president to adopt needed reforms to prevent government mistakes. Citizens also can support the many interest groups that lobby for good government, and can now keep their own watchful eye over government by visiting government Web sites and collecting information. There is an old saying in politics that Americans get the government they deserve. The more citizens demand better government, the better government they will get.

FIGURE 12.7 DOES THE FEDERAL GOVERNMENT HAVE TOO MUCH POWER?

Views of government power relate closely to party identification and other standard measures of political ideology. They also relate to the public's beliefs that the federal government is wasteful and inefficient, and their general distrust in their leaders.

SOURCE: The Gallup Poll, available at trump http://news.gallup.com/poll/220199/majority-say-federal-government-power.aspx.

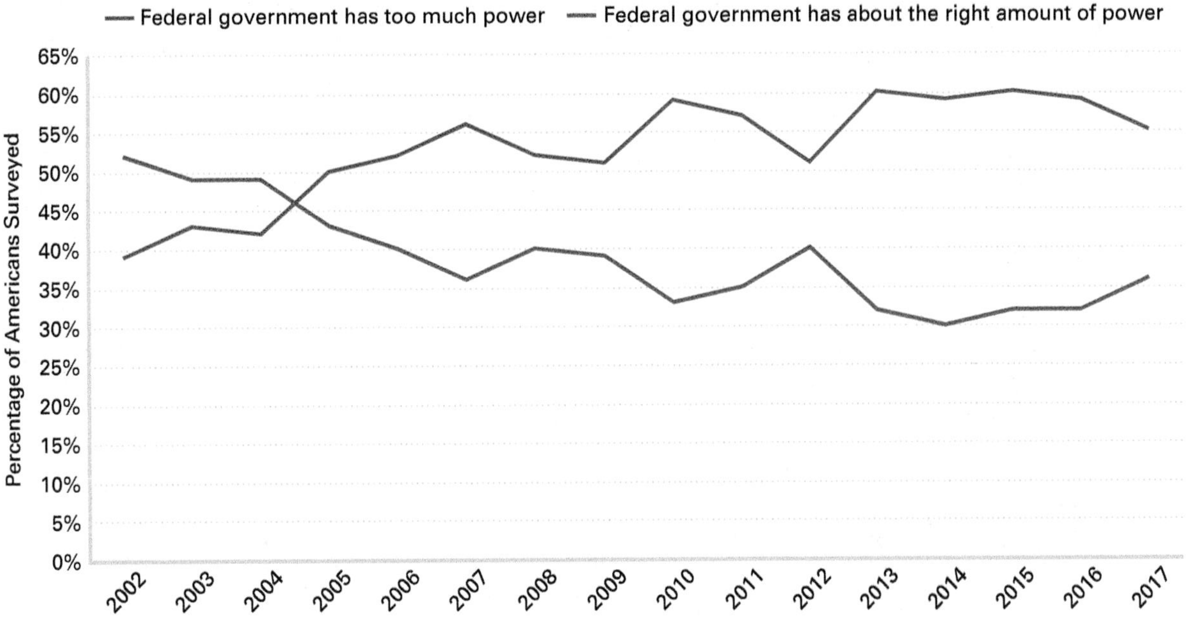

CONCLUSION

The federal bureaucracy's war against disease is far from over. Although it has won major battles against life-threatening communicable diseases such as polio, and made progress against some cancers, it has yet to conquer other forms of cancer and heart disease. It is also struggling to address the opioid epidemic as the death toll mounts in distraught states such as New Hampshire and West Virginia.

Public health programs have been successful in the past half-century in prolonging life for most Americans. This longer life has its costs, however, as diseases such as Alzheimer's, arthritis, and obesity take their toll. It is one thing to live a longer life, and quite another to live that life without pain, suffering, and loneliness. For the government and working-age persons especially, there is also the challenge of funding the social safety net for what some estimate will be more than 100 million Americans over 65 years old by 2050, compared to fewer than 50 million today.[57] Solutions will require a public willing to make compromises on policies like raising the retirement age, rewarding personal savings, and lowering medical costs. These problems are all solvable, but only if all generations come to the table. Younger Americans have been less involved in this issue and politics generally. You have a large stake in finding a workable solution to the policy consequences of our greater longevity.

REVIEW THE CHAPTER

The Constitutional Foundations of the Bureaucracy (Structure)

12.1 Outline the development of the federal bureaucracy, p. 362.

The Framers assumed that there would be a federal bureaucracy but that it would be small. The Constitution gives the presidency the power as administrator in chief to faithfully execute the laws, but gives Congress the power to pass the laws. The Framers assumed that the executive branch would contain primarily the departments that already had been created, and hence the bureaucracy would remain small. Nevertheless, the Framers appeared to agree with Hamilton that the bureaucracy would (1) have a big mission, (2) have a clear chain of command, (3) be led by talented senior officers, (4) act with "vigor and expedition," (5) recruit talented young Americans for the workforce, and (6) be open to inspection.

Organizing the Bureaucracy (Structure)

12.2 Describe how the federal bureaucracy is organized and staffed, p. 364.

The federal bureaucracy is organized into four different types of institutions: (1) departments, (2) independent stand-alone agencies, (3) independent regulatory commissions, and (4) government corporations. In turn, these organizations employ three types of bureaucrats: (1) presidential appointees, (2) senior executives, and (3) civil servants. Almost all civil servants today are selected by the merit system that replaced Andrew Jackson's spoils system, which awarded jobs to members of the ruling political party. Civil servants are governed by a set of rules under the Hatch Act that limit their participation in the election system.

The Bureaucracy's Job (Action)

12.3 Describe the roles and responsibilities of the federal bureaucracy, p. 375.

The federal bureaucracy generally makes rules, raises revenues, or spends money to implement the laws. Rules tell citizens what they can and cannot do and are enforced by the federal bureaucracy; taxes generate revenues and reward certain activities such as home ownership; and spending supports the purchase of goods and services and pays for benefits such as unemployment insurance. Most of the federal budget is uncontrollable, meaning that anyone who qualifies for programs such as Social Security, unemployment insurance, health care for the poor, and Medicare must be given benefits regardless of the impact on the federal budget.

Controlling the Federal Bureaucracy (Action)

12.4 Identify the means of controlling the federal bureaucracy, p. 379.

The federal bureaucracy has at least two immediate supervisors: Congress and the president. It must pay considerable attention as well to the courts and their rulings and to well-organized interest groups and public opinion. Despite their efforts to ensure accountability, Congress and the president frequently give vague instructions to the bureaucracy, which undermines faithful execution of the laws. The two branches often try to limit bureaucratic mistakes through oversight by the Office of Management and Budget and congressional committees.

Defining and Making Public Policy (Impact)

12.5 Explain public policy and identify the key steps in making public policy, p. 381.

Public policies are made through laws, presidential decisions, and judicial rulings, but are implemented by the bureaucracy. Public policies are attempts to solve significant national problems and come in two broad types: distributive (which provide benefits to all groups in society), and redistributive (which provide benefits to one group in society at the expense of another). But both types of policy involve a process that includes eight steps: (1) deciding to act; (2) making assumptions about the problem; (3) putting the problem on the agenda, which can involve nondecisions; (4) deciding how much to do; (5) choosing a solution to the problem; (6) deciding who will deliver the goods or services; (7) passing a law and making rules for implementation; and (8) running the program itself. The steps do not always occur in order. Some political scientists see problems, solutions, political actors, and so forth as "streams" that flow through the institutions of government and only occasionally come together.

Does the Bureaucracy Work? (Impact)

12.6 Identify the challenges the federal government faces in implementing public policy, p. 387.

Although many Americans approve of specific agencies such as NASA, many also have serious doubts about the size of government. Recent history suggests that the federal bureaucracy today violates all six of Hamilton's original principles for effective government in some way. The bureaucracy's mission is larger than its capacity to deliver, the chain of command is clouded with duplication and overlap, the presidential appointments process is slow, the bureaucracy is hobbled by budget cuts, young Americans are losing interest in government careers, and government may be keeping too many secrets. The result is that trust in Congress and the executive and legislative branches has fallen dramatically over time, which has made the federal bureaucracy a tempting target for budget cuts that further weaken its capacity to produce a good administration.

LEARN THE TERMS

bureaucracy, p. 362
bureaucrat, p. 362
inner cabinet, p. 366
outer cabinet, p. 366
independent regulatory commission, p. 367
Senior Executive Service, p. 371
civil service, p. 371
spoils system, p. 371
merit system, p. 372
Hatch Act, p. 374
implementation, p. 375
administrative discretion, p. 375
rule, p. 375
rule-making process, p. 375
Federal Register, p. 375
compliance costs, p. 376
deregulation movement, p. 376
budget deficit, p. 378
national debt, p. 378
progressive tax, p. 378
regressive tax, p. 378
uncontrollable spending, p. 378
entitlement programs, p. 378
discretionary spending, p. 378
tax expenditures, p. 379
oversight, p. 380
central clearance system, p. 380
police patrol oversight, p. 380
fire alarm oversight, p. 380
public policy, p. 381
distributive policy, p. 381
redistributive policy, p. 381
issue-attention cycle, p. 383
policy agenda, p. 384
incremental policy, p. 385
iron triangle, p. 386
issue network, p. 386

The Judiciary

CHAPTER 13

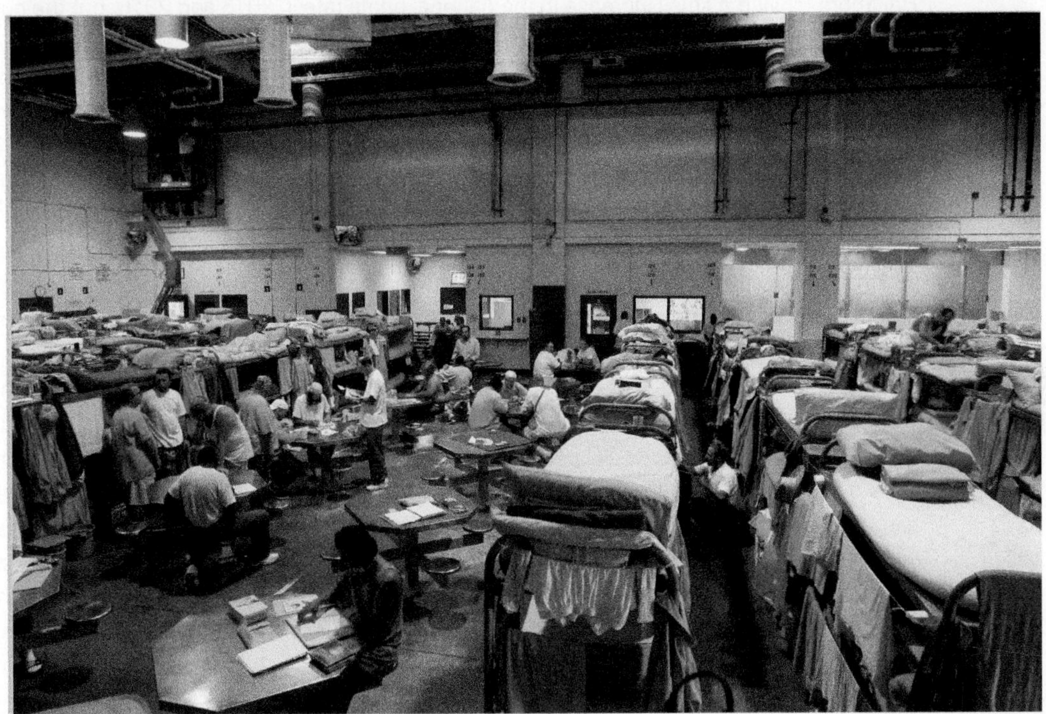

Criminal justice policies like mandatory minimums and three-strikes laws have resulted in prison overcrowding. In a case challenging conditions in California's state prisons, the Supreme Court held, in May 2011, that severe overcrowding can amount to conditions that violate the Eighth Amendment's prohibition on cruel punishment. The photo here shows how prison officials at Mule Creek State Prison turned a gymnasium into alternative housing for prisoners. In the wake of the Court's ruling, California had to release prisoners to bring their facilities in line with constitutional protections.

LEARNING OBJECTIVES

Reducing crime is one of the federal government's greatest achievements over the last quarter century. Violent crime hit a new high for the modern era in 1991 at a rate of about 750 instances per 100,000 people, but fell by over 50 percent to about 361 instances per 100,000 people in 2014. There was a slight increase in violent crime in 2015 and 2016, but a preliminary report for 2017 indicates a .8 percent decline over the previous year. Property crime declined as well. It had also peaked in 1991, at more than 5,000 instances per 100,000 Americans, but by 2016, that number had decreased by over 50 percent to 2,451.[1] During the 2016 election, then candidate Donald Trump frequently discussed the importance of crime fighting and severe sentencing. It is true that the rate of violent crime grew slightly in a few cities, particularly Chicago and Baltimore, driving a small increase in the national crime rate in 2015 and 2016, but the current rate still reflects a significant downward trend since 1991.

The federal government's largest crime-fighting investment has been in providing money to help states control both street crime and organized crime by the mafia and other criminal organizations. In 1968, for example, Congress passed the Crime Control and Safe Streets Act, which gave millions of dollars for the states to increase their police forces and to patrol the streets, and increased the minimum age to buy a handgun from 18 to 21. In 1994, Congress also passed the Violent Crime Control and Law Enforcement Act, which provided the funding to hire 100,000 new police officers, banned the sale of semi-automatic firearms, and allocated $1.6 billion to prevent and investigate violence against women (known as the Violence Against Women Act).

There is widespread agreement that lowering the crime rate benefits citizens and the economy of many formerly crime-ridden urban areas, such as New York City. But, scholars and policy experts alike disagree on what government policy or other factors should be credited with the decline. Some contend that new community policing strategies and improved surveillance technology are primarily responsible for the drop in crime, while others credit lengthy prison sentences, including now-controversial mandatory minimums, for keeping criminals behind bars and thus incapable of reoffending. Still others argue that changes in the drug market itself has contributed to the decline, as has an aging population that is no longer as likely to commit violent crime. And some scholars point to environmental factors, such as a link between childhood exposure to lead and increased aggression and criminal behavior in adulthood. According to this argument, the declining number of children exposed to lead paint and perhaps more importantly, emissions from vehicles burning leaded gasoline, contributed to the precipitous decrease in the crime rate.[2]

Amid disagreement over the causes for the drop in the crime rate there has been a renewed focus on reforming the criminal justice system. Policies such as mandatory minimum sentences for nonviolent drug offenses have resulted in a huge increase in the number of people incarcerated in state and federal prisons. And that increase has come with a high price tag. Beyond the financial burden such sentencing incurs, there is also significant evidence of racial bias in the criminal justice system, from racial profiling to harsher penalties for African-American defendants.

Many of these issues are now in the spotlight as the nation confronts police shootings, mass incarceration, and longstanding concerns about equal treatment under the law. And you are part of the debate. You may have watched the news about a shooting, or participated in a conversation on your campus. You may have talked about systemic racism, or been the victim of a crime or harassment. You may have had discussions about challenges law enforcement officers face when they so frequently need to make important decisions quickly. These are tough issues to talk about, but you are an important part of the conversation.

The courts have also been addressing other criminal justice issues, such as whether to impose the death penalty on juvenile offenders or those who are mentally impaired, or whether to impose life sentences without the possibility of parole for juvenile offenders. On these issues, the U.S. Supreme Court has reached decisions that are largely favorable to criminal defendants by banning the death penalty for both groups of offenders and requiring the possibility of review when juveniles are given life sentences.

This chapter will help you understand the judiciary's central role in criminal justice and so many other issues that are raised in this book. You will learn about the structure of the judicial branch, how it takes action on the cases that it resolves, and the impact it creates when it makes a decision. If you want to make a difference on these issues, you must know how the system works. By understanding the judiciary's institutional structure, actions, and impact, you can make a difference on the controversial issues you and your peers are talking about on campus and in your neighborhoods today.

Understanding the Federal Judiciary (Structure)

13.1 Explain the differences between criminal and civil cases and the role of the adversarial system in resolving disputes.

The Framers viewed the federal judiciary as an important check against both Congress and the president. But the judiciary lacked the institutional resources of the elected branches. As Alexander Hamilton wrote, "The Executive not only dispenses the honors, but holds the sword of the community. The legislature not only commands the purse, but prescribes the rules by which the duties and rights of every citizen are to be regulated. The judiciary, on the contrary, has no influence over either the sword or the purse."[3] So, in order to ensure the judicial check, the Framers insulated the judiciary against both public opinion and the rest of government.

The Framers rejected direct judicial election to protect the federal judiciary from shifts in public opinion. That was the method used to select many judges in the colonies, and it is still used today to choose many state and local judges. The Framers also excluded the House, the more representative of the two bodies of Congress, from any role in either selecting or confirming federal judges. To protect the judiciary from Congress as a whole, no limits were allowed on judicial terms. Federal judges serve during good behavior, which typically means for life. And finally, to prevent Congress from assessing a financial penalty against the judiciary, judges' salaries cannot be reduced once confirmed.

These early structural decisions were essential to protect the judiciary's independence. Because the judiciary has no army or police force to enforce its will or make people obey its decisions, it must rely on the public's respect for the court to implement its decisions.[4] This is sometimes a challenge, particularly when resolving controversial issues such as abortion rights or the rights of prisoners of war. But, even in the face of these challenges, it is crucial that the judiciary maintain its independence.

However, state judges who are chosen through popular elections are presumed to be accountable to the public. Although judicial elections arguably add accountability, some contend that because business, labor, and other interests often spend millions of dollars to elect or defeat judges, the real accountability is to the groups and corporations that contribute money to the judges' election campaigns, not to average citizens.[5] This is only one of the potential problems in systems that provide for greater accountability at the expense of judicial independence.

Characteristics of the Federal Judiciary

Just as the structure of the executive and legislative branches shapes the actions executives and legislators take, as well as the ways individuals and groups can act within that structure to impact policy, the federal judicial structure frames the

judicial review
The power of a court to review laws or governmental regulations to determine whether they are consistent with the U.S. Constitution, or in a state court, the state constitution.

adversary system
A judicial system in which the court of law is a neutral arena where two parties argue their differences.

criminal law
A law that defines crimes against the public order.

civil law
A law that governs relationships between individuals and defines their legal rights.

prosecutor
A government lawyer who tries criminal cases, often referred to as a district attorney or a U.S. attorney.

defendant
In a civil or criminal action, the person or party accused of an offense.

plea bargain
An agreement between a prosecutor and a defendant that the defendant will plead guilty to a lesser offense to avoid having to stand trial for a more serious offense.

plaintiff
The party instigating a civil lawsuit.

work of its judges and those who bring their cases before it. Understanding that structure is essential for participating in it and for understanding the decisions it reaches.

CIVIL AND CRIMINAL LAW Federal judges play a central role in U.S. life. They rule on controversial issues such as partial-birth abortion and affirmative action, and they often decide whether laws are constitutional. Many of these decisions are based on Chief Justice John Marshall's successful claim of **judicial review**—the power to interpret the Constitution. When it does so, only a constitutional amendment or a later Supreme Court can modify the Supreme Court's earlier decisions.

Several important characteristics distinguish the judiciary from Congress, the presidency, and the federal bureaucracy. First, the federal judiciary is an **adversary system**, based on the theory that arguing over law and evidence guarantees fairness.[6] The courts provide a neutral arena in which two parties argue their differences and present evidence supporting those views before an impartial judge. Because the two parties in a case must bring their arguments before the judge, judges may not go looking for cases to decide. The adversary system thus imposes restraints on judicial power. It also depends on you and your fellow citizens taking action to bring important issues to the courts for resolution, and in recognizing that voting in elections determines who is appointed and confirmed to be a federal judge.

The courts handle many kinds of legal disputes that fall into one of two broad categories: **criminal law**, which defines crimes against the public order and provides for punishment, and **civil law**, which governs relations between individuals and defines their legal rights. There are several important distinctions between criminal and civil law:

- In a criminal trial, a person's liberty is at stake (those judged guilty can be imprisoned); in a civil case, penalties are predominantly monetary.
- Criminal defendants who cannot afford attorneys are provided counsel by the government, but there is no right to a government-provided attorney in civil cases.
- Defendants generally have the right to a jury in criminal trials, but there is no constitutional right to a jury in state civil trials.

U.S. prosecutors working for the federal government, not the judiciary, bring all federal criminal cases to court; the federal government can also be a party to a civil action, and the federal judiciary decides the cases. For example, when Martha Stewart was tried for securities fraud and obstruction of justice, **prosecutors**, acting on behalf of the public, brought the case. Prosecutors decide whether and how to pursue a case against criminal **defendants** who may have violated the law. In some cases, they may decide to offer a **plea bargain**, an arrangement in which a defendant agrees to plead guilty to a lesser offense than he or she was charged with, to avoid having to face trial for a more serious offense and a lengthier sentence.

Undocumented immigrants enter the U.S. judicial system after being arrested in June 2018 and charged with entering the United States illegally. Under federal law, illegal entry is a federal crime punishable by prison and/or deportation. These undocumented immigrants worked for a large Ohio flower, garden, and landscaping company.

John Minchillo/AP Images

The federal government also brings civil cases to court, but so do individuals, state governments, cities, corporations, and any other party alleging a violation of federal law or the U.S. Constitution. These parties are known as **plaintiffs**, and begin a civil suit by filing a complaint requesting a judgment. They can do so, however, only if they have standing—which means they have experienced or are in immediate danger of experiencing direct and personal injury.

CASES AND CONTROVERSIES Unlike the legislative and executive branches, the federal judiciary is a passive and reactive branch. It does not instigate cases or conduct its own investigations, nor can it resolve every issue that comes before it. Federal judges decide only

justiciable disputes—according to the Constitution, they are to decide *cases* and *controversies* that have not been resolved by the parties or are not moot because one or both parties have died or dropped the case. It is not enough that a judge believes a particular law to be unconstitutional; a real case must be litigated for a judge to reach that decision. Hypothetical harm is also not enough to warrant court review. In an adversary system like ours, it is essential that each side bring forth the best possible arguments before the judge or jury. Because the decision makers depend on the adversaries to bring all the relevant information before them, if one side does not truly have a stake in the outcome, the adversarial process breaks down.

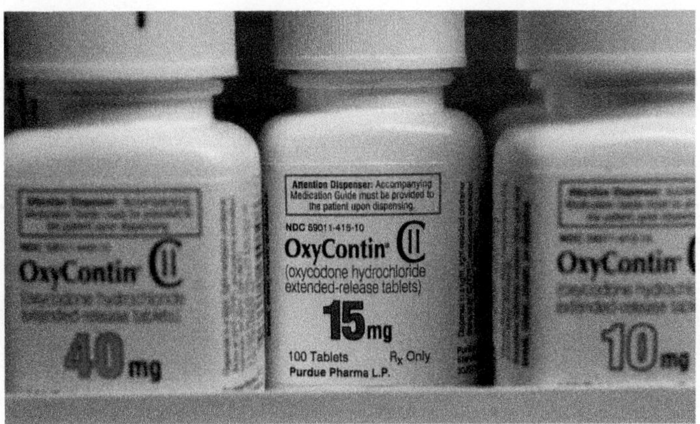

George Frey/Bloomberg/Getty Images

In a somewhat novel approach to the opioid epidemic in her state, Massachusetts Attorney General Maura Healey filed suit against the producer of OxyContin, Purdue Pharma. The state alleges that Purdue Pharma's representatives urged doctors to keep patients on higher doses for longer periods of time, meaning greater sales, without regard for the risk of addiction.

The federal judiciary has also been reluctant to hear disputes on powers the Constitution explicitly assigns to Congress or the president. It resists intervening in foreign policy questions, respecting the power to declare war or economic questions such as the fairness of the federal tax system. The federal judiciary does decide questions about whether the federal government followed the laws, but it generally allows Congress and the president to resolve their differences through the normal legislative process.

Prosecuting Cases

The U.S. Department of Justice is responsible for prosecuting federal criminal and civil cases. The **U.S. attorney general** leads the department, and is assisted by the **solicitor general**, 93 U.S. attorneys (at least one in each state), and approximately 1,200 assistant U.S. attorneys. The solicitor general represents the federal government whenever it has a case before the Supreme Court, whereas U.S. attorneys represent the government whenever it is party to a case in a lower federal court. The president appoints U.S. attorneys with the advice and consent of the Senate, whereas the attorney general appoints each of the assistant U.S. attorneys after consulting with the U.S. attorneys in each district. Some districts have as few as 10 assistant U.S. attorneys, as does the U.S. Attorney's Office for the district of North Dakota; the largest, the U.S. Attorney's Office for the District of Columbia, has more than 350.

The federal judiciary also provides help to defendants who cannot afford their own attorneys in criminal trials. Traditionally, private attorneys have been appointed to provide assistance, but many state and federal courts employ a **public defender system**. This system provides lawyers to any defendant who needs one and is supervised by the federal judiciary to ensure that public defenders are qualified for their jobs.

justiciable dispute
A dispute growing out of an actual case or controversy that is capable of settlement by legal methods.

U.S. attorney general
The chief law enforcement officer in the United States and the head of the Department of Justice.

solicitor general
The third-ranking official in the Department of Justice who is responsible for representing the United States in cases before the U.S. Supreme Court.

public defender system
An arrangement whereby public officials are hired to provide legal assistance to people accused of crimes who are unable to hire their own attorneys.

The Three Types of Federal Courts (Structure)

13.2 Describe the structure of the federal judiciary.

Article III of the Constitution is the shortest of the three articles establishing the institutions of government. Yet, as brief as it is, it instructs the judiciary to resolve several kinds of cases, including, for example, those to which the United States is a party in enforcing the laws and disputes between citizens of two or more states.

Article III is not the only part of the Constitution dealing with the federal judiciary, however. In Article I, the Framers also gave Congress the power to establish "all tribunals inferior to the Supreme Court," which meant that Congress could establish the lower courts we discuss next.

TABLE 13.1 ORGANIZATION OF THE FEDERAL JUDICIARY

The three-tiered structure of the federal courts includes trial courts, where most cases originate, mid-level appellate courts that hear arguments concerning particular error(s) alleged to have occurred at the trial level, and the Supreme Court, which hears a very small number of original cases per its Article III, Section 2 jurisdiction, but which predominantly hears appeals of lower court decisions through which a party requests the applicable law or constitutional provision be clarified.

Level	Court	Type of Jurisdiction	Categories of Cases	Case Examples
Level One	District Courts	Original Jurisdiction	District courts hear civil and criminal trials involving federal law or the U.S. Constitution.	A trial court hears a trial in which the plaintiff alleges the federal government deprived him of his religious liberties by refusing to let him wear religious icons while in federal prison.
Level Two	Circuit Courts of Appeals	Appellate Jurisdiction	Circuit courts hear appeals from federal district courts located in the states within each circuit.	The Court of Appeals for the Fifth Circuit considers a party's assertion that the district court judge erred in applying the wrong standard to evaluate a claim of race discrimination.
Level Three	U.S. Supreme Court	Original and Appellate Jurisdiction	The U.S. Supreme Court must hear cases brought to it on original jurisdiction as detailed in Article III, Section 2 of the Constitution. It also has discretion to hear appeals coming from the lower federal courts or a state high court, if it involves federal law or the U.S. Constitution.	Original Jurisdiction: The state of Montana sues the state of Wyoming for holding back too much water from the Tongue River. Appellate Jurisdiction: A criminal defendant asserts that a lower federal court judge admitted his confession in violation of the defendant's Fifth Amendment rights.

district courts
Courts in which criminal and civil cases are originally tried in the federal judicial system.

circuit courts of appeals
Courts with appellate jurisdiction that hear appeals from the decisions of lower courts.

U.S. Supreme Court
The court of last resort in the United States. It can hear appeals from federal circuit courts or state high courts.

original jurisdiction
The authority of a court to hear a case "in the first instance."

appellate jurisdiction
The authority of a court to review decisions made by lower courts.

The first Congress used this power to create a hierarchy of federal courts. Under the Judiciary Act of 1789, the first law Congress passed, the federal judiciary was divided into a three-tiered system that exists to this day (see Table 13.1). The lower tier consists of **district courts**, the middle tier of **circuit courts of appeals**, and the highest tier of only one court, the **U.S. Supreme Court**. The Supreme Court has **original jurisdiction**, the authority to hear a case essentially as a trial court would, only in cases involving ambassadors and other consuls, and cases in which a state or states are a party. In all other cases, the Supreme Court has **appellate jurisdiction** and reviews decisions of other federal courts and agencies, as well as appeals from state supreme court decisions that raise questions of federal law.

In general, federal courts may decide only cases or controversies arising under the Constitution, a federal law, a treaty, or admiralty and maritime law; cases brought by a foreign nation against a state or the federal government; and diversity suits—lawsuits between citizens of different states—if the amount of the controversy exceeds $75,000. As we discuss later in this section, each state also has its own court system that predates the development of the federal courts. Like the federal courts, most state court systems also include a trial level, an appellate level, and a high court.

Level One: District Courts

Although the Supreme Court and its justices receive most of the public attention and news coverage, district courts are the workhorses of the federal judiciary. These courts operate in each state, the District of Columbia, and U.S. territories. In 2017, they heard nearly 268,000 civil cases and just over 77,000 criminal cases.[7] There are 678 judgeships in the 94 district courts across the country, at least one in every state.

District courts are the trial courts where nearly all federal cases begin. They make decisions on the death penalty, drug crimes, and a range of civil law violations. District court judges normally hold trials and decide cases individually. However, because reapportionment of congressional districts and voting rights are so important to the nation, they hear cases concerned with these issues in three-judge panels made up of at least one district court judge, one circuit court judge, and one other judge who may be a district or circuit court judge, typically from the appellate circuit in which the case originated.

Level Two: Circuit Courts of Appeals

District court decisions can be *appealed,* or taken to a higher court for further review, should the losing party allege that an error occurred during a trial. For example, the losing party might contend that the trial judge issued inappropriate jury instructions or that evidence was erroneously admitted. It is not sufficient for a party to appeal simply because they did not like the trial court's decision, nor can the government appeal a not-guilty verdict in a criminal proceeding. Nearly all appeals are reviewed by federal courts of appeals. Judges in these courts are bound by **precedent**, or decisions previously made by courts of appeals and the Supreme Court, but they have considerable discretion in applying these earlier decisions to new cases. Although most of their cases come up from federal district courts, federal regulatory commissions bring their cases to the courts of appeals directly. For example, Federal Energy Regulatory Commission decisions can be appealed to the U.S. Court of Appeals for the District of Columbia Circuit. The decision of that court can be appealed to the U.S. Supreme Court.

Courts of appeals are located geographically in 11 *judicial circuits* that include all of the states and U.S. territories (see Figure 13.1 for a map of the states included in each of the circuits). In addition, there is also a circuit solely for the District of Columbia as well as the Court of Appeals for the Federal Circuit, the latter of which has nationwide jurisdiction over a number of subjects, such as patents and international trade. The District of Columbia Circuit hears the largest number of cases challenging federal statutes, regulations, and administrative decisions. Circuit courts normally operate as panels of three judges; in 2017, they decided more than 50,000 cases.

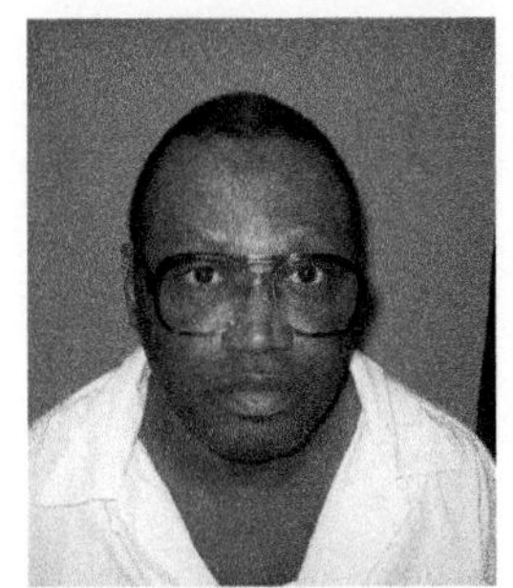

Vernon Madison, an inmate on Alabama's death row, was convicted of killing a police officer in April 1985. Supreme Court precedent holds that executing a person who is legally insane violates the Eighth Amendment. The Court has agreed to hear Madison's appeal during the October 2018 term at which time it will have to decide how to apply that precedent to a case in which the prisoner suffers from vascular dementia, causing multiple strokes that have left him without a memory of his crime.

precedent
A decision made by a higher court such as a circuit court of appeals or the Supreme Court that is binding on all other federal courts.

FIGURE 13.1 THE U.S. CIRCUIT COURTS OF APPEALS

The federal system has 13 circuit courts of appeals. Eleven are determined by geography; these courts of appeals hear appeals from federal district courts located in each of the states that make up the circuit. In addition, the District of Columbia Circuit handles appeals from the federal district court for the District of Columbia, and a Federal Circuit hears specialized cases such as those involving patent law or those decided by the U.S. Court of International Trade.

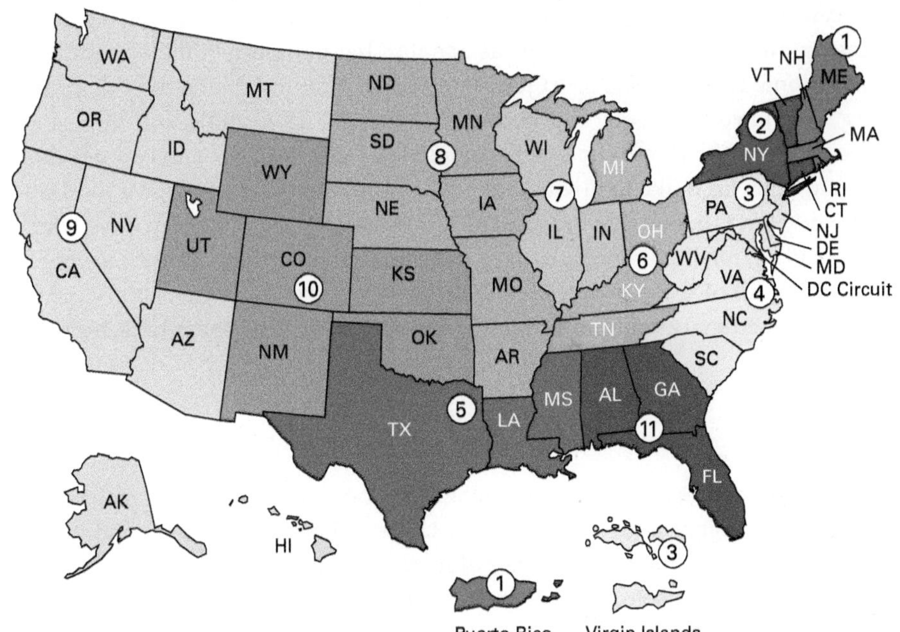

Except in unusual circumstances, courts of appeals can resolve only cases that have been decided by district courts. Nevertheless, their decisions are usually final. Less than 1 percent of their decisions are appealed to the Supreme Court. To learn more about the federal courts, visit the Web site of the Administrative Office of the U.S. Courts (www.uscourts.gov).

Level Three: The Supreme Court

The Constitution established only one court of appeals for the entire nation: the Supreme Court, or the "court of last resort." Once the Supreme Court makes a decision, the dispute or case is over.

Compared with Congress and the presidency, the Supreme Court has changed the least since its creation. There are nine seats on the Supreme Court today, compared with six in 1789, and the Court moved into its own building only in 1935. Before then it had shared space with the House and Senate in the U.S. Capitol building. Unlike the current practice in both houses of Congress, oral arguments before the Court are not televised, and the justices still appear in robes. Many of the Court's unique characteristics persist due to the constitutional protections the Framers put in place. Given its importance, we will turn to a more in-depth discussion of the Supreme Court later in this chapter.

OTHER FEDERAL COURTS The national government has a set of additional specialized courts that deal with mostly administrative matters. These can include legal issues like bankruptcy, taxes, and veterans appeals. Similarly, individuals having legal claims regarding Social Security, patents, or copyright will appear before an administrative law judge who specializes in cases involving these issues. There are also specialized federal courts which determine when the government can conduct surveillance of citizens the government has reason to believe may be spies or terrorists. There are also territorial courts for places like Samoa, Guam, or the Virgin Islands.

Immigration courts also have specialized jurisdiction. For example in 2018, when President Trump ordered a policy of separating parents from children of immigrants seeking asylum in the United States, one of the issues was how long the parents would have to wait to make their case before an immigration court judge. These courts already had a two-year backlog including about 700,000 active cases, or about 2,000 cases per judge. The number of pending cases has increased by 25 percent since President Trump took office.[8] Given the tremendous backlog and increasing number of new cases, Texas Senator Ted Cruz urged the appointment of 375 additional immigration court judges. President Trump dismissed this proposal, saying "We have to have a real border, not judges. Thousands and thousands of judges they want to hire. Who are these people? . . . Seriously, what country does it? They said, 'Sir, we'd like to hire about 5,000 or 6,000 more judges.' Five thousand or 6,000. Now, can you imagine the graft that must take place?"[9] Trump days later sent a tweet calling for the immediate deportation of even asylum seekers, saying: "We cannot allow all of these people to invade our Country. When somebody comes in, we must immediately, with no Judges or Court Cases, bring them back from where they came."[10]

Judicial Federalism: State and Federal Courts

Unlike most countries, which have a single national judicial system that makes all decisions on criminal and civil laws, the United States has both federal and state courts. Each state maintains a judiciary of its own, and many large cities and counties have judicial systems as complex as those of the states. As in the federal system, state judicial power is divided between trial courts (and other special courts such as traffic courts) and one or more levels of appellate courts. State courts hear the overwhelming majority of cases in the U.S. legal system—in 2009, overall state civil and criminal caseloads numbered more than 100 million, though that figure has dropped closer to 95 million in the years since then.[11]

State courts primarily interpret and apply their state constitutions and law. When their decisions are based solely on state law, their rulings may not be appealed to or reviewed by federal courts. Only when a decision raises a federal question requiring the application of the Bill of Rights or other federal law is a federal court able to review it. Federal courts do have **writ of *habeas corpus*** jurisdiction, or the power to release persons from custody if a judge determines they are being detained unconstitutionally, and may review criminal convictions in state courts if they believe that an accused person's federal constitutional and legal rights have been violated. Except for *habeas corpus* jurisdiction, the Supreme Court is the only federal court that may review state court decisions, and only in cases presenting a conflict with federal law.

writ of *habeas corpus*
A court order requiring explanation to a judge of why a prisoner is being held in custody.

Other than the original jurisdiction the Constitution grants to the Supreme Court, no federal court has any jurisdiction except that granted to it by an act of Congress. Congress controls the Supreme Court's appellate jurisdiction (as we discuss later in the chapter) and, as mentioned earlier, also established the three-tiered structure of the federal court system through legislation, beginning with the Judiciary Act of 1789. Congress could technically eliminate the lower federal courts, but that is entirely unlikely given their heavy caseloads.

The Politics of Appointing Federal Judges (Structure)

13.3 Explain the criteria for selecting and the process of approving federal judges and Supreme Court justices.

The Constitution sets absolutely no requirements for serving on the Supreme Court, nor did the first Congress create any requirements for the lower courts. Because judges were to be appointed by the president with the advice and consent of the Senate, the Framers assumed that judges would be experienced in the law. As Alexander Hamilton explained, "there can be but few men in the society who will have sufficient skill in the laws to qualify them for the stations of judges. And making the proper deductions for the ordinary depravity of human nature, the number must be still smaller of those who unite the requisite integrity with the requisite knowledge."[12]

Much as the Framers believed that the judiciary should be independent, the appointment process gives presidents and the Senate ample opportunity to influence the direction of the courts. Indeed, George Washington established two precedents in judicial appointments. First, his appointees were his political and ideological allies—all of Washington's appointees belonged to his Federalist Party. Second, every state was represented on some court somewhere, thereby ensuring at least some judicial representation across the nation.

Presidents have continued to follow Washington's lead on these two points. They nominate judges who are likely to agree with them on the key issues before the courts and tend to nominate judges from their own party. Presidents see these nominations as one of the most important legacies of their time in office. Indeed, if a president is able to appoint a 50-year-old justice, that person could continue to affect law in the United States for 30 years or more beyond the president's term.

TABLE 13.2 MOVING UP TO THE SUPREME COURT

U.S. Supreme Court justices tend to be chosen from among the ranks of prominent lower federal or state court judges, but may also have political or executive branch experience.

Job Experience	Number of Appointees	Most Recent Example
Federal Judges	33	Brett Kavanaugh, 2018
Practicing Lawyers	22	Lewis F. Powell, 1971
State Court Judges	18	Sandra Day O'Connor, 1981
Cabinet Members	8	Labor Secretary Arthur Goldberg, 1962
Senators	7	Harold H. Burton (R-OH), 1945
Attorneys General	6	Tom C. Clark, 1949
Governors	3	Earl Warren (D-CA), 1953
Other	15	Solicitor General Elena Kagan, 2010

SOURCE: *CQ Weekly*, October 10, 2005, p. 2701, updated by authors.

Presidents also routinely rely on the senators in a given state to recommend judicial candidates, especially for district court appointments. As Table 13.2 shows, federal court experience is the most common preparation for Supreme Court justices—in fact, 12 of the last 18 Supreme Court justices were lower federal court judges at the time of their nomination. All of the current U.S. Supreme Court justices, with the exception of Justice Kagan, have federal appeals court experience in particular.

Making the Initial Choices

Article II of the Constitution gives the president the power to appoint federal judges with the advice and consent of the Senate. Although that language may seem straightforward, it has caused great controversy over the Senate's appropriate role. The bitter fight over former D.C. Circuit Court of Appeals Judge Brett Kavanaugh's appointment to replace Justice Anthony Kennedy evinces such controversy. Senate Democrats' strong objections to his appointment got even stronger when, late in the confirmation process, allegations of sexual assault against Kavanaugh when he was a teenager were made public. The extreme partisan rancor that resulted was unprecedented in the confirmation process and draws into question how or whether the federal judicial appointment process can be depoliticized, if only by degree.

senatorial courtesy

The presidential custom of submitting the names of prospective appointees for approval to senators from the states in which the appointees are to work.

The process through which the president consults with members of Congress is complex and may differ from one appointment to the next, but one particularly important norm is **senatorial courtesy**—the custom of submitting the names of prospective judges for approval to the senators from the states in which the appointees are to work. The home-state senators, particularly if they are of the president's party, may also develop a list of candidates for the president's consideration, especially for federal district court nominations. If the senators approve the nomination, all is well. But if negotiations are deadlocked between them, or between the senators and the Department of Justice, a federal court seat may stay vacant for years.[13] For example, Senator Jesse Helms (R-NC) consistently blocked President Bill Clinton's nominees to the Fourth Circuit Court of Appeals because Clinton, upon taking office in 1992, had failed to nominate one of the Senator's former aides.[14]

The custom of senatorial courtesy is not observed with Supreme Court appointments, but presidents do strategically consult with members of Congress, as President Clinton did on his 1993 and 1994 appointments of Justices Ruth Bader Ginsburg and Stephen Breyer. Clinton was especially willing to consult with Republican senator Orrin Hatch, then the Senate Judiciary Committee chair, because Republicans controlled the Senate and he needed their support. Before selecting Solicitor General Elena Kagan as his candidate to replace Justice Stevens on the Supreme Court, President Obama met with Senate leaders and consulted with every member of the Senate Judiciary Committee.

However, as we mention above, such consultation with Senate leaders as well as rank-and-file members does not always carry the day. Almost immediately upon the announcement of Justice Scalia's unexpected death on February 13, 2016, Senate Republicans launched a media campaign arguing that President Obama, in his last year of his second term in office, should not appoint a successor. Instead, they argued, the seat should remain vacant until the winner of the November 2016 election took office. Indeed, during the Republican primary debate that evening, Donald Trump said it was up to Senate Majority Leader Mitch McConnell to "delay, delay, delay."[15]

In addition to congressional consultation, presidents also are advised by their own White House staffs and the Justice Department in compiling a list of potential nominees. In recent administrations, the Justice Department's Office of Legal Policy and the White House Counsel's Office began formulating lists of potential court appointees as soon as the president assumed office.

In addition to this process within the government, nongovernmental actors try to influence the selection process. The American Bar Association (ABA) has historically rated candidates being considered for appointment. However, conservative groups' concern that the ABA rankings were biased in favor of more liberal judges led the Bush (43) administration to end the ABA's preappointment involvement in favor of consulting with The Federalist Society, a conservative legal group. The ABA resumed its role during the Obama administration.

In the Trump administration, the Federalist Society is again advising the White House on judicial appointments. In fact, its role has expanded. During the presidential election race, Trump knew that one reason many Republicans were concerned about his candidacy was their fear of whom he would appoint to the open seat on the U.S. Supreme Court, as well as to many other open seats on the lower federal courts. To help assuage that concern, Trump worked with several leaders of the Federalist Society and the Heritage Foundation, a conservative Washington, D.C. think tank, to develop a list of candidates from which he would select his nominee for appointment to the vacant seat on the Supreme Court. He went back to that list after Justice Anthony Kennedy announced his retirement at the end of June 2018. This degree of involvement and developing a list of candidates for the president's consideration, is unmatched among interest groups.[16]

Liberal and conservative interest groups also provide their own views of nominees' qualifications for appointment. People for the American Way and the Alliance for Justice often support liberal nominees and oppose conservatives, whereas the Heritage Foundation and a coalition of 260 conservative organizations called the Judicial Selection Monitoring Project often support conservative judges and oppose liberals. These organizations once waited to express their opinions until after the president had sent the name of a nominee to the Senate, but now they are active before the choice is known, informing the media of their support for or opposition to potential nominees.

Senate Advice and Consent

The normal, but arguably declining, presumption is that the president should be allowed considerable discretion in the selection of federal judges. Even so, the Senate takes seriously its responsibility in confirming nominations, especially when the party controlling the Senate is different from that of the president. Historically, individual senators could threaten or actually mount a filibuster.

Judicial nominations are referred to the Senate Judiciary Committee for a hearing and a committee vote before consideration by the entire Senate. Like laws, judges are confirmed with a majority vote. Even before they receive a hearing, however, all district court nominees must survive a preliminary vote, historically at least, by the nominee's two home-state senators. Each senator receives a letter on blue paper, called a blue slip, from the committee asking for approval. In the past, if either home-state senator declines to return the slip, the nomination is dead and no hearing will be held. However, Senate Judiciary Committee Chair Chuck Grassley (R-IA) has allowed some federal appeals court nominees to proceed to the committee hearing with the approval of only one of those senators. Combined with the filibuster-rules change discussed below, for appeals court nominees in particular, there are very few checks the opposing party can levy against the president.[17]

The threat of filibuster long served as a significant constraint on judicial nominations.[18] But, in November 2013, due to the difficulty experienced by the last several administrations, Senate Democrats used a rare parliamentary procedure to change the Senate rules so that lower federal court (and executive office) nominations cannot be filibustered, though the filibuster remained an option for Supreme Court nominations until Republicans changed that rule in April 2017.[19]

As we learned throughout much of 2016, senators in the majority who oppose a president's choice may simply refuse to consider a nomination, even for a vacancy on the U.S. Supreme Court. In spite of Senate Republicans' threats to neither hold hearings nor vote on any candidate President Obama might appoint, he announced his Supreme Court nominee on March 16, just over a month after Justice Scalia's death. After significant consultation with senators as well as other political actors, President Obama chose Merrick Garland, the Chief Judge of the District of Columbia Circuit Court of Appeals, for the open seat. But, Senate Leader Mitch McConnell and Judiciary Committee Chair Chuck Grassley maintained their position that they would not consider his candidacy. Not surprisingly, when President Trump named Neil Gorsuch for Justice Scalia's seat, Senate Democrats mounted a filibuster, even in the face of Republicans' threats to use the "nuclear option," that is to remove the filibuster as an option in the confirmation of Supreme Court appointments. Republicans followed through on their threat and after a procedural vote eliminating the filibuster in votes on Supreme Court nominations, confirmed Gorsuch by a vote of 54-45.

recess appointment

A type of presidential appointment that allows the president to appoint federal judges when the Senate is recessed.

Even if the Senate delays or rejects a nomination, however, presidents have the option of making **recess appointments** after the Senate adjourns at the end of a session. Presidents have made more than 300 recess appointments to the federal courts since 1789, including 15 Supreme Court justices who were initially seated as recess appointments.[20] But, with the Supreme Court's 2014 decision on challenges to President Obama's recess appointments to the National Labor Relations Board, presidents' power to staff administrative and judicial vacancies during short Senate recesses was greatly diminished. The Court ruled that only when the Senate is recessed for 10 days or longer is the president permitted to make such appointments.[21] Given that most Senate recesses are far shorter than that, there will be little potential for recess appointments to be made going forward.

The confirmation process today is daunting at the Supreme Court level, and it is increasingly so for federal district and appellate court nominees; "now that lower-court judges are more commonly viewed as political actors, there is increasing Senate scrutiny of these nominees."[22] However, President Trump has enjoyed a Senate controlled by his own party during his tenure in office, and thus a process that is significantly smoother than that enjoyed by President Obama. By November 2018, 84 of Trump's judicial nominees had been confirmed: two Supreme Court justices, 29 courts of appeals judges, and 53 district court judges. At a pro-life event in May 2018, Trump heralded his court appointments saying, "We've appointed a record number of judges who will defend our Constitution and interpret the law as written," he continued that he would likely have the "all-time record for the appointment of judges."[23]

Due to their prominence, Supreme Court nominees are less likely to have their candidacies delayed in the Senate Judiciary Committee, but that norm may change with the unprecedented delay by Senate Republicans in 2016. Supreme Court candidacies are typically more heavily scrutinized than are lower court nominees, and the Judiciary Committee hearings are certainly subject to greater media coverage. The Senate has refused to confirm 31 of the 154 presidential nominations for Supreme Court justices since the first justice was nominated in 1789.

The difficulty that presidents face in making appointments to the federal courts is not going away, particularly if their party does not control the Senate. Presidents of both parties have been faced with Senate obstruction and delay; current conditions are likely to worsen given the treatment of Judge Garland's Supreme Court nomination. This is a problem many years in the making and it will be up to your generation to find a solution. Will it require a constitutional amendment to change the appointment process? Would you be willing to be appointed to the federal bench if your nomination was likely to languish for years in the Judiciary Committee, perhaps affecting your law practice and reputation?

Ideology and Diversity

Presidents so seldom nominate judges from the opposing party (only 10 percent of judicial appointments since the time of Franklin Roosevelt have gone to candidates from the opposition party) that partisan considerations are taken for granted. But, presidents want to pick the "right" kind of Republican or "our" kind of Democrat to serve as a judge. Thus judges picked by Republican presidents tend to be conservatives, and judges picked by Democratic presidents are more likely to be liberals. Both orientations are tempered by the need for judges to go through a senatorial confirmation process that requires bipartisan support.

Just as President Barack Obama selected Justices Sonia Sotomayor and Elena Kagan, who are each reflective of his more liberal ideology, President Trump's choices of Neil Gorsuch and Brett Kavanaugh were chosen to appeal to the Republican Party's conservative base. The appointments of these new justices have shaped the Supreme Court in important ways over the last decade. Justice Kavanaugh's appointment to fill the seat left vacant by Justice Kennedy's retirement will likely have the most significant effect on the Court's opinions, as Justice Kennedy was often the swing vote in closely divided cases. The Roberts Court is one that is substantially more favorable to businesses and corporations, and less receptive to affirmative action policies aimed at diversifying educational institutions, than its predecessors, although Justice Kennedy's 2016 vote proved decisive in upholding the use of affirmative action in university admissions.[24]

Today, substantial attention is paid to diversifying the federal bench.[25] Although white males have long dominated the federal judiciary, diversity has been increasing, particularly since the Carter administration. President Obama appointed the most diverse judicial candidates in history. Among his appointments were two new female U.S. Supreme Court justices: Sonia Sotomayor, who is also the first Hispanic justice on the Supreme Court, and Elena Kagan, only the fourth woman ever to serve on the Court. He also appointed diverse candidates to the district and appellate courts. Of his appointees, 19 percent are African American, 9 percent are Hispanic, and nearly 6 percent are Asian American. Approximately 42 percent are women. President Obama also diversified the federal bench in terms of sexual orientation; he appointed 11 LGBTQ judges to the federal courts, including Todd Hughes and Edward DuMont, both appeals court judges.[26] President Trump's appointments, however, have been an exception to that trend. As of October 2018, only 10 percent of Trump judicial appointees were racial or ethnic minorities and only 28 percent were women.

For the first time in the Supreme Court's history, three of the court's nine justices are women: Justices Ginsburg, Sotomayor, and Kagan. President Trump's two Supreme Court nominees, Justices Gorsuch and Kavanaugh, are also pictured here.

The Role of Judicial Philosophy

A candidate's judicial philosophy also influences the selection process. Does a candidate believe that judges should interpret the Constitution to reflect what the Framers intended or what its words literally say? Or does the candidate believe that the Constitution should be adapted to reflect current conditions and philosophies? Differences in constitutional interpretation can produce vastly different outcomes on the same legal question.

In its 1803 decision in *Marbury* v. *Madison,* the Court stated that "[i]t is emphatically the province and duty of the judicial department to say what the law is."[27] This decision, providing for judicial review, has led to substantial debate over the appropriate role of the courts. Does the candidate believe that the courts should strike down acts of the elected branches if they violate broad norms and values that might not be explicitly stated in the Constitution? That is, does the candidate espouse the view of **judicial activism**? Or does the candidate believe in **judicial restraint**, which deems it appropriate for the courts to strike down popularly enacted legislation only when it clearly violates the letter of the Constitution? At the heart of this debate are competing conceptions of the proper balance between government authority and individual rights, and between the power of democratically accountable legislatures and that of courts and unelected judges. And, although discussions of judicial activism are politically charged, the term can be appropriately applied to both liberal and conservative judges.

judicial activism
A philosophy proposing that judges should freely strike down laws enacted by the democratically elected branches.

judicial restraint
A philosophy proposing that judges should strike down the actions of the elected branches only if they clearly violate the Constitution.

The politics of judicial selection may shock those who like to think judges are picked strictly on the basis of legal merit and without regard for ideology, party, gender, or race. But as a former Justice Department official observed, "When courts cease being an instrument for political change, then maybe the judges will stop being politically selected."[28]

How the Supreme Court Decides (Action)

13.4 Outline the process by which the Supreme Court makes decisions and the factors that influence judicial decision making.

The Supreme Court is a unique institution. Its term runs from the first Monday in October through the end of June. The justices listen to oral arguments for two weeks each month from October to April and then adjourn for two weeks to consider the cases and to write opinions. By agreement, at least six justices must participate in each decision. Cases are decided by a majority vote. In the event of a tie, the decision of the lower court is sustained. A closely divided Court operating without its full membership, such as the Supreme Court in the wake of Justice Scalia's death, might well end up in a tie in one or more cases. Rather than hearing cases where a tie is likely, the Court can reschedule those cases to be heard at a later time, or even schedule reargument in a case in which arguments have already been heard.

The Eight Steps to Judgment

When citizens vow to take their cases to the highest court of the land even if it costs their last penny, they underestimate the difficulty of securing Supreme Court review and misunderstand the Court's role. The rules for appealing a case are established by the Supreme Court and Congress. Since 1988, when Congress passed the Act to Improve the Administration of Justice, the Supreme Court has not been obligated to grant review of most cases that come to it on appeal. Its *appellate jurisdiction* is almost entirely up to its own discretion; the overwhelming majority of cases appealed to the Court will be denied review. At least partly because of its power to decide which appeals it reviews, the U.S. Supreme Court's process is substantially different from that of other federal courts. Below we discuss each step of that process.

STEP 1. REVIEWING APPEALS Many appeals come to the Court by means of a petition for a **writ of *certiorari*,** a formal petition requesting the Court's review, or through an in forma pauperis ("as a pauper") petition, which avoids the payment of Court fees. The great majority of ***in forma pauperis*** petitions come from prisoners. In either case, the appeal may arise from any state supreme court or from the federal court system (see Figure 13.2 for a simplified description of the two paths to the Supreme Court).

writ of *certiorari*
A formal writ used to bring a case before the Supreme Court.

in forma pauperis
A petition that allows a party to file "as a pauper" and avoid paying Court fees.

Petitions for review have increased significantly since the 1970s as citizens have brought more lawsuits, states have imposed more death sentences (which are often appealed), federal regulation has increased, and federal punishment for crimes has become more severe. As the number of appeals has grown, however, the Supreme Court's discretion to decide which cases it will review has allowed it to hear fewer and fewer cases (see Figure 13.3 representing the size of the Supreme Court's docket over time).[29]

STEP 2. GRANTING THE APPEAL The Supreme Court will review a case only if the claim raises a substantial question of federal or constitutional law with broad public significance—for example, what kinds of affirmative action programs are permissible, whether individuals have a right to doctor-assisted suicide, or under what conditions women may have abortions. Alternatively, cases in which only the two parties involved are affected by the outcome, such as a civil suit between neighbors, are not likely to be heard by the Court. The Court also tends to review cases in which the courts of appeals disagree. Or a case may raise a constitutional issue on which a state supreme court has presented an interpretation with which the Court disagrees.

The Court decides whether to move forward based on the rule of four. If four justices are sufficiently interested in a petition, it will be granted and the case brought up for review. The justices' law clerks work as a group, in what is known as the *cert pool,* to read the petitions and write a memorandum on each, recommending whether a review should be granted. These memos circulate to all the justices except Justice Samuel Alito, who opted out of the cert pool in September 2008, and Justice Neil

FIGURE 13.2 HOW MOST CASES RISE TO THE SUPREME COURT

Most cases heard on appeal by the U.S. Supreme Court have come up either through a state high court (as long as there is a federal statutory or constitutional question involved) or through one of the federal circuit courts of appeals.

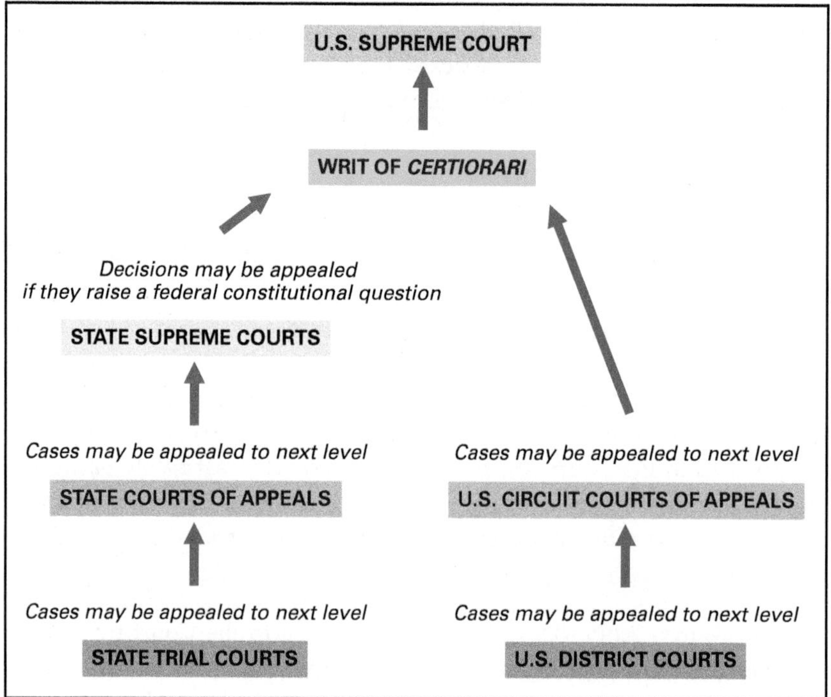

Gorsuch who decided not to join the pool upon being confirmed to the Court in April 2017. The justices seem to be more comfortable with a process that includes at least one justice's chamber working outside of the cert pool. For his entire tenure on the Court, Justice Stevens opted out of the pool; Stevens, who was appointed in 1975, served on

FIGURE 13.3 THE SUPREME COURT CASELOAD

Although the number of petitions for *certiorari* has increased greatly since the 1940s, the number of cases the Court actually hears on appeal has declined by more than half over the same time period.

SOURCE: Lee Epstein, Jeffrey A. Segal, Harold J. Spaeth, and Thomas G. Walker, *The Supreme Court Compendium: Data, Decisions, and Developments* (CQ Press, 2007), updated by the authors.

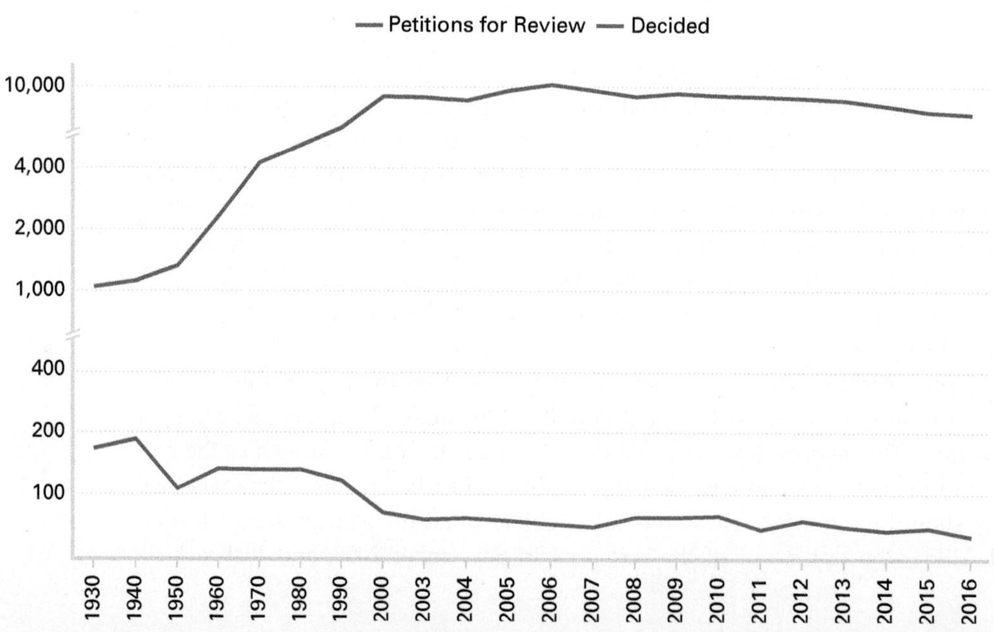

the Court before the practice developed and he never opted to join it. Realizing that Justice Stevens was likely to retire soon (and he did in 2010), Justice Alito began opting out in 2008.

Contrary to the way it is often portrayed in the press, denying a writ of *certiorari* does not mean the justices agree with the decision of the lower court, nor does it establish precedent. Refusal to grant a review can indicate all kinds of possibilities. The justices may wish to avoid a political "hot potato," or they may be so divided on an issue that they are not yet prepared to take a stand, or they may want to let an issue "percolate" in the federal courts so that the Court may benefit from their rulings before it decides.

STEP 3. BRIEFING THE CASE After a case is granted review, each side prepares written briefs presenting legal arguments, relevant precedents, and historical background for the justices and their law clerks to study and on which to base their decisions. Prior decisions by the U.S. Supreme Court itself are most highly desirable as precedent; however, the Court may also consider cases decided by the lower federal courts as well as state supreme courts in reaching its decision, depending on the issue presented.

In writing these briefs, the appellants are often aware of the justices' views or concerns about their case, and they attempt to address those concerns. Indeed, attorneys readily admit that they sometimes frame their briefs to appeal to a particular justice on the Court, one they suspect may be the swing, or deciding, vote in the case. Often, outside groups interested in the case file ***amicus curiae* briefs** (Latin for "friend of the court"), through which they can make arguments specific to their members and of interest to the justices.

***amicus curiae* brief**
Literally a "friend of the court" brief, filed by an individual or organization to present arguments in addition to those presented by the immediate parties to a case.

STEP 4. HOLDING THE ORAL ARGUMENT After the Court grants review, a case is set for oral arguments—these arguments are usually heard within three to four months. Lengthy oratory before the Supreme Court, once lasting for several days, is a thing of the past. As a rule, counsel for each side is usually allowed only 30 minutes. In order to ensure compliance with this rule, lawyers use a lectern with two lights: a white light flashes five minutes before time is up. When the red light goes on, the lawyer must stop, even in the middle of a sentence.

Although the format, particularly for the attorneys arguing before the Court, is quite formal, the environment for the justices can seem informal. Sometimes, to the annoyance of attorneys, justices talk among themselves or consult briefs or books during oral arguments. Other times, if justices find a presentation particularly bad, they will tell the attorneys so. Justices freely interrupt the lawyers to ask questions and request additional information. Commenting on the justices' verbosity, Fourth Circuit Court of Appeals Judge J. Harvie Wilkinson referred to a "hot bench" as one that asks a lot of questions. He said, "[t]he Supreme Court bench seems to me to get hotter and hotter and hotter."[30] Hence, the 30-minute time limit can be a problem, especially when the solicitor general participates because his or her time usually comes out of the 30 minutes of the party he or she is supporting.

If a lawyer is having a difficult time, the justices may try to help out with a question. Occasionally, justices bounce arguments off an attorney and one another. There are instances in which the justices are so busy posing questions to one another that the attorney may have a difficult time even getting in on the discussion. For example, before one attorney could even begin his 2007 oral argument before the Court, Justices Breyer, Scalia, Stevens, and Ginsburg each spoke, and Breyer's question included a lengthy hypothetical with a discussion of metaphysics.[31] Justice Ginsburg is a particularly persistent questioner, as was Justice Scalia before his death in 2016. In contrast, Justice Clarence Thomas almost never speaks at oral argument, although in 2016, he asked a question for the first time in 10 years.[32]

Because no cameras are allowed in the U.S. Supreme Court during oral arguments, artists provide the only visual record of the arguments. This rendering shows attorney Paul Clement making his arguments before the U.S. Supreme Court on the question of Congress's power to enact health care reform in March 2012.

STEP 5. MEETING IN CONFERENCE When in session, the justices meet on Friday mornings to discuss the cases they heard that week. These conference meetings are private; no one is allowed in the room except the justices themselves. As a result, much of what we know about the justices' conferences comes from their own notes taken during the meetings.

The conferences are typically a collegial but vigorous give-and-take. The chief justice presides, usually opening the discussion by stating the facts, summarizing the questions of law, and suggesting how to dispose of each case. Each justice, in order of seniority, then gives his or her views and conclusions. The justices typically do not view this as a time to convince others of their views on the case; that will come later as drafts of the opinion are circulated between chambers. After each justice has given his or her view of the case, the writing of the majority opinion is assigned. By practice, if the chief justice is in the majority, he can either assign the opinion to a justice also in the majority or choose to write the opinion himself. If he is not in the majority, the most senior justice in the majority makes that determination.

opinion of the Court
An explanation of a decision of the Supreme Court or any other appellate court.

STEP 6. EXPLAINING THE DECISION The Supreme Court announces and explains its decisions in **opinions of the Court**, and a case is not decided, nor votes counted, until the opinion of the court is announced. These opinions are the Court's principal method of expressing its views and reasoning to the world. Their primary function is to instruct state and federal court judges how to decide similar cases in the future.

Although the writing is assigned to one justice, the opinion must explain the reasoning of the majority. Consequently, opinions are negotiated documents that require the author to compromise and at times bargain with other justices to attain agreement.[33]

dissenting opinion
An opinion disagreeing with the majority in a Supreme Court ruling.

A justice is free to write a **dissenting opinion**. Dissenting opinions are, in Chief Justice Charles Evans Hughes's words, "an appeal to the brooding spirit of the law, to the intelligence of a future day."[34] Dissenting opinions are quite common, as justices hope that someday they will command a majority of the Court. If a justice agrees with the majority on how the case should be decided but differs on the reasoning, that justice may write a **concurring opinion**.

concurring opinion
An opinion that agrees with the majority in a Supreme Court ruling but differs on the reasoning.

Judicial opinions may also be directed at Congress or the president. If the Court regrets that "in the absence of action by Congress, we have no choice but to…" or insists that "relief of the sort that petitioner demands can come only from the political branches of government," it is asking Congress to act.[35] Justices also use opinions to communicate with the public. A well-crafted opinion may increase support for a policy the Court favors.[36]

STEP 7. WRITING THE OPINION Writing the opinion of the Court is an exacting task. The document must win the support of at least four—and more, if possible—intelligent, strong-willed persons. Assisted by the law clerks, the assigned justice writes a draft and sends it to colleagues for comments. If the justice is lucky, the majority will accept the draft, perhaps with only minor changes. If the draft is not satisfactory to the other justices, the author must rewrite and recirculate it until a majority reaches agreement.

The two weapons that justices can use against their colleagues are their votes and the threat of dissenting opinions attacking the majority's opinion. Especially if the Court is closely divided, one justice may be in a position to demand that a certain point or argument be included in, or removed from, the opinion of the Court as the price of his or her vote. Sometimes such bargaining occurs even though the Court is not closely divided. An opinion writer who anticipates that a decision will invite critical public reaction may want a unanimous Court and compromise to achieve unanimity. For this reason, the Court delayed declaring school segregation unconstitutional, in *Brown* v. *Board of Education* (1954), until unanimity was secured.[37] The justices understood that any sign of dissension on this major social issue would be an invitation to evade the Court's ruling.

STEP 8. RELEASING THE OPINION In the past, justices read their entire opinions from the bench on "opinion days." Now, they generally give only brief summaries of the decision and their opinions. Occasionally, when they are unusually unhappy with an opinion, justices read portions of their dissenting opinions from the bench, as Justice Stevens did in *Citizens United* v. *Federal Election Commission.*[38] Copies of the Court's opinions are immediately made available to reporters and the public and published in the official *United States Supreme Court Reports.*[39]

Influences on Supreme Court Decisions

Given the importance of cases that reach the U.S. Supreme Court, the complexity of the Court's decision-making process is not surprising. Supreme Court precedent is a primary influence, but if it were the only one, the lower courts could resolve the question themselves. Typically, there is conflicting precedent, and justices must decide which applies most closely to the legal question at hand.

Outside groups and other legal actors can influence the Court's decisions. Interest groups' *amicus curiae* briefs may influence a justice's view of the case or the implications of a particular outcome. The chief justice can also affect decision making by the way he frames a case at the conference as well as by his choice of the justice to write the opinion based on the conference vote. Law clerks, too, can affect the Court's decisions by the advice they give their justices, as well as by their role in reviewing the cases appealed to the Court.

THE CHIEF JUSTICE Like all lower-level federal judges and the rest of the Supreme Court justices, the chief justice of the United States is appointed by the president and confirmed by the Senate. Yet the chief justice heads the entire federal judiciary; as a result, he (so far in our history, all have been men) has greater visibility than if selected by rotation of fellow justices, as in the state supreme courts, or by seniority, as in the federal courts of appeals. The chief justice has special administrative responsibilities in overseeing the operation of the judiciary, such as assigning judges to committees, responding to proposed legislation that affects the judiciary, and delivering the Annual Report on the State of the Judiciary.

But within the Supreme Court, the chief justice is only "first among equals," even though periods in Court history (such as the Warren Court) are often named after the chief justice. As Rehnquist said when he was still an associate justice, the chief deals not with "eight subordinates whom he may direct or instruct, but eight associates who, like him, have tenure during good behavior, and who are as independent as hogs on ice."[40] As one political scientist has observed, "The Chief Justiceship does not guarantee leadership. It only offers its incumbent an opportunity to lead." Yet the chief justice "sets the tone, controls the conference, assigns the most opinions, and usually, takes the most important, nation-changing decisions for himself."[41]

LAW CLERKS Beginning in the 1920s and 1930s, federal judges began hiring the best recent graduates of law schools to serve as clerks for a year or two. As the judicial workload increased, more law clerks were appointed, and today, each Supreme Court justice is entitled to four. These are young people who have graduated from a leading law school and have previously clerked for a federal or state court. Securing a Supreme Court clerkship enhances the career of those chosen and many federal judges were themselves once clerks. In fact, five of the current U.S. Supreme Court justices, Chief Justice John Roberts and Associate Justices Stephen Breyer, Elena Kagan, Neil Gorsuch, and Brett Kavanaugh were Supreme Court clerks early in their careers. When Justice Gorsuch joined the Court in April 2017, it marked the first time a former clerk served on the Court with the justice for whom he had worked, in this case, Justice Kennedy.

Each justice picks his or her own clerks and works closely with them throughout the term. In addition to screening writs of *certiorari*, clerks prepare draft opinions for the justices. As the number of law clerks and use of computers has increased, so has the number of concurring and dissenting opinions. Today's opinions are longer and have more footnotes and elaborate citations of cases and law review articles. This is the result of the greater number of law clerks and the operation of justices' chambers like "nine little law firms," often practicing against each other.[42]

Debate swirls about the degree to which law clerks influence the Court's decisions.[43] Some scholars contend that law clerks have too much influence, especially as they help write early drafts of their justices' opinions. Others contend that justices select clerks with views very similar to their own, so to the extent law clerks are able to advance their views, they reflect those of the justice they serve. Regardless of this disagreement, however, there is widespread acceptance of law clerks' influence in the decision to grant *certiorari*, which surely provides them with an opportunity at least to influence the Court's docket.

THE SOLICITOR GENERAL Attorneys in the Department of Justice and other federal agencies participate in more than half of the cases the Supreme Court agrees to decide and therefore play a crucial role in setting the Court's agenda. As noted earlier in this chapter, the solicitor general is responsible for representing the federal government before the Supreme Court and is sometimes called the "tenth justice." Because

Supreme Court clerks typically have life-long relationships with the justices for whom they work. Here, 180 current and former law clerks line the Supreme Court's steps while court police carry Justice Scalia's casket into the building on February 19, 2016.

the U.S. government may not appeal any case upward without the solicitor general's approval, the solicitor general has significant influence over the kinds of cases the Supreme Court eventually sees.[44]

The solicitor general also files *amicus curiae* briefs in cases in which the federal government is not a party. The practice of filing *amicus curiae* briefs guarantees that the Department of Justice is represented if a suit questions the constitutionality of an act of Congress or the executive branch. The solicitor general may also use these briefs to bring to the Court's attention the views of the current administration.

The U.S. Solicitor represents the U.S. government in cases before the U.S. Supreme Court. Here, Paul Clement (left) and Donald Verrilli (right), solicitor generals for President George W. Bush and President Barack Obama respectively, participate on a panel at Georgetown Law School.

CITIZENS AND INTERESTED PARTIES Citizens, interest groups, and organizations may also file *amicus curiae* briefs if they claim to have an interest in the case and information of value to the Court.[45] An *amicus* brief may help the justices by presenting arguments or facts the parties to the case have not provided. In recent decades, interest groups have increasingly filed such briefs in an effort to influence the Court and to counter the positions of the solicitor general and the government. For example, in *Obergefell* v. *Hodges* (2015) the marriage equality case, a record 147 *amicus* briefs were filed. Although this case is an outlier, *amicus* briefs are regularly filed in cases before the U.S. Supreme Court. Between 1990 and 2001, at least one *amicus* brief was filed in nearly 90 percent of the cases. Cases involving civil liberties are particularly likely to result in *amicus* participation.[46] Interest groups may also file *amicus curiae* briefs to encourage the Supreme Court to review a case, although this strategy has almost no influence on how the case is decided.[47]

After the Court Decides

Victory in the Supreme Court does not necessarily mean that winning parties get what they want. Although the Court resolves many issues, it also sometimes remands the case, sending it back to the lower court with instructions to act in accordance with its opinion. The lower court often has considerable leeway in interpreting the Court's mandate as it disposes of the case.

The impact of a particular Supreme Court ruling on the behavior of individuals who are not immediate parties to a lawsuit is more uncertain. The most important rulings require a change in the behavior of thousands of administrative and elected officials. Given the Supreme Court's inability to implement its own decision without the support of the other branches, its pronouncements may simply be ignored, particularly if they are unpopular at the time. For example, despite the Court's holding that it is unconstitutional for school boards to require students to pray in school, some schools continue this practice.[48] And for years after the Supreme Court held public school segregation unconstitutional, many school districts refused to integrate, and some even closed their public school systems, as in Prince Edward County, Virginia, so as to avoid integration.[49]

Power and Its Limits (Impact)

13.5 Evaluate the role of the Supreme Court in national policy making.

Although the Framers worked hard to create an independent federal judiciary, judges are limited in that they cannot ignore earlier decisions unless they have a clear reason to break with the past.

Adherence to Precedent

stare decisis
The rule of precedent whereby a rule or law contained in a judicial decision is commonly viewed as binding on judges whenever the same question is presented.

Just because judges make independent decisions does not mean they are free to do whatever they wish. They are subject to a variety of limits on what they decide—some imposed by the political system of which they are a part and some imposed by higher courts and the legal profession. Among these constraints is the norm of ***stare decisis***, the rule of precedent.

Stare decisis pervades our judicial system and promotes certainty, uniformity, and stability in the law. Drawn from the Latin phrase "to stand by that which is decided," the term means that judges are expected to abide by previous decisions of their own courts and by rulings of superior courts. However, the doctrine is not very restrictive.[50] Indeed, lower-court judges sometimes apply precedent selectively, to raise additional questions about an earlier higher-court decision or to give the higher courts a chance to change precedent entirely.

Stare decisis is even less controlling in the field of constitutional law. Because the Constitution itself, rather than any one interpretation of it, is binding, the Court can reverse a previous decision it no longer wishes to follow, as it has done hundreds of times. Supreme Court justices are therefore not seriously restricted by *stare decisis*. Justice William O. Douglas, for one, maintained that *stare decisis* "was really no sure guideline because what did the judges who sat there in 1875 know about, say, electronic surveillance? They didn't know anything about it."[51] Anticipating Justice Stevens's strong dissent in *Citizens United* v. *Federal Election Commission*, in which the Court overturned two of its previously decided cases, Chief Justice Roberts wrote that if *stare decisis* were an "inexorable command" or "mechanical formula of adherence to the latest decision ... segregation would still be legal, minimum wage laws would be unconstitutional, and the Government could wiretap ordinary suspects without first obtaining warrants."[52] Since 1789, the Supreme Court has reversed nearly 200 of its own decisions and overturned nearly 180 acts of Congress, as well as nearly 1,300 state constitutional and legislative provisions and municipal ordinances.[53]

Congressional and Presidential Action

Individual judges are protected from Congress and the president by their life tenure, but the judiciary as a whole can be affected by legislative decisions that alter both the number and the composition of the courts. Because the district and circuit courts are both created through legislation, they can be expanded or altered through legislation.

"PACKING" THE COURT When a political party takes control of both the White House and Congress, it may see an opportunity to increase the number of federal judgeships. With divided government, however, when one party controls Congress and the other holds the White House, a stalemate is likely to occur, and the possibility for new judicial positions is greatly diminished. During Andrew Johnson's administration, Congress went so far as to reduce the size of the Supreme Court to prevent the president from filling two vacancies. After Johnson left the White House, Congress returned the Court to its former size to permit Ulysses S. Grant to fill the vacancies.

In 1937, President Franklin Roosevelt proposed an increase in the size of the Supreme Court by one additional justice for every member of the Court over the age of 70, up to a total of 15 members. Ostensibly, his proposal to "pack" the court with new supporters was aimed at making the Court more efficient. In fact, Roosevelt and his advisers were frustrated because the Court had declared much of the early New Deal legislation unconstitutional. Despite Roosevelt's popularity, his "court-packing scheme" aroused intense opposition and his proposal failed. Although he lost the battle, the Court began to sustain some important New Deal legislation, and subsequent retirements from the bench enabled him to make eight appointments to the Court.

CHANGING THE JURISDICTION Congressional control over the structure and jurisdiction of federal courts has been used to influence the course of judicial policy making. Although unable to get rid of Federalist judges by impeachment, in 1802 Jefferson's Republican Party abolished the circuit courts created by Federalists just before they lost control of Congress. In 1869, Radical Republicans in Congress altered the Supreme Court's appellate jurisdiction in order to remove a case it was about to review weighing the constitutionality of Reconstruction legislation.[54]

Each year, a number of bills are introduced in Congress to eliminate the jurisdiction of federal courts over cases relating to abortion, school prayer, and school busing, or to eliminate the appellate jurisdiction of the Supreme Court over such matters. These attacks on federal court jurisdiction spark debate about whether the Constitution gives Congress authority to take such actions. Congress has not yet decided to do so because it would amount to a fundamental shift in the relationship between Congress and the Supreme Court.

Judicial Power in a Constitutional Democracy

An independent judiciary is one of the hallmarks of a constitutional democracy and a free society. As impartial dispensers of equal justice under the law, judges should not depend on the executive, the legislature, parties to a case, or the electorate. But judicial independence is often criticized when judges make unpopular decisions. Perhaps in no other society do the people resort to litigation as a means of making public policy as much as they do in the United States. For example, the National Association for the Advancement of Colored People (NAACP) turned to litigation to get relief from segregation practices in the 1930s, 1940s, and 1950s. More recently, an increasing number of women's organizations, gay rights' groups, and religious and conservative organizations have also turned to the courts.[55]

Whether judges are liberal or conservative, defer to legislatures or not, try to apply the Constitution as they think the Framers intended or interpret it to conform to current values, there are links between what judges do and what the people want. The people never speak with one mind and the links are not direct, but they are at the heart of the matter.[56] In the first place, the president and the Senate are likely to appoint justices whose decisions reflect their values. Therefore, elections matter because the views of the people who nominate and confirm the judges are reflected in the composition and decisions of the courts.

For instance, in *Planned Parenthood* v. *Casey* in 1992, the Supreme Court refused, by a 5-to-4 vote, to overturn *Roe* v. *Wade* and upheld its core ruling—that the Constitution protects the right of a woman to an abortion—although it also upheld state regulations that do not "unduly burden" that right.[57] This close vote made it clear that presidential elections could determine whether the right to abortion would continue to be protected. How do you determine which candidate to support in presidential and congressional elections? Even though Supreme Court justices are appointed, you have the power to affect who occupies those nine seats and in turn impact the kinds of decision the Court reaches.

If you oppose the Court's decisions, you have several avenues through which you can make your opposition known. You can communicate with members of Congress to pressure them to pass legislation that limits the Court's ruling. You can organize to support or oppose a particular nomination to the federal judiciary. And, you can vote for a presidential candidate who will appoint the kinds of judges you would like to see on the federal judiciary. You can support changes in the Constitution that would limit the tenure of Supreme Court justices to 10 years or mandate retirement at age 70 or 75. In these ways and others, you can impact our federal courts. The Court's power rests, as former Chief Justice Edward White observed, "solely upon the approval of a free people."[58] No better standard for determining the legitimacy of a governmental institution has been discovered.

CONCLUSION

The judicial branch plays an integral role in our political system. The federal judiciary is insulated in many ways from the other branches with features like life tenure for federal judges and the power of the courts to interpret the Constitution. Protections like these are widely understood to be necessary to ensure an independent judiciary, a hallmark of a democratic society. But these features do not mean the federal courts are unaccountable to the public.

Without question, the judiciary will make many decisions related to criminal justice in the next few years. With the Supreme Court's decision ending sentences of life without the possibility of parole for juveniles, other questions concerning juvenile justice will emerge. The courts are likely to examine the extent to which juveniles may be tried as adults, whether they can be placed in adult prisons, and whether penalties such as solitary confinement are appropriate for juveniles. Continued challenges to the use and implementation of the death penalty are also likely. Although the Supreme Court has rejected the death penalty for juveniles and the mentally impaired, it has reaffirmed its constitutionality for adults convicted of capital murder. However, there are initiatives in a number of states to create an exception for the seriously mentally ill, and due to concerns about race bias in capital sentencing and the discovery of evidence leading to exonerations of convicted felons, the courts are also likely to face further challenges to capital punishment.

With your understanding of the judicial branch, you know there are many ways you can impact the federal courts. For example, you have a voice in determining the appropriate balance between maintaining safety and low rates of crime while protecting individual liberties, even the liberties of individuals convicted of breaking the law. You might express your views as a member of a victims' rights advocacy group to bring attention to the need for harsh penalties; or, you might work to support a presidential candidate who favors reforming the criminal justice system to have a greater focus on rehabilitation instead of lengthy periods of incarceration. The key is that you act to get your views represented. It is you and your children who will enjoy a continued low rate of violent crime, or who will suffer the consequences of a return to the higher crime rates of the 1980s and 1990s. Should we do away with mandatory minimum sentencing? If we do so, the judges appointed to the courts will have greater discretion in levying individual sentences. If we do not, how will we accommodate offenders in increasingly crowded prisons? What action will you take?

CHAPTER 13

REVIEW THE CHAPTER

Understanding the Federal Judiciary (Structure)

13.1 Explain the differences between criminal and civil cases and the role of the adversarial system in resolving disputes, p. 395.

The courts provide a neutral arena in which two adversaries argue their differences and present evidence supporting those views before an impartial judge. As a result, the courts are largely *reactive;* judges have to wait for parties to a case to bring issues before the courts. Civil cases are typically brought by an individual or company, but criminal cases are prosecuted by the state.

The Three Types of Federal Courts (Structure)

13.2 Describe the structure of the federal judiciary, p. 397.

There are three levels of federal courts: (1) district courts, which hear original trials; (2) circuit courts of appeals, which can only review the process by which district courts made their decisions; and (3) the Supreme Court, which makes the final decision.

The Politics of Appointing Federal Judges (Structure)

13.3 Explain the criteria for selecting and the process of approving federal judges and Supreme Court justices, p. 401.

Partisanship and ideology are important factors in the selection of all federal judges. In making appointments to the federal courts, presidents must also consider the confirmation environment. They act strategically in selecting a candidate and consulting with Congress. In recent decades, candidates for the presidency and the Senate have made judicial appointments an issue in their election campaigns.

How the Supreme Court Decides (Action)

13.4 Outline the process by which the Supreme Court makes decisions and the factors that influence judicial decision making, p. 406.

The Supreme Court has almost complete control over the cases it chooses to review as they come up from the state courts, courts of appeals, and district courts. Law clerks and the solicitor general play important roles in determining the kinds of cases the Supreme Court agrees to decide. The nine justices on the Court dispose of thousands of cases, but most of their time is concentrated on the fewer than 80 cases per year they accept for review. The Court's decisions and opinions establish guidelines for lower courts and the country.

In addition to Supreme Court precedent and justices' own preferences, a number of actors may influence the decision-making process. Law clerks often write early drafts of justices' opinions. *Amicus curiae* participants and the solicitor general's office sometimes affect the opinion-writing process through the briefs they file, as well as through points made during oral argument before the Court.

Power and Its Limits (Impact)

13.5 Evaluate the role of the Supreme Court in national policy making, p. 413.

Although the federal judiciary is largely independent, factors such as *stare decisis*, the appointment process, congressional control over its structure and jurisdiction, and the need for the other branches of government to implement its decisions limit the degree to which the courts can or are likely to act without the support of the other branches. As impartial dispensers of equal justice under the law, judges should not depend on the executive, the legislature, the parties to a case, or the electorate. But judicial independence is often criticized when judges make unpopular decisions.

LEARN THE TERMS

judicial review, p. 396
adversary system, p. 396
criminal law, p. 396
civil law, p. 396
prosecutor, p. 396
defendant, p. 396
plea bargain, p. 396
plaintiff, p. 396
justiciable dispute, p. 397
U.S. attorney general, p. 397
solicitor general, p. 397
public defender system, p. 397
district courts, p. 398
circuit courts of appeals, p. 398
U.S. Supreme Court, p. 398
original jurisdiction, p. 398
appellate jurisdiction, p. 398
precedent, p. 399
writ of *habeas corpus*, p. 401
senatorial courtesy, p. 402
recess appointment, p. 404
judicial activism, p. 406
judicial restraint, p. 406
writ of *certiorari*, p. 407
in forma pauperis, p. 407
amicus curiae brief, p. 409
opinion of the Court, p. 410
dissenting opinion, p. 410
concurring opinion, p. 410
stare decisis, p. 414

Civil Liberties

CHAPTER
14

Jose Luis Magana/AP Images

Hundreds of thousands of people joined the March for Our Lives rally in Washington, D.C., on March 24, 2018. The march was organized by Parkland, Florida's Marjory Stoneman Douglas High School students who had survived a shooting in their school that left 17 others dead.

LEARNING OBJECTIVES

14.1 Explain the roots of civil liberties in the Constitution and their development in the Bill of Rights (Structure), p. 421.

14.2 Distinguish between the establishment and the free exercise clauses of the First Amendment (Structure, Action, and Impact), p. 424.

14.3 Outline the First Amendment rights to and limitations on the freedoms of speech, press, assembly, and petition (Structure, Action, and Impact), p. 426.

14.4 Explain how the Constitution protects property rights and the right to bear arms (Structure, Action, and Impact), p. 431.

14.5 Explain the origin and significance of the right to privacy (Structure, Action, and Impact), p. 433.

14.6 Outline the constitutional rights of defendants and the issues involved in protecting defendants' rights (Structure, Action, and Impact), p. 436.

Columbine High School, Santana High School, Chardon High School, Red Lake Senior High School, Sandy Hook Elementary School. Add to that list Marjory Stoneman Douglas High School in Parkland, Florida. Just three months later, we must add Santa Fe High School in Santa Fe, Texas. The list is not one on which any parent, teacher, or student wants their school to appear: each has been the site of a mass shooting. In February 2018, a former student opened fire in Stoneman Douglas High School, killing 17 and injuring another 17. In May 2018, a student killed 10 and injured another 10 when he attacked his peers and teachers at Santa Fe High School in Texas. The list gets much longer if we include college shootings and/school shootings in which fewer than three people were killed or wounded.

Despite these many shootings and the subsequent demands for addressing these tragedies, calls for measures limiting access to guns, and particularly assault style rifles, have gone unanswered. With the shooting in Florida, there seemed to be a shifting dynamic on the issue. The surviving students themselves almost immediately pressed for new gun control legislation at the state and national levels.

They lobbied the Florida state legislature to enact gun control. The students were successful; the Florida legislation included a ban on bump stocks, after-market devices which when attached to semiautomatic rifles allow them to shoot at speeds closer to a fully automatic rifle. It also raised the minimum age requirement to own a firearm from 18 to 21. While the first two legislative features appealed to traditional gun control proponents, the third did not. Florida also allocated funding to programs providing teachers with firearms to defend themselves and their students.

The students also organized a march to protest gun violence in schools. The March for Our Lives led hundreds of thousands of Americans to Washington, D.C., and cities around the country held their own marches to call for action to stop school gun violence. The primary reason regulating firearms is so difficult is because Americans' right to own them is protected by the Second Amendment to the U.S. Constitution. When the government seeks to limit a constitutionally protected liberty, the courts require that it must have a compelling interest in doing so and that law must be narrowly tailored to meet that interest. Most of the time, the courts find that there is some other policy the government can pursue besides limiting that civil liberty. For example, some judges might think that protecting students from gun violence in schools is a compelling government interest, but that a law increasing the minimum age requirement for buying a firearm is not narrowly tailored enough to meet that interest. In contrast, the same judges might understand that a law prohibiting firearms within 1,000 feet of a public school meets the government's compelling interest and does so in the least restrictive manner possible. The judges would strike down the first law as impermissibly infringing on the Second Amendment, but uphold the latter.

Are there other policies the state and federal governments might pursue to improve students' safety in our public schools that would not burden the constitutionally protected right to bear arms? Is some burden on that liberty permissible in light of securing our children's safety in our public schools? If so, how much? The problem of gun violence in our elementary and secondary schools is unlikely to go away. The school shooting in Santa Fe, Texas, just three months after the Parkland, Florida shooting is evidence of that. Your generation will deal with the issue and perhaps you have been or will be directly affected by gun violence in your lifetime.

In this chapter, we examine the fundamental liberties protected in a free society. The state and federal courts play a key role in protecting civil liberties, and as we discuss in the next chapter, civil rights. The U.S. Constitution protects Americans from impermissible government restriction on those liberties and provides our federal court system's structure. State laws and constitutions provide a similar structure at the state level. But, courts are reactive bodies, meaning that they depend on people like you acting individually or in groups to bring issues before them. When you do, the courts establish case law, which affects Americans' lives and continues to shape the structure of government. But, even more so than in other areas of government, your willingness to act is essential in protecting civil liberties. If you and your fellow citizens do not challenge the government when you think it has impermissibly infringed on essential freedoms, these liberties mean nothing. Unless you act as caretakers of your liberties, you lose them.

The organization of this chapter is a bit different from most of those that have preceded it. In the first section we lay out the development of the constitutional structure protecting civil liberties in the United States. But in the following sections, rather than moving through individual sections focused on an explanation of structure, action, or impact, we touch on all three of these factors within each substantive section. Because legal rules derived from the court system focus on particular issues, it is most clear to address each of the liberties in turn. We do so below by discussing the structure underlying the protection of each liberty, the cases individuals and groups have brought before the courts, and the impact of those decisions.

The Basis for Our Civil Liberties (Structure)

14.1 Explain the roots of civil liberties in the Constitution and their development in the Bill of Rights.

Before we discuss freedoms, we need to clarify several terms—civil liberties, civil rights, and legal privileges—often used interchangeably when discussing rights and freedoms. The constitutional structure provides the basis for each. **Civil liberties** are the constitutional protections of all persons against governmental restrictions on the freedoms of conscience, religion, and expression. Civil liberties are protected by various provisions in the Bill of Rights and the due process clauses of the Fifth and Fourteenth Amendments.

civil liberties
The constitutional protections of all persons against impermissible governmental restrictions on the freedoms of conscience, religion, and expression, due process guarantees, and fair trial procedures.

Civil rights are the constitutional rights of all persons to due process and the equal protection of the laws: the right to be free from irrational discrimination such as that based on race, religion, sex, or ethnic origin. Civil rights are protected by the due process and equal protection clauses of the Fifth and Fourteenth Amendments and by the civil rights laws of national and state governments. **Legal privileges** like the right to welfare benefits or to have a driver's license are granted by governments and may be subject to conditions or restrictions.

civil rights
The constitutional rights of all persons to due process and the equal protection of the laws these include the rights of all people to be free from irrational discrimination such as that based on race, religion, sex, or ethnic origin.

legal privileges
Rights granted by governments that may be subject to substantial conditions or restrictions, such as the right to welfare benefits or to have a driver's license.

Rights in the Original Constitution

Even though most of the Framers did not think a bill of rights was necessary, they considered certain rights important enough to spell them out in the original Constitution (see Table 14.1).

TABLE 14.1 RIGHTS IN THE ORIGINAL CONSTITUTION

Rights and liberties are not only protected in the Bill of Rights, they are also found in the text of the unamended Constitution.

1. *Habeas corpus*
2. No bills of attainder (legislative act that sentences a person or group to punishment without a trial)
3. No *ex post facto* laws
4. No titles of nobility (aristocratic titles that had also been barred by the Articles of Confederation)
5. Trial by jury in national courts
6. Protection for citizens as they move from one state to another, including the right to travel
7. Protection against using the crime of treason to restrict other activities; limitation on punishment for treason
8. Guarantee that each state has a republican form of government
9. No religious test oaths as a condition for holding a federal office
10. Protection against the impairment of contracts (forbids states from passing laws that effectively invalidate contracts)

writ of *habeas corpus*

A court order requiring explanation to a judge as to why a prisoner is being held in custody.

Foremost among constitutional rights, and deserving of particular mention here, is the **writ of *habeas corpus***. Literally meaning "you have the body" in Latin, this writ is a court order directing any official holding a person in custody to produce the prisoner in court and explain why the prisoner is being held. Throughout the years, it developed into a remedy for any illegal confinement. People who are incarcerated have the right to appeal to a judge, usually through an attorney, stating why they believe they are being held unlawfully and should be released. The judge then orders the jailer or a lower court to justify why the writ should not be issued. If a judge finds that a petitioner is detained unlawfully, the judge may order the prisoner's immediate release.

Habeas corpus became an especially prominent issue during the War on Terror as the United States captured, detained, and tried alleged terrorists. The Supreme Court made several decisions underscoring the fundamental nature of the right to a writ of *habeas corpus*. In spite of opposition from the executive branch, the Court, for example, ruled that detainees at Guantanamo Bay and elsewhere have the right to pursue *habeas* review in the federal courts.[1]

Although the Court has emphasized the importance of *habeas corpus* generally, it has restricted its use, particularly for *habeas* appeals made by prisoners in the state criminal justice system. In appealing convictions for violating state laws, the number of permissible appeals has been restricted and the federal courts must defer to state judges unless their decisions were clearly "unreasonable."[2]

***ex post facto* law**

A retroactive criminal law that works to the disadvantage of a person.

The Constitution also bars ***ex post facto* laws**, any law that defines an act as a crime after it was committed, increases the punishment for a crime after it was committed, or reduces the proof necessary to convict someone of a crime after it was committed. However, the prohibition does not restrict retroactive application of a law that benefits an accused person, such as decreasing the punishment for a particular crime; nor does it apply to civil laws.

The Bill of Rights and the States

Most of the liberties we address in this chapter did not appear in the original Constitution. The Constitution drawn up in Philadelphia included guarantees of a few basic rights discussed previously, but it lacked a specific bill of rights similar to those in most state constitutions. Our civil liberties are primarily found in the Bill of Rights, which is composed of the first 10 amendments to the Constitution, ratified in 1791.

The Bill of Rights originally applied only to the national government, not to state governments.[3] Why not to the states? The Framers were confident that citizens could control their own state officials, and most state constitutions already had bills of rights. Furthermore, it would not have been politically feasible for the new Constitution to restrict state governments in this way. It was the new and distant central government the people feared.

due process clause

A clause in the Fifth Amendment limiting the power of the national government; a similar clause in the Fourteenth Amendment prohibits state governments from depriving any person of life, liberty, or property without due process of law.

It was not until the Fourteenth Amendment was adopted in 1868 that there became a way for the limits on government action found in the Bill of Rights to be applied to the states. Because the Fourteenth Amendment applies explicitly to the states, supporters contended that its **due process clause**—declaring that no state shall deprive a person of life, liberty, or property without due process of law—limits states in precisely the same way the Bill of Rights limits the national government. But for decades, the Supreme Court refused to interpret the Fourteenth Amendment in this way. The Court reversed this trend in *Gitlow* v. *New York* (1925) when it decided that when fundamental liberties, such as the "freedom of speech and of the press—which are protected by the First Amendment from abridgment by Congress"—are at stake, the due process clause of the Fourteenth Amendment prohibits the state from infringing on those liberties, just as the First Amendment prohibits Congress.[4]

Gitlow v. *New York* was a revolutionary decision. For the first time, the U.S. Constitution was interpreted to protect freedom of speech from abridgment by state and local governments. This landmark decision changed the balance of federalism in the United States. State action that deprived citizens of fundamental liberties could now be challenged as a violation of the U.S. Constitution. In the 1930s and continuing at an accelerated pace during the 1960s, the Supreme Court enforced the most important of these liberties against the states.[5] The Court did so through the process of **selective incorporation** in which provisions of the Bill of Rights are applied to the states using the due process clause of the Fourteenth Amendment.

selective incorporation
The process by which provisions of the Bill of Rights are brought within the scope of the Fourteenth Amendment and so applied to state and local governments.

Today, the Fourteenth Amendment imposes on the states all the provisions of the Bill of Rights the Court has deemed essential to ordered liberty (see Figure 14.1). After more than 50 years without having incorporated any other protections in the Bill of Rights, the Court incorporated the Second Amendment protection of the right to bear arms to the states in 2010.[6] As a result, state restrictions on handguns and other arms are now subject to strict constitutional review. Although the Supreme Court ruled that states have to abide by the Second Amendment, it did not spell out whether and what type of gun control regulation might survive that review.

Selective incorporation of most, but not all, provisions of the Bill of Rights into the Fourteenth Amendment is one of the most significant constitutional developments that has occurred since the Constitution was written. It has profoundly altered the relationship between the national government and the states, giving greater power to the national government. It has made the federal courts, under the guidance of the Supreme Court, the most important protectors of our liberties—not the individual states. It has also created a consistent national standard for interpreting the rights and liberties found in the Bill of Rights. The Supreme Court will soon determine whether another one of the clauses in the Bill of Rights should be applied to the states, the Eighth Amendment's restriction on excessive fines. Increasingly, states are assessing fines and forfeitures in cases involving relatively minor offenses. If the Eighth Amendment's clause applied to the states, their ability to do so would be restricted.

Otis McDonald, a resident of Chicago, Illinois, asked the U.S. Supreme Court to require states to abide by the protections of the Second Amendment in the 2010 landmark case, *McDonald* v. *Chicago*. As a result of the Court's decision, the Second Amendment was incorporated to the states, making it much more difficult for states to enforce gun control legislation.

FIGURE 14.1 TIMELINE OF SELECTIVE INCORPORATION

Over the course of the twentieth century, the Supreme Court applied most of the protections in the Bill of Rights to the states.

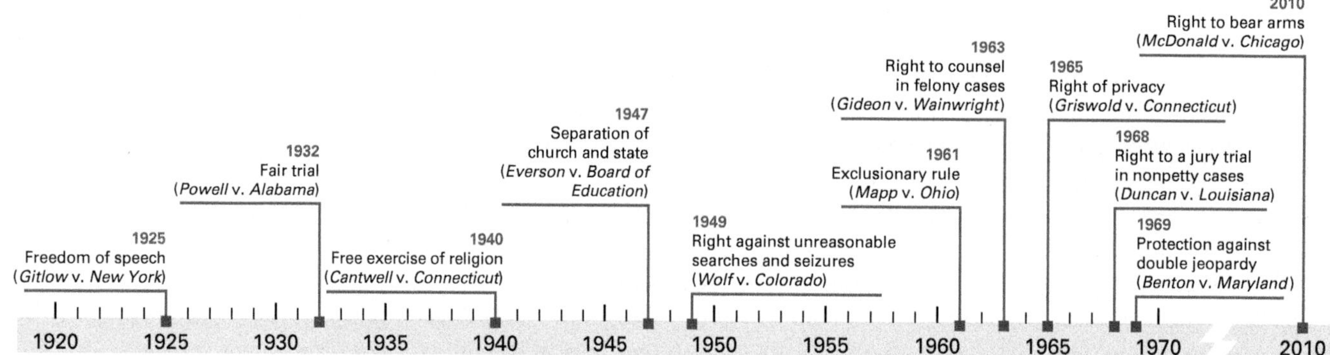

Religious Liberties: Establishment and Exercise (Structure, Action, and Impact)

14.2 Distinguish between the establishment and the free exercise clauses of the First Amendment.

The opening words of the First Amendment are emphatic and concise: "Congress shall make no law respecting an establishment of religion, or prohibiting the free exercise thereof." The amendment contains two important clauses concerning religion: the establishment clause and the free exercise clause. Part of what makes religious liberties questions so interesting and difficult is that the structure of the religion clauses creates some tension between them. Does a state scholarship provided to a student who decides to attend a college to become a clergy member violate the establishment clause by indirectly aiding religion? Or would denying the scholarship violate the student's free exercise of religion? In dealing with the questions posed here, the Supreme Court ruled that providing such scholarship benefits does not go so far as to violate the establishment clause, but neither does the free exercise clause require that states provide the benefits.[7]

The Establishment Clause

establishment clause

A clause in the First Amendment stating that Congress shall make no law respecting an establishment of religion. The Supreme Court has interpreted this to forbid direct governmental support to any or all religions.

In writing what has come to be called the **establishment clause**, the Framers were reacting to the English system, wherein the Crown was (and still is) the head of both the government and of the established church—the Church of England—and public officials were required to take an oath to support the established church as a condition of holding office. At least partly because of the brevity of the establishment clause, there is much debate as to its meaning. Some, such as the late Chief Justice William Rehnquist, contend it means only that the government cannot establish an official national religion nor prefer one sect or denomination to another.[8] Others argue that it requires the government to maintain neutrality, not only among religious denominations but also between religion and nonreligion.

When a party files a suit concerning the separation of church and state, they tend to emphasize the structure of the establishment clause in making their arguments. Those who favor government neutrality regarding religion use the metaphor, coined by Thomas Jefferson, of a "wall of separation" to explain the strict separation between government and religion the clause requires. The metaphor was the basis for the Supreme Court's decision in *Everson* v. *Board of Education of Ewing Township* (1947). The Court's 5-4 decision in the case, allowing government funds to reimburse parents

The presence of nativity scenes on public property has led to constitutional challenges by those arguing that a reasonable observer might understand it to be government sponsorship of religion. Here, Christian activists, who believe such scenes are consistent with the First Amendment, portray a living nativity scene in front of the U.S. Supreme Court. The Court has generally upheld holiday displays that include representations of a variety of religious traditions along with secular holiday symbols, such as a Christmas tree or Santa Claus.

for transporting children to private religious schools, is indicative of the confusion over the establishment clause. All nine justices agreed on conceiving of the establishment clause as a wall separating government from religion; but, they divided five to four on whether the township's action violated that test.[9]

Since *Everson* the Court has, with little success, attempted to clarify its interpretation of the establishment clause. In *Lemon* v. *Kurtzman* (1971), the Court established a three-part test, known as the *Lemon* test. According to the *Lemon* test, to withstand a constitutional challenge, a law must: (1) have a secular legislative purpose, (2) neither advance nor inhibit religion, and (3) avoid "excessive government entanglement with religion."[10] But, the Court has not consistently applied the *Lemon* test. Instead the Court developed other tests forbidding practices a reasonable observer would consider to be a government endorsement of religion (the endorsement test)[11] and requiring that government not favor any particular religion or favor religion to nonreligion and vice versa (the no preference test).[12] There are also justices who contend that there should be strict separation between religion and the state.[13] They generally argue that even indirect aid to religion, such as scholarships or teaching materials for students attending private religious schools, crosses the line that should separate the government from religion. But today, this latter view does not command a majority on the Court.

The Free Exercise Clause

The right to hold any or no religious belief is one of our few absolute rights because it occurs solely within each person. The **free exercise clause** affirms that no government can compel us to accept any creed or to deny us any right because of what we do or do not believe. Requiring religious oaths as a condition of public employment or as a prerequisite for running for public office is unconstitutional. In fact, the original Constitution states, "No religious Test shall ever be required as a Qualification to any Office or public Trust under the United States" (Article VI).

free exercise clause
A clause in the First Amendment stating that Congress shall make no law prohibiting the free exercise of religion.

Although carefully protected, the right to practice a religion, which typically requires some action such as proselytizing or participating in a religious ritual, is more likely to be restricted than the right to hold particular beliefs. Before 1990, the Supreme Court carefully scrutinized laws allegedly infringing on religious practices and insisted that the government provide some compelling interest to justify actions that might burden someone's religious practice. Then, in *Employment Division* v. *Smith* (1990), the Court significantly altered the interpretation of the free exercise clause when it determined that the government does not always need to show a compelling interest if its laws infringe on religious exercise.[14] For example, if a generally applicable law like a restriction on a controlled substance indirectly affects a citizen's ability to practice her religion, the state need only show that the law is reasonable to be consistent with the First Amendment. As long as a general law is not targeted at particular religious groups or practices, the law may be applied to conduct even if it burdens a particular religious practice.[15] However, should a law that targets the practices of a particular religious group be challenged, the Court would apply strict scrutiny to its review of the law, the impact of which will likely be that the legislation will be declared unconstitutional.

First Amendment Freedoms (Structure, Action, and Impact)

14.3 Outline the First Amendment rights to and limitations on the freedoms of speech, press, assembly, and petition.

Government by the people is based on every person's right to speak freely, to organize in groups, to question the decisions of the government, and to campaign openly against them. Essentially, the First Amendment's structure provides protection for your actions (to speak, to write, to protest alone or with a group, etc.) as you attempt to impact public policy. Only through free and uncensored expression of opinion can government be kept responsive to the electorate and political power be transferred peacefully. Elections, separation of powers, and constitutional guarantees are meaningless unless all persons have the right to speak frankly and to hear and judge the worth of what others have to say.

Even though the First Amendment explicitly denies Congress the power to pass any law abridging freedom of speech, the courts have never interpreted the amendment in absolute terms. Like almost all rights, the freedoms of speech and of the press are limited. In discussing the constitutional power of government to regulate speech, we distinguish among belief, speech, and action.

At one extreme is the right to believe as we wish. Despite occasional deviations in practice, the traditional view is that government should not punish a person for beliefs or interfere in any way with freedom of conscience. At the other extreme is action, which the government may restrain. As the old saying goes, "Your right to swing your fist ends where my nose begins."

libel
Written defamation of another person. For public officials and public figures, the constitutional tests designed to restrict libel actions are especially rigid.

obscenity
The quality or state of a work that, taken as a whole, appeals to a prurient interest in sex by depicting sexual conduct in a patently offensive way and that lacks serious literary, artistic, political, or scientific value.

fighting words
Words that by their very nature inflict injury on those to whom they are addressed or incite them to acts of violence.

Speech stands somewhere between belief and action. It is not an absolute right, like belief, but it is not as easily restricted as is action. Some kinds of speech—libel, obscenity, and fighting words, for example—are not entitled to constitutional protection. **Libel** refers to a published falsehood that damages a person's reputation. A book or film might be considered **obscene** if as a whole it appeals to a prurient interest in sex in a patently offensive way, and lacks socially redeeming value. **Fighting words** are words directed at a person that the speaker should reasonably understand are likely to result in violence. Although these definitions might seem fairly straightforward, problems arise in distinguishing between words that do or do not fit into the category of unprotected speech. It usually falls to the courts to decide what free speech means and to defend the right of individual and minority dissenters to exercise it.

Judges must answer a variety of questions when they confront a free speech case: What was said? If it is considered obscene, the government may restrict it. In what context and how was it said? General "time, place, and manner" restrictions typically meet constitutional muster, meaning the government can determine the times, places, and modes of speech, though it may not deny speech because leaders dislike the message.

For example, your local city council can permissibly limit the time for protests to daylight hours. It may not, however, limit the demonstration to only criticism of the national government, while restricting criticism of the city council itself. Judges might also consider how the government is attempting to regulate the speech—by prior restraint (censorship) or by punishment after the speech? If the restriction is made to preempt publication (prior restraint), it is likely to fail. Why is the government regulating the speech—to preserve the public peace or to prevent criticism of the people in power? Although the courts tend to be receptive to restrictions on speech that genuinely threatens public safety, restrictions on criticism are likely to fail.

Debates over free speech rights continue to occur, such as the controversy over protests held by Westboro Baptist Church members at the funerals of U.S. military servicemen and women killed in Iraq and Afghanistan. In a 2011 decision, the Supreme Court protected their lawful but unpopular protests (*Snyder* v. *Phelps*, 562 U.S. 443, 2011). The protester in this photo is Westboro Baptist Church member and former spokesperson, Shirley Phelps-Roper, one of the individuals named in the lawsuit.

Courts have also recognized that different kinds of speech are subject to different levels of protection. For example, political speech is strictly protected. Indeed, restrictions on speech (as paid for through campaign spending) have typically been declared unconstitutional.[16] However, the Court has allowed greater governmental restriction on **commercial speech**, particularly that which is misleading, though its willingness to allow these restrictions seems to be waning.[17]

This is a change from the Court's position at the beginning of the twentieth century, when it variously relied on one of three tests: the **bad tendency test** that generally allowed restricting speech that would tend to corrupt society or encourage crime; the **clear and present danger test** that allowed government to restrict only speech presenting an immediate danger; and the **preferred position doctrine** that rarely, if ever, allowed government to restrict speech or expression because of its importance in our constitutional structure. Today, there is no one single test that is applied to speech cases; however, the Court's reluctance to allow restrictions on speech persists as it evaluates the government's interest in limiting speech along lines similar to the clear and present danger test and the preferred position doctrine.

Protected Speech

Of all the forms of governmental interference with expression, judges are most suspicious of those that impose **prior restraint**—censorship before publication, broadcast, or utterance. Prior restraints include governmental review and approval before a speech can be made, before a motion picture can be shown, or before a newspaper can be published. The Court ruled that "[a]ny system of prior restraints of expression comes to this Court bearing a heavy presumption against its constitutional validity."[18] About the only prior restraints the Court has allowed relate to military and national security matters—such as the disclosure of troop movements[19]—and to high school authorities' control over student newspapers.[20]

Even for an important purpose, a legislature may not pass a law that impinges on First Amendment freedoms if other, less drastic means are available. For example, a state may protect the public from unscrupulous lawyers not by forbidding attorneys from advertising their fees for simple services, but, for example, by disbarring lawyers who mislead their clients.

Political speech has long been considered fundamental and courts have shown a desire to limit it as little as possible. One of the major expansions of free speech was *Citizens United* v. *Federal Election Commission* where the Court reaffirmed that political speech, such as that made possible through campaign expenditures, is essential to democracy and is protected by the First Amendment. Such speech is not given less protection because it is paid for by a corporation or union, rather than an individual.

commercial speech
Advertisements and commercials for products and services; they receive less First Amendment protection, primarily to discourage false and misleading ads.

bad tendency test
An interpretation of the First Amendment that would permit legislatures to forbid speech encouraging people to engage in illegal action.

clear and present danger test
An interpretation of the First Amendment holding that the government cannot interfere with speech unless the speech presents a clear and present danger that it will lead to evil or illegal acts.

preferred position doctrine
An interpretation of the First Amendment that holds that freedom of expression is so essential to democracy that governments should not punish persons for what they say, only for what they do.

prior restraint
Censorship imposed before a speech is made or a newspaper is published; usually presumed to be unconstitutional.

Jim Rogash/Getty Images

Members of the New England Patriots kneel during the national anthem in September 2017. Many National Football League players began taking a knee during the anthem to protest police shootings of unarmed black men. President Trump attacked the players' protest in the fall of 2017 and called on team owners to punish players who would not stand for the anthem. Although many thought that, under the First Amendment, the players should be able to express their views without interference, the amendment applies to government restrictions, not decisions made by private employers, such as NFL owners.

Laws that regulate some kinds of speech but not others, or that regulate speech expressing some views but not others, are likely to be struck down. But those that are called **content neutral or viewpoint neutral**—that is, laws that apply to all kinds of speech and to all views—are more likely to be safe. For example, laws may prohibit posting handbills on telephone poles. However, laws prohibiting only religious handbills or only handbills advocating racism or sexism would probably be declared unconstitutional because they would limit the content of handbills rather than restrict all handbills regardless of what they say.

Prior to becoming president, Donald Trump lost a libel suit against Timothy O'Brien, the author of *TrumpNation: The Art of Being The Donald.* O'Brien wrote that Trump's net worth was between $150 and $250 million. Trump asserted that his net worth exceeded $7 billion. Because Trump was and is a "public figure," to win a libel suit, he needed to provide evidence that the author was intentionally printing falsehoods. Since O'Brien cited three sources in making the claim about Trump's net worth, the court ruled that there was no evidence of actual malice.

Unprotected Speech

Unprotected speech lacks redeeming social value and is not essential to democratic deliberations and self-governance. As noted, the Supreme Court holds that all speech is protected unless it falls into one of three narrow categories: libel, obscenity, or fighting words. This does not mean that the constitutional issues relating to these kinds of speech are simple. How we prove libel, how we define obscenity, and how we determine which words are fighting words remain hotly contested issues.

LIBEL At one time, newspaper publishers and editors had to take considerable care about what they wrote to avoid prosecution by the government or lawsuits by individuals for libel, published falsehoods that harm a person's reputation. Today, as a result of gradually rising constitutional standards, it has become more difficult to win a libel suit against a newspaper or magazine, especially if the person alleging libel is a public official or a public figure. Neither can collect damages unless comments made about them were made with actual malice, meaning that the "statements were made with a knowing or reckless disregard for the truth."[21] Nor can they collect damages even when subject to outrageous, clearly inaccurate parodies and cartoons. Such was the case when *Hustler* magazine printed a parody of the Reverend Jerry Falwell; the Court held that parodies and cartoons cannot reasonably be understood as describing actual facts or events.[22]

OBSCENITY Publications deemed to be obscene are not entitled to constitutional protection, but members of the Supreme Court, like everyone else, have difficulty defining obscenity. As Justice Potter Stewart put it, "I know it when I see it."[23] But, the Court did develop a three-part standard indicating that a work is legally obscene if (1) an average person applying contemporary community standards would find the work as a whole appeals to a prurient, or excessive, interest in sex; (2) the work depicts or describes in a patently offensive way sexual conduct specifically defined by the applicable law, meaning that the legislature must carefully and explicitly define by law each obscene act; and (3) the work as a whole lacks serious literary, artistic, political, or scientific value.[24] Relying on this standard, cities such as New York use zoning laws to regulate the location of adult theaters and bookstores,[25] and they may ban totally nude dancing in adult nightclubs.[26]

content or viewpoint neutrality
Laws that apply to all kinds of speech and to all views, not only that which is unpopular or divisive.

unprotected speech
Libel, obscenity, and fighting words, which are not entitled to constitutional protection in all circumstances.

FIGHTING WORDS Fighting words were held to be outside the scope of constitutional protection because when directed at an individual, "their very utterance may inflict injury or tend to incite an immediate breach of peace."[27] That the words are abusive, offensive, and insulting or that they create anger, alarm, or resentment is not sufficient. Thus, a four-letter word worn on a sweatshirt was not judged to be a fighting word in the constitutional sense, even though it was offensive and angered some people. The word was not aimed at any individual, and those who were offended could look away.[28] However, the Court has struck down statutes criminalizing fighting words or "hate speech" due to vagueness. But, hate crime statutes, which do not limit a person's expression but instead allow courts to consider motive in criminal sentencing, have been broadly upheld.[29]

Freedom of the Press

Although courts are immediately skeptical of prior restraints and have carefully protected the right to publish information, no matter how journalists get it, they have not recognized additional protections allowing journalists to withhold information from grand juries or legislative investigating committees. Without this right to withhold information, reporters insist they cannot assure their sources of confidentiality, and they will not be able to get the information they need to keep the public informed.

The Supreme Court, however, has refused to acknowledge that reporters, and presumably scholars, have a constitutional right to ignore legal requests such as subpoenas and to withhold information from governmental bodies.[30] In 2005, *New York Times* reporter Judith Miller was jailed for two months for refusing to disclose her sources to a grand jury. Many states have passed reporter shield laws providing some protection for reporters from state court subpoenas, but similar legislation has failed to succeed in the U.S. Congress. Despite these difficulties, supporters continue to lobby for a federal shield law. Press sources are not guaranteed protection either. Edward Snowden, the National Security Agency contractor who leaked classified documents to the press, fled the United States and has been granted indefinite asylum in Russia to avoid federal prosecution for violating the 1917 Espionage Act. Snowden is simultaneously lauded as a First Amendment hero and attacked as an enemy of the state.

BROADCAST AND CABLE COMMUNICATIONS When the First Amendment was written, freedom of the press referred to leaflets, newspapers, and books. Today, the amendment protects other media as well, and much debate centers on the degree of protection that should be afforded to broadcast media and the Internet. Despite the rise of the Internet, television remains an important means of distributing news and appealing for votes. Yet of all the mass media, broadcasting receives the least First Amendment protection. The Federal Communications Commission (FCC) regulates the broadcast system by granting licenses and regulating their use, and imposing fines for indecent broadcasts.

The First Amendment would prevent censorship if the FCC tried to impose it. It does not, however, prevent the FCC from refusing to renew a license if, in its opinion, a broadcaster does not serve the public interest. However, stricter enforcement of revitalized FCC regulations in the last 10 years have led to disputes over whether the FCC can regulate indecent material that is "fleeting," such as Bono's use of a four-letter word in an award show acceptance speech. But, the Court has not ruled conclusively as to the FCC's power to restrict such expletives.[31] And, even though the Court has continued to uphold restrictions on the broadcast media, cable operators are given greater latitude in their programming.[32]

THE INTERNET The Internet presents an interesting problem in determining the appropriate level of First Amendment protection. In many ways, it functions as a newspaper—providing news and information critical to an informed citizenry. But it is also a commercial marketplace where millions of U.S. consumers buy books, clothing, jewelry, airplane tickets, stocks, and bonds.

In general, attempts to regulate Internet content have been unsuccessful. In its major ruling on First Amendment protection of Internet content, *Reno* v. *American Civil Liberties Union* (1997), the Court struck down provisions of the Communications Decency Act of 1996. In doing so, the Court emphasized the unique character of the Internet, holding that it is less intrusive than radio and broadcast television.[33] Although Congress passed additional restrictions aimed at protecting children from sexually explicit material on the Internet, the Supreme Court has continued to strike down such legislation. The majority has reasoned that rather than assessing criminal penalties, Congress could achieve its goal of blocking minors' access to sexually explicit sites through less drastic means such as the use of Internet filters or adult oversight.[34]

Freedom of Assembly

The Occupy Wall Street movement began in mid-September 2011 with protestors gathering in Manhattan's Zuccotti Park. Those involved in the movement protested economic inequality and corporate influence; similar Occupy movements soon sprang up across the United States.[35] The First Amendment protection of peaceable assembly was essential to Occupy groups' ability to march, and those involved that September evening were soon joined by thousands of others. However, by mid-November, New York's Mayor Bloomberg, and other leaders in cities across the United States, began to crack down on Occupy protestors who had been camping in parks and public spaces in cities for several months. Courts typically uphold these actions, citing city regulations against camping in parks.[36] The First Amendment protected the protestors' right to peaceably protest in the parks, but did not allow the Occupy groups to essentially set up residence in these public areas.

TIME, PLACE, AND MANNER REGULATIONS The Constitution protects the right to speak, but it does not give people the right to communicate their views to everyone, in every place, at every time they wish. As the evictions of Occupy protestors made clear, no one has the right to block traffic or to hold parades or make speeches in public streets or on public sidewalks whenever he or she wishes. Governments may not censor what can be said, but they can make "reasonable" time, place, and manner regulations for protests or parades. It is essential, however, that any restriction be applied evenhandedly and that the government not act because of what is being said, but how or where it is being said.

civil disobedience
Deliberate refusal to obey a law or comply with the orders of public officials as a means of expressing opposition.

The right to peaceful assembly does not include the right to violate a law deliberately, even if it is in the form of a nonviolent protest. **Civil disobedience**, even if

Clergy protesting the Trump administration's policy separating immigrant parents and children blocked the road in front of a Los Angeles federal building in June 2018. The First Amendment does not extend to civil disobedience and the clergy were arrested.

peaceful, is not a protected right. When Martin Luther King Jr. and his followers refused to comply with a state court's injunction forbidding them to parade in Birmingham, Alabama, without first securing a permit, the Supreme Court sustained their conviction, even though there was serious doubt about the constitutionality of the injunction and the ordinance on which it was based.[37] And, as discussed previously, courts have also upheld evictions of Occupy groups. The structure of the First Amendment provides protection to those acting legally to express their views, such as the more than one million people participating in the Women's Marches that took place in many cities across the United States on the day after President Trump's inauguration but not when protests occur in violation of neutral time, place, and manner restrictions.

First Amendment freedoms are crucial for the survival of our republican form of democracy. It is of utmost importance that individuals be able to make their voices heard regardless of the political views they wish to express. However, these freedoms alone do not provide full protection from arbitrary or impermissible government infringements on our liberties more generally. Next, we turn our attention to amendments in the Bill of Rights protecting property, due process, privacy, and the rights of criminal suspects.

Fundamental Liberties: Property and Arms (Structure, Action, and Impact)

14.4 Explain how the Constitution protects property rights and the right to bear arms.

Historically, the structure of U.S. political institutions has emphasized the close connection between liberty and owning property, and between property and power. An important difference between the colonists and the people in England and Europe was that the opportunity to own property was much greater in America. One of the Framers' central goals was to establish a government strong enough to protect people's rights to use and enjoy their property.

Because of their experiences under British rule, these were crucial issues for the Framers. It was not at all unusual that English colonial legislatures took private property without compensating the owner. For example, if the owner did not keep up his property, the legislature would transfer property to another person.[38] The Framers' experience with the British practice of seizing arms also meant they wanted to protect the right to bear arms and have state militias.[39] Some were also concerned that they protect the right to bear arms in order to preserve the people's ability to fight a tyrannical government, should it become necessary.[40]

Property

property rights
The rights of an individual to own, use, rent, invest in, buy, and sell property.

eminent domain
The power of a government to take private property for public use; the U.S. Constitution gives national and state governments this power and requires them to provide just compensation for property so taken.

regulatory taking
A government regulation that effectively takes land by restricting its use, even if it remains in the owner's name.

Property does not have rights; people do. People have the right to own, use, rent, invest in, buy, and sell property. The Constitution has a variety of clauses protecting **property rights**, particularly the Fifth Amendment takings clause. Although the right of property ownership is highly regarded, both the national and state governments have the power of **eminent domain**—the power to take private property for public use—but the owner must be fairly compensated. Typically, a "taking" must be direct, and a person must lose title and control over the property. But sometimes, especially in recent years, the courts have found that even when the title is left in the owner's name, if a governmental action renders a property unusable, the government must still compensate its owners.[41] These are called **regulatory takings**, meaning the regulation has effectively taken the land by restricting its use. Thus, compensation is required when government creates landing and takeoff strips for airplanes over property adjacent to an airport, which makes the land unsuitable for its original use (say, raising chickens).[42] The government may, however, impose land use and environmental regulations, temporarily prohibiting the development of a property, without compensating the owners.[43]

In 2005, the Supreme Court upheld the government's power of eminent domain to condemn and take private property, with just compensation, for the purpose of advancing the economic development of a community. In *Kelo* v. *City of New London* (2005), the Court held that "public use" was not limited to eminent domain to build a road or a bridge but includes "promoting economic development," even if the property was taken and sold for development to private developers.[44] Public reaction to the Court's decision in *Kelo* was extremely negative. In a clear reminder that the Court is only one instrument of government, many states and localities acted swiftly to pass laws that barred authorities from taking private property for such purposes.

"Just compensation" is not always easy to define. When there is a dispute over compensation, the courts make the final resolution based on the rule that "the owner is entitled to receive what a willing buyer would pay in cash to a willing seller at the time of the taking."[45] An owner is not entitled to compensation for the personal value of an old, broken-down, dearly loved house—just the value of the old, broken-down house.

The Right to Bear Arms

The Second Amendment's protection of the right to bear arms has not been widely litigated at the U.S. Supreme Court. Perhaps surprisingly, when the Supreme Court ruled on the right in 2008, it was the first time in over 70 years that the amendment had been addressed at the Court. But, when it heard the case challenging the District of Columbia's restrictive gun control law, it clarified a central question that had long been debated: whether the right to own guns was a right that belonged to each person individually, or whether it was a collective right, meaning the right of an individual to have a gun as a member of a group, such as a state militia.[46] The Court ruled decisively that the right belonged to each individual and as such struck down the District's gun control law.

Two years later, when the Court heard a similar case concerning a Chicago gun control law, discussed briefly in the section on incorporation, it reached the same conclusion.[47] The majority reasoned that the preamble in the Second Amendment,

"A well-regulated militia, being necessary for the security of a free state," did not modify "the right of the people to keep and bear arms" so as only to provide a collective right. And, more importantly for the present case, the Court decided that the right was essential and thus required protection not only from the federal government, but also the states.

The Supreme Court's decisions in these two cases set precedent on the appropriate interpretation of the Second Amendment. The conclusion that it protects an individual right to own firearms means it is much more difficult for the government to restrict than if it were a collective right. As a result, even when there is overwhelming support for restricting access to guns, the Constitution constrains lawmakers' ability to do so. Add to that the immense power of anti-gun control interest groups, such as the NRA as we discuss in Chapter 5, and the prospect for meaningful gun control reform seems particularly dim. The restrictions passed by the Florida legislature in the wake of the Stoneman Douglas High School shootings discussed at the beginning of the chapter, provide evidence that it is *possible*. But, on the same day Governor Rick Scott signed the bill into law, the NRA sued the state of Florida arguing the law violated the Second Amendment. And, in the month after the Florida school shooting, the NRA raised $2.4 million, the largest single-month total in nearly 20 years.[48]

Privacy Rights and Due Process (Structure, Action, and Impact)

14.5 Explain the origin and significance of the right to privacy.

Perhaps the most difficult parts of the Constitution to understand are the clauses in the Fifth and Fourteenth Amendments forbidding the national and state governments from denying any person life, liberty, or property without "due process of law." By extension these provisions have been interpreted to also mean individuals have a right to privacy in particular respects. Cases involving these guarantees have resulted in hundreds of Supreme Court decisions. Even so, it is impossible to explain due process precisely. In fact, the Supreme Court has refused to do so and has emphasized that "due process, unlike some legal rules, is not a technical conception with a fixed content unrelated to time, place, and circumstances."[49] We define **due process** as rules and regulations that restrain those in government who exercise power. There are, however, basically two kinds of due process: procedural and substantive.

due process
Established rules and regulations that restrain government officials.

Procedural Due Process

Traditionally, **procedural due process** refers not to the law itself but to how a law is applied. To paraphrase Daniel Webster's famous definition, the due process of law requires a procedure that hears before it condemns, proceeds upon inquiry, and renders judgment only after a trial or some kind of hearing. Originally, procedural due process was limited to criminal prosecutions, but it now applies to most kinds of governmental proceedings.

procedural due process
A constitutional requirement that governments proceed by proper methods; limits how government may exercise power.

The liberties that due process protects include "the right of the individual to contract, to engage in any of the common occupations of life, to acquire useful knowledge, to marry, to establish a home and bring up children, to worship God according to the dictates of his own conscience, and generally to enjoy those common law privileges long recognized as essential to the orderly pursuit of happiness by free men."[50]

Substantive Due Process

substantive due process
A constitutional requirement that governments act reasonably and that the substance of the laws themselves be fair and reasonable; limits what a government may do.

Procedural due process limits how governmental power may be exercised; **substantive due process** limits what a government may do. Procedural due process mainly limits the executive and judicial branches because they apply the law and review its application; substantive due process mainly limits the legislative branch because it enacts laws. Substantive due process means that a law, even if properly passed and properly applied, can be unconstitutional. It means that governments should not be allowed to do certain things, such as restricting a person's right to express political views.

Substantive due process has deep roots in concepts of natural law and a long history in U.S. constitutional tradition. For most citizens most of the time, it is not enough merely to say that a law reflects the wishes of the popular or legislative majority. We also want our laws to be just, and we rely heavily on judges to decide what is just.

Finding a Constitutional Right to Privacy

The most important extension of substantive due process in recent decades has protected the right of privacy, especially marital privacy. Although the Constitution does not mention the right to privacy, in *Griswold* v. *Connecticut* (1965), a case concerning contraception, the Supreme Court pulled together elements of the First, Third, Fourth, Fifth, Ninth, and Fourteenth Amendments to recognize that personal privacy is one of the rights the Constitution protects.[51] The decision remains controversial because the Bill of Rights does not specifically enumerate a right to privacy. Instead, the Court ruled that the right to privacy was implied by the rights listed above.

This right has three aspects: (1) the right to be free from governmental surveillance and intrusion, especially with respect to intimate decisions on sexuality; (2) the right not to have the government make private affairs public; and (3) the right to be free in thought and belief from governmental regulations.[52] Thus, the right underlies our discussion later in this chapter of unreasonable searches and seizures, government surveillance, and self-incrimination. The right to privacy also encompasses two controversial issues: state regulation of abortion and private, adult, consensual sexual conduct.

FAMILY PLANNING In *Roe* v. *Wade* (1973), the Supreme Court ruled that the right to privacy extended to a woman's decision, in consultation with her physician, to terminate her pregnancy. According to *Roe*'s "trimester framework," during each three months of a woman's pregnancy, the state's interest in protecting the woman's health grows. (1) In the first trimester, the decision to terminate a pregnancy is entirely up to a woman and her physician, but during the second, (2) the procedure can be regulated because of the state's interest in the woman's health, which might be at greater risk during a second trimester abortion than during one performed in the first trimester, and the state can make reasonable regulations about how, where, and when abortions might be performed. (3) And during the third trimester, when the fetus becomes capable of surviving outside of the womb, which the Court called "viability," the state's interest in protecting the unborn child is so important that the state can prohibit abortion altogether, except when necessary to preserve the life and health of the woman.[53]

Roe led to decades of heated public debate and attempts by Presidents Ronald Reagan and George H. W. Bush to select Supreme Court justices who might reverse it. Nonetheless, *Roe* v. *Wade* was reaffirmed in *Planned Parenthood* v. *Casey* (1992). In a 5-4 decision, the bitterly divided Court upheld *Roe*'s central tenet: the due process clause of the Constitution protects a woman's liberty to choose an abortion prior to the fetal viability outside the womb. However, the Court also held that the right may be subject to state regulation that does not "unduly burden" the woman's liberty. In other words, the Court threw out the trimester framework and permitted states to make "reasonable regulations" on how a woman exercises her right to an abortion, so long as they do not prohibit any woman from making the ultimate decision on whether to

FIGURE 14.2 PUBLIC OPINION ON ABORTION ACCESS

Although there is great controversy over the issue of abortion, when asked "Do you think abortions should be legal under any circumstances, legal only under certain circumstances, or illegal in all circumstances?" a majority of Americans has consistently agreed that abortion access should be "legal only under certain circumstances." The Supreme Court's precedent in abortion cases leads to outcomes that are largely consistent with those views.

SOURCE: Gallup Poll, "Abortion," Gallup News Service, June 10, 2018.

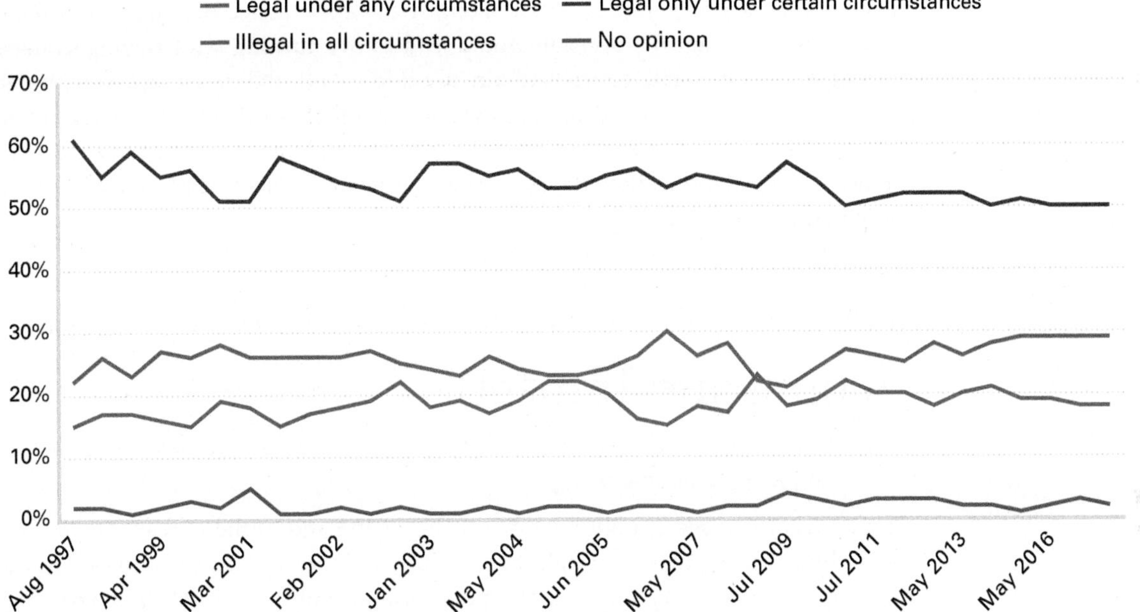

terminate a pregnancy before viability.[54] (See Figure 14.2 above for U.S. public opinion on abortion.)

Applying the undue burden test, the Court has held, on the one hand, that states can prohibit the use of state funds and facilities for performing abortions; states may make a minor's right to an abortion conditional on her first notifying at least one parent or a judge; and states may require women to sign an informed-consent form and wait 24 hours before having an abortion. On the other hand, a state may not condition a woman's right to an abortion on her first notifying her husband. And, in 2007, the Court upheld (by a 5-to-4 vote) a federal ban on "partial-birth" abortion procedures that, for the first time, did not include an exception for cases where the woman's health was at risk. It reasoned that because of "medical uncertainty" about the banned procedure's necessity, Congress was not required to include a health exception.[55]

In 2016, the Supreme Court reviewed a Texas state law requiring modifications in clinics in which abortions were performed as well as requiring that physicians performing abortions have admitting privileges at a hospital within 30 miles of the clinic. The required modifications effectively shut down over half of the abortion clinics in the state of Texas. The Court ruled that the requirements imposed by Texas went so far as to pose an undue burden for women pursuing an abortion and thus, according to its rule in *Casey*, the Texas requirements were struck down.[56]

INTIMATE RELATIONSHIPS Although there is general agreement on how much constitutional protection is provided for marital privacy, in *Bowers* v. *Hardwick* (1986), the Supreme Court refused to extend such protection to private relations between gay couples.[57] By a 5-to-4 vote in *Bowers*, the Court upheld a Georgia law prohibiting consensual sodomy, determining that the law did not violate privacy rights.

Although the federal courts did not protect intimate relationships between consenting adults, several state supreme courts, including Georgia's, protected privacy rights for gay couples based on their own state constitutions rather than relying on the U.S. Constitution. Nearly two decades later, in *Lawrence* v. *Texas* (2003),[58] the Court struck down the Texas law making consensual homosexual sodomy a crime. Writing for the Court and noting the trend in state court decisions refusing to follow *Bowers*, Justice Kennedy held that the Texas law violated personal autonomy and the right of privacy. Dissenting, Justice Scalia, along with Chief Justice Rehnquist and Justice Thomas, warned that the decision would lead to overturning laws barring same-sex marriages, as some state courts had already done. And, the dissenters were, in fact, correct. But, rather than challenging state and federal laws restricting marriage to heterosexual couples as a violation of privacy, the challenges have asserted that such laws violate the equal protection clause of the Fourteenth Amendment, and we discuss those in the civil rights chapter.

Rights of Criminal Suspects (Structure, Action, and Impact)

14.6 Outline the constitutional rights of defendants and the issues involved in protecting defendants' rights.

Despite what you see in police dramas on television and in the movies, law enforcement officers have no general right to break down doors and invade homes. They are not supposed to search people except under certain conditions, and they have no right to arrest them except under certain circumstances. They also may not compel confessions, and they must respect other procedural guarantees aimed at ensuring fairness and the rights of the accused. Persons accused of crimes are guaranteed these and other rights under the Fourth, Fifth, Sixth, Eighth, and Fourteenth Amendments.

Freedom from Unreasonable Searches and Seizures

According to the Fourth Amendment, "The right of the people to be secure in their persons, houses, papers, and effects, against unreasonable searches and seizures, shall not be violated, and no Warrants shall issue, but upon probable cause, supported by Oath or affirmation, and particularly describing the place to be searched, and the persons or things to be seized."

search warrant

A writ issued by a magistrate that authorizes the police to search a particular place or person, specifying the place to be searched and the objects to be seized.

Protection from unreasonable searches and seizures sometimes requires police to obtain a valid **search warrant**, issued by a magistrate after the police indicate under oath that they have probable cause to justify it. The warrant must specify the place to be searched and the things to be seized. General search warrants—warrants that authorize police to search a particular place or person without limitation—are unconstitutional. A search warrant is usually needed to search a person in any place he or she has an "expectation of privacy that society is prepared to recognize as reasonable," including, for example, in a hotel room, a rented home, or a friend's apartment.[59] In short, the Fourth Amendment protects people, not places, from unreasonable governmental intrusions.[60] But, the Fourth Amendment does not always require a warrant; it is entirely possible for a search completed without a warrant to be reasonable and thus permissible. The key is whether a person's consent to a search is coerced or whether an officer's or the public's safety is at risk.

The Supreme Court also upheld, in *Terry* v. *Ohio* (1968), a stop and frisk exception to the warrant requirement when officers have reason to believe someone is armed and dangerous, or has committed or is about to commit a criminal offense. The *Terry* search is limited to a quick pat-down to check for weapons that may be used to assault the arresting officer, to check for contraband, to determine identity, or to maintain the status quo while obtaining more information.[61] If individuals who are stopped for questioning refuse to identify themselves, they may be arrested, although police must have a reasonable suspicion that they are engaged in criminal activities.[62] If an officer stops and frisks a suspect to look for weapons and finds criminal evidence that may justify an arrest, the officer can make a full search.[63]

Technological advances have further complicated the Court's Fourth Amendment rulings. Even as the Supreme Court has increasingly allowed exceptions to warrant requirements, it has been reluctant to allow advancing technology to subvert the purposes of the Fourth Amendment. For example, without a warrant, law enforcement officials cannot use thermal imaging devices to gather evidence that a suspect is growing marijuana in his enclosed garage.[64] Nor may they use GPS tracking devices on a suspect's vehicle[65] nor obtain cell-tower information which can give information about a cellphone user's location absent a warrant.[66] However, given that these decisions often turn on a person's reasonable expectation of privacy, as these technological advances continue, the Court will have to revisit the matter to redefine whether electronic intrusions are reasonable and what, if any, limits should be imposed.[67]

THE EXCLUSIONARY RULE Before the development of the exclusionary rule, evidence obtained in violation of the Fourth Amendment could still be used at trial against a defendant. The remedy in such cases was the opportunity for the defendant to sue law enforcement. However, suing afterward did not resolve the denial of Fourth Amendment protection in the criminal action.

This changed in the federal courts in 1911 and was applied to the states in 1961. In *Mapp* v. *Ohio* (1961), the Supreme Court adopted a rule excluding from criminal trial evidence that the police obtained unconstitutionally or illegally.[68] This **exclusionary rule** was adopted to eliminate any incentive for police misconduct. Police officers know that if they obtain evidence in violation of the Fourth Amendment, it cannot be used against a defendant at trial. Critics question why criminals should go free just because of police misconduct or ineptness,[69] but the Supreme Court has refused to abandon the rule. It has made some exceptions to it, however, such as cases in which police relied in "good faith" on a search warrant that subsequently turned out to be defective or granted improperly.[70]

exclusionary rule
A requirement that evidence unconstitutionally or illegally obtained be excluded from a criminal trial.

Full-body scanners used at airports led to concerns that travelers were being subject to unreasonable searches under the Fourth Amendment. Courts have ruled that the scanners do not violate the amendment.

PROTECTIONS IN AN AGE OF TERROR Although the courts have established standards for what makes a search constitutional and have developed the exclusionary rule to deal with evidence obtained in violation of those standards, debate over adequate protections for individual liberties is ongoing. Today, there is particular concern about how to protect those liberties in the face of terrorist threats. For example, after several law enforcement attempts to access criminal suspects' iPhones, Apple announced in June 2018 that it would close a software loophole through which the authorities have hacked into iPhones. As Justice Oliver Wendell Holmes once wrote, "when a nation is at war, many things that might be said in a time of peace" will not be permissible "so long as men fight."[71] How do we find the correct balance between preserving national security and protecting civil liberties?

Ensuring protection against another terrorist attack would be much easier if the government had open access to listen in on our conversations, search our possessions, and detain or question suspects without having to show cause for doing so. The need to protect national security and gather foreign intelligence presents a special problem for Fourth Amendment protections. In response to concerns about domestic surveillance in the interest of foreign security, Congress created the Foreign Intelligence Surveillance Court in 1978, often referred to as FISA Courts in reference to the act that created them (the Foreign Intelligence Surveillance Act). The court consists of federal district court judges and meets in secret. During the George W. Bush administration, the court reviewed many requests for approval of warrantless wiretaps and physical searches of foreign agents.

The USA PATRIOT Act of 2001 (Uniting and Strengthening America by Providing Appropriate Tools Required to Intercept and Obstruct Terrorism) expanded the size of the court, lowered the requirement to approve warrants in cases involving terrorism, and permitted searches for foreign intelligence and evidence of terrorist activities. Congress overwhelmingly voted to extend the PATRIOT Act, and in June 2015, President Obama signed a four-year extension of the Act into law. However, the law has been changed to end bulk phone data collection by the National Security Agency's (NSA) domestic surveillance program, in no small part due to former NSA contractor Edward Snowden's leak of over one-and-a-half million classified documents.

The Right to Remain Silent

During the seventeenth century, special courts in England forced confessions from religious dissenters by torture and intimidation. The British privilege against self-incrimination developed in response to these practices. Because they were familiar with this history, the Framers of our Bill of Rights included in the Fifth Amendment the provision that persons shall not be compelled to testify against themselves in criminal prosecutions. This protection against self-incrimination is designed to strengthen the fundamental principle that no person has an obligation to prove innocence. Rather, the burden is on the government to prove guilt.

THE MIRANDA WARNING Police questioning of suspects is a key procedure in solving crimes. Approximately 90 percent of all criminal convictions result from guilty pleas and never reach a full trial. Police questioning, however, can easily be abused. Police officers sometimes forget or ignore the constitutional rights of suspects, especially those who are frightened and ignorant. Unauthorized detentions and lengthy interrogations to wring confessions from suspects, common practice in police states, have also occurred in the United States.

To put an end to such practices, the Supreme Court, in *Miranda* v. *Arizona* (1966), announced that no conviction could stand if evidence introduced at the trial had been obtained by the police during "custodial interrogation" unless suspects were notified that they have a right to remain silent and that anything they say can and will be used against them; to terminate questioning at any point; to have an attorney present during questioning by police; and to have a lawyer appointed to represent them if they

The case of Ernesto Miranda (right) led to the Supreme Court decision in 1966 requiring suspects in police custody to be advised of their constitutional right to remain silent and to have an attorney present during questioning.

cannot afford to hire their own attorney.[72] If suspects answer questions in the absence of an attorney, the burden is on prosecutors to demonstrate that suspects knowingly and intelligently gave up their right to remain silent. As is the case with Fourth Amendment cases, the Court has allowed evidence obtained contrary to *Miranda* guidelines to be used to attack the credibility of defendants who offer testimony at trial that conflicts with their statements to the police. But, as recently as 2000, the Court has reaffirmed *Miranda*'s constitutional necessity.[73]

The Right to an Attorney

Prior to 1963, states were not required to provide attorneys to criminal defendants who could not afford them unless there were "special circumstances" like the defendant being illiterate or mentally challenged.[74] Most states had some system for representing poor defendants, but the Supreme Court had not yet ruled that they were required to do so under the Sixth Amendment. But, in *Gideon* v. *Wainwright* the Court did just that; the Supreme Court ruled that because of the complexities of the legal system and the potential for being deprived of one's basic liberty, the government must provide an attorney to a criminal defendant who cannot afford one.[75] Legal representation is particularly important in an adversarial legal system such as we have in the United States, where the judge or jury, as a neutral decision maker, depends on the attorneys to bring forth all of the relevant evidence in a case.

Providing a defense for poor persons accused of a crime is essential for fulfilling the requirements of the Sixth Amendment, and the Supreme Court's decision in 1963 provided the basis for protecting criminal suspects' rights across the United States. In 2013, the most recent year for which comprehensive state data is available, nearly 15,000 attorneys across the United States closed over 2.5 million cases involving indigent clients.[76]

The Supreme Court's decision in *Gideon* and the development of extensive federal and state indigent defense systems has resulted in much better protection of Sixth Amendment rights than existed prior to 1963. But, there are still many concerns about the quality of representation provided to indigent defendants by public defense attorneys often saddled with large caseloads and insufficient funding.

The Orleans Parish Defender's Office in New Orleans, Louisiana, offers a stark example of the kinds of problems that often confront public defenders' offices. In 2014, the office handled more than 22,000 cases, including 8,000 felonies and nine death penalty cases; with 51 attorneys in the office, each attorney handled, on average, 431 cases.

Attorneys representing clients in felony cases found themselves handling around 300 of those cases annually, twice as many as the American Bar Association recommends an attorney handle in a given year.[77] In an unusual move, Derwyn Bunton, the parish's chief public defender, announced in January 2016 that the office would no longer accept certain felony cases where defendants faced long sentences because it simply did not have the resources to represent those clients. In an attempt to force the state legislature to appropriate adequate funds to the public defender's office, the American Civil Liberties Union (ACLU) filed suit against the office for denying indigent defendants their Sixth Amendment right to counsel. A federal judge dismissed the case in February 2017 saying that while the state was not providing the office with sufficient funds, it was up to the Louisiana legislature to do so, not the federal courts.

Fair Trial Procedures

Many people, perhaps believing that they will never find themselves accused of criminal wrongdoing, consider the rights of the criminally accused to be less important than other rights. Nonetheless, these rights guarantee that all persons accused of crimes will have the right to representation by counsel throughout each stage of the criminal process and to a fair trial by an impartial jury. Procedural protections are guaranteed at each of the phases in the criminal process: (1) pretrial, (2) trial, (3) sentencing, and (4) appeal.

Before a person can be forced to stand trial for a criminal offense (except for members of the armed forces or foreign terrorists), they must be indicted by a grand jury, or before a judge in what is called an information proceeding. A **grand jury** is concerned not with a person's guilt or innocence, as a **petit jury** would be, but merely with whether there is enough evidence to warrant a trial. The grand jury has wide-ranging investigatory powers and "is to inquire into all information that might possibly bear on its investigations until it has identified an offense or has satisfied itself that none has occurred."[78] The strict rules that govern trial proceedings, and the exclusionary rule to enforce the Fourth Amendment, do not apply, and the grand jury may consider hearsay evidence. If a majority of the grand jurors agree that a trial is justified, they return a true bill, or **indictment**.

grand jury
A jury of 12 to 23 persons, depending on state and local requirements, who privately hear evidence presented by the government to determine whether persons shall be required to stand trial. If the jury believes there is sufficient evidence that a crime was committed, it issues an indictment.

petit jury
A jury of 6 to 12 persons that determines whether a defendant is found guilty in a civil or criminal action.

indictment
A formal written statement from a grand jury charging an individual with an offense; also called a *true bill*.

plea bargain
An agreement between a prosecutor and a defendant that the defendant will plead guilty to a lesser offense to avoid having to stand trial for a more serious offense.

The Constitution guarantees the accused the right to be informed of the nature and cause of the accusation so that he or she can prepare a defense. After indictment, prosecutors and the defense attorney usually discuss the possibility of a **plea bargain** whereby the defendant often pleads guilty to a lesser offense that carries a lesser penalty. Prosecutors, facing more cases than they can handle, like plea bargains because they save the expense and time of going to trial and they result in a conviction. Likewise, defendants are often willing to agree to a plea deal for a lesser offense to avoid the risk of more serious punishment for the original indictment.

After indictment and preliminary hearings that determine bail and what evidence will be used against the accused, the Constitution guarantees a speedy and public trial. Do not, however, take the word speedy too literally. Defendants are given time to prepare their defense and often ask for delays because time often works to their advantage. In contrast, if the government denied the accused a speedy trial, not only is the conviction reversed, but the case must also be dismissed outright.

An impartial jury, one that meets the requirements of due process and equal protection, consists of persons who represent a fair cross section of the community. Although defendants are not entitled to juries that reflect their own race, sex, religion, or national origin, government prosecutors cannot strike people from juries because of race or sex, and neither can defense attorneys use what are called peremptory challenges to keep people off juries because of race, ethnic origin, or sex.[79]

During the trial, the defendant has a right to obtain witnesses in his or her favor and to have the judge subpoena, or order, witnesses to appear at the trial and testify. Both the accused and witnesses may refuse to testify on the grounds that their testimony would tend to incriminate themselves. If witnesses testify, both the prosecution and the defense have the right to confront and cross-examine them.

The sentencing phase begins with the conclusion of the trial. Here, the jury recommends, or a judge decides on, a verdict of guilty or not guilty. If the accused is found guilty, the judge usually hands down the sentence, although in some cases juries impose the sentence according to the judge's instructions. The Eighth Amendment forbids levying excessive fines and inflicting cruel and unusual punishment.

Prison overcrowding and the high costs associated with incarcerating a huge number of Americans has led to some reconsiderations of the way in which we sentence convicted felons. There is increasingly bipartisan support for sentencing reform and, at the federal level, removing harsh mandatory minimum requirements for low-level offenders. However, there is still support for what are known as "three strikes and you're out" laws, such as those in California, Virginia, Washington, and several other states. In some states, the felonies must be for violent crimes; in others, any three felonies will do. For example, the Supreme Court in *Ewing* v. *California* (2003) upheld California's tough law for committing three felonies, ruling that a 25-years-to-life sentence for a nonviolent third felony conviction for stealing three golf clubs did not violate the prohibition against cruel and unusual punishment.[80] However, the Supreme Court has eliminated mandatory life without parole sentences for juveniles, first in non-homicide cases (*Graham* v. *Florida* (2010)) and two years later, in cases involving murder (*Miller* v. *Alabama* (2012)). In *Graham*, Justice Kagan, writing for the majority, reasoned that in cases involving juveniles, the offenders must be given some opportunity to have their sentences reconsidered based on "demonstrated maturity and rehabilitation."[81]

In the final stage of the criminal process, defendants may appeal their convictions if they claim they have been denied some constitutional right of due process or equal protection of the law. The Fifth Amendment also provides that no person shall be "subject for the same offense to be twice put in jeopardy of life or limb." **Double jeopardy** does not prevent punishment by the national and the state governments for laws pertaining to the same offense or for successive prosecutions for the same crime by two states. Nor does the double jeopardy clause forbid a civil suit, where a party could sue another for damages resulting from some action, even after a person has been acquitted in a criminal trial for the same alleged wrongdoing.[82] For example, after O.J. Simpson was acquitted of the 1994 murder of his ex-wife and her friend, he was found civilly liable for their deaths in 1997 and ordered to pay their families $8.5 million in damages.

double jeopardy
Trial or punishment for the same crime by the same government; forbidden by the Constitution.

Across the United States, innocence projects, which are often associated with law schools, fight for the release of men and women who claim they were wrongly convicted. Here, an attorney with the California Innocence Project and her client, Luis Lorenzo Vargas, appear in Los Angeles County Court. Vargas, who spent 16 years in jail for three rape convictions, was exonerated by new DNA evidence and released at the end of 2015. Visit the innocence project at https://www.innocenceproject.org.

The Death Penalty

The Eighth Amendment's prohibition of cruel and unusual punishment has never been interpreted by a majority of the Supreme Court to bar the death penalty. Death was an available punishment when the Constitution was ratified and the language of the Fifth Amendment's due process clause indicating that a person not be denied of "*life*, liberty, or property, without due process of law" (emphasis added) provides further evidence that those voting to ratify the document understood that a person's life could be taken as long as the government adhered to procedural safeguards.

However, in the early 1970s the U.S. Supreme Court ruled that the mechanism by which most states meted out the death penalty failed to meet the standards required by the Eighth Amendment. In response to the Court's ruling, states modified their capital systems and the Court upheld the new capital sentencing structure developed by the state of Georgia. In doing so it ruled that the death penalty does not violate the Eighth Amendment when imposed for crimes that resulted in a victim's death, if the courts "ensure that death sentences are not meted out wantonly or freakishly," and if these processes "confer on the sentencer sufficient discretion to take account of the character and record of the individual offender and the circumstances of the particular offense to ensure that death is the appropriate punishment in a specific case."[83]

In the wake of the Supreme Court's 1976 decision upholding Georgia's revised death penalty statute,[84] many states followed Georgia's lead and revised their own statutes, and the federal government increased the number of crimes for which the death penalty could be imposed. As a result, the number of persons on death row increased dramatically. Since capital punishment was reinstated in 1976, nearly 1,500 people have been executed nationwide; today more than 2,700 are on death row (see Figure 14.3). Concerns have grown about the fairness with which capital punishment is imposed. Furthermore, there is ample evidence of racial bias in applying the death penalty. Not only do black defendants make up a disproportionate percentage of defendants executed, the death penalty is also disproportionately carried out when murder victims are white.[85] DNA tests that have established the innocence of a sizable number of those convicted of murder have increased these concerns as well.[86] Since 1973, 164 people who were convicted of murder and sentenced to death have been exonerated.[87]

FIGURE 14.3 NUMBER OF EXECUTIONS BY YEAR, 1976–2018

After reaching a high of 98 executions in 1999, the number of executions in the United States has fallen dramatically as has the number of death sentences meted out each year. In 1998, 295 capital defendants were given a death sentence, but by 2017 that figure had dropped to 39.

SOURCE: "Death Penalty Information Center: Facts about the Death Penalty," Death Penalty Information Center, http://www.deathpenaltyinfo.org/.

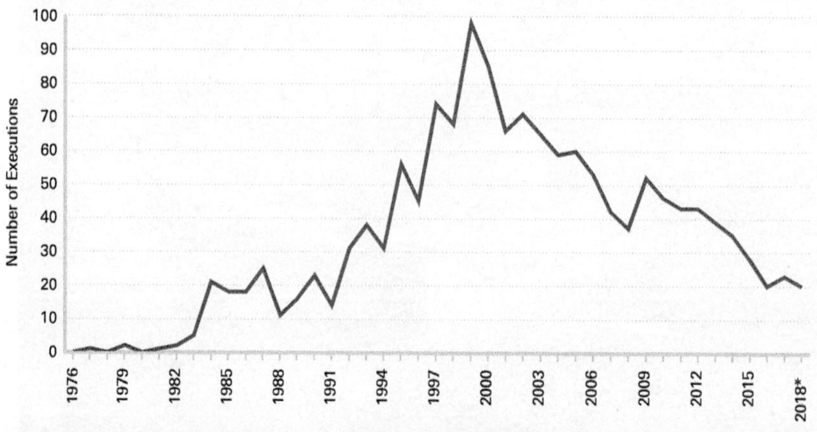

The prohibition against cruel and unusual punishment also forbids punishments grossly disproportionate to the severity of the crime. In recent years, the Supreme Court has narrowed the types of crimes for which the death penalty can be considered. It is no longer permissible to execute the mentally impaired,[88] minors,[89] or defendants convicted of child rape (the Court had previously eliminated defendants convicted of adult rape).[90]

Finally, and perhaps ironically, the mode of execution has become more controversial as states have largely abandoned firing squads and hanging as the means of execution and have turned to the theoretically more humane method of lethal injection. Although lethal injection's constitutionality has been challenged, the Supreme Court, in 2008, did not find it to be cruel or unusual, and therefore upheld it;[91] it also refused to rule out particular drugs from use in that process.[92] The drugs used in lethal injection have become scarcer as some manufacturers who have supplied the drugs in the past have refused to do so based on their own opposition to the death penalty. Indeed, the most recent case addressing the use of lethal injections, *Glossip* v. *Gross* (2015), resulted from an Oklahoma case in which Charles Lockett was executed by lethal injection but awoke after being given the drug that was supposed to render him unconscious, and he did not die until 40 minutes later.

CONCLUSION

Protecting each of the civil liberties described above requires significant effort on the part of individuals like you and your classmates. The judiciary is a reactive institution and cannot investigate or make rulings on alleged constitutional infringements on its own. Someone, individually or as a member of a group, has to step forward and provide evidence to the court that the government has acted in a way so as to impermissibly limit free speech, or has failed to provide adequate legal representation to a person charged with criminal activity.

In protecting these liberties, the Supreme Court must also balance the needs of all Americans against protecting the rights of the individual. For example, in the wake of the Parkland, Florida shooting, the Florida legislature and its Governor argued that limitations must be placed on the right to own firearms in order to protect the state's children during the school day. Several northeastern states are working to coordinate their gun control policies, other states and localities have established bans on bump stocks and have made it more difficult for individuals who have restraining orders against them to purchase firearms. As we discussed above, the NRA is challenging some of these policy changes to ensure that an individual's right to bear arms is protected.

What is the appropriate balance between protecting Second Amendment liberties while also protecting children in our schools? This is a question on which you and your peers will have input. As the high school students from Parkland, Florida have shown, you do not have to wait until you finish college or are elected to local government to make a difference on this question. Stoneman Douglas High School students organized one of the biggest gun control rallies ever held. They lobbied their state legislature and governor for stricter limits on gun ownership and met with the president of the United States to discuss their concerns.

Should firearms be further regulated? Is arming school administrators and teachers the solution to gun violence in the schools? Should policymakers focus attention on the availability of mental health services as a primary or even tertiary strategy in dealing with gun violence? Should states instead focus their financial resources on equipping schools with the latest technology in metal detectors and on-campus surveillance? Your generation must confront these difficult questions. By understanding the structure of the Constitution's civil liberties' protections you can plan to act strategically within it to achieve your goals.

CHAPTER 14

REVIEW THE CHAPTER

The Basis for Our Civil Liberties (Structure)

14.1 Explain the roots of civil liberties in the Constitution and their development in the Bill of Rights, p. 421.

Anti-Federalists were concerned that the new national government would infringe on individual rights. Although many state constitutions already protected civil liberties, the Bill of Rights was created to prevent the national government from infringing on civil liberties. However, with the ratification of the Fourteenth Amendment, there was a vehicle that allowed for incorporating the protections in the Bill of Rights to the states. The Court did so through the process of selective incorporation.

Religious Liberties: Establishment and Exercise (Structure, Action, and Impact)

14.2 Distinguish between the establishment and the free exercise clauses of the First Amendment, p. 424.

The First Amendment forbids the establishment of religion and guarantees its free exercise. In many cases, these two freedoms are in tension with each other and represent conflicting notions of what is in the public interest. There are a number of tests the Supreme Court used to determine whether the government has impermissibly restricted religious liberties, including the *Lemon* test and the no preference test for establishment clause cases, and the test of general applicability when reviewing an exercise clause claim.

First Amendment Freedoms (Structure, Action, and Impact)

14.3 Outline the First Amendment rights to and limitations on the freedoms of speech, press, assembly, and petition, p. 426.

The amendment includes protections for speech, the press, and the right of assembly. However, each of these are limited: not all speech is protected, members of the press have no greater rights than do ordinary citizens, and the right to peaceably assemble is subject to reasonable time, place, and manner restrictions. However, government restrictions based on the content of speech and prior restraints on publications are likely to be struck down as impermissible.

Fundamental Liberties: Property and Arms (Structure, Action, and Impact)

14.4 Explain how the Constitution protects property rights and the right to bear arms, p. 431.

The Framers saw private property rights and the right to bear arms as fundamental for maintaining a republican system of government in which the people remained a real check on the power of government. If the government takes private property for public use, it must provide adequate compensation, and the government must observe the individual right to own guns.

Privacy Rights (Structure, Action, and Impact)

14.5 Explain the origin and significance of the right to privacy, p. 433.

The Constitution imposes limits not only on the procedures government must follow but also on the ends it may pursue. These protections refer to procedural and substantive due process, respectively. Some legislation is unconstitutional no matter what procedures are followed because of what is being regulated. Legislation that violates the constitutional right to privacy is one example. The right to privacy is implied by a number of the protections in the Bill of Rights, including protections against unreasonable searches and seizures, the protection against self-incrimination, and the right to associate (and not associate) with those you choose. It also protects a woman's right to terminate pregnancy and intimate relationships between consenting adults, regardless of sexual orientation.

Rights of Criminal Suspects (Structure, Action, and Impact)

14.6 Outline the constitutional rights of defendants and the issues involved in protecting defendants' rights, p. 436.

The Framers knew from their own experiences that in their zeal to maintain power and to enforce the laws, especially in wartime, public officials are often tempted to infringe on the rights of persons accused of crimes. To prevent such abuse, the Bill of Rights requires federal officials to follow detailed procedures in making searches and arrests and in bringing people to trial.

LEARN THE TERMS

civil liberties, p. 421
civil rights, p. 421
legal privileges, p. 421
writ of *habeas corpus*, p. 422
ex post facto law, p. 422
due process clause, p. 422
selective incorporation, p. 423
establishment clause, p. 424
free exercise clause, p. 425
libel, p. 426
obscenity, p. 426
fighting words, p. 426
commercial speech, p. 427
bad tendency test, p. 427
clear and present danger test, p. 427
preferred position doctrine, p. 427
prior restraint, p. 427
content or viewpoint neutrality, p. 428
unprotected speech, p. 428
civil disobedience, p. 430
property rights, p. 432
eminent domain, p. 432
regulatory taking, p. 432
due process, p. 433
procedural due process, p. 433
substantive due process, p. 433
search warrant, p. 436
exclusionary rule, p. 437
grand jury, p. 440
petit jury, p. 440
indictment, p. 440
plea bargain, p. 440
double jeopardy, p. 441

Civil Rights

CHAPTER 15

On June 12, 2018, a U.S. Border Patrol agent and a local police officer, watch over a group of migrants near the U.S.-Mexico border in McAllen, Texas. The migrants were taken to a U.S. Custom and Border Control processing center where, under the Trump administration's "zero tolerance" policy, family members may have been separated as adults were criminally charged and taken to detention facilities. Over the period of about six weeks in May and June 2018, the administration's policy resulted in separating nearly 2,500 children from their parents.

LEARNING OBJECTIVES

15.1 Explain why the concept of equality is integral to our understanding of civil rights (Structure), p. 448.

15.2 Explain the concept of citizenship and the rights of U.S. citizens (Structure), p. 449.

15.3 Compare and contrast the efforts of various groups to obtain equal protection of the law (Action), p. 452.

15.4 Evaluate the standards by which civil rights are protected today (Structure and Impact), p. 461.

15.5 Trace the evolution of voting rights and analyze the protections provided by the 1965 Voting Rights Act (Structure), p. 464.

15.6 Describe congressional legislation forbidding discrimination in housing, employment, and accommodations (Structure), p. 466.

15.7 Evaluate the history of school integration and the current state of affirmative action (Impact), p. 469.

When we think about civil rights in the United States, we often think about the struggle to end racial segregation in the Little Rock, Arkansas public schools or at lunch counters in Montgomery, Alabama. Our thoughts might also turn to the fight for marriage equality that culminated in the U.S. Supreme Court's decision in *Obergefell* v. *Hodges,* ending state bans on same-sex marriage. But another important aspect of civil rights is the rights of noncitizens. The Framers of the U.S. Constitution did not understand the structure it provided as belonging only to United States citizens. The Framers believed that all human beings possessed natural rights or, as we discuss in Chapter 3 and below, what we commonly refer to as human rights. These are rights all humans possess and they include the basic protections afforded by the Bill of Rights.

Mass migration presents challenges to the countries where the migrants arrive, especially in an era with heightened concern about terrorism. Determining how to protect national security while also ensuring human rights is proving challenging around the world. Migration from Central and South America has certainly presented that challenge in the United States. Donald Trump's 2016 presidential campaign focused on the issue, promising to solve the immigration crisis and to build a wall across the southern U.S. border to keep migrants from entering the United States illegally.[1] These same ideas became part of his "four pillars" of immigration reform which he provided in his 2018 State of the Union Address.[2] The Trump administration is not the first one to deal with this issue. Presidents George W. Bush and Barack Obama also dealt with concerns of rising numbers of undocumented immigrants entering the United States and those detained for long periods awaiting hearings to determine whether they qualified for political asylum in the United States or would be sent back to their countries of origin. Many of these migrants claimed to have come to the United States due to violence and safety concerns in Central American countries such as Guatemala, El Salvador, and Honduras.

In April 2018, the Trump administration announced what they called a "zero tolerance" program for any migrants who did not cross a U.S. border at an official port of entry. Attorney General Jeff Sessions's announcement made formal a policy that had been in place, despite administration denials, since the previous summer.[3] The zero tolerance program meant that, regardless of whether they were seeking asylum, anyone who crossed into the United States anywhere other than a port of entry would be criminally prosecuted and, if they were traveling with their children, they would be separated.[4] This program differed in several ways from that of previous administrations. First, under the Obama administration, which was also criticized for the way it handled immigration at the southern border, individuals, particularly those with children, who illegally crossed into the United States were detained and then released pending a review of their civil (not criminal) immigration violation. Because of the backlog of immigration cases, those migrants might wait up to several years for a hearing and critics of that policy asserted that it amounted to a type of amnesty for migrants entering the country illegally.

How do we go about solving the issue of migrants at the U.S. border without treating them in a way that many argue deprives them of basic human rights and likely does long-term damage to children, often very young, who are separated from their families in a country in which they cannot speak the language, and do not understand why they have been taken from their parents? At the same time, how do we go about securing our borders without stemming the tide of undocumented immigrants entering the United States? The issue was prominent in electing President Trump and one with which many Americans are concerned.

The issue of immigration has long caused divisions in the United States, a country that prides itself on being a country built by immigrants. It also still struggles to square that narrative with one in which our predecessors treated the native population inhumanely, taking the land as they pushed Native Americans further and further westward and into "reservations" where they were routinely stripped of their culture and where their children too, were taken from them and enrolled in so-called Indian boarding schools where they were to assimilate into white American culture.

After several attempts to get comprehensive immigration reform during the first year of his administration, particularly after he announced he would end the Deferred Action for Childhood Arrivals (DACA) program on March 5, 2018, President Trump has been unsuccessful in getting an agreement on how to treat the "dreamers," as DACA program participants are often called. In the most recent efforts to deal with public backlash at his zero tolerance program, Trump initially claimed only Congress could fix the problem through legislation, then announced an executive order ending family separation but with no direction for reuniting some 2,500 children who had already been separated from their parents. And then, in a tweet, the president told congressional Republicans to "stop wasting their time on Immigration" until after the November 2018 elections when Trump predicted they would have greater numbers in the House and Senate.[5] The president's tweet likely ended any possibility for compromise between Republicans and Democrats since there is such a low probability that the president would actually sign a compromise bill.

The Trump administration argued that its 'zero tolerance' policy was not new; rather the administration was acting to enforce previously enacted law and deter illegal immigrants, especially those who smuggled children into the United States. Zero tolerance was deemed to be essential in protecting U.S. citizens from gangs like MS-13 and drug smugglers. Further, the administration and particularly Attorney General Jeff Sessions, argued that immigrants could keep from being separated from their children by simply waiting their turn to enter the United States lawfully. The attorney general emphasized that immigrants were being treated no differently than U.S. citizens who broke the law and were sent to prison, and thus separated from their children.[6]

As mentioned above, there was significant public backlash against Trump's policy of separating immigrating parents from their children. Opposition has come from many corners including civil rights leaders who see immigration as another front in the battle for equal protection in the United States. In addition to the 2018 crisis at the southern border, undocumented immigrants in the United States often suffer from poor working conditions and meager wages because their lack of documentation means they cannot challenge those conditions. Civil rights leaders recall Dr. Martin Luther King, Jr. words that "Injustice anywhere is a threat to justice everywhere."[7] But what is meant by equal protection? How do we guarantee it? When have we, as a country, fallen short on that responsibility?

We begin this chapter by discussing equality and equal rights. Most Americans value equality, but they often differ in their understanding of the concept. Next, we discuss citizenship rights and the kinds of protections that can be denied based on citizenship. As discussed above, these issues have become increasingly important, particularly in the debate about immigration reform. We then discuss several groups' efforts to secure their civil rights and examine what is meant by "equal protection of the law." In doing so, we will pay particular attention to two laws essential to securing civil rights protections: the Civil Rights Act of 1964 and the Voting Rights Act of 1965. Finally, we wrap up by examining how early decisions on affirmative action have shaped the current debate. As the 2018 immigration crisis illustrates, the debate over civil rights is far from finished, and how you resolve it today will establish the boundaries of civil rights in the future.

Equality and Equal Rights (Structure)

15.1 Explain why the concept of equality is integral to our understanding of civil rights.

civil rights
The constitutional rights of all persons to due process and the equal protection of the laws; include the rights of all people to be free from irrational discrimination such as that based on race, religion, sex, or ethnic origin.

The tension between protecting religious liberties and same-sex marriage highlights the United States' continuing dilemma of how to best ensure equality without violating the Constitution. In this case, the **civil rights** of religious practitioners—their right not to be discriminated against because of race, religion, gender, or ethnic origin—are potentially at odds with LGBTQ rights. The Constitution protects civil rights in two ways. First, it ensures that government officials do not impermissibly discriminate against us; second, it grants national and state governments the power to protect these civil rights against interference by private individuals.

The Constitution does not make any reference to "equality"; the Declaration of Independence proclaims "that all men are created equal," but equality is not mentioned in the Constitution or in the original Bill of Rights. We know, however, that the Framers believed all men—at least all white adult men—were equally entitled to life, liberty, and the pursuit of happiness. Although it took many years for the concept of equality to be extended to all people, the Framers did create a system of government designed to protect what they called natural rights. (Today, we speak of human rights, but the idea is basically the same.) By **natural rights**, the Framers meant that every person, by virtue of being a human being, has an equal right to protection against arbitrary treatment and an equal right to the liberties the Bill of Rights guarantees.

natural rights
The rights of all people to dignity and worth; also called human rights.

Citizens of the United States are committed to equality. "Equality," however, is an elusive term. How do you understand it? The understanding of equality on which we have the greatest consensus is that everyone should have equality of opportunity regardless of race, ethnic origin, religion and, in recent years, sex and sexual orientation. There is not much equal opportunity if one person is born into a well-to-do family, lives in a safe suburb, and receives a good education, while another is born into a poor, broken family, lives in a run-down inner-city neighborhood, and attends inferior schools. Some argue that providing equalizing opportunities for the disadvantaged through federal programs such as Head Start, which helps prepare preschool children from poor families for elementary school, is necessary to bridge this gap.

Traditionally, Americans have focused on individual achievement, but in recent decades some politicians and civil rights leaders shifted attention to the concept of equality between groups. When large disparities in wealth and advantage exist between groups—as between black and white people or between women and men—equality becomes a highly divisive political issue. Those who are disadvantaged might emphasize economic and social factors that exclude them from the mainstream. They champion programs like **affirmative action** that are often designed to increase diversity for the benefit of all students. Programs that take these group factors into account, as with affirmative action, have been and continue to be controversial.

affirmative action
Remedial action designed to overcome the effects of discrimination against minorities and women.

Finally, equality can also mean equality of results. A perennial debate is whether social justice and genuine equality can exist in a nation in which people of one class have so much and others have so little, and in which the gap between them is growing wider.[8] There is considerable support for guaranteeing a minimum floor below which no one should be allowed to fall, but American adults generally do not support guaranteeing an equality of results.

Citizenship and the Rights It Affords (Structure)

15.2 Explain the concept of citizenship and the rights of U.S. citizens.

Although, as discussed above, the natural rights the Framers envisioned do not depend on citizenship, important legal rights come with it. Citizenship determines nationality and defines who is a member of, owes allegiance to, and is a subject of the nation. But in a constitutional democracy, citizenship is also an office, and like other offices, it carries with it certain powers and responsibilities. How citizenship is acquired and retained is therefore important.

The basic right of citizenship was not given constitutional protection until 1868, when the Fourteenth Amendment was adopted; before that, each state determined citizenship. The Fourteenth Amendment states, "All persons born or naturalized in the

Immigrants are important members of American society. During this 2010 naturalization ceremony sponsored by U.S. Forces-Iraq, in which 50 service members took the oath of allegiance, U.S. Army Pfc. Yiraldy Aloma, a native of Panama City, Panama, wipes a tear from her eye. Military service has provided one path to citizenship for dreamers with specialized medical or language skills the military has deemed vital.

United States, and subject to the jurisdiction thereof, are citizens of the United States and of the State wherein they reside." This language has generally been understood to mean that all persons born in the United States, except children born to foreign ambassadors and ministers, are citizens of this country regardless of the citizenship of their parents.

Naturalized Citizens

naturalization
A legal action conferring citizenship on an immigrant.

People can also acquire citizenship by **naturalization**, a legal act conferring citizenship on an immigrant—someone who is living in the United States but is not a citizen. Congress determines naturalization requirements (see Table 15.1 for the list of requirements). Today, with minor exceptions, immigrants who are over 18 years of age, have been lawfully admitted for permanent residence, and who have resided in the United States for at least five years and in the state for at least six months are eligible for naturalization. Any state or federal court in the United States or the U.S. Citizenship and Immigration Services (USCIS) can grant citizenship. USCIS, with the FBI's help, makes the necessary investigations. Any person denied citizenship after a hearing before an immigration officer may appeal to a federal district judge.

TABLE 15.1 OFFICIAL WORDING OF U.S. CITIZENSHIP AND IMMIGRATION SERVICES INSTRUCTIONS FOR APPLICATION FOR NATURALIZATION

You may apply for naturalization when you meet all the requirements to become a U.S. citizen. General eligibility requirements are the following:

1. you are at least 18 years of age at the time of filing (except active-duty members of the U.S. Armed Forces);
2. you are a permanent resident of the United States for a required period of time;
3. you have lived within the state or USCIS district where you claim residence for at least three months prior to filing;
4. you have demonstrated physical presence within the United States for a required period of time;
5. you have demonstrated continuous residence for a required period of time;
6. you demonstrate good moral character;
7. you demonstrate an attachment to the principles and ideals of the U.S. Constitution;
8. you demonstrate a basic knowledge of U.S. history and government (also known as "civics") as well as an ability to read, write, speak, and understand basic English; and
9. you take an Oath of Allegiance to the United States. Some applicants may be eligible for a modified oath.

SOURCE: Instructions for Application for Naturalization, Department of Homeland Security, USCIS, https://www.uscis.gov/n-400.

Because each nation has complete authority to define nationality for itself, two or more nations may consider a person a citizen. **Dual citizenship** is not unusual, especially for people from nations that do not recognize the right of individuals to renounce their citizenship, called the **right of expatriation**. Children born abroad to U.S. citizens may also be citizens of the nation in which they were born. Children born in the United States of parents from a foreign nation may also be citizens to their parents' country.

dual citizenship
Citizenship in more than one nation.

right of expatriation
The right to renounce one's citizenship.

Rights of U.S. Citizens

A person becomes a citizen of one of the 50 states merely by residing in that state. Residence as understood in the Fourteenth Amendment means the place a person calls home. The legal status of residence is not the same as physical presence. Many of you may be currently living in a different state than what you consider home and you may have retained your legal status in your home state.

Many of our important rights flow from state citizenship. In the *Slaughter-House Cases* (1873), the Supreme Court carefully distinguished between the privileges of U.S. citizens and those of state citizens.[9] It held that the only privileges of national citizenship are those that "owe their existence to the Federal Government, its National Character, its Constitution, or its laws." These privileges have never been completely specified, but they include the right to use the navigable waters of the United States and to protection on the high seas, to assemble peacefully and petition for redress of grievances, to vote if qualified to do so under state laws and have your vote counted properly, and to travel throughout the United States.

In times of war, the rights and liberties of citizenship are tested and have been curbed, but not all attempts have been successful. The Supreme Court overruled President Abraham Lincoln's use of military courts to try civilians during the Civil War,[10] but it upheld the World War II internment of Japanese Americans in "relocation camps"[11] and has approved the use of military tribunals to try captured foreign saboteurs[12] who were held abroad. However, it also ruled that citizens may not be subject to courts-martial or denied the guarantees of the Bill of Rights.[13]

In the war against international terrorism, President George W. Bush issued orders declaring U.S. citizens "enemy combatants" for plotting with the Al-Qaeda network and authorized their detention, along with that of other captured foreign nationals, in military compounds without counsel or access to a court of law. However, even in these cases, prisoners have a right to have their detention reviewed, and the Court's decision in *Boumediene* v. *Bush* (2008) reinforced this right.[14] The tension over protecting citizens' rights while fighting the War on Terror continued during the Obama administration. From Faisal Shahzad's arrest for attempting to detonate a car bomb in Times Square in May 2010 to Dzhokhar Tsarnaev's arrest for detonating a bomb near the finish line of the 2013 Boston Marathon, the federal court system has been the venue for recent terrorism trials against U.S. citizens. Under the Court's ruling in *Boumediene*, Shahzad's case was heard in the federal court system where, in October 2010, he was sentenced to life in prison without the possibility of parole. Dzhokhar Tsarnaev was convicted of using and conspiring to use a weapon of mass destruction in April 2015 and was sentenced to death by lethal injection. He is currently appealing his conviction and sentence. Tsarnaev's brother and co-conspirator Tamerlan was killed as the brothers tried to leave Boston in the wake of the attacks.

Rights of Lawful Permanent Residents

During periods of suspicion and hostility toward immigrants, the protections of citizenship are even more precious. Congress enacted the Enemy Alien Act of 1798, which remains in effect, authorizing the president to detain and expel citizens of a country with which we are at war. U.S. citizens may not be expelled from the country, but noncitizens may be expelled for even minor infractions.[15] The Supreme Court also upheld the 1996 amendments to the Immigration and Nationality Act, which require mandatory detention during deportation hearings of immigrants accused of certain crimes,[16] though they may not be detained indefinitely.[17] As the average stay in immigration detention facilities reaches one year, the Court in 2018 ruled that current immigration law does not require periodic bond hearings to determine whether they pose a flight risk or a danger to public safety.[18] The Court did, however, send the case back to the Court of Appeals for the Ninth Circuit for them to determine if the Constitution itself required such review.

Only citizens may run for elective office and vote in national elections, but all other rights are not so literally restricted. Still, the Constitution protects many rights of all *persons*, not only of American citizens. Neither Congress nor the states can deny to immigrants the rights of freedom of religion or freedom of speech. Nor can any government deprive any person of the due process of the law or equal protection under the laws.[19]

However, Congress and the states may deny or limit welfare and many other kinds of benefits to immigrants. Congress has denied most federally assisted benefits to undocumented immigrants and has permitted states to deny them many other benefits, making an exception only for emergency medical care, disaster relief, and some nutrition programs. The Court has also upheld laws barring the employment of immigrants as police officers, schoolteachers, and probation officers.[20] Although states have considerable discretion over what benefits they give to immigrants, the Supreme Court has held that states cannot constitutionally exclude children of undocumented immigrants from the public schools or charge their parents tuition.[21] In a 2012 challenge to a controversial Arizona law requiring that law enforcement officers check the immigration status of individuals they stop or detain, the Supreme Court struck down most of its provisions because they violated the federal government's "broad, undoubted power over immigration. . . ."[22] But, it did uphold the immigration check provision as long as state law enforcement had a legitimate basis for making the stop or detention.

The Quest for Equal Justice (Action)

15.3 Compare and contrast the efforts of various groups to obtain equal protection of the law.

Citizenship rights have been prominent throughout our country's history, but not all people in the United States were originally granted full rights of citizenship. Here, we review the political history and social contexts in which constitutional challenges to laws and other government actions relating to civil rights for women and minorities arose. This history involves more than court decisions, laws, and constitutional amendments, however. It encompasses the entire social, economic, and political system. And although the struggles of all groups are interwoven, they are not identical, so we deal with each briefly and separately.

Racial Equality

U.S. citizens had a painful confrontation with the problem of race during the Civil War (1861–1865). As a result of the northern victory, the Thirteenth, Fourteenth, and Fifteenth Amendments became part of the Constitution. The Thirteenth Amendment ended slavery, the Fourteenth guarantees equal treatment of all people and establishes citizenship, and the Fifteenth Amendment protects citizens' voting rights. During Reconstruction in the late 1860s and 1870s, Congress passed civil rights laws to implement these amendments and established programs to provide educational and social services for the freed slaves. But the Supreme Court struck down many of these laws, and it was not until the 1950s and 1960s that legal progress was again made toward ensuring black Americans their civil rights.

SEGREGATION AND WHITE SUPREMACY Before Reconstruction programs could have any significant effect, the white southern political leadership regained power, and by 1877, Reconstruction ended. Northern political leaders abandoned blacks to their fate at the hands of their former white masters; presidents no longer concerned themselves with enforcing civil rights laws, and Congress enacted no new ones. The Supreme Court either declared old laws unconstitutional or interpreted them so narrowly that they were ineffective. The Court also gave such limited construction to the Thirteenth, Fourteenth, and Fifteenth Amendments that they failed to accomplish their intended purpose of protecting the rights of blacks.[23]

For nearly a century after the Civil War, white supremacy went unchallenged in the South, where most blacks then lived. They were kept from voting; they were forced to accept menial jobs; they were denied educational opportunities; they were segregated in public and private facilities.[24] Blacks were also subjected to terrible violence; in the late 1800s, an average of one black person was lynched every three to four days, a practice that continued into the 1960s.[25]

During World War I (1914–1918), blacks began to migrate to northern cities to seek jobs in war factories. The Great Depression of the 1930s and World War II in the 1940s accelerated their relocation. Although discrimination continued, more jobs became available, and blacks made social gains. As their migration from the rural South shifted the racial composition of cities across much of the United States, the black vote became important in national elections. These changes created a black middle class opposed to segregation as a symbol of servitude and a cause of inequality. There was a growing demand to abolish color barriers, and by the mid-twentieth century, urban blacks in the North were active and gaining political clout.

SLOW GOVERNMENT RESPONSE By the 1930s, blacks were challenging the doctrine of segregation in the courts, and after World War II, civil rights litigation began to have a major impact. Beginning with the landmark 1954 ruling in *Brown* v. *Board of Education of Topeka,* the Supreme Court prohibited racially segregated public schools[26] and subsequently struck down most of the devices that state and local authorities had used to keep blacks from voting.[27] We discuss *Brown* and voting

The "Great Migration" between 1910 and 1970 saw roughly 6 million blacks leaving southern states and relocating to northern and Midwestern cities. This 1942 photo shows some of the nearly 200,000 new black residents in New York City's Harlem neighborhood.

rights in detail later in the chapter. Although the Court struck down legalized segregation, achieving a significant level of desegregation required the other branches of government to act.

In the late 1940s and 1950s, Presidents Harry S. Truman and Dwight D. Eisenhower used their executive authority to fight segregation in the armed services and the federal bureaucracy. They directed the Department of Justice to enforce whatever civil rights laws were on the books, but Congress still held back. In the late 1950s, an emerging national consensus in favor of governmental action to protect civil rights, plus the political clout of blacks in the northern states, began to influence Congress. In 1957, northern and western members of Congress from both parties overrode a southern filibuster in the Senate and enacted the first federal civil rights laws since Reconstruction, the Federal Civil Rights Act of 1957, which made it a crime to intimidate or threaten blacks exercising their right to vote.

A TURNING POINT Even after the Court's decisions and congressional action, there was widespread resistance to integration in the South. As we discuss in detail later in the chapter, many legal barriers to equal rights had fallen, yet most blacks still could not buy houses where they wanted, compete fairly for the jobs they needed, send their children to well-equipped schools, eat in "whites only" restaurants, or walk freely on the streets of "white neighborhoods." While racial discrimination was most pronounced in the eleven former Confederate states, it also existed nationally. In fact, the landmark school desegregation case was actually a group of five cases that the Court consolidated under the name of *Brown* v. *Board of Education*. The cases came out of school districts in Kansas, Virginia, South Carolina, Delaware, and the District of Columbia. And in most states, blacks faced discriminatory practices such as redlining, which maintained segregated neighborhoods by denying them mortgages. The 1968 Fair Housing Act forbade redlining, but many argue the practice continues, if more subtly today than in the past.

Change came by way of a massive social, economic, and political movement. A major turning point came in Montgomery, Alabama, on December 1, 1955, when Rosa Parks, a black seamstress, refused to give up her seat to a white man on a bus as

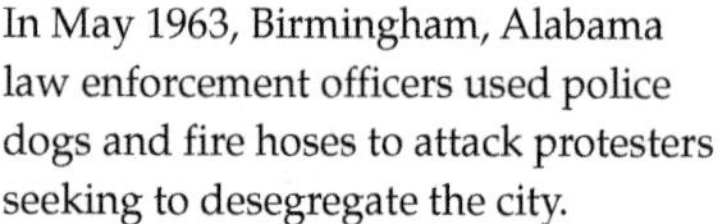

In May 1963, Birmingham, Alabama law enforcement officers used police dogs and fire hoses to attack protesters seeking to desegregate the city.

the law required her to do. She was removed from the bus, arrested, and fined. The black community responded by boycotting city buses.

The boycott worked and a charismatic national civil rights leader emerged, the Dr. Martin Luther King, Jr. Through his doctrine of nonviolent resistance, King gave a new dimension to the struggle. Following a peaceful 1963 demonstration in Birmingham, Alabama, that was met with fire hoses, police dogs, and mass arrests, more than a quarter of a million people converged on Washington, D.C., to hear King and other civil rights leaders speak. By the time the summer was over, hardly a city, North or South, had not been the site of demonstrations, protests, or sit-ins; some cities erupted in violence.

This direct action had an effect. Many cities enacted civil rights ordinances, more schools were desegregated, and President John F. Kennedy urged Congress to enact a comprehensive civil rights bill. Late in 1963, the nation's grief over the assassination of President Kennedy, who had become identified with civil rights goals, added political fuel to the drive for decisive federal action to protect civil rights.[28] President Lyndon B. Johnson made civil rights legislation his highest priority. On July 2, 1964, after months of divisive debate, he signed into law the Civil Rights Act of 1964, which forbids discrimination on the basis of race, color, religion, sex, or nationality.[29]

The 1964 Civil Rights Act was a monumental legal change in providing equal protection under the law. But as discussed in Chapter 4 and in the beginning of the chapter, it was not the end of the struggle for civil rights. Other important actions included the Twenty-fourth Amendment, which banned poll taxes and was ratified in January 1964, the Voting Rights Act of 1965, and Supreme Court decisions barring the use of racial gerrymandering and literacy tests as a means to deprive blacks of the right to vote.

The landmark 1964 and 1965 civil rights legislation has had a profound impact on the United States. Americans today take for granted that persons of all races can stay in hotels, purchase homes, and dine in restaurants. The same is true for admission to college, applying for jobs, and interracial marriage. And yet before the 1964 legislation blacks were routinely denied access. In a similar way, the 1965 Voting Rights Act and the Twenty-fourth Amendment meant that the voting discrimination that had gone on for decades was legally ended and large numbers of citizens, particularly blacks, were allowed to vote. More subtle barriers to effective political participation persist, as does discrimination more generally. But, the action of the federal courts, Congress, and the president in roughly a decade between the Court's 1954 decision in *Brown* v. *Board of Education* striking down racial segregation in public schools and the 1964 and 1965 federal legislation constitutes a historic turning point in U.S. history. We turn to a more thorough discussion of these concepts in the section on equal protection of the laws.

AT THE END OF THE EDMUND PETTUS BRIDGE On November 4, 2008, American voters elected Barack Obama president of the United States, the first time a black candidate has been elected to the office. The historic election was one where the candidates, more so than at any time in the past, represented the diversity of the United States electorate. That diversity was a direct result of the hard-won successes in our country's long battle over race and sex equality. Indeed, Congressman John Lewis, a longtime civil rights activist who was beaten by Alabama state police as he marched across Selma's Edmund Pettus Bridge in 1965, remarked that "Barack Obama is what comes at the end of that bridge in Selma."[30]

Women's Rights

The 2008 election broke barriers besides race. The Democrats' other major contender for the presidential nomination was Hillary Clinton, who would have been the first woman nominated by a major party for the presidency. Because of the historic nature

Congressman John Lewis (D-GA), then the chair of the Student Nonviolent Coordinating Committee, led civil rights activists in a 1965 march across the Edmund Pettus Bridge in Selma, Alabama. Lewis was elected to the U.S. Congress in 1977 and continues to serve today.

of the Obama candidacy, less attention was paid to the fact that Senator Clinton was herself breaking barriers in her string of primary election victories and near majority of elected delegates. And, in 2016, she won her party's nomination for president. Although Clinton went on to win the popular vote, she lost the Electoral College race, and thus the presidency, to Republican Donald Trump.

These developments came more than 165 years after the Seneca Falls Women's Rights Convention (1848), which launched the women's movement. That convention attracted men and women who actively campaigned to abolish slavery and to secure the rights of blacks and women. But as the Civil War approached, women were urged to abandon their own cause and devote their energies to ending slavery.[31] The Civil War effectively brought the women's movement to a halt.

women's suffrage
The right of women to vote.

By the turn of the twentieth century, however, a vigorous campaign was under way for **women's suffrage**—the right of women to vote. The first victories came in western states, where Wyoming led the way in 1869. But many suffragists were dissatisfied with this state-by-state approach. They wanted a decisive victory—a constitutional amendment that would force all states to allow qualified women to vote. Finally, in 1919, Congress proposed the Nineteenth Amendment. Many southerners opposed the amendment because it gave Congress enforcement power, which might bring federal officials to investigate elections to ensure that it was being obeyed—an interference that could call attention to how blacks were being kept from voting.

Women won the right to vote with the ratification of the Nineteenth Amendment in 1920, but they were still denied equal pay and equal rights, and national and state laws imposed many legal disabilities on them, such as the lack of comparable pay and health benefits. In the 1970s and 1980s, the unsuccessful struggle to secure the adoption of the Equal Rights Amendment occupied much of the movement's attention. Since then women have mobilized their political clout behind issues that range from equal pay to world peace, an end to sexual harassment, abortion rights, and the election of more women to office.[32]

The Supreme Court has been reluctant to expand the level of Fourteenth Amendment protection against sex discrimination as it has against racial discrimination. Even so, it has struck down many state laws that discriminate based on sex. For example, it held that Virginia could not create a separate military academy for women instead of admitting them into the all-male Virginia Military Institute, a 150-year-old state-run institution.[33]

And the courts have increasingly enforced the prohibition against sex discrimination found in the 1964 Civil Rights Act and expanded it to forbid sexual harassment in the workplace. In 1986, the Supreme Court applied the Act to "quid pro quo" sexual harassment, in which an employer requires sexual favors from a person as a condition of employment (in hiring, promotions, and continued employment).[34] It has since ruled that the Civil Rights Act also forbids a "hostile environment," defined as a workplace "permeated" with intimidation, ridicule, and insult that is severe and pervasive, and this includes same-sex harassment.[35]

Protests against sexual harassment and violence against women took center stage in 2017 and 2018, propelled by the actions and comments of powerful men including President Donald Trump, Hollywood movie producer Harvey Weinstein, comedian Bill Cosby, and many others. The #MeToo movement in which women are encouraged to speak out about their own experiences with harassment, assault, or rape, spread nationwide and women's marches in Washington, D.C. and throughout the country were held to protest the president and his administration's policies. Of course not all those who experience assault or harassment are women; men have also spoken out about the abuse they suffered. Many women's rights activists also encouraged women to run for office; 2018 saw a record-setting number of women, 417, running for seats in the House of Representatives and the Senate. Most of the female candidates are Democrats (310 compared to 107 Republicans). In primary races held by early June 2018, Democratic women were successful in half of the races in which they had run (63 out of 126) and Republican women won about one-third of their races (11 of 33).[36]

Even with these advancements, evidence of a "glass ceiling" preventing women's advancement in large corporations persists.[37] The number of female Fortune 500 CEOs reached an all-time high in 2017 when women led 32 of these companies. But, by 2018, that number dropped by 25 percent to 24.[38] But progress has been made, with more and more women going to graduate and professional schools and into the media and business. Indeed, during the past three decades, more women have graduated from colleges and universities than men (see Figure 15.1 on the next page).

Hispanics

The struggle for civil rights has not been limited to women and blacks. Throughout U.S. history, many native-born citizens have considered new waves of immigrants suspect, especially if the newcomers were not white or English speaking. Formal barriers of law and informal barriers of custom combined to deny these groups equal rights. But as they established themselves—first economically and then politically—most barriers were swept away, and the newcomers or their children enjoyed the same constitutionally guaranteed rights as other citizens.

On January 20, many gathered on the Mall in Washington, D.C. for the 2018 Women's March.

FIGURE 15.1 PERCENTAGE OF BACHELOR'S DEGREES AWARDED BY SEX

The number of women graduating from bachelor's degree programs increased dramatically during the twentieth century and into the twenty-first. For the first time in the 1981–1982 academic year, more than half of the bachelor's degrees awarded went to women, and that percentage has been growing ever since.

SOURCE: *Digest of Education Statistics*, 2012, Table 310. National Center for Education Statistics. Data updated by the authors using Table 301.10 in the 2013–2016 reports; 2015 data is most recent available. https://nces.ed.gov/programs/digest/d12/tables/dt12_310.asp.

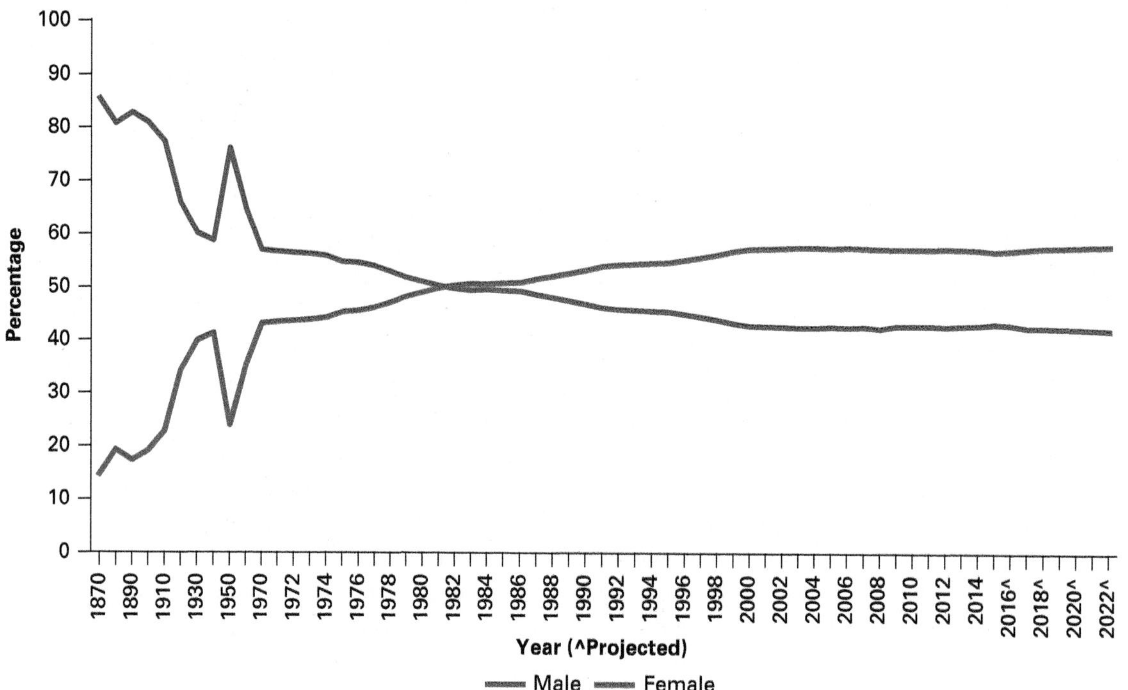

In many parts of the United States today, Hispanic immigrants are met with suspicion; the discussion concerning the immigration crisis at the beginning of the chapter illustrates the magnitude of the problem. But, the issue is not new. In 1954, the Immigration and Naturalization Service began a program known as "Operation Wetback," through which hundreds of thousands of Mexican immigrants were forcibly deported, sometimes with their U.S.–born children.[39] Deportation continues today and reached record highs in recent years.[40] As mentioned previously, most of Arizona's 2010 immigration legislation was struck down, including the provision making it a crime to fail to carry immigration documentation. But, the Supreme Court did uphold the so-called "show me your papers" provision requiring state law enforcement officers to check the immigration status of individuals they stop or detain for a legitimate purpose.[41] Conditions for Hispanic immigrants have become more tenuous under the Trump administration. The administration ended DACA in March 2018, but multiple judges have enjoined any action against "dreamers" while the legal challenges to the administration's actions make their way through the federal courts. At the same time, many undocumented immigrants are being detained pending review of their immigration status. Due to a significant backlog in immigration courts, undocumented immigrants seeking asylum in the United States face lengthy detentions prior to getting their cases resolved.[42]

Hispanics Americans have not always been able to translate their numbers into comparable political clout because of political differences among them and because many are not citizens or registered to vote. However, after California adopted Proposition 187 in 1994, which denied medical, educational, and social services to illegal immigrants, and Congress amended the federal welfare laws to curtail benefits to noncitizens, many immigrants rushed to become naturalized. Half of all Hispanic Americans live in two states: California and Texas. In 2000, California became the first large state in which white people are in the minority, and Texas followed in 2004; a majority of the population is made up of racial minorities (majority–minority) in Hawaii, New Mexico, Nevada, and the District of Columbia as well.[43]

Asian Americans

The term "Asian American" describes approximately 10 million people from many different countries and ethnic backgrounds. Most do not think of themselves as Asians but as U.S. citizens of Chinese, Japanese, Indian, Vietnamese, Cambodian, Korean, or other specific ancestry. Although Asian Americans are often considered a "model minority" because of their successes in education and business, the U.S. Civil Rights Commission found in 1992 that "Asian Americans do face widespread prejudice, discrimination, and barriers to equal opportunity" and that racially motivated violence against them "occurs with disturbing frequency."[44] Discrimination against Asian Americans is, unfortunately, nothing new. The Naturalization Act of 1906, for example, made it impossible for any Asian American to become a U.S. citizen. Although the Act was challenged, the Supreme Court upheld its provision that only white persons and aliens of African nativity or descent were eligible for citizenship.[45] As we discuss, it took decades for these restrictions to be repealed.

CHINESE AMERICANS The Chinese were the first Asians to come to the United States. Beginning in 1847, when young men came to the American West to escape poverty and to work in mines, on railroads, and on farms, the Chinese encountered economic and cultural fears by the white majority, who did not understand their language or their culture. Chinese Americans were recruited by the Central Pacific Railroad to work on the transcontinental railroad, but anti-Chinese sentiment grew. By the 1870s, attacks on "Chinatowns" began in cities throughout the United States. The Chinese Exclusion Act of 1882 restricted Chinese immigration and excluded Chinese immigrants already in the United States from the possibility of citizenship. It was not until 1943 that Congress repealed the Chinese Exclusion Act and opened the door to citizenship for Chinese Americans.

The 1965 amendments to the Immigration and Nationality Act went further to end the nationality criteria and thus equalize immigration criteria across race and ethnicity. Since that time, Chinese Americans have moved into the mainstream of U.S. society, and they have begun to run for and win local political offices. Gary Locke, a Democrat and a graduate of Yale and Boston University Law School, became the first Chinese American to become governor of a continental state (Washington in 1996) and later was the American ambassador to China.

JAPANESE AMERICANS Japanese immigrants first arrived in Hawaii in the 1860s and then California in the 1880s. By the beginning of the twentieth century, they faced overt hostility. In 1905, white labor leaders organized the Japanese and Korean Exclusion League, and in 1906, the San Francisco Board of Education excluded all Chinese, Japanese, and Korean children from neighborhood schools. Some western states passed laws denying the right to own land to immigrants who were ineligible to become citizens—meaning Asian immigrants.

During World War II, anti-Japanese hysteria led to interning many Japanese Americans living on the west coast—most of whom were loyal U.S. citizens guilty of no crimes—in prison camps in California, Colorado, and other states. Their property was often sold at below-market rates, and many of them lost their businesses, jobs, and incomes. Although Japanese Americans challenged the internment policies, the U.S. Supreme Court upheld the government's actions. In *Korematsu* v. *United States* (1944), the Court ruled that under the threat to national security, it could not reject congressional and military judgment that disloyalty existed and must be segregated.[46] Following the war, the exclusionary acts were repealed, though discrimination against

In *Korematsu* v. *United States* (323 U.S. 214 (1944)), the Supreme Court upheld the internment of Japanese American citizens in camps in California and Colorado, among other states, during World War II. But, it was later revealed that the military misrepresented information to the Court about the potential threat they posed. It was not until 1988 that the U.S. government officially apologized for its actions, and Congress awarded reparations to those interned during the war. Even more recently, the Supreme Court arguably overturned *Korematsu*. Writing for the majority, Chief Justice Roberts upheld President Trump's travel ban, but made clear that "*Korematsu* was gravely wrong the day it was decided" and "has no place in law under the Constitution" (*Trump* v. *Hawaii*, 585 U.S. ____ (2018)).

Japanese Americans persisted, such as the limits placed on Japanese American student enrollment at many colleges and universities. In 1988, President Ronald Reagan signed a law providing $20,000 restitution to each of the approximately 60,000 surviving World War II internees.

Native Americans

Approximately 20 percent of the nearly 3 million Native Americans in the United States live on or near a *reservation*—a tract of land given to tribal nations through treaties with the federal government.[47] The history of discrimination against Native Americans in the United States is a great stain on our human rights record. Although discrimination against blacks often gets more attention in civil rights discussions, legally sanctioned discrimination against Native Americans followed a similar path. Efforts that forcibly moved Native American tribes off their land and farther west as more whites migrated to the Midwest and western states are well known. The Indian Removal Act, passed in 1830, required that all Native American tribes be moved from the East and Southeast. The Act also authorized the use of force to meet its goals. As a result, approximately 4,000 of the 18,000 Cherokee Indians forced to move west into what became eastern Oklahoma in the late 1830s died on the "Trail of Tears."[48]

The Supreme Court decided cases on the constitutionality of government actions towards Native Americans soon after enactment of the Indian Removal Act and affirmed that tribes were "dependent nations," effectively under the control of the U.S. government, and that the federal, not state, government had the authority to deal with Indian nations.[49] The practices of seizing territory once inhabited by Native Americans continued as the U.S. government waged war on Indian tribes, taking land and forcing survivors to move to reservations in inhospitable lands in South Dakota and New Mexico. In the twentieth century, the government attempted to restrict American Indian culture and to eliminate indigenous languages and traditional celebrations.

Native American rights organizations, including the American Indian Movement, protested discrimination against Native Americans in housing, employment, and health care. Over time, other civil rights groups, such as the American Civil Liberties Union (ACLU), have joined the fight to protect Native American civil rights. In recent years the federal courts have approved settlements in class action lawsuits regarding the equal treatment of Native American students in the public schools[50] and discrimination against Native American farmers by the U.S. Department of Agriculture, the latter of which required the USDA to pay $680 million in damages to thousands of Native Americans and to forgive another $80 million in outstanding farm loans.[51]

As a result of these efforts and of a greater national consciousness, most citizens are now aware that many Native Americans continue to face discrimination and live in poverty. About one-fourth of all Native American children live in poverty, compared to almost 13 percent of the rest of the nation; their substance abuse rates are higher than the national average and they are twice as likely to die by age 24 than any other race.[52] Some reservations lack adequate health care facilities, schools, housing, and jobs. Congress has started to compensate Native Americans for past injustices and to provide more opportunities to develop tribal economic independence, and judges are showing greater vigilance in enforcing Indian treaty rights.

Equal Protection of the Laws: What Does It Mean? (Structure and Impact)

15.4 Evaluate the standards by which civil rights are protected today.

The **equal protection clause** of the Fourteenth Amendment declares that no state (including any subdivision thereof) shall "deny to any person within its jurisdiction the equal protection of the laws." Although no parallel clause explicitly applies to the national government, courts have interpreted the Fifth Amendment's **due process clause**, which prevents any person from being "deprived of life, liberty, or property, without due process of law," to impose the same restraints on the national government as the equal protection clause imposes on the states.

equal protection clause
A clause in the Fourteenth Amendment that forbids any state to deny to any person within its jurisdiction the equal protection of the laws. By interpretation, the Fifth Amendment imposes the same limitation on the national government. This clause is the major constitutional restraint on the power of governments to discriminate against persons because of race, national origin, or sex.

due process clause
A clause in the Fifth Amendment limiting the power of the national government; a similar clause in the Fourteenth Amendment prohibits state governments from depriving any person of life, liberty, or property without due process of law.

Note that the clause applies only to the actions of governments, not to those of private individuals. If a private person discriminates, that action does not violate the Constitution. It may, however, violate federal and state laws, like the 1964 Civil Rights Act, passed to protect people from unjust discrimination by private parties.

The equal protection clause does not, however, prevent governments from discriminating in all cases. What the Constitution forbids is unreasonable classifications. In general, a classification is unreasonable when there is no relationship between the classes it creates and permissible governmental goals. A law prohibiting redheads from voting, for example, would be unreasonable. In contrast, laws denying persons under the age of 18 the right to vote, to marry without the permission of their parents, or to apply for a driver's license appear to be reasonable (at least to most people over the age of 18).

Constitutional Classifications and Tests

One of the most difficult constitutional questions is how to distinguish between constitutional and unconstitutional classifications. The Supreme Court uses three tests for this purpose: the *rational basis* test, the *strict scrutiny* test, and the *heightened scrutiny* test.

THE RATIONAL BASIS TEST The traditional test to determine whether a law complies with the equal protection requirement—the **rational basis test**—places the burden of proof on the parties attacking the law. The person alleging discrimination must show that the law has no rational or legitimate governmental goal. Traditionally, the rational basis test applied only to legislation affecting economic interests and, with only two exceptions in the last 70 years, the Court has upheld the legislation and deferred to legislative judgments.[53] But more recently, the Court has applied the test when noneconomic interests are challenged.[54] Overwhelmingly in those cases, the

rational basis test
A standard developed by the courts to test the constitutionality of a law; when applied, a law is constitutional as long as it meets a reasonable government interest.

legislation is upheld, though there are exceptions. For example, when the Court struck down an amendment to the Colorado state constitution that excluded sexual orientation as a protected category in antidiscrimination laws, it did so using the rational basis test.[55] We will discuss laws discriminating based on sexual orientation later in this chapter.

strict scrutiny test

A test applied by the court when a classification is based on race; the government must show that there is a compelling reason for the law and no other less restrictive way to meet the interest.

SUSPECT CLASSIFICATIONS AND STRICT SCRUTINY When a law is subject to the **strict scrutiny test**, the burden shifts; for the law to be constitutional, the government must show that there is both a "compelling governmental interest" to justify the classification and no less restrictive way to meet this compelling interest. The Court applies the strict scrutiny test to suspect classifications. A suspect classification is one through which people have been deliberately subjected to severely unequal treatment or that society has used to render people politically powerless.[56] When a law classifies based on race or national origin, it immediately raises a red flag, regardless of whether it is intended to aid or inhibit a particular race or nationality. For example, the Supreme Court has held that laws that give preference for public employment based on race are subject to strict scrutiny.

heightened scrutiny test

This test has been applied when a law classifies based on sex; to be upheld, the law must meet an important government interest.

QUASI-SUSPECT CLASSIFICATIONS AND HEIGHTENED SCRUTINY To sustain a law under the **heightened scrutiny test**, the government must show that its classification serves "important governmental objectives." Heightened scrutiny is a standard first used by the Supreme Court in 1971 to declare classifications based on sex unconstitutional. As Justice William J. Brennan Jr. wrote for the Court: "There can be no doubt that our nation has had a long and unfortunate history of sex discrimination. Traditionally, such discrimination was rationalized by an attitude of 'romantic paternalism,' which in practical effect put women, not on a pedestal, but in a cage."[57] In recent years, the Supreme Court has struck down most laws brought before it that were alleged to discriminate against women, but has largely done so based on federal statutes like the 1964 Civil Rights Act.

POVERTY AND AGE Just as race and sex classifications receive elevated scrutiny, some argue that economic and age classification ought to be subject to some heightened review. The Supreme Court rejected the argument "that financial need alone identifies a suspect class for purposes of equal protection analysis."[58] However, some state supreme courts (Texas, Ohio, and Connecticut, among others) have ruled that unequal funding for public schools, as a result of "rich" districts spending more per pupil than "poor" districts, violates their state constitutional provisions for free and equal education.[59] More recently, the focus of such litigation has centered on requirements to provide an "adequate" or "suitable" education, based on state constitutions' education clauses.[60]

Age is not a suspect classification. Many states have laws that discriminate based on age: obtaining a driver's license, marrying without parental consent, attending schools, buying alcohol or tobacco, and so on. Many governmental institutions have age-specific programs: for senior citizens, for adult students, and for people in mid-career. As Justice Sandra Day O'Connor observed, "States may discriminate on the basis of age without offending the Fourteenth Amendment if the age classification in question is rationally related to a legitimate state interest."[61]

Although the Court has been unwilling to extend heightened protection to individuals who have experienced age discrimination, Congress has acted to provide statutory protection, particularly with the Age Discrimination in Employment Act (1967). In 1974, Congress attempted to extend the protections against age discrimination to cover state employees, but the Supreme Court ruled that Congress lacks the constitutional authority to open the federal courts to suits by state employees for alleged age discrimination. State employees are limited to recovering monetary damages under state laws in state courts.[62]

SEXUAL ORIENTATION In the United States, discrimination based on sexual orientation has never received the heightened protection against discrimination applied to classifications made on the basis of race or sex. The Supreme Court has ruled that the government needs only a reasonable basis for legislating in order to permissibly classify individuals based on sexual orientation. Traditionally, legislation meant to uphold basic values and morals, even laws targeting gay couples, would pass such a test; "morals and values" legislation has included prohibitions on consensual, intimate adult sexual activity occurring in the privacy of the home.

But, in 1996, the U.S. Supreme Court made the unusual move of striking down a law using only rational basis review. In *Romer* v. *Evans*, the Court struck down an amendment to the Colorado constitution that prohibited the state's local governments from protecting individuals from discrimination based on sexual orientation.[63] The Court ruled that the provision violated the equal protection clause because it lacked any rational basis and simply represented prejudice against gay people. Although in cases like *Romer* (1996) and *Lawrence* v. *Texas* (2003), a case in which the Court struck down a Texas ban on same-sex sodomy, the Court found that discriminatory laws targeting gay people violated the U.S. Constitution, it did not elevate the level of scrutiny with which it reviews such classifications.

During the 2000s, a number of gay rights activists took their cases to state courts, arguing that their state constitutions required at least the right to legal recognition of same-sex civil unions, and increasingly, the right to marriage equality. And, in 2013, the U.S. Supreme Court struck down the federal Defense of Marriage Act (DOMA) on the basis that states are responsible for defining marriage.[64] Thus, if the state recognized same-sex marriage, the federal government would do so as well.

In addition to the Court's decision to invalidate the key section of the federal DOMA, the justices also reached a decision on a procedural question of standing that effectively favored marriage equality in California.[65] In the wake of the Supreme Court's decisions in these cases, proponents of marriage equality began challenging a number of state same-sex marriage bans in federal district courts. It was one of those cases that the U.S. Supreme Court heard, *Obergefell* v. *Hodges*,[66] in late April 2015. The Court announced on June 26, 2015, that the due process and equal protection clauses of the Fourteenth Amendment require states to allow same-sex couples to marry and to recognize same-sex marriages performed in other states.

Although the Court settled the question of whether states could forbid same-sex marriage, they did not resolve that other types of discrimination based on sexual orientation were prohibited. In the wake of *Obergefell*, several states enacted religious freedom reform bills protecting, on the basis of religious beliefs, the right of individuals and groups to refuse service to gay couples. For example, in March 2016, Florida enacted legislation that protects churches, religious organizations, and individuals from having to solemnize any marriage or provide goods or services for a wedding if doing so would violate their sincerely held religious beliefs. Some states even enacted such "religious freedom restoration acts" in anticipation of the Supreme Court's decision. In Michigan, the legislature enacted several bills in early June 2015 that permitted private faith-based adoption agencies that received state funding to refuse to serve gay couples.[67]

In 2018, the Court had the opportunity to decide a case where a Colorado cake shop owner refused to make a cake for a same-sex couple's wedding because doing so would violate his religious beliefs. *Masterpiece Cakeshop, Ltd.* v. *Colorado Civil Rights Commission* was one of the most anticipated decisions of the Court's October 2017 term. The Court's ruling favored the baker, but on very narrow grounds that essentially left open the question of how to balance one person's religious liberties with another's right to be free from impermissible discrimination. In the present case, the Court ruled that the Colorado Civil Rights Commission did not genuinely consider the baker's religious beliefs and as such violated his religious exercise.[68]

Jim Obergefell, the named plaintiff in the same-sex marriage case heard by the Supreme Court in April 2015, arrives at the Court with members of the Human Rights Campaign. They brought over 200,000 copies of the "People's Brief," which calls for nationwide marriage equality. The Court agreed with Obergefell and struck down state bans on same-sex marriage.

FUNDAMENTAL RIGHTS AND STRICT SCRUTINY The Court also strictly scrutinizes laws impinging on fundamental rights. What makes a right fundamental in the constitutional sense? It is not the importance or the significance of the right but whether it is explicitly or implicitly guaranteed by the Constitution. Under this test, the rights to privacy and to vote have been held to be fundamental. Rights to education, to housing, or to welfare benefits have not been deemed fundamental. Important as they may be, no constitutional provisions specifically protect them from governmental regulation.

As mentioned previously, the Constitution, and particularly the Fourteenth Amendment's equal protection clause, is only one of the legal bases for civil rights protections in the United States. Although we often think of court decisions when we think of the civil rights movement, many of the courts' rulings upholding the civil rights of racial minorities and women were based on congressional legislation. Two pieces of legislation were particularly important to the civil rights movement: the Voting Rights Act of 1965 and the Civil Rights Act of 1964. We turn to these next.

Voting Rights (Structure)

15.5 Trace the evolution of voting rights and analyze the protections provided by the 1965 Voting Rights Act.

Under our Constitution, the states, not the federal government, regulate elections and voting qualifications. However, Article I, Section 4, gives Congress the power to supersede state regulations as to the "Times, Places, and Manner" of elections for representatives and senators. Congress has used this authority, along with its power under Article II, Section 2, to set the date for selecting electors, to set age qualifications and residency requirements to vote in national elections, to establish a uniform day for all states to hold elections for members of Congress and presidential electors, and to give citizens who live outside the United States the right to vote for members of Congress and presidential electors in the states in which they are legal residents.

In spite of these protections, officials seeking to deny blacks the right to vote enacted poll taxes, required literacy tests, developed biased registration requirements, and even turned to intimidation and violence. Reports of violence and intimidation against black voters were frighteningly prevalent, and national attention was drawn to them in the 1960s. One representative from Alabama described the efforts to deprive blacks of the right to vote this way: "At first, we used to kill them to keep them from voting; when we got sick of doing that, we began to steal their ballots; and when stealing their ballots got to troubling our consciences, we decided to handle the matter legally, fixing it so they couldn't vote."[69]

In many southern areas, **literacy tests** were used to discriminate against blacks and poor whites. Although poor white people often avoided registering out of fear of embarrassment from failing a literacy test, the tests were more often used to discriminate against blacks.[70] White people were often asked simple questions; black people were asked questions that would baffle the college educated. "In the 1960s, southern registrars were observed testing black applicants on such matters as the number of bubbles in a soap bar, the news contained in a copy of the Peking Daily, the meaning of obscure passages in state constitutions, and the definition of terms such as *habeas corpus*."[71]

literacy test
A literacy requirement some states imposed as a condition of voting, generally used to disqualify black voters in the South; now illegal.

Local officials were also able to keep black voters from participating through the use of the **white primary**. In the one-party South of the early twentieth century, the Democratic Party would hold whites-only primaries, effectively disenfranchising black voters because, in the absence of viable Republican candidates, the winner of the Democratic primary was guaranteed to win the general election.

white primary
A Democratic Party primary in the old "one-party South" that was limited to white people and essentially constituted an election; ruled unconstitutional in *Smith* v. *Allwright* (1944).

Protecting Voting Rights

After years of refusing to overturn racially discriminatory voting requirements, the Supreme Court in the 1940s began to strike down one after another of the devices that states and localities had used to keep blacks from voting. In *Smith* v. *Allwright* (1944), the Court declared the white primary unconstitutional.[72] Later, it struck down other methods of vote suppression. In 1960, the Court held that **racial gerrymandering**—drawing election districts to ensure that blacks would be a minority in all districts—was contrary to the Fifteenth Amendment.[73] In 1964, the Twenty-fourth Amendment eliminated the **poll tax**—payment required as a condition for voting—in presidential and congressional elections. In 1966, the Court held that the Fourteenth Amendment forbade the poll tax as a condition in any election.[74]

racial gerrymandering
Drawing election districts so as to ensure that members of a certain race are a minority in the district; ruled unconstitutional in *Gomillion* v. *Lightfoot* (1960).

poll tax
Tax required to vote; prohibited for national elections by the Twenty-fourth Amendment (1964) and ruled unconstitutional for all elections in *Harper* v. *Board of Elections* (1966).

The Voting Rights Act of 1965

For two decades after World War II, under the leadership of the Supreme Court, many limitations on voting were declared unconstitutional, but, as has often been the case, the Court acting alone was unable to open the voting booth to blacks. Finally, Congress acted by passing the Voting Rights Act of 1965. It was renewed in 1982, and in 2006 it was extended for another 25 years (for a list of congressional civil rights legislation see Table 15.2 on the next page).

The Voting Rights Act prohibits voting qualifications or standards that result in a denial of the right of any citizen to vote on account of race or color. The law also bars any form of threats or intimidation aimed at preventing citizens from voting. Under the Act, the Department of Justice must also review changes in voting practices or laws that may dilute the voting power of these groups,[75] such as changes in candidacy requirements and qualifications or boundary lines of voting districts.[76] However, challenges to key provisions of the Voting Rights Act have diluted its authority. In 2009, the Court upheld the preclearance provision,[77] but signalled that the requirement must be justified based not on historical evidence of discrimination, but on current needs. Then, in 2013, the Court invalidated Section 4 of the Act, which contained the formula used to identify states and localities required to undergo preclearance.[78] Until Congress develops a new formula, the prospects for which are dim, no states or

TABLE 15.2 MAJOR CIVIL RIGHTS LAWS

In addition to landmark Supreme Court decisions requiring that people be treated equally under the law, congressional action has been essential in protecting voting rights and prohibiting discrimination in employment, housing and education.

Civil Rights Act, 1957	Makes it a federal crime to prevent persons from voting in federal elections
Civil Rights Act, 1964	Bars discrimination in employment or in public accommodations on the basis of race, color, religion, sex, or national origin; created the Equal Employment Opportunity Commission
Voting Rights Act, 1965	Authorizes the appointment of federal examiners to register voters in areas with a history of discrimination
Age Discrimination in Employment Act, 1967	Prohibits job discrimination against workers or job applicants ages 40 through 65 and prohibits mandatory retirement
Fair Housing Act, 1968	Prohibits discrimination on the basis of race, color, religion, or national origin in the sale or rental of most housing
Title IX, Education Amendment of 1972	Prohibits discrimination on the basis of sex in any education program receiving federal financial assistance
Rehabilitation Act, 1973	Requires that recipients of federal grants greater than $2,500 hire and promote qualified handicapped individuals
Fair Housing Act Amendments, 1988	Gives the Department of Housing and Urban Development authority to prohibit housing bias against the handicapped and families with children
Americans with Disabilities Act, 1990	Prohibits discrimination based on disability and requires that facilities be made accessible to those with disabilities
Civil Rights Act, 1991	Requires that employers justify practices that negatively affect the working conditions of women and minorities or show that no alternative practices would have a lesser impact; also established a commission to examine the "glass ceiling" that keeps women from becoming executives and to recommend how to increase the number of women and minorities in management positions.

localities are required to get Justice Department pre-approval for changes that might well dilute minority voting power.

majority–minority district
A congressional district created to include a majority of minority voters; ruled constitutional so long as race is not the main factor in redistricting.

In a series of cases beginning with *Shaw* v. *Reno* (1993), the Supreme Court announced that state legislatures could consider race when they drew electoral districts to increase the voting strength of minorities. However, the Court ruled that states could not make race the sole or predominant reason for drawing district lines. A test case examined the North Carolina legislature's creation of a **majority–minority district**, which came to be known as the "I-85 district," following the 1990 census and 1992 redistricting; it was 160 miles long through the central region of the state and in some places only an interstate highway wide. The Supreme Court ruled that it was wrong to force states to create as many majority–minority districts as possible. To comply with the Voting Rights Act, the Court explained, states must provide for districts roughly proportional to the minority voters' respective shares in the voting-age population.[79] However, when challenging district boundaries, the Court clarified in 2018, plaintiffs bear the burden of showing that a legislature intended to discriminate when it drew the district lines.[80]

Rights to Equal Access: Accommodations, Jobs, and Homes (Structure)

15.6 Describe congressional legislation forbidding discrimination in housing, employment, and accommodations.

In 1883, the Supreme Court declared unconstitutional an act of Congress that made it a federal offense for any operator of a public conveyance (such as a train or bus), hotel, or theater to deny accommodations to any person because of race or color, on the grounds that the Fourteenth Amendment does not give Congress such authority.[81] Until the Supreme Court finally moved to strike down such laws in the 1950s, southern states had made it illegal for white and black people to ride in the same train cars, attend the same theaters, go to the same schools, be born in the same hospitals, drink from the same water fountains, or be buried in the same cemeteries. **Jim Crow laws**, as they came to be called, blanketed southern life.

Jim Crow laws
State laws formerly pervasive throughout the South requiring public facilities and accommodations to be segregated by race; ruled unconstitutional.

The Court reinforced legalized segregation under the Fourteenth Amendment's equal protection clause in *Plessy* v. *Ferguson* (1896). In *Plessy*, the Supreme Court endorsed the view that government-imposed racial segregation in public transportation, and presumably in public education, did not necessarily constitute discrimination if "equal" accommodations were provided for the members of both races.[82] But the "equal" part of the formula was meaningless. Blacks were segregated in unequal facilities and lacked the political power to protest effectively.

Beginning in the 1960s, Congress began to act to prevent such segregation. Its constitutional authority to legislate against discrimination by private individuals is no longer an issue because the Court has broadly construed the **commerce clause**—which gives Congress the power to regulate interstate and foreign commerce—to justify action against discriminatory conduct by individuals. Congress has also used its power to tax and spend to prevent not only racial discrimination but also discrimination based on ethnic origin, sex, disability, and age.

commerce clause
The clause of the Constitution (Article I, Section 8, Clause 3) that gives Congress the power to regulate all business activities that cross state lines or affect more than one state or other nations.

Civil Rights Act of 1964 and Places of Public Accommodation

The key step in establishing rights of equal access was the Civil Rights Act of 1964. Title II of the Act makes it a federal offense to discriminate against any customer or patron in a place of public accommodation because of race, color, religion, or national origin. It applies to any inn, hotel, motel, or lodging establishment (except those with fewer than five rooms and where the proprietor also lives—in other words, small boarding houses); to any restaurant or gas station that serves interstate travelers or sells food or products that are moved in interstate commerce; and to any movie house, theater, concert hall, sports arena, or other place of entertainment that customarily hosts films, performances, athletic teams, or other sources of entertainment that are moved in interstate commerce. Within a few months after its adoption, the Supreme Court upheld the constitutionality of Title II.[83] As a result, public establishments, including those in the South, opened their doors to all customers.

Federal law has not yet extended protections against discrimination based on sexual orientation. However, in the wake of their success in attaining marriage equality, gay rights activists have now turned greater attention to gaining protections in public accommodations, employment, and housing. In terms of public accommodations, as of 2018, only 23 states and the District of Columbia provide protection against discrimination on the basis of sexual orientation, and just 21 (and the District) do so on the basis of gender identity.[84]

Civil Rights Act of 1964 and Employment

In addition to dealing with equal access in public accommodations, the Civil Rights Act also barred discrimination in employment. Title VII of the 1964 Civil Rights Act made it illegal for any employer or trade union in any industry affecting interstate commerce and employing 15 or more people (and, since 1972, any state or local agency such as a school or university) to discriminate in employment practices against any person because of race, color, national origin, religion, or sex. Employers must create workplaces that avoid abusive environments. Related legislation made it illegal to discriminate against persons with physical handicaps, veterans, or persons over the age of 40. There is no federal protection for those whom employers discriminate against based on their sexual orientation, although 24 states and the District of Columbia provide such protection. Another 22 states and the District of Columbia provide protections based on gender identity.[85]

There are a few exceptions. Religious institutions such as parochial schools may use religious standards. Employers may take into account the age, sex, or handicap of prospective employees when occupational qualifications are absolutely necessary to the normal operation of a particular business or enterprise—for example, hiring only women to work in women's locker rooms.

class action suit

A lawsuit brought by an individual or a group of people on behalf of all those similarly situated.

The Equal Employment Opportunity Commission (EEOC) was created under the Act to enforce Title VII. The commission works together with state authorities to try to ensure compliance with the Act and may seek judicial enforcement of complaints against private employers. The attorney general prosecutes Title VII violations by public agencies. Not only can aggrieved persons sue for damages for themselves, but they can also sue for other persons similarly situated in a **class action suit**. The courts decide whether the persons in the class are similar enough that they may appropriately file a class action claim. For example, in 2011, the Supreme Court rejected a class action lawsuit alleging sex discrimination against Wal-Mart because the plaintiffs had not established that their cases were similar enough to proceed as a single class.[86] However, in October 2011, the plaintiffs again filed suit against Wal-Mart, but in direct response to the Supreme Court's concerns, they limited their claim to the chain's California stores.[87] The vigor with which the EEOC and the attorney general have acted has varied throughout the years, depending on the commitment of the president and the willingness of Congress to provide an adequate budget for the EEOC.[88]

The Fair Housing Act and Amendments

restrictive covenant

A provision in a deed to real property prohibiting its sale to a person of a particular race or religion. Judicial enforcement of such deeds is unconstitutional.

Housing is the last frontier of the civil rights crusade, the area in which progress is slowest and genuine change most remote. Even after legal restrictions on segregated housing have been removed, housing patterns continue to be segregated. The degree to which housing also affects segregation in employment and the public schools makes it a particularly important issue. In 1948, the Supreme Court made racial or religious **restrictive covenants** (a provision in a deed to real property that restricts to whom it can be sold) legally unenforceable.[89] The 1968 Fair Housing Act forbids discrimination in housing, with a few exceptions similar to those mentioned in public accommodations. Owners may not refuse to sell or rent to any person because of race, color, religion, national origin, sex, or physical handicap or because a person has children. Discrimination in housing also covers efforts to deny mortgage loans to minorities. In addition to the federal prohibitions on housing discrimination, 24 states and the District of Columbia also have laws that bar housing discrimination based on sexual orientation, and 22 states and Washington, D.C. prohibit discrimination on the basis of gender identity as well.[90]

The Department of Justice has filed hundreds of cases, especially against large apartment complexes, yet blacks and Hispanics still face discrimination in housing. Some real estate agents steer blacks and Hispanics toward neighborhoods that are not predominantly white and require minority renters to pay larger deposits than white renters. Yet victims complain about less than 1 percent of these actions because discrimination is so subtle that they are often unaware they are being discriminated against. However, more aggressive enforcement has increased the number of discrimination complaints the Department of Housing and Urban Development and local and state agencies receive.

Education Rights (Impact)

15.7 Evaluate the history of school integration and the current state of affirmative action.

After the Court's decision in *Plessy*, segregated public as well as private facilities became the norm. Separate public schools, buses, and bathrooms were commonplace. However, in the late 1930s, blacks started to file lawsuits challenging *Plessy*'s "separate but equal" doctrine. The National Association for the Advancement of Colored People's (NAACP) Legal Defense Fund (LDF) was active in challenging segregated educational facilities. The LDF cited facts to show that in practice separate was anything but equal and generally resulted in discrimination against blacks.

Initially, the LDF showed that so-called equal facilities were in fact not equal, or simply not provided. Many of their early successes addressed inequality in higher education. States were forced to either provide separate graduate and law schools for blacks students, or integrate those they already had. A major success that laid the groundwork for the LDF's challenge in public secondary and elementary schools came when the Court ruled that not only did segregated facilities themselves have to be equal, but they also had to provide the same quality of benefits to black students as their white counterparts.[91]

The End of "Separate but Equal": *Brown* v. *Board of Education*

Once the LDF had adequately established that segregated facilities were far from equal, it challenged the *Plessy* doctrine of "separate but equal" head on. And, in *Brown* v. *Board of Education of Topeka* (1954), the Court finally agreed, ruling that "separate but equal" is a contradiction in terms. Segregation is itself discrimination.[92]

The question before the Court in *Brown* was whether separate public schools for black and white students violated the Fourteenth Amendment's equal protection clause. Relying heavily on arguments addressing the harm to all schoolchildren, black and white, caused by racial segregation, the Court struck down segregation in the public schools and, in so doing, overturned *Plessy* v. *Ferguson* (1896). A year later, the Court ordered school boards to proceed with "all deliberate speed to desegregate public schools at the earliest practical date."[93]

But many school districts moved slowly or not at all, and in the 1960s, Congress and the president joined forces to more directly fight school segregation. Title VI of the Civil Rights Act of 1964, as subsequently amended, stipulated that federal dollars under any grant program or project must be withdrawn from an entire school or institution of higher education (including private schools) that discriminates "on the ground of race, color, or national origin," sex, age, or disability, in "any program or activity receiving federal financial assistance."

From Segregation to Desegregation—but Not Yet Integration

School districts that had operated separate schools for white children and black children now had to develop plans and programs to move from segregation to integration. Schools failing to do so were placed under court supervision to ensure that they were doing what was necessary and proper to overcome the evils of segregation. Simply doing away with laws mandating segregation would not be enough; school districts needed to actively integrate their schools.

Thurgood Marshall (center), George C. E. Hayes (left), and James Nabrit Jr. (right) argued and won *Brown* v. *Board of Education of Topeka* before the Supreme Court in 1954. Marshall went on to serve as a Supreme Court Justice between 1967 and 1991.

But because most white and black people continued to live in separate neighborhoods, merely removing legal barriers to school integration did not by itself integrate the schools. To overcome this residential clustering by race, some federal courts mandated busing across neighborhoods, moving white students to once predominantly black schools and vice versa.[94] Busing students was unpopular and triggered protests in many cities.

de jure segregation
Segregation imposed by law.

de facto segregation
Segregation resulting from economic or social conditions or personal choice.

The Supreme Court sustained busing only if it was undertaken to remedy the consequences of officially sanctioned segregation, **de jure segregation**. The Court refused to permit federal judges to order busing to overcome the effects of **de facto segregation**, segregation that arises as a result of social and economic conditions such as housing patterns.

After a period of vigorous federal court supervision of school desegregation programs, the Supreme Court in the 1990s restricted the role of federal judges.[95] It instructed some of them to restore control of a school system to the state and local authorities and to release districts from any busing obligations once a judge concludes that the authorities "have done everything practicable to overcome the past consequences of segregation."[96]

Political support for busing and for other efforts to integrate the schools also faded.[97] Many school districts eliminated mandatory busing and many others have been released from court-enforced integration, with the result that *Brown*'s era of court-ordered desegregation drew to a close. As a result, the percentage of southern black students attending white-majority schools fell from a high of 44 percent in 1988 to 30 percent in 2001, or approximately the same level it had been in 1969.[98] In the wake of such resegregation, some school districts have attempted to increase integration through race-conscious school assignment plans. However, in 2007, the Supreme Court ruled that such plans in Seattle, Washington, and Louisville, Kentucky, violated the Fourteenth Amendment's Equal Protection Clause.[99] Another method some schools have pursued, which is presumably constitutional based on court decisions, is integration based on socioeconomic factors rather than race.[100]

The Affirmative Action Controversy

When white majorities were using government power to discriminate against black, civil rights advocates cited with approval the famous words of Justice John Marshall Harlan when he dissented from the *Plessy* decision: "Our Constitution is color-blind and neither knows nor tolerates class among citizens."[101] But by the 1960s, a new set of constitutional and national policy debates raged. Many people began to assert that government neutrality is not enough. If governments, universities, and employers simply stopped discriminating but nothing else changed, individuals previously discriminated against would still be kept from equal participation in U.S. life. Furthermore, when barriers to equality in education and employment advancement exist, we all suffer from a lack of diversity in society. Because discrimination had so disadvantaged some people and groups, they suffered disabilities that white males did not share in competing for openings in medical schools, for skilled jobs, or for their share of government grants and contracts.

Supporters call remedies to overcome the consequences of discrimination against blacks, Hispanics, Native Americans, and women affirmative action; opponents call these efforts reverse discrimination. The Supreme Court's first major statement on the constitutionality of these programs came in a celebrated case relating to university admissions. Allan Bakke—a white male, a top student at the University of Minnesota and at Stanford, and a Vietnam War veteran—applied in 1973 and again in 1974 to the medical school of the University of California at Davis. In each of those years, the school admitted 100 new students, 84 in a general admissions program and 16 in a special admissions program created for minorities who had previously been underrepresented. Bakke was rejected in both years, while applicants with lower grade-point averages, test scores, and interview ratings were admitted through the special admissions program.

The Supreme Court ruled the UC-Davis plan unconstitutional[102] because it created a quota—a set number of admissions from which whites were excluded solely because of race. However, a state university may properly take race and ethnic background into account as "a plus," as one of several factors in choosing students, because of its compelling interest in achieving a diverse student body.

For many years following the *Bakke* decision, the Court refused to hear challenges to affirmative action in higher education, despite conflicting lower-court decisions leading to uncertainty about how colleges and universities could pursue diverse student bodies. But, in 2003 the Supreme Court reaffirmed *Bakke* in two University of Michigan cases, upholding the law school's holistic admission policy, which considered race as one of many "plus" factors, while striking down the undergraduate program's more formulaic point system.

State policies and court rulings on the use of affirmative action in university admissions are in a state of flux as a number of affirmative action lawsuits make their way through the federal courts. In 2013, the Supreme Court affirmed that maintaining diversity in higher education is a compelling state interest, but it rejected the notion that courts should simply defer to universities as to how they define and meet their goals for diversity.[103] In 2014, the Court upheld the Michigan constitutional amendment barring affirmative action in university admissions. That decision went a step further and illustrates that the Court is willing to defer to a political determination not to use affirmative action to increase diversity.[104] When the Supreme Court granted review of the University of Texas's affirmative action program for the second time in 2015, many believed the justices had done so to finally eliminate an applicant's race as a permissible consideration in university admissions. But, with only seven justices participating (due to Justice Scalia's death and Justice Kagan's recusal in the case), the Court narrowly upheld as constitutional, universities' consideration of race for the purpose of maintaining a diverse educational environment.[105] Justice Kennedy, who announced his retirement from the Court in June 2018, wrote the 4-to-3 majority opinion in *Fisher* v. *Texas* (579 U.S. _____ (2016)). As he was retiring, another affirmative action case was making its way through the courts. If the newly constituted Court hears Asian-American students' challenge to Harvard's admissions policy, it seems likely the decision will go the other way.

CONCLUSION

Today, civil rights legislation, executive orders, and judicial decisions have lowered, if not fully removed, legal barriers to full and equal participation in society. Important as these victories are, enacting the legislation, issuing an order, or ruling on a case does not, in and of itself, remove the barriers. Groups and individuals who disagree with the law or ruling may try to keep it from being fully implemented.

As discussed above, all people are entitled to civil rights guaranteed in the Constitution. Longstanding battles on appropriate treatment of undocumented immigrants continue to rage as Americans disagree on the appropriate balance between protecting our borders and protecting the basic human rights of migrants. The structure of our government provides multiple avenues for participation by groups and individuals. If you belong to a group with the resources to effectively lobby the legislature or get an initiative on the ballot, you might target your efforts in those directions to achieve the impact you desire. For groups and individuals who have a different set of resources, the state or federal courts provide another avenue through which they might act to achieve their policy goals. And, in the aftermath of any resulting impact, those who disagree with the policy change might reassert their interests elsewhere in the structure. We see this dance played out in the ongoing fight for civil rights protection at the border.

One of the many important lessons of the civil rights movement is that individuals, alone or working in groups, can impact policy. Without people willing to challenge the law, like the many immigration lawyers working to reunite migrants' families at the border, President Trump may not have issued the executive order to stop separating migrant families. Nor would we have experienced the monumental changes in our country's protection of all citizens' rights that we have seen during the last 100 years. By acting through the democratic structure and challenging the status quo, you each play a part in impacting equal rights for all citizens.

REVIEW THE CHAPTER

Equality and Equal Rights (Structure)

15.1 Explain why the concept of equality is integral to our understanding of civil rights p. 448.

Although there is no single agreed-upon definition of equality in the United States, there is general consensus that everyone should have an equal opportunity to succeed. Every person has the right to be free from invidious discrimination based on factors such as their race, sex, religion, and national origin. These civil rights are protected through important legislation as well as key court decisions.

Citizenship and the Rights It Affords (Structure)

15.2 Explain the concept of citizenship and the rights of U.S. citizens, p. 449.

The Constitution protects the acquisition and retention of citizenship. It protects the basic liberties of citizens as well as immigrants, although in times of war, foreign terrorists may be detained and tried without the rights accorded to citizens and other immigrants.

The Quest for Equal Justice (Action)

15.3 Compare and contrast the efforts of various groups to obtain equal protection of the law, p. 452.

Although blacks' rights were finally recognized under the Thirteenth, Fourteenth, and Fifteenth Amendments, the government failed to act to prevent racial discrimination for nearly a century thereafter. The women's rights movement was born partly out of the struggle to abolish slavery, and the women's movement learned and gained power from the civil rights movements of the 1950s and early 1960s. Concern for equal rights under the law continues today for blacks and women as well as other groups, including Hispanics, Asian Americans, and Native Americans.

Equal Protection of the Law: What Does It Mean? (Structure and Impact)

15.4 Evaluate the standards by which civil rights are protected today, p. 461.

The Supreme Court uses a three-tiered approach to evaluate the constitutionality of laws that may violate the equal protection clause. The Court upholds most laws if they simply help accomplish a legitimate government goal. It sustains laws that classify people based on sex only if they serve important government objectives. It subjects laws that touch fundamental rights or classify people because of race or ethnic origin to strict scrutiny and sustains them only if the government can show that they serve a compelling public purpose.

Voting Rights (Structure)

15.5 Trace the evolution of voting rights and analyze the protections provided by the 1965 Voting Rights Act, p. 464.

A series of constitutional amendments, Supreme Court decisions, and laws passed by Congress have now secured the right to vote to all citizens age 18 and older. As a result of the Voting Rights Act of 1965, the Justice Department oversees practices in locales with a history of discrimination. Recent Supreme Court decisions have refined the lengths to which legislatures can go, or are obliged to go, in creating majority–minority districts.

Rights to Equal Access: Accommodations, Jobs, and Homes (Structure)

15.6 Describe congressional legislation forbidding discrimination in housing, employment, and accommodations, p. 466.

By its authority under the interstate commerce clause (Article I, Section 8), Congress has passed important legislation barring discrimination in housing and accommodations. The Civil Rights Act of 1964 outlawed discrimination in public accommodations. This Act also provided for equal employment opportunity. The Fair Housing Act of 1968 and its 1988 amendments prohibited discrimination in housing.

Education Rights (Impact)

15.7 Evaluate the history of school integration and the current state of affirmative action, p. 469.

Brown v. *Board of Education of Topeka* (1954) struck down the "separate but equal" doctrine that had justified segregated schools, but school districts responded slowly. Full integration has proven elusive, as housing patterns and schools continue to be segregated. Affirmative action programs remain controversial and subject to judicial scrutiny. Although the Supreme Court upheld a Michigan state constitutional amendment barring affirmative action in the state's public universities' admissions decisions, it also upheld, in 2016, the University of Texas's right to consider race as a factor in its admission process so as to maintain a diverse educational environment.

LEARN THE TERMS

civil rights, p. 448
natural rights, p. 449
affirmative action, p. 449
naturalization, p. 450
dual citizenship, p. 451
right of expatriation, p. 451
women's suffrage, p. 456
equal protection clause, p. 461
due process clause, p. 461
rational basis test, p. 461
strict scrutiny test, p. 462
heightened scrutiny test, p. 462
literacy test, p. 465
white primary, p. 465
racial gerrymandering, p. 465
poll tax, p. 465
majority–minority district, p. 466
Jim Crow laws, p. 467
commerce clause, p. 467
class action suit, p. 468
restrictive covenant, p. 468
de jure segregation, p. 470
de facto segregation, p. 470

CHAPTER

Economic and Social Policy 16

In April 1964, President Lyndon Johnson developed his War on Poverty after spending time in the poorest regions of the Appalachian Mountains that run from West Virginia to Georgia. His 1964 "poverty tours" showed him the despair associated with the deep, seemingly unsolvable poverty in the isolated communities located deep in the foothills that had lost jobs and hope over the decades. Here, a mother and child walk the train tracks in Kentucky 50 years after Johnson launched his War on Poverty. Although his initiative reduced poverty in many regions of the country, the hills of Kentucky still hold many of the poorest Americans in the nation.

LEARNING OBJECTIVES

16.1 Describe the constitutional foundations and competing philosophies of economic and social policy (Structure), p. 477.

16.2 Describe the five measures used in making economic and social policy (Structure), p. 479.

16.3 Analyze the basic tools used to make economic and social policy (Action), p. 482.

16.4 Describe the evolution and goals of economic policy (Action), p. 490.

16.5 Describe the evolution and goals of social policy (Action), p. 495.

16.6 Assess the future of economic and social policy (Impact), p. 503.

The federal government has always been concerned about the economy and a small list of social issues such as public health and education, but generally relied on charities and local associations to care for the poor as the nation grew. The federal government did not ignore great economic and social crises such as the Civil War, but believed that its greatest obligation was holding the nation together against foreign and domestic threats, not helping unemployed Americans find jobs, food, and shelter.

The federal government's attitude changed almost overnight when the stock market crashed in 1929 and the Great Depression took hold. With the economy frozen and one quarter of Americans out of work, the federal government created dozens of new programs to ease poverty and despair, including unemployment insurance for the jobless, Social Security for older Americans, aid to families with needy children, food assistance for the hungry, and a host of economic reforms designed to create jobs, build homes, and strengthen the banking system.

These and other federal programs helped pull the nation through the Great Depression, but poverty still plagued the Appalachian Mountains and many of the nation's largest cities. Moved by his own "poverty tours" across the nation, President Lyndon Johnson declared "unconditional War on Poverty in America" in January 1964. "It will not be a short or easy struggle," he told Congress in his State of the Union Address. "No single weapon or strategy will suffice, but we shall not rest until that war is won. The richest nation on earth can afford to win it. We cannot afford to lose it."[1]

Johnson launched his "War on Poverty" with proposals to create preschool education programs, health insurance for older Americans, food and nutrition support for the poor, and college loans for low-income Americans, all of which remain in place today. Some programs, like Head Start for preschool children, have won support from liberals and conservatives alike, and there is widespread agreement that the persistence of poverty is a problem. But disagreements persist between the two parties on how much the federal government should spend, who should be eligible for assistance, how the support should be delivered, and whether beneficiaries should have to work in return for benefits.[2] Because new programs are often created without links to past initiatives, the War on Poverty now involves about 80 antipoverty programs, including 5 that provide cash assistance, 24 that focus on education and training, 17 that address hunger and nutrition, 8 that involve health care, and 20 that support housing.[3]

Despite this enormous effort, the War on Poverty was still being fought in 2017 when the Trump era began; if measured by the number of Americans who fall below the poverty line—meaning they cannot cover the cost of adequate food, housing, and other essentials for low-income families—almost one in six Americans today are in poverty. Poverty has only declined from 19 percent of the population in 1964 to 16 percent 50 years later.

At the same time, some Americans fared better during the first 50 years of the war than others. The number of older Americans who lived below the poverty line dropped from 35 percent to 9 percent, in large part because of Social Security, Medicare, and a new program for especially poor older Americans called Supplemental Security Income. On the other hand, poverty among children has been persistently high at 22–24 percent.[4]

Children who live in single-parent households are particularly vulnerable to poverty, in part because government support is based on the number of adults and children in a household. Children are also hard to reach because their parents may have a low-paying job that cuts into their government support, or because their parents may have expenses that are not covered in the federal government's estimate of what people need to stay above the poverty line. And children may be poor through circumstances entirely beyond their parents' control.

You will have to decide how to balance these facts against the real costs of helping America's citizens get out of poverty. Should the federal government give more cash assistance to the poor, create new jobs in poor neighborhoods, provide greater access to childcare so parents can take jobs, encourage marriage, and/or give single parents more job training? Every option has its supporters, but you will have to make the choice as you balance your own financial needs and President Johnson's belief that the richest nation on earth cannot leave so many of its citizens behind.

This chapter will give you the knowledge to assess these options. You will learn about the structure of economic and social policy, the ways that government uses both kinds of policy to accomplish goals such as stabilizing the economy and reducing poverty, and the impacts of the specific decisions it makes. The debate over the War on Poverty is almost certain to continue far into the future, but your decisions about what America should do to help the poor will come every year when the president's budget proposal reaches Congress.

The Constitutional Foundations of Economic and Social Policy (Structure)

16.1 Describe the constitutional foundations and competing philosophies of economic and social policy.

The Constitution's preamble is often cited as evidence that the Framers wanted government to provide the economic and social policies needed to promote the general welfare. After all, the preamble promises: "We the People of the United States, in Order to form a more perfect Union, establish Justice, insure domestic Tranquility, provide for the common defense, promote the general Welfare, and secure the Blessings of Liberty to ourselves and our Posterity, do ordain and establish this Constitution for the United States of America."[5]

Even though the preamble is part of the Constitution's text, it does not make any enforceable promises that shape the laws.[6] James Madison even implied that it was a "parchment barrier" against tyranny in *The Federalist*, No. 48, meaning that the preamble does not make any commitments that guarantee action.[7]

The federal courts have supported Madison's view that the preamble does not create enforceable constitutional rights of any kind. Rather, the preamble set a broad framework for understanding the Constitution that followed—it was more of an introduction, perhaps even an advertisement of a kind to the government the Framers were about to create. "Although one of the declared objects of the Constitution was to secure the blessings of liberty to all under the sovereign jurisdiction and authority of the United States," Chief Justice John Marshall Harlan, in 1905, wrote for the majority in *Jacobsen* v. *Commonwealth of Massachusetts*, "no power can be exerted to that end by the United States unless, apart from the Preamble, it be found in some express delegation of power or in some power to be properly implied therefrom."[8]

The Constitution itself gave Congress and the president control over the economy. Article I gives Congress the express powers to borrow, coin, and print money; regulate commerce among the states and with foreign nations; "lay and collect Taxes, Duties, Imposts, and Excises"; and to appropriate money and audit government spending. Article I also gives Congress the authority to protect inventions with patents and trademarks, and set standards for the weights and measures used in common trade.

In turn, Article II gives the president the power to appoint the officers of government who administer economic and social policy, demand their opinions in writing, report to the nation on the state of the union, and negotiate treaties with other nations. It is, however, the president's role as administrator in chief that provides the office's greatest influence over economic and social policy, especially through the power to shape the budget.

President Trump sent his first full budget to Congress on February 12, 2018. The budget proposal contained $4.4 trillion, and was presented to the House and Senate budget committees in three documents—the president's formal budget message making the case for enactment, a 500-page program-by-program analysis of each spending item, and a 1,500-page appendix on specific initiatives such as strengthening small business programs. The "FY19" on each document refers to Fiscal Year 2019. Each fiscal year is numbered by the year in which it expires. Here, the House Budget Committee prepares to distribute the budget to every member of Congress.

The Competing Philosophies of Economic and Social Policy

Economic and social policies are guided by competing philosophies of how much government should do in regard to making laws to stimulate the economy and protect those who are less fortunate than others. Some Americans believe that people are poor because of circumstances beyond their control, while others believe that people are poor because they do not work hard enough. These disagreements clearly shape how economic and social policy is made.

THE ECONOMIC POLICY DEBATE The Great Depression prompted a long-running debate between two groups of economists on how to keep the economy operating smoothly through good times and bad. The first group urged the government to leave the economy to correct itself during good and bad times, and opposed strong action to push the economy one direction or the other. These economists favored what is called **laissez-faire economics**. Republicans tend to support this approach, but have been known to favor strong government intervention to protect financial institutions such as the large banks that they said were too big to be allowed to fail during the 2008 economic crisis.

laissez-faire economics
A theory that opposes governmental interference in economic affairs beyond what is necessary to protect life and property.

The second group urged government to do the opposite. Influenced by English economist John Maynard Keynes,[9] this group recommended that government take a much more active role in stimulating the economy during desperate times. These economists favored what is called **Keynesian economics**. Democrats generally support this more aggressive approach, and provided the votes to pass the Obama administration's $800 billion package of increased federal spending to counteract the 2009 economic slowdown.[10]

Keynesian economics
An economic theory based on the principles of John Maynard Keynes stating that government spending should increase during business slumps and be curbed during booms.

As the growth in the federal budget suggests, Keynesians prevailed, although remnants of the debate continue today. The federal government injected vast amounts of money into the economy during the 1930s by creating dozens of new programs to create jobs, help the poor, and regulate the economy. They saw government spending as a stimulus to jump-start the economy during economic crisis, and developed sophisticated theories showing the relationship between tax cuts and spending increases on the one hand, and new jobs on the other.

THE SOCIAL POLICY DEBATE Social policy is also buffeted by two competing philosophies of how to protect the less fortunate from hardship. One group believes that people are often poor through no fault of their own, making them the "worthy poor"—hence, government must step in to create the jobs and provide the assistance needed to survive. The other group argues that people are responsible for their own situation in life and that people are poor because they do not want to work, making them the "unworthy poor"—hence, government should reduce or eliminate assistance to create the incentive to work.

Americans were sharply divided between the two groups until recently.[11] At the start of Johnson's War on Poverty, for example, about a third of Americans said that people are poor because of a lack of effort, another third said people are poor because of circumstances beyond their control, and a final third said both explanations are right. By 2016, however, about one half of Americans said people were poor because of circumstances beyond their control, while about a third still said people were poor because of a lack of effort. As the figures suggest, Americans were becoming increasingly concerned about how the economy works for some people, but not others.

Measuring Economic and Social Conditions (Structure)

16.2 Describe the five measures used in making economic and social policy.

Congress and the president use dozens of measures to structure the assessment of the nation's economic and social needs. In fact, the problem in making economic and social policy is not a lack of statistics, but a deluge that can create a murky picture of what is actually happening in real life.

For example, the Trump administration's 2019 budget was based on 96 different measures of the nation's economic and social health: 24 on general economic conditions including jobs, inventions, and national savings rates; 14 on demographic and civic trends such as total population, births to unmarried women, charitable giving, reading, and volunteering; 19 on social and economic trends such as reading achievement, savings, housing ownership, and number of hungry or "food insecure" families; 14 on health such as life expectancy, infant mortality, obesity, and the number of smokers; 7 on safety such as crime per 100,000 households, safety belt use, and number of military personnel on active duty; and 8 on the environment and energy such as greenhouse gas emissions, energy use per person, and air and water pollution. All of these measures are based on information collected by the U.S. government.[12]

Despite all the options they have for tracking economic and social policy, Congress and the president focus on four basic measures in reviewing economic and social problems: (1) unemployment, (2) inflation, (3) poverty rate, and (4) gross domestic product. Recent movement in these measures can be tracked in Figure 16.1 on the next page.

Unemployment

A first measure used in economic and social policy is **unemployment**, which the government defines as the number of people who (1) do not have a job, (2) have actively looked for work in the last four weeks, and (3) are ready to work if they are offered a job. The measure does not count the number of people who have given up on finding a job, which reduces the real unemployment rate by as much as half.

unemployment
The number of Americans who are out of work but actively looking for a job.

Unemployment is often the most visible problem during economic contraction and recession when the demand for goods and services falls below supply, thereby leading employers to cut jobs to save money. Unemployment passed the 10 percent mark following the 2008 financial collapse but eventually fell below 4 percent in April 2018 where it stayed through the rest of the year.

FIGURE 16.1 FOUR MEASURES OF U.S. ECONOMIC PERFORMANCE, 2000–2016

Economic policy is based on a broad inventory of measures for the state of the economy. Some measure the economy's overall performance through measures such as gross domestic product and poverty, while others look at more specific symptoms of trouble such as unemployment or inflation. Economic policy tries to balance the strengths and weaknesses to create a full picture of where the economy is today, and where it might be tomorrow. In today's complex global economy, there are many economic futures ahead that the United States can and cannot predict.

SOURCE: Bureau of Labor Statistics, Census Bureau, Bureau of Economic Analysis.

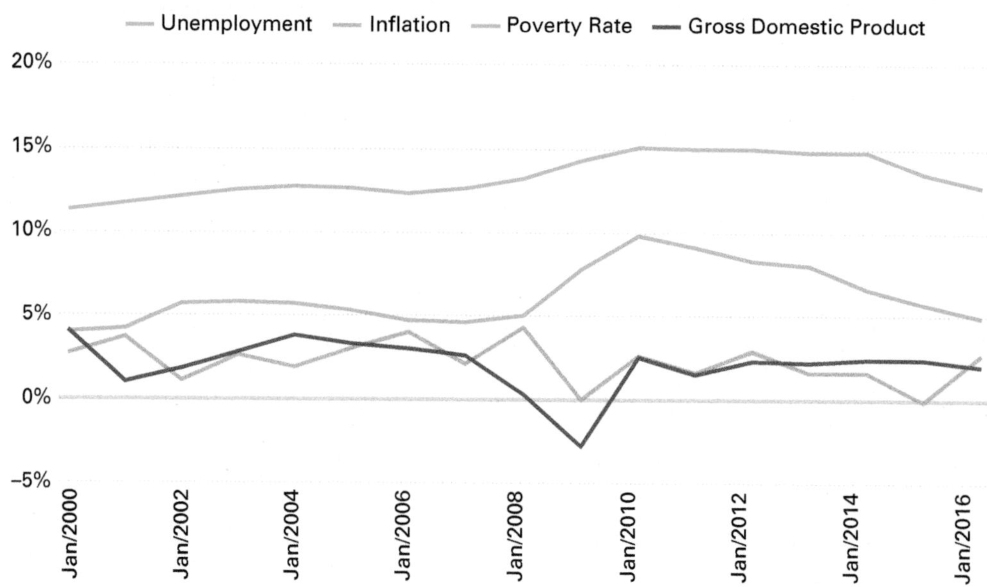

There are several different ways to measure unemployment, however. One alternative measurement is based on the number of Americans who have stopped looking for work either because they believe that there are no jobs available in their communities or that they will never be hired because they are too young, too old, or unqualified for any available jobs. Although the number of discouraged workers has also dropped in recent years, it still stands at about eight million potential workers.[13]

Unemployment is generally viewed as a "lagging," or trailing measure of economic performance, meaning that it surfaces later than other indicators and lasts longer as the economy recovers.[14] Businesses often wait to create the new jobs until they are more confident that the economy is improving. If the upward movement is uncertain or slow, unemployment will persist well beyond the end of an economic crisis. Without confidence in the future, businesses simply will not act, and the unemployed will not search for work.

Inflation

inflation
A rise in the general price of a market basket of products.

consumer price index (CPI)
A means of measuring inflation that shows how much more or how much less consumers are paying for the same goods and services over time.

A second measure used in making economic and social policy is **inflation**, which is the general increase in the market price of basic goods and services such as food, shelter, fuel, clothing, transportation, and medical care. Economists measure inflation with the **consumer price index (CPI)**, which shows how much more or how much less consumers are paying for the same goods and services over time. Inflation is the primary risk during economic expansion when the demand for goods and services exceed supply, thereby allowing producers to raise prices.

Although CPI is the most commonly used measure of inflation, it can overstate the rise in prices due to unexpected events that affect one or two products that carry heavier weight in the market basket. Droughts can cause a surge in milk prices, for example, while a surplus in oil supplies can simultaneously lower the cost of gasoline and put millions of oil workers out of work here in the United States and abroad. The resulting fear of inflation or unemployment can lead to major economic upheavals that heat or cool the economy.[15]

Poverty

A third measure used in economic and social policy is **poverty**, which is generally defined as the lack of enough money to maintain a minimum quality of life.[16] The most widely used poverty measure was first employed in 1965, and it has been used to calculate poverty annually by the U.S. Census Bureau ever since. The measure is based on the amount of income needed to purchase a healthy "food plan" in 1963 multiplied by a factor of three, and adjusted each year to reflect inflation in setting the overall poverty threshold, or line.[17] In 2018, this threshold was set at $12,140 a year for a single person living alone, and $25,100 for a family of four living together.[18]

poverty
A measure used in economic and social policy that is generally defined as the lack of enough money to maintain a minimum quality of life.

Concerns about the age of this measure prompted the Census Bureau to develop a new measure of poverty based on a broader set of goods and services.[19] This new measure is designed in part to show the impact of government assistance on poverty. According to the new measure, the War on Poverty has not been won, but government has reduced the number of Americans who suffer from the effects of poverty. According to the Stanford University Center on Poverty and Inequality, the federal government provides about one-third of the income that low-income individuals and families need to rise above the poverty line, and government programs have cut the poverty rate by a third.[20]

Gross Domestic Product

A fourth measure used in making economic and social policy is **gross domestic product (GDP)**. A nation's GDP is defined as the amount of goods and services its economy produces in any given year. This measure is used to assess the overall

gross domestic product (GDP)
The value of all goods and services produced by an economy during a specific period of time such as a year.

Dozens of oil rigs sat idle in Dickinson, North Dakota, in February 2016 as oil supplies exceeded demand. Lower oil prices are good for consumers, but too much supply can weaken an industry and cause higher unemployment. In classic economic theory, demand and supply move in opposite directions to create economic growth and decline—as demand rises, supplies decline and inflation takes hold, but as demand falls, supplies rise, and unemployment rises. The shutdowns produced a drop in supply that pushed oil prices upward in 2018, which led the Trump administration to push Saudi Arabia and other international suppliers to produce more oil to reduce oil prices.

performance of the economy, as well as measure significant changes in the economy's basic condition. It is also generally used as a measure of economic growth.

recession
Negative GDP that lasts two quarters or more.

The U.S. Bureau of Economic Analysis measures GDP at the end of each calendar quarter. The nation is considered to be in a **recession** when GDP falls for two consecutive quarters, and out of a recession when GDP rises for two consecutive quarters. According to this definition, the economy entered a recession in the fourth quarter of 2008, and came out of it in the last quarter of 2009. Even though the recession was technically over according to this definition in 2009, the growth was not enough to offset high unemployment and meager consumer confidence until 2013.

Choosing Measures

income inequality
The difference in wealth between the richest and poorest Americans as measured by the sum of an individual's cash, property, investments, retirement support, and other economic instruments.

Politics and ideology affect the choice of one of these measures of the economy over another, and often influence the budget, legislation, and election campaigns. Liberals tend to focus most on poverty, unemployment, and **income inequality**, for example, while conservatives tend to pay more attention to inflation and gross domestic product. Economic policy makers worry that any pressure to cool down the economy might increase the number of discouraged and marginally attached workers, while social policy makers worry that such action will increase the costs of basic benefits such as health insurance, food, and housing.

Policy makers also pay attention to short-term indicators of potential economic and social instability such as consumer confidence in the economy, debt burdens, loan defaults, bankruptcies, and stock market turmoil. The U.S. stock market is the most visible of these short-term indicators—stock market crashes often lead the news as Americans wonder whether a sharp drop is a sign of an impending recession, while upward spikes are often touted by presidents as a sign of their economic success. Trump often pointed to the rising stock market increases in 2017 as a sign of his success, but stopped talking about the market when it began to falter after he began raising tariffs, meaning taxes, on imports from Canada, China, and many European countries in 2018.

The Tools of Economic and Social Policy (Action)

16.3 Analyze the basic tools used to make economic and social policy.

Economic and social policies were frequent topics at the Constitutional Convention. The Framers spent weeks talking about how to pay back the Revolutionary War debt, and *The Federalist Papers* are laden with references to commerce, debts, revenues, and taxes. As Alexander Hamilton wrote in *The Federalist,* No. 30, money is "the vital principle of body politic; as that which sustains its life and motion, and enables it to perform its most essential functions."[21]

The Framers also talked about how to unite their sharply divided nation, and promised to create "extensive and arduous enterprises for the public benefit." And even though he was in France during the Constitutional Convention, Thomas Jefferson was always a strong advocate of education as the path to enlightenment, so he deserves at least some credit for the federal and state education policies of today. As Jefferson is often quoted, "An educated citizenry is a vital requisite for our survival as a free people."[22]

fiscal policy
Government spending and taxation policies that affect economic performance.

monetary policy
Government policies designed to control the supply of money through the economy.

Economic Policy Tools

Even as the federal government gives individuals and businesses freedom to create wealth through new ideas and hard work, it protects the nation from economic chaos through two types of policy: (1) **fiscal policy**, which uses federal taxes and spending to stimulate or slow the economy; and (2) **monetary policy**, which increases or decreases the supply of money and access to credit that individuals and businesses can use to make investments and purchases.

Congress and the president use these two tools to create what economists call the normal business cycle as it moves through four stages: (1) expansion, which can produce moderate to high inflation; (2) contraction, which can produce moderate unemployment; (3) recession, which can produce high unemployment; and (4) recovery, which can rebalance the economy at both low inflation and low unemployment.

In the best of conditions, the economy expands at a reasonable pace—not too fast, but not too slow, either. But in the worst of conditions, the economy can collapse into a **depression**, which lasts much longer than the normal one-to-two-year recession and creates much greater unemployment. The U.S. economy entered what is now known as the "Great Depression" following the stock market crash on "Black Friday," October 29, 1929, and only began to rebound 10 years later at the start of World War II as federal defense spending ignited an economic recovery.

depression
A much deeper form of a recession that lasts longer and is more destructive.

The Obama-era economic turmoil was not considered a depression, but is often referred to as the "Great Recession" because of its length and very high levels of unemployment. The recession began in 2008 with the collapse of the U.S. housing market, and soon expanded to other industries. Although economic activity began to increase in 2011, the U.S. economy was threatened by another slowdown in 2016, when the Chinese economy collapsed and oil prices plunged.

The 2016 economic scare had faded by the time the Trump administration took office in 2017. Although Trump had promised to cut federal spending during his campaign, he used fiscal policy to cut federal taxes by $1.5 trillion in 2017 and signed a federal budget bill that included another $1.5 trillion in increased spending. The combination of tax cuts and increased spending pushed the federal budget deficit to record levels, which stimulated the economy with more demand for goods and services, which in turn created more inflationary pressure.

FISCAL POLICY Congress and the president make fiscal policy by raising and spending money. In general, lower taxes, higher borrowing, and increased spending are considered ways to stimulate employment during periods of sluggish economic performance, while higher taxes, lower borrowing, and decreased spending are considered ways to reduce inflation during periods of rapid economic growth. Lower taxes and more spending put more money in the pockets of consumers, which increases demand for goods and services, which in turn increases inflation and reduces unemployment. Conversely, higher taxes and lower spending take money away from consumers, which reduces demand for goods and services, which in turn reduces inflation and increases unemployment.

The federal budget is considered the most powerful tool of fiscal policy because it mixes taxes and spending together in a single policy document that allocates the federal government's funding. In turn, the budget determines whether the nation faces a deficit that must be covered by higher taxes, lower spending, or more borrowing. Borrowing raises the national debt, which raises the amount of interest the United States must pay its lenders.

Congress and the president must make difficult choices in balancing where the money comes from and where the money goes. As Figure 16.2 on the next page shows, most of the federal government's money comes from individual Americans in the form of income and payroll taxes, and goes out in the form of spending for human service programs such as Social Security and Medicare. Although some of this money eventually finds its way back to each taxpayer through federal benefits such as better highways, Social Security, and student loans, many Americans believe that they are paying more than their fair share of taxes, and more than half believe government is almost always wasteful and inefficient.[23]

FIGURE 16.2 WHERE THE FEDERAL INCOME CAME FROM AND WHERE IT WENT IN THE 2019 BUDGET

The federal government has many ways to collect revenues, and many ways to spend it. However, the most important change in spending over the past three decades has been a sharp rise in interest on the national debt. As the federal budget has grown, while taxes have remained steady, the federal government has borrowed more money to cover the difference.

SOURCE: *Budget of the U.S. Government, Fiscal Year 2019* (U.S. Government Printing Office, 2018), Historical Tables, Table 3.1 available at http://www.whitehouse.gov/omb/budget/Historicals.

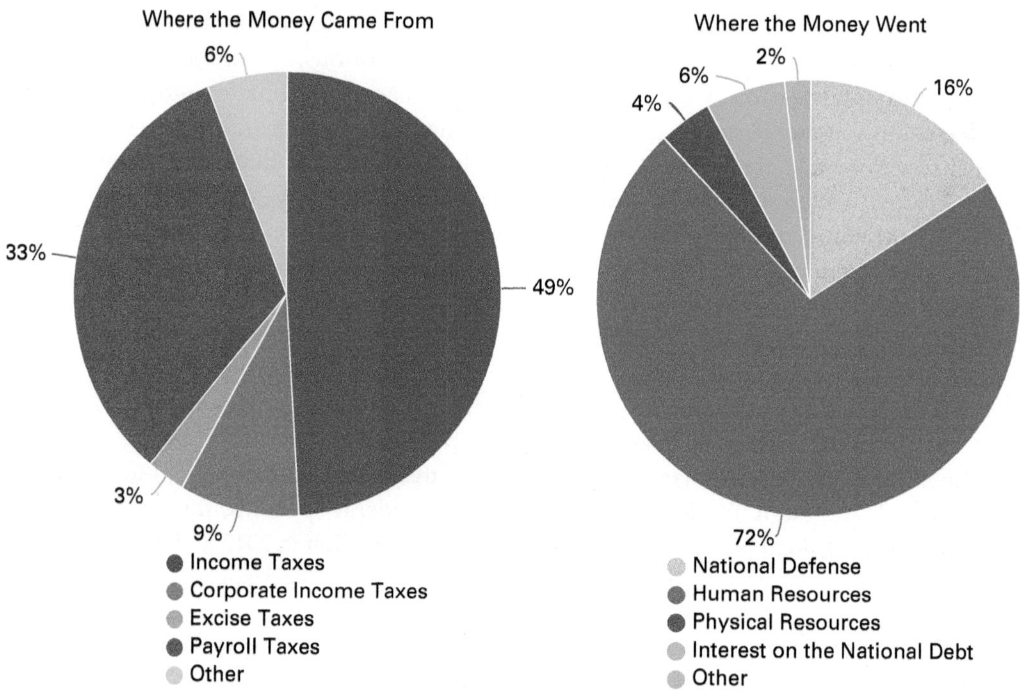

The government's fiscal year (FY) begins on October 1 of each calendar year, but it is numbered by its end on the following September 30, meaning that the FY 2019 budget will last from October 1, 2018 to September 30, 2019. However, the budget process for FY 2019 actually began in 2017, when the federal bureaucracy presented its proposed funding levels to the president.

At first glance, the federal budget process can seem overwhelming (see Figure 16.3). It involves budget resolutions, spending bills, and even new legislation. It also involves repeated votes in both chambers, and presidential signatures on more than a dozen separate bills. Although the bills are sometimes combined into one massive spending package, the president still has to take care that the priorities are right.

The process is not only difficult to follow, but it is nearly impossible to complete on time. The congressional budget committees often complain that the process has too many deadlines, and too many opportunities for delay. Partisanship also intervenes along the way to stall action on key bills, which almost always leads to omnibus spending bills that contain every appropriations bill in a huge package that is almost impossible to absorb in the time available. As the partisan polarization has grown in recent years, stalemates have become the norm, and Congress failed to complete the budget process five times in a row in 2011–2015. Although the system worked reasonably well from its creation in 1974, it now requires a series of tough votes to succeed, and gives ideological coalitions such as the conservative House Freedom Caucus the opportunity to sidetrack action with relatively small complaints.

Despite all its complexity, the budget process breaks down into three relatively straightforward tasks that must be completed before the new fiscal year begins.[24]

1. *The president proposes.* The president makes the first move in the budget process by submitting a formal budget proposal between the first Monday in January

FIGURE 16.3 THE BUDGET PROCESS IN DETAIL

The budget process is very complex. The House and Senate must agree on the budget spending and revenue targets, authorizing committees must change the laws if the targets require cuts in benefit formulas or revenue increases, and the powerful appropriations committees and subcommittees that control spending must produce detailed legislation outlining exactly how much each federal department and agency can spend on a program or activity. The federal budget is divided into 12 categories that cover different priorities such as defense, education, and transportation. Congress uses these categories as the basis for the 12 appropriations bills that must be enacted for each fiscal year.

SOURCE: Author edits on composite drawing from the *American Association for the Advancement of Science, American Institute of Physics, E&ENews Publications, House Committee on Appropriations, Library of Congress, Senate Committee on Appropriations, Washington Post, and the White House Office of Management and Budget (OMB).* Original framework supplied by the American Geological Institute and used with their permission.

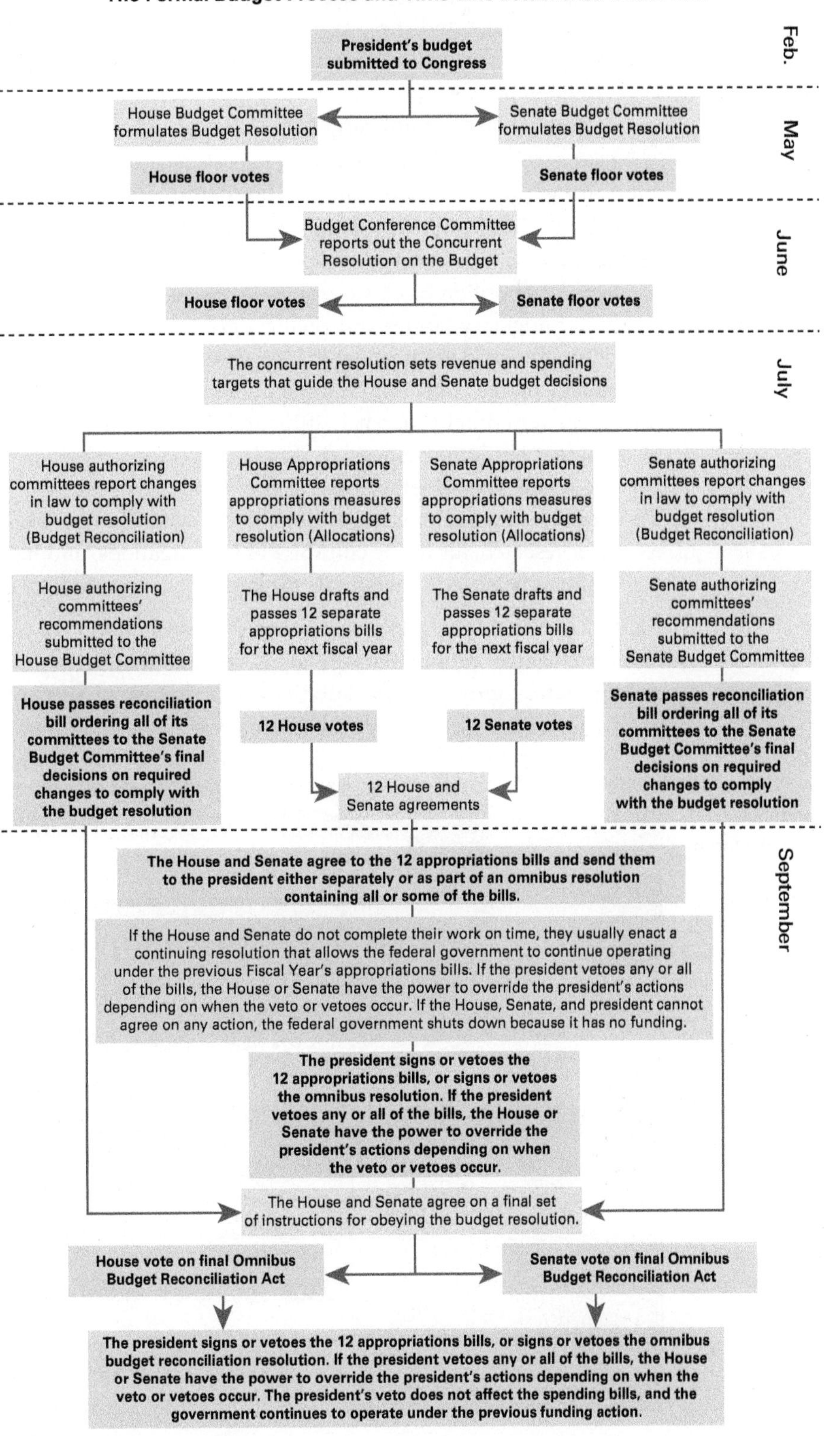

Office of Management and Budget (OMB)

The presidential staff agency that serves as a clearinghouse for budgetary requests and management improvements for government agencies.

Congressional Budget Office (CBO)

An agency of Congress that analyzes presidential budget recommendations and estimates the costs of proposed legislation.

and the first Monday in February. The proposal is drafted by the president's **Office of Management and Budget (OMB)** after negotiating with every department and agency about the coming year.

2. *The Congress rejects or revises.* Congress makes the second move in the budget process by passing the 12 appropriations bills that fund each of the major functions of the federal government. These bills are reviewed by the **Congressional Budget Office (CBO)**, which was created in 1974 to give Congress independent information in making its own budget decisions.[25] Prior to 1974, Congress had to rely on the president's information to develop its appropriations bills.
3. *The president approves.* The budget process is presumed to end with congressional passage and the president's approval of all 12 appropriations bills separately or in various combinations, such as an omnibus spending resolutions that Congress increasingly uses to keep government running while it fights to reach agreement on spending targets.[26]

Congress and the president have two alternatives if they miss the final deadline: (1) they can approve a continuing resolution that funds the government at the previous year's level until the 12 bills are passed; or (2) they can cut the discretionary budget by a fixed percentage under a "sequestration" process created in 1985.[27]

This latter option has been used only twice since 1985, in large part because it is a sign of budgetary failure and political gridlock. Both causes played a role in 2012, when Congress and the president failed to reach an agreement to cut $1.2 trillion from the federal budget over the following 10 years. The first sequestration order went into effect at midnight March 1, 2013, and was replaced five days later with a short-term budget resolution. Although it only lasted for a moment in budgetary time, the precedent was set—whether destructive or not, the sequester became a new tool in the effort to cut government spending. It also wreaked havoc on federal services such as cancer research, air traffic control, FBI investigations, and has even forced national parks, monuments, and memorials to close for short periods of time.

MONETARY POLICY Monetary policy is the second tool for managing the economy. The core element of monetary policy is the idea that prices, incomes, and economic stability reflect growth in the supply of money that circulates through the economy at any time. Increasing the supply of money tends to reduce unemployment by creat-

The U.S. Federal Reserve Board has great power over the economy by setting the "price" of money by raising or lowering the interest rates that banks and consumers must pay for credit. The price of money also affects the rate of return on any United States debt that individuals, banks, and even foreign countries own from buying the debt. This debt grew rapidly over the past two decades as the United States has borrowed money to pay for spending increases and tax cuts. Here, Federal Reserve Chair Jerome Powell testifies before Congress in 2018 as a national debt clock ticks in the background. The House Financial Services Committee had the clock installed to remind witnesses that the debt is a serious national issue.

ing more consumer demand and business investment, but it can ignite inflation; conversely, tightening or reducing the supply of money tends to increase unemployment by raising the cost of money, but it reduces inflation. Advocates of aggressive monetary policy contend that the money supply is the key factor affecting the economy's performance.

Monetary policy is made and executed by the **Federal Reserve Board** (often called the "Fed"), which is an independent regulatory commission. As leaders of America's most important bank, the Federal Reserve Board's chair and the six members of its board of governors are appointed by the president, with Senate consent, to 14-year terms; a different member's term expires every two years. Like all independent regulatory commissions, the Federal Reserve Board is effectively insulated from politics.

Federal Reserve Board
The independent regulatory commission created by Congress in 1913 to establish banking practices and regulate currency in circulation and the amount of credit available. The "Fed" consists of 12 regional banks supervised by a chair and a board of governors.

The current Federal Reserve Board chair is Jerome Powell who was serving on the Board of Governors of the Federal Reserve System before he was appointed chair by President Trump in 2018. Before his appointment to the Federal Reserve System, he worked in the private sector and at a think tank. Upon becoming chair he instantly became one of the most powerful economic leaders in the world and may have more say over economic performance than either the president or Congress. His predecessor, Janet Yellen, was the first Democrat appointed to the post since 1979. Nominated by President Obama and confirmed by the Senate in 2014. Yellen was also the first woman ever appointed to the post.

The Federal Reserve Board's most visible policy tool is the **federal funds rate**. The federal funds rate sends a signal to the economy about the cost of money. It is also used with other measures such as the discount rate to set the price for loans for cars, mortgages, college loans, and other consumer goods. The prime interest rate is closely monitored by financial institutions and tells the nation how much money will be available in the future. Increasing the federal funds rate slows down the economy by increasing the cost of borrowing, while lowering the rate stimulates the economy by making more

FIGURE 16.4 HOW INTEREST RATES AFFECT DIFFERENT KINDS OF LOANS, 2018

The federal funds rate matters to every interest rate we pay. Because the interest rate is passed on to consumers, the Federal Reserve Board's decision to raise or lower the rate raises or lowers the rate on different types of loans. Some loans cost less in interest because they cover long periods of time, while others are more expensive because they cover very short periods of time. But they all rise and fall with the funds rate depending on how long a given loan will last. The lowest interest rates in early 2018 covered long-term mortgages, while the highest rates covered monthly credit card bills.

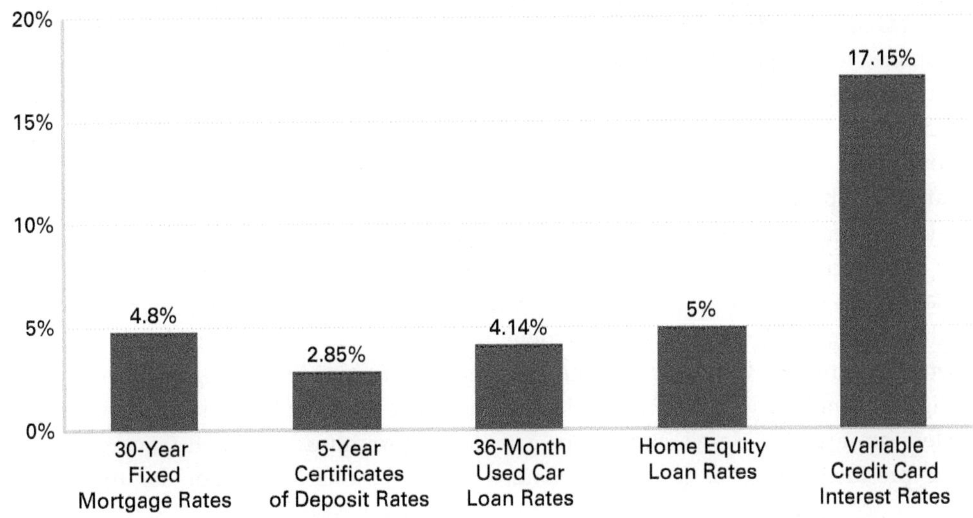

federal funds rate
The prime rate of interest that premier banks have to pay the Federal Reserve to borrow money.

money available for investment and growth. (Figure 16.4 shows the variation in interest rates that banks and other institutions set based on the Federal Reserve policy.)

The cost of borrowing money is linked to the interest rate that banks charge for short-term loans. In turn, this prime interest rate determines how much the federal government charges for many of its loans to new industries and college student loans, and flows down to bank home mortgages, car loans, and credit card debt. From 2008–2014, the Fed lowered the federal funds rate to near 0 percent in an effort to stimulate economic activity. By increasing the flow of money, the Fed pumped more money into home loans, small business start-ups, and hiring, which brought the economy back to life. Congress and the president also pumped more money into the economy through increased government spending for new roads. The economy sprung back to life in 2012 and unemployment began to fall. As the economy began to grow, the Fed started to raise interest rates to "tap the brakes" on the economic cycle.

Social Policy Tools

social safety net
The intent of federal programs that are designed to protect individuals and families that face economic hardship; programs to help the needy and less fortunate.

Social policy is designed to create a **social safety net** for protecting individuals and families against economic hardship. This "net" is designed to catch people as they suffer hardships from economic downturns, and the lack of access to health care, education, jobs, housing, and other essentials for building a healthy, productive life. But regardless of each program's purpose, the safety net relies on three basic tools for providing protection against hardship: (1) categorical programs for specific groups of individuals and families, (2) entitlement programs that establish a legal right to support, and (3) means-tested programs that require individuals and families to prove their need for help.

Together, the three tools capture about 80 social policy programs, including 33 housing programs run by four cabinet departments, 21 food programs run by three departments and one independent agency, 8 health care programs run by five different agencies all within the same department, and 27 cash assistance programs run by six cabinet departments and five independent agencies.[28] Most of these programs involve partnerships with state and local governments for two reasons. First, state and local governments have a history of protecting their citizens against hardship and have more public trust than the federal government. Second, state and local governments have the administrative skills and connections to deliver federal aid to the right people.

Because states vary greatly in their generosity and resources, however, most federal assistance is designed to set a minimum floor of support that individual states can add to if they wish. The most generous states in the country tend to be located in the Northeast and West, where legislatures are more liberal, whereas the least generous tend to be found in the South, where legislatures are more conservative.

categorical aid
Programs that are designed to provide benefits to groups or categories of individuals.

CATEGORICAL AID Most of the social programs discussed in this chapter are restricted to specific groups of citizens. As such, these programs are often described as a form of **categorical aid**. Simply typing a search term online such as "students," "elderly," "children," "disabled," "employees," "farmers," "women," or "veterans" reveals just how much help the federal government provides in each category. Although some categorical programs date back to early efforts to help mothers and children, most are relatively recent.

Some categorical grants involve discretionary, or controllable, spending, which means that Congress and the president can cut or increase spending as they wish, while other categorical grants involve mandatory, or uncontrollable, spending, which means that Congress and the president must provide funding to cover every eligible beneficiary unless they change the basic law itself. Social Security and Medicare are considered mandatory categorical programs; although Congress and the president can change these programs, the programs are so popular that they are considered untouchable. Social Security provides monthly income checks to eligible older Americans based on the taxes they paid into the program in the past, while Medicare provides health care and prescription drug coverage to the same beneficiaries.

Categorical aid for social policy involves two broad types of programs. The first type is called **social insurance**, which is defined as guaranteed government support for use at some future point in time, be it after hitting legal retirement age, losing a job, or returning home from war. The second type of categorical aid is much more loosely described as direct payments to individuals in need.

social insurance
Social programs that guarantee government support for use at some future point in time. Most, but not all, social insurance programs require contributions such as paying taxes in advance.

As discussed later, social insurance is available only to individuals and families who have done something to earn it, such as paying Social Security taxes or serving in the military, while direct payments are generally available only to individuals and families who qualify because of hardship. Even here, however, there is confusion about the difference between social insurance and direct payments—some social insurance such as Medicaid is available only to the poor, while some direct payments such as unsubsidized student loans are available to everyone who seeks them.[29]

ENTITLEMENT AID Many categorical programs provide support to anyone who fits a specific profile related to their personal circumstances. As such, these programs are often called **entitlement aid**. According to the Office of Management and Budget's glossary of budget concepts, the term "refers to a program in which the Federal Government is legally obligated to make payments or provide aid to any person who, or State or local government that, meets the legal criteria for eligibility."[30]

entitlement aid/entitlement programs
Programs such as unemployment insurance, disaster relief, and disability payments that provide benefits to all eligible citizens.

Large entitlement programs such as Social Security and Medicare are often described as untouchable, but Congress and the president can change the terms of an entitlement program at any time. Social Security and Medicare, however, are often described as "sacred cows" that cannot be cut. Many Americans pay Social Security taxes for decades before applying for benefits, for example, and consider their monthly checks as a guaranteed return on their investment.

These large programs are so ingrained in public life that many Americans do not consider the assistance to be part of the government's safety net. According to an exhaustive 2008 study, 57 percent of Americans say they have never used a government social program, even though all but 4 percent have used one or more. They just do not see their entitlements as social programs, in part because they believe they earned the checks and assistance through hard work, and in part because many social policy programs are disguised through the use of terms such as "insurance" instead of "assistance" or "aid."[31]

With Social Security and Medicare off the table for annual review, Congress has limited options to reduce spending for other entitlement programs. Under rules created in 1990, Congress must pay for any new spending by either reducing spending elsewhere in the budget or raising revenue. Because raising revenue is seen as much more painful than cutting spending, this **pay-as-you-go rule (PAYGO)** helped Congress and the president balance the budget in 1998 by cutting smaller entitlements and federal employment.[32] The rules expired in 2002 as the surplus evaporated after the Bush administration's 2001 tax cuts and the start of the costly Iraq War, but were reestablished in 2010 as the deficits soared to record levels.

pay-as-you-go rule (PAYGO)
A rule created in 1990 that requires Congress to pay for any new spending by either reducing spending elsewhere in the budget or raising revenue.

Congress and the president are also free to alter the limits on access to some entitlement programs based on income and need. Access to **means-tested entitlement aid** is based on a thorough assessment of an individual or family's financial resources to make sure that all recipients are truly needy. Most means tests are tied to the Census Bureau's poverty measure—potential beneficiaries must prove that they do not receive enough pay, have enough savings, and own enough assets, such as a car, to cross the 133 percent above the poverty limit.[33]

means-tested entitlement aid
Programs such as Medicaid and the Supplemental Nutrition Assistance Program that provide aid only to individuals or families that can show they do not have any other means to assist themselves.

The federal government spends almost $100 billion a year on agriculture and farm programs such as the SNAP that provides food stamps to needy families. The SNAP program came under fire in 2018 when House Republicans demanded changes that would require all SNAP recipients to either work, look for a job, or participate in a work training program at least 20 hours a week to receive assistance. The requirement has been tried before with mixed results, but won House passage in late June before being set aside in a compromise with the Senate. Here, a small group of Virginians protest the provision in a town hall meeting with their member of Congress.

Many of today's 80 means-tested entitlements are administered by the states, which means that the tests can vary greatly depending on the philosophy that guides the application. In Nevada, for example, a family of four cannot qualify for either Supplemental Nutrition Assistance Program (SNAP) or Temporary Assistance for Needy Families (TANF) if it makes more than $2,021 a month.[34] Individuals and families that qualify for one program such as SNAP automatically qualify for many others.

Spending on all of the nation's means-tested entitlement programs has expanded rapidly over the past two decades. According to the CBO, for example, between 1990 and 2016 the cost of nutrition assistance doubled, housing assistance tripled, and income security programs more than quadrupled as more people qualified for benefits and the number and size of benefits increased. More beneficiaries + more and larger benefits = higher costs.[35] Although the increases may seem large, means-tested entitlements are expected to grow more slowly over the next decade than non-means-tested entitlements such as Social Security, Medicare, and military retirement, which will rise steadily as the nation grows older.[36]

This growth confirms the wide reach of today's social safety net. Although some conservatives argue that spending has created incentives for being poor, past CBO research suggests that the safety net protects a very large number of vulnerable Americans.[37] Nevertheless, one-quarter to one-third of Americans—and even higher percentages of millennials and people of color—continue to experience direct economic hardship, and a majority of Americans have a direct personal connection to poverty.[38]

The Evolution and Goals of Economic Policy (Action)

16.4 Describe the evolution and goals of economic policy.

Federal economic policy is designed to do more than smooth the roller coaster called the business cycle. It also tries to promote economic growth, often measured by the number of new jobs or businesses created. This effort involves five broad goals:

(1) promote business, (2) expand international trade, (3) ensure competition, (4) protect employees from harm, and (5) police the stock markets.

Promote Business

Congress and the president often promote industries that are particularly important to the economy and or the public. And the more important the industry in terms of jobs, economic growth, and the incumbency advantage, the more likely it will be to have its own sources of government support, such as start-up grants, special tax credits, and even advice on how to succeed. Although economic policy involves a great deal of regulation, Congress and the president know that industry is the source of jobs, and jobs are always at or near the top of the electoral agenda.

The Department of Agriculture is an example of a department created to promote a major industry. Formally created in 1887, the department remains a powerful advocate of the farming industry, and a faithful provider of price supports for basic products such as corn, barley, oats, wheat, soybeans, cotton, and rice. In 2014 alone, the department spent more than $20 billion in federal crop support by either guaranteeing a minimum price for products or paying fees to farmers for not planting fields. By altering the supply and price of crops while promoting new products such as "biofuels" made from corn, sugar cane, and other crops, these subsidies simultaneously increase the cost of items such as bread, eggs, and milk, and provide steady earnings for farmers.

Regardless of their standing in the bureaucracy, all industries rely on the U.S. Patent and Trademarks Office to protect their ideas and inventions. Businesses and individuals would be less likely to bring new ideas to the market if others could copy their products without penalty. Drawing on the Constitution's promise to promote "Science and the Useful Arts," the office grants legal title to words and symbols through trademarks, and to inventions through patents. The office reviews each application for a trademark or patent to assure that the idea or invention is truly new, and gives inventors exclusive right to their "writings and discoveries," as the Constitution puts it, for a specific number of years.

The federal courts protect new ideas and scientific breakthroughs from theft, infringement, and abuse. In September 2012, for example, Apple won a $1 billion judgment against Samsung for copying several design features of the iPhone, including its "tap to zoom" option and rounded corners. The penalty was cut to $400 million in late 2013, but Samsung nonetheless appealed the judgment in 2016 when it asked the U.S. Supreme Court to review the case. In December 2016, the Supreme Court rejected the $400 million penalty, but sent the case back to the federal appeals court to develop an appropriate legal standard for adjudicating design patents.[39]

Expand International Trade

Nations have many options for gaining an unfair edge in today's highly competitive global economy. Some nations put high taxes, duties, and tariffs on the imports of certain products from other countries to protect their own industries from outside competition; others dump low-priced goods on other nations in an effort to kill foreign industries; and still others subsidize their own industries so their exports cost less than the fair-market price in other countries, or impose quotas or outright bans on foreign products.

These practices are all forms of **protectionism**, which insulates a domestic industry from international competition. Protectionism not only raises the costs of global goods and services, but also often provokes retaliation from affected countries and stalls needed economic reforms within the offending nations.

protectionism
A policy of erecting trade barriers to protect domestic industry.

balance of trade
The ratio of imports to exports. A negative balance of trade is called a trade deficit, while a positive balance of trade is a trade surplus.

Protectionism protectionism has been blamed for the nation's negative **balance of trade** in recent decades, which is a term based on a the value of imports minus exports. When imports exceed exports, the effect on the balance of trade is called a trade deficit; when exports exceed imports, the result is a trade surplus. The United States has been running large trade deficits for decades; generally it is seen as an innovative nation that pays too much for labor and regulation, and therefore charges too much for its products.

The international community currently uses two methods to create free trade: (1) lowering the barriers to free trade, and (2) encouraging international cooperation.

LOWER THE BARRIERS TO TRADE Nations have long debated the best way to protect and promote their own industries. Some nations believe that their industries are best supported when they compete against other nations on a level trading field, while others place taxes on imports from other countries to protect their own industries from competition. Although most nations now believe that open trade is the best way to create strong economies, they occasionally impose import taxes for political and economic advantage. In 2018, for example, the Trump administration imposed import fees on steel manufactured by some foreign countries as a way to protect the U.S. steel industry.

North American Free Trade Agreement (NAFTA)
An agreement signed by the United States, Canada, and Mexico in 1992 to form the largest free trade zone in the world.

Many nations pursue open markets through treaties with their largest trading partners. In 1992, for example, the United States, Canada, and Mexico signed the **North American Free Trade Agreement (NAFTA)**, forming the largest geographical free trade zone in the world. Although George H. W. Bush signed NAFTA near the end of his presidency, the agreement sparked intense opposition from U.S. labor unions and Democrats, and was not approved by Congress until December 1993. (A free trade agreement requires majority approval by both houses of Congress, and the president's signature.)

Although trade within the North American Free Trade Zone is not absolutely "free," the agreement has produced benefits for all three countries. By 2014, Mexico had become the third most important trading partner with the United States, while the United States had become the most important trading partner of Mexico. Critics remain concerned because Mexican antipollution laws are significantly less stringent than those in the United States, and Mexican employees receive considerably lower

Despite occasional skirmishes over specific industries and unfair competition, most of the world's economic leaders continue to embrace the broad goal of free trade. In 2018, however, the Trump administration imposed import taxes on a long list of Chinese products used by the U.S. robotics, information technology, and aerospace industries, which prompted the Chinese government to impose its own taxes on U.S. products such as soybeans, cars, pork, whiskey, and Harley Davidson motorcycles. Concerns about a possible trade war between the two giant economies drove the U.S. stock market down sharply in the months and weeks that followed. In July 2018, Harley Davidson announced that it was moving some of its U.S. jobs to Europe to reduce production costs associated with increased taxes. President Trump slammed the company on Twitter as disloyal to U.S. values and promised to impose higher costs on Harley Davidson plants in the United States. Chinese Harley Davidson riders prepare for a rally near Shanghai, which will soon be made in a factory in Thailand. Harley Davidson motorcycles have carved a niche in the Chinese market wages. Both of these factors make relocation to Mexico attractive to many U.S. companies seeking to reduce labor and pollution control costs.

Following NAFTA, Congress approved free trade agreements with Colombia Costa Rica, the Dominican Republic, El Salvador, Guatemala, Honduras, Nicaragua, Panama, and South Korea. The United States completed negotiations on the Trans-Pacific Partnership in 2016, but the Senate had not ratified the agreement by election day. All of these agreements came under close review once the Trump administration entered office. Trump often warned Canada, Mexico, and Latin America that he would remove the United States from NAFTA if they did not ease restrictions on American products.

ENCOURAGE COOPERATION The second path to free trade involves international agreements to enforce the broad outlines of the General Agreement on Tariffs and Trade (GATT) that was signed just after World War II. Although GATT was generally successful in reducing tariffs around the world, it was unable to produce lasting free trade agreements, and was eventually absorbed by the newly created **World Trade Organization (WTO)** in 1994.

World Trade Organization (WTO)
An international organization with more than 170 members that seeks to encourage free trade by setting rules for fair competition.

With 177 members as of 2014, the WTO has become a powerful international institution for negotiating further trade agreements and resolving disputes among its members. Many of these disputes take the form of legal cases filed by one or more countries against another. The WTO investigates each case, and has the power to direct any member nation to change its laws or policies into compliance with the underlying agreement on tariffs and trade.

In 2013, for example, the United States won a case against China for subsidizing its exports of precious metals used in computer chips, television monitors, and other high-tech products. According to the case, China's prices were so low that they crowded out all foreign competition, thereby smothering the mining industries in other nations. The WTO agreed with the United States, and ordered China to stop "dumping" cheap metals on the global economy. The Trump administration cited the case as an example of unfair trade practices when it announced import taxes on many Chinese products in 2018. The administration also warned that it would withdraw the United States from the WTO if Europe and China did not lower their trade barriers.

China is the world's largest supplier of the rare-earth metals that are used in sophisticated technologies such as computer flash drives, airplane engines, medical scanning systems, television screens, and nuclear reactors. Given its 97 percent share of the market, China decided to place quotas on its rare-earth exports in 2011 to drive up prices. The United States asked the WTO to order China to remove the quotas as an unfair restriction on free trade, and won the case in 2012. However, the United States had to go back to the WTO in 2015 to secure an order forcing China to begin implementing the ruling. Here, a mining truck carries precious metals to an extraction facility at China's Bayan Obo mine in Mongolia.

Ensure Competition

monopoly

Domination of an industry by a single company; also the company that dominates the industry.

Perhaps government's most important responsibility in a free-market economy is to guarantee competition. When one company gains a **monopoly**, or several companies create what is known as an "oligopoly," companies can raise their prices and stifle innovation. These tightly controlled trusts exist entirely to control a market.

Faced with a rising number of trusts in the oil, sugar, whiskey, and steel industries, progressive reformers convinced Congress to pass the Sherman Antitrust Act in 1890. Despite its grand promise of faithful protection of the markets, this first antitrust law had little immediate impact; presidents made few attempts to enforce it, and the Supreme Court's early interpretation of the act limited its scope.[40] Although the U.S. Federal Trade Commission continues to monitor large mergers such as the Comcast/Time Warner cable merger, it has become reluctant to interfere in economic activity that might strengthen the economy.

Business regulation increased in three major waves during the past century. The first wave came in the 1910s, the second in the 1930s, and the third in the late 1960s through 1980. In each case, changing circumstances gave rise to the legislation.

Protect Employees from Harm

The federal government has long protected employees from being harmed by their employers, but many of the most significant protections were enacted during the Great Depression when unemployment was high, employee wages low, and working conditions unsafe.

In 1935, for example, Congress enacted the National Labor Relations Act (often called the Wagner Act), which was the first major law to guarantee the basic right to form employee unions, and prohibited businesses from discriminating against union members or refusing to bargain in good faith on wages and working conditions.[41] Three years later in 1938, Congress also enacted the Fair Labor Standards Act of 1938, which established the 40-hour workweek, prohibited child labor, and required that employers pay overtime beyond the 40-hour limit.

Congress and the president did not turn from employee protections after the depression, either. In 1956, for example, Congress created Social Security disability insurance to help employees who could not work due to what the law described as "an impairment of mind or body" that renders employment impossible. And almost 15 years later, in 1970, Congress passed the Occupational Safety and Health Act of 1970, which created the first comprehensive workplace safety standards. The act also created the Occupational Safety and Health Administration (OSHA) to enforce the standards.

Most experts believe that the most important employment policy is the minimum wage, which was created under the Wagner Act in 1935 and now stands at $7.25 an hour. President Obama asked Congress in 2014 to raise the minimum wage for all workers in all states from $7.25 to $10.10, but received little support because of potential effects on the economy. According to the CBO, an increase might boost consumer spending by creating larger paychecks, but it also might reduce employment by 500,000 jobs as employers seek to absorb the costs by cutting jobs.[42] Having failed to win the increase, President Obama issued an executive order in February 2014 requiring that companies that work for the federal government pay their employees no less than $10.10 an hour.[43]

However, many states are free to raise the minimum wage above the federal mark within their own borders. As of January 2018, Washington, D.C., had the nation's highest minimum hourly wage at $13.25, followed by Washington State at $11.50, and California and Massachusetts at $11.00. Ten other states have set a minimum wage of $10 or higher. States are also free to raise minimum wages for specific groups of employees. In New York City, for example, businesses with 11 or more employees are required to pay at least $13.00 per hour and those with 10 or fewer employees must pay at least $11/hour. States may not lower their minimum wage below the federal level without violating the Constitution's Supremacy Clause.

Police the Stock Markets

The stock market crash of 1929 did more than devastate the U.S. economy and usher in the Great Depression. It also revealed deep problems in the way companies sold investment securities, or stocks, to investors. Millions of new investors entered the stock market in the 1920s, only to find that the companies in which they had invested were virtually worthless.

After a long investigation of the deceptive practices that led to the "Black Friday" crash, Congress and the president passed the 1934 Securities Exchange Act to police the stock markets that allow investors to buy and sell shares of a company's assets and earnings. The act required businesses to tell the truth about their fair-market value, and created an independent agency called the Securities and Exchange Commission (SEC) to monitor and punish deception. The SEC is also responsible for preventing and punishing "insider trading" by investors who have access to secret information about an investment.

Over the following decades, the SEC was given new powers to investigate schemes for selling worthless investments, but it failed to catch the deception that led to the 2008 financial collapse. The collapse was caused in part by the rise of almost worthless and confusing investment packages called derivatives, credit-default swaps, junk bonds, and securitized subprime mortgages.[44] The 2010 Wall Street Transparency and Accountability Act strengthened many of the protections in the wake of the 2008 financial collapse.

The Evolution and Goals of Social Policy (Action)

16.5 Describe the evolution and goals of social policy.

The nation's first social policy program was created during the Revolutionary War when the Continental Congress established programs to help veterans of war, but vast expansion in this area occurred under President Franklin Delano Roosevelt. Facing an

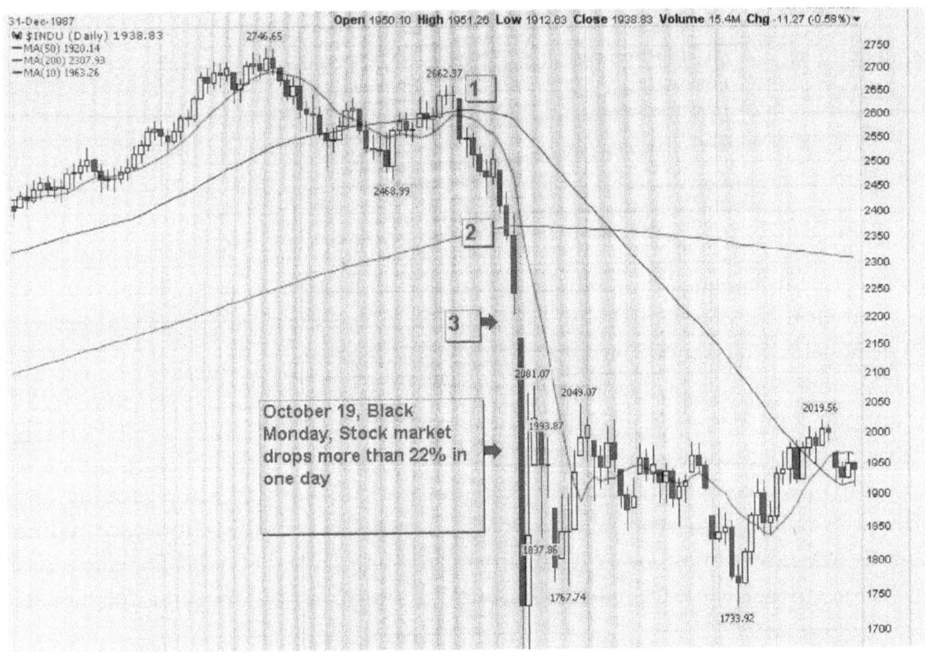

The U.S. stock markets fell almost a quarter of their value in a matter of hours on Monday, October 19, 1987. The crash was allegedly caused by automatic, or program, trading that tripped a nearly instantaneous series of trades that followed three days of downward movement in the market. The Federal Reserve Board and other federal financial regulators created a set of new rules that created "circuit breakers" to temporarily halt trading in the event of large price shocks. These circuit breakers exist to this day.

economic catastrophe in 1932, Roosevelt built a New Deal agenda of social policies to help retirees (Social Security), the jobless (unemployment insurance), and low-income Americans (Aid to Families with Dependent Children).

Before creating these programs, however, Roosevelt moved quickly to help low-income Americans. The first 100 days of 1933 produced the most significant list of social policy legislation ever passed in U.S. history, starting with cash grants to help unemployed Americans survive the long, hot summer. It is little wonder that scholars describe the New Deal as the "big bang" of social policy.[45]

Today's social policy agenda still covers many of the New Deal goals, but has grown to almost three-quarters of the federal budget. When Social Security, Medicare, and the War on Poverty programs are added, the social policy agenda in 2016 absorbed more than $2.7 trillion of the federal government's $3.5 trillion budget, and it is expected to grow larger every year into the foreseeable future.[46] Other nations have been able to lower their social spending somewhat, but the global economy has affected every corner of the world.

Using either social insurance or direct payments to individuals, federal social policy addresses five goals: (1) insure older Americans against financial hardship, (2) provide a safety net for Americans living at, below, or headed toward the poverty line, (3) insure working Americans against disability, (4) insure working Americans against unemployment, and (5) provide health care access to all Americans. Although the nation is still working toward each of these goals, its social policies have cut poverty almost in half. Figure 16.5 shows the effect by comparing the official, more accurate, measure of poverty with the amount of federal support included in the calculation to one without the federal support. As the figure clearly shows, the federal government and its state partners made a remarkable impact on the poverty rate.

Measuring these effects year-by-year back to Johnson's declaration of the War on Poverty, the Social Security program cut the percentage of Americans living below the alternative poverty line by 8 percent, while cashable tax credits pushed it down by 3 percent, food and nutrition aid by 1.6 percent, housing subsidies by 0.9 percent, and unemployment insurance by 0.8 percent. They could not drive it to zero. The federal government and the states did not win the war, but they made substantial progress breaking the enemy down. Without these and other social programs, almost a third of Americans would be living below the poverty line in 2016.[47]

Insure Older Americans Against Financial Hardship

The federal government uses social insurance to provide ongoing support for certain groups such as retirees and veterans. By using insurance rather than direct payments, government gives beneficiaries a sense of responsibility and fairness in collecting their checks because they have earned the support.

Social Security is arguably the most popular form of social insurance, and affects almost all of its beneficiaries without regard to their income or assets. Created in 1935, it is one of three programs to support eligible older Americans: (1) Social Security, (2) personal savings, and (3) employer-funded pensions.

As noted earlier in this chapter, Social Security provides guaranteed income to anyone who has paid into the program long enough to qualify for coverage. Supported by equal payroll tax contributions from employers and employees, the program now covers more than 90 percent of the U.S. workforce and provides benefits to 55 million Americans.[48] The program provides monthly checks to qualified beneficiaries, who must be at least 62 years of age and have paid Social Security taxes for at least 15 years (60 three-month quarters) before applying for benefits,

FIGURE 16.5 PERCENT OF AMERICANS LIVING AT OR BELOW THE POVERTY LINE

Most social policy makers rely on the official poverty rate to make decisions about help for the poor. However, the real poverty rate depends in part on how it is measured. The amount of poverty increases dramatically when the official rate is recalculated to remove government benefits from the total. Although conservatives have argued that the War on Poverty has failed, the adjusted rate in this figure shows that government reduced poverty significantly, but still not enough to declare victory in the war.

SOURCE: 1990–2012 measures, Christopher Wimer, Liana Fox, Irv Garfinkel, Neeraj Kaushal, and Jane Waldfogel, "Trends in Poverty with an Anchored Supplemental Poverty Measure," Columbia Population Research Center, working paper CPRC13-01, December 5, 2013; post-2012 measures, U.S. Census Bureau, https://www.census.gov/library/publications/2017/demo/p60-261.html.

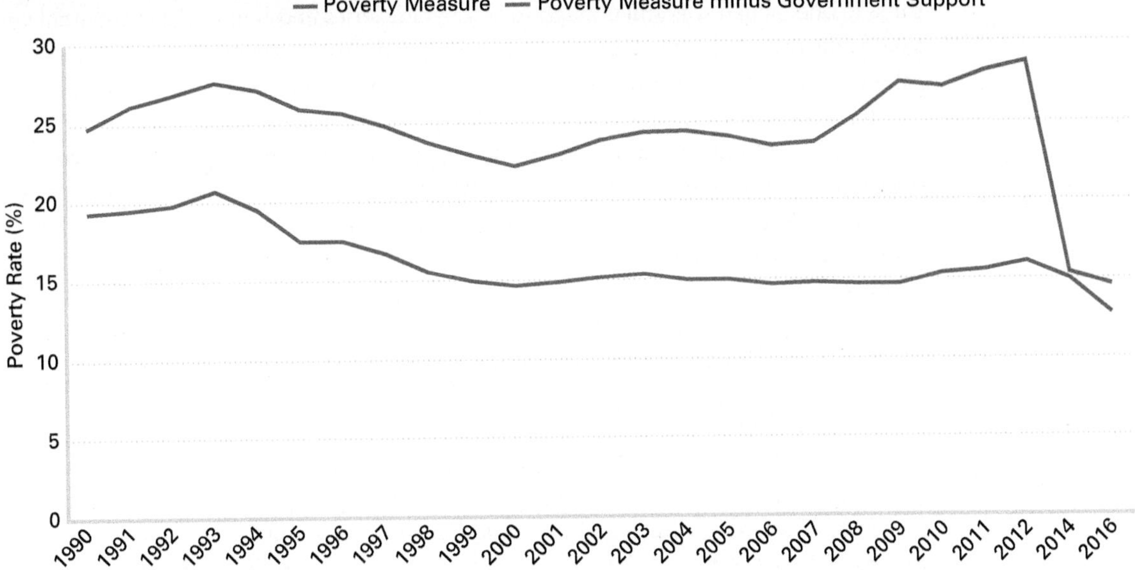

but do not have to work the years one after the other. Nor do they have to meet the requirement in full-time employment. In fact, some beneficiaries collect the quarters here and there over the years in part-time jobs. You almost certainly have a handful of quarters already in the system, but need to go into your local Social Security Administration office to find out just how many you have—the administration is not currently equipped to deal with Internet requests unless you are already drawing down benefits.

Employees and employers pay equal amounts of the federal government's Social Security payroll tax. People who work in the so-called "gig," or self-employed, economy must pay the whole amount. Except for certain groups of employees such as some state and local government employees, and student employees at many colleges and universities, the FICA tax is deducted automatically from every paycheck, and covers all earnings up to a certain mark that is raised every year to keep pace with inflation—the tax covered all earnings up to $128,400 in 2018, for example. Most workers now pay more in annual Social Security payroll taxes than in income tax.

Social Security was expanded in 1939 to help the families of deceased Social Security beneficiaries, and again and again over the years as Congress used the increases to protect constituents, which is one of several incumbency advantages. These discretionary increases became so frequent and expensive that Congress stopped itself from further bidding wars by indexing benefits to rise under an automatic cost-of-living adjustment (COLA), based on the consumer price index.[49] As of January 1, 2018, the maximum monthly Social Security benefit was $2,788, the average was $1,404, and the minimum was only $39.90 for someone with the minimum amount of time in the workforce.[50] Under legislation enacted in 1983, the Social Security retirement age for the full benefit will reach 67 in the year 2027.

The link between today's payroll taxes and tomorrow's benefits creates a sense that the benefits are already being set aside in numbered accounts at the Social Security Administration. However, the program was designed as a "pay-as-you-go" system that spends today's payroll taxes on today's benefits. Your current payroll taxes will generate future benefits only if there are enough taxpayers to cover your costs.

However, current estimates suggest that there may not be enough taxpayers in the workforce to cover the costs. In 1960, for example, there were five taxpayers paying into the program for every beneficiary, which was more than enough to pay beneficiaries and even store up a small surplus for future use. By 2000, the ratio was down to about three to one, which was still enough to pay beneficiaries and build up a substantial surplus as the huge baby boom generation built up a nearly $3 trillion surplus. By 2040, the ratio will drop to two to one, and the baby boom's $2.5 trillion surplus will be gone.[51]

If current trends hold, Congress and the president will either have to raise the payroll tax for you and others in the workforce, raise the retirement age to keep you and others working longer, cut benefits for wealthier retirees, create a much faster path to citizenship for new taxpayers, encourage families to have more children who will grow up to pay taxes, or pump general tax revenues into the program to cover the annual shortfall.[52]

Provide a Safety Net for Americans at, Below, or Headed Toward the Poverty Line

Franklin Roosevelt's New Deal agenda stimulated a remarkable expansion in the federal government's social domestic policy role. Although the federal government had long relied on charities and others to help the poor, the Great Depression forced Roosevelt to act. Although he added dozens of programs to the new social safety net, he started by asking Congress to provide **public assistance** to low-income families with children, and some adults.[53] Over time, public assistance became known as welfare.

public assistance
A traditional term used to describe government programs to aid the poor.

States established the nation's first public assistance programs in the late 1800s to help low-income single mothers and their children, and the federal government soon followed with the Infancy and Maternity Protection Act of 1921. Supported by many of the same women's groups that had just won ratification of the Nineteenth Amendment, which gave women the right to vote, the act gave the newly created federal Children's Bureau funds to encourage states to create new maternal, infant, and early childhood health programs.

This precedent eventually produced the Aid to Families with Dependent Children (AFDC) program in 1935.[54] Like most public assistance today, AFDC was designed as a state program primarily funded by the federal government. However, states only received the funding under two conditions: (1) they had to match the federal funds with some contribution of their own, and (2) they had to establish a means test for all families that would receive benefits.

AFDC remained relatively unchanged until 1996 when President Clinton decided to "end welfare as we know it."[55] Working with the new Republican congressional majority elected in 1994, Clinton persuaded Congress to pass the Personal Responsibility and Work Opportunity Reconciliation Act in 1996, which replaced the New Deal's AFDC with Temporary Assistance for Needy Families (TANF).

TANF contains three requirements that have changed the definition of welfare from indefinite to temporary. First, states cannot use federal funds to provide cash assistance to any family for more than 60 months total—hence, the name "temporary." Second, parents are required to do some kind of work for at least 30 hours a week or risk losing their benefits. And third, states are encouraged to use TANF funds to pursue four goals: (1) help families care for their children in their homes, not childcare centers; (2) promote job training, work, and marriage; (3) prevent and reduce unmarried pregnancies; and (4) encourage the formation of two-parent families.[56]

Dinner is served at the St. Anthony Foundation's soup kitchen in San Francisco during the economic recession in 2010. Measured in percentages, African Americans and Hispanics are at a higher risk of poverty than whites. Measured in absolute numbers, however, whites accounted for two-thirds of all Americans at or below the poverty line. Similarly, African American and Hispanic women had higher poverty rates than white women, but white women were more likely to have the largest numbers at or below the poverty line. Despite these numbers, African Americans and Hispanics are often pictured in stories about poverty.

The welfare reforms worked in reducing caseloads and encouraging work, but were not enough to stem the rising tide of child poverty during the late 2010s. Welfare applications fell dramatically during the first 15 years of the program, which suggests that the new work rules and tighter state rules deterred some families from seeking support. At the same time, TANF left many children behind—fewer cases meant more children at risk as the economy declined.

TANF is not the only program for Americans below the poverty line or headed down toward it. According to a recent report from the Government Accountability Office, the federal government has about 80 safety-net programs that were created during the New Deal, the Great Society, the early 1970s, the mid-1980s, the mid-1990s, and 2009–2012. Four of these expansions came under Democratic presidents, and the other two under Republican presidents.[57]

The 80 programs accounted for about $750 billion in the 2019 budget, with the largest share spent on health care (Medicaid); food support through a debit card that can be used at grocery stores for milk, bread, and other staples but not for cigarettes, alcohol, or other unhealthy products (Supplemental Nutrition Assistance Program, or SNAP); the Supplemental Security Income program (SSI), which gives an extra level of protection to older, blind, and disabled Americans through benefit checks that covered more than five million Americans in 2019;[58] a tax credit for the low-income workers that often creates a refund they can cash out to keep them out of poverty (the Earned Income Tax Credit); access to subsidized, rent-controlled housing; Pell Grants for low-income college students; and pre-kindergarten education through the Head Start program, which helps low-income children catch up on the basics they need to succeed in elementary school.[59] All of these programs are means-tested entitlements.

Liberals tend to applaud the inventory, but some conservatives, such as former Speaker of the U.S. House, Paul A. Ryan (R-WI), believe it isolates low-income Americans from the tailored support they need, and focuses the federal government on raising benefits, not ending poverty. Citing the 15 percent of Americans who still live in poverty 50 years after Johnson's declaration, Ryan argued that low tax rates on rich Americans was not the problem: "The problem is that Washington is holding too many people back. The problem is that they're cut off from three crucial sources of support: education, work, and family." Ryan also argued that the Great

Society had created "a hodgepodge of programs that are so disorganized and dysfunctional, they pull families closer to government and away from society."[60]

The Trump administration asked Congress to cut almost every one of these programs in 2018. Health care for the poor and children was slated for a $616 billion 10-year cut, loans for low-income college students were listed for another $311 billion, food assistance for children and families for $189 billion, and disability coverage for injured employees for $50 billion.

The budget proposal also asked Congress to set work requirements for all able-bodied recipients of financial assistance. "We need people to go to work," the president's budget director said in late May. "If you're on food stamps, and you're able-bodied, we need you to go to work. If you're on disability insurance and you're not supposed to be—if you're not truly disabled, we need you to go back to work. We need everybody pulling in the same direction."

Insure Working Americans Against Disability

Under the disability insurance program mentioned above, employees can apply for federal assistance if they are no longer able to work, and are eligible as soon as they become disabled. The process for earning a disability payment, which covers part of a worker's monthly salary, is very strict. Only 20 percent of applications are approved. The worker has to present detailed evidence that the disability was not caused by age, and must prove that the disability is long term. Approximately nine million disabled Americans received disability support in January 2018, with an average monthly benefit of $1,197.

Insure Working Americans Against Unemployment

The Great Society produced the first federal protection for the unemployed. As with Social Security, the protection came in the form of insurance, in part to reduce the stigma of receiving help for losing a job. Federal unemployment insurance is jointly administered by the federal government and the 50 states and is covered by monthly premiums that are automatically deducted from paychecks. Employers also pay monthly premiums for their employees.

Unemployment insurance is available to workers who have lost their jobs through no fault of their own because of economic conditions, harassment, or discrimination. Workers cannot receive benefits if they quit their jobs by their own choice—for example, if they have children, get married, move to another part of the country—or are fired for poor performance or being absent without good reason.

Both levels of government collect unemployment taxes, but the federal government sets broad rules about who qualifies for coverage, while states set their own maximum weekly benefits. As might be expected, less-prosperous states provide lower benefits. In 2018, for example, Mississippi's maximum payment was $235 a month, compared with $742 in Massachusetts.[61] During normal economic times, the benefit is paid for 26 weeks, although there are exceptions to the length of coverage. Coverage was extended several times during the deep recession, when 17 million Americans collected unemployment payments.

Provide Health Care Access to All Americans

The United States mostly relied on charity health care to help Americans in hardship until the 1960s. Although Roosevelt tried to provide health insurance to older Americans in his Social Security bill, and President Harry S. Truman pushed for action in 1946, neither could find enough support to win passage of a comprehensive law. As a result, Congress and presidents have built the current health care system one piece at time starting with veterans of war in 1789, older Americans and Americans below the poverty line in 1965, and children in 1997. Whether the 2010 effort to cover all uninsured Americans will survive the recent campaign to repeal and replace the national health insurance program is yet to be settled.

INSURE OLDER AMERICANS AGAINST POOR HEALTH Medicare was created in 1965 as part of President Johnson's Great Society. Johnson knew he could not convince Congress to enact health insurance for all Americans, and decided to take the easier path to cover older Americans as a natural extension of the Social Security insurance model.[62]

Fifty years later, Medicare has expanded into the second largest social policy, and now reaches 50 million older Americans. It covers all reasonable hospital, medical, and prescription drug expenses. The hospital insurance is funded by a 1.42 percent tax on employees and employers. Medicare pays for inpatient hospital care, skilled nursing care, and other services. Individuals can purchase additional Medicare insurance to cover some expenses not traditionally covered by Medicare. As of 2018, about 60 million Americans received Medicare benefits. As an entitlement program, Medicare provides benefits only to Americans who are at least 65 years old and have paid Medicare taxes for at least 10 years (40 quarters).[63]

PROVIDE HEALTH CARE ACCESS TO AMERICANS AT OR BELOW THE POVERTY LINE Medicaid was also created in 1965 to provide basic health services for poor families. The program is administered and partially funded by state governments and covers items such as hospital care and family planning. Medicaid provided access to care for 74 million Americans in 2018 at a cost of $625 billion.[64]

Federal and state governments fund Medicaid jointly, but the federal government covers about 75 percent of the total, and also makes many of the decisions about how states spend the combined total. For example, states must cover inpatient and outpatient hospital services, laboratory tests and X-rays, federally qualified health center access, and family planning. States can choose, however, not to provide physical therapy, optometry services, chiropractic treatments, end-of-life hospice care, and speech, hearing, and language help. Moreover, states are free to deny coverage to individuals without dependent children, and may not cover individuals under 65 years of age.

REDUCE THE NUMBER OF UNINSURED AMERICANS All of the health care programs described above rely on a single stream of government funding. The funding might mix federal and state dollars for a program such as Children's Health Insurance, or collect payroll taxes to cover future benefits for a program such as Medicare. The funding might also require beneficiaries to bear some of the costs for their care in a program such as Medicaid, or simply flash an ID card to prove their eligibility for a program such as geriatric care at a Veterans Affairs hospital.

However, just because the bills are paid by a single stream of government funding does not mean government must deliver the health care. With the exceptions of programs such as military and veterans health care, the federal government pays private doctors, nurses, pharmacists, clinics, and hospitals to provide the services. It also allows private insurers to charge premiums or to close gaps in coverage in a program such as Medicare.

In theory, these kinds of modified **single-payer systems** should be able to demand lower prices for health care. In practice, however, they generally offer higher benefits and cover more expensive patients who enter the system later in life or with long-neglected illness. More importantly, all of the federal government's single-payer programs were designed for specific groups of Americans—veterans, military families, retirees, children, and people who live below the poverty line. As of 2009 when the Obama administration entered office, 51 million Americans did not qualify for any of the government's traditional health care programs, and the number was rising as the economy collapsed.[65]

single-payer system
A payment system that involves one source of funding, such as the federal government.

Having promised to press forward on national health insurance during his presidential campaign, Obama had to choose among the many options for reform, including Medicare reform to reduce soaring health care costs, more regulation of private health insurance, expanded Medicaid coverage for Americans just above the poverty line, tax credits for small businesses that provide insurance for their employees, penalties on the "young invincibles" who refused to buy the affordable insurance at their command, and the creation of new options for Americans who wanted protection.

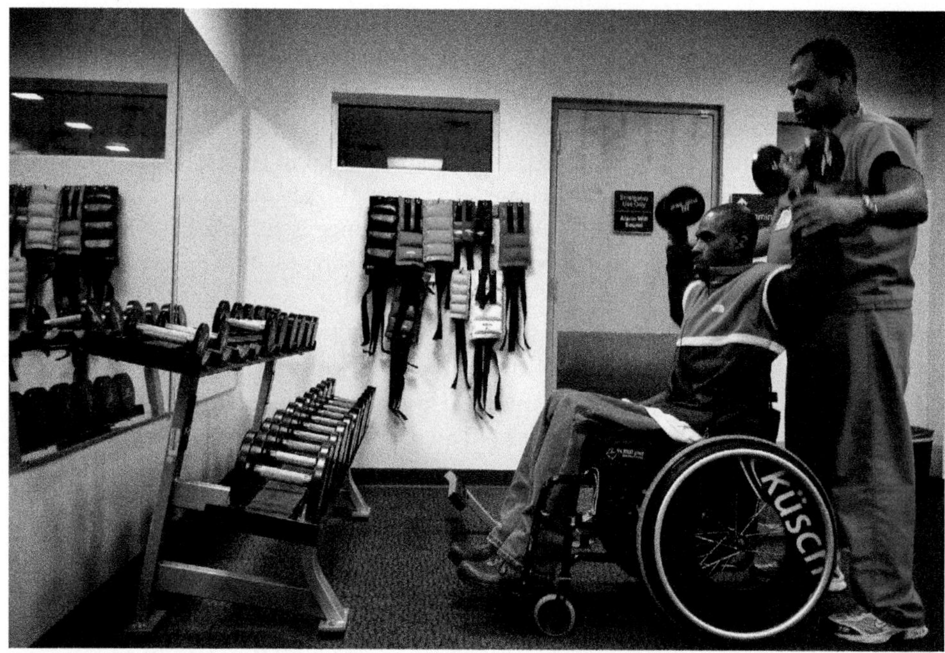

The federal government has been caring for veterans of war since the Revolutionary War, and currently operates 153 veterans hospitals and more than 700 clinics across the nation. It is one of the very few federal health care programs where government is the single funder and the single provider. Here, Army Staff Sergeant Eugene Simpson (retired) receives physical therapy at the Washington, D.C., Veterans Hospital. Sergeant Simpson was paralyzed on patrol during the Iraq War. Like all veterans, Sergeant Simpson automatically received access to veterans care because of his service.

After months of legislative struggle, Congress and the president blended a single-payer system with private delivery and health insurance into the Patient Protection and Affordable Care Act of 2010, which is usually shortened to the Affordable Care Act, and often called "Obamacare." Backed by CBO estimates, the act promised to enroll 21 million uninsured Americans by 2016, passed through the House and Senate on party-line votes, was signed into law on March 10, 2010, and survived a Supreme Court test in 2012 mostly intact.[66] The act weighed in at 906 pages, and produced 10,353 pages of regulations designed to implement a vast array of reforms that are now in full effect:

- Individuals are now required to show proof that they have purchased insurance for themselves and their families and must provide proof when they file their annual federal tax returns or pay a substantial tax penalty.[67]
- Individuals who cannot meet Medicare or Medicaid eligibility tests may purchase insurance from a private company such as Blue Cross Blue Shield, or enroll either through their state government's insurance exchange, if it has one, or the federal exchange at https://www.healthcare.gov. As of 2016, 24 states had insurance exchanges of some kind, while the rest relied on https://www.healthcare.gov.[68]
- Individuals can choose the benefits they wish with the deductibles, co-pays, and premium they are willing to pay, but must be offered 10 essential benefits such as emergency care, maternity and newborn care, mental health and addiction treatment, laboratory services, and preventive care.[69]
- Individuals who live well below the poverty line but are not eligible for Medicare or Medicaid may qualify for a federal insurance subsidy of up to 40 percent of the insurance cost.
- Insurance companies cannot deny coverage to any person for any reason, and without regard to preexisting conditions, such as high blood pressure, cancer, diabetes, or mental illness.
- Insurance companies must allow children to remain on their parent or guardian's insurance until they are 26 years of age.
- As noted below, the federal government will pay 100 percent of state Medicaid expansion for the first three years, and 90 percent thereafter, provided that the coverage is available to all citizens under 65 years of age who live at 133 percent of the poverty line and below, and regardless of their employment or marital status.

- Health care providers will no longer be paid a fee for each separate service they provide, but in a single bundle that will allow the federal and state governments to see and therefore control the overall cost of care.
- The Affordable Care Act also gives the federal government significant authority to discipline hospitals for high patient readmission and infection rates, both of which signal poor operating discipline and inadequate follow-up after discharge, and both of which generate higher costs.

Under the 2010 Affordable Care Act, Congress and the president encouraged states to expand their Medicaid programs by offering 100 percent reimbursement for the first three years after expansion, and 90 percent thereafter. The only requirement was that states had to admit individuals with incomes up to 133 percent of the poverty line, and could no longer exclude adults without children. The incentive may have seemed irresistible to its designers, but 13 states were still unwilling to accept the deal as of February 2016, and another six were still bargaining over the details or just starting the conversation. Moreover, Florida and Texas remain adamantly opposed to expansion, which will keep 1.5 million of their citizens among the uninsured.[70]

Republicans had opposed the Affordable Care Act at every step toward passage and implementation in 2009, and pushed to honor Trump's campaign promise to "repeal and replace" the program in 2017. Having voted more than 50 times between 2010 and 2016 to reverse the program, they finally saw a chance to repeal and replace the program as Congress took action on budget and tax reform only months after the president's inauguration.

Conservative Republicans soon realized that repealing and replacing Obama's signature program was easier promised than done. Although the Republican House succeeded in a broad repeal by a vote of 217 to 2013 in July, the bill soon stalled in the Senate when Sen. John McCain provided the final vote needed to stop action. Nonetheless, conservatives were able to strip the mandate to buy health insurance from the law in late December when they passed the president's $1.5 trillion tax cut, but the law remained largely intact. In addition, several states including New Jersey soon took action to create their own insurance mandates for all of their citizens.

The Economic and Social Policy Future (Impact)

16.6 Assess the future of economic and social policy.

Despite continued philosophical disagreements, Democrats and Republicans can find ample evidence that the nation's economic and social health is thriving. Patents, life expectancy, and high school graduations are all up since 1960, while infant mortality, cigarette smoking, and poverty rates among older Americans are all down.[71] If economic and social policies are measured in terms of creating a more prosperous and healthy society, the United States can be very proud of its accomplishments.

However, economic and social challenges remain. Income inequality appears to be rising; the number of children who live in poverty has barely changed since the War on Poverty began; and the nation's economy continues to struggle with relatively high unemployment, high budget deficits, and a growing national debt. Although the CBO estimates that the GDP will grow during the next decade, it also foresees continued deficits and rising interest payments on the national debt. These payments may be the most serious consequence of the debt if only because the money could be spent on other priorities such as tax cuts.

At some point, the interest payments will become so large that they will cut into other programs such as Social Security, veterans' care, and the national defense. Although there is great disagreement about how to lower the debt, the interest will continue to rise

TABLE 16.1 TRENDS IN THE FEDERAL GOVERNMENT'S EIGHT HIGHEST-COST PROGRAMS (IN BILLIONS OF DOLLARS)

Program	2008	2012	2016	2020 estimate
Social Security	620	778	933	1,168
National Defense	696	681	615	608
Medicare	407	484	602	703
Medicaid	201	251	367	450
Interest on the National Debt	253	220	240	523
Assorted Income Security Programs	167	124	184	211
Federal Retirement	110	124	142	159
Food and Nutrition	61	115	111	113
Total of the Eight Programs as a Percent of the Federal Budget	75%	80%	80%	90%

SOURCE: *Budget of the U.S. Government, Fiscal Year 2019* (U.S. Government Printing Office, 2018), Historical Tables, Table 5.1 available at http://www.whitehouse.gov/omb/budget/Historicals.

until the debt is paid down. Like the interest on your own credit cards, the bills you skip each month gather interest until you have to pay up or declare bankruptcy. (See Table 16.1 for a comparison of the federal government's eight highest-cost programs over time.)[72]

The Debt Problem

This is not the first time in history that the federal government has faced such a large gap between its revenues and spending. The federal government generated huge deficits during the Civil War, World War I, and World War II. The explanation is obvious: wars are expensive. The current deficit was affected by the costly wars in Iraq and Afghanistan, but also was driven by the 2008 economic calamity. More people were out of work; more people and families needed help through unemployment insurance and other public assistance; and more businesses failed.[73] Even though today's deficit is not the first in history, the current deficit is by far the largest, and will produce $880 billion in interest payments by 2024, which is more than Social Security costs today.

The consequences of the mounting debt were already clear in 2010 just before the Republicans recaptured the House. As the president's National Commission on Fiscal Responsibility and Reform reported shortly after the elections, Congress and the president needed to act: "Our challenge is clear and inescapable: America cannot be great if we go broke. Our businesses will not be able to grow and create jobs, and our workers will not be able to compete successfully for the jobs of the future without a plan to get this crushing debt burden off our backs."[74] Despite its dire assessment and a $4 trillion plan for cutting the debt, the commission failed to garner enough support for action. President Obama walked away from the package of painful tax increases and spending cuts, and neither Congress nor the president has returned to the negotiating table since that time.[75]

While the National Commission's recommendations were not pursued, the report offered an expansive agenda of 45 specific suggestions, including cuts in defense spending, a cap on discretionary spending to reduce programs such as agriculture price subsidies, the elimination of almost all tax deductions, and Social Security and Medicare reform. The plan involved a long list of "sacred cows," meaning programs that have high public and political support that make them untouchable.

Repairing Social Security and Medicare for the Future

Congress and the president face two equally difficult problems surrounding Social Security and Medicare. According to the Social Security and Medicare Board of Trustees that oversees the huge programs, the most likely future is gloomy at best.[76] Neither program is collecting enough money through payroll taxes to cover future costs, and both are starting to carve into their once impressive trust funds at an alarming pace. Based on the best available estimates of the economic and social policy future, Medicare and Social

Security are already spending more on benefits than they are receiving from taxes, and will run out of their cash reserves by about 2030. Social Security and Medicare will either have to raise more revenues in some way through higher taxes or debt, or they will have to cut or constrain benefits in some other way, both of which are very painful options.

Both of these programs are easier to fix now than at the last minute when older Americans are on the precipice of no funds for their retirement years. According to the Social Security and Medicare Board of Trustees, it would be much easier to trim the two huge programs now. "If lawmakers take action sooner rather than later, more options and more time will be available to phase in changes so that the public has adequate time to prepare. Earlier action will also help elected officials minimize adverse impacts on vulnerable populations, including lower-income workers and people already dependent on program benefits."[77]

The two programs may be headed toward the same funding crisis, but the difficulties are being driven by very different problems. Social Security is straining under the wave of baby-boom retirements, while Medicare is buckling under rising health care costs. Although some advocates suggest that both programs can be repaired with minor tinkering, the balance of evidence suggests that tinkering will not be sufficient, especially if Congress and the president want to restore public confidence that the two programs will be there when younger Americans retire.

There are four options for repairing Social Security, which must absorb a much larger number of beneficiaries using taxes from a much smaller workforce:

1. *Increase the legal retirement age to keep up with gains in life expectancy.* After all, life expectancy has grown six years since Social Security issued its first benefit checks in 1940, but the retirement age has been raised by only two years. Some argue that a simple increase starting in 2023 would be enough to keep the program from crisis.[78]
2. *Change the way Social Security calculates its annual cost-of-living adjustment (COLA).* Under current practice, Social Security uses what some experts believe is a relatively expensive market basket of goods and services to set the increase when a more realistic basket for retirees would be more appropriate. Merely changing the market basket could shave the annual increase by a full percentage point, which would push the crisis date back by a decade or more.
3. *Expand the Social Security tax base.* Under current laws, the Social Security tax is collected only on the first $128,400 that individuals earn in any given year. However, research shows that about 5 percent of all individuals earn more than $128,400, meaning they stop paying FICA taxes well before the end of each year. Removing this cap on coverage not only would generate a significant increase in revenues, but also would reduce income inequality by exposing the top 5 percent of individuals to higher taxes. The total revenue from this option depends on the number of Americans who reach the top 5 percent.
4. *Create a Social Security means test.* Experts already know that 75 percent of all Social Security benefits go to beneficiaries who make less than $20,000 a year, and some believe the figure should be 100 percent. Denying some portion of the maximum benefit to anyone over the poverty threshold would save billions each year, and could be done easily simply by changing the benefit formula to cut the maximum benefit for upper-income retirees. Unlike the three other proposals above, however, this one would convert Social Security from an entitlement program for all to a means-tested entitlement program for some, which might undermine its popularity as an insurance program that gives everyone a rate of return on their taxes.[79]

As this list suggests, none of the options will be particularly popular, but they just might work if they are combined into a package that asks for sacrifices from everyone. Shared sacrifice has worked in past Social Security crises, and it may be the only way to convince the public to touch the program. According to the reports cited above, the means test would save the most money over the next 75 years, followed by creating a more accurate COLA, expanding the Social Security tax base, and increasing the retirement age.

The same strategy might work for Medicare, where health care costs are the major problem. Although health care spending has slowed somewhat since 2012, it is still headed upward, and Medicare is already paying more in benefits than it collects in taxes, and will exhaust its reserves in 2030. Moreover, it is not clear that Americans are getting the best health care for their dollars. Other nations spend much less on health care but have much healthier citizens.[80]

As with Social Security, there are four options for reducing health care costs, and therefore reducing the Medicare spending flow. The difference, as compared with Social Security, is that the U.S. health care system is extremely complicated, which makes Medicare cost savings difficult to calculate.

1. *Encourage greater competition among health care providers.* Today's complicated health care system encourages many patients to stay with the same physicians and providers regardless of performance, but this loyalty reduces the competition that might lower costs. If patients had greater freedom to choose their health care providers on the basis of health care quality, the resulting competition could produce significant savings and would likely enhance health care quality.
2. *Support prevention and wellness programs.* Every American seems to believe in preventing disease, but too many still smoke, avoid the gym, and eat fatty foods. Although there are few estimates of the cost savings from prevention at all stages of life, there is little doubt that the U.S. health care system invests large sums of money in curing diseases that could have been prevented or delayed by providing small incentives for healthy living.[81]
3. *Reduce medical mistakes and overbilling.* Although the Affordable Care Act addressed several of the most visible threats to patient safety such as infections, it did not focus on the medical mistakes and misdiagnoses that cost lives and money. Recent studies estimate that more than 400,000 Americans die of medical mistakes each year, which adds up to as much as $100 billion in direct health care costs, another $1 trillion in indirect economic costs, and immeasurable pain and suffering.[82] "Quality care is less expensive care," a recent study suggests. "It is better, more efficient, and by definition, less wasteful. It is the right care, at the right time, every time. Whatever the measure, poor quality is costing payers and society a great deal."[83] At the same time, many providers overbill Medicare for costs, sometimes because they simply lose track of costs, and other times because they set very high prices for seemingly inexpensive services and supplies such as catheters, bandages, and even socks.

Health costs remain a serious concern within the U.S. health system and have become the focus of ongoing protests among health professionals, political leaders, and private insurers. Here, a group of California nurses rally in support of a 2016 ballot initiative to limit the prices that state agencies pay for prescription drugs. The initiative failed, but continues to gain support in California and other states as health providers try to provide services as costs rise across the health industry.

4. *Coordinate care after patients leave the hospital through inexpensive visits and phone check-ins by nurses and other public health experts.* Research suggests that one-fifth of all hospital patients return to the emergency room within 30 days after they leave. This "churning" cost, as it is called, amounts to $15–$20 billion a year in immediate health care billings, and untold billions in economic costs through lost productivity, absenteeism, and insurance premiums.

It is not clear how much these reforms would save, largely because Medicare is only one component of the nation's huge health care system. The entire health care system, not Medicare benefits and taxes, is the cause of the problem. Therefore, the only way to save Medicare for future generations is to slow down the cost increases that affect all Americans, which would also reduce the costs for Medicare beneficiaries.

Nor is it clear just how to achieve these Social Security and Medicare reforms: although there are savings within reach, neither party wants to be criticized for cutting these popular programs. Nevertheless, Congress and the president will have to act eventually. After all, Social Security and Medicare will face inadequate funding, which provides ample reason for action, as younger Americans rightly wonder why they are paying such high payroll taxes for insurance that may not be available when they retire.

CONCLUSION

Your views of the War on Poverty may have changed as you have read this chapter. You now know that the poverty rate has gone down with federal support, but is far from zero. You also know that the Fed can only do so much to stimulate the economy, and that Congress and the president often fail to make fiscal decisions on time. And you know that the federal government's safety net is much more complicated than most of us imagine.

So given all that you now know about the structure, action, and impact of economic and social policy, you might ask yourself why so many Americans live in or near poverty: a lack of effort on the person's part or circumstances beyond her or his control?

The answer depends in part on your own political preferences and personal experience. Liberals tend to argue that economic circumstances such as slowdowns and recessions are mostly to blame for poverty, while conservatives tend to argue that many people in poverty could find a job if they only tried harder. As you now know, the answer may be a mix of the two. Economic conditions drove poverty upward during the nation's most recent recession, while some Americans might get work if they were willing to take very low wages.

However, former U.S. House Speaker Paul Ryan has a very different theory. Calling the War on Poverty a "stalemate" as of 2016, Ryan argues that it has been more a cause of further poverty than a success. "There are many different kinds of poverty," he has said. "But what a lot of them share in common is, people are cut off from the community. They don't have the support they need to grow, whether it's a counselor, or a teacher, or a boss. What they need is someone they can trust, someone who can help them learn new skills. And by discouraging work, the federal government is isolating the poor."[84]

Ryan could be right, but community is difficult to find in the isolated areas where poverty often thrives. Ryan could also be right that Congress and the president should combine many of the government's antipoverty programs to eliminate wasteful duplication and bureaucracy. And he certainly knows that raising taxes or cutting benefits to stabilize Social Security and Medicare could produce intergenerational warfare between your generation, your parents, and even your grandparents. As for his own battle against the War on Poverty, Ryan decided to retire from Congress at the end of 2018 to pursue other avenues for political impact.

These are all very tough issues, but here is the catch: the decisions need to be made sooner rather than later. People already in retirement or near retirement need time to adjust to benefit cuts, and you need time to think about how to balance higher taxes with all the other financial issues you face. As we often say, you will decide what to do. In this case, you will need to decide soon to give your parents a chance to prepare.

REVIEW THE CHAPTER

The Constitutional Foundations of Economic and Social Policy (Structure)

16.1 Describe the constitutional foundations and competing philosophies of economic and social policy, p. 477.

The Constitution's preamble promises that government will promote the general welfare, but the power to do so is embedded in Articles I and II. The Constitution gives Congress the authority to regulate commerce, raise revenues, and grant patents, for example, while giving the president the authority to oversee the government agencies that implement economic and social policy. Two competing philosophies guide economic policy: (1) the laissez-faire view that government should stay out of the way, and (2) the Keynesian view that government should take strong action to regulate the economy, especially when the economy needs stimulus. Two different philosophies also guide social policy: (1) the view that the poor face hardship because of circumstances, making them the worthy poor; and (2) the view that the poor face hardship because they do not try hard enough to advance, making them the unworthy poor.

Measuring Economic and Social Conditions (Structure)

16.2 Describe the five measures used in making economic and social policy, p. 479.

Congress and the president focus on four basic measures in reviewing economic and social problems: (1) unemployment, which measures the number of people who do not have a job, are currently looking for work and are ready to work if they are offered a job; (2) inflation, which measures the cost of goods and services determined by the consumer price index; (3) poverty, which measures the number of people who do not have the means to purchase a standard market basket of food; and (4) gross domestic product, which measures economic output and is tracked to show economic growth, or the lack of it.

The Tools of Economic and Social Policy (Action)

16.3 Analyze the basic tools used to make economic and social policy, p. 482.

Economic and social policies rely on very different tools to promote the general welfare. Economic policy uses two tools: (1) fiscal policy, and/or (2) monetary policy. Fiscal policy involves decisions about government spending and revenues, while monetary policy involves decisions about the supply of money that flows through the economy. Congress and the president make fiscal policy, while the Federal Reserve Board makes monetary policy.

Social policy uses three tools: (1) categorical aid, which is reserved for specific categories of people and organizations in society; (2) entitlement aid, which is guaranteed for anyone who is eligible regardless of income; and (3) means-tested entitlement aid, which is provided to anyone who meets a strict test of "means," usually based on earnings and other assets such as savings.

The Evolution and Goals of Economic Policy (Action)

16.4 Describe the evolution and goals of economic policy, p. 490.

Economic policy is designed to smooth the business cycle, but also seeks to achieve five other economic goals: (1) promote business through representation in the federal bureaucracy and patents and trademarks protection; (2) expand international trade by lowering the barriers to free trade and creating international competition; (3) regulate competition by preventing monopolies; (4) protect employees from harm through disability insurance, the minimum wage, and occupational safety programs; and (5) police the stock markets by assuring that companies tell investors the truth about their financial condition, while preventing illegal activities such as insider trading.

The Evolution and Goals of Social Policy (Action)

16.5 Describe the evolution and goals of social policy, p. 495.

Social policy is designed to create a social safety net to protect individuals and families against economic hardship. Using either social insurance or direct payments to individuals, this spending is dedicated to five broad goals: (1) assist the poor by providing public assistance or welfare through the Temporary Assistance for Needy Families program and other means-tested entitlements; (2) insure Americans for the future through Social Security; (3) protect the disabled through disability insurance; (4) support the unemployed through unemployment insurance, job training programs, and temporary assistance; and (5) provide health care to all Americans through Medicare, Medicaid, and the Patient Protection and Affordable Care Act.

The Economic and Social Policy Future (Impact)

16.6 Assess the future of economic and social policy, p. 503.

The nation's economic and social policies have improved the quality of life for most Americans since the War on Poverty began in 1964, but they also have generated a very large national debt. As the debt grows, so do interest payments to the federal government's lenders, but Congress and the president have not been able to agree on the spending cuts and tax increases needed to reduce the growing budget deficit. Nor have they been able to agree on how to repair the Social Security and Medicare programs, both of which are facing serious cash flow problems in the coming decades. Although there are several compelling solutions at hand, including an increased retirement age for Social Security beneficiaries and a sharp reduction in medical errors for patients, the public has shown little interest in reform.

LEARN THE TERMS

laissez-faire economics, p. 478
Keynesian economics, p. 478
unemployment, p. 479
inflation, p. 480
consumer price index (CPI), p. 480
poverty, p. 481
gross domestic product (GDP), p. 481
recession, p. 482
income inequality, p. 482
fiscal policy, p. 482
monetary policy, p. 482
depression, p. 483
Office of Management and Budget (OMB), p. 486
Congressional Budget Office (CBO), p. 486
Federal Reserve Board, p. 487
federal funds rate, p. 488
social safety net, p. 488
categorical aid, p. 488
social insurance, p. 489
entitlement aid/entitlement programs, p. 489
pay-as-you-go rule (PAYGO), p. 489
means-tested entitlement aid, p. 489
protectionism, p. 491
balance of trade, p. 492
North American Free Trade Agreement, p. 492
World Trade Organization, p. 493
monopoly, p. 494
public assistance, p. 498
single-payer system, p. 501

CHAPTER

17

Foreign and Defense Policy

The United States became the first and only nation in history to use nuclear weapons in war when it dropped its "Little Boy" bomb on Hiroshima, Japan, on August 6, 1945, and its "Fat Man" bomb on Nagasaki, Japan, three days later. The Japanese surrendered within a week. Here, one of the last buildings left standing after the Hiroshima blast has become a World Heritage reminder of the power of nuclear war. Barack Obama became the first sitting president in history to visit Hiroshima when he traveled to Japan in August 2016. Obama did not apologize for the bombing, which historians believe ended World War II, but did promise to pursue the elimination of all nuclear weapons in the world. "We must have the courage to escape the logic of fear and pursue a world without them." Donald Trump did not endorse global arms reduction as president, but did warn North Korea in 2017 to stop its nuclear weapons program or risk "fire and fury like the world has never seen." Trump secured a broad commitment to North Korea's denuclearization in June 2018 but was still waiting for a formal agreement at the end of 2018.

LEARNING OBJECTIVES

17.1 Understand the constitutional foundations and current philosophies that guide foreign and defense policy (Structure), p. 512.

17.2 Evaluate the options for achieving foreign and defense policy goals (Action), p. 520.

17.3 Outline the structure of the foreign and defense policy bureaucracy (Action), p. 525.

17.4 Assess the goals and impacts of America's foreign policy (Impact), p. 533.

17.5 Assess the goals and impacts of America's defense policy (Impact), p. 537.

The United States has worked long and hard to reduce the threat of nuclear war that began with its bombings of Hiroshima and Nagasaki at the end of World War II. The Soviet Union soon had its own nuclear weapons, and the "arms race" between the two giant adversaries was on. Over the next half-century, they built thousands of nuclear weapons, and the sophisticated nuclear triad of air, land, and submarine launch systems needed to unleash nuclear war anywhere in the world. Driven by the theory that mutual destruction was the only way to deter a first strike, the nations spent billions upon billions to create the most threatening weapons ever deployed.

However, both nations knew that the risk of a nuclear war was far too great to accept, and have been negotiating arms reduction agreements since the 1950s.[1]

- In 1972, the United States and Soviet Union agreed to cap the number of nuclear weapons and limit the number of missiles, bombers, and submarines that could launch the weapons each nation already had.
- In 1979, they also agreed to cap the total number of these "delivery vehicles" at 2,250.
- In 1991, they agreed to reduce the number of delivery vehicles to 1,600 and cap the total number of nuclear warheads to no more 6,000.
- In 2002, they agreed to reduce the total number of warheads to 1,700–2,200 and to dismantle the weapons needed to meet the targets.
- In 2010, they agreed to limit each nation to no more than 1,550 bombs and warheads and to dismantle the warheads to meet the targets again.[2]

The total number of delivery vehicles and warheads is still more than enough to destroy the world many times over, but the agreements mark great progress in avoiding global nuclear war. However, even as the United States and Russia have reduced the risk of war, other nations such as North Korea have been working hard to develop their own nuclear weapons. According to the nonpartisan Arms Control Association, India, Israel, and Pakistan almost certainly have nuclear weapons, while North Korea, Iran, and Syria either have weapons or are producing nuclear materials and launch systems, and another 25 nations have announced their plans to build nuclear power plants that can produce weapons-grade materials by 2030.[3]

Efforts to control nuclear weapons through international agreements have also faded in recent years.[4] In the spring of 2018, for example, the Trump administration withdrew the United States from an international agreement to end Iran's nuclear development program. Under the eight-nation agreement signed in 2015, Iran agreed to stop developing enriched nuclear weapons material in return for an end to tough economic pressure from the world's leading powers. The Trump administration alleged that Iran was secretly violating the agreement and was already preparing to restart its weapons program when the agreement expired. "This was a horrible one-sided deal that should have never, ever been made," Trump said in the White House in withdrawing the United States on May 8. "It didn't bring calm, it didn't bring peace, and it never will."[5]

This rising risk of nuclear war has clear implications for you and your families. Will the United States become a target for a future dictator able to obtain both a weapon and delivery system for that weapon? Will terrorists finally gain access to a "dirty bomb" that could spread radiation across a city? Will your children have to practice the "duck-and-cover" drills that your grandparents learned in school during the height of the arms race?

This chapter is designed to help you make a difference in answering these and other tough questions about foreign and defense policy. By learning the structure, action, and impact of foreign and defense policy, you can play a role in shaping U.S. policies designed to promote a healthy, peaceful, and hopeful world. Although you face dangerous challenges such as nuclear proliferation, you also have enormous power of your own to create a positive future.

The Constitutional Foundations of Foreign and Defense Policy (Structure)

17.1 Understand the constitutional foundations and current philosophies that guide foreign and defense policy.

The primary goal of American foreign and defense policy is to protect the nation from international threats, such as terrorism, hostile governments, piracy, and attacks against our homeland. Although more than half of the public now say the nation should "mind its own business internationally and let other nations do the best they can on their own," an even higher percentage wants the U.S. government to provide a strong defense and protect the national interest.[6]

Moreover, even if the United States could seal itself off from the rest of the world by building impenetrable borders and the strongest military in the world, it would still have to interact with other nations. The United States needs access to international markets, consumers, and suppliers to keep its economy growing, and has long supported new democracies as a way to assure the blessings of liberty to all global citizens. Although the nation is still committed to international cooperation on many issues, the Trump administration has pursued an "America First" agenda on most global issues, such as trade, immigration, and foreign aid.[7]

Constitutional Foundations

The Framers had extensive arguments during the Constitutional Convention about how to separate foreign and defense powers. Although they saw the judiciary as an occasional actor in some foreign and defense disputes, they clearly believed that Congress and the president would be the central participants in the nation's defense.

Some of the Framers, such as John Jay, argued that foreign and defense policy are too important to give to the executive branch of government, largely because the temptations to make war as a path to popular acclaim are too great for any branch. As Jay wrote in *The Federalist*, No. 4, "absolute monarchs will often make war when their nations are to get nothing by it, but for purposes and objects merely personal, such as a thirst for military glory, revenge for personal affronts, ambition, or private compacts to aggrandize or support their particular families or partisans."[8] Therefore, the Framers checked these ambitions by dividing the power to make war between Congress and the presidency.

Others, such as future Supreme Court Chief Justice John Marshall, argued that the president must speak for the entire government on foreign and defense policy. "The President is the sole organ of the nation in its external relations, and its sole representative with foreign nations. Of consequence, the demand of a foreign nation can only be made on him. He possesses the whole Executive power. He holds and directs the force of the nation. Of consequence, any act to be performed by the force of the nation is to be performed through him."[9]

sole organ doctrine
A belief that the president is the sole voice in making foreign and defense policy.

Most contemporary legal scholars have rejected this **sole organ doctrine**. They note that Marshall's remarks referred to the president's power to negotiate treaties. And they also note that Marshall continued his analysis by outlining the congressional checks on all presidential foreign and defense decisions, sometimes to the point of frustrating presidential action on important issues such as immigration reform.[10]

Presidents have a different view and often use executive actions—such as executive orders, memorandums, and informal instructions—to shape foreign and defense policy. President Obama took a series of executive actions to address the "children's crossing" of 2014, when almost 1 million children crossed the border from Mexico into the United States.[11]

Many of the children were driven across the border by violence in their home countries, but Texas and 25 other states argued that Obama had created an undue burden on their budgets by protecting the children from being deported. Although the crossing was widely viewed as a humanitarian crisis, the states argued that Obama's executive action had exceeded his authority to act as the nation's administrator-in-chief. The program was suspended in 2016 when the Supreme Court could not reach a decision on Obama's other executive actions on immigration reform.

Despite this decision, which may yet be reconsidered, future presidents retain significant authority to act with "energy and dispatch" in foreign and defense policy. However, the president cannot act with complete freedom. The Constitution gives Congress significant checks against presidential power—Congress, not the president, has the power to declare war, raise armies, confirm the senior leaders of government, reorganize the bureaucracy, ratify treaties, conduct oversight, overturn vetoes, and provide the dollars needed to execute foreign and defense policy. The power to declare war is the most significant of these powers, but presidents regularly evade this important congressional check by using quick military strikes against specific targets such as terrorist training camps.

In turn, the Constitution orders the president to take care to execute all laws, including foreign and defense policy, negotiate treaties, appoint ambassadors, and wage wars. The president does not make foreign and defense policy alone, but is responsible for negotiating treaties and waging wars. Although the constitutional system of checks and balances limits these powers, presidents have occasionally asserted what they see as their inherent powers to protect the nation in desperate situations such as the September 11, 2001, terrorist attacks on New York City and Washington, D.C. As John Jay wrote in *The Federalist*, No. 4, the "safety of the people of America against dangers from **FOREIGN** force depends not only on their forbearing to give **JUST** causes of war to other nations, but also on their placing and continuing themselves in such a situation as not to **INVITE** hostility or insult; for it need not be observed that there are **PRETENDED** as well as just causes of war."

Even though the Constitution does not mention inherent powers, presidents argue that they need these murky powers to protect the nation against great threats. President George W. Bush drew upon these inherent powers to justify the use of

A child being taken into custody after crossing the Rio Grande into the United States near Mission, Texas, on July 24, 2014. Most of the children were embraced by local charitable organizations such as Catholic Charities, but many ended up in federal government detention centers before placement. Similar images produced a surge of public pressure in June 2018 as the Trump administration came under fire for separating families that had crossed into the United States illegally. Under pressure from Democrats and Republicans alike, the administration eventually suspended its "zero-tolerance" policy on illegal entry and began reuniting the 2,500 children who had been separated from their parents.

"enhanced interrogation techniques"—such as waterboarding, depriving prisoners of sleep, and physical torture to extract information from suspected terrorists—though he eventually abandoned the policy under congressional and public pressure.[12]

Nevertheless, his decision sparked an intense debate about how much presidents can do during national emergencies. Although President Obama rejected the use of enhanced interrogation techniques, he used implied powers in picking targets for secret drone attacks on suspected terrorists. He also approved the secret 2011 raid on Osama bin Laden's hiding place in a small Pakistani city, and gave the order to "take him out."[13] Bin Laden had approved the September 11 terrorist attacks on New York City and Washington, D.C., and had managed to hide for almost a decade. The decision to authorize the raid is cited as another example of a president's use of inherent power to protect the nation.[14]

The Competing Philosophies of Foreign and Defense Policy

Just like economic and social policy, foreign and defense policy is guided by four complicated questions about how the United States should promote its national interest at home and abroad. Although there is no right answer to the four questions, they create a philosophical debate that is always changing as foreign and defense problems arise:

1. Should the United States accept the world as it is (realism) or lead it toward democracy and justice (idealism)?
2. Should the United State isolate itself from the rest of the world (isolationism) or do its part in solving global problems (internationalism)?
3. Should the United States act on its own when conflicts arise (unilateralism) or work with its allies to achieve mutual goals (multilateralism)?
4. Should the United States strike first when it sees a threat (preemption) or try to contain the threat until it can find a way to solve it (containment)?

Before turning to these questions in more detail, it is first important to note that foreign and defense policy is generally viewed as a bipartisan issue. Although Democrats and Republicans often disagree about the foreign policy and defense agenda, they usually come together to support a unified position on major issues such as war and peace. This does not mean the two parties agree about how to promote the national interest, however. After all, foreign and defense decisions often put the nation and its people at risk. The two parties almost always stand together at the start of a war or military intervention, for example, but often come apart if the action goes badly. Democrats and Republicans engaged in bitter debates as the wars in Korea, Vietnam, Iraq, and Afghanistan dragged on with no end in sight, but neither side had enough votes to bring the costly conflicts to an end. Moreover, neither party wanted to be portrayed as being "weak" on communism or terrorism, or send the world mixed signals about the nation's willingness to act.[15]

realism

A theory of international relations that suggests a nation's primary goal is to maintain its power and security.

REALISM VERSUS IDEALISM America's foreign and defense policy has been shaped by two seemingly contradictory views of the world. The first is based on **realism**, which claims that the individual nations are primarily concerned with their own power and success. They may also care about peace and global development, but survival comes first. "The realist school does not reject the importance of ideals or values," writes former Secretary of State Henry A. Kissinger. "It does, however, insist on a careful, even unsentimental, weighing of the balance of material forces, together with an understanding of the history, culture and economics of the societies comprising the international system—above all, our own."[16] Realists contend that the United States should have recognized the deeply rooted ethnic and religious rivalries in Iraq and Afghanistan, which have made securing peace and stability in both countries difficult even after many years of U.S. military and economic assistance.

Trump is also committed to realism. He won the 2016 election in part by promising to put America first in every decision. He also promised to force U.S. allies to pay their fair share for international military alliances, prevent nations such as Iran and North Korea from developing nuclear weapons, strengthen the nation's southern border with Mexico, send undocumented immigrants home, rebuild the military, cancel bad trade deals, bring jobs back from foreign countries, and protect the economy from what he referred to as the global warming hoax.

Trump changed his mind on some of these promises once in office as he learned more about the issues, but he also pushed forward to make better deals with other nations. His 10-day foreign trip in May 2018 involved negotiations with Saudi Arabia about driving terrorism from the Middle East, discussions with Israel about solving the long conflict with the Palestinians, and conversations with Pope Francis about environmental policy. He met with U.S. allies in Europe, pushed for economic concessions at an international summit, and sold $100 billion in American-made weapons along the way. He was still a realist when Air Force One brought him home, but he developed a deeper understanding of how to negotiate with friends and adversaries. He also learned that being president is difficult saying, "This is more work than in my previous life," just before his 100th day as president. "I thought it would be easier."

Critics of realism argue that nations should seek cooperation and stability, not power. This second view is built on **idealism**, a hopeful view that nations can work together to solve common problems such as global hunger and poverty with peace, not war, as the ultimate aim. Idealists view national power as a tool for good and for promoting democracy in other nations, not merely as a way to amass more military and economic resources. In contrast to the harsh forces that make international conflict a fact of life, idealists tend to believe that foreign and defense policy can be used to build new governments, promote justice and equality, and reduce the hunger and disease that plague so many nations.[17]

idealism
A theory of international relations that focuses on the hope that nations will act together to solve international problems and promote peace.

Although realism and idealism are often presented as competing visions of foreign and defense policy, they are often blended together in the day-to-day decisions that shape international action. Thus, the United States could be realistic about the need to work with dictators (realism) yet still believe that democracy is the best form of government (idealism). As President Bush argued in the months leading to the war in Iraq, the United States had to be realistic about Iraq's hatred of the United States and its longstanding pursuit of **weapons of mass destruction (WMD)** that can kill millions of people through a single biological, chemical, or nuclear attack.

weapon of mass destruction (WMD)
Biological, chemical, or nuclear weapons that can cause a massive number of deaths in a single use.

Yet, even as he promised Americans that he would take Osama bin Laden "dead or alive," Bush was very much an idealist in launching the broader war on terrorism as a fight between good and evil.[18] Bush often talked about the need to restore international justice and freedom abroad, and fully expected the Iraq War to end with a new democratic government that would spark a wave of reform across the Middle East. Bush's idealism might have been "inept" and "militarized," as some historians have argued, but it was built on the notion that war could lead to a democratic peace that would produce a more enlightened world.[19]

The Obama administration's approach drew more heavily on realism than the Bush administration had before it. According to Slate.com reporter Fred Kaplan, much as Obama expressed broad idealist "sympathy" for past efforts to create a more ethical, democratic world, his actual foreign and defense policy was described by some of his advisers as "hard-nosed," even "cold."[20] Contrary to the Bush administration, Obama was particularly careful to avoid long-term commitments to creating new democracies, the hallmark of the Bush administration's foreign and defense policy. He refused to put U.S. troops at risk as dictatorships came under fire in the Middle East and rejected pressure for military engagement in the bloody Syrian civil war that began in 2011. Although he drew a "red line" in the sand promising action if Syria ever used chemical weapons against its people, he used this threat of force to pressure action rather than destroy the

Syrian weapons stockpile with unilateral action from U.S. Navy ships positioned far off shore. He understood that such military action would undermine international diplomacy and might entangle the United States in another costly war.[21]

Obama's realism did not mean he was reluctant to use military force, however. Realism requires action in the face of cold opportunities to defeat threats to the United States. Thus, Obama launched the "drone war" against terrorist leaders hiding abroad and approved the risky raid to kill Osama bin Laden despite opposition from his own vice president.[22] Finally, if he had any thoughts about creating a majestic "Valhalla" in Afghanistan as U.S. troops came home, he quickly set them aside as he evaluated the long-term odds of continued corruption and religious conflict that would remain after the last U.S. troops leave.[23]

isolationism
The desire to avoid international engagement altogether.

ISOLATIONISM VERSUS INTERNATIONALISM Whether based on realism or idealism, U.S. foreign and defense policy has also reflected very different views of how America should respond to the rest of the world. Some Americans support **isolationism**, which is a belief that the United States should stay out of international affairs unless other nations constitute a direct threat to its existence. As noted, the delayed and limited U.S. response to the war in Syria reflected the view that the U.S. public was weary of Middle East wars.

Isolationism also remains alive and well in the debate about whether and how the United States should address the spread of terrorism to nations like Somalia and Yemen. On the one hand, isolationists argue that the United States should follow George Washington's advice to avoid international "entanglements," stay out of wars that can-not be won, never put its troops at risk unless there is an imminent threat to homeland security, and stop providing foreign aid to the world's neediest nations. Simply put, isolationists argue that the United States should always focus first on its own interests and leave the rest of the world alone.

internationalism
The belief that nations must engage in international problem solving.

Other Americans support **internationalism**, which is a belief that the nation must engage in international affairs to protect its interests. Realists and idealists may disagree on the goals of U.S. foreign and defense policy, but they can still agree that the United States should engage the world on economic, political, and social issues such as human rights for oppressed people, global hunger, and the War on Terrorism. Internationalists tend to view themselves as citizens of both the United States and the world. They think there are times when the United States should intervene, even when not directly threatened by another nation. From 2014 to today for example, the United States, NATO, and a long list of other nations have joined together to fight the terrorist forces of the Islamic State in Iraq and Syria (ISIS). After almost two years of air strikes, this international coalition reclaimed all but a fragment of the ISIS territory and could safely claim victory. However, ISIS continues to support terrorist attacks in other nations, and has established a presence in Africa.[24]

unilateralism
A philosophy that encourages individual nations to act on their own when facing threats from other nations.

UNILATERALISM VERSUS MULTILATERALISM Even as internationalists argue for active engagement, they do not always agree that the United States should seek support from other nations. Supporters of **unilateralism** believe that America has the right to act alone in response to threats, even if other nations are unwilling to help. They argue that the United States should never give other nations a veto over its actions, even if that means acting alone in using its great military power. The problem is that unilateralism is expensive to American taxpayers and often alienating to other countries.

multilateralism
A philosophy that encourages nations to act together when facing threats from other nations.

In contrast, supporters of **multilateralism** argue that America should generally seek broad support for its agenda. They believe that the United States is always stronger when it has the support of its allies, especially when its allies provide troops, equipment, and financing for large military operations such as the Iraq War. Supporters of multilateralism know that the United States may on occasion be forced to go it alone, but for them the presumption should be to try to form alliances.

President Obama and his advisers gathered in the White House "situation room" with his foreign and defense policy team to watch a night-vision video feed as Navy Seals worked their way into Osama bin Laden's compound just after midnight on May 2, 2011. Bin Laden was shot and killed on the third floor of the compound's guesthouse, and was buried at sea. Seated at the table from left to right are Vice President Joe Biden, President Barack Obama, General Marshall "Brad" Webb, Deputy National Security Advisor Dennis McDonough, Secretary of State Hillary Clinton, and Defense Secretary Robert Gates. Secretary Gates, a Republican, served in the same position in the George W. Bush administration.

Historically, the United States has leaned toward multilateralism whenever possible, but has been perfectly willing to act on its own when it has faced immediate threats. President Bush did just that immediately after the September 11 attacks. He was willing to launch the War on Terrorism without the help of any other nations, but nonetheless built a small international coalition before the United States attacked Iraq on March 20, 2003. Alliances, coalitions, and international organizations were thought to be potentially helpful, but not essential to the task.[25] After all, the United States had more than enough military might to fight the terrorists, and did not need foreign intelligence or bases to get the job done. "At some point, we may be the only ones left," he said. "That's okay with me. We are America."[26] In unmistakable unilateralist tones, Bush promised that America would act alone even if its allies said "no."

Obama echoed this unilateralism at times, but he had a deeper commitment to multilateralism than Bush. He worked to bring U.S. allies together to impose sharp penalties on Russia after its impetuous leader, Vladimir Putin, annexed Ukraine's Crimean peninsula in 2014; he frequently worked to forge broad international consensus to build support against the Iranian and North Korean nuclear weapons program; and he provided modest military backing for the 2011 Libyan revolution. One enduring problem with multilateralism is that it takes time to negotiate a shared view of a problem along with a workable solution. Sometimes there is not time to achieve those objectives, as when a threat may be imminent. This may push the United States to take unilateral action.

Trump's approach was even more unilateralist than his predecessors. He campaigned on an "America-first" platform that put United States' interests ahead of broad international problems such as climate change. He criticized U.S. allies for not paying their fair share as members of U.S. alliances such as the North Atlantic Treaty Organization, and threatened trading partners—such as China—with import taxes and tariffs if they did not open their markets to American goods. He also questioned many of the Obama administration's decisions and agreements, even withdrawing from hard-fought agreements, such as the 2015 Iran nuclear agreement.

PREEMPTION VERSUS CONTAINMENT Foreign policy involves more than direct action such as war. Containment and preemption also provide options for preventing conflict. **Containment** is a strategy for reducing the threat of war or expansion by strengthening friendly nations and diplomatic pressure, while **preemption** involves military action to prevent another nation from launching a first strike.

containment
A strategy for reducing the threat of war or expansion by strengthening friendly nations and diplomatic pressure.

preemption
A strategy for attacking adversaries who might otherwise attack first.

The United States and NATO used containment to prevent the Soviet Union from expanding its control of Eastern and Central Europe immediately after World War II. The United States and allies made clear that an attack on any of them was an attack on all of them and would result in all-out war. The conflict between the super powers of the United States and Soviet Union was called the Cold War (1947–1991) because there was never a bullet fired but there was a protracted period when war was possible at any moment.

The United States also worked to contain the Soviet Union by strengthening the economies of war-torn Europe through the Marshall Plan. The plan was named in honor of General George C. Marshall, the Army's chief of staff during World War II. The Marshall Plan invested billions of dollars in rebuilding Germany, Italy, and other nations that would contain the Soviet Union's advance in the event of another world war.[27]

Bush Doctrine

A policy adopted by the Bush administration in 2001 that asserts America's right to attack any nation that has weapons of mass destruction that may be used against U.S. interests at home or abroad.

In contrast, the Bush administration used preemption to take action against Iraq in 2003. Convinced that Iraq had inspired the terrorist attacks on New York City and Washington, D.C., the administration developed what came to be known as the **Bush Doctrine**, warning the world that the United States would strike first whenever it believed it was at risk of attack.[28] The Bush administration issued the warning in 2002 through a series of speeches and documents that made the case for preemptive war.[29] After arguing that nations such as the United States are free to defend themselves against "imminent danger," the administration argued that containment did not work in a world of "shadowy terrorist networks" and "unbalanced dictators" who were willing to inflict massive casualties without warning:

> We must adapt the concept of imminent threat to the capabilities and objectives of today's adversaries. Rogue states and terrorists do not seek to

The Marshall Plan did more than rebuild the factories, roads, and railroads of war-torn Europe. It also helped children and families rebuild their lives. Here, a young Austrian boy clutches his new shoes that just arrived, shoes purchased with funding from the Marshall Plan. Foreign policy experts often refer to the Marshal Plan in proposals to provide economic aid to struggling nations.

> attack us using conventional means...Instead, they rely on acts of terror and, potentially, the use of weapons of mass destruction—weapons that can easily be concealed, delivered covertly and used without warning. The United States has long maintained the option of preemptive actions to counter a sufficient threat to our national security. The greater the threat, the greater is the risk of inaction—and the more compelling the case for taking anticipatory action to defend ourselves, even if the uncertainty remains as to the time and place of the enemy's attack. To forestall or prevent such hostile acts by our adversaries, the United States will, if necessary, act preemptively.[30]

Compressed into a single sentence, the Bush Doctrine promised that the nation would not remain idle while dangers gather: America will act first.[31]

The Iraq War is an example of preemption. Convinced that Iraq was preparing to use its weapons of mass destruction against us, the Bush administration decided to launch a war before the dictator, Saddam Hussein, could use his alleged weapons of mass destruction against us.

The president's National Security Advisor and future Secretary of State, Condoleezza Rice, also argued that the United States had a moral obligation to remove Hussein from power, even if doing so meant war. "This is an evil man who, left to his own devices, will wreak havoc again on his own population, his neighbors, and, if he gets weapons of mass destruction and the means to deliver them, on all of us," Rice told the British Broadcasting Corporation in August 2002 in coupling idealism with preemption. "There is a very powerful moral case for regime change. We certainly do not have the luxury of doing nothing."[32]

Obama generally embraced the Bush Doctrine but never used his predecessor's "kill-or-be-killed" language. Although he made many decisions to kill terrorists before they could strike, he also worked to end the wars in Iraq and Afghanistan and did not take preemptive action against the "rogue," ungoverned nations that had or were developing weapons of mass destruction.

Nevertheless, Obama did not accept the Bush Doctrine's broad rejection of containment as a way to stop terrorism. Unlike nations, terrorists do not have borders to defend or citizens to protect, and they are ready and willing to give their own lives to kill others. Terrorists do not respond to traditional diplomacy, nor are they interested in modifying their behavior in return for economic or humanitarian assistance. Like Bush, Obama believed terrorists must be killed and he took action to do so.[33]

The Structure of Public Opinion on Foreign and Defense Policy

Public opinion is part of the structure of foreign and defense policy. It frames the philosophical choices just described and sets limits on the use of the tools described in the next section of this chapter. When public opinion is firm, Congress and the president must pay attention, but they may be frozen when public opinion is mixed or unclear.

At least in recent years, public opinion seems to be drifting toward an uneasy blend of internationalism and isolationism. According to the Pew Research Center, more than half of Americans have come to believe that the United States is less important and powerful today than it was 10 years ago, and a similar percentage says that the nation should "mind its own business internationally and let other countries get along the best they can on their own."[34] As Figure 17.1 also suggests, Americans are losing confidence in U.S. leadership in the world, and believe that the world is losing confidence in us.

Many foreign policy experts believe these opinions reflect "war fatigue" from the long, costly Iraq and Afghanistan wars. Americans are tired of the fighting, the costs, and the casualties. In a very real sense, they want a break from the constant headlines about international conflict and the demand for action by the United States, especially when others are unwilling to become involved.

FIGURE 17.1 THE ROLE OF THE UNITED STATES IN THE WORLD

Americans are currently reconsidering the idea that the United States should let other nations make it on their own given the rise of these global threats and the need for allies in defeating terrorism. Americans had become more isolationist during and after the Vietnam and Iraq wars but are becoming more divided on the need for international engagement in the face of serious threats to the world from the Islamic State in Iraq and Syria. Why did Americans become more willing to say that the United States should mind its own business dealing with the rest of the world between 1964 and 2018? Why have they become less supportive of U.S. engagement with the rest of the world in recent years?

SOURCE: Pew Research Center, "Public Uncertain, Divided over America's Place in the World," May 2016.

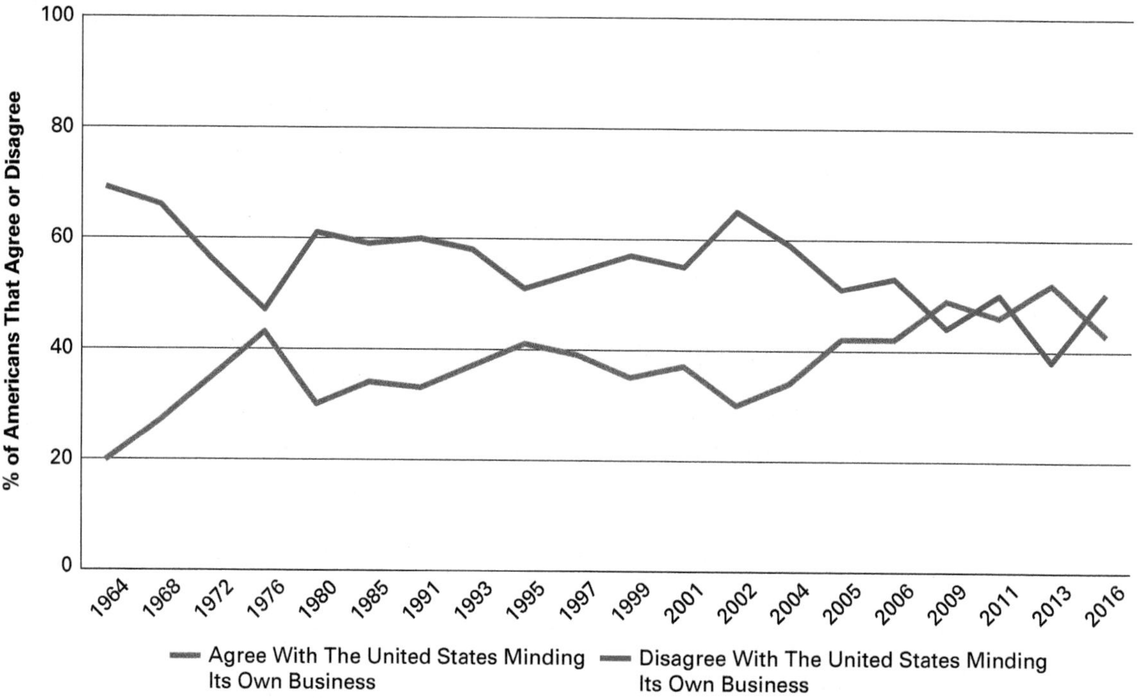

The Tools of Foreign and Defense Policy (Action)

17.2 Evaluate the options for achieving foreign and defense policy goals.

soft power
The use of encouragement, persuasion, and recognition to show other countries the value of American ideals, culture, and values.

hard power
The use of military and economic action to achieve foreign and defense policy goals.

The United States has two sets of tools to convert its foreign and defense aims into action. The first is based on the use of **soft power** (carrots) such as foreign assistance and diplomacy to attract other nations to cooperate with U.S. wishes, while the second uses **hard power** (sticks) such as military action.[35] Soft power is about attracting another nation to a common cause such as nuclear arms control or finding a path to peace in a divided region, while hard power is about using military strength, or the threat thereof, to accomplish U.S. goals.

These two forms of power may seem at odds with each other, but they actually work together as America pursues its goals. As explained by Joseph S. Nye, the key thinker behind the hard/soft power concept, a strong army is rarely enough to convince other nations to cooperate, but it does help make cooperation more attractive.[36] And graceful diplomacy may not be enough to secure deep concessions, but it does help light the path to peace.

Soft Power

Soft power is sometimes viewed as a more peaceful way to create international cooperation and prosperity, but using the tools of soft power requires just as much determination and toughness as using the tools of hard power. The United States must know where it stands as it enters a negotiation, how much it is willing to give as a price for agreement, and what it must do to protect the nation's interests. These decisions affect the three soft-power tools discussed below: (1) diplomacy, (2) global communications, and (3) foreign aid.

DIPLOMACY Soft power relies on efforts to convince other nations to accept the U.S. position on international issues, and diplomacy is a key form of making the case. Members of the U.S. Foreign Service and the nation's nearly 200 Senate-confirmed ambassadors make most of the arguments, but rely on the president and the foreign policy bureaucracy to help shape the case, set the priorities, negotiate the treaties that provide the details, and secure a two-thirds vote of the Senate as explained in *The Federalist*, No. 75. Even though traditional diplomacy appears more subdued and somewhat less vital in this era of personal leader-to-leader communication by telephone, fax, and teleconferencing, it is still an important, if slow, process by which nations can gain information, talk about mutual interests, and try to resolve disputes.

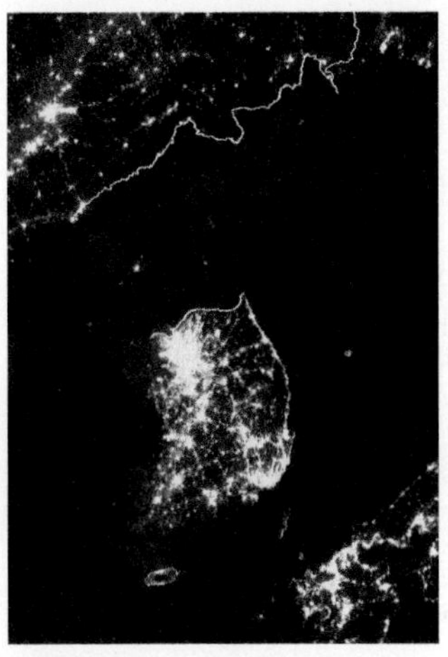

Journalists and commentators often discuss economic pressure as a form of soft power, but experts and academics view economic pressure as hard power because of the implied threat to injure other nations by denying access to consumer goods and economic growth. Here, a satellite photo shows North and South Korea at night—economic sanctions against North Korea have forced its citizens into deep poverty with little access to electricity, heat and light, fuel, medical supplies, and food. U.S. economic sanctions helped force North Korea to the bargaining table in 2018.

Conventional diplomacy can become hard power when the United States breaks diplomatic relations with another nation as it did with Cuba in 1961 and Iran in 1980. Doing so greatly restricts tourist and business travel to a country and in effect curbs economic as well as political relations with the nation. Breaking diplomatic relations is a next-to-last resort (force is the last resort), for it undermines the ability to reason with a nation's leaders or use other diplomatic strategies to resolve conflicts. It also hampers our ability to get valuable information about what is going on in a nation and to have a presence there.

The **United Nations** is one of the most important arenas for traditional diplomacy. Established in 1945 by the victors of World War II, it now has 193 member nations who try to work together to resolve disputes and maintain peace. Despite its promise as a forum for world peace, the United Nations has been frustrated in achieving progress during past decades. Critics contend that the United Nations has either avoided crucial global issues or has been politically unable to tackle them. During much of that time, the U.N. General Assembly was dominated by a combination of nations hostile to many U.S. interests.

United Nations

An international organization composed of the 193 nations that was established in 1945 to help the world resolve disputes and maintain peace.

More recently, the five permanent members of the U.N. Security Council—the United States, China, Russia, Britain, and France—have usually worked in harmony to resolve pressing global crises. Moreover, the United Nations' assumption of responsibilities after the 1990 Persian Gulf War and its extensive peacekeeping missions in Cyprus and Lebanon have been notable examples of the effort to build respect for the United Nations.

Each of the five permanent members has a veto on every Security Council resolution, including the assignment of armed peacekeeping forces to protect endangered citizens from harm. These forces are strictly prohibited from using their weapons except in defense, but they nonetheless stand in the way of hostile forces by representing the will of other nations.

Several of the United Nations' specialized agencies—including the World Health Organization, the United Nations High Commission for Refugees, and the World Food Program—are considered major successes in fighting poverty and diseases. But the review is much more mixed with respect to the United Nations' 63 peacekeeping efforts throughout its history. As of early 2014, the United Nations was engaged in 18 different peacekeeping missions around the world, including the continuing effort to help Haiti recover from a 2010 hurricane.

GLOBAL COMMUNICATIONS Only months after the September 11 attacks, the Bush administration created the White House Office of Global Communications to enhance the United States' reputation abroad. Created to win the war of words between the United States and its adversaries, the office was eventually absorbed by the State Department as a new division of public diplomacy and public affairs.[37] Although its mission is still to promote a more democratic world, the division is also responsible for countering negative press about the nation's conduct across the globe.[38] In short, global communication is a form of public relations designed to convince the world that the United States can be trusted to honor its promises.

Bush was not the first president to worry about the U.S. image abroad. President Franklin Roosevelt created the Office of War Information early in World War II, which in turn established the Voice of America program to broadcast pro-U.S. information into Nazi Germany. President Harry Truman followed suit early in the **Cold War** with the Soviet Union by launching the Campaign of Truth, which eventually led to the creation of the U.S. Information Agency in 1953 when Dwight D. Eisenhower became president. Both agencies exist today and are being strengthened as part of the "new public diplomacy."

Cold War
The 40-year war between the United States and Soviet Union that never involved a direct confrontation.

FOREIGN AID The federal government spent $32 billion in 2016 helping poor nations improve the lives of their citizens. Although the Trump administration proposed deep cuts in foreign assistance for 2019, Congress rejected the cuts in bipartisan votes on the State Department's budget. Most of this aid went to poor nations in Africa, Central and South America, and Southeast Asia.

The State Department spent the assistance on five foreign policy goals: (1) assuring peace and security ($9 billion), (2) investing in people by improving global health and education ($11.5 billion), (3) strengthening democracy, human rights, and governance ($3 billion), (4) encouraging economic growth ($4 billion), and (5) providing humanitarian assistance to victims of natural disasters, war, and crises such as the spread of the Zika virus that started in 2016 ($5.5 billion).[39]

Much as they support these broad priorities, many Americans believe the United States spends too much on foreign aid.[40] Asked for their views in 2015, 56 percent of Americans say the federal government spends "too much" on foreign aid, compared to 24 percent who say the federal government spends "about the right amount," and 11 percent who say "too little." Asked to estimate how much the government actually spends, the average American believes 26 percent of the federal budget is spent on foreign aid.[41]

Americans change their opinions about foreign aid once they learn the specific amounts. Told that the federal government spends about 1 percent on foreign aid, the percentage of Americans who say the figure is too much falls from 56 percent to 28 percent, while the percentage of Americans who say the figure is too little jumps from 11 percent to 26 percent.[42]

Ask your friends to take the test, and see who comes closest to the 1 percent mark. If your friends are like most Americans, the liberals will be closer to the real mark than the conservatives, but both will be wrong. Even liberal Democrats overestimate how much the nation spends on foreign aid and tend to think the figure is about right until they get the real number. Most also think the United States is the most generous country in the world and are surprised to discover that the United Arab Emirates is the global leader in foreign aid measured as a percentage of gross domestic product (GDP).[43]

Many Americans may have the wrong estimates, but they are not alone in wondering whether the United States is spending too much. Although most foreign policy experts believe foreign aid is an important source of soft power, there is growing concern that too much of the spending supports corrupt governments that oppress their citizens. Some experts, such as Nobel Prize winning economist Angus Deaton, argue that governments determine the structure that nurtures or denies prosperity and growth and can manipulate foreign aid to support their own political ambitions. "Foreign aid, especially when there is a lot of it, affects how institutions function and how they change," Deaton argues. "Politics has often choked off economic growth, and even in the world before aid, there were good and bad political systems. But large inflows of foreign aid change local politics for the worse and undercut the institutions needed to foster long-run growth." Aid can also be used to undermine the democratic rights that might produce governments that work on behalf of all the people, not just a dictator's allies."[44]

Deaton and his fellow critics never argue that the United States should use foreign aid to punish its adversaries, and rarely question the effectiveness of specific programs to improve health, education, and opportunity. But they do question the impact of aid as a form of incumbency advantage for dictators—that is, a way to buy off supporters and starve opponents. Instead of asking how much the United States gives, they urge all of us to ask about what the people actually get. And the answer is almost never "freedom."[45]

Hard Power

Hard power is often viewed as a blunt force to be used only when necessary. The United States must know where to attack, how much force to apply, which weapons to deploy, how much killing is enough, and when to stop. The United States must also know which of the three types of hard power to use: (1) economic sanctions that deny access to international markets and goods, (2) the threat of limited military action such as air strikes, and (3) outright war itself. If sanctions fail, the next step is the threat of war; if the threat fails, then war is almost inevitable. As with the tools of soft power, these three tools reinforce each other. The threat of war and economic sanctions are only effective if the United States is truly serious about enforcing its position, which means that it must have a credible military ready to act.

economic sanctions
Denial of export, import, or financial relations with a target country in an effort to change that nation's policies.

ECONOMIC SANCTIONS The United States frequently uses **economic sanctions** to punish other nations by cutting off access to international markets, goods, and services. Although sanctions come in different sizes, including denying access to food, fuel, and even medical supplies, all sanctions are designed to weaken another nation by strangling its exports and imports, disrupting communications, and even restricting access to food and fuel.

The United States has used economic sanctions more than 100 times since the end of World War II, but has an uneven record of success. Sanctions against South Africa doubtless helped end the racial discrimination called apartheid, while sanctions against Iran produced a deal to limit its nuclear weapons program. Some would say that sanctions against Cuba created movement toward a reopening of trade and travel with the isolated Caribbean nation in 2016. At the same time, recent sanctions against Russia have made little impact thus far toward ending its war against Ukraine or reducing its meddling in U.S. elections.[46]

Moreover, sanctions can hurt the United States by slowing down the global economy, and are especially unpopular among businesses that lose access to international

The world was shocked in late 2015 when a terrorist cell killed 130 Parisians in a coordinated attack. Here, a Parisian places a candle at a memorial near one of the restaurants that was randomly selected as one of the terrorist targets. The world reacted to the attack by using hard power to attack the Islamic State in Iraq and Syria. Similar attacks continue to occur across the world, including the use of cars and trucks to kill civilians in Nice, France, London, New York City, Stockholm, Sweden, and at Ohio State University.

markets. Sanctions can also harm the wrong people—dictators rarely suffer when food and medicines are cut off, but their people do. Finally, sanctions are relatively easy to evade by using hidden sources of economic goods, and help from friendly nations.[47]

At the same time, sanctions can work if they last long enough, do enough damage, and involve multilateral enforcement. However, they are much less likely to work if they abuse the citizens of the target nation by cutting off needed supplies such as medicines, which often generates foreign outrage and efforts to break the sanction.

THE THREAT OF WAR Hard power involves military strength and the willingness to use it. It also involves the ability to deter adversaries from taking the first step toward war. This **theory of deterrence** was originally developed during the Cold War as a way to prevent a global nuclear war between the United States and Soviet Union.[48] "Thus far the chief purpose of our military establishment has been to win wars," a senior defense expert explained in a book titled *The Absolute Weapon*. "From now on its chief purpose must be to avert them."[49]

theory of deterrence
The belief that massive military force will deter other nations from threatening the nation. Originally developed to deter nuclear war between the United States and Soviet Union during the Cold War.

According to the theory of deterrence, neither nation would ever launch its missiles if it believed the other nation would survive long enough to launch an equally devastating number of missiles in response. The only way to prevent a nuclear apocalypse was to build enough missiles to guarantee **mutual assured destruction (MAD)**, which would mean the end of the world. Although both nations did their best to hide their weapons on submarines, trucks, and aircraft, the United States and Soviet Union knew they would never survive a counterattack.[50]

mutual assured destruction (MAD)
A theory of deterrence that is based on creating enough nuclear weapons that warring nations would survive early strikes long enough to fire back, thereby assuring the end of the world.

The theory fell out of favor after the Soviet Union collapsed in 1989, but has returned to the forefront of defense planning as a way to deter the use of biological, chemical, and nuclear weapons by other nations. As ever-more-dangerous weapons spread to unstable nations, the core principal of deterrence still stands.[51]

WAR Military action is the ultimate expression of hard power, and reflects the breakdown of soft power. The United States has used military force in other nations on the average of almost once a year since 1789, although usually in short-term initiatives such as NATO's military activities in Bosnia and Kosovo. Alexander Hamilton described this power in *The Federalist*, No. 41 as absolutely essential for defending the nation, and so obviously needed that no one would question its significance. Nor would anyone question the power to raise armies, build fleets, and maintain both in wartime and peace—one as a source of hard power, and the other as a source of deterrence from attack.

The Trump administration used hard power in early April 2017 to punish the Syrian government for using chemical weapons to kill more than 80 men, women, and children trapped in the territory held by anti-government forces. Moved by photos of children writhing in pain after the attack, Trump ordered a cruise missile attack on the Syrian airbase where the chemical weapon attack was launched. The attack was Trump's first use of hard power as president and served as a signal to the world that he was willing to launch an attack; it illustrated that the president embraced realism and hard power in action. Trump returned to hard power again in mid-April 2018 to punish Syria for another attack, which raised the question of whether the 2017 response had been strong enough to compel an end to the use of chemical weapons.

Many of these unilateral military interventions were launched without congressional approval, let alone notification. And although critics have often argued that the Iraq War was the first time in history the United States had gone to war because it chose to, not because it had to, the country has actually sent forces into combat many times without a clear threat. It did not have to go to war against Spain in 1898 or send troops to Cuba, Haiti, the Dominican Republic, Lebanon, Mexico, Nicaragua, Somalia, South Vietnam, or even Europe in World War I.[52] (See Table 17.1 for the number of troops killed in America's major wars.)

Military action is not always visible to the public, nor is the intended target always revealed. Covert, or secret, intervention such as attacks on terrorist leaders are often

TABLE 17.1 THE COSTS OF WAR, 1776–2018

As Table 17.1 shows, wars are extremely expensive not just in dollars, but more significantly in lives. Although the number of lives lost has declined with the advent of better protection, more precise weapons, and much faster battlefield care, it still involves "boots on the ground" that put U.S. soldiers at great risk.

War in Historical Order	Length of War	Cost (adjusted to equal 2010 dollars)	Number of U.S. Troops Killed
Revolutionary War	8.4 years	2.4 million	4,435
War of 1812	2.6 years	1.6 million	2,260
Civil War	5 years	60 million	214,939
Spanish-American War	8 months	9 million	385
World War I	1.6 years	334 billion	53,402
World War II	3.7 years	4.1 trillion	291,557
Korean War	3.1 years	341 billion	35,516
Vietnam War	10.2 years	738 billion	58,516
Persian Gulf War	5 months	102 billion	382
Iraq War	8.8 years	815 billion	4,500
Afghanistan War	14 years	686 billion	2,381

SOURCE: Amy Belasco, "The Cost of Iraq, Afghanistan, and Other Global War on Terror Operations Since 9/11," Congressional Research Service, December 8, 2014; Stephen Daggett, "Costs of Major U.S. Wars," Congressional Research Service, June 29, 2010; updated through April 2018.

planned and executed without any notice at all until the operation is over, if the attacks are ever announced at all. The United States engaged in dozens of covert operations during the Cold War, including some that are no doubt still secret, while others such as a series of failed CIA assassination attempts on Cuba's communist dictator, Fidel Castro, were grist for congressional investigations and tighter congressional control.

Administering Foreign and Defense Policy (Action)

17.3 Outline the structure of the foreign and defense policy bureaucracy.

Foreign and defense policy is converted into action by a large bureaucracy spread across government. This bureaucracy spends more than $750 billion a year and employs almost 2 million civil servants and uniformed members of the armed forces. Although the number of employees and military personnel began to decline after the Cold War ended, the foreign and defense policy budget increased steadily until 2012 when it dropped slightly.

Congress and the president share control over the bureaucracy through the budget and appointments process. Congress is responsible for overseeing the bureaucracy, approving its budget, and confirming the president's appointees, while the president directs the bureaucracy's actions during war and peace.

While the two branches share broad control of the bureaucracy, the president is the Commander in Chief of the military. The president is free to ask the military for its advice about foreign and defense policy and is responsible for assuring the military's readiness for war. However, the military's duty is to follow the president's orders, not make them. As such, the military operates under what experts call **objective civilian control,** which emphasizes its role as a professional force to be selected and trained solely on the basis of merit. According to Political Scientist Samuel P. Huntington, the military has to be "immune to politics and respected for its military character."[53] Otherwise, it could become a tool for tyranny. Thus, neither Congress nor the president is allowed to interfere in the recruitment or promotion of military officers, and Congress may not call military officers to testify or report to its committees without presidential permission.

objective civilian control
The general philosophy that the military should be insulated from political interference of any kind.

Congress and the president exert more control over presidential appointees, but generally maintain objective, not subjective, control of the civil service. They can ask the bureaucracy to rethink its estimates and conclusions, and have been known to pressure intelligence agencies on estimates of foreign threats, but the foreign and defense bureaucracy works hard to maintain its independence in providing information and advice.[54] Like the military, civil servants have the same responsibility to steer clear of making policy.

Officially, the president's principal foreign policy adviser is the Secretary of State and principal defense adviser is the Secretary of Defense. In turn, the departments of state and defense implement foreign and defense policy through their separate bureaucracies. Although these two departments have the greatest influence on policy action, Congress and the president also rely on the National Security Council (NSC) and the intelligence community for advice and information on potential threats such as terrorism. These two advisory bodies do not make policies, but shape final decisions nonetheless.

The Foreign and Defense Advisory System

Congress and the president make foreign and defense policy based in part on advice and information from their own institutions and the federal government. Congress tends to give wide latitude to the president, but also depends on its own high-level committees on foreign affairs, homeland security, and intelligence for detailed information. In turn, presidents rely on the NSC and secret intelligence collected by the federal government's substantial intelligence bureaucracy. Although Congress holds the power of the purse on both of these executive advisory units, they report directly to the president, and can arrange a presidential briefing on a moment's notice.

National Security Council (NSC)

The White House group that is responsible for advising the president on key foreign and defense policy. The Council is headed by the National Security Advisor, who sits just down the hall from the president.

THE NATIONAL SECURITY COUNCIL The **National Security Council (NSC)** is the president's most visible source of foreign and defense policy advice. The NSC was created by law in 1947 to coordinate the nation's increasingly complex foreign and defense bureaucracy and is composed of the vice president, the Secretaries of State, Defense, Treasury, and Homeland Security, the attorney general, and representatives of the intelligence community and armed forces.[55]

The National Security Advisor supports the NSC. Operating from a West Wing office just down the hall from the president and supported by a small staff, the National Security Advisor monitors all of the foreign and defense information that flows through the White House, briefs the president on the international situation every morning, and is often described as the most important foreign and defense policy adviser in Washington.

Despite their impact, national security advisors are appointed as White House staff members without being confirmed by the Senate, and they never testify before Congress. Nevertheless, they are often the most visible foreign and defense policy advisers in Washington, and often act as "gatekeepers" who write the briefing books that shape presidential action, and occasionally become the Secretary of State or defense later in an administration. They are also frequent guests on the Sunday television news shows, and occasionally reveal new policies in off-the-record conversations with newspaper and Internet reporters.[56]

The Trump administration had three different national security advisors in its first 17 months. The president's first advisor was forced to resign after only a month on the job after he misled the vice president about his contacts with the Russian government after the 2016 election, while the second was forced out of his job in March 2018, over disagreements with the president about foreign policy. Trump's third advisor, John Bolton joined the White House staff in April. Turnover in other key foreign and defense policy positions was also high in the early Trump administration. Secretary of State Rex Tillerson was replaced by CIA Director Mike Pompeo, he in turn was replaced by Gina Haspel at the CIA. Of the key advisors in this policy area only former General James Mattis, was still in office in July 2018, and he was rumored to be leaving after the midterm elections.

THE INTELLIGENCE COMMUNITY The federal government's large and mostly hidden collection of intelligence agencies play a central role in virtually every foreign and defense policy decision.[57] Informally called the **intelligence community**, the 16 member agencies provide detailed information on who is doing what, where the next attack might come from, what our adversaries might be planning, and when the United States needs to act. Measured either by budget or visibility, the Central Intelligence Agency, Defense Intelligence Agency, Federal Bureau of Investigation, and National Security Administration are the most important organizations within the community. The director of national intelligence leads this broad community and has the authority to make recommendations regarding the annual budgets across the community. The director is also responsible for coordinating the movement of information across the 16 member agencies.[58]

intelligence community
The group of 16 intelligence agencies that provide information on threats to the nation.

According to secret documents leaked to the *Washington Post* in 2013, the intelligence community spends more than $52 billion a year and employs more than 100,000 civilian, military, and contract analysts.[59] According to the same documents, the community spends almost $5 billion a year on secret operations such as an electronic surveillance program that "scraped" information from millions of emails and cell phone records.

Intelligence collection involves three basic activities: (1) collection, (2) analysis, and (3) dissemination. Collection is based on close and rigorous observation of developments around the world; analysis is the attempt to detect meaningful patterns in what was observed in the past and to understand what appears to be going on now; dissemination means getting the right information to the right people at the right time. These activities sum up what experts call the "tradecraft" of intelligence analysis.[60]

However, coordination is not a substitute for careful tradecraft. In summer 2016, a lone terrorist killed dozens of innocent citizens in an Orlando, Florida, night club. Although he had been a suspected terrorist several years before, he managed to purchase the weapons and ammunition used in the attack with ease.

Orlando was just one of several recent failures in tradecraft. Two years earlier, the community lost track of the two brothers who planned the deadly Boston Marathon bombing even though one was on a U.S. government terrorist "watch list." "Of course it is an intelligence failure," a former White House intelligence adviser described the attack 10 days later. "It is every investigator's worst nightmare—to have your eyes on a person, allow them to drop from your attention, and then they carry out a terrorist attack. But what we do not yet know is the cause of this failure."[61] The answer appears to be a blend of poor tradecraft and a lack of coordination.

Finally, the intelligence community clearly missed the warning signs that led to the September 11 terrorist attacks on New York and Washington, D.C.: the federal government had information to prevent the attacks, but never thought terrorists might use hijacked airplanes as bombs against the World Trade Center and the Pentagon. The intelligence community had plenty of "dots" of information about the impending attacks, but not the management, capacity, leadership, and imagination to analyze and disseminate a desperate warning that might have prevented the death of 3,000 Americans and perhaps even the wars in Iraq and Afghanistan.[62]

The State Department

The State Department is at the center of the foreign policy bureaucracy. Organized around a series of "desks" that are responsible for monitoring different parts of the world, the department has diplomats in every corner of the world. But more than a year into the Trump administration scores of ambassadorships remained vacant, including most notably South Korea. In May 2018, President Trump finally nominated Admiral Harry Harris to that important position; Harris had served since 2015 as head of the Pacific Command. One group that tracks appointments found at the same point in their administrations that President Obama had appointed 131 ambassadors or other senior officials in the State Department and President Trump had appointed 88.[63] Created in 1789, the department has been led by some of the most distinguished citizens in United States history, including Thomas Jefferson, Daniel Webster, William Jennings Bryan, Henry Kissinger, Madeline Albright, Condoleezza Rice, and Hillary Clinton. Seven Secretaries of State eventually became presidents of the United States, and several became presidential nominees, such as former Secretary of State Hillary Clinton. As noted, former Central Intelligence Agency Director Mike Pompeo was confirmed as the Trump administration's second Secretary of State in April 2018.

The State Department has one of the federal government's most complicated missions but one of its smallest budgets. It had a $50 billion budget and just 13,000 employees in 2017 but administered a dense agenda of mostly soft-power foreign policy priorities that included efforts to expand democracy across the globe, provide humanitarian aid in the wake of natural disasters, manage the flow of visitors, and promote global health, prosperity, and human rights.[64]

The State Department is also responsible for helping U.S. citizens prove their U.S. citizenship whenever they leave or enter the country, and for providing entry visas for tourists, foreign students, and guest workers with special skills needed in the economy. In 2018, the State Department issued more than 15 million passports to U.S. citizens and millions of visas to foreign visitors and students. The department has a budget that is just one-tenth as large as the Defense Department's total, but has been largely successful because of two very different sets of employees: (1) ambassadors, and (2) the U.S. Foreign Service.

AMBASSADORS An ambassador heads every United States embassy in the world. About one-third of the nation's 180 ambassadors are political appointees confirmed by the Senate who are handpicked by the president for a blend of expertise, loyalty, and party service, while the other two-thirds are career members of the U.S. Foreign Service who advance to the posts through presidential appointments as well. All U.S. ambassadors must be U.S. citizens.

Wealthy friends of the president and major donors to the president's election campaign often fill the most glamorous, prestigious ambassadorships. Some of these jobs involve a great deal of entertaining and relatively few substantive responsibilities in nations such as England, France, Italy, and the Vatican. Most of the other political ambassadors have more significant responsibilities, such as navigating trade and policy issues with allies and potential adversaries. These are highly prized jobs, too, but require the substantial foreign policy experience needed to negotiate with tough nations such as China, Israel, Japan, and Russia.

Senior officers of the State Department's Foreign Service fill the final two-thirds of the ambassadorships. These posts are usually found in distant, little-known countries that present relatively few challenges to the United States. Nevertheless, these jobs often involve tough decisions about issues such as terrorism, and are also subject to presidential appointment and Senate confirmation.

These jobs are often very dangerous. In 2011, for example, U.S. Ambassador to Libya J. Christopher Stevens and three other Americans were killed in a terrorist attack at their Benghazi compound. These "high-risk posts" demand intense protection, but the State Department failed to provide adequate support despite repeated requests for extra security. The failure prompted a series of congressional investigations that matched former Secretary of State Hillary Clinton against a House of Representatives special committee for an 11-hour exchange.[65]

THE FOREIGN SERVICE The U.S. Foreign Service is composed of 4,000 highly trained civil servants who execute many of the State Department's most important foreign policy programs. Members of the Foreign Service are expected to take assignments anywhere in the world on short notice, and help U.S. citizens living or vacationing abroad deal with problems such as lost passports, access to emergency services,

The State Department is responsible for overseeing the nation's foreign aid programs, including efforts to help victims of war. Here, Iraqis help unload aid supplies delivered by the U.S. Agency for International Development in the town of Daquq just north of Baghdad. They will eventually reach hundreds of Iraqi citizens caught in the wars in Iraq and Syria.

and even securing a visa for their betrothed to get married in the United States. They also represent the United States in negotiations over issues such as economic aid, immigration, trade, human trafficking, adoptions, and even evacuating U.S. citizens in the event of terrorist threats.

Foreign service officers can choose among five different career tracks: (1) consular officers who help U.S. citizens with emergencies, (2) economic officers who deal with larger policy issues involving the U.S. economy, (3) management officers who handle the day-to-day issues in running an embassy, (4) political officers who keep track of issues that might raise policy concerns in the United States, and (5) public diplomacy officers who promote the United States abroad. Two-thirds of U.S. ambassadors are Foreign Service officers, while the rest are presidential appointees.[66] Foreign Service officers tend to serve as ambassadors in small, less prestigious posts, but have all the responsibilities of ambassadors to represent their country.[67]

The Foreign Service is under pressure to adjust to a more uncertain world, and change some of its old habits. Critics claim that the Foreign Service stifles creativity, attracts officers who worry more about their status and tenure than serving the nation, and takes too long in giving new recruits significant responsibilities. Moreover, the Foreign Service is still struggling to recruit officers with Arabic-language skills, which clearly weakens each agency's ability to collect and interpret intelligence about the terrorist networks that have emerged in the Middle East and Asia.[68]

The Defense Department

Compared to the State Department, the Defense Department has one of the least complicated missions in government: to prepare for war. The mission may be simple, but the bureaucracy is anything but. The department has the largest number of civilian employees in the federal bureaucracy, and is housed in the Pentagon just across the Potomac from the White House.

Trump promised to make the Defense Department even larger during his 2016 campaign and followed through on his promise when he asked Congress to add 10 percent to the Defense Department's $550 billion annual budget. Although the United States was already spending twice as much on defense as China and Russia combined, Trump argued that the increase was essential for repairing the nation's "depleted military."

The only challenge was to find the funding. With Trump's tax and social-policy cuts likely to provoke intense opposition, the administration decided to propose a $20 billion cut in the State Department's budget. The total was tiny compared to the Defense Department's half-trillion annual budget but amounted to a 30 percent cut in soft-policy programs such as global communication and foreign aid.

THE DEFENSE BUREAUCRACY The defense bureaucracy is not just the largest in government, but is also one of the most complicated. It is the only federal department that has a secretary of the entire department, as well as secretaries of the Army, Air Force, and Navy, a senior council of top military officers, and the chiefs of nine combat commands located in America, the Pacific, Europe, and Africa.

The secretary of defense also oversees a long list of separate offices for personnel and readiness, intelligence collection, advanced research, weapons development, and purchasing, as well as the military academies at West Point, Annapolis, and Colorado Springs. The secretary of defense always has the final word on policy, but the military and its nine combat commands must implement the decisions.

Joint Chiefs of Staff
The committee composed of the military heads of the armed forces that serves as the principal source of military advice to the president, the National Security Council, and the secretary of defense. The chairman of the Joint Chiefs is the highest-ranked military adviser in the United States.

THE JOINT CHIEFS OF STAFF The **Joint Chiefs of Staff** serves as the principal source of military advice to the president, the National Security Council, and the secretary of defense. The group is composed of the heads of the Air Force, Army, Navy, and Marine Corps, and the chair and vice chair of the Joint Chiefs, and is appointed by the president with Senate confirmation. This appointment process helps remind the armed forces that they are under civilian control, and can neither take action without presidential action nor go to war without a congressional declaration.

The Department of Defense Reorganization Act of 1986 shifted considerable power to the chair of the Joint Chiefs. Reporting through the secretary of defense, the chair now advises the president on military matters, exercises authority over the forces in the field, and is responsible for overall military planning. In theory, the chair of the Joint Chiefs can even make a military decision that the chiefs of the other services oppose.

Note, however, that the chairman of the Joint Chiefs is *not* the head of the military. Under law, the chairman is the principal adviser to the secretary of defense and the president, but has no direct authority to order the armed forces into battle. The president is the Commander in Chief, and must weigh military action or inaction against the larger foreign and security interests of the nation.

THE ARMED FORCES The Constitution authorizes Congress to do what is "necessary and proper" in order to "raise and support Armies," "to provide and maintain a Navy," and "to provide for calling forth the Militia." The president and the three political appointees who serve as secretaries of the Air Force, Army, and Navy oversee the 1.5 million soldiers who currently serve in what the founders might call the national militia. In turn, the joint chiefs of staff oversee the armed forces. The Secretary of the Navy also oversees the Marine Corps.

Successful hard power depends on having enough soldiers, sailors, pilots, marines, and special operations forces needed to fight and win wars. As Figure 17.2 shows, the size of the armed forces has been declining over the past decades largely because the nature of war has been changing. Whereas massive armies fought World War I, World War II, the Korean War, the Persian Gulf War, and the wars in Iraq and Afghanistan face to face, future wars are likely to involve more precise engagements and the use of sophisticated technologies such as unmanned drones. Hence, the Defense Department argues that there will be less need for infantry soldiers, and more need for fighter pilots, drone experts, hackers, and naval ships that act as offshore military bases. Although courage is still the essential ingredient of success, the size of the armed forces

FIGURE 17.2 THE DEFENSE WORKFORCE, 1984–2018

As Figure 17.2 shows, defense contractors now employ more workers than the department itself. When the armed forces are added to the total number of people who make and implement defense policy, contractors have accounted for more than half of the bureaucracy for decades.

SOURCE: Paul C. Light, *The Government-Industrial Complex: Tracking the True Size of Government, 1984–2018* (New York, NY: Oxford University Press, 2018).

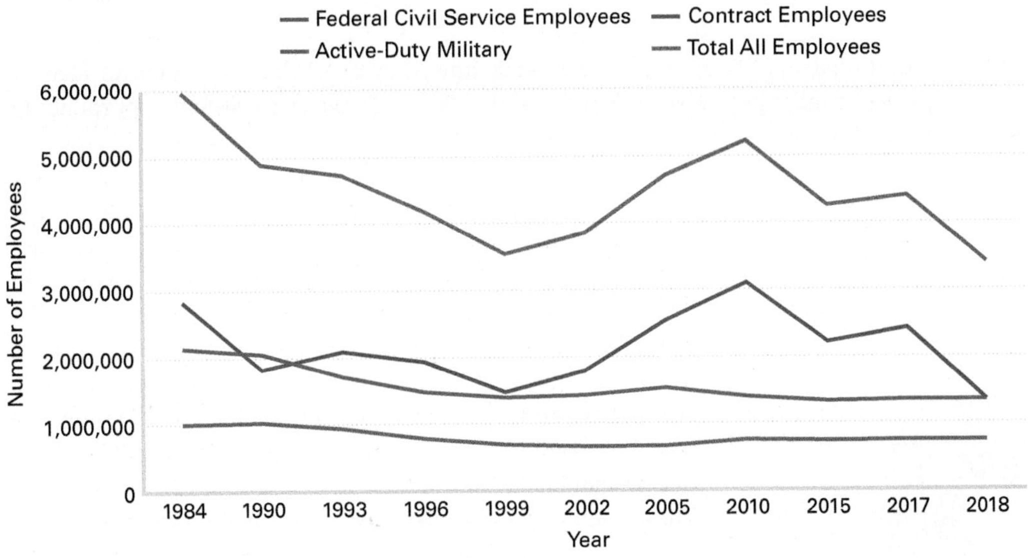

is far less important today than the technological savvy and precision weaponry that shape the field of battle.

There will always be a need for armed forces, however, which means that there will always be a need to entice individuals to serve their country. Until World War I, the United States generally relied on citizen volunteers to fight its battles. However, World War I demanded so many troops that the United States had to impose a **draft** to force large numbers of civilians to serve. By definition, a draft involves some element of chance for selection, which is usually created by a lottery of some kind for choosing young men at random. The United States stopped using a draft at the end of the Vietnam War in 1973, but still requires all men between the ages of 18 and 25 to register with their local draft boards just in case the military needs a vast infusion of troops to fight a future war.[69] Given the changes described below, it is just a matter of time before women will be required to register as well.

draft
Also known as conscription, the draft is a method for recruiting military troops by forcing all American males to register for service.

With or without a draft, the military still needs what it calls "warfighters" and "warriors," and now uses incentives to draw young Americans into the **All Volunteer Force (AVF)**. This recruiting system uses benefits such as advanced job training, health and family benefits, higher pay, college loans, and access to low-cost housing. It also uses advertising that reminds young Americans that they can make a difference in the world by helping others through humanitarian assistance such as fighting the Ebola crisis in 2014.[70]

All Volunteer Force (AVF)
The replacement for the draft (conscription) for recruiting members of the armed services.

The United Sates created the AVF for three reasons.[71] First, the demand for draftees was falling rapidly as the Vietnam War ended, and there was little reason to believe that the United States would need so many troops in the future. Second, the Vietnam War was so unpopular that some young men avoided service by leaving the country in protest, thereby undermining public confidence in both the draft and the military. Third, and most importantly, the draft contained so many escape routes through deferments and exemptions that it earned a reputation for targeting lower-income Americans. Even the U.S. Army came to oppose the draft due to difficulties of motivating draftees to take risks on the battlefield. As one historian argues, the Army was ready for a change, and the volunteer option provided the answer.[72]

The AVF has been generally successful in meeting the military's annual targets for enlistment. However, the AVF tends to have its greatest success recruiting African Americans, in part because many see it as a path to improved career and educational opportunities. At the same time, however, the AVF tends to face its greatest challenges recruiting women, in part because of persistent reports about sexual harassment.[73]

Women have played a significant role at or near the battlefront dating back to the Revolutionary War, but had to wait until 1917 to enlist in the military as nurses and staff, 1948 to make the military a career, 1976 to be admitted to the military academies at West Point and Annapolis, and 2016 to be allowed in combat. They have given their lives to service in every war the nation has fought. Between 2003 and 2018, for example, 150 women died in Iraq and Afghanistan, with the largest numbers of casualties coming from Texas, Florida, New York, and Pennsylvania. Despite increased acceptance and more active duty in combat zones, women still confront discrimination in the military and report sexual harassment. These complaints have declined somewhat in recent years, but still present barriers to service for many talented soldiers, sailors, and pilots.

Dr. Mary Edwards Walker was the first and last woman to receive the Medal of Honor, which is the highest military honor given. She was awarded the medal for her service as a military surgeon in a field hospital during the Civil War. She won the medal as a civilian. Women are now allowed to serve in combat positions, and one will no doubt become the second woman to win the medal for battlefield bravery in the not-too-distant future.

LGBTQ citizens have also fought hard to serve in the military, but had to keep their orientation secret until 2010 when Congress overturned the "don't ask, don't tell" rules on LGBTQ service created in 1993. Prior to 1993, LGBTQ service members who hid their orientation during the enlistment process were subjected to harsh discipline, confinement, and dishonorable discharge if their orientation were discovered. Although the military services now acknowledge the important role that all soldiers play in protecting the nation, a series of presidential tweets in July 2017 left transgender service members' status murkier. In those tweets, President Trump stated that transgender individuals would no longer be able to serve in the military. Because the statements came via tweet, it was not clear to military leaders or service members whether there was an official policy change. That confusion persisted until August 25, 2017, when the White House finally issued an official policy memo instituting a full ban on transgender military service effective March 2018. But, the right of transgender individuals to serve remains uncertain. After several federal district and appellate courts issued orders preventing the August 2017 policy from going into effect, Trump responded with a new ban disqualifying from service those who "require or have undergone gender transition." This "qualified" ban was quickly challenged and a federal court judge issued yet another injunction preventing it, too, from going into effect. Thus, uncertainty for presently enlisted transgender service members and those who seek to serve their country continues.

THE DEFENSE INDUSTRY Defense policy depends on more than its own soldiers, sailors, Marines, and pilots. It also depends on weapons, technology, equipment, communication systems, meals, and even housing that must be bought using contracts with private companies such as Lockheed Martin (fighter planes), General Dynamics (tanks, ships, and ammunition), Raytheon (missiles and electronics), United Technologies (helicopters), Computer Sciences Corporation (technology), Huntington Ingalls (ships), and even Booz Allen Hamilton (management consulting).[74]

This contracting is a major source of American jobs, and is protected by the members of Congress back home. Yet, contractors also blur the lines between the military and civilian sectors of society. As Eisenhower warned the nation just before he left office in 1960, the United States must be wary of the **military-industrial complex** that supports increased defense spending as a way to protect jobs. Eisenhower's words are well worth reading today:

military-industrial complex
The collection of government defense agencies and the private firms who supply key equipment, advice, supplies, and contractors.

> The creation of an immense military establishment and a large arms industry is new in the American experience. The total influence—economic, political, and even spiritual—is felt in every city, every State house, and every office of the Federal government. We recognize the imperative need for this development. Yet we must not fail to comprehend its grave implications. Our toil, resources, and livelihood are all involved; so is the very structure of our society.
>
> In the councils of government, we must guard against the acquisition of unwarranted influence, whether sought or unsought, by the military industrial complex. The potential for the disastrous rise of misplaced power exists and will persist.[75]

Despite Eisenhower's warning, the military-industrial complex has grown since 1960, and now consists of an estimated 3 million workers and more than $500 billion in annual spending (see Figure 17.2 earlier in this section.) Although recent research suggests that the federal government often pays too much for weapons and services, contract workers often make the ultimate sacrifice for the nation.[76] Four hundred contract workers were killed in the Iraq War, for example, and the vast majority are deeply committed to the nation's security.[77]

Foreign Policy Goals (Impact)

17.4 Assess the goals and impacts of America's foreign policy.

Many international problems are difficult to resolve. Nevertheless, the United States continues to produce impact on its four major foreign policy goals: confront global climate change, build new democracies, find peace in the Middle East, and reduce global poverty and disease. Each will be explained below.

Confront Global Climate Change

The United States has a mixed record in efforts to control the global climate change often associated with greenhouse gases that trap heat in the environment and raise the world's temperature. Much of the recent increase in greenhouse gases is related to the release of carbon dioxide from the burning of fossil fuels such as gasoline and coal by automobiles and power plants.

Experts do not all agree that global warming is a problem; there is considerable debate today regarding the scientific evidence underpinning the call for action on global warming. However, rising temperatures appear to threaten the world's climate in two ways. First, as the average temperature rises, the polar ice caps and glaciers melt. As the water melts, the oceans rise, threatening low-lying areas across the world. By some estimates, New York City, the states of Washington, Florida, Louisiana, and other coastal areas could be completely under water within several hundred years.

Second, as the average temperature rises, the world's weather becomes more unpredictable and potentially severe. Some experts attribute the recent increase in violent hurricanes such as Hurricane Katrina to global warming and predict more violent storms in the future.[78]

The world acknowledged these problems when it adopted an international treaty called the Kyoto Protocol in 1997. Under the treaty, all participating nations agreed to steadily reduce their greenhouse gas emissions over the coming decades. Although 85 nations signed the agreement and 190 have ratified it, the United States never ratified the treaty, and it has never taken hold.

The United States returned to the climate-change negotiating table almost 20 years later, however, and helped broker the Paris agreement on global climate change just before Christmas 2015. Under the agreement, 196 nations agreed to take action to reduce global warming to no more than 2 degrees Celsius above the levels that existed before the industrial age began in the late 1800s. Although the agreement marked the first breakthrough in almost two decades, most experts agreed that the negotiators had not gone far enough, suggesting that the agreement was only the beginning of what would have to be even more aggressive reductions in the greenhouse gases produced by power plants, automobiles, airplanes, and even animals.[79]

The world was already moving too slowly to meet the first round of targets when Trump pulled the United States out of the accord in mid-2017, but the decision created an even greater worry that the effects of rising temperatures will be felt faster than predicted. Thus, even more aggressive steps may be needed soon, along with an effective implementation process created to make sure all nations, including the United States, move quickly.[80] Although Trump said the United States was willing to consider a return to the accord if other nations shared more of the cost of reducing greenhouse gases, he remained broadly opposed to environmental protection during his first years in office, and showed little interest in reopening negotiations as the nation turned toward the 2020 presidential campaign.

Build New Democracies

nation building
A foreign policy goal to promote democracy by helping individual nations create democratic government.

Approximately 60 years after the United States completed its effort to rebuild Europe following the massive destruction of World War II, it continues to engage in **nation building**, which is generally defined as the effort to convert dictatorships into

Secretary of State John Kerry holds his granddaughter as he signs the Paris Climate Accords on December 15, 2015. President Trump withdrew the United States from the accord in June 2017. "The bottom line is that the Paris accord is very unfair at the highest level to the United States," he said in announcing the decision. He also claimed that the accord would undermine the economy, and "effectively decapitate our coal industry."

democracies. This exercise of both soft and hard power has been particularly visible in recent years. It was part of the Bush administration's idealistic rationale for the wars in Iraq and Afghanistan in 2003, and supported the "Arab Spring" of uprisings against the dictatorships in Tunisia, Egypt, and Libya in 2011–2012.

Building democracies is a very difficult task. After all, the United States needed a decade to win its independence, ratify the Constitution, and bring its new government to order. Today's efforts to spark democracy often take longer, in part because of deep divisions within countries formerly led by dictators. Dictators use their power while in office to build strong support within their countries and often use heavy military force to suppress calls for democracy from their citizens. Once freed to pursue democracy, citizens are often resistant to U.S. involvement, frequently because the United States used military force or economic sanctions to overthrow the dictatorship.

Nation building involves much more than removing a dictator from control, however. Once a nation is free from tyranny, it must create new democratic institutions such as a legislature, presidency, and judiciary. It must also write a constitution, hold free and fair elections, create a free press, and allow peaceful protests. The United States often provides aid in the form of health care, education, and food, some of which is provided by volunteers from charitable organizations such as Doctors without Borders. The U.S. military also provides humanitarian assistance when a crisis such as the 2014 Ebola outbreak in Africa becomes too large for local governments to handle.

Find Peace in the Middle East

Long before the September 11 attacks, the United States was working to secure peace between Israel and its neighbors, in part because the Middle East is such an important source of the world's oil and in part because the United States has long considered Israel an ally. However, despite decades of U.S. efforts to promote peace in the

Myanmar rejoined the ranks of democratic nations when it held its first national elections in 50 years in November 2015. The United States applauded the election, and has been a long supporter of Nobel Prize winner and democratic activist Aung San Suu Kyi. Here, voters stand in line to cast their ballots in Yangon. Two years later, however, the Myanmar government launched a series of brutal attacks on members of its Rohingya ethnic minority population, driving nearly 700,000 people into exile, killing thousands along the desperate journey to safety. Aung San Suu Kyi was widely criticized for her role in what human rights advocates described as an "ethnic cleansing."

region, the Middle East remains locked in a violent struggle over Israel's right to exist. Progress toward peace has been threatened by ongoing conflict with the Palestinian Authority that represents citizens immediately to the east of Jerusalem. Without a resolution, the region could become a battlefield that could draw the United States into another major war.

There was a brief moment of hope for peace in 2003 when the United States, Israel, and the Palestinian Authority embraced the "Road Map for Peace." Under this road map, Israel and its neighbors agreed to take two broad steps toward peace. The Palestinian Authority agreed to arrest, disrupt, and restrain individuals and groups that plan and conduct violent attacks on Israel. Israel in turn agreed to start dismantling settlements of Israeli citizens in the occupied territories to its south and east. Israel honored part of its end of the agreement starting in 2005 by beginning to dismantle settlements and turn over control of these territories to the Palestinian Authority. Despite this initial progress, the peace process collapsed in 2015 as Israel went to war against the Palestinians living in the Gaza Strip along the Mediterranean. Although the conflict was eventually settled, tensions remain high today as terrorism increases across the world and sporadic attacks take place inside Israel.

As of 2018, the road map for peace remained unresolved as the brutal war in Syria continued with chemical attacks against civilians, while Turkey launched an assault on Kurdish rebels on its border with Iraq. Although the Islamic State in Iraq and Syria was almost over after a decade of U.S. attacks and allied attacks, the Middle East remained on edge as Israel, Iran, and Syria sought to protect their advantage in the post-Iraq War era.

Reduce Global Poverty and Disease

The United States believes that global poverty and disease violate its values. Poverty, disease, corruption, and intolerance are proven causes of economic inequality, high death rates, dictatorship, and anger toward the United States and other wealthy nations of the world. People in poverty barely have the strength to live, let alone the commitment to democratic life, but often turn their anger toward the United States, which is sometimes called the "Great Satan" by its most aggressive enemies.

The United States accepted a major role in addressing these global challenges when it joined 189 other nations in 2002 in a long campaign to eliminate the most extreme forms of poverty, provide universal elementary education for all children, reduce child mortality from preventable disease, and eradicate hunger among the world's nearly 900 million starving people.[81] Although the world made significant progress on all of the goals by 2017, there is still more work to be done.[82]

The United States and its partners began this second round of goal setting in 2016 by embracing an even longer list of goals to eliminate all poverty, stop global climate change, ensure access to health care for all citizens, improve government performance, and assure freedom and equality in all nations, all by 2030. With a price tag of $4 trillion and just 15 years to reach the goals, the new Sustainable Development Goals put the world's wealthier nations to work on creating a much healthier, freer, and hopeful world.[83]

The United States will need maximum soft power to reach these goals, starting with a significant increase in its foreign aid budget. It will also need aggressive partnerships with nations that it might have fought in the past, and might be challenging in the present or sometime in the not-too-distant future. The United States and its partners will also need help from global philanthropies such as the Gates, Ford, MacArthur, Rockefeller, and Zuckerberg-Chan foundations. And they will need help from you, including your willingness to take simple steps such as turning off your lights, letting your hair dry naturally, calculating and cutting your carbon footprint, putting the pressure on your college and university to turn down the temperature, and increasing the recycling.

And you might even consider a tour of duty in the Peace Corps, a program created to help citizens in other nations achieve their development goals on their own.[84]

Ending global distress is also supported by hard power when it is used to remove corrupt, abusive dictators. The United States was deeply involved in the "Arab Spring" uprisings that began in 2011 with the uprising in Tunisia and quickly spread to Egypt, Syria, and Yemen. The United States also joined with its allies in the North Atlantic Treaty Organization (NATO) in the air war over Libya, which began in March 2011 after the Libyan public rose up against Muammar Gaddafi. Although Gaddafi was caught and killed on October 20, 2011, Libya has drifted away from its initial commitment to democracy as its people have broken into religious and ideological factions that refuse to cooperate in building a stable nation. As in Iraq, removing a dictator is not enough to create a democracy.

Defense Policy Goals (Impact)

17.5 Assess the goals and impacts of America's defense policy.

Defense policy is based almost entirely on military power and the readiness to use it to achieve impact in attaining four goals: reduce the spread of weapons of mass destruction, win the War on Terrorism, reduce wasteful defense spending, and learn the lessons from the Iraq War.

Reduce the Threat of Weapons of Mass Destruction

The United States is using both soft and hard power to reduce the spread of chemical, biological, and nuclear weapons across the world. As noted earlier in this chapter, these weapons have the potential to cause mass casualties and appear to be spreading to hostile nations such as North Korea and Iran. The United States has been working to negotiate stronger sanctions against the spread of the basic materials used in manufacturing these weapons, but has considered using conventional military strikes to eliminate these kinds of threats before they are used against allies such as Israel, South Korea, and Japan.

The United States is also working with Russia to dismantle the huge inventory of nuclear weapons manufactured during the Cold War. The two adversaries started this **nuclear disarmament** process even before the end of the long conflict in 1989, and are making progress toward reducing their arsenals. In 2010, for example, they agreed to reduce each nation's number of nuclear warheads by a third.[85] Even with the 2010 reductions, each nation still has over 1,500 warheads each, and neither has proposed a reduction to zero.

nuclear disarmament
The effort to reduce the number of nuclear weapons.

Biological and chemical weapons also threaten the world with mass casualties. Although chemical weapons were outlawed by international agreement after World War I, at least nine nations are known to have chemical weapons that kill on contact, another (North Korea) has developed a nuclear weapon and is working feverishly to build long-range missiles to deliver it, and still another (Iran) is building the capacity to manufacture the nuclear material needed for a weapon. All of these nations are violating international agreements that prohibit the development of weapons of mass destruction, but have been mostly unwilling to unwind their programs.[86]

Syria used chemical weapons during its long civil war by firing artillery shells containing deadly sarin gas into small towns held by rebels. On August 21, 2013, it launched a particularly lethal strike on a small town called Ghouta, killing between 300 and 1,800 men, women, and children. The United States and France responded by promising a military strike unless the Syrian government agreed to destroy its stockpile under international supervision. Under pressure from its long-time ally and arms supplier, Russia, Syria agreed to the proposal and joined the Chemical Weapons Convention banning the use of chemical weapons.[87]

Win the War on Terrorism

war on terrorism
The effort to attack and destroy terrorist networks and leaders.

The **war on terrorism** is a broad term used to describe efforts to prevent terrorist acts either sponsored by other nations or launched by independent groups that operate without any connection to a government. As hard as the United States and its allies work to destroy terrorist cells through drone strikes and military raids, terrorism is so strongly rooted in deep religious and ideological beliefs and so attractive to young converts that it tends to rebound quickly.

The war against terrorism is most often associated with Osama bin Laden and his Al-Qaeda terrorist organization, but it now involves dozens of other terrorist organizations. These groups have carried out bombings in Istanbul, London, Madrid, Moscow, Paris, the Middle East, and throughout Southeast Asia, including Thailand, Malaysia, the Philippines, and Indonesia, where terrorists have carried out several bombings at or near popular tourist hotels. The attacks have also come to the streets of America as "home-grown" terrorists have taken up arms to kill innocent Americans in ordinary towns such as San Bernardino, California, where a U.S. citizen and his wife killed 14 people and wounded another 22 in December 2015.

These attacks showed the power of violence as a tool of terrorism, and the media's widespread coverage of terrorist incidents like these also (unwittingly or not) spreads this fear. Groups that were once small and unknown can achieve widespread notoriety, which helps with fund-raising and recruiting. As a result, Americans are increasingly worried about terrorism and increasingly discouraged by the federal government's response. By the start of 2016, almost half of Americans were very or somewhat worried that they or a family member would be a victim of a terrorist attack planned or inspired by the Islamic State in Iraq or Syria, while two-fifths were very or somewhat worried that they or a family member would be the victim of a mass shooting.[88]

The challenge is not just to fight terrorists when they show themselves, however. The terrorism must also be deterred through a blend of hard and soft power. The direct approach is to continue the war on terrorist leaders or impose sanctions on the families and friends of terrorists, while the indirect approach is to strengthen homeland security, increase intelligence gathering, and never negotiate with terrorists.[89]

Former U.S. Ambassador to the United Nations, Nikki Haley urged the U.N. to condemn the Syria chemical attack on civilians on April 7, 2018. "Who does this?" she asked the assembly. "Only a monster does this. Only a monster targets civilians and then ensures that there are no ambulances to transfer the wounded, no hospitals to save their lives, no doctors or medicine to ease their pain." The United States joined with Britain and France to attack Syria's chemical weapons facilities four days later.

FIGURE 17.3 REDUCING THE THREAT OF TERRORISM

This figure shows responses to recent public opinion surveys that asked respondents how well the federal government is doing to reduce the threat of terrorism. Note the slow decline in confidence from 2001 to 2016 and ask why a substantial number of Americans remain concerned about the government's performance.

SOURCE: Pew Research Center, "Government Gets Lower Ratings for Handling Health Care, Environment, Disaster Response," December 14, 2017.

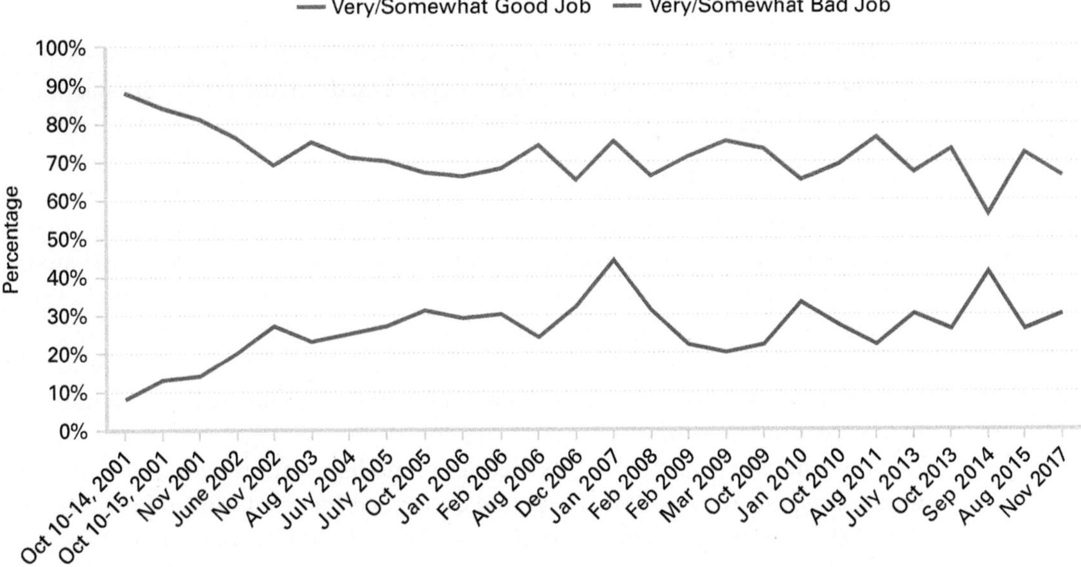

All of these approaches have been used in the past, but rarely in combination. Although they could be more effective in combination, they cannot succeed without strengthening the intelligence community, which has failed repeatedly to detect impending threats such as the 2009 Christmas Day bombing attempt on a Detroit-bound airliner. As noted above, intelligence is the Achilles' heel of the war on terrorism.[90]

Figure 17.3 gives a sense of public confidence in the government's ability to reduce terrorism.

Reduce Defense Spending

The United States spends more on defense than any other nation in the world, which raises questions about waste and inefficiency. Does the United States need all the weapons and soldiers it has, and is it getting the right weapons at the best cost? (See Figure 17.2, The Defense Workforce, 1984–2018.)

The public is unsure of the answer. On the one hand, Americans applauded the Trump administration's 2018 budget increases for defense spending. On the other hand, Americans also accepted Trump's own description of defense spending as wasteful. According to ongoing public opinion surveys, Americans believe there is a great deal of waste in the defense budget, and majorities believe Congress and the president should take action to save money.[91] Americans were clearly inconsistent in their views on whether to spend more or less money on defense, as was the president.

The next question is how and where to make further cuts. Some advocates argue that Congress and the president should impose an across-the-board spending cap on all defense programs. Others argue that the department should eliminate missions such as research on nonmilitary issues, schools for children of military families, grocery stores (commissaries) that offer lower prices than Walmart and Costco, and tuition assistance for officers who have already graduated from college and graduate school.[92] But whatever the approach, even the secretary of defense acknowledges that it is time for cutting and strongly supports a careful trimming of obsolete and wasteful weapons systems. Thus far, Congress has expressed little interest in such winnowing, largely because the defense industry is such a strong lobbying force on Capitol Hill and provides so much campaign funding to incumbents.

Learn the Lessons from Iraq

The end of war only marks the start of the fight for peace. This was true after World War I, World War II, and Vietnam, and it is now true about the Iraq War. The Iraq War ended in 2011, for example, but has yet to settle into a stable peace.

Iraq was a controversial and expensive war from its very beginning. The war was launched with congressional approval largely based on the Bush administration's claim that Iraq's brutal dictator Saddam Hussein was involved in the September 11 terrorist attacks, and also had biological, chemical, and even nuclear weapons that could be used against the United States and its allies, especially Israel.

Despite the administration's claim that the war would be quickly won, it lasted almost nine years and eventually claimed the lives of 4,500 U.S. troops, left another 32,000 wounded, and cost more than $1 trillion that was added to the growing national debt. The cost will continue to climb as U.S. military advisers help train the new Iraq Army, and the Department of Veterans Affairs continues to care for wounded U.S. soldiers, including many who suffered traumatic brain injuries from hidden road-side bombs.

The war clearly tested the U.S. theories of modern warfare. Many of our sophisticated weapons were of little use as Iraq descended into civil war, and experts questioned the original decision to launch a war in such an unstable region. Despite its early military success, the United States soon discovered that it did not have enough troops to police the nation and lacked the international support needed to rebuild the economy. The United States also lacked an "exit strategy" for withdrawal from its increasingly dangerous effort to win the peace.

Now it must convert the lesson into new policy for choosing where and when to fight. The United States also learned painful lessons about its flawed intelligence system. The United States never found Iraq's alleged weapons of mass destruction, nor did it find any link between Iraq's brutal dictator Saddam Hussein and the September 11 terrorist attacks. Moreover, even as U.S. troops came home from Iraq after the longest war in history, the internal violence began to heat up again, threatening the fragile democracy.[93]

CONCLUSION

The emerging threats to the Nuclear Non-proliferation Treaty have prompted a series of proposed remedies. Some experts recommend military strikes, including the use of so-called "bunker buster" bombs designed to destroy underground nuclear facilities. Israel has allegedly considered air strikes on Iran as news reports of its nuclear program spread in 2012, while the United Nations has warned North Korea repeatedly to dismantle its nuclear program with little effect.[94]

Other experts argue that the United States should modernize and reposition its nuclear arsenal on rogue states such as North Korea.[95] It is one thing to threaten nuclear retaliation against easily identifiable targets, and quite another to even find a target against fast-moving targets such as the Islamic State. These experts also worry about Russia's and China's current efforts to develop new, smaller, and more accurate nuclear weapons that would arrive so quickly on target that they could not be stopped.[96]

Still other experts argue that the United Nations has already provided the answer to proliferation in its Sustainable Development Goals. What if the world ended poverty in all its forms everywhere? What if it also ended hunger, improved nutrition, and promoted sustainable agriculture? What if it ensured access to water and sanitation for all? What if it kept the oceans clean and saved endangered coral reefs? And what if it ended sex trafficking, stopped the flow of nuclear arms components, reduced corruption and bribery in all their forms, and gave all citizens the freedom to vote in free, fair, competitive elections?

You do not have to choose between these hard and soft power options, but you will have to decide whether you favor candidates more inclined to soft or hard power. Are you more supportive of trying diplomacy and foreign aid, or do you think military action yields better results? Foreign and defense policies clearly come at a price, and you will have to make the choices about the right blends and be prepared to live with the consequences. Moreover, you will have to balance foreign and defense priorities against economic and social needs, and you will need to decide how you will make your own difference in guaranteeing a safer world for yourself, your family, and your community. Will you join the Peace Corps at some point? What about the armed forces for a two-year tour? What about working for a socially responsible investment firm, a public school, or a charitable organization that delivers humanitarian aid?

Millennials are one of the most socially conscious generations in history.[97] They care about who they work for and with, and why. And they have their own ways of shaping public policies of all kinds.[98] Now you have a much better understanding about the structure, action, and impact of U.S. public policy. Now you get to set the balance.

REVIEW THE CHAPTER

The Constitutional Foundations of Foreign and Defense Policy (Structure)

17.1 Understand the constitutional foundations and current philosophies that guide foreign and defense policy, p. 512.

The primary goal of foreign and defense policy is to protect the nation from international threats. The Constitution divides responsibilities for achieving this goal between Congress and the presidency, but presidents argue that they have inherent powers to protect the nation whenever it is threatened. Foreign and defense policy is also divided among three different philosophies about its role in the world: (1) realism versus idealism, (2) isolationism versus internationalism, and (3) unilateralism versus multilateralism. Public opinion is also divided, even confused about these questions. However, recent surveys suggest that Americans are moving toward isolationism as they search for answers to domestic problems such as jobs and the budget.

The Tools of Foreign and Defense Policy (Action)

17.2 Evaluate the options for achieving foreign and defense policy goals, p. 520.

The United States uses both soft and hard power to achieve its foreign and defense policy goals. Soft power (carrots) involves the use of incentives such as foreign aid to attract other nations toward cooperation, while hard power (sticks) involves the use of military force to force other nations to follow U.S. directions. Soft power is about attracting another nation to a common cause such as international peace, while hard power is about raw strength and endurance. The three tools of soft power are (1) diplomacy, (2) global communications, and (3) foreign assistance, while the three tools of hard power are (1) war, (2) the threat of war, and (3) economic sanctions. Soft and hard powers are often used together to lead other nations toward the U.S. position on major problems and opportunities.

Administering Foreign and Defense Policy (Action)

17.3 Outline the structure of the foreign and defense policy bureaucracy, p. 525.

Foreign and defense policy is converted into action by a large bureaucracy spread across government, including the National Security Council, defense and state departments, and the intelligence community. The National Security Council is a unit within the Executive Office of the President that advises the president on key foreign and defense issues, and is headed by the National Security Advisor. The State Department is the lead executive branch organization in making and managing foreign policy, and secures much of its impact through its ambassadors and the Foreign Service. The intelligence community is composed of 16 agencies, including the Central Intelligence Agency, and is supervised by the director of national intelligence. The Defense Department is the largest organization in the federal government, and contains a long list of organizations dedicated to military readiness. The military is highly dependent on the defense industry, which President Eisenhower described as the military-industrial complex.

Foreign Policy Goals (Impact)

17.4 Assess the goals and impacts of America's foreign policy, p. 533.

The United States has four foreign policy goals. First, the United States is trying to reduce global climate change by working with the rest of the world to reduce the greenhouse gasses that are driving temperatures higher. Second, the United States is working to build new democracies around the world. This effort, or nation building, is designed to convert authoritarian governments into democratic states, but is expensive and difficult. Third, the United States is continuing to pursue peace in the Middle East, which has also proven to be difficult. Despite past agreements to follow a road map to peace, the region remains locked in bitter conflict. Fourth, the United States is investing in efforts to reduce global poverty and disease through its foreign aid.

Defense Policy Goals (Impact)

17.5 Assess the goals and impacts of America's defense policy, p. 537.

The United States has four defense policy goals. First, the United States is working to reduce the world's growing inventory of weapons of mass destruction. It is currently trying to invent new methods of policing these weapons and deterring their use. Second, the United States continues to fight the War on Terrorism, which also involves new direct and indirect methods for imposing costs and denying benefits to countries that help terrorists. Third, the United States is moving toward the sharp cuts in wasteful defense spending that the public supports and both Congress and the president need. Fourth, the United States is trying to learn the lessons from the Iraq War, especially in developing new techniques for choosing where and when to fight.

LEARN THE TERMS

Appendix

The Declaration of Independence

Drafted mainly by Thomas Jefferson, this document adopted by the Second Continental Congress, and signed by John Hancock and 55 others, outlined the rights of man and the rights to rebellion and self-government. It declared the independence of the colonies from Great Britain, justified rebellion, and listed the grievances against George III and his government. What is memorable about this famous document is that it not only declared the birth of a new nation, but also set forth, with eloquence, our basic philosophy of liberty and representative democracy.

In Congress, July 4, 1776

(The unanimous Declaration of the Thirteen United States of America)

Preamble

When, in the course of human events, it becomes necessary for one people to dissolve the political bands which have connected them with another, and to assume, among the powers of the earth, the separate and equal station to which the laws of nature and of nature's God entitle them, a decent respect to the opinions of mankind requires that they should declare the causes which impel them to the separation.

New Principles of Government

We hold these truths to be self-evident; that all men are created equal, that they are endowed by their Creator with certain unalienable rights, that among these are life, liberty, and the pursuit of happiness.

That, to secure these rights, governments are instituted among men, deriving their just powers from the consent of the governed.

That whenever any form of government becomes destructive of these ends, it is the right of the people to alter or to abolish it, and to institute new government, laying its foundation on such principles, and organizing its powers in such form, as to them shall seem most likely to effect their safety and happiness. Prudence, indeed will dictate that governments long established should not be changed for light and transient causes; and accordingly all experience hath shown that mankind are more disposed to suffer while evils are sufferable, than to right themselves by abolishing the forms to which they are accustomed. But when a long train of abuses and usurpations, pursuing invariably the same object, evinces a design to reduce them under absolute despotism, it is their right, it is their duty, to throw off such government, and to provide new guards for their future security.

Reasons for Separation

Such has been the patient sufferance of these colonies; and such is now the necessity which constrains them to alter their former systems of government. The history of the present king of Great Britain is a history of repeated injuries and usurpations, all having in direct object the establishment of an absolute tyranny over these states. To prove this, let facts be submitted to a candid world.

He has refused his assent to laws, the most wholesome and necessary for the public good.

He has forbidden his governors to pass laws of immediate and pressing importance unless suspended in their operation till his assent should be obtained; and when so suspended, he has utterly neglected to attend to them.

He has refused to pass other laws for the accommodation of large districts of people, unless those people would relinquish the right of representation in the legislature, a right inestimable to them, and formidable to tyrants only.

He has called together legislative bodies at places unusual, uncomfortable, and distant for the depository of their public records, for the sole purpose of fatiguing them into compliance with his measures.

He has dissolved representative houses repeatedly, for opposing, with manly firmness, his invasions on the rights of people.

He has refused, for a long time after such dissolutions, to cause others to be elected; whereby the legislative powers incapable of annihilation, have returned to the people at large for their exercise; the state remaining, in the meantime, exposed to all the dangers of invasion from without and convulsions within.

He has endeavored to prevent the population of these states; for that purpose obstructing the laws of naturalization of foreigners, refusing to pass others to encourage their migration hither, and raising the conditions of new appropriations of lands.

He has obstructed the administration of justice, by refusing his assent to laws for establishing judiciary powers.

He has made judges dependent on his will alone for the tenure of their offices, and the amount and payment of their salaries.

He has erected a multitude of new offices, and sent hither swarms of officers to harass our people and eat out their substance.

He has kept among us, in times of peace, standing armies, without the consent of our legislature.

He has affected to render the military independent of, and superior to, the civil power.

He has combined with others to subject us to jurisdiction foreign to our constitution and unacknowledged by our laws, giving his assent to their acts of pretended legislation:

For quartering large bodies of armed troops among us;

For protecting them, by a mock trial, from punishment for any murders which they should commit on the inhabitants of these states;

For cutting off our trade with all parts of the world;

For imposing taxes on us without our consent;

For depriving us, in many cases, of the benefits of trial by jury;

For transporting us beyond seas, to be tried for pretended offenses;

For abolishing the free system of English laws in a neighboring province, establishing therein an arbitrary government, and enlarging its boundaries, so as to render it at once an example and fit instrument for introducing the same absolute rule into these colonies;

For taking away our charters, abolishing our most valuable laws, and altering, fundamentally, the forms of our governments;

For suspending our own legislatures, and declaring themselves invented with power to legislate for us in all cases whatsoever.

He has abdicated government here, by declaring us out of his protection and waging war against us.

He has plundered our seas, ravaged our coasts, burned our towns, and destroyed the lives of our people.

He is at this time transporting large armies of foreign mercenaries to complete the works of death, desolation, and tyranny already begun with circumstances of cruelty and perfidy scarcely paralleled in the most barbarous ages and totally unworthy of the head of a civilized nation.

He has constrained our fellow-citizens, taken captive on the high seas, to bear arms against their country, to become the executioners of their friends and brethren, or to fall themselves by their hands.

He has excited domestic insurrections among us, and has endeavored to bring on the inhabitants of our frontiers the merciless Indian savages, whose known rule of warfare is an undistinguished destruction of all ages, sexes, and conditions.

In every stage of these oppressions we have petitioned for redress in the most humble terms; our repeated petitions have been answered only by repeated injury. A prince whose character is thus marked by every act which may define a tyrant is unfit to be the ruler of a free people.

Nor have we been wanting in attention to our British brethren. We have warned them, from time to time, of attempts by their legislature to extend an unwarrantable jurisdiction over us. We have reminded them of the circumstances of our emigration and settlement here. We have appealed to their native justice and magnanimity; and we have conjured them, by the ties of our common kindred, to disavow these usurpations, which would inevitably interrupt our connections and correspondence. They, too, have been deaf to the voice of justice and of consanguinity. We must, therefore, acquiesce in the necessity which denounces our separation, and hold them, as we hold the rest of mankind, enemies in war, in peace, friends.

We, therefore, the representatives of the United States of America, in General Congress assembled, appealing to the Supreme Judge of the world for the rectitude of our intentions, do, in the name and by authority of the good people of these colonies, solemnly publish and declare, that these united colonies are, and of right ought to be, free and independent states; that they are absolved from all allegiance to the British crown, and that all political connection between them and the state of Great Britain is, and ought to be, totally dissolved; and that, as free and independent states, they have full power to levy war, conclude peace, contract alliances, establish commerce, and do all other acts and things which independent states may of a right do. And, for the support of this declaration, with a firm reliance on the protection of Divine Providence, we mutually pledge to each other our lives, our fortunes, and our sacred honor.

The Federalist, No. 10, James Madison

***The Federalist*, No. 10, written by James Madison soon after the Constitutional Convention, was prepared as one of several dozen newspaper essays aimed at persuading New Yorkers to ratify the proposed constitution. One of the most important basic documents in American political history, it outlines the need for and the general principles of a democratic republic. It also provides a political and economic analysis of the realities of interest group or faction politics.**

To the People of the State of New York: Among the numerous advantages promised by a well-constructed union, none deserves to be more accurately developed than its tendency to break and control the violence of faction. The friend of popular governments, never finds himself so much alarmed for their character and fate, as when he contemplates their propensity of this dangerous vice. He will not fail, therefore, to set a due value on any plan which, without violating the principles to which he is attached, provides a proper cure for it. The instability, injustice, and confusion introduced into the public councils, have, in truth, been the mortal diseases under which popular governments have everywhere perished; as they continue to be the favorite and fruitful topics from which the adversaries to liberty derive their most specious declamations. The valuable improvements made by the American constitutions on the popular models, both ancient and modern, cannot certainly be too much admired; but it would be an unwarrantable partiality, to contend that they have as effectually obviated the danger on this side, as was wished and expected. Complaints are everywhere heard from our most considerate and virtuous citizens, equally the friends of public and private faith, and of public and personal liberty, that our governments are too unstable; that the public good is disregarded in the conflicts of rival parties; and that measures are too often decided, not according to the rules of justice, and the rights of the minor party, but by the superior force of an interested and overbearing majority. However anxiously we may wish that these complaints had no foundation, the evidence of known facts will not permit us to deny that they are in some degree true. It will be found, indeed, on a candid review of our situation, that some of the distresses under which we labor have been erroneously charged on the operations of our governments; but it will be found, at the same time, that other causes will not alone account for many of our heaviest misfortunes; and, particularly, for that prevailing and increasing distrust of public engagements, and alarm for private rights, which are echoed from one end of the continent to the other. These must be chiefly, if not wholly, effects of the unsteadiness and injustice, with which a factious spirit has tainted our public administrations.

By a faction, I understand a number of citizens, whether amounting to a majority or minority of the whole, who are united and actuated by some common impulse of passion, or of interest, adverse to the rights of other citizens, or to the permanent and aggregate interests of the community.

There are two methods of curing the mischiefs of faction: the one, by removing its causes; the other, by controlling its effects.

There are again two methods of removing the causes of faction: the one, by destroying the liberty which is essential to its existence; the other, by giving to every citizen the same opinions, the same passions, and the same interests.

It could never be more truly said, than of the first remedy, that it was worse than the disease. Liberty is to faction what air is to fire, an aliment without which it instantly expires. But it could not be a less folly to abolish liberty, which is essential to political life, because it nourishes faction, than it would be to wish the annihilation of air, which is essential to animal life, because it imparts to fire its destructive agency.

The second expedient is as impracticable, as the first would be unwise. As long as the reason of man continues fallible, and he is at liberty to exercise it, different opinions will be formed. As long as the connection subsists between his reason and his self-love, his opinions and his passions will have a reciprocal influence on each other; and the former will be objects to which the latter will attach themselves. The diversity in the faculties of men, from which the rights of property originate, is not less an insuperable obstacle to an uniformity of interests. The protection of these faculties is the first object of government. From the protection of different and unequal faculties of acquiring property, the possession of different degrees and kinds of property immediately results; and from the influence of these on the sentiments and views of the respective proprietors, ensues a division of the society into different interests and parties.

The latent causes of faction are thus sown in the nature of man; and we see them everywhere brought into different degrees of activity, according to the different circumstances of civil society. A zeal for different opinions concerning religion, concerning government, and many other points, as well of speculation as of practice; an attachment to different leaders ambitiously contending for preeminence and power; or to persons of other descriptions whose fortunes have been interesting to the human passions, have, in turn, divided mankind into parties, inflamed them with mutual animosity, and rendered them much more disposed to vex and oppress each other, than to cooperate for their common good. So strong is this propensity of mankind, to fall into mutual animosities, that where no substantial occasion presents itself, the most frivolous and fanciful distinctions have been sufficient to kindle their unfriendly passions and excite their most violent conflicts. But the most common and durable source of factions, has been the various and unequal distribution of property. Those who hold, and those who are without property, have ever formed distinct interests in society. Those who are creditors, and those who are debtors, fall under a like discrimination. A landed interest, a manufacturing interest, a mercantile interest, a moneyed interest, with many lesser interests, grow up of necessity in civilized nations, and divide them into different classes, actuated by different sentiments and views. The regulation of these various and interfering interests forms the principal task of modern legislation, and involves the spirit of the party and faction in the necessary and ordinary operations of the government.

No man is allowed to be a judge in his own cause; because his interest will certainly bias his judgment, and, not improbably, corrupt his integrity. With equal, nay, with greater reason, a body of men are unfit to be both judges and parties at the same time; yet what are many of the most important acts of legislation, but so many judicial determinations, not indeed concerning the right of single persons, but concerning the rights of large bodies of citizens? And what are the different classes of legislators, but advocates and parties to the causes which they determine? Is a law proposed concerning private debts? It is a question to which the creditors are parties on one side, and the debtors on the other. Justice ought to hold the balance between them. Yet the parties are, and must be, themselves the judges; and the most numerous party, or, in other words, the most powerful faction, must be expected to prevail. Shall domestic manufacturers be encouraged, and in what degree, by restrictions on foreign manufacturers? Are questions which would be differently decided by the landed and the manufacturing classes; and probably by neither with a sole regard to justice and the public good. The apportionment of taxes, on the various descriptions of property, is an act which seems to require the most exact impartiality; yet there is, perhaps, no legislative act, in which greater opportunity and temptation are given to a predominant party to trample on the rules of justice. Every shilling, with which they overburden the inferior number, is a shilling saved to their own pockets.

It is in vain to say, that enlightened statesmen will be able to adjust these clashing interests, and render them all subservient to the public good. Enlightened statesmen will not always be at the helm, nor, in many cases, can such an adjustment be made at all, without taking into view indirect and remote considerations, which will rarely prevail over the immediate interest which one party may find in disregarding the rights of another, or the good of the whole.

The inference to which we are brought is, that the causes of faction cannot be removed; and that relief is only to be sought in the means of controlling its effects.

If a faction consists of less than a majority, relief is supplied by the republican principle, which enables the majority to defeat its sinister views, by regular vote. It may clog the administration, it may convulse the society; but it will be unable to execute and mask its violence under the forms of the Constitution. When a majority is included in a faction, the form of popular government, on the other hand, enables it to sacrifice to its ruling passion or interest, both the public good and the rights of other citizens. To secure the public good, and private rights, against the danger of such a faction, and at the same time to preserve the spirit and the form of popular government, is then the great object to which our inquiries are directed. Let me add, that it is the great desideratum, by which alone this form of government can be rescued from the opprobrium under which it has so long laboured, and be recommended to the esteem and adoption of mankind.

By what means is this object attainable? Evidently by one of two only. Either the existence of the same passion or interest in a majority, at the same time, must be prevented; or the majority, having such coexistent passion or interest, must be rendered, by their number and local situation, unable to concert and carry into effect schemes of oppression. If the impulse and the opportunity be suffered to coincide, we well know that neither moral nor religious motives can be relied on as an adequate control. They are not found to be such on the injustice and violence of individuals, and lose their efficacy in proportion to the number combined together; that is, in proportion as their efficacy becomes needful.

From this view of the subject, it may be concluded, that a pure democracy, by which I mean a society consisting of a small number of citizens, who assemble and administer the government in person, can admit of no cure for the mischiefs of faction. A common passion or interest will, in almost every case, be felt by a majority of the whole; a communication and concert, results from the form of government itself; and there is nothing to check the inducements to sacrifice the weaker party, or an obnoxious individual. Hence, it is, that such democracies have ever been spectacles of turbulence and contention; have ever been found incompatible with personal security, or the rights of property; and have in general been as short in their lives, as they have been violent in their deaths. Theoretic politicians, who have patronized this species of government, have erroneously supposed, that by reducing mankind to a perfect equality in their political rights, they would, at the same time be perfectly equalized and assimilated in their possessions, their opinions, and their passions.

A republic, by which I mean a government in which the scheme of representation takes place, opens a different prospect, and promises the cure for which we are seeking. Let us examine the points in which it varies from pure democracy, and we shall comprehend both the nature of the cure and the efficacy which it must derive from the union.

The two great points of difference, between a democracy and a republic, are, first, the delegation of the government, in the latter, to a small number of citizens, elected by the rest; secondly, the greater number of citizens, and greater sphere of country, over which the latter may be extended.

The effect of the first difference is, on the one hand, to refine and enlarge the public views, by passing them through the medium of a chosen body of citizens, whose wisdom may best discern the true interest of their country, and whose patriotism and love of justice, will be least likely to sacrifice it to temporary or partial considerations. Under such a regulation, it may well happen, that the public voice, pronounced by the representatives of the people, will be more consonant to the public good, than if pronounced by the people themselves, convened for the purpose. On the other hand the effect may be inverted. Men of factious tempers, of local prejudices, or of sinister designs, may by intrigue, by corruption, or by other means, first obtain the suffrages, and then betray the interest of the people. The question resulting is, whether small or extensive republics are most favourable to the election of proper guardians of the public weal; and it is clearly decided in favour of the latter by two obvious considerations.

In the first place, it is to be remarked that, however small the republic may be, the representatives must be raised to a certain number, in order to guard against the cabals of a few; and that however large it may be, they must be limited to a certain number, in order to guard against the confusion of a multitude. Hence, the number of representatives in the two cases not being in proportion to that of the constituents, and being proportionally greatest in the small republic, it follows, that if the proportion of fit characters be not less in the large than in the small republic, the former will present a greater option, and consequently a greater probability of a fit choice.

In the next place, as each representative will be chosen by a greater number of citizens in the large than in the small republic, it will be more difficult for unworthy candidates to practice with success the vicious arts, by which elections are too often carried; and the suffrages of the people being more free, will be more likely to centre in men who possess the most attractive merit, and the most diffusive and established characters.

It must be confessed, that in this, as in most other cases, there is a mean, on both sides of which inconveniences will be found to lie. By enlarging too much the number of electors, you render the representatives too little acquainted with all their local circumstances and lesser interests; as by reducing it too much, you render him unduly attached to these, and too little fit to comprehend and pursue great and national objects. The federal constitution forms a happy combination in this respect; the great and aggregate interests being referred to the national, the local and particular to the state legislatures.

The other point of difference is, the greater number of citizens, and extent of territory, which may be brought within the compass of republican, than of democratic government; and it is this circumstance principally which renders factious combinations less to be dreaded in the former, than in the latter. The smaller the society, the fewer probably will be the distinct parties and interests composing it; the fewer the distinct parties and interests, the more frequently will a majority be found of the same party; and the smaller the number of individuals composing a majority, and the smaller the compass within which they are placed, the more easily will they concert and execute their plans of oppression. Extend the sphere, and you take in a greater variety of parties and interests; you make it less probable that a majority of the whole will have a common motive to invade the rights of other citizens; or if such a common motive exists, it will be more difficult for all who feel it to discover their own strength, and to act in unison with each other. Besides other impediments, it may be remarked, that where there is a consciousness of unjust or dishonourable purposes, communication is always checked by distrust, in proportion to the number whose concurrence is necessary.

Hence, it clearly appears, that the same advantage, which a republic has over a democracy, in controlling the effects of faction, is enjoyed by a large over a small republic—is enjoyed by the union over the states composing it. Does this advantage consist in the substitution of representatives, whose enlightened views and virtuous sentiments render them superior to local prejudices, and to schemes of injustice? It will not be denied that the representation of the union will be most likely to possess these requisite endowments. Does it consist in the greater security afforded by a greater variety of parties, against the event of any one party being able to outnumber and oppress the rest? In an equal degree does the increased variety of parties, comprised within the union, increase the security? Does it, in fine, consist in the greater obstacles opposed to the concert and accomplishment of the secret wishes of an unjust and interested majority? Here, again, the extent of the union gives it the most palpable advantage.

The influence of factious leaders may kindle a flame within their particular states, but will be unable to spread a general conflagration through the other states; a religious sect may degenerate into a political faction in a part of the confederacy; but the variety of sects dispersed over the entire face of it, must secure the national councils against any danger from that source: a rage for paper money, for an abolition of debts, for an equal division of property, or for any other improper or wicked project, will be less apt to pervade the whole body of the union than a particular member of it; in the same proportion as such a malady is more likely to taint a particular county or district, than an entire state.

In the extent and proper structure of the union, therefore, we behold a republican remedy for the diseases most incident to republican government. And according to the degree of pleasure and pride we feel in being republicans, ought to be our zeal in cherishing the spirit, and supporting the character of federalists.

The Federalist, No. 51, James Madison

The Federalist, No. 51, also written by Madison, is a classic statement in defense of separation of powers and republican processes. Its fourth paragraph is especially famous and is frequently quoted by students of government.

To what expedient, then, shall we finally resort, for maintaining in practice the necessary partition of power among the several departments as laid down in the Constitution? The only answer that can be given is that as all these exterior provisions are found to be inadequate the defect must be supplied, by so contriving the interior structure of the government as that its several constituent parts may, by their mutual relations, be the means of keeping each other in their proper places. Without presuming to undertake a full development of this important idea I will hazard a few general observations which may perhaps place it in a clearer light, and enable us to form a more correct judgment of the principles and structure of the government planned by the convention.

In order to lay a due foundation for that separate and distinct exercise of the different powers of government, which to a certain extent is admitted on all hands to be essential to the preservation of liberty, it is evident that each department should have a will of its own; and consequently should be so constituted that the members of each should have as little agency as possible in the appointment of the members of the others. Were this principle rigorously adhered to, it would require that all the appointments for the supreme executive, legislative, and judiciary magistracies should be drawn from the same fountain of authority, the people, through channels having no communication whatever with one another. Perhaps such a plan of constructing the several departments would be less difficult in practice than it may in contemplation appear. Some difficulties, however, and some additional expense would attend the execution of it. Some deviations, therefore, from the principle must be admitted. In the constitution of the judiciary department in particular, it might be inexpedient to insist rigorously on the principle: first, because peculiar qualifications being essential in the members, the primary consideration ought to be to select that mode of choice which best secures these qualifications; second, because the permanent tenure by which the appointments are held in that department must soon destroy all sense of dependence on the authority conferring them.

It is equally evident that the members of each department should be as little dependent as possible on those of the others for the emoluments annexed to their offices. Were the executive magistrate, or the judges, not independent of the legislature in this particular, their independence in every other would be merely nominal.

But the great security against a gradual concentration of the several powers in the same department consists in giving to those who administer each department the necessary constitutional means and personal motives to resist encroachments of the others. The provision for defense must in this, as in all other cases, be made commensurate to the danger of attack. Ambition must be made to counteract ambition. The interest of the man must be connected with the constitutional rights of the place. It may be a reflection on human nature that such devices should be necessary to control the abuses of government. But what is government itself but the greatest of all reflections on human nature? If men were angels, no government would be necessary. If angels were to govern men, neither external nor internal controls on government would be necessary. In framing a government which is to be administered by men over men, the great difficulty lies in this: you must first enable the government to control the governed; and in the next place oblige it to control itself. A dependence on the people is, no doubt, the primary control on the government; but experience has taught mankind the necessity of auxiliary precautions.

This policy of supplying, by opposite and rival interests, the defect of better motives, might be traced through the whole system of human affairs, private as well as public. We see it particularly displayed in all the subordinate distributions of power, where the constant aim is to divide and arrange the several offices in such a manner as that each may be a check on the other—that the private interest of every individual may be a sentinel over the public rights. These inventions of prudence cannot be less requisite in the distribution of the supreme powers of the State.

But it is not possible to give to each department an equal power of self-defense. In republican government, the legislative authority necessarily predominates. The remedy for this inconveniency is to divide the legislature into different branches; and to render them, by modes of election and different principles of action, as little connected with each other as the nature of their common functions and their common dependence on the society will admit. It may even be necessary to guard against dangerous encroachments by still further precautions. As the weight of the legislative authority requires that it should be thus divided, the weakness of the executive may require, on the other hand, that it should be fortified. An absolute negative on the legislature appears, at first view, to be the natural defense with which the executive magistrate should be armed. But perhaps it would be neither altogether safe nor alone sufficient. On ordinary occasions it might not be exerted with the requisite firmness, and on extraordinary occasions it might be perfidiously abused. May not this defect of an absolute negative be supplied by some qualified connection between this weaker department and the weaker branch of the stronger department, by which the latter may be led to support the constitutional rights of the former, without being too much detached from the rights of its own department?

If the principles on which these observations are founded be just, as I persuade myself they are, and they be applied as a criterion to the several State constitutions, and to the federal Constitution, it will be found that if the latter does not perfectly correspond with them, the former are infinitely less able to bear such a test.

There are, moreover, two considerations particularly applicable to the federal system of America, which place that system in a very interesting point of view.

First. In a single republic, all the power surrendered by the people is submitted to the administration of a single government; and the usurpations are guarded against by a division of the government into distinct and separate departments. In the compound republic of America, the power surrendered by the people is first divided between two distinct governments, and then the portion allotted to each subdivided among distinct and separate departments. Hence a double security arises to the rights of the people. The different governments will control each other, at the same time that each will be controlled by itself.

Second. It is of great importance in a republic not only to guard the society against the oppression of its rulers, but to guard one part of the society against the injustice of the other part. Different interests necessarily exist in different classes of citizens. If a majority be united by a common interest, the rights of the minority will be insecure. There are but two methods of providing against this evil: the one by creating a will in the community independent of the majority—that is, of the society itself; the other, by comprehending in the society so many separate descriptions of citizens as will render an unjust combination of a majority of the whole very improbable, if not impracticable. The first method prevails in all governments possessing an hereditary or self-appointed authority. This, at best, is but a precarious security; because a power independent of the society may as well espouse the unjust views of the major as the rightful interests of the minor party, and may possibly be turned against both parties. The second method will be exemplified in the federal republic of the United States. Whilst all authority in it will be derived from and dependent on the society, the society itself will be broken into so many parts, interests and classes of citizens, that the rights of individuals, or of the minority, will be in little danger from interested combinations of the majority. In a free government the security for civil rights must be the same as that for religious rights. It consists in the one case in the multiplicity of interests, and in the other in the multiplicity of sects. The degree of security in both cases will depend on the number of interests and sects; and this may be presumed to depend on the extent of country and number of people comprehended under the same government. This view of the subject must particularly recommend a proper federal system to all the sincere and considerate friends of republican government, since it shows that in exact proportion as the territory of the Union may be formed into more circumscribed Confederacies, or States, oppressive combinations of a majority will be facilitated; the best security, under the republican forms, for the rights of every class of citizen, will be diminished; and consequently the stability and independence of some member of the government, the only other security, must be proportionally increased. Justice is the end of government. It is the end of civil society. It ever has been and ever will be pursued until it be obtained, or until liberty be lost in the pursuit. In a society under the forms of which the stronger faction can readily unite and oppress the weaker, anarchy may as truly be said to reign as in a state of nature, where the weaker individual is not secured against the violence of the stronger; and as, in the latter state, even the stronger individuals are prompted, by the uncertainty of their condition, to submit to a government which may protect the weak as well as themselves; so, in the former state, will the more powerful factions or parties be gradually induced, by a like motive, to wish for a government which will protect all parties, the weaker as well as the more powerful. It can be little doubted that if the State of Rhode Island was separated from the Confederacy and left to itself, the insecurity of rights under the popular form of government within such narrow limits would be displayed by such reiterated oppressions of factious majorities that some power altogether independent of the people would soon be called for by the voice of the very factions whose misrule had proved the necessity to it. In the extended republic of the United States, and among the great variety of interests, parties, and sects which it embraces, a coalition of a majority of the whole society could seldom take place on any other principles than those of justice and the general good; whilst there being thus less danger to a minor from the will of a major party, there must be less pretext, also, to provide for the security of the former, by introducing into the government a will not dependent on the latter, or, in other words, a will independent of the society itself. It is no less certain that it is important, notwithstanding the contrary opinions which have been entertained that the larger the society, provided it lie within a practicable sphere, the more duly capable it will be of self-government. And happily for the *republican cause,* the practicable sphere may be carried to a very great extent by a judicious modification and mixture of the *federal principle.*

The Constitution of the United States

The Preamble

We the People of the United States, in Order to form a more perfect Union, establish Justice, insure domestic Tranquility, provide for the common defence, promote the general Welfare, and secure the Blessings of Liberty to ourselves and our Posterity, do ordain and establish this Constitution for the United States of America.

Article I—The Legislative Article

Legislative Power

SECTION 1 All legislative Powers herein granted shall be vested in a Congress of the United States, which shall consist of a Senate and House of Representatives.

House of Representatives: Composition; Qualifications; Apportionment; Impeachment Power

SECTION 2

Clause 1 The House of Representatives shall be composed of Members chosen every second Year by the People of the several States, and the Electors in each State shall have the Qualifications requisite for Electors of the most numerous Branch of the State Legislature.

Clause 2 No Person shall be a Representative who shall not have attained to the Age of twenty five Years, and been seven Years a Citizen of the United States, and who shall not, when elected, be an inhabitant of that State in which he shall be chosen.

Clause 3 Representatives and direct Taxes[1] shall be apportioned among the several States which may be included within this Union, according to their respective Numbers, which shall be determined by adding to the whole Number of free Persons, including those bound to Service for a Term of Years, and excluding Indians not taxed, three-fifths of all other Persons.[2] The actual Enumeration shall be made within three Years after the first Meeting of the Congress of the United States, and within every subsequent Term of ten Years, in such Manner as they shall by Law direct. The Number of Representatives shall not exceed one for every thirty Thousand, but each State shall have at Least one Representative; and until such enumeration shall be made, the State of New Hampshire shall be entitled to chuse three, Massachusetts eight, Rhode-Island and Providence Plantations one, Connecticut five, New-York six, New Jersey four, Pennsylvania eight, Delaware one, Maryland six, Virginia ten, North Carolina five, South Carolina five, and Georgia three.

[1]Modified by the Sixteenth Amendment

[2]Replaced by Section 2, Fourteenth Amendment

Clause 4 When vacancies happen in the Representation from any State, the Executive Authority thereof shall issue Writs of Election to fill such Vacancies.

Clause 5 The House of Representatives shall chuse their Speaker and other Officers; and shall have the sole Power of Impeachment.

Senate Composition: Qualifications, Impeachment Trials

SECTION 3

Clause 1 The Senate of the United States shall be composed of two Senators from each State, chosen by the Legislature thereof,[3] for six Years; and each Senator shall have one Vote.

Clause 2 Immediately after they shall be assembled in Consequence of the first Election, they shall be divided as equally as may be into three Classes. The Seats of the Senators of the first Class shall be vacated at the Expiration of the second Year, of the second Class at the Expiration of the fourth Year, and of the third Class at the Expiration of the sixth Year, so that one-third may be chosen every second Year; and if Vacancies happen by Resignation, or otherwise, during the Recess of the Legislature of any State, the Executive thereof may make temporary Appointments until the next Meeting of the Legislature, which shall then fill such Vacancies.[4]

Clause 3 No person shall be a Senator who shall not have attained to the Age of thirty Years, and been nine Years a Citizen of the United States, and who shall not, when elected, be an Inhabitant of that State for which he shall be chosen.

Clause 4 The Vice President of the United States shall be President of the Senate, but shall have no Vote, unless they be equally divided.

Clause 5 The Senate shall chuse their other Officers, and also a President pro tempore, in the Absence of the Vice President, or when he shall exercise the Office of President of the United States.

Clause 6 The Senate shall have the sole Power to try all Impeachments. When sitting for that Purpose, they shall be on Oath or Affirmation. When the President of the United States is tried, the Chief Justice shall preside: And no Person shall be convicted without the Concurrence of two-thirds of the Members present.

Judgment in Cases of Impeachment shall not extend further than to removal from Office, and disqualification to hold and enjoy any Office of honor, Trust or Profit under the United States: but the Party convicted shall nevertheless

[3]Repealed by the Seventeenth Amendment

[4]Modified by the Seventeenth Amendment

be liable and subject to Indictment, Trial, Judgment and Punishment, according to Law.

Congressional Elections: Times, Places, Manner

SECTION 4 The Times, Places and Manner of holding Elections for Senators and Representatives, shall be prescribed in each State by the Legislature thereof; but the Congress may at any time by Law make or alter such Regulations, except as to the Places of chusing Senators.

The Congress shall assemble at least once in every Year, and such Meeting shall be on the first Monday in December, unless they shall by Law appoint a different Day.[5]

Powers and Duties of the Houses

SECTION 5

Clause 1 Each House shall be the Judge of the Elections, Returns and Qualifications of its own Members, and a Majority of each shall constitute a Quorum to do Business; but a smaller Number may adjourn from day to day, and may be authorized to compel the Attendance of absent Members, in such Manner, and under the Penalties as each House may provide.

Clause 2 Each House may determine the Rules of its Proceedings, punish its Members for disorderly Behaviour, and, with the Concurrence of two-thirds, expel a Member.

Clause 3 Each House shall keep a Journal of its Proceedings, and from time to time publish the same, excepting such Parts as may in their Judgment require Secrecy; and the Yeas and Nays of the Members of either House on any question shall, at the Desire of one-fifth of those Present, be entered on the Journal.

Clause 4 Neither House, during the Session of Congress, shall, without the Consent of the other, adjourn for more than three days, nor to any other place than that in which the two Houses shall be sitting.

Rights of Members

SECTION 6

Clause 1 The Senators and Representatives shall receive a Compensation for their Services, to be ascertained by Law, and paid out of the Treasury of the United States. They shall in all Cases, except Treason, Felony and Breach of the Peace, be privileged from Arrest during their Attendance at the Session of their respective Houses, and in going to and returning from the same; and for any Speech or Debate in either House, they shall not be questioned in any other Place.

Clause 2 No Senator or Representative, shall, during the Time for which he was elected, be appointed to any civil Office under the Authority of the United States, which shall have been created, or the Emoluments whereof shall have been encreased during such time; and no Person holding any Office under the United States, shall be a Member of either House during his Continuance in Office.

Legislative Powers: Bills and Resolutions

SECTION 7

Clause 1 All Bills for raising Revenue shall originate in the House of Representatives; but the Senate may propose or concur with Amendments as on other Bills.

Clause 2 Every Bill which shall have passed the House of Representatives and the Senate, shall, before it become a Law, be presented to the President of the United States; if he approve he shall sign it, but if not he shall return it, with his Objections to that House in which it shall have originated, who shall enter the Objections at large on their Journal, and proceed to reconsider it. If after such Reconsideration two-thirds of that House shall agree to pass the Bill, it shall be sent, together with the Objections, to the other House, by which it shall likewise be reconsidered, and if approved by two-thirds of that House, it shall become a Law. But in all such Cases the Votes of both Houses shall be determined by yeas and Nays, and the Names of the Persons voting for and against the Bill shall be entered on the Journal of each House respectively. If any Bill shall not be returned by the President within ten Days (Sundays excepted) after it shall have been presented to him, the Same shall be a Law, in like Manner as if he had signed it, unless the Congress by their Adjournment prevent its Return, in which Case it shall not be a Law.

Clause 3 Every Order, Resolution, or Vote to which the Concurrence of the Senate and House of Representatives may be necessary (except on a question of Adjournment) shall be presented to the President of the United States; and before the Same shall take Effect, shall be approved by him, or being disapproved by him, shall be repassed by two-thirds of the Senate and House of Representatives, according to the Rules and Limitations prescribed in the Case of a Bill.

Powers of Congress

SECTION 8

Clause 1 The Congress shall have Power To lay and collect Taxes, Duties, Imposts and Excises, to pay the Debts and provide for the common Defence and general Welfare of the United States; but all Duties, Imposts and Excises shall be uniform throughout the United States;

To borrow Money on the credit of the United States;

To regulate Commerce with foreign Nations, and among the several States, and with the Indian Tribes;

To establish an uniform Rule of Naturalization, and uniform Laws on the subject of Bankruptcies throughout the United States;

To coin Money, regulate the Value thereof, and of foreign Coin, and fix the Standard of Weights and Measures;

[5]Changed by the Twentieth Amendment

To provide for the Punishment of counterfeiting the Securities and current Coin of the United States;

To establish Post Offices and post Roads;

To promote the Progress of Science and useful Arts, by securing for limited Times to Authors and Inventors the exclusive Right to their respective Writings and Discoveries;

To constitute Tribunals inferior to the supreme Court;

To define and punish Piracies and Felonies committed on the high Seas, and Offences against the Law of Nations;

To declare War, grant Letters of Marque and Reprisal, and make Rules concerning Captures on Land and Water;

To raise and support Armies, but no Appropriation of Money to that Use shall be for a longer Term than two Years;

To provide and maintain a Navy;

To make Rules for the Government and Regulation of the land and naval Forces;

To provide for calling for the Militia to execute the Laws of the Union, suppress Insurrections and repel Invasions;

To provide for organizing, arming, and disciplining the Militia, and for governing such Part of them as may be employed in the Service of the United States, reserving to the States respectively, the Appointment of the Officers, and the Authority of training the Militia according to the discipline prescribed by Congress;

Clause 2 To exercise exclusive Legislation in all Cases whatsoever, over such District (not exceeding ten Miles square) as may, by Cession of particular States, and the Acceptance of Congress, become the Seat of the Government of the United States, and to exercise like Authority over all Places purchased by the Consent of the Legislature of the State in which the Same shall be, for the Erection of Forts, Magazines, Arsenals, dock-Yards; and other needful Buildings;—And

Clause 3 To make all Laws which shall be necessary and proper for carrying into Execution the foregoing Powers, and all other Powers vested by this Constitution in the Government of the United States, or in any Department or Officer thereof.

Powers Denied to Congress

SECTION 9

Clause 1 The Migration or Importation of such Persons as any of the States now existing shall think proper to admit, shall not be prohibited by the Congress prior to the Year one thousand eight hundred and eight, but a Tax or duty may be imposed on such Importation, not exceeding ten dollars for each Person.

Clause 2 The privilege of the Writ of *Habeas Corpus* shall not be suspended, unless when in Cases of Rebellion or Invasion the public Safety may require it.

Clause 3 No Bill of Attainder or ex post facto law shall be passed.

Clause 4 No Capitation, or other direct, Tax shall be laid, unless in Proportion to the Census or Enumeration herein before directed to be taken.[6]

Clause 5 No Tax or Duty shall be laid on Articles exported from any State.

Clause 6 No Preference shall be given by any Regulation of Commerce or Revenue to the Ports of one State over those of another; nor shall Vessels bound to, or from, one State, be obliged to enter, clear, or pay Duties in another.

Clause 7 No Money shall be drawn from the Treasury, but in Consequence of Appropriations made by Law; and a regular Statement and Account of the Receipts and Expenditures of all public Money shall be published from time to time.

Clause 8 No Title of Nobility shall be granted by the United States: And no Person holding any Office of Profit or Trust under them, shall, without the Consent of Congress, accept of any present, Emolument, Office, or Title, of any kind whatever, from any King, Prince, or foreign State.

Powers Denied to the States

SECTION 10

Clause 1 No State shall enter into any Treaty, Alliance, or Confederation; grant Letters of Marque and Reprisal; coin Money; emit Bills of Credit; make any Thing but gold and silver Coin a Tender in Payment of Debts; pass any Bill of Attainder, ex post facto law, or Law impairing the Obligation of Contracts, or grant any Title of Nobility.

Clause 2 No State shall, without the Consent of the Congress, lay any Imposts or Duties on Imports or Exports, except what may be absolutely necessary for executing its inspection Laws: and the net Produce of all Duties and Imposts, laid by any State on Imports or Exports, shall be for the Use of the Treasury of the United States; and all such Laws shall be subject to the Revision and Controul of the Congress.

Clause 3 No State shall, without the Consent of Congress, lay any Duty of Tonnage, keep Troops, or Ships of War in time of Peace, enter into any Agreement or Compact with another State, or with a foreign Power, or engage in War, unless actually invaded, or in such imminent Danger as will not admit of Delay.

Article II—The Executive Article

Nature and Scope of Presidential Power

SECTION 1

Clause 1 The executive Power shall be vested in a President of the United States of America. He shall hold

[6]Modified by the Sixteenth Amendment

his Office during the Term of four Years and, together with the Vice President, chosen for the same Term, be elected as follows:

Clause 2 Each State shall appoint, in such Manner as the Legislature thereof may direct, a Number of Electors, equal to the whole Number of Senators and Representatives to which the State may be entitled in the Congress: but no Senator or Representative, or Person holding an Office of Trust or Profit under the United States, shall be appointed an Elector.

Clause 3 The Electors shall meet in their respective States, and vote by Ballot for two Persons, of whom one at least shall not be an Inhabitant of the same State with themselves. And they shall make a List of all the Persons voted for, and of the Number of Votes for each; which List they shall sign and certify, and transmit sealed to the Seat of the Government of the United States, directed to the President of the Senate. The President of the Senate shall, in the Presence of the Senate and House of Representatives, open all the Certificates, and the Votes shall then be counted. The Person having the greatest Number of Votes shall be the President, if such Number be a Majority of the whole Number of Electors appointed; and if there be more than one who have such Majority and have an equal Number of Votes, then the House of Representatives shall immediately chuse by Ballot one of them for President; and if no Person have a Majority, then from the five highest on the List the said House shall in like Manner chuse the President. But in chusing the President, the Votes shall be taken by States, the Representation from each State having one Vote; A quorum for this Purpose shall consist of a Member or Members from two-thirds of the States, and a Majority of all the States shall be necessary to a Choice. In every Case, after the Choice of the President, the Person having the greatest Number of Votes of the Electors shall be the Vice President. But if there should remain two or more who have equal Vote, the Senate shall chuse from them by Ballot the Vice President.[7]

Clause 4 The Congress may determine the Time of chusing the Electors, and the Day on which they shall give their Votes; which Day shall be the same throughout the United States.

Clause 5 No Person except a natural born citizen, or a Citizen of the United States, at the time of the Adoption of this Constitution, shall be eligible to the Office of President; neither shall any Person be eligible to that Office who shall not have attained to the Age of thirty five Years, and been fourteen Years a Resident within the United States.

Clause 6 In Case of the Removal of the President from Office, or of his Death, Resignation, or Inability to discharge the Powers and Duties of the said Office, the Same shall devolve on the Vice President, and the Congress may by Law provide for the Case of Removal, Death, Resignation, or Inability, both of the President and Vice President, declaring what Officer shall then act as President, and such Officer shall act accordingly, until the Disability be removed, or a President shall be elected.[8]

Clause 7 The President shall, at stated Times, receive for his Services, a Compensation, which shall neither be increased nor diminished during the Period of which he shall have been elected, and he shall not receive within that Period any other Emolument from the United States, or any of them.

Clause 8 Before he enter on the Execution of his Office, he shall take the following Oath or Affirmation:—"I do solemnly swear (or affirm) that I will faithfully execute the Office of President of the United States, and will to the best of my Ability, preserve, protect and defend the Constitution of the United States."

Powers and Duties of the President

SECTION 2

Clause 1 The President shall be the Commander in Chief of the Army and Navy of the United States, and of the Militia of the several States, when called into the actual Service of the United States; he may require the Opinion, in writing, of the principal Officer in each of the executive Departments, upon any Subject relating to the Duties of their respective Offices, and he shall have the Power to grant Reprieves and Pardons for Offences against the United States, except in Cases of Impeachment.

Clause 2 He shall have Power, by and with the Advice and Consent of the Senate to make Treaties, provided two-thirds of the Senators present concur; and he shall nominate, and by and with the Advice and Consent of the Senate, shall appoint Ambassadors, other public Ministers and Consuls, Judges of the supreme Court, and all other Officers of the United States, whose Appointments are not herein otherwise provided for, and which shall be established by Law: but the Congress may by Law vest the Appointment of such inferior Officers, as they think proper, in the President alone, in the Courts of Law, or in the Heads of Departments.

Clause 3 The President shall have Power to fill up all Vacancies that may happen during the Recess of the Senate, by granting Commissions which shall expire at the End of their next Session.

SECTION 3 He shall from time to time give to the Congress Information of the State of the Union, and recommend to their Consideration such Measures as he shall judge necessary and expedient; he may, on extraordinary Occasions, convene both Houses, or either of them and in Case of Disagreement between them, with Respect to the Time of

[7]Changed by the Twelfth and Twentieth Amendments

[8]Modified by the Twenty-fifth Amendment

Adjournment, he may adjourn them to such Time as he shall think proper; he shall receive Ambassadors and other public Ministers; he shall take Care that the Laws be faithfully executed, and shall Commission all the Officers of the United States.

Section 4 The President, Vice President and all civil Officers of the United States, shall be removed from Office on Impeachment for, and Conviction of, Treason, Bribery, or other high Crimes and Misdemeanors.

Article III—The Judicial Article

Judicial Power, Courts, Judges

Section 1 The judicial Power of the United States shall be vested in one supreme Court, and in such inferior Courts as the Congress may from time to time ordain and establish. The Judges, both the supreme and inferior Courts, shall hold their Offices during good Behaviour, and shall, at stated Times, receive for their Services a Compensation, which shall not be diminished during their Continuance in Office.

Jurisdiction

Section 2 The judicial Power shall extend to all Cases, in Law and Equity, arising under this Constitution, the Laws of the United States, and Treaties made, or which shall be made, under their Authority;—to all Cases affecting Ambassadors, other public Ministers and Consuls;—to all Cases of admiralty and maritime Jurisdiction;—to Controversies to which the United States shall be a Party;—to Controversies between two or more States; between a State and Citizens of another State;[9]—between Citizens of different States;—between Citizens of the same State claiming Lands under Grants of different States, and between a State, or the Citizens thereof, and foreign States, Citizens, or Subjects.

In all Cases affecting Ambassadors, other public Ministers and Consuls, and those in which a State shall be Party, the supreme Court shall have original Jurisdiction. In all the other Cases before mentioned, the supreme Court shall have appellate Jurisdiction, both as to Law and Fact, with such Exceptions, and under such Regulations as Congress shall make.

The Trial of all Crimes, except in Cases of Impeachment, shall be by Jury; and such Trial shall be held in the State where the said Crimes shall have been committed; but when not committed within any State, the Trial shall be at such Place or Places as the Congress may by Law have directed.

Treason

Section 3 Treason against the United States, shall consist only in levying War against them, or in adhering to their Enemies, giving them Aid and Comfort. No Person shall be convicted of Treason unless on the Testimony of two Witnesses to the same overt Act, or on Confession in open Court.

The Congress shall have Power to declare the Punishment of Treason, but no Attainder of Treason shall work Corruption of Blood, or Forfeiture except during the Life of the Person attainted.

Article IV—Interstate Relations

Full Faith and Credit Clause

Section 1 Full Faith and Credit shall be given in each State to the public Acts, Records, and judicial Proceedings of every other State. And the Congress may by general Laws prescribe the Manner in which such Acts, Records and Proceedings shall be proved, and the Effect thereof.

Privileges and Immunities; Interstate Extradition

Section 2

Clause 1 The Citizens of each State shall be entitled to all Privileges and Immunities of Citizens in the several States.

Clause 2 A Person charged in any State with Treason, Felony or other Crime, who shall flee from Justice, and be found in another State, shall on Demand of the executive Authority of the State from which he fled, be delivered up, to be removed to the State having Jurisdiction of the Crime.

Clause 3 No person held to Service or Labour in one State, under the Laws thereof, escaping into another, shall, in Consequence of any Law or Regulation therein, be discharged from such Service or Labour, but shall be delivered up on Claim of the Party to whom such Service or Labour may be due.[10]

Admission of States

Section 3 New States may be admitted by the Congress into this Union; but no new State shall be formed or erected within the Jurisdiction of any other State; nor any State to be formed by the Junction of two or more States, or Parts of States, without the Consent of the Legislatures of the States concerned as well as of the Congress.

[9] Modified by the Eleventh Amendment

[10] Repealed by the Thirteenth Amendment

The Congress shall have Power to dispose of and make all needful Rules and Regulations respecting the Territory or other Property belonging to the United States; and nothing in this Constitution shall be so construed as to Prejudice any Claims of the United States, or of any particular State.

Republican Form of Government

SECTION 4 The United States shall guarantee to every State in this Union a Republican Form of Government, and shall protect each of them against Invasion; and on Application of the Legislature, or of the Executive (when the Legislature cannot be convened) against domestic Violence.

Article V—The Amending Power

The Congress, whenever two-thirds of both Houses shall deem it necessary, shall propose Amendments to this Constitution, or, on the Application of the Legislatures of two-thirds of several States, shall call a Convention for proposing Amendments, which, in either Case, shall be valid to all Intents and Purposes, as Part of this Constitution, when ratified by the Legislatures of three-fourths of the several States, or by Conventions in three-fourths thereof, as the one or the other Mode of Ratification may be proposed by the Congress; Provided that no Amendment which may be made prior to the Year One thousand eight hundred and eight shall in any Manner affect the first and fourth Clauses in the Ninth Section of the first Article; and that no State, without its Consent, shall be deprived of its equal Suffrage in the Senate.

Article VI—The Supremacy Act

Clause 1 All Debts contracted and Engagements entered into, before the Adoption of this Constitution, shall be as valid against the United States under the Constitution, as under the Confederation.

Clause 2 This Constitution, and the Laws of the United States which shall be made in Pursuance thereof; and all Treaties made, or which shall be made, under the Authority of the United States, shall be the supreme Law of the Land; and the Judges in every State shall be bound thereby, any Thing in the Constitution or Laws of any State to the Contrary notwithstanding.

Clause 3 The Senators and Representatives before mentioned, and the Members of the several State Legislatures, and all executive and judicial Officers, both of the United States and of the several States, shall be bound by Oath or Affirmation, to support this Constitution; but no religious Test shall ever be required as a Qualification to any Office or public Trust under the United States.

Article VII—Ratification

The Ratification of the Conventions of nine States, shall be sufficient for the Establishment of this Constitution between the States so ratifying the Same.

Done in Convention by the Unanimous Consent of the States present the Seventeenth Day of September in the Year of our Lord one thousand seven hundred and Eighty seven and of the Independence of the United States of America the Twelfth In Witness whereof We have hereunto subscribed our Names.

Amendments

The Bill of Rights

[The first ten amendments were ratified on December 15, 1791, and form what is known as the "Bill of Rights."]

Amendment 1—Religion, Speech, Assembly, and Politics

Congress shall make no law respecting an establishment of religion, or prohibiting the free exercise thereof; or abridging the freedom of speech, or of the press; or the right of the people peaceably to assemble, and to petition the government for a redress of grievances.

Amendment 2—Militia and the Right to Bear Arms

A well-regulated Militia, being necessary to the security of a free State, the right of the people to keep and bear Arms, shall not be infringed.

Amendment 3—Quartering of Soldiers

No Soldier shall, in time of peace be quartered in any house, without the consent of the Owner, nor in time of war, but in manner to be prescribed by law.

Amendment 4—Searches and Seizures

The right of the people to be secure in their persons, houses, papers, and effects, against unreasonable searches and seizures, shall not be violated, and no Warrants shall issue, but upon probable cause, supported by Oath or affirmation, and particularly describing the place to be searched, and the persons or things to be seized.

Amendment 5—Grand Juries, Self-Incrimination, Double Jeopardy, Due Process, and Eminent Domain

No person shall be held to answer for a capital, or otherwise infamous crime, unless on a presentment or indictment of a Grand jury, except in cases arising in the land or naval forces, or in the Militia, when in actual service in time of War or public danger; nor shall any person be subject for the same offence to be twice put in jeopardy of life or limb;

nor shall be compelled in any criminal case to be a witness against himself, nor be deprived of life, liberty, or property, without due process of law; nor shall private property be taken for public use, without just compensation.

Amendment 6—Criminal Court Procedures

In all criminal prosecutions, the accused shall enjoy the right to a speedy and public trial, by an impartial jury of the State and district wherein the crime shall have been committed, which district shall have been previously ascertained by law, and to be informed of the nature and cause of the accusation; to be confronted with the witnesses against him; to have compulsory process for obtaining Witnesses in his favor, and to have the Assistance of Counsel for his defence.

Amendment 7—Trial by Jury in Common Law Cases

In Suits at common law, where the value in controversy shall exceed twenty dollars, the right of trial by jury shall be preserved, and no fact tried by a jury shall be otherwise re-examined in any Court of the United States, than according to the rules of the common law.

Amendment 8—Bail, Cruel and Unusual Punishment

Excessive bail shall not be required, nor excessive fines imposed, nor cruel and unusual punishments inflicted.

Amendment 9—Rights Retained by the People

The enumeration in the Constitution, of certain rights, shall not be construed to deny or disparage others retained by the people.

Amendment 10—Reserved Powers of the States

The powers not delegated to the United States by the Constitution, nor prohibited by it to the States, are reserved to the States respectively, or to the people.

Amendment 11—Suits Against the States [Ratified February 7, 1795]

The Judicial power of the United States shall not be construed to extend to any suit in law or equity, commenced or prosecuted against one of the United States by Citizens of another State, or by Citizens or Subjects of any Foreign State.

Amendment 12—Election of the President [Ratified June 15, 1804]

The Electors shall meet in their respective states, and vote by ballot for President and Vice-President, one of whom, at least, shall not be an inhabitant of the same state with themselves; they shall name in their ballots the person voted for as President, and in distinct ballots the person voted for as Vice-President, and they shall make distinct lists of all persons voted for as President, and of all persons voted for as Vice-President, and of the number of votes for each, which lists they shall sign and certify, and transmit sealed to the seat of the government of the United States, directed to the President of the Senate;—The President of the Senate shall, in presence of the Senate and House of Representatives, open all the certificates and the votes shall then be counted;—The person having the greatest number of votes for President, shall be the President, if such number be a majority of the whole number of Electors appointed; and if no person have such majority, then from the persons having the highest numbers not exceeding three on the list of those voted for as President, the House of Representatives shall choose immediately, by ballot, the President. But in choosing the President, the votes shall be taken by states, the representation from each state having one vote; a quorum for this purpose shall consist of a member or members from two-thirds of the states, and a majority of all states shall be necessary to a choice. And if the House of Representatives shall not choose a President whenever the right of choice shall devolve upon them, before the fourth day of March next following, then the Vice-President shall act as President, as in the case of the death or other constitutional disability of the President.[11] The person having the greatest number of votes as Vice-President, shall be the Vice-President, if such a number be a majority of the whole numbers of Electors appointed, and if no person have a majority, then from the two highest numbers on the list, the Senate shall choose the Vice-President; a quorum for the purpose shall consist of two-thirds of the whole number of Senators, and a majority of the whole number shall be necessary to a choice. But no person constitutionally ineligible to the office of President shall be eligible to that of Vice-President of the United States.

Amendment 13—Prohibition of Slavery [Ratified December 6, 1865]

Section 1 Neither slavery nor involuntary servitude, except as a punishment for crime whereof the party shall have been duly convicted, shall exist within the United States, or any place subject to their jurisdiction.

Section 2 Congress shall have power to enforce this article by appropriate legislation.

Amendment 14—Citizenship, Due Process, and Equal Protection of the Laws [Ratified July 9, 1868]

Section 1 All persons born or naturalized in the United States, and subject to the jurisdiction thereof, are citizens of the United States and of the State wherein they reside. No State shall make or enforce any law which shall

[11] Changed by the Twentieth Amendment

abridge the privileges or immunities of citizens of the United States; nor shall any State deprive any person of life, liberty, or property, without due process of law; nor deny to any person within its jurisdiction the equal protection of the laws.

SECTION 2 Representatives shall be apportioned among the several States according to their respective numbers, counting the whole number of persons in each State, excluding Indians not taxed. But when the right to vote at any election for the choice of electors for President and Vice President of the United States, Representatives in Congress, the Executive and Judicial officers of a State, or the members of the Legislature thereof, is denied to any of the male inhabitants of such State, being twenty-one[12] years of age, and citizens of the United States, or in any way abridged, except for participation in rebellion, or other crime, the basis of representation therein shall be reduced in the proportion which the number of such male citizens shall bear to the whole number of male citizens twenty-one years of age in such State.

SECTION 3 No person shall be a Senator or Representative in Congress, or elector of President and Vice President, or hold any office, civil or military, under the United States, or under any State, who, having previously taken an oath, as a member of Congress, or as an officer of the United States, or as a member of any State legislature, or as an executive or judicial officer of any State, to support the Constitution of the United States, shall have engaged in insurrection or rebellion against the same, or given aid or comfort to the enemies thereof. But Congress may by a vote of two-thirds of each House, remove such disability.

SECTION 4 The validity of the public debt of the United States, authorized by law, including debts incurred for payment of pensions and bounties for services in suppressing insurrection or rebellion, shall not be questioned. But neither the United States nor any State shall assume or pay any debt or obligation incurred in aid of insurrection or rebellion against the United States, or any claim for the loss or emancipation of any slave; but all such debts, obligations and claims shall be held illegal and void.

SECTION 5 The Congress shall have power to enforce, by appropriate legislation, the provisions of this article.

Amendment 15—The Right to Vote [Ratified February 3, 1870]

SECTION 1 The right of citizens of the United States to vote shall not be denied or abridged by the United States or by any State on account of race, color, or previous condition of servitude.

[12]Changed by the Twenty-sixth Amendment

SECTION 2 The Congress shall have power to enforce this article by appropriate legislation.

Amendment 16—Income Taxes [Ratified February 3, 1913]

The Congress shall have power to lay and collect taxes on incomes, from whatever source derived, without apportionment among the several States, and without regard to any census or enumeration.

Amendment 17—Direct Election of Senators [Ratified April 8, 1913]

The Senate of the United States shall be composed of two Senators from each State, elected by the people thereof, for six years; and each Senator shall have one vote. The electors in each State shall have the qualifications requisite for electors of the most numerous branch of the State legislatures.

When vacancies happen in the representation of any State in the Senate, the executive authority of such State shall issue writs of election to fill such vacancies: Provided, That the legislature of any State may empower the executive thereof to make temporary appointment until the people fill the vacancies by election as the legislature may direct. This amendment shall not be so construed as to affect the election or term of any Senator chosen before it becomes valid as part of the Constitution.

Amendment 18—Prohibition [Ratified January 16, 1919. Repealed December 5, 1933, by Amendment 21]

SECTION 1 After one year from the ratification of this article the manufacture, sale, or transportation of intoxicating liquors within, the importation thereof into, or the exportation thereof from the United States and all territory subject to the jurisdiction thereof for beverage purposes is hereby prohibited.

SECTION 2 The Congress and the several states shall have concurrent power to enforce this article by appropriate legislation.

SECTION 3 This article shall be inoperative unless it shall have been ratified as an amendment to the Constitution by the legislatures of the several states, as provided in the Constitution, within seven years from the date of the submission hereof to the States by the Congress.[13]

Amendment 19—For Women's Suffrage [Ratified August 18, 1920]

The right of the citizens of the United States to vote shall not be denied or abridged by the United States or by any State on account of sex.

[13]Repealed by the Twenty-first Amendment

Congress shall have power, by appropriate legislation, to enforce the provision of this article.

Amendment 20—The Lame Duck Amendment [Ratified January 23, 1933]

Section 1 The terms of the President and Vice President shall end at noon on the 20th day of January, and the terms of the Senators and Representatives at noon on the 3rd day of January, of the years in which such terms would have ended if this article had not been ratified, and the terms of their successors shall then begin.

Section 2 The Congress shall assemble at least once in every year, and such meeting shall begin at noon on the 3rd day of January, unless they shall by law appoint a different day.

Section 3 If, at the time fixed for the beginning of the term of the President, the President elect shall have died, the Vice President elect shall become President. If a President shall not have been chosen before the time fixed for the beginning of his term, or if the President elect shall have failed to qualify, then the Vice President elect shall act as President until a President shall have qualified; and the Congress may by law provide for the case wherein neither a President elect nor a Vice President elect shall have qualified, declaring who shall then act as President, or the manner in which one who is to act shall be selected, and such person shall act accordingly until a President or Vice President shall have qualified.

Section 4 The Congress may by law provide for the case of the death of any of the persons from whom the House of Representatives may choose a President whenever the right of choice shall have devolved upon them, and for the case of the death of any of the persons from whom the Senate may choose a Vice President whenever the right of choice shall have devolved upon them.

Section 5 Sections 1 and 2 shall take effect on the 15th day of October following the ratification of this article.

Section 6 This article shall be inoperative unless it shall have been ratified as an amendment to the Constitution by the legislatures of three-fourths of the several States within seven years from the date of its submission.

Amendment 21—Repeal of Prohibition [Ratified December 5, 1933]

Section 1 The eighteenth article of amendment to the Constitution of the United States is hereby repealed.

Section 2 The transportation or importation into any State, Territory, or Possession of the United States for delivery or use therein of intoxicating liquors, in violation of the laws thereof, is hereby prohibited.

Section 3 This article shall be inoperative unless it shall have been ratified as an amendment to the Constitution by conventions in the several States, as provided in the Constitution, within seven years from the date of the submission hereof to the States by the Congress.

Amendment 22—Number of Presidential Terms [Ratified February 27, 1951]

Section 1 No person shall be elected to the office of the President more than twice, and no person who has held the office of President, or acted as President, for more than two years of a term to which some other person was elected President shall be elected to the office of the President more than once. But this Article shall not apply to any person holding the office of President when this article was proposed by the Congress, and shall not prevent any person who may be holding the office of President, or acting as President, during the term within which this Article becomes operative from holding the office of President or acting as President during the remainder of such term.

Section 2 This Article shall be inoperative unless it shall have been ratified as an amendment to the Constitution by the legislatures of three-fourths of the several states within seven years from the date of its submission to the States by the Congress.

Amendment 23—Presidential Electors for the District of Columbia [Ratified March 29, 1961]

Section 1 The District constituting the seat of government of the United States shall appoint in such manner as the Congress may direct:

A number of electors of President and Vice President equal to the whole number of Senators and Representatives in Congress to which the District would be entitled if it were a State, but in no event more than the least populous State; they shall be in addition to those appointed by the States, but they shall be considered for the purposes of the election of President and Vice President, to be electors appointed by a State; and they shall meet in the District and perform such duties as provided by the twelfth article of amendment.

Section 2 The Congress shall have power to enforce this article by appropriate legislation.

Amendment 24—The Anti-Poll Tax Amendment [Ratified January 23, 1964]

Section 1 The right of citizens of the United States to vote in any primary or other election for President or Vice President, for electors for President or Vice President, or for Senator or Representative in Congress, shall not be denied or abridged by the United States or any state by reason of failure to pay any poll tax or other tax.

SECTION 2 The Congress shall have power to enforce this article by appropriate legislation.

Amendment 25—Presidential Disability, Vice Presidential Vacancies [Ratified February 10, 1967]

SECTION 1 In case of the removal of the President from office or his death or resignation, the Vice President shall become President.

SECTION 2 Whenever there is a vacancy in the office of the Vice President, the President shall nominate a Vice President who shall take the office upon confirmation by a majority vote of both Houses of Congress.

SECTION 3 Whenever the President transmits to the President pro tempore of the Senate and the Speaker of the House of Representatives his written declaration that he is unable to discharge the powers and duties of his office, and until he transmits to them a written declaration to the contrary, such powers and duties shall be discharged by the Vice President as Acting President.

SECTION 4 Whenever the Vice President and a majority of either the principal officers of the executive departments, or of such other body as Congress may by law provide, transmit to the President pro tempore of the Senate and the Speaker of the House of Representatives their written declaration that the President is unable to discharge the powers and duties of his office, the Vice President shall immediately assume the powers and duties of the office as Acting President.

Thereafter, when the President transmits to the President pro tempore of the Senate and the Speaker of the House of Representatives his written declaration that no inability exists, he shall resume the powers and duties of his office unless the Vice President and a majority of either the principal officers of the executive departments, or of such other body as Congress may by law provide, transmit within four days to the President pro tempore of the Senate and the Speaker of the House of Representatives their written declaration that the President is unable to discharge the powers and duties of his office. Thereupon Congress shall decide the issue, assembling within forty-eight hours for that purpose if not in session. If the Congress, within twenty-one days after receipt of the latter written declaration, or, if Congress is not in session, within twenty-one days after Congress is required to assemble, determines by two-thirds vote of both houses that the President is unable to discharge the powers and duties of his office, the Vice President shall continue to discharge the same as Acting President; otherwise, the President shall resume the powers and duties of his office.

Amendment 26—Eighteen-Year-Old Vote [Ratified July 1, 1971]

SECTION 1 The right of citizens of the United States, who are 18 years of age, or older, to vote shall not be denied or abridged by the United States or by any state on account of age.

SECTION 2 The Congress shall have power to enforce this article by appropriate legislation.

Amendment 27—Congressional Salaries [Ratified May 7, 1992]

No law, varying the compensation for the services of the Senators and Representatives, shall take effect, until an election of Representatives shall be intervened.

Glossary

24/7 news cycle News is now constantly updated and presented via Internet sites like the *New York Times* or *Wall Street Journal* and cable news sources like CNN, Fox News, and MSNBC.

A

administrative discretion Authority given by Congress to the federal bureaucracy to use reasonable judgment in implementing the laws.

adversary system A judicial system in which the court of law is a neutral arena where two parties argue their differences.

affirmative action Remedial action designed to overcome the effects of discrimination against minorities and women.

All Volunteer Force (AVF) The replacement for the draft (conscription) for recruiting members of the armed services.

American dream A complex set of ideas that holds that the United States is a land of opportunity where individual initiative and hard work can bring economic success.

American exceptionalism The view that due to circumstances of history, the Constitution, and liberty, the United States is different from other nations.

***amicus curiae* brief** Literally a "friend of the court" brief, filed by an individual or organization to present arguments in addition to those presented by the immediate parties to a case.

Anti-Federalists Opponents of ratification of the Constitution and of a strong central government generally.

appellate jurisdiction The authority of a court to review decisions made by lower courts.

apportionment A general term used to describe the assigning of the 435 House seats to the states based on the total U.S. population. All states are guaranteed at least one seat regardless of population.

Articles of Confederation The first governing document of the confederated states, drafted in 1777, ratified in 1781, and replaced by the present Constitution in 1789.

articles of impeachment The formal House document that lists the charges against the president for treason, bribery, or high crimes and misdemeanors.

attitudes An individual's propensity to perceive, interpret, or act toward a particular object in a particular way.

attentive public Citizens who follow public affairs carefully.

B

bad tendency test An interpretation of the First Amendment that would permit legislatures to forbid speech encouraging people to engage in illegal action.

balance of trade The ratio of imports to exports. A negative balance of trade is called a trade deficit, while a positive balance of trade is a trade surplus.

Bible Belt The region of states in the South and states bordering the South with a large number of strongly committed Protestants who see a public role for religion.

bicameralism The division of the legislative branch into two chambers that have the power to check and balance each other.

Bill of Rights The first 10 amendments to the Constitution that provide a guarantee of individual liberties and due process before the law.

Bipartisan Campaign Reform Act (BCRA) Largely banned party soft money, restored a long-standing prohibition on corporations' and labor unions' use of general treasury funds for electoral purposes, and narrowed the definition of issue advocacy.

budget deficit The result of a budget with lower revenues than spending.

bundling A tactic in which PACs collect contributions from like-minded individuals (each limited to $2,000) and present them to a candidate or political party as a "bundle," thus increasing the PAC's influence.

bureaucracy A form of organization that operates through impersonal, uniform rules and procedures.

bureaucrat A negative term for describing a government employee.

Bush Doctrine A policy adopted by the Bush administration in 2001 that asserts America's right to attack any nation that has weapons of mass destruction that may be used against U.S. interests at home or abroad.

C

cabinet An informal advisory group composed of cabinet heads and a handful of agency administrators who meet with the president on occasion.

candidate appeal The tendency in elections to focus on the personal attributes of a candidate, such as his or her strengths, weaknesses, background, experience, and visibility.

capitalism An economic system based on private property, competitive markets, economic incentives, and limited government involvement in the production, pricing, and distribution of goods and services.

casework A source of incumbent advantages based on member efforts to help constituents receive better service and benefits from the federal bureaucracy.

categorical aid Programs that are designed to provide benefits to groups or categories of individuals.

caucus A meeting of local party members to choose party officials or candidates for public office and to decide the platform.

central clearance system The Office of Management and Budget process for overseeing all executive branch communication with Congress.

centralists People who favor national action over action at the state and local levels.

checks and balances A constitutional grant of powers that enables each of the three branches of government to check some acts of the others and therefore ensures that no branch can dominate.

circuit courts of appeals Courts with appellate jurisdiction that hear appeals from the decisions of lower courts.

civil disobedience Deliberate refusal to obey a law or comply with the orders of public officials as a means of expressing opposition.

civil law A law that governs relationships between individuals and defines their legal rights.

civil liberties The constitutional protections of all persons against impermissible governmental restrictions on the freedoms of conscience, religion, and expression, due process guarantees, and fair trial procedures.

civil rights The constitutional rights of all persons to due process and the equal protection of the laws; these include the rights of all people to be free from irrational discrimination such as that based on race, religion, sex, or ethnic origin.

civil service A term that describes federal employees who are hired under a competitive, nonpolitical selection process.

class action suit A lawsuit brought by an individual or a group of people on behalf of all those similarly situated.

clear and present danger test An interpretation of the First Amendment holding that the government cannot interfere with speech unless the speech presents a clear and present danger that it will lead to evil or illegal acts.

closed primary A primary election in which only persons registered in the party holding the primary may vote.

closed shop A company with a labor agreement under which union membership can be a condition of employment.

cloture A procedure for terminating filibusters in the Senate.

coattail effect The boost that candidates may get in an election because of the popularity of candidates above them on the ballot, especially the president.

coattails The ability of a winning presidential candidate to pull party members into Congress by running ahead of them and creating coattails in the general election.

Cold War The 40-year war between the United States and Soviet Union that never involved a direct confrontation.

collective action How groups form and organize to pursue their goals or objectives, including how to get individuals and groups to participate and cooperate. The term has many applications in the various social sciences such as political science, sociology, and economics.

collective bargaining The process in which a union represents a group of employees in negotiations with the employer about wages, benefits, and workplace safety.

commerce clause The clause in the Constitution (Article I, Section 8, Clause 3) that gives Congress the power to regulate all business activities that cross state lines or affect more than one state or other nations.

commercial speech Advertisements and commercials for products and services; they receive less First Amendment protection, primarily to discourage false and misleading ads.

communism A belief that the state owns property in common for all people and a single political party that represents the working classes controls the government.

compliance costs The costs involved in obeying a federal rule.

concurrent powers Powers that the Constitution gives to both the national and state governments, such as the power to levy taxes.

concurring opinion An opinion that agrees with the majority in a Supreme Court ruling but differs on the reasoning.

confederation A constitutional arrangement in which sovereign nations or states, by compact, create a central government but carefully limit its power and do not give it direct authority over individuals.

conference committee A committee appointed by the presiding officers of each chamber to adjust differences on a particular bill passed by each chamber in different form.

Congressional Budget Office (CBO) An agency of Congress that analyzes presidential budget recommendations and estimates the costs of proposed legislation.

Congressional committee Separate units of each chamber of Congress composed of a specific number of members and chartered to examine legislative proposals and conduct oversight of past decisions in specific areas of concern such as appropriations, taxation, the budget, foreign policy, and domestic issues.

Connecticut Compromise The compromise agreement by states at the Constitutional Convention for a bicameral legislature with a lower house in which representation would be based on population and an upper house in which each state would have two senators.

consensus A substantial percentage of a sample that agrees on an issue.

conservatism A belief in private property rights and free enterprise.

Constitutional Convention The convention in Philadelphia, from May 25 to September 17, 1787, that debated and agreed on the Constitution of the United States.

constitutional democracy A government that enforces recognized limits on those who govern and allows the voice of the people to be heard through free, fair, and relatively frequent elections.

consumer price index (CPI) A means of measuring inflation that shows how much more or how much less consumers are paying for the same goods and services over time.

containment A strategy for reducing the threat of war or expansion by strengthening friendly nations and diplomatic pressure.

content or viewpoint neutrality Laws that apply to all kinds of speech and to all views, not only that which is unpopular or divisive.

criminal law A law that defines crimes against the public order.

cross-cutting cleavages Divisions within society that cut across demographic categories to produce groups that are more heterogeneous or different.

crossover voting Voting by a member of one party for a candidate of another party.

D

dealignment Weakening of partisan preferences that point to a rejection of both major parties and a rise in the number of Independents.

decentralists People who favor state or local action rather than national action.

de facto segregation Segregation resulting from economic or social conditions or personal choice.

defendant In a civil or criminal action, the person or party accused of an offense.

de jure segregation Segregation imposed by law.

delegate A person selected by local citizens to represent them in selecting party leaders and nominees, and in deciding party positions.

delegated powers Powers given to the national government.

deliberation The idea of people coming together, listening to each other, exchanging ideas, learning to appreciate each other's differences, and defending their opinions.

democracy Government by the people, where citizens through free and frequent elections elect those who govern and pass laws or where citizens vote directly on laws.

demography The study of the characteristics of human populations.

depression A much deeper form of a recession that lasts longer and is more destructive.

deregulation movement The effort starting in the late 1970s to reduce rules in the airline, trucking, railroad, banking, and other heavily regulated industries.

devolve To return national powers to the states.

direct democracy Government in which citizens vote on laws and select officials directly.

direct primary An election in which voters choose party nominees.

discretionary spending The portion of the federal budget that is spent on programs that Congress and the president can change from year to year.

dissenting opinion An opinion disagreeing with the majority in a Supreme Court ruling.

distributive policy A public policy such as Social Security that provides benefits to all groups in society.

district courts Courts in which criminal and civil cases are originally tried in the federal judicial system.

divided government Governance divided between the parties, especially when one holds the presidency and the other controls one or both houses of Congress.

double jeopardy Trial or punishment for the same crime by the same government; forbidden by the Constitution.

draft Also known as conscription, the draft is a method for recruiting military troops by forcing all American males to register for service.

dual citizenship Citizenship in more than one nation.

due process Established rules and regulations that restrain government officials.

due process clause A clause in the Fifth Amendment limiting the power of the national government; a similar clause in the Fourteenth Amendment prohibits state governments from depriving any person of life, liberty, or property without due process of law.

E

earmarks Special spending projects that are set aside on behalf of individual members of Congress for their constituents.

economic sanctions Denial of export, import, or financial relations with a target country in an effort to change that nation's policies.

Electoral College The electoral system used in electing the president and vice president, in which voters vote for electors pledged to cast their ballots for a particular party's candidates.

eminent domain The power of a government to take private property for public use; the U.S. Constitution gives national and state governments this power and requires them to provide just compensation for property so taken.

entitlement aid/entitlement programs Programs such as unemployment insurance, disaster relief, and disability payments that provide benefits to all eligible citizens.

enumerated powers Powers that are specifically given to a branch of the national government; sometimes called "express powers."

equal opportunity All individuals, regardless of race, gender, or circumstance, have the opportunity to participate in politics, self-government, and the economy.

equal protection clause A clause in the Fourteenth Amendment that forbids any state to deny to any person within its jurisdiction the equal protection of the laws. By interpretation, the Fifth Amendment imposes the same limitation on the national government. This clause is the major constitutional restraint on the power of governments to discriminate against persons because of race, national origin, or sex.

establishment clause A clause in the First Amendment stating that Congress shall make no law respecting an establishment of religion. The Supreme Court has interpreted this to forbid direct governmental support to any or all religions.

ethnicity A social division based on national origin, religion, language, and often race.

ethnocentrism Belief in the superiority of one's nation or ethnic group.

exclusionary rule A requirement that evidence unconstitutionally or illegally obtained be excluded from a criminal trial.

executive action A presidential directive to a federal government agency or agencies that tells government how to faithfully interpret and execute the laws. The term covers a range of formal and informal presidential decisions that can change the government's direction; some executive actions involve signed orders that carry the force of law in telling the government exactly what it should or should not do regarding a specific issue.

executive agreement A binding pact between the U.S. president and an international leader or leaders that does not require Senate approval.

executive memorandum A formal instruction that acts like an executive order, but that is much less visible to the public and potentially more significant in shaping broad policies.

executive order A presidential directive to a federal government agency or agencies that implements or interprets a federal statute, a constitutional provision, or a treaty.; executive orders carry the force of law but can be revoked by the next president.

Executive Office of the President (EOP) Created in 1939, the EOP contains the president's most important staff support, including the Office of the White House, National Security Staff, and Office of Management and Budget.

executive privilege A constitutionally supported right that allows presidents the right to keep executive communications confidential.

ex post facto law A retroactive criminal law that works to the disadvantage of a person.

evolutionary approach A method used to interpret the Constitution that understands the document to be flexible and responsive to the changing needs of the times.

F

faction A term the founders used to refer to political parties and special interests or interest groups.

faithless elector In the Electoral College an elector who does not vote for the candidate who should receive the electoral vote based on the popular vote in the presidential election in his or her state or district is a faithless elector.

Federal Election Commission (FEC) A commission created by the 1974 amendments to the Federal Election Campaign Act to administer election reform laws. It consists of six commissioners appointed by the president and confirmed by the Senate. Its duties include overseeing disclosure of campaign finance information, public funding of presidential elections, and enforcing contribution limits.

federal funds rate The prime rate of interest that premier banks have to pay the Federal Reserve to borrow money.

federalism A constitutional arrangement in which power is distributed between a central government and states, which are sometimes called provinces in other nations. Both the national government and the states exercise direct authority over individuals.

Federalists A group that argued for ratification of the Constitution, including a stronger national government at the expense of states' power. They controlled the new federal government until Thomas Jefferson's election in 1800.

The Federalist Essays promoting ratification of the Constitution, published anonymously by Alexander Hamilton, John Jay, and James Madison in 1787 and 1788.

Federal Register An official document, published every weekday that lists the new and proposed regulations of executive departments and regulatory agencies.

Federal Reserve Board The independent regulatory commission created by Congress in 1913 to establish banking practices and regulate currency in circulation and the amount of credit available. The "Fed" consists of 12 regional banks supervised by a chair and a board of governors.

fighting words Words that by their very nature inflict injury on those to whom they are addressed or incite them to acts of violence.

filibuster A procedural practice in the Senate whereby a senator refuses to relinquish the floor and thereby delays proceedings and prevents a vote on a controversial issue.

fire alarm oversight Oversight that is triggered by urgent events or highly visible government failures.

fiscal policy Government spending and taxation policies that affect economic performance.

franking privilege A free postage Congressional members receive by simply putting their signature, or frank, on any mail back home.

free exercise clause A clause in the First Amendment stating that Congress shall make no law prohibiting the free exercise of religion.

free rider An individual who does not join a group representing his or her interests yet receives the benefit of the group's influence.

full faith and credit clause The clause in the Constitution (Article IV, Section 1) requiring each state to recognize the civil judgments rendered by the courts of the other states and to accept their public records and acts as valid.

fundamentalists Conservative Christians who, as a group, have become more active in politics in the last two decades and were especially influential in the 2000 and 2004 presidential elections.

G

gender gap The difference between the political opinions or political behavior of men and of women.

general election Election in which voters elect officeholders.

gerrymandering The drawing of legislative district boundaries to benefit a party, group, or incumbent.

going public A presidential strategy for increasing public approval by reaching out to congressional constituents by going over the heads of the Washington media and interest groups.

government The processes and institutions through which binding decisions are made for a society.

grand jury A jury of 12 to 23 persons, depending on state and local requirements, who privately hear evidence presented by the government to determine whether persons shall be required to stand trial. If the jury believes there is sufficient evidence that a crime was committed, it issues an indictment.

gross domestic product (GDP) The value of all goods and services produced by an economy during a specific period of time such as a year.

H

Hatch Act A federal statute barring federal employees from active participation in certain kinds of politics and protecting them from being fired on partisan grounds.

hard money Political contributions given to a party, candidate, or interest group that are limited in amount and fully disclosed. Raising such limited funds was harder than raising unlimited soft money, hence the term *hard money*.

hard power The use of military and economic action to achieve foreign and defense policy goals

heightened scrutiny test This test has been applied when a law classifies based on sex; to be upheld, the law must meet an important government interest.

honeymoon The first six months or so of a new presidential administration when the president enjoys generally positive relations with the press and Congress, his or her supporters are still celebrating victory, and the public focuses on the inaugural festivities and presidential agenda.

horse race A close contest; by extension, any contest in which the focus is on who is ahead and by how much rather than on substantive differences between the candidates.

I

idealism A theory of international relations that focuses on the hope that nations will act together to solve international problems and promote peace.

impeachment A process for removing the president, judges, and other civil officials from office for committing treason, bribery, and other high crimes and misdemeanors. The House is responsible for approving the articles of impeachment by a majority vote, while the Senate is responsible for convicting or acquitting the president by a two-thirds vote.

impeachment power The formal charges of treason, bribery, or other high crimes and misdemeanors against the president, judges and other civil officials enacted by the House by majority vote.

implementation The process of putting a law into practice through bureaucratic rules or spending.

implied powers Broad and unwritten powers that Congress uses to carry out its enumerated powers.

impoundment A decision by the president not to spend money appropriated by Congress, now prohibited under federal law.

income inequality The difference in wealth between the richest and poorest Americans as measured by the sum of an individual's cash, property, investments, retirement support, and other economic instruments.

incremental policy A policy that makes small-scale adjustments to an existing public policy or the budget.

incumbency advantage The electoral strength that incumbent members of Congress gain through increased visibility, popularity, and campaign funding.

independent expenditures The Supreme Court has ruled that individuals, groups, and parties can spend unlimited amounts in campaigns for or against candidates as long as they operate independently from the candidates. When an individual, group, or party does so, they are making an independent expenditure.

independent regulatory commission A government agency or commission with regulatory power whose independence is protected by Congress.

indictment A formal written statement from a grand jury charging an individual with an offense; also called a *true bill.*

inflation A rise in the general price of a market basket of products.

in forma pauperis A petition that allows a party to file "as a pauper" and avoid paying Court fees.

inherent powers Broad and unwritten powers of the national government essential for protecting the nation from domestic and foreign threats. An unwritten extension of the take care clause that presidents occasionally use to claim authority to take action without congressional or judicial authority.

initiative A procedure whereby a certain number of voters may, by petition, propose a law or constitutional amendment and have it submitted to the voters.

inner cabinet The four departments of government that are most important to the president: Defense, Justice, Treasury, and State.

intelligence community The group of 16 intelligence agencies that provide information on threats to the nation.

intensity A measure of how strongly an individual holds a particular opinion.

interest group A collection of people who share a common interest or attitude and seek to influence government for specific ends. Interest groups usually work within the framework of government and try to achieve their goals through tactics such as lobbying.

internationalism The belief that nations must engage in international problem solving.

iron triangle A policy-making instrument composed of a tightly related alliance of a congressional committee, interest groups, and a federal department or agency.

isolationism The desire to avoid international engagement altogether.

issue advocacy Promoting a particular position or an issue paid for through unlimited and undisclosed spending by interest groups or individuals but not candidates. Much issue advocacy is often electioneering for or against a candidate, avoiding words like "vote for" or "vote against," and until 2004 had not been subject to any regulation.

issue-attention cycle The movement of public opinion toward public policy from initial enthusiasm for action to realization of costs and a decline in interest.

issue network Relationships among interest groups, congressional committees and subcommittees, and the government agencies that share a common policy concern.

J

Jim Crow laws State laws formerly pervasive throughout the South requiring public facilities and accommodations to be segregated by race; ruled unconstitutional.

Joint Chiefs of Staff The committee composed of the military heads of the armed forces that serves as the principal source of military advice to the president, the National Security Council, and the secretary of defense. The chairman of the Joint Chiefs is the highest-ranked military adviser in the United States.

judicial activism A philosophy proposing that judges should freely strike down laws enacted by the democratically elected branches.

justiciable dispute A dispute growing out of an actual case or controversy that is capable of settlement by legal methods.

judicial restraint A philosophy proposing that judges should strike down the actions of the elected branches only if they clearly violate the Constitution.

judicial review The power of a court to review laws or governmental regulations to determine whether they are consistent with the U.S. Constitution, or in a state court, the state constitution.

K

Keynesian economics An economic theory based on the principles of John Maynard Keynes stating that government spending should increase during business slumps and be curbed during booms.

L

laissez-faire economics A theory that opposes governmental interference in economic affairs beyond what is necessary to protect life and property.

latency Political opinions that are held but not yet expressed.

legal privileges Rights granted by governments that may be subject to substantial conditions or restrictions, such as the right to welfare benefits or to have a driver's license.

libel Written defamation of another person. For public officials and public figures, the constitutional tests designed to restrict libel actions are especially rigid.

liberalism A belief that government can bring about justice and equality of opportunity.

libertarianism Would limit government to such vital activities as national defense while fostering individual liberty. Unlike conservatives, libertarians oppose all government regulation, even of personal morality.

line item veto A form of veto that allows the president to strike, or veto, specific provisions within a bill before signing it into law. The line item veto was declared unconstitutional in 1998.

literacy test A literacy requirement some states imposed as a condition of voting, generally used to disqualify black voters in the South; now illegal.

lobbyist A person who is employed by and acts for an organized interest group or corporation to try to influence policy decisions and positions in the executive and legislative branches.

lobbying Engaging in activities aimed at influencing public officials, especially legislators, and the policies they enact.

M

majority–minority district A congressional district created to include a majority of minority voters; ruled constitutional so long as race is not the main factor in redistricting.

majority rule Governance according to the expressed preferences of the majority.

mandate A postelection claim that the public has given its support to the president's agenda for action, but a claim that is credible only if the president has enough election votes to prove it, and the public approval and party seats in Congress to enforce it.

manifest destiny A notion held by nineteenth-century Americans that the United States was destined to rule the continent, from the Atlantic to the Pacific.

manifest opinion A widely shared and consciously held view, such as support for abortion rights or for homeland security.

margin of error The range of percentage points in which the sample accurately reflects the population.

means-tested entitlement aid Programs such as Medicaid and the Supplemental Nutrition Assistance Program that provide aid only to individuals or families that can show they do not have any other means to assist themselves.

member caucus A meeting of the members of a party in a legislative chamber to select party leaders and to develop party policy.

merit system A system of public employment in which selection and promotion depend on demonstrated performance rather than political patronage.

midterm election Election held midway between presidential elections.

military-industrial complex The collection of government defense agencies and the private firms who supply key equipment, advice, supplies, and contractors.

minor party A small political party that persists over time that is often composed of ideologies on the right or left, or centered on a charismatic candidate. Such a party is also called a *third party*.

monetary policy Government policies designed to control the supply of money through the economy.

monopoly Domination of an industry by a single company; also the company that dominates the industry.

multilateralism A philosophy that encourages nations to act together when facing threats from other nations.

mutual assured destruction (MAD) A theory of deterrence that is based on creating enough nuclear weapons that warring nations would survive early strikes long enough to fire back, thereby assuring the end of the world.

N

name recognition Incumbents have an advantage over challengers in election campaigns because voters are more familiar with them, and incumbents are more recognizable.

nation building A foreign policy goal to promote democracy by helping individual nations create democratic government.

national debt The cumulative amount of money the federal government owes for past borrowing.

national mandates Requirements the national government imposes as a condition for receiving national funds.

national party convention A national meeting of delegates elected in primaries, caucuses, or state conventions who assemble once every four years to nominate candidates for president and vice president, ratify the party platform, elect officers, and adopt rules.

National Security Council The White House group that is responsible for advising the president on key foreign and defense policy. The Council is headed by the National Security Advisor, who sits just down the hall from the president.

national tide The inclination to focus on national issues, rather than local issues, in an election campaign. The impact of a national tide can be reduced by the nature of the candidates on the ballot who may have differentiated themselves from their party or its leader if the tide is negative, as well as competition in the election.

naturalization A legal action conferring citizenship on an immigrant.

natural rights The rights of all people to dignity and worth; also called *human rights.*

Necessary and Proper Clause The constitutional authority given to Congress to make all laws deemed necessary and proper for executing its duties.

New Jersey Plan The proposal at the Constitutional Convention made by William Paterson of New Jersey for a central government with a single-house legislature in which each state would be represented equally.

news media Means of communication about the news that reach the public, including newspapers and magazines, radio, television (broadcast, cable, and satellite), and electronic communication.

nongovernmental organization (NGO) A nonprofit association or group operating outside government that advocates and pursues policy objectives.

nonpartisan election An election in which candidates are not selected or endorsed by political parties, and party affiliation is not listed on ballots.

North American Free Trade Agreement (NAFTA) An agreement signed by the United States, Canada, and Mexico in 1992 to form the largest free trade zone in the world.

nuclear disarmament The effort to reduce the number of nuclear weapons.

O

objective civilian control The general philosophy that the military should be insulated from political interference of any kind.

obscenity The quality or state of a work that, taken as a whole, appeals to a prurient interest in sex by depicting sexual conduct in a patently offensive way and that lacks serious literary, artistic, political, or scientific value.

Office of Management and Budget (OMB) The presidential staff agency that serves as a clearinghouse for budgetary requests and management improvements for government agencies. The OMB drafts the president's annual budget message to Congress and oversees the basic operations of the executive branch.

open primary A primary election in which any voter, regardless of party, may vote.

open shop A company with a labor agreement under which union membership cannot be required as a condition of employment.

opinion of the Court An explanation of a decision of the Supreme Court or any other appellate court.

original jurisdiction A court's authority to hear a case for the first time, as a trial.

originalist approach An approach to constitutional interpretation that envisions the document as having a fixed meaning that might be determined by a strict reading of the text or the Framers' intent.

outer cabinet The departments of government that are less important to the president than those in the inner cabinet.

oversight Legislative or executive review of a particular government program or organization that can be in response to a crisis of some kind or part of routine review.

P

parliamentary government A form of government in which the chief executive is the leader of the majority party in the legislature.

partisanship Strong allegiance to one's own political party, often leading to unwillingness to compromise with members of the opposing party.

party convention A meeting of party delegates to vote on matters of policy and, in some cases, to select party candidates for public office.

party identification An affiliation with a political party that most people acquire in childhood. The best predictor of voting behavior in partisan candidate elections.

party-independent expenditures Spending by political party committees that is independent of the candidate. The spending occurs in relatively few competitive contests and is often substantial.

party registration The act of declaring party affiliation; required by some states to vote in a party's primary.

patronage The dispensing of government jobs to persons who belong to the winning political party.

pay-as-you-go rule (PAYGO) A rule created in 1990 that requires Congress to pay for any new spending by either reducing spending elsewhere in the budget or raising revenue.

petit jury A jury of 6 to 12 persons that determines whether a defendant is found guilty in a civil or criminal action.

plaintiff The party instigating a civil lawsuit.

platform Every four years the national political parties draft a document stating the policy positions of the party. This party platform details general party-wide issue stances. The process sometimes engenders disputes among fellow partisans but is rarely an election issue and often is written to avoid controversy.

plea bargain An agreement between a prosecutor and a defendant that the defendant will plead guilty to a lesser offense to avoid having to stand trial for a more serious offense.

pluralism A theory of government that holds that open, multiple, and competing groups can check the asserted power of any one group.

plurality rule The candidate or party with the most votes wins an election, not necessarily more than half.

pocket veto A veto exercised by the president after Congress has adjourned; if the president takes no action for 10 days, the bill does not become law and is not returned to Congress for a possible override.

polarized A wide, intense difference between two opposing sides regarding an issue; often used to describe public opinion regarding an issue.

police patrol oversight Oversight that is triggered by regular, noncontroversial contact with the federal bureaucracy through the authorization and appropriations process.

policy agenda The list of congressional and presidential priorities that are being considered for action.

political action committee (PAC) The political arm of an interest group that is legally entitled to raise funds on a voluntary basis from members, stockholders, or employees to contribute funds to candidates or political parties.

political capital The political influence a president can use to push forward on the legislative agenda; it is generally composed of public approval and party seats in Congress, and is expended over time.

political culture The widely shared beliefs, values, and norms citizens hold about their relationship to government and to one another.

political ideology A constant pattern of ideas or beliefs about political values and the role of government, including how it should work and how it actually does work.

political party An organization that seeks political power by electing people to office so that its positions and philosophy become public policy.

political socialization The process—most notably in families and schools—by which we develop our political attitudes, values, and beliefs.

politician An individual who participates in politics and government, often in the service of a group or political community.

politics The process by which decisions are made and carried out within and among nations, groups, and individuals.

poll tax Tax required to vote; prohibited for national elections by the Twenty-fourth Amendment (1964) and ruled unconstitutional for all elections in *Harper* v. *Board of Elections* (1966).

popular consent The idea that a just government must derive its powers from the consent of the people it governs.

popular sovereignty The idea that ultimate political authority rests with the people.

poverty A measure used in economic and social policy that is generally defined as the lack of enough money to maintain a minimum quality of life.

power of the purse The congressional power to appropriate and raise money for government programs and administration.

precedent A decision made by a higher court such as a circuit court of appeals or the Supreme Court that is binding on all other federal courts.

preemption A policy of taking action before the United States is attacked rather than waiting for provocation (in foreign and defense policy); the right of a national law or regulation to preclude enforcement of a state or local law or regulation (in federalism).

preferred position doctrine An interpretation of the First Amendment that holds that freedom of expression is so essential to democracy that governments should not punish persons for what they say, only for what they do.

presidential election Election held in a year when the president is on the ballot.

presidential support score The most frequently used measure of a president's success in convincing Congress to act; the score measures the president's percentage of victories on key votes.

presidential ticket A requirement created under the Twelfth Amendment in 1803 that requires the presidential and vice presidential candidates of the same party to run for election as a single choice.

primary election Election in which voters determine party nominees.

prime minister In the United Kingdom, the leader of a parliamentary government elected by the majority party in the House of Commons, which is the lower house of the parliament.

prior restraint Censorship imposed before a speech is made or a newspaper is published; usually presumed to be unconstitutional.

procedural due process A constitutional requirement that governments proceed by proper methods; limits how government may exercise power.

professional associations Groups of individuals who share a common profession and are often organized for common political purposes related to that profession.

progressive tax A tax that falls more heavily on individuals with higher incomes.

property rights The rights of an individual to own, use, rent, invest in, buy, and sell property.

proportional representation An election system in which each party running receives the proportion of legislative seats corresponding to its proportion of the vote.

prosecutor Government lawyer who tries criminal cases, often referred to as a district attorney or a U.S. attorney.

prospective issue voting Voting based on what a candidate pledges to do in the future about an issue if elected.

protectionism A policy of erecting trade barriers to protect domestic industry.

public assistance A traditional term used to describe government programs to aid the poor.

public choice Synonymous with "collective action," specifically studies how government officials, politicians, and voters respond to positive and negative incentives.

public defender system An arrangement whereby public officials are hired to provide legal assistance to people accused of crimes who are unable to hire their own attorneys.

public opinion The distribution of individual preferences for or evaluations of a given issue, candidate, or institution within a specific population.

public policy A specific course of action that government takes to address a problem.

Q

R

race A grouping of human beings with distinctive characteristics determined by genetic inheritance.

racial gerrymandering Drawing election districts so as to ensure that members of a certain race are a minority in the district; ruled unconstitutional in *Gomillion* v. *Lightfoot* (1960).

rally point A significant jump in presidential approval that occurs during a national crisis; the term refers to the tendency of Americans to "rally 'round the flag" and the chief executive when the nation is in trouble.

random sample In this type of sample, every individual has a known and equal chance of being selected.

rational basis test A standard developed by the courts to test the constitutionality of a law; when applied, a law is constitutional as long as it meets a reasonable government interest.

realigning election An election during periods of expanded suffrage and change in the economy and society that proves to be a turning point, redefining the agenda of politics and the alignment of voters within parties.

realism A theory of international relations that suggests a nation's primary goal is to maintain its power and security.

reapportionment The reassignment of the 435 House seats to the states based on the most recent census of the U.S. population.

recall A procedure for submitting to popular vote the removal of officials from office before the end of their term.

recess appointment A type of presidential appointment that allows the president to appoint principal officers of government when the Senate is recessed.

recession Negative GDP that lasts two quarters or more.

redistributive policy A policy that provides to one group of society while taking away benefits from another through policy solutions such as tax increases to pay for job training.

redistricting The division of the total number of House seats within a state into specific districts based on an equal number of citizens per district. State legislatures are responsible for redistricting.

referendum A procedure for submitting to popular vote measures passed by the legislature or proposed amendments to a state constitution.

regressive tax A tax that falls equally on all taxpayers regardless of income.

regulatory taking A government regulation that effectively takes land by restricting its use, even if it remains in the owner's name.

reinforcing cleavages Divisions within society that reinforce one another, making groups more homogeneous or similar.

representative democracy Government in which the people elect those who govern and pass laws; also called a republic.

republic Government in which the power is held by the people and their elected representatives.

reserve powers All powers not specifically delegated to the national government by the Constitution. The reserve power can be found in the Tenth Amendment to the Constitution.

restrictive covenant A provision in a deed to real property prohibiting its sale to a person of a particular race or religion. Judicial enforcement of such deeds is unconstitutional.

retrospective issue voting Holding incumbents, usually the president's party, responsible for their records on issues, such as the economy or foreign policy.

revolving door An employment cycle in which individuals who work for government agencies that regulate interests eventually end up working for interest groups or businesses with the same policy concern.

right of expatriation The right to renounce one's citizenship.

rural Sparsely populated territory and small towns, often associated with farming.

rule A precise statement of how a law is implemented.

rule making process The detailed process for drafting a rule.

Rust Belt States in the Midwest once known for their industrial output, which have seen factories close and have experienced relatively high unemployment.

S

safe seat An elected office that is predictably won by one party or the other, so the success of that party's candidate is almost taken for granted.

salience An individual's belief that an issue is important or relevant to him or her.

search warrant A writ issued by a magistrate that authorizes the police to search a particular place or person, specifying the place to be searched and the objects to be seized.

Section 501(c) groups Section 501(c) groups are organized under this section of the Internal Revenue Code. Some of these groups have spent heavily in recent campaigns. Because donors to these groups are not disclosed they are attractive to some donors.

selective exposure Individuals choosing to access media with which they agree or avoiding media with which they disagree.

selective incorporation The process by which provisions of the Bill of Rights are brought within the scope of the Fourteenth Amendment and so applied to state and local governments.

selective perception The process by which individuals perceive what they want in news media messages.

senatorial courtesy The presidential custom of submitting the names of prospective appointees for approval to senators from the states in which the appointees are to work.

Senior Executive Service Established by Congress in 1978 as a flexible, mobile corps of senior career executives who work closely with presidential appointees to manage government.

seniority rule A legislative practice that assigns the chair of a committee or subcommittee to the member of the majority party with the longest continuous service on the committee.

separation of powers Constitutional division of powers among the legislative, executive, and judicial branches, with the legislative branch making law, the executive applying and enforcing the law, and the judiciary interpreting the law.

Shays' Rebellion A rebellion led by Daniel Shays of farmers in western Massachusetts in 1786–1787 protesting mortgage foreclosures. It highlighted the need for a strong national government just as the call for the Constitutional Convention went out.

single-member district An electoral district in which voters choose one representative or official.

single-payer system A payment system that involves one source of funding, such as the federal government.

signing statement A statement issued by a president refusing to implement a provision of a law deemed unconstitutional or a violation of presidential powers.

social capital The value of social contacts, associations, and networks individuals form that can foster trust, coordination, and cooperation.

social conservatives Focus less on economics and more on morality and lifestyle.

social insurance Social programs that guarantee government support for use at some future point in time. Most, but not all, social insurance programs require contributions such as paying taxes in advance.

socialism A governmental system where some of the means of production are controlled by the state and where the state provides key human welfare services like health care and old-age assistance. Allows for free markets in other activities.

social movement A large body of people interested in a common issue, idea, or concern that is of continuing significance and who are willing to take action. Movements seek to change attitudes or institutions, not just policies.

social safety net The intent of federal programs that are designed to protect individuals and families that face economic hardship; programs to help the needy and less fortunate.

socioeconomic status (SES) A division of population based on occupation, income, and education.

soft money Money raised in unlimited amounts by political parties for party-building purposes. Now largely illegal except for limited contributions to state or local parties for voter registration and get-out-the-vote efforts.

soft power The use of encouragement, persuasion, and recognition to show other countries the value of American ideals, culture, and values.

sole organ doctrine A belief that the president is the sole voice in making foreign and defense policy.

solicitor general The third-ranking official in the Department of Justice who is responsible for representing the United States in cases before the U.S. Supreme Court.

Speaker of the House The presiding officer in the House of Representatives, formally elected by the House but selected by the majority party.

spoils system A system of public employment based on rewarding party loyalists and friends.

stare decisis The rule of precedent, whereby a rule or law contained in a judicial decision is commonly viewed as binding on judges whenever the same question is presented.

states' rights Powers expressly or implicitly reserved to the states.

strict scrutiny test A test applied by the court when a classification is based on race; the government must show that there is a compelling reason for the law and no other less restrictive way to meet the interest.

substantive due process A constitutional requirement that governments act reasonably and that the substance of the laws themselves be fair and reasonable; limits what a government may do.

suburban An area that typically surrounds the central city, is often residential, and is not as densely populated.

Sun Belt The region of the United States in the South and Southwest that has seen population growth relative to the rest of the country and which, because of its climate, has attracted retirees.

superdelegate Delegates to national party nominating conventions who are not selected through the normal caucus or primary process. They are often state or local party leaders or elected officials.

Super PAC Independent expenditure-only PACs are known as Super PACs because they may accept donations of any size and can endorse candidates. Their contributions and expenditures must be periodically reported to the FEC

supremacy clause Contained in Article IV of the Constitution, the clause gives national laws the absolute power even when states have enacted a competing law.

T

take care clause A constitutional requirement that presidents take care that the laws are executed faithfully.

tax expenditures Spending that occurs through tax deductions and incentives that are largely hidden from public view.

theocracy A form of government in which a deity is recognized as the supreme civil ruler, but the deity's laws are interpreted by ecclesiastical authorities.

theory of deterrence The belief that massive military force will deter other nations from threatening the nation. Originally developed to deter nuclear war between the United States and Soviet Union during the Cold War.

three-fifths compromise The compromise between northern and southern states at the Constitutional Convention that three-fifths of the slave population would be counted for determining direct taxation and representation in the House of Representatives.

treaty A formal agreement between the United States and other nations that requires a two-thirds vote of approval from the Senate.

trustees An official who is expected to vote independently based on his or her judgment of the circumstances; one interpretation of the role of the legislator.

turnout The proportion of the voting-age public that votes, sometimes defined as the number of registered voters that vote.

U

uncontrollable spending The portion of the federal budget that must be spent on programs that provide guaranteed benefits.

unemployment The number of Americans who are out of work but actively looking for a job.

unified government Governance in which one party controls both the White House and both houses of Congress.

unilateralism A philosophy that encourages individual nations to act on their own when facing threats from other nations.

unitary executive An assertion that presidents have complete authority to exercise any and all powers they deem appropriate to protect the nation from imminent threats.

unitary system A constitutional arrangement that concentrates power in a central government.

United Nations An international organization composed of the 193 nations that was established in 1945 to help the world resolve disputes and maintain peace.

universe The group of people whose preferences we try to measure by taking a sample; also called population.

unprotected speech Libel, obscenity, and fighting words, which are not entitled to constitutional protection in all circumstances.

urban A densely settled territory that is often the central part of a city or metropolitan area.

U.S. attorney general The chief law enforcement officer in the United States and the head of the Department of Justice.

U.S. Supreme Court The court of last resort in the United States. It can hear appeals from federal circuit courts or state high courts.

V

vesting clause A constitutional provision in Article II that gives the president authority to execute the laws.

veto A formal decision to reject a bill passed by Congress.

Virginia Plan The initial proposal at the Constitutional Convention made by the Virginia delegation for a strong central government with a bicameral legislature dominated by the big states.

voter registration A system designed to reduce voter fraud by limiting voting to those who have established eligibility to vote by submitting the proper documents, including proof of residency.

W

war on terrorism The effort to attack and destroy terrorist networks and leaders.

War Powers Resolution A 1973 law that limits the presidential use of U.S. military power without (1) a prior declaration of war by Congress, (2) a congressional resolution approving the use of force, or (3) an emergency.

weapons of mass destruction Biological, chemical, or nuclear weapons that can cause a massive number of deaths in a single use.

White House chief of staff The president's most trusted staff aide in the White House.

white primary A Democratic Party primary in the old "one-party South" that was limited to white people and essentially constituted an election; ruled unconstitutional in *Smith* v. *Allwright* (1944).

winner-take-all system An election system in which the candidate with the most votes wins.

women's suffrage The right of women to vote.

World Trade Organization (WTO) An international organization with more than 170 members that seeks to encourage free trade by setting rules for fair competition.

writ of *certiorari* A formal writ used to bring a case before the Supreme Court.

writ of *habeas corpus* A court order requiring explanation to a judge of why a prisoner is being held in custody.

Notes

CHAPTER 1

1. Mayflower Compact (1620), http://avalon.law.yale.edu/17th_century/mayflower.asp.
2. Louis Hartz, *The Liberal Tradition in America* (New York: Harcourt, Brace, and World, Inc., 1955), p. 63; see also Jack Citrin, "Political Culture," in Peter H. Schuck and James Q. Wilson, eds., *Understanding America: The Anatomy of an Exceptional Nation* (New York: Public Affairs, 2008), pp. 147–148.
3. *New African Magazine*, "Nigeria: Nine Constitutions in 24 Years of Democracy!" November 23, 2013, http://newafricanmagazine.com/nigeria-nine-constitutions-in-24-years-of-democracy/. For a summary of constitutions across nations see: Webster University, "Lists of Constitutions and Some Provisions," http://faculty.webster.edu/corbetre/haiti/misctopic/constitution/listof.htm.
4. Thomas Jefferson, *The Works of Thomas Jefferson, vol. 5 (Correspondence 1786–1789)*, p. 256. Edited by Paul Leicester Ford. Published 1905. Accessed online at http://oll.libertyfund.org/titles/jefferson-the-works-vol-5-correspondence-1786-1789.
5. David Boaz, "The Man Who Would Not Be King," *CATO Institute*, February 20, 2006, http://www.cato.org/pub_display.php?pub_id=5593.
6. Russell J. Dalton, "Citizenship Norms and Political Participation in America: The Good News Is ... the Bad News Is Wrong," Center for the Study of Democracy, June 2006.
7. Pew Research Center, "Beyond Distrust: How Americans View Their Government," November 23, 2015, available at http://www.people-press.org/2015/11/23/beyond-distrust-how-americans-view-their-government/.
8. *Strauss* v. *Horton*, 46 Cal. 4th 364, 93 Cal. Rptr. 3d 591, 207 P.3d 48 (2009).
9. *Perry* v. *Schwarzenegger*, 704 F. Supp. 2d 921 (N.D. Cal. 2010); *Hollingsworth* v. *Perry*, 570 U.S. _____ (2013).
10. *Reitman* v. *Mulkey*, 387 U.S. 369 (1967).
11. Aristotle, *Politics* (Oxford University Press, 1998); and George Huxley, "On Aristotle's Best State," *History of Political Thought*, vol. 6 (Summer 1985), pp. 139–149.
12. John Locke, *Two Treatises of Government and a Letter Concerning Toleration* (Yale University Press, 2003); and Virginia McDonald, "A Guide to the Interpretation of Locke the Political Theorist," *Canadian Journal of Political Science*, vol. 6 (December 1973), pp. 602–623.
13. Thomas Hobbes, *Leviathan* (Oxford University Press, 1998); and Frank M. Coleman, "The Hobbesian Basis of American Constitutionalism," *Polity*, vol. 7 (Autumn 1974), pp. 57–89.
14. Charles de Montesquieu, *The Spirit of the Laws* (Cambridge University Press, 1989); and E. P. Panagopoulos, *Essays on the History and Meaning of Checks and Balances* (University Press of America, 1986).
15. Clinton Rossiter, *Conservatism in America* (Vintage Books, 1962), p. 72.
16. Bernard Bailyn, *The Ideological Origins of the American Revolution* (Belknap Press, 1967); Gordon S. Wood, *The Creation of the American Republic, 1776–1787* (University of North Carolina Press, 1969); and Jack Citrin, "Political Culture," in Peter H. Schuck and James Q. Wilson, eds., *Understanding America: The Anatomy of an Exceptional Nation* (New York: Public Affairs, 2008), pp. 160–161.
17. Jeremy Rifkin, *The European Dream* (Penguin, 2005).
18. James Madison, "The Federalist #10," in *The Federalist Papers* (New York: Penguin Books, 1987), p. 124.
19. Pew Research Center, "Millennials in Adulthood: Detached from Institutions, Networked with Friends," March 7, 2014, http://www.people-press.org/2015/11/23/beyond-distrust-how-americans-view-their-government/.
20. When adjusted using the consumer price index (CPI), the percentage of households earning more than $75,000 a year has risen from 10.1 percent in 1970 to 22.6 percent in 1999. U.S. Bureau of the Census, *Statistical Abstracts of the United States, 2001* (U.S. Government Printing Office, 2001), table 661; see also Julia Isaac, "Economic Mobility of Black and White Families," Brookings Institution, Economic Mobility Project, November 2007.
21. See Michael B. Katz, *The "Underclass" Debate* (Princeton University Press, 1993); Theodore Dalrymple, *Life at the Bottom: The Worldview That Makes the Underclass* (December 2001); and Charles A. Murray, *The Underclass Revisited* (AEI Press, 1999).
22. Yoram Meital, "The Struggle over Political Order in Egypt: The 2005 Elections," *Middle East Journal*, vol. 60, no. 2 (Spring 2006), pp. 257–279.
23. Anthony Shadid, "Crackdown in Egypt Widens but Officials Offer Concessions," *The New York Times*, February 3, 2011, http://www.nytimes.com/2011/02/04/world/middleeast/04egypt.html?pagewanted=all (accessed May 9, 2016).
24. Ian Black, "Mohamed Morsi: The Egyptian Opposition Charge Sheet," the *Guardian*, July 3, 2013, https://www.theguardian.com/world/2013/jul/03/mohamed-morsi-egypt-president-opposition (accessed May, 9 2016).
25. Charles Tiefer, "Al-Sisi's Undemocratic Egyptian Election May Disappoint U.S. Government Critics." Forbes, November 9, 2015. https://www.forbes.com/sites/charlestiefer/2015/11/09/al-sisis-undemocratic-egyptian-election-may-disappoint-u-s-government-critics/#48fc94e7ea2d
26. Gret Gotelho, Paul Hancocks, and Kocha Olarn, "Thai Military Takes Over in Coup—Again," CNN, http://www.cnn.com/2014/05/22/world/asia/thailand-martial-law.
27. Katherine Lam, "Cuban Leader Raul Castro to Remain in Office Until April, Elections PostPostponed." Fox News. https://www.forbes.com/sites/charlestiefer/2015/11/09/al-sisis-undemocratic-egyptian-election-may-disappoint-u-s-government-critics/#48fc94e7ea2d
28. John Mukum Mbaku, "The Postponed DRC Electons: What Does the DRC's Situation Look Like Now?" Brookings. https://www.brookings.edu/blog/africa-in-focus/2016/11/22/the-postponed-drc-elections-what-does-the-drcs-situation-look-like-now/; "DRC Sets Elections for December 2018." News24. https://www.news24.com/Africa/News/drc-sets-elections-for-december-2018-20171106
29. Yomi Kazeem, "Liberia's Presidential Election Run-off Has Been Postponed Indefitely." Quartz Africa. November 6, 2017. https://qz.com/1121288/liberia-elections-delayed-by-court-george-weah-and-joseph-boakai-will-have-to-wait/.
30. "Venezuela Presidential Election Postponed to May." BBC News. March 2, 2018. https://www.bbc.com/news/world-latin-america-43241884.
31. Chris Buckley and Adam Wu, "Ending Term Limits for China's Xi Is a Big Deal. Here's Why." *The New York Times*, March 10, 2018. https://www.nytimes.com/2018/03/10/world/asia/china-xi-jinping-term-limit-explainer.html.
32. *Marbury* v. *Madison*, 5 U.S. 137 (1803).
33. David B. Magleby, *Direct Legislation: Voting on Ballot Propositions in the United States* (Johns Hopkins University Press, 1984), p. 119.
34. Sheri Berman, "Civil Society and the Collapse of the Weimar Republic," *World Politics*, vol. 49, no. 3 (April 1997), pp. 410–429.

35. Seymour Martin Lipset, "The Social Requisites of Democracy Revisited," *American Sociological Review*, vol. 59 (1994), pp. 1–22.
36. For a discussion of the importance for democracy of such overlapping group memberships, see David Truman's seminal work, *The Governmental Process*, 2nd ed. (New York: Knopf, 1971).
37. Lesli J. Favor, *The Iroquois Constitution: A Primary Source Investigation of the Law of the Iroquois* (New York: Rosen, 2003), p. 60.
38. Joyce Appleby, "The American Heritage: The Heirs and the Disinherited," *Journal of American History*, vol. 74 (December 1987), p. 808.
39. Kevin Butterfield, "What You Should Know about the Declaration of Independence," *St. Louis Post-Dispatch*, July 4, 2000, p. F1.
40. Richard L. Hillard, "Liberalism, Civic Humanism, and the American Revolutionary Bill of Rights, 1775–1790," paper presented at the annual meeting of the Organization of American Historians, Reno, NV, March 26, 1988.
41. Robert W. Hoffert, *A Politics of Tensions: The Articles of Confederation and American Political Ideas* (University Press of Colorado, 1992); see also Merrill Jensen, *The Articles of Confederation: An Interpretation of the Social-Constitutional History of the American Revolution, 1774–1781* (University of Wisconsin Press, 1970).
42. *The Federalist*, No. 40.
43. Quoted in Charles L. Mee Jr., *The Genius of the People* (New York: Harper & Row, 1987), p. 51.
44. Charles A. Beard, *An Economic Interpretation of the Constitution of the United States* (New York: Macmillan, 1913).
45. Robert Brown, *Charles Beard and the Constitution: A Critical Analysis of "An Economic Interpretation of the Constitution"* (Princeton University Press, 1956).
46. Declaration of Congress, February 21, 1787; and Worthington C. Ford et al., eds., *Journals of the Continental Congress, 1774–1789*, vol. 32 (Washington, D.C., 1904–1937), p. 74.
47. Seymour Martin Lipset, "George Washington and the Founding of Democracy," *Journal of Democracy*, vol. 9 (October 1998), p. 31.
48. Michael P. Zuckert, "Federalism and the Founding: Toward a Reinterpretation of the Constitutional Convention," *Review of Politics*, vol. 48, no. 2 (Spring 1986), pp. 166–210.
49. David O. Stewart, *The Men Who Invented the Constitution: The Summer of 1787* (New York: Simon & Schuster, 2007). Only 11 states participated because the New Hampshire delegation did not arrive in time and Rhode Island boycotted the convention. On New Hampshire, see http://www.usconstitution.net/constcmte.html and http://law2.umkc.edu/faculty/projects/ftrials/conlaw/marrynewhamp.html; on Rhode Island, see http://usinfo.org/enus/government/overview/convention.html.
50. See the essays in Thomas E. Cronin, ed., *Inventing the American Presidency* (University Press of Kansas, 1989); see also Richard J. Ellis, ed., *Founding the American Presidency* (Lanham, MD: Rowman & Littlefield, 1999).
51. David McKay, *American Politics and Society* (Hoboken, NJ: Wiley-Blackwell, 2009); see also Saul Cornell "Aristocracy Assailed: The Ideology of Backcountry Anti-Federalism," *Journal of American History*, vol. 76 (March), p. 1156, www.jstor.org/stable/pdfplus/2936593.pdf.
52. Charles A. Beard and Mary R. Beard, *A Basic History of the United States* (New York: New Home Library, 1944), p. 136.
53. W. B. Allen and Gordon Lloyd, eds., *The Essential Antifederalist* (Lanham, MD: University Press of America, 1985), pp. xi–xiii.
54. See Herbert J. Storing, ed., abridgment by Murray Dry, *The Anti-Federalist: Writings by the Opponents of the Constitution* (University of Chicago Press, 1985).
55. On the role of the promised Bill of Rights amendments in the ratification of the Constitution, see Leonard W. Levy, *Constitutional Opinions* (Oxford University Press, 1986), Chapter 6.
56. James Madison, "The Federalist #10," in *The Federalist Papers* (New York: Penguin Books, 1987), p. 3.
57. James Madison, "The Federalist #51," in *The Federalist Papers* (New York: Penguin Books, 1987), p. 1.

CHAPTER 2

1. Elaina Plott, "Trump Vents His Anger Over Border-Wall Funding," *The Atlantic*, March 21, 2018.
2. *Book of the States 2015*, The Council of State Governments, www.knowledgecenter.csg.org.
3. Sanford Levinson, *Constitutional Faith* (Princeton University Press, 1988), pp. 9–52.
4. "Americans Know Surprisingly Little About Their Government, Survey Finds," *The Annenberg Public Policy Center*, September 17, 2014.
5. Alexander Hamilton, James Madison, and John Jay, in Clinton Rossiter, ed., *The Federalist Papers* (New York: New American Library, 1961).
6. Quoted in Alpheus T. Mason, *The Supreme Court: Palladium of Freedom* (University of Michigan Press, 1962), p. 10.
7. Lydia Saad, "Americans Fault Mental Health System Most for Gun Violence: Half Say Gun Laws Should Be Stricter, Down from 58% After Newtown," *Gallup Politics* (September 20, 2013), http://www.gallup.com.
8. Jeffrey M. Jones, "U.S. Preference for Stricter Gun Laws Highest since 1993," *Gallup Politics* (March 14, 2018), http://www.gallup.com.
9. *District of Columbia* v. *Heller*, 554 U.S. 570 (2008); *McDonald* v. *Chicago*, 561 U.S. 3025 (2010).
10. Hamilton, Madison, and Jay, *The Federalist Papers*.
11. Ibid.
12. Ibid.
13. Justice Brandeis dissenting in *Myers* v. *United States*, 272 U.S. 52 (1926).
14. Charles O. Jones, "The Separate Presidency," in Anthony King, ed., *The New American Political System*, 2nd ed. (AEI Press, 1990), p. 3.
15. Morris P. Fiorina, "An Era of Divided Government," *Political Science Quarterly* vol. 107 (1992), p. 407.
16. David R. Mayhew, *Divided We Govern: Party Control, Lawmaking, and Investigations, 1946–1990* (Yale University Press, 1991), p. 4; see also James A. Thurber, ed., *Divided Democracy: Presidents and Congress in Cooperation and Conflict* (CQ Press, 1991).
17. Charles O. Jones, *Separate but Equal Branches: Congress and the Presidency* (Chatham House, 1995).
18. Judith A. Best, *The Choice of the People? Debating the Electoral College* (Lanham, MD: Rowman & Littlefield, 1996).
19. Alex T. Williams and Martin Shelton, "What Drove Spike in Public Comments on Net Neutrality? Likely, a Comedian," *Pew Research Center*, September 5, 2014.
20. James Risen and Eric Lichtblau, "Bush Lets U.S. Spy on Callers Without Courts," *The New York Times*, December 16, 2005.
21. Hamilton, Madison, and Jay, *The Federalist Papers*.
22. See Alec Stone Sweet, Wayne Sandholtz, and Neil Fligstein, *The Institutionalization of Europe* (Oxford University Press, 2001); Alec Stone Sweet, *Governing with Judges: Constitutional Politics in Europe* (Oxford University Press, 2000); and Anne-Marie Slaughter, Alec Stone Sweet, and J. H. H. Weiler, *The European Court and National Courts—Doctrine, Jurisprudence: Legal Change in Its Social Context* (Hart, 1998).
23. *Marbury* v. *Madison*, 5 U.S. 137 (1803).
24. Dumas Malone, *Jefferson the President: First Term, 1801–1805* (Little, Brown, 1970), p. 145.
25. *Burwell v. Hobby Lobby*, 573 U.S. _____ (2014).
26. J. W. Peltason, *Federal Courts in the Political Process* (Random House, 1955).
27. Lyle Denniston, "Analysis: Health Care's Mandate—Part I," *SCOTUS blog*, December 1, 2011, http://www.scotusblog.com/2011/12/analysis-health-cares-mandate-part-i/.
28. *National Federation of Independent Business* v. *Sebelius*, 567 U.S. 519 (2012).
29. Richard E. Neustadt, *Presidential Power* (Free Press, 1990), pp. 180–181.
30. *Marbury* v. *Madison*, 5 U.S. 137 (1803).
31. *Brown* v. *Board of Education*, 347 U.S. 483 (1954).
32. *Griswold* v. *Connecticut*, 381 U.S. 479 (1965).

33. *District of Columbia* v. *Heller*, 554 U.S. 570 (2008).
34. *Texas* v. *Johnson*, 491 U.S. 397 (1989).
35. *United States* v. *Eichman*, 496 U.S. 310 (1990).
36. John A. Clark and Kevin T. McGuire, "Congress, the Supreme Court, and the Flag," *Political Research Quarterly* vol. 49 (1996), pp. 771–781.
37. Senate Joint Resolution 12, 109th Congress, 2d session.
38. Ann Stuart Diamond, "A Convention for Proposing Amendments: The Constitution's Other Method," *Publius* vol. 11 (Summer 1981), pp. 113–146; and Wilbur Edel, "Amending the Constitution by Convention: Myths and Realities," *State Government* vol. 55 (1982), pp. 51–56.
39. Russell L. Caplan, *Constitutional Brinksmanship: Amending the Constitution by National Convention* (Oxford University Press, 1988), p. x; see also David E. Kyvig, *Explicit and Authentic Acts: Amending the U.S. Constitution, 1776–1995* (University Press of Kansas, 1996), p. 440.
40. Samuel S. Freedman and Pamela J. Naughton, *ERA: May a State Change Its Vote?* (Wayne State University Press, 1979).
41. Kyvig, *Explicit and Authentic Acts*, p. 286; and *Dillon* v. *Gloss*, 256 U.S. 368 (1921).
42. Mark R. Daniels, Robert Darcy, and Joseph W. Westphal, "The ERA Won—At Least in the Opinion Polls," *P.S.: Political Science and Politics* (Fall 1982), p. 583.
43. National Organization for Women, http://www.now.org/issues/-economic/eratext.html.
44. Kristy N. Kamarck, "Women in Combat: Issues for Congress," Congressional Research Service, December 3, 2015, available at https://fas.org/sgp/crs/natsec/R42075.pdf.
45. Bureau of Labor Statistics Report 1059, "Women in the Labor Force: A Databook," December 2015.
46. Bureau of Labor Statistics Report 1059, "Highlights of Women's Earnings in 2012," December 2015.

CHAPTER 3

1. Visit the U.S. Bureau of Transportation Statistics for details on the system at. https://www.rita.dot.gov/bts/sites/rita.dot.gov.bts/files/publications/state_transportation_statistics/state_transportation_statistics_2012/html/fast_facts.html.
2. Paul C. Light, *Government's Great Achievements: From Civil Rights to Homeland Security* (Washington, D.C.: Brookings Institution, 2002), pp. 93–96.
3. Jennifer Erickson, "Top 10 U.S. Government Investments in 20th Century American Competitiveness," Center for American Progress, January 2012.
4. American Society of Civil Engineers, *2017 Report Card for America's Infrastructure* (American Society of Civil Engineers, 2017).
5. U.S. Council of Economic Advisers, "An Economic Analysis of Transportation Infrastructure Investment," The White House, 2014.
6. Ron Nixon, "Human Cost Rises as Old Bridges, Dams and Roads Go Unrepaired," *The New York Times*, November 5, 2015, available at http://nyti.ms/1XTgjLT.
7. See Pew Charitable Trusts, "Funding Challenges in Highway and Transit: A Federal-State-Local Analysis," February 24, 2015, available at http://www.pewtrusts.org/en/research-and-analysis/analysis/2015/02/24/funding-challenges-in-highway-and-transit-a-federal-state-local-analysis.
8. Congressional Budget Office, "Spending and Funding for Highways," Economic and Budget Issue Brief, January 2011.
9. William H. Stewart, *Concepts of Federalism* (Center for the Study of Federalism/University Press of America, 1984); see also Preston King, *Federalism and Federation*, 2nd ed. (New York: Cass, 2001).
10. There is some debate about whether the decision to leave out the word *expressly* from the phrase "powers not delegated" showed the true intention of the Framers to eclipse the states. It was a word that featured prominently in the Supreme Court's *McCulloch* v. *Maryland* decision, and is carefully addressed in Kurt T. Lash, "The Original Meaning of an Omission: The Tenth Amendment, Popular Sovereignty, and 'Expressly' Delegated Power," *Notre Dame Law Review*, vol. 83 (2008), pp. 1890–1956.
11. See Caleb Nelson, "Preemption," *Virginia Law Review*, vol. 86 (2000), pp. 225–305, for the leading analysis of preemption in recent years.
12. Elizabeth Harris, "Connecticut to Ban Gun Sales to Those on Federal Terrorism Lists," *The New York Times*, December 10, 2015.
13. Charles Evans Hughes, "War Powers Under the Constitution," *ABA Reports*, vol. 62 (1917), p. 238.
14. *National Association of Independent Businesses* v. *Sebelius*, 567 U.S. ____ (2012).
15. See Michael S. Greve, *Real Federalism: Why It Matters, How It Could Happen* (American Enterprise Institute, 1999).
16. *Printz* v. *United States*, 521 U.S. 898 (1997); see also *New York* v. *United States*, 505 U.S. 144 (1992).
17. See the *Washington Post*'s ongoing coverage of the "Faces of the Fallen" for the most accurate numbers on the death tolls in Iraq and Afghanistan, available at http://apps.washingtonpost.com/national/fallen/.
18. See *Franchise Tax Board of California* v. *Hyatt*, 538 U.S. 488 (2003).
19. *California* v. *Superior Courts of California*, 482 U.S. 400 (1987).
20. David C. Nice, "State Participation in Interstate Compacts," *Publius*, vol. 17 (Spring 1987), p. 70; see also *Interstate Compacts and Agencies*, Council of State Governments (Author, 1995), for a list of compacts by subject and by state with brief descriptions.
21. Alexander Hamilton, James Madison, and John Jay, *The Federalist Papers*, available at http://thomas.loc.gov/home/histdox/fedpaper.txt.
22. See *Arizona* v. *United States*, 132 S.Ct. 2492 (2012). For an accessible description of the case, see "*Arizona* v. *United States*," *SCOTUSblog*, available at http://www.scotusblog.com/case-files/cases/arizona-v-united-states/.
23. U.S. Census Bureau, *2012 Census of Governments* (Government Printing Office, 2012), available at https://www.census.gov/govs/go/.
24. Morton Grodzins, "The Federal System," in *Goals for Americans: The Report of the President's Commission on National Goals* (Columbia University Press, 1960).
25. Thomas R. Dye, *American Federalism: Competition Among Governments* (Lanham, MD: Lexington Books, 1990), pp. 13–17.
26. For a history and evaluation of Race to the Top, see Ulrich Boser, "Race to the Top: What Have We Learned from the States So Far? A State-by-State Evaluation of Race to the Top Performance," Center for American Progress, 2012.
27. Michael D. Reagan and John G. Sanzone, *The New Federalism* (Oxford University Press, 1981), p. 175.
28. Bruce Katz, "Nixon's New Federalism 45 Years Later," Brookings Institution, August 11, 2014.
29. Richard Nathan, "There Will Always Be a New Federalism," *Journal of Public Administration Research and Theory*, vol. 16 (2006), pp. 499–510.
30. See American Enterprise Institute, "A Policymaker's Guide to No Child Left Behind Reauthorization," February 27, 2015, available at https://www.aei.org/publication/policymakers-guide-no-child-left-behind-reauthorization/.
31. Kevin Carey, "Requiem for a Failed Education Policy: The Long Slow Death of No Child Left Behind," *The New Republic*, July 13, 2012.
32. *McCulloch* v. *Maryland*, 4 Wheaton 316 (1819).
33. Oliver Wendell Holmes, Jr., *Collected Legal Papers* (New York: Harcourt, 1920), pp. 295–296.
34. *Gibbons* v. *Ogden*, 22 U.S. 1 (1824).
35. *Reno* v. *Condon*, 528 U.S. 141 (2000).
36. *Champion* v. *Ames*, 188 U.S. 321 (1907).
37. *Caminetti* v. *United States*, 242 U.S. 470 (1917).
38. *Federal Radio Commission* v. *Nelson Brothers*, 289 U.S. 266 (1933).
39. *Obergefell et al.* v. *Hodges*, 576 U.S. ____ (2015).
40. For a summary of the case and highlights from the ruling, see Adam Liptak, "Supreme Court Ruling Makes Same-Sex Marriage a Right Nationwide," *The New York Times*, June 26, 2015.

41. Adam Liptak, "Supreme Court Strikes Down Texas Abortion Restrictions," *The New York Times*, July 27, 2016.
42. National Federation of Independent Business et al. v. Sebelius, 567 U.S. _____ (2012). Kathleen Sebelius was the Secretary of the Department of Health and Human Services at the time the case was filed, and was responsible for implementing Obamacare. Hence, she was the logical administration official to sue.
43. Henry J. Kaiser Family Foundation at http://kff.org/health-reform/state-indicator/state-activity-around-expanding-medicaid-under-the-affordable-care-act/#.
44. *National Federation of Independent Business et al.* v. *Sebelius*, 567 U.S. _____ (2012), p. 18.
45. The term *devolution revolution* was coined by Richard P. Nathan in testimony before the Senate Finance Committee, quoted in Daniel Patrick Moynihan, "The Devolution Revolution," *The New York Times*, August 6, 1995, p. B15.
46. William H. Riker, *The Development of American Federalism* (Academic Press, 1987), pp. 14–15. Riker contends not only that federalism does not guarantee freedom, but also that the Framers of our federal system, as well as those of other nations, were animated not by considerations of safeguarding freedom but by practical considerations of preserving unity.
47. *New State Ice Company* v. *Liebmann*, 285 U.S. 262 (1932), Brandeis dissenting.
48. *Massachusetts* v. *Environmental Protection Agency*, 549 U.S. 497 (2007).
49. These figures come from *Budget of the U.S. Government, Fiscal Year, 2014*, Historical Tables, President's Budget for Fiscal Year 2014, and can be found in Table 12.1 available at https://www.gpo.gov/fdsys/browse/collection.action?collectionCode=BUDGET&browsePath=Fiscal+Year+2014&searchPath=Fiscal+Year+2014&leafLevelBrowse=false&isCollapsed=false&isOpen=true&packageid=BUDGET-2014-TAB&ycord=0.
50. Cited by the U.S. Commission on National Security/21st Century, *Road Map for National Security: Imperative for Change: The Phase III Report* (Government Printing Office, 2001), n. 145.
51. John E. Chubb, "The Political Economy of Federalism," *American Political Science Review*, vol. 79 (December 1985), p. 1005.
52. Donald F. Kettl, *The Regulation of American Federalism* (Johns Hopkins University Press, 1987), pp. 154–155.
53. See Paul J. Posner, *The Politics of Unfunded Mandates: Whither Federalism?* (Georgetown University Press, 1998).
54. See National Conference of State Legislatures, Mandate Monitor, at http://www.ncsl.org/state-federal-committees/scbudg/mandate-monitor-overview.aspx.
55. Aaron Wildavsky, "Bare Bones: Putting Flesh on the Skeleton of American Federalism," in *The Future of Federalism in the 1980s* (Advisory Commission on Intergovernmental Relations, 1981), p. 79.
56. Dye, *American Federalism*, p. 199.
57. The grade came from former Pennsylvania governor, Ed Rendell, who is the cochairman of the infrastructure advocacy group Building America's Future (bffuture.org). The group provides detailed assessments on all aspects of the infrastructure problem, and has a long list of reform ideas. Rendell was quoted in Jason Plautz, "Congress Finally Does a Highway Bill, But Can't Clear Decks for the Next President," *National Journal*, December 3, 2015.
58. See Keith Miller, Kristina Costa, and Donna Cooper, "Creating a National Infrastructure Bank and Infrastructure Planning Council," Center for American Progress, September 2012, for a study of how long-term goals and more federalism would help solve the infrastructure problem.

CHAPTER 4

1. Michael D. Shear and Julie Hirshfeld Davis, "Trump Moves to End DACA and Calls on Congress to Act." *The New York Times*. September 5, 2017. https://www.nytimes.com/2017/09/05/us/politics/trump-daca-dreamers-immigration.html.
2. Matt Zapotosky, "The Trump Administration Said it Feared Legal Fight Over DACA. Ending the Program Will Bring New Challenges. *Washington Post*, September 5, 2017. https://www.washingtonpost.com/world/national-security/the-trump-administration-said-it-feared-legal-fight-over-daca-ending-the-program-will-bring-new-challenges/2017/09/05/bbc8d7fc-925d-11e7-8754-d478688d23b4_story.html?noredirect=on&utm_term=.eb292db50e13.
3. Adam Liptak and Michael D. Shear, "Supreme Court Turns Down Trump's Appeal in Dreamers' Case." *The New York Times*, February 26, 2018. https://www.nytimes.com/2018/02/26/us/politics/supreme-court-trump-daca-dreamers.html.
4. Michael D. Shear and Julie Hirschfield Davis, "Trump Moves to End DACA and Calls on Congress to Act." September 5, 2017. https://www.nytimes.com/2017/09/05/us/politics/trump-daca-dreamers-immigration.html.
5. Jeremy W. Peters, "Trump Gets What He Wants in Immigration Debate: Quiet on the Right." *The New York Times*, February 15, 2018. https://www.nytimes.com/2018/02/15/us/politics/conservatives-immigration-trump.html; see also, Jessica Taylor, "Conservatives Fume Over DACA Deal As Trump Tries to Mollify His Base." NPR, September 14, 2017. https://www.npr.org/2017/09/14/551053707/conservatives-fume-over-daca-deal-as-trump-tries-to-mollify-his-base.
6. David Cook-Martin and David Scott Fitzgerald, "How Legacies of Racism Persist in the U.S. Immigration Policy" Scholars Strategy Network. June 20, 2014. https://scholars.org/brief/how-legacies-racism-persist-us-immigration-policy.
7. Alexis de Tocqueville, *Democracy in America*, ed. J. P. Mayer, trans. George Lawrence (Doubleday, 1969), p. 278. Originally published 1835 (Vol. 1) and 1840 (Vol. 2). https://www.nbcnews.com/politics/elections/u-s-intel-russia-compromised-seven-states-prior-2016-election-n850296.
8. John Lewis Gaddis, *Surprise, Security, and the American Experience* (Harvard University Press, 2005).
9. Cynthia McFadden, William M. Arkin, Kevin Monahan, and Ken Dilanian, "U.S. Intel: Russia Compromised Seven States Prior to 2016 Election." NBC News. February 28, 2018. https://www.nbcnews.com/politics/elections/u-s-intel-russia-compromised-seven-states-prior-2016-election-n850296.
10. Shane Harris, Damien Paletta, and Carol E. Lee, "Intelligence Agencies Say Russia Ordered 'Influence Campaign' to aid Donald Trump in Election." *The Wall Street Journal*, January 6, 2017. https://www.wsj.com/articles/donald-trump-continues-attacks-on-intelligence-agencies-ahead-of-classified-briefing-on-russia-1483728966. see also, Jeremy Diamond, "Intel report: Putin directly ordered effort to influence election." CNN. January 06, 2017. Accessed March 12, 2018. https://www.cnn.com/2017/01/06/politics/intelligence-report-putin-election/index.html.
11. This excludes the Japanese attack on the U.S. territory of Hawaii in 1941 and other attacks on U.S. embassies or territories.
12. World Trade Organization, International Trade Statistics 2014, p. 54, https://www.wto.org/english/res_e/statis_e/its2014_e/its14_toc_e.htm.
13. Gavin Wright, "The Origins of American Industrial Success, 1879–1940." *The American Economic Review*, Vol. 80, No. 4, (Sep. 1990), pp. 651–668.
14. Earl Black and Merle Black, *The Rise of Southern Republicans* (Cambridge, MA: The Belknap Press of Harvard University Press, 2002), pp. 1–5.
15. Stephanie McCrummen, Beth Reinhard and Alice Crites, "Woman Says Roy Moore Initiated Sexual Encounter When She Was 14, He was 32." *Washington Post*. November 9, 2017. https://www.washingtonpost.com/investigations/woman-says-roy-moore-initiated-sexual-encounter-when-she-was-14-he-was-32/2017/11/09/1f495878-c293-11e7-afe9-4f60b5a6c4a0_story.html?utm_term=.934a68194437, see also, Jonathan Martin, and Sheryl Gay Stolberg. "Roy Moore Is Accused of Sexual Misconduct by a Fifth Woman." *The New York Times*. November 13, 2017.

Accessed March 12, 2018. https://www.nytimes.com/2017/11/13/us/politics/roy-moore-alabama-senate.html.

16. Calculated by author from http://history.house.gov/Institution/Election-Statistics/Election-Statistics/. Used 2014 election results and included all states categorized in the Southern region by the U.S. census.
17. Calculated by author. Used 2014 election results and included all states categorized in the Southern region by the U.S. census; Ballotpedia, 2016; "Partisan composition of state houses" and "Partisan composition of state senates," *The Encyclopedia of American Politics*, Web, https://ballotpedia.org/Partisan_composition_of_state_houses and https://ballotpedia.org/Partisan_composition_of_state_senates.
18. http://www.nga.org/files/live/sites/NGA/files/pdf/directories/GovList2016.pdf.
19. The term was coined by H.L. Mencken, who included it in an article in the *Chicago Daily Tribune* and then reported in a letter to a friend that he was proud of this phrase. See: http://www.aaa.si.edu/collections/items/detail/h-l-mencken-letter-to-charles-green-shaw-9819.
20. Robert S. Erikson, Gerald C. Wright, and John P. McIver, *Statehouse Democracy: Public Opinion and Policy in the American States* (Cambridge University Press, 1993).
21. U.S. Census Bureau, "Quick Facts." https://www.census.gov/quickfacts/fact/table/US,CA/PST045217PST045216.
22. U.S. Bureau of the Census, "2010 Census Urban and Rural Classification and Urban Area Criteria," HYPERLINK "http://www.census.gov/geo/reference/ua/urban-rural-2010.html" www.census.gov/geo/reference/ua/urban-rural-2010.html.
23. Ibid.
24. Albert Einstein, quoted in Laurence J. Peter, *Peter's Quotations* (Morrow, 1977), p. 358.
25. Deborah Amos, "The U.S. Has Accepted Only 11 Syrian Refugees This Year." NPR. April 12, 2018. https://www.npr.org/sections/parallels/2018/04/12/602022877/the-u-s-has-welcomed-only-11-syrian-refugees-this-year.
26. Liam Stack, "Trump's Executive Order on Immigration: What We Know and What We Don't" *The New York Times*, January 29, 2017. https://www.nytimes.com/2017/01/29/us/trump-refugee-ban-muslim-executive-order.html.
27. Glen Thrush, "Trump's New Travel Ban Blocks Migrants from Six Nations, Sparring Iraq." *The New York Times*, March 9, 2017. https://www.nytimes.com/2017/03/06/us/politics/travel-ban-muslim-trump.html.
28. Arianede Vogue, "Appeals Court Rules Against Latest Trump Travel Ban." CNN. March 27, 2018. https://www.cnn.com/2018/02/15/politics/travel-ban-ruling/index.html.
29. Adam Liptak and Michael D. Shear, "Trump's Travel Ban Is Upheld by Supreme Court." *The New York Times*, June 26, 2018. https://www.nytimes.com/2018/06/26/us/politics/supreme-court-trump-travel-ban.html.
30. Nadia Abu El-Haj, "The Genetic Reinscription of Race," *Annual Review of Anthropology*, 36 (2007), pp. 283–300.
31. David R. Harris and Jeremiah Joseph Sim, "Who Is Multiracial? Assessing the Complexity of Lived Race," *American Sociological Review* (August 2002), p. 615.
32. U.S. Census Bureau, "Race," State and County QuickFacts, https://www.census.gov/quickfacts/fact/table/US/PST045217
33. United States' Census Bureau, State & County QuickFacts, https://www.census.gov/quickfacts/fact/table/US#viewtop.
34. United States' Census Bureau, State & County QuickFacts, https://www.census.gov/quickfacts/fact/table/US#viewtop; Krogstad, Jens Manuel. "U.S. Hispanic Population Growth Has Leveled Off." Pew Research Center. August 3, 2017.
35. United States' Census Bureau, State & County QuickFacts, https://www.census.gov/quickfacts/fact/table/US#viewtop.
36. Sandra L. Colby and Jennifer M. Ortman, "Projections of the Size and Composition of the U.S. Population: 2014 to 2060," *US Census Bureau News*, March 2015, https://www.census.gov/content/dam/Census/library/publications/2015/demo/p25-1143.pdf.
37. On South Dakota see James Meader and John Bart, "The More You Spend, the Less They Listen: The South Dakota U.S. Senate Race," in David B. Magleby and J. Quin Monson, eds., *The Last Hurrah? Soft Money and Issue Advocacy in the 2002 Congressional Elections* (Brookings Institution Press, 2004), p. 173; and Elizabeth Theiss Smith and Richard Braunstein, "The Nationalization of Local Politics in South Dakota," in David B. Magleby and J. Quin Monson, eds., *Dancing Without Partners: How Candidates, Parties, and Interest Groups Interact in the New Campaign Finance Environment* (Center for the Study of Elections and Democracy, 2005), pp. 241–242; on Alaska see Kim Murphy, "Lisa Murkowski Claims Victory in Alaska Senate Election," *Los Angeles Times*, November 18, 2010, http://articles.latimes.com/2010/nov/18/nation/la-na-alaska-senate-20101118; and Yereth Rosen, "Lisa Murkowski Ahead in Alaska, but Long Count of Write-ins Looms," *Christian Science Monitor*, November 4, 2010, http://www.csmonitor.com/USA/Elections/Senate/2010/1104/Lisa-Murkowski-ahead-in-Alaska-but-long-count-of-write-ins-looms.
38. United States' Census Bureau, Profile America Facts for Features https://www.census.gov/content/dam/Census/newsroom/facts-for-features/2017/cb17-ff20.pdf.;.
39. U.S. Department of Health & Human Services, "Profile: American Indian/Alaska Native," Minority Population Profiles, https://minorityhealth.hhs.gov/omh/browse.aspx?lvl=3&lvlid=62.
40. Sonya Rastogi, Tallese D. Johnson, Elizabeth M. Hoeffel, and Malcolm P. Drewery, Jr., "The Black Population: 2010; 2010 Census Briefs," U.S. Census Bureau, September 2011, https://www.census.gov/prod/cen2010/briefs/c2010br-06.pdf; see also, Robert D. Ballard, "Introduction: Lure of the New South," in Robert D. Ballard, ed., *In Search of the New South: The Black Urban Experience in the 1970s and 1980s* (University of Alabama Press, 1989), p. 5; *Statistical Abstract, 2008*, p. 449.
41. Sonya Rastogi, Tallese D. Johnson, Elizabeth M. Hoeffel, and Malcolm P. Drewery, Jr., "The Black Population: 2010; 2010 Census Briefs," U.S. Census Bureau, September 2011, http://www.census.gov/prod/cen2010/briefs/c2010br-06.pdf.
42. Reniqua Allen, "Racism Is Everywhere, So Why Not Move South?" *The New York Times*, July 8, 2017. https://www.nytimes.com/2017/07/08/opinion/sunday/racism-is-everywhere-so-why-not-move-south.html.
43. U.S. Department of Labor, Bureau of Labor Statistics, News Release. April 13, 2018. https://www.bls.gov/news.release/pdf/wkyeng.pdf.
44. U.S. Bureau of the Census, "Families Below Poverty Level and Below 125 Percent of Poverty By Race and Hispanic Origin: 1980 to 2014 [Selected Years]," ProQuest Statistical Abstract of the U.S. 20162014 Online Edition. Ed. ProQuest, 20162014. Web: ProQuest Statistical Abstract, March 2016, http://statabs.proquest.com/sa/docview.html?table-no=735&acc-no=C7095-1.13&year=2016&z=6FE99C0D5ECFBD43E7527292D45DA0F937C00780>14.
45. U.S. Bureau of the Census, "Money Income of Households—Percent Distribution by Income Level, Race, and Hispanic Origin, in Constant (2016) Dollars: 2000 to 2016 [Selected Years]," ProQuest Statistical Abstract of the U.S. 2018 Online Edition. Ed. ProQuest, 2018. Web: ProQuest Statistical Abstract, May 2018, https://statabs.proquest.com/sa/docview.html?table-no=716&acc-no=C7095-1.13&year=2018&z=0A8B18562F4BA6E080F725A87E165F6252BD0FE6&rc=1&seq=1&y=current.
46. Based on 3-year moving averages. See National Center for Education Statistics, Percent of Recent High School Completers Enrolled in 2- and 4-year Colleges, by Race/Ethnicity: 1960 through 2015. https://nces.ed.gov/programs/digest/d16/tables/dt16_302.20.asp.
47. Camille L. Ryan and Kurt Bauman, U.S. Bureau of the Census, "Educational Attainment in the United States: 2015. Table 1. https://www.census.gov/content/dam/Census/library/publications/2016/demo/p20-578.pdf.

48. https://factfinder.census.gov/faces/tableservices/jsf/pages/productview.xhtml?src=CF
49. Jeremy D. Mayer, *Running on Race* (Random House, 2002), pp. 4, 297. See also Mark R. Levy and Michael S. Kramer, *The Ethnic Factor: How America's Minorities Decide Elections* (Simon & Schuster, 1973); and Mark Stern, "Democratic Presidency and Voting Rights," in Lawrence W. Mooreland, Robert P. Steed, and Todd A. Baker, eds., *Blacks in Southern Politics* (Praeger, 1987), pp. 50–51.
50. For 1984–2000, see Harold W. Stanley and Richard G. Niemi, *Vital Statistics on American Politics, 2000–2001* (CQ Press, 2001), p. 122; for 2004, see Harold W. Stanley and Richard G. Niemi, *Vital Statistics on American Politics, 2005–2006* (CQ Press, 2006), p. 124. For more recent years see CNN exit polls. https://www.cnn.com/election/2016/results/exit-polls.
51. BBC News, "The U.S. Election in Figures," at http://news.bbc.co.uk/2/hi/americas/us_elections_2008/7715914.stm.
52. For 2000 see https://ropercenter.cornell.edu/polls/us-elections/how-groups-voted/how-groups-voted-2000/. Survey by Voter News Service, a consortium ABC News, CBS News, CNN, FOX News, NBC News, and the Associated Press. Sample of 13,225 voters as they left voting booths on election day, November 7, 2000. Oregon residents were interviewed by telephone October 29–November 4, 2000; for 2004 see https://ropercenter.cornell.edu/polls/us-elections/how-groups-voted/how-groups-voted-2004/. Survey by Edison Media Research/Mitofsky International for the National Election Pool (ABC News, Associated Press, CBS News, CNN, Fox News, NBC News). Sample of 13,719 voters consisted of 11,719 voters as they left the voting booths on Election Day November 2, 2004, and a telephone absentee/early voters survey of 2,000 respondents conducted October 25–31, 2004.
53. "How Groups Voted 2016." Roper Center. https://ropercenter.cornell.edu/polls/us-elections/how-groups-voted/groups-voted-2016/.
54. Howard W. Stanley and Richard G. Niemi, *Vital Statistics on American Politics, 2015–2016*, (CQ Press, 2016), pp. 56–57.
55. Howard W. Stanley and Richard G. Niemi, *Vital Statistics on American Politics, 2015–2016*, (CQ Press, 2016), pp. 56–57.
56. "Black-American Representatives and Senators by Congress, 1870-Present." United States House of Representaties: History, Art & Archives. http://history.house.gov/Exhibitions-and-Publications/BAIC/Historical-Data/Black-American-Representatives-and-Senators-by-Congress/.
57. Matt Barreto, Rodolfo O. de la Garza, Jongho Lee, Jaesung Ryu, and Harry P. Pachon, "Latino Voter Mobilization in 2000," Tomás Rivera Policy Institute (2000), pp. 4–5, www.trpi.org/PDFs/Voter_mobiliz_2.pdf. See also Matt Barreto and Gary M Segura, *Latino America: How America's Most Dynamic Population Is Poised to Transform the Politics of the Nation* (Public Affairs, 2014).
58. U.S. Bureau of the Census, "Resident Population by Hispanic Origin and State: 2016 [as of July 1]," *ProQuest Statistical Abstract of the U.S. 2018 Online Edition*. Ed. ProQuest, 2018. Web: *ProQuest Statistical Abstract*, May 2018, https://statabs.proquest.com/sa/docview.html?table-no=19&acc-no=C7095-1.1&year=2018&z=FA9EF54CA2C3CC8BA7F9C6E3A5B5AD05627E438A&rc=1&seq=6&y=current.
59. Jens Manuel Krogstad and Mark Hugo Lopez, "Hillary Clinton Won Latino vote but Fell Below 2012 Support for Obama," *Pew Research Center*, November 29, 2016 http://www.pewresearch.org/fact-tank/2016/11/29/hillary-clinton-wins-latino-vote-but-falls-below-2012-support-for-obama/ (Accessed April 9, 2018).
60. Francisco I. Pedraza and Bryan Wilcox-Archuleta, "Did Latino Voters Actually Turn Out for Trump in the Election? Not really." *Los Angeles Times*, January 11, 2017. http://www.latimes.com/opinion/op-ed/la-oe-pedraza-latino-vote-20170111-story.html.
61. U.S. Bureau of the Census, "Foreign-Born Population by Citizenship Status and Place of Birth: 2013," *ProQuest Statistical Abstract of the U.S. 2016 Online Edition*. Ed. ProQuest, 2016. Web: ProQuest Statistical Abstract, March 2016, https://statabs.proquest.com/ftv2/4c4e0000025ec0332016.pdf.
62. Department of Homeland Security, "Estimated Unauthorized Immigrants by Selected States and Countries of Birth: 2000 to 2012 [Selected Years, as of January]," *ProQuest Statistical Abstract of the U.S. 2016 Online Edition*, http://statabs.proquest.com/sa/docview.html?table-no=45&acc-no=C7095-1.1&year=2016&z=49D7085367686B391544EAF8871FA38237AC7B8C.
63. U.S. Bureau of the Census, "Resident Population by Race, Hispanic Origin, and Age: 2010 and 2014 [April 1, 2010, and July 1, 2014]," *ProQuest Statistical Abstract of the U.S. 2016 Online Edition. Ed. ProQuest, 2016. Web: ProQuest Statistical Abstract*, March 2016, http://statabs.proquest.com/sa/docview.html?table-no=9&acc-no=C7095-1.1&year=2016&z=58613C46D25109671B8F5B4ACCD3663BEB2E896D01/14.
64. Philip Bump, "Ted Cruz Gets It Very Wrong on Recent Presidents' Deportation Numbers." *Washington Post*, December 16, 2015. https://www.washingtonpost.com/news/the-fix/wp/2015/12/16/the-numbers-ted-cruz-cited-on-past-deportations-during-the-cnn-debate-were-way-off/?utm_term=.0988ba7317f6
65. Corasaniti, Nick. "Donald Trump Releases Plan to Combat Illegal Immigration." *The New York Times*, August 16, 2015. Accessed May 23, 2018. https://www.nytimes.com/2015/08/17/us/politics/trump-releases-plan-to-combat-illegal-immigration.html.
66. Elaina Plott, "Trump's Immigraton Plan Receives a Chilly Reception." *The Atlantic* January 31, 2018. https://www.theatlantic.com/politics/archive/2018/01/trump-bets-on-immigration-in-the-state-of-the-union/551936/
67. Arelis R. Hernandez and Steven Mufson, "Getting Relief Supplies to Puerto Rico Ports Is Only Half the Problem." *Washington Post*, September 28, 2017. https://www.washingtonpost.com/business/economy/getting-relief-supplies-to-puerto-rico-ports-is-only-half-the-problem/2017/09/28/9ff558a6-a460-11e7-8cfe-d5b912fabc99_story.html?utm_term=.30ee6a1b1b00
68. Camila Domonoske, "In Puerto Rico, Containers Full of Goods Sit Undistributed at Ports." NPR, September 28, 2017. https://www.npr.org/sections/thetwo-way/2017/09/28/554297787/puerto-rico-relief-goods-sit-undistributed-at-ports. On the estimated dead, the government initially reported 112 dead, but other estimates placed the number much higher. see, https://www.npr.org/sections/health-shots/2018/05/29/615120123/study-puts-puerto-rico-death-toll-at-5-000-from-hurricane-maria-in-2017 https://www.cnn.com/2018/05/29/us/puerto-rico-hurricane-maria-death-toll/index.html https://www.nejm.org/doi/full/10.1056/NEJMsa1803972
69. U.S. Census Bureau. "Data." Educational Attainment in the United States: 2017. December 14, 2017. Accessed March 23, 2018. https://www.census.gov/data/tables/2017/demo/education-attainment/cps-detailed-tables.html
70. Janelle Wong, S. Karthick Ramakrishnan, Taeku Lee, and Jane Junn, *Asian American Political Participation: Emerging Constituents and Their Political Identities* (Russell Sage Foundation: 2011).
71. Zoltan L. Hajnal and Taeku Lee, *Why Americans Don't Join the Party: Race, Immigration, and the Failure (of Political Parties) to Engage the Electorate* (Princeton, NJ: Princeton University Press, 2011).
72. 2004 totals can be found in Roper Center, "U.S. Elections: How Groups Voted in 2004," https://ropercenter.cornell.edu/polls/us-elections/how-groups-voted/how-groups-voted-2004/.
73. The 2012 totals can be found in "President Exit Polls," *The New York Times*, https://www.nytimes.com/elections/2012/results/president/exit-polls.htm; the 2008 totals can found in Roper Center, "U.S. Elections: How Groups Voted in 2008," https://ropercenter.cornell.edu/polls/us-elections/how-groups-voted/how-groups-voted-2008/; the 2004 totals can be found in Roper Center, "U.S. Elections: How Groups Voted in 2004," https://ropercenter.cornell.edu/polls/us-elections/how-groups-voted/how-groups-voted-2004/; and the 2000 totals can be found in Roper Center, "U.S. Elections: How Groups Voted in 2000,"

https://ropercenter.cornell.edu/polls/us-elections/how-groups-voted/how-groups-voted-2000/.

74. "How Groups Voted 2016." Roper Center. https://ropercenter.cornell.edu/polls/us-elections/how-groups-voted/groups-voted-2016/.
75. Patrick J. Buchanan, "The GOP's New Minority," *The American Conservative*, June 14, 2013, http://www.theamericanconservative.com/articles/the-gops-new-minority/.
76. Karl Rove, "More White Voters Alone Won't Save the GOP," *Wall Street Journal*, June 26, 2013, https://www.wsj.com/articles/SB10001424127887323873904578569480696746650.
77. Growth and Opportunity Project, Republican National Committee. 2012. p. 12. https://gop.com/growth-and-opportunity-project.
78. For a different view on the religious roots of this conflict see, Steven A. Cook, "Why the Myth of Sunni-Shia Conflict Defines Middle East Policy—and Why It Shoudn't." Council on Foreign Relations, May 8, 2017. https://www.cfr.org/blog/why-myth-sunni-shia-conflict-defines-middle-east-policy-and-why-it-shouldnt.
79. Leni Yahil, *The Holocaust: The Fate of European Jewry* (Oxford University Press, 1990).
80. Stephen C. LeSuer, *The 1838 Mormon War in Missouri* (University of Missouri Press, 1987), pp. 151–153.
81. Nicholas Jay Demerath, *Crossing the Gods: World Religions and Worldly Politics* (Rutgers University Press, 2001).
82. Robert Booth Fowler, Allen D. Hertzke, Laura R. Olson, and Kevin R. Den Dulk, *Religion and Politics in America: Faith, Culture and Strategic Choices* (Westview, 2014). See also Ronald Inglehart and Wayne E. Baker, "Looking Forward, Looking Back: Continuity and Change at the Turn of the Millennium," *American Sociological Review* (February 2000), pp. 29, 31.
83. http://www.cbsnews.com/elections/2016/primaries/republican/iowa/exit/.
84. Kenneth D. Wald and Allison Calhoun-Brown, *Religion and Politics in the United States*, 5th ed. (New York: Rowman and Littlefield, 2011), pp. 9–10.
85. PewResearch, Religious Landscape Study, "Attendance at Religious Services," Pew Research Center Religion and Public Life, http://www.pewforum.org/religious-landscape-study/attendance-at-religious-services/.
86. PewResearch, Religious Landscape Study, "Religions," Pew Research Center Religion and Public Life, http://www.pewforum.org/religious-landscape-study/#religions.
87. PewResearch, Religious Landscape Study, "Religions," Pew Research Center Religion and Public Life, http://www.pewforum.org/religious-landscape-study/#religions.
88. PewResearch, Religious Landscape Study, "Religions," Pew Research Center Religion and Public Life, http://www.pewforum.org/religious-landscape-study/#religions.
89. PewResearch, Religious Landscape Study, Pew Research Center Religion and Public Life, http://www.pewforum.org/religious-landscape-study/.
90. *2000 American National Election Study* (Center for Political Studies, 2000); *2004 American National Election Study* (Center for Political Studies, 2004). 2008 American National Election Study (Center for Political Studies, 2008); 2012: The American National Election Study (ANES; www.electionstudies.org). The ANES 2012 Time Series Study [dataset]. Stanford University and the University of Michigan [producers]. Post-election surveys often overestimate the vote, and that appeared to be especially the case in the 2004 National Election Study. See Morris Fiorina and Jon Krosnick, "*Economist/YouGov Internet Presidential Poll*," www.economist.com/media/pdf/Paper.pdf; and Michael P. McDonald and Samuel Popkin, "The Myth of the Vanishing Voter," *American Political Science Review* 95 (2001), pp. 963–974.
91. Pew Forum on Religion and Public Life, "How the Faithful Voted: 2012 Preliminary Analysis," November 7, 2012, http://www.pewforum.org/2012/11/07/how-the-faithful-voted-2012-preliminary-exit-poll-analysis/.
92. 2012: The American National Election Study (ANES; www.electionstudies.org). The ANES 2012 Time Series Study [dataset]. Stanford University and the University of Michigan [producers].
93. 2016 American National Election Study (ANES; www.electionstudies.org). The ANES 2016 Time Series Study [dataset]. https://electionstudies.org/project/2016-time-series-study/.
94. James West Davidson, William E. Gienapp, Christine Leigh Heyrman, Mark H. Lytle, and Michael B. Stoff, *Nation of Nations* (McGraw-Hill, 1990), pp. 833–834.
95. Margaret C. Trevor, "Political Socialization, Party Identification, and the Gender Gap," *Public Opinion Quarterly* 63 (Spring 1999), p. 62.
96. U.S. Bureau of the Census, "Voting-Age Population—Reported Registration and Voting by Selected Characteristics: 2000 to 2014 [By Age, Sex, Race, Region, Education, and Employment Status, Presidential and Congressional Election Years, as of November]," ProQuest Statistical Abstract of the U.S. 20162014 Online Edition. Ed. ProQuest, 2016. Web: ProQuest Statistical Abstract March 2016, http://statabs.proquest.com/sa/docview.html?table-no=430&acc-no=C7095-1.7&year=2016&z=56CF1635C1E6F1F037BE726164CB7A5271FB5358; see also Sue Tolleson-Rinehard and Jyl J. Josephson, eds., *Gender and American Politics* (Sharpe, 2000), pp. 77–78; Center for American Women and Politics, "Gender Differences in Voter Turnout," 2017, http://www.cawp.rutgers.edu/sites/default/files/resources/genderdiff.pdf. Danielle Paquette, "The Unexpected Voters Behind the wildest Gender Gap in Recorded Election History." *Washington Post*, November 9, 2016. https://www.washingtonpost.com/news/wonk/wp/2016/11/09/men-handed-trump-the-election/?utm_term=.de7075c87e61
97. Sue Tolleson-Rinehard and Jyl J. Josephson, eds., Gender and American Politics (Sharpe, 2000), pp. 232–233. See also Cindy Simon Rosenthal, ed., *Women Transforming Congress* (University of Oklahoma Press, 2002), pp. 128–139.
98. Richa Chaturvendi, "A Closer Look at the Gender Gap in Presidential Voting." Pew Research Center, July 28, 2016. http://www.pewresearch.org/fact-tank/2016/07/28/a-closer-look-at-the-gender-gap-in-presidential-voting/; for data on gender and presidential voting in 2016 see, CNN, Exit polls, 2016. https://www.cnn.com/election/2016/results/exit-polls
99. Office of the Clerk, "People Search," 2016, http://history.house.gov/People/Search?filter=6.
100. National Conference of State Legislators, "Women in State Legislatures for 2015," http://www.ncsl.org/legislators-staff/legislators/womens-legislative-network/women-in-state-legislatures-for-2015.aspx.
101. Center for the American Woman and Politics, 2017, "The Gender Gap: Voting Choices in Presidential Elections," January, Web, http://www.cawp.rutgers.edu/sites/default/files/resources/ggpresvote.pdf.
102. Alec Tyson and Shiva Maniam, Behind Trump's Victory: Divisions by Race, Gender, Education. Pew Research Center, November 9, 2016. http://www.pewresearch.org/fact-tank/2016/11/09/behind-trumps-victory-divisions-by-race-gender-education/
103. Georgina Waylen, Karen Celis, Johanna Kantola, and S. Laurel Weldon, *The Oxford Handbook of Gender and Politics* (Oxford University Press, 2013).
104. Pew Research Center, "Gender Gap on Importance of Abortion, Birth Control, Inequality, Environment," U.S. Politics and Policy, September 12, 2014, http://www.people-press.org/2014/09/12/wide-partisan-differences-over-the-issues-that-matter-in-2014/9-12-2014_07/.
105. U.S. Bureau of the Census, "Money Income of People—Selected Characteristics by Income Level: 2014 [By Sex, Age, Region, Education, and Housing Tenure]," *ProQuest Statistical Abstract of the U.S. 2016 Online Edition*. Ed. ProQuest, 2016. Web: ProQuest Statistical Abstract March 2016 https://statabs.proquest.com/sa/docview.html?table-no=724&acc-no=C7095-1.13&year=2016&z=55CB5ACA0E155D778C661242BCAEDB8D6F1DA2B4&rc=1&seq=0&y=2016&q=money%20income%20of%20people.

106. "Income and Poverty in the United States: 2016," United States Census Bureau, September 2017, https://www.census.gov/library/publications/2017/demo/p60-259.html.
107. Catherine Rampell, "As Layoffs Surge, Women May Pass Men in Job Force," *The New York Times*, February 5, 2009, http://www.nytimes.com/2009/02/06/business/06women.html.
108. Jeff Hayes and Heidi Hartmann, "Women and Men Living on the Edge: Economic Insecurity after the Great Recession," an IWPR/Rockefeller Survey of Economic Security, September 2011.
109. Anna Quindlen, "Some Struggles Never Seem to End," *The New York Times*, November 14, 2001, p. H24.
110. Anna Brown, "5 Key Findings About LGBT Americans." Pew Reseracy Center. June 13, 2017. http://www.pewresearch.org/fact-tank/2017/06/13/5-key-findings-about-lgbt-americans/
111. Elisabeth Bumiller, "Obama Ends 'Don't Ask, Don't Tell' Policy," *The New York Times*, July 22, 2011, https://www.nytimes.com/2011/07/23/us/23military.html
112. Jacqueline Klimas and Bryan Bender, "Trump Moves to Ban Most Transgender Troups." *POLITICO*, March 23, 2018. https://www.politico.com/story/2018/03/23/trump-transgender-troops-ban-483434
113. *Obergfell* v. *Hodges*, 135 S.Ct. 2071 (2015).
114. *Masterpiece Cakeshop* v. *Colorado Civil Rights Commission*, 584 U.S. _____ (2018).
115. Renee Stepler, Number of U.S. Adults Cohabiting with a Partner Continues to Rise, Especially Among Those 50 and Older." Pew Research Center, April 6, 2017. http://www.pewresearch.org/fact-tank/2017/04/06/number-of-u-s-adults-cohabiting-with-a-partner-continues-to-rise-especially-among-those-50-and-older/
116. U.S. Bureau of the Census, "Table 72: Opposite And Same-Sex Unmarried-Partner Households By Region 2016," ProQuest Statistical Abstract of the U.S. 2018 Online Edition. Ed. ProQuest, 2086. Web: ProQuest Statistical Abstract, March 2016, http://statabs.proquest.com/sa/docview. https://statabs.proquest.com/sa/docview.html?table-no=72&acc-no=C7095-1.1&year=2018&z=9E46C0D42AA888DAB99C52E2D6927521198BC483&rc=1&seq=0&y=current&q=Opposite%20And%20Same-Sex%20Unmarried-Partner%20Households%20By%20Region%202016.
117. U.S. Bureau of the Census, "Historical Marital Status Tables, 2107." https://www.census.gov/data/tables/time-series/demo/families/marital.html
118. U.S. National Center for Health Statistics, "82: Live Births, Birth Rates, And Fertility Rates By Hispanic Origin: 2010 to 2016 [Selected Years]," United States Statistical Abstract: Online Edition 2018, https://statabs.proquest.com/sa/docview.html?table-no=82&acc-no=C7095-1.2&year=2018&z=75E1153BE7C73B0D63B22712C34D8F02765E22C9&rc=1&seq=0&y=current&q=fertility.
119. Statistical Abstract of the United States, 2018. Table 82. https://statabs.proquest.com/sa/docview.html?table-no=82&acc-no=C7095-1.2&year=2018&z=75E1153BE7C73B0D63B22712C34D8F02765E22C9&rc=1&seq=1&y=current
120. U.S. National Center for Health Statistics, "Table 138: Marriage And Divorce Rates By State: 1990 To 2016 [Selected Years]," United States Statistical Abstract: Online Edition 2018, https://statabs.proquest.com/sa/docview.html?table-no=138&acc-no=C7095-1.2&year=2018&z=D5F2934EC99B2ED05817DF90F95BB148238B45A6&rc=1&seq=1&y=current&q=Divorce.
121. Thomas Jefferson to P. S. du Pont de Nemours, April 24, 1816, in Paul L. Ford, ed. *The Writings of Thomas Jefferson* (Putnam, 1899), vol. 10, p. 25.
122. U.S. Bureau of the Census, "School Enrollment in the United States: October 2016—Detailed Tables." August 23, 2017. https://www.census.gov/data/tables/2016/demo/school-enrollment/2016-cps.html
123. *Statistical Abstract, 2012*, p. 152.
124. U.S. Bureau of the Census. "Highest Educational Levels Reached by Aduts in the U.S. Since 1940." March 30, 2017. Release Numbder CB17-51. https://www.census.gov/newsroom/press-releases/2017/cb17-51.html
125. Herbert McClosky and John Zaller, *The American Ethos: Public Attitudes Toward Capitalism and Democracy* (Harvard University Press, 1984), p. 261.
126. "Graying of America," PBS Sunset Story, http://www.pbs.org/independentlens/sunsetstory/graying.html.
127. Family Caregiver Alliance, "Selected Long-Term Care Statistics." https://www.caregiver.org/selected-long-term-care-statistics. For additional information on the demographic aging, see Jennifer M. Ortman and Victoria A. Velkoff, "An Aging Nation: The Older Population in the United States," U.S. Census Bureau Current Population Reports, May 2014, https://www.census.gov/prod/2014pubs/p25-1140.pdf.
128. U.S. Census Bureau, "Quick Facts." https://www.census.gov/quickfacts/fact/table/US/AGE775216#viewtop; Medical Expenditure Panel Survey, "Concentration of Health Expenditures in the U.S. Civilian Noninstitutionalized Population, 2014," https://meps.ahrq.gov/data_files/publications/st497/stat497.pdf; see also, Emily M. Mitchell and Steven R. Machlin, "Concentration of Health Expenditures and Selected Characteristics of High Spenders, U.S. Civilian Noninstitutionalized Population, 2015. Agency for Healthcare Research and Quality, December 2017. https://meps.ahrq.gov/data_files/publications/st506/stat506.pdf
129. https://www.census.gov/content/dam/Census/library/publications/2014/demo/p23-212.pdf, Table 4.1, p. 104.
130. Michael McDonald, United States Elections Project, Voter Turnout Demographics. This cite uses data from the Census Bureau's Current Population Survey. November Voting and Registration Supplement. http://www.electproject.org/home/voter-turnout/demographics.
131. CIRCLE, "Youth Voting," Center for Information and Research on Civic Learning and Engagement, 2016, http://civicyouth.org/quick-facts/youth-voting/.
132. Nicholas L. Danigelis, Stephen J. Cutler, and Melissa Hardy, "Population Aging, Intracohort Aging, and Sociopolitical Attitudes," *American Sociological Review* 72 (October 2007), p. 816.
133. Lily Rothman, "50 Years Ago This Week: How Young People Changed the World," Time Magazine, January 2, 2017, http://time.com/4607270/1967-january-6-anniversary/
134. Douglas Main, "Who Are the Millennials?" LiveScience, September 8, 2017. https://www.livescience.com/38061-millennials-generation-y.html
135. Pew Research Center, "Millennials: A Portrait of Generation Next," February 2010, www.pewsocialtrends.org/files/2010/10/millennials-confident-connected-open-to-change.pdf.
136. Neil Howe and William Strauss, "The New Generation Gap," *Atlantic*, December 1992, www.theatlantic.com/magazine/archive/1992/12/the-new-generation-gap/536934/.
137. Derek Robertson and Tim Henderson, "The United States of Millennials," *Politico Magazine*, April 26, 2018, www.politico.com/magazine/story/2018/04/26/millennials-cities-where-they-live-218059.
138. Alex Williams, "Move Over, Millennials, Here Comes Generation Z." *The New York Times*, September 18, 2015. https://www.nytimes.com/2015/09/20/fashion/move-over-millennials-here-comes-generation-z.html
139. Shiva Maniam and Samantha Smith, "A Wider Partisan and Ideological Gap Between Younger, Older Generations." Pew Research Center. Factank: News in Numbers. March 20, 2017. http://www.pewresearch.org/fact-tank/2017/03/20/a-wider-partisan-and-ideological-gap-between-younger-older-generations/.
140. Joel Stein, "Millennials: The Me Me Me Generation," *Time Magazine*, May 20, 2013, http://time.com/247/millennials-the-me-me-me-generation/.
141. Jeremy Rifkin, *The European Dream* (Penguin, 2005).
142. Raymond E. Wolfinger, Fred I. Greenstein, and Martin Shapiro, *Dynamics of American Politics*, 2d ed. (Prentice Hall, 1980), p. 19.
143. Harold W. Stanley and Richard G. Niemi, *Vital Statistics on American Politics, 2015–2016* (CQ Press, 2016), pp. 362–363.

144. These numbers can be found at the Department of Health and Human Services Web site, https://aspe.hhs.gov/poverty-guidelines, January 18, 2018. See also U.S. National Center for Health Statistics, "Births: Final Data for 2016," National Vital Statistics Reports January 2018, https://www.cdc.gov/nchs/data/nvsr/nvsr67/nvsr67_01.pdf.
145. Yang Jiang, Mercedes Ekono, and Curtis Skinner, "Basic Facts about Low-Income Children: Children under 18 Years," National Center for Children in Poverty, Columbia University, February 2016, multiple pages.
146. Drew Desilver, "U.S. Income inequality, on rise for decades, is now highest since 1928," Pew Research Center Fact Tank, December 5, 2013, http://www.pewresearch.org/fact-tank/2013/12/05/u-s-income-inequality-on-rise-for-decades-is-now-highest-since-1928/.
147. Jill Mislinski, "U.S. Household Incomes: A 50-Year Perspective," *Advisor Perspectives*, September 19, 2017, https://www.advisorperspectives.com/dshort/updates/2017/09/19/u-s-household-incomes-a-50-year-perspective. See also (source data) U.S. Bureau of the Census, "Table H-3 All Races," Historical Income Tables: Income Inequality," September 2015, https://www.census.gov/data/tables/time-series/demo/income-poverty/historical-income-inequality.html.
148. "Income and Poverty in the United States: 2016," United States Census Bureau, September 2017, https://www.census.gov/library/publications/2017/demo/p60-259.html.
149. Larry M. Bartels, *Unequal Democracy: The Political Economy of the New Gilded Age* (Princeton: Princeton University Press, 2008), p. 3.
150. Larry M. Bartels, *Unequal Democracy: The Political Economy of the New Gilded Age* (Princeton: Princeton University Press, 2008), pp. 2, 15.
151. Arthur M. Okun, *Equality and Efficiency: The Big Tradeoff* (Washington, D.C.: Brookings Institution, 1975).
152. Derek Thompson, "Why the GOP Tax Cut Will Make Wealth Inequality So Much Worse." The Atlantic, December 19, 2017. https://www.theatlantic.com/business/archive/2017/12/gop-tax-bill-inequalilty/548726/.
153. Robert A. Dahl, *Dilemmas of Pluralist Democracy: Autonomy vs. Control* (New Haven, CT: Yale University Press, 1982), p. 175.
154. Gary Burtless, "Has Rising Inequality Brought Us to the 1920s? It Depends on How We Measure Income," Brookings Institution, May 20, 2014, https://www.brookings.edu/blog/up-front/2014/05/20/has-rising-inequality-brought-us-back-to-the-1920s-it-depends-on-how-we-measure-income/.
155. David Brooks, "The Populist Myths on Income Inequality," *The New York Times*, September 7, 2006, http://www.nytimes.com/2006/09/07/opinion/07brooks.html?hp.
156. Larry M. Bartels, *Unequal Democracy: The Political Economy of the New Gilded Age* (Princeton: Princeton University Press, 2008), p. 54.
157. Scott Horsley, "Republicans Say They Delivered Tax Cuts, Democrats Say Not So Fast." NPR, December 23, 2017. https://www.npr.org/2017/12/23/573142592/republicans-say-they-delivered-on-tax-cuts-democrats-say-not-so-fast.
158. United States Department of Labor, "Wage and Hour Division," January 1, 2018, http://www.dol.gov/whd/minwage/america.htm.
159. Minimum Wage on the Ballot. Ballotopedia. https://ballotpedia.org/Minimum_wage_on_the_ballot.
160. Jonathan Martin and Michael D. Shear, "Democrats Turn to Minimum Wage as 2014 Strategy: Effort to Tap Populism," *The New York Times* (December 30, 2013), p. A1.
161. Christina D. Romer, "The Business of the Minimum Wage," *The New York Times*, March 2, 2013, https://www.nytimes.com/2013/03/03/business/the-minimum-wage-employment-and-income-distribution.html
162. Ezra Klein, "This graph is the best argument for raising the minimum wage," *Washington Post*, February 14, 2013, http://www.washingtonpost.com/blogs/wonkblog/wp/2013/02/14/this-graph-is-the-best-argument-for-raising-the-minimum-wage/.
163. U.S. Bureau of Labor Statistics, "Characteristics of Minimum Wage Workers, 2017." BLS Reports. March 2018. Occupational Employment and Wages Summary," United States Department of Labor, March 30, 2016, available at http://www.bls.gov/news.release/ocwage.nr0.htm; for a list of current and scheduled minimum wage levels by state, see the calculator at https://raisetheminimumwage.com/minimum-wage-state.
164. Economic Policy Institute, "It's Time to Raise the Minimum Wage," Fact Sheet, April 23, 2015; see also Heidi Shierholz, "Fix It and Forget It: Index the Minimum Wage to Growth in Average Wages," Economic Policy Insti-tute Briefing Paper, December 17, 2009.
165. Bureau of Labor Statistics "Characteristics of Minimum Wage Workers, 2017." BLS Reports. March 2018. https://www.bls.gov/opub/reports/minimum-wage/2017/home.htm
166. U.S. Department of Commerce, Bureau of Economic Analysis, "Real Gross Domestic Product," April 27, 2018, https://fred.stlouisfed.org/series/GDPC1.
167. Daniel Bell, *The Coming of Post-Industrial Society: A Venture in Social Forecasting* (Basic Books, 1973), p. xviii.
168. U.S. Department of Commerce, Bureau of Economic Analysis, SA25N Total Full-Time and Part-Time Employment by NAICS Industry 1, https://www.bea.gov/iTable/iTable.cfm?reqid=70&step=30&isuri=1&7022=4&7023=0&7024=naics&7033=-1&7025=0&7026=00000&7027=2013&7001=44&7028=-1&7031=0&7040=-1&7083=levels&7029=30&7090=70#reqid=70&step=30&isuri=1&7022=4&7023=0&7033=-1&7024=naics&7025=0&7026=00000&7027=-1&7001=44&7028=-1&7031=0&7040=-1&7083=levels&7029=30&7090=70.SeealsoWorld Bank, http://data.worldbank.org/indicator/SL.AGR.EMPL.ZS?page=6&order=wbapi_data_value_2012%20wbapi_data_value%20wbapi_data_value-last&sort=asc.
169. U.S. Department of Commerce, Bureau of Economic Analysis, SA25N Total Full-Time and Part-Time Employment by NAICS Industry 1, https://www.bea.gov/iTable/iTable.cfm?reqid=70&step=30&isuri=1&7022=4&7023=0&7024=naics&7033=-1&7025=0&7026=00000&7027=2013&7001=44&7028=-1&7031=0&7040=-1&7083=levels&7029=30&7090=70#reqid=70&step=30&isuri=1&7022=4&7023=0&7033=-1&7024=naics&7025=0&7026=00000&7027=-1&7001=44&7028=-1&7031=0&7040=-1&7083=levels&7029=30&7090=70.
170. U.S. Department of Commerce, Bureau of Economic Analysis, SA25N Total Full-Time and Part-Time Employment by NAICS Industry 1, https://www.bea.gov/iTable/iTable.cfm?reqid=70&step=30&isuri=1&7022=4&7023=0&7024=naics&7033=-1&7025=0&7026=00000&7027=2013&7001=44&7028=-1&7031=0&7040=-1&7083=levels&7029=30&7090=70#reqid=70&step=30&isuri=1&7022=4&7023=0&7033=-1&7024=naics&7025=0&7026=00000&7027=-1&7001=44&7028=-1&7031=0&7040=-1&7083=levels&7029=30&7090=70.
171. U.S. Department of Commerce, Bureau of Economic Analysis, Table 1.1.5 Gross Domestic Product, https://www.bea.gov/iTable/iTable.cfm?reqid=19&step=2#reqid=19&step=2&isuri=1&1921=survey&1903=5.
172. Gabriel A. Almond, G. Bingham Powell, Jr., Russell J. Dalton, and Kaare Strøm, eds., *Comparative Politics Today: A World View*, 9th ed. (Pearson Longman, 2008), p. 54.
173. Harold Hongju Koh, "On American Exceptionalism," *Stanford Law Review* 55 (May 2003), p. 1481.
174. James Madison, *Federalist*, No. 10: "The Same Subject Continued: The Union as a Safeguard Against Domestic Faction and Insurrection," *New York Daily Advertiser*, November 22, 1787.
175. "Romney's Speech from Mother Jones Video," September 19, 2012, *The New York Times*, http://www.nytimes.com/2012/09/19/us/politics/mitt-romneys-speech-from-mother-jones-video.html?pagewanted=all.
176. Bernie Sanders, "Bernie's Announcement," Bernie 2016, May 26, 2015, https://berniesanders.com/bernies-announcement/.
177. http://time.com/4640707/donald-trump-inauguration-speech-transcript/

CHAPTER 5

1. Robert Maguire, "Audit Shows NRA Spending Surged $100 Million Amidst Pro-Trump Push in 2016." Center for Responsive Politics, November 15, 2017. https://www.opensecrets.org/news/2017/11/audit-shows-nra-spending-surged-100-million-amidst-pro-trump-push-in-2016/
2. Ellen Brait, "Candidates' NRA Ratings: A Telling Reflection of Reactions to San Bernardino Shooting." *The Gurardian*, December 3, 2015. http://www.theguardian.com/us-news/2015/dec/03/san-bernardino-shooting-presidential-candidates-responses-nra-ratings
3. Center for Responsive Politics, "2016 Outside Spending by Group." https://www.opensecrets.org/outsidespending/summ.php?cycle=2016&chrt=V&disp=O&type=A
4. David Smiley, "Parkland Parents Launch a Super PAC to Go After Politicians and the NRA." *Miami Herald*, May 30, 2018. http://www.miamiherald.com/latest-news/article212173729.html
5. Jim Puzzanghera, "Equifax CEO Steps Down after Data Breach; He'll Still Get $18 Million Pension." *Los Angeles Times*, September, 26 2017. http://www.latimes.com/business/la-fi-equifax-ceo-20170926-story.html
6. Elizabeth Pennisi, "How Humans Became Social," *Science*, November 9, 2011, http://www.sciencemag.org/news/2011/11/how-humans-became-social.
7. Henri Tajfel, *Human Groups and Social Categories* (Cambridge University Press, 1981).
8. League of Women Voters, "History," League of Women Voters, http://lwv.org/history.
9. James Madison, *The Federalist*, No. 10, November 23, 1787, in Isaac Kramnick, ed., *The Federalist Papers* (Penguin, 1987), pp. 122–128.
10. Peter B. Clark and James Q. Wilson, "Incentive Systems: A Theory of Organizations," *Administrative Science Quarterly*, vol. 6, no. 2, (September 1960), pp. 129–166.
11. David S. Meyer, "The Parkland Teens Started Something. How Can It Become a Social Movement." *Washington Post*, April 13, 2018. https://www.washingtonpost.com/outlook/2018/04/13/392feb24-3e55-11e8-974f-aacd97698cef_story.html?utm_term=.eda2ac0e70c8
12. Jonathan Weisman, "Senate Blocks Drive for Gun Control," *The New York Times*, April 17, 2013, http://www.nytimes.com/2013/04/18/us/politics/senate-obama-gun-control.html?pagewanted=all&_r=.
13. Maggie Astor, "Florida Gun Bill: What's In It, and What Isn't" *The New York Times*, March 8, 2018. https://www.nytimes.com/2018/03/08/us/florida-gun-bill.html
14. See Robert Dahl, *Who Governs?* (Yale University Press, 1961).
15. Center for Responsive Politics, "Microsoft Corp: Donor Profile," http://www.opensecrets.org/orgs/summary.php?id=D000000115.
16. Gabriel A. Almond, G. Bingham Powell, Jr., Russell J. Dalton, and Kaare Strøm, *Comparative Politics Today*, 9th ed. (Pearson Longman, 2008), p. 70.
17. Change to Win, "About Us," 2010, http://www.changetowin.org/about.
18. Office of Labor Management Standards, Union Reports, and Constitutions, http://www.dol.gov/olms/regs/compliance/rrlo/lmrda.htm.
19. Michael P. McDonald and Thomas F. Schaller, "Voter Mobilization in the 2008 Presidential Election," in *The Change Election*, edited by David B. Magleby (Philadelphia: Temple University Press), p. 80.
20. Bureau of Labor Statistics, "Economic News Release: Union Members Summary," United States Department of Labor, January 24, 2014, http://www.bls.gov/news.release/union2.nr0.htm. See also AFL-CIO, "About Us: Union Facts," www.aflcio.org/aboutus/faq/.
21. U.S. Bureau of Labor Statistics, www.bls.gov/cps/cpsaat40.pdf.
22. Brian C. Mooney, "Nation's Two Biggest Unions to Wait on Presidential Endorsement," *Boston Globe* (September 11, 2003), p. A3.
23. https://www.opensecrets.org/pacs/indexpend.php?cycle=2016&cmte=C00490375.
24. Alison Grant, "Labor Chief Sees Anti-Union Efforts Growing Bolder," (Cleveland) *Plain Dealer* (November 22, 2005), p. C1.
25. James MacGregor Burns and Stewart Burns, *A People's Charter: The Pursuit of Rights in America* (Knopf, 1991).
26. Chris W. Cox, "Who We Are, and What We Do," National Rifle Association, 2011, www.nraila.org/About/.
27. Laura Longhine, "Display Cases," *Legal Affairs*, November 2005, http://www.legalaffairs.org/issues/November-December-2005/scene_longhine_novdec05.msp.
28. https://www.humanrightsfirst.org/campaigns/close-guantanamo
29. The American Israel Public Affairs Committee, "What Is AIPAC?" http://www.aipac.org/about/how-we-work.
30. "AIPAC Statement on Opening of U.S. Embassy in Jerusalem." May 14, 2018. http://www.aipac.org/learn/resources/aipac-publications/publication?pubpath=PolicyPolitics/Press/AIPAC%20Statements/2018/05/AIPAC%20Statement%20on%20Opening%20of%20US%20Embassy%20in%20Jerusalem
31. National Education Association, "Our History," 2016, http://www.nea.org/home/1704.htm.
32. Lyndsey Layton, "Teachers Union Endorses Clinton for 2016 Democratic Nomination," *Washington Post*, https://www.washingtonpost.com/local/education/teachers-endorse-clinton-in-2016-primary-bid/2015/10/03/e1c9d71e-69f9-11e5-9ef3-fde182507eac_story.html.
33. Ben Kamisar, "Nation's Largest Police Union Endorses Trump." *The Hill*, September 16, 2016. http://thehill.com/blogs/ballot-box/presidential-races/296342-nations-largest-police-union-endorses-trump
34. Kellan Howell, "National Border Patrol Council Endorses Donald Trump" *The Washington Times*, March 30, 2016. https://www.washingtontimes.com/news/2016/mar/30/national-border-patrol-council-endorses-donald-tru/
35. See Mancur Olson, *The Logic of Collective Action* (Harvard University Press, 1971).
36. Kenneth J. Arrow, "A Difficulty in the Concept of Social Welfare," *Journal of Political Economy*, 58 (August), pp. 328–346; see also David Austen-Smith and Jeffrey S. Banks, "Social Choice Theory, Game Theory, and Positive Political Theory," *Annual Review of Political Science*, 1 (June), pp. 259–287.
37. See the work of Peter Clark and James Q. Wilson, "Incentive System: A Theory of Organization," *Administrative Science Quarterly* 6 (1961), pp. 129–166.
38. Center for Responsive Politics, "Revolving Door: Former Members of the 113th Congress," http://www.opensecrets.org/revolving/departing.php; and Center for Responsive Politics, "Revolving Door: Former Members of the 114th Congress," www.opensecrets.org/revolving/departing.php?cong=114
39. Hugh Heclo, "Issue Networks and the Executive Establishment," in Anthony King, ed., *The New American Political System* (American Enterprise Institute, 1978).
40. Jane Mayer, Dark Money, *The Hidden History of the Billionaires Behind the Rise of the Radical Right* (Doubleday, 2016) p. 169.
41. BIPAC, "Our Model for Political Success," http://bipac.net/bipac_public/initial.asp; see also David B. Magleby, Anthony Corrado, and Kelly D. Patterson, *Financing the 2004 Election* (Brookings Institute Press, 2006); and David B. Magleby, J. Quin Monson, and Kelly Patterson, *Electing Congress: New Rules for an Old Game* (Pearson Prentice Hall, 2007).
42. Andrew Chadwick, "Digital Network Repertoires and Organizational Hybridity," *Political Communication*, 24 (July–September 2007), p. 284.
43. R. Kenneth Godwin, *One Billion New Rules for an Old Game* (Prentice Hall, 2006); see also David B. Magleby, J. Quin Monson, and Kelly D. Patterson, *Dancing Without Partners: How Candidates, Parties, and Interest Groups Interact in the Presidential Campaign* (Rowman & Littlefield, 2007); and David B. Magleby and Kelly D. Patterson, eds., *The Battle for Congress: Iraq, Scandal, and Campaign Finance in the 2006 Election* (Paradigm, 2008).

44. See Jose Antonio Vargas, "Obama Raised Half a Billion Online," *Washington Post*, November 20, 2008, http://voices.washingtonpost.com/44/2008/11/obama-raised-half-a-billion-on.html.
45. The *Federal Register* is published every weekday. You can find it at the library or on the Internet at http://www.federalregister.gov/.
46. Lucius J. Barker, "Third Parties in Litigation: A Systemic View of the Judicial Function," *Journal of Politics*, 29 (February 1967), pp. 41–69; and Jethro K. Lieberman, *Litigious Society*, rev. ed. (Basic Books, 1983).
47. *National Federation of Independent Business, et al.* v. *Sebelius, Secretary of Health and Human Services, et al.*, 567 U.S. 11-393 (2012).
48. Gregory A. Caldeira and John R. Wright, "Organized Interests and Agenda Setting in the U.S. Supreme Court," *American Political Science Review*, 82 (December 1988), pp. 1109–1127; see also Gregory A. Caldeira and John R. Wright, "*Amici Curiae* Before the Supreme Court: Who Participates, When, and How Much?" *Journal of Politics*, 52 (August 1990), pp. 782–806.
49. National Public Radio, "Understanding the Impact of Citizens United," February 23, 2012; Federal Election Committee, "Ongoing Legislation: *Speechnow.org* v. *FEC*"; *Federal Election Commission* v. *Wisconsin Right to Life, Inc.*, 551 U.S. 449 (2007).
50. Gregory A. Caldeira and John R. Wright, "Amici Curiae Before the Supreme Court: Who Participates, When and How Much?" *The Journal of Politics* (August 1990).
51. Nina Totenberg. "Record Number of Amicus Briefs Filed in Same-Sex Marriage Cases," National Public Radio, April 28, 2015.
52. John Cassidy, "The Women's Marches Could Have More Lasting Consequences Than the Government Shutdown." *The New Yorker.* January 22, 2018. https://www.newyorker.com/news/our-columnists/the-womens-marches-could-have-more-lasting-consequences-than-the-government-shutdown
53. John Eligon, "One Slogan, Many Methods: Black Lives Matter Enters Politics," *The New York Times*, November 18, 2015, https://www.nytimes.com/2015/11/19/us/one-slogan-many-methods-black-lives-matter-enters-politics.html.
54. Hansi Lo Wang, "For Black Activists, Charlottesville is Part of A Long History of Racial Strife." NPR, August 17, 2017. https://www.npr.org/2017/08/17/544081153/charlottesville-magnified-issues-with-white-nationalists-black-activists-say
55. See Kenneth Klee, "The Siege of Seattle," *Newsweek* (December 13, 1999), p. 30.
56. For evidence of the impact of PAC expenditures on legislative committee behavior and legislative involvement generally, see Richard L. Hall and Frank W. Wayman, "Buying Time: Moneyed Interests and the Mobilization of Bias in Congressional Committees," *American Political Science Review*, 84 (September 1990), pp. 797–820.
57. http://www.irs.gov/charities-non-profits/other-non-profits/social-welfare-organizations.
58. Michael R. Bloomberg, "The Risk I Will Not Take," *Bloomberg View*, March 7, 2016, http://www.bloomberg.com/view/articles/2016-03-07/the-2016-election-risk-that-michael-bloomberg-won-t-take.
59. Michelle Ye Hee Lee, "Bloomberg to Spend $80 Million, Largely to Support Democrats' Effort to Gain House Majority," *Washington Post*, June 20, 2018, http://www.washingtonpost.com/politics/bloomberg-to-spend-80-million-largely-to-support-democrats-effort-to-gain-house-majority/2018/06/20/e19740a2-74b3-11e8-9780-b1dd6a09b549_story.html?utm_term=.bdf3ffe6ff6b
60. Ethan Bronner, *Battle for Justice: How the Bork Nomination Shook America* (Norton, 1989), pp. 50–55.
61. David B. Magleby, ed., *The Change Election: Money, Mobilization, and Persuasion in the 2008 Federal Elections* (Temple University Press, 2011), p. 47.
62. Jim Rutenberg, "Rove Returns, with Team, Planning G.O.P. Push," *The New York Times*, September 25, 2010, http://www.nytimes.com/2010/09/26/us/26rove.html?pagewanted=all&_r=0; See also, Jane Mayer, *Dark Money: The Hidden History of the Billionaires Behind the Rise of the Radical Right* (New York: Doubleday, 2016) pp. 248-53.
63. Nish Acharya, "The Women's March After Trump's Inauguration Is A Perfect Example of Social Entrepreneurship." *Forbes* (January 19, 2017) https://www.forbes.com/sites/nishacharya/2017/01/19/womens-march-is-social-entrepreneurship-at-its-best/#7668f3b048f7; Planned Parenthood in its annual report for 2016-17 stated, "Since November 2016, we have grown to more than 10 million supporters. More than 700,000 new donors have stepped up to support Planned Parenthood. More than 250,000 people have become new volunteers. "Planned Parenthood: 100 Years." pp. 2-3. https://www.plannedparenthood.org/uploads/filer_public/71/53/7153464c-8f5d-4a26-bead-2a0dfe2b32ec/20171229_ar16-17_p01_lowres.pdf
64. David Mayhew, *Congress: The Electoral Connection* (Yale University Press, 1974), p. 45.
65. John R. Wright, "Contributions, Lobbying, and Committee Voting in the U.S. House of Representatives," *American Political Science Review*, 84 (June 1990), pp. 417–438.
66. Stephen Lacey, "Koch and Exxon Pay to Write State Legislation Repealing Climate Change Laws," *Think Progress*, July 21, 2011, http://thinkprogress.org/climate/2011/07/21/275206/koch-exxon-state-legislation-climate-change-laws/#.
67. Dan Eggen, "Expecting Final Push on Health Care Reform, Interest Groups Rally for Big Finish," *Washington Post*, February 28, 2010, http://www.washingtonpost.com/wp-dyn/content/article/2010/02/27/AR2010022703253.html.
68. *McConnell* v. *Federal Elections Commission*, 124 S. Ct. 621 (2003).
69. Federal Election Commission, https://transition.fec.gov/press/summaries/2016/tables/pac/PAC1_2016_24m.pdf
70. Federal Election Commission, https://transition.fec.gov/press/summaries/2016/tables/pac/PAC1_2016_24m.pdf
71. Open Secrets, "Business Associations," April 25, 2011, http://www.opensecrets.org/pacs/industry.php?txt=N00&cycle=2010.
72. David B. Magleby and Jay Goodliffe, "Interest Groups," in David B. Magleby, ed. *Financing the 2016 Election* (Washington, D.C.: Brookings Institution Press, forthcoming).
73. *Citizens United* v. *Federal Election Commission*, 130 S. Ct. 866 (2010).
74. David B. Magleby and Jay Goodliffe, "Interest Groups," in David B. Magleby, ed. *Financing the 2016 Election* (Washington, D.C.: Brookings Institution Press, forthcoming).
75. Center for Responsive Politics, "2016 Outside Spending by Super PAC" https://www.opensecrets.org/outsidespending/summ.php?cycle=2016&disp=R&pty=A&type=S
76. It is important to note that corporations and unions are still prohibited from contributing money to candidates' campaigns from their profits or general funds.
77. Super PAC spending is not complete. Final amounts could be higher. See https://www.washingtonpost.com/graphics/politics/2016-election/campaign-finance/.
78. David B. Magleby and Jay Goodliffe, "Interest Groups," in David B. Magleby, ed. *Financing the 2016 Election* (Washington, D.C.: Brookings Institution Press, forthcoming)
79. Calculated by author from Federal Election Commission, David B. Magleby and Jay Goodliffe, "Interest Groups," in David B. Magleby, ed. *Financing the 2016 Election* (Washington, D.C.: Brookings Institution Press, forthcoming)
80. Thomas Frank, "What Is K Street's Project?" *The New York Times*, August 19, 2006, http://www.nytimes.com/2006/08/19/opinion/19frank.html?_r=0
81. Federal Election Commission, Table 2: PAC Contributions 2009–2010 Through December 31, 2010, http://www.fec.gov/updates/fec-summarizes-campaign-activity-of-the-2011-2012-election-cycle/.
82. Calculated by author from Federal Election Commission, "PAC Contributions to Candidates, January 1, 2011–December 31, 2012," http://www.fec.gov/updates/fec-summarizes-campaign-activity-of-the-2011-2012-election-cycle/.
83. Diana Dwyre and Robin Kolodny, "Party Money in the 2016 Elections." In David B. Magleby, ed., *Financing the 2016 Election* (Washington, D.C.: Brookings Institution, forthcoming).

84. David B. Magleby and Jay Goodliffe, "Interest Groups," in David B. Magleby, ed. *Financing the 2016 Election* (Washington, D.C.: Brookings Institution Press, forthcoming)
85. David B. Magleby and Jay Goodliffe, "Interest Groups," in David B. Magleby, ed. *Financing the 2016 Election* (Washington, D.C.: Brookings Institution Press, forthcoming); on donors to 45 Committee, see Kenneth P. Vogel, "Secret Money to Boost Trump: A Former Anti-Trump Financier Offers GOP Mega-donors Who Are Embarrassed by Trump the Chance to Help Him Anonymously," *Politico*, September 28, 2016 (www.politico.com/story/2016/09/secret-money-to-boost-trump-228817).
86. J. Quin Monson, "Get On TeleVision vs. Get On the Van: GOTV and the Ground War in 2002," in David B. Magleby and J. Quin Monson, eds., *The Last Hurrah* (Brookings Institution Press, 2004), p. 108.
87. Ruth Marcus, "Labor Spent $119 Million for '96 Politics, Study Says; Almost All Contributions Went to Democrats," *Washington Post* (September 10, 1997), p. A19.
88. David B. Magleby, ed., *Outside Money: Soft Money and Issue Advocacy in the 1998 Congressional Elections* (Rowman and Littlefield, 2000), p. 3; David B. Magleby, ed., *The Other Campaign: Soft Money and Issue Advocacy in the 2000 Congressional Elections* (Rowman and Littlefield, 2003), p. 1; David B. Magleby and J. Quin Monson, eds., *The Last Hurrah? Soft Money and Issue Advocacy in the 2002 Congressional Elections* (Brookings Institution Press, 2004), pp. 1–3.
89. David B. Magleby and Nicole Carlisle Smith, "Party Money in the 2002 Congressional Elections," in David B. Magleby and J. Quin Monson, eds., *The Last Hurrah* (Brookings Institution Press, 2004), p. 54; David B. Magleby and Eric A. Smith, "Party Soft Money in the 2000 Congressional Elections," in David B. Magleby, ed., *The Other Campaign* (Rowman & Littlefield, 2003), pp. 34–35; Marianne Holt, "The Surge in Party Money," in David B. Magleby, ed., *Outside Money* (Rowman & Littlefield, 2000), p. 36; and David B. Magleby, "Conclusions and Implications," in David B. Magleby, ed., *Outside Money* (Rowman & Littlefield, 2000), p. 214.
90. *Federal Election Commission* v. *Wisconsin Right to Life Inc.*, 551 U.S. 449 (2007).
91. *Citizens United* v. *Federal Election Commission*, 130 S. Ct. 876 (2010).
92. Elise Viebeck, "'Washington Cartel': The Ups and Downs of a Cruz Catchphrase," *Washington Post*, August 12, 2015, https://www.washingtonpost.com/news/powerpost/wp/2015/08/12/washington-cartel-the-ups-and-downs-of-a-cruz-catchphrase/.
93. Jenna Johnson, "At Miami Debate, Donald Trump Settles on a Somewhat Reserved Pitch to Voters," *Washington Post*, March 11, 2016, https://www.washingtonpost.com/news/post-politics/wp/2016/03/11/at-miami-debate-donald-trump-settles-on-a-polished-pitch-to-voters/.
94. https://www.hillaryclinton.com/issues/campaign-finance-reform/.
95. https://berniesanders.com/issues/money-in-politics/.
96. Jill Ornitz and Ryan Struyk, "Donald Trump's Surprisingly Honest Lessons About Big Money in Poitics." ABC News. August 11, 2016. https://abcnews.go.com/Politics/donald-trumps-surprisingly-honest-lessons-big-money-politics/story?id=32993736
97. David B. Magleby and Kelly D. Patterson, "Campaign Consultants and Direct Democracy: Politics of Citizen Control," in James E. Thurber and Candice J. Nelson, eds., *Campaign Warriors: The Role of Political Consultants in Elections* (Brookings Institution Press, 2000).
98. Ronald Reagan, "Remarks to Administration Officials on Domestic Policy," December 13, 1988, *Weekly Compilation of Presidential Documents*, 24 (December 1988), pp. 1615–1620.
99. Sylvia Tesh, "In Support of Single-Interest Politics," *Political Science Quarterly*, 99 (Spring 1984), pp. 27–44.
100. Center for Responsive Politics, Lobbying, https://www.opensecrets.org/lobby/.
101. Executive Order 13490—Ethics Commitments. See https://oge.gov/web/oge.nsf/Executive%20Orders/A70F962587DAC28F85257E96006A90F2/$FILE/23a5e4eeaffd4e14b4387b40b0eae5963.pdf?open.
102. Isaac Arnsdorf, "Trump Lobbying Ban Weakens Obama Rules." *Politico*, January 28, 2017. http://www.politico.com/story/2017/01/trump-lobbying-ban-weakens-obama-ethics-rules-234318
103. U.S. Constitution, Article I, Section 9, Clause 8.
104. "Judge Allows Part of Emoluments Lawsuit Against Trump to Move Forward." CBS News. March 28, 2018. http://www.cbsnews.com/news/judge-allows-emoluments-clause-lawsuit-against-trump-to-move-forward/
105. Eric Lipton, Steve Eder, Lisa Friedman, and Hiroko Tabuchi, "For Pruitt Aides, the Boss's Personal Life Was Part of the Job." *The New York Times*, June 15, 2018. https://www.nytimes.com/2018/06/15/us/politics/scott-pruitt-epa-aides.html; for a listing of several of the ethics violations see, Oliver Milman, "A Scandal for All Seasons: Scott Pruitt Ethics Violations in Full." *The Guardian*, June 10, 2018. https://www.theguardian.com/environment/2018/jun/10/scott-pruitt-epa-administrator-scandal-list
106. Coral Davenport, Lisa Friedman and Maggie Haberman, "Mired in Scandal, Pruitt Is Pushed to Exit E.P.A. Post" *The New York Times*, July 6, 2018, p. A1.
107. Federal Election Commission, "Appendix 4: The Federal Election Campaign Laws: A Short History," https://transition.fec.gov/info/appfour.htm.
108. Matthew Ericson, Haeyoun Park, Alicia Parlapiano, and Derek Willis, "Who's Financing the 'Super PACs,'" *The New York Times*, May 7, 2012, https://archive.nytimes.com/www.nytimes.com/interactive/2012/01/31/us/politics/super-pac-donors.html?hp
109. Shane Goldmacher, "Marco Rubio's Secret (Money) Legacy: The Senator's Allies Found a Way to Spend Millions to Support His Presidential Campaign While Remaining Anonymous—Forever," *Politico*, March 28, 2016, http://www.politico.com/story/2016/03/marco-rubio-secret-money-legacy-221218

CHAPTER 6

1. John Mueller, "Choosing Among 133 Candidates," *Public Opinion Quarterly*, Fall 1970, pp. 395-402.
2. E. E. Schattschneider, *Party Government* (Holt, Rinehart and Winston, 1942), p. 1.
3. George Washington, Farewell Address, September 17, 1796, https://founders.archives.gov/documents/Washington/99-01-02-00963.
4. John Adams, letter to Jonathan Jackson, October 2, 1789, http://www.thefederalistpapers.org/founders/adams/john-adams-letter-to-jonathan-jackson-october-1780.
5. See Scott Mainwaring, "Party Systems in the Third Wave," *Journal of Democracy* (July 1998), pp. 67–81.
6. Benjamin Franklin, George Washington, and Thomas Jefferson, quoted in Richard Hofstadter, *The Idea of a Party System* (University of California Press, 1969), pp. 2, 123.
7. For concise histories of the two parties, see Jules Witcover, *Party of the People: A History of the Democrats* (Random House, 2003); and Gould, *Grand Old Party*.
8. See V. O. Key, Jr., "A Theory of Critical Elections," *Journal of Politics*, 17 (February 1955), pp. 3–18; Walter Dean Burnham, *Critical Elections and the Mainsprings of American Politics* (Norton, 1970), pp. 1–10; and E. E. Schattschneider, *The Semisovereign People: A Realist's View of Democracy in America* (Holt, Rinehart and Winston, 1975), pp. 78–80.
9. See Walter Dean Burnham, *Critical Elections and the Mainsprings of American Politics* (New York: W. W. Norton, 1970), pp. 131–134; and Gerald M. Pomper, "The Decline of the Party in American Elections," *Political Science Quarterly*, 92 (Spring 1977), p. 41.

10. William E. Gienapp, *The Origins of the Republican Party, 1852–1856* (Oxford University Press, 1987).
11. Gould, *Grand Old Party*, p. 88.
12. Ibid.
13. David W. Brady, "Election, Congress, and Public Policy Changes, 1886–1960," in Bruce A. Campbell and Richard Trilling, eds., *Realignment in American Politics: Toward a Theory* (University of Texas Press, 1980), p. 188.
14. L. Sandy Maisel, *Parties and Elections in America: The Electoral Process* (Rowman & Littlefield, 2002), pp. 48–49.
15. Gerald Pomper, "Classification of Presidential Elections," *Journal of Politics*, 29 (August 1967), p. 538.
16. During periods of one-party dominance, the other party occasionally wins, as happened with the election of Woodrow Wilson in 1912 and 1916. See Gerald Pomper, "Classification of Presidential Elections," *Journal of Politics*, 29, no. 3 (August 1976): pp. 535–566.
17. see also U.S. Bureau of the Census, Historical Statistics of the United States, Colonial Times to 1957 (Washington, D.C., 1960), https://www.census.gov/library/publications/1960/compendia/hist_stats_colonial-1957.html
18. Earl Black and Merle Black, *The Rise of Southern Republicans* (Belknap Press, 2003).
19. Ross Douthat, "The Obama Realignment," *The New York Times*, November 7, 2012, http://campaignstops.blogs.nytimes.com/2012/11/07/douthat-the-obama-realignment/.
20. "The Center for the Study of the American Electorate" put 2012 voter turnout at 57.5% of all eligible voters, compared to 62.3% who voted in 2008 and 60.4% who cast ballots in 2004," See Curtis Gans, "National Party Turnout Hits New Record Low in States." Center for the Study of the American Electorate, October 10, 2012. https://docs.google.com/file/d/0B5A1lFQvBa-iSkZERUZJSDA2ZVE/edit
21. "2018 United States election results," Associated Press, November 8, 2018.
22. Theda Skocpol and Vanessa Williams, *The Tea Party and the Remaking of the Republican Conservatism* (Oxford Press, 2012).
23. Joseph A. Schlesinger, *Political Parties and the Winning of Office* (University of Michigan Press, 1994).
24. Jill Lepore, "Rock, Paper, Scissors: How We Used to Vote," *New Yorker*, October 13, 2008, http://www.newyorker.com/magazine/2008/10/13/rock-paper-scissors,
25. Jill Lepore, "Rock, Paper, Scissors: How We Used to Vote," *New Yorker*, October 13, 2008, http://www.newyorker.com/magazine/2008/10/13/rock-paper-scissors
26. Robert R. Alford and Eugene C. Lee, "Voting Turnout in American Cities," *American Political Science Review*, 62 (September), pp. 809–810.
27. "2018 United States election results," Associated Press, November 8, 2018.
28. Gary W. Cox and Mathew D. McCubbins, *Legislative Leviathan: Party Government in the House* (University of California Press, 1993).
29. David W. Brady and Craig Volden, *Revolving Gridlock: Politics and Policy from Carter to Clinton* (Westview Press, 1998); James A. Thurber, ed., *Divided Democracy: Cooperation and Conflict Between the President and Congress* (CQ Press, 1991); James A. Thurber, ed., *Rivals for Power: Presidential–Congressional Relations* (CQ Press, 1996); Charles O. Jones, *Separate but Equal Branches: Congress and the Presidency* (Chatham House, 1995), Chapters 5 and 6; and Jon R. Bond and Richard Fleisher, *The President in the Legislative Arena* (University of Chicago Press, 1990).
30. James A Barnes and Jerrick Adams, "2016 Presidential Nominations: Calendar and Delegate Rules." Ballotpedia. https://ballotpedia.org/2016_presidential_nominations:_calendar_and_delegate_rules
31. Fox & Friends, "Donald Trump: Slams 'Crooked System' after Cruz Wins Colorado," April 11, 2016.
32. Yamiche Alcindor, "Bernie Sanders Says Super Delegates Should Follow Voters' Will in Landslide States," *The New York Times*, May 1, 2016, http://www.nytimes.com/politics/first-draft/2016/05/01/bernie-sanders-says-superdelegates-should-follow-voters-will-in-landslide-states/.
33. David Weigel, "Democrats Take First Step Toward Curtailing Superdelegates." *Washington Post*, March 10, 2018. https://www.washingtonpost.com/powerpost/democrats-take-first-step-toward-curtailing-superdelegates/2018/03/10/1ba4eeb6-23f6-11e8-badd-7c9f29a55815_story.html?utm_term=.bd0ac27490a3
34. David Weigel and Erica Werner, "Pelosi Defends Party Intervention in Democratic Primaries." *Washington Post*, April 26, 2018. https://www.washingtonpost.com/news/powerpost/wp/2018/04/26/pelosi-defends-party-intervention-in-democratic-primaries/?utm_term=.32b65e88adc0
35. Author's calculations from data provided by the United States Election Project, http://www.electproject.org/home/voter-turnout/voter-turnout-data.
36. *California Democratic Party* v. *Jones*, 530 U.S. 567 (2000).
37. George Skelton, "California Open Primaries? Give Them a Chance," *Los Angeles Times*, February 11, 2010, http://articles.latimes.com/2010/feb/11/local/la-me-cap11-2010feb11.
38. For California, see http://www.sos.ca.gov/elections/primary-elections-california/; and for Washington, see https://www.sos.wa.gov/elections/faqcandidates.aspx.
39. RNC, Growth & Opportunity Project, 2013, https://gop.com/growth-and-opportunity-project.
40. Rachel Weiner, "Reince Priebus Gives GOP Prescription for Future," *Washington Post*, March 18, 2013, http://www.washingtonpost.com/blogs/post-politics/wp/2013/03/18/reince-priebus-gives-gop-prescription-for-future/.
41. Evan Halper, "Fallout from Data Breach Threatens Bernie Sanders' Campaign," *Los Angeles Times*, December 18, 2015, http://www.latimes.com/nation/politics/la-na-sanders-campaign-data-breach-20151218-story.html.
42. John Wagner, Abby Phillips, and Rosalind S. Helderman, "Accord Reached After Sanders Sues the DNC Over Suspended Access to Critical Voter List," *Washington Post*, https://www.washingtonpost.com/politics/sanders-threatens-to-sue-dnc-if-access-to-voter-list-isnt-restored/2015/12/18/fa8d6df8-a5a2-11e5-ad3f-991ce3374e23_story.html.
43. Joe Uchill, "Gucifer 2.9 Releases New DNC Docs." The Hill. July 13, 2016.
44. David B. Magleby, J. Quin Monson, and Kelly D. Patterson, "The Lingering Effects of a Night Spent Dancing," in David B. Magleby, J. Quin Monson, and Kelly D. Patterson, eds., *Dancing Without Partners: How Candidates, Parties, and Interest Groups Interact in the Presidential Campaign* (Lanham, MD: Rowman & Littlefield, 2007), pp. 163–167; and David B. Magleby, ed., *The Change Election: Money, Mobilization, and Persuasion in the 2008 Federal Election* (Temple University Press, 2011).
45. The early Republican efforts and advantages over the Democrats are well documented in Thomas B. Edsall, *The New Politics of Inequality* (Norton, 1984); and Gary C. Jacobson, "The Republican Advantage in Campaign Finances," in John E. Chubb and Paul E. Peterson, eds., *New Direction in American Politics* (Brookings Institution Press, 1985), p. 6; see also David B. Magleby and Kelly D. Patterson, "Rules of Engagement: BCRA and Unanswered Questions," in David B. Magleby and Kelly D. Patterson, eds., *The Battle for Congress: Iraq, Scandal, and Campaign Finance in the 2006 Election* (Paradigm, 2008), pp. 33–36.
46. David C. King, "The Polarization of American Political Parties and Mistrust of Government," in Joseph S. Nye, Philip Zelikow, and David C. King, eds., *Why People Don't Trust Government* (Harvard University Press, 1997); and National Election Study, "Important Difference in What Democratic and Republican Parties Stand For, 1952–2000," http://www.electionstudies.org/nesguide/toptable/tab2b_4.htm.
47. Kelly D. Patterson, *Political Parties and the Maintenance of Liberal Democracy* (Columbia University Press, 1996), pp. 30–31.
48. Tom Shales, "Bush, Bringing the Party to Life; From the New Nominee, a Splendid Acceptance Speech," *Washington Post*, August 19, 1988, p. C1.
49. See James L. Gibson, Cornelius P. Cotter, John F. Bibby, and Robert J. Huckshorn, "Assessing Party Organizational Strength," *American Journal of Political Science*, 27 (May 1983), pp. 193–222;

see also Cornelius P. Cotter, James L. Gibson, John F. Bibby, and Robert Huckshorn, *Party Organizations in American Politics* (University of Pittsburg Press, 1989).

50. Paul S. Herrnson, *Party Campaigning in the 1980s: Have the National Parties Made a Comeback as Key Players in Congressional Elections?* (Harvard University Press, 1988), p. 122.
51. *Marbury* v. *Madison*, 1 Cranch 137 (1803).
52. Nine percent of all voters were Pure Independents in 1956 and 1960; Keith et al., *The Myth of the Independent Voter*, p. 51. In 1992, the figure was also 9 percent; *1992 National Election Study* (Center for Political Studies, University of Michigan, 1992).
53. *McCutcheon* v. *Federal Election Committee*, 572 U.S. _____ (2014).
54. Robert Barnes, "Supreme Court Strikes Down Limits on Overall Federal Campaign Donations" *Washington Post*, April 2, 2014, http://www.washingtonpost.com/politics/supreme-court-strikes-down-limits-on-federal-campaign-donations/2014/04/02/54e16c30-ba74-11e3-9a05-c739f29ccb08_story.html.
55. Jonathan S. Krasno and Daniel E. Seltz, *Buying Time: Television Advertising in the 1998 Congressional Elections*, report of a grant funded by the Pew Charitable Trusts (1998).
56. "Top Individual Contributors to Joint Fundraising Committees." OpenSecrets. https://www.opensecrets.org/jfc/top_individuals.php.; see also, Michael Beckel, "Clinton's Super-Sized Fundraising Machine Pushes Legal Boundaries." https://www.publicintegrity.org/2016/11/07/20437/clinton-s-super-sized-fundraising-machine-pushes-legal-boundaries The Center for Public Integrity, November 7, 2016.
57. Sidney Milkis, "Parties versus Interest Groups," in *Inside the Campaign Finance Battle: Court Testimony on the New Reforms*, edited by Anthony Corrado, Thomas E. Mann and Trevor Potter (Washington, D.C.: Brookings Institution) 2003, pp. 40-48, for a different defence of party soft money see also, Stephen Ansolabehere and Shanto Iyengar, *Going Negative: How Political Advertisements Shrink & Polarize the Electorate.* (New York: Free Press, 1995). pp. 145–158.
58. Michael Bloomberg, "The Risk I Will Not Take," *Bloomberg News*, March 7, 2016, http://www.bloombergview.com/articles/2016-03-07/the-2016-election-risk-that-michael-bloomberg-won-t-take.
59. Steven J. Rosenstone, Roy L. Behr, and Edward H. Lazarus, *Third Parties in America: Citizen Response to Major Party Failure*, 2d ed. (Princeton University Press, 1996); see also Xandra Kayden and Eddie Mahe, Jr., *The Party Goes On: The Persistence of the Two-Party System in the United States* (Basic Books, 1985), pp. 143–144. The Republican Party, which started as a third party, was one of the two major parties by 1860, the year Republican Abraham Lincoln won the presidency; see Lewis L. Gould, *Grand Old Party: A History of the Republicans* (Random House, 2003), pp. 3–17.
60. Dean Lacy and Quin Monson, "The Origins and Impact of Voter Support for Third-Party Candidates: A Case Study of the 1998 Minnesota Gubernatorial Election," *Political Research Quarterly*, 55(2), pp. 409–437.
61. On the impact of third parties, see Howard R. Penniman, "Presidential Third Parties and the Modern American Two-Party System," in William J. Crotty, ed., *The Party Symbol* (Freeman, 1980), pp. 101–117; see also Frank Smallwood, *The Other Candidates: Third Parties in Presidential Elections* (University Press of New England, 1983).
62. For an analysis of the potential effects of different electoral rules in the United States, see Todd Donovan and Shawn Bowler, *Reforming the Republic: Democratic Institutions for the New America* (Prentice Hall, 2004).
63. William H. Riker, "The Two-Party System and Duverger's Law: An Essay on the History of Political Science," *American Political Science Review*, 76 (December 1982), pp. 753–766. For a classic analysis, see E. E. Schattschneider, *Party Government* (Holt, Rinehart and Winston, 1942).
64. Maurice Duverger, *Party Politics and Pressure Groups* (Nelson, 1972), pp. 23–32.
65. "Nevada," *The New York Times*, 2012, http://elections.nytimes.com/2012/results/states/nevada.
66. "Exit polls," *CNN*, 2016, http://edition.cnn.com/election/results/exit-polls/national/president.
67. Abigail Geigere and Lauren Kent. "Number of Women Leaders around the World Has Grown, but They're Still a Small Group." Pew Research Center. March 08, 2017. Accessed May 10, 2018. http://www.pewresearch.org/fact-tank/2017/03/08/women-leaders-around-the-world/.
68. See Angus Campbell, Philip E. Converse, Warren E. Miller, and Donald E. Stokes, *The American Voter* (University of Chicago Press, 1960); Norman A. Nie, Sidney Verba, and John R. Petrocik, *The Changing American Voter*, enlarged ed. (Harvard University Press, 1979); and Warren E. Miller and J. Merrill Shanks, *The New American Voter* (Harvard University Press, 1996).
69. Marchant, Bristow and Avery G. Wilks, "Arrington blames Sanford for stunning loss to Cunningham in SC Congress race," The State, November 8, 2018. https://www.thestate.com/news/politics-government/article221285930.html.
70. Campbell et al., *The American Voter*, pp. 121–128.
71. Ibid.
72. Bruce E. Keith et al., *The Myth of the Independent Voter* (University of California Press, 1992).
73. Ros Krasney and Arit John, "Sanders Vows Contested Convention, Makes Case for Superdelegate Flips," *BloombergPolitics*, May 1, 2016, http://www.bloomberg.com/politics/articles/2016-05-01/bernie-sanders-vows-contested-convention-makes-case-for-superdelegate-flips.
74. John Sides, "Everything You Need to Know About Delegate Math in the Presidential Primary," *Washington Post*, February 16, 2016, https://www.washingtonpost.com/news/monkey-cage/wp/2016/02/16/everything-you-need-to-know-about-delegate-math-in-the-presidential-primary/.
75. Paul S. Herrnson, *Party Campaigning in the 1980s* (Harvard University Press, 1988), pp. 80–81.
76. Diana Dwyre and Robin Kolodny, "Party Money in the 2012 Elections," in David B. Magleby, ed., *Financing the 2012 Election* (Washington, D.C.: The Brookings Institution, forthcoming).
77. Diana Dwyre and Robin Kolodny, "Party Money in the 2016 Elections." In David B. Magleby, ed. *Financing the 2016 Election* (Washington, D.C.: Brookings Institution, forthcoming).
78. V. O. Key, Jr., *Political Parties and Pressure Groups*, 5th ed. (International, 1964); see also Marjorie Randon Hershey, *Party Politics in America*, 12th ed. (Longman, 2006).
79. Hershey, *Party Politics in America.*

CHAPTER 7

1. Richard Nixon, "Statement About Ratification of the 26th Amendment," June 30, 1971, http://www.presidency.ucsb.edu/ws/?pid=3065.
2. David C. Colby, "The Voting Rights Act and Black Registration in Mississippi," *Publius*, 16 (1986), pp. 129–130.
3. Center for American Women and Politics, Eagleton Institute of Politics, "Gender Differences in Voter Turnout," http://www.cawp.rutgers.edu/sites/default/files/resources/genderdiff.pdf.
4. "Voting Restrictions in Place for First Time in Presidential Election in 2016," Brennan Center for Justice, April 4, 2016.
5. Adam Liptak and Michael D. Shear, "Supreme Court Upholds Trump's Travel Ban, Delivering Endorsement of Presidential Power." *The New York Times*, June 26, 2018. https://www.nytimes.com/2018/06/26/us/politics/supreme-court-trump-travel-ban.html
6. Robert Coles, *The Political Life of Children* (Atlantic Monthly Press, 2000), pp. 24–25; see also Stephen M. Caliendo, *Teachers Matter: The Trouble with Leaving Political Education to the Coaches* (Greenwood Press, 2000).
7. Robert D. Putnam, "Bowling Alone: America's Declining Social Capital," *Journal of Democracy*, 6 (January 1995), pp. 65–78; see also Robert D. Putnam, *Bowling Alone: The Collapse and Revival*

of American Community (Simon & Schuster, 2000); and Robert D. Putnam, "Bowling Together," *The American Prospect*, 13 (February 2002), p. 20.

8. Christine B. Williams, "Introduction: Social Media, Political Marketing, and the 2016 U.S. Election." *Journal of Political Marketing*. June 2017. https://www.tandfonline.com/doi/full/10.1080/15377857.2017.1345828
9. Adam Entous and Ellen Nakashima, "FBI in Agreement with CIA That Russia Aimed to Help Trump Win White House." *Washington Post*. December 16, 2016, https://www.washingtonpost.com/politics/clinton-blames-putins-personal-grudge-against-her-for-election-interference/2016/12/16/12f36250-c3be-11e6-8422-eac61c0ef74d_story.html?utm_term=.f40f3748e1ec.
10. Eric Uslaner, "The Real Reason Why Millennials Don't Trust Others," *Washington Post*, March 17, 2014, https://www.washingtonpost.com/news/monkey-cage/wp/2014/03/17/the-real-reason-why-millennials-dont-trust-others/.
11. Caliendo, *Teachers Matter*, pp. 16–17; Robert Daniel Hess,and Judith V. Torney-Purta. The Development of Political Attitudes in Children. Transaction Publishers, 2005.
12. Kent M. Jennings, Laura Stoker, and Jake Bowers, "Politics Across Generations: Family Transmission Reexamined," *The Journal of Politics*, 71, no. 3 (July 2009). See also Christopher H. Achen, "Parental Socialization and Rational Party Identification," *Political Behavior*, 24, no. 2 (June 2002).
13. Gabriel A. Almond and Sidney Verba, eds., *The Civic Culture Revisited* (Little Brown, 1980), p. 13.
14. J. L. Glanville, "Political Socialization or Selection? Adolescent Extracurricular Participation and Political Activity in Early Adulthood," *Social Science Quarterly*, 80 (1999), p. 279.
15. National Association of Secretaries of State, *New Millennium Project, Part I: American Youth Attitudes on Policies, Citizenship, Government, and Voting* (Author, 1999); and Shaena Engle, "Political Interest on the Rebound Among the Nation's Freshmen, UCLA Survey Reveals," UCLA Newsroom, January 26, 2004, http://newsroom.ucla.edu/releases/Political-Interest-on-the-Rebound-4860.
16. Margaret Stimmann Branson, "Making the Case for Civic Education: Educating Young People for Responsible Citizenship," paper presented at the Conference for Professional Development for Program Trainers, Manhattan Beach, California, February 25, 2001.
17. Amy Mitchell, Jeffrey Gottifried, and Katerina Eva Matsa, "Political Interest and Awareness Lower Among Millennials," Pew Research Center, June 1, 2015, http://www.journalism.org/2015/06/01/political-interest-and-awareness-lower-among-millennials/; Russell Dalton, "Why Don't Millennials Vote?" *Washington Post*. March 22, 2016. https://www.washingtonpost.com/news/monkey-cage/wp/2016/03/22/why-dont-millennials-vote/?noredirect=on&utm_term=.cced3ad8f594; On turnout in 2008 see, Michael Winerip, "Boomers, Millennials and the Ballot Box." *The New York Times*, October 29, 2012, https://nyti.ms/2iGzjDn; for 2016 see, "Millennial and Gen X Voter Turnout Increased in 2016: and Among Millennials, Black Turnout Decreased." Pew Research Center, May 17, 2017. http://www.pewresearch.org/fact-tank/2017/05/12/black-voter-turnout-fell-in-2016-even-as-a-record-number-of-americans-cast-ballots/ft_17-05-12_voterturnout_millennialnew/
18. Russell J. Dalton, *The Good Citizen: How a Younger Generation Is Reshaping American Politics, Second Edition* (Washington, D.C.: CQ Press, 2008), pp. 66, 73, 162.
19. B. Bradford Brown, Sue Ann Eicher, and Sandra Petrie, "The Importance of Peer Group ("Crowd") Affiliation in Adolescence," *Journal of Adolescence*, 9 (March 1986), pp. 73–96.
20. Kenneth Feldman and Theodore M. Newcomb, *The Impact of College on Students*, vol. 2 (Jossey-Bass, 1969), pp. 16–24, 49–56; see also David O. Sears and Nicholas A. Valentino, "Politics Matters: Political Events as Catalysts for Preadult Socialization," *American Political Science Review*, 91 (March 1997), pp. 45–65.
21. Jody C. Baumgartner and Jonathan S. Morris, "MyFaceTube Politics: Social Networking Web Sites and Political Engagement of Young Adults," *Social Science Computer Review*, 28 (2010), pp. 24–44.
22. Daniel B. German, "The Role of the Media in Political Socialization and Attitude Formation Toward Racial/Ethnic Minorities in the U.S.," in Robert F. Farnen, ed., *Nationalism, Ethnicity, and Identity: Cross National and Comparative Perspective* (Transaction, 2004), p. 287.
23. James G. Gimpel, J. Celeste Lay, and Jason E. Schuknecht, *Cultivating Democracy: Civic Environments and Political Socialization in America* (Brookings Institution Press, 2003), p. 127 (see Chapter 5).
24. Robert D. Putnam, "The Rebirth of American Civic Life," *Boston Globe*, March 2, 2008, p. D9.
25. For a general discussion of political knowledge, see Michael Delli Carpini and Scott Keeter, *What Americans Know About Politics and Why It Matters* (Yale University Press, 1996).
26. Elizabeth Mendes, "Americans Down on Congress, OK with Own Representative," Gallup, May 9, 2013, http://www.gallup.com/poll/162362/americans-down-congress-own-representative.aspx.
27. Erikson and Tedin, *American Public Opinion*, p. 304.
28. Joe Concha, "Survey: Only 43 Percent Can Name a Supreme Court Justice." *The Hill*, March 20, 2017. http://thehill.com/homenews/media/324834-survey-only-43-percent-can-name-a-supreme-court-justice
29. http://anesold.isr.umich.edu/nesguide/toptable/tab6d_5.htm
30. *The 2004 National Election Study* (Center for Political Studies, University of Michigan, 2004).
31. James Marson, Alan Cullison and Alexander Kolyandr, "Ukraine President Viktor Yanukovych Driven from Power" *Wall Street Journal*, February 23, 2014, http://www.wsj.com/articles/SB10001424052702304914204579398561953855036.
32. International Republican Institute, "Public Opinion Survey of Residents of Ukraine, November 15–December 14, 2017. http://www.iri.org/sites/default/files/2018-1-30_ukraine_poll_presentation.pdf
33. Sarah Dutton, Jennifer De Pinto, Fred Backus, Kabir Khanna and Anthony Salvanto. "CBS News Poll: State of the Race the Day Before the Election," https://www.washingtonpost.com/news/the-fix/wp/2016/11/10/how-much-did-polls-miss-the-mark-on-trump-and-why/?utm_term=.09a0ba492b68. Other polls had different predictions and the Gallup Poll did not release any pre-election poll. Steven Shepard, "Gallup Gives Up the Horse Race," http://www.politico.com/story/2015/10/gallup-poll-2016-pollsters-214493.
34. American Association for Public Opinion Research, "An Evaluation of 2016 Election Polls in the United States." https://www.aapor.org/getattachment/Education-Resources/Reports/AAPOR-2016-Election-Polling-Report.pdf.aspx
35. Scott Clement, "The 2016 National Polls Are looking Less Wrong After Final Election Tallies." *Washington Post*. February 6, 2017. https://www.washingtonpost.com/news/the-fix/wp/2016/11/10/how-much-did-polls-miss-the-mark-on-trump-and-why/?utm_term=.09a0ba492b68" www.washingtonpost.com/news/the-fix/wp/2016/11/10/how-much-did-polls-miss-the-mark-on-trump-and-why/?utm_term=.09a0ba492b68
36. Thomas D. Snyder, Sally A. Dillow, and Charlene M. Hoffman, "Number of Persons Age 18 and Over, by Highest Level of Education Attained, Age, Sex, and Race/Ethnicity: 2005," *Digest of Education Statistics 2007* (U.S. Government Printing Office, 2008), p. 24.
37. Quoted in Hadley Cantril, *Gauging Public Opinion* (Princeton University Press, 1944), p. viii.
38. John G. Geer, *From Tea Leaves to Opinion Polls: A Theory of Democratic Leadership* (Columbia University Press, 1996).
39. Norman J. Ornstein and Amy S. Mitchell, "The Permanent Campaign: The Trend Toward Continuous Campaigning Stems from Advances in Technology and the Proliferation of Public Opinion Polls," *World and I*, 12 (January 1997): pp. 48–55.
40. "Do You Approve or Disapprove of the Way George W. Bush Is Handling the Situation with Iraq?" CBS News and *The New York Times* Poll, May 3, 2003; and May 20, 2004, http://www.pollingreport.com/iraq2.htm.

41. CBS News and *The New York Times*, "Looking Ahead to the General Election," http://www.cbsnews.com/htdocs/pdf/apr08b_genelec.pdf.
42. Gallup, "Gallup Daily: Obama Job Approval," http://www.gallup.com/poll/113980/gallup-daily-obama-job-approval.aspx.
43. http://www.gallup.com/poll/116500/presidential-approval-ratings-george-bush.aspx.
44. Lawrence R. Jacobs and Robert R. Shapiro, *Politicians Don't Pander* (University of Chicago Press, 2000), p. 3.
45. Robert S. Erikson and Kent L. Tedin, *American Public Opinion: Its Origins, Content, and Impact*, 6th ed. (Longman, 2001), pp. 272–273. On the centrality of the reelection motive, see David R. Mayhew, *Congress: The Electoral Connection* (Yale University Press, 1974).
46. ANES Guide to Public Opinion and Electoral Behavior, "Liberal-Conservative Self-Identification 1972–2008," available at http://anesold.isr.umich.edu/nesguide/toptable/tab3_1.htm.
47. McCloskey and Zaller, *The American Ethos: Public Attitudes Toward Capitalism and Democracy* (Cambridge: Harvard University Press, 1984), p. 190.
48. McCloskey and Zaller, *The American Ethos: Public Attitudes Toward Capitalism and Democracy* (Cambridge: Harvard University Press, 1984), p. 190.
49. See Samuel G. Freedman, "Santorum's Catholicism Proves a Draw to Evangelicals," *The New York Times*, March 23, 2012, https://www.nytimes.com/2012/03/24/us/santorums-catholicism-draws-evangelicals.html.
50. Jonathan Rauch, "The Accidental Radical," *National Journal*, July 26, 2003, pp. 2404–2410.
51. Kathleen Day, *S&L Hell: The People and the Politics Behind the $1 Trillion Savings and Loan Scandal* (Norton, 1993).
52. Yuluya Demyanyk and Otto Van Hemert, "Understanding the Subprime Mortgage Crisis," *Review of Financial Studies*, 24 (2011), pp. 1846–1880.
53. Sylvia Nasar, "Even Among the Well-Off, the Rich Get Richer," *The New York Times*, March 5, 1992, p. A1.
54. Robert Pear and Jennifer Steinhauer, "Tax Cut Extension Passes; Everyone Claims a Win," *The New York Times*, February 17, 2012, https://www.nytimes.com/2012/02/18/us/politics/congress-acts-to-extend-payroll-tax-cut-and-aid-to-jobless.html.
55. Jackie Calmes, "Obama Goes on Offensive Over Taxes on Wealthy," *The New York Times*, April 10, 2012, https://nyti.ms/2N765Mp.
56. Irving Howe, *Socialism and America* (Harcourt, 1985); and Michael Harrington, *Socialism: Past and Future* (Arcade, 1989).
57. Daniel Yergin and Joseph Stanislaw, *The Commanding Heights: The Battle Between Government and the Marketplace That Is Remaking the Modern World* (Simon & Schuster, 1998).
58. Gallup, Inc. "Americans' Views of Socialism, Capitalism Are Little Changed." Gallup.com. May 06, 2016. Accessed June 06, 2018. http://news.gallup.com/poll/191354/americans-views-socialism-capitalism-little-changed.aspx.
59. Senator Bernie Sanders, "Prepared Remarks on Democratic Socialism in the United States," November 19, 2015, Georgetown University, https://berniesanders.com/democratic-socialism-in-the-united-states/.
60. John Zogby, "Ron Paul and the Libertarians Can't Be Discounted," *Forbes*, November 9, 2011, http://www.forbes.com/sites/johnzogby/2011/11/09/paul-libertarians-cant-be-discounted/.
61. Nicole B. Ellison, Charles Steinfield, and Cliff Lampe, "The Benefits of Facebook 'Friends': Social Capital and College Students' Use of Online Social Network Sites," *Journal of Computer-Mediated Communication*, 12 (2007), Art. 1.
62. Data from the American National Election Studies, Center for Political Studies, University of Michigan, 1948–2004, https://www.icpsr.umich.edu/icpsrweb/ICPSR/studies/7281.
63. As many as 48 percent reported that they tried to influence how another person voted in 2004. In 2008 the proportion so reported dropped to 45 percent, and in 2012 it was 40 percent. Available at http://anesold.isr.umich.edu/nesguide/toptable/tab6b_1.htm.
64. *The 2008 National Election Study.*
65. Hadas Gold, "Sanders Bests Clinton on Social Media," *Politico*, March 5, 2016, http://www.politico.com/blogs/on-media/2016/03/social-media-2016-elections-220286.
66. Tessa Berenson, "The Secret of Ben Carson's Campaign Success: Facebook," *Time*, September 8, 2015, http://time.com/4025577/ben-carson-facebook-campaign/.
67. Frank R. Parker, *Black Votes Count: Political Empowerment in Mississippi After 1965* (University of North Carolina Press, 1990), p. 3.
68. Bernard Grofman and Lisa Handley, "The Impact of the Voting Rights Act on Black Representation in Southern State Legislatures," *Legislative Studies Quarterly*, 16 (February 1991), pp. 111–128.
69. Jennifer E. Manning, "Membership of the 114th Congress: A Profile," *Congressional Research Service*, October 31, 2015, https://www.fas.org/sgp/crs/misc/R43869.pdf.
70. Raymond E. Wolfinger and Steven J. Rosenstone, "The Effect of Registration Laws on Voter Turnout," *American Political Science Review*, 72 (March 1978), p. 41.
71. International Institute for Democracy and Electoral Assistance, "Voter Turnout Database," https://www.idea.int/data-tools/data/voter-turnout.
72. Ibid. p. 24.
73. Raymond E. Wolfinger and Steven J. Rosenstone, *Who Votes?* (Yale University Press, 1980), pp. 78, 88.
74. Adam Liptak, "Supreme Court Upholds Ohio's Purge of Voting Rolls," *The New York Times*, June 11, 2018. https://nyti.ms/2Mh1LWX
75. Federal Election Commission, "The Impact of the National Voter Registration Act on Federal Elections 1999–2000," http://www.fec.gov" www.fec.gov.
76. See Raymond E. Wolfinger and Ben Highton, "Estimating the Effects of the National Voter Registration Act of 1993," *Political Behavior* (June 1998), pp. 79–104; and Raymond E. Wolfinger and Jonathan Hoffman, "Registering and Voting with Motor Voter," *PS: Political Science & Politics* (March 2001), pp. 85–92.
77. Marjorie Randon Hershey, "What We Know About Voter-ID Laws, Registration, and Turnout," *PS: Political Science and Politics*, 42 (2009), pp. 87–91, http://journals.cambridge.org/action/displayFulltext?type=6&fid=3260784&jid=PSC&volumeId=42&issueId=01&aid=3260780&bodyId=&membershipNumber=&societyETOCSession=&fulltextType=BT&fileId=S1049096509090234.
78. Quin Monson and Lindsay Nielson, "Mobilizing the Early Voter," paper presented at the annual meeting of the Midwest Political Science Association, Chicago, Illinois, April 3–6, 2008; and Michael P. McDonald and Thomas Schaller, "Voter Mobilization in the 2008 Presidential Election," in David B. Magleby, ed., *The Change Election: Money, Mobilization, and Persuasion in the 2008 Federal Elections* (Temple University Press, 2011).
79. 2012 Election Administration and Voting Survey, pp. 8–10, http://www.eac.gov/assets/1/Page/990-050%20EAC%20VoterSurvey_508Compliant.pdf; 2016 data at: https://www.eac.gov/assets/1/6/2016_EAVS_Comprehensive_Report.pdf.
80. David B. Magleby, "The Death of Voting Booths: America Is Changing the Way We Vote," *Forbes*, December 4, 2014, http://www.forbes.com/sites/datafreaks/2014/12/04/the-death-of-voting-booths-america-is-changing-the-way-we-vote/#1006405224e8.
81. David B. Magleby, "Participation in Mail Ballot Elections," *Political Research Quarterly*, 40 (1987), p. 81.
82. Allison Terry, "Voter Turnout: The 6 States That Rank Highest, and Why," *The Christian Science Monitor*, November 6, 2012, https://www.csmonitor.com/USA/Elections/2012/1106/Voter-turnout-the-6-states-that-rank-highest-and-why/Oregon; see also Paul Gronke, Eva Galanes-Rosenbaum, and Peter A. Miller, "Early Voting and Turnout," *PS: Political Science & Politics*, 40 (2007), pp. 639–645.

83. National Conference of State Legislatures, "Absentee and Early Voting," http://www.ncsl.org/research/elections-and-campaigns/absentee-and-early-voting.aspx.
84. Brennan Center for Justice, "Voting Restrictions in Place for 2016 Presidential Election." August 2, 2016.
85. *Shelby County* v. *Holder*, 570 U.S. _____ (2013).
86. Wendy R. Weiser and Lawrence Norden, Brennan Center for Justice, "Voting Law Changes in 2012," New York University School of Law, available at http://www.brennancenter.org/page/-/d/download_file_39242.pdf.
87. National Conference of State Legislatures, "Voter Identification Requirements," April 11, 2016, http://www.ncsl.org/research/elections-and-campaigns/voter-id.aspx.
88. Justin Grimmer, Eitan Hersh, Marc Meredith, Jonathan Mummolo, and Clayton Nall. "Comment on 'Voter Identification Laws and the Suppression of Minority Votes.'" *Manuscript*, August 7, 2017. https://stanford.edu/~jgrimmer/comment_final.pdf
89. David Cottrell, Michael C. Herron, and Sean J. Westwood, "An Exploration of Donald Trump's Allegations of Massive Voter Fraud in the 2016 General Election." *Electoral Studies*, February 2018, pp. 123-42. https://www.sciencedirect.com/science/article/pii/S026137941730166X
90. David Schultz, "Less than Fundamental: The Myth of Voter Fraud and the Coming of the Second Great Disenfranchisement," *William Mitchell Law Review*, 34, no. 2 (2007), pp. 483–532, 501.
91. Michael Tackett and Michael Wines, "Trump Disbands Commission on Voter Fraud." *The New York Times*, January 3, 2018. https://www.nytimes.com/2018/01/03/us/politics/trump-voter-fraud-commission.html
92. For a discussion of the differences in the turnout between presidential and midterm elections, see James E. Campbell, "The Presidential Surge and Its Midterm Decline in Congressional Elections, 1868–1988," *Journal of Politics*, 53 (May 1991), pp. 477–487.
93. David E. Rosenbaum, "Democrats Keep Solid Hold on Congress," *The New York Times*, November 9, 1988, p. A24; Louis V. Gerstner, "Next Time, Let Us Boldly Vote as No Democracy Has Before," *USA Today*, November 16, 1998, p. A15; and Michael P. McDonald and Thomas Schaller, "Voter Mobilization in the 2008 Presidential Election," in David B. Magleby, ed., *The Change Election: Money, Mobilization, and Persuasion in the 2008 Federal Elections* (Temple University Press, 2011), p. 89.
94. http://www.electproject.org/2016g
95. Christopher Ingraham, "About 100 Million People Couldn't Be Bothered to Vote This Year." *Washington Post*. November 12, 2016. Accessed June 06, 2018. https://www.washingtonpost.com/news/wonk/wp/2016/11/12/about-100-million-people-couldnt-be-bothered-to-vote-this-year/?utm_term=.540e014bdba0; and "2016 November General Election Turnout Rates." United States Elections Project. Accessed June 06, 2018. http://www.electproject.org/2016g.
96. http://www.idea.int/data-tools/data/voter-turnout/compulsory-voting.
97. Wolfinger and Rosenstone, *Who Votes?*, p. 102.
98. Roper Center, "U.S. Elections: How Groups Voted in 2012," https://www.ropercenter.uconn.edu/elections/how_groups_voted/voted_12.html; For a discussion of mobilization efforts and race, see Jan Leighley, *Strength in Numbers? The Political Mobilization of Racial and Ethnic Minorities* (Princeton University Press, 2001).
99. Jens Manuel Krogstad and Mark Hugo Lopez, "Black Voter Turnout Fell in 2016, Even As A Record Number of Americans Cast Ballots." Pew Research Center, May 12, 2017. http://www.pewresearch.org/fact-tank/2017/05/12/black-voter-turnout-fell-in-2016-even-as-a-record-number-of-americans-cast-ballots/
100. U.S. Census Bureau, "Reported Voting and Registration by Race, Hispanic Origin, Sex, and Age Groups: November 1964 to 2008," *Voting and Registration*, July 2009, https://www.census.gov/population/socdemo/voting/tabA-1.xls
101. Ibid.
102. http://www.cnn.com/election/2012/results/race/president/.
103. http://pewresearch.org/pubs/1790/2010-midterm-elections-exit-poll-hispanic-vote.
104. Jens Manuel Krogstad and Mark Hugo Lopez, "Hispanic Voters in the 2014 Election: Democratic Advantage Remains, but Republicans Improve Margin in Some States," Pew Research Center, November 7, 2014, http://www.pewhispanic.org/2014/11/07/hispanic-voters-in-the-2014-election/.
105. Jens Manuel Krogstad, and Mark Hugo Lopez. "Black Voter Turnout Fell in 2016, Even as a Record Number of Americans Cast Ballots." Pew Research Center. May 12, 2017. Accessed June 06, 2018. http://www.pewresearch.org/fact-tank/2017/05/12/black-voter-turnout-fell-in-2016-even-as-a-record-number-of-americans-cast-ballots/; and Jens Manuel Krogstad, and Mark Hugo Lopez. "Hillary Clinton Won Latino Vote but Fell below 2012 Support for Obama." Pew Research Center. November 29, 2016. Accessed June 06, 2018. http://www.pewresearch.org/fact-tank/2016/11/29/hillary-clinton-wins-latino-vote-but-falls-below-2012-support-for-obama/.
106. Howard W. Stanley and Richard G. Niemi, *Vital Statistics on Politics, 2015–2016* (Sage/CQ Press, 2015), pp. 118–120.
107. http://www.time.com/time/politics/article/0,8599,1708570,00.html; and Heather Smith, Rock the Vote Executive Director, interview with David B. Magleby, March 25, 2009.
108. The Center for Information & Research on Civic Learning and Engagement, "CIRCLE: An Estimated 24 Million Young People Voted in 2016 Election." CIRCLE RSS. https://civicyouth.org/an-estimated-24-million-young-people-vote-in-2016-election/.
109. Walbert Castillo, Michael Schramm, and University Of Michigan. "How We Voted - by Age, Education, Race and Sexual Orientation." USA Today. http://college.usatoday.com/2016/11/09/how-we-voted-by-age-education-race-and-sexual-orientation/.
110. http://www.cnn.com/election/2012/results/main/.
111. David B. Magleby, ed., *The Change Election: Money, Mobilization, and Persuasion in the 2008 Federal Elections* (Temple University Press, 2011).
112. http://www.cnn.com/election/2008/results/polls/.
113. U.S. Census Bureau, "Voting and Registration in the Election of November 2000," http://www.census.gov/prod/2002pubs/p20-542.pdf.
114. Christopher R. Ellis, Joseph Daniel Ura, and Jenna Ashley-Robinson, "The Dynamic Consequences of Nonvoting in American National Elections," *Political Research Quarterly*, 59 (June 2006), pp. 232–233.
115. Austin Ranney, "Nonvoting Is Not a Social Disease," *Public Opinion* (October–November 1983), pp. 16–19.
116. Sidney Verba, "Would the Dream of Political Equality Turn Out to Be a Nightmare?" *Perspectives on Politics*, 4 (December 2003), pp. 667–672.
117. E. E. Schattschneider, *The Semisovereign People* (Dryden Press, 1975), p. 96.
118. David B. Magleby, Candice J. Nelson, and Mark C. Westlye, "The Myth of the Independent Voter Revisited," in Paul Sniderman and Benjamin Highton, eds., *Facing the Challenge of Democracy: Explorations in the Analysis of Public Opinion and Political Participation* (Princeton: Princeton University Press, 2011), pp. 238–263.
119. Ibid.
120. 2016 American National Election Study (ANES; www.electionstudies.org). The ANES 2016 Time Series Study [dataset]. https://electionstudies.org/project/2016-time-series-study/.
121. Travis Mitchell, "2016 Party Identification Detailed Tables." Pew Research Center for the People and the Press. September 13, 2016. Accessed June 06, 2018. http://www.people-press.org/2016/09/13/2016-party-identification-detailed-tables/.
122. http://www.whitehouse.gov/history/presidents/.
123. David Menefee-Libey, *The Triumph of Campaign-Centered Politics* (Chatham House/Seven Bridges Press, 2000).
124. Jennifer de Pinto, "From Trump to Terrorism, the Year in Polls." December 30, 2016. http://www.cbsnews.com/news/from-trump-to-terrorism-the-year-in-polling/

125. J. Merrill Shanks and Warren E. Miller, "Policy Direction and Performance Evaluation: Complementary Explanations of the Reagan Elections," *British Journal of Political Science*, 20 (1990), pp. 143–235; and Warren E. Miller and J. Merrill Shanks, "Policy Direction and Performance Evaluation: Comparing George Bush's Victory with Those of Ronald Reagan in 1980–1984," paper presented at the annual meeting of the American Political Science Association, Atlanta, Georgia, August 31–September 2, 1989.
126. Amihai Glazer, "The Strategy of Candidate Ambiguity," *American Political Science Review*, 84 (March 1990), pp. 237–241.
127. Robert S. Erikson and David W. Romero, "Candidate Equilibrium and the Behavioral Model of the Vote," *American Political Science Review*, 84 (December 1990), p. 1122.
128. Morris P. Fiorina, *Retrospective Voting in American National Elections* (Yale University Press, 1981).
129. Roper Center, "How Groups Voted in 2000," https://ropercenter.cornell.edu/polls/us-elections/how-groups-voted/how-groups-voted-2000/.
130. Gerald H. Kramer, "Short-Term Fluctuations in U.S. Voting Behavior, 1896–1964," *American Political Science Review*, 65 (March 1971), pp. 131–143; see also Edward R. Tufte, "Determinants of the Outcomes of Midterm Congressional Elections," *American Political Science Review* (September 1975), pp. 812–826; and Andrew E. Busch, *Horses in Midstream: U.S. Midterm Elections and Their Consequences* (University of Pittsburgh Press, 1999).
131. John R. Hibbing and John R. Alford, "The Educational Impact of Economic Conditions: Who Is Held Responsible?" *American Journal of Political Science*, 25 (August 1981), pp. 423–439; and Morris P. Fiorina, "Who Is Held Responsible? Further Evidence on the Hibbing-Alford Thesis," *American Journal of Political Science* (February 1983), pp. 158–164.
132. David B. Magleby, "Electoral Politics as Team Sport: Advantage to the Democrats," in John C. Green and Daniel J. Coffey, eds., *The State of the Parties: The Changing Role of Contemporary American Parties* (Rowman & Littlefield, 2011). See also David B. Magleby, "The 2012 Election as Team Sport," in David B. Magleby, ed. *Financing the 2012 Election* (Brookings Institution Press, 2014) pp. 1–45.

CHAPTER 8

1. Jake Miller, "Trump: Putting Gorsuch on Supreme Court "best Moment" of First 100 Days." CBS News. May 01, 2017. Accessed May 29, 2018. https://www.cbsnews.com/news/trump-putting-gorsuch-on-supreme-court-best-moment-of-first-100-days/.
2. U.S. Census Bureau, "Number of Elected Officials Exceeds Half Million—Almost All Are with Local Governments," press release, January 30, 1995.
3. U.S. Senate, http://www.senate.gov/general/contact_information/senators_cfm.cfm.
4. Jennie Bowser, "Constitutions: Amend with Care," State Legislatures Magazine, September 2015, http://www.ncsl.org/research/elections-and-campaigns/constitution-amend-with-care.aspxt.
5. See, Voter Registration in North Dakota," http://www.dmv.org/nd-north-dakota/voter-registration.php.
6. Daniel P. Tokagi, "Voter Registration and Election Reform," *William and Mary Bill of Rights Journal*, vol. 17, Issue 2 (2008), pp. 453–506, http://scholarship.law.wm.edu/cgi/viewcontent.cgi?article=1027&context=wmborj.
7. Gregory Korte and Jackie Kucinich, "Paul Ryan Loses Vice Presidential Bid, Keeps House Seat," *USA Today*, November 7, 2012, http://www.usatoday.com/story/news/politics/2012/11/06/paul-ryan-had-the-least-to-lose-on-election-night/1687899/.
8. National Conference of State Legislatures, "The Term-Limited States," NCSL, February 11, 2013, http://www.ncsl.org/research/about-state-legislatures/chart-of-term-limits-states.aspx.
9. *U.S. Term Limits Inc.* v. *Thornton*, 514 U.S. 799 (1995).
10. For an insightful examination of electoral rules, see Bernard Grofman and Arend Lijphart, eds., *Electoral Laws and Their Political Consequences* (Agathon Press, 1986).
11. Eric Ostermeier, "Lisa Murkowski Becomes 1st Three-Time U.S. Senate Plurality Winner." *Smart Politics*, November 22, 2016. http://editions.lib.umn.edu/smartpolitics/2016/11/22/lisa-murkowski-becomes-1st-three-time-us-senate-plurality-winner/
12. Arend Lijphart, "The Political Consequences of Electoral Laws, 1945–85," *American Political Science Review*, 84 (June 1990), pp. 481–495; see also David M. Farrell, *Electoral Systems: A Comparative Introduction* (Macmillan, 2001).
13. There was one faithless elector in 2000 from the District of Columbia who abstained rather than cast her vote for Al Gore in order to protest the lack of congressional representation for Washington, D.C. See, Bob Franken and Art Harris, "Electoral College to Meet Monday." CNN, December 15, 2000. http://www.cnn.com/2000/ALLPOLITICS/stories/12/15/electoral.college/index.html. The Electoral College vote in 2004 had one faithless elector, an elector from Minnesota who voted for John Edwards instead of John Kerry.
14. Kiersten Schmidt and Wilson Andrews, "A Historic Number of Electors Defected, and Most Were Supposed to Vote for Clinton." *The New York Times* December 19, 2016. https://www.nytimes.com/interactive/2016/12/19/us/elections/electoral-college-results.html?_r=0
15. As noted, one of Gore's electors abstained, reducing his vote from 267 to 266; www.cnn.com/2001/ALLPOLITICS/stories/01/06/electoral.vote/index.html.
16. Paul D. Schumaker and Burdett A. Loomis, *Choosing a President: The Electoral College and Beyond* (Seven Bridges Press, 2002), p. 60; see also George Rabinowitz and Stuart Elaine MacDonald, "The Power of the States in U.S. Presidential Elections," *American Political Science Review*, 80 (March 1986), pp. 65–87; and Dany M. Adkison and Christopher Elliott, "The Electoral College: A Misunderstood Institution," *PS: Political Science and Politics*, 30 (March 1997), pp. 77–80.
17. "States with New Voting Restrictions Since 2010 Elections," *Brennan Center for Justice*, April 4, 2016, https://www.brennancenter.org/sites/default/files/analysis/Restrictive_Appendix_Post-2010.pdf.
18. Ryan L. Claasen, David B. Magleby, J. Quin Monson, and Kelly D. Patterson, "At Your Service: Voter Evaluations of Poll Worker Performance," *American Politics Research*, 36 (July 2008), pp. 612–634.
19. *Husted* v. *A. Philip Randolph Institute*, 584 U.S. ____ (2018); Adam Liptik, "Supreme Court Upholds Ohio's Purge of Voting Rolls." *The New York Times*, June 11, 2018. https://www.nytimes.com/2018/06/11/us/politics/supreme-court-upholds-ohios-purge-of-voting-rolls.html
20. Trump tweet at: https://twitter.com/realdonaldtrump/status/787995025527410688?lang=en
21. Charles Stewart III, "Trump's Controversial Election Integrity Commission Is Gone. Here's What Comes Next." *Washington Post*, January 4, 2018. https://www.washingtonpost.com/news/monkey-cage/wp/2018/01/04/trumps-controversial-election-integrity-commission-is-gone-heres-what-comes-next/?utm_term=.281b21a22a12
22. *Buckley* v. *Valeo*, 424 U.S. 1 (1976).
23. John C. Fortier and Norman J. Ornstein, "The Absentee Ballot and the Secret Ballot: Challenges for Election Reform," *University of Michigan Journal of Law Reform*, 36 (Spring 2003), pp. 483–517.
24. Jerrold G. Rusk, "The Effect of the Australian Ballot Reform on Split Ticket Voting: 1876–1908," *American Political Science Review*, 64 (December 1970), pp. 1220–1238.
25. Fortier and Ornstein, "The Absentee Ballot and the Secret Ballot."
26. Lewis L. Gould, *Grand Old Party: A History of the Republicans* (Random House, 2003), p. 236.
27. David B. Magleby and Candice J. Nelson, *The Money Chase: Congressional Campaign Finance Reform* (Brookings Institution Press, 1990), pp. 13–14.

28. David B. Magleby, "The 2012 Election as Team Sport," in David B. Magleby, *Financing the 2012 Election* (Brookings, 2014), pp. 7–16.
29. https://www.opensecrets.org/pres08/summary.php?cid=n00000286&cycle=2008 In 2016, Donald Trump stated that he planned on spending $100 million of his own money on his campaign. The actual amount he spent was $66 million. [Cite: https://www.opensecrets.org/pres16/candidate?id=n00023864]
30. https://www.opensecrets.org/pres16/candidate?id=n00023864
31. Anthony Corrado, Thomas E. Mann, Daniel R. Ortiz, and Trevor Potter, eds., *The New Campaign Finance Sourcebook* (Brookings Institution Press, 2005).
32. *Davis* v. *FEC*. 128 S.Ct. 2759. (2008).
33. Elizabeth Drew, *The Corruption of American Politics: What Went Wrong and Why* (Carol, 1999), pp. 7–8; Robert Longley, "Campaign Contribution Laws for Individuals," About.com, http://usgovinfo.about.com/od/thepoliticalsystem/a/contriblaws.htm; Federal Election Commission, "Contribution Limits for 2011–2012," http://www.fec.gov/info/contriblimits1112.pdf; Federal Election Commission, "How Much Can I Contribute?" http://www.fec.gov/ans/answers_general.shtml#How_much_can_I_contribute.
34. Marta Gold, "Justices Strike Limit on Donors," *Washington Post*, April 3, 2014, p. A20.
35. Diana Dwyre and Robin Kolodny, "Party Money in the 2016 Elections" in David B. Magleby, ed., *Financing the 2016 Election* (Washington, D.C.: Brookings Institution, forthcoming).
36. Gould, *Grand Old Party*, pp. 389–391; and Jules Witcover, *Party of the People: A History of the Democrats* (Random House, 2003), pp. 589–590.
37. Anthony Corrado, "Money and Politics: A History of Campaign Finance Law," in *Campaign Finance Reform: A Sourcebook* (Brookings Institution Press, 1997), p. 32.
38. See David B. Magleby, ed., *Outside Money: Soft Money and Issue Advocacy in the 1998 Congressional Elections*, (Lanham, MD: Rowman & Littlefield, 2000); David B. Magleby, ed. *The Other Campaign: Soft Money and Issue Advocacy in the 2000 Congressional Elections*, (Lanham, MD: Rowman & Littlefield, 2003); David B. Magleby and J. Quin Monson, eds. *The Last Hurrah? Soft Money and Issue Advocacy in the 2002 Congressional Elections*, (Washington, D.C.: Brookings Institution, 2004).
39. See Senate Committee on Governmental Affairs, "1997 Special Investigation in Connection with the 1996 Federal Election Campaigns," http://hsgac.senate.gov/sireport.htm.
40. *Buckley* v. *Valeo*, 424 U.S. 1 (1976).
41. David B. Magleby and Nicole Carlisle Squires, "Party Money in the 2002 Congressional Elections," in *The Last Hurrah?* p. 45, Figure 2–2.
42. David B. Magleby and Eric A. Smith, "Party Soft Money in the 2000 Congressional Elections," in David B. Magleby, ed., *The Other Campaign: Soft Money and Issue Advocacy in the 2000 Congressional Elections* (Rowman & Littlefield, 2003), p. 29, 38; and David B. Magleby and Nicole Carlisle Squires, "Party Money in the 2002 Congressional Elections," in David B. Magleby and J. Quin Monson, eds., *The Last Hurrah? Soft Money and Issue Advocacy in the 2002 Congressional Elections* (Brookings Institution Press, 2004), pp. 44–45, Figure 2–2, http://hsgac.senate.gov/sireport.htm.
43. *McConnell* v. *Federal Election Commission*, 540 U.S. 93 (2003).
44. Corrado, Mann, Ortiz, and Potter, *The New Campaign Finance Sourcebook*, p. 79.
45. David B. Magleby, ed., *The Last Hurrah* (Brookings Institution Press, 2004), pp. 44–45.
46. Ibid., p. 46.
47. David B. Magleby, "Change and Continuity in the Financing of Federal Elections," in David B. Magleby, Anthony J. Corrado, and Kelly D. Patterson, eds., *Financing the 2004 Elections* (Brookings Institution Press, 2006), p. 15.
48. Open Secrets, "2014 Outside Spending, by Race," https://www.opensecrets.org/outsidespending/summ.php?cycle=2014&disp=R&pty=A&type=A
49. Center for Responsive Politics, "2012 Outside Spending, by Group," *OpenSecrets.org*, http://www.opensecrets.org/outsidespending/summ.php?cycle=2012&disp+kR&pty=pty=A&type=A.
50. David B. Magleby, "Continuity and Change in the Financing of U.S. Federal Elections" in David B. Magleby, ed. *Financing the 2016 Election* (Washington, D.C.: Brookings Institution, forthcoming).
51. Bipartisan Campaign Reform Act of 2002, 107th Cong., 1st sess., H.R. 2356.
52. Federal Election Commission, "Independent Expenditure Table 1. https://transition.fec.gov/press/summaries/2016/tables/ie/IE1_2016_24m.pdf; See also, Theodore Schleifer, "Billboard Magnate Pours Fortune Into Unusual Single-Handed Effort for Trump." CNN, September 11, 2016. https://www.cnn.com/2016/09/10/politics/trump-billboards-stephen-adams/index.html
53. *Citizen's United* v. *Federal Election Commission, 558 U.S.* (2010).
54. Nicholas Confessore and Jess Bidgood, "Little to Show for Cash Flood by Big Donors," *The New York Times*, November 9, 2012, http://www.nytimes.com/2012/11/08/us/politics/little-to-show-for-cash-flood-by-big-donors.html?_r=0.
55. David B. Magleby and Jay Goodliffe, "Interest Groups," In David B. Magleby, ed., *Financing the 2012 Election* (Brookings, 2014).
56. Matt Waldrip, deputy national finance director, Romney for President, Inc., Interviewed by David Magleby, March 12, 2013.
57. David B. Magleby, ed., *The Change Election* (Philadelphia: Temple University Press), p. 13.
58. David B. Magleby, Jay Goodliffe, and Joseph Olsen, "How the Internet, BCRA, and Super PACs Have Affected Donor Attitudes, Behavior, and Campaigns," paper presented at the 2014 annual meeting of the Midwest Political Science Association, Chicago, IL (April 3–6, 2014).
59. Jose Antonio Vargas, "Campaign USA," *Washington Post*, April 1, 2008, http://www.washingtonpost.com/wp-dyn/content/article/2008/03/31/AR2008033102856.html.
60. Kenneth P. Vogel, "How Bernie Built a Fundraising Juggernaut," *Politico*, February 10, 2016, http://www.politico.com/story/2016/02/bernie-sanders-fundraising-219112.
61. Kenneth P. Vogel, "How Bernie Built a Fundraising Juggernaut," *Politico*, February 10, 2016, http://www.politico.com/story/2016/02/bernie-sanders-fundraising-219112.
62. Amy Chozich and Jason Horowitz, "Small Gifts to Bernie Sanders Challenge Hillary Clinton Fund-Raising Model," *The New York Times*, February 13, 2016, http://www.nytimes.com/2016/02/14/us/politics/small-gifts-to-bernie-sanders-challenge-hillary-clinton-fund-raising-model.html?_r=2.
63. Nick Gass, "Clinton Outraises Sanders in April," *Politico*, May 2, 2016, http://www.politico.com/blogs/2016-dem-primary-live-updates-and-results/2016/05/hillary-clinton-april-fundraising-totals-222695.
64. Nicholas Confessore and Nick Corasanti, "Fueled by Small Donations, Donald Trump Makes Up Major Financial Ground." *The New York Times*, August 3, 2016. https://www.nytimes.com/2016/08/04/us/politics/trump-fundraising.html
65. Campaign Finance Institute, "President Trump, with RNC Help, Raised More Small Donor Money than President Obama; As Much as Clinton and Sanders Combined." February 21, 2017. http://www.cfinst.org/Press/PReleases/17-02-21/President_Trump_with_RNC_Help_Raised_More_Small_Donor_Money_than_President_Obama_As_Much_As_Clinton_and_Sanders_Combined.aspx
66. See, for example, David R. Mayhew, *Congress: The Electoral Connection* (Yale University Press, 1974); Richard F. Fenno, Jr., *Home Style: House Members in Their Districts* (Little, Brown, 1978); and James E. Campbell, "The Return of Incumbents: The Nature of Incumbency Advantage," *Western Political Quarterly*, 36 (September 1983), pp. 434–444.

67. Gary King and Andrew Gelman, "Systemic Consequences of Incumbency Advantage in U.S. House Elections," *American Journal of Political Science*, 35 (February 1991), pp. 110–137.
68. Alan I. Abramowitz, "Economic Conditions, Presidential Popularity, and Voting Behavior in Midterm Congressional Elections," *Journal of Politics*, 47 (February 1985), pp. 31–43; see also Gary C. Jacobson, *The Politics of Congressional Elections*, 5th ed. (Addison-Wesley, 2001), pp. 146–153.
69. See Edward R. Tufte, *Political Control of the Economy* (Princeton University Press, 1978); see also his "Determinants of the Outcomes of Midterm Congressional Elections," *American Political Science Review*, 69 (September 1975), pp. 812–826. For a more recent discussion of the same subject, see Jacobson, *Politics of Congressional Elections*, pp. 123–178.
70. Alan I. Abramowitz and Jeffrey A. Segal, "Determinants of the Outcomes of U.S. Senate Elections," *Journal of Politics*, 48 (1986), pp. 433–439.
71. Harold W. Stanley and Richard G. Niemi, *Vital Statistics on American Politics 2015–2016* (CQ Press, 2015), p. 32.
72. Linda L. Fowler and Robert D. McClure, *Political Ambition: Who Decides to Run for Congress* (Yale University Press, 1989); and Paul S. Herrnson, *Congressional Elections: Campaigning at Home and in Washington*, 5th ed. (CQ Press, 2007), p. 45.
73. Linda Feldman, "Lisa Murkowski of Alaska Bows Out, Is Seventh Losing Incumbent," *Christian Science Monitor*, September 1, 2010, http://www.csmonitor.com/USA/Elections/Senate/2010/0901/Lisa-Murkowski-of-Alaska-bows-out-is-seventh-losing-incumbent.
74. Gregory Giroux, "Congressional Primaries End with Most House Defeats Since 1992," *Bloomberg*, September 12, 2012, http://go.bloomberg.com/political-capital/2012-09-12/congressional-primaries-end-with-most-house-defeats-since-1992/.
75. Karen Tumulty, "'Republicans Don't Want the Tweet I Got'": Mark Sanford Says Trump Sealed His Loss." *Washington Post*, June 13, 2018. https://www.washingtonpost.com/opinions/republicans-dont-want-the-tweet-that-i-got-mark-sanford-says-trump-sealed-his-loss/2018/06/13/d36a9fe2-6f0e-11e8-afd5-778aca903bbe_story.html?utm_term=.80659c0cc0c4&wpisrc=nl_popns&wpmm=1
76. Jane C. Timm, "'Stunned and Grateful': Katie Arrington, Republican who Beat Sanford, Credits Trump with Win." NBC News., June 13, 2018. https://www.nbcnews.com/politics/politics-news/stunned-grateful-katie-arrington-republican-who-beat-sanford-credits-trump-n882796
77. Shane Goldmacher and Jonathan Martin, "Aleandria Ocasio-Cortez Defeats Joseph Crowley in Major Democratic House Upset." https://www.nytimes.com/2018/06/26/nyregion/joseph-crowley-ocasio-cortez-democratic-primary.html?hp&action=click&pgtype=Homepage&clickSource=story-heading&module=a-lede-package-region®ion=top-news&WT.nav=top-news
78. Eric Bradner, "Tensions Flare Among Democrats As Primaries Approach." CNN, February 28, 2018. https://www.cnn.com/2018/02/28/politics/tensions-democratic-primaries/index.html
79. David McKay, *American Politics and Society*, 7th ed. (Riley-Blackwell, 2009), p. 147; see also Kathleen Hall Jamieson, *Everything You Think You Know About Politics . . . and Why You're Wrong* (Basic Books, 2000), p. 38.
80. For a discussion of different explanations of the impact of incumbency, see Keith Krehbiel and John R. Wright, "The Incumbency Effect in Congressional Elections: A Test of Two Explanations," *American Journal of Political Science*, 27 (February 1983), p. 140.
81. Harold W. Stanley and Richard G. Niemi, *Vital Statistics on American Politics 2015–2016* (CQ Press, 2015), pp. 43–47, for 2016 see Center for Responsive Politics, "Reelection Rates Over the Years." https://www.opensecrets.org/overview/reelect.php
82. Federal Election Commission, "Financial Activity of General Election Congressional Candidates from 1992 to 2010," includes activity through December 31, 2010, https://www.fec.gov/press/2010_Full_summary_Data.shtml. In 2012, the differences were even slimmer. Incumbents outspent challengers two to one in the House and incumbents only spent 15 percent more than challengers in the Senate. See, Federal Election Commission, "House and Senate Financial Activity," includes activity through December 31, 2012, https://transition.fec.gov/press/summaries/2012/ElectionCycle/24m_CongCand.shtml.
83. Federal Election Commission, "House and Senate Financial Activity", includes activity through 12/31/14, https://transition.fec.gov/press/summaries/2014/ElectionCycle/24m_CongCand.shtml.
84. David B. Magleby and Jay Goodliffe, "Interest Groups," in David B. Magleby, ed. *Financing the 2012 Election* (Brookings, 2014). For an account of the tone of outside money advertising before BCRA, see David B. Magleby and J. Quin Monson, eds., *The Last Hurrah: Soft Money and Issue Advocacy in the 2002 Congressional Elections* (Brookings Institution Press, 2004), p. 6.
85. Corrado, Mann, Ortiz, and Potter, *The New Campaign Finance Sourcebook*, pp. 74–76.
86. Data compiled by author from FEC data.
87. Ashley Balcerzak, "Leftover Campaign Cash Can Signal Future Plans." Center for Responsive Politics, February 2017. https://www.opensecrets.org/news/2017/02/leftover-campaign-cash/
88. Candice J. Nelson, "Spending in the 2000 Elections," in David B. Magleby, ed., *Financing the 2000 Election* (Brookings Institution Press, 2002), pp. 28–30.
89. Jonathan S. Krasno, *Challengers, Competition, and Reelection: Comparing Senate and House Elections* (Yale University Press, 1994), p. 2.
90. Alan I. Abramowitz, "Explaining Senate Election Outcomes," *American Political Science Review*, 82 (June 1988), pp. 385–403.
91. Manu Raju, "GOP Civil War: A Coup in Colorado," *Politico*, March 27, 2014, http://politi.co/1duuyUv.
92. Matt Volz, "Baucus Casts Wide Shadow Over Montana Senate Race," *The Kansas City Star*, April 18, 2014, http://www.kansascity.com/2014/04/18/4968565/baucus-casts-wide-shadow-over.html.
93. Sheryl Gay Stolberg and Jonathan Martin, "With a Nevada Senate Candidates Exit, The Bannon Revolt Fizzles" *The New York Times*, March 16, 2018. https://www.nytimes.com/2018/03/16/us/politics/bannon-republican-senate-primary-challengers.html
94. Lee Fang, "Secretly Taped Audio Reveals Democratic Leadership Pressuring Progressive to Leave Race." The Intercept. April 26, 2018. https://theintercept.com/2018/04/26/steny-hoyer-audio-levi-tillemann/
95. David B. Magleby, "More Bang for the Buck: Campaign Spending in Small State U.S. Senate Elections," paper presented at the annual meeting of the Western Political Science Association, Salt Lake City, Utah (March 30–April 1, 1989).
96. Scott Shepard, "Politicians Already Looking to 2008 Election," *Austin (Texas) American-Statesman*, February 6, 2005; and Associated Press, "Former Bush Aide: 2008 Democratic Nomination Belongs to Hillary," April 30, 2005.
97. Chris Morris, "Trump Kicks Off Re-Election Campaign Earlier Than Any President in History" *Fortune*, February 27, 2018. http://fortune.com/2018/02/27/donald-trump-2020-reelection-campaign/
98. Arthur Hadley, *Invisible Primary* (Prentice Hall, 1976).
99. Nick Gass, "Jeb Bush to Announce 2016 Bid on June 15," *Politico*, June 4, 2015, http://www.politico.com/story/2015/06/jeb-bush-to-announce-2016-intentions-on-june-15-118626.
100. Nicholas Confessore, "Jeb Bush Outstrips Rivals in Fund-Raising as 'Super PACs' Swell Candidates' Coffers." *The New York Times*. July 9, 2015. http://www.nytimes.com/2015/07/10/us/politics/jeb-bush-races-past-rivals-in-fund-raising-aided-by-super-pac-cash.html
101. Zachary A. Goldfarb, "Gingrich Fails to Win Spot on Virginia Primary Ballot, *Washington Post*, December 24, 2011, http://www.washingtonpost.com/politics/gingrich-fails-to-win-spot-on-virginia-primary-ballot/2011/12/24/gIQAnErBGP_story.html.

102. Joe Hallett, "Santorum Loses 9 Ohio Delegates," *Columbus Dispatch*, February 16, 2012, http://www.dispatch.com/content/stories/local/2012/02/16/santorum-loses-9-ohio-delegates.html.
103. Unless otherwise indicated, the following section draws all of its data on delegate allocation, delegate type, and primary type from the following sources: For general information regarding primary types, see James W. Davis, *Presidential Primaries*, rev. ed. (Greenwood Press, 1984), Chapter 3, pp. 56–63 for specifics on each state (and Puerto Rico). This material is used with the permission of the publisher. For specific allocation of delegates for the 2016 Democratic National Convention see, https://ballotpedia.org/wiki/images/c/ce/Appendix_B_-_Allocation_Chart_1.29.16.pdf.pdf. See also Delegate Selection Materials for the 2016 Democratic National Convention, December 15, 2014, http://demrulz.org/wp-content/files/12.15.14_2016_Delegate_Selection_Documents_Mailing_-_Rules_Call_Regs_Model_Plan_Checklist_12.15.14.pdf. For specific allocation of delegates for the Republican Party and the type of primary by state, see 2016 Presidential Nominating Process of the Republican National Committee, https://prod-static-ngop-pbl.s3.amazonaws.com/media/documents/2016%20PRESIDENTIAL%20NOMINATING%20PROCESS%20BOOK_1443803140.pdf.
104. To calculate these numbers, three sites were used: "America's Primary Agenda: 2016 Election Calendar," *The Economist*, May 4, 2016, http://www.economist.com/blogs/graphic-detail/2016/05/primary-season; "2016 Democratic National Convention Delegate/Alternative Allocation," Democratic National Committee, August 23, 2014, https://ballotpedia.org/wiki/images/c/ce/Appendix_B_-_Allocation_Chart_1.29.16.pdf.pdf; "Choosing the Nominee," GOP.com, https://www.gop.com/2016-gophq/event_schedule/?schedule_type=primary.
105. The Green Papers Republican Detailed Delegate Allocation—2016, http://www.thegreenpapers.com/P16/D-PU.phtml?sort=u, and http://www.thegreenpapers.com/P16/R-PU.phtml?sort=u.
106. Domenico Montanaro, "Clinton Has a 45-to-1 'Superdelegate' Advantage Over Sanders," *NPR Politics*, November 13, 2015, http://www.npr.org/2015/11/13/455812702/clinton-has-45-to-1-superdelegate-advantage-over-sanders.
107. David Byler, "California Moved Its Primary Up. What Does that Mean for 2020?" FiveThirtyEight, https://fivethirtyeight.com/features/california-moved-its-primary-up-what-does-that-mean-for-2020/. By combining the presidential primary vote with the regularly scheduled June 2012 primary the state saved approximately $100 million. See Jeff Zeleny, "Primary Calendar Stirs Republican Anxiety," *The New York Times*, July 25, 2011, http://www.nytimes.com/2011/07/26/us/politics/26primary.html?pagewanted=all.
108. Lesley Clark, "DNC Votes to Strip Florida of Delegates: Florida's Status as a Key Presidential Prize Is in Doubt, with National Democratic Party Leaders Rejecting a State Plan to Hold an Early Primary," *Miami Herald*, August 26, 2007; see also "Campaign Briefing: On the Trail," *Newsday*, December 2, 2007, p. A3.
109. Rosalind S. Helderman, "Florida Takes Blame for Nasty GOP Race," *Washington Post*, February 5, 2012, Suburban Edition.
110. Peter Hamby, "GOP Adopts Changes to 2016 Presidential Primary Process," *CNNPolitics Blog*, January 24, 2014, http://politicalticker.blogs.cnn.com/2014/01/24/gop-adopts-changes-to-2016-presidential-primary-process/.
111. 2016 Presidential Primaries, Caucuses, and Conventions Chronologically, The Green Papers, http://www.thegreenpapers.com/P16/events.phtml?s=c.
112. *California Democratic Party et al., Petitioners* v. *Bill Jones, Secretary of State of California et al.*, 530 U.S. 567 (2000).
113. David Redlawsk and Arthur Sanders, "Groups and Grassroots in the Iowa Caucuses," in David B. Magleby, ed., *Outside Money in the 2000 Presidential Primaries and Congressional Elections*, in *PS: Political Science and Politics* (June 2001), p. 270; see also Iowa Caucus Project 2004, http://www.iowacaucus.org.
114. 2016 Presidential Primaries Results, http://www.politico.com/2016-election/results/map/president.
115. CNN Exit Polls, http://www.cnn.com/ELECTION/2012/primaries.html.
116. Public Opinion Strategies, "Turnout by Party and Year Among States Where Both Parties Have Held Primaries/Caucuses," April 27, 2016.
117. David A. Graham, "Democrats Debate the Debates: The Party Announced Its Slate of Six Meetings for 2016 Candidates, and Martin O'Malley and Bernie Sanders are Not Pleased." *The Atlantic* August 6, 2015. https://www.theatlantic.com/politics/archive/2015/08/democrats-in-disarray/400682/
118. Nicholas Confessore and Karen Yourish, "Measuring Donald Trump's Mammoth Advantage in Free Media," *The New York Times*, March 15, 2016, http://www.nytimes.com/2016/03/16/upshot/measuring-donald-trumps-mammoth-advantage-in-free-media.html?_r=0.
119. The viewership of conventions has declined as the amount of time devoted to conventions dropped. In 1988, Democrats averaged 27.1 million viewers and Republicans 24.5 million. By 1996, viewership for the Democrats was 18 million viewers on average; for the Republicans, it was 16.6 million. See John Carmody, "The TV Column," *Washington Post*, September 2, 1996, p. D4. Viewership figures improved somewhat in 2000: Democrats averaged 20.6 million viewers and Republicans 19.2 million. See Don Aucoin, "Democrats Hold TV Ratings Edge," *Boston Globe*, August 19, 2000, p. F3; and Jim Rutenberg and Brain Stelter, "Conventions, Anything but Dull, Are a TV Hit," *The New York Times*, September 6, 2008.
120. Nicolas Groom, "Obama Draws Biggest Convention TV Audience, Twitter Record," *Reuters*, September 7, 2012, http://www.reuters.com/article/us-usa-campaign-media-idUSBRE88619220120907.
121. David Bauder, "Donald Trump Speech Beats Hillary Clinton in TV Viewership," *Washington Post, July* 29, 2016.
122. Barry Goldwater, speech to the Republican National Convention accepting the Republican nomination for president, July 16, 1964, www.washingtonpost.com/wp-srv/politics/daily/may98/goldwaterspeech.htm.
123. http://www.presidency.ucsb.edu/ws/?pid=25970
124. Jeff Fishel, *Presidents and Promises* (CQ Press, 1984), pp. 26–28.
125. W. H Lawrence, "Johnson Is Nominated for Vice President: Kennedy Picks Him to Placate the South," *The New York Times*, July 15, 1960, https://partners.nytimes.com/library/politics/camp/600715convention-dem-ra.html.
126. Alexander Burns and Maggie Haberman, "How Donald Trump Finally Settled on Mike Pence." *The New York Times*, July 15, 2016. https://www.nytimes.com/2016/07/16/us/politics/mike-pence-donald-trump-vice-president.html
127. National Association of Secretaries of State, "State Laws Regarding Presidential Ballot Access for the General Election, Reviewed February 2016," https://www.nass.org/node/134
128. "First Presidential Debate Draws 84 Million Viewers." Nielson, September 27, 2016. http://www.nielsen.com/us/en/insights/news/2016/first-presidential-debate-of-2016-draws-84-million-viewers.html
129. Jessica Taylor, "Fireworks in St. Louis: Trump, Clinton Trade Barbs in Heated Debate" NPR, October 9, 2016. https://www.npr.org/2016/10/09/497314611/trump-clinton-debate-for-first-time-since-leaked-audio
130. Daniel White, "Read the Transcript of the Second Presidential Debate." *Time*, October 10, 2016. http://time.com/4523325/read-the-transcript-of-the-second-presidential-debate/
131. "Clinton Wins Third Debate, Gains Ground as 'Presidential.'" Gallup News. October 24, 2016. http://news.gallup.com/poll/196643/clinton-wins-third-debate-gains-ground-presidential.aspx
132. Commission on Presidential Debates "The Commission on Presidential Debates: An Overview. http://www.debates.org/index.php?page=overview.

133. Ibid.
134. Adam Nagourney, Ashley Parker, Jim Rutenberg, and Jeff Zeleny, "How a Race in the Balance Went to Obama," *The New York Times*, November 7, 2012, http://www.nytimes.com/2012/11/08/us/politics/obama-campaign-clawed-back-after-a-dismal-debate.html.
135. "The Great Ad Wars of 2004," *The New York Times*, November 11, 2004, http://www.nytimes.com/imagepages/2004/11/01/politics/20041101_CAMP_GRAPHIC.html.
136. University of Wisconsin Advertising Project, "Political Advertising in 2008," March 17, 2010, http://wiscadproject.wisc.edu/wiscads_report_031710.pdf.
137. Wesleyan Media Project, "Presidential Ad War Tops 1M Airings," *Wesleyan Media Project*, November 2, 2012, http://mediaproject.wesleyan.edu/2012/11/02/presidential-ad-war-tops-1m-airings/.
138. Erika Franklin Fowler, Michael M. Franz, and Travis N. Ridout. *Political Advertising in the United States* (Westview Press. 2016) p. 3; for 2016 see Erika Franklin Fowler, Travis N. Ridout, and Micahel M. Franz, "Political Advertising in 2016: The Presidential Election as Outlier?" *The Forum*. 2016. p. 447.
139. David B. Magleby, ed., *The Change Election* (Temple University Press, 2011); Institute of Politics, John F. Kennedy School of Government, Harvard University, *Campaign for President: The Managers Look at 2012* (Lanham, Md.: Rowman and Littlefield, 2013).
140. David B. Magleby, "Continuity and Change in the Financing of U.S. Federal Elections." in David B. Magleby, *Financing the 2016 Election*. (Washington, D.C.: Brookings Institution, forthcoming)
141. http://www.cnn.com/election/results/exit-polls.
142. Robert S. Erikson, "Economic Conditions and the Presidential Vote," *American Political Science Review*, 83 (June 1989), pp. 567–575. Class-based voting has also become more important. See Robert S. Erikson, Thomas O. Lancaster, and David W. Romers, "Group Components of the Presidential Vote, 1952–1984," *Journal of Politics*, 51 (May 1989), pp. 337–346.
143. Alec Tyson and Shiva Maniam, "Behind Trump's Victory: Divisions by Race, Gender, Education," November 9, 2016, http://www.pewresearch.org/fact-tank/2016/11/09/behind-trumps-victory-divisions-by-race-gender-education/.
144. *Citizens United* v. *FEC*, 558 U.S. 310 (2010) and *McCutcheon* v. *FEC*, 572 U.S. _____ (2014).
145. Ben Freeman, *The Foreign Policy Auction: Foreign Lobbying in America* (United States: CreateSpace, 2012), 1.
146. Anne Farris, "Unfolding Story Swelling Like a Sponge," April 6, 1997, https://www.washingtonpost.com/wp-srv/politics/special/campfin/stories/story.htm.
147. Terry Frieden, "Former Democratic Fund-raiser John Huang Pleads Guilty." *CNN*.com, August 12, 1999, http://www.cnn.com/ALLPOLITICS/stories/1999/08/12/huang.sentence/.
148. Adam Entous and Ellen Nakashima, "FBI in Agreement with CIA That Russia Aimed to Help Trump Win White House." *Washington Post*. December 16, 2016, https://www.washingtonpost.com/politics/clinton-blames-putins-personal-grudge-against-her-for-election-interference/2016/12/16/12f36250-c3be-11e6-8422-eac61c0ef74d_story.html?utm_term=.f40f3748e1ec.
149. Callum Borchers, "Analysis | What We Know about the 21 States Targeted by Russian Hackers." *Washington Post*. September 23, 2017, https://www.washingtonpost.com/news/the-fix/wp/2017/09/23/what-we-know-about-the-21-states-targeted-by-russian-hackers/?noredirect=on&utm_term=.2b361eeb88c7.
150. Evan Perez and Daniella Diaz, "Russia Sanctions Announced by White House," *CNN.com*, January 03, 2017, https://www.cnn.com/2016/12/29/politics/russia-sanctions-announced-by-white-house/index.html.
151. Anne Gearan, Philip Rucker, and Abby Phillip, "DNC Chairwoman Will Resign in Aftermath of Committee Email Controversy." *Washington Post*. July 24, 2016, https://www.washingtonpost.com/politics/hacked-emails-cast-doubt-on-hopes-for-party-unity-at-democratic-convention/2016/07/24/a446c260-51a9-11e6-b7de-dfe509430c39_story.html?utm_term=.a221e98e1a1e.
152. Max Fisher, "Donald Trump's Appeal to Russia Shocks Foreign Policy Experts." *The New York Times*, January 20, 2018, https://www.nytimes.com/2016/07/29/world/europe/russia-trump-clinton-email-hacking.html.
153. "Inside the Internet Research Agency's Lie Machine." *The Economist*" February 22, 2018, https://www.economist.com/briefing/2018/02/22/inside-the-internet-research-agencys-lie-machine.
154. Anne Claire Stapleton, "No, You Can't Vote by Text Message." *CNN.com*, November 07, 2016, https://www.cnn.com/2016/11/07/politics/vote-by-text-message-fake-news/index.html.
155. Mark Mazzetti, Ronen Bergman, and David Kirkpatrick, "Trump Jr. and Other Aides Met with Gulf Emissary Offering Help to Win Election." *The New York Times*, May 19, 2018, https://www.nytimes.com/2018/05/19/us/politics/trump-jr-saudi-uae-nader-prince-zamel.html.
156. Federal Election Commission, "House Campaign Activity by State and District," http://www.fec.gov/press/summaries/2012/ElectionCycle/24m_CongCand.shtml.
157. Lynda W. Powell, "The Influence of Campaign Contributions on Legislative Policy," *The Forum: A Journal of Applied Research in Contemporary Politics*, 11, no. 3 (October 2013), pp. 339–355, http://www.cfinst.org/pdf/papers/02_Powell_Influence.pdf.
158. New Jersey Election Law Enforcement Commission, "Candidate Disclosure Report," http://www.elec.state.nj.us/ELECReport/StandardSearch.aspx.
159. John C. Green, "Financing the 2016 Presidential Nomination Campaigns," in David B. Magleby, ed., *Financing the 2016 Election*, (Washington, D.C.: Brookings Institution, forthcoming).
160. https://www.opensecrets.org/pres08/summary.php?cid=n00000286&cycle=2008 In 2016, Donald Trump stated that he planned on spending $100 million of his own money on his campaign. The actual amount he spent was $66 million. [Cite: https://www.opensecrets.org/pres16/candidate?id=n00023864]
161. Federal Election Commission, herndon1.sdrdc.com/fecimg/srssea.html; see also FEC, "Congressional Candidates Spend $1.16 Billion During 2003–2004," press release, June 9, 2005, https://classic.fec.gov/press/press2005/20050609candidate/20050609candidate.html.
162. Erin Durkin, "Bernie Sanders Shakes His Head at New York's Closed Primary as He Takes One Last Campaign Stroll Through Times Square," *New York Daily News*, April 19, 2016, http://www.nydailynews.com/news/politics/bernie-sanders-slams-closed-n-y-primary-times-square-article-1.2607146.
163. Tom LoBianco, "Trump Children Unable to Vote for Dad in New York Primary," *CNN.com*, April 12, 2016, http://www.cnn.com/2016/04/11/politics/donald-trump-ivanka-vice-president/.
164. See Todd Donovan and Shawn Bowler, *Reforming the Republic: Democratic Institutions for a New America* (Prentice Hall, 2004).
165. Louis Nelson, "Trump Pushes To Swap Electoral College for Popular Vote." *Politico*, April 26, 2018. https://www.politico.com/story/2018/04/26/trump-electoral-college-popular-vote-555148
166. Curtis B. Gans, director, Committee for the Study of the American Electorate, personal communication, September 22, 2004.
167. The President's Commission for a National Agenda for the Eighties, in *A National Agenda for the Eighties* (U.S. Government Printing Office, 1980), p. 97, proposed holding four presidential primaries, scheduled approximately one month apart.

CHAPTER 9

1. Jasmine C. Lee and Kevien Quealy, "The 446 People, Places and Things Donald Trump Has Insulted on Twitter: A Complete List." *New York Times*, April 13, 2018. https://www.nytimes.com/interactive/2016/01/28/upshot/donald-trump-twitter-insults.html
2. Seth Brown, "Online 'Trolls' Target Baptists." BRnow.org. https://brnow.org/News/February-2018/Online-trolls-target-Baptists
3. Josh Hafner, USA Today, Nov. 1, 2017 https://www.usatoday.com/story/news/politics/onpolitics/2017/11/01/onpolitics-today-army-jesus-how-russia-messed-americans-online/823842001/
4. Shane Harris, Damien Paletta, and Carol E. Lee, "Intelligence Agencies Say Russia Ordered 'Influence Campaign' to aid Donald Trump in Election." *The Wall Street Journal*, January 6, 2017. https://www.wsj.com/articles/donald-trump-continues-attacks-on-intelligence-agencies-ahead-of-classified-briefing-on-russia-1483728966
5. Issie Lapowsky, "Facebook Doesn't Know How Many People Followed Russians on Instagram." *Wired* March 2, 2018. https://www.wired.com/story/facebook-does-not-know-how-many-followers-russian-trolls-had-on-instagram/
6. Callum Borchers, "What We Know About the 21 States Targeted by Russian Hackers." *The Washington Post*, September 23, 2017. https://www.washingtonpost.com/news/the-fix/wp/2017/09/23/what-we-know-about-the-21-states-targeted-by-russian-hackers/?utm_term=.7e4c160cc941
7. Cynthia McFadden, William M. Arkin, Kevin Monahan, and Ken Dilanian, "U.S. Intel: Russia Compromised Seven States Prior to 2016 Election." NBC News. February 28, 2018. https://www.nbcnews.com/politics/elections/u-s-intel-russia-compromised-seven-states-prior-2016-election-n850296
8. The New York Times, "Full Transcript and Video: James Comey's Testimony on Capitol Hill," *The New York Times*, June 8, 2017. https://www.nytimes.com/2017/06/08/us/politics/senate-hearing-transcript.html
9. See Gordon S. Wood, *The American Revolution: A History* (Modern Library, 2002), pp. 55–56.
10. Eugene Volokh, "Freedom for the Press as an Industry, or for the Press as a Technology? From the Framing to Today," *University of Pennsylvania Law Review*, 160 (2012), p. 465.
11. Benjamin Franklin, "Apology for Printers," *The Pennsylvania Gazette*, June 10, 1731, National Humanities Center: Resource Toolbox, Becoming American: The British Atlantic Colonies, 1690–1763, http://nationalhumanitiescenter.org/pds/becomingamer/ideas/text5/franklinprinting.pdf.
12. Benjamin Franklin, "Statement of Editorial Policy," *The Pennsylvania Gazette*, July 24, 1740, National Humanities Center: Resource Toolbox, Becoming American: The British Atlantic Colonies, 1690–1763, http://nationalhumanitiescenter.org/pds/becomingamer/ideas/text5/franklinprinting.pdf.
13. *First National Bank of Boston* v. *Bellotti*, 435 U.S. 765 (1978) p. 800, note 5.
14. Eugene Volokh, "Freedom for the Press as an Industry, or for the Press as a Technology? From the Framing to Today," *University of Pennsylvania Law Review*, 160 (2012), p. 466.
15. *New York Times Co.* v. *United States*, 403 U.S. 713 (1971).
16. William Rivers, *The Other Government* (Universe Books, 1982); Douglas Cater, *The Fourth Branch of Government* (Houghton Mifflin, 1959); Dom Bonafede, "The Washington Press: An Interpreter or a Participant in Policy Making?" *National Journal*, April 24, 1982, pp. 716–721; and Michael Ledeen, "Learning to Say 'No' to the Press," *Public Interest* 73 (Fall 1983), p. 113.
17. Potter Stewart, "Or of the Press," *Hastings Law Journal*, 26 (1975), p. 634.
18. See Robert A. Rutland, *Newsmongers: Journalism in the Life of the Nation, 1690–1972* (Dial Press, 1973).
19. Leslie G. Moeller, "The Big Four: Mass Media Actualities and Expectations," in Richard W. Budd and Brent D. Ruben, eds., *Beyond Media: New Approaches to Mass Communication* (Transaction Books, 1988), p. 15.
20. David Paul Nord, *Communities of Journalism* (University of Illinois Press, 2001), pp. 80–89.
21. Christine Haughney and Michael J. De Le Merced, "Gannett, Owner of USA Today, to Split Its Print and Broadcast Businesses," *The New York Times, August* 5, 2014, http://dealbook.nytimes.com/2014/08/05/gannett-to-spin-off-its-print-business/?_r=0.
22. Paul Farhi, "Los Angeles Times Owner Sells Paper to Local Billionaire Patrick Soon-Shiong, Ending a Long Troubled Relationship." *The Washington Post*, February 7, 2018. https://www.washingtonpost.com/lifestyle/style/los-angeles-times-owner-will-sell-paper-ending-a-long-troubled-relationship/2018/02/06/60f5f42e-0b5f-11e8-95a5-c396801049ef_story.html?utm_term=.d36f2d6d46de
23. Joe Flint and John McKinnon, "Sinclair Faces Federal Resistance Over Proposed Purchase of Tribune Media: Regulator Pushes Back Against Potential Buyers of TV Stations Sinclair Plans to Unload to Gain Approval for the Deal." *The Wall Street Journal*, April 10, 2018. https://www.wsj.com/articles/sinclair-faces-fcc-resistance-over-tribune-purchase-1523387359.
24. Frank Ahrens, "Murdoch Seizes Wall Street Journal in $5 Billion Coup," *Washington Post*, August 1, 2007, http://www.washingtonpost.com/wp-dyn/content/article/2007/07/31/AR2007073100896_pf.html.
25. Karla Adam and Paul Fahri, "News of the World to Close Amid Phone-Hacking Scandal," *Washington Post*, July 7 2011, https://www.washingtonpost.com/lifestyle/style/phone-hacking-scandal-closes-news-of-the-world/2011/07/07/gIQAy5RA2H_story.html; See also John F. Burns, "Murdoch, Center Stage, Plays Powerless Broker," *The New York Times*, April 25, 2012, p. A1, http://www.nytimes.com/2012/04/26/world/europe/rupert-murdoch-testimony-leveson-inquiry.html.
26. Sydney Ember, "In Sheldon Andelson's Newsroom, Looser Purse Strings and a Tighter Leash," *The New York Times*, May 22, 2016, http://www.nytimes.com/2016/05/23/business/media/in-adelsons-newsroom-looser-purse-strings-and-a-tighter-leash.html?_r=0. See also, Ken Doctor, "Sheldon Adelson Tightens Grip on Review-Journal," *Politico*, February 4, 2016, http://www.capitalnewyork.com/article/media/2016/02/8590189/sheldon-adelson-tightens-grip-review-journal.
27. Ruth Eglash, "How U.S. Billionaire Sheldon Adelson Is Buying Up Israel's Media," *Washington Post*, May 1, 2014, https://www.washingtonpost.com/news/worldviews/wp/2014/05/01/how-u-s-billionaire-sheldon-adelson-is-buying-up-israels-media/.
28. Richard Pérez-Peña, "As Cities Go from Two Papers to One, Talk of Zero," *The New York Times*, March 11, 2009, http://www.nytimes.com/2009/03/12/business/media/12papers.html?pagewanted=all.
29. Leichtman Research Group, Inc., "Overall, 87% Still Subscribe to a Multi-Channel Video Service," *FierceCable*, July 5, 2012, http://www.fiercecable.com/press-releases/overall-87-still-subscribe-multi-channel-video-service.
30. Seth Schiesel, "FCC Rules on Ownership Under Review," *The New York Times*, April 3, 2002, p. C1.
31. Tony Romm and Brian Fung, "AT&T –Time Warner Merger Approved, Setting the State for More Consolidation Across Corporate America" *Washington Post*, June 12, 2018. https://www.washingtonpost.com/news/the-switch/wp/2018/06/12/att-time-warner-decision/?noredirect=on&utm_term=.697325dbd6c7http://www.pewglobal.org/2018/01/11/publics-globally-want-unbiased-news-coverage-but-are-divided-on-whether-their-news-media-deliver/
32. Donna Britt, "Janet's 'Reveal' Lays Bare an Insidious Trend," *Washington Post*, February 4, 2004, p. B1.
33. "An FCC 'Data-Driven' Double Standard?" *Net Competition*, http://www.netcompetition.org/resource-center/competitive-evidence/an-fcc-data-driven-double-standard#sthash.m2r3cW2f.dpuf.
34. *FCC* v. *Fox Television Stations, Inc.*, 567 U.S. ______ (2012).

35. Amy Mitchell, Katie Simmons, Katerina Eva Matsa and Laura Silver, "Publics Globally Want Unbiased News Coverage, but Are Divided on Whether Their News Media Deliver.' Pew Research Center, January 11, 2018.
36. Pew Research Center for the People & the Press, "In Changing News Landscape, Even Television Is Vulnerable: Section 1: Watching, Reading and Listening to the News," September 27, 2012, http://www.people-press.org/2012/09/27/section-1-watching-reading-and-listening-to-the-news-3/.
37. Jeffrey Herbst, "The Algorithm Is an Editor," *Wall Street Journal*, April 14, 2016, p. A15.
38. John Gramlich, "5 Facts about Americans and Facebook." Pew Research Center, April 10, 2018. http://www.pewresearch.org/fact-tank/2018/04/10/5-facts-about-americans-and-facebook/
39. Vindu Goel and Mike Isaac, "Facebook Moves to Ban Private Gun Sales on Its Site and Instagram," *New York Times*, January 29, 2016, http://www.nytimes.com/2016/01/30/technology/facebook-gun-sales-ban.html.
40. Mack Nicas, "Want a Political Ad on Facebook? Now, You Must Reveal Yourself." *New York Times*, April 7, 2018. p. A1.
41. From *Scribner's* Monthly, June 1872 (Vol. IV, p. 204), quoted in Frank Luther Mott, *American Journalism*, 3d ed. (Macmillan, 1962), p. 412.
42. CBS News, "Abuse of Iraqi POWs by GIs Probed: 60 Minutes II Has Exclusive Report on Alleged Mistreatment," April 28, 2004, http://www.cbsnews.com/stories/2004/04/27/60II/main614063.shtml.
43. Dana Priest, "CIA Holds Terror Suspects in Secret Prisons," *Washington Post*, November 2, 2005, p. A01.
44. Glenn Greenwald, "NSA Collecting Phone Records of Millions of Verizon Customers Daily," *Guardian*, June 5, 2013, http://www.theguardian.com/world/2013/jun/06/nsa-phone-records-verizon-court-order.
45. Glenn Greenwald, Ewan MacAskill, and Laura Poitras, "Edward Snowden: The Whistleblower Behind the NSA Surveillance Revelations," *Guardian*, June 9, 2013, http://www.theguardian.com/world/2013/jun/09/edward-snowden-nsa-whistleblower-surveillance.
46. David E. Sanger and Mark Mazzetti, "Allegation of U.S. Spying on Merkel Puts Obama at Crossroads," *New York Times*, October 24, 2013, http://www.nytimes.com/2013/10/25/world/europe/allegation-of-us-spying-on-merkel-puts-obama-at-crossroads.html.
47. Stephanie McCrummen, Beth Reinhard and Alice Crites, "Woman Says Roy Moore Initiated Sexual Encounter When She Was 14, He Was 32." *The Washington Post*. November 9, 2017. https://www.washingtonpost.com/investigations/woman-says-roy-moore-initiated-sexual-encounter-when-she-was-14-he-was-32/2017/11/09/1f495878-c293-11e7-afe9-4f60b5a6c4a0_story.html?utm_term=.b65ffa97dcf3
48. Chris Snyder and Linette Lopez. "Tarana Burke on Why She Created the #MeToo movement—and Where It's Headed." *Business Insider*, December 13, 2017. http://www.businessinsider.com/how-the-metoo-movement-started-where-its-headed-tarana-burke-time-person-of-year-women-2017-12
49. CBS/AP. "More than 12M "Me Too" Facebook posts, comments, reactions in 24 hours." *CBS News*, October 17, 2017. https://www.cbsnews.com/news/metoo-more-than-12-million-facebook-posts-comments-reactions-24-hours/
50. Fred Emery, *Watergate: The Corruption of American Politics and the Fall of Richard Nixon* (Touchstone, 1995).
51. Bob Woodward and Carl Bernstein, *All the President's Men* (Simon & Schuster, 1994).
52. Mark Felt, John D. O'Connor, and W. Mark Felt, *A G-Man's Life: The FBI, Being 'Deep Throat' and the Struggle for Honor in Washington* (Public Affairs Press, 2006).
53. Jeffrey Gottfried and Elisa Shearer, "Americans' Online News Use Is Closing in on TV News Use." Pew Research Center, September 7, 2017. http://www.pewresearch.org/fact-tank/2017/09/07/americans-online-news-use-vs-tv-news-use/
54. Internet Live Stats, "Internet Users," http://www.internetlivestats.com/internet-users/.
55. Michael Barthel, "Despite Subscription Surges for Largest U.S. Newspapers, Circulation and Revenue Fall for Industry Overall." Pew Research Center, June 1, 2017. http://www.pewresearch.org/fact-tank/2017/06/01/circulation-and-revenue-fall-for-newspaper-industry/
56. Pew Research Center, "State of the News Media," April 15, 2015, available at http://www.journalism.org/2015/04/29/state-of-the-news-media-2015/.
57. Paul Farhi, "Washington Post to Be Sold to Jeff Bezos, the Founder of Amazon," *Washington Post*, August 5, 2013, http://www.washingtonpost.com/national/washington-post-to-be-sold-to-jeff-bezos/2013/08/05/ca537c9e-fe0c-11e2-9711-3708310f6f4d_story.html.
58. Paul Farhi, "Washington Post to Be Sold to Jeff Bezos, the Founder of Amazon," *Washington Post*, August 5, 2013, http://www.washingtonpost.com/national/washington-post-to-be-sold-to-jeff-bezos/2013/08/05/ca537c9e-fe0c-11e2-9711-3708310f6f4d_story.html.
59. Janet Asteroff, "A Progress Report on Jeff Bezos Transforming the Washington Post," *Mediashift*, January 14, 2015, http://www.journalism.org/media-indicators/newspaper-readership-by-age/.
60. Eric Pfanner, "Papers Worldwide Embrace Web Subscriptions: More Newspapers Are Making Web Readers Pay," *New York Times*, March 31, 2013, http://www.nytimes.com/2013/04/01/business/media/more-newspapers-are-making-web-readers-pay.html?_r=0.
61. Nat Ives, "Publishers: Why Count Only People Who Pay?" *Advertising Age*, November 12, 2007, p. 8.
62. Michael Barthiel, "Newspapers: Fact Sheet," Pew Research Center, April 29, 2015, http://www.journalism.org/2015/04/29/newspapers-fact-sheet/.
63. The Pew Research Center's Project for Excellence in Journalism, "The State of the News Media 2013," http://stateofthemedia.org/, p. 12.
64. The Pew Research Center's Project for Excellence, "The State of the News Media 2013: An Annual Report on American Journalism, Overview," p. 4.
65. Rick Edmond, Emily Guskin, Amy Mitchell, and Mark Jurkawitz, "Newspapers by the Numbers," Pew Research Center's Project for Excellence in Journalism, "The State of the News Media 2013," May 7, 2013, http://stateofthemedia.org/2013/newspapers-stabilizing-but-still-threatened/newspapers-by-the-numbers/.
66. Katerina Eva Matsa, "Gibbs Takes Over a Troubled Time Magazine," Pew Research Center, September 24, 2013, http://www.pewresearch.org/fact-tank/2013/09/24/gibbs-takes-over-a-troubled-time-magazine/.
67. David Kaplan, "WaPo Sells Newsweek to Harman; Announcement Coming This Afternoon," paidContent.org, August 2, 2010, http://paidcontent.org/article/419-wapo-sells-newsweek-to-harman-announcement-coming-this-afternoon/.
68. The Associated Press, "Newsweek Magazine to Hit the Presses Again," *NBC News*, December 4, 2013, http://www.nbcnews.com/business/newsweek-magazine-hit-presses-again-2D11690931.
69. Statista, "Reach of Popular Magazines in the United States in February 2018" based on data from MPA, comScore, and Gfk Nielsen. https://www.statista.com/statistics/208807/estimated-print-audience-of-popular-magazines/
70. "The Twenties in Contemporary Commentary: Radio," *America in Class*, http://americainclass.org/sources/becomingmodern/machine/text5/colcommentaryradio.pdf. See also, Michael X Delli Carpini, "Radio's Political Past," University of Pennsylvania Developmental Papers (ASC), July 1993, http://repository.upenn.edu/cgi/viewcontent.cgi?article=1022&context=asc_papers.
71. Frances Perkins, quoted in James MacGregor Burns, *Roosevelt: The Lion and the Fox* (Harcourt, 1956), p. 205.
72. Pew Research Center, "Audio and Podcasting Fact Sheet" June 16, 2017. http://www.journalism.org/fact-sheet/audio-and-podcasting/

73. Pew Research Center, "State of the News Media 2015," http://www.journalism.org/files/2015/06/Millennials-and-News-FINAL-7-27-15.pdf, p. 57.
74. Pew Research Center, "State of the News Media 2015," http://www.journalism.org/files/2015/06/Millennials-and-News-FINAL-7-27-15.pdf, p. 5.
75. Nick Corasanti, "Campaigns Turn to a Cheaper Medium to Get Voters' Ears: Radio." *New York Times*, December 3, 2015. http://www.nytimes.com/2015/12/04/us/politics/campaigns-turn-to-a-cheaper-medium-to-get-voters-ears-radio.html?ref=topics&_r=2.
76. Ed Pilkington, "Battle for Ohio: Campaigns Micro-target Their Message in State's Four Corners: Obama and Romney Take Localized Campaigning to the Next Level with Distinct Battlegrounds in Race for State's Electoral Votes," *Guardian*, October 25, 2012, http://www.theguardian.com/world/2012/oct/25/battle-ohio-campaigns-micro-target.
77. Laura Santhanam, Amy Mitchell, and Kenny Olmstead, "Audio: Digital Drives Listener Experience," in Pew Research Center's Project for Excellence in Journalism, "The State of the Mews Media 2013: An Annual Report on American Journalism," http://stateofthemedia.org/, p. 9.
78. "NPR Ratings at All-Time High." *NPR Press Room*, March 15, 2017, https://www.npr.org/about-npr/520273005/npr-ratings-at-all-time-high.
79. "The Top Talk Radio Audiences: March 2018," *Talkers*, April 2018, http://www.talkers.com/top-talk--audiences/.
80. The Pew Research Center's Project for Excellence in Journalism, "The State of the News Media 2013," http://stateofthemedia.org/, p. 22.
81. See Doris A. Graber, "Say It with Pictures: The Impact of Audiovisual News on Public Opinion Formation," paper presented at the annual meeting of the Midwest Political Science Association, April 1987, Chicago; and Benjamin I. Page, Robert Y. Shapiro, and Glenn R. Dempsey, "What Moves Public Opinion?" *American Political Science Review* 76 (March 1987), pp. 23–43.
82. The Nielsen Company, 2011, "State of the Media: Trends in TV Viewing—2011 TV Upfronts," http://www.nielsen.com/content/dam/corporate/us/en/newswire/uploads/2011/04/State-of-the-Media-2011-TV-Upfronts.pdf.
83. Nick Corasaniti and Josh Keller, "Party, Gender, Whiskey: How Campaigns Place Ads to Reach New Hampshire Voters," *New York Times*, February 9, 2016, http://www.nytimes.com/interactive/2016/02/09/us/politics/campaign-ad-tracking.html?_r=1.
84. The Pew Research Center's Project for Excellence in Journalism, "The State of the News Media 2013: An Annual Report on American Journalism, Overview," p. 10.
85. Kathleen Hall Jamieson and Joseph N. Cappella, *Echo Chamber: Rush Limbaugh and the Conservative Media Establishment* (Oxford University Press, 2008); see also Alessandra Stanley, "How MSNBC Became Fox's Liberal Evil Twin," *New York Times*, August 31, 2012, http://www.nytimes.com/2012/08/31/us/politics/msnbc-as-foxs-liberal-evil-twin.html.
86. Douglas Blanks Hindman and Kenneth Wiegand, "The Big Three's Prime-Time Decline: A Technological and Social Context," *Questia.com*, https://www.questia.com/library/journal/1G1-177361653/the-big-three-s-prime-time-decline-a-technological.
87. Pew Research Center, "State of the News Media 2015," http://www.journalism.org/files/2015/06/Millennials-and-News-FINAL-7-27-15.pdf, p. 36.
88. Pew Research Center, "State of the News Media 2015," http://www.journalism.org/files/2015/06/Millennials-and-News-FINAL-7-27-15.pdf, pp. 32–33.
89. Arthur L. Norberg and Judy E. O'Neill, *Transforming Computer Technology: Information Processing for the Pentagon, 1962–1986* (Johns Hopkins University Press, 1996).
90. Jesse Alpert and Nissan Hajaj, "We Knew the Web Was Big...," *Google Official Blog*, July 25, 2008, http://googleblog.blogspot.com/2008/07/we-knew-web-was-big.html.
91. Barry Schwartz, "Google's Search Knows About over 130 Trillion Pages." *Search Engine Land*, November 14, 2016. https://searchengineland.com/googles-search-indexes-hits-130-trillion-pages-documents-263378
92. Aaron Smith and Monica Anderson, "Social Media Use in 2018: A Majority of Americans Use Facebook and YouTube, but Young Adults are Especially Heavy Users of Snapchat and Instagram." Pew Research Center, March 1, 2018. http://assets.pewresearch.org/wp-content/uploads/sites/14/2018/03/01105133/PI_2018.03.01_Social-Media_FINAL.pdf
93. Aaron Smith and Monica Anderson, "Social Media Use in 2018: A Majority of Americans Use Facebook and YouTube, but Young Adults are Especially Heavy Users of Snapchat and Instagram." Pew Research Center, March 1, 2018. http://assets.pewresearch.org/wp-content/uploads/sites/14/2018/03/01105133/PI_2018.03.01_Social-Media_FINAL.pdf
94. Aaron Smith, "U.S. Smartphone Use in 2015," Pew Research Center, April 1, 2015, http://www.pewinternet.org/2015/04/01/us-smartphone-use-in-2015/.
95. Pew Research Center, "Mobile Fact Sheet" February 5, 2018. http://www.pewinternet.org/fact-sheet/mobile/
96. Shan Wang, "85 Percent of Americans Use Mobile Devices to Access News-and Seniors Are Driving that Number Up." NiemanLab, June 12, 2017. http://www.niemanlab.org/2017/06/85-percent-of-americans-use-mobile-devices-to-access-news-and-seniors-are-driving-that-number-up/
97. Dave Chaffey, "Mobile Marketing Statistics Compilation." Smart Insights. January 30, 2018. https://www.smartinsights.com/mobile-marketing/mobile-marketing-analytics/mobile-marketing-statistics/
98. Andrea Caumont, "12 Trends Shaping Digital News," Pew Research Center, October 16, 2013, http://www.pewresearch.org/fact-tank/2013/10/16/12-trends-shaping-digital-news/.
99. John B. Horrigan, "The Numbers Behind the Broadband 'Homework Gap.'" Pew Research Center, April 20, 2015. http://www.pewresearch.org/fact-tank/2015/04/20/the-numbers-behind-the-broadband-homework-gap/
100. Monica Anderson, "Digital Divide Persists Even as Lower Income Americans Make Gains in Tech Adoption." Pew Research Center. March 22, 2017. http://www.pewresearch.org/fact-tank/2017/03/22/digital-divide-persists-even-as-lower-income-americans-make-gains-in-tech-adoption/
101. Cass Sunstein, *Republic.com* (Princeton University Press, 2001), pp. 73–75; see also Philippe J. Maarek, *Campaign Communication and Political Marketing* (Wiley-Blackwell, 2011).
102. Elisa Shearer, "5 Key Takeaways About Twitter, Facebook and News Use," Pew Research Center, July 14, 2015, http://www.pewresearch.org/fact-tank/2015/07/14/5-key-takeaways-about-twitter-facebook-and-news-use/.
103. Jesse Holcomb, Amy Mitchell, and Tom Rosentiel, "Cable: Audience vs. Economics," Pew Research Center's Project for Excellence in Journalism, "The State of the News Media 2011," http://stateofthemedia.org/2011/cable-essay/.
104. Ashley Parker, "For Campaigns, Twitter is Both an Early-Warning System and a Weapon," *New York Times*, January 29, 2011, p. A15.
105. Republican National Committee, 2014, "Growth and Opportunity Project," http://goproject.gop.com/RNC_Growth_Opportunity_Book_2013.pdf.
106. Ben Branstetter, "Can the 2016 Election Help Save Twitter?" *The Daily Dot*, February 4, 2016, http://www.dailydot.com/opinion/can-2016-election-help-save-twitter/.
107. Nicholas Confessore and Karen Yourish, "$2 Billion Worth of Free Media for Donald Trump," *New York Times*, March 15, 2016 (https://nyti.ms/2jQTVYm).
108. Niv Sultan, "Election 2016: Trump's Free Media Helped Keep Cost Down, But Fewer Donors Provided More of the Cash," *Center for Responsive Politics*, April 13, 2017 (www.opensecrets.org/news/2017/04/election-2016-trump-fewer-donors-provided-more-of-the-cash/).

109. Dan Mangan, "Rex Tillerson Found Out He Was Fired as Secretary of State from President Donald Trump's Tweet," *CNBC*, March 13, 2018. https://www.cnbc.com/2018/03/13/tillerson-learned-he-was-fired-from-trumps-tweet.html
110. Callum Borchers, "Donald Trump Knows Exactly What He's Doing on Twitter, Says His Spokesman." *The Washington Post*, January 5, 2017, https://www.washingtonpost.com/news/the-fix/wp/2017/01/05/donald-trump-knows-exactly-what-hes-doing-on-twitter-says-his-spokesman/?utm_term=.46d4f692822a
111. Anna Everet, "The Civil Rights Movement and Television," *Archive of American Television*, http://emmytvlegends.org/interviews/topics/civil-rights-movement-c-1960s.
112. "Tempers Flare as Christie, Rubio Exchange Attacks," *Politico*, February, 6, 2016, http://www.politico.com/blogs/new-hampshire-primary-2016-live-updates/2016/02/chris-christie-marco-rubio-2016-debate-218872.
113. Shanto Iyengar, Mark D. Peters, and Donald R. Kinder, "Experimental Demonstrations of the 'Not-So-Minimal' Consequences of Television News Programs," *American Political Science Review* 76 (December 1982), pp. 848–858.
114. Ibid.; Maxwell E. McCombs and Donald L. Shaw, "The Agenda-Setting Function of the Mass Media," *Public Opinion Quarterly* 36 (1972), pp. 176–187; Maxwell E. McCombs and Sheldon Gilbert, "News Influence on Our Pictures of the World," in Jennings Bryant and Dolf Gillman, eds., *Perspectives on Media Effects* (Erlbaum, 1986), pp. 1–15; and Iyengar and Kinder, *News That Matters*.
115. Quoted in Michael J. Robinson and Margaret A. Sheehan, *Over the Wire and on TV: CBS and UPI in Campaign '80* (Russell Sage Foundation, 1983), p. xiii.
116. ABC News, http://abcnews.go.com/US/story?id=92498&page=1.
117. Thomas E. Patterson, "News Coverage of the 2016 General Election: How the Press Failed the Voters." Shorenstein Center on Media, Politics, and Public Policy. December 2016. https://shorensteincenter.org/wp-content/uploads/2016/12/2016-General-Election-News-Coverage-1.pdf?x78124
118. Shane Goldmacher, "Trump Treads on Tradition in New Hampshire." *Politico*, December 2, 2015. https://www.politico.com/story/2015/12/donald-trump-new-hampshire-retail-politics-216338
119. North Woods Advertising, "Fast Paced Paul—Paul Wellstone for U.S. Senate (MN)," http://www.youtube.com/watch?v=aTiW0YCMM0g.
120. Garrett M. Graff, "What the FBI Files Reveal About Hillary Clinton's Email Server." *Politico* September 30, 2016. https://www.politico.com/magazine/story/2016/09/hillary-clinton-emails-2016-server-state-department-fbi-214307
121. Statement by FBI Director James B. Comey on the Investigation of Secretary Hillary Clinton's Use of a Personal E-Mail System." FBI, Washington, D.C. July 5, 2016. https://www.fbi.gov/news/pressrel/press-releases/statement-by-fbi-director-james-b-comey-on-the-investigation-of-secretary-hillary-clinton2019s-use-of-a-personal-e-mail-system
122. 2016 Exit Polls, CNN, https://www.cnn.com/election/2016/results/exit-polls
123. Daniel Victor, "'Access Hollywood' Reminds Trump: 'The Tape Is Very Real.'" *The Washington Post* November 28, 2017. https://www.nytimes.com/2017/11/28/us/politics/donald-trump-tape.html
124. Paul T. David, Ralph M. Goldman, and Richard C. Bain, *The Politics of the National Party Conventions* (Brookings Institution Press, 1960), pp. 300–301.
125. Mark Z. Barabak, "Party Conventions Still Matter as a Political Reality," *Los Angeles Times*, August 20, 2012, http://articles.latimes.com/2012/aug/20/nation/la-na-do-2012-conventions-matter-20120820.
126. Maggie Haberman and Michael Barbaro, "How Melania Trump's Speech Veered Off Course and Caused an Uproar," *The New York Times*, July 19, 2016, http://www.nytimes.com/2016/07/20/us/politics/melania-trump-convention-speech.html.
127. Jonathan Allen & Amie Parnes, *Shattered: Inside Hillary Clinton's Doomed Campaign*. (New York: Crown, 2017. p. 297.
128. Frank I. Lutz, *Candidates, Consultants, and Campaigns* (Blackwell, 1988), Chapter 7.
129. Romney's data science team was less than one-tenth the size of Obama's analytics department. According to Issenberg, the Obama camp spent $52 million on online ads through mid-October to the Romney camp's $26 million. Sasha Issenberg, "A More Perfect Union: How President Obama's Campaign Used Big Data to Rally Voters," *MIT Technology Review*, December 19, 2012, http://www.technologyreview.com/featuredstory/509026/how-obamas-team-used-big-data-to-rally-voters/; see also Sasha Issenberg, *Victory Lab: The Secret Science of Winning Campaigns* (New York: Crown, 2012).
130. Joshua Green and Sasha Isenberg, "Inside the Trump Bunker, With Days to Go." Bloomberg. October 27, 2016. https://www.bloomberg.com/news/articles/2016-10-27/inside-the-trump-bunker-with-12-days-to-go
131. Mayhill Fowler, "Obama: No Surprise That Hard-Pressed Pennsylvanians Turn Bitter." *The Huffington Post*, April 11, 2008. http://www.huffingtonpost.com/mayhill-fowler/obama-no-surprise-that-ha_b_96188.html; and, Katherine Q. Seelye and Jeff Zeleny, "On the Defensive, Obama Calls His Words Ill-Chosen." *The New York Times*, April 13, 2008. http://www.nytimes.com/2008/04/13/us/politics/13campaign.html.
132. Michael D. Shear and Michael Barbaro, "In Video Clip, Romney Calls 47% 'Dependent' and Feeling Entitled," *The New York Times*, September. 17, 2012, http://thecaucus.blogs.nytimes.com/2012/09/17/romney-faults-those-dependent-on-government/.
133. Mike Isaac and Sydney Ember, "For Election Day Influence, Twitter Ruled Social Media" *The New York Times*, November 9, 2016, http://www.nytimes.com/2016/11/09/technology/for-election-day-chatter-twitter-ruled-social-media.html.
134. Hadas Gold, "#Hillary #Ted Cruz rule," *Politico*, December 4, 2015, http://www.politico.com/story/2014/12/hillary-clinton-ted-cruz-social-media-2016-elections-113310.
135. Larry J. Sabato, "Gerald Ford's 'Free Poland' Gaffe—1976," *Washington Post*, http://www.washingtonpost.com/wp-srv/politics/special/clinton/frenzy/ford.htm.
136. Arlette Saenz, "Rick Perry's Debate Lapse: 'Oops'—Can't Remember Department of Energy," ABC News, November 9, 2011, http://abcnews.go.com/blogs/politics/2011/11/rick-perrys-debate-lapse-oops-cant-remember-department-of-energy/.
137. Larry J. Sabato, *The Rise of Political Consultants* (Basic Books, 1981); Alexis Rice, "Campaigns Online: The Profound Impact of the Internet, Blogs, and E-Technologies in Presidential Political Campaigning," Center for the Study of American Government at Johns Hopkins University, January 2004, http://www.campaignsonline.org/reports/online.pdf.
138. See Thurber and Nelson, Campaign Warriors: Political Consultants in Elections (Brookings, 2000).
139. Quoted in Sabato, *Rise of Political Consultants*, p. 144.
140. John R. Zaller, *The Nature and Origins of Mass Opinion* (Cambridge University Press, 1992); Jennings Bryant and Mary Beth Oliver, eds., *Media Effects: Advances in Theory and Research*, 3rd ed. (Routledge, 2009).
141. Shanto Iyengar and Donald R. Kinder, *News that Matters: Television and American Opinion* (University of Chicago Press, 1987), p. 2.
142. Richard J. Semiatin, *Campaigns on the Cutting Edge*, 3rd ed. (Sage, 2017), pp. 127–145.
143. John H. Aldrich, *Before the Convention* (University of Chicago Press, 1980), p. 65; see also Patterson, *Mass Media Election*.
144. John Foley et al., *Nominating a President: The Process and the Press* (Praeger, 1980), p. 39. For the press's treatment of incumbents, see James Glen Stovall, "Incumbency and News Coverage of the 1980 Presidential Election Campaign," *Western Political Quarterly*, 37 (December 1984), p. 621.
145. Wesleyan Media Project, "Super PACs Dominate Airwaves," Wesleyan Media Project, December 15, 2015, http://www.mediaproject.wesleyan.edu/releases/super-pacs-airwaves/.

146. Wesleyan Media Project, "2014 General Election Advertising Opens Even More Negative Than 2010 or 2012," Wesleyan Media Project, September 16, 2014, http://www.mediaproject.wesleyan.edu/releases/2014-general-election-advertising-opens-even-more-negative-than-2010-or-2012/; see also Wesleyan Media Project, "Ad Spending in 2014 Elections Poised to Break $1 Billion," Wesleyan Media Project, October 14, 2014, http://www.mediaproject.wesleyan.edu/releases/ad-spending-in-2014-elections-poised-to-break-1-billion/.
147. Erika Franklin Fowler, Travis N. Ridout and Michael M. Franz, "Political Advertising in 2016: The Presidential Election as Outlier?" *The Forum*, 2016 pp 445-69. https://www.degruyter.com/downloadpdf/j/for.2016.14.issue-4/for-2016-0040/for-2016-0040.pdf
148. Stephen Ansolabehere and Shanto Iyengar, *Going Negative: How Political Advertisements Shrink and Polarize the Electorate* (Free Press, 1995).
149. John G. Geer, *In Defense of Negativity: Attack Ads in Presidential Campaigns* (University of Chicago Press, 2006); and Richard R. Lau, Lee Sigelman, and Ivy Brown Rovner, "The Effects of Negative Political Campaigns: A Meta-Analytic Reassessment," *Journal of Politics*, 69 (November 2007), pp. 1176–1209.
150. Kevin Collins, "Who Gives? Political Messages, Activist Motivations, and Campaign Contribution Behavior," paper presented at the annual meeting of the American Political Science Association, Seattle, WA, September 1–4, 2011. Revised version of paper provided by author, May 23, 2012.
151. Thomas Patterson, *Mass Media Election*: How Americans Choose Their President (New York: Praeger, 1980). pp. 115–117.
152. Michael Traugott, Benjamin Highton, and Henry E. Brady, *A Review of Recent Controversies Concerning the 2004 Presidential Election Exit Polls*, March 10, 2005, http://elections.ssrc.org/research/ExitPollReport031005.pdf; see also Michael Traugott, "The Accuracy of the National Preelection Polls in the 2004 Presidential Election," *Public Opinion Quarterly* 69 (Special Issue 2005), pp. 642–654.
153. Lewis Wolfson, *The Untapped Power of the Press* (Praeger, 1985), p. 79.
154. Trudy Lieberman, "Dropped Coverage: How the Media Missed the Two Biggest Obamacare Screw-Ups," *PoliticoMagazine*, December 2, 2013, http://www.politico.com/magazine/story/2013/12/dropped-coverage-media-obamacare-100546.html#.Ut7RghDn-70.
155. Lloyd Cutler, "Foreign Policy on Deadline," *Foreign Policy* 56 (Fall 1984), p. 114.
156. Eli Rosenberg, "White House Takes Down 'We the People' Petitions Site Before Responding to a Single One." *The Washington Post*, December 19, 2017. https://www.washingtonpost.com/news/the-fix/wp/2017/12/19/white-house-takes-down-we-the-people-petitions-site-without-responding-to-a-single-one/?utm_term=.29e57a76468e
157. Eli Rosenberg, "The White House Has Finally Restored a Petitions Site That Is Critical of President Trump." *The Washington Post*, February 1, 2018. https://www.washingtonpost.com/news/the-fix/wp/2018/01/31/the-white-house-promised-to-restore-a-petitions-site-that-was-critical-of-trump-it-hasnt/?utm_term=.60ada7a574bb
158. Dan Froomkin, "After Two Years, White House Finally Responds to Snowden Pardon Petition—With a 'No'" *The Intercept*. July 28, 2015. https://theintercept.com/2015/07/28/2-years-white-house-finally-responds-snowden-pardon-petition/
159. We the People, Your Voice in the White House. https://petitions.whitehouse.gov/
160. Stephen Hess, *Live from Capitol Hill!* (Brookings Institution, 1991), pp. 62–76; and Timothy E. Cook, *Making Laws and Making News* (Brookings Institution, 1989), pp. 81–86; Congress.org, "Congressional Staff Roles," 2012, http://www.congress.org/congressorg/issues/basics/?style=staff.
161. Susan Heilmann Miller, "News Coverage of Congress: The Search for the Ultimate Spokesperson," *Journalism Quarterly* 54 (Autumn 1977), pp. 459–465.
162. See Stephen Hess, *Live from Capitol Hill: Studies of Congress and the Media* (Brookings Institution Press, 1991), pp. 102–110; and Jonathan S. Morris and Rosalee A. Clawson, "Media Coverage of Congress in the 1990s: Scandals, Personalities, and the Prevalence of Policy and Process," *Political Communication*, 22:3, pp. 297–313, http://www.tandfonline.com/doi/pdf/10.1080/10584600591006546.
163. Jonathan S. Morris and Rosalee A. Clawson, "Media Coverage of Congress in the 1990s: Scandals, Personalities and the Prevalence of Policy and Process." *Political Communication* 22 (2005), pp. 297–313.
164. For a discussion of the Supreme Court and public opinion, see Thomas R. Marshall, *Public Opinion and the Supreme Court* (Unwin Hyman, 1989); and Gregory Caldiera, "Neither the Purse nor the Sword: Dynamics of Public Confidence in the Supreme Court," *American Political Science Review* 80 (December 1986), pp. 1209–1228.
165. For a discussion of the relationship between the Supreme Court and the press, see Richard Davis, "Lifting the Shroud: News Media Portrayal of the U.S. Supreme Court," *Communications and the Law* 9 (October 1987), pp. 43–58; and Elliot E. Slotnick, "Media Coverage of Supreme Court Decision Making: Problems and Prospects," *Judicature* (October–November 1991), pp. 128–142.
166. See, for example, Jack Dennis, "Preadult Learning of Political Independence: Media and Family Communications Effects," *Communication Research* 13 (July 1987), pp. 401–433; and Olive Stevens, *Children Talking Politics* (Robertson, 1982).
167. See Angus Campbell, Philip E. Converse, Warren E. Miller, and Donald E. Stokes, *The American Voter* (Wiley, 1960).
168. Pew Research Center for the People & the Press, Survey Reports, "News Audiences Increasingly Politicized," June 8, 2004, http://people-press.org/reports/display.php3?ReportID=215.
169. Pew Research Center for the People & the Press, "In Changing News Landscape, Even Television Is Vulnerable: Section 1: Watching, Reading and Listening to the News," September 27, 2012, http://www.people-press.org/2012/09/27/section-1-watching-reading-and-listening-to-the-news-3/.
170. Paul Lazarsfeld, Bernard Berelson, and Hazel Gaudet, *The People's Choice: How the Voter Makes Up His Mind in a Presidential Campaign*, 3d ed. (Columbia University Press, 1968); and Bernard Berelson, Paul Lazarsfeld, and William McPhee, *Voting: A Study of Opinion Formation in a Presidential Campaign* (University of Chicago Press, 1954).
171. Stuart Oskamp, ed., *Television as a Social Issue* (Sage, 1988); James W. Carey, ed., *Media, Myths, and Narratives: Television and the Press* (Sage, 1988).
172. Times Mirror Center for the People and the Press, "Times Mirror News Interest Index," press releases, January 16 and February 28, 1992.
173. The Rush Limbaugh Show, "This Show Forced Liberal Media to Drop the Pretense of Objectivity," April 19, 2010, http://webtest1.rushlimbaugh.com/home/daily/site_041910/content/01125111.member.html.
174. Rick Lyman, "Multimedia Deal: The History; 2 Commanding Publishers, 2 Powerful Empires," *The New York Times*, March 14, 2000, p. C16.
175. For two perspectives on this see Bernard Goldberg, *Bias* (Regnery Publishing, Inc., 2002); and David Halberstam, *The Powers That Be* (University of Illinois Press, 2000).
176. FAIR: Fairness & Accuracy in Reporting, http://www.fair.org/index.php?page=121.

CHAPTER 10

1. U.S. Office of Management and Budget, Historical Tables: Budget of the U.S. Government, Fiscal Year 2016 (U.S. Government Printing Office, 2015), Table 3.1.
2. The figure comes from the Stockholm International Peace Research Institute, *SIPRI Military Expenditure Database*, April 2015;

see also Maurice R. Greenberg, *Trends in U.S. Military Spending*, Council on Foreign Relations, July 15, 2014.

3. See Dakota L. Wood, ed., *2016 Index of U.S. Military Strength* (Heritage Foundation, 2016) for a sobering assessment of the marginal condition of the armed services.
4. See Benjamin H. Friedman and Justin Logan, "Why the U.S. Military Budget Is 'Foolish and Sustainable,'" CATO Institute, Spring 2012.
5. Visit opensecrets.org to find out what the defense industry gave to candidates in the most recent campaign, and how much it spent on lobbying.
6. Alexander Hamilton, James Madison, and John Jay, *The Federalist Papers*, available at http://thomas.loc.gov/home/histdox/fedpaper.txt.
7. Ibid.
8. See Roger H. Davidson and Walter J. Oleszek, *Congress and Its Members*, 10th ed. (CQ Press, 2005).
9. Alexander Hamilton, James Madison, and John Jay, *The Federalist Papers*, available at http://thomas.loc.gov/home/histdox/fedpaper.txt.
10. Cass Sunstein, *Impeachment: A Citizen's Guide* (Harvard University Press, 2017).
11. Alexander Hamilton, James Madison, and John Jay, *The Federalist Papers*, available at http://thomas.loc.gov/home/histdox/fedpaper.txt
12. Charles Warren, *The Making of the Constitution* (Little, Brown, 1928), p. 195.
13. See Chris Cazilla, "People Hate Congress. But Most incumbents Get Re-elected. What Gives?" *Washington Post*, May 9, 2013, available at http://www.washingtonpost.com/blogs/the-fix/wp/2013/05/09/people-hate-congress-but-most-incumbents-get-re-elected-what-gives/.
14. This story comes from the U.S. Senate historian, available at http://www.senate.gov/legislative/common/briefing/Senate_legislative_process.htm.
15. *Bush* v. *Vera*, 517 U.S. 952 (1996).
16. Based on author projections based on CQ.com, "A Demographic Divide in the House," available at http://media.cq.com/pub/2013/demographic-divide/.
17. Thomas E. Mann, *Unsafe at any Margin: Interpreting Congressional Elections* (American Enterprise Institution, 1978).
18. See David B. Magleby, *Last Hurrah? Soft Money and Issue Advocacy in the 2002 Elections* (Brookings Institution Press, 2004).
19. See Citizens Against Government Waste at www.cagw.org for the latest information on earmarks.
20. http://www.washingtonpost.com/blogs/2chambers/post/toomey-mccaskill-to-call-for-permanent-earmark-ban/2011/11/29/gIQAlZAu8N_blog.html.
21. Center for Responsive Politics, "The Dollars and Cents of Incumbency," available at https://www.opensecrets.org/overview/incumbs.php?cycle=2014&type=A&party=A.
22. Matthew Eric Glassman, Jacob R. Straus, and Colleen J. Shogan, "Social Networking: Members' Use of Twitter and Facebook During a Two-Month Period in the 112th Congress," Congressional Research Service, March 22, 2013.
23. Jennifer E. Manning, "Membership of the 115th Congress: A Profile," Congressional Research Service, January 17, 2018.
24. Jonathan Weisman and Jennifer Steinhauer, "Senate Women Lead in Effort to Find Accord," *New York Times*, October 14, 2013, available at http://www.nytimes.com/2013/10/15/us/senate-women-lead-in-effort-to-find-accord.html.
25. These comparisons were constructed by merging Jennifer Manning's 2015 profile of Congress with R. Eric Petersen, Ida A. Brudnick, R. Sam Garrett, Jennifer E. Manning, Jacob R. Strauss, and Amber Hope Wilhelm, "Representatives and Senators: Trends in Member Characteristics Since 1945," Congressional Research Service, January 27, 2014.
26. For discussion of the modern Speakership, see Barbara Sinclair, "House Majority Party Leadership in an Era of Legislative Constraint," in Roger H. Davidson, ed., *The Postreform Congress* (St. Martin's Press, 1992), pp. 91–111; and Ronald M. Peters, Jr., ed., *The Speaker: Leadership in the U.S. House of Representatives* (CQ Press, 1995).
27. For an insightful set of essays on Senate leadership, see Richard A. Baker and Roger H. Davidson, eds., *First Among Equals: Outstanding Senate Leaders of the Twentieth Century* (CQ Press, 1991).
28. Sarah A. Binder and Steven S. Smith, *Politics or Principles? Filibustering in the United States Senate* (Brookings Institution Press, 1997).
29. Despite their earlier opposition to the change, the Republican majority elected in 2014 decided not to "defuse" the nuclear option, perhaps because they hoped the next president would be a Republican who might need it. United States Senate, "Senate Action on Cloture Motions," available at http://www.senate.gov/pagelayout/reference/cloture_motions/clotureCounts.htm.
30. For an insider's perspective on the option and how it might be used in the future, see Orrin G. Hatch, "How 52 Senators Made 60 = 51," *Stanford Law & Policy Review* Online, March 19, 2014. Senator Hatch (R-UT) was the senior Republican on the Senate Judiciary Committee when the change was made.
31. For more information on conference committees, see Walter J. Oleszek, "*Whither the Role of Conference Committees: An Analysis,*" Congressional Research Service, February 2009.
32. Reagan made the analogy in a December 18, 1982, interview with the Independent Radio Network. The transcript can be found at Gerhard Peters and John T. Woolley, The American Presidency Project, http://www.presidency.ucsb.edu/ws/?pid=42130.
33. The complete list of member caucuses as of April 2012 can be found at http://cha.house.gov/sites/republicans.cha.house.gov/files/documents/cmo_cso_docs/cmo_112th_congress.pdf.
34. Joel D. Aberbach, *Keeping a Watchful Eye: The Politics of Congressional Oversight* (Brookings, 1991).
35. Ida A. Brudnick, "Congressional Salaries and Allowances: In Brief," Congressional Research Service, December 30, 2014.
36. These numbers come from the second session of the 113th Congress, which ended on November 7, 2012, available at http://www.-senate.gov/reference/resources/pdf/Resumes/current.pdf.
37. For the full details of the House legislative process, see John V. Sullivan, *How Our Laws Are Made* (U.S. Government Printing Office, 2007); for the full details of the Senate legislative process, see Robert B. Dove, *Enactment of a Law* (U.S. Senate Parliamentarian's Office, 1997). Both authors were parliamentarians of their chamber when they wrote these guides.
38. See Robert B. Dove, *Enactment of a Law* (U.S. Senate Parliamentarian's Office, 1997) for more details on Senate amendments.
39. For a history of the early Congresses, see James Sterling Young, *The Washington Community, 1800–1828* (Columbia University Press, 1966).
40. Davidson and Oleszek, *Congress and Its Members*, p. 30.
41. Nelson Polsby, "The Institutionalization of the U.S. House of Representatives," *American Political Science Association* (March 1968), pp. 144–168.
42. Herbert Asher, "The Learning of Legislative Norms," *American Political Science Review* 67 (June 1973), pp. 499–513.
43. See the case studies in Richard F. Fenno, Jr., *Senators on the Campaign Trail: The Politics of Representation* (University of Oklahoma Press, 1996), p. 331; see also Benjamin Bishin, "Constituency Influence in Congress: Does Subconstituency Matter?" *Legislative Studies Quarterly* (August 2000), pp. 389–415.
44. Stephen A. Jessee and Sean M. Theriault, "The Two Faces of Congressional Roll-Call Voting," *Party Politics*, June 2012.
45. Bill Bradley, *Time Present, Time Past: A Memoir* (Knopf, 1996), Chapter 4.
46. Martin Gilens and Benjamin I. Page, "Testing Theories of American Politics: Elites, Interest Groups, and Average Citizens," *Perspectives on Politics* (September 2014), p. 575.
47. Richard E. Cohen, "Vote Ratings," *National Journal*, February 21, 2005, p. 426.
48. Joseph I. Lieberman, *In Praise of Public Life* (Simon & Schuster, 2000), p. 109.

49. This information comes from the Center for Responsive Politics, available at opensecrets.org.
50. Lynda Powell, "The Influence of Campaign Contributions on Legislative Policy," *The Forum: A Journal of Applied Research in Contemporary Politics* (October 2013), pp. 339–355.
51. Lee Drutman and Alexander Furnas, "How Revolving Door Lobbyists are Taking Over K Street," *Sunlight Foundation blog post*, January 22, 2014, available at http://sunlightfoundation.com/blog/2014/01/22/revolving-door-lobbyists-take-over-k-street/.
52. Catherine Richert, "Party Unity: United We Stand Opposed," *Congressional Quarterly Weekly*, January 14, 2008, p. 143.
53. Eliza Newlin Carney, "Standing Together Against Any Act," *National Journal*, March 16, 2005.
54. CQ Vote Studies: Presidential Support," *CQ Magazine*, February 12, 2018.
55. Senate S. 1, *Honest Leadership and Open Government Act of 2007*, passed September 14, 2007.
56. See Kimberly Kindy, Scott Higham, David S. Falls, and Dan Keating, "Lawmakers Reworked Financial Portfolios After Talks with Fed, Treasury Officials," *Washington Post*, June 24, 2012, available at http://www.washingtonpost.com/politics/lawmakers-reworked-financial-portfolios-after-talks-with-fed-treasury-officials/2012/06/24/gJQAnQPg0V_story.html?hpid=z11. The story contains detailed information on each of the 34 senators and representatives who moved their money in advance of public knowledge.
57. Pollster Patrick Caddell may have been the first to use this term in work he did for Jimmy Carter in 1976; see Joe Klein, "The Perils of the Permanent Campaign," *Time*, October 5, 2005. Journalist and later advisor to President Bill Clinton used the term as title of his 1982 book. See Sidney Blumenthal, *The Permanent Campaign* (New York: Simon and Schuster, 1982).

CHAPTER 11

1. Journalist's Resource, "The Health Effects and Costs of Air Pollution," December 7, 2015, http://journalistsresource.org/studies/environment/pollution-environment/health-effects-costs-air-pollution-research-roundup.
2. Johannes Lelieveld, John S. Evans, Mohammed Fnais, Despina Glannadaki, and Andrea Pozzer, "The Contribution of Outdoor Air Pollution Sources to Premature Mortality on a Global Scale," *Nature*, September 2015.
3. Monica Anderson, "Partisans Differ Sharply on Power Plan Emissions Limits, Climate Change," Pew Research Center, August 3, 2015.
4. Michael Greshko, Laura Parker, and Brian Clark Howard, "A Running List of How Trump Is Changing the Environment," *National Geographic*, https://news.nationalgeographic.com/2017/03/how-trump-is-changing-science-environment/. The list is regularly updated.
5. [55]Alexander Hamilton, James Madison, and John Jay, *The Federalist Papers*, No. 68, available at http://thomas.loc.gov/home/histdox/fedpaper.txt.
6. Alexander Hamilton, James Madison, and John Jay, *The Federalist Papers*, No. 70, available at http://thomas.loc.gov/home/histdox/fedpaper.txt.
7. Michael Nelson, "Constitutional Qualifications for President," *Presidential Studies Quarterly*, vol. 17, no. 2 (Spring, 1987), pp. 383–399.
8. Brooks Jackson, "Donald, You're Fired: Trump Repeats Claims About Obama's Birthplace," FactCheck.org, April 9, 2011, available at http://www.factcheck.org/2011/04/donald-youre-fired/. See also Michael Barbaro, "Donald Trump Clung to 'Birther' Lie for Years, and Still Isn't Apologetic," *New York Times*, September 16, 2016.
9. http://www.publicpolicypolling.com/main/2015/08/trump-supporters-think-obama-is-a-muslim-born-in-another-country.html.
10. Kathryn Dunn Tenpas, "Why Is Trump's Staff Turnover Higher Than the 5 Most Recent Presidents?" Brookings Institution, January 19, 2018, updated on March 7, https://www.brookings.edu/research/why-is-trumps-staff-turnover-higher-than-the-5-most-recent-presidents/.
11. Donald J. Trump, "Remarks by President Trump and Prime Minister Löfven of Sweden in Joint Press Conference," March 6, 2018, available at https://www.whitehouse.gov/briefings-statements/remarks-president-trump-prime-minister-lofven-sweden-joint-press-conference/
12. Alexander Hamilton, James Madison, and John Jay, *The Federalist Papers*, No. 70, available at http://thomas.loc.gov/home/histdox/fedpaper.txt.
13. See the U.S. Senate's history of the Jefferson vice presidency at http://www.senate.gov/artandhistory/history/common/generic/VP_Thomas_Jefferson.htm.
14. Jeffrey Crouch, Mark J. Rozell, and Mitchel A. Sollenberger, "The Unitary Executive Theory and President Donald J. Trump," *Presidential Studies Quarterly*, September 2017.
15. Ryan J. Barilleaux and Christopher S. Kelley, eds., *The Unitary Executive and the Modern Presidency* (Texas A&M University Press, 2010).
16. Richard Pious, *The American Presidency* (Basic Books, 1978).
17. This history of presidential powers draws heavily on Sidney M. Milkis and Michael Nelson, *The American Presidency: Origins and Development, 1976–2000*, 4th ed. (CQ Press, 2003).
18. Letter from Abraham Lincoln to his Illinois law partner W. H. Herndon, February 15, 1848, in *Abraham Lincoln, Speeches and Writings, 1832–1858* (Library of America, 1989), p. 175.
19. Barbara Salazar Torreon, "Instances of Use of United States Armed Forces Abroad, 1798–2015," Congressional Research Service, October 15, 2015.
20. Louis Fisher, *Congressional Abdication on War and Spending* (Texas A&M University Press, 2000), p. 184.
21. Matthew C. Weed, "The War Powers Resolution: Concepts and Practice," Congressional Research Service, April 3, 2015.
22. Miles A. Pomper, "Bush Hopes to Avoid Battle with Congress over Iraq," *CQ Weekly*, August 31, 2002, p. 2251.
23. Stephen Daggett, "Costs of Major U.S. Wars," Congressional Research Service, June 29, 2010.
24. Saba Hamedy, and Joyce Tseng, "All the Times President Trump has Insulted North Korea," CNN, March 9, 2018, available at https://www.cnn.com/2017/09/22/politics/donald-trump-north-korea-insults-timeline/index.html.
25. Haeyuon Park, "Children at the Border: Q. and A.," *New York Times*, October 21, 2014, available at http://www.nytimes.com/interactive/2014/07/15/us/questions-about-the-border-kids.html. See also, Caitlin Dickerson, "What Is DACA? Who Are the Dreamers? Here Are Some Answers," *The New York Times*, January 23, 2018, available at https://www.nytimes.com/2018/01/23/us/daca-dreamers-shutdown.html.
26. Haeyuon Park, "Children at the Border: Q. and A.," *The New York Times*, October 21, 2014, available at http://www.nytimes.com/interactive/2014/07/15/us/questions-about-the-brder-kids.html.
27. "For Bush, the Fun Begins at Recess," *Washington Post*, June 29, 2007, p. A19; for a scholarly argument about this power, see the paper by Michael B. Rappaport, "The Original Meaning of the Recess Appointments Clause," October 6, 2004, at http://ssrn.com/abstract=601563.
28. See Paul C. Light, *Thickening Government: Federal Hierarchy and the Diffusion of Accountability* (Brookings Institution, 1995), for a discussion of how this very small number of appointees actually controls the very large federal workforce.
29. *National Labor Relations Board* v. *Noel Canning*, 573 US _____ (2014).
30. See Gerhard Peters and John T. Wooley, "Executives Orders" The American Presidency Project, edited by John T. Wooley and Gerhard Peters (Santa Barbara, 1999–2016).
31. Alan Levin, and Jesse Hamilton, "Trump Takes Credit for Killing Hundreds of Regulations That Were Already Dead," *Bloomberg*

Businessweek, December 11, 2017, https://www.bloomberg.com/news/features/2017-12-11/trump-takes-credit-for-killing-hundreds-of-regulations-that-were-already-dead

32. An indexed list of all executive orders dating back to 1933 can be found at http://www.archives.gov/federal-register/executive-orders/disposition.html.
33. Kenneth S. Lowande, "After the Orders: Presidential Memoranda and Unilateral Action," *Presidential Studies Quarterly* (December 2014).
34. See http://www.whitehouse.gov/briefing-room/presidential-actions/presidential-memoranda for Obama's list.
35. Gregory Korte, "Obama Issues Executive Orders by Another Name," *USA Today*, December 17, 2014.
36. Elena Kagan, "Presidential Administration," *Harvard Law Review*, April 2001.
37. *United States* v. *Texas*, 579 ______ (2016).
38. Tai Kopan, Trump Administration Reverses DAPA in 'House Cleaning,'" CNN, June 16, 2017, https://www.cnn.com/2017/06/16/politics/dhs-scraps-dapa-keeps-daca-deferred-action/index.html.
39. A detailed look at current federal spending can be found at http://www.USAspending.gov.
40. Clinton et al. v. New York City et al., 524 U.S. 417 (1998).
41. Raoul Berger, *Executive Privilege: A Constitutional Myth* (Harvard University Press, 1974).
42. Mark J. Rozell, "The Law: Executive Privilege—Definition and Standards of Application," *Presidential Studies Quarterly* (December 1999), p. 924.
43. *United States* v. *Nixon*, 418 U.S. 683 (1974).
44. The speech can be read at http://www.presidency.ucsb.edu/ws/?pid=26805.
45. The veto numbers come from Kevin R. Kosar, "Regular Vetoes and Pocket Vetoes: An Overview," Congressional Research Service, April 22, 2013.
46. Thomas Kaplan, "Congress Approves $1.3 Trillion Spending Bill, Averting a Shutdown," March 22, 2018, available at https://www.nytimes.com/2018/03/22/us/politics/house-passes-spending-bill.html.
47. For a history of signing statements, see Todd Garvey, "Presidential Signing Statements: Constitutional and Institutional Implications," Congressional Research Service, September 17, 2007.
48. "Statement on Signing the National Defense Authorization Act for Fiscal Year 2013," January 2, 2013, Daily Compilation of Presidential Documents, available at http://www.whitehouse.gov/the-press-office/2013/01/03/statement-president-hr-4310.
49. Harold C. Relyea, "The Executive Office of the President: A Historical Overview," Congressional Research Service, November 26, 2008.
50. For a general discussion of these methods and a specific review of President Obama's approach, see James P. Pfiffner, "Decision Making in the Obama White House," *Presidential Studies Quarterly*, vol. 41, no. 2 (June 2011), pp. 244–262.
51. Philip Rucker, and Robert Costa, "'Tired of the Wait Game': White House Stabilizers Gone, Trump Calling His Own Shots," *Washington Post*, March 31, 2018, https://www.washingtonpost.com/politics/unhinged-or-unleashed-white-house-stabilizers-gone-trump-calling-his-own-shots/2018/03/31/19447ae2-343b-11e8-8bdd-cdb33a5eef83_story.html?utm_term=.def09a3b35be.
52. See Irving Janis, *Groupthink* (Houghton Mifflin, 1982).
53. Mitchel A. Sollenberger and Mark J. Rozell, "The Origins and Development of Executive Branch Czars," *Journal of Policy History*, vol. 25, no. 4 (2013), pp. 639–664.
54. See Donald F. Kettl, *Team Bush* (McGraw-Hill, 2003), for a discussion of George W. Bush's management style.
55. The President's Committee on Administrative Management, "Report of the President's Committee on Administrative Management," Government Printing Office, January 1937, p. 1.
56. Biographies of all White House staff are available at http://www.whorunsgov.com/Departments/White_House_Organizational_Chart.
57. Arthur Schlesinger, Jr., "Is the Vice Presidency Necessary?" The *Atlantic*, May 1974, available at http://www.theatlantic.com/magazine/archive/1974/05/is-the-vice-presidency-necessary/305732/.
58. See Paul C. Light, *Vice Presidential Power* (Johns Hopkins University Press, 1984).
59. McCay Coppins, "God's Plan for Mike Pence," *The Atlantic*, January/February, 2018.
60. Rep. Rahm Emanuel (D-Ill.) was Obama's first chief of staff in 2009, but left in 2010 to run for mayor of Chicago. Emanuel was replaced by Bill Daley, a former Secretary of Commerce who left in 2012 to consider a run for governor of Illinois. Daley was replaced by Jack Lew, Obama's Management and Budget director who left in 2013 to serve as Treasury secretary. And Lew was replaced by Denis McDonough, the chief of staff at the National Security Council, who was still in the job at the start of 2014.
61. David Gergen, a highly placed White House aide in several administrations, shares his views on presidents and the White House staff in *Eyewitness to Power: The Essence of Leadership, Nixon to Clinton* (Touchstone, 2000).
62. See Shelley Lynne Tomkins, Inside OMB: Politics and Process in the President's Budget Office (Sharpe, 1998).
63. Annie Lowrey, and Stephen Johnson, "The Trump Administration's Gender Gap Is Both Broad and Deep," *Government Executive*, March 28, 2018.
64. José D. Villalobos, Justin S. Vaugh, and Julia R. Azari, "Politics or Policy: How Rhetoric Matters to Presidential Leadership of Congress," *Presidential Studies Quarterly*, vol. 42, no. 3 (September 2012), pp. 549–550.
65. James W. Beck, Alison E. Carr, and Philip T. Walmsley, "What Have You Done for Me Lately? Charisma Attenuates the Decline in U.S. Presidential Approval Over Time," *Leadership Quarterly*, vol. 2, no. 2 (September 2011), pp. 934–942.
66. Samuel Kernell, *Going Public: New Strategies of President Leadership*, 3rd ed. (Congressional Quarterly Press, 1997).
67. Andrew W. Barrett, "Gone Public: The Impact of Going Public on Presidential Legislative Success," *American Politics Research*, vol. 32, no. 3 (May 2004), pp. 338–370.
68. The Editors, "The Trump Tweet Tracker," *The Atlantic*, June 4, 2017, https://www.theatlantic.com/liveblogs/2017/06/donald-trump-twitter/511619/.
69. Eugene Scott, "More White Evangelicals Believe Stormy Daniels, and That Could Have Some Long-Term Implications," *Washington Post*, March 27, 2018, https://www.washingtonpost.com/news/the-fix/wp/2018/03/27/more-white-evangelicals-believe-stormy-daniels-and-that-could-have-some-long-term-implications/?utm_term=.a6ef0a6ac5ea.
70. See "Inside the White House: Letters to the President," available at https://www.youtube.com/watch?v=eG00mM8QEGk
71. Michael D. Shear, and Sheryl Gay Stolberg, "Conceding to N.R.A., Trump Abandons Brief Gun Control Promise," *New York Times*, March 12, 2018, available at https://www.nytimes.com/2018/03/12/us/politics/trump-gun-control-national-rifle-association.html.
72. David R. Mayhew, Divided We Govern: Party Control, Lawmaking, and Investigations, 1946–2002, 2nd ed. (Yale, 2005).
73. The phrase "power to persuade" is from Richard Neustadt, Presidential Power and the Modern Presidents: The Politics of Leadership from Roosevelt to Reagan (Free Press, 1990), p. 7.
74. Matthew Eshbaugh-Soha, and Thomas Miles, "Presidential Speeches and the Stages of the Legislative Process," *Congress & the Presidency*, vol. 38, no. 3 (September–December 2011), pp. 301–321.
75. See the article cited earlier by José D. Villalobos, Justin S. Vaugh, and Julia R. Azari on "Politics or Policy: How Rhetoric Matters to Presidential Leadership of Congress" for more detail on this list.
76. Congressional Quarterly, "CQ Vote Studies: 2016 Presidential Support," *CQ Weekly*, October 17, 2016.
77. Brandon Rottinghaus, and Justin S. Vaughn, "How Does Trump Stack Up Against the Best—and Worst—Presidents?" *New York*

Times, February 19, 2018, available at https://www.nytimes.com/interactive/2018/02/19/opinion/how-does-trump-stack-up-against-the-best-and-worst-presidents.html?smid=tw-share.
78. Greg Jaffe, "In State of the Union, Obama Takes on Country's Anger and Anxiety," *Washington Post*, January 12, 2016, http://www.washingtonpost.com/pb/politics/in-state-of-the-union-obama-takes-on-countrys-anger-and-anxiety/2016/01/12/c8b-f04ce-b94a-11e5-b682-4bb4dd403c7d_story.html.

CHAPTER 12

1. Colin D. Mathers, Gretchen A. Stevens, Ties Bowman, Richard A. White, and Martin I. Tobias, "Cause of International Increases in Older Age Life Expectancy," *The Lancet*, February 7, 2015.
2. Harry J. Helman, and Samantha Artiga, "Beyond Health Care: The Role of Social Determinants in Promoting Health and Health Equity," Kaiser Family Foundation, November 4, 2015, available at https://www.kff.org/disparities-policy/issue-brief/beyond-health-care-the-role-of-social-determinants-in-promoting-health-and-health-equity/.
3. Max Weber, *Economy and Society* (University of California Press, 1978). The original version of the book was published in German in 1922 after Weber's death.
4. See Stanley Elkins and Eric McKitrick, *The Age of Federalism* (Oxford University Press, 1993), pp. 50–51.
5. See John A. Rohr, *To Run a Constitution: The Legitimacy of the Administrative State* (University of Kansas Press, 1986).
6. Alexander Hamilton, James Madison, and John Jay, *The Federalist Papers*, available at http://thomas.loc.gov/home/histdox/fedpaper.txt.
7. Ibid.
8. Ibid.
9. Forest McDonald, *Alexander Hamilton: A Biography* (W.W. Norton, 1982), p. 218.
10. Max Farrand, ed., *The Records of the Federal Convention* (Yale University Press, 1966), I, p. 82.
11. See Stephen Skowronek, *Building a New American State: The Expansion of National Administrative Capacities, 1877–1920* (Cambridge University Press, 1982), for a discussion about how motivations changed with civil service reform in 1883.
12. Alexander Hamilton, James Madison, and John Jay, *The Federalist Papers*, available at http://thomas.loc.gov/home/histdox/fedpaper.txt.
13. Leonard White, *The Federalists* (Macmillan, 1956), p. 1.
14. These quotes can be found in Paul C. Light, *A Government Ill Executed: The Decline of the Federal Service and How to Reverse It* (Harvard University Press, 2008), pp. 9–14.
15. See Paul C. Light, *Forging Legislation* (W.W. Norton, 1992), for the history of the VA elevation to department rank.
16. James Fesler and Donald Kettl, *The Politics of the Administrative Process* (Chatham House, 1991).
17. See Robert Puentes, Adie Tomer, and Joseph Kane, "A New Alignment: Strengthening America's Commitment to Passenger Rail," Brookings Institution, March 2013.
18. For a review of the USPS/Amazon relationship, see John Kruel, "Trump Takes Aim at Amazon in Barded Tweet. What Are the Facts?" *Politifact*, August 16, 2017, at http://www.politifact.com/truth-o-meter/article/2017/aug/16/trump-takes-aim-amazon-barbed-tweet/. See also Manuela Tobias, "No, the Postal Service Isn't Losing a Fortune on Amazon," *Politifact*, April 2, 2018, at http://www.politifact.com/truth-o-meter/statements/2018/apr/02/donald-trump/trump-usps-postal-service-amazon-losing-fortune/.
19. Paul C. Light, *A Government Ill Executed*, Chapter 7.
20. See Paul C. Light, "The State of the Federal Service," Brookings Institution Press, October 2001, and "The Troubled State of the Federal Service," Brookings Institution Press, May 2002.
21. Paul C. Light, *A Government Ill Executed*, p. 127.
22. For an analysis of the use and abuse of the civil service system in the early twentieth century, see Stephen Skowronek, *Building a New American State* (Cambridge University Press, 1982).
23. Congressional Budget Office, "Comparing the Compensation of Federal and Private-Sector Employees," January 2012.
24. U.S. Government Accountability Office, "Results of Studies on Federal Pay Varied Due to Differing Methodologies," June 2012.
25. See Joseph A. McCarin, *Collision Course: Ronald Reagan, the Air Traffic Controllers, and the Strike That Changed America* (Oxford University Press, 2011).
26. For pre-Iraq and Afghanistan War estimates, see Carey Luse, Christopher Madeline, Landon Smith, and Stephen Starr, *An Evaluation of Contingency Contracting: Past, President, and Future*, MBA Professional Report, Naval Postgraduate School, December 2005. The Iraq and Afghanistan estimates can be found at U.S. Library of Congress, Congressional Research Service, *Department of Defense Contractor and Troop Levels in Iraq and Afghanistan: 2007-2017*, by Heidi M. Peters, Moshe Schwartz, and Lawrence Kapp, R44116 (2017). For a discussion of private military contractors as an emerging profession, see Scott L. Efflandt, "Military Professionalism & Private Military Contractors," *Parameters*, 44, no. 2 (2014).
27. Paul C. Light, *The Government-Industrial Complex: Tracking the True Size of Government, 1984-2018*, (Oxford University Press, 2018).
28. These figures build upon the 2014 trends highlighted in U.S. government statistics.
29. For analysis of the number of women at senior levels in the federal government, see U.S. Office of Personnel Management, "Women in Federal Service: A Seat at Every Table," March 2015, available at https://www.fedview.opm.gov/2014files/2014_Womens_Report.pdf; for analysis of the number of minority group members at senior levels of government, see U.S. Office of Personnel Management, "Federal Equal Opportunity Recruitment Program Report to Congress, Fiscal Year 2014," February 2016.
30. Partnership for Public Service, "Federal Hiring," 2014.
31. Partnership for Public Service, "Improving the Employee Experience: What Agencies and Leaders Can Do to Manage Talent Better," August 2015.
32. See Jeanne Ponessa, "The Hatch Act Rewrite," *CQ Weekly*, November 13, 1993, pp. 3146–3147.
33. Theodore J. Lowi, Jr., *The End of Liberalism*, 2nd ed. (Norton, 1979).
34. Scott Menchin, "Trump's 'Best People' and Their Dubious Ethics," *New York Times*, February 18, 2018, available at https://www.nytimes.com/2018/02/18/opinion/trump-best-people-ethics.html.
35. John S. and James L. Knight Foundation, *"Decoding the Net Neutrality Debate: An Analysis of Media, Public Comment and Advocacy on Open Internet,"* December 11, 2014, available at http://knightfoundation.org/features/netneutrality/.
36. Coral Davenport, and Lisa Friedman, "In His Haste to Roll Back rules, Scott Pruitt, E.P.A. Chief, Risks His Agenda," *New York Times*, April 7, 2018, https://www.nytimes.com/2018/04/07/climate/scott-pruitt-epa-rollbacks.html?hp&action=click&pgtype=Homepage&clickSource=story-heading&module=first-column-region®ion=top-news&WT.nav=top-news.
37. The story of the rescue is told in Andrew Ross Sorkin, *Too Big to Fail: The Inside Story of How Wall Street and Washington Fought to Save the Financial System—and Themselves* (Penguin, 2011).
38. See Richard H. Thaler and Cass R. Sunstein, *Nudge: Improving Decisions About Health, Wealth, and Happiness* (Penguin, 2009), for new forms of low-cost regulation.
39. These figures come from Office of Management and Budget, *Budget of the U.S. Government, Fiscal Year 2014*, Historical Tables (U.S. Government Printing Office, February 2013), Table 2.2, pp. 34–35, available at http://www.whitehouse.gov/sites/default/files/omb/budget/fy2013/assets/hist.pdf.
40. Quoctrung Bui, "See Everyone the U.S. Government Owes Money to, in One Graph," National Public Radio, October 10, 2013, available

at http://www.npr.org/blogs/money/2013/10/10/230944425/everyone-the-u-s-government-owes-money-to-in-one-graph.

41. Office of Management and Budget, *Budget of the U.S. Government, Fiscal Year 2014*, Historical Tables (U.S. Government Printing Office, February 2013), pp. 157–164, available at http://www.whitehouse.gov/sites/default/files/omb/budget/fy2013/assets/hist.pdf.
42. See *Budget of the U.S. Government, Fiscal Year 2014* (U.S. Government Printing Office, 2014), Analytical Tables, Table 16.3, available at http://www.whitehouse.gov/omb/budget/analytical_perspectives.
43. Morris P. Fiorina, "Flagellating the Federal Bureaucracy," *Society* (March–April 1983), p. 73.
44. Mathew D. McCubbins and Thomas Schwartz, "Congressional Oversight Overlooked: Police Patrols Versus Fire Alarms," *American Journal of Political Science*, vol. 28, no. 1, pp. 165–179.
45. The original types of public policy were developed by Theodore J. Lowi, "American Business, Public Policy, Case Studies, and Political Theory," *World Politics*, vol. 16 (1964), pp. 677–715.
46. See Frank R. Baumgartner, "Some Thoughts on Reform Miracles," unpublished paper available at https://www.unc.edu/~fbaum/papers/Baumgartner_Reform_Miracles.pdf.
47. Peter Bachrach and Morton S. Baratz, "Two Faces of Power," *American Political Science Review*, vol. 56, no. 4 (December 1962), p. 918.
48. Anthony Downs, "The 'Issue-Attention Cycle,'" *Public Interest*, vol. 28 (Summer 1972), p. 38.
49. William Greider, "The Education of David Stockman," *Atlantic* (1981), p. 296.
50. John Kingdon, *Agendas, Alternatives, and Public Policies* (Little, Brown, 1984), p. 3.
51. James L. True, Bryan D. Jones, and Frank R. Baumgartner, "Punctuated-Equilibrium Theory: Explaining Stability and Change in Public Policymaking," in Paul A. Sabatier, ed., *Theories of the Policy Process* (Westview Press, 2007), p. 157.
52. Lester Salamon and Michael Lund, "The Tools Approach: Basic Analytics," in L. Salamon, ed., *Beyond Privatization: The Tools of Government Action* (Urban Institute Press, 1989).
53. See James E. Anderson, *Public Policymaking: An Introduction* (Houghton Mifflin, 2003), pp. 1–34.
54. See Paul C. Light, *A Government Ill Executed: The Decline of the Federal Service and How to Reverse It* (Harvard University Press, 2008).
55. Hugh Heclo, "Issue Networks and the Executive Establishment," in A. King, ed., *The New American Political System* (American Enterprise Institute, 1978), pp. 87–124.
56. Government Accountability Office, "Opportunities to Reduce Potential Duplication in Government Programs, Save Tax Dollars, and Enhance Revenue," Report GAO-11-318SP. The report has been updated every year since its first publication.
57. Mark Mather, Linda A. Jacobsen, and Kelvin M. Pollard, "Aging in the United States," *Population Bulletin*, June 2015; 2016 figures updated by Mark Mather.

CHAPTER 13

1. The Federal Bureau of Investigation, Uniform Crime Reports, 2016, https://ucr.fbi.gov/crime-in-the-u.s/2016/crime-in-the-u.s.-2016/topic-pages/tables/table-1.
2. "Michael Hawthorne. "Studies Link Childhood Lead Exposure, Violent Crime," *The Chicago Tribune*, June 6, 2015.
3. Roy P. Fairfield, ed., *The Federalist Papers* (Johns Hopkins University Press, 1981), p. 227.
4. Robert Dahl, "Decision Making in a Democracy: The Supreme Court as a National Policy Maker," *Journal of Public Law*, vol. 6 (1957), pp. 279–295.
5. Madhavi McCall, "The Politics of Judicial Elections: The Influence of Campaign Contributions on the Voting Patterns of Texas Supreme Court Justices, 1994–1997," *Politics & Policy*, vol. 31 (June 2003), pp. 314–343.
6. Jerome Frank, *Courts on Trial: Myth and Reality in American Justice* (Princeton University Press, 1949), pp. 80–103; see also Martin Shapiro, *Courts* (University of Chicago Press, 1981); and Robert P. Burns, *A Theory of the Trial* (Princeton University Press, 1999).
7. Many of these workload statistics can be found in the Supreme Court's annual *Year-End Report on the Federal Judiciary* (U.S. Government Printing Office, December 31, 2015).
8. Laura Meckler and Alicia A. Caldwell, "The Glitch in Trump's Immigration Campaign: Overloaded Courts" *The Wall Street Journal*, May 23, 2018. https://www.wsj.com/articles/u-s-immigration-courts-long-crowded-are-now-overwhelmed-1527089932
9. Mike DeBonis, Philip Rucker, Sueung Min Kim, and John Wagner, "Trump Urges House GOP to Fix Immigration System, Expresses No Strong Preference on Rival GOP Bills Amid Uproar Over His Family Separations." *Washington Post*, June 20, 2018. https://www.washingtonpost.com/powerpost/trump-is-defiant-as-border-crisis-escalates-prepares-to-lobby-house-gop-on-immigration-bills/2018/06/19/e20a108e-73c1-11e8-805c-4b67019fcfe4_story.html?utm_term=.8617358278e0
10. Katie Rogers and Sheryl Gay Stolberg, "Trump Wants No Due Process At U.S. Border: Constitutional Worries After a Fiery Attack." *New York Times* June 25, 2018. p. A-1.
11. "Examining the Work of State Courts: An Overview of 2012 State Trial Court Caseloads," Court Statistics Project (National Center for State Courts, 2014).
12. Fairfield, *The Federalist Papers*, p. 228.
13. Harold W. Chase, *Federal Judges: The Appointing Process* (University of Minnesota Press, 1972); and Sheldon Goldman, *Picking Federal Judges: Lower Court Selection from Roosevelt Through Reagan* (Yale University Press, 1997).
14. Sarah Wilson, "Appellate Judicial Appointments During the Clinton Presidency: An Inside Perspective," *Journal of Appellate Practice and Process*, vol. 5, no. 1 (Spring 2003), pp. 36–39.
15. Nick Corasaniti, "At Debate, Donald Trump Calls on Republicans to 'Delay, Delay, Delay'" *New York Times*, February 13, 2016.
16. Baum, Lawrence and Neal Devins. *The Company They Keep: How Partisan Divisions Came to the Supreme Court.* (Oxford University Press, 2018).
17. Slattery, Elizabeth, "Two Obstacles for Trump's Judicial Nominees to Overcome," *The Heritage Foundation.* April 25, 2018. (https://www.heritage.org/courts/commentary/two-obstacles-trumps-judicial-nominees-overcome).
18. See David M. O'Brien, "Ironies and Disappointments: Bush and Federal Judgeships," in Colin Campbell and Bert A. Rockman, eds., *The George W. Bush Presidency* (CQ Press, 2004), pp. 133–157; and Brannon P. Denning, "The Judicial Confirmation Process and the Blue Slip," *Judicature* (March–April 2002), pp. 218–226.
19. Jeremy W. Peters, "In Landmark Vote, Senate Limits Use of the Filibuster," *New York Times*, November 21, 2013.
20. Scott E. Graves and Robert M. Howard, *Justice Takes a Recess: Judicial Appointments from George Washington to George W. Bush* (Lexington Books, 2009).
21. *National Labor Relations Board* v. *Noel Canning*, 573 U.S. ______, 2014.
22. Lisa M. Holmes and Roger E. Hartley, "Increasing Senate Scrutiny of Lower Federal Court Nominees," *Judicature* (May–June 1997), p. 275.
23. Christine Rousselle, "President Trump at Pro-Life Event: 'Vote for Life.'" *National Catholic Register*, May 23, 2018. http://www.ncregister.com/daily-news/president-trump-at-pro-life-event-vote-for-life
24. *Fisher* v. *Texas* 579 U.S. ______ (2016).
25. Barbara A. Perry and Henry J. Abraham, "A 'Representative' Supreme Court? The Thomas, Ginsburg, and Breyer Appointments," *Judicature* (January–February 1998), pp. 158–165.
26. Judicial Selection Dashboards, Alliance for Justice, up-dated February 5, 2016, http://www.afj.org/judicial-selection-dashboards.

27. *Marbury* v. *Madison*, 5 U.S. 137 (1803).
28. Donald Santarelli, quoted in Jerry Landauer, "Shaping the Bench," *Wall Street Journal*, December 10, 1970, p. 1.
29. Lee Epstein, Jeffrey A. Segal, Harold J. Spaeth, and Thomas G. Walker, *The Supreme Court Compendium: Data, Decisions, and Developments* (CQ Press, 2007), figures updated by the authors.
30. Adam Liptak, "A Most Inquisitive Court? No Argument There," *New York Times*, October 7, 2013.
31. Timothy R. Johnson, Ryan C. Black, and Justin Wedeking, "Pardon the Interruption: An Empirical Analysis of Supreme Court Justices' Behavior During Oral Arguments," *Loyola Law Review*, vol. 55 (2009), pp. 331–351.
32. You can listen to oral arguments at www.oyez.org, and argument transcripts are now made available on the Court's Web site on the same day as the case is heard (www.supremecourt.gov).
33. Forrest Maltzman, James F. Spriggs III, and Paul Wahlbeck, *Crafting Law on the Supreme Court: The Collegial Game* (Cambridge University Press, 2000).
34. Charles Evans Hughes, *The Supreme Court of the United States* (Columbia University Press, 1966), p. 68.
35. Daniel M. Berman, *It Is So Ordered: The Supreme Court Rules on School Segregation* (Norton, 1986), p. 114; and David M. O'Brien, *Storm Center: The Supreme Court in American Politics*, 7th ed. (Norton, 2005), pp. 262–272.
36. Charles H. Franklin and Liane C. Kosaki, "The U.S. Supreme Court, Public Opinion, and Abortion," *American Political Science Review* (September 1989), pp. 751–771.
37. *Brown* v. *Board of Education of Topeka*, 347 U.S. 483 (1954).
38. *Citizens United* v. *Federal Election Commission*, 558 U.S. 50 (2010).
39. Since April 2000, the Court has made its opinions immediately available on its Web site (www.supremecourt.gov).
40. William H. Rehnquist, quoted in John R. Vile, "The Selection and Tenure of Chief Justices," *Judicature* (September–October 1994), p. 98.
41. David Danelski, "The Influence of the Chief Justice in the Decisional Process of the Supreme Court," in Thomas P. Jahnige and Sheldon Goldman, eds., *The Federal Judicial System: Readings in Process and Behavior* (Holt, Rinehart and Winston, 1968), p. 148.
42. O'Brien, *Storm Center*, Chapter 3.
43. Artemus Ward and David L. Weiden, *Sorcerers' Apprentices: 100 Years of Law Clerks at the United States Supreme Court* (New York University Press, 2006); and Todd C. Peppers, *Courtiers of the Marble Palace: The Rise and Influence of the Supreme Court Law Clerk* (Stanford University Press, 2006).
44. Lincoln Caplan, *The Tenth Justice: The Solicitor General and the Rule of Law* (Knopf, 1987); and Rebecca Mae Salokar, *The Solicitor General: The Politics of Law* (Temple University Press, 1992).
45. Gregory A. Caldeira and John R. Wright, "Organized Interest and Agenda Setting in the U.S. Supreme Court," *American Political Science Review*, vol. 82 (December 1988), p. 1110; and Donald R. Songer and Reginald S. Sheehan, "Interest Group Success in the Courts: *Amicus* Participation in the Supreme Court," *Political Research Quarterly*, vol. 46 (June 1993), pp. 339–354.
46. Paul M. Collins, Jr., *Friends of the Supreme Court: Interest Groups and Judicial Decision Making* (Oxford University Press, 2008).
47. Caldeira and Wright, "Organized Interest and Agenda Setting," *American Political Science Review*, vol. 82 (December 1988), p. 1118; and Songer and Sheehan, "Interest Group Success in the Courts," *Political Research Quarterly*, vol. 46 (June 1993).
48. Gerald N. Rosenberg, *Hollow Hope: Can Courts Bring About Sound Change?* (University of Chicago Press, 1991).
49. J. W. Peltason, *Fifty-Eight Lonely Men: Southern Federal Judges and School Desegregation* (University of Illinois Press, 1971); and Gary Orfield and Chungmei Lee, *Brown at 50: King's Dream or Plessy's Nightmare* (Civil Rights Project, Harvard University, 2004).
50. See Benjamin N. Cardozo, *The Nature of the Judicial Process* (Yale University Press, 1921)—a classic.
51. William O. Douglas, quoted in O'Brien, *Storm Center*, p. 184.
52. *Citizens United* v. *Federal Election Commission*, 558 U.S. 50 (2010), C. J. Roberts concurring.
53. Lee Epstein, Jeffrey A. Segal, Harold J. Spaeth, and Thomas G. Walker, *The Supreme Court Compendium: Data, Decisions, and Developments*, 4th ed. (CQ Press, 2007). Data through 2005–2006 Supreme Court term.
54. Ex parte *McCardle*, 74 U.S. 506 (1869).
55. See Shawn Francis Peters, *Judging the Jehovah's Witnesses* (University of Kansas Press, 2002); Clyde Wilcox, *Onward, Christian Soldiers? The Religious Right in American Politics* (Westview Press, 1996); Mark Tushnet, *The NAACP's Legal Strategy Against Segregated Education, 1925–1950* (University of North Carolina Press, 1987); and Karen O'Connor, *Women's Organizations' Use of the Court* (Lexington Books, 1980).
56. J. W. Peltason, "The Supreme Court: Transactional or Transformational Leadership," in Michael R. Beschloss and Thomas E. Cronin, eds., *Essays in Honor of James MacGregor Burns* (Prentice Hall, 1988), pp. 165–180; and Valerie Hoekstra, *Public Reactions to Supreme Court Decisions* (Cambridge University Press, 2003).
57. *Planned Parenthood* v. *Casey*, 505 U.S. 833 (1992).
58. Edward White, "The Supreme Court of the United States," *American Bar Association Journal*, vol. 7 (1921), p. 341.

CHAPTER 14

1. *Boumediene* v. *Bush*, 553 U.S. 723 (2008).
2. *Felker* v. *Turpin*, 518 U.S. 651 (1996); *Winthrow* v. *Williams*, 507 U.S. 680 (1993); *McCleskey* v. *Zant*, 499 U.S. 467 (1991); and *Stone* v. *Powell*, 428 U.S. 465 (1976).
3. *Barron* v. *Baltimore*, 7 Peters 243 (1833).
4. *Gitlow* v. *New York*, 268 U.S. 652 (1925).
5. Richard C. Cortner, *The Supreme Court and the Second Bill of Rights: The Fourteenth Amendment and the Nationalization of Civil Liberties* (University of Wisconsin Press, 1981).
6. *McDonald* v. *Chicago*, 561 U.S. 3025 (2010).
7. *Witters* v. *Washington Department of Services for the Blind*, 474 U.S. 481 (1986); and *Locke* v. *Davey*, 540 U.S. 712 (2004).
8. *Wallace* v. *Jaffree*, 472 U.S. 38 (1985).
9. *Everson* v. *Board of Education of Ewing Township*, 333 U.S. 203 (1947).
10. *Lemon* v. *Kurtzman*, 403 U.S. 602 (1971).
11. *Capital Square Review Board* v. *Pinette*, 515 U.S. 753 (1995).
12. *Mitchell* v. *Helms*, 530 U.S. 793 (2000).
13. *Agostini* v. *Felton*, 521 U.S. 74 (1997).
14. *Employment Division of Human Resources of Oregon* v. *Smith*, 494 U.S. 872 (1990).
15. *Church of Lukumi Babalu Aye* v. *City of Hialeah*, 508 U.S. 520 (1993).
16. *Buckley* v. *Valeo*, 424 U.S. 1 (1976); *McConnell* v. *FEC*, 540 U.S. 93 (2003); *Citizens United* v. *FEC*, 558 U.S. 50 (2010).
17. *44 Liquormart* v. *Rhode Island*, 517 U.S. 484 (1996); *Sorrell* v. *IMS Health*, 131 S. Ct. 2653 (2011).
18. *New York Times Company* v. *United States*, 403 U.S. 670 (1971).
19. Ibid., *Near* v. *Minnesota*, 283 U.S. 697 (1930).
20. *Hazelwood School District* v. *Kuhlmeier*, 484 U.S. 260 (1988).
21. *New York Times* v. *Sullivan*, 376 U.S. 254 (1964).
22. *Hustler Magazine* v. *Falwell*, 485 U.S. 46 (1988).
23. Potter Stewart, concurring in *Jacobellis* v. *Ohio*, 378 U.S. 184 (1964).
24. *Miller* v. *California*, 413 U.S. 15 (1973).
25. *Young* v. *American Mini Theatres*, 427 U.S. 51 (1976); *Renton* v. *Playtime Theatres, Inc.*, 475 U.S. 41 (1986); and *City of Los Angeles* v. *Alameda Books, Inc.*, 535 U.S. 425 (2002).
26. *Barnes* v. *Glen Theatre, Inc.*, 501 U.S. 560 (1991); and *City of Erie* v. *Pap's A.M.*, 529 U.S. 277 (2000).
27. *Chaplinsky* v. *New Hampshire*, 315 U.S. 568 (1942).
28. *Cohen* v. *California*, 403 U.S. 115 (1971).
29. *Wisconsin* v. *Mitchell*, 508 U.S. 476 (1993).
30. *Branzburg* v. *Hayes*, 408 U.S. 665 (1972).
31. *Federal Communications Commission* v. *Fox Television Stations, Inc.*, 567 U.S. 502 (2012).

32. *United States* v. *Playboy Entertainment Group*, 529 U.S. 803 (2000); and *Denver Area Educational Television* v. *Federal Communications Commission*, 518 U.S. 727 (1996).
33. *Reno* v. *American Civil Liberties Union*, 521 U.S. 844 (1997).
34. *Ashcroft* v. *ACLU*, 542 U.S. 656 (2004).
35. Heather Gautney, "What Is Occupy Wall Street? This History of Leaderless Movements," *Washington Post*, October 10, 2011.
36. Andrew Grossman, Alison Fox, and Sean Gardiner, "Wall Street Protestors Evicted from Camp," *Wall Street Journal*, November 16, 2011.
37. *Walker* v. *Birmingham*, 388 U.S. 307 (1967).
38. William Michael Treanor, "The Origins and Original Significance of the Just Compensation Clause of the Fifth Amendment," *Yale Law Journal*, vol. 94 (1985), pp. 694–716.
39. Stephen P. Halbrook, "Encroachments of the Crown on the Liberty of the Subject: Pre-Revolutionary Origins of the Second Amendment," *University of Dayton Law Review* (Fall 1989), pp. 91–124.
40. Adam Winkler, *Gunfight: The Battle over the Right to Bear Arms* (New York: W. W. Norton & Company, 2011).
41. *First English Evangelical* v. *Los Angeles County*, 482 U.S. 304 (1987); see Richard A. Epstein, *Taking: Private Property and the Power of Eminent Domain* (Harvard University Press, 1985).
42. *Lucas* v. *South Carolina Coastal Commission*, 505 U.S. 647 (1992).
43. *Tahoe-Sierra Council, Inc.* v. *Tahoe Regional Planning Agency*, 535 U.S. 302 (2002).
44. *Kelo* v. *City of New London*, 545 U.S. 469 (2005).
45. *United States* v. *554 Acres of Land*, 441 U.S. 506 (1979).
46. *District of Columbia* v. *Heller*, 554 U.S. 570 (2008).
47. *McDonald* v. *Chicago*, 561 U.S. 3025 (2010).
48. Ingraham, Christopher, "After Parkland Shooting, NRA Posts Biggest Fundraising Haul in Nearly 20 Years," *Washington Post.* April 24, 2018.
49. *Mathews* v. *Eldridge*, 424 U.S. 319 (1976), restated in *Connecticut* v. *Doeher*, 501 U.S. 1 (1991).
50. *Meyer* v. *Nebraska*, 262 U.S. 390 (1923).
51. *Griswold* v. *Connecticut*, 381 U.S. 479 (1965).
52. Philip B. Kurland, *Some Reflections on Privacy and the Constitution* (University of Chicago Center for Policy Study, 1976), p. 9. A classic and influential article about privacy is Samuel D. Warren and Louis D. Brandeis, "The Right to Privacy," *Harvard Law Review* (December 15, 1890), pp. 193–220.
53. *Roe* v. *Wade*, 410 U.S. 113 (1973).
54. *Planned Parenthood of Southeastern Pennsylvania* v. *Casey*, 505 U.S. 833 (1992).
55. *Gonzales* v. *Carhart*, 550 U.S. 124 (2007).
56. *Whole Woman's Health* v. *Hellerstedt*, 579 U.S. ______ (2016).
57. *Bowers* v. *Hardwick*, 478 U.S. 186 (1986).
58. *Lawrence* v. *Texas*, 539 U.S. 558 (2003).
59. But see *Washington* v. *Chrisman*, 445 U.S. 1 (1982); and compare *Georgia* v. *Randolph*, 126 547 U.S. 103 (2006).
60. *Katz* v. *United States*, 389 U.S. 347 (1967).
61. *Terry* v. *Ohio*, 392 U.S. 1 (1968).
62. *Hiibel* v. *Sixth Judicial District of Nevada*, 542 U.S. 177 (2004).
63. *Minnesota* v. *Dickerson*, 508 U.S. 366 (1993).
64. *Kyllo* v. *United States*, 533 U.S. 27 (2001).
65. *United States* v. *Jones*, 565 U.S. 400 (2012).
66. *Carpenter* v. *United States*, 585 U.S. ______ (2018).
67. Barry Friedman, "Privacy, Technology and the Law," *New York Times*, January 28, 2012.
68. *Mapp* v. *Ohio*, 367 U.S. 643 (1961).
69. Senate Committee on the Judiciary, the Jury, and the Search for Truth: The Case Against Excluding Relevant Evidence at Trial, Hearing Before the Committee, 104th Cong., 1st sess. (U.S. Government Printing Office, 1997).
70. *United States* v. *Leon*, 468 U.S. 897 (1984); and *Arizona* v. *Evans*, 514 U.S. 1 (1995).
71. *Schenck* v. *United States*, 249 U.S. 47 (1919).
72. *Miranda* v. *Arizona*, 384 U.S. 436 (1966); but see *Yarborough* v. *Alvarado*, 541 U.S. 652 (2004).
73. *Dickerson* v. *United States*, 530 U.S. 428 (2000).
74. *Betts v. Brady*, 316 U.S. 455 (1942).
75. Gideon v. Wainwright, 372 U.S. 335 (1963).
76. U.S. Department of Justice, Bureau of Justice Statistics, "State-Administered Indigent Defense Systems, 2013," revised May 3, 2017.
77. Jed Lipinski, "The Trials and Travails of a New Orleans Public Defender," The Times-Picayune, NOLA.com, March 30, 2016.
78. *United States* v. R. (title should be "R. Enterprises, Inc." *Enterprises, Inc.*, 498 U.S. 292 (1991).
79. *J. E. B.* v. *Alabama ex rel T. B.*, 511 U.S. 127 (1994); *Batson* v. *Kentucky*, 476 U.S. 79 (1986); *Powers* v. *Ohio*, 499 U.S. 400 (1991); *Hernandez* v. *New York*, 500 U.S. 352 (1991); and *Georgia* v. *McCollum*, 505 U.S. 42 (1990).
80. *Ewing* v. *California*, 538 U.S. 11 (2003).
81. Graham v. Florida, 560 U.S. 48 (2010) and Miller v. Alabama, 567 U.S. 460 (2012).
82. *Benton* v. *Maryland*, 395 U.S. 784 (1969); see also *Kansas* v. *Hendricks*, 521 U.S. 346 (1997).
83. *Graham* v. *Collins*, 506 U.S. 461 (1993).
84. *Gregg* v. *Georgia*, 428 U.S. 153 (1976).
85. Death Penalty Information Center, "Facts About the Death Penalty," Updated March 28, 2014, www.deathpenaltyinfo.org/documents/FactSheet.pdf.
86. Barry Scheck, Peter Neufeld, and Jim Dwyer, *Actual Innocence: Five Days to Execution and Other Dispatches from the Wrongly Convicted* (Doubleday, 2000); and Timothy Kaufman-Osborn, *From Noose to Needle: Capital Punishment and the Late Liberal State* (University of Michigan Press, 2002).
87. Death Penalty Information Center, "Facts About the Death Penalty," Updated May 17, 2018, www.deathpenaltyinfo.org/documents/FactSheet.pdf.
88. *Atkins* v. *Virginia*, 536 U.S. 304 (2002).
89. *Roper* v. *Simmons*, 543 U.S. 551 (2006).
90. *Kennedy* v. *Louisiana*, 554 U.S. 407 (2008).
91. *Baze* v. *Rees*, 553 U.S. 35 (2008).
92. *Glossip* v. *Gross*, 576 U.S. ______ (2015).

CHAPTER 15

1. Dominic Tierney, "Trump's Unspeakable Strategy to Erase His Past," *The Atlantic*, February 10, 2016.
2. Elaina Plott, "Trump's Immigration Plan Receives A Chilly Reception." *The Atlantic*, January 31, 2018. https://www.theatlantic.com/politics/archive/2018/01/trump-bets-on-immigration-in-the-state-of-the-union/551936/
3. Richard Gonzales, "Sessions Says 'Zero Tolerance' For Illegal Border Crossers, Vows to Divide Families," *National Public Radio.* May 7, 2018. https://www.npr.org/sections/thetwo-way/2018/05/07/609225537/sessions-says-zero-tolerance-for-illegal-border-crossers-vows-to-divide-families.
4. Jonathan Blitzer, "How the Trump Administration got Comfortable Separating Immigrant Kids from their Parents," *The New Yorker*, May 30, 2018. https://www.newyorker.com/news/news-desk/how-the-trump-administration-got-comfortable-separating-immigrant-kids-from-their-parents
5. @realDonaldTrump. "Republicans should stop wasting their time...." *Twitter.* June 22, 2018. https://twitter.com/realdonaldtrump/status/1010116816998490113?lang=en
6. "Attorney General Jeff Sessions Delivers Remarks Before Media Availability in El Paso, Texas," U.S. Department of Justice. April 20, 2017. https://www.justice.gov/opa/speech/attorney-general-jeff-sessions-delivers-remarks-media-availability-el-paso-texas
7. Martin Luther King, Jr. *Letter from Birmingham Jail.* April 13, 1963.
8. Andrew Hacker, *Two Nations: Black and White, Separate, Hostile, Unequal* (Scribner, 1992). Lane Kenworthy, *Jobs With Equality* (Oxford University Press, 2008).
9. *Slaughter-House Cases*, 83 U.S. 36 (1873).
10. Ex Parte *Milligan*, 71 U.S. 2 (1866).

11. *Korematsu* v. *United States*, 323 U.S. 214 (1944).
12. Ex Parte *Quirin*, 317 U.S. 1 (1942).
13. *Reid* v. *Covert*, 354 U.S. 1 (1957).
14. *Boumediene* v. *Bush*, 553 U.S. 723 (2008)
15. *Mathews* v. *Diaz*, 426 U.S. 67 (1976); and *Shaughnessy* v. *United States ex rel. Mezei*, 345 U.S. 206 (1953).
16. *Demore* v. *Kim*, 538 U.S. 510 (2003).
17. *Zadvydas* v. *Davis*, 533 U.S. 678 (2001).
18. *Jennings* v. *Rodriguez*, 583 U.S. ______ (2018).
19. *Yick Wo* v. *Hopkins*, 118 U.S. 356 (1886); *Kwong Hai Chew* v. *Colding*, 344 U.S. 590 (1953); *Zadvydas* v. *Davis*, 533 U.S. 678 (2001); *Rasul* v. *Bush*, 542 U.S. 466 (2004); and *Hamdi* v. *Rumsfeld*, 542 U.S. 507 (2004).
20. *Foley* v. *Connelie*, 435 U.S. 291 (1978); *Ambach* v. *Norwick*, 441 U.S. 68 (1979); *Cabell* v. *Chavez-Salido*, 454 U.S. 432 (1982).
21. *Plyler* v. *Doe*, 457 U.S. 202 (1982).
22. *Arizona* v. *United States*, 567 U.S. 387 (2012).
23. *Slaughter-House Cases*, 83 U.S. 36 (1873); and *Civil Rights Cases*, 109 U.S. 3 (1883).
24. *Plessy* v. *Ferguson*, 163 U.S. 537 (1896).
25. Susan B. Carter, Scott Sigmund Gartner, Michael R. Haines, Alan L. Olmstead, Richard Sutch, and Gavin Wright, *Historical Statistics of the United States, Millennial Edition Online* (Cambridge University Press, 2006).
26. *Brown* v. *Board of Education of Topeka*, 347 U.S. 483 (1954); and *Brown* v. *Board of Education of Topeka*, 349 U.S. 294 (1955).
27. *Gomillion* v. *Lightfoot*, 364 U.S. 339 (1960).
28. Taylor Branch, *Parting the Waters: America in the King Years, 1954–1963* (Simon & Schuster, 1988); see also Harris Wofford, *Of Kennedys and Kings: Making Sense of the Sixties* (Farrar, Straus, & Giroux, 1980).
29. See Charles Whalen and Barbara Whalen, *The Longest Debate: A Legislative History of the 1964 Civil Rights Act* (Mentor, 1985); and Hugh Davis Graham, *The Civil Rights Era* (Oxford University Press, 1990).
30. David Remnick, *The Bridge: The Life and Rise of Barack Obama* (Knopf, 2010).
31. Ellen Carol Du Bois, *Feminism and Suffrage: The Emergence of an Independent Women's Movement in America, 1848–1869* (Cornell University Press, 1978); and Joan Hoff-Wilson, "Women and the Constitution," *News for Teachers of Political Science* (Summer 1985), pp. 10–15.
32. Susan M. Hartmann, *From Margin to Mainstream: American Women and Politics Since 1960* (Temple University Press, 1989); and Susan Gluck Mezey, *In Pursuit of Equality: Women, Public Policy, and the Federal Courts* (St. Martin's Press, 1992).
33. *United States* v. *Virginia*, 518 U.S. 515 (1996); see also Philippa Strum, *Women in the Barracks: The VMI Case and Equal Rights* (University Press of Kansas, 2002).
34. *Meritor Savings Bank, FBD* v. *Vinson*, 477 U.S. 57 (1986).
35. *Oncale* v. *Sundowner Offshore Services*, 523 U.S. 75 (1998); *Faragher* v. *City of Boca Raton*, 524 U.S. 775 (1998); and *Burlington Industries* v. *Ellerth*, 524 U.S. 742 (1998).
36. Domenico Montenaro, "4 Lessons from the 2018 Primaries So Far," *National Public Radio*, June 5, 2018.
37. David A. Cotter, Joan M. Hermsen, Seth Ovadia, and Reeve Vanneman, "The Glass Ceiling Effect," *Social Forces*, vol. 80, no. 2 (2002), pp. 655–681.
38. Valentina Zarya, "The Share of Female CEOs in the Fortune 500 Dropped by 25% in 2018," *Fortune*, May 21, 2018.
39. Avi Astor, "Unauthorized Immigration, Securitization, and the Making of Operation Wetback," *Latino Studies*, 7 (2009), pp. 5–29.
40. Ann Gonzalez-Barrera and Jens Manuel Krogstad, "U.S. Deportations of Immigrants Reach Record High In 2013," Pew Research Center, October 2, 2014, http://www.pewresearch.org/fact-tank/2014/10/02/u-s-deportations-of-immigrants-reach-record-high-in-2013/.
41. *Arizona* v. *United States*, 567 U.S. 387 (2012).
42. Anna O. Law, "This is How Trump's Deportations Differ from Obama's, *Washington Post*, May 3, 2017.
43. Dudley L. Poston, Jr. and Rogelio Sáenz. "U.S. Whites Will Soon be the Minority in Number, But not Power," *The Baltimore Sun*. August 8, 2017.
44. Celia W. Dugger, "U.S. Study Says Asian Americans Face Widespread Discrimination," *New York Times*, February 29, 1992, p. 1, reporting on U.S. Civil Rights Commission, *Civil Rights Issues Facing Asian Americans in the 1990s* (U.S. Government Printing Office, 1992).
45. *Takao Ozawa* v. *United States*, 260 U.S. 178 (1922).
46. *Korematsu* v. *United States*, 323 U.S. 214 (1944).
47. "The American Indian and the Alaska Native Population: 2010," *2010 Census Briefs*, issued January 2012.
48. "Assimilation, Relocation, Genocide: The Trail of Tears," *Indian Country Diaries*, PBS, November 2006, http://www.pbs.org/indiancountry/history/trail.html.
49. *Cherokee Nation* v. *Georgia*, 30 U.S. 5 (1831); *Worchester* v. *Georgia*, 31 U.S. 515 (1832).
50. *Antoine et al.* v. *Winner School District*, (D.S.D. 2006).
51. *Keepseagle* v. *Vilsack* (D.D.C. 2011).
52. Sari Horwitz, "The Hard Lives—And High Suicide Rates—Of Native American Children on Reservations," *Washington Post*, March 9, 2014.
53. *Morey* v. *Doud*, 354 U.S. 459 (1957); and *Allegheny Pittsburgh Coal Co.* v. *County Commission*, 488 U.S. 336 (1989).
54. *City of Cleburne, Texas* v. *Cleburne Living Center*, 473 U.S. 432 (1985); *Heller* v. *Doe*, 509 U.S. 312 (1993); and *Romer* v. *Evans*, 517 U.S. 620 (1996).
55. *Romer* v. *Evans*, 517 U.S. 620 (1996).
56. *San Antonio School District* v. *Rodriguez*, 411 U.S. 1 (1973).
57. *Frontiero* v. *Richardson*, 411 U.S. 677 (1973).
58. *San Antonio School District* v. *Rodriguez*, 411 U.S. 1 (1973); and Douglas Reed, *On Equal Terms: The Constitutional Politics of Educational Opportunity* (Princeton University Press, 2001).
59. Matthew Bosworth, *Courts as Catalysts: State Supreme Courts and Public School Finance Equity* (State University of New York Press, 2001).
60. Molly A. Hunter, "Requiring States to Offer a Quality Education to All Students," *Human Rights* (Fall 2005), pp. 10–12.
61. Sandra Day O'Connor, in *Kimel* v. *Florida Board of Regents*, 528 U.S. 62 (2000).
62. Ibid.
63. *Romer* v. *Evans*, 517 U.S. 620 (1996).
64. *United States* v. *Windsor*, 570 U.S. ______ (2013).
65. *Hollingsworth* v. *Perry*, 570 U.S. ______ (2013).
66. *Obergefell* v. *Hodges*, 576 U.S. ______ (2015).
67. Alana Samuels, "Should Adoption Agencies Be Allowed to Discriminate Against Gay Parents?" *The Atlantic*. September 23, 2015.
68. *Masterpiece Cakeshop, Ltd.* v. *Colorado Civil Rights Commission*, 584 U.S. ______ (2018)." (2018).
69. Leon F. Litwack, *Trouble in Mind: Black Southerners in the Age of Jim Crow* (1998), p. 227, as cited in James W. Fox Jr., "Intimations of Citizenship: Repressions and Expressions of Equal Citizenship in the Era of Jim Crow," *Howard University Law Journal* (Fall 2006).
70. Harold W. Stanley, *Voter Mobilization and the Politics of Race: The South and Universal Suffrage*, 1952–1984 (Praeger, 1987).
71. Abigail M. Thernstrom, *Whose Votes Count? Affirmative Action and Minority Voting Rights* (Harvard University Press, 1987), p. 15.
72. *Smith* v. *Allwright*, 321 U.S. 649 (1944).
73. *Gomillion* v. *Lightfoot*, 364 U.S. 339 (1960).
74. *Harper* v. *Virginia Board of Elections*, 383 U.S. 663 (1966).
75. Thernstrom, *Whose Votes Count?* For a contrary view, see Bernard Grofman, Lisa Handley, and Richard G. Niemi, *Minority Representation and the Quest for Voting Equality* (Cambridge University Press, 1992).
76. *Morse* v. *Republican Party of Virginia*, 517 U.S. 116 (1996).
77. *Northwest Austin Municipal Utility District Number One* v. *Holder*, 557 U.S. 193 (2009).
78. *Shelby County* v. *Holder*, 570 U.S. ______ (2013).
79. *Shaw* v. *Reno*, 509 U.S. 630 (1993).

80. *Abbott* v. *Perez*, 585 U.S. (2018).
81. *Civil Rights Cases*, 109 U.S. 3 (1883).
82. *Plessy* v. *Ferguson*, 163 U.S. 537 (1896).
83. *Heart of Atlanta Motel* v. *United States*, 379 U.S. 421 (1964).
84. Movement Advancement Project, Non-discrimination Laws, June 21, 2018. http://www.lgbtmap.org/equality-maps/non_discrimination_laws.
85. Movement Advancement Project, Non-discrimination Laws, June 21, 2018. http://www.lgbtmap.org/equality-maps/non_discrimination_laws.
86. *Wal-Mart Stores, Inc.* v. *Dukes*, 564 U.S. 338 (2011).
87. Andrew Martin, "Female Wal-Mart Employees File New Bias Case," *New York Times*, October 27, 2011.
88. Darryl Van Duch, "Plagued by Politics, EEOC Backlog Grows," *Recorder* (August 18, 1998), p. 1; and David Rovella, "EEOC Chairman Casellas: 'We Are Being Selective,'" *National Law Journal* (November 20, 1995), p. 1.
89. *Shelley* v. *Kraemer*, 334 U.S. 1 (1948).
90. Movement Advancement Project, Non-Discrimination Laws, June 21, 2018. http://www.lgbtmap.org/equality-maps/non_discrimination_laws.
91. *Sweat* v. *Painter*, 339 U.S. 629 (1950).
92. *Brown* v. *Board of Education of Topeka*, 347 U.S. 483 (1954); see also J. W. Peltason, *Fifty-Eight Lonely Men: Southern Federal Judges and School Desegregation* (University of Illinois Press, 1971), p. 248.
93. *Brown* v. *Board of Education of Topeka*, 349 U.S. 294 (1955).
94. *Swann* v. *Charlotte-Mecklenburg Board of Education*, 402 U.S. 1 (1971).
95. *Freeman* v. *Pitts*, 503 U.S. 467 (1992); and *Missouri* v. *Jenkins*, 515 U.S. 70 (1995).
96. See Gary Orfield, Susan E. Eaton, and the Harvard Project on School Desegregation, *Dismantling Desegregation: The Quiet Reversal of Brown* v. *Board of Education* (New Press, 1996).
97. Raymond Hernandez, "NAACP Suspends Yonkers Leader After Criticism of Usefulness of School Busing," *New York Times*, November 1, 1995, p. A13.
98. Gary Orfield and Chungmei Lee, *Brown at 50: King's Dream or Plessy's Nightmare?* (Civil Rights Project, January 1, 2004), http://civilrightsproject.ucla.edu/research/k-12-education/integration-and-diversity/brown-at-50-king2019s-dream-or-plessy2019s-nightmare/?searchterm=brown%20at%2050; see also Charles Clotfelter, *After Brown: The Rise and Retreat of School Desegregation* (Princeton University Press, 2004).
99. *Parents Involved in Community Schools* v. *Seattle School District No. 1*, 551 U.S. 701 (2007).
100. Richard Kahlenberg, *All Together Now: Creating Middle-Class Schools Through Public School Choice* (Brookings Institution Press, 2003).
101. John Marshall Harlan, dissenting in *Plessy* v. *Ferguson*, 163 U.S. 537 (1896).
102. *University of California Regents* v. *Bakke*, 438 U.S. 265 (1978); see also Howard Ball, *The Bakke Case* (University Press of Kansas, 2000).
103. *Fisher* v. *Texas*, 570 U.S. _____ (2013).
104. *Schuette* v. *Coalition to Defend Affirmative Action*, 572 U.S. _____ (2014).
105. *Fisher* v. *Texas*, 579 U.S. _____ (2016).

CHAPTER 16

1. Lyndon B. Johnson, "Annual Message to the Congress on the State of the Union," January 8, 1964, available online in Gerhard Peters and John T. Woolley, *The American Presidency Project*, at http://www.presidency.ucsb.edu/ws/?pid=26787.
2. The Earned Income Tax Credit is one of the most popular programs across the ideological spectrum. The program gives lower-income working Americans a credit that lowers their tax obligations. The credit often exceeds the amount of taxes they owe, which means that these Americans receive a tax refund that will help them stay out of poverty. President Ronald Reagan once called the EITC "the best antipoverty, the best pro-family, the best job creation measure to come out of Congress." See Thomas L. Hungerford and Rebecca Thiess, "The Earned Income Tax Credit: History, Purpose, Goals, and Effectiveness," Economic Policy Institute, September 25, 2013. For a summary of the Earned Income Tax Credit and its impact on poverty, see Center for Budget and Policy Priorities, "Policy Basics: The Earned Income Tax Credit," updated January 30, 2014, available at http://www.cbpp.org/files/policybasics-eitc.pdf.
3. See U.S. Government Accountability Office, "Federal Low-Income Programs Target Diverse Populations and Needs," GAO-15-516, July 2015.
4. The percent of children classified as in poverty fell to 14 percent in 1969, but then rose again, Drew Desilver, "Who's Poor in America? 60 Years into the 'War on Poverty,' A Data Portrait," Pew Research Center, January 13, 2014, available at http://www.pewresearch.org/fact-tank/2014/01/13/whos-poor-in-america-50-years-into-the-war-on-poverty-a-data-portrait/.
5. See Liav Orgad, "The Preamble in Constitutional Interpretation," *International Journal of Constitutional Law*, vol. 714 (Winter 2011), pp. 714–738, available in early draft form at http://papers.ssrn.com/sol3/papers.cfm?abstract_id=1686745.
6. See Sanford Levinson, "Do Constitutions Have a Point? Reflections on 'Parchment Barriers' and Preambles," *Social Philosophy and Policy Foundation*, vol. 28 (2010), pp. 50–178, for a discussion of how to rescue the preamble as a force of law.
7. Alexander Hamilton, James Madison, and John Jay, *The Federalist Papers*, available at http://thomas.loc.gov/home/histdox/fedpaper.txt.
8. See *Jacobson* v. *Massachusetts*, 197 U.S. 11 (1905), p. 2.
9. The debate over Keynes and his economic theories is still alive in the United States. See Donald E. Moggridge, *Maynard Keynes: An Economist's Biography* (Routledge, 1992).
10. "How to Spend $787 Billion," *New York Times*, May 27, 2016, http://projects.nytimes.com/44th_president/stimulus.
11. Joel F. Handler, *The Poverty of Welfare Reform* (Yale University Press, 1995), p. 21.
12. Office of Management and Budget, *Budget of the U.S. Government, Fiscal Year 2019* (U.S. Government Printing Office, 2018), Analytical Tables, Table 6-1, pp. 49-51, available at https://www.whitehouse.gov/wp-content/uploads/2018/02/spec-fy2019.pdf.
13. For further information on different measures of unemployed, see Federal Reserve Board of Philadelphia, "Alternative Unemployment Rates: Their Meaning and Their Measure," March 12, 2014, available at https://www.philadelphiafed.org/-/media/&/aur2014march.pdf?la=en.
14. Linda Levine, "Economic Growth and the Unemployment Rate," Congressional Research Service, January 7, 2013, available at http://www.fas.org/sgp/crs/misc/R42063.pdf.
15. Marc Labonte, "Inflation: Causes, Costs, and Current Status," Congressional Research Service, July 26, 2011, available at https://www.fas.org/sgp/crs/misc/RL30344.pdf.
16. Bruce D. Meyer and J. X. Sullivan, "Identifying the Disadvantaged: Official Poverty, Consumption Poverty, and the New Supplemental Poverty Measure," *Journal of Economic Perspectives*, vol. 26 (Fall 2012), pp. 111–135.
17. This definition was originally created in 1963, and was based on a simple calculation of how much money an individual or individuals would need to purchase what the Department of Agriculture defined in 1962 as an economy food plan. Poverty was defined as income at below the cost of the economy food plan multiplied by a factor of three, and it is still defined that way today. See Gordon M. Fisher, "The Development and History of the U.S. Poverty Thresholds—A Brief Overview," *Newsletter of the Government Statistics Section and the Social Statistics Section of the American Statistical Association* (Winter 1997), pp. 6–7, available at

http://aspe.hhs.gov/poverty/papers/hptgssiv.htm. According to Fisher's history, a senior economist at the Social Security Administration named Mollie Orshansky created the measure as follows:

Orshansky knew from the Department of Agriculture's 1955 Household Food Consumption Survey (the latest available such survey at the time) that families of three or more persons spent about one third of their after-tax money income on food in 1955. Accordingly, she calculated poverty thresholds for families of three or more persons by taking the dollar costs of the economy food plan for families of those sizes and multiplying the costs by a factor of three—the "multiplier." In effect, she took a hypothetical average family spending one third of its income on food, and assumed that it had to cut back on its expenditures sharply. She assumed that expenditures for food and non-food would be cut back at the same rate. When the food expenditures of the hypothetical family reached the cost of the economy food plan, she assumed that the amount the family would then be spending on non-food items would also be minimal but adequate. (Her procedure did not assume specific dollar amounts for any budget category besides food.) She derived poverty thresholds for two-person families by multiplying the dollar cost of the food plan for that family size by a somewhat higher multiplier (3.7) also derived from the 1955 survey. She derived poverty thresholds for one-person units directly from the thresholds for two-person units, without using a multiplier. The base year for the original thresholds was calendar year 1963.

18. These numbers can be found at the Department of Health and Human Services Web site, https://aspe.hhs.gov/poverty-guidelines, January 15, 2016.
19. See Christopher Wimer, Liana Fox, Irv Garfinkel, Neeraj Kaushal, and Jane Waldfogel, "Trends in Poverty with an Anchored Supplemental Poverty Measure," Columbia Population Research Center, working paper CPRC13-01, December 5, 2013.
20. David B. Grusky, "4 Myths About Poverty," *Chronicle of Higher Education*, February 24, 2014, available at http://chronicle.com/article/4-Myths-About-Poverty/144819/.
21. Alexander Hamilton, James Madison, and John Jay, *The Federalist Papers*, available at http://thomas.loc.gov/home/histdox/fedpaper.txt.
22. It is not entirely clear that Jefferson ever made such a statement, though it does appear to be a faithful interpretation of his later writings. See the analysis of the quote at http://www.monticello.org/site/jefferson/educated-citizenry-vital-requisite-our-survival-free-people-quotation.
23. See Pew Research Center, "Beyond Distrust: How Americans View Their Government," November 23, 2015, for the specific questions about government taxes and waste, available at http://www.people-press.org/2015/11/23/beyond-distrust-how-americans-view-their-government/.
24. For a discussion of the budgetary cycle, see Allen Schick, *The Federal Budget: Politics, Policy, Process*, rev. ed. (Brookings Institution Press, 2000).
25. For an accessible summary of the act, see Nooree Lee, "Congressional Budget and Impoundment Control Act of 1974, Reconsidered," Harvard Law School, Federal Budget Policy Seminar, Briefing Paper No. 34, March 4, 2008.
26. Ryan Alexander, "See Appropriations Dysfunction Isn't Going Anywhere," *U.S. News & World Report*, January 15, 2014, available at http://www.usnews.com/opinion/blogs/economic-intelligence/2014/01/15/congress-is-likely-to-continue-appropriations-bill-dysfunction.
27. See Karen Spar, "Budget 'Sequestration' and Selected Program Exemptions and Special Rules," Congressional Research Service, June 13, 2013, for details on the sequestration process and rules, available at https://www.fas.org/sgp/crs/misc/R42050.pdf.
28. Michael D. Tanner, "A New War on Poverty," Cato Institute, January 8, 2014, available at http://www.cato.org/publications/commentary/new-war-poverty.
29. Visit studentaid.gov for the options at http://studentaid.ed.gov/sites/default/files/federal-loan-programs.pdf.
30. Office of Management and Budget, *Budget of the U.S. Government, Fiscal Year 2015* (U.S. Government Printing Office, 2014), Analytical Tables, p. 137, available at http://www.whitehouse.gov/omb/budget/analytical_perspectives.
31. Julianna Koch and Suzanne Mettler, "Who Perceives Government's Role in Their Lives? Assessing the Impact of Social Policy on Visibility," unpublished research paper, revised version, January 23, 2012. Mettler's broader findings can be found in *The Submerged State: How Invisible Government Policies Undermine American Democracy* (University of Chicago Press, 2011).
32. Committee for a Responsible Federal Budget, "Lawmakers Must Abide by PAYGO ... Here's Why," blog post, December 10, 2013, available at http://crfb.org/blogs/lawmakers-must-abide-paygoheres-why.
33. Automobiles are rarely counted as an asset, but can be used if they are used exclusively for transportation to a job.
34. See the eligibility requirements at http://www.fns.usda.gov/snap/eligibility#Income.
35. Congressional Budget Office, "Growth in Means-Tested Programs and Tax Credits for Low-Income Households," February 2013, available at http://www.cbo.gov/publication/43934.
36. See Douglas W. Elmendorf, "Letter Report to the Hon. Tom Price, Chairman, U.S. House Committee on the Budget," Congressional Budget Office, March 13, 2015, available at https://www.cbo.gov/sites/default/files/114th-congress-2015-2016/reports/MeansTestedLtrTomPrice.pdf.
37. Robert Rector, "Examining the Means-Tested Welfare State: 79 Programs and $927 Billion in Annual Spending," Testimony before the Committee on the Budget, U.S. House of Representatives, April 17, 2012, available at http://www.heritage.org/research/testimony/2012/05/examining-the-means-tested-welfare-state.
38. Center for American Progress, "Half in Ten: 50 Years After LBJ's War on Poverty," January 2014, available at http://www.americanprogress.org/wp-content/uploads/2014/01/WOP-PollReport2.pdf.
39. *Samsung Electronics Co.* v. *Apple Inc.*, 580 US ___ (2016).
40. *United States* v. *E. C. Knight Co.*, 156 U.S. 1 (1895).
41. Steven Greenhouse, "Union Membership in U.S. Fell to 70-Year Low Last Year," *New York Times*, January 21, 2011, available at http://www.nytimes.com/2011/01/22/business/22union.html.
42. See Congressional Budget Office, "The Effects of a Minimum-Wage Increase on Employment and Family Income," Congressional Budget Office, February 2014, available at http://www.cbo.gov/sites/default/files/cbofiles/attachments/44995-MinimumWage.pdf.
43. Executive Order—Minimum Wage for Contractors, February 12, 2014.
44. There are too many books on the causes and consequences of the crisis to mention here, but the PBS Frontline series titled "Money, Power & Wall Street" provides a compelling summary in four parts. The series ran on April 24 and May 1, 2012, and is available at http://www.pbs.org/wgbh/pages/frontline/money-power-wall-street/.
45. See, for example, Margaret Weir, "Political Parties and Social Policymaking," in Margaret Weir, ed., *The Social Divide: Political Parties and the Future of Activist Government* (Brookings Institution Press, 1998).
46. See *Budget of the U.S. Government, Fiscal Year 2015* (Government Printing Office, 2014), Historical Tables, Table 3.1, available at http://www.whitehouse.gov/sites/default/files/omb/budget/fy2014/assets/hist.pdf.
47. See Vox, "Fifty Years of Poverty," January 4, 2014, for the figures and links to the underlying information.
48. Self-employed workers must cover both amounts, and many state and local government workers are not required to participate.
49. Martha Derthick, "No More Easy Votes for Social Security," *Brookings Review*, vol. 10 (Fall 1992), pp. 50–53.
50. Visit htpp://ssa.gov for details on benefits and coverage, and Social Security Administration "Special Minimum Benefits,"

https://www.ssa.gov/cgi-bin/smt.cgi for specifics on program spending and benefit levels in 2016.

51. Social Security and Medicare Boards of Trustees, "A Summary of the 2015 Annual Reports," Social Security Administration, July 2015.
52. Gayle R. Reznik, Dave Shoffner, and David A. Weaver, "Coping with the Demographic Challenge: Fewer Children and Living Longer," *Social Security Bulletin*, 2005/2006.
53. For an essential guide to all public assistance programs and eligibility, visit the Economic Progress Institute at http://www.economicprogressri.org/GuidetoGovernmentAssistance/GuidetoGovernmentAssistanceOverview/tabid/210/Default.aspx. The Web site provides lists of programs for adults without children living with them, and programs for families with children 18 and under.
54. See Theda Skocpol, *Protecting Soldiers and Mothers: The Political Origins of Social Policy in the United States* (Belknap Press, 1992), Chapter 9, for a history of the act.
55. William J. Clinton, acceptance speech, Democratic National Convention, Chicago, July 6, 1992.
56. Center on Budget and Policy Priorities, "Policy Basics: An Introduction to TANF," December 4, 2012.
57. Government Accountability Office, "Federal Low-Income Programs: Multiple Programs Target Diverse Populations and Needs," Report GAO-15-516, July 2015.
58. This statistic comes from the Social Security Administration, April 2018, available at https://www.ssa.gov/oact/cola/SSIamts.html; additional information about the program can be found at Center on Budget and Policy Priorities, "Introduction to the Supplemental Security Income (SSI) Program," January 20, 2011, available at http://www.cbpp.org/files/1-10-11socsec.pdf.
59. U.S. Department of Health and Human Services Administration for Children and Families, "Head Start Impact Study," January 2010.
60. "Ryan Opening Statement: A Progress Report on the War on Poverty," House of Representatives Committee on the Budget, January 28, 2014, available at http://budget.house.gov/news/documentsingle.aspx?DocumentID=367880.
61. See http://www.savingtoinvest.com/maximum-weekly-unemployment-benefits-by-state/ for a summary of maximum weekly benefits in 2015–2016.
62. For a definitive history and current assessment of Medicare, see Patricia A. Davis, Scott R. Talaga, Cliff Binder, Jim Hahn, Suzanne M. Kirchhoff, Paulette C. Morgan, and Sibyl Tilson, "Medicare Primer," Congressional Research Service, January 31, 2013, available at https://www.fas.org/sgp/crs/misc/R40425.pdf.
63. Centers for Medicare and Medicaid Services, "FY2016 Budget in Brief," U.S. Department of Health and Human Services, available at http://www.hhs.gov/about/budget/budget-in-brief/cms/medicare/index.html.
64. See Julia Paradise, "Medicaid Moving Forward," The Henry J. Kaiser Foundation, March 9, 2015, for an introduction to the program.
65. Carmen DeNavas-Walt, Bernadette D. Proctor, and Jessica C. Smith, *Income, Poverty, and Health Insurance Coverage in the United States: 2009*, U.S. Census Bureau, 2010.
66. Congressional Budget Office, "Estimates for the Insurance Coverage Provisions of the Affordable Care Act Updated for the Recent Supreme Court Decision," July 2012, available at http://cbo.gov/sites/default/files/cbofiles/attachments/43472-07-24-2012-CoverageEstimates.pdf.
67. To see whether you are required to buy insurance see http://kff.org/infographic/the-requirement-to-buy-coverage-under-the-affordable-care-act/.
68. You can keep track of the options in your own state at http://kff.org/health-reform/state-indicator/state-health-insurance-marketplace-types/.
69. The 10 essential benefits are listed at http://obamacarefacts.com/essential-health-benefits/.
70. Find the current state-by-state count at http://kff.org/health-reform/state-indicator/state-activity-around-expanding-medicaid-under-the-affordable-care-act/; for an analysis of the characteristics of the potential enrollees in states that have yet to accept the federal government's deal, see Rachael Garfield, and Anthony Damico, "The Coverage Gap: Uninsured Poor Adults That Do Not Expand Medicaid, an Update," The Henry J. Kaiser Foundation, January 21, 2016.
71. This inventory can be found at Paul C. Light, "Endeavors, Achievements, and Breakdowns," unpublished memo written for the Salzburg Seminar sponsored by the Volcker Alliance for Effective Governance, August 2013, Table 3.
72. All but two of the programs identified in the figure are identified within the federal budget as "subfunctions," meaning separate programs. The exceptions were Medicaid, which had to be pulled out of the health services subfunction to generate a true reading of its size, and national defense, which had too many large subfunctions to be presented without distorting the trend shown in the figure.
73. Daniel L. Thornton, "The U.S. Deficit/Debt Problem: A Longer-Run Perspective," *Federal Reserve Bank of St. Louis Review*, vol. 94, no. 6 (November/December 2012), pp. 441–444, available at http://research.stlouisfed.org/publications/review/12/11/Thornton.pdf.
74. National Commission on Fiscal Responsibility and Reform, *The Moment of Truth*, December 2010, p. 4, available at http://www.fiscalcommission.gov/sites/fiscalcommission.gov/files/documents/TheMomentofTruth12_1_2010.pdf.
75. Eric Pianen, "Super Flaw: If Only Obama Had Upheld Bowles-Simpson," *Financial Times*, November 11, 2011, available at http://www.thefiscaltimes.com/Articles/2011/11/22/Super-Flaw-If-Only-Obama-Had-Upheld-Bowles-Simpson.aspx#page1.
76. Social Security and Medicare Boards of Trustees, "A Summary of the 2013 Annual Reports," Social Security Administration, May 2013, available at http://www.ssa.gov/oahttp://www.actuary.org/files/Means_Testing_SS_IB.pdfct/trsum/.
77. Social Security and Medicare Boards of Trustees, "A Summary of the 2013 Annual Reports," Social Security Administration, May 2013, available at http://www.ssa.gov/oact/trsum/.
78. Dawn Nuschler, "Social Security Reform: Current Issues and Legislation," Congressional Research Service, November 28, 2012, p. 17, available at http://www.fas.org/sgp/crs/misc/RL33544.pdf.
79. See Dean Baker and Hye Jin Rho, "The Potential Savings to Social Security from Means Testing," Center for Economic and Policy Research, March 2011, available at http://www.cepr.net/documents/publications/ss-2011-03.pdf; see also American Academy of Actuaries, "Means Testing for Social Security," December 2012, available at http://www.actuary.org/files/Means_Testing_SS_IB.pdf.
80. Bipartisan Policy Center, "What Is Driving Health Care Spending: America's Unsustainable Health Care Cost Growth," September 2012, p. 4, available at http://bipartisanpolicy.org/sites/default/files/BPC%20Health%20Care%20Cost%20Drivers%20Brief%20Sept%202012.pdf.
81. National Commission to Build a Healthier America, *Time to Act: Investing in the Health of Our Children and Communities*, Robert Wood Johnson Foundation, 2014, available at http://www.rwjf.org/en/research-publications/find-rwjf-research/2014/01/recommendations-from-the-rwjf-commission-to-build-a-healthier-am.html.
82. John T. James, "A New, Evidence-Based Estimate of Patient Harms Associated with Hospital Care," *Journal of Patient Safety*, vol. 9 (September 2013), pp. 122–128, available at http://journals.lww.com/journalpatientsafety/Fulltext/2013/09000/A_New,_Evidence_based_Estimate_of_Patient_Harms.2.aspx#.
83. Charles Andel, Stephen L. Davidow, Mark Hollander, and David A. Moreno, "The Economics of Health Care Quality and Medical Errors," *Journal of Health Care Finance*, vol. 39 (Fall 2012), p. 48.
84. Paul Ryan, "Expanding Opportunity," Remarks at the Kemp Forum, January 9, 2016, available at https://medium.com/@PRyan/expanding-opportunity-kempforum16-11fe61f733d2#.8z9sdn6gv.

CHAPTER 17

1. Lisa M. Schenck and Robert A. Youmans, "From Start to Finish: A Historical Review of Nuclear Arms Control Treaties and Starting Over with the New Start," *Cardozo Journal of International and Comparative Law*, 2012, pp. 399–436.
2. For an interactive timeline of these starts and stops, visit the Council on Foreign Relations online slideshow at http://www.cfr.org/nonproliferation-arms-control-and-disarmament/us-russia-arms-control/p21620.
3. Kelsey Davenport and Marcus Taylor, "Assessing Progress on Nuclear Nonproliferation and Disarmament: Updated Report Card: 2010–2013," Arms Control Association Report, 2013.
4. Alexei Arbatov, "An Unnoticed Crisis: The End of History for Nuclear Arms Control," Carnegie Moscow Center, June 2015.
5. Jon Greenberg, John Kruzel, and Amy Sherman, "Trump Withdraws U.S. from the Iran Nuclear Deal--Here's What You Need to Know," *Politifact*, May 8, 2018, http://www.politifact.com/truth-o-meter/article/2018/may/08/trump-withdrew-us-iran-nuclear-deal-heres-what-you/.
6. Pew Research Center, "Public Sees U.S. Power Declining as Support for Global Engagement Slips: America's Place in the World, 2013" (Pew Research Center, December 3, 2013), p. 10, available at http://www.people-press.org/2013/12/03/public-sees-u-s-power-declining-as-support-for-global-engagement-slips/.
7. For a timeline of Trump administration foreign policy decisions, see the Council on Foreign Relations timeline at https://www.cfr.org/timeline/trumps-foreign-policy-moments.
8. Alexander Hamilton, James Madison, and John Jay, *The Federalist Papers*, available at http://thomas.loc.gov/home/histdox/fedpaper.txt.
9. Marshall made the statement as a member of the House of Representatives in 1800. Louis Fisher, "*The Law*: Presidential Inherent Power: The 'Sole Organ' Doctrine," *Presidential Studies Quarterly* 37 (March 2007), p. 141, available at http://www.loc.gov/law/help/usconlaw/pdf/SoleOrgan-March07.pdf.
10. As Louis Fisher argues, the federal courts sometimes make mistakes in interpreting history, which is what may have happened with the sole-organ doctrine. See Fisher, "Judicial Errors That Magnify Presidential Power," *The Federal Lawyer* 67 (January/February 2014), available at http://www.constitutionproject.org/wp-content/uploads/2014/02/fisher-TFL-updated.pdf.
11. William A. Kandel, coordinator, "Unaccompanied Alien Children: Potential Factors Contributing to Recent Immigration," Congressional Research Service, 2014, available at https://fas.org/sgp/crs/homesec/R43628.pdf.
12. For a summary of these arguments, see John Yoo, *Crisis and Command: A History of Executive Power from George Washington to George W. Bush* (New York: Kaplan, 2009). Yoo was the key Justice Department official who drafted the documents justifying advanced interrogation techniques.
13. For an alternative, highly critical account of the bin Laden raid, see Seymour M. Hersh, "The Killing of Osama bin Laden," *London Review of Books*, May 2015.
14. Louis Fisher, "The Unitary Executive and Inherent Executive Power," *Journal of Constitutional Law* 12 (February 2010), pp. 569–591, available at https://www.law.upenn.edu/journals/conlaw/articles/volume12/issue2/Fisher12U.Pa.J.Const.L.569%282010%29.pdf.
15. Dina Smeltz, Ivo Daalder, Karl Friedhoff, and Craig Kafura, "America Divided: Political Partisanship and U.S. Foreign Policy: Results of the 2015 Chicago Council Survey of American Public Opinion and US Foreign Policy," The Chicago Council on Foreign Affairs, 2015.
16. Henry A. Kissinger, "Realists v. Idealists," *The New York Times*, May 11, 2005, available at http://www.nytimes.com/2005/05/11/opinion/11iht-edkissinger.html?pagewanted=all.
17. For a defining article on these terms, see Thomas I. Cook and Malcolm Moos, "Foreign Policy: The Realism of Idealism," *The American Political Science Review*, vol. 46, no. 2. (June 1952), pp. 343–356.
18. See James M. Lindsay, "George W. Bush, Barack Obama and the Future of U.S. Global Leadership," *International Affairs*, 82 (2011), pp. 767–779.
19. Jacob Weisberg, "What Is Obama's Foreign Policy?" *Slate.com*, May 24, 2011, available at http://www.slate.com/articles/news_and_politics/the_big_idea/2011/05/what_is_obamas_foreign_policy.html.
20. Fred Kaplan, "The Realist: Barack Obama's a Cold Warrior Indeed," *Politico Magazine*, February 27, 2014, available at http://www.politico.com/magazine/story/2014/02/barack-obama--realist-foreign-policy-103861_full.html?print#.U3L5DI7yHG6.
21. Obama's decision not to act is explained in detail in Jeffrey Goldberg, "The Obama Doctrine," *Atlantic*, April 2016.
22. David Jackson, "Obama Notes That Biden Opposed Bin Laden Raid," *USA Today*, October 23, 2012, available at http://www.usatoday.com/story/theoval/2012/10/23/obama-biden-bin-laden-raid-foreign-policy-debate/1651377/.
23. Richard N. Haass, "The Return of American Realism," Council on Foreign Relations, May 3, 2009, available at http://www.cfr.org/history-and-theory-of-international-relations/return-american-realism/p19304.
24. Ross Douthat, "A War Trump Won," *The New York Times*, December 16, 2017, https://www.nytimes.com/2017/12/16/opinion/sunday/war-trump-islamic-state.html. See also Eric Schmitt, "Thousands of ISIS Fighters Flee in Syria, Many to Fight Another Day," *The New York Times*, February 4, 2018, https://www.nytimes.com/2018/02/04/world/middleeast/isis-syria-al-qaeda.html.
25. James M. Lindsay, "George W. Bush, Barack Obama and the Future of U.S. Global Leadership," p. 766.
26. Bob Woodward, *Bush at War* (New York: Simon & Schuster, 2002), p. 81.
27. Jacob Magid, "The Marshall Plan," *Advances in Historical Studies*, December 2012.
28. Robert J. Delahunty and John Yoo, "The 'Bush Doctrine': Can Preventive War Be Justified?" *Harvard Journal of Law & Public Policy* 32 (Summer 2009), pp. 833–834.
29. See Michael E. O'Hanlon, Susan E. Rice, and James B. Steinberg, "The New National Security Strategy and Preemption," The Brookings Institution, Policy Brief #113, December 2002, available at http://www.brookings.edu/research/papers/2002/12/terrorism-ohanlon.
30. The President of the United States, *The National Security Strategy of the United States*, September 2002, p. 15.
31. See Robert S. Litwak, "The New Calculus of Pre-Emption," *Survival*, 44 (Winter 20 (2003)), pp. 53-80, available at http://www.wilsoncenter.org/sites/default/files/newcalc.pdf.
32. Condoleezza Rice, quoted in Glenn Kessler, "Rice Lays Out Case for War in Iraq," *Washington Post*, August 16, 2002, p. A1.
33. For an assessment of Obama's position, see Micah Zenko, *Reforming U.S. Drone Strike Policies* (Council on Foreign Relations Press, 2013), available at http://www.cfr.org/wars-and-warfare/reforming-us-drone-strike-policies/p29736.
34. Pew Research Center, "Public Sees U.S. Power Declining as Support for Global Engagement Slips: America's Place in the World, 2013" (Pew Research Center, December 3, 2013), pp. 4–5, available at http://www.people-press.org/2013/12/03/public-sees-u-s-power-declining-as-support-for-global-engagement-slips/.
35. Colin S. Gray, *Hard Power and Soft Power: The Utility of Military Force as an Instrument of Policy in the 21st Century* (Strategic Studies Institute, U.S. Army War College, April 2001), available at http://www.strategicstudiesinstitute.army.mil/pdffiles/PUB1059.pdf.
36. See Joseph Nye, *Soft Power: The Means to Success in World Politics* (Public Affairs, 2005).

37. P. W. Singer, "Winning the War of Words: Information Warfare in Afghanistan," *Brookings Analysis Paper No. 5*, October 2001.
38. These responsibilities fall to the Bureau of Public Affairs, which can be visited at http://www.state.gov/r/pa/index.htm.
39. U.S. State Department, "FY 2017: Congressional Budget Justification-Department of State, Foreign Operations, and Related Programs," available at http://www.state.gov/s/d/rm/rls/ebs/2017/pdf/index.htm.
40. Asked in 2013 whether they favored an increase, decrease, or no change in spending for 19 different public policies, Americans wanted an increase or no change for all but one policy, aid to the world's needy. According to this Pew Research Center poll, 48 percent of Americans favored a decrease in foreign aid, 21 percent favored an increase, and the rest said they wanted to keep spending the same. See the Pew Research Center for the People & the Press, "As Sequester Deadline Looms, Little Support for Cutting Most Programs," February 22, 2013, available at http://www.people-press.org/2013/02/22/as-sequester-deadline-looms-little-support-for-cutting-most-programs/.
41. Kaiser Family Foundation, *Survey of Americans on the U.S. Role in Global Health*, 2015, available at http://kff.org/global-health-policy/poll-finding/data-note-americans-views-on-the-u-s-role-in-global-health/.
42. Bianca DiJulio, Jamie Firth, and Mollyann Broder, "Data Note: Americans' Views on the U.S. Role in Global Health," Kaiser Family Foundation, January 23, 2015, available at http://kff.org/global-health-policy/poll-finding/data-note-americans-views-on-the-u-s-role-in-global-health/.
43. Visit the Borgen Project at borgenproject.org/foreign-aid/ to get more facts and figures on U.S. foreign aid.
44. Angus Deaton, *The Great Escape: Health, Wealth, and the Origins of Inequality* (Princeton, 2013), pp. 204–205.
45. See William Easterly, "Response to Reviewers on 'The Tyranny of Experts,'" *Review of Austrian Economics*, July 24, 2015.
46. See Jon Hovi, Robert Huseby, and Detief F. Sprinz, "When Do (Imposed) Economic Sanctions Work?" *World Politics* 57 (July 2005), pp. 479–499.
47. Gary Clyde Hufbauer, Jeffrey J. Schott, Kimberly Ann Elliott, and Barbara Oegg, *Economic Sanctions Reconsidered* (Peterson Institute for International Economics, 2009).
48. The war was called "cold" because the United States and Soviet Union never engaged in face-to-face combat. Rather, they used surrogates such as Vietnam to wage wars. Nevertheless, the fear of a nuclear Armageddon was real, and lasted from the end of World War II to the fall of the Berlin Wall in 1989.
49. Bernard Brodie, ed., *The Absolute Weapon: Atomic Power and World Order* (reprinted by Harcourt Brace Jovanovich, 1972).
50. For a history of MAD, see Henry D. Sokolski, ed., *Getting Mad: Nuclear Mutual Assured Destruction, Its Origins and Practice* (Strategic Studies Institute, U.S. Army War College, November 2004), available at http://www.strategicstudiesinstitute.army.mil/pdffiles/pub585.pdf.
51. Thérèse Delpech, *Nuclear Deterrence in the 21st Century: Lessons from the Cold War for a New Era of Strategic Piracy* (RAND, 2012), p. 1., available at http://www.rand.org/content/dam/rand/pubs/monographs/2012/RAND_MG1103.pdf.
52. See Robert Kagan, "The Kerry Doctrine," *Washington Post*, August 1, 2004, for this argument.
53. Samuel P. Huntington, The Soldier and the State: The Theory and Politics of Civil-Military Relations (Belknap, 1957), p. 464.
54. See Paul R. Pillar, "Intelligence, Policy, and the War in Iraq," *Foreign Affairs* 85 (March/April, 2006), pp. 15–27, for a discussion of the Bush administration's alleged efforts to manipulate the intelligence that led Congress to approve the Iraq War. As Pillar argues at page 19, the administration did not force the intelligence community to alter its estimates, but "selected pieces of raw intelligence to use in its public case for war, leaving the intelligence community to register varying degrees of private protest when such use started to go beyond what analysts deemed credible or reasonable."
55. See Richard A. Best, Jr., "The National Security Council: An Organizational Assessment," Congressional Research Service, December 28, 2011, for details on how the NSC has changed since its creation, available at http://www.fas.org/sgp/crs/natsec/RL30840.pdf.
56. John P. Burke, Honest Broker? The National Security Advisor and Presidential Decision Making (Texas A&M University Press, 2009).
57. For a history of U.S. intelligence operations, see Mark M. Lowenthal, *Intelligence: From Secrets to Policy* (CQ Press, 2011).
58. These authorities are summarized in Richard A. Best, Jr., "Director of National Intelligence Statutory Authorities: Status and Proposals," Congressional Research Service, December 16, 2011, available at http://www.fas.org/sgp/crs/intel/RL34231.pdf.
59. The CIA budget is technically "black," meaning it is secret. The *Washington Post* received a copy of the budget from Edward Snowden in August 2013, and produced a full report on the federal intelligence community. See Barton Gellman and Greg Miller, "U.S. Spy Network's Successes, Failures and Objectives Detailed in 'Black Budget Summary," *Washington Post*, August 29, 2013, available at http://www.washingtonpost.com/world/national-security/black-budget-summary-details-us-spy-networks-successes-failures-and-objectives/2013/08/29/7e57bb78-10ab-11e3-8cdd-bcdc09410972_story.html.
60. Gregory F. Treverton and C. Bryan Gabbard, *Assessing the Tradecraft of Intelligence Analysis* (RAND, 2008).
61. Council on Foreign Relations, "Domestic Intelligence and the Boston Bombings," interview with Richard A. Falkenrath, April 25, 2013, available at http://www.cfr.org/counterterrorism/domestic-intelligence-boston-bombings/p30557.
62. National Commission on Terrorist Attacks on the United States, *The 9/11 Commission Report* (Norton, 2004), p. 12.
63. Charles S. Clark, "Trump's Pace of Naming Ambassadors Trails That of Predecessors." *Government Executive*, January 25, 2018. https://www.govexec.com/management/2018/01/trumps-pace-naming-ambassadors-trails-predecessors/145485/
64. U.S. Department of State, "Congressional Budget Justification, Fiscal Year 2017," February 9, 2016, available at http://www.state.gov/documents/organization/252179.pdf.
65. The entire hearing is available at http://www.c-span.org/video/?328699-4/hillary-clinton-testimony-house-select--committee-benghazi-part-4.
66. These options are explained on an interactive Web site with videos about each track at https://careers.state.gov/work/foreign-service/officer/career-tracks.
67. See J. Robert Moskin, *American Statecraft: The Story of the U.S. Foreign Service* (Thomas Dunne Books, 2013) for a history of the Foreign Service. Also visit http://careers.state.gov/officer/ for basic information on how to become a Foreign Service Officer.
68. Government Accountability Office, "Comprehensive Plan Needed to Address Persistent Foreign Language Shortfall," September 2009.
69. Beth Bailey, America's Army: Making the All-Volunteer Force (Belknap, 2009).
70. Visit http://myarmybenefits.us.army.mil/ for the Army's list of benefits for soldiers, https://www.navy.com/joining/benefits.html for the Navy's list, https://www.airforce.com/careers/pay-and-benefits for the Air Force's list, and https://www.marines.com/being-a-marine/benefits for the Marine's list.
71. Bernard Rostker, *I Want You: The Evolution of the All-Volunteer Force* (RAND, 2006), available at http://www.rand.org/pubs/monographs/MG265.html.
72. Much of this history is contained in a study by the Congressional Budget Office titled "The All-Volunteer Military: Issues and Performance," July 2007, available at http://www.cbo.gov/sites/default/files/cbofiles/ftpdocs/83xx/doc8313/07-19-militaryvol.pdf.
73. Mickey R. Dansby, James B. Steward, and Schuyler C. Webb, eds., Diversity in the Military: Research Perspectives from the Defense Equal Opportunity Management Institute (Transaction Publishers, 2012).

74. P.W. Singer, Corporate Warriors: The Rise of the Privatized Military Industry (Cornell University Press, 2007).
75. *Public Papers of the Presidents, Dwight D. Eisenhower* (U.S. Government Printing Office, 1960), pp. 1035–1040.
76. See Scott H. Amey, "Public Comments on the Use of Cost Comparisons," letter to the U.S. Office of Federal Procurement Policy, April 15, 2013, for a discussion of the cost of purchasing government services from private contractors, available at http://pogoarchives.org/m/co/pogo_comment_ofpp_cost_comparison_20130416.pdf.
77. See Rod Nordland, "Risks of Afghan War Shift from Soldiers to Contactors," *The New York Times*, February 11, 2012, available at http://www.nytimes.com/2012/02/12/world/asia/afghan-war-risks-are-shifting-to-contractors.html?scp=1&sq=%2522Risks%20of%20Afghan%20War%2522&st=cse.
78. Intergovernmental Panel on Climate Change, "Climate Change 2014: Synthesis Report," January 11, 2016, available at https://www.ipcc.ch/news_and_events/docs/misc/160111_PR_AR5_Synthesis_Report_language_versions_final.pdf; also available in Arabic, Chinese, French, Russian, and Spanish.
79. Coral Davenport, Justin Gillis, Sewell Chan, and Melissa Eddy, "Inside the Paris Climate Deal," December 12, 2015, interactive and related article, available at http://www.nytimes.com/interactive/2015/12/12/world/paris-climate-change-deal-explainer.html.
80. Suzanne Goldenberg, "Paris Climate Deal: Counties with About Half of Global Emissions to Join This Year," *Guardian*, April 25, 2016.
81. The United Nations explains the Millennium Development goals at http://www.un.org/millenniumgoals/.
82. See United Nations, *The Millennium Development Goals Report, 2013* (United Nations, 2013), available at http://www.un.org/millenniumgoals/pdf/report-2013/mdg-report-2013-english.pdf.
83. Danielle Renwick, "Sustainable Development Goals: A CFR Backgrounder," Council on Foreign Relations, September 28, 2015.
84. For more information, visit the Peace Corps Web site, http://www.peacecorps.gov. For a useful study of the Peace Corps, see Elizabeth Cobbs Hoffman, *All You Need Is Love: The Peace Corps and the Spirit of the 1960s* (Harvard University Press, 1998).
85. For the Republican reaction to the proposal, see "U.S. Weighing Options for Future Cuts in Nuclear Weapons, Including 80% Reduction," February 14, 2012, available at http://www.thespec.com/news-story/2237687-us-weighing-options-for-future-cuts-in-nuclear-weapons-including-80-reduction/.
86. Alexei Arbatov, *An Unnoticed Crisis: The End of History for Nuclear Arms Control* (Carnegie Moscow Center, June 2015).
87. See Seymour M. Hersh, "Whose Sarin?" *London Review of Books*, December 2013, for allegations that both sides in the Syrian civil war had chemical weapons, available at http://www.lrb.co.uk/v35/n24/seymour-m-hersh/whose-sarin.
88. Art Swift, "Americans More Worried About Terrorism Than Mass Shootings," The Gallup Poll, December 16, 2015, available at http://www.gallup.com/poll/187688/americans-worried-terrorism-mass-shootings.aspx.
89. Matthew Kroenig and Barry Pavel, "How to Deter Terrorism," *The Washington Quarterly*, 35 (Spring 2012), pp. 21–36, available at http://csis.org/files/publication/TWQ_12Spring_Kroenig_Pavel.pdf.
90. See Kenneth Lieberthal, *The U.S. Intelligence Community and Foreign Policy: Getting Analysis Right* (Brookings, 2009), available at http://www.brookings.edu/research/papers/2009/09/intelligence-community-lieberthal.
91. The Center for Public Integrity, "Public Overwhelmingly Supports Large Defense Spending Cuts," February 25, 2013, available at http://www.publicintegrity.org/2012/05/10/8856/public-overwhelmingly-supports-large-defense-spending-cuts.
92. Senator Tom A. Coburn, "Department of Everything," November 2012, available at http://www.coburn.senate.gov/public/index.cfm?a=Files.Serve&File_id=00783b5a-f0fe-4f80-90d6-019695e52d2d.
93. There are many books on the lessons from Iraq, but the most thorough studies come from the RAND Corporation. These studies are easy to search and download at http://rand.org. See, for example, Rick Brennan, Jr., Charles P. Ries, Larry Hanauer, Ben Conable, Terrence K. Kelly, Michael J. McNearey, Stephanie Your, Jason H. Campbell, and K. Scott McMahon, *Smooth Transitions: Lessons Learned from Transferring U.S. Military Responsibilities to Civilian Authorities in Iraq* (RAND, 2013), available at http://www.rand.org/pubs/research_briefs/RB9749.html.
94. Ronen Bergman, "Will Israel Attack Iran?" *The New York Times Magazine*, January 25, 2012. Bergen predicted that Israel would attack sometime in 2012, but the attack was never launched.
95. Thérèse Delpech, *Nuclear Deterrence in the 21st Century: Lessons from the Cold War for a New Era of Strategic Piracy* (RAND Corporation, 2012).
96. William J. Broad and David E. Sanger, "Race for the Latest Class of Nuclear Arms Threatens to Revive Cold War," *The New York Times*, April 16, 2016.
97. Pew Research Center, "Millennials: A Portrait of Generation Next," February 2010, available at http://www.pewsocialtrends.org/2010/02/24/millennials-confident-connected-open-to-change/.
98. Russell J. Dalton, "Citizenship Norms and Political Participation in America: The Good News Is...The Bad News Is Wrong," Center for the Study of Democracy, Occasional Paper, 2006.

Credits

Chapter 1 001: Blend Images/Hill Street Studios/Brand X Pictures/Getty Images; 003: Library of Congress Prints and Photographs Division Washington, D.C. 20540 USA [LC-DIG-ppmsca-07842]; 005: Lautaro/Alamy Stock Photo; 006: Rich Pedroncelli/AP Images; 007: Ian Dagnall/Alamy Stock Photo; 008: Toby Talbot/AP Images; 012: Olamikan Gbemiga/AP Images; 017: Sergiy Palamarchuk/Shutterstock; 018: Everett Collection Inc/Alamy Stock Photo; 019: dbtravel/dbimages/Alamy Stock Photo; 026: Morgan Hill/Alamy Stock Photo

Chapter 2 031: Chip Somodevilla/Getty Images; 033: Michael Ventura/Alamy Stock Photo; 038: Jacquelyn Martin/AP Images; 040: Buyenlarge/Getty Images; 043: Sun-Sentinel/ZUMA Press, Inc./Alamy Stock Photo; 045: Drew Angerer/Getty Images; 049: whitehouse.gov

Chapter 3 051: David Denney/ZUMA Press, Inc./Alamy Stock Photo; 054: Albin Lohr-Jones/Pacific Press/Alamy Stock Photos; 055: Mark Wallheiser/AP Images; 056: United States Department of Labor; 059: Erik S. Lesser/EPA/Newscom; 063: Jeffrey Rotman/Alamy Stock Photo; 066: Jim West/Alamy Stock Photo; 071: Justin Cooper/Cal Sport Media/Alamy Stock Photo; 073: David McNew/Getty Images; 074: Jim West/Alamy Stock Photo

Chapter 4 079: Jacquelyn Martin/AP Images; 083: Archive PL/Alamy Stock Photo; 085: Tom Till/Alamy Stock Photo; 091: Gerald Herbert/AP Images; 091: Bebeto Matthews/AP Images; 094: Cliff Owen/AP Images; 097: Scott G Winterton/The Deseret News/AP images; 100: James Leynse/Corbis Historical/Getty Images; 102: Rachel La Corte/AP Images; 105: David Bleeker - London/Alamy Stock Photo

Chapter 5 108: Sue Ogrocki/AP Images; 112: Rick Kern/Stella Artois/Getty Images; 113: Jim West/Alamy Stock Photo; 118: David Zalubowski/AP Images; 119: Gary Cameron/Reuters; 122: Ronen Tivony/Sipa USA/AP Images; 123: David McNew/Getty Images; 127: Sarah Edwards/WENN Ltd/Alamy Stock Photo; 133: Alex Brandon/AP Images

Chapter 6 141: Alex Brandon/AP Images; 145: AP Images; 149: Ethan Miller/Getty Images; 150: Michael B. Thomas/AFP/Getty Images; 153: Paul Sancya/AP Images; 161: Maurizio Gambarini/picture-alliance/dpa/AP Images; 163: Kathryn Ziesig/ The Post And Courier/AP Images; 168: APA/Hulton Archive/Getty Images; 170: Ron Sachs/CNP/ZUMA Press, Inc./Alamy Stock Photo; 170: Richard Ellis/Planetpix/Alamy Stock Photo

Chapter 7 174: Charles Moore/Black Star/Alamy Stock Photo; 179: Jon Elswick/AP Images; 182: Bulent Kilic/AFP/Getty Images; 183: Michael Reynolds/epa european pressphoto agency b.v./Alamy Stock Photo; 185: Gerald Herbert/AP Images; 190: Elizabeth Flores/ Star Tribune/AP Images; 191: Tom Williams/CQ Roll Call/AP Images; 192: Joshua Lott/Getty Images News/Getty Images; 193: Chip Somodevilla/Getty Images News/Getty Images; 194: Charles Ommanney/Getty Images News/Getty Images; 200: Travis Morisse/The Hutchinson News/AP Images; 204: Don Ryan/AP Images; 206: Main; 208: Pete Souza/White House/The LIFE Picture Collection/Getty Images

Chapter 8 214: Rich Pedroncelli/AP Images; 219: Michael Dinneen/AP Images; 220: MPI/Archive Photos/Getty Images; 223: Robert King/Newsmakers/Getty Images; 224: CSU Archives/Everett Collection Historical/Alamy Stock Photo; 226: Dpa picture alliance/Alamy Stock Photo; 233: MSNBC/AP Images; 238: Virginia Sherwood/MSNBC/NBCUniversal/Getty Images; 242: Michael Ciaglo/Pool/Getty Images; 244: Richard Ellis/Planetpix/Alamy Stock Photo; 244: Li Muzi/Xinhua/Alamy Stock Photo; 248: Pablo Martinez Monsivais/AP Images; 250: Naira Davlashyan/AP Images

Chapter 9 259: Jon Elswick/AP Images; 262: Sam Aronov/Alamy Stock Photo; 264: Peter Morgan/Reuters; 267: Evan Agostini/AP Images; 267: Theo Wargo/Getty Images; 267: Matt McClain/The Washington Post/Getty Images; 268: Pictorial Press Ltd/Alamy Stock Photo; 270: World History Archive/Alamy Stock Photo; 273: M4OS Photos/Alamy Stock Photo; 275: Paul Schutzer/The LIFE Picture Collection/Getty Images; 278: AP Images; 278: The Washington Post/Getty Images

Chapter 10 291: Win Mcnamee/picture-alliance/dpa/AP Images; 293: Jacquelyn Martin/AP Images; 298: Ron Sachs/picture-alliance/dpa/AP Images; 299: Corey Lowenstein/The News & Observer/AP Images; 303: Alex Edelman/dpa picture alliance/Alamy Stock Photo; 304: Steve Helber/AP Images; 305: Saul Loeb/AFP/Getty images; 306: Office of the Secretary of the Senate; 312: usa.gov; 315: Manuel Balce Ceneta/AP Images; 318: Win McNamee/Getty Images North America/Getty Images; 319: Olivier Douliery/ Abaca Press/AP Images

Chapter 11 325: John Glaser/Cal Sport Media/Alamy Stock Photo; 330: Lenscap/Alamy Stock Photo; 332: Richard Ellis/Alamy Stock Photo; 335: Andrew Milligan/AP Images; 336: Everett Collection/Alamy Stock Photo; 340: White House Photo/Alamy Stock Photo; 346: NASA Photo/Alamy Stock Photo; 348: J. Scott Applewhite/AP Images; 355: Carolyn Kaster/AP Images; 327: Andrey Borodulin/Newzulu/Crowdspark/Alamy Stock Photo

Chapter 12 360: Spencer Platt/Getty Images; 368: Justin Sullivan/Getty Images News/Getty Images; 371: Jocelyn Augustino/FEMA; 372: Evan Vucci/AP Images; 374: Al Drago/Congressional Quarterly/CQ-Roll Call Group/Getty Images; 382: Dennis Brack/Danita Delimont/Alamy Stock Photo; 385: WorldFoto/Alamy Stock Photo; 388: Mario Tama/Reportage Archive/Getty Images

Chapter 13 393: Justin Sullivan/Getty Images News/Getty Images; 396: John Minchillo/AP Images; 397: George Frey/ Bloomberg/Getty Images; 399: Alabama Department of Corrections/AP Images; 406: WDC Photos/Alamy Stock Photo; 410: Dana Verkouteren/AP Images; 412: Chip Somodevilla/Getty Images News/Getty Images; 413: Haraz N. Ghanbari/AP Images

Chapter 14 419: Jose Luis Magana/AP Images; 423: Haraz N Ghanbari/AP Images; 425: Alex Wong/Getty Images News/Getty Images; 427: Nati Harnik/AP Images; 428: David Becker/Getty Images News/Getty Images; 428: Jim Rogash/Getty Images; 431: Newzulu/CrowdSpark/Alamy Stock Photo; 437: Scott Olson/Getty Images News/Getty Images; 439: Bettmann/Getty Images; 441: Francine Orr/Los Angeles Times/Getty Images

Chapter 15 446: John Moore/Getty Images; 450: 615 collection/Alamy Stock Photo; 453: National Archives/Hulton Archive/Getty Images; 454: Bill Hudson/AP Images; 456: Francis Miller/The LIFE Picture Collection/Getty Images; 457: Cheriss May/NurPhoto/Getty Images; 458: Carl Mydans/The LIFE Picture Collection/Getty Images; 464: Andrew Harnik/AP Images; 470: AP Images

Chapter 16 475: Roger Tiley/Alamy Stock Photo; 478: Bill Clark/CQ Roll Call/AP Images; 481: Andrew Cullen/Reuters; 486: Jacquelyn Martin/AP Images; 490: Sarah Silbiger/CQ Roll Call/AP Images; 492: Jack/ImagineChina/AP Images; 493: Bert van Dijk/Moment/Getty Images; 495: Itani/Alamy Stock Photo; 499: Justin Sullivan/Getty Images News/Getty Images; 502: Jeff Hutchens/Getty Images News/Getty Images; 506: Nick Ut/AP Images

Chapter 17 510: Humeau Guy/Sagaphoto.com/Alamy Stock Photo; 513: John Moore/Getty Images News/Getty Images; 517: WDC Photos/Alamy Stock Photo; 518: The George C. Marshall Research Library; 521: Planet Observer/Universal Images Group North America LLC/Alamy Stock Photo; 523: Gautier Stephane/Alamy Stock Photo; 529: Marwan Ibrahim/AFP/Getty Images; 532: Apic/Hulton Archive/Getty Images; 534: Andy Katz/Pacific Press/LightRocket/Getty Images; 535: Philip Heijmans/Newzulu/Alamy Stock Photo; 538: Luiz Rampelotto/EuropaNewswire/picture-alliance/dpa/AP Images

Text Credits

Chapter 1 Thomas Jefferson, The Works of Thomas Jefferson, vol. 5 (Correspondence 1786-1789), p. 256. Edited by Paul Leicester Ford. Published 1905. Accessed online at http://oll.libertyfund.org/titles/jefferson-the-works-vol-5-correspondence-1786-1789.; James Madison, 1787, in The Federalist, No. 10. https://www.congress.gov/resources/display/content/The+Federalist+Papers#TheFederalistPapers-10; Thomas Jefferson's famous words in the Declaration of Independence. https://www.archives.gov/founding-docs/declaration-transcript; *Marbury* v. *Madison*, 5 U.S. 137 (1803).; Joyce Appleby, "The American Heritage: The Heirs and the Disinherited," Journal of American History, vol. 74 (December 1987), p. 808.; Letter of George Washington To David Humphreys, December 26, 1786. In National Historical Publications and Records Commission (NHPRC). https://founders.archives.gov/GEWN-04-04-02-0408; The Federalist, No. 4; John Adams to Abigail Adams. Quoted in Charles L. Mee, Jr., The Genius of the People (NY: Harper & Row, 1987), p. 51; James Madison, The Writings of James Madison, comprising his Public Papers and his Private Correspondence, including his numerous letters and documents now for the first time printed, ed. Gaillard Hunt (New York: G.P. Putnam's Sons, 1900). Vol. 3. 7/5/2018. http://oll.libertyfund.org/titles/1935; Seymour Martin Lipset, "George Washington and the Founding of Democracy," Journal of Democracy, vol. 9 (October 1998), p. 31.; Winton U. Solberg (1990) "The Constitutional Convention and the Formation of the Union," University of Illinois Press; David K. Watson, LL.B., LL.D. (1910) The Constitution of the United States, it's history, application, and construction. Callaghan & Company; J. Franklin Jameson, ed. "Papers of Dr. James McHenry on the Federal Convention of 1787," American Historical Review 11 (April 1906), 595-624.; Saul Cornell "Aristocracy Assailed: The Ideology of Backcountry Anti-Federalism," Journal of American History, vol. 76 (March), p. 1156, www.jstor.org/stable/pdfplus/2936593.pdf.; Charles A. Beard and Mary R. Beard, A Basic History of the United States (NY: New Home Library, 1944), p. 136.; Patrick Henry quoted. In James MacGregor Burns (1982) "The vineyard of liberty." Knopf; Patrick Henry, March 23, 1775. In William Wirt (1817) "Sketches of the Life and Character of Patrick Henry." ; James Madison, "The Federalist #10," in *The Federalist Papers* (New York: Penguin Books, 1987), p. 3.; James Madison, "The Federalist #51," in *The Federalist Papers* (New York: Penguin Books, 1987), p. 1.

Chapter 2 Statue of Liberty inscription from "The New Colossus," sonnet by Emma Lazarus, November 2, 1883. Manuscript at the Library of Congress. https://www.loc.gov/exhibits/haventohome/images/hh0041s.jpg; Thomas Jefferson. Quoted in Alpheus T. Mason, The Supreme Court: Palladium of Freedom (University of Michigan Press, 1962), p. 10.; Morris P. Fiorina, "An Era of Divided Government," Political Science Quarterly vol. 107 (1992), p. 407; U.S. Constitution, Second Amendment. Library of Congress. https://www.loc.gov/law/help/second-amendment.php; Richard E. Neustadt, Presidential Power (Free Press, 1990), pp. 180–181. Alexander Hamilton & James Madison, "Federalist No. 51: The Structure of the Government Must Furnish the Proper Checks and Balances Between the Different Departments," The Independent published on February 8, 1788; Zoe Tillman and Lissandra Villa, "House Conservatives Introduced Articles Of Impeachment Against The Deputy Attorney General," BuzzFeed, July 25, 2018. https://www.buzzfeednews.com/article/zoetillman/house-conservatives-introduced-articles-of-impeachment; Alexander Hamilton, "Federalist No. 78: The Judiciary Department" The Independent published on May 28, 1788.

Chapter 3 Charles Evans Hughes, "War Powers Under the Constitution," ABA Reports, vol. 62 (1917), p. 238; The commerce clause (Article I, Section 8, Clause 1. The National Constitution Center. https://constitutioncenter.org/interactive-constitution/articles/article-i; *California* v. *Superior Courts of California*, 482 U.S. 400 (1987).; Alexander Hamilton, James Madison, and John Jay, *The Federalist Papers*, available at http://thomas.loc.gov/home/histdox/fedpaper.txt.; Oliver Wendell Holmes, Jr., Collected Legal Papers (New York: Harcourt, 1920), pp. 295–296.; *Obergefell et al.* v. *Hodges*, 576 U.S. _____ (2015).; *National Federation of Independent Business et al.* v. *Sebelius*, 567 U.S. _____ (2012), p. 18.; Aaron Wildavsky, "Bare Bones: Putting Flesh on the Skeleton of American Federalism," in The Future of Federalism in the 1980s (Advisory Commission on Intergovernmental Relations, 1981), p. 79.; Thomas R. Dye (1990) "American Federalism: competition among governments.", Lexington Books p. 199.;

U.S. Constitution, The Tenth Amendment. Passed by Congress September 25, 1789. Ratified December 15, 1791. The first 10 amendments form the Bill of Rights. https://constitutioncenter.org/interactive-constitution/amendments/amendment-x; William J. Clinton: "Address Before a Joint Session of the Congress on the State of the Union," January 23, 1996. Online by Gerhard Peters and John T. Woolley, The American Presidency Project. http://www.presidency.ucsb.edu/ws/?pid=53091. Remarks of President Donald J. Trump - As Prepared for Delivery "The Inaugural Address" The White House, January 20, 2017. https://www.whitehouse.gov/briefings-statements/the-inaugural-address/; Gregory Korte and Alan Gomez, "Trump ramps up rhetoric on undocumented immigrants: 'These aren't people. These are animals.'" USA Today, May 16, 2018.

Chapter 4 Adam Liptak and Michael D. Shear, "Supreme Court Turns Down Trump's Appeal in Dreamers' Case." The New York Times, February 26, 2018. https://www.nytimes.com/2018/02/26/us/politics/supreme-court-trump-daca-dreamers.html; Alexis de Tocqueville, Democracy in America, ed. J. P. Mayer, trans. George Lawrence (Doubleday, 1969), p. 278. Originally published 1835 (Vol. 1) and 1840 (Vol. 2).; Arianede Vogue, "Appeals Court Rules Against Latest Trump Travel Ban." CNN. March 27, 2018. https://www.cnn.com/2018/02/15/politics/travel-ban-ruling/index.html.; U.S. Census Bureau, "Race," State and County QuickFacts, https://www.census.gov/quickfacts/fact/table/US/PST045217; Patrick J. Buchanan, "The GOP's New Minority," The American Conservative, June 14, 2013, http://www.theamericanconservative.com/articles/the-gops-new-minority/.; Karl Rove, "More White Voters Alone Won't Save the GOP," Wall Street Journal, June 26, 2013, http://online.wsj.com/news/articles/SB10001424127887323873904578569480696746650.; Thomas Jefferson to P. S. du Pont de Nemours, April 24, 1816, in Paul L. Ford, ed. The Writings of Thomas Jefferson (Putnam, 1899), vol. 10, p. 25.; Raymond E. Wolfinger, Fred I. Greenstein, and Martin Shapiro, Dynamics of American Politics, 2nd ed. (Prentice Hall, 1980), p. 19; James Madison in The Federalist, No. 10; Larry M. Bartels, Unequal Democracy: The Political Economy of the New Gilded Age (Princeton: Princeton University Press, 2008), pp. 2, 15.; Robert A. Dahl, Dilemmas of Pluralist Democracy: Autonomy vs. Control (New Haven, CT: Yale University Press, 1982), p. 175.; Jonathan Martin and Michael D. Shear, "Democrats Turn to Minimum Wage as 2014 Strategy: Effort to Tap Populism," The New York Times (December 30, 2013), p. A1.; Daniel Bell, The Coming of Post-Industrial Society: A Venture in Social Forecasting (Basic Books, 1973), p. xviii.; Harold Hongju Koh, "On American Exceptionalism," Stanford Law Review 55 (May 2003), p. 1481.; "Romney's Speech from Mother Jones Video," September 19, 2012, The New York Times, http://www.nytimes.com/2012/09/19/us/politics/mitt-romneys-speech-from-mother-jones-video.html?pagewanted=all.; James Madison, Federalist, No. 10: "The Same Subject Continued: The Union as a Safeguard Against Domestic Faction and Insurrection," New York Daily Advertiser, November 22, 1787.; James Madison, Federalist, No. 10: "The Same Subject Continued: The Union as a Safeguard Against Domestic Faction and Insurrection," New York Daily Advertiser, November 22, 1787.; "Read Donald Trump's Full Inauguration Speech" http://time.com/4640707/donald-trump-inauguration-speech-transcript/.

Chapter 5 IRS Issues Guidelines for the Tax-Exempt Groups Engaged in Public Advocacy. The Internal Revenue Service [https://www.irs.gov/charities-non-profits/other-non-profits/political-campaign-activities-business-leagues]; David Mayhew, Congress: The Electoral Connection (Yale University Press, 1974), p. 45.; David B. Magleby and Jay Goodliffe, "Interest Groups," in David B. Magleby, ed. Financing the 2016 Election (Washington, D.C.: Brookings Institution Press, forthcoming); Elise Viebeck, "'Washington Cartel': The Ups and Downs of a Cruz Catchphrase," Washington Post, August 12, 2015, https://www.washingtonpost.com/news/powerpost/wp/2015/08/12/washington-cartel-the-ups-and-downs-of-a-cruz-catchphrase/.; "Hillary Clinton proposes campaign finance overhaul to limit influence of big donors." The Guardian. https://www.theguardian.com/us-news/2015/sep/08/hillary-clinton-proposes-campaign-finance-overhaul-limit-influence-big-donors; "Getting Big Money Out of Politics and Restoring Democracy," https://berniesanders.com/issues/money-in-politics/.; U.S. Constitution, Article I, Section 9, Clause 8. https://constitutioncenter.org/interactive-constitution/articles/article-i; Jill Ornitz and Ryan Struyk, "Donald Trump's Surprisingly Honest Lessons About Big Money in Politics." ABC News. August 11, 2016. https://abcnews.go.com/Politics/donald-trumps-surprisingly-honest-lessons-big-money-politics/story?id=32993736.

Chapter 6 Sam Levine, "Hillary Clinton: 'I'm A Progressive, But I'm A Progressive Who Likes To Get Things Done'," Huffington Post, October 13, 2015. https://www.huffingtonpost.com/entry/hillary-clinton-progressive_us_561dafabe4b050c6c4a35c32.

Chapter 7 Margaret Stimmann Branson, "Making the Case for Civic Education: Educating Young People for Responsible Citizenship," paper presented at the Conference for Professional Development for Program Trainers, Manhattan Beach, California, February 25, 2001. http://www.civiced.org/papers/articles_mb2001.html.; Gabriel A. Almond and Sidney Verba, eds., The Civic Culture Revisited: Analytic Study (Little Brown, 1980), p. 13.; Robert S. Erikson and Kent L. Tedin, "American Public Opinion," Longman, 2011, p. 314.; ANES Guide to Public Opinion and Electoral Behavior, "Liberal-Conservative Self-Identification 1972–2008," available at http://www.electionstudies.org/nesguide/toptable/tab3_1.htm.; Quoted in Hadley Cantril, Gauging Public Opinion (Princeton University Press, 1944), p. viii.; Senator Bernie Sanders, "PREPARED REMARKS Senator Bernie Sanders on Democratic Socialism in the United States," November 19, 2015, Bernie, https://berniesanders.com/democratic-socialism-in-the-united-states/.; 2016 American National Election Study (ANES; www.electionstudies.org). The ANES 2016 Time Series Study [dataset]. http://electionstudies.org/studypages/download/datacenter_all_datasets.php.; Bernard Grofman and Lisa Handley, "The Impact of the Voting Rights Act on Black Representation in Southern State Legislatures," Legislative Studies Quarterly, 16 (February 1991), pp. 111–128.; Frank R. Parker, Black Votes Count: Political Empowerment in Mississippi After 1965 (University of North Carolina Press, 1990), p. 3.; David Schultz, "Less than Fundamental: The Myth of Voter Fraud and the Coming of the Second Great Disenfranchisement," William Mitchell Law Review, 34, no. 2 (2007), pp. 483–532, 501. James Madison,

"The Utility of the Union as a Safeguard Against Domestic Faction and Insurrection" The Independent, November 22, 1787; Brown University. (1999). President's Fourth of July declaration on the civic responsibility of higher education. Providence, RI: Brown University, Campus Compact; National Association of Secretaries of State. (1999). New millennium project, part 1: American youth attitudes on policies, citizenship, government, and voting. Washington, D.C.: Author 34-38.

Chapter 8 Trump tweet at: https://twitter.com/realdonaldtrump/status/787995025527410688?lang=en; Jerrold G. Rusk, "The Effect of the Australian Ballot Reform on Split Ticket Voting: 1876–1908," American Political Science Review, 64 (December 1970), pp. 1220–1238.; Anthony Corrado, Thomas E. Mann, Daniel R. Ortiz, Trevor Potter, "The New Campaign Finance Sourcebook," Brookings Institution Press, 2006 p. 79.; Jose Antonio Vargas, "Campaign USA," Washington Post, April 1, 2008, http://www.washingtonpost.com/wp-dyn/content/article/2008/03/31/AR2008033102856_2.html.; Kenneth P. Vogel, "How Bernie Built a Fundraising Juggernaut," Politico, February 10, 2016, http://www.politico.com/story/2016/02/bernie-sanders-fundraising-219112.; Karen Tumulty, "'Republicans Don't Want the Tweet I Got'": "Mark Sanford Says Trump Sealed His Loss." Washington Post, June 13, 2018. https://www.washingtonpost.com/opinions/republicans-dont-want-the-tweet-that-i-got-mark-sanford-says-trump-sealed-his-loss/2018/06/13/d36a9fe2-6f0e-11e8-afd5-778aca903bbe_story.html?utm_term=.80659c0cc0c4&wpisrc=nl_popns&wpmm=1; Jane C. Timm, "'Stunned and Grateful': Katie Arrington, Republican who Beat Sanford, Credits Trump With Win." NBC News., June 13, 2018. https://www.nbcnews.com/politics/politics-news/stunned-grateful-katie-arrington-republican-who-beat-sanford-credits-trump-n882796; Barry Goldwater, speech to the Republican National Convention accepting the Republican nomination for president, July 16, 1964, www.washingtonpost.com/wp-srv/politics/daily/may98/goldwaterspeech.htm.; Adam Nagourney, Ashley Parker, Jim Rutenberg, and Jeff Zeleny, "How a Race in the Balance Went to Obama," The New York Times, November 7, 2012, http://www.nytimes.com/2012/11/08/us/politics/obama-campaign-clawed-back-after-a-dismal-debate.html.; Louis Nelson, "Trump Pushes To Swap Electoral College For Popular Vote," Politico, April 26, 2018. https://www.politico.com/story/2018/04/26/trump-electoral-college-popular-vote-555148.

Chapter 9 The New York Times, "Full Transcript and Video: James Comey's Testimony on Capitol Hill," The New York Times, June 8, 2017. URL: https://www.nytimes.com/2017/06/08/us/politics/senate-hearing-transcript.html; William Blackstone, Commentaries, 1769 [https://scholarship.law.upenn.edu/cgi/viewcontent.cgi?referer=https://www.google.com/&httpsredir=1&article=1043&context=penn_law_review]; First Amendment, U.S. Constitution. https://constitutioncenter.org/interactive-constitution/amendments/amendment-i; Benjamin Franklin, "Apology for Printers," The Pennsylvania Gazette, June 10, 1731, National Humanities Center: Resource Toolbox, Becoming American: The British Atlantic Colonies, 1690–1763, http://nationalhumanitiescenter.org/pds/becomingamer/ideas/text5/franklinprinting.pdf.; Article I, U.S. Constitution. https://constitutioncenter.org/interactive-constitution/articles/article-i; First National Bank of *Boston* v. *Bellotti*, 435 U.S. 765 (1978) p. 800, note 5.; Eugene Volokh, "Freedom for the Press as an Industry, or for the Press as a Technology? From the Framing to Today," University of Pennsylvania Law Review, 160 (2012), p. 466.; Potter Stewart, "Or of the Press," Hastings Law Journal, 26 (1975), p. 634.; L. Gordon Crovitz (August 1, 2007) "A Report to Our Readers," The Wall Street Journal. https://www.wsj.com/articles/SB118592510130784008; John Gramlich, "5 Facts about Americans and Facebook." Pew Research Center, April 10, 2018. http://www.pewresearch.org/fact-tank/2018/04/10/5-facts-about-americans-and-facebook/; Jack Nicas, "Want a Political Ad on Facebook? Now, You Must Reveal Yourself," The New York Times, April 7, 2018. p. A1. https://www.nytimes.com/2018/04/06/business/facebook-verification-ads.html ; Actress Alyssa Milano tweeted a screenshot of #MeToo with the message (October 15, 2017) available at, https://twitter.com/alyssa_milano/status/919659438700670976?lang=en; The Pew Research Center's Project for Excellence in Journalism, "The State of the News Media 2013," http://assets.pewresearch.org.s3.amazonaws.com/files/journalism/State-of-the-News-Media-Report-2013-FINAL.pdf; Lucinda Southern (May 9, 2018) "How the Economist's new app tries to keep people from unsubscribing," Digiday, https://digiday.com/media/economists-new-app-tries-keep-people-unsubscribing/; Frances Perkins, quoted in James MacGregor Burns, Roosevelt: The Lion and the Fox (Harcourt, 1956), p. 205.; The Pew Research Center's Project for Excellence in Journalism, "The State of the News Media 2013," Available at, http://assets.pewresearch.org.s3.amazonaws.com/files/journalism/State-of-the-News-Media-Report-2013-FINAL.pdf; Donald Trump Tweet; Callum Borchers, "Donald Trump knows exactly what he's doing on Twitter, says his spokesman." Washington Post, January 5, 2017, https://www.washingtonpost.com/news/the-fix/wp/2017/01/05/donald-trump-knows-exactly-what-hes-doing-on-twitter-says-his-spokesman/?; Daniel Politi (February 7, 2016) "The Other Problem With Marco Rubio's Broken Record: 'Dispel With' Isn't a Thing," Slate Magazine. The Slate Group http://www.slate.com/news-and-politics/2018/07/canvassing-while-black-police-called-on-oregon-state-rep-janelle-bynum-for-campaigning-door-to-door.html; "Tempers Flare as Christie, Rubio Exchange Attacks," Politico, February, 6, 2016, Politico LLC https://www.politico.com/blogs/new-hampshire-primary-2016-live-updates/2016/02/chris-christie-marco-rubio-2016-debate-218872.; Quoted in Michael J. Robinson and Margaret A. Sheehan, Over the Wire and on TV: CBS and UPI in Campaign '80 (Russell Sage Foundation, 1983), p. xiii.; ABC News, (September 14, 2018) "Bush Visits WTC; Material Witness Held" ABC News http://abcnews.go.com/US/story?id=92498&page=1.; North Woods Advertising, "Fast Paced Paul—Paul Wellstone for U.S. Senate (MN)," http://www.youtube.com/watch?v=aTiW0YCMM0g; Statement by FBI Director James B. Comey on the Investigation of Secretary Hillary Clinton's Use of a Personal E-Mail System. FBI, Washington, D.C. July 5, 2016. https://www.fbi.gov/news/pressrel/press-releases/statement-by-fbi-director-james-b-comey-on-the-investigation-of-secretary-hillary-clinton2019s-use-of-a-personal-e-mail-system; Mayhill Fowler, "Obama: No Surprise that Hard-Pressed Pennsylvanians Turn Bitter." The Huffington Post, April 11, 2008. http://www.huffingtonpost.com/mayhill-fowler/obama-no-surprise-that-ha_b_96188.html; Katherine Q. Seelye and Jeff Zeleny, "On the Defensive, Obama Calls His Words Ill-Chosen." The New York Times, April 13, 2008. http://www.nytimes.com/2008/04/13/us/

politics/13campaign.html.; Larry Sabato (1981) "The Rise of Political Consultants: New Ways of Winning Elections," Basic Books; Shanto Iyengar and Donald R. Kinder, News that Matters: Television and American Opinion (University of Chicago Press, 1987), p. 2.; John H. Aldrich, Before the Convention (University of Chicago Press, 1980), p. 65; From Scribner's Monthly, June 1872 (Vol. IV, p. 204), quoted in Frank Luther Mott, American Journalism, 3rd ed. (Macmillan, 1962), p. 412.

Chapter 10 Alexander Hamilton, James Madison, and John Jay, *The Federalist Papers*, available at http://thomas.loc.gov/home/histdox/fedpaper.txt.; Alexander Hamilton, James Madison, and John Jay, *The Federalist Papers*, available at http://thomas.loc.gov/home/histdox/fedpaper.txt.; Article I, Section 8, U.S. Constitution. National Constitution Center. https://constitutioncenter.org/interactive-constitution/articles/article-i; Alexander Hamilton, James Madison, and John Jay, *The Federalist Papers*, available at http://thomas.loc.gov/home/histdox/fedpaper.txt; Thomas Wentworth Higginson, "The Birth of a Nation," Harper's New Monthly Magazine 68, no. 4 (1884): 242. Text available online at Cornell University's Making of America Collection.; This story comes from the U.S. Senate historian, available at http://www.senate.gov/legislative/common/briefing/Senate_legislative_process.htm.; Jonathan Weisman and Jennifer Steinhauer, "Senate Women Lead in Effort to Find Accord," The New York Times, October 14, 2013, available at http://www.nytimes.com/2013/10/15/us/senate-women-lead-in-effort-to-find-accord.html.; Reagan made the analogy in a December 18, 1982, interview with the Independent Radio Network. The transcript can be found at Gerhard Peters and John T. Woolley, The American Presidency Project, http://www.presidency.ucsb.edu/ws/?pid=42130.; (March 23, 2018) "Remarks by President Trump at Signing of H.R. 1625". https://www.whitehouse.gov/briefings-statements/remarks-president-trump-signing-h-r-1625/; Martin Gilens and Benjamin I. Page, "Testing Theories of American Politics: Elites, Interest Groups, and Average Citizens," Perspectives on Politics (September 2014), p. 575.; Joseph I. Lieberman, In Praise of Public Life (Simon & Schuster, 2000), p. 109.

Chapter 11 Alexander Hamilton, James Madison, and John Jay, *The Federalist Papers*, No. 68, available at http://thomas.loc.gov/home/histdox/fedpaper.txt.; Donald J. Trump, "Remarks by President Trump and Prime Minister Löfven of Sweden in Joint Press Conference," March 6, 2018, available at https://www.whitehouse.gov/briefings-statements/remarks-president-trump-prime-minister-lofven-sweden-joint-press-conference/; U.S. Senate's history of the Jefferson vice presidency at http://www.senate.gov/artandhistory/history/common/generic/VP_Thomas_Jefferson.htm; Presidential Oath of Office. Article II, Section 1, U.S. Constitution. National Constitution Center. https://constitutioncenter.org/interactive-constitution/articles/article-ii; Remarks by the President at Memorial Service for Fallen Dallas Police Officers. U.S. Embassy in Chad https://td.usembassy.gov/remarks-president-memorial-service-fallen-dallas-police-officers/; Philip Rucker, and Robert Costa, "'Tired of the Wait Game': White House Stabilizers Gone, Trump Calling His Own Shots," Washington Post, March 31, 2018, https://www.washingtonpost.com/politics/unhinged-or-unleashed-white-house-stabilizers-gone-trump-calling-his-own-shots/2018/03/31/19447ae2-343b-11e8-8bdd-cdb33a5eef83_story.html?utm_term=.def09a3b35be.; The President's Committee on Administrative Management, "Report of the President's Committee on Administrative Management," Government Printing Office, January 1937, p. 1.; "Inside the White House: Letters to the President," available at https://www.youtube.com/watch?v=eG00mM8QEGk; Michael D. Shear, and Sheryl Gay Stolberg, "Conceding to N.R.A., Trump Abandons Brief Gun Control Proposal," The New York Times, March 12, 2018, available at https://www.nytimes.com/2018/03/12/us/politics/trump-gun-control-national-rifle-association.html.; Greg Jaffe, "In State of the Union, Obama Takes on Country's Anger and Anxiety," Washington Post, January 12, 2016, http://www.washingtonpost.com/pb/politics/in-state-of-the-union-obama-takes-on-countrys-anger-and-anxiety/2016/01/12/c8bf04ce-b94a-11e5-b682-4bb4dd403c7d_story.html.; Arthur Schlesinger, Jr., "Is the Vice Presidency Necessary?" The Atlantic, May 1974, available at http://www.theatlantic.com/magazine/archive/1974/05/is-the-vice-presidency-necessary/305732/.; The Editors, "The Trump Tweet Tracker," The Atlantic, June 4, 2017, https://www.theatlantic.com/liveblogs/2017/06/donald-trump-twitter/511619/.

Chapter 12 U.S. Surgeon General Jerome Adams told NPR. In Rachel Martin (April 5, 2018) "Surgeon General Urges More Americans To Carry Opioid Antidote" https://www.npr.org/sections/health-shots/2018/04/05/599538089/surgeon-general-urges-more-americans-to-carry-opioid-antidote; "Surgeon General's Advisory on Naloxone and Opioid Overdose" https://www.surgeongeneral.gov/priorities/opioid-overdose-prevention/naloxone-advisory.html; Alexander Hamilton, James Madison, and John Jay, *The Federalist Papers*, available at http://thomas.loc.gov/home/histdox/fedpaper.txt.; Thomas Jefferson, first Inaugural Address, 1801. In The Avalon Project at Yale Law School. Lillian Goldman Law Library. http://avalon.law.yale.edu/19th_century/jefinau1.asp; Paul C. Light, A Government Ill Executed: The Decline of the Federal Service and How to Reverse It (Harvard University Press, 2008), pp. 9–14.; Coral Davenport, and Lisa Friedman, "In His Haste to Roll Back Rules, Scott Pruitt, E.P.A. Chief, Risks His Agenda," The New York Times, April 7, 2018, https://www.nytimes.com/2018/04/07/climate/scott-pruitt-epa-rollbacks.html?hp&action=click&pgtype=Homepage&clickSource=story-heading&module=first-column-region®ion=top-news&WT.nav=top-news.; William Greider, "The Education of David Stockman," Atlantic (1981), p. 296.; John Kingdon, Agendas, Alternatives, and Public Policies (Little, Brown, 1984), p. 3. Gunnar E. Kvaran, "A Study of the News Coverage of the International Whaling Ban in The New York Times and the Los Angeles Times" San Jose State University, 1994 p.13.

Chapter 13 David Lat, "No, Justice Anthony M. Kennedy Is Not Retiring Tomorrow" Above the Law, June 25, 2017 https://abovethelaw.com/2017/06/no-justice-anthony-m-kennedy-is-not-retiring-tomorrow/; Alexander Hamilton, "Federalist No. 78: The Judiciary Department," The Independent published on May 28, 1788; Brett Samuels, "Trump rejects calls for more immigration judges: 'We have to have a real border, not judges'" Capitol Hill Publishing Corp., June 19, 2018 https://thehill.com/homenews/administration/393031-trump-rejects-calls-for-additional-immigration-judges-we-have-to-have; Alexander Hamilton,

"Federalist No. 78: The Judiciary Department," The Independent published on May 28, 1788.

Chapter 15 Martin Luther King, Jr. "Letter from Birmingham Jail," April 13, 1963. Available at, https://web.cn.edu/kwheeler/documents/Letter_Birmingham_Jail.pdf.; The Fourteenth Amendment to the U.S. Constitution; Justice Miller delivered the opinion of the Court, "SLAUGHTER-HOUSE CASES" DECEMBER 1872, Term. Available at, http://law2.umkc.edu/faculty/projects/ftrials/conlaw/slaughter.html; U.S. Supreme Court "*Arizona* v. *United States*, 567 U.S. 387 (2012)". No. 11–182. Argued April 25, 2012—Decided June 25, 2012; David Remnick, "The Bridge: The Life and Rise of Barack Obama" (Knopf, 2010).; United States Commission on Civil Rights," "Civil Rights Issues Facing Asian Americans in the 1990s," February 1992; Celia W. Dugger, "U.S. Study Says Asian Americans Face Widespread Discrimination," The New York Times, February 29, 1992, p. 1, reporting on U.S. Civil Rights Commission, Civil Rights Issues Facing Asian Americans in the 1990s; *Trump* v. *Hawaii*, 585 U.S. _____ (2018); equal protection clause of the Fourteenth Amendment declares; Fifth Amendment's due process clause,; *Frontiero* v. *Richardson*, 411 U.S. 677 (1973).; Sandra Day O'Connor, in *Kimel* v. *Florida Board of Regents*, 528 U.S. 62 (2000). Available at, https://supreme.justia.com/cases/federal/us/528/62/; Abigail M. Thernstrom, "Whose Votes Count? Affirmative Action and Minority Voting Rights," (Harvard University Press, 1987), p. 15.; Leon F. Litwack, Trouble in Mind: Black Southerners in the Age of Jim Crow (1998), p. 227, as cited in James W. Fox, Jr., "Intimations of Citizenship: Repressions and Expressions of Equal Citizenship in the Era of Jim Crow," Howard University Law Journal (Fall 2006).; *Brown* v. *Board of Education of Topeka*, 349 U.S. 294 (1955).; 42 U.S. Code § 2000d; See Gary Orfield, Susan E. Eaton, and the Harvard Project on School Desegregation, Dismantling Desegregation: The Quiet Reversal of *Brown* v. *Board of Education* (New Press, 1996).; John Marshall Harlan, dissenting in *Plessy* v. *Ferguson*, 163 U.S. 537 (1896).

Chapter 16 Lyndon B. Johnson, "Annual Message to the Congress on the State of the Union," January 8, 1964, available online in Gerhard Peters and John T. Woolley, The American Presidency Project, at http://www.presidency.ucsb.edu/ws/?pid=26787.; Alexander Hamilton, James Madison, and John Jay, *The Federalist Papers*, available at http://thomas.loc.gov/home/histdox/fedpaper.txt.; Office of Management and Budget, "Fiscal Year 2016 Analytical Perspectives: Budget of the U. S. Government," (Government Printing Office, 2015); William J. Clinton, acceptance speech, Democratic National Convention, Chicago, July 6, 1992 available at http://www.presidency.ucsb.edu/ws/?pid=25958; "6 Things to Know About President Trump's New Budget" available at, http://fortune.com/2017/05/22/donald-trump-white-house-budget/; Charles Andel, Stephen L. Davidow, Mark Hollander, and David A. Moreno, "The Economics of Health Care Quality and Medical Errors," Journal of Health Care Finance, vol. 39 (Fall 2012), p. 48. Available at, http://www.wolterskluwerlb.com/health/resource-center/articles/2012/10/economics-health-care-quality-and-medical-errors; "Ryan Opening Statement: A Progress Report on the War on Poverty Opening Remarks, as Prepared for Delivery," House of Representatives Committee on the Budget, January 28, 2014, available at http://budget.house.gov/news/documentsingle.aspx?DocumentID=367880.

Chapter 17 President Barrack Obama's Speech in Hiroshima, Japan (May 27, 2016).; President Donald Trump's interview against North Korea in Bridgewater, New Jersey. (August 8, 2018).; Whitehouse "Remarks by President Trump on the Joint Comprehensive Plan of Action," May 8, 2018. Available at, https://www.whitehouse.gov/briefings-statements/remarks-president-trump-joint-comprehensive-plan-action/; Pew Research Center, "Public Sees U.S. Power Declining as Support for Global Engagement Slips: America's Place in the World, 2013," (Pew Research Center, December 3, 2013), p. 10, available at http://www.people-press.org/2013/12/03/public-sees-u-s-power-declining-as-support-for-global-engagement-slips/.; Alexander Hamilton, James Madison, and John Jay, *The Federalist Papers*, (Federalist No.4) available at http://thomas.loc.gov/home/histdox/fedpaper.txt.; For an alternative, highly critical account of the bin Laden raid, see Seymour M. Hersh, "The Killing of Osama bin Laden," London Review of Books, May 2015.; Henry A. Kissinger "Henry A. Kissinger: Realists v. Idealists," The New York Times, May 12, 2005, available at http://www.nytimes.com/2005/05/11/opinion/11iht-edkissinger.html?pagewanted=all.; Stephen J. Adler, Jeff Mason, and Steve Holland, "Exclusive: Trump says he thought being president would be easier than his old life" April 28, 2017. Available at, https://www.reuters.com/article/us-usa-trump-100days/exclusive-trump-says-he-thought-being-president-would-be-easier-than-his-old-life-idUSKBN17U0CA?utm_campaign=trueAnthem:+Trending+Contentutm_content=5902feb704d3013925c95855utm_medium=trueAnthemutm_source=twitter; Bob Woodward, "Bush at War," (New York: Simon & Schuster, 2002), p. 81.; Pew Research Center, "Public Sees U.S. Power Declining as Support for Global Engagement Slips: America's Place in the World, 2013," (Pew Research Center, December 3, 2013), pp. 4–5, available at http://www.people-press.org/2013/12/03/public-sees-u-s-power-declining-as-support-for-global-engagement-slips/.; Bernard Brodie, "The Absolute Weapon: Atomic Power and World Order," (Harcourt, Brace, 1946).; Samuel P. Huntington, "The Soldier and the State: The Theory and Politics of Civil-Military Relations," Belknap Press of Harvard University Press, 1957 (Belknap Press, 1957), p. 464.; Council on Foreign Relations, "Domestic Intelligence and the Boston Bombings," interview with Richard A. Falkenrath, April 25, 2013, available at http://www.cfr.org/counterterrorism/domestic-intelligence-boston-bombings/p30557.; President Donald Trump announces the Decision to leave Paris climate accord in Rose Garden The White House on June 09, 2017; U.S. Ambassador Nikki Halley speaks on the suspected chemical weapon attack in Syria, April 09, 2018. Available at, https://twitter.com/cnn/status/983442623032709122?lang=en.

Index

Note: Page numbers followed by *f* indicates a figure; *t* indicates a table; *p* indicates a picture or its caption; *m* indicates a map.

A

B

C

G

H

I

N

Q

R

T

Z